SECOND EDITION

Human Behavior in the Social Environment

▲ ▲ ▲ ▲ ▲ ▲ ▲ ▲ ▲ ▲ ▲ ▲ ▲ ▲ ▲

A Multidimensional Perspective

José B. Ashford
Arizona State University

Craig Winston LeCroy
Arizona State University

Kathy L. Lortie
*University Medical Center
at the University of Arizona Health Sciences Center*

Brooks/Cole
Thomson Learning™

Australia • Canada • Mexico • Singapore • Spain • United Kingdom • United States

Executive Social Work Editor: Lisa Gebo
Assistant Editors: Susan Wilson and JoAnne von Zastrow
Editorial Assistant: Sheila Walsh
Marketing Manager: Caroline Concilla
Project Editor: Susan Walters
Print Buyer: Karen Hunt
Permissions Editor: Joohee Lee

Production Service: Johnston Associates
Text Designer: Adriane Bosworth
Photo Researcher: Susie Friedman
Copy Editor: Stacey Sawyer
Cover Designer: Bill Stanton
Compositor: ColorType
Text and Cover Printer: R. R. Donnelley, Crawfordsville

Library of Congress Cataloging-in-Publication Data
Ashford, José B.
    Human behavior in the social environment:
a multidimensional perspective/José B. Ashford,
Craig Winston LeCroy, Kathy L. Lortie.—2nd ed.
        p.   cm.
    Includes bibliographical references and index.
    ISBN 0-534-35915-9
    1. Developmental psychology. 2. Social psychology.
I. LeCroy, Craig W.   II. Lortie, Kathy L., 1953-.   III. Title.
BF713 .A82   2001
302—dc21   00-033690

For more information, contact
Wadsworth/Thomson Learning
10 Davis Drive
Belmont, CA 94002-3098
USA
http://www.wadsworth.com

International Headquarters
Thomson Learning
International Division
290 Harbor Drive, 2nd Floor
Stamford, CT 06902-7477
USA

UK/Europe/Middle East/South Africa
Thomson Learning
Berkshire House
168-173 High Holborn
London WC1V 7AA
United Kingdom

Asia
Thomson Learning
60 Albert Street, #15-01
Albert Complex
Singapore 189969

Canada
Nelson Thomson Learning
1120 Birchmount Road
Toronto, Ontario M1K 5G4
Canada

 This book is printed on acid-free recycled paper.

Contents

CHAPTER 4

The Social Dimension for Assessing Social Functioning   103

CHAPTER 5

Pregnancy, Birth, and the Newborn   153

CHAPTER 7

Early Childhood   251

CHAPTER 8

Middle Childhood   301

CHAPTER 10

Young Adulthood   413

CHAPTER 12

Late Adulthood   527

Preface

The most challenging aspect of writing a textbook on Human Behavior in the Social Environment (HBSE) is selecting what to include and what to omit. Students do not benefit when they are overwhelmed with unconnected bits of information, whether this information is conceptual or theoretical in nature. We challenged ourselves to write a comprehensive textbook, applied and integrated, that would be of value in both graduate and undergraduate programs.

In preparing the first edition, we were aware that few textbooks being used in undergraduate programs were also being adopted at the graduate level. It was commonly believed that graduate students require more advanced content than that traditionally offered to undergraduates. Yet comparability of content in foundation courses is a major concern in accreditation by the Council of Social Work Education. Issues of comparability are particularly germane where students can use undergraduate courses to achieve advanced standing in graduate school. In the first edition, we decided to address the demands on undergraduates for foundation knowledge by presenting the material in a user-friendly fashion without ducking difficult conceptual and theoretical issues.

Thus, we introduced students to a multidimensional framework for assessing concerns about human behavior that was then applied in each of the developmental chapters. The application of this framework, along with the careful balancing of human development and social systems, was well received by both colleagues and students. We appreciate the support received by the first edition and are delighted to offer this revision, which builds on the unique strengths of our first effort.

Key Changes in the Second Edition

Maintaining the original spirit and intent, in the second edition we keep pace with the rapid progress of knowledge in the biological, psychological, health, and social sciences. Thus, there are many new references in this edition, including seminal writings on theory. In addition, every chapter has been revised to include developments in research and theory that focus on variability in social environments. For instance, we have introduced a number of strategies for addressing the causes and consequences of macroenvironmental variability on life course. These include:

- Increased coverage on the effects of variations in social structure (groups, families, communities, organizations, and institutions) on key developmental transitions across the life-span

- More about communities

- New focus sections on social issues and policy considerations

- New material on the roles of communities, cohorts, institutions, and other environmental variables in identifying potential changes in life course

- New coverage of life-course theory and principles from sociology; this emphasis on life-course development allowed us to increase our focus on socialization issues across the life-span as well as to devote more attention to the effects of sociohistorical contexts on life-course variability

In this new edition we were able to incorporate a number of suggestions from colleagues who adopted the first edition. These include:

- Chapter-by-chapter integration of new focus sections on spirituality

- Chapter-by-chapter integration of new focus sections presenting personal narratives; these narratives deal with racism, poverty, sexual orientation, youth, ageism, and other topics related to the impact of human diversity on development

- Increased attention to the role of empirical knowledge in addressing prevention issues (primary, secondary, and tertiary)
- Critiques of existing biological and psychological models of human development that fail to recognize the profoundly interactive nature of person-environment transactions and the influences of cultural diversity
- Introduction in Chapter 2 of a new case (Raul Salazar) that illustrates the multidimensional framework throughout Chapters 2, 3, and 4
- Redesigned openers for the developmental chapters, where templates present issues, tasks, risks, and opportunities distinct to each phase of development
- Chapter-by-chapter suggested websites
- Access to *InfoTrac® College Edition* and abstracting resources

Chapter 1, which introduces the multidimensional framework, was revised substantially to provide students with a broader orientation to the profession of social work and its view of HBSE. The chapter begins with a macro case about the conflicts in a Latino agency in Los Angeles. This chapter helps students to differentiate between case and situation conceptualizations. The first edition linked foundational knowledge with direct practice, and now we go further in challenging students to understand the connections between theory and the kinds of situations they will confront as practitioners in *indirect* areas of practice. Chapter 1 includes more on crisis theory and on the differences between life-span and life-course perspectives; this content is linked with strengths and competency models of social work. Thus, the chapter provides a general overview relating issues of change and development to social work's view of HBSE. New developmental concepts, including *transitions, trajectories,* and *life course,* are linked to a review of the role of prevention in the practice of social work.

Chapter 2, the biophysical dimension, now includes the case study mentioned earlier that is designed to guide students throughout Chapters 2, 3, and 4. In response to reviewers, we eliminated detailed content on medication side effects, neurotransmitter systems, and gene expression of inherited traits.

Chapter 3, the psychological dimension, encourages students to see the multidimensionality of client issues, beginning with a look at the case presented in Chapter 2. Also new is content on ego functions and the superego, as well as on issues of memory, attitudes, and emotions.

Chapter 4, the social dimension—and the last chapter that introduces the multidimensional framework—includes questions designed to guide the application of the social dimension to the case of Raul Salazar. Also new is content on groups, including group value theory, social identity theory, and definitions of social conflict. A major addition to the chapter is a review of community as system, including various ways of conceptualizing community.

Chapter 5, on pregnancy and childbirth, includes the couvade syndrome, the role of the social workers in abortion, the use of epidurals in the birth process, gestational diabetes, assisted reproductive technology, perinatal transmission of HIV infections in children, ethical issues surrounding the Human Genome Project, genetic counseling, effects of multiple gestation births, and home visitation programs.

Chapter 6, on infancy, includes new information on information processing and cross modal transfer, infant temperment, assessment and interventions of infant mental health, playing with a baby, understanding different cultural beliefs, environmental context and child development, programs targeted at children living in poverty, and infant abuse.

Chapter 7, on early childhood, includes new content on asthma in early childhood, preschoolers who are bilingual, resilience and emotion coaching, signs of aggression in children, low-income parents, and quality of time. A number of focus sections relate directly to practice.

Chapter 8, on middle childhood, includes new material on emotional intelligence, refugee children, the Ashenbach child behavior checklist, and rites of passage for African-American youth.

Chapter 9, on adolescence, includes new content on implications for practice, delinquency, and prevention of drug abuse.

Chapter 10, on young adulthood, includes new material on rational emotive therapy, the Americans with Disabilities Act, depression and job loss, marital expectations and myths, implication for practice, internalized homophobia, blending religions, parenting children's spirituality, the Million Man March, and spiritual growth in women with AIDS.

Chapter 11, on middle adulthood, contains an updated section on menopause, including new material on hormone replacement therapy. There is additional new content on prostate cancer, menopause and multiculturalism, the hard of hearing adult, and there are a number of new narratives.

Chapter 12 is on late adulthood. This last chapter updates material on adults 85 and older, sexuality in later life, AIDS in persons over 50, alcoholism in late adulthood, the issue of friendships, persons who are dying, and introduces new content on spirituality, retirement, and cognitive interventions.

On a final note, we increased the number of narratives in this edition because we believe they are an excellent devise for helping students link theoretical content to reality. The narrative themes vary, but most of them focus on topics that can enhance student appreciation of issues of diversity and their consequences for the personal experiences of individuals.

New Text Design Reflects Integrative Approach

The second edition was redesigned to more closely reflect our integrative approach to understanding human development across social and cultural contexts. We continue to believe that a major issue confronting students in HBSE is how to apply knowledge about dimensions of human functioning while respecting variations in gender, race, ethnicity, and sexual orientation. To this end, the new design includes templates that appear at the beginning of each developmental chapter. These templates offer students an integrated framework for approaching each developmental stage.

Supplements for Instructors

INSTRUCTOR'S MANUAL/TEST BANK

This is a comprehensive guide that includes an overview of the history of HBSE in social work, multiple-choice and essay questions, ideas for class projects, guidelines for teaching, and discussion questions.

EXAMVIEW (INCLUDING ONLINE TESTING)

Create, deliver, and customize tests (both print and online) in minutes with this easy-to-use assessment and tutorial system for both Windows and Macintosh systems. This cross-platform CD-ROM offers both a *Quick Test Wizard* and an *Online Test Wizard* to guide you step by step through the process of creating tests, while its unique WYSIWYG (what you see is what you get) capability allows you to see your test on the screen exactly as it will print or display online. You can build tests of up to 250 questions using up to twelve question types. Using ExamView's complete word processing capabilities, you can enter an unlimited number of new questions or edit existing questions.

Supplements for Students

ONLINE QUIZZES

Use the Web to help study and review! With online quizzing, you can answer questions corresponding to each text chapter any time, day or night, at your convenience. Five multiple-choice questions from the Instructor's Manual are included for each chapter. Online Quizzes can be accessed through the Brooks/Cole Helping Professions Resource Center website at *http://helpingprofs.Wadsworth.com.*

INFOTRAC® COLLEGE EDITION

This fully searchable online database gives you immediate access to full-text articles from scholarly and popular publications. *InfoTrac College Edition* offers authoritative sources, updated daily, and dating back as far as four years. You will be able to conduct searches and narrow the scope of term-paper topics quickly and easily. You can even print out articles at your convenience. In North America, four months' FREE access to this virtual library is provided with new copies of the second edition of *Human Behavior in the Social Environment.* It's a fast, efficient way to expand your course beyond the pages of the text and actually do research as you read.

Acknowledgments

Our second edition could not have been completed without the work of many dedicated people. Special thanks to Beth Auerbach-Dixon, who worked tirelessly on research and assisted with course supplements. Thanks also to Shirley Patterson for the chapter on late adulthood and for her constant encouragement throughout. We could not have completed this project on time without Jayne Cooper's work on middle childhood. Kathy Olson and Mary Lutes provided timely assistance with mailings and manuscript preparation. Special thanks to Renita Benally for her work on permissions and other time-consuming tasks.

For their contributions to focus sections in this edition, we wish to thank Jill Littrell, Georgia State University; Barry Oblas, Margaret Waller, and Hubert Johnston, Arizona State University; and Sarah and Daniel Brosmer. The diligent research of Misha Marvel requires special mention. We are sincerely grateful for her contribution of a number of focus sections and, especially, the book's indexes.

No book can be successful without the help of reviewers who offer suggestions, constructive criticism, and encouragement. Special thanks to Paula Nurius, many of whose suggestions were included in this edition and were well received by subsequent reviewers. We thank especially the following reviewers of this edition: Kim Haynes, David Lipscomb University; Sally Mathiesen, Florida State University; Munira Merchant, Aurora University; Carolyn Pryor, Wayne State University; William Roberts, Glenville State College; Louise Stanger, San Diego State University.

In preparing this second edition, we have been most fortunate to work with Lisa Gebo, who is an amazingly patient and supportive editor. Lisa offered excellent guidance and helped assure that the book remained user-friendly. The rest of the acquisitions staff—Susan Wilson, JoAnne von Zastrow, and Sheila Walsh—were invaluable in keeping the book on schedule and in facilitating communications among project members. Susan Walters, our project editor, has overseen a complex project with great aplomb. Production services provided by Judy Johnstone were invaluable, and she maintained good spirits despite tight deadlines and unexpected changes. Photo researcher Susan Friedman dealt smoothly with authors who had difficulties translating concepts into visual images. Copyeditor Stacey Sawyer provided many helpful suggestions for improving the readability of the text. All of these people have been splendid colleagues during this process.

Thanks, finally, to our mates and families for their support and encouragement during this project. We appreciated their willingness to listen whenever we wanted to talk about the latest findings in the literature.

José B. Ashford
Craig W. LeCroy
Kathy L. Lortie

José B. Ashford, Arizona State University, is a professor of human behavior in the social environment in the School of Social Work and a professor of social science and law in the Interdisciplinary Doctoral Program in Justice Studies. His previous books include *Introduction to Social Work and Social Welfare* (with Mary Macht) and *Treating of Adult and Juvenile Offenders with Special Needs* (with Bruce D. Sales and William H. Reid). His forthcoming books include *Assessing Mitigating and Aggravating Circumstances* and *Mental Health Policy and Law.* He is currently the principle investigator for the Family Drug Court grant, funded by the Governor's Division of Drug Policy, and a planning grant funded by the U.S. Office of Justice Programs–Drug Courts Program Office. In addition, Professor Ashford is the program evaluator for: (1) a grant dealing with the conditional discharge of dually diagnosed offenders from Maricopa County Jail System, and (2) the Safe and Stable Families program of the Navajo Nation. He is widely published in areas dealing with the assessment, classification, and treatment of special need offenders, juvenile aftercare, and forensic social work. Professor Ashford testifies across the country as an expert in the assessment of mitigating factors in capital murder cases.

Craig Winston LeCroy is a professor in the School of Social Work at Arizona State University. Professor LeCroy is author of *Social Skills Training for Children and Youth, Case Studies in Social Work Practice,* and *Handbook of Child and Adolescent Treatment Manuals.* His forthcoming books include *Go Girls: A Strength-Building Program For Teenage Girls, Case Studies in Child and Adolescent Counseling,* and *The Call to Social Work.* Professor LeCroy has directed several child and adolescent projects including a National Institute of Mental Health Training Grant for emotionally disturbed children and adolescents; Youth Plus: Positive Socialization for Youth, a substance abuse prevention project; and a primary prevention program for adolescent girls. Professor LeCroy has published widely in the areas of children's mental health, social skills training, risk and needs assessment with juvenile offenders, and adolescent treatment and program evaluation.

Kathy L. Lortie is a pediatric social worker at University Medical Center, University of Arizona, Health Sciences Center. She co-teaches Social Work in Health Care, a graduate course at Arizona State University. A certified childbirth educator, she has taught classes on childbirth, parenting, and infant care and has worked as a labor assistant. She is also the author of *Special Delivery: A Labor Guide for Expectant Parents.* Her current interests include child abuse prevention, infant mental health, and coping with chronic illness in adolescence.

lieve are responsible for the problems. However, they don't want to fire any of the Mexican-American assistants, because this could weaken further the program's ability to reach members of the Mexican-American community. The director of the program told an outside consultant that "Mexicans are not really bad, but they are somewhat lazy and must be taught to change their ways." He doubts that they would ever be able to run things by themselves. Thus he assumes that if he can change the employees in his program, then the agency would start doing a better job of selling the program in the Mexican-American community.

The teaching assistants from the Mexican-American community believe that both the board and the teachers are at fault for the inability of the program to enroll sufficient numbers of students. They do not believe that the board is willing to spend the kind of money needed to pay for classes with adequate student/teacher ratios. They also agree with the teachers that the program is in need of newer teaching materials. Several assistants who plan to leave the agency also pointed out that many of the teachers "really don't like us and accept us as Mexicans." One assistant told a consultant that "they want to make us like them." Another assistant said "We often feel that we are being used by everyone. Why don't they give us the money, and we will do it all; it's our money too" (adapted from Ziegler, 1994).

Which statement offers the best understanding of El Centro's situation? Explain your choice.

A. This agency's board is suffering the consequences of what some organizational theorists have termed "bureapathic behavior." This behavior begins with a need for persons in authority to control those in subordinate positions. Moreover, the director has a bureaucratic personality and harbors biases toward Mexican-Americans that are affecting his relationships with staff.

B. The teachers in the agency are displacing their anger and frustration onto their assistants because of feelings of powerlessness. They also resent their dependence on their assistants in recruiting students for the program.

C. El Centro has teachers and administrators who have learned stereotypes about Mexicans that influence their behavior toward students and em-

ployees; this contributes to much of the conflict in this setting.

D. The social institutions in this agency are not functioning well. In these institutions, people learn structured ways of relating to one another. Each group's norms are in conflict with the others', triggering anger, frustration, and evidence of breakdown in institutional or socially structured patterns of relating.

E. El Centro has not adopted a system of service delivery that recognizes the strengths of its target populations.

▼ ▼ ▼

CASE B
Jean Davis

Jean Davis is a 19-year-old woman who is experiencing difficulties in college. She moved out of the dorm because she thought other students were out to ruin her life. Her former roommate said that Jean would stay up all night reading the Bible and laughing inappropriately. Jean claims that other students in the dorm were jealous of her because of her special powers. She will not tell anyone what these powers are; when asked, she just smiles strangely. Her mother recently learned that Jean stopped attending classes. Neighbors have complained about hearing Jean pace the floor of her apartment throughout the night. Whenever the mother talks to her daughter, Jean tells her mother that she needs to prepare because the end is near. Jean told the social worker that God speaks to her all the time, telling her that she needs to be prepared. But Jean says that she cannot tell anyone what she is preparing for. Her mother is frightened because this is not like the Jean she previously knew. She is concerned because Jean is not eating and is disturbing her neighbors.

Which statement offers the best understanding of Jean's situation? Explain your choice.

A. Jean is suffering from schizophrenia.

B. Jean has developed an extreme fear of others and is seeking refuge in her spiritual beliefs.

C. Jean has learned to adapt to the stresses of college and young adulthood by withdrawing from others.

D. The lack of support in Jean's school environment caused her to seek refuge in fantasy and other escapist activities.

E. Jean is acting irresponsibly so that she can avoid the stressful expectations in her everyday life.

▼ ▼ ▼

CASE C

Jeff Johnson

Jeff Johnson is a 27-year-old man who was arrested for two counts of sexually inappropriate behavior. He was accused of having sex with two boys from his scouting troop. Jeff had been previously arrested and convicted for sex with minors, but he was placed on probation on the condition that he obtain treatment. Jeff has virtually no relationships with persons his own age. He lives with his parents and is currently employed as a truck driver for a company that collects old newspapers. His probation officer eventually learned that Jeff keeps this low-paying job primarily because it is near an area with underprivileged children whom he has often paid for sexual favors.

When Jeff was 12 years old, he became involved in a sexual relationship with an older man. He was in this sexual relationship for approximately five years. He also recalled being fondled in a closet by an older boy at his school when he was around 8 years old and being ambivalent about the experience. Jeff reports no relationships with a female or a male over 16 years of age since he stopped seeing the older man. He prefers having sex with young boys and provides vivid descriptions of what stimulates him about them physically.

Which statement offers the best understanding of Jeff's situation? Explain your choice.

A. Jeff is suffering from a mental disorder called paraphilia of the pedophilia type.

B. Jeff's inappropriate sexual orientation is due to his immature personality.

C. Jeff learned his interest in molesting children from his own experience of molestation.

D. Jeff's social situation does not provide him with effective social outlets.

E. Jeff's behavior is morally "disgusting" or bad.

▼ ▼ ▼

CASE D

Tim Lad

Tim Lad is a 7-year-old boy who was referred by the school counselor for running away from school and for constantly fighting with other students. Tim lives with his brother, sister, and mother in a poor section of a small southwestern town. Tim's father deserted the family when Tim was 2½ years old. His father was an alcoholic and had a history of trouble with the law. Tim is very impulsive and has difficulties controlling his behavior. His teachers say that he often misinterprets the actions of others. For instance, he bumped into a boy the other day in class, and the boy told him to be careful. Tim responded with "no one tells me what to do" and proceeded to attack the other youth. Tim also has difficulties reading and sitting still in class. Tim's mother works long hours and says she is exhausted when she gets off from her restaurant job. She reports that she is not sure she can control him any longer. Ms. Lad reported that Tim has always had a bad temper but is generally sorry for whatever he does. When the social worker met with Tim, he was very cooperative and friendly throughout the interview.

Which statement offers the best understanding of Tim's situation? Explain your choice.

A. Tim has attention deficit hyperactivity disorder and a possible conduct disorder.

B. Tim is acting out his need for love.

C. Tim has learned that the only way to get what he desires is to act on impulse. He has not learned to reflect on his actions.

D. Tim is acting out because he is in a school system without adequate special education resources.

His school situation needs to provide him with a substitute father figure to replace the loss of his father.

E. Tim is a bad child who needs to learn discipline and responsibility.

▼ ▼ ▼

In selecting appropriate statements to describe each of the preceding cases, some of you may have believed that all the descriptions applied. Others may have thought that none applied. Indeed, all the descriptions may apply to some degree; they were taken from established approaches for assessing human behavior with roots in biological, psychological, and social theory. Each of these theories includes concepts of use to social workers in assessing individual and social issues.

Case or *situation conceptualizations* in social work assessments provide a description of what a client and his or her situation are like as well as an explanation of why the client and the situation are the way they are (Berman, 1997; Eells, 1997). They offer hypotheses about the effects of biological, psychological, and social factors on behavior as it occurs at individual, group, organizational, community, and societal levels. In some contexts, case or situation conceptualizations are referred to as *case formulations* (Eells, 1997). Like any other type of formulation, they offer a systematic way of coming to an explanation or understanding of a problematic situation.

Case or situation formulations vary in terms of the concepts or theories used. There is no one concept for guiding conceptualizations of cases in social work or any other human service profession. "All assessment is guided by some conception that tells investigators where to look, even if it is silent about what they will find" (Peterson, 1992, p. 128). Based on the findings from the hypotheses generated in case formulations, practitioners of social work design plans of prevention and intervention for individuals, families, groups, communities, organizations, and societies.

There are no universal concepts or theories that must be used in conceptualizing persons, behaviors, problems, and situations (Peterson, 1992). However, research has documented that practitioners commonly apply preferred theoretical orientations in developing case formulations (Beutler & Harwood, 1995). Not very long ago, case or situation formulations in social work were guided by grand theories of change and development typically named after their originators: Freud, Erikson, Mead, Merton, Parsons, Perlman, Rank, Richmond, and so on. They were considered grand theories because each provided powerful frameworks that guided all the questions used by practitioners in gathering information needed to understand issues involving human behavior (Renninger & Amsel, 1997). However, "competing theories have existed side by side, and integration of theories has seldom or ever taken place" (Magnusson & Torestad, 1992, p. 89).

The presenting problems and social issues encountered by social work practitioners can be extremely complex. Any single theory will almost certainly be incapable of accounting for the whole range of forces influencing a person's behavior in the social environment (Lyons, Wodarski, & Feit, 1998). Various approaches to assessing human behavior have guided the activities of social work professionals. These approaches include medical, psychoanalytic, social-learning, social-group, community and organizational, normative, and ecological systems. They direct the way practitioners define problems and seek solutions.

The following Focus section reviews theories of social functioning relevant to the cases used in opening this chapter.

FOCUS ON THEORY

▼

Approaches to Assessing Social Functioning

Some of you may have noticed a pattern in the descriptions of the cases that opened the chapter. All the "A" statements are similar; all the "B" statements are similar; and so on.

The (A) descriptions represent the *medical approach*. This approach is directed toward treatment of identified diseases and disorders. The medical approach implies that "health" is the absence of a disorder or disease. Diagnosis of a problem is based on criteria that define disorders in the *Diagnostic and*

Statistical Manual of the American Psychiatric Association, Fourth Edition (DSM-IV). Although the first case does not have a DSM-IV diagnosis, the A statement in that case does assume the presence of a disorder attributed to organizations; that is, it relies on a disease metaphor in structuring its description of the organizational difficulties expressed in this case illustration.

Limitations: The major drawback of this approach is its focus on prevention or treatment of disorder or disease; problems of living are essentially ignored. Thus the danger ensues that a problem of living may be treated as a disease or a medical condition. For example, normal anxiety over a divorce could be treated with medication designed for anxiety disorders in spite of the absence of an actual anxiety disorder. The medical approach is also basically person-centered; it ignores many personal troubles that are fundamentally a result of variables in a person's external environment.

(B) statements represent the *psychodynamic approach.* This approach, of course, is based on the work of Freud and the theoretical modifications in analytical traditions including ego psychology. The focus is on identifying causes of symptom behavior, and the different approaches in this tradition debate the fundamental causes of many human-behavior problems. Assessment focuses on symptoms and identifying the causes of the symptoms. Such causes could be traumatic life events or past experiences; for example, depression could be attributed to loss of a loved one or to anger turned inward. Intervention is concerned with eliminating symptom behavior.

Limitations: The danger of this approach is that it may increase the number of pathological labels assigned to clients based on questionable assumptions about theoretical **etiology,** or the study of the origins and causes of diseases. That is, the focus of this approach is on identifying causes of symptoms rather than on describing the presences of clusters of signs and symptoms associated with an established system of disease classification, such as in the case of A responses.

The (C) statements represent the *learning approach.* This approach assumes that people learn adaptive and maladaptive functioning. Intervention is based on the client's learning new behavior by manipulating events and consequences that maintain adaptive and maladaptive forms of behavior.

Limitations: The learning approach focuses only on behavior. It does not take into account affective dimensions that are considered an important component of the human experience, and it ignores the role emotions can play in motivating behavior. It also overlooks the contributions of genetics and other biological determinants of human behavior that place individuals, families, and groups at risk for developing a number of negative life outcomes.

(D) statements represent *social, group, community, and organizational approaches.* The focus in each of these approaches is on the contributions of the structure and function of social relationships on problems in human behavior. That is, these approaches assess how conflicts in the normative environment contribute to problem behaviors. In addition, they focus on how relations with other persons influence individual, family, group, and societal behavior.

Limitations: The problem with these approaches is that explanations for behavior are limited to factors extrinsic to the person. An individual's intrinsic factors are often held constant and are not assumed to play a pivotal role in variations in observed behavior. In other words, these approaches exclude from consideration the contributions of biological factors and other important individual differences intrinsic to an individual's biological and psychological systems. To state this another way: Interventions based on these approaches focus on changing external factors without consideration of important intrinsic personal characteristics.

(E) responses represent the *normative,* or *utopian, approach.* This approach is also often referred to in the social and behavioral science literature as the *moral model.* Here the focus is on moral expectations or ideals as defined by some utopian view of people and their behavior.

Limitations: There is little agreement about what is considered moral, ideal, or normal behavior. For instance, members of some cultures may think female circumcision is the ideal way to protect a women's position in society, while other cultures see this behavior as a form of oppression. In this approach, making judgments about behavior is not based on knowledge but on values or ideals.

If all persons and situations were alike, applications of grand theories would be sufficient to guide social work activities in conceptualizing cases. However, in social work, we know that all individuals and their situations have unique characteristics that are subject to principles of diversification. Diversification involves any processes that contribute to the variations observed in people and environments. People come from different ethnic backgrounds; have different likes and dislikes; convey various attitudes and prejudices; are different colors, shapes, and sizes; have different predispositions and vulnerabilities; and come with distinct developmental histories. Individuals and their environments cannot escape processes of diversification, especially those relating to time (age, history, and timing considerations). Indeed, diversification in people and their environments makes the world interesting (Duffy & Wong, 1996). However the complexity of diversification processes forces social workers to address factors like sexual orientation, gender, cultural background, personal biographies, and so on in designing change strategies. Such factors contribute to observed variations in behavior not addressed by many of the grand theories of human behavior.

One of the fundamental threats to the integration of theories in conceptualizing human behavior is the practice of seeking the determinants of human behavior either in external social conditions or in the internal dispositions of persons (Bronfenbrenner, 1996; The Carolina Consortium on Human Development, 1996; Magnusson & Cairns, 1996; Magnusson & Torestad, 1992). This book takes issue with accepting any one particular approach to human behavior, whether it be person-centered or environment-centered. A key theme in this book is that human behavior cannot be understood by isolating the internal variables of persons from the external variables in their environments. This dual focus on internal and external variables in transactions is an orientation to conceptualizing human behavior that has dominated the thinking of social workers since the 1950s (Boehm, 1958; Butler, 1959; Hyde & Murphy, 1955; Perlman, 1959) and is what distinguishes social work from many other professions and disciplines in the social sciences.

The following Focus section uses current events to illustrate that behavior cannot be understood by isolating people or events from their environment.

FOCUS ON THE SOCIAL ENVIRONMENT

School Shootings and Noticeable Gaps in the News

When white middle-class kids kill, there is always an outcry of why and a search for what went wrong, but when inner-city minority kids kill, the public is warned of demons and superpredators."—Alvin Poussaint, M.D. (Dowdy, 1998)

In October of 1997, Luke Woodham killed his mother and then went to school and killed three students and wounded seven in Pearl, Mississippi. In that same year, Michael Carneal killed three students at a high school prayer meeting in West Paducah, Kentucky. This trend of school shootings did not end in 1997. In March of 1998, Mitchell Johnson and Andrew Golden killed four students and a teacher in Jonesboro, Arkansas. This tragedy was followed by a shooting in Edinboro, Pennsylvania at an eighth-grade graduation dance. This dance ended when a 14-year-old boy named Andrew Wurst shot and killed a teacher and wounded another teacher and two students. On May 21, 1998, Kip Kinkel walked into a school cafeteria in Springfield, Oregon and shot 24 students; two of these students died.

James Garbarino (1999), who is an expert on human development in areas of violence and trauma, considers the year between 1997 and 1998 a turning point in our country's experience and understanding of kids who murder. All the incidents we just listed were committed by white youths from the suburbs or small rural towns. The public is now recognizing that violence is not limited to urban areas with high concentrations of minority youths.

What is it about a society and its media that ignores similar violent tragedies involving youths from racial and ethnic minority populations? What about the Hispanic youth who opens fire on a street full of children with an automatic weapon, or the African-American kid who shoots two boys who made fun of his shoes, or the Asian-American kids who open fire on a store where other kids from school are hanging out? We rarely see demands by the media and other social institutions to make sense of these acts of violence. "Is it easier for the media and the general public to forget or demonize the low-income minority kids who kill?" (Garbarino, 1999; p. 3).

Since the publication of James Garbarino's book *Lost Boys: Why Our Sons Turn Violent and How We Can Save Them,* there have been additional school shootings in Colorado and in Georgia. The most noteworthy of these events is probably the Columbine High School shootings in the town of Littleton, Colorado in which 14 people were killed, including the two perpetrators. The two assailants in this tragedy were members of a group of outcasts known in the school as the Trenchcoat Mafia. Although this group is considered to be a youth gang by some theorists, its upper-middle-class members have escaped being branded with many of the negative labels commonly assigned to members of urban gangs.

The differences in the ways various groups in society respond to events involving violent human behavior illustrate that social workers cannot underestimate the role played by social environmental factors in understanding social and behavioral issues.

The field of social work has historically assumed that social problems, such as school shootings, cannot be understood by limiting analysis to the inner life of the perpetrators and their relationships to family or close friends. Events of this nature are not isolated errors in socialization processes or the result of intrinsically bad individuals. Such perpetrators are part of an environment that influences their behavior, as well as how we react to them.

Why Do Social Workers Study Human Behavior and the Social Environment?

What influences our behavior? What makes us act in certain ways? Is it our biological makeup, our psychological characteristics, or our social setting? As you will learn in this book, human behavior takes place in a diverse array of physical, psychological, and social contexts. In these contexts, people confront biological, psychological, and social demands that require effective human responses. The ability to respond effec-

tively to these demands on individuals, families, and groups is known as **adaptation.**

Understanding the process of adaptation is vital to practice in any human-service profession. In the field of social work, Human Behavior and the Social Environment (HBSE) is the curriculum area that provides the foundation of knowledge needed for a basic understanding of human adaptation.

The study of adaptation in social work focuses on identifying concepts that can aid practitioners in improving the fit between the behavior of people and the demands and constraints imposed on them by their environments. The kinds of person-environment relations that are of most interest to social workers are the ones most likely to enhance or inhibit adaptation. In spite of this commitment to understanding adaptation, some forms of adaptation are of less interest to social-work professionals than others. For instance, the issues and mechanisms of change involved in the adaptation of transplanted fetal cells to the brains of persons with Parkinson's disease is of less substantive interest to social-work practitioners than are issues involving changes in various forms of social adaptation.

Social work, unlike many other human-service professions, sees social adaptation as one of its primary areas of expertise. In social life, people must adapt to many occurrences and situations. "Personal relationships, changes in work schedules and living habits, and major happenings such as war, a poor economy, or a natural disaster are some of the events that require good coping skills from almost everyone, no matter how healthy or disabled" (Duffy & Wong, 1996, p. 94). Adaptation to such factors can be enhanced by expanding the niche (suitable life space) in the person's environment or by increasing the person's behavioral competence in adapting to environmental factors.

Human behavior in social work is often viewed as the adaptation of people to resources and circumstances. Resources are an important component of many practice perspectives in social work. Altering the availability of resources allows for corrections in adaptations through (a) the creation of new services to enhance adaptations and (b) the identification of strengths in people or their social networks so that conditions can be changed to enhance the use of these available resources (Levine & Perkins, 1997). For example, "the increasing number of young, unemployed

African-American males, the correlated absent father families and the concentration of social problems such as crime in certain urban areas can be attributed at least in part to a changed job market and to the loss of access to jobs, a critical resource for favorable adaptation" (Levine & Perkins, 1997; p. 5). In other words, social workers and other human-service professionals attempt to develop or improve the personal and the social resources of their clients.

Most students of social work have taken courses in anthropology, economics, human biology, psychology, political science, and sociology. These courses present a variety of approaches, concepts, and frames of reference for understanding human behavior, the social environment, and problems in living. Some texts focus on understanding the attributes and characteristics of people, as well as the kinds of changes they undergo across the life span, while others focus on explaining changes in peoples' environments and how these changes affect individual human behavior. These texts are fine as far as they go. However, social workers also need a framework for practice to help them organize the rapidly expanding body of knowledge from the behavioral, social, and health sciences to be able to assess whether behavior is adaptive or maladaptive.

This book introduces social work students to a multidimensional framework for integrating knowledge and theory from the *biological, psychological,* and *social perspectives* on human behavior. We stress the need for social workers to take into account the interactions of these three dimensions in assessing social functioning. Of course, other dimensions remain relevant to understanding behavior—for example, the spiritual and ecological (physical environmental) dimensions. We include these dimensions, but only as domains or variables relevant to assessing variations in behavior due to issues of *diversity* in persons and environments. For instance, the Focus sections cover the subjects of ethics, personal narratives, policy, research, and theory, and deal with spirituality, sexual orientation, ethnic background, and so on. These variables are important in explaining and understanding many forms of adaptation encountered by the clients of social workers. As an example, the following Focus section, written by a social work educator, addresses important issues involving the role of spirituality in assessing human behavior.

FOCUS ON SPIRITUALITY

The Spiritual Dimension in Assessing Human Behavior

What do we mean by "spirituality"? Why is it important for social workers to understand people's **spiritual dimension** of experience along with the biological, psychological, and social dimensions?

Spirituality is the domain of human experience that pertains to the human essence, the very core of personhood and its relationship to something greater than oneself. Human beings call this "something" by many names. Whatever name we use, it is our relationship to something greater than ourselves and the way each of us perceives it that enable us to make sense of our lives and provide us with a sense of stability, guidance, power, and direction (Bullis, 1996; Schuster & Ashburn, 1992).

Whereas "spirituality" refers to subjective experiences of relationship to something greater than ourselves, religion refers to formal, institutionalized systems of belief that include dogmas, creeds, denominational identity, and rituals (Bullis, 1996; Zastro & Kirst-Ashman, 1990). Most religions maintain that human beings experience a process of spiritual development over time (Swinburne, 1986). Depending on the religion, this development may take place over the course of one or many lifetimes. Some human-development theorists (Erikson, 1988; Fowler, 1981; Goldman, 1968) have adopted this developmental view of spirituality and have attempted to describe stages of spiritual development that parallel stages of development in the biological, psychological, and social domains.

The word "psychology" comes from the Greek word *psyche* meaning "spirit" or "soul." Taken literally, "psychology" means the study of the spirit or soul. These linguistic connections reflect a belief, common to many cultures and religions, that spirituality and human development are inextricably intertwined.

There are several reasons why the spiritual domain is relevant to social work practice. First, contemporary social work is informed by the idea that individuals create spiritual belief systems that give meaning and organization to their experience (Anderson &

Goolishian, 1992; Dudley & Helfgott, 1990). Theologian and social work theorist Ronald Bullis (1996) concludes that, in a clinical sense, our beliefs about ourselves and our world are the "spirits" that inform our feelings and actions and ultimately become our personal realities. Similarly, cognitive theory, which is based on constructivism, maintains that attention to the "unique private meanings the client holds in relation to the problem and its context validates the client and provides the shared awareness and meaning base from which the client and the social worker collaboratively proceed" (Granvold, 1995, p. 526). This is why giving thoughtful attention to clients' spiritual concerns is central to the empowerment model of social work practice (Hartman, 1994). Conversely, if social workers do not recognize the importance of spiritual beliefs and their significance, clients' constructions of their own experience may be subjugated to "expert" professional interpretations. If such subjugation occurs, social workers are perpetuating oppressive conditions rather than empowering their clients (Foucault, 1980; Pinderhughes, 1994).

Second, attention to the spiritual as well as the biopsychosocial domains of human behavior completes the holistic approach required by the ecological perspective of social work (Hartman, 1994). The life challenges that bring individuals to helping professionals may also cause them to seek meaning and guidance in spiritual beliefs and practices, which raises spiritual issues. For example, a study by Greif & Porembski (1988) found that a renewed or continued faith in God was an important factor for individuals, families, and friends coping with AIDS.

Third, because of the perceived spiritual basis of their physical and psychological symptoms, many individuals will consult a religious or folk healer for spiritual healing instead of or in addition to seeking help from a health care professional. In fact, the use of healers in the non-Western world is so widespread that it is the backbone of the rural health care system (Gupta, 1993). In the United States, several studies have indicated that Americans overall are much more likely to pray, read scripture, or talk to a religious healer than to seek help from a mental health professional (Gallup & Castelli, 1989; Gurin, Veroof, & Felds, 1960; Mollica et al., 1986). A holistic approach requires that social workers be prepared to explore spiritual issues and

remedies. Social workers must also be prepared to consult, coordinate services with, and collaborate with religious and folk healers who may be clients' primary source of mental health care. Otherwise, important information and coping resources will remain untapped.

A fourth reason for social workers to attend to the spiritual domain is that doctrines that condemn people who believe differently continue to be a major source of intolerance, discrimination, and oppression. Accordingly, social workers attempting to understand and counteract oppression must be sensitive to the oppressive aspects of spiritual beliefs, beginning with their own (Zastrow & Kirst-Ashman, 1997).

Fifth, many contemporary social issues have religious dimensions. For example, in working with client's concerns related to abortion, use of contraceptives, acceptance of gays and lesbians, cloning, reproductive technology, roles of women, prayer in public schools, and physician-assisted suicide, social workers must be prepared to include discussion of spiritual concerns (Bullis, 1996).

Finally, given the central role of spirituality in many cultures, the spiritual domain will have an effect on what takes place between social worker and client (Green, 1994), whether or not spirituality is openly discussed (Canda, 1989). If client and social worker come from different spiritual orientations, language and behavior may have different meanings. Therefore, understanding the client's spiritual beliefs is essential to culturally competent practice (Green, 1994).

Historically, social work has deep roots in religious tradition. The 19th-century charitable and philanthropical organizations that became the foundation of the social work profession were inspired by Judeo-Christian beliefs. Nevertheless, social work has evolved as a secular profession, and social workers have chosen to treat religion and spiritual issues as private concerns beyond the scope of the biopsychosocial perspective (Sanzenbach, Canda, & Joseph, 1989). Accordingly, the topic of spirituality has received little attention in the social work literature and curriculum. Although some social work theorists have argued that spirituality should be considered part of the discipline (Canda, 1989; Joseph, 1988; Sheridan et al., 1992; Siporin, 1986), and journals such as *Spirituality and Social Work* have emerged, the social work literature generally fails to acknowledge the importance of spirituality to social work practice (Lowenberg, 1988). With few exceptions, social work human-behavior texts either make no mention of spirituality as a factor in human development or mention spirituality only in the context of particular ethnic groups or life situations.

Several possible explanations exist for the fact that social workers have generally overlooked the spiritual domain of their clients' experience (Green, 1994). First, the field of social work developed in a historical period in which the social sciences and the helping professions were dominated by logical positivism, which maintained that scientific approaches to addressing human problems required objectively measuring and quantifying human experience. Because the spiritual domain could not be quantified, its usefulness in explaining and solving human problems was discounted. Second, social work followed the lead of the medical model, which historically has treated spiritual beliefs as delusions or as evidence of immaturity, escapism, or neurosis (Freud, 1953; Stenfels, 1994). Although the latest version of the American Psychiatric Association's DSM-IV recognizes spiritual problems as "a category of concern distinct from any mental disorder," it is still "pathologizing" spiritual dilemmas as "other conditions that may be a focus of clinical attention" (American Psychiatric Association, 1994). Third, a significant spiritual gap exists between helping professionals and the general population. For example, separate studies indicated that only 43% of the American Psychiatric Association's membership (American Psychiatric Association, 1995) and 66% of psychologists (Meyers & Jeeves, 1987) believe in God, whereas an overwhelming 94% of the general population reports believing in God (Gallup & Castelli, 1989). A more recent study indicated that social workers are much less likely than their clients to rely on spiritual beliefs and practices (Bullis, 1996).

Although social work has evolved as a secular profession, in recent years social workers have become increasingly aware of the relevance of the spiritual domain to the field. This increasing awareness is reflected in the most recent Curriculum Policy Statement of the Council on Social Work Education (1992), which requires that accredited baccalaureate and master's programs provide practice content related to spirituality. Attention to the spiritual dimension of human behavior is also becoming more apparent in the social work lit-

erature. For example, a recent study of Virginia social workers found that a relatively high percentage of social workers addressed spiritual issues in practice: 62% explored their clients' spiritual backgrounds; 24% recommended spiritual books; 41% recommended participation in spiritual programs; and 45% helped clients explore spiritual values. Sheridan, Bullis, Adcock, Berlin, and Miller (1992) studied the extent to which social workers and clients consider spiritual concerns to be either problematic or helpful. Berthold (1989) identified the sources of illnesses attributed to spiritual causes. Other writers have described ways to incorporate into interventions spiritual practices such as meditation (Bullis, 1996; Keefe, 1986), prayer (Canda, 1990), shamanism, (Canda, 1983), and spiritism (Berthold, 1989).

In her classic, *Common Human Needs,* Charlotte Towle asserted that spiritual needs "must be seen as distinct needs, and they must also be seen in relation to other human needs" (Towle, 1945, p. 8). Many years later, the social work profession, long estranged from its spiritual roots, is now beginning to come full circle and reawaken to the importance of the spiritual dimension of human experience.

Margaret Waller

DIMENSIONS OF HUMAN BEHAVIOR AND THE SOCIAL ENVIRONMENT

What are appropriate measures for assessing human behavior? Are there different measures for assessing the social environment (Friedman & Wachs, 1999)? Social work practitioners must be clear about how they will systematically assess, measure, or describe the characteristics of their clients and their various life troubles. These activities are significantly influenced by the perspective of the social worker. As Anderson and Carter (1998) note, any viewpoint is relative to one's own perceptions and to the system being described, as well as to its environment. Social work professionals seek a perspective of human behavior that is consistent with the principles of their professional code of ethics, their commitments to respecting individual uniqueness, the strengths and empowerment perspectives, ecological theory, and principles from general systems theory.

Many terms can be used to classify or define the dimensions of individuals and their environments. Sciences also have systems for classifying and measuring areas of interest. The science of social work practice is no exception. Practitioners from this profession are expected to use empirically validated classifications of behavior that transcend the biases associated with "common sense" and other forms of "conventional wisdom." These scientific classifications are needed to make important distinctions about client functioning. If practitioners lack categories or classifications for making such distinctions, they are unlikely to understand their clients' needs and concerns. Although social work has not established a unified system of human behavior classification, it has advocated the use of a biopsychosocial approach to understanding human behavior and the social environment.

The framework that we use in this textbook subscribes to this approach. It is conceived of as a perspective and not as a theory. This perspective offers practitioners a way to consider various points of view and to integrate these points of view in their assessments of human behavior as it occurs at individual, family, group, organizational, community and societal levels. The biopsychosocial approach is based on principles from systems thinking that assume that "[e]ach person is composed of molecules, cells and organs; each person is also a member of a family, community, culture, nation and world" (Eisendrath, 1988, p. 36). The fundamental assumptions underlying this framework are as follows:

1. There are three basic dimensions for assessing human behavior and the social environment: biophysical, psychological, and social.

2. These three dimensions are conceptualized as a system of biopsychosocial functioning.

3. This system involves multiple systems that are organized in a hierarchy of levels from the smallest (cellular) to the largest (social).

4. This ascending hierarchy of systems is in a constant state of interaction with other living systems and with other nonliving components of the system's physical environment.

We assume that the multiple systems in this framework are needed to guide practitioners in understanding human behavior. They incorporate units of analysis

for assessing the interaction of person-in-environment transactions. "The interactive process takes place at various levels from micro to macro at the same time, and at all these levels it can be analyzed theoretically and empirically using two perspectives: current and developmental" (Magnusson & Torestad, 1992, p. 91). While the **current perspective** involves assessing how biological, psychological, and social systems influence current states of affairs, the **developmental perspective** focuses on how these systems interact in leading up to the current state of affairs. These dimensions provide perspectives on human behavior that form the bases for various kinds of intervention strategies. They also allow social workers to maintain their commitment to taking into account strengths and competencies in person–environment transactions in designing intervention strategies. Practitioners all too often focus on presenting problems and fail to zero in on areas of strength that can facilitate change in a person's situation (Saleebey, 1992b).

A framework for assessment that includes multiple dimensions is much more likely to recognize individuals in their totality than is a framework that focuses on only one dimension. When individuals are seen in their totality, there is less of a danger that issues involving client strengths will be ignored in planning change efforts. Frameworks that see individuals in their totality are also consistent with social work's distinct commitment to an emphasis on ameliorating problems involving social functioning.

WHAT IS SOCIAL FUNCTIONING?

Werner Boehm (1958) made a major contribution to social work's knowledge base by clarifying social work's focus. Before the late 1950s, the profession lacked an explicit focus for understanding *persons, problems, and behavior* that was different from that of other human-service professionals. Boehm (1958, p. 14) wrote that "both the complexity of man's [sic] functioning and the increase of scientific specialization have made it necessary for each profession to take one aspect of man's [sic] functioning as the primary focus of its activities." In Boehm's view, whereas the physician focuses on enhancing the client's physical functioning, the social worker should focus on enhancing the client's social functioning.

Werner Boehm, the developer of the social functioning framework.

Social functioning is a technical term in social work that supports the profession's focus on person-in-environment transactions. Social functioning "involves addressing common human needs that must be adequately met to enable individuals to achieve a reasonable degree of fulfillment and to function as productive and contributing members of society" (Hepworth & Larsen, 1993, p. 5).

The concept of social functioning developed by Boehm had roots in social interaction theory and role theory. These theories assume that through the performance of social roles people achieve a sense of self-worth and belonging with others. When people fail to locate themselves correctly in their social environment, this violates the expectations of others. "Failure and disappointment with oneself and the reactions of others to oneself are critical in locating oneself within the 'normative' ecology (i.e., to answering the question 'How well am I doing')" (Levine & Perkins, 1997, p. 206). When the person concludes that he or she is not doing well, then this forces him or her to make appropriate adaptations (Levine & Perkins, 1997). The social-functioning perspective directs social workers to focus on factors relevant to the performance

of roles expected of individuals by virtue of their participation in various social groups. In this perspective, the point of connection between persons and environments is the social role. In other words, the social role is the structure that links individuals with various social systems. This emphasis on role behavior allows for a shift in focus from the individual to the interaction of the individual with various social systems in assessing human behavior concerns. This shift in the orientation of the social work assessment opened the door for developing other perspectives that took into account social roles and other components of interactional theory.

The following Focus section describes the dual perspective, which was developed by Norton and other social work educators to integrate knowledge about the multiple role expectations experienced by minority clients within the context of the dominant culture.

The Dual Perspective

The **dual perspective** is a cognitive approach for understanding the behavior, attitudes, and response patterns of minority clients within the context of the dominant culture. This approach seeks to acknowledge the fact that every person is a member of two systems: the dominant societal system and the system involving the client's immediate emotional, physical, and social environment. According to the dual perspective, these two systems are referred to as the *sustaining system* and the *nurturing system*. (See Figure 1.1.) Social workers need to understand this duality. These systems represent the experiences of all minority persons, and practitioners have the duty of assessing the degrees of convergence and divergence between these systems.

As stated, social workers must understand the normal expectations for behavior, attitudes, and values in the sustaining system as well as in the nurturing system. Normal expectations for childhood in the sustaining system may differ from expectations in the nurturing system. For example, children from ethnic minority homes and children in the majority culture will experience different processes that influence self-development. These different developmental processes affect children's views of themselves and how they evaluate themselves against their peers to establish a sense of self-esteem. If these differences are ignored, interventions are not likely to address children's real psychosocial needs, and the children's engagement in appropriate intervention plans will likely be inhibited.

Latino children live in the Latino community and the wider American community. The problems they and other minority group members encounter require social workers to be sensitive to the dual perspective. This perspective provides a cognitive device for increasing the awareness of the experiences, values, and beliefs of these persons; however, it cannot be implemented without a solid foundation of facts, events, and issues about various ethnic and racial groups. The developers of this perspective assumed that the appropriate content should be provided in Human Behavior and the Social Environment courses.

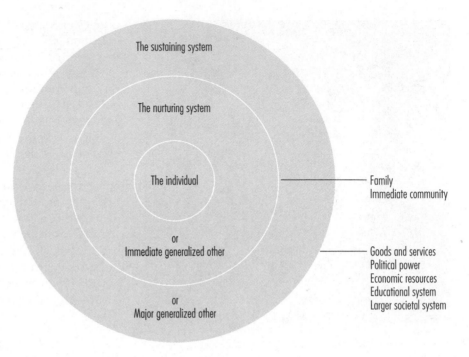

FIGURE 1.1   Key systems in the dual perspective (Norton et al., 1978)

SOCIAL COMPETENCE MODELS AND STRENGTHS PERSPECTIVE

Boehm's (1959, p. 31) social functioning framework led to the formulation of five major educational objectives for social workers in the curriculum area of Human Behavior and the Social Environment:

1. Understanding biological endowment (genes, dispositions, and so forth) as the source of the potential for human functioning

2. Understanding environmental forces that may enhance or endanger the potential for social functioning

3. Understanding interaction of endowment and environmental forces as enhancing or endangering the potential for social functioning

4. Understanding the person's response to change and stress

5. Understanding assessment of the potential for social functioning

This social functioning framework is often reflected in social competence models of human behavior. Wine and Smye (1981) pointed out that, in competence models, humans are seen as growing, changing, learning, and in continuous interaction with their environments. "While defect models tune their users to the observation of pathology, the users of competence models are more likely to be alert to positive behaviors and capacities in individuals. . . . People are seen as at least potentially capable of setting goals, identifying needs, and developing skills that will allow them to cope more effectively with stress" (pp. 24–25).

Competence models focus on helping people achieve their potential and on understanding the normal stresses and demands that environmental transactions place on people. "The defining characteristic of competence approaches is a concern with the effectiveness of the individual's interactions with the environment" (Wine & Smye, 1981, p. 24). Exponents of competence models are more likely to subscribe to what Garvin and Seabury (1984) have termed a *nature metaphor*. In this meta-phor, the focus is on issues of growth and decay and not on deviations. Interventions derived from this metaphor focus on balancing, fitting, and matching human capabilities with environmental demands (Garvin & Seabury, 1984). This metaphor differs from disease metaphors, which stress treatment and the elimination of causes of disease. The social functioning framework eventually developed by Ruth Butler (1970) is highly compatible with the nature metaphor. In fact, it was developed to replace frameworks in the social and the behavioral sciences that rely strictly on disease and/or pathology metaphors.

Psychiatry and psychology have historically focused on the weaknesses and problems of individuals. Robert White (1959) was the first theorist to write about the concept of competence in psychology. By **competence,** he meant a person's sense of mastery or control when interacting with the environment. His conception of competence assumes that it is a basic desire or motive for people to seek a sense of competence. No one likes to feel incompetent; instead people like to feel a sense of strength that comes from mastering the demands of the environment (Duffy & Wong, 1996). For instance, you may recall the enjoyment you felt when you first learned how to ride a bike unassisted by training wheels or a nearby adult. The joy experienced in such circumstances of mastery is due to what White (1959) termed *competence*.

Social work also supports competence conceptions, but there are increased calls in the social work literature for the addition of a "strengths perspective" (Weick, 1992). "Central to this view is a belief in people's inherent capacity to transform themselves by getting in touch with their own natural resources" (Weick, 1992, pp. 22–23). How the **strengths perspective** differs from competence perspectives is in the history of their respective origins and their acceptance of professional expertise. Strengths perspectives in social work are less hospitable to approaches to change that rely on expertise external to the people or persons in need. As a consequence, they are also less supportive of problem-solving models of practice. However, both of these perspectives recognize the important role played by resources in the adaptations of people to various conditions in their environment.

Tasks and Life Demands

The emphasis in a social competence model is on helping clients realize their potential. Social workers need to understand the demands and life tasks that people encounter if they are to help people realize their personal and social aspirations. To this end, Bartlett (1970) suggested the concept of tasks to assist workers in assessing their clients' life situations. The

This college student's life in a dorm illustrates how she is part of two distinct cultures with different perspectives—the dominant society's system and her own Latin cultural background.

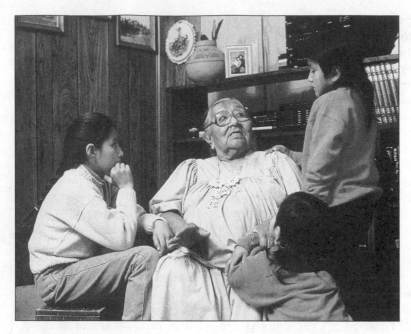

Grandparents transmit the wisdom of their generation to their grandchildren by teaching them stories, songs, customs, and beliefs. This wisdom is an important strength that social workers cannot overlook. (Newman & Newman, 1999)

concept of tasks plays a key role in social functioning and in social competence frameworks. By asking the question "What tasks are confronting my client?" the worker can focus on key biopsychosocial demands. For instance, what biopsychosocial demands confront a half-Asian youth in America in achieving a sense of identity during adolescence? What tasks confront a 16-year-old girl who is losing her hair while undergoing chemotherapy? Each adolescent is confronting distinct biopsychosocial demands. The social worker must understand all these demands to help each youth adapt to the social environment.

The concept of developmental tasks was introduced into scientific discourse by Havighurst (1948; 1954). Since his work in this area, many attempts have been made by developmental scientists to provide an inventory of the developmental tasks individuals need to complete during the course of their life (Heymans, 1994). However, these efforts have been criticized by some developmentalists because the concept presupposes what it is also supposed to explain (Heymans, 1994). In fact, the concept of developmental tasks went

out of favor for a while in the field of psychology but witnessed a major revival during the 1980s in the field of life-span development (Heymans, 1994). The newer versions of developmental tasks do not merely provide descriptions of tasks that people must complete; they also offer concepts that provide explanations of factors or processes that lead to specific developmental outcomes. One such approach to developmental tasks is embodied in Heymans's (1986) *Symbolic Structuring of Lives,* which employs a number of assumptions from Harré's (1983) dramaturgical model of human performances. This model assumes that successful completion of tasks rest with whether a person can successfully convince an audience of his or her competence.

Maluecio (1981) points out that competence is also a theme present in the writings of several pioneers in social work education, including Mary Richmond (1917) and Bertha Reynolds (1942). Although these pioneers addressed competence concerns, competence was primarily an implicit component of their approaches. In response to this lack of specificity, Maluccio (1981) introduced an ecological approach to competence that supercedes many of the prior conceptual frameworks on this topic in social work. His ecological competence model has three major components: capacities and skills, motivational aspects, and environmental qualities. These components represent Maluccio's attempt to conceptualize the multiple dimensions of competence and their dynamic interplay. For many social workers, this model provides an excellent conceptual approach for assessing person–environment transactions. In fact, we believe that the ecological systems theory is the best overall framework for social work practice (LeCroy, 1999).

If social workers are to focus their activities on enhancing individuals' responses to their life tasks, should they also understand disease and pathology metaphors? That is, should practitioners direct their activities toward treating and correcting client deviations or pathologies? We believe that the answer to this question is yes. We take this position because illness and pathology often affect a person's social functioning.

For instance, clients with schizophrenia have significantly impaired effectiveness in role functioning. Practitioners must understand how this disorder affects the clients' abilities. Equipped with this knowledge, social workers can better focus their activities on enhancing clients' skills to meet the demands of their environment. The social worker's duty, regardless of the particular field of practice, is to select the right view of behavior for the right circumstance.

See the following Focus section on diversity for a critical assessment of the consequences of psychiatric diagnosis on persons from different cultural backgrounds written by a social work professor.

FOCUS ON DIVERSITY

▼

Psychiatric Diagnosis and Cultural Diversity

Psychiatric diagnosis has been controversial for many years. Some of the most enduring criticisms revolve around issues of stigmatization, definitions of mental illness, and the unreliability of the DSM system. Given these issues, psychiatric diagnosis is an important topic for social work professionals.

The reliability of psychiatric diagnosis has been severely challenged over the years. The DSM has also been criticized because of its inadequate scientific foundation and unreliability (Kirk & Kutchins, 1992). Kirk and Kutchins (1994) wrote, "[t]he psychiatric bible is filled with nonsense and applies no coherent standard of what constitutes a mental disorder."

Perhaps the best-known study attesting to the unreliability of psychiatric diagnosis and the inability to identify mental illness was conducted by Rosenhan (1973). His study devastated the psychiatric community. This study looked at admissions procedures at mental hospitals around the country. Rosenhan wanted to know what would happen if normal individuals applied for psychiatric admission. He made arrangements for his associates to present themselves at 12

different hospitals and gave them instructions on how to behave (for example, complain of hearing voices). All pseudopatients were diagnosed as severely disordered and admitted. When they acted normal none of the hospital staff noticed or realized that they should not have been admitted. The only people who became aware of the experiment were the real patients. The pseudopatients were hospitalized for an average of 19 days. One woman became so frustrated with the situation that she began taking notes about her experiences. She was given an additional diagnosis of having "compulsive handwriting."

After Rosenhan's study was published, he alerted another mental hospital that he would be sending pseudopatients to the hospital between January and March. This hospital admitted 193 patients during this period, and 43 were classified as pseudopatients. However, Rosenhan had not sent any pseudopatients (Rosenhan, 1973).

A study conducted by Morey and Ochoa (1989) provides further evidence that psychiatric diagnosis can be unreliable and biased. When clinicians in this study were asked to make a diagnosis of borderline personality disorder, clinicians who were either less experienced or female diagnosed this disorder more frequently than the criteria indicated. Experienced clinicians and male clinicians made the diagnosis of the borderline personality disorder less frequently than the criteria indicated. In addition, when the patients were white, female, or poor, they were diagnosed with borderline personality disorder more frequently than the criteria indicated (Morey & Ochoa, 1989).

Cultural diversity becomes a serious issue when social workers try to apply mainstream assessment tools to culturally diverse populations. For this reason, the APA is experimenting with methods for integrating the role of social and cultural variables into the diagnostic process. Cultural assessment assumes that we cannot ignore the interaction between the clinician and the client and their respective cultures in making a diagnosis. To accomplish this goal, one may wish to consider the following questions: (1) What is the primary cultural reference group of the patient? (2) Does the patient use descriptions from his or her original culture to describe the disorder? (3) What kinds of "disabilities" are and are not acceptable in a given culture? (4) Does the clinician understand the first language of the patient as well as the cultural significance of the disorder (Kearney, Weyermann, & Durand, 1995, p. 45)?

Kleinman (1988, pp. 43–44) has also devised a model for eliciting information from a client that focuses on the client's perception of the nature of the problem. He stated that clinicians need to ask: (1) Why has the problem affected you? (2) Why has the illness had its onset now, and what course do you think the illness will follow? (3) How does the illness affect you? (4) What treatment do you think is appropriate, and what treatment do you want? (5) What do you fear most about the illness and its treatment?

Disease-centered psychiatrists are not necessarily receptive to Kleinman's approach, because the client may be viewed as having too much control over the helping process (Castillo, 1997). Traditional training programs in psychiatry teach students to assess and diagnose based on symptomatology and prescribe appropriate medications (Castillo, 1997). There may have been some instances when so-called appropriate medications may not have been so appropriate. To deviate from traditional psychiatric training/practice may raise the issue of heresy. However, these newer approaches to the diagnostic process are consistent with social work's commitment to principles of client empowerment.

Hubert Johnston

The next section describes a model developed by social workers for examining the person in his or her environment that considers social roles an important factor to examine in assessing person–environment transactions.

THE PERSON-IN-ENVIRONMENT SYSTEM

The **person-in-environment (PIE) system** was designed to assess problems in social functioning. It provides social workers with a common classification system for communicating about client problems (Williams, Karls, & Wandrei, 1989). This system uses four factors to describe client problems:

- Factor I: Social-role problems
- Factor II: Environmental problems
- Factor III: Mental disorders
- Factor IV: Physical disorders

All four factors are considered necessary for describing a client's problems. The first two factors address the components in a social-functioning assessment handled primarily by the social work practitioner. In this system, *social functioning* refers to the client's ability to accomplish the tasks necessary for daily living (such as obtaining food, shelter, and transportation) and to fulfill his or her major social roles as defined by the client's community or subculture (Williams, Karls, & Wandrei, 1989). This system sets up explicit categories for identifying problems in social-role functioning and for establishing a list of environmental systems and problem areas. Factor III addresses mental disorders, and Factor IV includes any medical conditions that might affect social functioning.

In the PIE framework, the social worker describes the problems, their severity, and their duration. This framework uses the established categories and codes defined in the manual for describing client problems. Like the DSM-IV, this system operationally defines the categories, terms, and codes used in classifying client problems. Use of this system might increase social workers' reliability in defining social-functioning concerns. Without reliable definitions of social-functioning problems, we cannot accurately assess whether problems are increasing or decreasing. We also lack a shared system for communicating about problems. The PIE system has undergone field tests similar to those applied to the DSM-IV. With the benefit of a universal definition of social functioning, researchers will have an easier task trying to assess the prevalence rates of problems in social functioning typically found in the practice of social work.

The following example illustrates how a complete case would look when the PIE system is applied (based on Williams, Karls, & Wandrei, 1989). This case involves a 68-year-old woman who was admitted to the hospital with fever and confusion. Neighbors reported that the confusion had been increasing over the last few weeks. The patient was diagnosed with a urinary tract infection and was treated with intravenous antibiotics. However, when the medical problem was resolved, the confusion and disorientation was not. Because of this situation, the hospital staff determined that it would not be safe for the woman to return to her apartment alone. But the woman had no savings and only a limited income from social security, so she was unable to afford in-home care. The woman's son wanted to help out, but because of his lifestyle as a musician and single father, he was unable to care for his mother in his own home. The patient was adamant about returning to her own apartment. The social worker obtained a psychiatric evaluation of the woman, which determined that she was suffering from dementia and was unable to make her own decisions. On discharge from the hospital, the social worker and the son, against the patient's wishes, placed the woman in an assisted-living home that was willing to accept the social security payments in exchange for care. Over the next two weeks, the woman, who had always been proud of her independence and strength, became increasingly despondent over her living arrangements.

FACTOR I

Social-role category: other nonfamilial (tenant)

Social-role problem: status/status change

Severity: 4, high

Duration: 5, two weeks or less

Coping skills: 4, inadequate

FACTOR II

Environmental system: economic/basic needs

Environmental problem: shelter and care (unable to care for self in own apartment)

Severity: 4, high

Duration: 5, two weeks or less

FACTOR III

Dementia

FACTOR IV

Urinary tract infection, resolved

On Factor I, the worker indicates the role relationship in which the client is having a problem. The worker also establishes the type of role problem, its severity, and its duration. On Factor II, the worker identifies the physical or social environmental systems affecting the client and the type of problem, its severity, and duration.

A key benefit anticipated from this system, besides research, is a shared approach for communicating and defining client problems that results in improved treatment effectiveness. Other applied models exist for examining person and environment interactions. These other models focus on preventing normal stressors and other life events from turning into negative life destinations or outcomes.

Problems in Living

In addition to recognizing the need for practitioners to understand the consequences of pathology on social functioning, we also assume that social workers should have knowledge of life troubles as normative aspects of everyday life. No one can avoid normal life troubles such as losing a job, losing a friend or family member, having an illness, experiencing interpersonal conflicts, and so on. Human life is just not without troubles, a fact that is also recognized by writers of soap operas. Soap operas "chronicle for the American public the impact of death, disease, divorce, crime and sundry tragedies in the everyday lives of fictional characters" (Levine & Perkins, 1997, p. 12). These chronicles teach people a number of lessons about life including the fact that many problems are inevitable but not insurmountable (Levine & Perkins, 1997).

As social workers, we need to adopt perspectives for assessing these troubles that do not ignore the role played by the wider social context in the creation of many personal troubles. All too often persons are assigned inappropriate moral blame for troubles that are caused by problems in structured social arrangements that are characteristic of the society in which they live. Social work, as a profession, has had a long history of asserting that many troubles that are considered personal are better defined as social problems.

How do we differentiate personal problems from social problems? Are there specific criteria that can help professionals in the human services to define social problems? Unfortunately, there are no simple answers. Problems of life can be defined and experienced at many different levels. A person who falls from his bicycle and scars his face has a problem. But, what kind of problem? Is this a personal problem or a social problem? A problem is considered personal: (a) if it affects only the individual; and (b) if the individual is responsible for the problem. However, many conditions and experiences initially appear as if they affect only an individual but indeed result in part from events and situations that immediately surround that individual.

The following Focus section on narrative demonstrates how personal descriptions of troubles in the lives of ordinary people are connected to variables in their social and economic environment.

This woman, from French-speaking Louisiana, is confronting a personal problem, having lost her husband. Her responses are influenced by socially prescribed customs and coping styles related to death and burial practices.

Life's Troubles

American society embodies a way of life that is not good for all of its members. The structured social arrangements that characterize the way people eat, establish dreams, raise families, make a living, manage conflicts, and engage in love relationships are created by social processes that characterize our society during a particular period of history. The lives of women, persons of color, and the poor are influenced by structured social arrangements that are distinct to our society and the period of history in which such people find themselves. Ethnicity, race, class, and power are all forms of structured social arrangements in the wider social environment that play a fundamental role in the descriptions provided by ordinary people of their lives, needs, and troubles. These factors cannot be ignored by social workers.

For example, Marilyn, a homeless woman, offers a description of the context that low-wage workers encounter in our society in trying to make a living.

> We went and worked on this job a week. The boss said he'd pay us at the end of the week. We were there the day he got $2,500. And he took us to the Tamale House and said he was going to go to the bank and cash the check and come back and pay us, but he never came back and nobody got their money. See, he was a subcontractor and there was four of us working for him. And we got the job done and we were down there waiting for him to come back and pay us.

Homeless persons like Marilyn are easily exploited because they lack the resources to fight the injustices within existing institutions. The relationships of domination and exploitation that are entrenched in our society shape the lives of the less powerful in many different ways.

Frank, age 53, was laid off from five full-time jobs. Each job he was laid off from paid less than the last job did. He held jobs like microwave test supervisor and senior engineering technician. He now earns the minimum wage.

> I come home now and I just don't know what to say to my wife, or to my daughter. I know it's not anything I did wrong. But you have this overpowering sense, this sick feeling that somehow you let everybody down. You have fear.

More and more members of our society are part of what is often termed a *contingent work force,* made up of temporary, part-time, and contract workers. Frank's self-development is highly dependent on changes in the wider economic relationships that influence his quality of life and that of his family.

Safety is another major issue that many workers confront in trying to make a living in our society. Francisco, a disabled assembly-line worker, is now on worker's compensation. His description illustrates how his problems are further compromised by other structured social arrangements that contribute to his troubles.

> I made 2,300 golf clubs a day. I worked 40 hours a week for 10 years . . . I told them about the pain. They said, "if you don't work, you'll get fired." My supervisor would shake his finger at me. He would kick me. He would tell me, "I don't like you because you are Latino." . . . I worked for two years with the pain [because I needed the $5.50 an hour to support my family]. I went to a doctor who told me that little by little the bone had worn away. He said I have a frozen shoulder.

These descriptions of personal troubles all involve some kind of stratification issue. Stratification refers to "the relation of domination and subordination in which powerful people control a disproportionate share of such resources as property and wealth and thus shape the lives of the less powerful." Many forms of racial, class, and gender stratification have been present in our society from its beginnings. Social work, as a profession, is committed to achieving *social and economic justice.* As a consequence, it takes issue with approaches to assessing the relationships between people's troubles and their environments that attribute blame for these problems solely to the individual without consideration of the role played by social and other environmental factors.

(Adapted from Feagin & Feagin, 1997)

During the 1970s, William Ryan (1971) published his book *Blaming the Victim,* which criticized the application of pathological orientations to social problems. This book had a major effect on many social workers. It sensitized them to the limitations of individually oriented views of behavior that placed responsibility for social problems on individuals rather than on defective social institutions. Blaming the victim generally occurs when well-intentioned practitioners set out to identify the causes or differences in the individual that explain personal problems. Approaches that adhere to a blaming-the-victim ideology generally avoid the wider social origins of problems. Individuals are assigned responsibility for a situation that was essentially out of their control. Recognition of the dangers of a blaming-the-victim ideology and of preoccupation with pathology prompted movements in social work toward alternative models.

MODELS OF STRESS AND COPING

Stress is another major concept that plays a fundamental role in understanding many forms of human adaptation. Monat and Lazarus (1977, p. 3) have pointed out that **stress** represents "any event in which environmental demands, internal demands, or both tax or exceed the adaptive resources of an individual, social system, or tissue system." However, *stress* has been defined and used in different ways, depending on the aims of theorists (Weiten, 2000). This complex concept was first studied by Hans Selye (1936; 1956; 1982), a Canadian scientist who spent his entire career researching the body's physical responses to stress. His model of the body's responses to stress is known as the **general adaptation syndrome (GAS).** Professor Selye identified three stages that are associated with this syndrome: the alarm stage, the resistance stage, and the exhaustion stage. In the *alarm stage,* the sympathetic nervous system is activated, which increases the heart rate, respiration, and other physiological processes needed to combat the challenges to the body's adaptive processes. This response has also been characterized as the *fight-or-flight response* (Weiten, 2000). The second stage, the *resistance phase,* involves the body trying to resist the stress when it persists over a period of time. During this phase, it appears as if the individual is doing fine. However, the person's bodily defenses are actually beginning to erode (Duffy & Wong, 1996). In the final stage, *exhaustion* is reached. Exhaustion occurs because the body's resources for combating stress are limited. After the exhaustion is reached, arousal decreases and so does one's capacity for resistance, which results in disease as an adaptation to the biological threat or challenge (Weiten, 2000). (See Table 1.1.)

Other theorists have focused primarily on psychological and emotional responses to stress. When under stress, people typically confront two problems. "One is to manage the internal stress, anxiety, tension,

TABLE 1.1	Stress Responses

Stress responses vary according to:

1. physiological reactions, such as ulcers, asthma, and high blood pressure;
2. psychological reactions, such as avoidance of a stressful event in the future;
3. serious mental conditions, such as learned helplessness, anxiety disorders, and dissociative disorders.

TABLE 1.2	Sources of Stress

There are three sources of stress in the environment:

1. a person's position in the social structure;
2. characteristics of the physical environment;
3. life changes.

depression, anger, restlessness, difficulty in concentrating, sleeplessness, and fatigue and the associated thought content, self doubt, and self blame"(Levine & Perkins, 1997, pp. 215–216). This first problem requires what has been termed a form of **emotion-focused coping** (Folkman & Lazarus, 1980). The second problem involves what a person should do in response to the stress or stressor. This kind of response is generally termed **problem-focused coping.** Problem-focused coping strategies seek to deal directly with the source of the stress, while emotion-focused coping seeks to reduce one's emotional response to the stress. People use both of these types of coping in stressful situations and can vary in the amounts and types employed (Heller et al., 1984).

As social workers, we are interested in understanding all forms of stress experienced by people that place them at risk for developing poor adaptations, poor health, and other negative life outcomes. These forms of stress include factors in the physical and social environments of people that are sources of stress. Poverty, social class, sexism, racism, and unemployment are examples of factors in a person's environment that are known human stressors. These factors are often highly correlated with a person's position or location in the social structure. In addition, factors such as high population density, air pollution, heat, noise, and toxic chemicals are recognized by environmental psychologists as major contributors to stress (Heller et al., 1984; Wapner et al., 1997). (See Table 1.2.)

Barbara Dohrenwend (1978) has developed a model of stress that takes into account both person and environment. She assumes that what determines how people respond to stress are **moderating factors** such as one's personal characteristics and one's

social resources. "A moderating factor is considered to be operative when, if in its presence, the relationship of stress to illness (mental or physical) is weaker than in its absence (Duffy & Wong, 1996, p. 99). In the Dohrenwend model, having sufficient psychological and situational mediators is what reduces a person's vulnerability to stress and risk of developing health impairments (Dohrenwend, 1998). **Crisis theory** is compatible with the model of stress developed by Barbara Dohrenwend. In crisis theory, differences in outcome from stressors is a function of the environmental supports and psychological mediators available to the person who is coping. Figure 1.2 shows an illustration of Barbara Dohrenwend's (1978) model of how psychosocial stress induces psychopathology and clarifies for readers the potential role psychological and situational mediators can play in this process.

Crisis theory originated with the work of Eric Lindemann (1944). He is known for his follow-up of the relatives of victims of a tragic nightclub fire in Boston at the Coconut Grove Dance Hall in 1941. Lindemann learned from his study of the survivors' grief responses that the survivors had to change by detaching in some manner from the relationships they had previously had with the deceased and starting new attachments. Those who did not adapt developed some form of disabling mental disorder. **Crisis** refers in this context to "any rapid change or encounter that provides an individual with a "no exit" challenge, no choice but to alter his or her conduct in some manner" (Levine & Perkins, 1997, p. 207). Gerald Caplan, Lindemann's colleague at Harvard School of Public Health, recognized that not just loss events involving extreme stress placed people at risk for developing serious mental disorders. From his research, he concluded that normative life changes are also capable of producing symptoms of psychopathology. His definition of *crisis* includes any significant change in a person's life situation. Such a change be-

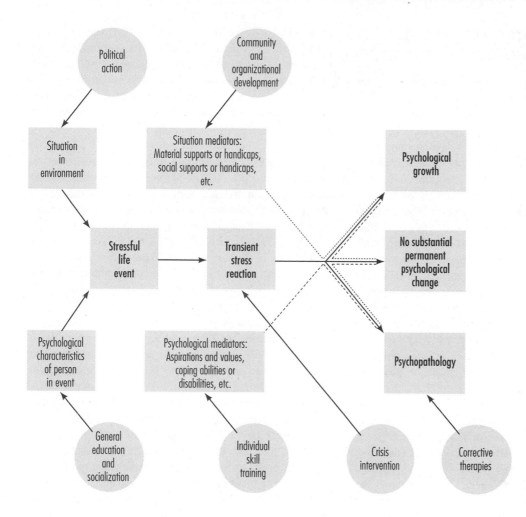

FIGURE 1.2
Model of the process whereby psychosocial stress induces psychopathology and some conceptions of how to counteract this process (Dohrenwend, 1978)

comes a crisis when internal adjustment or external adaptation is beyond the person's capacity. His research inspired a growing field of inquiry presently known as *life events research*. As a result of this body of research, we now know that change associated with non-extreme events in life also contributes to stress and can place persons at risk for developing serve mental disturbances (Dohrenwend, 1998; Gotlib & Wheaton, 1997).

The word *crisis* comes from a Greek root word meaning "to decide." In some contexts, it refers to a point in a disease or disorder process that is "decisive" for recovery or death (Levine & Perkins, 1997). In a more general sense, it refers to a critical turning point in the progress of some type of process in which a decisive change for better or worse is approaching. To some extent, this is the meaning adopted by Erikson in his theory of psychosocial crisis. For Erikson, a crisis is considered a challenge or turning point at which there are opportunities for individuals to choose between polarities associated with key developmental tasks such as trust or mistrust (Newman & Newman, 1999).

In crisis theory, winning the lottery is viewed as a challenge to the person's previous state of adaptation. Accepting a new job or becoming the boss also involves changes that require new adaptations that tax personal and social resources. To understand these challenges, social workers are expected to have a theoretical and an empirical understanding of crisis theory and of life changes resulting from normal developmental processes.

LIFE-SPAN VERSUS LIFE-COURSE PERSPECTIVES ON HUMAN DEVELOPMENT

The curriculum in social work education has historically looked to the developmental sciences for knowledge of change processes in people and their environments (Hutchison & Charlesworth, 1998). Development as an area of science focuses on the causes and consequences of biopsychosocial changes. These changes contribute to positive and negative outcomes in human behavior, as well as positive and negative patterns in peoples' lives. Traditionally, psychologists have focused in their research on understanding changes in behavior across a person's life span with a particular focus on clarifying the contributions of age to understanding biopsychosocial changes. Sociologists, in contrast have taken a different focus in their research and theory construction. Their focus is on understanding the contributions of social changes to the age-differentiated life course (Clausen, 1986; Dannefer, 1984).

Social workers need to place in proper perspective what each of these academic traditions bring to our understanding of changes in persons and environments. "That people change across life is not a particularly contentious issue. However, precisely how and why people change similarly or differently has been the topic of many a debate in the 20th century (Dixon & Lerner, 1999, p. 4). Life-span development is a major theme in this book. Most research and writing in the life-span tradition adheres to one of two styles. The first is the study of behaviors, dispositions, skills, and traits over a substantial period of the life span. For example, Terri Moffitt and her colleagues have studied the traits of emotionality, constraint, and intelligence over time in birth cohorts in New Zealand and in the United States (Hagan, 1995). Their research specifically tracks the role of the continuity of individual differences in explaining deviant behaviors (see Moffitt et al., 1993). The second style of research in life-span studies focuses on clarifying how specific psychological functions, traits, and skills in one stage of development compare with other stages (Lyons, Wodarski, & Feit, 1998). In other words, life-span perspectives focus on providing a description and an explanation of age-related biological, psychological, and behavioral changes from birth to death (Hutchison & Charlesworth, 1998). The life-

course perspective, on the other hand, originated in sociology and is considered both a concept and a theoretical perspective (Bronfenbrenner, 1996; 1999; Clausen, 1986). The **life course** is defined as age-differentiated life patterns embedded in social institutions and subject to historical changes (Elder, 1991; 1996; Laub & Sampson, 1993). This approach to change focuses on understanding changes in patterns of life. It studies people's lives by using the concept of trajectory to understand the paths followed by people in key life domains: work, marriage, crime, and parenthood (Elder, 1996). Life-course theorists are also interested in understanding the causes of other life destinations or outcomes (Gotlib & Wheaton, 1997; Paternoster & Brame, 1997; Robins & Rutter, 1990). They want to describe and explain life destinations in terms of trajectories and transitions. A **trajectory** is defined by Wheaton and Gotlib (1997, p. 2) as "the stable component of a direction toward a life destination and is characterized by a given probability of occurrence." A *trajectory* refers in this context to a specific path or line of development followed by a person to a specific life outcome, regardless of whether the outcome is positive or negative.

In the life-course perspective, it is assumed that transitions are embedded in trajectories and that both the transitions and the trajectories can be analyzed at either micro or macro levels. They are also conceptualized in many writings as a series of linked states (Elder, 1996). When there is a change from one of these states to another state it constitutes what is technically termed in the life-course literature as a *transition*. *Transitions* are defined as short-term state changes that are marked by life events. Each life trajectory is marked by an ordered sequence of life events and transitions embedded within a specific life trajectory such as work, crime, or marriage (Elder, 1991; Paternoster & Brame, 1997).

The following Focus section presents narratives that describe school transitions to illustrate the use of different methods for obtaining knowledge about life transitions. Personal narratives are an important source of knowledge. For instance, *Reflections: Narratives of Professional Helping* is a journal published by the California State University at Long Beach that examines narratives of special interest to members of the social work profession.

High School and College Transitional Experiences

Starting High School: Sarah's Apprehensions

I was nervous and excited to go to high school. I was coming from a small grade school where I knew everyone and going to a high school with 600 students where I only knew a few people. I was also moving to the bottom of the totem pole since I was going to be a lowly freshman instead of a great big eighth grader. I would have to work my way up in the ranks once again.

While still in eighth grade, my classmates and I discussed what we worried most about. The two main things were having no one to sit with or where to sit at lunch and arriving late for class or going to the wrong classroom. On my first day of class, I confronted many of these issues. During the first homeroom, besides learning everyone's name, we quickly looked at our schedules to see who had lunch together. People with the same lunch would plan where to meet so they could sit together and not have to worry about eating alone. The plan worked, and when we entered the huge cafeteria the first day, we all felt secure and calm. Luckily, the school had put plastic tablemats on certain tables that were reserved only for freshmen. They left these on for the first two weeks and it also gave us a sense of security. It was also helpful because we also did not need to worry about whether we were sitting at a senior's table.

My first day of classes ran smoothly. I found all of my classrooms easily and was not late for any of them. Of course, I had highlighted what path I would take to get to each classroom on the map that we had received from the school. I knew what direction to go in and what staircase I would take. Although I was okay, some of my friends weren't as lucky. I was in English class after lunch the second day and the teacher was assigning seats. Everyone was standing at the back of the room waiting for their seat assignment. Everyone's name was called except my friend who was standing alone in the back of the room. The teacher asked for her name and it was not on the list. Then the teacher asked for her schedule. By now, everyone in class was staring at her, and she was turning different shades of red. It turns out she had English the next period and was supposed to be in History. My teacher gave her a

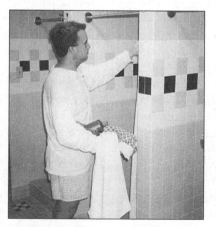

Examples of Common College Transitions These young adults depict some of the transitions experienced by students in changing from the home environment to the college environment.

late pass and she left. She never made the same mistake again.

Sarah Brosmer

Handling College's Freedoms

A teenager's transition into college life can be very exciting; yet very stressful and confusing at the same time. After living at home for 18 years with the security provided by my parents, I was thrown into a whole new world with as little as a few weeks' time for making an adjustment. Time flew by so fast that I had to try very hard to get a firm grasp on my personal situation before everything passed me by.

In preparing for my first Fall Semester, I was really concerned about my future roommates. I was going to live in one room with three other guys. I considered this a double-edged sword. However, the positives proved to outweigh the anticipated negatives. Rather than the four of us constantly getting on each other's nerves, instead we got to know each other very quickly and were constantly together. This, of course, did not come without patience and the kinds of generosity that all roommates must put forth if they are to get along. When one roommate is playing the guitar, the second is talking on the phone, and the third is watching television, sacrifice is definitely in great need.

Meeting new friends was the best thing about my first year at college. My friend Paul was a very zany personality just as I am, so when we first met that fall, I thought that he was absolutely hilarious. We distinctly remember our first two months as friends because every time we saw each other, we simply laughed ourselves silly. Also, after having a girlfriend for most of my senior year, it was nice not having a 'significant other' during my freshman year. I could go out and meet as many people as I could, and I made several female friends that I know I'll be close to for a long time. One of my roommates started dating a girl the first week of school, and when they broke up with each other after a couple of weeks, he hardly knew anyone. He spent all of his time with her, and probably missed getting to know many people.

Another change that naturally evolved pertained to my relationship with my parents. My mother was pretty open-minded about the 'whole college thing.' She actually expected me to start drinking, even though I did not. When I came home for breaks and the following summer, my parents automatically gave me more responsibility, as the word 'curfew' was never even mentioned. When one of my friends discovered the same thing, her response was, 'What happened to my old parents?' Because of the family atmosphere of my dorm and the friends that I met, I felt very comfortable being an eleven-hour drive away from home. I called home every Sunday night to keep in touch with the home front, and I often e-mailed my father to update him on little things, but I honestly never really missed my parents this past year. Although it sounds sort of insensitive, I think that it shows that I grew up as an individual. At college, I enjoyed the freedom that I received, and I believe that I used it in a responsible manner. It really made me more mature and more ready to handle the life ahead of me.

Daniel Brosmer

Life-course researchers have also studied emotion and health trajectories over life in terms of early life experiences (Robins & McEvoy, 1990). For example, considerable research has been devoted to studying individuals under conditions of maximum adversity such as the Holocaust (Levav, 1998), natural or human disasters (Giel, 1998), and childhood victimization (Widom, 1998). Research using this perspective has devoted substantial attention as well to trying to understand how the life course as a socialization institution is influenced by processes of social change (Heinz, 1996). Elder's (1974) seminal work on the effects of the Great Depression on life patterns is an excellent example. (See also Clausen's 1986 and 1993 research on children of the Great Depression.) What sets these researchers apart from other developmentalists is their interest in how developmental changes are influenced by period or history effects. In the life-course perspective, issues of time and timing often shift from focusing on the characteristics of the person to features of the environment (Bronfrenbrenner, 1999; Friedman & Wachs, 1999.

In essence, the life-course perspective from sociology offers a different view of the role of time in human change from that of life-span models of psychology. Biographical time (the life span) in the life-course perspective is conceived as a socially constructed pathway. Researchers who use this approach are interested in explaining how the biographical timing of events is influenced by social institutions and historical changes (Weymann & Heinz, 1996). Thus, a benefit of the life-course perspective is that it allows for an examination of the multiple dimensions of time—biographical time, social time, and historical time—in understanding human behavior (Weymann & Heinz, 1996).

A number of European scholars have pointed out that scholarship in America on life-span development often treats social structure as a given (Hagestad, 1991b; Heinz, 1991b). This kind of approach has been challenged by Dannefer (1984) and other sociologists. They adopt approaches to development that assume that social policy and other sources of social change can influence institutions of training, employment, kinship, and socialization that have implications for the life course (Laub & Sampson, 1993). This focus on policy assumes, of course, that the timing of change in the life course can be subject to the influences of social processes. In other words, change in this approach is not limited to modifications in the organism's physical structure.

By focusing on understanding developmental changes, social workers are better equipped to engage in prevention. The science of prevention is becoming a key component of practice in social work. Many social workers are involved in primary, secondary, and tertiary prevention.

A good way to think about prevention is in terms of end states to be prevented: delinquency, divorce, HIV, and so on. **Primary prevention** seeks to prevent a problem or situation from occurring in the first place. It involves any interventions instituted before a psychological or social dysfunction, illness, or problem occurs. The aim is to focus on populations that have not developed problems or to focus on groups of people at risk for developing an identified end state—for example, children of divorce or alcoholics, individuals growing up in poverty, survivors of a recent loss, and so on. **Secondary prevention** is designed to intervene as early as possible in a problem situation, before it becomes severe or persistent. **Tertiary prevention** involves reducing the complications or negative consequences of a problem situation in terms of preventing handicaps or impairments that are known consequences of identified problem situations.

In the practice of social work, practitioners need knowledge of factors that place individuals at risk for developing negative life destinations. They also must be cognizant of what internal and external factors serve as turning points. A **turning point** is defined as "a change in direction in the life course, with respect to a previously established trajectory, that has the long-term impact of altering the probability of a life destination" (Wheaton & Gotlib, 1997, p. 5). A turning point is a useful concept to social workers because it "implies alternative pathways that have real and important differences in life chances attached to them—whether or not the alternative pathway seemed to differ only slightly from each other at the time of the point of choice" (Wheaton & Gotlib, 1997, pp. 3–4).

In sum, the developmental sciences recognize that some of the changes in people's behavior and lives are ordered forms of change. These predictable changes that are tied to a person's age are termed **normative age-graded influences.** Other changes with degrees of predictability can be caused by what is often termed **normative history-graded influences.** These kinds of changes are caused by factors or forces operating during a particular historical era or period. They are also termed in the literature **cohort effects** or **period effects.** A *cohort* consists of individuals who have birth years in the same generation. A *generation* refers here to a time period of approximately 20 to 30 years. Some of the generations that have been studied by developmental scientists include: the GI-Generation, which consists of persons born between 1901 and 1920; the Silent Generation, with individuals born between 1925 and 1942; the Boomer Generation; with individuals born between 1946 and 1964; the X Generation, with individuals born between 1961 and 1981; and the Millennium Generation, with individuals born between 1982 and 2003.

However, many changes observed in people and their environments are caused by non-normative events. **Non-normative events** encompass all our chance encounters that do not happen to everyone in terms of any predictable timetable (Lemme, 1995). We lack knowledge of the sequencing of these events and their causes relative to issues of time and place. They also cannot be timed-based on assessments of either a person's age or cohort years.

FIGURE 1.3
Multilevel concept of human development

An emerging paradigm in the developmental sciences recognizes a need for integrating the sociological, psychological, and biobehavioral approaches to understanding developmental concerns (The Carolina Consortium on Human Development, 1996). In this paradigm, patterns of adaptation represent interactions across levels within and without the person. Figure 1.3 illustrates a multilevel concept of human development.

This book adopts the assumptions stressed in this new synthesis by emphasizing that development cannot be understood without taking into account biopsychosocial interactions across multiple levels.

THE BIOPSYCHOSOCIAL INTERACTION

Individuals and their environment represent multiple systems that extend from the biochemical to the psychosocial realm (Nurcombe & Gallagher, 1986; Puri, Laking, & Treasaden, 1996). The biological realm of an individual extends from the molecular to the molar; the psychological realm extends from the emotional to the behavioral. The social realm of an individual includes the family and groups, the neighborhood, the cultural setting, and the context of society. Such multiple sources of influence can be described as a person within a body, within a family, within a state, within a country, within the world, within the solar system, within the galaxy, and within the universe.

A person's *constitution* refers to who he or she is individually (genetic makeup, past learning, and so forth) and socially or environmentally (the social forces in the environment). *Behavior* is the result of interactions between the person and the environment. A person's biological makeup can limit his or her capacity to respond to the environment in certain ways.

No single factor can be solely responsible for causing a behavioral response. Multiple factors, within a

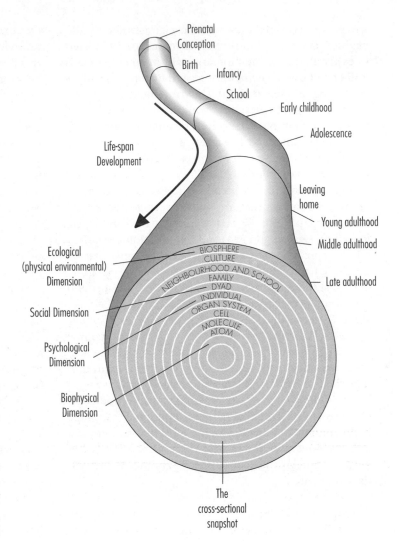

Prenatal
Conception

Birth

Infancy

School

Early childhood

Adolescence

Life-span
Development

Leaving
home

Young adulthood

Middle adulthood

Ecological
(physical environmental)
Dimension

BIOSPHERE
CULTURE
NEIGHBOURHOOD AND SCHOOL
FAMILY
DYAD
INDIVIDUAL
ORGAN SYSTEM
CELL
MOLECULE
ATOM

Late adulthood

Social Dimension

Psychological
Dimension

Biophysical
Dimension

The
cross-sectional
snapshot

complex system, interact to produce specific behaviors. When we think of the biopsychosocial interaction, we recognize that certain biological problems, cognitive processes, and/or certain environments can increase our prediction that a particular behavioral response will develop.

Human behavior has a multidimensional aspect. For example, attention deficit disorder in children can have a strong genetic component. However, some children who possess this genetic component will not develop attention deficit disorder, indicating that biological factors do not completely determine who will develop it. We must also consider psychological and social or environmental variables in accounting for people's behavior. A parent's interaction with a child can exert a profound amount of influence. A child with a small tendency toward hyperactivity may be influenced by a parent in such a way as to reinforce and promote more hyperactive behavior. A child exposed to high amounts of lead, through lead-based paint, can develop symptoms of attention deficit disorder.

Social workers must understand that explanations of human behavior need to be multidimensional to adequately explain human behavior. This requirement, however, makes it difficult to plan prevention and intervention strategies. Systems explanations are useful for understanding the total picture of the client but are not specific enough to be helpful for designing an intervention. Social workers must break the system into separate parts, considering each part's contribution to the client's problem, while at the same time keeping in mind the total system.

In social work we seem either to emphasize the total picture through a systems model or to focus on specific components for assessing and planning interventions. Unfortunately, neither approach is adequate. As a social worker, you must take into consideration the broad picture in assessing a client and then move to an understanding of some of the relevant factors that could be influencing your client's behavior. To become more adept at examining independent factors, we suggest that you learn how to formulate hypotheses within a framework for understanding human behavior. In our framework we move from individual factors to social and environmental factors. It is our expectation that this will help you think about human behavior from a multidimensional perspective.

In using this approach to conceptualizing cases, whether they involve an individual or some larger social system, we recommend two procedures. The first is to establish hypotheses for each dimension of the multidimensional framework. This procedure clarifies in a concise fashion the main concerns in the case situation. The second procedure is to provide a detailed case analysis that provides evidence that backs up the statements contained in the initial hypotheses. This activity should include a comprehensive analysis of strengths (strong points, positive features, successes, coping strategies, skills, factors that can augment

change efforts) and weaknesses (concerns, issues, problems, symptoms, intervention barriers, and so forth) from the questions systematically covered in the multidimensional framework (Berman, 1997).

Such an analysis should also include consideration of the age-appropriateness of the client's physical and psychological development as well as consideration of the differential roles played by peers, caregivers, and others in the development of the people whom you are assessing. These developmental issues need to be addressed to insure that we attend to issues of diversity and uniqueness in our case assessment that might best be explained by age or history considerations. In addition to this developmental domain, practitioners must also consider other domains that are sensitive to diversity, such as sexual orientation, gender, culture, class, and violence. Violence should be included in any practice-oriented framework involving assessment, because social workers are ethically and legally obligated to make judgments about the potential danger to clients and others. In our framework, the domains addressing diversity considerations are included in the section of the framework that focuses on multicultural and gender considerations.

Multidimensional Framework

The **biophysical dimension** of the multidimensional framework consists of the biochemical systems, cell systems, organ systems, and physiological systems (Nurcombe & Gallagher, 1986). This dimension looks at an individual's physical growth and development and is described in Chapter 2. The functioning of this system refers to the balanced exchange of energy among its biophysical components. Any change in this dimension will have corresponding changes in the other dimensions inside and outside this system. Therefore, this dimension also considers physical hazards that may affect an individual's behavior.

The **psychological dimension** represents the systems that contribute to the organization of the individual's mental processes. This dimension involves several functions designed to help the person achieve a sense of satisfaction of his or her needs. These psychological functions involve the systems of information processing and cognitive development, communication, attitudes and emotions, regulation and social cognition, and psychological hazards. These systems are described in detail in Chapter 3.

The **social dimension** refers to the systems of social relationships that a person interacts with individually or in a group (Nurcombe & Gallagher, 1986). This dimension is described in Chapter 4. The social groups and relationships included in this system are families, communities, other support systems, gay and lesbian relationships, cultural groups, ethnic groups, and social institutions such as churches, political parties, schools, and health care and welfare institutions.

APPLYING THE MULTIDIMENSIONAL FRAMEWORK

To understand a person's total functioning, the social worker makes an assessment of all aspects of the person's life and experience. It is helpful to take a hypotheses approach to each primary dimension and its underlying functions. Hypotheses from the biophysical, psychological, and social dimensions are posed in order to examine possible etiology and explanations of the client's functioning. Social workers can use a hypotheses approach to help guide questioning and data gathering during the assessment phase.

The following outline suggests specific areas of questioning to consider for each hypothesis in making an evaluation of a client.

I. Biophysical hypotheses
   a. Biophysical growth and development
   b. Biophysical hazards
II. Psychological hypotheses
   a. Cognitive development and information processing
   b. Communication
   c. Attitudes and emotions
   d. Social cognition and regulation
   e. Psychological hazards
III. Social hypotheses
   a. Families, groups, support systems, and contexts (communities, organizations, institutions)
   b. Multicultural and gender considerations
   c. Social hazards

We expand on this outline by presenting a brief overview of how this framework can be applied in gathering data in an assessment. But first, we provide examples of some potential assessment considerations to use in making your evaluation. This is not a conclusive list of assessment questions; other information can and should be considered. Each of the developmental chapters in this book goes into further detail and provides other considerations for you to use. When reading the case study at the end of each developmental chapter, keep these suggested considerations in mind. Also, think of other questions you would want to ask or obtain answers to when evaluating the client's problem in each case study.

BIOPHYSICAL HYPOTHESES

Physical or biological hypotheses refer to assumptions about the client's functioning as a result of a biological catalyst. Examples include influences from the autonomic nervous system, the neuroendocrine system, physical dependence on a drug, or a biological reaction to an environmental event. The social worker should seek to understand the client's general physical condition. Assess information about the client's medical history including any diseases, neurological impairments, physical impairments, current physical condition, and any medications being taken. A client's problem may be related to or a direct result of the following biological determinants.

Biophysical Growth and Development

Prenatal Growth and Development Assessment considerations include mother's nutritional status during pregnancy; mother's health status; father's health status; length of gestation; prenatal substance abuse by mother; pregnancy complications; family genetic history; genetic abnormalities; chromosomal abnormalities; and physical birth defects (cleft palate, heart defects).

Client's History of Attaining Developmental Milestones Assessment considerations include when did client take first steps; say first word; feed self; dress self; achieve toilet training; have first menses or first nocturnal emission; and develop sex characteristics.

Client's General Health Status Assessment considerations include stability of weight; regularity of menstrual periods; regularity of sleep-wake cycle; level of physical activity and level of nutrition; presence of biochemical imbalances; presence of physically handicapping conditions; use of substances such as tobacco, alcohol, and drugs; assessment of client's general appearance (does client look his or her stated age); and client's ability to perform activities of daily living (ADLs).

Biophysical Hazards

Problems with General Health Status, Including Problems with Any Major Organ System Assessment considerations include family history of heart disease; respiratory problems; cancer; diabetes; health status of close relatives; cause of death of close relatives and age of death of those relatives; client's current and past health status; and presence of symptoms related to a major illness.

PSYCHOLOGICAL HYPOTHESES

The social worker must consider many relevant psychological hypotheses when making an assessment in this dimension. Psychological data can be gathered through a variety of means. Most relevant to the social worker is the individual or family interview. In addition to the traditional psychosocial interview, social workers are making use of semistructured interviews as well as psychological tests, behavioral observations, personality tests, and rapid assessment instruments.

A client's problem may be either related to or a direct result of the following psychological determinants.

Cognitive Development and Information Processing

Client's Attention Span, Memory, Concentration, and Capacity for Abstract Thought Assessment considerations include ability to focus attention; ability to complete tasks appropriate to age; and capacity for memory.

Client's Learning Abilities and Performance Assessment considerations include school performance; problem-solving abilities; and capacity for insight and reflection.

Communication

Client's Language Ability and Vocabulary Assessment considerations include bilingual expectations; use of language; and general verbal and nonverbal abilities in self-expression.

Attitudes and Emotions

Client's Self-Perception Assessment considerations include negative and positive perceptions of self; view of self with others; comparison of self with expectation of others; and perception of what others think about the person.

Client's Emotional Responses Assessment considerations include full range of emotions evident and excessive emotions such as anger, sadness, and frustration.

Client's Self-Statements Assessment considerations include content of self-talk; amount of irrational ideas present; and relationship between self-talk and problem behavior (for example, fear and hopelessness).

Client's Perception of Others Assessment considerations include client's view of others; client's view of others' expectations of client; and extent to which perception is reality based.

Social Cognition and Regulation

Client's Social Knowledge About Others Assessment considerations include client's understanding of social interactions; client's view of friendship; and client's expectations of others.

Client's Capacity for Empathy Assessment considerations include client's capacity for perspective taking; client's sense of morality; and client's interpersonal understanding of others.

Client's Reality Base Assessment considerations include client's cognitive functioning; client's ability to discern reality; and content of client's thoughts and perceptions.

Client's Social Skills Assessment considerations include appropriateness of client's social interactions; client's knowledge of social skills; and client's ability to communicate effectively.

✳ *Client's Social Problem-Solving Skills* Assessment considerations include client's ability to generate solutions to problems; client's ability to think of consequences; and client's means–ends thinking (steps needed to solve problems).

✳ *Client's Maladaptive Behavior Patterns* Assessment considerations include client's behavioral response to problem situations; client's patterns of behavior that lead to difficulties for self, others, or society; and client's desired behavior changes and patterns.

Psychological Hazards

✳ *Client's Experience of Past Life Events* Assessment considerations include client's description of significant events in childhood; client's experience with parents and other adult figures (especially whether any physical or sexual abuse occurred); client's experience with peers; client's psychosocial living environment; client's history of past diagnosis of a mental disorder; and history of use of antidepressants or antipsychotics.

✳ *Client's Experience with Recent Life Events* Assessment considerations include client's description of significant life events in recent years; client's recent experiences with adult and peer figures in his or her life (especially events such as divorce or parent's divorce, death of a loved one); present use of antidepressants or antipsychotics; and use of other prescription drugs.

SOCIAL HYPOTHESES

The social worker's assessment extends beyond the biological and the psychological dimensions to include the social dimension. Social factors include the family, community and other social support systems, access to resources, and the impinging social environment. What are the client's social relationships? And what is the environmental context of the client's social relationships? For example, does the client live in poverty; does the client face racism on a daily basis? The social worker must assess how the client is viewed by society, by the social systems he or she interacts with, and by the individuals directly involved with the client on a daily basis, such as friends and family.

A client's problem may be related to or a direct result of the following sociological or environmental determinants.

Families, Groups, Support Systems, and Context

✳ *Family's Boundaries, Systems, and Subsystems* Assessment considerations include open or closed family system; family structure (for example, enmeshed or disengaged); and how the family defines itself.

✳ *Family's Patterns of Communication* Assessment considerations include content and process of interaction; patterns of conflict; and verbal and nonverbal expressions of affect.

✳ *Family's Roles* Assessment considerations include role assignments within the family; satisfaction with roles; expectations and definitions of roles; allocation of power; and role strain and support.

✳ *Groups the Client Interacts With* Assessment considerations include patterns of interaction in peer and work groups; influence of group norms and other group dynamics; and behavior of the individual in the group.

✳ *Support Systems Available to the Client* Assessment considerations include social supports (family, friends, extended family, social support and self-help groups); institutional supports (child support, welfare, health benefits); access to resources (day care, recreational facilities, police protection); barriers to support systems; and need for new resources and support systems.

✳ *Community and Other Environmental Contributions to the Client's Problem* Assessment considerations include who in the external environment perceives the client's responses as maladaptive; external factors likely to influence client behavior (such as loss of job, aging, relocation); and stressful factors in the environment (poverty, racism, underemployment); client's sense of community, sense of neighborliness, feeling of connection with an identified ethnic group; and other senses of group membership.

Multicultural and Gender Considerations

✳ *Cultural and Gender Context of the Client's Life* Assessment considerations include ethnic or gender identity; degree of acculturation; sexual orientation; language barriers; amount of interaction within and outside the ethnic group; and expectations influenced by cultural, gender, or sexual-orientation considerations.

Social Hazards

✳ Social Context of the Client's Life Assessment considerations include high rates of unemployment; divorce; poverty; discrimination; inadequate social institutions; and impoverished neighborhoods.

SELECTING INTERVENTIONS BASED ON HYPOTHESES

When you select a hypothesis as a way of explaining a person's behavior, that hypothesis should help you select an appropriate intervention. For example, if your assessment suggests that the best hypothesis for understanding a person's behavior is based on his or her biochemical makeup or brain chemistry, then an intervention that changes an individual's physiology should be considered. If a client is diagnosed as having a schizophrenic disorder that you believe is caused by biological factors, then that person should be referred for psychotropic drug treatment. Of course, the client might also need psychosocial treatment as well.

If you develop a hypothesis that a person's difficulty is due to inappropriate social learning, then the intervention will focus on providing the client with a new learning experience. For example, if the person has developed a serious phobic disorder of open spaces (agoraphobia), and you believe it is related to some negative learning experiences, then the intervention will attempt to provide the client with some new, positive learning experiences. The intervention might use contact desensitization, whereby the goal is to induce a state of relaxation and then expose the client gradually to the feared stimulus. This procedure provides a new learning experience for the client.

If you develop a hypothesis that the person's problems are related to the environment, then the intervention should be one that focuses on environmental changes. For example, you may be working with a child with extreme withdrawal behavior and discover that the child is suffering from serious physical abuse. The determinant of the child's problem is primarily environmental. Here, the intervention is to change the child's environment. You may make arrangements for the state child welfare department to remove the child from his or her home environment. By giving the child a new environment—placement in a foster home, for example—you control the child's environment and provide new experiences to meet the child's needs for safety and proper development.

Behavior can also be changed by helping the client access new resources. Often clients simply need information and resources. For example, a client may need help in obtaining housing or material resources. The intervention consists either of providing the information or resources or making a referral so the client can access the resources.

In summary, hypotheses help you think about the various determinants of human behavior. We encourage you to think about human behavior in terms of different hypotheses. In this way, you will become better skilled in assessment. And the better you are in assessment, the more effective you will be in providing services.

✳ Overview ✳

In the first part of this book we describe theoretical and conceptual themes that influence development within the biophysical, psychological, and social dimensions of human behavior. In the second part of the book, on life-span development, each life stage is introduced with a review of developmental themes. These sections reflect Erik Erikson's view that each stage contains certain life tasks that need to be achieved for optimal development. Each developmental chapter then discusses in-depth factors that affect behavior in the biophysical, psychological, and social dimensions. Each of the dimensions in this framework provides a distinct outlook on problems in social functioning; each also suggests different strategies for intervention that must be synthesized for an appropriate response to a client's problem. For example, a client suffering from a severe psychosis needs interventions directed at multiple levels. Biological concepts from neurobiology suggest psychopharmacological interventions to address the psychotic systems, psychological concepts to deal with the client's expectancies regarding his or her condition, and social concepts to address the supportiveness of the individual's environment. These various strategies are needed because of the complexity of the problem situations encountered in the practice of social work. Social workers do not have the luxury of limiting their description of problems to a single dimension. Using a single dimension to assess social functioning ignores the total person; it also implies the existence of a unified theory of human behavior. Because there is no unified theory of social functioning, practitioners must not adhere to a single explanation of social functioning.

Our multidimensional framework cannot be considered comprehensive. Other dimensions can be used to assess social-functioning concerns. However, we will review only those dimensions that have received the profession's sanction and are supported by established scientific disciplines. This does not mean that you should ignore other dimensions in your evaluations of client functioning. In fact, careful evaluation of information from these specified dimensions will sensitize you to additional issues relevant to assessing social functioning concerns.

A person is more than the sum of his or her parts. Each dimension of human behavior is in constant interaction with other dimensions.

 ## ✳ Summary ✳

Social workers need a multidimensional framework for integrating the knowledge and theory from biological, psychological, and social perspectives on human development. No single theory or approach to intervention can account for the whole range of forces influencing social functioning. A multidimensional framework includes the following assumptions: (1) There are three dimensions for assessing human behavior—biophysical, psychological, and social; (2) these dimensions constitute a system of biopsychosocial functioning; (3) systems are organized in a hierarchy of levels from smallest to largest; and (4) each system is in constant interaction with other systems.

Social functioning is the primary focus of a social worker's orientation to human development. Social functioning takes a person-in-environment perspective, which suggests that common human needs must be met for individuals to function effectively in society. How individuals perform their roles in order to participate in society represents the interaction of the individual with the environment. The social-functioning framework is similar to social-competence models. In

the social-competence model, the focus is on helping people achieve their potential and on understanding the normal stresses and demands on people in their interactions with the environment. A useful way of looking at this is to examine the tasks that confront people in adapting to their environmental situation. In addition, how people respond to these tasks can be better understood by looking at their coping abilities. The PIE system was specifically designed by social workers to assess problems in social functioning.

System explanations are useful in alerting us to the multidimensional nature of human behavior. When combined with a hypotheses approach, a multidimensional perspective allows us systematically to evaluate the effects that different dimensions and their complexity have on client functioning. This perspective also ensures that practitioners focus their attention on the person's whole situation, including his or her personal and environmental hazards and strengths. The multidimensional framework includes the following components.

I. Biophysical dimension
 a. Biophysical growth and development
 b. Biophysical hazards
II. Psychological dimension
 a. Cognitive development and information processing
 b. Communication
 c. Attitudes and emotions
 d. Social cognition and regulation
 e. Psychological hazards
III. Social dimension
 a. Families, groups, communities and other support systems, and context considerations
 b. Multicultural and gender considerations
 c. Social hazards

✸ Online Resources

Bronfenbrenner Life Course Center
http://www.blcc.cornell.edu
 This site contains information on research projects on the life course at the Bronfenbrenner Life Course Center. This center is located in the Cornell University's College of Human Ecology.

Slave Narratives
http://www.umkc.edu/lib/instruction/
> This is an excellent resource provided by the University of Kansas for studying the history of American slavery through narratives.

Hazards and Human Adaptations
http://www.colorado.edu/hazards
> This site, which provides information on natural hazards, is housed at the Natural Hazards Center at the University of Colorado, Boulder, which is a national clearinghouse on natural hazards and human adjustment to hazards and disasters.

Environment and Community Psychology
http://www.Tulsa.Oklahoma.net
> This site links you to other sites that deal with ways psychological processes interact with natural and man-made environments.

 InfoTrac® College Edition

For interesting materials related to what you have just read, please go to the *InfoTrac College Edition* website and search using the following key words:

life course	social competence
social functioning	life paths
stress	generations

Key Terms

adaptation
biophysical dimension
cohort (period) effects
competence
crisis
crisis theory
current perspective
developmental
   perspective
disease
disorder
dual perspective
emotion-focused coping
etiology
general adaptation
   syndrome (GAS)
illness
life course
life-span development
moderating factors
normative age-graded
   influences

normative history-graded
   influences
non-normative events
person-in-environment
   (PIE) system
primary prevention
problem-focused coping
psychological dimension
secondary prevention
signs
spiritual dimension
social dimension
social functioning
strengths perspective
stress
symptoms
syndrome
tertiary prevention
trajectory
transition
turning point

CHAPTER 2

The Biophysical Dimension for Assessing Social Functioning

What biological processes affect human growth and development? Exactly how do these processes affect aspects of an individual's behavior? What information do social workers need to understand how biology affects behavior? Since the inception of social work as a profession, biological knowledge has been recognized as a fundamental foundation for effective practice (Schwitalla, 1930). Yet the knowledge base of social workers in clinical and other areas of practice has been virtually unaffected by the veritable explosion of knowledge in the biological sciences (Saleebey, 1985). Social workers tend to be better versed in the psychological and social facets of the profession's biopsychosocial framework (Johnson et al., 1990).

Yet, many functions performed by social workers require biological knowledge. These functions include screening, referral, coordinating services with medical and psychiatric caregivers, case monitoring and advocacy, and psychotherapy (Johnson et al., 1990). It follows that, without relevant biological knowledge, practitioners can make bad referrals or engage in inappropriate screening and other care-giving activities. Most reviews of the social work curriculum during the 1980s revealed minimal evidence that the profession was translating biological knowledge into assessment, intervention, prevention, and education strategies (Saleebey, 1985). This problem was particularly acute in the area of clinical practice (Cohen, 1988; Gerhart & Brooks, 1993; Libassi, 1990; Littrell & Ashford, 1994). As a result, the Council on Social Work Education (CSWE) took specific actions aimed at increasing the social work student's knowledge of adverse effects of psychotropic medication on patients (Ashford & Littrell, 1998; Libassi, 1990). Of course, there are other reasons social workers need to understand brain-and-behavior relationships and their biochemical substrates (Lyons, Wodarski, & Felt, 1998). As Allen-Meares and DeRoos (1997, p. 380) point out, "in the 21st century, the health and mental health issues that will confront social workers will be far more likely to involve matters of biochemistry, neuroscience, and biotechnology than they do today" (Roobeek, 1995).

The case of Raul Salazar includes a number of elements that require some biological knowledge to place them in proper perspective. This case history will be used in the next three chapters to illustrate the independent contributions of each of the dimensions in our multidimensional framework.

CASE

Raul Salazar

Raul Salazar has just started the fourth grade. He was referred to the school's multidisciplinary team because of reports of difficulties in school and concerns about his home situation. Teachers are questioning whether he has a learning disability. They are also asking the team to determine whether he is an appropriate candidate for medications. He often does not follow instructions well. However, his current teacher is "surprised by his vocabulary." It is "much better than many of the other Puerto Rican kids in his class." However, his performance in school has steadily deteriorated. He especially has problems with reading and mathematics and on occasion comes to school with dirty clothing and falls asleep in class.

His performance in the first grade was average, but his records indicate that the teachers at the other school considered him to be a very anxious child. These teachers reported that Raul constantly moved in his seat and had problems with writing but did well in other fine-motor tasks.

Another fact that stands out in his school history is that his performance was better when he was attending a smaller parochial school. Raul's father works for the city of New York as a painter, and his mother is a teaching assistant. She completed two years of college but had to leave her education because she got pregnant with their oldest son. Raul has two other siblings. There is a three-year difference in age between Raul and his older brother, and there is a twelve-month difference between Raul and his younger sister.

Raul's mother's family moved to the mainland when she was 8 years of age. Her father was a teacher and they were not very pleased when she "had to marry" Raul's father. Raul's father's family came from a poor rural area on the island. His own father had a history of alcoholism and left the family when Mr. Salazar was very young.

Mrs. Salazar reported to the social worker that she had serious problems with her nerves throughout her life and that they became worse whenever she was pregnant. Otherwise she felt her pregnancy with Raul had been normal. However, school staff learned that there had been some fear that she might lose Raul during the pregnancy, and this is why she was prescribed bed rest during the last trimester.

Mrs. Salazar's third child, her daughter Maria, was born prematurely, but Mrs. Salazar did not have any problems with her first pregnancy. She told the social worker that her daughter's prematurity really hit the family hard because Maria required so much care when she finally came home.

Unfortunately, Mr. Salazar was released from his job shortly after Maria's birth. The mother reports this was possibly the most stressful period in her life. When Maria was about 4 months old, Mrs. Salazar's doctor considered placing her on medication after she had a seizure. However, testing did not reveal any evidence of the presence of a seizure disorder. She reports a history of fainting and other seizure-like experiences when she was a teenager.

Mrs. Salazar says that she has always had problems with her nerves and has been very sickly throughout her life. She also told the social worker that "she was always the weakest one in her family." When Raul was about 18 months old, Mrs. Salazar's closest brother was killed in a car accident. She reports not being able to get out of bed for weeks following the news of his death. Raul's medical records indicate that it was approximately around this time that he started banging his head in order to fall asleep. This habit continued until he was about 6 years of age. He also developed some other habits that persist to this date. He still bites his fingernails, and did bite his toenails when he was younger. Raul's history also reveals that he was extremely frightened of the dark as a child and has an extreme startle response for which he is often teased by his brother and father.

Raul's father is a strict disciplinarian. He told workers that he often loses his temper and yells at the children, but he says that he has never physically abused them. He reported to the social worker that he cannot tolerate the kids being noisy. When he comes home from his new job, his wife is often in bed, and things are a mess. Mr. Salazar is under lots of pressure at work. His supervisor does not like Puerto Ricans and gives him all the worst job assignments. The family no longer lives near other family members because they moved for Mr. Salazar to get his city job. Mrs. Salazar started working as a teaching assistant, but Mr. Salazar believes that this job is not necessary because the kids need her at home. He is hoping to apply for a transfer to a position with higher pay. Mr. Salazar told the social worker that the family is willing to pay for any services that will help his son do well in school.

We hope that Raul Salazar's case has stimulated your interest in trying to figure out what factors are contributing to his difficulties in school and in other areas of social functioning. If you were performing a multidimensional assessment of this case, you would need to begin by generating biological hypotheses.

▼ ▼ ▼

This chapter reviews the biophysical dimension that is included in our multidimensional framework for assessing social functioning. It looks at aspects of cell systems, genes, and organ systems involved in human growth and development. Does Raul have any problems that are genetically based? What role is inheritance playing in this case history if any? This chapter also examines the neurons, the brain, and their development. Did any areas in his history pose threats to his neuronal or brain development either prenatally or during his postnatal life? If so, what are they, and how do they explain why he is experiencing certain kinds of problems? Are there critical periods in the development of Raul's brain that could have been affected by risk factors in his environment? If so, what are they?

This chapter also covers several theories concerning the biological aspects of development, beginning with the following Focus section on evolution and evolutionary psychology.

FOCUS ON THEORY

▼

Evolution and Evolutionary Psychological Assumptions

Evolution is an early biological theory that has played a significant role in creating a biological basis for behavior. This theory seeks to help us understand the mech-

anisms and factors that have contributed to the development of humans as a species. Evolution tries to identify how much the species has changed over time and to explain why these changes have occurred. A key concept in this field of study is *variation*.

Variations are differences between individual organisms that affect their functioning. Some variations in organisms are caused by outside conditions involving the physical and social environment—for example, weather, rich soil, availability of nutritious food, effective social supports, presence of predators, and other external factors. The variations or differences in organisms produced by these factors are considered acquired developmental characteristics.

There is an entire area of psychology that focuses on individual differences; it is concerned with explaining variations observed in behavior patterns caused by evolutionary processes. However, the abuse of individual-differences research in areas of race and gender contributed to the demise of evolutionary thinking in many sectors of scientific psychology and the other social and behavioral sciences.

David Buss (1996) has refocused attention on the role of evolutionary processes in psychology. He is advocating a new theoretical paradigm for psychology known as *evolutionary psychology* (Buss, 1995). This paradigm assumes that evolution caused by natural selection, as described below, is the only known causal process that can account for the complex organic mechanisms associated with adaptation (Buss, 1995).

Buss points out that, "as Symons (1987) phrased it, 'we're all Darwinians' in the sense that all (or nearly all) psychologists believe that evolution is responsible for who we are today. If another causal process exists that is capable of producing complex psychological and physiological mechanisms, it has not been made generally known to the scientific community" (1995, p. 2). One such disproved theory for explaining variations in psychological and physiological mechanisms is Lamarkism (Buss, 1995). Lamark, an early evolutionary theorist, assumed that acquired traits could be passed from generation to generation. In other words, as an explanation for why a particular tribe of people eats a certain plant, Lamark's theory might assume the people in the tribe learn to eat the plant because it is abundant and tastes good. The knowledge to eat this food would then be inherited by offspring of the tribe.

Lamark's thesis was challenged by Charles Darwin in his book, *The Origin of Species* (1859/1958). Because of Darwin's work, we now know that acquired developmental characteristics cannot be inherited. Instead, Darwin established the principle of natural selection as the key mechanism underlying variations observed in species. This mechanism selects traits that are useful to the survival of the species. According to natural selection, a tribe would eat a certain plant not only because it is plentiful and tastes good but also because the tribe possesses an enzyme that allows them to digest that plant and use it as food. This digestive ability would be inherited, and persons who possess this enzyme would be able to utilize a plentiful food supply and therefore have a greater chance of survival than would those who do not possess the enzyme.

The principle of natural selection offers a general explanation of how humans changed from lower to higher forms. Yet natural selection does not offer an explicit description of the specific mechanisms involved in the process of inheritance. This mechanism was not discovered until Gregor Mendel's (1822–1884) work on genetics was rediscovered (Vale, 1980). It was not until we understood genes that variations in organisms were understood. For example, people in a tribe choose a particular plant as food because tribe members possess a gene that produces the enzyme that allows them to digest the plant. They would pass that gene to their offspring, giving them a survival advantage over another group of individuals who did not possess the gene and could not eat this plentiful food source.

Darwin's theory was not easily accepted. Before Darwinism, humans were perceived as being special creatures distinguished from animals on the basis of their intelligence. This fundamental notion was turned upside down when Darwin linked the development of humans to the development of animals. This linkage involved the connection of animals to intelligence and, by logical extension, of humans to instincts (Vale, 1980). Thus Darwin's contribution not only increased our understanding of human development but also challenged cherished conceptualizations of human nature.

Like Darwin, current evolutionary psychologists are challenging cherished notions about behavioral topics like mate selection, parental investment, and language development. Evolutionary psychologists are attempting to describe and understand the specific adaptive problems that a behavioral pattern was selected by nature to solve. For example, evolutionary psychologists contend that observed visual-spatial differences between males and females are associated with specific adaptive functions. In their opinion, women have better spatial location memory than males primarily because of their responsibility for gathering food in early modes of social organization. Men perform better on visual tasks that involve mental rotation of images, map reading, and maze learning, which is better adapted to the hunting responsibilities of earlier societies (Weiten, 2000). In other words, evolutionary psychologists attend to the evolutionary significance of observed behavioral variations in humans. They assume that all our current psychological functions can be described and explained in terms of their adaptive function. Researchers in this field have applied this approach to domains in psychology as diverse as reasoning, social exchange, language, aggression, jealousy, and sex and status (Buss, 1995). Evolutionary thinking and principles is also witnessing a rebound in other areas of social and behavioral science (Petrinovich, 1995).

Biophysical Growth and Development

The growth and development of the biophysical person play a central role in the study of human behavior, and social workers are expected to understand how changes occur in biophysical processes. Growth is the technical term that refers to the addition of new biophysical components, such as new cells, or an increase in body size (Schuster & Ashburn, 1992). Hyperplasia refers to the type of growth observed in the fetal and early phases of development, which involves an increase in the number of cells (Schuster & Ashburn, 1992). It is eventually replaced by **hypertrophic growth,** or growth involving an increase in the size of cells. Most of our growth after adolescence involves hypertrophic growth.

Development refers in the biophysical dimension to the refinement or improvement of body components. Most adherents of a maturational view of human development assume that any species will follow a typical path of development that is limited by genetic processes. The process by which persons inherit general pathways that constrain their growth and developmental processes is referred to as **canalization.** Some aspects of human development seem to be canalized, or genetically determined, and regardless of environmental conditions, these predetermined pathways limit the degree of variation observed in a species. For instance, most normal human infants will learn to walk. This ability is genetically determined, and only a severely deprived environment would alter the development of walking in a normal infant.

In a biological sense, development can be studied from a hierarchical perspective. The biophysical dimension in our framework is part of the larger biopsychosocial system. This larger system represents the person in the social environment and is organized in a hierarchy from the smallest (biological) to the largest (social). Biological systems can also be organized from the smallest to the largest, beginning at the cellular level and progressing to tissues, organs, and organ systems. The study of physical development can follow this progression.

Cells are the smallest unit of living matter known to scientists. Most cells are too small to be seen without the aid of a microscope. When cells are grouped together, they form *tissues,* which have varying characteristics according to their function. Examples include connective tissue, muscular tissue, nervous tissue, and epithelial tissue (the outer surface of the skin) (DiMatteo, 1991). Tissues combine to form organs. Organs serve specific functions in the body's system but do not work independently of one another. They combine to form systems that serve various functions in maintaining life forms. Each of our organs is assumed to experience optimal growth periods. If in an optimal growth spurt the organism is subjected to adverse conditions, then there is a danger of serious impairment; that is, body tissue is most sensitive to permanent damage in these periods of rapid growth (Schuster & Ashburn, 1992).

We will begin our discussion of how biophysical growth and development can affect human behavior by looking first at genetic transmission and its implications for understanding diversity. This is followed by a description of neurons and how they change during brain development. We also explore in this discussion specific biochemical processes in the nervous system. First, however, the next Focus section looks at what sociobiology has contributed to our understanding of variations in social organization and diversity in animal behavior with implications for human behavior.

FOCUS ON THEORY

What Is Sociobiology?

The discipline of sociobiology involves studying the biological contributions to the social aspects of behavior observed in animals. In 1975, E. O. Wilson published *Sociobiology.* This book has as its primary focus the objective of understanding animal behavior, but it also offers some controversial speculations about the contributions of biological processes to the social aspects of human behavior. Wilson summarized his book in a well-quoted phrase: "Genes hold the culture on a leash." Wilson and other sociobiologists believe that important similarities exist between the way people act and the "unthinking" behavior of animals. Did you ever wonder why animals and even insects display courtship rituals before mating? Lower animals also commit "crimes" similar to those committed by humans. Mallard ducks commit rape; chimpanzees form groups that conduct warlike raids on neighboring tribes; and ant colonies have a social hierarchy that includes slaves. Lower animals also commit acts of altruism not unlike those of people. For example, bees will die to save the beehive, and birds will often warn of an oncoming predator even though the warning most likely will result in the bird's death. Wilson's work was significantly influenced by the principle of *genetic altruism.* William D. Hamilton, an entomologist, put forth this principle in 1964 (Maxwell, 1991), which is referred to elsewhere in the literature as the "selfish gene." "The key point is that altruism is not 'really' performed for the good of others; it is performed for the good of the gene that selfishly 'wants' to be included in future generations" (Maxwell, 1991,

p. 6). For entomologists, this principle explained altruistic behaviors observed in insects and animals. Thus, when a mother runs back into a burning house to save her two sons, sociobiologists believe she is compelled at a biological level. This self-sacrificing, altruistic behavior is simply a gene's way of working to ensure continued existence, which, sociobiologists argue, is the resut of billions of years of evolution. Basically, we got to where we are today on the basis of our genes through the process of natural selection. This explains how altruistic behavior may have evolved as an adaptation (Kalat, 1995).

Wilson's *Sociobiology* was initially seen as a new form of social Darwinism. *Social Darwinism* refers to the social-theoretical movement that ascribed the domination of one group over another to the selection by nature of the fittest group, a process commonly referred to as "survival of the fittest." Many researchers approached social Darwinism with grave suspicion. Yet, this idea stimulated them to explore a number of issues involving the relationship between genes and culture. It eventually led to the collaboration of Lumsden and Wilson (1981) in developing a theory of gene-culture co-evolution. This theory addressed a number of interesting problems. Why do very distant cultures have many characteristics in common? How did cultures originate? The emphasis was on trying to understand the genetic bases for many cross-cultural universals observed in human behavior.

Ideas stimulated by this theory have been some of the most controversial issues of the nature-versus-nurture debate. Some argue that the theory is too simplistic, that genes do not plan and scheme on their own accord. Instead, it could be argued that people learn new ways to behave in response to situations, and they pass these learned behaviors on. Also, if selfish genes do exist, social norms would be likely to conquer them. Other theories, like behaviorism, contend that people act certain ways based on what they have learned from the environment. The ideas of co-evolution bring the nature-nurture controversy into perspective. People are not just all genes. Yet, a "gene's-eye" view of behavior suggests that genes have the power to influence behavior but not directly control it. Genetic evolution occurs because a form of behavior is selected for its adaptive function. In the end,

behavior is a combination of genes, culture, and environment—however, their proportions remain a topic of debate.

GENETICS AND HUMAN BEHAVIOR

Social workers require some basic knowledge of cellular growth, because they encounter many people with dysfunctions or defects in cellular processes. These breakdowns in natural growth processes can occur in formative or growth phases of development or after the organism has reached maturation. Such defects can play a significant role in many aspects of a person's behavior. Inadequate growth can place the person at definite risk for behavioral dysfunctions and for disease. For this reason, we will provide a brief overview of cellular growth processes from a genetic perspective. We chose a genetic perspective primarily because it represents one of nature's key control mechanisms for directing the kinds and amounts of cells needed for effective adaptation.

Genetic information is contained within each cell of the human body. This information is located on chromosomes—threadlike structures found in the nucleus of the cell (see Figure 2.1). Specific traits of an individual, such as hair color, eye color, and height, are coded in genes located on the chromosomes. Each body cell contains 46 chromosomes.

Mitosis is the cellular process by which a body cell reproduces itself by dividing and producing two new daughter cells, each with 46 chromosomes. When cells reproduce themselves, they do so at varying rates. For instance, blood cells reproduce as rapidly as every 10 hours (Schuster & Ashburn, 1992), whereas muscle cells can wait several years before reproducing, and nerve cells do not reproduce at all once a full complement has been established. It is through these processes of cell division that growth and development occur.

The cell division that creates the reproductive, or sex, cells is called **meiosis.** The sperm and egg cells (also known as *gametes*) formed in this process have only half the parent cell's genetic material, or 23 chromosomes. At conception, the mother and father each provide 23 chromosomes through each gamete. The offspring then develops from a single cell formed by

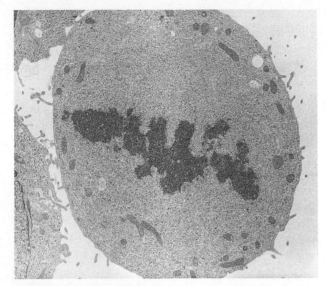

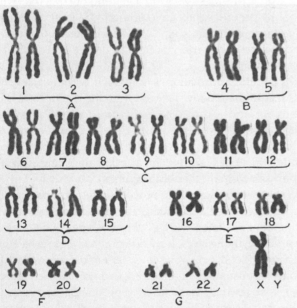

FIGURE 2.1 **The top portion of the figure shows chromosomes during mitosis. The bottom portion shows matched and sorted chromosomes.**

the union of these two gametes—one from each of the parents—a sperm and an egg. The single cell formed from this union contains 46 chromosomes, or 23 pairs of chromosomes. Of these pairs, 22 pairs are **auto-somes.** Autosomes are any chromosomes other than

sex chromosomes. The pair of sex chromosomes consists of two X chromosomes in females and one X and one Y chromosome in males (so named because of their shape). Each of these autosome and sex chromosome pairs consists of many genes, which represent the basic units of inheritance.

If the human species has evolved through variations caused by genetic inheritance, how have these variations occurred? One source of variation observed in humans involves problems in cell division. In this variation, one parent contributes "something other than exactly one copy of each chromosome" (Kalat, 1995, p. 462). Any process that affects this copying of chromosomes from each of the parents contributes to major variation in an organism's characteristics. Chromosome disorders occur when an alteration takes place either in the structure or the number of chromosomes.

As we have discussed, in the process of fertilization, male and female gametes should unite 23 single chromosomes from each parent and produce a single cell containing 46 chromosomes. However, errors can occur in which the offspring has more or fewer than the normal 46 chromosomes. Problems with chromosomes that affect growth and development are discussed in the section on chromosome disorders.

Problems that affect development can also occur with the genes located on the chromosomes. When two parents unite in a reproductive effort, there are approximately 1 million genes available for forming a new progeny (Beck, Rawlins, & Williams, 1988). This potential for the recombination of genes is why offspring have a new combination of genes that differ from their parents. *Recombination* is a major source of the variations observed in offspring. Variations in organisms can also be caused by changes in a gene. This process is referred to as **mutation.** Mutations are random and rare events that can distort key characteristics in an organism's growth and development.

We will explore various types of genetic disorders and their causal mechanisms in the following sections of this chapter. This discussion is intended to sensitize you to the types of disorders commonly encountered in direct practice. Basic knowledge of these disorders is needed to counsel family members and make appropriate referrals for genetic counseling.

The three fundamental types of genetic disorders are single-gene, multifactorial, and chromosomal.

Single-gene disorders refer to inherited dysfunctions or defects that result from dominant, recessive, or X chromosome-linked genes.

Single-Gene Disorders

Dominant Single-Gene Disorders   **Huntington's chorea** is a disorder involving a dominant autosomal gene. This disorder has a 50-50 chance of occurrence in an offspring of a person carrying the gene. Because the gene for Huntington's chorea is dominant, we will refer to that gene as *H* and the recessive, or non-Huntington's, gene as *h*. An affected individual will have a genotype of *Hh* and a phenotype of having the disease. When this affected individual produces a child with another person, the chance of that child inheriting the dominant, or *H*, gene is 50%. Each parent contributes a gene to the offspring. The affected person with the genotype of *Hh* might contribute the dominant *H* or the recessive *h* gene. When the parent with this allele contributes a recessive *h* rather than the dominant *H*, the child will have an *hh* pair and avoid the disorder. However, when the parent with the *Hh* allele contributes the dominant *H*, then the offspring will have Huntington's chorea. This disorder is serious; it is characterized by progressive chorea (purposeless motions) and the eventual development of dementia (mental deterioration). This disorder is of particular concern because it often does not manifest itself until the fourth decade of life. By this time, the affected individual most likely will have already had children before discovering that he or she has the disease. And some of these children may also have the disease.

Some dominant genes that are present with a recessive gene do not entirely control the inherited characteristic. This condition is called *incomplete dominance*. For instance, the dominant gene for red blood cells that are round does not totally mask the effects of a recessive gene for *sickle-cell disease*. Individuals with sickle-cell disease have sickle-shaped blood cells that tend to clump together. This clumping causes severe pain for the individual. These sickle-shaped cells also distribute less oxygen through the circulatory system than normal cells (Sigelman & Shaffer, 1991). Sickle-cell disease occurs most often in African-Americans and does not have a cure (Rauch, 1988). Some individuals who are carriers of this disease can have many round cells but are likely also to have some sickle cells. These sickle cells do not have an effect on the person's functioning except in stressful circumstances. In stressful situations, persons with this condition of incomplete dominance may experience some symptoms of the disease.

Sickle-cell disease is often encountered by persons working with members of the African-American community. One out of every 12 African-Americans carries the gene for this condition (Rauch, 1988). This condition also occurs in persons of Mediterranean extraction, from Greece, Italy, and Turkey, and has been found in persons from malarial regions of the world such as Indo-China and China. A prominent feature of this disease is anemia. A person with sickle-cell disease has a life expectancy that is significantly compromised, but many adults with this condition have lived well into their 70s. Social workers involved with persons affected by this condition seek to reduce the stresses that place the affected individuals at risk for serious health complications.

Recessive Single-Gene Disorders   Most single-gene disorders affect some aspect of the body's structure and are often serious and life threatening (Rauch, 1988). Single-gene disorders are not limited to those caused by dominant genes. Autosomal recessive genes also contribute to genetic disorders. We all carry abnormal recessive genes. These genes will cause no ill effects unless we mate with a person who is also carrying an abnormal gene. If two persons carry the same abnormal gene, the chance is 1 in 4 that their offspring will inherit two of these recessive genes (Abuelo, 1983). For example, 1 in 20 African-Americans and 1 in 30 whites carry the recessive gene for cystic fibrosis on chromosome 7. If two people with this recessive gene marry and have a child, each parent has a genotype of *Cc*—one dominant gene that does not cause the disease and one recessive gene that does. Because the dominant gene overpowers the recessive gene, the parents do not have this disease. However, when these parents have a baby, there is a 25% chance that the child will have a genotype of two dominant genes *CC* and will not have the disorder; a 50% chance that the child will have the genotype *Cc* and, like the parents, not have the disease; but a 25% chance that the baby will inherit two recessive genes *cc* and have cystic fibrosis.

Cystic fibrosis is a serious disease of the exocrine glands that causes secretion of excess, thick, body fluids. The disease occurs in 1 out of 1,600 to 1 out of 3,600 live births. The affected individual has difficulties with lung function and digestion, among other problems. In years past, many children died of cystic fibrosis, but with improved medical care, children with this disease are living into adulthood. The average life span in 1993 was 29.4 years. As adults, individuals with CF are still quite ill and often are limited in their ability to function. These individuals may require the services of a social worker, especially in coping with chronic illness and reduced life expectancy as a young adult.

The risk of both parents carrying a recessive abnormal gene is increased for persons who are related by blood. First cousins are at a substantially higher risk of having a child with birth defects because they have one-eighth of their genes in common (Abuelo, 1983). For example, the risk in the general population of having an offspring with mental retardation is approximately 3%–4%, whereas the risk of mental retardation for the offspring of cousins is approximately 6%–8% (Abuelo, 1983). (Please note that this is a population statistic for individuals whose genotype is unknown. The risk for people related by blood of each having a recessive gene is higher, but for any two individuals, related or not, where both are known to have a recessive gene, the risk of the offspring having the disorder is 25%.)

The prevalence of abnormal recessive genes is often higher in certain ethnic groups. For instance, Ashkenazi (Eastern European) Jews have a 1 in 30 chance of being a carrier of the recessive disorder Tay-Sachs disease. **Tay-Sachs disease** is a neurodegenerative disorder characterized by progressive mental and physical retardation. Most children with this disease die between 2 and 4 years of age. The chances of occurrence of this disorder are 1 in 300 in the general population (Abuelo, 1983).

Whenever social workers encounter a rare genetic disorder, they should take a genetic history and explore whether the parents are related. In isolated rural areas and on islands, the gene pool is reduced, which results in individuals running the risk of sharing a common ancestor without knowing it. Careful questioning is needed to discern any indication of potential consanguinity. Also, it should be noted that the risk for abnormalities in offspring from an incestuous relationship rises as much as 30%, whether it involves father and daughter or brother and sister (Abuelo, 1983). Thus, social workers should rule out the possibility of incest whenever there is a history for a rare recessive disorder and a teenage mother is involved.

X Chromosome–Linked Disorders   The third form of single-gene disorders involves any condition that is associated with X chromosome–linked genes. That is, these disorders are influenced by a single gene that is probably located on the X chromosome. Y chromosomes are shorter than X chromosomes and, as a result, have fewer genes. The genes on the X chromosome then have no corresponding allele on the Y chromosome that could possibly overpower the effects of a harmful gene on the X chromosome. For instance, red-green color blindness occurs most often in males. This scenario is most probable if a male has a recessive gene for color blindness on his X chromosome, because it cannot be overpowered by a matching dominant gene on the Y chromosome. Thus, males are more likely to have red-green color blindness because they lack a gene for this trait on the Y chromosome. Females can have this condition only if they have recessive genes for color blindness on both of their X chromosomes (Sigelman & Shaffer, 1991).

Hemophilia is a condition caused by a defective gene on the X chromosome that creates a problem with blood coagulation. This condition is often referred to as the "bleeder's disease." Hemophilia also occurs mostly in males, who have no corresponding gene on the Y chromosome to overcome the effects of this X chromosome–linked gene. **Duchenne muscular dystrophy** is another form of X-linked genetic disorder. However, "[n]ot all types of muscular dystrophy are X-linked recessive; some are *autosomal dominant* or *autosomal recessive.* In other cases, there is no family history of muscular dystrophy; these so-called sporadic cases are thought to be due to a change in a gene (mutation)" (Rauch, 1988, p. 62).

Lesch-Nyhan syndrome is another disorder that involves a gene on the X chromosome. It is characterized by mental retardation, spasticity, and self-mutilation (Abuelo, 1983). Children with this condition often bite their fingers and lips and have abnormal physical development. This genetic disorder creates an inborn error in the metabolism of purine. Infants with this condition appear normal at birth. In fact, the first sign of difficulty emerges when the primary caregiver discovers orange sand in the infant's diapers. This sand is crystals of uric acid that result from the infant's inability to metabolize purine (Abuelo, 1983). Children with this condition often stand out in terms of their aggressiveness. **Fragile X syndrome** is another disorder linked to the X chromosome. However, it is considered a chromosome disorder and therefore will be discussed in that section.

Multifactorial Disorders

This second major group of genetics disorders is called **multifactorial disorders** and is characterized by the interaction of multiple genes and environmental factors. The mechanisms underlying these disorders are poorly understood, and. it is difficult to isolate the effects of environmental factors on multifactorial conditions. The environment can play a significant role in the presentation of multifactorial disorders. For instance, if the environment prevents the person from reaching a given threshold necessary for the appearance of a condition, then the person will not develop the characteristics of a particular genetic aberration. Evidence has been increasing that indicates that persons who contract certain multifactorial disorders have relatives with the condition. However, such a genetic liability does not mean that they will get the disorder (Rauch, 1988). An excellent example of this principle is seen in cancer. Many individuals with relatives who have had cancer do not develop the condition.

A group of disorders known to be associated with multifactorial inheritance is *neural tube defects.* These disorders involve conditions in which a child has an open defect in the brain or spinal cord. Included in this group are anencephaly, encephalocele, and spina bifida. (Neural tube defects are described in more detail in Chapter 5). These are serious conditions that are usually accompanied by severe mental retardation and that sometimes result in death (Abuelo, 1983). In the United States, the risk for neural tube defects is 1 in 500. The condition with the best prognosis among neural tube defects is spina bifida. In fact, percentages of persons with this condition who have developed severe mental retardation have decreased in recent years. Surgical advancements have greatly improved the prognosis for persons with this condition. Although some cases of anencephaly and other neural

defects may have a genetic basis, others may have solely environmental causes, such as lack of folic acid in the mother's diet during pregnancy.

In effect, multifactorial disorders have a genetic component, but this component is dependent on the environment for its presentation. For instance, some fetuses may be at greater risk for developing structural abnormalities in utero as the result of a minimal exposure to alcohol than others. Thus, the interaction of many variables are involved in the causation of multifactorial disorders, and one, two, or more of these variables will be genetic. Careful assessment is needed, because it is difficult to isolate the genetic component(s)of many forms of multifactorial conditions.

Chromosome Disorders

Chromosome disorders represent the last major class of genetic disorders. These disorders are caused by a variety of problems in cell division; translocation and nondisjunction are the most common problems.

Meiotic errors, during the process of forming gametes, can occur in the formation of either the sperm or the egg and are not hereditary. Remember that during meiosis the pairs of chromosomes must separate to form sex cells with only 23 chromosomes each. During this process, a piece of a chromosome may break off and attach to another chromosome. This is called *translocation,* or *deletion.* The remaining chromosome fragment, which lacks genetic material, causes defects that are contingent on what genetic information was deleted from the chromosome.

Chromosome disorders are often a result of too many or too few chromosomes—for example, 45 or 47 chromosomes rather than the normal 46. Failure of paired chromosomes to separate during meiosis is called *nondisjunction.* Nondisjunction can cause three chromosomes in one cell (trisomy) or only one chromosome in a cell (monosomy). These types of abnormalities underlie many of our identified chromosomal disorders.

Down syndrome, or *Trisomy 21,* was the first chromosome abnormality identified by scientists (Foster, Hunsberger, & Anderson, 1989). About 95% of Down syndrome cases result from an extra number-21 chromosome. At conception, the newly formed cell has three number-21 chromosomes because chromosome 21 did not separate during meiosis. Thus the offspring received one number-21 chromosome from one parent and two number-21 chromosomes from the other. Risk for this problem is highly associated with advancing maternal age. After age 35, the risk increases and remains about the same up to about age 40. At 40, the risk increases dramatically. The reason for this association between age and increased risk for Down syndrome is unknown. One plausible explanation is associated with the aging of the body's system. That is, the body fails, as a result of age, to recognize and spontaneously abort chromosomal abnormalities. Another explanation often given in the literature is that the eggs are exposed to environmental threats for longer periods of time and accordingly are more likely to encounter errors in the meiotic process.

Down syndrome is not the only type of disorder resulting from an additional chromosome. There are two syndromes with a lower frequency of occurrence that are associated with extra chromosomes: *Trisomy 18* (Trisomy D) and *Trisomy 13* (Trisomy E). Trisomy 18 is the second most common autosomal disorder, with an incidence of 1 in 3,000 live births. It is characterized by multiple deformities and severe mental retardation. This disorder is more prevalent in females, and survival is generally for no more than three months. Trisomy 13 occurs in approximately 1 in 5,000 births and is present on rare occasions on chromosome 14 or 15. This disorder is associated with many types of central nervous system abnormalities. Newborns with this syndrome rarely live beyond six months.

The last major type of chromosomal disorder that we will discuss in this overview involves the X chromosome. The **fragile X syndrome** is a form of serious mental retardation that is identified in karyotype studies (microscopic study of the chromosomes) by a constriction at the end of the long arm of the X chromosome. In some circumstances, the portion below this constriction is broken, which is why the disorder is labeled fragile X syndrome. Although the exact incidence of this condition is unknown, fragile X is be-

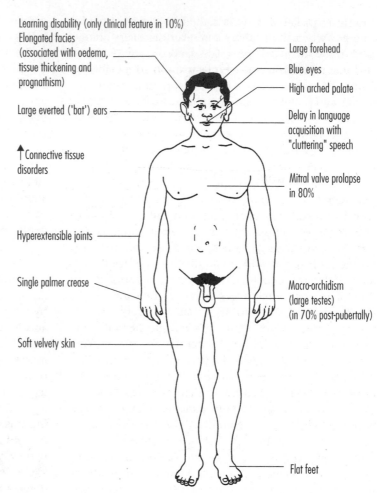

FIGURE 2.2 Clinical features of Fragile X syndrome

lieved to be second only to Down syndrome as a genetic contributor to mental retardation. This syndrome, which occurs in males, is characterized by nonspecific mental retardation, large testes, speech defects, and large, protuberant ears (Foster, Unsberger, & Anderson, 1989). Figure 2.2 provides an illustration of the clinical features of fragile X syndrome.

Many gender-linked defects in chromosomes are undetected until early adolescence because some of these disorders are identified only by an individual's failure to develop secondary sex characteristics. Klinefelter's and Turner's syndromes are distinct examples. In **Klinefelter's syndrome,** the most common of the sex-chromosome disorders, the child is born with an extra X chromosome (XXY). Males with this condition have gynecomastia, or female-like breasts, mild mental retardation, underdeveloped testes, and attendant personality difficulties involving body-image problems. It is the most common condition associated with male infertility.

Turner's syndrome is the chromosomal disorder resulting from only one X chromosome, and it occurs in 1 out of 3,000 live female births. That is, females with this condition have an XO genotype and a number of physical stigmata that are correlated with a lack of secondary sexual characteristics (Lemeshow, 1982). Women with this condition are short in stature, have a webbed neck, and often have congenital heart problems and kidney difficulties. However, mental retardation is not necessarily a characteristic, and, when present, it is generally mild. Doctors have begun treating these women with estrogen during adolescence to enhance their development of secondary sex characteristics. Most persons with Turner's syndrome will achieve an adult height of 5 feet. Genetic counseling is needed when a mother has a child with this condition to identify future risk for additional children and to clarify any misconception about the etiology of a syndrome (Foster, Hunsberger, & Anderson, 1989).

Implications for Practice

Social workers often deal with clients who have irrational beliefs about the causes of disabilities observed in their children. Parents may unnecessarily blame each other for the child's problem or blame themselves for behaviors that have no bearing on the true cause of the child's problem. Social workers must understand the different types of genetic disorders in order to make effective referrals and dispel many of the misconceptions clients have. In fact, many parents operate on a number of false assumptions that are easily addressed by exposing the parents to relevant educational materials. It is shocking how many families have been destroyed by misinformation about developmental and physical disabilities.

Social workers are also operating more and more in autonomous capacities (Lebassi, 1990). In these situations, social workers end up determining whether clients are referred for genetic counseling. Genetic counseling is an essential service from which many clients can benefit. This counseling helps family members identify the risk of occurrence of a given genetic disorder and make plans about having children. Genetic counseling also provides information and advice about options available to a couple, given each partner's family history. When parents have a disabled child, some of the stress associated with deciding to have additional children can be minimized if they learn that their child has a disorder with a low probability of reoccurrence. Often, parents are in a state of shock when they are given the initial diagnosis. Thus, the genetic counselor or social worker can play a major role in clarifying information that is unintentionally distorted by family members.

Social workers also need to focus on genetic issues in their assessments to help clarify the etiology of many of the problems encountered in practice. If social workers do not consider family genetic history in their investigations, they may fail to identify patterns that can provide essential clues to the causes of various behavioral and developmental disturbances. Many conditions with a genetic basis often follow similar patterns among family members. (See Focus on Genetics: Genetic and Environmental Effects on Human Behavior, below.) This information may be overlooked unless the social worker obtains family background information.

FOCUS ON GENETICS

Genetic and Environmental Effects on Human Behavior

Jim Springer and Jim Lewis are identical twins, separated just 6 weeks after they were born. Reunited 39 years later in a study of twins conducted at the University of Minnesota, they discovered that they had married and divorced women named Linda, married second wives named Betty, and named their first sons James Allan and James Alan, respectively. That's not all: They both drove the same model blue Chevrolet, often vacationed at the same small beach in St. Petersburg, Florida, and owned dogs named Toy (Begley, 1988, p. 80).

These two male twins share a genetic history with their great grandmother.

Are the striking similarities between these two brothers the result of similar environmental influences, pure coincidence, or the fact that they share the same genes? And what accounts for their differences? To what extent does one's genetic makeup influence behavior, and to what extent is the environment a factor? This issue is commonly referred to as *nature versus nurture.*

There are two major methods for studying whether family resemblance is a result of shared heredity or shared environment. The first method is *twin study,* in which researchers examine whether identical twins raised in the same environment are more similar to each other on particular attributes than are fraternal twins raised in the same environment. If heredity is an important prerequisite for the occurrence of a trait, identical twins, because they share the same genotype, should be more alike than fraternal twins (Plomin, 1990).

The other common family study is *adoption study,* which focuses on siblings who are adopted and reared apart from each other. An example would be our identical twins who were adopted into different homes at birth and raised in different environments. The degree to which these twins are alike reveals the effect of heredity; the degree to which they are like members of the family in which they were raised reveals the effect of environment.

Family researchers suggest that about 50% of the differences between people on IQ scores are the results of genetics (Plomin, 1990). Personality characteristics, such as extroversion and neuroticism, show heritability of about 40%. Various forms of psychopathology, such as schizophrenia, also show evidence of genetic transmission—about 30%. Genetics also seems to influence such behaviors as delinquent and criminal activity.

Recent research by Robert Plomin (1994) indicates a significant genetic influence in human social development for such attributes as empathy, attachment, and social competence. In fact, Plomin predicts that, in the not too distant future, researchers will no longer have to rely on twin and adoption studies but will be able to pinpoint specific genes that directly affect genetic variability among individuals. Just recently, in fact, scientists have found a link between a particular gene and the personality trait of novelty seeking. Persons with a gene for novelty seeking score higher on such traits as impulsiveness, excitability, quick temper, and extravagance (Ritter, 1996).

According to recent research, therefore, one-third to one-half of all behavioral characteristics can be attributed to genetics. This means, however, that most differences in human behavior are a result of the environment. How, then, does the environment shape behavior?

Previously, researchers believed that shared environment contributed to similarities among family members. *Shared environment* refers to the physical environment of the home, the family's socioeconomic status, parents' style of parenting, and so on. Research now seems to indicate that shared environment has almost no influence on differences in behavior among siblings (Tellegen et al., 1988). Thus, when family members behave similarly, this resemblance is due to genetics.

Family members are different because of their non-shared environment—those aspects of the environment that they do not share. Examples of non-shared environmental influences include parental response to a child's gender, birth order, and temperament. In other words, parents respond differently to an easy-going, first-born female than they do to an intense, demanding younger son. Another source of non-shared environmental influence is the interaction among siblings. An older sibling with the responsibility for caring for younger siblings may develop more assertive, responsible behaviors; a younger sibling may learn to be more passive and cooperative. Other examples of non-shared environment include outside influences particular to each family member, such as interactions with teachers and peers.

According to this research, you are similar to your siblings because you share similar genes. You are different from your siblings because you experience different environmental influences through your interactions with parents, siblings, peers, and others.

To what extent, then, do genetics and environment interact in determining human behavior? A current popular belief is that genes influence behavior by determining the type of environment that people choose. People seek out environments that match their genetic preferences (Bouchard et al., 1990; Scarr & McCartney, 1983). As children grow older, they are less influenced by their parents and freer to choose their own environmental influences. In reality, research shows that siblings become less alike the longer they live together (Plomin & Daniels, 1987). Athletic, outgoing children may choose team sports, whereas more withdrawn children may choose reading or playing computer games by themselves. Because of genetic preferences, these two types of children experience very different environments.

Research by Scarr and McCartney (1983) indicates that the non-shared environmental influences that children experience may also result from the fact that

their different genetic make-up causes them to elicit different reactions from others. Parents may respond more positively to an alert, smiling baby than to a fussy, demanding one. An extroverted child may have more positive interactions with peers than a shy, withdrawn child. It would appear then, that a child's genetic make-up determines, to some extent, that child's non-shared environmental influences.

Research by Thomas Bouchard and his colleagues (1990) seems to indicate that twins reared apart are similar because their genetic make-up causes them to choose similar environments. This research states that, although it does indeed appear that most psychological variance is the result of learning through experience, the experiences are self-selected. We choose our environment based on our genetic preferences. According to this theory, the twins in our story are alike not because of coincidence or because they ended up in similar homes, but because they have the same genes, which caused them to choose similar environments and experiences and to elicit similar responses from the people in their environments. Therefore, it is less appropriate to talk of nature versus nurture than to study "nature via nurture" (Bouchard et al., 1990).

BIOCHEMICAL SYSTEMS AND BEHAVIOR

After exploring biophysical growth and development at the cellular level, we will now turn to biochemical processes in the nervous system that can have a significant effect on behavior. We will first focus on the brain, because it is the key organ in our nervous system. In addition, we will review the characteristics of our autonomic nervous system and the structure and function of nerve cells and processes involved in their development. This should provide you with the necessary foundation for understanding biochemical subsystems that contribute to the functioning of key psychological processes.

Anatomy of the Brain

It is difficult to understand brain functions without some fundamental understanding of neuroanatomy, the study of structure and function of the nervous system.

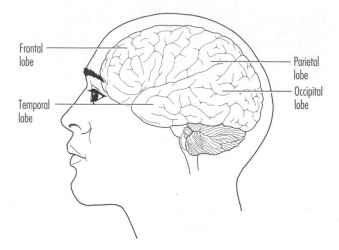

FIGURE 2.3   The parts of the brain (Heller, 1996)

The brain's cerebral cortex (its covering) is divided into two hemispheres, and each of these hemispheres is divided into four lobes. These four lobes were named after bones in the human skull: frontal, parietal, occipital, and temporal (see Figure 2.3). The **frontal lobe** involves the portion of the brain that participates in body movements, thinking, feeling, imagining, and making decisions. It is the lobe that includes the largest portion of the brain. It also plays a critical role in social inhibitions and emotional expressiveness (Kalat, 1998). Persons with impairments in this area of brain functioning may have marked changes in personality and in planning abilities. The left side of the frontal lobe also contains an area known as Broca's area, which plays an important role in speech production (see Figure 2.4).

The **parietal lobe** is primarily involved in the process of integrating sensory information. This lobe is located next to the motor components of the frontal lobe. When individuals have damage in this area, they generally have some type of difficulty involving the ability to interpret sensory information. For instance, they may not be able to identify objects by touch and may have a poor sense of coordination. The **occipital lobe** is located below the parietal lobe and is involved in the receiving and sending of visual information.

Last, the **temporal lobe** is involved in emotions and human motivation. "Damage to the temporal lobes can lead to unprovoked laughter, joy, anxiety or violent behavior" (Kalat, 1995). The left side of the temporal lobe contains an area referred to as Wernicke's area, which has been identified as being important for language comprehension (see Figure 2.4).

The brain has three major divisions besides the four lobes: the forebrain, midbrain, and hindbrain (see Figure 2.5). The *forebrain,* or cerebrum, is the largest portion of the human brain. This area of the brain includes important structures such as the pituitary gland, which regulates certain hormones; the basal ganglia, which control certain aspects of movement; and the limbic system, which regulates such behaviors as eating, drinking, sexual activity, anxiety, and aggression (Kalat, 1998). The *midbrain* is the portion of the brain that includes aspects of the brainstem (that portion of the brain above the spinal cord). The midbrain also includes the reticular system, which monitors the state of the body through connections with the motor and sensory tracks. The third and final division of the brain is the *hindbrain.* This portion of the brain includes the *medulla oblongata* and the *cerebellum.* The medulla is considered a portion of the spinal cord and is involved in controlling heart rate, vomiting, salivation, and other vital reflexes (Andreasen, 1984; Kalat, 1998). The cerebellum is the portion of the brain concerned with a person's sense of balance.

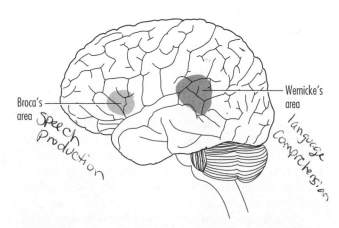

FIGURE 2.4   Broca's area and Wernicke's area (Goldstein, 1994)

FIGURE 2.5
Structures and areas in the human brain

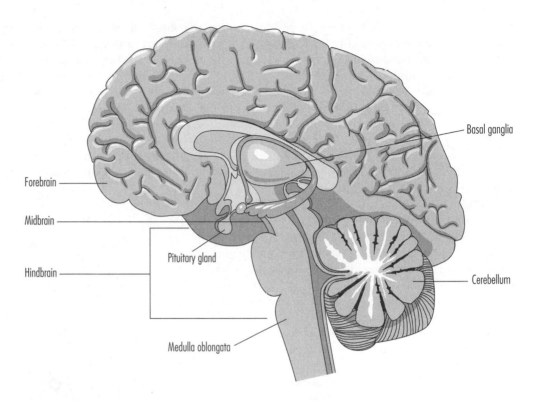

Basal ganglia

Forebrain

Midbrain

Pituitary gland

Hindbrain

Cerebellum

Medulla oblongata

Autonomic Nervous System

The autonomic nervous system involves the **sympathetic** and the **parasympathetic nervous systems** (see Figure 2.6). The autonomic nervous system controls glands, internal organs, smooth muscles, the stom-ach, and intestines. It is the system that plays a significant role in the human stress response. It is also the system that contributes to many of the symptoms and signs observed in persons with anxiety disorders. Under stress, the sympathetic nervous system prepares the body to participate in the fight-or-flight response. This system speeds up the heart rate, increases the blood supply to the body's organs and skeletal muscles, and prepares the body to respond to a perceived sense of threat (DiMatteo, 1991).

The parasympathetic system counteracts the stimulatory effects of the sympathetic system; that is, it serves the opposite function (DiMatteo, 1991). This system is called the parasympathetic nervous system because it consists of nerves that are next to the sympathetic nerve pathways.

Sympathetic		Parasympathetic
Pupils dilated, dry; far vision	**Eyes**	Pupils constricted, moist; near vision
Dry	**Mouth**	Salivating
Goose bumps	**Skin**	No goose bumps
Sweaty	**Palms**	Dry
Passages dilated	**Lungs**	Passages constricted
Increased rate	**Heart**	Decreased rate
Supply maximum to muscles	**Blood**	Supply maximum to internal organs
Increased activity	**Adrenal glands**	Decreased activity
Inhibited	**Digestion**	Stimulated

FIGURE 2.6   **Autonomic nervous system (Goldstein, 1994)**

Biochemical Processes in the Nervous System

We currently know that the brain consists of various groupings of neurochemical systems (Andreasen & Black, 1991). These systems vary depending on the function they perform in the nervous system. Social work practitioners cannot directly assess these biochemical systems and are not expected to do so. However, they should understand how these systems operate and how they relate to various forms of human behavior.

The structural organization of any true living system has the cell as its basic unit of organization. This fundamental unit consists of three kinds of molecules: proteins, lipids and nucleic acids. Proteins are the fundamental substances involved in the building of cells, muscles, skin, and internal organs. In fact, the term *protein* is derived from the Greek word *proteious,* "of first rank" (Page, 1981). **Proteins** are defined as any organic compound that has a large combination of amino acids. Scientists have identified over 100 amino acids, 20 of which are the building blocks for forming proteins. Eight of the amino acids must be obtained from dietary sources: isoleucine, leucine, lysine, methionine, phenylalanine, threonine, tryptophan, and valine. These eight amino acids are referred to as *essential amino acids.* Any dietary deficiency in these amino acids contributes to many of the problems observed in social work involving delayed growth and development, emotional disturbance, and various physical conditions. Protein molecules also include a class of biochemical catalysts called *enzymes.* Enzymes facilitate chemical reactions in cells and aid proteins in achieving their structural and transport functions in the cell processes of human organisms (Steiner & Pomerantz, 1981). The other key molecules in living organisms are the *nucleic acids.* The two kinds of nucleic acids important in the study of development are deoxyribonucleic acid (DNA) and ribonucleic acid (RNA). These nucleic acids are important in the transmission of genetic information and in the synthesis of proteins (Steiner & Pomerantz, 1981, p. 3). In this section, we will explore the influence of biochemical processes by examining the biochemical aspects of our nervous system.

Although proteins are involved in all processes of growth and development, social workers need to understand their functions in the **central** and **peripheral nervous systems** (see Figure 2.7). The central nervous system (CNS) consists of the neural cells and their attendant chemical processes that are located within the brain or the spinal cord. The peripheral nervous system (PNS), in contrast, involves all the neural cells and cell processes that lie outside the brain and the spinal cord (Hoyenga & Hoyenga, 1988). Our entire nervous system

consists of thousands of nerve cells, and each nerve cell receives information from about one thousand other nerve cells (Hoyenga & Hoyenga, 1988).

There are two kinds of cells in our nervous system: glia and neurons. **Glia** cells make up the bulk of our brain. There are various kinds of glia in our nervous system. They are often referred to as "supporting cells" (Kalat, 1998). Their exact nature and function are still being debated (Hoyenga & Hoyenga, 1988). However, we know that they do not covey information

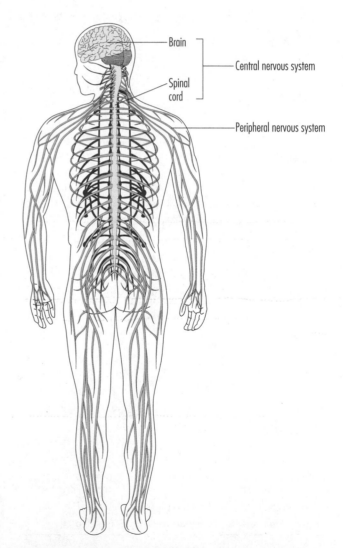

FIGURE 2.7   **Central and peripheral nervous systems (Goldstein, 1994)**

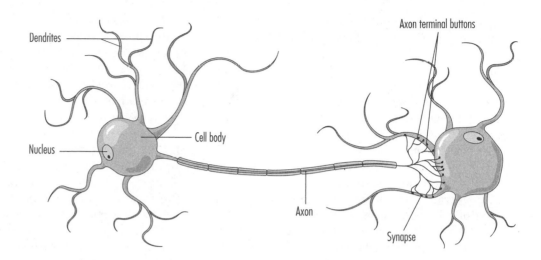

from one cell to another and are not as plentiful in the brains of non-human species (Kalat, 1995).

Neurons are generally what people refer to when they speak of nerve cells (see Figure 2.8). Neurons are the cells involved in conveying information from one cell to another. Some of these cells are long and have branched extensions that diverge from their bodies. The single long extensions are called *axons,* and the short extensions are called *dendrites* (Lickey & Gordon, 1983). **Axons** are long fibers that carry the impulses from the cell body of a neuron to other cells. **Dendrites** perform the opposite function. They are the branched fibers on a cell body that bring messages to the cell body of the neuron. Neurons are the only cells in the human body that are separate from one another (Maxmen & Ward, 1995). Since neurons are separate, they need to communicate across the open spaces between individual neurons and between neurons and other cells. The space between any two neurons or a neuron and another cell is called the **synaptic cleft** (see Figure 2.9).

How are messages transmitted across this synaptic cleft from one cell to another? At the tip of the axon is a small bulblike swelling called the *axon terminal* (Lickey & Gordon, 1983, p. 18). An axon terminal is generally found near a dendrite of another cell body. The axon terminal of the neuron sending the message is referred to as the *presynaptic terminal,* and the receiving portion of the neuron is referred to as the *postsynaptic membrane.* Conveying information from the transmitting cell to the receiving cell across the synaptic cleft requires mechanisms, known as *synapses,* for

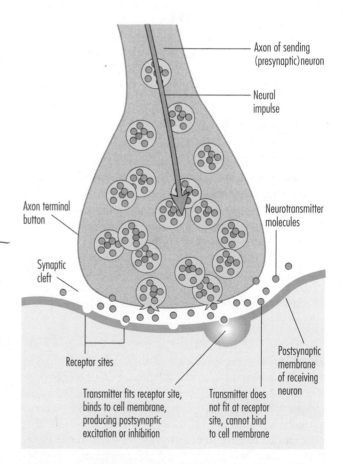

FIGURE 2.9 **Synapse (Weiten, 1995)**

communicating the impulse or the message. There are different types of synapses, some chemical and others electrical (Grebb, Reus, & Freimer, 1988). Chemical synapses involve the signaling of information from one cell to another by means of chemical substances. Different cells in the nervous system release different kinds of chemical substances to transmit the information across the synaptic cleft. In our discussion, we will focus on the actions of one type of chemical substance, the neurotransmitters, because they play a central role in current treatments of mental disorders.

Neurotransmitters are chemicals that are synthesized inside the neuron. "Each neuron synthesizes its neurotransmitters from materials in the blood" (Kalat, 1998; p. 55). Dozens of chemicals function as neurotransmitters. Some of their names are:

amino acids acids containing an amine group (NH-2) such as glutamate, GABA, and others

peptides chains of amino acids such as endorphins, substance P, neuropeptide Y, and others (A protein is a also a chain of amino acids; the term *peptide* is generally used for short chains, *protein* for long chains)

acetylcholine a "one-member family": similar to an amino acid, except that the NH-2 group has been replaced by an N(CH-3)3 group

monoamines non-acidic neurotransmitters containing an amine group (NH-2) formed by a metabolic change of certain amino acids: serotonin (indoleamines), dopamine, norepinephrine, and epinephrine (catecholamines)

purines adenosine and several of its derivatives, ATP, and others.

gases nitric oxide and possibly others (see, Kalat, 1998; p 56)

These neurotransmitters are released from the axon's end or presynaptic terminal, where they swim across the synaptic cleft and bind onto receptors on the membranes (or edges) of adjacent cells (the postsynaptic terminal) (Maxmen & Ward, 1995). Neurons actually act like a wet sponge. When they fire, they contract to release neurotransmitters; when not firing, they expand and reabsorb the neurotransmitters (Maxmen & Ward, 1995).

Receptors, located on postsynaptic membranes, are the special protein molecules to which neurotransmitters attach, much like a lock and a key relationship. When a neurotransmitter is released from one nerve cell, swims across the cleft, and attaches to a receptor site on another cell, that process is called *binding.* This binding process activates chemical changes in the receiving neuron. Sometimes the chemical change encourages the production of a nerve impulse, and other times it discourages nerve impulses. When the chemical process encourages the production of a nerve impulse, this is called *synaptic excitation;* when the chemical process in the membrane discourages an impulse, it is called *synaptic inhibition.*

In sum, a transmitting neuron releases a chemical substance known as a neurotransmitter from the presynaptic terminal. This chemical crosses the space between the cells and binds onto the postsynaptic membrane of the receiving cell. The chemical then either encourages the receiving cell to fire a nerve impulse or discourages the cell from firing an impulse.

GROWTH AND DEVELOPMENT OF NEURONS

Neurons develop very rapidly before we are born; 250,000 neurons are added each minute during many phases of prenatal development. When a child is born, it has a full complement of neurons. Nature provides us with perhaps twice as many neurons as we need (Sheibel, 1997). A newborn infant's nerve cells appear much like a mass of unconnected electrical wires. Imagine having the job of trying to connect all these neurons! Fortunately, no one is individually responsible for this monumental task, but we do know that a connection is made among these nerve cells every time the infant is touched, held, or has some other form of experience with primary caregivers. In other words, the nurture part of the nature-versus-nurture expression plays an important role in how our brains are wired and organized. In fact, most of the development of the brain following birth involves the wiring and rewiring of different neuronal systems. "Our genes set up an enormous number of neurons, connections, and potential connections, and then experience determines how many and which ones will survive" (Kalat, 1995; p. 151).

A conservative estimate is that the newborn's brain consists of about 100 billion nerve cells that are in need of being connected (Nash, 1997). The infant's brain at this point has been described as being like "the Pentium chips in a computer before the factory preloads the software. They are pure and almost infinite potential, unprogrammed circuits that might one day compose rap songs and do calculus, erupt in fury and melt in ecstasy" (Begley, 1996; p. 54). The "programming" of these "chips" is provided by the infant's experiences. In fact, we now know that the growth and development of the brains of children suffer serious consequences if they are deprived of stimulating environments during the first three years of their development. (See Focus on Theory: Neurons in their Environment, this page, which was written by a social worker who also is a neuroscientist. This Focus section examines additional information in the research literature about the role of the environment in neuronal systems.) "Early stimulation with toys in an enriched environment dramatically alters brain structure, resulting in greater branching of nerve cells, and increased number of supporting gila. Stimulated lab animals developed 25% more synapses per nerve cell and 80% more blood vessels to nourish each cell" (*Los Angeles Times,* 1996). Thus experience plays a major role in the formation of the synapses and connections between neurons that are characteristic of the major neuronal systems that make up the human brain. This includes the systems responsible for enabling us to learn a second language, play an instrument, and learn mathematics. In fact, we now know that there are critical periods for a number of human functions that develop during the early years of a child's life: emotional control, ages 0–2; vocabulary, ages 0–3; social attachment, ages 0–2; math/logic, ages 1–4; music, ages 3–10; and second language, ages 0–10 (Begley, 1996; Rutter & Rutter, 1993).

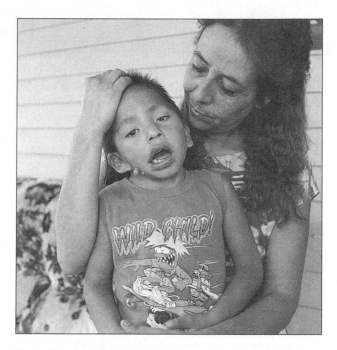

Some of the typical features of children suffering from fetal alcohol syndrome include a small non-symmetrical head, a short nose, a flattened area between the eyes, oddly shaped eyes, and a thin upper lip.

FOCUS ON THEORY

Neurons in Their Environment (NIE)

In the person-in-the-environment approach to practice, social workers examine how behavior and personality are influenced by biological factors, such as genetics, along with psychosocial environmental circumstances, such as the nuclear family and the community in which one is raised. In a similar manner, neuronal development can be examined by focusing on the molecular properties of individual nerve cells that make up the "community" in which they develop. This community includes other nerve cells and extracellular fluid surrounding each cell, along with various biochemicals, minerals, and nutrients. Just as factors in a person's family, community, and physical environment influence individual development, neurons, too, are influenced by their "neighbors."

Within the brain, spinal cord, and peripheral nervous system, there are billions of neurons connected to one another at junctures called *synapses.* These connections make up the circuitry, or hard wiring, of the nervous system that allows us to perceive our internal and external environment and make necessary changes via the motor component of the nervous system. In addition, our neuronal circuitry is responsible for uniquely human behavior such as acquisition of language, ability to emote and problem solve, abstract thinking, and the creation of art, technology, and science—which, of course, allow us to contemplate, for example, how our nervous system is designed and how it develops!

Since nerve cells are particularly active and most vulnerable during embryonic development, it is especially important to understand how we can optimize the neuronal environment during early life. We are equally concerned about identifying risk factors, such as street drugs, alcohol, nicotine, exposure to HIV, and malnutrition, that can impede neuronal development. To fully appreciate the importance of early neuronal development, we will now consider some of the highlights that take place during this period.

During the first trimester of pregnancy, primitive nerve cells divide and connect with one another, thus differentiating into specific structures like brain, spinal cord, and sense organs. Nerve cells continue to proliferate in the second and third trimesters. At the birth of the infant, although cell division ceases, existing nerve cells increase in size (hypertrophy), and synaptic formation increases dramatically. Within a relatively short time after birth, the brain increases dramatically in size, and higher cortical functions such as learning, memory, and problem solving take place.

Numerous studies have revealed that early-childhood experiences with nurturing and stimulation can have a profound effect on infant and child development. For example, a five-year study at the University of North Carolina involving low-income children revealed that an intensive educational program for both child and parent raises IQ scores by almost 20%, compared with a control group not given the program. This study underscores the malleability of the developing nervous system and the importance of providing early intervention before the "windows of opportunity" close. (The neural circuitry necessary for intellectual development is essentially completed by late adolescence.) The more stimulating the environment is, the more efficiently the infant brain develops. According to Dr. Bruce Perry, a psychiatrist at Baylor University College of Medicine, the brain develops in a "use-dependent" manner: It modifies itself according to experience. The more an infant is exposed to sensory experience, such as being held, played with, talked to, and touched, the more neuronal connections will be made, thus promoting the necessary circuitry for the child's acquisition of language skills, learning, memory, socialization, and emotional development.

Now, let us briefly examine a different scenario—that is, when developing neurons are deprived of sensory input, critical nutrients, and are exposed to in-utero alcohol. Consider the case of Stephan, a 7-year-old boy who spent the first four years of his life in an Eastern European orphanage. Stephan was born prematurely to an alcoholic mother, was given up for adoption shortly after birth, and was subsequently raised in an orphanage characterized by staff shortages, lack of proper nutrition and medical care, and a gross lack of sensory stimulation. At 4 years of age he was malnourished (in the lowest 1% on the growth curve) and weak. He was adopted by an American couple when he was 4 and has had the following conditions: ADD, Fetal Alcohol Effects, Reactive Attachment Disorder (failure to bond with primary caregiver), Oppositional Defiant Disorder, possible PTSD, and borderline microencephaly (small brain size). This case illustrates what can happen to a child who is exposed to a hostile neuronal environment. Prevention of cases like Stephan's is possible if social workers and other health care providers begin working on increasing the levels of interventions that promote childhood stimulation and proper nutrition, as well as on eliminating many of the risk factors associated with childhood neglect and abuse.

Barry Oblas

Unlike most other human organs, the brain has two major growth spurts (Rutter & Rutter, 1993). The first major growth spurt occurs during the last trimester of the prenatal phase of development. If the fetus has inadequate intake of protein and calories during this last trimester, the number of brain cells can be reduced by as much as 40% (Kalat, 1998). Figure 2.10 provides an illustration of five stages of brain development that indicates how much growth occurs during the final trimester, in comparison with the other two trimesters. This figure also provides an illustration of a child's brain at age 1, which represents the status of the brain at the conclusion of its second major growth spurt.

FIGURE 2.10
Five stages of brain development (photo courtesy of Dana Copeland, in Kalat, 1998)

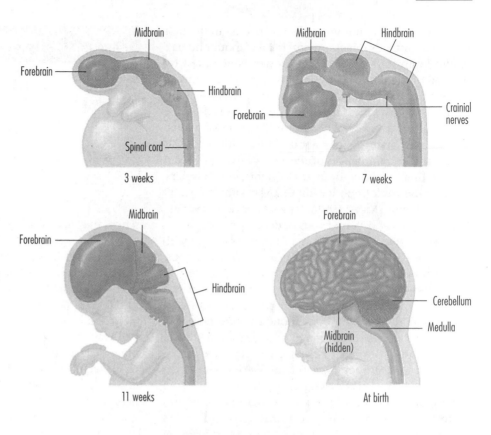

3 weeks

7 weeks

11 weeks

At birth

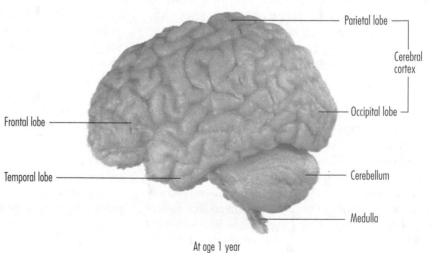

At age 1 year

The second major growth spurt occurs in the first year of an infant's development. In fact, about one half of the brain's entire postnatal growth is achieved by the end of the first year. By as early as 6 months, the infant's brain has reached half of its final mature weight. Most of the growth during this spurt is caused by the formation of synapses and the myelination of axons. The human brain weighs about 350 to 400 grams at birth. At the completion of the first year of postnatal life, the brain weighs about 1,000 grams, which is very close to the adult brain weight of approximately 1,200 to 1,400 grams (Kalat, 1998). Table 2.1 reviews average brain weights at different ages of development.

Assessments of variations in brain weight at various stages of development stimulate a number of questions about brain growth and developmental processes. For example, how does the brain continue to grow if it does not produce any new neurons after birth? Do changes in brain weight correspond to other noteworthy psychological or behavioral changes? For instance, does the onset of object permanence, concrete operations, and formal operations (cognitive developmental structures identified by Piaget, see Chapters 3, 6, 7, 8) correspond with any observable changes in the brain's neuronal structures? We have learned over the years that students are better equipped to answer many of these questions, as well as frame new ones, once they have developed a general understanding of the four stages involved in the development of neurons: *proliferation, migration, differentiation, and myelination.*

The **proliferation** stage involves all the processes involved in the production of new cells. We have devoted an entire chapter to the prenatal phase of development, which covers many proliferation processes. For this reason, in this chapter we will not address all the threats in the environment that can harm genetic and other biological mechanisms involved in the proliferation of neurons in the brain or other components of the nervous system. This does not mean that proliferation is not an important stage of neuronal development. In fact, a sizable proportion of social work's involvement in areas of prevention should be devoted to eliminating the occurrence of conditions in a person's environment that can destroy or impede the formation of needed neurons.

Neurons created in the proliferation process divide to make new cells. "Some of these new cells remain

TABLE 2.1   Brain Weights at Different Ages of Development

Age	Brain Weight (Grams)
20 weeks gestation	100
Birth	400
18 months	800
3-year-old	1,100
Adult	1,300–1,400

where they are, continuing to divide and redivide. Others become primitive neurons and gila that migrate (move) toward their eventual destination in the brain" (Kalat, 1995, p. 147). Some of these neurons use fibers from the gila and axons of other nerve cells to migrate to the brain's outer layers. "By studying normal neuron migration and factors that can disrupt it, scientists may find ways of preventing or treating epilepsy and many other developmental brain disorders" (Society for Neuroscience, 1995, p. 1). The **migration** of some neurons covers great distances. This is especially true of the neurons that form the outer layers of the cortex. Researchers are trying to understand how these neurons know which destinations to migrate to in the brain. Scientists do know that they migrate from the inside out, or from the center of the brain outward, but they do not completely understand factors that drive this process. What they do know is that genetic mutations, drugs such as cocaine and alcohol, and radiation can interfere with processes of neuronal migration (Society for Neuroscience, 1995). "For instance, many people who received radiation in the womb during the atomic explosions at Hiroshima and Nagasaki had incomplete neuron migration leading to brain abnormalities (Society of Neuroscience, 1995, p. 2).

After neurons migrate to their destinations in the brain, they start to differentiate. In the **differentiation** phase, they start forming axons and dendrites. In general, the axon grows before the dendrite, but some axons grow while the neuron is still migrating (Kalat, 1998). The last stage in the developmental process involves **myelination.** This is the stage in which axons are insulated by sheaths of myelin. These sheaths are composed mainly of fat that serves as an insulator. The insulation provided by the myelin sheaths lets signals travel through axons about 100 times faster than through an unmyelinated axon. This is important because, the better myelinated the axons are in your brain, the more likely your brain is capable of working at a fast rate. That is, myelin speeds up the circuits in your brain and thus makes certain activities easier for you to learn or perform.

We now know that different regions of the brain become myelinated at different stages of an individual's development. For instance, Wernicke' area in the brain, which deals with language comprehension, becomes myelinated about six months before Broca's area even starts. [Recall that Broca's area deals with processes involving language production. This component of language acquisition logically should follow the formation of processes involving language-comprehension abilities (Markezich, 1996).]

When you are reading the chapters on development that follow, try to note when the brain is undergoing increased processes of myelination, because this can help mark other forms of developmental changes in behavior or cognition. That is, these processes form the bases for many cognitive and other mental abilities observed in humans across the life course.

Implications for Practice

Social workers play a critical role in service-delivery systems for traumatized youth, for persons with serious mental disabilities, and for persons suffering from various types of brain injuries. In each of these areas, knowledge of the brain and how it is compromised by threats in the environment is essential to designing corrective and preventive interventions. Bruce Perry and his associates estimate that the number of children exposed to a traumatic event in the United States is well above 4 million. Included in this conservative estimate are children exposed to physical or sexual abuse, living in the fallout zone of domestic or community violence, being a party to a serious car accident, and so on (Perry et al., 1995). Perry and his associates have concluded that such traumatic situations can dramatically influence the brain during periods of vulnerability, when brain systems are organizing. This research on brain development is contributing to reforms in public policy that recognize that children are not as resilient as we once thought (Perry et al., 1995). Extreme traumatic experiences can contribute to life-long traits

of personal disturbance. In other words, children will not necessarily get over bad or toxic social environments that they are exposed to during their early life (Garbarino, 1995).

Knowledge of the brain and its development is also critical for the design of appropriate forms of early intervention. If practitioners can develop interventions that reduce the intensity and severity of a child's response to trauma then there is less danger that he or she will develop a negative use-dependent response. That is, the more a child is in a fear state, the greater the probability becomes that he or she will begin to carry around a hyperarousal or dissociative response that will be transferred across situations and time (Perry et al., 1995).

Understanding the brain and how it develops also has implications for the design of programs intended to prevent child abuse and neglect, such as Healthy Families America. Society needs more of these programs that target risk for abuse and neglect during critical periods of brain growth and development. In addition, research on the use-dependent features of brain organization points to the significance of providing support services for new mothers at risk for developing serious mental disorders. Depressed mothers are not available for their children; this fact can affect their responses to normal threats in their environment. This is especially true during windows of opportunity for the development of social attachment, emotional regulation, and so forth.

In sum, practitioners in direct and indirect services are obtaining more information about the role of biological factors in forming many traits and life destinations that social work is committed to eliminating. The profession is unlikely to realize this objective if it does not consider the biological threats to brain development.

Biophysical Hazards

We currently know that any deficits or dysfunctions in physiological structures will have some bearing on a person's social functioning. The social worker's duty is to assess how these physiological impairments influence the person's capacity to meet life tasks. Before appropriate support services can be identified, the social work professional must have a general understanding of the person's disease, impairment, or disability. This generalized understanding is not possible without a basic understanding of key human biological systems.

This understanding of biological systems is markedly improved whenever the social worker has a basic understanding of disease and health terminology. In fact, many social workers, in addition to health social workers, are expected to review the client's health status and history when doing background studies. This common expectation requires an understanding of human biosystems and health-related concepts. This section provides a brief, rather than a comprehensive, overview of biologically related concepts encountered in multiple-practice contexts. Further discussion of these topics is systematically provided in each subsequent chapter on developmental content under the heading "Biophysical Hazards." Our multidimensional framework seeks to make you aware of the need for having a developmental perspective on relevant biological hazards. This knowledge is needed for assessment in direct practice and in planning contexts involved in preventive programming. This section cannot cover all the relevant biosystems; that task is beyond the scope of this book. Instead, we hope to sensitize you to the various types of medical and physical information you will need in your practice. Additional information on biosystems is addressed in the biophysical sections of our chapters on life-span development.

CANCER

Any living organism can get cancer. Cancer is a serious disease that involves improper cell growth, indeed, the purposeless growth of cells. As we have discussed, our cells grow by the orderly process of cell division known as *mi-*

tosis. Mitosis involves one cell dividing into two cells, two cells becoming four, and so forth. The process of cell division is normally controlled by other natural processes. Any process that interferes with nature's controls can lead to massive cell growth. Rampant cell growth can lead to the buildup of masses of purposeless tissue referred to as a **tumor.** Self-contained tumors are called *benign* tumors; tumors that are spreading, or are not self-contained, are generally referred to as **malignant tumors.** The spread of these cells to other areas of the body is known as *metastasis*. When cancer metastasizes, the cells then begin to grow in other organs, and the disease is much more difficult to cure.

Though progress has been made in the diagnosis and treatment of cancer, this disease remains a leading cause of death, surpassed only by heart disease.

CARDIOVASCULAR SYSTEM PROBLEMS

The heart is a hollow "muscular pump" that provides the energy needed to force a person's blood through the body. It is one of the few human organs that works con-

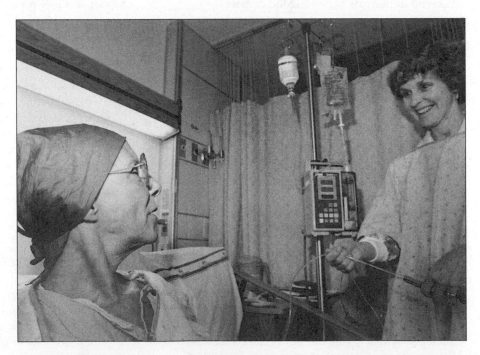

There are many psychosocial aspects of having cancer. For example, adjustment to hair loss is difficult both for people with cancer and for those around them.

stantly. This necessity for continuous work makes the heart vulnerable to a wide variety of injuries and abnormalities (Meyers, 1972). The heart is divided into four chambers: two *atria* and two *ventricles* (see Figure 2.11). The wall that runs down the center of the heart is called the *septum.* There are two chambers on each side of the septum. The top chambers are atria and the bottom chambers are ventricles. The structures that control the flow of blood through these chambers are *valves.* Blood gets into the heart by means of *veins.* The *arteries* carry blood from the heart to the rest of the body.

The heart is about the size of a human fist. It is enclosed in a thin sac called the **pericardium,** which covers the middle muscular layer of the heart. This important muscle is known as the *myocardium.* The function of the heart and its valves may be impaired by a variety of processes. For example, the heart or any of its components may be malformed at birth, a condition known as a *congenital heart disease.* Numerous factors may contribute to a congenital heart condition. Many of these factors will be discussed in our presentation of prenatal development. Also, the heart can be exposed to infections or other factors that damage or injure the heart's muscle (**myocarditis**) or its valves (**endocarditis**) (Meyers, 1972). There is also a technical term used when the sac surrounding the entire heart is diseased: *pericarditis.*

The most common lesion in valvular heart disease involves a condition known as *mitral valve insufficiency.* In this condition, the valve fails to prevent the regurgitation of processed blood. *Mitral stenosis* is another valvular disease involving the hardening or narrowing of the mitral valve, which is located between the left atrium and left ventricle. Social workers in mental health may encounter persons with severe anxiety symptoms that result from a condition known as **mitral valve prolapse.** This valvular disease involves the protrusion of one or both cusps of the mitral valve back into the left atrium. This protrusion can contribute to a backflow of blood. Common symptoms are chest pain, palpitations, fatigue, or dyspnea (shortness of breath and labored respiration). This is one of the conditions that a mental health worker should be aware of in performing differential assessments. The worker may need to make a referral to have this condition ruled out by a physician because it is often con-

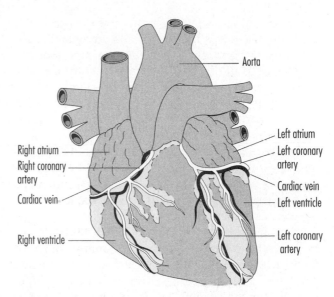

FIGURE 2.11   Cardiovascular system (Brannon & Feist, 1997)

fused with anxiety disorders and other forms of psychological distress.

The force of the blood moving through the heart may also injure any component of the cardiovascular system: heart, arteries, veins, capillaries. This force of the blood moving through the body is known as *blood pressure.* Normal blood pressure is expressed in two numbers, the **systolic pressure** and the **diastolic pressure.** The systolic pressure involves a measure of the heart when it is contracting and pumping blood out and through the body. This is the highest number, or measure of the blood's force through the heart. Normal blood pressure in a young adult is about 120 mm Hg (*hydrargyrum,* a measurement using mercury) systolic and 70 to 90 mm Hg diastolic (DiMatteo, 1991, p. 25). Diastolic pressure is the measure of the blood's flow during the relaxation, or diastole, of the heart. When a person's systolic pressure is above 140, or if the diastolic pressure is above 90, the person is considered to have *hypertension,* or high blood pressure. Essential hypertension refers to having a chronically elevated blood pressure over a long period of time.

Angina pectoris is a coronary condition involving pain and a tightness in the chest. This condition results when the heart muscle does not receive sufficient oxygen. When insufficient oxygen is directed to the heart's muscle, resulting in the death of part of the heart's tissue, this is referred to as a **myocardial infarction,** or heart attack. A number of processes can contribute to the blockage of arteries and to a myocardial infarction. For example, arteriosclerosis, a condition contributing to decreased blood supply, is a common condition that contributes to heart attacks. This condition is often associated with aging and may be referred to as hardening of the arteries. Atherosclerosis, a form of arteriosclerosis, involves the buildup of plaque on the walls of the arteries. Plaque is produced by a fatty substance known as *cholesterol;* it clogs up the arteries and impedes appropriate blood flow.

The heart beats at a rate of 60 to 80 beats per minute. A heart beat of 100 beats per minute or above following normal activities is an indicator of potential difficulties. An elevated heartbeat can indicate structural or functional impairment or the influence of some type of psychoactive substance. The heart rate, or *pulse,* must change to respond to the body's demands for oxygen. The heart generally beats faster when an individual is involved in a strenuous activity. However, it also beats faster when a person is angry, anxious, or emotionally excited. During pregnancy, the heart works harder because it is also handling the needs of the fetus. This is one of the major reasons some women experience secondary heart complications during pregnancy.

The blood flowing through the heart and cardiovascular system consists of several formed elements— *red cells (erythrocytes), white cells (leukocytes),* and *platelets (thrombocytes)*—in a liquid medium known as plasma. The number of red blood cells ranges from about 4.5 to 5.5 million per cubic milliliter of blood (Meyers, 1972). If a person has a red blood count of below 4 million or a blood hemoglobin (protein compound in the blood) below 12 grams, he or she is considered to have anemia. *Anemia* is a condition that involves inadequate red-blood-cell production. Red blood cells are responsible for carrying oxygen from the lungs to various tissues in the body. Anemia then may result in less oxygen being available to the body and cause fatigue and dizziness.

White cells number about 5,000 to 10,000 per cubic milliliter and protect the body against infections and other foreign substances. The platelet number is approximately 200,000 to 400,000 per milliliter. Platelets play a critical role in blood clotting. Platelet problems can result in difficulties with excess bleeding.

RESPIRATORY SYSTEM PROBLEMS

The respiratory system handles the inhalation of oxygen and the exhalation of carbon dioxide. This system consists of the lungs, diaphragm, major air pathway (trachea, or windpipe), and other air pathways (Meyers, 1972) (see Figure 2.12). The chief organ involved in the respiration process is the lungs. The lungs are two pyramid-shaped structures that lie in the chest cavity. The lungs consist of spongy tissue that is divided into numerous small air sacs called *alveoli.* These air sacs have in their walls a network of tiny blood vessels called *capillaries.* These capillaries cover the alveoli and take the oxygen from the air into the bloodstream. *Bronchial asthma* is a condition of the lungs characterized by intermittent attacks of shortness of breath. The cause is often an allergic response associated with the constriction of the *bronchioles,* tubes that carry air from the trachea to the air sacs, or alveoli. During an asthma attack, the bron-

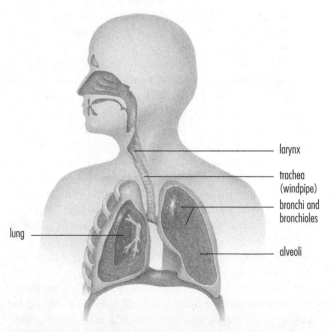

larynx

trachea (windpipe)

bronchi and bronchioles

lung

alveoli

FIGURE 2.12   **Respiratory system (Ingraham & Ingraham, 1995)**

FIGURE 2.13
Endocrine system
(Goldstein, 1994)

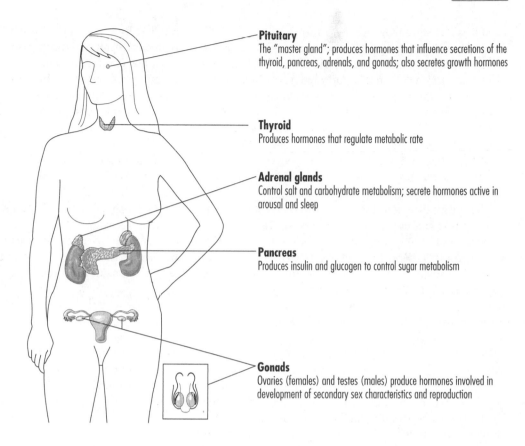

Pituitary
The "master gland"; produces hormones that influence secretions of the thyroid, pancreas, adrenals, and gonads; also secretes growth hormones

Thyroid
Produces hormones that regulate metabolic rate

Adrenal glands
Control salt and carbohydrate metabolism; secrete hormones active in arousal and sleep

Pancreas
Produces insulin and glucogen to control sugar metabolism

Gonads
Ovaries (females) and testes (males) produce hormones involved in development of secondary sex characteristics and reproduction

chial muscle constricts and thick, sticky mucus is produced. This mucus further obstructs air pathways. Air intake may be normal, but only partial expiration is achieved. In severe attacks, mucus can plug or block the bronchi.

Acute bronchitis is a disorder involving a bacterial infection of the bronchi, whereas *chronic bronchitis* is a progressive inflammatory disease that is caused by exposure to irritants (Wilson, 1987). Chronic bronchitis is a disorder that develops in middle age, often in persons with a history of chronic smoking. This disorder contributes to extreme difficulty in breathing, or dyspnea. The condition is aggravated by damp and cold. If the alveolar walls are ruptured because of chronic bronchitis, the person will develop emphysema or chronic obstructive pulmonary disease. This condition destroys the walls between the alveoli and decreases the surface within the lung that can be used to exchange gases (DiMatteo, 1991, p. 29).

ENDOCRINE SYSTEM PROBLEMS

The endocrine system is a system of ductless glands that is controlled by the autonomic nervous system. The endocrine system consists of the pituitary, the thyroid, the adrenal, and the sex glands (or gonads), as well as the pancreas, and other glands (Meyers, 1972) (see Figure 2.13). These glands release chemical substances called *hormones* into the bloodstream. The stimuli that cause the release of these hormones are controlled by the nervous system, which is linked to the endocrine system by means of the pituitary gland and its connections with the hypothalamus (DiMatteo, 1991).

DiMatteo (1991) has summarized this process in relation to stress. When the sympathetic nervous system becomes aroused in response to an emergency, the hypothalamus chemically stimulates the pituitary to release ACTH (adrenocorticotropic hormone) into the blood. ACTH stimulates other hormones in response to stress. The adrenal glands, located on top of the kidneys, are stimulated to produce epinephrine and norepinephrine (adrenaline and noradrenaline), which speed up the heart and respiration and increase the liver's output of sugar to the muscles. Cortisol is also released by the adrenal glands during perceived emergencies to help control swelling should injury occur (p. 36). The role the pituitary plays in stress responses is just one example of the important roles played by endocrine glands in human emotions and behavior.

The pituitary gland consists of three lobes and is located just below the hypothalamus. The posterior pituitary collects vasoprine, an antidiuretic hormone, and oxytocin. Vasoprine is involved in the regulation of water reabsorption by the kidneys and oxytocin with contraction of involuntary muscles in the uterus (Green, Beatty, & Arkin, 1984). The thyroid gland is located at the front of the neck and secretes the hormone thyroxin. This hormone is essential for normal body growth and development. Hyperthyroidism is a condition that results from overactivity of the thyroid gland. The gland in this condition is generally enlarged. Hyperthyroidism is clinically characterized by nervousness, tremor, constant hunger, heat intolerance, hyperactivity, and insomnia. The pancreas is another important ductless gland that is located below the stomach. It secretes substances such as digestive enzymes, insulin, and glucagon.

Problems with insulin production and utilization lead to the disease *diabetes mellitus*. Insufficient production of insulin or inadequate use of insulin results in body cells being unable to absorb glucose or sugar from the blood for metabolism. As a result, glucose builds up in the blood and causes high blood sugar and the problems associated with diabetes mellitus. This disease occurs in two forms: Type I, or juvenile-onset diabetes (insulin dependent), and Type II, or adult-onset diabetes. Type I diabetes is caused by failure of the pancreas to produce sufficient insulin. Persons with this type of diabetes must have daily insulin injections to replace what the body fails to produce. In adult-onset diabetes, the body has decreased ability to utilize the insulin produced, so the pancreas must produce more insulin to compensate. Blood sugar also builds up, causing problems. Diabetes, especially juvenile-onset, can lead to many complications, including blindness,

renal failure, and infections in the lower extremities that can result in amputations. Persons with diabetes must pay careful attention to diet and weight and must carefully regulate their blood sugar levels. Regulation of blood sugar often requires finger sticks to check the blood. Social workers may be involved in helping diabetes mellitus sufferers adjust to the lifestyle changes necessary to maintain good health.

The other hormones produced by the endocrine system also play vital roles in human functioning. For example, researchers are exploring the role played by hormones in sexual and aggressive behavior.

Abnormalities in systemic processes can be major contributors to emotional disturbances and should not be ignored by social work practitioners in assessing dysfunctions in the affective domain.

Implications for Practice

Health status is significantly related to a person's sense of well-being. As a result, practitioners must be knowledgeable about conditions that threaten key health functions. They must also understand the effects of various conditions on a person's sense of self, behavior, and expectations. Biological defects in organ systems or diseases can significantly change how people perceive who they are and how they relate to others. For instance, persons who have had a heart attack will make substantial changes in how they approach many aspects of their everyday lives. They may (1) develop new approaches to handling stress, (2) change their lifestyle, (3) eliminate previous coping behaviors that contributed to their heart attack, and (4) change diet and exercise practices. They also may develop new maladaptive responses to fears that have no realistic basis in their recovery process. Thus, it is essential for the social worker to appreciate these conditions as well as develop a basic understanding of the organ systems affected by common disease processes. With such information, social workers are better equipped to engage in effective education, prevention, and treatment.

In health social work, practitioners also need to have a basic understanding of illness behavior. Illness behavior refers to how people respond to their subjective realization that they have an illness. Illness behavior can vary directly with the biological systems involved in the client's illness. Some clients have better adaptive coping skills for dealing with physical disorders and distress than other clients do. And, although some people do not handle physical illnesses well, these people may have excellent skills for handling mental disorders. The social worker must understand how basic biological systems function and how these systems affect human behavior processes in order to improve client responses to physical and mental disturbances.

Overview

Social workers who ignore the biophysical dimension will compromise the quality of both their theory and their practice in their efforts to understand human behavior (Saleebey, 1992). As Saleebey has argued, "the profession of social work has given only superficial attention to taking into account the body's urges, promptings and energies" (1992, p. 112). We have attempted to compensate for this limitation by examining key biophysical systems that play a fundamental role in understanding human behavior. We assume that the body-mind-environment connection requires the integration of each of the biological subsystems examined in this chapter.

Individual variations in biological systems must be identified in social work assessments. Social workers must not hold biological variables constant in their practical assessments, and practitioners must be as diligent about assessing biological dimensions as they are about assessing social and psychological dimensions. If social workers do not take into account these biological variations, they run the risk of subscribing to abstract conceptions of client concerns and run the additional risk of ignoring vital biological sensations or needs that make up the fundamental characteristics of the human experience.

Summary

BIOPHYSICAL GROWTH AND DEVELOPMENT

Any understanding of human growth and development must take into account key biophysical systems. Human growth includes all the processes that contribute to the addition of new components of a person's physical structure, including biophysical components like cells that result in increased size of a person's body. Growth differs from development, which refers to all the processes that contribute to the improvement or change in body components.

Cells represent the smallest unit of living physical matter. Basic cellular functions are under the control of DNA and RNA, the nucleic acids that determine our hereditary characteristics. A gene is a small portion of the DNA molecule that provides the blueprint for the other nucleic acids that control the fundamental properties of human organisms.

Chromosomes are located in the nucleus of every cell and contain sets of genes from each of the parents. The mother and father each provide 23 chromosomes to the zygote, or fertilized egg. These chromosomes contain many genes that influence our inherited characteristics.

Social workers must understand the fundamental processes that influence variations in inherited characteristics in order to help clients understand inherited physical and developmental processes. The fundamental kinds of inherited disorders encountered by social work practitioners include single-gene disorders (dominant, autosomal recessive, sex-linked recessive), multifactorial disorders, chromosomal disorders (Down syndrome, Trisomy 18 and 13), and sex chromosomal disorders. Cell-division problems occur in both meiotic and mitotic processes. Translocation and nondisjunction are the most common problems in cell division. Each of these problems influences biophysical growth and development.

Biochemical processes, especially those in the central and peripheral nervous systems, influence many aspects of human behavior. The central nervous system (CNS) consists of the nerve cells (neurons) and their attendant chemical processes located within the brain and spinal cord. The peripheral nervous system involves all the nerve cells and cell processes that lie outside the brain and spinal cord. The nervous system consists of thousands of nerve cells, and each nerve cell receives information from about 1,000 other nerve cells through biochemical substances called neurotransmitters. The growth and development of neurons have optimum windows for the establishment of specific functions. Many traits in humans are influenced by factors in the environment that determined how key neuronal systems were programmed.

BIOPHYSICAL HAZARDS

Impairments in any organ or physiological system have significant implications for social functioning. Cardiovascular-system problems are a major concern at various stages of the life cycle. There are many ways to measure the cardiovascular organ system's functioning. Blood pressure represents the force of blood moving through the body, and it is expressed in two numbers: systolic pressure and diastolic pressure. Social workers should know the ranges of normal blood pressure at various stages of development and in various social situations. The heart rate, which is typically 60 to 80 beats per minute, changes in response to the body's demands for oxygen and is measured as a pulse. Abnormalities in the heart, respiratory, and endocrine systems can contribute to many forms of emotional disturbance.

Social workers need a basic understanding of the range of physical conditions that contribute to emotional and behavioral disturbances in each of the key organ systems outside the nervous system.

🜨 Online Resources

Brain Networks
http://www.brainnet.org
    The central nervous system and brain disorders network and Alliance of the National Foundation of Brain Research has links on this site.

Neurotransmitters
http://www.letsfindout.com/subjects/body/rfilocke.html
    This is a resource for searching on neurotransmitter issues.

Brain Development
http://www.unol.org/bb
    This site presents a curriculum for the promotion of balanced care relevant to brain development.

Diabetes Among Native Americans
http://www.aaip.com/resources/diabetesrisk.html
    This site provides data on diabetes as a growing problem for Native Americans.

InfoTrac® College Edition

For interesting materials related to what you have just read, please go to the *InfoTrac College Edition* website and search using the following key words:

nature and nurture	gene therapy
mental retardation	behavior genetics

Key Terms

acetylcholine	mitral valve prolapse
amino acid	monoamine
angina pectoris	multifactorial disorder
autosomes	mutation
axon	myelination
canalization	myocardial infarction
central nervous system	myocarditis
chromosome disorder	neuron
cystic fibrosis	neurotransmitter
dendrite	occipital lobe
development	parasympathetic nervous
diastolic pressure	system
differentiation	parietal lobe
dominant gene	peptide
Down syndrome	pericardium
endocarditis	peripheral nervous
fragile X syndrome	system
frontal lobe	phenotype
genotype	proliferation
glia	protein
growth	purine
hemophilia	recessive gene
Huntington's chorea	single-gene disorder
hyperplasia	sympathetic nervous
hypertrophic growth	system
Klinefelter's syndrome	synaptic cleft
Lesch-Nyhan syndrome	systolic pressure
malignant tumor	Tay-Sachs disease
meiosis	temporal lobe
migration	tumor
glia	Turner's syndrome
mitosis	

The Psychological Dimension for Assessing Social Functioning

CHAPTER CONTENTS

What do we mean by the term *psychological*? Although we can have an intuitive understanding of psychological processes, we often find it difficult to define our psychological characteristics and functioning. Although the discipline of psychology is relatively new, questions and concerns about the mind's operations have interested humans since the inception of human history (Hothersall, 1984). Our ancestors explored dreams, memory, ideas, perception, and other key mental functions. They were also curious about what we would refer to today as *personality*, or individual differences.

What factors account for patterns we observe in our character and our behavior? How is each one of us unique? Can we differentiate ourselves from others around us? These are questions commonly addressed by psychologists with an interest in personality concerns. What is the role of intuition and subjective experience in understanding the mind or cognition? What determines the formation of our individual personalities? What are common human needs and emotions? How do people learn and forget information? What motivates people to behave as they do? How is information represented and stored in our minds? A multitude of questions reflect the interest in the psychological dimension of human behavior.

This chapter addresses the psychological dimension of psychosocial functioning. The psychological system serves the purpose of mobilizing our biological and social resources to attain goals (Anderson & Carter, 1984; 1990). Anderson and Carter (1984) have pointed out that the function of goal attainment is what differentiates the psychological system from the other major systems of psychosocial functioning. The psychological system also plays a critical role in helping avoid danger.

The psychological dimension includes many subsystems with key concepts of use to social workers in assessing the psychological contributions to problems of social functioning. Each of these subsystems includes concepts that are useful in assessing psychological contributions to human behavior. For instance, what psychological systems are useful in assessing Raul Salazar's case, introduced in the last chapter? Is Raul experiencing any difficulties in his emotions, attitudes, or perceptual abilities? Does Raul have problems with concentration or attention? What is the difference? Are Raul's reported activity levels a function of problems with behavior or emotions? Are Raul's behavioral problems learned?

Answers to these questions involve systematically gathering data about key psychological functions covered in this chapter. Knowledge of these functions is also useful in differentiating the psychological system from the social and biological systems in our multidimensional framework. Several theories pertain to how the psychological system affects functioning. The following Focus sections examine Freud's psychodynamic theory and Erikson's psycho-social development approach, which expanded Freud's ideas by covering the entire life-span.

FOCUS ON THEORY

Psychodynamic Theory

Sigmund Freud, a physician and neurologist, developed the first major theory of personality during the late 19th century. He became interested in patients with mental problems and encouraged his clients to explore their childhood experiences. He believed that all behavior was determined by events that happened in childhood. His contributions to psychology are perhaps unmatched in terms of their overall influence (Leahey, 1987). His concepts and views of human nature are incorporated in popular culture, most areas of social science, literature, and the humanities. He clarified for practitioners how we can study the unconscious by observing its clinical manifestations.

All human behavior, according to Freud, is driven by a special kind of energy referred to as the **libido.** The libido is in constant search of pleasure. This "libido theory" is considered the cornerstone of contemporary psychoanalysis (Gaylin, 1986). "With this theory, all human behavior could be related to the driving force of the sexual instinct and the counterforces that kept it in check" (Gaylin, 1986, p. 47). The libido is associated with instinctual drives like hunger, elimination, and sex, which are biologically determined. These drives must be released in order to reduce tension, and this release is experienced as pleasure. These drives

operate according to the *pleasure principle,* which insists on immediate gratification of urges. Even an infant's behavior is motivated by these unconscious, pleasure-seeking urges (Frosh, 1987). The **id,** one of the three components of personality, is the instinctive component and operates from the basis of the pleasure principle. The **id** is often referred to as the storehouse of psychic energy. This psychic energy is limited to **primary process thinking,** which is based on irrational, illogical, and fantasy-oriented notions; it is disconnected from reality.

The **ego** saves us from being victims of our own pleasure. It is the executive branch of one's personality and makes rational decisions. It is able to postpone pleasure until an appropriate time. The ego operates within the context of the *reality principle* by bringing individual pleasure within the boundaries of reality. The ego must create balance between the other two personality components, the id and the superego. In attempting to create a balance, the ego is sensitive to the desires for immediate gratification and also acknowledges social realities such as norms, rules, and customs that influence behavior. The ego is responsible for mediating between the id and the superego. Mastery of this task leads to mature and adaptive behavior. Such adaptive behavior is referred to as **secondary process thinking,** which is based on realistic and rational approaches to problem solving. The ego desires to avoid any negative consequences from society and thus helps the person conform to society's rules. The ego is an abstract concept that is often defined by its functions. These functions represent the way a person adapts to his or her environment (Goldstein, 1984).

The **superego** is the moral guidance that helps balance the drives associated with the id. It represents the social standards derived from society and the family. As children grow up they are exposed to moral standards for behavior. The id and the superego are not too friendly with each other, because each is oriented toward a different goal—one pleasure and the other moral standards. The ego mediates between these two components, taking into account instinctual impulses and moral values. Freud assumes that the superego emerges from the ego at about 3–5 years of age.

For Freud, the superego emerges from the ego through identification with intimate authority figures or from the selective reactions of an individual's environment to certain behaviors (Andrews & Bonta, 1998). In many of his writings, he considered the process of identification to be the most important determinant of moral conduct. Freud also assumed that the superego consists of two elements: the conscience and the ego-ideal. The **conscience** involves internalized mental representations of conduct that are subject to punishment, whereas the **ego-ideal** is considered the mental representation of conduct that is positively valued by the environment (Andrews & Bonta, 1994; 1998).

From a Freudian perspective, how does personality develop? Psychoanalytic theory is based on a stage theory of development. We move through various stages, and how well we master those stages forms the basis of our personality. As children mature, their sexual energy (urges for physical pleasure) is invested in biologically predetermined areas of the body. Each stage in Freud's psychosexual development represents a different area of sexual focus that influences our adult personality. Infants are dominated by an oral focus, early childhood moves through an anal and phallic focus, middle childhood is represented by a latency period, and the psychosexual stages end at puberty when the focus is on one's genitals.

Personality depends on how each of these stages is handled. Children may experience excessive gratification or excessive frustration while in one of the stages. When this happens, *fixation* occurs, whereby the child cannot move on to the next stage of development. Fixation can be apparent during the adult years. For example, many people are familiar with the label "anal." A person is referred to as "anal" because his or her fixation is exhibited by compulsiveness. Table 3.1 presents Freud's stages of psychosexual development.

According to Freud, early childhood development is critical in the development of personality. In fact, personality is laid down by the age of 5 or 6 as the child completes the primary psychosexual stages. The

TABLE 3.1	Freud's Stages of Psychosexual Development		
Stage	Sexual Focus	Key Tasks	Fixations
Oral (0–1)	Mouth	Weaning from breast or bottle	Obsessive eating, talking, smoking, drinking
Anal (1–3)	Anus	Toilet training	Obstinacy, compulsiveness, possessiveness
Phallic (3–6)	Genitals	Oedipal crisis, identification with adult role models	Homosexuality, narcissism, arrogance, adult role models flamboyance
Latency (6–12)	None	Focus on social relationships	
Genital (puberty)	Genitals (intercourse)	Development of intimate relationships	

last two phases of development are latency and genital. During the latency stage, a child's sexual energy subsides. During the genital stage in adolescence, the conflicts of early childhood are revived. If they have been mastered appropriately, then the child moves into normal heterosexual relationships. This foundation of one's personality is re-experienced in adulthood, whereby adult conflicts are related to early crises that occurred in childhood. Many theorists did not like Freud's notion that personality development is confined to the early years. Most notable is Erik Erikson, who believes that personality evolves across the lifespan. His work, as well as Freud's, is criticized for its emphasis on heterosexual relationships.

Anna Freud (1895–1982) is known for her work on defense mechanisms and how defensive reactions determine our behavior. Because of the focus in her work on the adaptations of the ego to the demands of the environment, she is seen by some as the first proponent of the modern-day field of **ego-psychology,** or **self-theory** (Barlow & Durand, 1995). These approaches focus on understanding how the self copes with the demands of the environment. For ego-psychologists, ego functioning is determined by assessing a person's *impulse control, frustration tolerance, and affect regulation.* Data on these functions provides mental health professionals with information about the quality of ego functioning and about the defenses a person utilizes to cope with stressful circumstances (Stoudemire, 1994).

Erikson's Psychosocial Development

Erik Erikson is noted for having developed a psychosocial approach to human development. Before immigrating to the United States in 1933, Erikson worked with Sigmund Freud. But Erikson's work includes several key departures from Freud's thinking. In Erikson's view, Freud attached far too much emphasis to the role of biological and sexual forces on human development. This resulted in Freud's neglect of development after adolescence. Erikson, in contrast, was interested in explaining development from birth through death.

Erikson assumed that people follow a sequence of stages of development from birth through death. These developmental stages include tasks that result from both biological forces and age-related social or cultural expectations. The biological forces follow a built-in plan that governs when and how aspects of the biological system arise. This plan is technically referred to in the literature as the **epigenetic principle.** It refers to the biological blueprint that dictates how the organism grows and reaches maturity. This plan guiding the biological forces combines with the changes in the social expectations of a society to structure the person's adaptation to his or her environment.

Erikson has identified eight psychosocial stages of human development, as shown in Figure 3.1. Each of these stages is marked by differential tasks. "They are

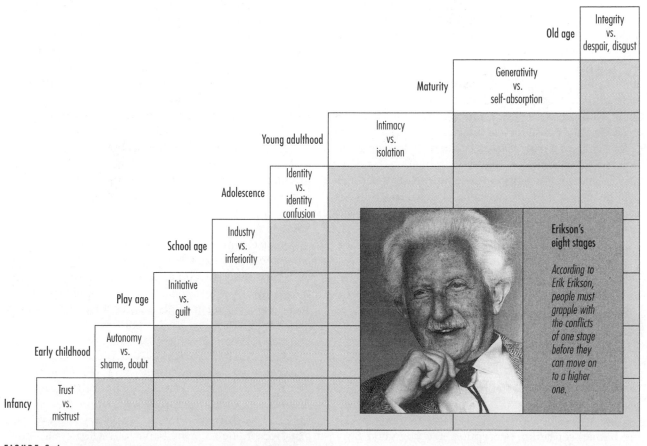

FIGURE 3.1   Erikson's eight psychosocial stages (Erikson, 1976)

patterned sequences of stages encompassing appropriate physical, emotional, and cognitive tasks that the individuals must master in the struggle to adjust to the demands of the social environment" (Okun, 1984, p. 16). This patterned sequence of changes is not considered complete in adulthood; it continues across the lifespan. A fundamental issue underlying this sequence of changes is how individuals define their sense of identity.

For Erikson, each of the eight stages of development should be viewed as a psychosocial crisis or psychosocial conflict. "Whether the conflict of a particular stage is successfully resolved or not, the individual is pushed by both biological maturation and social demands into the next stage" (Sigelman & Shaffer, 1995, p. 269). These conflicts involve bipolar tasks, such as trust versus mistrust. With the successful resolution of each of these conflicts, the person acquires new ego strengths. For instance, a person develops a healthy balance during the first stage of development between trust and mistrust. For our survival, we cannot be too trusting or distrusting but need an appropriate balance between these opposite life tasks.

In many of our discussions of developmental themes, we refer to Erikson's psychosocial tasks, which have influenced theory and research on human development. His approach has appealed to social workers because of its sensitivity to the effect of social and cultural variables on processes of human development. But the age-grading associated with many of his identified stages is not without controversy. Many individuals do not adhere to the age-grading implied in his stages of psychosocial development. Furthermore, his stages reflect a historical bias toward heterosexuality, marriage, dual-parent families, and other social formations that differ from many of our current realities. Nonetheless, his approach directs us to look at the influence of historical, social, and cultural factors on human development.

Cognitive Development and Information Processing

Cognitive psychologists investigate processes involving human sensation, perception, and cognition. **Sensation** refers to the processes by which the organism detects internal and external stimulation at its various receptor sites. **Perception,** in contrast, refers to the interpretation of this sensory input. It involves the use of signals and symbols to understand and differentiate among sensations. **Cognition** is the process of obtaining, organizing, and using sensory and perceptual information from the environment, from past experience, and from other mental activities such as plans and strategies (Kietzman, Spring, & Zubin, 1985). All these processes are examined by cognitive psychologists. Prominent among cognitive psychologists is Jean Piaget, whose concepts about cognitive development are widely applied in various areas of cognitive science and influence many areas of social work practice.

JEAN PIAGET'S STRUCTURAL APPROACH TO COGNITION

Piaget was formally trained as a biologist, and his biological perspective influenced his eventual work in cognitive psychology. He published his first scholarly work at age 10 on an albino sparrow that he observed in a park (Cohen, 1983). An important benefit of this accomplishment was his introduction to Paul Godet, a zoologist and a curator of the Museum of Natural History in Neuchatel, Switzerland. After Godet saw Piaget's one-page article, he invited him to go on walks in the countryside where Godet showed Piaget how to make observations. By age 16, Piaget was given the job of curator of mollusks at the local museum of natural history. He continued research in this area and completed his doctoral thesis on the habits and habitat of Valais mollusks (Cohen, 1983).

Piaget's interest turned to psychology, and he collaborated with Alfred Binet on the development of intelligence tests. In conducting these tests with children, Piaget was intrigued about how children reason about their wrong answers. Rather than study how to measure intelligence, he became interested in how children *use* their intelligence.

Piaget built his career on studying the relationship between how we develop and how we learn. He believed that we mature into logic rather than learn it. It was because of this important distinction that some of his early works were ignored by American psychologists. According to many behaviorists, logic and other knowledge skills are products of learning. Many behaviorists consider the mind at birth to be a blank slate that is written on by experience. But Piaget assumed that there are inborn, invariant processes in humans that play a fundamental role in understanding reality. These processes are *adaptation* and *organization.*

The concepts of adaptation and organization are critical components of Piaget's theory of cognitive development. People use schema (plural schemata) or cognitive structures in the process of adapting to and organizing their world. A **schema** is a unit of information that an individual possesses; **adaptation** deals with the individual's relation to the external world and the ability to change or adapt to that world. The process of adaptation involves the twin processes of **assimilation** and **accommodation.** According to Piaget, what we perceive in the external world does not always fit our internal schema or what we know. So we can assimilate new information into our existing schema or thought structures and thereby change what we perceive (assimilation). Or we can accommodate our thought patterns to what we perceive, in other words, change what we think (accommodation).

Organization is the other invariant feature of human cognition. "Organization is the tendency for all members of a species to systematize their processes into coherent systems, physical or psychological" (Ginsburg, 1985, p. 180). It is the way we make sense out of what we perceive. To understand this concept, it is often helpful to keep in mind Piaget's biological perspective on the role of heredity in human development. In Piaget's view, individuals are endowed with physical structures that are species-specific. In other words, each species has distinctive physical structures, and, as humans, we inherit several key

physical structures that are specific to our species. Thus, through heredity, everybody possesses the same basic nervous systems, perceptual structures, and other similar attributes (Ginsburg, 1985).

This concept suggests that the *specific heredity* of humans guarantees that they have in common a universal potential for acquiring a specific type of cognitive development. The expression of this potential requires an adequate environment. For instance, humans have the inherited potential for abstract thought, but they will not develop this psychological function without an environment that stimulates the need for the development of abstract adaptations.

This tendency toward organization is what Piaget's theory of cognitive development seeks to explain. He provided a stage description of the developmental variations in the systems or structures of thought observed in humans. In his approach to cognition, he proposed that individuals go through a series of mental stages: (1) the sensorimotor period (from birth to about age 2), (2) the preoperations period (ages 2 to 7), (3) the concrete operations period (ages 7 to 11), and (4) the formal operational period (ages 11 and above). These stages illustrate why we observe variations in knowledge between children and young adults. These variations are not due merely to children

Children under the age of 7 intuitively assume that a volume of liquid increases when it is poured from a short, wide container into a taller, thinner one.

lacking facts, experience, or information; children think differently because of the mental structures that define their stage of development. The role played by mental structures in his theory of cognitive development led to Piaget being termed a *structuralist*.

Piaget's structural approach has significantly affected how clinicians work with children. In the past, minimal attention had been given to a systematic approach for working with children from a cognitive developmental perspective. Today, cognitive development is gaining recognition as a critical consideration in choosing appropriate interventions for children.

Although adults recognize that children lack the capacity to understand many events in their lives, Piaget's work provides an invaluable base for explaining observations that are often taken for granted. For instance, throughout history the limitations in the abilities of children have been recognized. But these developmental abilities are often ignored in actual interventions. An excellent example of the dangers associated with ignoring cognitive developmental abilities is addressed in the work of Berrick and Gilbert (1991) on the child sexual-abuse prevention movement.

Berrick and Gilbert argue that prevention services were created to respond to the perceived epidemic of sexual abuse without regard for potential consequences and age appropriateness. In fact, the first child sexual-abuse prevention program relied heavily on principles from rape prevention programming developed for adults (Ashford, 1994). In these adult programs, the concept of empowerment was a key organizing principle. This principle, coupled with the now well-recognized "good and bad touches" continuum, were incorporated into the early child sexual-abuse prevention programs. Berrick and Gilbert's assessment of these prevention strategies indicates that efforts to sensitize preschool children to be assertive in their responses to good and bad touches is developmentally inappropriate. The researchers offer a different approach to this problem that takes children's developmental needs into account. Many of these needs involve cognitive considerations requiring actual prevention efforts by adults. Their suggestions are consistent with many of Piaget's propositions. It is now becoming widely known among clinical professionals that they should use a cognitive developmental approach when planning interventions for children.

In addition, social workers are often asked to counsel children about very complex emotional or traumatic events. In fact, this was a key role played by social workers following the bombing of the federal building in Oklahoma City in 1995. Members of the media asked mental health specialists, including social workers, to provide consultation to parents about how they should explain this horrible event to their children. Piaget's theoretical approach offers some general guidelines for this type of practice task. It cautions practitioners to be sensitive to children's cognitive abilities. In his theoretical approach, it is assumed that the preoperational child cannot understand the notions of cause and effect commonly understood by adults. In fact, one of the fundamental aims of many of Piaget's experiments was to understand how children develop these fundamental notions of causality. These developmental differences in understanding the causes of events must be taken into account in trying to explain complex issues (such as why people would kill children with a bomb) to children.

At what age is it reasonable to assume that children can self-monitor their own behavior? Do preschool children have understandings of death, divorce, war, and other events similar to those of adolescents and adults? The answers to many of these questions will be covered in the developmental chapters of this book, and propositions from Piaget's cognitive theory of development are useful in answering these questions.

Though Piaget's work provides valuable insight into cognitive development, more recent research has shown that we cannot make accurate assessments of key cognitive functions without understanding the information-processing system. This system and its subsystems play a fundamental role in most of our cognitive activities. Today, social workers cannot rely on just one theory of cognition to address the multifaceted problems they encounter in their practice situations.

INFORMATION PROCESSING

For social workers to assess the mental functioning of their clients, they must have a basic understanding of human **information processing.** The goal of most human information-processing approaches is to understand how stimuli generated internally or externally enter the perceptual awareness of individuals and result in some kind of response. Information processing examines the uptake, selection, coding, and storage of information (Weinman, 1987). This perspective assumes that a sequence of stages takes place between the initial stimulus and the subsequent response. These stages follow procedures analogous to those followed by the computer, as shown in Figure 3.2.

Each stage of information processing contains many substages and concepts that must be understood by social workers. Deficits or problems in any of these areas will contribute to impairments in cognitive functioning. For this reason, we will briefly review several key functions in the information-processing subsystem: (1) consciousness and orientation, (2) perception, (3) attention, (4) learning, (5) memory, (6) comprehension, and (7) reasoning and judgment (Nurcombe & Gallagher, 1986).

Consciousness and Orientation

Consciousness is considered the most fundamental and essential element of our cognitive activities, and it is defined as our awareness of internal or external stimuli. This includes awareness of self, others, and various aspects of the physical environment (Ludwig, 1986). Healthy individuals experience a wide zone of aware-

ness in their day-to-day activities, from alertness to sleep. Although consciousness can be described in many ways, it is difficult to operationalize.

One approach, other than the sleep-wake cycle, for dealing with the definitional problems associated with consciousness is to examine levels of consciousness along a continuum from coma to full alertness. Coma represents a mental state in which verbal, motor, or other responses cannot be elicited even with noxious stimuli. Alertness, in contrast, refers to the ability to respond to any emotionally meaningful, noxious, or novel stimulus (Ludwig, 1986).

Social workers can test a client's level of consciousness by evaluating the individual's response to various types of stimuli. Have you ever called out the name of a person who is seriously intoxicated? Such persons may respond to your efforts to arouse their awareness, but immediately after your efforts they drift back into a state of unawareness of their surroundings. Persons in deep sleep can also experience difficulties in being made aware of their surroundings. These states of low alertness affect a person's potential for many kinds of cognitive processes. These states of consciousness are called **disoriented states** whenever individuals experience significant deviations in their lev-

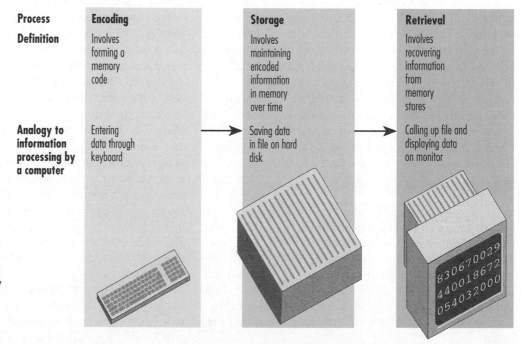

FIGURE 3.2
Computer as an analogy to information processing (Weiten, 1995)

Process	Encoding	Storage	Retrieval
Definition	Involves forming a memory code	Involves maintaining encoded information in memory over time	Involves recovering information from memory stores
Analogy to information processing by a computer	Entering data through keyboard	Saving data in file on hard disk	Calling up file and displaying data on monitor

FIGURE 3.3
Distinction between sensation and perception (Weiten, 1995)

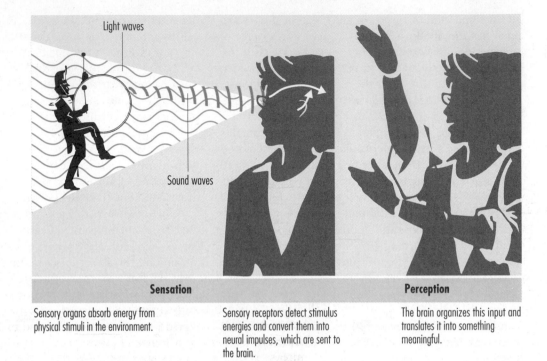

Light waves

Sound waves

Sensation		**Perception**
Sensory organs absorb energy from physical stimuli in the environment.	Sensory receptors detect stimulus energies and convert them into neural impulses, which are sent to the brain.	The brain organizes this input and translates it into something meaningful.

els of awareness. In a disoriented state, a person loses specific levels of awareness: awareness of time, place, and person.

Disorientation can be indicative of an organically based mental disorder. Generally, if a person's sensory registers are clouded or restricted, then the individual is likely to have problems in orientation. Social workers employed in nursing facilities and in situations in which they encounter persons suffering from serious mental disorders often see orientation difficulties. Orientation, therefore, is a form of consciousness that social workers assess in determining the status of a client's mental processes by asking clients questions about the time, hour, day, date, month, year, place, city, and so forth.

Perception

Our knowledge of our physical and social realities rests on the functioning of our senses. Can we have pure knowledge of these sensory experiences? This puzzle has intrigued philosophers and scientists throughout human history. What are the differences between sensations and perceptions? Sensation refers to the process in which receptors detect information that is transmitted to the brain. We currently know that infants detect light, sound, and other stimuli at birth, but they do not understand what this information means. They cannot make sense of this information. Perception is the interpretation of this sensory input (see Figure 3.3). There are very few things people do that do not involve perception. As a result, a number of theories about perception have developed in the field of psychology. We will briefly discuss two of these theories: enrichment theory and differentiation theory.

Enrichment theory is often associated with Jean Piaget. In Piaget's view, the information received by our sensory receptors is formless. For this reason, Piaget assumed that we must enrich this fragmented information to make sense of it. Figure 3.4 illustrates this point. At first glance you will probably see a young woman looking back over her shoulder. However, you might also see an older woman with her chin placed on her chest (the young woman's ear becomes the older woman's eye). People who are led to expect to see a young woman or an older woman generally end up seeing what they expect (Weiten, 1995). Our cognitive expectations enrich this visual sense experience; that is, our perceptions help us construct interpreta-

FIGURE 3.4
Exercise in perception (based on Boring, 1930)

A famous reversible figure

Unambiguous drawings of the young and old woman

tions of our reality. In social work, many individuals we encounter in practice situations have faulty perceptions that are rooted in negative life experiences. For instance, many children of abuse often misperceive the actions of other children. They will perceive hostile intentions from neutral acts like someone accidentally bumping into them.

In contrast, **differentiation theory** contends that all the information we need is contained in the sensations themselves. Our task is to differentiate the various aspects in the stimulations that were there all along. These two theories hold different understandings of how we make sense of reality. Many factors can influence human perceptions. In fact, the same situation will trigger different perceptual responses among different individuals. Our aim is to understand what

factors are contributing to these different perceptions. As social workers, we must understand how individuals perceive objects and persons. Different factors can be involved in each of these processes. Social psychology devotes substantial attention to trying to discern the factors that influence our perceptions of other human beings in our environment. Other areas of psychology focus on perceptual difficulties in dealing with physical objects in reality.

Attention

Attention is a fundamental cognitive function that plays an important role in memory. Although clients can demonstrate levels of alertness in their functioning, this does not mean that they are attentive. **Attention** differs from alertness in that "it pertains to the

Aggressive children have been found to perceive events in such a way that they overattribute the actions of others as hostile.

ability to focus on a specific stimulus without distraction by irrelevant stimuli" (Ludwig, 1986, p. 17). Attention is often evaluated in clinical practice by having clients perform what is known as serial 7s. Serial 7s give an indication of the client's ability to attend and indications of special memory functions. The client is asked, on interview, to subtract 7s in a repeated fashion from 100. To accomplish this task, the client must focus on the remainder while performing the serial subtractions. Some workers prefer to have clients spell words like "world" backward to test an individual's attentional abilities. Another test is to ask a client to recite the months of the year backward. Clinical scientists have identified other aspects of attention with

significance in human behavior assessment—vigilance and concentration.

Vigilance differs from attention in that an individual must be able to sustain outward attention over a prolonged period of time. In dangerous or unpredictable situations, this is a very important cognitive function. Individuals must be able to scan the environment with a high degree of vigilance to guard against potentially harmful events. Individuals with disorders like post-traumatic stress disorder and other anxiety disorders often engage in this process in circumstances in which it serves no function. **Hypervigilance** refers to an excessive focus on outward factors in the environment. For example, persons suffering from post-traumatic stress disorder are hypervigilant about scanning their environment for danger.

Concentration is another cognitive function that involves attentional abilities. It refers to a person's ability to sustain inner mental operations without disruption (Ludwig, 1986). When social workers encounter persons with attention problems, they must distinguish the type of deficit in the client's attentional processes when describing the problem for other professionals.

Learning

The issue of how people learn new information has fascinated humans since the time of Aristotle. In fact, Aristotle is noted for having instituted a special tradition in philosophy that continues to have influence on the field of learning psychology—associationism. Association is probably one of the oldest and most influential constructs in the field of psychology (Bourne, Ekstrand, & Dominowski, 1971). It involves the formation of mental associations that are registered or stored in the mind (Richardson, 1988). These associations are the result of three fundamental factors: continuity, similarity, and repetition.

Continuity refers to associations occurring in the mind because two events occur together in time or space. For instance, if a person connects the sensory experience of furriness with a dog, this can lead to the lasting association between furriness and the concept *dog*. Other associations occur in memory because of the principle of similarity. This principle refers to associations being formed because events or ideas that occur close together have features that are similar. Associationists also believe that ideas are likely to become associated when they occur together often. This process is referred to as repetition.

Some associationists have made a distinction between sensory association and stimulus-response association. Sensory association assumes that there is a direct connection between the experience of an event and the sensation of that event in the brain. This sensation of the event in the brain is called an *idea*, or *image*. This viewpoint suggests that the connection in the brain is what contributes to ideas being associated with one another. This form of associationism was eventually replaced by stimulus-response associationism. It was believed that stimulus-response associa-

tions were easier to study. In a stimulus-response approach, learning involves the development of chains of stimulus-response associations, or connections in the mind.

Interest in studying processes of association led researchers to discover another major factor contributing to the learning process—reinforcement. Classical conditioning and instrumental, or operant, conditioning are two fundamental models of learning that employ a slightly different definition of reinforcement. In classical conditioning, reinforcement involves the strengthening of an association between a stimulus and a response through the presentation of a second stimulus. For example, a dog can learn to flex its paw in response to a bell (first stimulus) that is associated with a second stimulus (a shock). In operant conditioning, reinforcement refers to the acquisition of new responses because of their effect on the environment. For instance, if a response solves a problem for a child, the child will repeat that response if provided with a similar situation because of the associated result. (See the following Focus section on learning theories.)

Other factors besides reinforcement contribute to learning in humans. A close relative of instrumental conditioning is learning through observation, or social-learning theory. In this approach, individuals learn by observing events that they do not directly experience. Bandura (1977) is one of the most noteworthy contributors to this learning theory. He has identified four fundamental components of observational learning: attentional, retentional, motor reproduction, and motivational processes. These processes explain how people can learn information without experiencing themselves the consequences of or reinforcement for their behavior. (See Focus on Theory: Social-Learning Theory, page 83.)

FOCUS ON THEORY

Learning Theories

John B. Watson brought behaviorism into the forefront of psychology in 1913 when he asserted that psychology must abandon its focus on subjective "mentalistic" concepts and instead focus exclusively on behavior. Watson is recognized as the father of *behaviorism,* a learning theory that is based on observable behavior. Watson was extreme in his position that we are born *tabula rasa*—as a blank slate. A well-known statement of his represents his thinking:

> Give me a dozen healthy infants, well formed, and my own specified world to bring them up in and I'll guarantee to take any one at random and train him to become any type of specialist I might select—doctor, lawyer, artist, merchant, chief, and yes, even beggar-man and thief, regardless of his talents, penchants, tendencies, abilities, vocations, and race of his ancestors. (Watson, 1925, p. 82)

Clearly, Watson believed that development depends on learning. Given the proper experiences, learning will proceed. This theory is quite different from the theories of Freud and Piaget, which assume that changes in behavior take place as children move through different stages. Furthermore, behaviorists reject notions like the id, ego, and superego because these mental functions cannot be observed and studied. Instead, they focus on studying observable stimuli and observable responses to the stimuli.

Watson demonstrated the importance of learning in an experiment designed to prove that children's fears are learned and not inborn. A child named Albert participated in an experiment whereby he learned to fear cute little white rats. The procedure was simple: Albert was presented with a stimulus, the cute white rat, and at the same time was exposed to a second stimulus, a loud, frightening sound. Through repeated associations Albert learned to associate the white rat with the frightening noise. It did not take long before just presenting Albert with a white rat led to a fearful reaction. Thus, Watson demonstrated that fears can be learned through experience.

This style of learning is referred to as *classical conditioning,* the term used to explain learning that occurs when a neutral stimulus acquires the capacity to elicit a response that was originally elicited by another stimulus. Classical conditioning is a widely accepted explanation for the acquisition of certain emotional responses, such as fear and anxiety. You can easily see how a phobia or fear could be developed in this manner. For example, if you got into a serious automobile accident you could develop a fear of driving. The previously neutral stimulus of driving a car is now associated with your frightening accident. So when you recover from the accident and get into the driver's seat again, you may not be able to drive the car without a heightened sense of fear and panic.

Although John Watson's name may not have been familiar to you, B. F. Skinner, who built on Watson's learning theory, is probably a familiar name. Skinner (1953) advanced the study of *operant conditioning,* a form of learning that occurs when responses are controlled by their consequences. Skinner observed that behavior is repeated when followed by positive consequences and that behavior is not repeated when followed by neutral or negative consequences. When consequences such as rewards and punishments are made contingent on behavior, they can have a powerful influence on behavior.

Two critical concepts in operant conditioning are reinforcement and punishment. *Reinforcement* refers to anything that follows a behavior and increases the likelihood of that behavior. *Punishment* is anything that follows a behavior and decreases the likelihood of that behavior. These concepts are really quite simple, and part of the attraction of operant conditioning is that it is a straightforward theory about behavior.

Two other operant learning processes contribute to how behavior is acquired. *Negative reinforcement* occurs when a behavior increases because it is followed by the withdrawal of an unpleasant stimulus. *Extinction* occurs when a conditioned response that was previously reinforced stops producing positive consequences.

Consider the following example: A child begins to whine at his mother, begging for a cookie before dinner. The child continues to whine and nag the mother until she eventually relents and gives the child a cookie. In this example, the child's whining is strengthened through positive reinforcement; the whining was followed by a positive consequence, the cookie. However, the mother's behavior is influenced by negative reinforcement. The child's whining, an aversive event, is terminated by the mother's giving in and rewarding the child with the cookie. The mother's giving-in behavior is an example of negative reinforcement because this response is strengthened by the termination of the aversive event.

From a developmental point of view, Skinner's theory of operant conditioning provides an understanding of how learning takes place. Our behavior can be influenced—over the life course—by the positive and negative consequences that we experience. Many theorists, while agreeing with Skinner about the influence of the environment on behavior, have argued that our beliefs or thought processes can also influence how we learn. Watson would be surprised to learn that many modern-day behaviorists have acknowledged a role for cognition in understanding behavior.

FOCUS ON THEORY

Social-Learning Theory

Foremost among the new cognitive behaviorists, more appropriately referred to as *social learning theorists,* is Albert Bandura. Bandura attempts to understand people as conscious, thinking beings who can have an influence over their environment. What is distinctive about his perspective is that, unlike Skinner, who believes learning is passive, Bandura believes that people can process information to actively influence how the environment controls them.

Bandura's cognitive emphasis in learning becomes obvious when we examine his perspective on how observation can lead to learning. *Observational learning* occurs when people observe role models and learn new behavior as a result of those observations. In this context, learning occurs without any reinforcement for imitating what is being observed. In essence, observational learning is a kind of indirect learning. The learning process is considered cognitive because people must pay attention to the role models and process this information in their memory.

According to social-learning theory, models are critical in the development of personality. How do children learn to develop aggressive tendencies? Bandura thinks it has a lot to do with the kind of social role models children are exposed to. In perhaps his most famous research experiment, Bandura demonstrated the dramatic influence of observational learning. He and his colleagues (Bandura, Ross, & Ross, 1963) exposed one group of children to a film that showed children displaying aggressive behaviors and exposed another group of children to a neutral film. Following the films, children were taken to a playroom and allowed to interact freely. Children who had seen the aggressive film and had been exposed to aggressive models engaged in more aggressive behavior than did children who had been exposed to the neutral film. This study became a classic because it demonstrated the negative influence that media can have on children's behavior.

An important aspect to Bandura's approach to social-learning theory is the notion of *self-efficacy* (Bandura, 1989). Self-efficacy refers to a person's belief about his or her ability to perform behaviors that lead to expected outcomes. When people have a strong belief in their ability to perform certain behaviors, their confidence is high. This confidence means they are likely to persist in their endeavor. When people have low self-efficacy, they are not very confident, and so are likely to give up easily. Thus, the decision to engage in a situation, as well as the intensity of the effort expended in the situation, is determined by a person's self-efficacy.

From a human-development perspective, self-efficacy is helpful in understanding how individuals adjust and adapt to new situations and roles. A strong sense of self-efficacy can help a person engage in new situations and persist. For example, if a person, say, a single woman, moved to a new city and did not know anyone, a strong sense of self-efficacy may help her adjust to the move. If she is confident in her ability to meet new people (has a strong sense of self-efficacy), she is more likely to pursue situations that give her the opportunity to meet people. Furthermore, her self-efficacy may help her persist in finding new friends—not an easy task, which may take repeated attempts.

Memory

In addition to the various reinforcement theories of learning, some cognitive approaches include information-processing theories. In the information-processing model, memory is considered the most critical component of the learning process. Clinical professionals have devised specific ways to describe the various components of our memory processes. These descriptions help practitioners identify areas of impairment in people's memory functions that affect their capacity to learn new information. We have already reviewed this approach for understanding memory in our discussion of information processing. We will now discuss some specific concepts used in the mental-status evaluation to assess human memory functions.

The first distinction made in clinical assessment is between *immediate memory* and *short-term memory.* **Immediate memory** refers to information that is retained for up to 10 seconds, and it is generally tested by having a person perform a digit span. A *digit span* is administered by having a person repeat a list of numbers given forward and backward. An unimpaired individual should be able to repeat five to six digits forward and up to four or five digits backward. Intermediate memory can also be tested by having the person repeat three pieces of information. Andreasen and Black (1991) offer the following example—the color green, the name Mr. Williams, and the address 1915 High Street. The objective is to assess whether the client can recall this information immediately after being told by the practitioner. This clinical test examines whether the client has any problems recalling the information.

In the information-processing approach, memory involves four stages: *registration, rehearsal, retention,* and *recall.* Ludwig (1986) refers to these four stages as the "Four Rs." Registration cannot occur without receptor elements being intact; we register or receive information through our senses (sensory registration). Injuries in the brain caused by a stroke or by a physical trauma can affect portions of the brain that play a major role in the registration of information. Short-term memory loss generally is caused by an impairment in some areas involving registration, rehearsal, or consolidation of information (Ludwig, 1986), whereas long-term memory loss is generally caused by a problem in recall or in the retrieval of the needed information. When assessing memory, social workers often warn clients that they will ask them within 5 minutes to recall the specific information they were given. After 5 minutes of pursuing other topics in the interview, the client will be asked to recall it.

Short-term memory has definite limits. It can maintain unrehearsed information for about 20 to 30 seconds; with rehearsal, between 5 and 10 minutes. Rehearsal, a critical strategy for retaining information, refers to the process of repeating by verbalization, im-

agery, or thought the information received from stimuli. When individuals cannot rehearse unfamiliar information, this information is easily lost from their short-term memory.

Short-term memory is also limited in the number of items it can hold. George Miller (1956) wrote a famous paper on this topic called "The Magical Number Seven, Plus or Minus Two: Some Limits on Our Capacity for Processing Information." As a result of Miller's research, we now have a better understanding about short-term memory capacity. When information is added to short-term memory, some of the older information will have to be displaced. For instance, if you are reciting a telephone number to yourself provided by the operator and stop to ask yourself where you placed your pencil, the additional information about where you placed the pencil will displace some of the information already in your short-term memory. (See Focus on Psychology: Information-Processing Functions in Remembering a Phone Number, page 102.) In fact, Miller discovered that, if you are memorizing ten items, the ninth or tenth item will knock out earlier items in your memory.

Think of short-term, or working, memory as containing seven slots or drawers. Each drawer can handle only a single item of information (Howard, 1983). This means that we cannot add additional information to these drawers without displacing the information already contained in them.

Long-term memory refers to the retention of information for days to months to years. Most individuals easily remember events from their past. In assessing long-term memory, social workers may ask clients to recall the last five presidents. Social workers can also ask about personally relevant information that was obtained before the interview. For example, they can ask about significant childhood experiences that they learned about from the client's relatives.

Long-term memory has an unlimited capacity for storing information. There are many views on the length of time that memory can be stored in our brains. One view is that long-term memory, unlike other types of memory, is permanent. Evidence of its permanence is often illustrated in cases of "flashbulb memories," memories involving vivid and detailed recollections. Examples include persons remembering explicit details about where they were and how they felt when they learned of the bombing of Pearl Harbor, the assassination of President Kennedy and of Martin Luther King, Jr., and the explosion of the Challenger spacecraft. Additional evidence of the permanency of memory is often found in cases involving exceptional forms of recall triggered by hypnosis. Penfield and Perot (1963) provided additional evidence in some of their early brain research. They found that they could trigger long-lost memories in experiments in which subjects had portions of their brains electrically stimulated.

In spite of various forms of evidence, many scientists are not certain that long-term memory is permanent (Weiten, 1995; Weiten, 2000). Some scientists use the analogy of a barrel to illustrate how memories are lost. The permanency view holds that memory is stored as if we were placing small stones in a barrel. In this view, all the stones remain. When people forget information, it is because they cannot retrieve or pull out the desired stones contained in the barrel; the problem has to do with how the information is organized in memory. This organizational problem makes it difficult to locate the stone, or the bit of information. The contrasting view assumes that some memories can vanish because the barrel is leaky and allows some of the stones to fall out of the storage area (Weiten, 1995; 2000).

Figure 3.5 provides an illustration of the key memory systems in our psychological system: sensory reg-

isters; short-term, or working, memory; and long-term memory. In particular, note that we register many forms of information in our sensory registers, but because our attention can focus on only a few items at a time, much of this information is not committed to long-term memory.

Practitioners also make distinctions between recent and remote memory in their evaluations of clients. **Recent memory** refers to retention of information individuals need to perform their daily functions. It is usually tested by asking a person about events occurring within the last 24 hours. Individuals should be able to recall, for example, what they did on the day before the interview, how they got to the interview, what they had for breakfast, and other immediate happenings in their daily life. **Remote memory** refers to information occurring several weeks or months in the past. (See the following Focus section.)

FOCUS ON THEORY

Implicit Memory: A Form of Remembering Without Awareness

Memory generally refers to awareness of events from our past. When we say we remember what we did this past weekend, we are saying that we know that the weekend was an explicit event that we experienced in the past and that we are currently thinking about that event. What we are thinking about right now reading this Focus section can stay in our mind for a few seconds before we forget what we were thinking about. Psychologists, philosophers and neuroscientists have questioned where this information goes when we are not thinking about it. When you remember a past event that you had not been thinking about, this kind of memory or re-awareness of the experience is referred to as **explicit memory** (Weiten, 2000).

Researchers have also identified another form of memory that involves changes in behavior or performance of a task because one has previously experienced an event. This other form of memory has been termed **implicit memory.** Jacoby and Witherspoon (1982) documented the existence of implicit memory

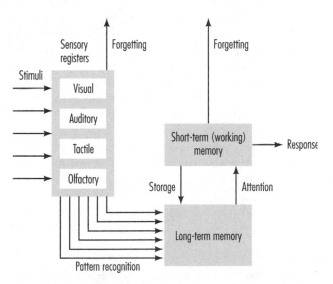

FIGURE 3.5   **Diagram of short-term and long-term memory (Howard, 1983)**

in a study of amnesiacs. They gave a series of tests to amnesiacs and normals that showed that performance on earlier tasks influenced performance on subsequent tasks. Subjects with amnesia were more likely to spell correctly a word for which they had a previous experience even though they could not recall the word itself. In this study, subjects were asked the following general-knowledge question: "Name an instrument that employs a reed." The next test involved asking the amnesiac to spell "reed." Jacoby and Witherspoon (1982) found that amnesiacs who had been asked about musical instruments that use reeds were more likely to spell "reed" correctly. They concluded that the prior experience primed the amnesiacs to perform better on the spelling test. These results have triggered research into the identification of factors that affect priming. What is distinct about implicit memory is that it is characterized by a lack of conscious awareness in the act of recollection. That is, when the information is being encoded, the person has no awareness that they are encoding it. This type of memory is a form of learning that is not affected by traditional variables in information-processing models of memory such as attention.

In assessing memory functions, social workers should consider in their evaluation recall of both auditory and visual information. At points, the social worker will need to capitalize on visual memory when auditory capacity is impaired. For instance, some individuals lose the capacity to remember verbal information but can remember how to read. In other words, if reading is preserved, then this capacity can be used to help the person remember specific information. *Visual memory* is usually tested by having a person reproduce a simple design. The clinician will draw a simple design and ask the client to reproduce the same design.

The assessment of memory functions has always played an important role in assessing psychological functioning. Social workers will probably experience increased demands for their expertise in handling memory impairments. As our population ages, social workers will have increased contact with persons suffering from various kinds of dementia. To assess the functioning of these individuals, they will need to determine the extent to which memory has deteriorated.

FOCUS ON PSYCHOLOGY

▼

Information-Processing Functions in Remembering a Phone Number

Let's look at the stages involved in the process of memory by considering the example of remembering a telephone number told to us by an operator. The first stage of information processing is referred to as *sensory registry*. At this stage, the phonetic sounds on the phone provided by the operator stimulate the listener's acoustic nerve. This information is then transmitted to the cortical area of the brain that deals with auditory information. Initially, this phonetic information is not necessarily categorized as a number or as any other signal or symbol value. The assignment of symbolic value does not occur until the second stage of processing. A sizable proportion of auditory sensations that we receive are not processed beyond the stage of sensory registration. Individuals must attend to the specifics of the sound in order to progress to the subsequent stages (Kietzman, Spring, & Zubin, 1985).

The next stage in information processing involves perception and is often referred to as *pattern recognition*. The attachment of meanings or symbols to the auditory sounds indicates that pattern recognition has taken place. In our case, when the sounds of the operator are recognized as numbers, then pattern recognition has occurred. Language and other factors associated with experience are located in long-term memory and play a significant role in this process. The pattern-recognition stage is followed by the short-term memory stage. Any deficits in these three processes can influence how information is stored in long-term memory.

The digits of the phone number fill up short-term memory. (Remember there are only seven drawers, the addition of any more information will knock one of the numbers out of its drawer.) Many people hold the number in short-term memory by saying or thinking (rehearsing) the number until they have entered it.

Remembering the phone number long enough to enter it is a short-term-memory issue only. Committing the number to long-term memory will require other memory functions such as association or learning through repetition.

Comprehension

Practitioners confront many problems caused by deficits in comprehension. For instance, social workers often encounter clients experiencing difficulties in the comprehension and expression of language, which is closely associated with memory impairment. Nurcombe and Gallagher (1986) point out some of the key areas in which comprehension and expression overlap. They both depend on the following:

1. amount of information in long-term memory (storage);

2. amount of information that can be retrieved from long-term memory (retrieval);

3. arrangement of information in long-term memory (organization); and

4. capacity to apply to problems the schematas, structures, scripts, or maps in long-term memory (p. 46).

Although comprehension and expression are intimately related, they are often differentiated by practitioners doing clinical assessments.

Deficits in human comprehension are represented in various forms of disorders commonly encountered in social-work practice. For example, clients suffering from brain damage caused by stroke, Alzheimer's disease, or trauma experience *aphasia,* which is a disorder that involves deficiencies in the comprehension or expression of language. There are two fundamental types of aphasia: sensory and motor. *Sensory aphasia* refers to language deficits that are caused by problems in the receptive mechanisms of the brain; *motor aphasia* refers to an inability to express one's thoughts through language. This is why motor aphasia is also referred to as an *expressive* form of aphasia.

Motor aphasia is often caused by some form of neurological impairment.

Reasoning and Judgment

People can understand stimuli in their environment; however, this does not mean that they will interpret this information effectively. Our mental functions also involve a number of other cognitive abilities. For example, *problem solving* and *abstract reasoning* differ in many ways from the cognitive functions previously discussed in this chapter. Scientists make important distinctions between thinking and other cognitive functions like remembering and comprehending. Although they define these functions differently, thinking cannot occur without them. In the field of cognitive psychology, thinking is often divided into three areas: problem solving, reasoning, and conceptual thinking.

We will begin this description of human thought processes by discussing *problem solving.* Social workers are interested in understanding why people cannot solve their life problems. To begin to understand this concern, first we need to define what we mean by the term *problem.* A problem is assumed to exist under the following conditions: "First, there is some initial state in which the person begins. Second, there is some goal state that is different from the initial state and which the person wishes to achieve. Third, the actions that are necessary to convert the initial state into the goal state are not immediately obvious" (Howard, 1983, p. 407). If any of these conditions are not present, then the situation is not considered a problem. We often desire to move from an initial state to another state, but the solution is obvious, in which case any initiated behavior would not be considered problem-solving activities.

Much of our everyday life involves a need to change our state of being. Cognitive scientists are interested in understanding why people fail to arrive at adequate solutions to these problems. One common factor is *rigidity.* We currently know that people often use a solution from their past that worked well in other situations to solve problems even though there might be a better way of solving the new problem. This represents a special form of rigidity referred to as a response set, so called because the person continues to use a response that worked well in other situations (Howard, 1983).

Rigidity in problem solving can be of concern. All too often humans use only one perspective in perceiving a problem. This represents a form of perceptual rigidity called a **perceptual set.** This type of set occurs whenever people perceive objects as having only their most common or recent functional significance. Duncker (1945) is known for describing a famous problem in psychology that illustrates this point. He asked individuals to figure out how to mount a candle on a plywood board so that it could act as a lamp. They were asked to solve this problem with a group of common items placed on a table. The items included candles, a box of matches, string, and some tacks. To solve this problem, the subjects needed to change their perspective about the objects on the table. The solution to this problem is illustrated in Figure 3.6.

People often have difficulties solving Duncker's problem because they fail to see the matchbox as having a function other than holding the matches. It is interesting that, when this experiment is repeated with the matches outside the box, subjects generally encounter fewer difficulties solving the problem. Solving the task is troublesome because of the common barrier in problem solving known as *functional fixed-*

FIGURE 3.6 Solution to Duncker's problem

ness. We cannot solve many problems in living without finding novel uses for known objects.

Another key barrier to problem solving in humans is the use of irrelevant information. This has been clearly illustrated in a number of psychological experiments. See if you can solve the following problem (Weiten, 1995): 15% of the people in Topeka have unlisted telephone numbers. You select 200 names at random from the Topeka phone book. How many of these people can be expected to have unlisted phone numbers? (p. 281)

The correct answer to this problem is "none," because you will not find anyone with an unlisted phone number in the phone book. If you had trouble answering this problem correctly, it was probably because you committed a common error in the human reasoning process. You focused on irrelevant information in the problem statement. The numerical information in this problem is not relevant to its solution.

Also, whether we can solve a problem depends on how it is mentally represented. We can represent a problem in many ways: verbally, visually, mathematically, or spatially. In fact, some problems are incapable of being solved unless we can properly represent them in our minds. This point is often illustrated by the Buddhist monk problem: At sunrise, a Buddhist monk sets out to climb a tall mountain. He follows a narrow path that winds around the mountain and up to a temple. He stops frequently to rest and climbs at varying speeds, arriving around sunset. After staying a few days, he begins his return journey. As before, he starts at sunrise, rests often, walks at varying speeds, and arrives around sunset. Prove that there must be a spot along the path that the monk will pass on both trips at precisely the same time of day.

Research has demonstrated that subjects who represent this problem verbally or mathematically have tremendous difficulties arriving at the correct solution. However, it is easy to solve this problem by using graphic representation. See Figure 3.7 for the solution to this problem.

Humans use a number of problem-solving strategies, one of the most noted being **trial and error.** This approach involves the sequential application of possible solutions to a problem. These solutions are tested and then eliminated when they do not work. Other approaches include means-ends analysis, changing the

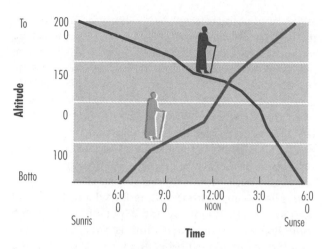

FIGURE 3.7   Solution to the Buddhist monk problem (Weiten, 1995)

representation of the problem, searching for analogies, and many others. In clinical practice, it is difficult to assess these mental functions. To this end, practitioners often examine specific types of problem-solving abilities. In particular, it is common for clinicians to ask their clients mathematically oriented problems involving the need for the client to complete a series of numbers. These problems are often referred to as series-completion problems (A, 3, B, 6, C, ?). To complete such series correctly, clients must have the ability to sort out relevant from irrelevant information and adopt a strategy or plan to solve the problem. They must also detect a pattern in the sequence. In fact, **problem solving** is defined as the "ability to sort out relevant from irrelevant information and to adopt a strategy or plan for completing the task" (Ludwig, 1986, p. 21).

Abstract thinking is another cognitive function that is difficult to assess. **Abstraction** involves the ability to recognize the meaning of symbols. For this reason, it is often tested by asking clients about similarities and differences among objects. This is also why psychiatrists often ask their clients to interpret commonly known proverbs. For example, they may ask clients if they have ever heard the saying "People in glass houses shouldn't throw stones." These simple questions can help the clinician determine whether the client can handle abstract tasks. Without the ability to abstract or problem solve, a person will have severe impairments in judgment. Clinicians often test this

function by asking clients to solve a simple life problem like "What would you do if someone jumped in front of you in line at the movies?" Persons with serious impairments in abstract thought processes will have difficulty solving this problem.

Communication

Communication is considered one of the most important elements in human affairs. It involves oral and written language, nonverbal gestures, and other forms of exchanging information. Throughout this book, we will examine various aspects of linguistic and nonlinguistic forms of communication. In particular, social workers need to have an understanding of speech and language acquisition. These two forms of communication play a pivotal role in understanding human behavior. We will assume in this discussion that when we communicate with language it involves two basic activities: speaking and listening. These two activities provide important clues about a person's psychological makeup and implications for his or her ability to interact with other human beings.

We cannot have any form of culture or civilization without some form of speech and language. Brown observed that language "is nothing less than an inventory of all the ideas, interests, and occupations that take up the attention of the community" (Brown, 1958, p. 156). Although this is a figurative description of the term, it does not provide a clear definition. Before providing a definition of *language,* we should point out that language and speech are not synonymous (DeVito, 1970). People can fail to develop speech but possess a system of symbols and rules that make up what we would call "language." As Saussure (1959) has pointed out, language is a social thing shared by an entire community, whereas speech is considered an individual product. (Saussure is a famous linguist who has significantly influenced many theoretical approaches to the study of language. He is one of the major contributors to the field of modern linguistics.)

As mentioned, speaking and listening are not the only way in which individuals communicate. We also communicate nonverbally and by writing. *Nonverbal communication* includes the facial expressions, gestures, and other actions intended to send a message to a receiver. These forms of communication have many characteristics in common with language systems.

However, unlike verbal communication, nonverbal communication has multiple channels for the transmission of messages. That is, information can be transmitted through gestures, facial expressions, eye movements, and other channels, whereas verbal communication is limited to one fundamental channel of communication (Weiten & Lloyd, 1997). In effect, human communication consists of four basic components: (1) the source, (2) the message, (3) the channel used to send the message, and (4) the receiver. In addition to these fundamental elements, communication theorists have added feedback as another major consideration. Clinical social workers are particularly interested in the role of feedback in understanding human communication.

Spoken language and written language are the two key elements in the human-communication process of interest to social workers. To understand them, researchers have developed several subfields in the language sciences: phonology, semantics, syntactics, and pragmatics. **Phonology** examines the system of sound in languages. Every language is made up of two basic units: *phonemes* and *morphemes*. The basic identifiable sound in the language system is known as a **phoneme.** We currently know that the simplest language has about 15 phonemes, and the most complex about 85. In English, each letter of the alphabet has a related phoneme, and some letters have more than one. For example, the letter *i* in "pipe" is different from the *i* in "pit." This is also true of other alphabets. Every word in the English language can be broken down into sound patterns, or phonemes. In English, we have a total of 45 phonemes. The smallest unit of meaning in any language system is called a **morpheme.** An example of a morpheme is *-ing*. There are approximately 50,000 morphemes in the English language.

Semantics is the area in language studies that deals with meaning. It is concerned with understanding how signs and symbols signify actual referents. Because speech and language serve the important function of communicating meaning, semantics are of interest to most social work professionals, who are often asked to decode client communications. In doing so, they must understand the role of symbols and signs within the individual's language system, culture, class position, and nationality. A **symbol** stands for things or ideas but does not necessarily have a direct relationship with them. For instance, the Spanish word *cielo* serves

as a symbol of the referent "sky." This word does not directly represent aspects of this object. The same is true of the symbol, or word, *sky* in English. That is, the symbol "sky" is no more blue than the symbol "cielo." A symbol does not relate directly to the object it is describing. In fact, the attribution of a symbol in a language is often arbitrary. DeVito illustrated this point clearly: "the word *small* is actually larger than the word *big,* and the symbol green—on this paper—is just as black as the symbols black and white" (DeVito, 1970, p. 7).

Signs differ from symbols in that they do bear a valid relationship with the thing for which they stand (DeVito, 1970). When we say a person has a fever, some linguists assume that there is a real rather than an arbitrary relationship between a sickness and the sign—fever. Although this viewpoint is controversial, it clarifies an important distinction that linguists often make between signs and symbols. Symbols are seen as being arbitrary and lacking clear relations with the objects they describe. Also, symbols are not limited to speech. They can include other substances like cloth, rock, metal, or sound, and these symbols are used in conjunction with clearly defined rules. Recall that language is considered a structured system that enables the speaker to produce an infinite number of messages with a set of agreed-on rules.

In the study of language, **syntax** focuses on the rules that govern the way words are combined to form sentences. We learn these rules quickly. With the exception of a few salutations and clichés, most of the sentences expressed by a person are made for the first time. Would any speaker of the English language accept the following string of words as fitting the rules of the English language? *Time break heard about and.* Even very young children intuitively know that this phrase is not legitimate communication. Linguists assume that children recognize that this phrase violates the fundamental rules of their language system. In fact, many linguists predict that children would show little hesitation in accepting a word string like *All mimsy were the borogoves, and the mome raths outgrabe* (Lewis Carroll) as being strange but would consider it a legitimate utterance (Vetter, 1969).

Grammar is the element of language that provides its coherent features and makes language a predictable process. The role of grammar in language studies has had a long and extensive history. In fact, grammar was considered a fundamental component of early Greek philosophy (Taylor, 1976). Most early linguists set out to uncover the units in each language system. However, the views of Noam Chomsky on transformational generative grammar (TGG) have revolutionized the field. TGG captures an element about language that is distinctive to human communication processes—generativity. When linguists state that human language is generative, they mean that humans can use a limited number of symbols in infinite ways. Although chimps can use symbols to communicate, very few studies have uncovered evidence of a generative grammar in their communication competence. Chimps have been taught to use symbols, but their messages often lack spontaneity.

The complexity of language acquisition has triggered significant investigation into a variety of issues. One topic that is gaining in popularity is the study of bilingualism. A *bilingual* individual is someone who can speak two languages that differ in sounds, vocabulary, and syntax (Taylor, 1976). Although Americans have seen bilingualism as an unusual occurrence, it is a more pervasive characteristic in the world community than many Americans realize. Many educated individuals from other countries speak more than one language. For instance, many people in Holland speak Dutch, English, and German. Moreover, English is becoming a second language in many parts of the world. The demand for bilingual skills in New York, Chicago, Los Angeles, Miami, Phoenix, San Francisco, and other major cities is on the increase. The social worker should understand how having two systems of grammar can influence basic psychological functions.

Pragmatics, the final major area in the language sciences, is the study of the rules that specify how language is used across social contexts. All human speakers must master what can and cannot be said to people in their environment. Grammar relates words to words, whereas pragmatics involves the study of the relationship between words and behavior in the social environment. What is polite or appropriate language behavior in relating to one's boss? Many clients avoid contact with individuals who communicate with them in a fashion suggesting a lack of respect. Issues of respect and politeness vary from language system to language system and from era to era. This area of linguistics crosses into social concerns often examined by sociolinguists and anthropologists.

Implications for Practice

Social workers must reflect constantly on the content of messages conveyed by the language and words used in all aspects of direct and indirect practice (Schriver, 1995). What should we call the place for providing services to persons with mental disorders? If we want to target a program for new mothers to prevent child abuse and neglect, then what should we call this program? Some names contain meanings that can alienate the very persons who need the services most. What is the best way to tell parents about their child's future? Why do foreign-born individuals often regress to their first language system following a stroke? What is the best way to enhance language acquisition in bicultural environments? The answers to these questions require knowledge of human communication processes, including aspects of speech and language development. Throughout this book, we will examine key developmental milestones that involve these basic communication functions.

Attitudes and Emotions

So far, we have looked at factors that play a critical role in cognitive development. Now we will look at parts of the psychological system that play a role in motivating behavior. We will explore the role of attitudes and emotions in human behavior. Attitudes and emotions have been subjected to substantial empirical and theoretical scrutiny by researchers in both social work and psychology. Students of human motivation are interested in solving many motivational puzzles: Why do some people have greater propensities toward altruism? What motivates individuals to be achievement oriented? Why do some people prefer antisocial over social activities? We will begin this discussion of motivational subsystems by examining the role of attitudes in human behavior.

THE NATURE AND FUNCTION OF ATTITUDES

What are attitudes? How do we form them? What purpose do they serve in our day-to-day activities? An **attitude** is defined as "a learned evaluative response, directed at specific objects, which is relatively enduring and influences and motivates our behavior toward these objects" (Lippa, 1994, p. 214). Gordon Allport (1935) considered attitudes "the keystone in the edifice of American social psychology" (p. 708). Social psychology is a branch of psychology that links the behavior, attitudes, and emotions of the individual to the broader social context of which the individual is a part. Language is one way of making this connection between the individual and society, and attitude is a common element of everyday language. All of us have at some time heard or made comments about other people's positive or negative attitudes.

The following Focus section reviews a summary of study by social work researchers on attitudes of African-American homeless men.

FOCUS ON RESEARCH

▼

Attitudes of African-American Homeless Men

In the well-publicized book *When Work Disappears,* sociologist William Julius Wilson reports on his research findings indicating that both white and African-American employers prefer to hire immigrants over inner-city African-Americans because they perceive African-Americans as harboring "bad attitudes" toward work. While Wilson knew of no quantitative data relevant to the accuracy of the view that poor, African-American men have bad work attitudes, he referenced ethnographic findings. These findings portray African-Americans as exhibiting a low threshold for perceiving prejudice from their employers, which fuels a readiness to abandon the job rather than endure the perceived injustice.

Our research applied quantitative methods to investigating the attitudes of homeless inner-city African-American men. We found that African-American homeless men were no more likely to believe they had ever been employed in a job where they were treated unfairly than were male students majoring in Criminal Justice and Business at a local university. Given a scenario in which an ambiguous boss was described, the homeless men were no more likely to be-lieve that the boss was behaving unfairly than were the college students. The African-American homeless men were more likely to endorse such statements as "In America, every child who wants to learn has the opportunity to do so." They were more likely to believe that homelessness is caused by "drugs and alcohol," but they did not differ from the college students in their tendency to blame homelessness on structural factors in the society. They were no more likely to believe that African-Americans are discriminated against in the work place and just as likely to perceive justice in the world. Thus, on a variety of measures, we found little support for the view that the homeless men had a low threshold for the perception of prejudice or that they left jobs because of perceived injustice. (However, for most of them, crack addiction was having a devastating effect on their ability to sustain employment.)

We also examined the psychological correlates associated with perceiving injustice. Greater belief that the world is just was associated with stronger reliance on God. Reliance on God constituted a prominent coping mechanism for our sample, with approximately 78% of the sample endorsing the most extreme values on a Likert scale. Those men who maintained a belief in a just world and who relied on God exhibited a higher sense of mastery and greater optimism. Thus, our findings suggested some psychological benefits associated with the failure to perceive injustice.

Jill Littrell

Some social psychologists attempt to distinguish attitudes from other mental structures like values and beliefs. **Values** are considered abstract goals that do not have specific objects or reference points (Deaux, Dane, & Wrightsman, 1993). Examples of values include abstract judgments about topics such as beauty, freedom, and health. These values can contribute to the development of attitudes and other belief systems. We also use values to evaluate information in making many of our decisions. In fact, attitudes play a mediating role in turning our values into action (Deaux, Dane, & Wrightsman, 1993).

We need to be able to distinguish beliefs from attitudes. Beliefs include information about objects. But what distinguishes a belief from an attitude? Technically speaking, **beliefs** are observations about the qualities of objects (Feld & Radin, 1982). For instance, we can have information or beliefs about the harmful consequences of smoking. Are these beliefs the same thing as an attitude? As this example points out, it is difficult to make distinctions between attitudes and other mental structures. Although we may hold beliefs, it does not mean that we will not smoke or behave in a particular fashion. It is assumed in social psychology that attitudes are more likely to influence behavior than general beliefs.

Fishbein and Ajzen (1975) addressed this issue directly in their *theory of reasoned action*. They set out to determine what factors, in addition to attitudes, influence our behavior. In their approach, they make an interesting distinction between attitudes and subjective norms. They suggest that *attitudes* refer to our evaluative feelings; for instance, negative internal feelings you may have about smoking reflect your attitude about this activity. **Subjective norms** would be your beliefs about what important people or significant others think about smoking (Lippa, 1994). That is, you may learn scientific information about smoking and its negative consequences, but this does not mean that you will develop a negative attitude. In Fishbein and Ajzen's (1975) theory, attitudes and subjective norms combine to influence our behavioral intention.

Behavioral intention refers to our subjective estimate of how likely we are to engage in a specific behavior. For instance, what is the likelihood that you will smoke in the next month? Fishbein and Ajzen's (1975) theory predicts that, in many circumstances, people's internal attitudes will better predict their behavioral intention than will their subjective norms. This theory allows for a comparison of internal and external influences on our behavior: Our attitudes represent the internal influences on our behavior, and our subjective norms represent the social or external influences.

Fishbein and Ajzen's theory is useful in understanding intentional behaviors: Do you intend to have a baby? Do you intend to increase your study time? These behavioral questions are influenced by some combination of your attitudes, subjective norms, and perceived behavioral control. But, in examining these factors, you should also consider the consequences of the behavior you are trying to predict, and you should personally evaluate these consequences. For instance,

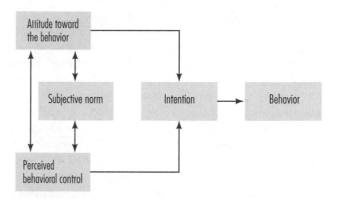

FIGURE 3.8   Relationship between attitudes and intentional behavior (Ajzen, 1987)

two people might agree on the consequences of increased studying—improved grades and less time with friends—but each may evaluate these outcomes differently (see Figure 3.8).

From research on Fishbein and Ajzen's (1975) theory, we know that attitudes are most likely to predict smoking among adults. Subjective norms, however, are more likely to predict the smoking behavior of adolescents; adolescents are more likely to be influenced by the subjective norms of their peers. Information of this nature is useful to social work professionals who assist in the development of preventive interventions. With the benefit of theories on attitudes, social workers are better equipped to develop effective programs intended to change client attitudes.

Attitudes differ from emotions in several important ways. Unlike attitudes, emotions do not have to be directed at a specific target or object. Furthermore, attitudes tend to be enduring. If you are opposed to racism today, you probably will be tomorrow. Emotions, however, can come and go in a matter of seconds. Although you are angry at your best friend today, this does not mean that you will be angry at him or her tomorrow. Attitudes differ in many respects from emotional responses.

However, there is a feeling, or affective component, to attitudes that we cannot ignore. Feld and Radin (1982) point out definitions of "attitude" that emphasize this point. Fishbein and Ajzen's (1975) theory includes a definition of "attitude" that stresses emotional reactions. In their theory, attitudes are considered emotional

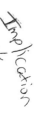

responses to objects in the form of favorable or unfavorable feelings. People have favorable feelings toward many objects in their environment. In fact, this is what many scientists attempt to capture in their research.

Regardless of how we define "attitude," social workers must be able to modify or change attitudes. While social psychologists debate the best definition of "attitude," social workers need validated theories to guide their efforts. In *Social Psychology for Social Work and the Mental Health Professions,* Feld and Radin (1982) have identified theories in social psychology that social workers may find helpful in achieving their practice objectives (for example, cognitive-dissonance theory and self-perception theory). Social workers need to develop a strong competency in understanding attitude formation and change. For this reason, we provide systematic coverage of factors in human development that contribute to the formation of attitudes. These attitudes are assumed to play a fundamental role in human motivation and development. (See the following Focus section.)

FOCUS ON THEORY

▼

Theories of Attitudes and Their Change

In social work, we assume that if we change the attitudes of our clients it will influence their behavior. This means we believe that we can predict behaviors from attitudes and that attitudes influence behavior. Although many studies have uncovered a relationship between attitudes and behavior, this relationship is not consistent. At an intuitive level, people expect consistency between attitudes and behavior. This assumption has contributed to the development of an entire group of theories on attitudes known as *consistency theories.*

Consistency theories in social psychology refer to the idea that people strive to maintain consistency in their views of themselves, their environment, and in their relations with others (Lindgren, 1969). People are motivated to keep their attitudes and behaviors consistent (Deaux et al., 1993). This implies that, if people have attitudes inconsistent with their behaviors, they feel uncomfortable. This sense of discomfort will motivate them toward reestablishing some form of balance or consistency between their attitudes and behavior.

Leon Festinger (1957) is known for proposing another important consistency theory known as *cognitive-dissonance theory.* "Cognitive dissonance" describes the feelings of anxiety that arise when a person is aware of two inconsistent cognitions, or a cognition and a behavior that are inconsistent. In his theory, whenever an attitude and a behavior are inconsistent, this inconsistency generates dissonance. Festinger assumes that this distress motivates individuals to reconcile the inconsistencies in their cognitions or between their cognition and their behavior. However, Festinger found that subjects would not always experience dissonance from conflicts between attitudes or cognition. In his view, they experience a sense of dissonance only if the thoughts or attitudes are relevant to one another. Conflicting cognitions that are not related to one another do not trigger a sense of personal dissonance.

Festinger's theory initially focused on inconsistencies in cognitions and predicted that dissonant cognitions would motivate a person to change one of his or her cognitions. In his early research, he discovered that change in behavior could trigger changes in attitudes. In fact, his theory predicts that people will change their attitudes to be consistent with performed behaviors. In his now-famous forced-compliance experiments, this finding occurred on a regular basis. He subjected individuals to dull tasks and paid them to lie to other students about how interesting they found the tasks. The individuals who participated in the dull tasks were then given a questionnaire to determine their private attitudes about the tasks. Some individuals had been paid $1 and others $20 to engage in these tasks. The individuals who were paid $1 experienced greater dissonance. Dissonance theory suggests that they became more motivated to believe that the tasks were really interesting because the justification for their actions—a measly dollar—was insufficient.

Self-perception theory, another theory about attitude changes, was developed by D. J. Bem (1967). It seeks to explain the same types of behavior addressed by cognitive-dissonance theory; however, it offers a different explanation for why a person might change an attitude after performing a behavior (Feld & Radin, 1982). Self-perception theory suggests that, when we are not sure of our attitudes about a certain topic, we infer them from our behaviors and from the context within which those behaviors occur. Using this theory, Bem set out to offer an alternative explanation of what occurred in Festinger's experiment. In Bem's view, the subjects defined the tasks as interesting not because of dissonance but because they had merely inferred their attitude from their actual behavior. "That is, one dollar is not enough money to induce someone to lie, so subjects in that condition looked back at their behavior and decided they must have enjoyed the experiment because they had said they enjoyed it; no inconsistency, no discomfort, no dissonance" (Deaux et al., 1993, p. 170). In his view, the individuals in the experiment were essentially asking themselves: "What must my attitude be if I am willing to behave in this fashion?"

Bem's theory has led to important findings widely used to obtain the cooperation of clients. His theory has also led to the discovery of what is known as the *foot-in-the-door effect,* or the tendency for individuals who have complied with a small request first to agree to a larger request later. Researchers thought that this phenomenon occurred because of individuals' changes in self-perception. Bem's theory predicts that, "if individuals observe themselves doing something out of free choice, the behaviors are attributed to their disposition, not to external forces, and the conclusion reached is that 'I am that sort of a person'" (Feld & Radin, 1982, p. 175). Some theorists also predict that persons who comply with small requests are also likely to conclude that "I am the type of individual who agrees to socially desirable requests." Thus, there are competing theories of why changes in behavior can result in changes in attitudes.

EMOTIONS

What are emotions? How can we explain our emotions and their role in human behavior? Are emotions caused by internal and bodily changes or by some form of cognitive appraisal? The answers to these questions are quite controversial. In this section, we will provide a brief overview of some of the different theoretical perspectives in psychology on human emotions.

The word *emotion* in its early history meant "to move or agitate in a physical sense" (Petri, 1986). It later came to mean "an agitated or aroused mental state." Although there is no commonly accepted definition of the term, there are a number of widely debated theories or models of human emotions.

The first person to write about the topic of emotional expression was Charles Darwin (1872), in his book *The Expression of Emotions in Man and Animals.* Darwin was the first theorist in modern times to assume that both emotions and their expression are innate. The bulk of his writings on the topic focused on the manner in which emotions are expressed. Today, there is still controversy as to whether there are universal ways to channel the expression of our emotions.

Although humans have expressed concerns about the control of emotions since ancient times, Ross Buck (1988) recently proclaimed that "psychology has rediscovered emotions." As we pointed out earlier, psychology shifted during the 1950s and 1960s to investigating cognitive functioning. This did not, however,

Fear plays an essential role in human functioning. The child appears frightened by something in the environment.

include studying emotions. Emotions were relegated to a second-class position in the psychological sciences. Shame, guilt, and anger were studied, but much of the research in this area was motivated by clinical or neuropsychological interests. Much of the controversy in this area of study dates back to the writings of William James (1884).

William James and Carl Lange arrived at a similar conclusion about emotions that challenged traditional assumptions. They identified the following order for describing emotions: perception to bodily change to emotion (Hilgard, 1987). This theory turned common sense upside down. "Everyday logic suggests that when you stumble onto a rattlesnake in the woods the conscious experience of fear leads to visceral arousal (the fight-or-flight responses)" (Weiten, 1992, p. 363). This means that the order of events is: perception to emotion to bodily expression (Hilgard, 1987). Independent of each other, James and Lange arrived at views that contradicted this assumption. James placed greater stress on perception of change in striate muscles, and Lange emphasized changes in heart rate and blood pressure. Their approach to emotions is referred to as the *James-Lange theory of emotions,* and it emphasizes the role of physiological determinants in the expression of emotions. (See the following Focus section.)

FOCUS ON SOCIOLOGICAL THEORY

Shame and the Sociology of Emotions

Sociologists have devoted increased attention in recent years to the study of the role of shame and other emotions in social interaction, called the **sociology of emotions.** This is particularly true of sociologists with an interest in social psychological concerns. Shame is one of the emotions that is alluded to in early sociological writings of Simmel, Cooley, Marx, and Goffman. However, their writings seem to take for granted how shame is defined (Scheff, 1999).

For instance, George Simmel (1904) in writing about fashion pointed out that the origins of fashion has roots in shame as a source. "People want variation and change, he argued, but they also anticipate shame if they stray from the behavior and appearance of others. Fashion is the solution to this problem, since one can change along with others, avoiding being isolated, and therefore shame" (Scheff, 1999, p. 4). As Scheff (1999) points out, Simmel assigns an important role to conformity of thought and behavior to expectations considered fashionable by a group. When people deviate from these group expectations they are vulnerable in Simmel's opinion to shame. But, Simmel never really defined "shame" in his writings about fashion.

Charles Horton Cooley (1922), known for his conception of the looking-glass self, also included shame in his writings, but, like Simmel, he never provided an explicit definition of this concept. For Cooley, pride and shame are important social emotions that rely heavily on self-monitoring processes. Cooley (1922, p. 184) pointed out that self-monitoring involves three steps: "the imagination of our appearance to the other person, the imagination of his judgment of that appearance, and some sort of self-feeling, such as pride or mortification."

Scheff (1999) has attempted to define "shame" through the lens of the sociological imagination. He wrote: "By shame I mean a large family of emotions that includes many cognates and variants, most notably embarrassment, humiliation, and related feelings such as shyness that involve reactions to rejection or feelings of failure or inadequacy. What unites all these cognates is that they involve the feeling of a *threat to the social bond*" (Scheff, 1999; p. 14). Scheff further points out that, if shame is the result of threat to the social bond, then shame should be considered the most social of the basic emotions.

An important piece of research on shame is included in the book *The Hidden Injuries of Class* by Sennett and Cobb (1973). These field researchers performed a participant observation study in Boston communities, schools, clubs, and bars of white working-class males of Italian and Jewish backgrounds. They found that these men felt that their class and occupational position were the reasons why they were not accorded respect by others. This lack of respect was experienced by the subjects of this study in many contexts, including interactions with teachers, bosses, and even their own children.

Structural contributions to negative emotions cannot be overlooked by social workers. Factors like class, race, and gender are the source of many forms of emotion that are the roots of many current social problems. For instance, issues of respect triggered by dominant group rejection plays a major role in gang formation in many communities. It also plays a pivotal role in many other forms of social conflict motivated by emotions with roots in social processes. In other words, the source of many emotional responses is rooted in social considerations that cannot be overlooked by social work professionals.

Emotions are experienced individually, but some emotions have deep roots in collective processes that are under increased scrutiny by sociologists. The American Sociological Association currently has a special section of its organizational structure that focuses on research topics involving emotions from a sociological perspective. This research body recognizes that emotions cannot be understood by strictly studying biological and psychological processes.

Adapted from *Shame and the Social Bond: A Sociological Theory* by Thomas Scheff (http://sscf.ucsb.edu/scheff/2.html/)

Stanley Schachter is noted for developing a two-factor theory that includes physiological explanations in looking at the experience of emotion. In his theory, the experience of emotion requires the two factors of autonomic arousal and cognitive interpretation of the visceral or autonomic arousal. In his approach, a person will experience physiological arousal and then search his or her environment for an explanation. If you are in a threatening situation, then your explanation of your arousal will probably fit the situation. Schachter's model was the first to stress the important role played by cognitive appraisal in experiencing emotions, but it stressed the need for both factors to be present.

Lazarus has argued, however, that cognition alone is sufficient for a person to experience emotions. In his experiments, he was able to alter the intensity of subjects' responses by modifying their appraisal process (Petri, 1986). He showed subjects movies and could change their emotional responses by changing the nature of the sound track. With the benefit of these findings, Lazarus has argued for the primacy of cognition in experiencing emotions.

Zajonc (1980) has argued for the primacy of affect in experiencing emotions. He (1984) bases his theory on observations of animals. He contends that emotion is a universal phenomenon in the animal kingdom, but the cognitive processes and systems observed in humans are not transferable to animals. "Indeed," as Zajonc noted, "a rabbit would rarely have time to assess all the attributes of a snake in order to decide whether to fear it; the rabbit feels fear and reacts. Such reactions may also occur in people" (Petri, 1986). That is, people probably acquired the same emotional mechanisms before the development of cognitive systems. Thus, Zajonc assumes that the emotions of humans have much in common with the emotions of animals. Another argument that he provides in support of the primacy of affect is that we cannot avoid emotions. If logic occurs before emotions, then logic should affect our emotional responses to stimuli. Yet this is not always what occurs. Overall, Zajonc argues that emotions are innate reactions that are part of our evolutionary makeup.

Evolutionary theories of emotion are once again regaining popularity in psychological research. The theorists in this area include Silvan Tomkins, Carroll Izard, and Robert Plutchik, who set out to identify the fundamental human emotions. These emotions are considered to be innate and to have evolved before cognition did. Tomkins, Izard, and Plutchik assume that people exhibit between eight and ten primary emotions. A summary of these emotions is presented in Table 3.2. Note the similarities between the elements in their

TABLE 3.2 Summary of Emotions According to Different Theorists		
Silvan Tomkins	**Robert Plutchik**	**Carroll Izard**
Fear	Fear	Fear
Anger	Anger	Anger
Enjoyment	Joy	Joy
Disgust	Disgust	Disgust
Interest	Anticipation	Interest
Surprise	Surprise	Surprise
Contempt	Sadness	Contempt
Shame	Acceptance	Shame
Distress	Sadness	

(Based on Mandler, 1984)

lists. These theorists do not assume that our emotions are limited to these primary emotions. Plutchik has pointed out that, from our primary emotions, we can develop many secondary blends of emotions.

Implications for Practice

Without emotions, individuals cannot develop meaningful responses to their environment. Social workers need to develop practical ways for describing changes in their clients' emotional states. From the theories discussed, we can distinguish between the *expression* of emotions and the *experience* of emotions. We experience our emotions within our central nervous sys-

Understanding a person's mood and affect is an important clinical skill. What emotion is the person displaying in this photograph?

tem and its attendant cognitive structures, but we express these emotions through our somatic and autonomic response systems.

Clinical social workers also distinguish between mood and affect. **Mood** can be defined as a prevailing and enduring emotional state. **Affect** refers to a person's instant emotional state. In assessing affect, social workers focus on determining the presence or absence of specific types of emotional states. For instance, **lability** refers to the rapid shift from one emotion to another within a very brief period of time. If these shifts are extreme, some clinicians label them as representing a form of emotional "incontinence" (Ludwig, 1986). Social workers must learn the characteristics of normal and abnormal presentations of emotion. They must also have an understanding of how people learn to use their emotions and behavior.

In the last subsystem of our framework, we will look more closely at the role of social cognition in controlling our emotions and behavior.

Social Cognition and Regulation

How do we acquire social knowledge? Is there a difference between social and nonsocial cognition? Does social knowledge acquisition differ from the acquisition of other forms of knowledge? These questions have helped psychologists clarify the nature of **social cognition.** Theorists in the field have devoted substantial ink to topics like: Do we employ different processes in acquiring knowledge about things than we employ in acquiring knowledge about people? These debates have led to some general conclusions. Now "social cognition" is widely considered to be cognition about people. It includes "thinking and knowledge about self and other individuals, about social relations between people, about social customs, groups, and institutions" (Flavell, 1985, p. 159). In fact, substantial attention is now being devoted to understanding the role of the self-system in all areas of human cognition. The self-system refers here to all the feelings, thoughts, and other elements that are associated with a person's sense of self.

In the mid-1970s, it was rare to encounter theorists with identified interests in social cognition. Social cognition is considered a newly discovered convergence of two distinct disciplines: social psychology and cognitive psychology. Developments in each of these disciplines have created major shifts in traditional approaches to scientific inquiry in psychology.

Social psychologists have identified many deficits in their approach to studying human behavior and judgment processes. Most of their early research focused on understanding the effects of situational and individual differences on various forms of social behavior. As disenchantment with stimulus-response models increased, social psychologists started to realize that this approach to research was not clarifying the fundamental psychological processes that underlie *social* behavior. To rectify this problem, they turned to cognitive theory (Wyer & Srull, 1984).

Many of the concepts introduced in this chapter that examine cognitive functions are now being employed in psychology to address a number of social processes. These same processes are examined in sociology and other fields of inquiry. We have included social cognition in our psychological dimension primarily because it employs a psychological orientation to studying social processes. The fundamental aim of social cognition, as a field of inquiry, is to understand the interdependence between cognition and social behavior (Ostrom, 1984). Isen and Hastorf (1982) refer to this field as "cognitive social psychology" instead of social cognition. This area of study in psychology focuses on individual-level explanations of social behavior. Anthropology and sociology also examine various aspects of social behavior but rely primarily on group-level explanations (Lippa, 1994).

In this book, we will explore various factors in social development that influence individuals' sense of self, their ability to control their behavior, and their sense of social competence. Because social cognition is a useful framework for examining each of these concerns, we cover topics from that field in each chapter.

Researchers in the field of social cognition have recognized that a significant component of social behavior is motivated by our innate need to control various aspects of our environment. Robert White (1959) refers to this as a form of *competence motivation.* "Competence" is the capacity to interact effectively with one's environment. In essence, the goal of this motive is to bring about a sense of efficacy for the individual. This assumption is also acknowledged by so-

cial workers in models of interaction that take into account principles of social cognition (Brower & Nurius, 1993).

The need for a sense of control has received further scrutiny by Richard deCharms. In his view, the primary motive at the root of most social behavior is the need to be effective in producing changes in our environment. He refers to this as a need to achieve a sense of personal causation.

As deCharms noted, we typically describe motivation in relation to the goals toward which a behavior leads: When hungry, we seek food; when thirsty, we seek water; and so on. Though we speak of the hunger motive, personal causation is the force requiring that we be able to respond in ways that will get us food. Thus, deCharms saw personal causation as the underlying principle of all motivated behaviors (Petri, 1986, pp. 298–299).

Regulation of behavior, emotions, and cognition is an important area of research developing in the field of social cognition. By employing principles of social cognition, it is possible to link processes of social regulation with individual cognitive processes. This linkage allows for the identification of external and internal factors contributing to the regulation of our emotions and behavior.

Regulation is an important human behavior function and will receive substantial attention in our developmental chapters. We now know that humans learn considerable information from others that helps in regulating various aspects of their behavior. The focus in social cognition research is on understanding how people acquire this information from other individuals.

Implications for Practice

Brower and Nurius (1993) have written on the utility of social cognition in what they have termed a cognitive-ecological model for direct practice. In their view, social cognition and social transactions serve as "the backdrop for understanding our clients' presenting problems and for developing change strategies that will positively build upon these normative processes" (Brower & Nurius, 1993, p. 3). They believe that social cognition plays an important mediating role between people and their environments. They contend that, if we integrate our knowledge of the self-system with information-processing knowledge and knowledge of human problem solving, we can deal more efficiently with clients' concerns.

By using their cognitive approach, we can better evaluate the effect of immediate and distant factors on specific forms of human behavior. Ecological and broader social influences are important, but the concepts of social cognition enable us to isolate key personal factors that play unique roles in an individual's behavioral choices. That is, social cognition is an approach that allows us to bring together important person-and-environment factors. In particular, it places tremendous emphasis on self-constructs that recognize the highly interdependent relationship between self and society. Unlike personality constructs, the self-system in social cognitive approaches does not artificially isolate persons from key social realities. Moreover, concepts and principles in the social cognitive approach are highly useful in achieving social work's commitment to making person-and-environment interactions central in its approach to understanding human behavior. It allows us to understand individual processes underlying our tendency to make selective appraisals of situations based on our personally constructed schemata and life images.

Psychological Hazards

Our psychological system facilitates our processing of information from our internal and external world and helps us communicate and respond to the demands of everyday life. It includes many processes and functions that are vulnerable to many kinds of hazards occurring at the biophysical, psychological, and social levels of functioning.

Psychological hazards include events, experiences, abilities, skill deficits, cognitive impairments, emotional impairments, and behavioral impairments that compromise the mental processes and functions employed by individuals to control their biopsychosocial system.

Individuals are exposed to many experiences that constitute risks to their mental functioning. A risk occurs whenever there is a lack of harmony in the person's psychological system. Individuals are also at risk when there is a lack of opportunity to develop mental and motor processes that enable them to meet the demands of their life circumstances.

A crisis presents a problem in living that requires more than habitual coping (Nurcombe & Gallagher, 1986). Whenever an individual cannot cope with problems, he or she is at risk for many kinds of psychological harm. This harm has many different forms of presentation: learning disabilities, mood disturbances, abstract reasoning deficits, perpetual disturbances, and many others.

Overview

This chapter provided a description of key developments in the cognitive and psychological sciences that help us understand individual-level explanations of human behavior. We reviewed concepts from major theoretical perspectives that assist us in understanding the cognitive and individual bases for human behavior. These factors play a critical mediating role between our biological and social systems. They involve many functions that people need in order to engage in planned behavior intended to resolve their life problems. Each of the subsystems in our psychological system also provides internal motivation for many of our activities. The psychological system consists of several key functions employed by humans in directing their behavior to achieve desired ends. These individual processes differ significantly from the social processes that will be described in our next chapter.

Summary

The objective of the psychological system is goal attainment. This system consists of many functions associated with our mental processes. These processes are needed to help people achieve their desired goals.

COGNITIVE DEVELOPMENT AND INFORMATION PROCESSING

Cognitive development is an approach to assessing cognitive functions. Piaget's structural approach is useful for social workers. It explains how cognition is organized or structured at various phases of development. Different mental structures direct cognitive processes for individuals at different stages of development.

The information-processing subsystem of the psychological system includes seven major functions: consciousness and orientation, perception, attention, learning, memory, comprehension, and reasoning and judgment. Information processing is not only a major function in the psychological system but also an established approach in psychology for studying human cognitive processes. Information processing resembles a computer and explains the uptake, selection, coding, and storage of information.

"Consciousness" involves the processes that allow us to be aware of internal and external stimuli. "Orientation" is a form of consciousness assessed by clinical professionals in evaluating the status of a person's mental functioning. "Perception" refers to the interpretation of information detected by our senses. "Attention" is the component of our information-processing system that pertains to the ability to focus on a specific stimulus without distraction by irrelevant stimuli. "Vigilance" involves the ability to sustain outward attention over a prolonged period of time. "Concentration" refers to a person's ability to sustain inner mental operations without disruption.

"Memory" is considered a key component of the learning process in our information-processing system. It consists of four stages: registration, rehearsal, retention, and recall. There are definite limits on our capacity for processing information. Our short-term, or working, memory is limited to the number of items it can hold (seven, plus or minus two). Unlike short-term memory, long-term memory has unlimited capacity to store information. Key processes, besides memory, assessed by social workers include problem solving, abstract reasoning, and judgment.

COMMUNICATION

"Communication" involves oral and written language, nonverbal gestures, and other forms of exchanging information. Language is a social product, but speech is an individual product. Human communication consists of four basic components: the source, the message, the channel used to send the message, and the receiver.

ATTITUDES AND EMOTIONS

Attitudes and emotions play a fundamental role in motivating behavior. "Attitude" refers to our evaluative feelings and other evaluative responses directed at specific norms. There are different theories of what influences changes in attitudes: consistency theories and self-perception theories. "Emotion" is difficult to define, but there are several noteworthy theoretical conceptualizations of emotions: the James-Lange theory, Schacter's two-factor theory, and evolutionary theories. Without emotions, individuals cannot develop meaningful responses to their environment.

SOCIAL COGNITION AND REGULATION

"Social cognition" refers to knowledge about people. Social and cognitive psychologists assume that acquisition of social knowledge differs from acquisition of other forms of knowledge. The norms learned from social cognitive processes constrain and regulate our behavior in social situations.

PSYCHOLOGICAL HAZARDS

"Psychological hazards" include anything that compromises mental functioning. A risk to mental functioning occurs when there is disharmony in the psychological system or a lack of opportunity to develop mental and motor processes needed to cope with the life's demands. When people have a crisis and cannot cope with life's demands, they are at increased risk of psychological harm.

🌐 Online Resources

Current Research in Social Cognition
http://www.uiowa.edu/grpproc/crisp/crisp.html
    Peer-reviewed electronic journal dealing with the whole of social cognition.

Psyche: An Interdisciplinary Journal of Research on Consciousness
http://psyche.cs.monash.edu.au
    Psyche is a refereed electronic journal dedicated to supporting the interdisciplinary exploration of

the nature of consciousness and its relation to the brain.

George A. Miller
http://www. cogsci.princeton.edu/~geo
Short-term memory. Miller is one of the founders of cognitive psychology.

Emotions and Emotional Intelligence
http://trochim.human.cornell.edu/gallen/young/emotio.htm
Offers a new theory to get rid of unwanted feelings.

InfoTrac® College Edition

For interesting materials related to what you have just read, please go to the *InfoTrac College Edition* website and search using the following key words:

Jean Piaget empathy
repressed memories social perception
problem solving

Key Terms

abstraction affect
accommodation assimilation
adaptation associationism

attitude organization
behavioral intention perception
beliefs perceptual set
classical conditioning phoneme
cognition phonology
concentration pragmatics
conscience primary process thinking
consciousness problem solving
continuity recent memory
differentiation theory remote memory
disoriented states repetition
ego schema
ego ideal secondary process
ego-psychology (self-theory) thinking
enrichment theory semantics
epigenetic principle sensation
explicit memory short-term memory
grammar sign
hypervigilance similarity
id social cognition
immediate memory social-learning theory
implicit memory sociology of emotions
information processing subjective norms
lability superego
libido symbol
long-term memory syntax
mood trial and error
morpheme values
operant conditioning vigilance

▲ ▲ ▲ ▲ ▲ ▲ ▲ ▲ ▲ ▲ ▲

The Social Dimension for Assessing Social Functioning

CHAPTER CONTENTS

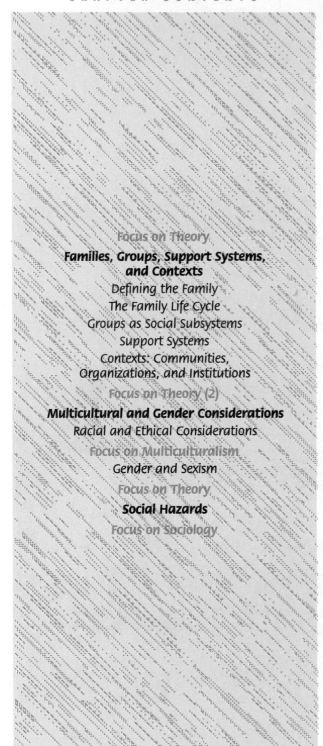

The aim of this chapter is to define and describe how social systems guide the multidimensional framework. A whole host of debates occur in the social sciences about the merits of micro versus macro approaches to social analysis. This kind of dualism, along with the dualisms of agency versus structure and individual versus society, is avoided in this chapter by using systems principles to describe the dimensions of social life.

For purposes of clarity, we treat the social systems and categories included in our framework as if they were independent of one another. However, you should keep in mind the following principles:

1. Any analysis of a social system must take into account the interactions of that system with other systems.

2. All social systems and structures are highly interrelated and have many points of intersection that are critical to understanding processes of social domination and other forms of social inequality.

3. Social structures are sources of both support and oppression.

4. Any analysis of social, cultural, and individual experience cannot ignore key multicultural foundations.

The preceding chapter covered the role of psychological systems in human development. However, these psychological processes do not occur in a vacuum. All forms of goal-directed activities involving humans take place in an established environment. If we are going to understand how the environment influences behavior, we need to have a framework that allows us to compare elements in one social context with those of another. To this end, our multidimensional framework provides a description of ways to conceptualize the key systems making up the social system. It also identifies variables and concepts that are useful for looking at different levels of social organization.

Before reading this chapter, revisit the case of Raul Salazar (page 39). What structural factors are contributing to his problems? Are there social institutions that are influencing how the school is responding to Raul and his family? Is there something about Raul's social location that is influencing teacher assessments of his functioning? What social systems are playing a role in his problems? Is there evidence of cultural conflicts in this case? What influence do social-system variables have on the etiology of his condition? The social dimension described in this chapter should help structure your assessment of Raul Salazar's case. We begin this description of the social dimension by defining the social system and its utility in studying human development.

Our approach to human behavior in social work deals not only with developmental events but also with the context in which these events take place. The term *context* in the social work literature is often used interchangeably with *space, setting, situation, territory, locus, milieu,* and *environment.* In this book, we define many forms of contexts in terms of systems principles. We subscribe to this approach because we assume that social workers must adhere to a *people-in-systems* approach to understanding human behavior. The following Focus section describes the relationship between ecological systems theory and social-work practice.

FOCUS ON THEORY

Ecological Systems Theory

According to Carol Germain (1991, p. 15), "ecology is the science that studies the relations between organisms and their environments." Critical to the ecological perspective is its holistic view of people. The ecological perspective is a metaphor that provides an understanding about the reciprocal transactions that take place between people and the social environment in which they function. Therefore, people and environments are part of a holistic system in which each shapes the other (Germain, 1991).

Following are some of the basic ideas of the ecological systems perspective (Germain, 1991; Hearn, 1979).

- Social work practice is based on a dual focus. This focus includes the person and situation, and the system and its environment.

- Social work practice occurs at the interface between the human system and its environment.

- Transactions occur at the interface between the system and the environment.

- In transactional relationships, both systems are influenced by change efforts.

- Social work practice is best conducted when the transactions promote growth and development of the organism while simultaneously being ameliorative to the environment, thus making it a better place for all systems that depend upon the environment for sustenance.

To understand the structure of various social contexts, you need a deep understanding of the social system. A **system** represents any set of elements that affect or influence one another. We cannot solve the problem of any system without taking into account

Carol Germain was a noted social work theorist who developed the ecological perspective for the practice of social work and furthered the understanding of human behavior in multiple environments.

all the factors that influence the system and its components (Bronfenbrenner, 1999; Churchman, 1978). A **social system** is a system in which the components are people. These people participate in a number of social systems that influence their development—family, school, work setting, neighborhood, community, nation, and so forth. We cannot understand human development by focusing merely on the psychological dimensions of individuals. For this reason, we need to develop knowledge of the key dimensions of social systems, their interrelations, and their environment.

Brim (1975) and Bronfenbrenner (1977) identified four categories, or levels, of systems that are useful to social workers: microsystems, mesosystem, exosystem, and macrosystem. **Microsystems** represent any systems that involve face-to-face or direct contact among the system participants. As social workers, we are interested in having categories that enable us to classify behavior that takes place in these systems. This type of analysis is limited, however, if it neglects the relations between the microsystem of primary attention and other key microsystems. If we have an understanding of how our multiple microsystems are interconnected, we can have a more informed understanding of the behavior in a particular microsystem. The **mesosystem** is the category systems theorists use to address this level of analysis. It refers to the network of personal settings in which we live our social lives. Each of our clients lives in a similar but different mesosystem. It is critical to have an understanding of the network of personal settings affecting a particular microsystem under investigation.

Individuals are members of a number of different microsystems. What happens to them in any one microsystem can influence their behavior in other settings. For example, if you are working with an adolescent, you should not ignore the fact that events in his or her peer group can influence the degree of conflict observed in his or her school or family setting. The makeup of the mesosystem must be taken into account in analyzing any identified microsystem issue.

The **exosystem** in Bronfenbrenner's scheme refers to the larger institutions of society that influence our personal systems. This includes institutions like government agencies in which we do not directly work but that have profound effects on our lives. Exosystems are considered to be any of the systems in which an individual is not directly involved. For instance, parents' work settings can affect the life of their children in many ways, yet the children have no direct involvement in the work settings of their parents. An exosystem level of analysis stresses the need to take into account the broader social environment of our clients by examining the influence of significant social institutions.

Last, the **macrosystem** represents the larger subcultural and cultural contexts in which the microsystems, mesosystem, and exosystem are located. This system has the most pervasive level of influence on social activities. **Culture** is defined as a system of meanings and values shared by a population and transmitted to future generations (Sigelman & Shaffer, 1995). It includes all the key artifacts developed during the history of a population—all its material and nonmaterial (symbolic) products. Every sociocultural group has its own history, but in recent years scholars of race, class, and gender studies have pointed out, through the voices metaphor, that many of these histories have been silenced. The voices metaphor comes from the efforts of scholars to challenge the silence that has surrounded the experiences of many groups in our society. These scholars focus on ignored aspects of diversity of our society in

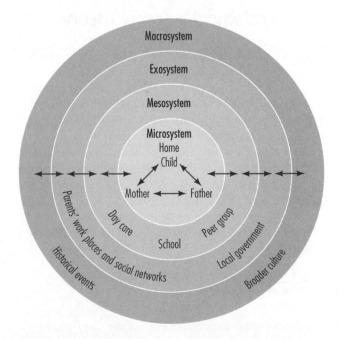

FIGURE 4.1   Bronfenbrenner's ecological model (adapted from Kopp & Krakow, 1982)

FIGURE 4.2
Ecomap (Jordan & Franklin, 1995)

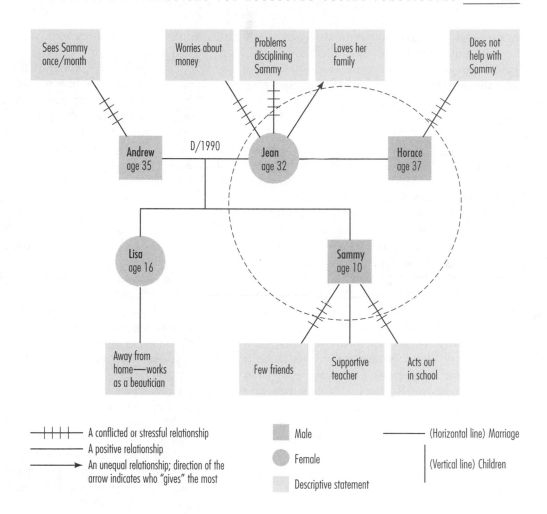

terms of "listening to the voices" of representatives of the silenced groups (Anderson & Collins, 1995; 1998). The goal of much of current multicultural scholarship is to help people think about the experiences of a multitude of previously silenced groups (Andersen & Collins, 1995; 1998). The material and symbolic aspects of culture influence all facets of our behavior, and they are given significant attention in the analysis of social systems by most practice frameworks in social work.

Bronfenbrenner used these four systems to describe the environmental contexts of human development. (See Figure 4.1.) These same systems have been adopted by social work scholars to conceptualize the environmental component of our professional focus on person-and-environment transactions. Before the

emergence of ecological systems thinking in social work, there were many simplistic views of the environment in the profession. These views frustrated most practitioners' efforts to achieve any objectives involving "environmental modification" (Grinnell, Kyte, & Bostwick, 1981). Grinnell and colleagues pointed out that these early concepts of environment represented "(1) social structures (for example, social class system, ethnicity); (2) social conditions (for instance, unemployment, discrimination); (3) social systems (for example, economic, health, and educational networks); and (4) specific neighborhood or community resources (for instance, schools, churches, day-care centers, job training programs)" (1981, p. 153). Many other dimensions and classifications have been used in social work to categorize the environment. However, ecological systems thinking, unlike the other approaches, enhanced our ability to look at the environment in a way that allowed its modification. This perspective redirected the attention of workers to the transactions between persons and environment, not to either person *or* environment variables.

Principles from systems theory direct social workers to identify relevant systems, their subsystems, and the suprasystems of which they are a part (Anderson & Carter, 1990). Social workers often achieve these ends by drawing an **ecomap.** Hartman and Laird (1983) are known in social work for having originally developed this tool for use by social workers in the field of child welfare. Ecomapping highlights the points of connection between systems influencing a person's life and facilitates the identification of points of conflict and points of support in a person's life space. Figure 4.2 presents a case example to illustrate the application of an ecomap to a social work situation.

To apply ecomaps and other systems-oriented concepts, one must be able to define the key social systems and their characteristics. We begin this process by describing the dimensions and characteristics of the family system. The family is a pivotal microsystem that influences many forms of social behavior.

Families, Groups, Support Systems, and Contexts

The **family** is increasingly being recognized as a "social system"—a whole composed of interrelated parts, each of which affects and is affected by one another, and each of which contributes to the functioning of the whole. This "systems perspective" helps us recognize that understanding a family is not as simple as understanding the mother-and-child relationship. Indeed, the family is influenced by many factors: the father and his relationship with the mother and baby, the grandparents and their relationships with the parents and the infant, and the environmental context—what kind of support does the family have from friends, church groups, and neighborhood? The important point about understanding families as systems is to recognize how different interactions within and outside the family system affect the family.

Garbarino and Abramowitz (1992a, p. 16) discuss an ecological approach to human development that emphasizes the *interaction* between the individual and environment. This view views the process of development as the expansion of the child's conception of the world and the child's ability to act on that world. An individual organism and the environment engage in reciprocal interaction: Each influences the other in an ever-changing interplay of biology and society, with intelligence and emotion as the mediators and identity and competence as the outcomes.

Belsky (1981) describes the family as a social system, wherein the family is bigger than the sum of its parts. Parents can influence the infant who can influence each parent and the marital relationship (see Figure 4.3). Consider the following example. An infant is interacting with its mother and is involved in a process of **reciprocal interaction.** It is reciprocal because the infant can influence the mother and the mother can influence the infant. If the mother responds to the infant's smile with a corresponding smile and high-pitched talk, the infant is likely to reciprocate with laughter. When the father walks into the room, the mother-infant dyad is transformed into a family system (Belsky, 1981). The family system can be affected by any pair in the family. For example, mothers are less likely to play with their infants when the fathers join the dyad. In addition, the marital relationship affects the relationship between the parent and child, and, in turn, each parent's relationship with the child affects the quality of the marriage.

Family practitioners and clinical social workers use a systems perspective to help them understand the social context of a family problem. When a family is seen for a child's problem, the assumption is that the child's problem cannot be understood separate from the family system. The problem is related to how the person is treated in the family system, and as such the solution to the problem involves changing the other members of the family system as well, not just changing the "problem" child.

No family system can be completely understood without also considering external factors and influences. So to the already complex family system we must add influences such as the extended family, the school

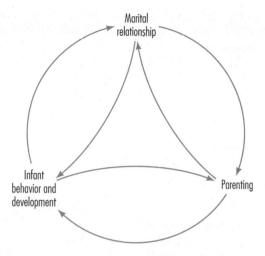

FIGURE 4.3 **Diagram of the family as a social system (Belsky, 1981)**

system, the neighborhood, the church or religious affiliation, the friends, the work environment, and so forth.

DEFINING THE FAMILY

What exactly is a family? How you answer this question can have important implications for how you practice social work. Indeed, how we as a society define" family" has important implications for the benefits and rights that family members receive. For example, if gay and lesbian couples are not considered to be families, that effects certain legal situations. For example, they may not be able to get married, make medical decisions for each other when the other person cannot do so, and receive shared benefits from health and life insurance companies. What about single-parent families? Shouldn't they be included in any definition of a family? The changing norms of society suggest that we must have changing definitions of families.

Schriver (1995) uses the term "familiness" to broaden the traditional concept of family. He states that "this concept reminds us as individuals and as members of particular families to think always about possible alternative structures and sets of functions that constitute *family* for others" (Schriver, 1995, p. 220).

Garbarino and Abramowitz (1992a) refer to the family as the "headquarters for human development." Families do make up the thread necessary to weave

human society together. "Through our families we are connected to the past—the distant times and places of our ancestors—and to the future—the hope of our children's children" (Garbarino & Abramowitz, 1992b, p. 72). Most discussions about the family include two related aspects of family: the family as the "headquarters for human development" and the family as a social institution.

Sociologists who attempt to answer the question "what is a family?" stress three functions: getting married, having children, and developing kinship ties. Reiss (1980, p. 29) summarized a global perspective regarding the family as "a small kinship-structured group with the key function of nurturant socialization." Duvall's (1971, p. 5) definition of the family is "a unit of interacting persons related by ties of marriage, birth, or adoption, whose central purpose is to create and maintain a common culture which promotes the physical, mental, emotional, and social development of each of its members." A less traditional definition of the family is offered by Hartman and Laird (1983, p. 576), who state that a family is created when "two or more people construct an intimate environment that they define as a family, an environment in which they generally will share a living space, commitment, and a variety of the roles and functions usually considered part of family life." Therefore, a family is a composition of people who decide to act as a family. This definition takes into account diverse forms of the family that might include homosexual couples, single-parent families, elderly persons not related by blood but living together as a family group, and other extended family groupings. Although the family is clearly changing, it remains a strong thread that ties together society as it functions to help provide socialization and companionship for diverse groups of people.

THE FAMILY LIFE CYCLE

One way of understanding family life is to consider the family life cycle—a sequence of developmental stages that families typically move through. Carter and McGoldrick (1988) have described a six-stage model of family development. An overview of the model is presented in Table 4.1.

As couples move through the family life cycle they have different sources of satisfaction and frustration. Some researchers have attempted to examine the effect

TABLE 4.1 Family Life Cycle

Stage of the Family Life Cycle	Key Developmental Task	Changes in Family Status Required to Proceed Developmentally
1. Between families: the unattached young adult	Accepting parent/offspring separation	Differentiation of self in relation to family of origin
		Development of intimate peer relations
		Establishment of self in work
2. The joining of families through marriage: the newly married couple	Commitment to new system	Formation of marital system
		Realignment of relationships with extended families and friends to include spouse
3. The family with young children	Accepting new members into the system	Adjusting marital system to make space for children
		Taking on parenting roles
		Realignment of relationships with extended family to include parenting and grandparenting roles
4. The family with adolescents	Increasing flexibility of family boundaries to include children's independence and grandparents' frailties	Shifting of parent-child relationships to permit adolescent to move in and out of system
		Refocus on midlife marital and career issues
		Beginning shift toward concerns for older generation
5. Launching children and moving on	Accepting a multitude of exits from and entries into the family system	Renegotiation of marital system as dyad
		Development of adult-to-adult relationships between grown children and their parents
		Realignment of relationships to include in-laws and grandchildren
6. The family in later life	Accepting the shifting of generational roles	Maintaining own functioning, couple functioning, or both, and interests in face of physiological decline; exploration of new familial and social-role options
		Support for a more central role for middle generations
		Making room in the system for the wisdom and experience of the elderly; supporting the older generation without overfunctioning for them
		Dealing with loss of spouse, siblings, and other peers and preparation for own death; life review and integration

(Adapted from Carter & McGoldrick, 1988)

of the life-cycle stage on various behaviors and attitudes. For example, how does the stage of the family life cycle affect marital satisfaction? In general, researchers (Belsky, 1990; Rollins & Feldman, 1970) have found a U-shaped relationship between life-cycle stage and marital satisfaction. Marital satisfaction starts high, with the newly married couple, and decreases to its lowest point at the stage where families have school-aged children.

The next stage, families with teenage children, begins the upward incline to the final stage, the aging family, where satisfaction reaches a level similar to that of the newly married couple. Figure 4.4 presents the U-shaped relationship across the family life-cycle stages.

Although the family life-cycle perspective helps us understand how families change over time, it also presents common patterns of the typical family. However,

It is increasingly recognized that "family" does not mean two heterosexual parents and a child—families represent great diversity, as this lesbian family demonstrates.

families today are not easily described using typical norms. Therefore, transitions from one stage to the next may depend on the unique aspects of the family and the family's previous experience. Indeed, changes in the "typical" family, such as divorce, working mothers, delayed childbirth, and blended families, add different sets of tasks and challenges that may be different from those of the traditional family.

The Changing Family

As we have seen, the family is a complex system; but it is not static, and as a developing system the family reflects a changing world. As we noted earlier, even the definition of "family" is changing to accommodate rapid changes that are taking place in our society. There-

fore, understanding the family includes staying informed about the numerous changes that have taken place with regard to families. Some recent changes include the following trends (Sigelman & Shaffer, 1991).

- More adults are living as singles today than in the past.
- Many young adults are delaying marriage while they pursue educational and career goals.
- After marriage, couples are having fewer children.
- An increasing number of couples are deciding to remain childless.
- Most women, including those who have children, work outside the home.
- Up to 50% of young people are expected to divorce sometime in their marriage.
- Up to 50% of children born in the 1980s will spend some time in a single-parent family.
- Because more couples are divorcing, more adults, about 75%, are remarrying.
- Adults today are spending more of their later years as couples or as single adults without children in the home primarily because people live longer than they used to.

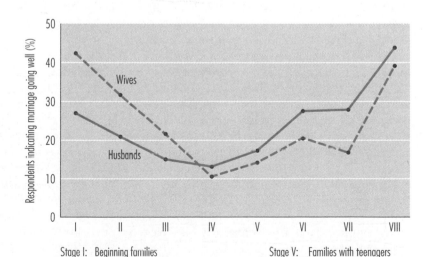

FIGURE 4.4
U-shaped relationship of marital satisfaction across the family life cycle (Rollins & Feldman, 1970)

Stage I: Beginning families
Stage II: Child-bearing families
Stage III: Families with preschool children
Stage IV: Families with school-aged children

Stage V: Families with teenagers
Stage VI: Families as launching centers
Stage VII: Families in the middle years
Stage VIII: Aging families

Learning to express anger and to deal with conflict are important in marriage. Conflicts test the communication, problem solving, and negotiation abilities of most couples.

The Family of Our Times

Tommy needs to eat at 6:00 because of a school function at 7:00. His sister, Martha, must be picked up from her field hockey game, but their mother, Sarah, has an office function and can't get home until after 8:00—thus, no dinner and no transportation. Sarah asks her husband, Rick, to come to the rescue, but he has to work late to prepare for a flight to Dallas the next morning. It is also Sarah's mother's birthday the next day, but Sarah is not prepared. Urgent messages await on the answering machine, one from a longtime friend of Rick's, in town for a day and wanting to drop by, and another from a close friend of Sarah's, in tears because of her floundering marriage (Gergen, 1991, p. 29).

This description of the modern family portrays what Gergen refers to as the "saturated family." Unlike family life a century ago, new technologies have infiltrated our lives and become necessities, with the effect that the individual's experience of the cultural and social world has expanded and become more complex. In this electronic age, which has brought new forms of communication—fax machines, copy machines, Internet connections, electronic mail—there is a new reality concerning our abilities to interact. At the social level, we confront a multiplicity of relationships. One result of all this, Gergen points out, is that it is increasingly difficult for people to discover what they believe in. This experience of the world and the self is referred to as "social saturation" (Gergen, 1991). We are simply bombarded with new causes, different inner voices, and mixed opinions, and it is increasingly difficult to get a sense of the "right way."

The preceding example of typical family life is characterized by what Gergen refers to as a "slapstick style of turmoil now so pervasive that it seems unremarkable" (Gergen, 1991, p. 29). Do families have consensual goals that provide direction in their lives? Gergen believes that the technologies of social saturation make this very difficult. "The ordinary, daily confluence of multiple lives within one household makes for a sense of fragmentation, as if the members of the family were being scattered by the centrifugal force of postmodern life" (Gergen, 1991, p. 29). This predicament leads to the inability to define "family." In fact, Gergen refers to the **floating family,** which is a formless array of familial relationships that are in a continuous state of flux. Such a lack of boundaries leads to a blurring of ideals, whereby there is no sense about what it means to be a "good" family. Because there is no shared sense of reality, the family often becomes the site of multiple confrontations and conflicts. Furthermore, the floating family must adapt to a loss in power structure. Traditional notions of hierarchy and authority structure are becoming increasingly less relevant.

Such changes have led to more intense discussions about what a family really is and how to function within a family. Gergen believes that in this new world "the postmodern family can provide a kind of emotional sustenance that seems uniquely suited to the needs of people in a saturated world" (p. 34). The home is not just a place where one can "be oneself," but it is a place where people can "be their many selves." So, although the family is undergoing many new adaptations, it remains an adaptive self-system.

GROUPS AS SOCIAL SUBSYSTEMS

How many groups do you belong to? To answer this question you need to think about what makes up a group. When you are together with your friends, is this a group? What about the members of the Human Behavior and Social Environment class you are presently taking: Is that a group? Are all the college students from your home town a group?

A *group* can de defined as "two or more persons who are interacting with one another in such a manner that each person influences and is influenced by each other person" (Shaw, 1981, p. 8). Brown (1991, p. 3) defines a group as "a small, face-to-face collection of persons who interact to accomplish some purpose." Therefore, although you have a lot in common with all the college students from your home town, they do not constitute a group in Brown's definition, because the people don't depend on one another to accomplish shared goals.

A definition of what constitutes a group depends on the focus of the theorist. Forsyth (1999) provides an overview of the range of definitions contained in the literature (see Table 4.2). Some of these definitions of groups highlight different variables such as influence, identity, and structure. However, they often ignore other important characteristics such as group size.

TABLE 4.2	Sampling of Definitions of *Group*
Central Feature	**Definition**
Communication	"We mean by a group a number of persons who communicate with one another, often over a span of time, and who are few enough so that each person is able to communicate with all the others, not at second hand, through other people, but face-to-face" (Homans, 1950, p. 1).
Influence	"Two or more persons who are interacting with one another in such a manner that each person influences and is influenced by each other person" (Shaw, 1981, p. 454).
Interaction	"A group is a social system involving regular interaction among members and a common group identity. This means that groups have a sense of "weness" that enables members to identify themselves as belonging to a distinct entity" (Johnson, 1995, p. 125).
Interdependence	"A group is a collection of individuals who have relations to one another that make them interdependent to some significant degree" (Cartwright & Zander, 1968, p. 46).
Interrelations	"A group is an aggregation of two or more people who are to some degree in dynamic interrelation with one another" (McGrath, 1984, p. 8).
Psychological significance	"Descriptively speaking, a psychological group is defined as one that is psychologically significant for the members, to which they relate themselves subjectively for social comparison and the acquisition of norms and values, . . . that they privately accept membership in, and which influences their attitudes and behavior" (Turner, 1987, pp. 1–2).
Shared identity	"A group exists when two or more people define themselves as members of it and when its existence is recognized by at least one other" (Brown, 1988, pp. 2–3).
Structure	"A group is a social unit which consists of a number of individuals who stand in (more or less) definite status and role relationships to one another and which possesses a set of values or norms of its own regulating the behavior of individual members, at least in matters of consequences to the group" (Sherif & Sherif, 1956, p. 144).

Shaw's definition of "group" defines the barest requirements of a group but leaves unanswered other questions about groups (Forsyth, 1999).

Groups are often classified as either formed or natural groups. **Formed groups** are created through an outside influence or intervention and are convened for a particular purpose; **natural groups** are created by naturally occurring events, interpersonal attraction, or the mutual needs of the individuals involved (Toseland & Rivas, 1995).

Belonging to a Group

People belong to particular groups for a variety of reasons. Why would you want to be a member of a particular group? Do you seek membership in groups because they provide you with a sense of security, intimacy, or identity? To what extent are groups a fundamental "bridge" between you and the society at large (Forsyth, 1999)? Clearly, there are a variety of reasons why people belong to groups. Schein (1980) suggests that these reasons revolve around five essential goals we want to accomplish in groups:

1. To fulfill our need for affiliation;

2. To increase our sense of identity and our self-esteem;

3. To obtain a source for social comparisons between ourselves and others;

4. To obtain a greater sense of security and power; and

5. To accomplish a particular task or set of tasks.

People can identify with and belong to a variety of small groups such as family, peer or friendship groups, ethnic groups, civil rights groups, and formal organizations. Membership in these groups is a major source of self-validation and standing. Tyler (1989) contends that people value membership in social groups because group identifications are psychologically rewarding. The groups to which we belong tell us about out status or our place in society. This is why self-esteem is so closely associated with how a person evaluates the groups to which he or she belongs. It is assumed in social-identity theory that people are motivated to overvalue their own groups and, by doing so, to enhance their self-esteem.

According to social-identity theory (Tajfel, 1978, 1982; Tajfel & Turner, 1986), identity in interpersonal interactions can be dependent completely on an individual's membership in a social group (social identity). This differs from circumstances involving a person's identity being determined by personal characteristics or traits (Stephan & Stephan, 1996). "A major premise of Tajfel's social-identity theory is that social identity creates and maintains attitudinal and behavioral discriminations favoring the ingroup" (Stephan & Stephan, 1996, p. 91). That is, Tajfel assumes that people are mo-

tivated to overvalue their own group and by doing so increase their own self-esteem. This includes (1) making positive comparisons between groups that individuals are members of and relevant outgroups and (2) seeing important differences in one's own group but assuming similarity or homogeneity in outgroup members (Stephan & Stephan, 1996).

Overvaluation of one's groups contributes to many forms of intergroup conflict. This includes actions by members of groups to exclude others from desired activities and resources. Social rejection is a form of social conflict that takes on many different faces and varies from context to context. Some theorists assume that this and other forms of social conflict are inevitable aspects of human existence but that intergroup conflict can be managed so that it results in constructive rather than destructive outcomes (Boardman & Horowitz, 1994).

We need groups to function effectively in society. All of us have special needs for affiliation and want to enhance our self-esteem. Groups also help us achieve important goals, like developing an increased sense of security and power. As Johnson and Johnson (1989) point out:

> From the moment we are born to the moment we die, relationships are the core of our existence. We are conceived within relationships, are born into relationships, live our lives within relationships. We are dependent on other people for the realization of life itself, for survival during one of the longest gestation periods in the animal kingdom, for food and cognitive development, for guidance in learning essential competencies required to survive in our world, and for fun, excitement, comfort, love, personal confirmation, and fulfillment. Our relationships with others form the context for all other aspects of our lives (p. 107).

Interdependence in our social relationships is significantly influenced by the social groups to which we belong. For this reason, we must make distinctions among groups to understand their contributions to human behavior.

Treatment and Task Groups

In social work, an important classification of groups is whether they are treatment oriented or task oriented (Toseland & Rivas, 1995). In general, the two types of groups serve different purposes. In **treatment groups** the purpose is to meet members' socioemotional needs. Different types of treatment groups include groups for support, education, therapy, growth, and socialization. In **task groups** the primary purpose is to complete the work for which the group was convened (Toseland & Rivas, 1995). The task group is not specifically linked to the needs of the members of the group. Using selected characteristics, Toseland and Rivas provide a comparison of treatment groups and task groups, as was shown in Table 4.2.

Although we have presented a distinction between two types of groups, treatment and task, many different group purposes exist within these two types of groups (Toseland & Rivas, 1995, p. 20):

- *Rehabilitation:* Restoring members to their former level of functioning;
- *Habilitation:* Helping members grow and develop;
- *Correction:* Helping members who are having problems with social laws or mores;
- *Socialization:* Helping members learn how to get along with others and do what is socially acceptable;
- *Prevention:* Helping members develop and function at an optimum level and helping them to prepare for events that are likely to occur;
- *Social action:* Helping members change their environment;
- *Problem solving:* Helping members resolve complex issues and concerns; and
- *Developing social values:* Helping members develop a humanistic approach to living.

Understanding How Groups Function

Groups can have a powerful influence on human behavior. What factors can account for this influence? To answer this question, we must understand *group dynamics,* or *group process.* These factors can influence the behavior of both the individual in the group and the group as a whole. In social work we direct our attention to the helpful influences of group dynamics. However, we must recognize that group dynamics can also unleash harmful forces (Galinsky & Schopler, 1977). The group dynamics that help explain these forces include *norms* that guide the behavior of group members; *roles* that members play in groups; *communication patterns,*

which influence the manner in which people interact; *power and status,* which affect the influence members have on one another; and *cohesiveness,* which determines how much sharing takes place in the group.

 ## Roles and Norms

Norms are expectations and beliefs regarding appropriate behavior in a group. When you are with your group of friends, there are certain informal, unwritten laws about what is appropriate behavior. For example, name-calling may or may not be appropriate depending on the norms of your particular group. In some groups, this is a sign of affection or expected behavior; however, in other groups, this would be considered inappropriate and rude behavior. How you decide whether to engage in behaviors like name-calling will depend on the norms of your group. Rosenblatt (1962) notes that the influence of norms on behavior will depend on the extent to which they are considered binding. In general, however, group norms exert powerful influence over the behavior of individuals. As Toseland and Rivas (1995, p. 81) point out, "soon it becomes clear that sanctions and social disapproval result from some behaviors and that praise and social approval result from other behaviors." The development of group norms can be helpful to the individuals and to the group itself. Norms provide a predictable group environment and add stability and security for members. Through the development of group norms, groups can develop procedures for coordinated action to reach goals (Toseland & Rivas, 1995). Alternatively, norms can develop destructive patterns of behavior that are harmful to others or unethical.

A **role** is a pattern of behavior that a person acts out in a group. It is a shared expectation about the functions of the individuals in the group. For example, there are role expectations about your status as a student, a mother, a spouse, and the many other roles you have in society. In groups, individuals also act according to certain roles, which can be important contributors to the group's effectiveness. "Roles are important for groups because they allow for division of labor and appropriate use of power" (Toseland & Rivas, 1995, p. 82). By accepting a particular role, individuals agree to behave in a certain manner.

Roles, like norms, can vary from being explicit to vague and informal. Bales (1958) has identified two categories of roles: task-related roles and socioemotional

BOX 4.1

Tasks and Socioemotional Roles in Groups

TASK ROLES

INFORMATION SEEKER: Emphasizes "getting the facts" by calling for background information

OPINION SEEKER: Asks for more qualitative types of data, such as attitudes, values and feelings

ELABORATOR: Gives additional information—such as rephrasing, implications—about points made by others

COORDINATOR: Shows the relevance of each idea and its relationship to the overall problem

ORIENTER: Refocuses discussion on the topic whenever necessary

EVALUATOR-CRITIC: Appraises the quality of the group's efforts in terms of logic, practicality, or method

ENERGIZER: Stimulates the group to continue when discussion lags

SOCIOEMOTIONAL ROLES

ENCOURAGER: Rewards others through agreement, warmth, and praise

HARMONIZER: Mediates conflicts among group members

COMPROMISER: Shifts his or her own position on an issue in order to reduce conflict in the group

GATEKEEPER OR EXPEDITER: Smoothes communication by setting up procedures and ensuring equal participation

STANDARD SETTER: Expresses or calls for discussion of standards for evaluating the quality of the group process

GROUP OBSERVER AND COMMENTATOR: Informally points out the positive and negative aspects of the group's dynamics and calls for change if necessary

FOLLOWER: Accepts the ideas offered by others and serves as an audience for the group

(Adapted from Benne & Sheats, 1948)

roles. *Task-related roles* refer to actions that move the group toward the completion of its goals. *Socioemotional roles* refer to actions that keep the interactions in the group positive, friendly, and supportive. Box 4.1 shows seven different task-related roles and seven different socioemotional roles that are used in groups.

Communication Patterns

Communication patterns reflect the nature of how the members in the group communicate—in both verbal and nonverbal ways. A communication process is always occurring in the group, because people communicate whenever they are together in a group. Communicating in a group has a number of functions (Kiesler, 1978):

- Understanding people and finding out where they stand in relation to other people;
- Persuading others;
- Gaining or maintaining power;
- Defending oneself;
- Provoking a reaction in others;
- Making an impression on others;
- Gaining or maintaining relationships; and
- Presenting a unified image to the group.

Communication patterns vary within a group and may be either centralized, whereby the leader is usually the central figure, or decentralized, whereby members share equally in communication and the pattern of interactions is more group-centered. What kind of communication pattern is best for groups? Research by McGrath (1984) found that, when problems are simple, centralized groups are efficient in resolving the problems. "Group-centered communication patterns tend to increase social interaction, group morale, and members' commitment to group goals" (Toseland & Rivas, 1995, p. 74). However, when problems are more complex, a decentralized pattern of communication is more effective. Group members have greater satisfaction in more decentralized groups.

 ## Status and Power

How do some group members obtain more status and power than other members? **Status** refers to the ranking of each group member's position in the group relative to the other members. **Power** refers to the potential ability of a member to influence the group's decision or the behavior of individuals in the group. Although status and power often go hand in hand, this is not necessarily the case. A person's status is based on two different factors. First, what is the person's prestige or position outside the group? Is the person recognized as a leader in the community? Second, what kinds of roles does the person assume when he or she becomes a member of a group? Is the person a coordinator and a standard setter, influencing how the group achieves its goals? Because status is defined relative to other group members, a person's status is influenced by how others in the group perceive him or her.

"Power" is a difficult concept to define, but French and Raven (1959), in a classic analysis, identify five sources of power in groups:

1. *Reward power:* Based on the person's ability to reward others as a means for obtaining power;

2. *Coercive power:* Based on the person's ability to apply sanctions such as punishments and threats toward others;

3. *Expert power:* Based on the person's ability to demonstrate superior skills and abilities as a means of influencing others;

4. *Referent power:* Based on the person's personal characteristics, such as likability and respect, that give him or her influence over others; and

5. *Legitimate power:* Based on the person's perceived legitimate right to make demands of other people.

Cohesiveness

A **cohesive group** is one in which individual members have strong bonds with one another and to the group itself. Group cohesion is the dynamic that compels individuals to remain part of the group (Festinger, 1950). Therefore, cohesive group members are often emotionally close, loyal to one another and to the group, and have a strong sense of camaraderie.

Fundamentally, the factors that make a group cohesive are those that promote positive, caring relationships among the members—for example, group members that are more similar in attitudes, have greater liking and respect for one another—and that are successful in achieving goals (Ridgeway, 1983). When members are attracted to a group, there is a greater likelihood of developing group cohesion. Attraction to the group is influenced by people's desire for affiliation, the group's access to resources and incentives, the expectations group members have about the outcomes that can be achieved in the group, and the relative comparison to other groups (Cartwright, 1968).

Group workers believe that an important skill for a group leader is the ability to influence group cohesion (Rose, 1989). This skill is important because a cohesive group has a number of benefits (Cartwright, 1968; Dion, Miller, & Magnan, 1970; Evans & Dion, 1991; Rose, 1989; Yalom, 1985):

- Members are more likely to stay in the group;

- Members are more likely to persevere in attempts to accomplish group goals;

- Attendance is higher;

- Members accept more responsibility for group functioning;

- Members are more satisfied;

- Members are less likely to feel psychological distress; and

- Members are more likely to have increased self-esteem and self-confidence.

Effect of Gender on Groups

How does gender influence small-group interactions? Not surprisingly, the small group is similar to what we experience in society. Therefore, status and power differentials in the larger society are reflected in the small group. As a result, gender roles can play an important function in how individuals and groups behave. Kanter (1977) believes that, when men and women are in mixed-gender groups, tension exists that places many women at a disadvantage. In essence, because men and women do not have equal power and status in society, there is little reason to believe that equal power status would exist in the small mixed-gender group.

Indeed, research on mixed-gender groups has found that, in line with traditional gender-role expectations, men are more likely to assume task-oriented roles, and women are more likely to assume socioemotional roles (Eagly & Wood, 1991; Wood, 1987). Wood (1987) further discovered that, when groups confront problems that require a task orientation, all-male groups do better; but when problems are based on complex social interactions, all-female groups do better.

Decision Making in Groups

Whatever the composition of the group, its members often have to confront group decision making, and social psychologists have discovered interesting theories about this topic. In a classic study, Stoner (1961) asked individuals and groups to make decisions under conditions of uncertainty. For example, one scenario involved an electrical engineer with a small family to support. He makes an adequate income and has good job security. After attending a conference, he is offered a job at a small new company with an uncertain future. However, if he takes the job, he can participate in a share of the ownership. Stoner compared how individuals and groups resolved such dilemmas and found that, overall, groups made riskier decisions than individuals did. This observation became known as *risky shift.*

Additional research found that the shift can occur in either direction. A group may start out mildly opposed to an idea, but, after discussion, the sentiment against the idea becomes stronger. In contrast, a group may start out favorably inclined toward an idea, but, after discussion, this sentiment becomes stronger. This shift toward the more extreme position is referred to as *group polarization.* Group polarization results when discussion strengthens a group's perspective and then shifts toward a more extreme position in the same direction.

Another important group phenomenon is **groupthink.** Groupthink occurs when a cohesive group emphasizes consensus at the expense of critical thinking when attempting to problem solve. The concept of groupthink is based on the keen observations of Irving Janis (1972; 1982), who described groupthink in an effort to explain how President John Kennedy and his advisers could so mistakenly decide to invade Cuba at the Bay of Pigs in 1961. Janis was amazed at how botched the invasion was. "How could bright men like John F. Kennedy and his advisers be taken in by such a stupid, patchwork plan as the one presented to them by the CIA representatives" (Janis, 1973, p. 16)?

Based on this question, Janis developed his model of groupthink, which is described in Box 4.2. When groupthink sets in, members of the group fail to use their own critical judgment. Because the group is cohesive, members develop group norms against dissent, and the pressure to conform becomes great. Also, the group's viewpoint is protected by "mind guards," who withhold information from the group if it contradicts the group's perspective.

If the group's view is challenged from the outside, then an *ingroup* and an *outgroup* are created. The ingroup includes everyone who agrees with the group perspective, and the outgroup is everyone who is not part of the ingroup. Via the perception of the outgroup as different from the ingroup, the outgroup can easily become the enemy, and an "us-versus-them" mentality develops. An additional symptom of groupthink is a biased approach to examining information and facts. Everything is seen from the viewpoint of supporting the group perspective.

The groupthink theory suggests that the way individuals in groups process information may not be the best approach to problem solving. Janis reports that groupthink was an underlying problem in President Roosevelt's lack of preparation for Pearl Harbor, President Johnson's continued involvement in the Vietnam War, and in President Nixon's cover-up of the Watergate scandal. However, as Weiten and Lloyd (1997)

BOX 4.2

Janis's Model of Groupthink

ANTECEDENT CONDITIONS

High cohesiveness

Insulation from the group

Lack of methodological procedures for search and appraisal

Directive leadership

High stress and a low degree of hope for finding a better solution than the one favored by the leader or other influential groups

CONCURRENCE-SEEKING TENDENCY

SYMPTOMS OF GROUPTHINK

Illusion of invulnerability

Collective rationalization

Belief in inherent morality of the group

Stereotypes of outgroups

Direct pressure on dissenters

Self-censorship

Illusion of unanimity

Self-appointed mind guards

SYMPTOMS OF DEFECTIVE DECISION MAKING

Incomplete survey of alternatives

Incomplete survey of objectives

Failure to examine risks of preferred choice

Poor information search

Selective bias in processing information at hand

Failure to reappraise alternatives

Failure to work out contingency plans

(Janis & Mann, 1977)

note, groupthink is likely to be observed in everyday life as groups struggle with the many decisions they have to make.

What would be the likely causes of groupthink? Janis notes three critical factors: first, the isolation of the group; second, the influence of directive leadership; and third, the use of unsystematic procedures for generating and evaluating decisions. Additional factors include the stress present in the situation, the particular characteristics of certain leaders, and the level of cohesiveness in the group. Although research has found that groupthink is not inevitable, it can occur and can lead to profoundly negative consequences (Weiten & Lloyd, 1997).

Research like Janis's has led to the implementation of new procedures in approaches to group decision making. For example, the Institute for Cultural Affairs, a nonprofit organization designed to empower people

to facilitate change, has developed a method called the Technology of Participation (Spencer, 1989). This process teaches people a specific method for focused conversation via four steps for groups to follow: be objective, reflective, interpretive, and decisional. Then group members use five steps of the Technology of Participation in decision making: (1) set the context; (2) brainstorm data and ideas; (3) order the data; (4) name the categories; and (5) evaluate the work and its implications.

SUPPORT SYSTEMS

Children and families do not develop in isolation. They grow and develop in interaction with many other systems, such as school systems, neighborhood systems, and extended family systems. These systems can offer a needed source of *social support*. Caplan (1974, p. 4) defines **social support systems** as "continuing social aggregates that provide individuals with opportunities for feedback about themselves and for validations for their expectations about others, which may offset deficiencies in these communications within the larger community context."

Germain (1991) classifies support systems into five different types: formal organizations, formed groups, self-help groups, social networks, and natural helpers. For our discussion, we are concerned primarily with informal support systems, which include self-help groups, social networks, and natural helpers. Understanding social support is important in social work because the notion of *social* support expresses the person-in-environment perspective and is critical to making a social work assessment (Germain, 1991). Silverman (1987a) notes that social support groups are important for people who are undergoing transitions in certain roles, which can be a critical time for change. Social support groups help people develop appropriate expectations and learn appropriate role behaviors for obtaining a new integration into society.

Self-Help and Mutual Aid Groups

Social support is offered through self-help or mutual-aid groups. These groups seek to offer mutual aid through the exchange that occurs when people share a common problem. Such exchanges may have strong biological and social roots. People are often drawn to small groups, and this may be because of the evolutionary benefit of being in such groups; groups provide emotional and physical security. As Dubos (1978) points out, evolution took place in the context of small groups, which provided security from predators. In a similar sense, small groups provide protection in contemporary life where we "experience urbanized mass society as stressful, despite its attractions and advantages. We protect ourselves by maintaining noninvolvement through depersonalized, detached interactions with those outside our own 'band'" (Germain, 1991, p. 77).

In self-help groups, people join together to help one another cope more effectively with shared problems. These groups are often a part of voluntary organizations in which members control the resources and policy decisions. In this sense, they are self-help organizations. Silverman (1987a) uses the term *mutual help* to describe these organizations, noting that the help goes two ways.

Mutual-aid groups can be classified into two basic types: social-change groups and personal-coping groups (Germain, 1991). Social-change groups may be involved in changing public laws or attitudes; examples are groups that support gay and lesbian issues and groups for parents with disabled children. These groups are often involved in awareness campaigns and efforts to ensure that group members receive the kind of services and treatment that they are entitled to. Personal-coping groups focus on getting help for individual members that will influence their behavior or personal growth. The best example is Alcoholics Anonymous, the oldest self-help organization of its kind. Both of these types of groups are examples of mutual help organizations because the "members retain control of resources and are actively involved in helping programs built on their own experience" (Silverman, 1987a, p. 171).

Characteristics of Self-Help or Mutual Aid Groups

What makes a self-help group different from other types of groups? One of the fundamental differences is that, in **self-help organizations,** the members control the resources and policies—that is, the groups are self-governing and self-regulating (Silverman, 1987). However, the nature of the organizations' structures varies considerably. For example, some very informal organizations have little or no organizational structure, and the members that participate control the organization. Other groups emulate voluntary organizations, using parliamentary procedures, establishment of committees, and election of officers (Silverman, 1987). For example, the La Leche League is a service organization for mothers who breast-feed, and local offices follow national leaders for directives in running the local chapters. Typically, such groups use dues from affiliated chapters that support the national office. Other self-help groups are less formally organized and use a consensus model in managing the activities of the group.

Functions of Self-Help Groups

Silverman (1987, p. 173) identifies three primary functions in a mutual self-help organization: "(1) Receive information on how to cope, (2) obtain material help when necessary, (3) feel cared about and supported." Self-help groups are fundamentally based on the idea that people with like experiences can offer the best information regarding these three functions. Silverman (1987, p. 173) describes the functions this way: The helper and the beneficiary become peers, if only in the sense that they share a common problem. As they discover that what seemed unusual is common to others in a similar situation, people no longer feel alone with their problems. Their emotions and experiences are legitimated, and a framework is provided for coping with the situation. They receive specific guidance on how to implement change, thus expanding their repertoire of appropriate coping strategies.

Each self-help group or organization has its own approach to helping its members. Alcoholics Anonymous is the best-known self-help organization, and its basic structure and philosophy are used as a model for similar self-help groups for addictive behavior and other personal problems. Examples of such groups include Overeaters Anonymous and Incest Survivors Anonymous.

The relationship between self-help groups and professional organizations has not always been cooperative. Indeed, self-help groups may be reluctant to associate with professionals, fearing their autonomy may be compromised. Furthermore, many people who use self-help groups may have had poor experiences with formal helping systems. Many professionals have attempted to intervene with self-help groups in an effort to impose their professional knowledge. As a result, there is often tension between professionals and the self-help organization. However, some research (Toseland & Hacker, 1982) has found strong connections between self-help groups and professionals. Social workers increasingly recognize that self-help groups can be an important resource that is often more flexible and responsive than formal service systems (Toseland & Rivas, 1995).

The number of self-help organizations has grown so rapidly that many people now refer to "self-help" as a movement. Box 4.3 presents only a sample of self-help groups that were available in one community. Germain (1991, p. 74) notes that "the rapid expansion of self-help reflects the readiness (always present, but until recently not acknowledged or recognized) of people in all segments of society to solve their own problems, in concert with others like themselves." Libraries, grocery stores, and community organizations list information about self-help groups. Computer access through the Internet has greatly increased people's ability to find others with like problems and join self-help groups electronically (Finn, 1995). Indeed, there are many computer-based self-help groups, such as those for sexual abuse survivors and for recovered substance abusers (Finn, 1996).

Why is the self-help movement gaining such popularity? Part of the answer to this question lies in the evolutionary benefit achieved by such groups. The growth may also be due to the expanding professionalism and the depersonalization of care being offered (Gartner & Riessman, 1977). Perhaps the rapid changes taking place in society are limiting the opportunities for people to obtain needed social support. The growth also parallels the consumer movement, which advocates greater personal involvement in one's care and less reliance on outside professionals. Silverman (1987) believes the growth in self-help reflects the fact that people want a different form of help that is simply not available in the existing service system. People often seek help that can be made available to them only through association with others who are similarly afflicted.

Natural Helpers

Closely related to self-help organizations are **natural helpers**—"central figures in a social network or in a neighborhood who have gained recognition for their unique wisdom, resourcefulness, and caring qualities" (Germain, 1991, p. 81). Pancoast, Parker, and Froland (1983) describe mutual help groups as natural helping networks, and Collins and Pancoast (1976) describe neighborhoods where natural helpers are a critical resource, providing social support to families at risk for child abuse and neglect.

Developing and using natural helpers may be critical in efforts to help people who are isolated and without access to traditional support services. For example, Patterson, Brennan, Germain, and Memmot (1988) found that natural helping in rural communities is characterized by reciprocity—helpers provide for

BOX 4.3

Some Support Groups and Anonymous Organizations

Adult Children of Alcoholics	OURS (for adoptive parents)
Adult Children of Sex Addicts	Overeaters Anonymous
Adults Recovering from Incest (women's group)	Parents Anonymous
Alcoholics Anonymous	Pills Anonymous
Al-Anon	PMS Peer Support group
Child Abusers Anonymous	RESOLVE: Infertility Education Support
Chronic Pain Outreach	Sex Addicts Anonymous
Cocaine Anonymous	Sex and Love Addicts Anonymous
Coc-Anon	Sexaholics Anonymous
Concerned United Birth Parents	Co-Sexaholics Anonymous
Eating Disorders	Shoplifters Anonymous
Emotions Anonymous	Smokers Anonymous
Families Anonymous	Spenders Anonymous
For Accountability in Religion	S-Anon
Gamblers Anonymous	Survivors of Incest Anonymous
Men for Sobriety	Twelve Steps for Christian Living group
Depressive and Manic-Depressive Association	Women for Sobriety
Narcotics Anonymous	Women with Multiple Addictions

friends and are in turn cared for by them. Germain (1991) quotes a natural helper's description of her role:

> He was abusive and very, very abusive of their son. When the divorce was finally completed, it made her very sad because it all started because of alcohol. She really still liked the guy, but she was determined this was it. As a result she was badly in need of friends. And that's where I thought I helped her—more for listening than anything else because I couldn't do anything else (p. 82).

Interest in natural-helping networks has grown as part of the larger interest in prevention, self-help, and community building at the local level (Pancoast & Collins, 1987). Informal helping is now a legitimate part of the continuum of helping strategies (Whittaker & Garbarino, 1983). The growth of this type of inter-

vention has led to the development of a new role for the social worker. The social worker is expected to be not an expert but instead a partner with the natural helpers. As Pancoast and Collins (1987) point out, "it is important for social workers to be careful not to usurp the position of the natural helper or to take on a customary professional position of leadership and direction" (p. 180).

CONTEXTS: COMMUNITIES, ORGANIZATIONS, AND INSTITUTIONS

Communities are key contexts for social work interventions (Fellin, 1995). As Heller and his colleagues (1984) point out, **community** is considered one of the most important environmental contexts for understanding human behavior and issues of personal and social well-being. Although we have known since Hippocrates that personal well-being is determined by contexts, the role of factors external to the individual or person are being newly appreciated by members of the scientific community in understanding human behavior (Gallagher, 1993). This is especially true of conceptions of community.

The concept of community means different things to different theorists. As Paul Hoggett (1997) points out, nowhere is the idea of community more dominant than in areas of contemporary public policy. "We hear of care in the community, community policing, community architecture, community development, community mental health, and, to add a very contemporary twist to our vocabulary, we now even hear of punishment in the community" (Hoggett, 1997, p. 3). In fact, many jobs held by social workers have the term *community* attached to the job description. Yet there is no agreed-on theory or conceptualization of "community." Some theorists focus on community as a place, while others focus on community as representing relationships. Still others focus on it as a source of identification, and others as a resource (Moffitt, 1996). We begin this discussion of community with the traditional focus on place or location.

Place as Community

Place has been a longstanding problem on the North American continent for many of its inhabitants. Many non-first-nation peoples in North America have a history of migratory spasms toward or away from some place (Pindell, 1995). These spasms include flight from the "Old World" to the new, followed by flight from ways of life in the newly formed cities to the frontier, followed by migrations from farms back to the cities and then from cities to the suburbs (Pindell, 1995). These shifts have produced a number of unforeseen consequences that are evident in many aspects of life in American society. As Pindell (1995) points out,

> It shows in locales with few physical edifices that last beyond a generation or two, as if all we know are beginnings, and so we frenetically tear down and pave over every last generation's best effort. It shows in the cities that the middle class has abandoned to the rich and the poor. It shows in the fallen suburban ideal

where we lived an isolated existence remote from the settings of human discourse (p. xiii).

Place as a community in current social life is being threatened by technological advances such as the Internet, video culture, and other technological developments that are transforming the importance of place in the lives of people. "Certainly in many urban areas the idea of community in its traditional sense, as something referring to as a place or neighborhood with which one feels some sense of identification, may well be waning" (Hoggett, 1997, p. 3). Some of the present-day threats to traditional notions of community were brought about by the development of the car. This invention allowed people to live in places other than where they worked, socialized, and shopped for basic necessities. Indeed, the suburbs do not provide the sense of identity, sense of belonging, or sense of significance that people require to provide them with a sense of direction in their lives. In other words, Lynd's (1929–1937) model of a community that used to exist in many areas of American society, in which people conducted virtually all their interactions and with whose location they strongly identified, no longer exists.

In premodern forms of social organization, community was considered the geographical location in which people carried out the majority of their activities. People in these traditional communities knew how to behave based on their positions within the community. Their behavior was predictable primarily because people in these communal societies shared a system of beliefs and values that tied them together. What ties people together if they lack shared beliefs and values? Is there a different sense of community in modern urban ways of life?

Communities were tied together by shared religious beliefs and a feudal system of social relationships in most early European societies. In France, these shared beliefs and values were destroyed when the authority of the church and aristocracy were challenged by the Jacobins, who played a major role in the French Revolution. In fact, a goal of the Jacobins was to replace traditional society, with its history of corruption and superstition, with a new order of solidarity or community based on principles of science and reason (Dennisoff & Waharman, 1979). This social movement contributed to the development of an individualistic libertarian community. "Solidarity in such communities is brought about because each individual within it realizes that community will safeguard the right of each individual to exercise his/her individual autonomy short of violating the autonomy of others" (Lowery, 1993, p. 43).

Following the French Revolution, many social thinkers questioned whether notions of community or solidarity were possible in France. "If people refused to take on unquestioningly the traditional moral standards of their ancestors, how would they behave?" (Dennisoff & Waharman, 1979, p. 14). Would the shift from rural-local communities to cities as a place to live mean that community would disappear? Debates on topics of this nature brought about the development of sociology as a science. Auguste Comte (1798–1857), who is often thought of as the father of sociology, did not believe that industrialization and the other social changes following the French Revolution would lead to the destruction of societies. However, he agreed with many of the conservative thinkers of his time that the primary problem facing society was the breakdown of the traditional shared system of beliefs and values that tied people together (Dennisoff & Wahrman, 1979). In its place, he called for a humanist religion led by priest-sociologists who worked at producing order and progress.

Emile Durkheim (1858–1917) supported Comte's view that industrialization would not necessarily destroy solidarity or community, but he believed that societies needed a new basis for social bonding that could replace the beliefs and values provided by the Catholic Church. Durkheim assumed that what would hold people together in industrialized societies would no longer be the similarities of its members. "What Durkheim called the *mechanical solidarity of the past* (based on similarity) had to be replaced, if society were to hold together, by some kind of new bond between people" (Dennisoff & Wahrman, 1979, p. 18). In his view, this new bond would be based on the characteristics of the emerging division of labor. "Division of labor" refers here to people performing distinct jobs that other people depend on for their survival. These relationships also involve contractual arrangements entered into by free individuals. This view of community has been questioned in the sociological literature, because it defines "community" in a way that is not too different from what many sociologists have termed a "society" (Moffitt, 1996). Indeed, it raises fundamental questions about whether there are qualitative differences between communal and other kinds of interpersonal connections that are characteristic of modern and post-modern societies.

Rousseau (1991) considers the controversy between contractual and communal theories of association a key element in understanding fundamental differences in views about what brings people in unity with one another. Contractual theorists focus on understanding the various kinds of agreements, negotiations, and other processes that characterize relationships in societies with high divisions of labor. This includes premarital agreements, labor contracts, and so forth (Rousseau, 1991). These relationships meet interests agreed on by individuals, but the people in these associations are not bonded in terms of deeper sentiments or in terms of the broader senses of identification traditionally attributed to many place communities. In other words, place communities involve mutual obligations among members involving a sense of commitment and identity not commonly observed in associations that are strictly contractual in nature. In fact, a number of social critics (for example, Etzioni, 1993; Bellah et al., 1996) are committed to a "**communitarian agenda**" that is designed to place responsibilities to others in balance with claims for individual rights.

Many people continue to search for places that will provide them with a better sense of community. They are seeking the benefits once found in traditional communal ways of life in the places where they desire to live. This is clearly evident in the growing trend in urban design toward what is termed *new urbanism,* or *neotraditionalism.* This movement seeks to recreate places in urban settings that offer opportunities for increased interaction among its residents. Examples of these designed communities include Seaside and Celebrity in Florida. These planned communities offer individuals a greater opportunity to achieve what psychologists have termed a **sense of community.** A sense of community involves the feeling an individual has for his or her relationship to the place or community of which he or she is a part. It can also include the sense of what it means to belong to a particular collective or location. A sense of community typically includes the following elements:

1. *Membership* means that people experience feelings of belonging in their community.

2. *Influence* signifies that people feel they can make a difference in their communities.

3. *Integration,* or fulfillment of needs, suggests that members of the community believe that their needs will be met by resources available in the community.

4. *Emotional connection* implies that community members have and will share history, time, places, and experiences" (Duffy & Wong, 1996, p. 18).

For many modern urban dwellers, neighborhoods have served as the bases for this sense of community. In fact, **neighboring** is a concept identified by Unger and Wanderman (1985) that is closely related to the notion of a "sense of community." Neighboring refers to an individual's "emotional, cognitive and social attachment to a neighborhood that makes him or her more likely to participate in neighborhood organizations" (Duffy & Wong, 1996, p. 18). Many adolescents in urban settings consider the "barrio" or "hood" the location that fulfills their sense of identity. However, there are many other forms of community that fulfill a person's sense of identity that are not limited to a geographical location.

Identificational and Interest-Oriented Communities

"Community" also refers to the perceived relationships associated with groups that define a person's social location within the broader society. For instance, social class is a social category in England that provides a sense of community for its members. Social class is also important in the states, but it has provided less of a symbolic identification for class members. Other kinds of identificational communities include racial and ethnic-group communities (the African-American community, Latino community, Mexican-American community, Jewish community, and so on), gay and lesbian communities, religious denominational communities, and professional communities. The sense of belonging

and value provided by these groups is what creates bonds between its members. Many theorists point out that the Balkan states lacked any fundamental sense of identity derived from the communist way of life that survived the fall of the Soviet Union. As a consequence, people in this region looked to their ethnic groups for a sense of identity beyond that which was afforded by the secular communities within which they had been living.

A person's **identificational community** often becomes a major resource for resistance and struggle against other opposition groups. This notion of community as a resource fits with another major conceptualization of community that defines it in terms of communicational networks. In this approach, one focuses on a person's informal social networks. "Informal social networks refer to a person's relations with relatives, friends, neighbors, co-workers, and acquaintances (Heller et al., 1984, p. 133). These relationships have important implications for a person's social and personal well-being. As Moffitt (1996, p. 217) points out, they offer "a new kind of life-sustaining and identificational mix." However, they are determined primarily by processes of affinity rather than proximity. In other words, a network definition of "community" consists of a web of functional activities and communicative interactions that are linked together in many ways other than via place. These linkages trigger different kinds of communal loyalties from those of traditional local communities, but the two can be equally satisfying. Informal networks are not the only contexts in which people have their needs met in modern societies. People also depend on relationships with formal organizations and other societal institutions that mediate their needs and obligations.

Organizations

Organizations are a special context in which humans live. Social workers and other social scientists assume that organizations can be studied apart from the people who make them up, because organizations continue even after their members die, quit, or retire (Ferrante, 1995). Much of our life takes place within these impersonal structures. Most of us begin life in a hospital; attend school in a formal organizational setting; eventually work in a bank, factory, office, or corporation; have contacts with members of governmental agencies; and depend on multinational organizations for meeting many of our other needs.

Formal organizations differ significantly from situations in which people have most of their needs met by primary groups. For instance, it was rare in many parts of traditional China for members of a rural village to come in contact with a governmental official or nonprimary group member (Giddens, 1989). They lived their lives for the most part in small group settings without the influence of formal organizations.

What Is a Formal Organization?

A formal organization is any large social group that is designed to achieve specific objectives rationally. Organizations have carefully designed structures that coordinate the activities of their members with an end in view of achieving the greatest possible efficiency. The relationships among the members of a formal organization are based on their position or location in the organization. The duties and rights associated with their position are attached to the office itself and not to the individuals. For most formal organizations, we can draw a chart that reflects the relationships of the various positions in this social system without making any reference at all to the actual individuals working in the organization.

Without a doubt, our way of life in a postindustrial society is still highly dependent on the existence of formal organizations. Although fewer and fewer individuals are working in large factories, most individuals have some form of affiliation with a formal organization, such as a governmental agency, multinational corporation, telecommunication organization, or educational system. In fact, formal organizations appear very natural to most individuals who were born and raised in an industrial society. During their lives, they have had very few opportunities to escape the influence of these designed social systems, which employ highly impersonal structures to achieve their specified aims.

In the preindustrial era, families and neighbors provided for most of an individual's needs. Primary groups were responsible for providing the food, instructing the children, and managing leisure-time activities. Today, most of our needs are met by persons whom we have never had an occasion to meet. In this type of social context, there is a need for extremely effective coordination of actions and resources. The most common structure used for achieving this objective is a bureaucracy.

What Is a Bureaucracy?

When organizations are large and complex, they often adopt what is known as a bureaucratic structure. Most modern organizations have bureaucratic qualities. The word **bureaucracy** was first coined in 1745 by Monsieur de Gournay. "He added to the word 'bureau,' meaning both an office and a writing table, a term derived from the Greek verb 'to rule.' 'Bureaucracy' is thus the rule of officials" (Giddens, 1989, p. 277). As Giddens points out, the term has been used in disparaging ways since its inception. De Gournay questioned the emerging power of governmental officials and even alluded to them as having an illness that he called bureaumania. Today, *bureaucracy* still carries negative connotations, and these connotations are not limited to governmental organizations. *Bureaucracy* conjures forth many images of excessive red tape, inefficiency, and alienation of its participants. Yet, Max Weber, who is the most influential writer on the topic, defined it as representing, in theory, a "rational organization" (Ferrante, 1995).

For Weber, rationalization was the major trend of the modern world. He identified four fundamental types of social action: instrumentally rational action, value-rational action, affective action, and traditional action (Waters, 1994). The following Focus section on Weber's Topology of Rational Action provides a description of each of these forms of action. Weber used these hypothetical types as ideals against which to evaluate any kind of intentional action. It was his view that instrumentally rational actions were, in the modern world, replacing actions guided by traditions, emotions, and other non-rational processes. He was interested in the transformation in Western societies from power structures based on claims of tradition to structures based on claims of reason. Weber extended this view of rational actions to his theory of bureaucracy and his widely known theory of authority relations.

For Weber, the bureaucracy is considered an **ideal type.** An ideal type refers to an abstract description derived from real cases that were analyzed to determine their essential features. A real agency will not necessarily conform in all respects to this type.

In Weber's view, a bureaucracy is an ideal type that has the following features:

- Its activities are governed by rules;
- It has a specific sphere of competence;
- It is organized hierarchically;
- Its members are specifically trained for their occupations;
- Its officers do not own the means of production;
- They do not own their jobs, but can be dismissed from them; and
- Its actions are recorded in files (Waters, 1994, p. 224).

For Weber, an organization with features that resemble these is likely to be efficient at coordinating the activities of its members and in achieving specific objectives.

FOCUS ON THEORY

Weber's Topology of Rational Action

In the theory of Max Weber, the meanings and intentions of actors play a central role. He is noted for the development of *Verstehen* (German for "understanding") sociology, an approach to sociological analysis that focuses on actors' reasons for their actions. Weber recognized that our reasons can vary, and he developed a well-known typology that classifies various forms of social action:

- *Instrumental rationality:* Involves action that is rational in relation to a goal. The individual selects the best means available to achieve an intended goal. It is also referred to as *goal-rational action.*
- *Value-rational action:* Involves action that is considered rational in relation to a value. The individual acts in terms of what is right: for instance, acting in relation to a commitment to a higher-order value like beauty, justice, or God.

- *Affective action:* Action that is determined by feelings, passions, psychological needs, or other emotional concerns.
- *Traditional action:* Any action that is dictated by custom; that is, it is performed because that is the way it has always been performed (Waters, 1994).

Scientific Management Traditions in Human Organizations

Shafritz and Whitbeck (1978) point out that any theory must be evaluated in the context of its time. This is also true of organizational theory. Early management theory, in this sense, originated before workers began to enjoy even limited rights. Times were harsh, and workers were seen merely as interchangeable parts in a highly impersonal "industrial machine." "Consequently, the first theories of organizations were concerned with the anatomy or structure of formal organizations. This is the hallmark of classical organization theory—a concern for organization structure that is premised upon the assumed rational behavior of its human parts" (Shafritz & Whitbeck, 1978, p. 1).

Within this context, the first notions of organizational principles were developed. It is often customary to begin discussion of the origins of management theory with the early writings of Adam Smith. In his famous work, *An Inquiry into the Nature and Causes of the Wealth of Nations* (1776), Smith looked at the optimum functioning of a factory in the chapter "Of the Division of Labor." This chapter clarifies how increased specialization of labor contributed to the enhanced productivity of a pin factory. In Smith's view, the factory represented the "most appropriate means of mass production." This view was shared by Frederick Winslow Taylor, who believed that factory workers could be even more productive if their jobs were scientifically designed. Taylor is considered by most authorities as the founder of *scientific management.*

For Taylor, there is "one best way" of accomplishing a job task, and the goal of the scientific manager is to ensure that the best way is followed by the employees of the organization. Taylor is noted for instituting time-and-motion studies and piece-rate wages. In 1954, Peter Drucker observed that scientific management "may well be the most powerful as well as the most lasting contribution America has made to Western thought since the Federalist Papers" (see Shafritz & Whitbeck, 1978, p. ix). In one sense, the major focus in the writings of Taylor was on issues of technology.

Management, as a separate discipline, emerged in the United States after World War I and was heavily influenced by scientific management principles. In fact, this approach is often referred to as "Taylorism." In 1937, Luther Gulick introduced the famous mnemonic *POSDCORB,* which defined the elements required to manage an organization: planning, organizing, staffing, directing, coordination, reporting, and budgeting. These elements are still examined today by modern organizational theorists.

Formal and Informal Relations in Organizations

Weber's approach to understanding organizations focused primarily on issues of formalization and structure. The more an agency is bureaucratized in its organization, the more formal its relationships are. In fact, Weber has very little to say about the role of informal relations in the operations of modern organizations. We now know that informal relationships and networks exist in most formal organizations. People in organizations know one another in many ways besides their official positions. They develop informal procedures for handling problems, negotiating their way through the hierarchy, and achieving assigned tasks. The Hawthorne studies at the Western Electric Company in 1932 documented these processes. In fact, the results of this research led to a specific approach in organizational studies known as the **human relations school.** This tradition in organizational studies focuses on understanding the influences of informal networks on all forms of organized activities.

The human relations school was in many senses a reaction to the overemphasis on structural rationality in the writings of Weber and members of the scientific management school (Netting, Kettner, & McMurtry, 1993). Chester Barnard (1938) proposed the first real theory on human relations that challenged the other classical approaches. He pointed out the important role of cooperation and other social processes in organizations. He is noted mostly for introducing researchers to the study of "natural groups within the organization,

upward communication, authority from below rather than from above, and leaders who functioned as a cohesive force" (Perrow, 1978, p. 315). His focus on cooperative processes was well timed because he was writing around the period of the Great Depression (Perrow, 1978), when there was significant labor unrest and conflict between labor and management.

The human relations school ushered in a wealth of research on the traits of effective leaders in organizations. Also, social psychologists in this tradition studied task groups to determine the effect of social factors on human efficiency. However, this school has not been without its critics. Netting and colleagues (1993) argue that several studies have shown that informal organizational structures might not be as prevalent in organizations as many human relations writers suggest. Furthermore, democratic leadership may have less to do with productivity than with other factors in human motivation, such as economic benefits. Nonetheless, this school has introduced many concepts in organizational research that encourage more humane treatment of organization members. In fact, it directs us to look at the assumptions about human nature included in any theory of organizations.

Douglas McGregor's work (1960) is an excellent example of theoretical work resulting from the shift from analysis of structure to analysis of participants' behavior in organizations. His work focused on understanding the factors that motivate employees. He identified two distinct approaches to leadership or management in organizations: Theory X and Theory Y. Theory X approaches to management assume that managers must adopt coercion in their style of leadership, because coercion is necessary to obtain good work performance by employees. McGregor (1960) argues that the theories of Taylor and Weber were highly supportive of this type of management style. He assumes that workers need to be controlled by the structure of the organization because: "(a) people have an inherent dislike for work; (b) they must be coerced in order to work; (c) the average worker prefers to be told what to do; and (d) monetary reward is the worker's primary motivator" (Netting et al., 1993, p 133). Theory Y approaches assume that, in trying to motivate workers, management needs to take into account many of the higher-order needs identified by Maslow. Theory Y's assumptions are as follows:

1. Work is as natural an activity as rest or play, thus people do not necessarily have to be forced to do it.

2. Workers will commit to organizational goals if they are able to meet their own needs in so doing.

3. Workers will accept responsibility for meeting goals that are congruent with their needs.

4. Organizational tasks should be structured to allow workers to exercise creativity and imagination in fulfilling these responsibilities (Netting et al., 1993, p. 133.)

Theory Y approaches are sensitive to individual worker needs but ignore the motivational needs of persons. To this end, William Ouchi (1981) developed an approach that he terms Theory Z. "Theory Z had its roots not in traditional Western assumptions about humans, but in assumptions about humans based on Japanese culture and reflected in many Japanese organizations and approaches to management" (Schriver, 1995, p. 421). Ouchi contrasted these approaches to management in Japan with approaches in the United States. (See Table 4.3.)

Social workers need knowledge not only of theories of organizations but also of management. But views of management cannot be limited to U.S. viewpoints. The United Nations estimates that there are approximately 35,000 multinational corporations worldwide. A disproportionate number of their headquarters are in the United States, Japan, and Western Europe. Corporations in Japan and Western Europe may sub-

scribe to distinctly different approaches to management and views of human nature, a fact that social workers cannot ignore. Multinational corporations are a special type of organization having characteristics that can contribute to many social problems encountered by social work professionals. When students are asked about how their lives are affected by our increased global contexts, we often learn the effect that multinational corporations are having on them and their families. That is, they can point out how their lives have changed because of some connection with a corporation that has significant international ties.

Social Institutions

Every society requires the formation of institutions in order to survive. Giddens (1989) considers these institutions the cement that holds together all forms of social life. They constitute the basic social arrangements within which people live most of their daily lives.

In social work, we rarely assess individuals without taking into account their behavior in larger social contexts, including key social institutions. In particular, we are interested in understanding the primary institutional arrangements that contribute to the health and welfare of our clients. Most societies have large social institutions that encompass and cut across many segments of their members' social life. The institutions of economy, kinship, education, law, polity, and religion are observed in most industrial or postindustrial societies. These institutions contribute to the stability of statuses, roles, and norms observed in the behavior of people in these communities. This relationship of structure to human behavior is what social scientists grapple with when they examine human behavior in terms of its structural or institutional properties (see the accompanying Focus section on Modern Functionalism).

William Graham Sumner (1906), in his classic work *Folkways,* examined how social institutions are formed in non-industrial societies. He contends that the first task of life is to survive, stating, "[n]eed was the first experience and it was followed by some blundering effort to satisfy it" (Sumner, 1906, pp. 17–18). In Sumner's view, the yardstick for measuring the success of these blundering efforts is pleasure and pain. Pleasure and pain underlie all our trial-and-error methods of testing solutions to our survival needs. Our early ancestors tried to profit from the successful experiences

TABLE 4.3 Japanese and U.S. Management Approaches	
Japanese Organization	**U.S. Organization**
Lifetime employment	Short-term employment
Slow evaluation and promotion	Rapid evaluation and promotion
Non-specialized career path	Specialized career paths
Implicit control mechanisms	Explicit control mechanisms
Collective decision making	Individual decision making
Collective responsibility	Individual responsibility
Holistic concern	Segmented concern

(Ouchi, 1981)

Participation in religious institutions is an important aspect of social life. This picture captures a family going to church together.

of other group members. The most expedient ways for achieving survival ends were generally adopted by the group, and these ways turned into what are known as customs. In effect, successful ways of doing things become institutionalized in any society. In Sumner's view, this is how **folkways** arise in natural group processes.

This concept of folkways is a key foundation underlying most of Sumner's theoretical observations (Cotterrell, 1984). For Sumner, folkways represent group ways of solving problems and of doing things. These ways are handed down through tradition, imitation, and authority. They "provide for all the needs of life: They specify the best way to make a fire, to cook meat, to greet one's neighbor, and to raise one's children" (Cotterrell, 1984, p. 20). Folkways are sanctioned in many premodern societies by fear of ancestors. That is, the ghosts of ancestors will seek vengeance if members of the community deviate from the ancient ways of doing things. This implies that folkways are transformed at some point in societal evolution from representing merely utilitarian ends to having a position of right or truth. When folkways start to be viewed in terms of right and wrong ways of doing things, they are elevated to what Sumner termed **mores.**

Folkways and mores prescribe the rules that govern the behavior of people in primary group relations. These rules exist prior to a person's birth and structure how life is to be lived. As societies change over time, traditional rules are gradually replaced by formal law. Formal law has proven to be the type of system capable of maintaining moral order in a complex society that has a high division of labor. In this system, "All citizens are, in theory, formally equal under the law. Law is also autonomous from other social institutions" (Horwitz, 1990, p. 2). That is, the law functions to maintain a culture and set of norms that are distinct from the rules of religion, political systems, and economic interests. This view differs from the views of law espoused earlier by Sumner.

In Sumner's view, the law needs to be rooted in the mores of the society, an assumption that has been challenged by other legal scholars. Many aspects of law are in opposition to the customs and mores of people. Civil rights law in the United States is an excellent example: The customs and mores of southern society were in violation of modern case law that made segregation illegal.

FOCUS ON THEORY

Modern Functionalism

Talcott Parsons and Robert Merton are two of the major contributors to functionalist thought in American sociology. Their work was significantly influenced by the early sociologists and the first functional anthropologists—Malinowski and Radcliffe-Brown. Talcott Parsons is considered "the most dominant theorist of his time" (Turner, 1991, p. 51), known for having established a general theory of social systems. Before developing this dominant analytical approach to the social system, he viewed social life as a matter of agency. *Agency* is a technical term in sociology that includes the idea that goal-oriented people act in intentional ways (Waters, 1994). Any theory of social behavior that examines the process of acting in relation to a set of meanings or intentions is referred to as a theory of agency.

To this end, Parsons considered action systems as being patterned by a series of alternative courses of action called *pattern variables*. These pattern variables prescribe the limited choices available to individuals in social situations.

In Parsons's scheme, actors can choose only one of the options in a pattern variable. For example, a person confronting another person in a situation can choose only one option from each pattern variable to judge the other person by—in terms of his or her performance (achievement) or in terms of his or her qualities (ascription). Because these choices influence the social arrangements in any given society, they were widely used to classify differences in social structures among societies.

Parsons modified his approach to studying the structure of social systems to give them a stronger functional focus, which led him to emphasize the importance of social systems. This change in his theory became known as *structural functionalism*. In this phase, Parsons identified four functional imperatives that are essential to the survival of any social system. These four requisites are referred to as the AGIL scheme after its initials:

Adaptation

Goal Attainment

Integration

Latent Pattern Maintenance

Any social system must meet these requisites if it is to survive. These requisites also help us understand the role played by key social systems in society. To illustrate this point, we will use the AGIL scheme to provide a conceptual description of the needs of the social system (Waters, 1994). These needs are represented as follows.

SOCIAL SYSTEM NEED	FULFILLED BY
1. Adaptation	The economy—money
2. Goal Attainment	The political system—power
3. Integration	The social system—social controls, norms, and legal rules
4. Pattern Maintenance	Socialization—family, schools

This classification scheme helps us make sense of the major social institutions in our society. Functional principles help us study our social institutions, and social institutions represent the final step in the process in which cultural values are translated into customary behavior. A social institution is technically defined as an "integrated set of social norms organized around the preservation of a basic society value" (Leslie, Larson, & Gorman, 1973, p. 109). Parsons and his followers identified five basic institutions: family, religion, education, economy, and government. Each of these institutions plays a critical role in the social system's survival. A common assignment for social work students is to examine the social welfare system using principles from Parsons' institutional conceptualizations.

How can we analyze social systems? Parsons also contributed a useful conceptual scheme for classifying the four layers of social organization that underpin the social system (Layder, 1994).

SYSTEM OR LEVEL	ASPECT OF EXPERIENCE
1. The physiological system	The body
2. The personality system	Individual psychology
3. The social system	Norms, roles, and positions
4. The cultural system	Knowledge, literature, art, and other human products

Robert Merton also looked at the functions of so-cial structures, but he extended his study of social sys-tems to include dysfunctions. For instance, he would analyze a system such as poverty in terms of its dys-functions but would also seek to uncover any of its al-ternative functions. According to Merton, we need to examine the manifest and latent functions of any social institution.

For example, Herbert Gans, a noted sociologist, set out to discover why poverty exists. To the surprise of some, he uncovered 15 functions that were served by poverty, including the provision of job opportunities for individuals who serve the needs of the poor. Some func-tionalists assume, therefore, that balanced approaches to understanding problems cannot be arrived at merely by looking at their functions. Instead they argue that ques-tions should also be asked about the manifest and la-tent functions, as well as the dysfunctions of any social system (Ferrante, 1995). These concepts provide social workers with a conceptual approach for thinking about the influence of social systems that identifies their key units. These units are included in the multidimensional framework presented in this book.

Multicultural and Gender Considerations

One of the most interesting aspects of the human species is its diversity. Yet this diversity contributes to significant intergroup conflict and social inequality. All societies have some way of making distinctions among its members. But some of these distinctions are used for purposes of discrimination. **Discrimination** is ap-plying prejudice or bias to a person based on some particular characteristic. Discriminations are often based on physical characteristics or cultural traits. In the United States, physical and cultural differences in-fluence the life chances and experiences of many women and persons of color. As a consequence, race, ethnicity, gender, sexual orientation, and able-bodiness are key variables in assessing social and interpersonal relations.

RACIAL AND ETHNIC CONSIDERATIONS

The United States is witnessing many demographic and cultural changes. "People of color constitute the fastest growing population in the United States" (Comas-Diaz & Greene, 1994, p. 3). If current trends in immigration and birth rates continue, the Hispanic/ Latino population will increase by an estimated 21%, the Asian-American population by about 22%, and the African-American population by approximately 12%, whereas projections for growth rates in the white pop-ulation are for an increase of about 2%. By the year 2056, it is projected that typical residents of the United States will trace their ancestry to Africa, Arab nations, Asia, Latin America, or the Pacific Islands (Takaki, 1993). These trends in birthrate projections and im-migration patterns suggest the arrival of increased cultural pluralism within the United States.

The United States has been pluralistic since its in-ception. Yet this fact is often overlooked in discussions about multiculturalism. Many early ethnic groups immi-grating to this country maintained their original group identities but incorporated customs and practices from other cultures into these identities to adapt to their new environment. In fact, this process is referred to in the West Indies and in Spanish and French settlements in the Americas as **creolization** (Ancelet, Edwards, & Pitre, 1991). Ancelet and colleagues point out that "migration, whether voluntary or not, caused a break in ancestral patterns. While individual cultures did preserve some of their old ways in the New World, the frontier environment also provided the opportunity for them to create new ways based on the old" (1991, p. xiv). These new ways contributed to many of the rich cultural traditions observed in Cuba, Haiti, Puerto Rico, Mexico, and Louisiana that include a blending of many different cultural influences.

Throughout American history, groups have inter-acted and intermarried with neighbors of different cul-tures and races. This blending produced some interest-ing cultural variations that make up our current ethnic landscape. *Cajuns* are a distinct ethnic group in this country that we will use to illustrate the process of creolization. When the Cajuns, originally from France, were exiled in 1755 from the region of Canada known as Acadia, some migrated to the French settlements in

Our society is becoming increasingly multicultural.

Louisiana. In Louisiana, they encountered new groups of Native Americans with traditions and customs different from those they were accustomed to in Canada. They also encountered persons born in Louisiana who were direct descendants of French-born individuals (Creoles). Some of the Acadian immigrants attempted to join the French plantation society. Others isolated themselves from this group and intermarried and interacted with Native Americans, African-Americans, and many different immigrants to this region, including German Alsatians, Spaniards, Anglo-Americans, the Irish, and the Scots. This blending of cultures and races produced a new cultural group with its own distinctive identity.

Today, many individuals in Louisiana identify with the Cajun ethnic group but can trace their ancestry to other groups outside of Canada. "This is why one finds people who call themselves Cajuns yet who have last names like Hoffpauir and Schexnayder, Ortego and Romero, Johnson and Reed, and McGee and Melancon" (Ancelet, Edwards, & Pitre, 1991, p. xv). The Acadians had significant interaction with Africans born in the region, who influenced their music, dancing, and cooking practices. Cajuns are members of an ethnic group whom many modern French-speaking Canadians and Europeans find difficult to understand. In fact, their culture has minimal points of commonality with persons from other more dominant French regions of the world. In particular, European and Canadian French "are surprised at the Cajun's love of fried chicken and iced tea, forgetting this is also the American South; at their love of hamburgers and Coke, forgetting this is the United States; at their love of cayenne and cold

beer, forgetting this is the northern tip of the West Indies (Ancelet, Edwards, & Pitre, 1991, pp. xvii–xviii).

In efforts to define America, historians have tended to ignore the experiences of Cajuns and other groups who don't support the *Anglo-conformity ideology* that underlies our espoused national identity (McLemore, 1991). This identity, although false, has supported the assumption that an American is a white person of European origin who has abandoned language ties and adopted a distinctive American culture. Ronald Takaki's (1993) book *A Different Mirror: A History of Multicultural America* points out that the histories of Asian-Americans, African-Americans, and other persons of color are not included in existing constructions of the American identity. He begins the book by describing an incident widely shared by Americans who are non-white and of non-European origins. He was riding in a taxi to a conference on multiculturalism in Norfolk, Virginia, when the taxi driver asked him how long he had been in this country. For Takaki, this situation illustrates the narrow view shared by many Americans about its history and its people. Takaki's family had lived in this country for well over 100 years, yet this driver adhered to a very narrow but commonsense definition of the American identity as "white" and primarily European in ancestry.

The changing racial and ethnic makeup of the country is threatening the identity of many Americans. As Takaki (1993) points out, the country has been racially diverse since its inception, but evidence of increased diversity is triggering fearful responses in many sectors of our society. Some long for "a more cohesive culture and more homogeneous America" (Takaki, 1993, p. 3). However, this view ignores the significant diversity in our country's past that was systematically purged from most major accounts of America's history. Because of this oversight, many universities are introducing curricula to assist students in obtaining a more accurate view of their country's history (Schoem et al., 1993). This approach to history has not been without controversy. In fact, the demands for increased multiculturalism in education are starting to retest the legitimacy of valued notions of tolerance previously considered the hallmark of most Western liberal societies (Horton, 1993b). This is clearly seen in students' objections and protests to multicultural courses that have been required on many college campuses.

Most modern liberal societies celebrate diversity and other forms of difference. In fact, this country considers tolerance of difference an important element underlying its reason for existence. Yet, "it has become an increasingly urgent issue of theory and practice as to how tolerant liberalism is, or can be, of cultural and religious groups which do not themselves subscribe universally or without qualification to what have been taken to be the basic values of liberalism" (Horton, 1993, p. 1). These values include liberty, equality, rights, neutrality, and autonomy. That is, all modern liberal societies are experiencing immigration patterns that involve cultures with distinct value traditions that are in opposition to the values of modern liberal thought. Does this mean that there are limits to what are considered acceptable or tolerable forms of cultural diversity in these societies?

Steven Lukes (1991) points out that liberalism was born out of religious conflict, and toleration was central to the development of liberalism. At the heart of this toleration is the notion that one will not interfere with other groups' cultural beliefs and behaviors. Does this view also apply to Jewish, Buddhist, and Islamic traditions? Muslims in France and England have asserted that Muslim girls ought to be educated in a context that prepares them for roles in Muslim society rather than in the values of secular liberalism. Muslims were also in violent disagreement with the kinds of free speech that permitted the vilification of their culture's most sacred beliefs with the publication of *The Satanic Verses* by Salman Rushdie. These examples illustrate situations in our liberal societies in which issues of tolerance are being reexamined. Current multicultural scholars are noticing that much of the acclaimed tolerance is not being extended to non-Christians or non-whites.

As Gundara (1993) points out, if we assume that the imposition of a single culture or value system in a country like Trinidad is improper, then these same principles should apply to American, British, and other European countries. Liberal critics have vigorously attacked countries that advocate a single-value orientation in Africa, Latin America, and Asia because of their totalitarian implications. Yet many new writings are emerging in our own society that promote intolerance toward ethnic, religious, and linguistic variations. In fact, a number of politicians are arguing for English as the official language in the United States. What is the implication of this from a multicultural perspective?

The "Intelligence Report," a publication of the Southern Poverty Law Center, chronicles the recent increases in violence toward immigrants in our society. The center reports that hostility toward immigrants is at the highest level it has been in 70 years. This view is supported by the findings of Jack McDevitt, associate director of the Center for Applied Research at Northeastern University and an expert on hate crimes. He has stated that attitudes toward immigrants in recent years are "frighteningly similar to those of the mid-1920s when the United States passed restrictive laws to halt massive immigration from southern Europe" (Southern Poverty Law Center, 1994, p. 3). Examples of hate crimes the Southern Poverty Law Center is tracking include the following:

- A 19-year-old Vietnamese American pre-med student in Coral Springs, Florida, was beaten to death by a mob of white youths who called him "chink" and "Vietcong."

- An Hispanic man in Alpine, California, was beaten with baseball bats by six white men at a camp for homeless migrant workers. The assailants later reportedly bragged about "kicking Mexican ass."
- An Hispanic immigrant activist in Davis, California, was assaulted twice in April 1993 by white men who wrote "wetback" on her body.
- An Indian immigrant in New York City was beaten and burned with a cigarette by three teenagers who reportedly told him they did not like Indians.
- Two lesbian organizers were killed in Medford, Oregon, by presumed hate groups.

Official government statistics are not completely accurate, but 4,558 hate crimes were reported in the United States in 1992 (FBI, 1993). Nakagawa (1993) reports that the number of hate crimes in Los Angeles increased about 31% between 1991 and 1992. Hate crimes are increasing not only in the United States; there were approximately 2,000 reported hate crimes in Germany in 1992, a remarkable number given the relative size of that country's population compared with the United States (Baldwin & Hecht, 1995).

The shameful intolerance of ethnic differences is a frightening but all too prevalent characteristic of our times. Understanding intolerance is, therefore, a significant issue that social workers in all areas of practice need to address. Baldwin and Hecht (1995) have adopted what they refer to as a *layering metaphor* for describing how intolerances develop. In their view, layering is a useful metaphor for illustrating that there are alternative ways of experiencing the world that

"are continually juxtaposed and played off of each other and/or blended together" (Hecht, 1993, p. 76). For instance, "the perception of a certain group begins at a young age, when people around the individual speak of group members in terms of their distinctiveness from the person's own group. Images and messages from parents, media, friends, textbooks, and teachers, as well as personal experiences with members of the 'other' group layer upon each other and interplay with one another to form the person's own, often inconsistent view of the 'others'" (Baldwin & Hecht, 1995, pp. 61–62). By examining these layers, we can get a better perception of what is happening at different levels of a person's experience. Each level of experience provides another clue to the puzzle of how prejudicial and hateful attitudes develop.

Prejudice and Discrimination

Although there has been much progress in human affairs during this century, it has been marked by horrible episodes of prejudice (Lippa, 1994). This century has seen the mass murder of Armenians by Turks, the Nazis' "final solution" in Europe for Jewish and other "non-Aryan" peoples, the "ethnic cleansing" by Serbs in Bosnia, the mass lynching of African-Americans in the first half of this century in the United States, and vicious attacks in New York at the Stonewall Bar that

Intolerance is mounting among white racist groups who perceive the advances of many racial and ethnic groups as a threat to their own interests.

triggered the gay rights movement. **Prejudice** is a generalized negative attitude directed toward another person's membership in a socially defined group. Like most attitudes, it occurs at the cognitive (beliefs), behavioral (overt action), and affective (emotional) levels. It can include negative emotional responses to a group of people resulting from intolerant, unfair, or unfavorable attitudes toward the targeted group (Deaux et al., 1993). It also can involve discriminatory actions or practices.

The cognitive component of prejudice involves the beliefs we hold about a target group. A structured set of beliefs about any identifiable social group is referred to as a **stereotype.** Stereotypes can be either positive or negative. A negative stereotype is highly interchangeable with what is known as prejudice. That is, stereotypes represent an important foundation on which prejudices are built.

Basow (1992) uses a familiar story to demonstrate the pervasiveness of stereotypes in modern life: A boy and his father were involved in a serious automobile accident. The father was killed instantly; the son was severely injured. An ambulance rushed him to the nearest hospital, and a prominent surgeon was called in to perform the operation. On entering the operating room, however, the surgeon exclaimed: "I can't operate on this boy. He's my son." How can this be (p. 2)?

If you came up with the answer of a stepfather, adopted father, or some other similar response, then you are not unlike most Americans. Most Americans see surgery as a predominately male field. As a result, you would have ignored the fact that the surgeon probably was the boy's mother. Stereotypes of this nature are highly prevalent in our society and can contribute to various types of discrimination. Stereotypes can be directed at any group: Hispanics, short people, physically disabled people, gay men and lesbians, and fundamentalist Christians. When individuals act on their prejudicial stereotypes, this leads to what is known as individual, or attitudinal, discrimination. *Individual discrimination* involves overt acts that treat members of a target group in an unfair manner. Generally, the bases for these discriminatory treatments have roots in negative stereotypes.

Some forms of discrimination in society are legal. In addition, many individuals justify discriminatory practices on what they consider moral grounds. For instance, in many societies "senior citizens" are allowed to pay cheaper rates for using public facilities: movies, buses, public parks, and museums. Publishers of some professional journals also engage in differential treatment of customers when they provide different subscription rates for people from different income categories. Are these practices unlawful or without moral justification? Although these forms of differential treatment are considered lawful, they are always open to moral challenge. This raises the important question of whether there are circumstances when it is legitimate to make differentiations in treatment of people in terms of race, sex, class, or age. What distinguishes differentiation from discrimination?

Most religions of the world do not think it is discriminatory to bar women from holding positions of leadership in their hierarchy. Yet many members of these same communities assume that these practices are without moral justification and are discriminatory. How do we determine whether this form of differential treatment is to be considered discriminatory? In most modern industrial societies, disputes involving issues of discrimination are handled by legal institutions. However, this is a relatively recent historical phenomenon. Notions of unlawful discrimination took a long time to develop in Western legal systems. Banton (1994) points out that the first recorded use of the term *discrimination* was in a speech by President Andrew Johnson in 1866. He used this term in discussing debates surrounding the denial of the benefits of full citizenship to African-Americans. Robert MacIver (1948), however, is known for educating the public "to distinguish between discrimination as a form of behavior and prejudice as an attitude" (Banton, 1994, pp. 6–8).

Most early considerations of discrimination in the United States involved issues of race; "discrimination" was not used in a more general sense to include other groups until around 1958. In that year, the International Labour Office (ILO) defined discrimination as "any distinction, exclusion or preference made on the basis of race, colour, sex, religion, political opinion, national extraction or social origin" (Banton, 1994, p. 7). In recent years, discrimination law has been extended to many other areas of life. However, the issue of discrimination in law focuses primarily on protecting people from unfair treatment in public life.

Discrimination law does not apply to private life or private decisions. "In Great Britain and the United States the main protected fields are those of the administration of justice, employment, education, housing, and the provision of goods, facilities and services" (Banton, 1994, p. 8). For instance, people may limit invitations to parties on the grounds of race or gender. As you might imagine, the legitimacy of such actions is a major societal concern. Still, there is substantial controversy about what ought to be considered private versus public spheres of life. Should the law protect individuals from unfair treatment by private clubs or other organizations? Should the law of discrimination apply to treatment in voluntary organizations like churches? For instance, should the law address actions within churches regarding issues of equality for women? Churches and other religious institutions are organizations that presently do not fall under the legal protections of antidiscrimination law. But this does not mean that these institutions do not violate moral definitions of discrimination shared by many members of a society.

In social work, we encounter many forms of discrimination that contribute to a diverse array of social disadvantage and other forms of inequality. For this reason, it is important that the social worker have a fundamental understanding of race, ethnicity, sex roles, and other areas in which persons can be subjected to unfair social practices. Our goal as social work professionals is to engage in activities that will reverse structural contributions to harmful discriminatory practices in voluntary social organizations and in public social institutions.

Institutional discrimination is a special type of discrimination derived from structural arrangements in the society. It refers to inequalities rooted in the normal operations of society and its social institutions. This form of discrimination has little to do with attitudes or prejudices. Even when we eliminate prejudice in a society, the inequalities between groups often remain because they are rooted in the everyday operations of existing social institutions. That is, discrimination can continue in a society even though its members are not intent on discriminating. For instance, a Mexican-American family can be denied access to housing that would lead to better schools not because of intentional bigotry by realtors but because their previous restriction to low-paying jobs inhibits their ability to purchase a home with access to superior schools. Institutional discrimination has much more subtle char-

acteristics than the more visible forms of attitudinal, or individual, discrimination. For example, in social service agencies, institutional racism may be present when supervisors assign low-income clients of color to MSW students and middle-income whites to senior staff. This is particularly problematic because low-income clients of color have higher dropout rates and may benefit more from an experienced social worker.

Race and Everyday Social Relations

What are the differences between race and ethnicity? **Race** is a social term used to refer to groups that are defined in terms of their physical characteristics. It is important to recognize that the characteristics used to define a racial group are socially defined; the word *race* is a fundamentally meaningless biological concept. Although humans can be traced back well over a million years, the racial differences of today are quite recent in origin (Robertson, 1977). "Whatever the seeming diversity of races in the modern world, all contemporary human beings trace their origin to ancestral populations that lived in east Africa about 200,000 years ago" (Green, 1995, p. 11).

People attach meanings to physical differences that are either real or imagined. "From a sociological point of view, then, a race is a large number of people who, for social or geographical reasons, have interbred over a long period of time; as a result, they have developed visible physical characteristics and regard themselves and are regarded by others as a biological unit" (Robertson, 1977, p. 262). However, it is not easy to classify humans into different races. In fact, determining race by blood sample would be impossible because human population groups are not distinct; rather, they form a continuum. This is why physical anthropologists prefer using terms like *population* or *gene pool* to explain physical differences to using terms like *race* (Green, 1995). For these scientists, "The genetic diversity within populations that share certain visible physical traits is as great as those between groups" (Giddens, 1989, p. 246). Accordingly, many scientists argue that race is not a useful concept and should no longer be used (Giddens, 1989).

The Anglo ideology of assimilation has always emphasized that immigrants should conform to the dominant culture and leave behind their ethnicity. "Full assimilation, in this view, is achieved when the

Multiracial families are on the rise.

many because of this emphasis on biology. Even though some African-Germans can demonstrate German ancestry, they are still discriminated against because they do not fit the German biological stereotype. Biracial individuals also have a confusing identity in the United States.

Although, by convention, people are assigned to one of three racial categories—Caucasoid, Mongoloid, or Negroid—many people do not easily fit into one of these groups. Even though these classifications are difficult to implement, people continue to apply them. In South Africa, the classification of races was still a major societal enterprise in the late 1980s. The following quotation illustrates the difficulties this society encountered in trying to classify persons racially. A woman classified as "Colored" reports:

> Under South-African law, I am officially considered Colored. But so is my light-skinned sister with brown hair and my brother who has kinky hair and skin even blacker than mine. The state determines what color you are. At 16, you have to fill out some forms, attach a photograph and send them to a state authority where your race will be decided. Differences in color are noted by official subdivisions. For example, I am a Cape Colored whereas my sister is called Indian Colored. Of course, many people categorized as Colored are of mixed Black and White ancestry. In fact, if you can prove having had a white grandparent or parent and are yourself very light skinned, you can even make an application to be reclassified from Colored to White (Chapkis, 1986, p. 69).

Sociologists are interested in negative classification schemes that include beliefs about the abilities or traits of a racial group. They are also interested in studying any actions a society takes to use racial classifications to subordinate members of a group on the basis of color or other biological characteristics. These societal classifications change in time and are products of many social, historical, and political forces. In the United States, we have had shifting relations of power that have influenced our racial classifications. In 1860, the three classifications for the census were whites, blacks, and mulattoes; in 1890, five additions were added (quadroon, octoroon, Chinese, Japanese, and Indian); in 1990, five different groups were listed (white; black, or African-American; Asian, or Pacific-Islander; American-Indian, Eskimo, or Aleut; and the ethnicity

descendants of the immigrants blend into the majority group and are no longer distinguishable from it" (McLemore, 1991, p. 106). But this ideology has not applied to persons of Indian, Asian, and African decent. Persons of color cannot blend into the societal matrix as do white ethnics. As Rushdie (1982) points out, there are two different worlds in Anglo societies, and which one you inherit depends on the color of your skin.

In Germany, individuals until recently were entitled to citizenship, regardless of their country of origin, if they could prove that they were of German ancestry. That is, the criterion for German citizenship was biological. This law made life difficult for persons who had lived their entire lives in Germany but who did not look German or who lacked German biological ancestry (Ferrante, 1995). Turks, Arabs, and East Indians were subjected to serious discrimination in Ger-

Hispanic). Each of these changes is indicative of key sociohistorical contingencies. The following Focus section poignantly describes one girl's reflections on being biracial or of mixed race.

FOCUS ON MULTICULTURALISM

One Girl's Reflection on Being Biracial

10:06 A.M. The buzz of an artificially lit classroom swarms around its third-hour occupants. Slouched in my chair at the back of the room, I try to ignore the sweat running into the collar of my T-shirt, the incessant tapping of my foot. I chew anxiously on my pen top, and the words on the paper before me swim around in a mocking blur.

No, I'm not struggling over a physics test, or an essay question in College English. This is simply a survey on student-teacher relationships given to the whole school, and I haven't made it past the first section.

Name _____ Okay, got that one. Age _____ Grade _____ Sex _____ Yeah, these are easy. Race _____ What? RACE. 1. White; 2. Black; 3. Oriental; 4. Hispanic; 5. American Indian. This is where my panic begins. I read my choices again, and my brow furrows. Basically, the problem is this: I'm racially mixed, and there is no option for me.

Now, this is not the first time this has happened. All my life, I've had to decide what race I am, which half of me to deny. I remember asking my sister one day in third grade which one I was. "We're mixed, Rach," she told me. Mixed. And for every survey, every technical form I received in every grade after, I looked for that word. The closest I ever found was "other." That always kind of amused me, but I tried it. Other; mixed. But my teachers came to me. "Mixed what, honey?" And they looked at me. "You're black. Next time, just put black, okay?" And I would go home to my mother, my single, cream-colored mother, who wanted nothing but to raise us well. Even as an intelligent 8-year-old, I was a bit confused.

My next practice, starting about seventh grade, was to circle both white and black. It made the most sense, really, but even here in high school I got in trouble. Again, the tender pressure: "Hon, you can't be *both*." So I ended up selecting "Caucasian" for the day. Recently, I went to my counselor and had that changed. See, I'm a junior, and considering colleges, and I know that as a "minority student" I'll be eligible for certain scholarships. Also, it will give me an edge at schools that are looking for a diverse student body. So I figure I'll be black for the next five years or so, and then go back to being myself.

But can I really go back? Can I really be comfortable with who I am if society ignores that people like me exist? Well, I can—but you must realize that I'm lucky. I grew up in Hyde Park (in Chicago), one of the most liberal integrated neighborhoods in America. My 14 years there taught me that I could exist as a mixed person, with both black and white friends. That I could be proud of my brown skin, even have fun with it. It's always great to see the look on people's faces when my mom and sister and I go out, especially with my white stepfather.

But for some kids, there is no joke. Only confusion, and the total lack of a sense of identity. These children are pressured to choose a group of friends, and in effect to choose a parent, a race, a way of life, a heritage—and to completely deny the other. But do black people really want a friend who's only half black, and vice versa?

That was the problem facing the first mixed kids—the children born of slaves and their owners. It should not exist now. In this age, the so-called "modern civilization" we're supposed to have reached, being racially mixed shouldn't be a dilemma, it should be considered a blessing. We are graced with the best of both worlds, exposure to two entirely different walks of life. In fact, our parents should be congratulated for creating a higher, enlightened race with such a large sphere of influences and possibilities. Instead, they have been scolded. God forbid we should pollute one race by adding another to it.

The world is a box of crayons. Though they're all different colors, they're all made of the same thing. And even though yellow and blue are combined to make green, once the wax has set, it's a green crayon, and that's all. It's never asked to make a choice between blue and yellow. One of the things my sister and I did together was draw pictures of the family, coloring them from our big box of Crayolas. And I always thought it was neat that a drawing of four people could use up three crayons—peach, light brown, and dark brown, when the other kids only got to use one.

(Morris & Leighninger, 1990)

Forms of Racism and Privilege

Racism is technically defined as a system of power and privilege that can be manifested in attitudes, actions, and/or institutional structures based on color characteristics of people (Anderson & Collins, 1998). Today, it is less socially acceptable to show blatant forms of racism than was once true. However, racism has remained in other more symbolic or subtle ways, which in the social psychology literature are called *modern racism.* Modern racists convey their negativity toward others by opposing issues that promise equality for the races. They do not blatantly attack persons on racial grounds, but they defend practices that maintain social privilege. For instance, they may oppose equal-opportunity hiring by arguing against the use of quotas, rather than by directly attacking individuals on presumed notions of inferiority (Deaux et al., 1993).

The systemic features of racism are a key part of social structures that social workers must understand. "In a racist system, well-meaning white people benefit from racism even if they have no intentions of acting or thinking like 'racists'" (Andersen & Collins, 1995, p. 60). That is, they might not question the built-in system of privilege for whites in our social system. Peggy McIntosh (1995) has pointed out in her groundbreaking essay "White Privilege and Male Privilege" that systems of privilege become invisible to the persons benefiting most from them. In her view, people are carefully socialized not to recognize these privileges.

After experiencing significant frustration with men who did not recognize male privilege, Peggy McIntosh set out to understand her own privileges as a white female. She wanted to know what advantages she had as a white person in our society. Through this exercise, she realized that her own difficulties facing privilege as a white person were similar to the difficulties faced by men in experiencing their own privilege. She wrote, "Only rarely will a man go beyond acknowledging that women are disadvantaged to ac-knowledging that men have unearned advantage . . ." (McIntosh, 1995, p. 77). In her view, white women and men have many layers of denial that prevent them from examining their unearned advantages. McIntosh (1995) identified these special circumstances and conditions as part of her day-to-day privileges as a white woman:

1. I can, if I wish, arrange to be in the company of people of my race most of the time.

2. I can avoid spending time with people whom I was trained to mistrust and who have learned to mistrust my kind or me.

3. If I should need to move, I can be pretty sure of renting or purchasing housing in an area that I can afford and in which I would want to live.

4. I can be reasonably sure that my neighbors in such a location will be neutral or pleasant to me.

5. I can go shopping alone most of the time, fairly well assured that I will not be followed or harassed by store detectives.

6. I can turn on the television or open to the front page of the paper and see people of my race widely and positively represented.

7. When I am told about our national heritage or about "civilization," I am shown that people of my color made it what it is.

8. I can be sure that my children will be given curricular materials that testify to the existence of their race.

9. If I want to, I can be pretty sure of finding a publisher for this piece on white privilege.

10. I can be fairly sure of having my voice heard in a group in which I am the only member of my race.

11. I can be casual about whether or not to listen to another woman's voice in a group in which she is the only member of her race.

12. I can go into a book shop and count on finding the writing of my race represented, into a supermarket and find the staple foods that fit with my cultural traditions, into a hairdresser's shop and find someone who can deal with my hair.

13. Whether I use checks, credit cards, or cash, I can count on my skin color not to work against the appearance that I am financially reliable.

14. I could arrange to protect our young children most of the time from people who might not like them.

15. I did not have to educate our children to be aware of systemic racism for their own daily physical protection.

16. I can be pretty sure that my children's teachers and employers will tolerate them if they fit school and workplace norms; my chief worries about them do not concern others' attitudes toward their race.

17. I can talk with my mouth full and not have people put this down to my color.

18. I can swear, or dress in secondhand clothes, or not answer letters, without having people attribute these choices to the bad morals, the poverty, or the illiteracy of my race.

19. I can speak in public to a powerful male group without putting my race on trial.

20. I can do well in a challenging situation without being called a credit to my race (McIntosh, 1995, pp. 79–81).

Although race is not a fact of nature, it continues to structure many aspects of social reality. Moreover, many Americans consider it to be an unchanging part of the natural world sanctioned by god (Green, 1995). These views sanction negativity toward the mixing of the races and the ascription of rank along selected racial lines. As social workers, we cannot ignore the fact that race influences social relations at all levels of social life. Also, people's experience with race will depend on their location in social space. That is, it will also vary with their social class, gender, age, sexuality, and other markers of social location (Andersen & Collins, 1995).

Ethnicity and Its Social Consequences

Ethnicity, like race, focuses on differences in people. But it is not always easy to identify true ethnic differences: "When we try to determine what differences mean, the idea of ethnicity becomes complex and frequently troublesome" (Green, 1995, p. 16). There are many definitions of ethnicity in the social sciences, and each definition captures a different layer of an ethnic group's experiences. Some definitions stress distinctive values underlying the behavior of group members, whereas others focus more on the association of ethnicity with social class, political processes, or other forms of social experience. Although these approaches to difference may be useful in many forms of social analysis, they often lead to the formation of needless stereotypes. For this reason, we subscribe to a more process or transactional definition of ethnicity developed for social service professionals by James Green.

Green (1995) contends that we should study ethnicity in terms of boundaries, control, and meaning construction. "Ethnicity has less to do with distinct and enduring groups than it does with the perceptions of boundaries, with how contrasts are manipulated, managed, denied, asserted, and proclaimed. With ethnicity, we are dealing, first, with meanings that define separateness, and, second, with the enforcement of meanings and separateness through power" (Green, 1995, p. 19). In other words, we need to understand how individuals assert their sense of ethnicity and how others treat this ethnicity in various social contexts. In particular, we need to understand how dominant-group individuals use ethnic differences to isolate or exclude individuals from inclusion in the most valued segments of social life.

Core Versus Surface Features of Ethnicity

Many surface aspects of ethnicity are used to identify various ethnic groups in our society. These include "clothing preferences, speech pattern, behavioral styles, physical characteristics, housing locations and types, living arrangements and decor, food items, and fam-ily and community rituals and celebrations" (Green, 1995, p. 19). These manifestations of ethnicity are used to distinguish outsiders from insiders. As Green (1995) points out, these aspects are what many Americans think of when making references to ethnic differences. But they should not be confused with what is truly ethnic about ethnicity. Pinder-hughes provides one of the more descriptive definitions of ethnicity that includes these core elements. She states: "Ethnicity refers to connectedness based on these commonalities that have evolved as a result of shared identity and history based on religion, nationality, and so on" (Pinderhughes, 1994, p. 265).

Nash (1989) has also tried to differentiate between surface and core elements of ethnicity. Core elements are the real grounds on which all forms of boundary maintenance rest. They represent the central psychic and social foundations that underlie human identification with group relationships. Nash has broken down these core elements into three fundamental components: kinship, commensality, and a common cult. He provides a definition of each of these components in his book *The Cauldron of Ethnicity in the Modern World.* He states:

> The most common ethnic boundary markers, in the ethnographic record, and the most pervasive, in any system of ethnic differentiation, are *kinship,* that is the presumed biological and descent unity of the group implying a stuff or substance continuity each group member has and outsiders do not; *commensality,* the propensity of eating together indicating a kind of equality, peership, and the promise of further kinship links stemming from the intimate acts of dining together, only one step removed from the intimacy of bedding together, and a *common cult,* implicating a value system beyond time and empirical circumstance . . . (1989, pp. 10–11).

The previous description of the core elements of ethnicity indicate the levels at which sentiments surrounding ethnic identity occur. They describe the dimensions that define people's sense of connection to their social context. Obviously, these senses of bondedness will vary with a person's position in the social structure and his or her life experiences. These fundamental elements of ethnicity can play a major role in the way clients respond to social work interventions.

Pinderhughes (1994) points out that "culture determines what clients see as a problem, how they express it (that is, whether symptoms are somatic, behavioral, or affective; what specific symptoms clients manifest), who they seek out for help, what they regard as helpful and the intervention strategies they prefer" (pp. 293–294). To respond to each of these levels, the social worker must be exposed to the life experiences of many different ethnic groups and to multiple representatives from these groups. This is critical

This adopted child from China is keeping connected with the traditions and dress of her ancestors.

because there is as significant a diversity within ethnic groups as there is between ethnic groups.

In this book, we assume that culture influences many aspects of behavior. For this reason, we will systematically review documented variations in human development involving cultural variables. We will not, however, provide a laundry list of key historical events or characteristics of ethnic group members. We believe that clients will situationally define and manage their ethnic boundaries and identity, ethnic boundaries being how individuals define their own sense of ethnicity. The relevance of historical events is contingent on individuals' current boundary-maintenance need; that is, time and other historical factors will be used differentially by clients in setting their ethnic boundaries. Some clients will seek a sense of revival of ethnic ties; others will struggle with their significance in current situations and contexts. Thus, our aim as social workers is to assess the factors contributing to ways in which contrasts are asserted by persons with ethnic differences and how dominant group members respond to these differences.

GENDER AND SEXISM

Can women perform on an equal basis with men as firefighters or police officers? Why or why not? Many women are currently employed in these and other professions previously dominated by men, including the military. The current debate about the role of women in the military reflects a larger debate about sex roles in our society. To place these debates in context, it might be useful to review recent history about the roles of women in our society.

As recently as the 19th century, women were denied the right to vote, to be a member of a jury, to have sole custody of their children, and to attend most institutions of higher education. Many of these practices were justified on false beliefs about differences between males and females. In fact, a major area of research in the social sciences focuses on the existence or non-existence of sex differences between males and females. Social scientists use the word **sex** to refer to the biological status of being female or male. These scientists research the structural and other biophysical characteristics that distinguish females from males. **Gender,** in contrast, refers to the social definitions of male and female. It represents a socially constructed concept and not a fact of nature with specific biological imperatives.

In assessing human behavior, social workers need to have a good understanding of the consequences of gender roles and beliefs. Gender issues incorporate all the factors that structure the relationships between women and men. This includes all the social processes that dictate how women are to behave in their social life. In work and other social contexts, the relations of women are structured differently from those of men. The specific structures that establish how they should behave are also a part of each of the other major social institutions in their lives. Sandra Lipsitz Bem (1993) has termed this process **gender polarization,** which refers to "the organizing of social life around the male-female distinction" (Bem, 1993, p. 192). In fact, in a gender-polarized society, every aspect of a person's life

is connected to his or her sex in some way. This includes "modes of dress, social roles, and even ways of expressing emotion and experiencing sexual desire" (Bem, 1993, p. 192).

Gender differences, like racial and cultural differences, can be used to distort many aspects of social life. "Anthropologists, for example, use the term *exotic bias* to refer to the investigators' tendency to focus only on those aspects of a group or society that differ from their own group or society" (Deaux et al., 1993, p. 350). This type of bias is often found in situations in which actual differences are noted in women. For instance, many studies have shown that the average male is more aggressive than the average female. But our biases can influence how we interpret the findings from these studies. Figure 4.6 presents a graph of male and female distributions of aggressiveness. As you can see, many of the females in these studies have aggressiveness scores that are higher than those of the males. Also, these distributions indicate that many of the women and men have similar aggressiveness scores.

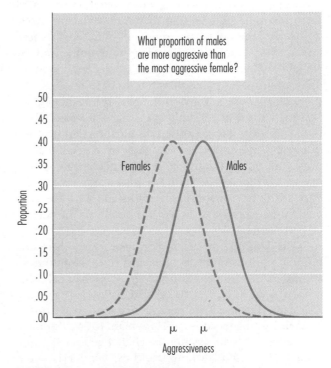

FIGURE 4.6   Overlapping distributions on aggressiveness for males and females (Deaux, Dane, & Wrightsman, 1993)

The information on averages can be used to distort the realities of many of the women and men in these studies by supporting the bias toward an assertion of fundamental difference between males and females.

Hooyman (1994) has identified three conceptual frameworks in social work for examining women's content: women's issues, nonsexist perspectives, and feminist perspectives. The *women's issues* approach has also been referred to as "add the women and stir," and it is probably the most dominant approach to education in social work. In this approach, separate attention is devoted to understanding the distinct issues that pertain to women. This approach is typically criticized because in many circumstances it perpetuates the treatment of women as "others." This means that they are treated as a special population in knowledge discourse rather than as a pivotal group representing 51% of the world population (Hooyman, 1994). As a group with special consideration, they are judged in relation to male criteria, and this perpetuates the structural features of many of their problems.

The second approach is the *nonsexist,* or *equal rights,* model. This approach does focus on structural factors within systems that maintain sexist practices, and it assumes that "the range of problems experienced by women are rooted in and influenced by societal expectations for women's behavior and in societal restrictions of life possibilities" (Hooyman, 1994, p. 321). In such a view, problems should not be assessed in terms of culturally prescribed sex-role behaviors. This view has important implications for practice because it indicates that behaviors by women that do not conform to traditional role expectations should not be considered deviant. For instance, women who choose not to care for their parents and who leave the task to their brothers should not be viewed as deviant or pathological.

The *feminist* model, in contrast, rejects many traditional notions about gender and starts from the assumption that current knowledge of human behavior is for the most part sexist. Social reality as we know it is shaped by the male perspective known as **androcentricity** (man as norm) (Hooyman, 1994). Essentialist thinking about gender is challenged in this approach. In essentialist approaches, gender is often considered absolute, or fixed in nature as a biological fact. The feminist perspective rejects the binary conceptualizations of males and females, or of white men and women, and sees gender as one "strain" among others in our layered experiences. This point of view "opens up the possibility of diversity among men and women in specific historical, social, and cultural constructs" (Hooyman, 1994, p. 325). It also allows analysis and action to focus on the experiences of women without neglecting the other "isms"—like racism and ageism—that threaten the well-being of humanity. In fact, feminism sees its fundamental aim as that of ending domination and resisting all forms of oppression (Van Den Bergh & Cooper, 1987).

Feminism is more than an analytical approach; it is also an ideology that involves a "call for transforming the world from competitive, hierarchical, and authoritarian relationships to a world based on gender and racial equality" (Van Den Bergh & Cooper, 1987, p. 611), and it has a long history in Western society. In fact, gender stratification is more deeply rooted in human history than are class distinctions and many other social categories of current oppression. Like class, gender stratification has varied over the ages, as has feminist ideology (Calvert & Calvert, 1992). The following Focus section discusses conflict theory, which is critical in understanding the role of power in social relationships.

FOCUS ON THEORY

Conflict Theories

Conflict theories focus on issues involving conflict, coercion, and the role of power in social relations. The best-known conflict theorist was Karl Marx—without a doubt the most influential thinker from this group of early 19th-century social theorists. His theory assumes that all of human history represents a struggle over material or monetary resources involving conflicts between the classes, and it places significant emphasis on understanding the material structures of production. For Marx, the relations of production are the fundamental organizing principles of human society. To illustrate this point, we need to review his key assumptions and theory of structural contradiction.

Marx considers production to be a fundamental quality of human nature. He contends in his materialist view of history that the first act of human history is to produce the necessary materials for survival. To achieve this end, humans enter into social relationships that are "independent of their will." "These are the relationships which surround the production process and which will vary according to the particular historical stage of development of the system of production—technically referred to as the *mode of production*. These relations of production are the foundation of society, its economic base" (Waters, 1994, p. 101). In Marx's view, this economic base is the fundamental determinant of the structure and development of social life. The social organization of production (referred to as the economic substructure) plays the determining role not only in the productive processes but also in the formation of the society's superstructure. The superstructure in Marxian theory includes all the idealist structures in society, such as religion, law, and philosophy (Timasheff, 1967). In his view, the characteristics of these superstructures are determined by the economic base of the society.

For Marx, social change occurs as a result of the contradictions between the material forces of production and the relations of production. He defines the forces of production as all the factors required in the production process—raw materials, technology, and so forth. The relations of production refer to the social organization of the production process, especially the relations surrounding ownership of the means of production. Waters (1994) contends that this conflict between the material forces of production and the social relations is the key form of structural contradiction within societies that Marx assumes contributes to changes in social relations.

Other conflict theorists identify other forms of conflict between groups that contribute to harmony and change in social systems, including interest-group conflicts, value conflicts, and conflicts in authority relations. Denisoff and Wahrman (1979) provide an overview of some of the basic assumptions in more modern conflict approaches:

1. Interests are basic elements of social life;
2. Social life involves coercion;
3. Social life involves groups with different interests;
4. Social life generates opposition, exclusion, and hostility;
5. Social life generates conflict;
6. Social differences involve power;
7. Social systems are not united or harmonious; and
8. Social systems tend to change.

This summary of assumptions indicates that stability is not of primary concern. In addition, it illustrates that an important issue in conflict is who is benefiting from a particular form of social arrangement. This perspective invites social workers to ask questions like, whose interests are involved and who will benefit or suffer from the existing social conditions? For social workers, this perspective is most helpful in studying issues of social inequality. Conflict theorists do not assume that inequality exists because it is functional for the society as a whole. Instead, they assume that these inequalities result from some group's ability to achieve power over another.

Sexual Status and Forms of Oppression

The ideology of sexism takes on many forms, but regardless of its form, sexism supports a system of oppressive gender relations for women. "Like racism, sexism is a system of beliefs and behaviors by which a group is oppressed, controlled, and exploited because of presumed gender differences" (Andersen & Collins, 1995, p. 67). For this reason, we need to approach issues of gender difference with extreme caution. Sexism pervades all aspects of our cultural symbols and ways of doing things. In fact, our language itself has supported the dominance of males in human relations. Until the 1960s, few questioned the use of terms like *mankind* when referring to humans or humanity. We also used the pronoun *he* when speaking of a person whose sex was unspecified, because the English language did not have a pronoun representing "he or she." Sexist language is being challenged, but its existence reflects the extent to which sexism is deeply rooted in our cultural traditions.

Sex-Role Stereotypes

What are sex-role stereotypes? Sex-role stereotypes involve beliefs about men and women that describe not how men and women *actually* differ but how societal members *believe* they differ (Rothblum & Franks,

1983). Baumgartner-Papageorgious (1982) asked a group of elementary and high school students how their lives would be different if they were a member of the opposite sex. These students' responses reflect many of the stereotypes within our society. In particular, it is interesting to note that boys perceived that the change would result in more negative consequences. This is a sample of some of their responses:

- "I would start to look for a husband as soon as I got into high school."
- "I would play girl games and not have many things to do during the day."
- "I'd use a lot of make-up and look good and beautiful ... I have to shave my whole body."
- "I'd have to know how to handle drunk guys and rapists."
- "I would not be able to help my dad fix the car and truck and his two motorcycles" (pp. 2–9).

Girls, however, anticipated more activity and less restrictiveness in their life if they were a member of the opposite sex:

- "I would have to stay calm and cool whenever something happened."
- "I could sleep later in the mornings since it would not take [me] very long to get ready for school."
- "My father would be closer because I'd be the son he always wanted."
- "I would not have to worry about being raped."
- "People would take my decisions and beliefs more seriously" (pp. 5–13).

Baumgartner-Papageorgious (1982) found similar beliefs among college students. This study points out how much of our lives are organized around male-female distinctions. In fact, the quotations from respondents in these studies indicate that there is even a gender belief system that influences how people make decisions (Ferrante, 1995).

The pressure to conform to established sex-role stereotypes can contribute to many psychological problems: depression, sexual dysfunction, obesity, and other clinical concerns (Rothblum & Franks, 1983). Women confront many dilemmas in the face of sex-role stereotypes. Their strategies for coping with these dilemmas are important for social work practitioners to understand. A number of other consequences should be taken into account as well. Gender influences self-esteem, psychological well-being, and physical health. In addition, it structures how and with whom we establish friendships and introduces many barriers in the social relationships between males and females. It also has important consequences for family relationships and forms of labor force participation. Throughout our discussion of human development, we will treat gender as a social category that affects each of these areas of social behavior. Also, we will try to provide a diverse sample of experiences that women encounter in their development. Without this knowledge, social workers cannot engage in activities designed to remove the key structural barriers that affect the liberty and life chances of women in our society.

Homophobia

Gender oppression is also closely linked with the other system of oppression involving gender: sexual orientation. **Homophobia** refers to the fear and hatred of sex with a same-sex partner. In our society, power and privilege are structured in terms of sexual orientation, and our system has institutionalized heterosexual forms of gender identity. In fact, a heterosexual gender identity has been considered the yardstick for determining normality and has contributed to the isolation and oppression of gays, lesbians, and bisexuals.

As feminists point out, women and men are not monolithic groups; they have significant withingroup diversity. One key withingroup variation in gender relations is *sexual orientation.* Sexual orientation is a critical life-span issue that has multiple dimensions and layers of experience that constitute an integral part of the human experience (Newman, 1994). For this reason, we will examine this topic using a life-span perspective. From this perspective, equal time should be allotted to the issue of sexual orientation as will be given to other gender issues like gender identity and gender roles. But biases in our research institutions have contributed to some regretful deficiencies in this area of our knowledge base, making this task more difficult.

Longres (1995) points out that gays and lesbians are not socialized into roles, values, and positions in society the way that heterosexuals are. As a consequence, gay males often have more in common with heterosexual males before they "come out." After coming out, gay males can learn the customs and ways of the homosexual community. The stigma associated with their sexual orientation also structures how they relate with gay and nongay persons in heterosexual (straight) interactions. How they negotiate this marginalization by the dominant society at various phases of their life becomes an important knowledge issue for social work professionals.

In sum, issues of diversity are highly complex and require close scrutiny by members of the social work community. You will be exposed to many studies in this book that suggest fundamental differences between males and females, between racial and ethnic groups, between heterosexual and homosexual persons, and between able-bodied people and people with disabilities. You must always approach the interpretation of the findings from these studies with extreme caution. Some researchers have a bias toward finding differences that perpetuate many forms of insensitivity or oppression. Thus, we advise that you take a critical stance in evaluating the social consequences of any findings suggesting behavioral tendencies that are attributable to any form of human difference. This is not to imply that there are not important physical, psychological, and social differences. Instead, our aim here is to sensitize you to the fact that you are responsible for making distinctions between real and false differences in people that are supported by compelling and unbiased evidence.

Social Hazards

Many social and cultural conditions in our lives place us at risk for many forms of harm. These include conditions of poverty, inequality, injustice, dependency, relative deprivation, segregation, powerlessness, underrepresentation, postindustrialism, postmodernism, and others.

Our economy has become more global in scope and is experiencing a major social transformation. Unemployment is rising in many industrial sectors of our economy, and technology is eliminating many positions in manufacturing and service sectors. These eco-

nomic pressures reduce available resources for sustaining our welfare systems. In fact, debates about the viability of welfare systems and of the welfare state are increasing in American society. Crime, substance abuse, domestic violence, homelessness, poverty, and urban decline are also increasing at exponential rates in various sectors of our society. Rivers and other sources of drinking water are diminishing, and pollution of our waterways and air are threatening the well-being of individuals and communities.

Other quality-of-life concerns are gaining the attention of more and more people in our major metropolitan areas. Natural resources are being depleted, and food shortages are increasing in sectors of our society and the world at large. Immigration is increasing, and public tolerance of difference is decreasing. Racial and ethnic tensions are mounting, and peaceful relations between the straight sector and gay and lesbians is in jeopardy in many communities. These conditions differ from the conditions encountered by other birth cohorts in our society's history and will contribute to distinct variations in life-span development.

One way of understanding how critical such factors can be to the well-being of a child is to examine them in the light of sociocultural risk. Garbarino and Abramowitz (1992a, p. 35) define sociocultural risk as "the impoverishing of the child's world so that the child lacks the basic social and psychological necessities of life." Children need many things to grow up happy and competent—for example, the basic necessities of food, water, and shelter; affection and love; proper medical care; proper educational stimulation; and positive social interactions. Without these things, children may end up "at risk" for impaired development (Garbarino & Abramowitz, 1992). Adults are also at risk for impaired development or other deficiencies if they are deprived of needed resources.

Two significant sources of sociocultural risk include *social impoverishment* and *cultural impoverishment*. Social impoverishment is the lack of critical social resources in a child's life, and cultural impoverishment refers to the values that undermine the child's healthy development. "Both of these forms of impoverishment find their most significant expression in the day-to-day content and structure of formal and informal support systems in a family's environment" (Garbarino & Abramowitz, 1992, p. 65).

These Lower East Side kids of New York City are playing in impoverished conditions that reflect many physical, social and cultural shortcomings.

Impoverishment of this nature is the result of unavailable, dysfunctional, eroded, or destroyed support systems. When institutional and community forces prevent supportive relationships from becoming established and being maintained, children and families are placed at increasing risk. This risk transcends the material resources and, in fact, is particularly destructive when accompanied by social deprivation. The combination of social deprivation and poverty produces devastating consequences (Garbarino & Abramowitz, 1992).

Sociocultural risk for children depends on the extent to which parents' functions are supported (Garbarino & Abramowitz, 1992). If parents are supported, encouraged, and helped by others who have a significant investment in the child's long-term future, then sociocultural risk is significantly reduced. Community efforts to create healthy living environments for children need to examine the support net that the community provides for parents and children. Reducing sociocultural risk is part and parcel of community development.

For example, community efforts to reduce child abuse need to examine the available support that can be offered to offset the sociocultural risks families face in their daily existence. Pregnancy complications can be reduced when support systems are made available to women (Nuckolls, Cassel, & Kaplan, 1972). Via support through home visitors, development can be enhanced for infants at high risk due to poverty, maternal depression, and caretaking inadequacy (Lyons-Ruth et al., 1990). Turner and Avison (1985) found that maternal adaptation to the parental role is distinguished, in part, by social support. In essence, women who do not obtain the needed level of social support have difficulty providing the most positive and healthy environment for their children. Social support enhances parental functioning by providing feedback about children and parenting, norms for nonabusive child-rearing, and increased opportunities for reducing stress and problem solving. Living in today's society has its challenges, as we will see in the following Focus section.

FOCUS ON SOCIOLOGY

What Is Postmodernism?

Many scholars define *postmodernism* by contrasting it with *modernism*. Postmodernism is considered the new phase of history that follows the period known as modernism. Brown (1994) argues that many scholars assume that there were two great events in human history: the appearance of horticulture and the emergence of "modern societies." We are now on the verge of a third major event, which involves the appearance of a "yet unnamed 'post modern' social and cultural formation" (Brown, 1994, p. 13).

Modern societies are characterized by industrial economies, territorial states, mass culture, and scientific rationality (Smart, 1993). Other theorists differentiate modern societies from other social formations by focusing on the relationship between modernism and the spirit of Enlightenment, or what is known as the *Age of Reason*. In this historical period, instrumental rationality replaced tradition and religious dogmas as the grounds for truth and knowledge. Modernity promotes instead the pursuit of innovation, novelty, and dynamism through the process of instrumental rationality (Kellner, 1990). This highly rational, changeable, and instrumental way of life associated with modernism did not emerge in human history until after feudalism, or the Middle Ages, around 1600.

The postmodern age, by contrast, is a "time of troubles" marked by the collapse of rationalism and the ethos of the Enlightment (Kellner, 1990). It is considered a period in which social engineering and other forms of scientific thought are looked upon with great suspicion. Most postmodernists are critical of views that support the notion that social work can solve the problems of social life with the aid of principles of science. In their view, this is an arrogant belief that is doomed to failure.

One of the major formulators of the postmodernist perspective is Jean-Francois Lyotard. Lyotard (1984) wrote *The Postmodern Condition,* wherein he states that "the status of knowledge is altered as societies enter what is known as the postindustrial age and culture enters what is known as the postmodern age" (p. 3). In the modern age, science is elevated to a position of high status because it replaces the fictions and myths of tradition with facts derived from the scientific method. For Lyotard, the idea of postmodernity represents a fundamental change in the ways in which we relate to science and knowledge. In the postmodern period, we relate to science as another language game of mythical narrative. The goals and values of Western culture are no longer considered universal, and they are not considered to be the primary points of reference for any form of social organization or knowledge. In the views of many postmodernists, the decentering of Western knowledge and values is reflected in many of the controversies of our times.

Overview

This chapter presents a way of conceptualizing the key systems that make up our social system, which integrates and regulates how we relate to one another.

The social system also involves all the processes and structures that contribute to various forms of social organization. In discussing these elements that make up the social system, we presented traditional and nontraditional concepts from the social work and social science literature. We also examined structures in social relationships that contribute to various forms of oppression and social support, and we described how these social structures are interrelated, as well as where they intersect. This form of knowledge is essential in trying to individualize the experiences of clients. Social workers need to understand the consequences of race, class, and gender on each aspect of human behavior.

In the next section of the book, we begin applying each of the dimensions in our framework to the many phases and events associated with the process of human development.

Summary

The social system serves the function of integrating people into a life shared with other people. Its key components are people in interaction with one another. The various contexts in our lives can be analyzed as separate systems, and there are four levels of subsystems: microsystems, mesosystems, exosystems, and macrosystems. These systems can be used to examine the environmental contexts of human development.

Principles from systems thinking help us identify relevant systems, subsystems, and the suprasystem of which problems, persons, and behaviors are a part. This approach is aided by drawing an ecomap. An ecomap highlights the points of connection between systems influencing a person's life and allows for the identification of points of conflict and points of support in a person's life space.

FAMILIES, GROUPS, SUPPORT SYSTEMS, AND CONTEXTS

The family is a key system within the larger social system. By treating the family as a system, the social worker can better understand the social context of family difficulties. The family is a system that is considered bigger than the sum of its parts. There are traditional and nontraditional definitions of the family. A useful definition that takes into account the conditions of our times is as follows: A family is a composition of people who decide to act like a family. Families, like individuals, experience a sequence of developmental stages. Carter and McGoldrick have described a six-stage model of family development that is useful in understanding how families change over time.

Examining family structure and function helps us understand how families work. Family structure refers to the manner in which each family organizes itself into interactional patterns. The key subsystems in a family are the couple subsystem, parental subsystem, sibling subsystem, and parent-child subsystem. Families function best when the subsystems maintain their own unique roles, identities, and boundaries. Family systems involve a number of key processes, such as homeostasis, information, and feedback, and communication plays a major role in family relations. Families are functional to the extent that they have good problem-solving, negotiation, and decision-making skills.

Another key context for understanding human behavior is the group. Groups are any small face-to-face collections of persons who interact to accomplish some purpose. Groups are often classified as (1) formed or natural and (2) treatment groups or task groups. Understanding how groups function requires knowledge of group dynamics and processes, including knowledge of norms, roles, communication patterns, power and status relationships, and cohesiveness. Most groups must resolve the issue of how they will make decisions.

Support systems are a special type of social context. They represent continuing social aggregates that provide individuals with opportunities for feedback about themselves and for validation of their expectations about others. There are five different types of support systems: formal organizations, formed groups, self-help groups, social networks, and natural helpers. Self-help groups are a major social trend. Closely related to self-help groups are natural helpers. Natural helpers are considered central figures in a social network or in a neighborhood who have gained recognition for their unique wisdom, resourcefulness, and caring qualities.

Organizations and institutions are other types of contexts within which humans live. A formal organization is any large social group that is designed to achieve specific objectives rationally. Some formal organizations develop bureaucratic structures. All forms of organization meet critical goals necessary for the survival of a society.

Another key social context that influences our lives is our social institutions. These include the institutions of economy, kinship, education, law, polity, and religion. They contribute to the stability of status, roles, norms, and power in our relationships. Our location in social space is significantly influenced by our social institutions. There are many terms employed by social scientists to describe variations in a person's location in social space: social distance, social integration, social marginality, and hierarchy.

MULTICULTURAL AND GENDER CONSIDERATIONS

We live in a multicultural world, which means that social workers must have knowledge of factors contributing to tolerance and intolerance in social relationships. Prejudice refers to a generalized negative attribute directed toward another individual's membership in a socially defined group. Discrimination involves overt acts that treat members of a target group in an unfair manner. Race is a social and not a biological concept, and it can be used to make distinctions that have unfair consequences. Ethnicity also focuses on differences in people, but it is not as easy to identify ethnic differences as it is to identify racial and sex differences. Ethnicity, gender, and sexual orientation should be examined in terms of acquired meaning. These meanings have little to do with distinct differences that can characterize each of these social categories.

SOCIAL HAZARDS

Many social conditions, such as poverty, inequality, and postindustrialism, place people at risk for many forms of harm. Major transformations in society continue to take place, affecting the status of social conditions. Examining sociocultural risk is one way of identifying and understanding conditions like poverty, inequality, and so on. Sociocultural risk occurs when a child's world is so impoverished that the child lacks basic social and psychological necessities, and it includes two aspects: social impoverishment and cultural impoverishment. Community efforts can be designed to increase support and reduce the risks families face.

🌐 Online Resources

Rethinking Marxism
http://www.Nd.edu/remarx
An interdisciplinary journal for discussion and debates both within the Marxist tradition and between Marxism and other forms of contemporary critical thought.

Anthropological theories
http://www.as.ua.edu/ant/faculty/murphy/function.htm
A guide prepared by students for students.

International Center for Research on Women
http://www.ICRW.org/
Promoting social and economic development with women's full participation.

Traveling through time on the family life cycle
http://www.askdrgayle.com/flc2.html
The latter stages of the family life cycle.

☞ InfoTrac® College Edition

For interesting materials related to what you have just read, please go to the *InfoTrac College Edition* website and search using the following key words:

intergroup relations	sexism
group identification	hate crimes

Key Terms

androcentricity	macrosystem
bureaucracy	mesosystem
cohesive group	microsystem
communication pattern	mores
communitarian agenda	natural groups
community	natural helpers
creolization	neighboring
culture	norms
discrimination	power
ecomap	prejudice
exosystem	race
family	racism
family structure	reciprocal interaction
floating family	role
folkways	self-help organizations
formal organizations	sense of community
formed groups	sex
gender	social distance
gender polarization	social identity theory
groupthink	social support systems
hierarchy	status
homeostasis	stereotype
homophobia	system
human relations school	task groups
ideal type	treatment groups
identificational community	

Developmental Themes

Accepting the reality of the pregnancy. Adjusting to the role of parenthood. Accepting the real baby vs. the fantasy baby.

Biophysical Dimension

Biophysical Growth and Development	Physical development of the fetus: germinal stage: rapid cell division; embryonic stage: internal organs develop; fetal stage: growth and weight gain; birth. The normal newborn, newborn evaluations: Apgar score.
Biophysical Hazards	Complications of pregnancy: hyperemesis, vaginal bleeding, toxemia, polyhydramnios, IUGR. Environmental effects on prenatal development: maternal age, multiple gestations, maternal nutrition, illness, drug use, smoking, stress. Prenatal testing. Complications of birth: meconium aspiration, malpresentation, prolonged labor. Cesarean births. Neonatal complications: prematurity, birth defects.

Psychological Dimension

Cognitive Development and Information Processing	Fetal responses to pain, light, touch, taste.
Communication	Fetal response to sound: habituation to sound. Fetal learning: newborn response to maternal voice.
Attitudes and Emotions	Effect of mother's emotional state on fetus. Parental interactions with fetus and newborn emotional health.
Social Cognition and Regulation	Newborn states, newborn reflexes. The Brazelton Neonatal Assessment Scale.
Psychological Hazards	Newborn attachment: question of a "sensitive period." The birth experience: LeBoyer "gentle" birth. The neonatal intensive care unit.

Social Dimension

Families, Groups, Support Systems and Communities	Prenatal intervention programs, postpartum early intervention programs.
Multicultural and Gender Considerations	Infant mortality: the black-white disparity. Cultural differences among newborns. Circumcision.
Social Hazards	Poverty's effect on prenatal development. Drug-exposed infants, fetal alcohol syndrome, domestic violence.

CHAPTER 5

Pregnancy, Birth, and the Newborn

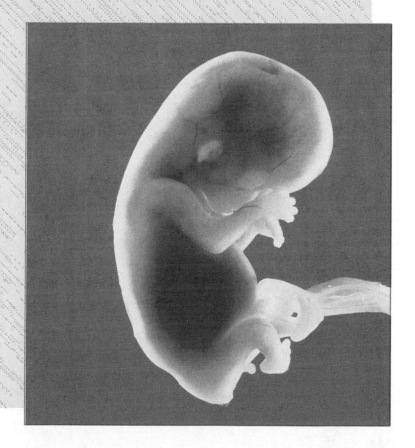

DEVELOPMENTAL THEMES

It has been said that pregnancy is an act of faith until the birth of the baby, when nine months of waiting culminate in a new life. Upon seeing their infant for the first time new mothers have been heard to exclaim, "Oh my God, it really is a baby!" Whether planned or unplanned, confirmation of pregnancy is often a shock. The first task for the expectant parents is to accept that the pregnancy is real and involves the growth of a real fetus.

Reva Rubin, who has researched the developmental tasks of pregnancy, describes two questions women ask throughout **gestation** (the length of pregnancy): "Now?" and "Who, me?" (Rubin, 1970). If the pregnancy is unplanned, the woman may have to decide whether to terminate it or continue it. (See the Focus section on Abortion—A Difficult Decision, page 155). Even if the pregnancy is expected, the woman may still wonder whether it is such a good idea at this time. She may have thoughts such as, "Wait, am I really ready for this?" Even the most wanted pregnancy can be a source of anxiety. The woman may worry about the birth process and wonder, "How is this baby going to get out, and how much will it hurt?" A young, single woman may ignore the reality of the pregnancy for months, refusing to admit even to herself that she is expecting.

As the pregnancy progresses and the woman feels the fetus move, hears the heartbeat, and perhaps sees the fetus via ultrasound, she usually becomes reconciled to the reality of the pregnancy. At this point, she may begin to integrate the baby as part of herself. Baby and mother become one. During this phase, the mother turns inward and becomes narcissistic and self-centered. She becomes preoccupied with her own thoughts and feelings. In later pregnancy, the baby begins to become a real and separate person. Now the mother begins to plan for the birth. She fantasizes about her baby, dreams about her baby, and plans for her baby. She may begin to think of her own childhood and her relationship to her family. Pregnancy can reactivate unresolved developmental conflicts for a woman (Schuster & Ashburn, 1992) and lead to the task of resolving identity confusions and assuming the role of mother. She may analyze her own identity, her relationship to her mother, and her relationship to her partner. She may worry about balancing career and family and about being a good mother without losing her own identity.

Pregnancy for the father is as much of an adjustment as it is for the mother. He also has many worries about his ability to parent, to provide for a family, to live up to his wife's expectations. The pregnancy is even less real for him, and his task often is to assimilate the fact that the fetus is real and is his. Feeling fetal movement, hearing the heartbeat, attending childbirth preparation classes, and being present at the birth all help to include the father in the pregnancy and birth process.

One example of a cultural practice that may serve to establish the man as the father of the baby is *couvade*. In certain tribal societies, the father behaves as if he were giving birth. While his wife is delivering the infant, the father goes to bed and may even complain of labor pains (Mason & Elwood, 1995). This custom symbolically establishes the man as the father of the baby and gives him legal rights as the parent. In modern societies, up to 65% of men report symptoms of pregnancy during their partner's gestation (May & Perrin, 1985), including nausea, fatigue, back pain, and even abdominal pain. Though many different reasons have been suggested for this phenomenon—an expression of underlying biological changes in the male, envy of the pregnant woman, somatic anxiety—its prevalence is not entirely understood. Could the modern version of couvade be the result of the male identifying strongly with his mate and thereby symbolically assuming responsibility for his role as father of their child? Could these symptoms help make the pregnancy more real for him? Some research suggests that couvade brings the father into a "paternal state" and that this might reduce the risk of the father abusing the child (Mason & Elwood, 1995). While there are no definitive answers about this syndrome, research indicates that men have psychological, emotional, and physical needs related to fatherhood that should be addressed.

Through the nine months of pregnancy, then, the couple faces the tasks involved in becoming a mother and a father. When the baby is born, both must give up the fantasy baby each has dreamed of for nine months and accept the very real baby that has been born.

The following Focus section discusses the difficulties a woman faces when deciding whether to keep or abort a fetus.

FOCUS ON ETHICS

Abortion—A Difficult Decision

For a woman of any age, the abortion decision is often one of the most difficult and distressing choices in her life. Abortion is a complicated and controversial issue with strong arguments both for and against. On the one hand, some pro-life advocates feel that termination of a pregnancy at any point for any reason is murder and is morally wrong. On the other hand, pro-choice advocates feel that a woman has the right to control her own reproductive process and determine her own fate.

The abortion question has a long history. In 1973, the Supreme Court in *Roe v. Wade* decided that states could not deny a woman her right to have an abortion. Since that time, however, several other laws and rulings have eroded that right. As early as 1976, the Hyde amendment stopped Medicaid funding for abortions, which made it more difficult for poor women to obtain abortions. Before that time, 33% of abortions were paid for by federal funds. In 1989, a more conservative Supreme Court ruled on *Webster v. Reproductive Health Services,* allowing states once again to limit abortions. The *Webster* ruling allowed states to ban abortions in public hospitals and clinics and prohibit public employees from assisting in abortions. Since then, the Supreme Court has accepted even more cases with the result that abortion is still legal but less available, especially to young, poor women. For instance, more than 30 states require girls under 18 to notify or get permission from their parents to obtain an abortion—in some states, permission is required even from a noncustodial parent. And employees of federally funded family planning clinics cannot discuss abortion with clients; only the doctor can mention abortion as an alternative or even offer abortion counseling (Guernsey, 1993). And fewer and fewer doctors are available who perform abortions. Some simply are untrained in the procedure, whereas others become discouraged over the violence associated with abortion protests. However, as of this writing, many women still have a choice.

How does a woman make such a difficult decision? She needs to explore honestly how she personally feels about abortion. She needs help in exploring alternatives such as putting the baby up for adoption, raising the child herself, or allowing a family member to raise the child. She needs to think through what each choice means for her now and in the future.

A social worker can play an important role in helping a woman make the abortion decision. But this is one instance in which it is vital to be able to separate personal from professional values. The most important consideration is that the woman needs to make the decision herself; no one can make it for her. In this situation, a social worker's role is a supportive one. In a Swedish study, more than one-third of the women studied felt that their social support system was inadequate, illustrating the need for social work intervention for women contemplating abortions (Hamark, Uddenberg, & Forssman, 1995). Though many women feel some guilt and depression after an abortion, most women have less regret and fewer emotional problems when the choice has not been forced on them by other people (Reeder, Mastroianni, & Martin, 1983). In fact, fewer than 10% of women experience psychological problems after an abortion (Lemkau, 1988; Olson, 1980). Women who do have a high incidence of emotional problems following abortion were more ambivalent before the procedure, felt coerced, or already had symptoms of personality problems (Schuster & Ashburn, 1992). However, women who have been denied an abortion may have more problems with the child born as a result of that denial. One study in Czechoslovakia (Matejcek, Dytrych, & Schuller, 1979) found that, at the age of 9, children born to women denied an abortion had more hospitalizations, poorer school grades, poorer relationships with peers, and more irritable dispositions than other children.

A woman who is encouraged to take some time and carefully analyze her options before coming to a decision will be better able to live with that decision. Counseling before and after the abortion can help a woman deal with her feelings about her choice. The goal is to help a woman make a decision that—whether she feels good or bad about it at the time—she ultimately believes is the right one.

BIOPHYSICAL DIMENSION

Biophysical Growth and Development

What will eventually become a baby begins as a single cell. About midway through her menstrual cycle, a woman produces a mature ovum, or egg, in a fluid-filled sac on one of her ovaries. At ovulation, the sac bursts and the mature ovum is swept into the fallopian tube to begin the journey to the uterus.

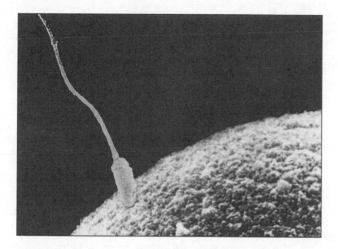

Sperm and egg: A magnified image of the process of conception.

PHYSICAL DEVELOPMENT OF THE FETUS

no one, not even the rain, has such small hands
— E. E. CUMMINGS

After eight weeks, the embryo begins to look quite human; it is 90% formed, with most of the basic structures, including a face, arms, legs, feet, and hands. From this point on, the embryo is referred to as a *fetus,* and this period is called the period of the fetus. Between 8 and 12 weeks, the chorionic villi develop into a functioning placenta attached to the mother's uterus, and the fetus is connected to the placenta by the umbilical cord. For the remainder of the pregnancy, the placenta acts as the fetus's lungs, digestive tract, kidneys, and liver. Oxygen and nutrients from the mother pass through this semipermeable membrane to the fetus, and carbon dioxide and other wastes pass from the fetus to the mother. It was once thought that the placenta acted as a barrier and protected the fetus from any harmful substances ingested by the mother. Now, however, we know that what the mother eats, drinks, sniffs, or inhales is passed on to the developing baby. The effects of these substances on the fetus will be discussed in a later section.

The fetus floats in amniotic fluid inside the amniotic sac, or bag of waters. This fluid regulates the temperature, cushions the fetus from injury, and allows freedom of movement. After 12 weeks, the fetus begins to move in this fluid, to drink this fluid, and to urinate into it. By this time, also, it is possible to determine the sex of the fetus.

By 20 weeks, the mother feels the first fetal movements, commonly described as "butterflies" fluttering in her lower abdomen. Often this is the time when the expectant parents first hear the fetal heartbeat on a prenatal visit. The fetus is covered with fine, downy hair called *lanugo.* Some babies are born with a substantial amount of this hair on their bodies, although many babies lose most of this body hair before birth.

By 24 weeks, the fetus resembles a tiny baby. This baby appears to be rather red and wrinkled, though, because it has not put on much fat. At this time, the fetus is covered with a substance called *vernix,* which looks a lot like shortening. This substance protects the skin from prolonged exposure to the amniotic fluid. Babies at term are sometimes born with some of this

When the ovum enters the fallopian tube, it is swept along toward the lower one-third of the tube. Sperm deposited in the vagina during intercourse swim up through the cervix, into the uterus, and then into the fallopian tube, where one sperm fertilizes the ovum.

The fertilized ovum is known as a *zygote.* After a brief rest of 24–36 hours, the zygote begins the process of regular cell division. It then takes three days for the zygote to travel down the fallopian tube and into the uterus. By the time the zygote enters the uterus, it has developed into a fluid-filled sphere of about 150 cells. The inner layer of cells develops into the embryo, and the outer layer of cells forms the *chorionic villi*—fingerlike tendrils that give the zygote a shaggy appearance. These chorionic villi burrow into the uterine lining (implant) and provide early nutrients. This process of implantation of the zygote, known as the *germinal period,* takes about two weeks. After implantation, the zygote, now known as an *embryo,* begins to secrete human chorionic gonadotrophin (HCG) to maintain the pregnancy. HCG can be detected in the mother's blood six to eight days after conception, and presence of this substance is the basis for early pregnancy testing. An at-home early pregnancy test can detect HCG in the mother's urine one day after the missed menstrual cycle. The next few weeks after conception, from two to eight weeks, is the embryonic period.

vernix still covering their skin. A fetus at 24 weeks makes breathing motions, hiccoughs (sometimes felt by the mother), responds to sound, and sleeps and wakes in noticeable cycles. With the advanced technology now available in high-level neonatal intensive care units (NICU), babies born at 24 weeks have a chance for survival.

If born at 28 weeks, the fetus has a good chance of survival. Now the fetus opens and closes its eyes and may even suck its thumb. A fetus usually assumes the head-down position in the uterus at this time, because the head is the heaviest part of the body.

During the last two months of pregnancy, the fetus stores fat and gains weight. The fetal lungs undergo important development, and each week the fetus remains in the uterus increases its chances of survival. Although today a premature baby has improved chances of survival at earlier and earlier stages of pregnancy, problems related to low birth weight and prematurity remain.

The fetus is full term and ready for life outside the uterine environment between 38 and 41 weeks. How is the "due date" determined? If pregnancy is defined as beginning at the time of conception, then birth occurs after 266 days, or 38 weeks. The mother's due date, however, is usually calculated according to Nagele's rule. To determine a woman's due date, count back three months from the first day of her last menstrual period and add seven days. According to this procedure, pregnancy begins on the first day of the last menstrual period and lasts 280 days, or 40 weeks. In most clinical situations, pregnancy is calculated in this way, so, for our discussion of prenatal development, pregnancy is based on menstrual dates and lasts 40 weeks.

THE BIRTH PROCESS

Doesn't it seem that, in popular media depictions of birth, labor begins with the woman doubling over in sudden, intense pain? This is followed by a frantic rush to get to the hospital in time for the birth. Although some cab drivers have delivered babies, in reality most women find that labor begins more slowly, allowing ample time to make it to the hospital.

Labor is divided into three stages (see Figure 5.1). During the first stage, the cervix opens up, or dilates, to 10 centimeters to allow the passage of the baby's head.

The average length of the first stage of labor is 12–14 hours. In early labor, the contractions can be up to 20 minutes apart and usually last less than 1 minute. Most women are pretty comfortable in the early part of labor and are excited about having the baby at last, though a little anxious over the process. As labor progresses, toward the end of the first stage, the contractions may come one right after another and last up to 2 minutes. During this phase, a laboring woman needs a lot of support and encouragement. And if she has not gone to the hospital or birthing center yet, now is the time to rush or hope the cab driver knows what he or she is doing.

When the cervix has fully dilated to 10 centimeters, the second stage of labor begins. During this stage, the baby is born. A woman can now actively participate in the birth process by pushing the baby down the birth canal. This process can take from 10 minutes to more than 3 hours, depending on how many previous births the woman has had and how much medication she has been given.

During the third stage of labor, the placenta is delivered, which usually takes from 5 to 30 minutes. At this time, the mother and her partner or support person are busy marveling over the baby. Sometimes a fourth stage of labor is included; this is the recovery time, 1 to 2 hours after birth. During this time, the mother is watched for excessive bleeding or other recovery problems. This is usually the time for the new family to get to know one another.

The following Focus section discusses significant changes that have taken place in preparing for childbirth.

FOCUS ON HISTORY

Prepared Childbirth

Having a baby involves some degree of pain. A popular comedienne describes the pain of childbirth: "Take your lower lip and pull it up over your head." Physically the pain comes from cervical dilation and the sensation of the baby's head pushing through the pelvis. Through the years, different methods have been used to help ease this pain.

FIGURE 5.1
Birth process (adapted from Moore, 1989)

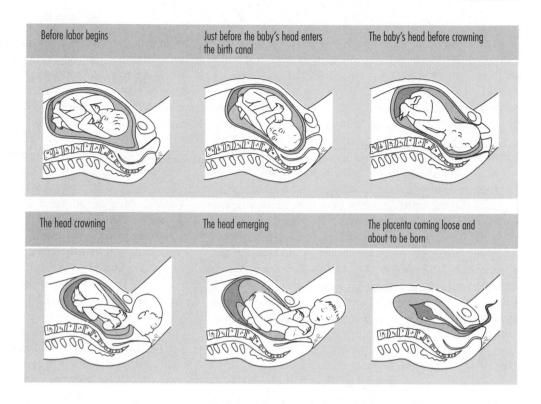

Before labor begins

Just before the baby's head enters the birth canal

The baby's head before crowning

The head crowning

The head emerging

The placenta coming loose and about to be born

Many of the early drugs given to relieve the pain of childbirth rendered most women unconscious during delivery. Because the mother was not awake and could not help push the baby out, the baby was usually delivered with a high degree of medical intervention. The mother's partner would wait in the fathers' waiting room. After birth, the baby was kept in the hospital nursery and brought to the mother only at scheduled feeding times. Understandably, women began to want more control over and participation in their birth experiences. Also, such a heavy reliance on drugs for pain relief during birth had major side effects for the baby. In response, other methods of pain relief, without drugs, were developed.

The most popular method of prepared childbirth was developed by a French obstetrician, Fernand Lamaze. In the Lamaze method, the father or other support person stays with the mother through her labor to provide help and encouragement. The mother and her support person attend classes where they learn about the birth process and specific relaxation techniques. Knowledge and relaxation help reduce fear

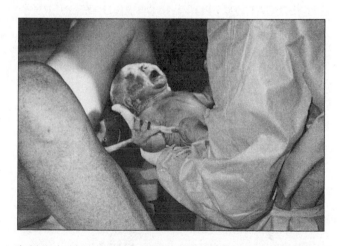

At birth, babies leave the comfort of the uterine environment and must immediately adapt to the outside environment.

and thereby reduce pain. The woman is taught to replace the normal responses to pain of fear and tension with more useful and distracting responses, such as patterned breathing and relaxation.

More recently, studies have shown that women who walk and move around during labor have shorter labors, experience less discomfort, and need less medication than women who lie down (Balaskas, 1992). Studies have also shown that the presence of a supportive female birth attendant, or doula, during labor results in less medication, less medical intervention, fewer birth complications, and a shorter labor (Klaus, Kennell, & Klaus, 1993).

Over the years, hospitals have attempted to make birth more family centered. Many hospitals have special birthing rooms, which resemble a regular bedroom. The mother is allowed to have any number of attendants present for the birth; even siblings may be included. After the birth, the baby is handed to the mother, and she can keep the baby in the room with her and feed it on demand. Birthing centers, outside the hospital setting, allow for homelike birth with the possibility of medical intervention if necessary. Some women choose to have their babies at home, but in case of last-minute complications, most obstetricians prefer to deliver babies in a hospital or a birthing center.

MEDICATIONS FOR LABOR AND DELIVERY

Development of prepared childbirth methods has allowed women to be awake and active participants in the birth process. Being rendered totally unconscious with drugs is now usually only an option during an emergency cesarean section. However, prepared childbirth does not eliminate the pain of labor. Today, "natural" childbirth does not necessarily mean unmedicated childbirth.

The most commonly used medications in labor today are narcotics and regional anesthesias. Narcotics, such as Demerol, are given before the end of the first stage of labor so that most of the drug will pass out of the baby's system before birth. If the baby is born with the narcotic in its system, it may experience difficulty breathing or sucking. Because the narcotic is sometimes given with a tranquilizer, the baby may also be sleepy at birth in contrast to unmedicated babies, who are more alert.

Regional anesthesias include the epidural. In the epidural, an anesthetic is injected into the mother's lower spine. Though little of this drug reaches the baby, its long-term effects on the baby are still unknown. Some studies show mild effects on early newborn behavior (Sepkoski, 1992), whereas others have found little or no effect. Over the years, some studies have indicated that there are effects on the birth process itself. For instance, the epidural may increase the length of labor and the need for medical intervention, including the use of forceps (a pair of instruments that resemble salad tongs used to guide the baby out of the birth canal when the mother is not able to push the baby out), and the possibility of a **cesarean section** (birth through an incision in the mother's abdomen) (Thorpe & Breedlove; 1996; Cohen, Yeast, & Hu, 1994). However, studies reviewed by Thorpe & Breedlove (1996) suggest that the epidural is the most safe and effective method of pain relief for women in labor, with associated benefits such as relaxing women and helping labor progress (see also Erickson, 1996).

Although most women who are prepared for childbirth use less medication than those who are not, the use of medication in labor in many hospitals remains quite high. In fact, in some hospitals the rate of epidural use approaches 85 to 90%. All obstetric medications given to the mother cross the placenta and alter the baby's environment in the uterus (Balaskas, 1992). Conclusive evidence of the long-term effects of these drugs is not yet available. Thus, use of medications during birth may still be an important factor to consider in making an assessment.

CHARACTERISTICS OF A NORMAL NEWBORN

How does a newborn infant look? Bill Cosby describes the experience of seeing his new baby for the first time, at which point he tells his wife, "Congratulations, dear. You have just given birth to a . . . lizard." Although most newborns bear little resemblance to reptiles, they are not exactly the "Gerber Baby."

Normal newborns at term weigh between 5½ pounds (2,500 grams) and 9½ pounds (4,300 grams). The head of a vaginally delivered newborn is often elongated or cone-shaped. This molding of the head results from the fact that the bones in a newborn's head are not fused together. These bones shift during birth, allowing the head to change shape to fit through the birth canal. (Infants delivered by cesarean section

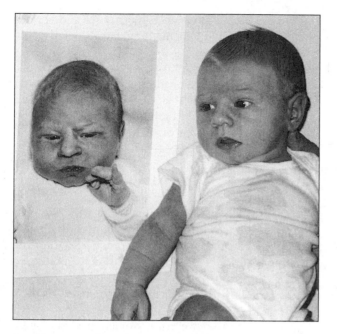

A striking comparison of the baby at birth and at 4 weeks. The newborn's head is elongated, and the baby's face shows the pressures that occurred during the birth process.

the physician evaluates the baby on skin color, heart rate, response to stimulation, muscle tone, and breathing effort. In each area, the physician gives the baby a score of 0, 1, or 2. Normal newborns usually lose a point or two for skin color, in that the hands and feet remain somewhat blue for a time after birth. (There is an old joke that only fellow obstetricians' babies receive a perfect score of 10.) At any rate, a score of 7-10 is considered good. A score of 5-7 is poor, and the baby may need some medical intervention. A score of 0-4 is very poor; the baby very likely requires resuscitation and has increased risk of mortality. A score of 0-4 at 5 minutes is significantly associated with increased risk of mortality and neurological defects.

Biophysical Hazards

Birth is as safe as life gets.
—Harriette Hartigan

As discussed in Chapter 2, when a social worker is gathering developmental data about a client for a psychosocial history, it may be helpful to obtain prenatal information about the client, including any problems or complications that occurred during the pregnancy or birth. These complications may have an effect on the individual's postnatal development. For instance, some early research (Colletti, 1979) suggested that children with learning disabilities had a significantly

have round heads.) Passage through the birth canal can also cause facial bruising and swelling. Many newborns have a bluish color to their skin until they begin breathing. After birth, the newborn's skin may be red, wrinkled, and scaling. But to the new parents, their newborn is usually a beautiful sight.

NEWBORN EVALUATIONS

One of the first questions asked by new parents at delivery is, "Is my baby OK?" One objective exam that looks at whether or not a newborn is OK is the **Apgar score** (see Table 5.1). In 1953, Virginia Apgar developed a scale that looks at the infant's adaptation to life outside the womb. A newborn is given an Apgar score at 1 minute and 5 minutes after birth. At these times,

TABLE 5.1	The Apgar Score		
	Score		
Sign	0	1	2
Heart rate	No heartbeat	Fewer than 100 beats per minute	100 to 140 beats per minute
Breathing	No breathing	Irregular shallow breathing	Strong breathing and crying
Reflex	No response	Weak reflexive response	Strong reflexive response (sneezing, coughing, grimacing)
Muscle tone	Limp	Weak flexion of arms and legs	Strong flexion of arms and legs
Color	Blue body	Body pink, blue extremities	Body and extremities pink

(Based on Apgar, 1953)

higher incidence of pregnancy and birth complications than did normal children. Other more recent evidence suggests a link between attention deficit disorder and pregnancy, birth, and neonatal complications (Sprich-Buckminster, 1993). In the next sections, we will discuss some of the possible complications of pregnancy and birth.

COMPLICATIONS OF PREGNANCY

Many women experience nausea, or morning sickness, during early pregnancy. This nausea and occasional vomiting usually clear up by the fourth month of gestation. If a woman vomits several times a day for a long period of time, however, she runs the risk of nutritional problems and dehydration. This frequent vomiting during pregnancy is called **hyperemesis gravidarum.** Some women have vomiting so severe that they require hospitalization.

A complication that can have serious consequences is **vaginal bleeding.** In early pregnancy, this bleeding can be the result of spontaneous abortion. Seventy-five percent of spontaneous abortions occur in the first 12 weeks of pregnancy. Not all incidences of first-trimester bleeding end in loss of the pregnancy, though. Sometimes the bleeding abates, and the pregnancy is carried to term. But, because many spontaneous abortions are the result of fetal abnormalities, it may be helpful to note instances of early-pregnancy bleeding.

Vaginal bleeding in later pregnancy may be an indication of placental problems. This bleeding is usually the result of a placenta located low in the uterus and covering the cervix (placenta previa) or a placenta that begins to separate from the wall of the uterus (abruptio placentae). Significant bleeding in late pregnancy due to these conditions can be very serious and threaten the survival of the mother and the baby.

Toxemia and eclampsia can also be serious complications of pregnancy. Early stages of toxemia are referred to as preeclampsia. In preeclampsia, the pregnant woman exhibits elevated blood pressure, swelling (especially of the hands and face), weight gain, and protein in her urine. These symptoms are not always easily noticed by the mother and are often caught at a prenatal visit. This is one reason that regular, consistent prenatal visits are so important to pregnancy outcome. If these early signs are not detected and treated,

the condition can advance to eclampsia and serious complications, including maternal death, fetal death, and fetal brain damage.

Diabetes is one of the most common metabolic abnormalities that occur during pregnancy. **Gestational diabetes,** defined as carbohydrate intolerance with onset or first recognition during pregnancy, makes up 80% of cases of diabetes in pregnancy. A woman diagnosed with diabetes before pregnancy is at an increased risk of both maternal and fetal complications and may require intensive medical management before, during, and after her pregnancy. A woman who develops gestational diabetes must monitor her blood glucose levels, controlling them through diet and possibly insulin injections. Women experiencing gestational diabetes should be routinely monitored by a physician postpartum, since up to 62% of these women develop diabetes after pregnancy (Pasui & McFarland, 1997).

Sometimes the pregnant woman has too much amniotic fluid, or **polyhydramnios.** This excess fluid can signal problems with the baby. Remember, the baby drinks the fluid. If for some reason the baby cannot drink the fluid, it builds up in the uterus, causing the mother to exhibit an overly large abdomen.

A good example of a complication of pregnancy that can be caused by factors in the maternal environment is **intrauterine growth retardation (IUGR).** This condition occurs when the fetal weight falls below the 10th percentile for gestational age. Many factors can affect the quality of the maternal uterine environment and result in this growth slowdown, including the mother's nutrition, weight gain, age, number and spacing of previous pregnancies, health status, level of environmental stress, and ingestion of substances such as cigarettes, alcohol, and drugs. In many instances, this growth reduction is in some way caused by intrauterine deprivation. Because of this deprivation, IUGR increases the risk of fetal death and the risk of problems for the infant after birth.

ENVIRONMENTAL EFFECTS ON PRENATAL DEVELOPMENT

The child is born into a family environment that will shape and influence his or her lifelong development. Even before birth, however, human development occurs in an "environment" that exerts significant influence on the growing fetus. The fetal environment exists inside the mother's uterus, and this environment can be influenced by numerous factors, such as the mother's health, her diet, her ingestion of substances such as alcohol and drugs, and her emotional state and level of stress. In this section we will discuss maternal health factors and practices that can adversely affect prenatal development.

Maternal Age

Problems in pregnancy attributable to maternal age arise in mothers under 18 and over 35. Older mothers have an increased risk for illness and for pregnancy complications. Specifically, the incidence of chromosomal abnormalities such as Down syndrome goes up significantly for older women. The risk of Down syndrome for a 21-year-old woman is 1:1,600, whereas the risk for a woman at age 41 is 1:83.

Teenage mothers may also have problems with pregnancy, including increased risk of infant death, pregnancy complications, and infant mental retardation. One contributing problem for teenage mothers may be that they are less likely to obtain prenatal care than are older women (Eberstadt, 1991).

For either end of the age spectrum, good medical management of the pregnancy through prenatal visits increases the likelihood of a successful outcome. Some outcomes, however, may not be what we expect. The following Focus section presents some research results that indicate that teens with low socioeconomic status (SES) may actually have healthier babies than older women of low SES.

FOCUS ON DIVERSITY

Low-SES Teens May Have Healthier Babies

One researcher (Geronimus, 1991, 1992) has discovered some interesting information about low-socioeconomic-status teens. This researcher found that economically disadvantaged women who give birth as teens have healthier babies than do comparable older women. In particular, in regard to birth outcomes for low-SES African-American sisters, those who gave birth as teenagers had healthier babies and more family support than did the sisters who gave birth in their 20s. One suggested explanation for this outcome is that low-SES women are healthier as teenagers. As they enter their 20s, the health of these women declines as a result of poor living conditions and unsafe health habits.

Multiple Gestations

A pregnancy involving more than one fetus increases the risk of complications of pregnancy, especially for IUGR and premature labor. Whereas the average gestational age for single fetuses is 39 weeks, for twins it is 35 weeks, triplets 33, and quadruplets 29. Multiple gestations are twice as likely to have birth defects (Feinbloom, 1993). These and other complicating factors often result in multiple-gestation infants spending more time in the hospital after birth compared with "singleton" infants (Wilcox, et al., 1996).

Assisted reproductive technology (ART), such as in vitro fertilization, has been a contributing factor to the increase in multiple gestation births. In fact, research estimates that ART-associated conception has contributed to an increase of approximately 38% of triplet and higher-order gestation births since the 1970s (Wilcox et al., 1996). Because of the increased risk of multiple gestation, women and couples interested in ART should receive information and counseling regarding the procedure.

Women who have several closely spaced pregnancies also experience increased problems with fetal health.

Maternal Nutrition

A pregnant woman needs an extra 300 calories a day of high-quality food for good nutrition. Physicians used to advise pregnant women to limit their weight gain to 15 to 18 pounds. Physicians now advise their patients to "eat to appetite" and to gain 25 to 30 pounds. Poor nutrition can result in IUGR and low birth weight. Lack of certain vitamins and minerals can cause problems; specifically, lack of folic acid has been linked to neural tube defects. Severe malnutrition increases the likelihood of congenital defects and fetal death. A good diet adequate in protein is most important during the last three months of pregnancy, when the baby is gaining weight and developing brain cells.

To help ensure adequate nutrition for low-income women during pregnancy, the government developed the Supplemental Food Program for Women, Infants and Children (referred to as WIC). This program provides vouchers to pregnant women and new mothers with children to age 5 for high-protein, iron-fortified food. The program also provides nutritional education and counseling.

FOCUS ON MULTICULTURALISM

Pica During Pregnancy

A nutritional problem for women in some communities is pica, the ingestion of nonfood substances such as paint chips, starch, dirt, clay, and ice. Sometimes the pregnant woman may ingest enough of these substances to interfere with her appetite for normal food. As a result, she may experience nutritional problems that can affect fetal growth and development. Though pica can be a craving for a particular substance, it can also be a cultural phenomenon. In some ethnic communities, women ingest nonfood substances with the belief that these substances will relieve the symptoms of pregnancy or benefit the fetus.

A study at a prenatal clinic in Washington, D.C., found that 8.1% of the African-American patients engaged in a form of pica called *pagophagia*—the ingestion of ice or freezer frost. These women ate up to two cups of ice a day and as a result showed a tendency toward anemia. This study suggested that these urban women ate ice chips to help alleviate stress. In fact, the authors found that pica was higher among women who had a poor social support network (Edwards et al., 1994). And, interestingly, the women who ate ice chips used fewer illegal drugs.

Maternal Illness

Several illnesses can cause serious problems with a pregnancy or for the fetus at birth. In particular, several nonbacterial infections referred to as the TORCH complex can cause multiple complications, including blindness, deafness, brain damage, miscarriage, fetal death, and mental retardation. These infections include toxoplasmosis, an infection caused by a parasite found in raw meat and cat feces; rubella, or German measles, a virus that can result in serious defects if contracted during the first three months of pregnancy; cytomegalovirus, a viral infection; and active herpes, a sexually transmitted virus.

Sexually transmitted diseases, such as syphilis, gonorrhea, and HIV, can have a profound effect on the fetus. Syphilis can be passed to the fetus through the placenta. Fetal infection with syphilis can result in miscarriage or eye, ear, bone, or brain damage. A woman with gonorrhea can pass the infection to her newborn during birth, resulting in blindness in the infant. As a safeguard, most hospitals treat a newborn's eyes with erythromycin ointment or silver nitrate. About 50% of mothers infected with HIV transmit the virus to their babies. In infected babies the disease progresses rapidly and kills 95% of infected children by the age of 3.

The Centers for Disease Control (1997) state that perinatal transmission accounts for almost all new HIV infections in children. However, progress has been made in reducing the incidence of mother-to-child transmission. From 1984 through 1992, the number of perinatally infected children with AIDS was on a steady increase, but a decline of 43% was seen between 1992 and 1996. What has caused this dramatic decline? HIV counseling, testing of mothers, and the increased use of AZT during pregnancy are factors that are thought to have made an important contribution to the reduced rate of transmission. What can be done to continue this trend? The CDC recommend that state and local outreach to pregnant women be intensified to further reduce the mother-to-child transmission rate. To assist with this task, the Ryan White CARE Act provides resources for care and services to HIV-infected individuals and also requires states to examine their perinatal HIV-prevention programs.

Diabetic mothers have increased risk of pregnancy and birth complications. Uncontrolled diabetes can result in miscarriage, fetal death, and birth defects. Also, babies born to diabetic mothers tend to be large, with an increased risk of birth injury because of their size. For this reason, infants of diabetic mothers are often delivered early, resulting in problems associated with prematurity.

Another problem that can have serious effects on pregnancy outcome is not a maternal illness but is related to a maternal characteristic—the mother's blood type. This problem is known as **Rh incompatibility.** This problem arises when a mother with Rh negative blood has a partner with Rh positive blood, bringing about the possibility that their fetus will have Rh positive blood. During pregnancy, the blood of the mother and fetus can sometimes mix through small tears in the placenta. If an Rh negative mother is exposed to fetal blood that is Rh positive, the mother forms antibodies against the fetal blood. During a first pregnancy this is usually not a problem. But in subsequent pregnancies, Rh negative mothers who have been sensitized to Rh positive blood will have these antibodies in their system. If these antibodies enter the fetal blood supply, they destroy fetal red blood cells, resulting in fetal anemia and possible death. A fetus that survives to birth is at risk for mental retardation. For this reason, Rh negative mothers are given Rho Gam, a drug that counteracts the Rh antibodies, within 72 hours of a delivery or miscarriage to prevent sensitization. A fetus with this Rh problem can sometimes be saved by a blood transfusion.

Maternal Drug Use

Substances that cause birth defects are known as **teratogens.** The serious effects of drugs as teratogens can be illustrated with the story of thalidomide. Thalidomide was a mild tranquilizer sold over the counter in the early 1960s for symptoms of morning sickness. The drug had been tested on pregnant laboratory rats and deemed safe for use by pregnant women. Although thalidomide was widely used in West Germany and Britain, the FDA never approved its use in the United States, "pending further study." Unfortunately, thousands of women who used the drug in early pregnancy gave birth to babies with birth defects. The most striking defect was short or missing limbs, so that hands and feet were attached to the torso. This story illustrates that the effects of a substance on a developing fetus cannot always be accurately assessed in the laboratory. A pregnant woman is now advised not to take any over-the-counter medications without consulting her physician. Table 5.2 lists several other drugs that have been identified as teratogens.

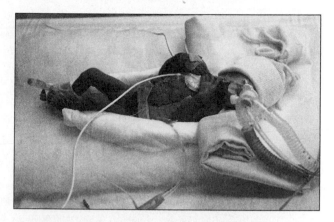

Drug-exposed infants differ significantly in appearance and behavior from normal newborns and require extensive care immediately after birth.

Though the long-term effects of illegal substances on development are still questionable, mothers addicted to street drugs, such as cocaine, heroin, and barbiturates, can give birth to addicted infants. These infants suffer the withdrawal problems associated with these drugs, including seizures, vomiting, agitation, tremors, and sleep disturbances. In addition, illicit drug use can increase the incidence of miscarriage, fetal death, hemorrhage, and low birth weight.

FOCUS ON SOCIOLOGY

Mandatory Drug Testing of Pregnant Women—Does It Work?

Laura arrived at the hospital emergency room in early labor. On questioning, Laura admitted that she had received no prenatal care. When the nurses requested a urine sample, Laura left. Three days later Laura returned, hemorrhaging, and an emergency cesarean section was performed. Because of the lack of prenatal care, Laura was screened for drug use, and her lab results showed positive for methamphetamines. Laura's baby was born lethargic, with low muscle tone and an irregular heartbeat. He was immediately transferred to the neonatal intensive care unit for further evaluation. The hospital notified Child Protective Services.

TABLE 5.2	Drugs That May Affect Prenatal Development
Alcohol	Prenatal/postnatal growth retardation; developmental delays; facial anomalies; microcephaly (small head); heart defects; hyperactivity; behavioral problems; mental retardation
Amphetamines	Premature birth; stillbirth; neonatal irritability; poor feeding in newborn
Antibiotics	
Streptomycin	Hearing loss
Tetracycline	Premature birth; stained teeth; short arms or legs; webbed hands; inhibited bone growth
Aspirin	Bleeding problems in mother or infant
Dilantin (seizure medicine)	Head and facial abnormalities; heart defects; cleft palate; mental retardation
Barbiturates	Fetal addiction with subsequent withdrawal symptoms, including seizures, vomiting, agitation; also can cause neurological problems
Hallucinogens (LSD, mescaline)	Possible chromosomal damage; miscarriage; possible behavioral abnormalities
Lithium	Heart defects; lethargic newborn
Cocaine	Low birth weight; seizures; microcephaly; SIDS, premature birth; IUGR; miscarriage
Heroin (methadone)	Toxemia; IUGR; miscarriage; premature birth; low birth weight; stillbirth; SIDS; neonatal addiction with withdrawal symptoms, including restlessness, vomiting, tremors
Hormones	
DES	Reproductive system anomalies; cancer of reproductive system
Estrogens	Feminization of males
Androgens	Masculinization of females
Tranquilizers (valium)	In first trimester, can cause cleft palate, respiratory distress, poor muscle tone, lethargy in newborn
Tobacco	IUGR; premature birth; stillbirth; low birth weight; miscarriage; SIDS; possible hyperactivity; possible learning problems
Vitamin A	Cleft palate; heart defects
Accutane (acne medicine)	Microcephaly; blindness; heart defects; miscarriage; fetal death
Caffeine	Low birth weight; IUGR; premature birth
Antihistamines	Anomalies; fetal death
Corticosteroids	Anomalies; cleft palate, IUGR

The effects of drug use in pregnancy take their toll on innocent infants. To help eliminate the occurrence of situations such as the one described above, many people favor laws that allow a pregnant woman to be tested and treated for substance use without her consent. These people believe that if the pregnant woman does not comply with treatment, she should be jailed. Although there can be little dispute over protecting unborn children from maternal drug abuse, how effective are mandatory testing and threatening a mother with possible jail as preventive measures? Jannke (1994) questions the ethics, legality, and effectiveness of these punitive laws.

First of all, is it ethical to test a woman without her consent? Such practices may undermine the relationship of health care providers with drug-using families. Such families often mistrust medical workers and fear these workers are trying to take their children away. Testing a woman without her consent with the intent of jailing her only further reinforces this fear and may lead these women to become more distrustful and ultimately to avoid contact with health providers (Jannke, 1994).

As to the question of legality, it should be noted that many of the women who would be tested for drugs or jailed are African-American. Although a study conducted in Florida found little difference in rates of abuse between private insurance patients and those on public assistance or between white and black clients, providers are less likely to suspect white, middle-class women with health insurance of drug abuse. In fact, a booklet produced by the U.S. Department of Health and Human Services states, "Reports indicate that a pregnant woman's race, ethnicity, and socioeconomic status have an overwhelming impact on whether or not she is screened" (Mitchell, 1993, p. 48). So, poor, ethnic minority women may be singled out by these laws.

How effective are these laws? Women who use drugs during pregnancy often know the risks to the fetus but are unable to stop the abuse because of the nature of addiction. Threat of prosecution only makes women avoid prenatal care. In fact, as described above, the mother may avoid reporting to the hospital when she is in labor, hoping that a delay will give her some time and reduce the possibility of a positive drug screen.

Is jail the answer? Drugs are readily available in jail, so imprisoning the mother may not protect the fetus at all. Also, adequate medical care for pregnant high-risk mothers is not available in most jails. Few prisons provide education for expectant mothers on childbirth and parenting (Jannke, 1994).

What about treatment? Often, even when the mother agrees to drug treatment, the treatment options are inadequate or not available. In fact, only 11% of pregnant addicts get into treatment (Cronin, Ludtke, & Willwerth, 1991). Many treatment programs have a long waiting list, many do not take pregnant women, and those that do often do not allow the woman to keep her other children with her during treatment. For an addicted mother, residential treatment, when available, can mean up to a year's separation from her family. Sometimes her children are placed in foster care. If the woman's partner is also abusing drugs, treatment for him is even more difficult to find. Programs that consider the needs of whole families are rare. Even in communities that do not prosecute and jail pregnant substance abusers, the women often experience neglect from the health care and service delivery systems.

The report entitled "Pregnant, Substance-Using Women" written in 1993 by a panel for the U.S. De-

Children with FAS can have many adjustment difficulties such as learning disorders, impulsiveness and lack of coordination.

partment of Health and Human Services states, "The Panel does not support the criminal prosecution of pregnant, substance-using women. Furthermore, there is no evidence that punitive approaches work" (Mitchell, 1993, p. 2). This report recommends that individuals who work with addicted mothers should provide counseling and education, drug treatment, and assistance in general living skills.

Maternal Alcohol Abuse

Though much attention has recently been given in the media to "crack babies," the leading known preventable cause of irreversible mental retardation in the Western world is a common legal drug—alcohol (Abel & Sokol, 1987). In the past, doctors recognized that some infants were born with an unidentified syndrome of facial abnormalities and behavioral problems. Having no other term to describe this particular set of abnormalities, physicians would enter "FLK" in the infant's chart. These initials did not specify a particular medical diagnosis, but reflected the doctors' bewilderment at the nature of the disorder; FLK stands for "Funny Looking Kid." Today, this set of abnormalities has been associated with infants born to alcoholic mothers. Mothers who drink heavily during pregnancy may give birth to newborns with that particular set of birth defects now recognized as **fetal alcohol syndrome (FAS).**

FAS is a set of birth defects with lasting consequences. As previously stated, alcohol abuse in pregnancy is the leading known preventable cause of mental retardation. The physical signs include facial abnormalities such as a small head, small eyes or short eye openings, poorly developed philtrum (that part of the face between the nose and upper lip), thin upper lip, short nose, and flattened midfacial area (Warren, 1985) (see Figure 5.2). Children with FAS have problems with learning, attention, memory, and problem solving along with lack of coordination, impulsiveness, and speech and hearing impairment. Adolescents and adults with FAS exhibit impulsiveness, lack of inhibitions, poor judgment, and a lack of understanding of socially appropriate sexual behavior (Mattson & Riley, 1998). These behavioral characteristics make it difficult for these individuals to hold a job or establish successful peer relationships.

Less severe birth defects that may be related to alcohol use are termed *fetal alcohol effects (FAE)*. The characteristics of FAE include low birth weight, irritability, and hyperactivity in the newborn, and short attention span and learning disabilities in the child (Little & Ervin, 1984). Having an abnormality that can be attributed to alcohol use is termed *an alcohol-related birth defect* (ARBD).

Maternal Smoking

Inhaling cigarette smoke increases the level of carbon monoxide in a pregnant woman's blood. This increase in maternal carbon monoxide blood level decreases oxygen to the fetus. Smoking increases the risk of prematurity, infant death, miscarriage, and other compli-cations of pregnancy and birth. Women who smoke during pregnancy risk retarding the growth and development of their fetus, often resulting in low-birth-weight infants (Jedrychowski & Flack, 1996). Smoking has also been suspected of causing a higher risk of sudden infant death syndrome (SIDS). Other research suggests that maternal smoking decreases inutero fetal responsiveness to external stimuli (Azar, 1997a). A growing number of studies now are showing that the effects of smoking during pregnancy may be long-term. Children of smokers are smaller and show problems with cognitive development and educational achievement; Drews, Murphy, Yeargin-Allsopp, and Decofle (1996) suggest that smoking during pregnancy increases the risk of mental retardation by 50% compared with nonsmoking mothers. Infants of smokers show differences in responsiveness by 1 week of age. Through the preschool years, these children scored lower on verbal tests than children of nonsmokers (Newman & Buka, 1991).

Maternal Stress

In the New England Journal of Medicine, Davidson (1992) states that we need to assess the role of stress in pregnancy as a contributing factor to premature and low-birth-weight infants. Other studies have shown a significant relationship between IUGR and stress (Goldenberg, 1991). In what exact ways does maternal stress contribute to complications of pregnancy?

A mother's physical response to stress could result in reduced blood flow to the uterus. This reduced blood flow, in turn, could decrease the amount of oxygen and nutrients to the fetus. Fetuses of women under stress exhibit different in-utero movement and heart rate patterns than fetuses of less stressed women (Azar, 1997a).

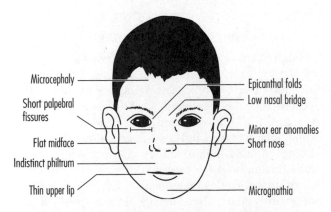

Microcephaly

Short palpebral fissures

Flat midface

Indistinct philtrum

Thin upper lip

Epicanthal folds

Low nasal bridge

Minor ear anomalies

Short nose

Micrognathia

FIGURE 5.2   Facial characteristics of fetal alcohol syndrome (Zigler & Stevenson, 1993)

More important, however, are the effects that stress can have on the mother's coping responses. Pregnant women may cope with environmental stress by engaging in poor health behaviors such as smoking, drinking, and using drugs—activities that have all been shown to increase the risk of premature birth and low birth weight (Brooks-Gunn, McCormick, & Heagarty, 1988).

PRENATAL TESTING

Several prenatal tests have been developed in recent years that allow genetic screening during pregnancy. It is now possible to determine before birth the sex of the fetus and whether the fetus has a specific genetic anomaly. The ability to obtain information about the sex and health of the fetus before birth brings up several legal and ethical issues. (See Focus on Ethics: Selecting for Perfection—Important Questions to Consider, this page.)

Ultrasound is now used almost routinely in prenatal care. During an ultrasound, or sonogram, high-frequency sound waves are passed through the mother's abdomen to form a picture of the developing pregnancy. The procedure is used often during pregnancy, in particular to determine the gestational age of the fetus, location of the placenta, whether there are multiple pregnancies, and to assess the growth and development of the fetus. Ultrasound can identify anomalies of the fetus and other pregnancy complications.

Another noninvasive procedure is **alpha-fetoprotein blood screening.** This procedure is used to detect neural tube defects including spina bifida, an opening in the spinal column. Alpha-fetoprotein (AFP) can leak out of this opening and be absorbed into the mother's bloodstream. The test is done at 16 weeks' gestation and detects the presence of AFP in the mother's blood.

A much more invasive procedure is **amniocentesis.** During this procedure, a needle is inserted through the mother's abdomen into the amniotic sac to collect a sample of amniotic fluid. This fluid contains fetal skin cells, which can be grown in a culture for genetic screening. The skin cells are used for a karyotype—a genetic picture of the fetal chromosomes. This procedure can detect chromosomal abnormalities such as Down syndrome and Trisomy 13. Amniocentesis can also determine the sex of the fetus.

Amniocentesis is usually performed at 15–16 weeks' gestation. Growing the cells for genetic testing takes another three weeks. This means that, by the time the mother receives the test results, she could be almost halfway through her pregnancy. She may have already felt the baby move. The decision to terminate the pregnancy for genetic reasons is a difficult one at this point because termination requires a second-trimester abortion. By the time the mother has the abortion, the baby may almost be viable, or able to live outside the womb. Another problem with amniocentesis is the slight risk of spontaneous abortion brought on by the procedure.

In contrast, a **chorionic villus sample (CVS)** can be performed at eight weeks of gestation. In this procedure, the physician inserts a catheter into the uterus through the cervix and obtains a piece of the chorionic villi—the developing placenta. These cells contain the same genetic material as the fetus. Because these cells are growing rapidly, chromosomal test results are available within a couple of days. The decision to terminate the pregnancy can be made early in the first trimester. CVS is thought to have a slightly higher risk of spontaneous abortion than amniocentesis.

FOCUS ON ETHICS

▼

Selecting for Perfection— Important Questions to Consider

Many parents who find out they are carrying a fetus with a major birth defect choose to have an abortion. This elective abortion of defective fetuses brings up many questions that social workers need to address.

Does this practice of elective abortion mean that living with a disabling condition is now unacceptable? How do these practices reflect our society's attitude toward people with disabilities? For example, there has been a recent increase in "wrongful life" and "wrongful birth" lawsuits allowed by courts. These suits are filed by parents who claim that the physician failed to recommend prenatal testing that would have detected a genetic abnormality. As a result, the parents want to hold the physician responsible for the birth of a child with disability and require the physician to pay damages. Do these actions endorse the notion that defective fetuses should be aborted and that life with a disability is not worth living (Lamb, 1994)?

Street and Soldan (1998) discuss the many psychosocial issues faced by parents undergoing genetic testing. They found that Rolland's psychosocial typology of chronic illness could also be applied to genetic conditions, since both involve the feature of uncertainty about outcome. Parents faced with the issue of whether to abort a fetus might think about these five factors regarding genetic conditions in making their decision: onset, course, outcome, incapacitation, and uncertainty. *Onset* refers to whether the condition is sudden or gradual. Huntington's disease is an example of a condition that is gradual but increases in severity. *Course* refers to whether a condition stays consistent, changes, or worsens over time. *Outcome:* How will the condition affect the life span of the child? The degree of incapacitation is also a factor: What degree of impairment will the child have? Finally, *uncertainty* refers to the unpredictability of the condition, or how much is known or not known about the nature of the condition and the rate of changes that might occur. A social worker might consider these factors when working with parents who have had or are considering genetic testing.

To what extent should prenatal testing be used to determine which characteristics are desirable? In some parts of the world, where male infants are preferred, prenatal testing is used for sex selection. If prenatal sex selection becomes acceptable in the United States, what other undesirable characteristics may be weeded out? A poll of New England couples showed that 11% would abort a fetus predisposed to obesity. How many couples would choose to abort a fetus destined for short stature or low IQ (Lamb, 1994)?

Another question that needs to be addressed concerns who receives prenatal testing. The tests are expensive and may not be available to lower-class families. Will this result in more disabled individuals among the lower classes?

Activists and ethicists urge us to carefully consider these questions concerning the use of prenatal tests before coming to the decision of who does and who does not live.

(Adapted from Lamb, 1994.)

COMPLICATIONS OF BIRTH

Birth complications have been linked with everything from schizophrenia (Verdoux, 1993) and violent crime (Raine, Brennan, & Mednick, 1994) to sleep disorders (Coren & Searleman, 1985) and left-handedness (Van Strien, Bouma, & Bakker, 1987). Other studies have failed to establish conclusively a connection between difficulties of birth and later problems. As we have already stated, some evidence exists, however, that suggests a link between learning disabilities and attention deficit disorder and pregnancy and birth complications. Further research may yet turn up relationships between abnormal development and problems during the birth process, so complications of birth may be an important factor to consider in making an assessment.

One birth complication that has an effect on development is **anoxia,** or insufficient oxygen to the fetus during delivery. Oxygen loss to the fetus can be caused by such problems as maternal blood loss, maternal overmedication, or umbilical cord compression. Lack of oxygen to the fetus during labor can cause fetal distress, which can be detected by an electronic fetal monitor that records the baby's heart rate during labor and birth. When the baby is in distress, the heart rate drops or fluctuates. Lack of oxygen can cause brain damage or, in some instances, death. One consequence of anoxia is cerebral palsy—a condition that can result in movement and speech problems. Even mild reduction in oxygen to the fetus during delivery has been shown to produce problems with early development.

Meconium aspiration can cause problems for the newborn baby. Meconium is the waste material in the baby's bowels at birth. It is black and tarry. If problems occur during delivery, the baby may have a bowel movement into the amniotic fluid during labor. If the baby inhales or aspirates amniotic fluid containing meconium, the baby can have respiratory problems at birth.

Another problem of birth is **malpresentation**. In 95% of deliveries, the fetus is in a head-down, or vertex, position, with the result that the head is the first part of the baby to be born. In 5% of births, however, some other part of the fetus presents for delivery. In a breech presentation, the feet or buttocks of the infant are the first part through the birth canal. Breech presentations carry a higher risk of injury and death for the baby. For this reason, many physicians deliver breech babies by cesarean section. Another presentation that requires a cesarean birth is transverse lie. Here the infant is across the mother's abdomen with a shoulder or arm presenting into the pelvis.

A **prolonged labor** is one lasting more than 24 hours for a first-time mother or more than 12 hours for a woman who has previously given birth. Long labors can leave a woman exhausted and dehydrated. The baby faces a risk of intracranial hemorrhage (bleeding in the brain) from prolonged pressure to the head during the long labor. A baby with severe intracranial bleeding can be stillborn or suffer from mental retardation or cerebral palsy.

FOCUS ON BIOPHYSICS

Cesarean Section

Jane and Gary expected that their first child's birth would be an uncomplicated vaginal delivery. Gary had actively participated with Jane in childbirth classes. As a graduation present, she had presented him with a dark blue T-shirt with COACH printed on the front. Jane's labor was long and slow. She spent most of her labor in bed with an epidural for pain relief. She never dilated beyond 6 centimeters. After 18 hours of labor, the baby was delivered by cesarean section. Now, six weeks after the birth of a beautiful baby girl, Jane is tired and weepy. In addition, she feels guilty about her sadness because she thinks she should be happy just to have a normal, healthy baby.

In the past, some of the complications of birth could result in fetal death or injury. Today, however, many babies are saved through birth by cesarean section. Though a c-section can be a life-saving solution to a birth complication, the procedure itself carries increased risks for the mother and the baby. A cesarean birth increases the mother's risk of pain, trauma, and surgical complications and has two to four times the risk of maternal mortality as a vaginal birth (Mutryn, 1993).

In addition, some studies have shown that women who give birth by cesarean suffer from depression more than do women who give birth vaginally (Edwards, Porter, & Stein, 1993; Gottlieb & Barrett, 1986). Depression is a common consequence of major surgery (Mutryn, 1993), and a c-section is major surgery. A woman who gives birth by cesarean not only must recover from surgery but also must care for a newborn infant. This experience may leave her feeling tired and drained, and her fatigue and depression may interfere with maternal-infant interactions.

Many fathers or support persons now attend cesarean births. It has been said that a c-section is the only circumstance in modern medicine under which an individual watches a loved one undergo major surgery. The support person may be a bit overwhelmed.

C-section births have increased over the past 30 years from around 5% to as much as 35%. This means that, in some hospitals, more than one-third of all babies are delivered surgically. Mutryn (1993) claims that, in recent years, because of the increased incidence of surgical births, cesarean delivery has been trivialized. Even childbirth educators describe a cesarean as "just another way to have a baby." This attitude may overlook the fact that surgery is one of life's most frightening experiences.

NEONATAL COMPLICATIONS— THE HIGH-RISK INFANT

One of the major risk factors for the newborn infant is low birth weight. A low-birth-weight infant is one born weighing less than 2,500 grams, or 5½ pounds. A low birth weight can be the result of **prematurity**—being born before the 38th week of gestation—or intrauterine growth retardation—having some sort of prenatal deprivation that retards growth. In the past, all babies born weighing less than 5½ pounds were considered premature. However, a baby born before 38 weeks to a diabetic mother can weigh 5½ pounds but still be premature and still encounter problems associated with early birth. A baby born at 40 weeks weighing less than 5½ pounds is mature but will encounter the problems associated with retarded fetal growth and development.

Intrauterine Growth Retardation (IUGR)

Growth retardation can occur at any point in the pregnancy. A fetus is considered growth retarded or small for gestational age (SGA) if its weight is less than the 10th percentile of the normal weight of an infant at that particular stage of gestational development. A premature baby whose weight is normal for gestational age has low birth weight because of being born too early; but a small-for-gestational-age baby is low birth weight because of abnormal growth. There is evidence that these babies are at risk for perinatal asphyxia, often requiring resuscitation after delivery (Nieto et al., 1998). As we have already seen, this abnormal prenatal growth can be caused by factors such as maternal illness, poor nutrition, and drug and alcohol abuse.

The problem for growth-retarded infants is not just that they are born small; they are small because some sort of prenatal deprivation affected their growth and development. In terms of long-term developmental problems, these children exhibit increased abnormal brain-wave patterns and an increased risk of learning disabilities (Reeder, Mastroianni, & Martin, 1983). In terms of long-term growth improvement, the outcome for growth-retarded infants is good. With appropriate medical care, most of these infants catch up in their growth during the first three months of life and tend to follow normal growth curves by one year of age (Vandenbosche & Kirchner, 1998).

Prematurity

Seven percent of births occur before the end of the 37th week of pregnancy and are classified as premature. Though premature babies may be growing and developing at a normal rate, they face the problems associated with low birth weight as the result of being born too early, such as respiratory difficulties, feeding problems, and jaundice. The lower the birth weight and the earlier the gestational age, the more likely it is that these problems will occur.

Problems Associated with Premature Birth

During the last month of pregnancy, the fetal lungs mature in preparation for birth. A baby born before the lungs are fully mature can suffer from respiratory distress syndrome (RDS). The baby may need supplemental oxygen, which needs to be carefully monitored, because it has been discovered that high oxygen levels can cause blindness (retinopathy of prematurity).

A baby with RDS may need a ventilator to assist with breathing. A baby on a ventilator has a breathing tube placed down his airway, or trachea. If the baby requires this breathing tube for a long period, scarring and narrowing of the airway may occur. If the narrowing becomes severe enough to prevent normal air intake, then to breathe on his own after being removed from the ventilator, the baby will require a tracheostomy. In this procedure, a small opening is made in the baby's throat and a small tube is placed in this opening so that the baby breathes through this tube instead of through the nose or mouth. Taking home a baby with a tracheostomy can be a scary experience for new parents. A baby with a tracheostomy cannot make a sound, so the parents cannot hear their baby cry. Long-term placement of a tracheostomy may interfere with development of speech.

After being removed from a ventilator, a premature baby can experience a respiratory problem called **bronchopulmary dysplasia (BPD).** BPD is diagnosed when a baby continues to require oxygen after reaching 36 gestational weeks. BPD develops as a result of lung injury, most often caused by mechanical forces, such as a ventilator (Bank et al., 1999). In other words, premature infants who require a ventilator can sustain lung damage that results in the long-term need for oxygen to ensure adequate respiration. BPD is the leading cause of lung disease in infants in the United States and the third leading cause of lung disease in children (Singer & Yamashita, 1997). There may even be long-term consequences for infants with BPD. Singer and Yamashita (1997) found BPD in infants to be a significant predictor of poor motor coordination at 3 years of age. Current respiratory therapies are assisting infants with BPD to have better outcomes.

Another breathing problem of premature infants that can cause distress to new parents is apnea, or periods when the baby stops breathing. Apnea is common among premature babies after periods of exertion, such as following a feeding. Babies experiencing apnea may need to be on a monitor to signal when breathing has stopped, so the baby can then be stimulated to resume respiration.

The reflexes of a premature infant are often weak or lacking. In particular, the sucking reflex is not well established until 34 weeks gestation. A baby born before 34 weeks, then, may have feeding problems and not be able to nurse or take a bottle. These babies must be fed through a tube passed through their noses, down their throats, and into their stomachs (gavage feeding). The baby then has to learn to suck in order to feed from a bottle or the breast.

Preterm infants have more problems with jaundice than do full-term infants. Before birth, the fetus has extra red blood cells circulating in the blood. After birth, when the baby begins to breathe, these extra red blood cells are not necessary and are broken down in the baby's body. As these cells break down, they produce a byproduct known as bilirubin. In a normal newborn, this bilirubin is broken down by the liver and excreted. A preterm infant's immature liver cannot effectively break down the excess bilirubin, so the substance builds up in the baby's system. Because bilirubin is orange-colored, this buildup results in a yellowish orange tint to the baby's skin, called *jaundice* (also known as hyperbilirubinemia). High levels of bilirubin deposited in the infant's brain can lead to a form of brain damage that can result in mental retardation. Babies with jaundice, or hyperbilirubinemia, are usually placed under lights because the light helps break down the bilirubin. A baby under these bili lights must wear a mask because the light can harm the baby's eyes.

Developmentally, premature babies need to be assessed according to their expected due date instead of their actual birth date. Therefore, babies born two months early will have the capabilities of newborns when they are two months old. With good care, many of the problems of premature infants discussed up to this point resolve in the first few years after birth, allowing the children to develop normally. But the smaller and more immature the infant, the greater the risk of long-range problems. With the high technology now available in neonatal intensive care units (NICU), smaller and smaller babies are surviving. With good care, 67% of infants born weighing between 750 and 999 grams (1 lb. 10 oz. to 2 lb. 3 oz.) live. What is even more amazing, up to 44% of babies weighing between 500 and 740 grams (1 lb. 2 oz. to 1 lb. 10 oz.) can be saved. What are the long-term developmental consequences of being born so small?

These very small babies run a high risk of central nervous system bleeding or infection, which can result in permanent disabilities such as mental retardation, seizure disorder, and cerebral palsy (Jason & van de Meer, 1989). Sometimes parents and practitioners face the very difficult decision of whether to use high-technology procedures and knowledge to save a very small infant who may later have severe handicaps, or to let the baby die.

Implications for Practice: The Premature Infant

A premature birth can be a difficult adjustment for new parents. Depending on gestational age and weight, the baby may spend several weeks or months in an isolette, an enclosed infant bed that helps regulate temperature and guard against infection. New parents may feel intimidated by the high-technological and medical atmosphere of the NICU. They may hesitate to interact with a small, fragile infant hooked up to an intravenous line, a feeding tube, and a ventilator. When the parents do interact with the baby, they may find the experience frustrating. It may be hard to attract and keep the baby's attention. Yet, too much stimulation can cause the baby to withdraw. Parents need help in learning to read their baby's cues and in learning to know when to interact and when to back off. The combination of an immature nervous system and a lengthy stay in an overstimulating hospital environment may make the baby irritable and difficult to parent (Jason & van de Meer, 1989).

In addition, many premature infants are born to young, poor, uneducated, single mothers. In fact, low-birth-weight births "are often associated with poverty and its cofactors (for example, low maternal education, high unemployment, and teenage motherhood), which are themselves associated with decreases in child well-being" (Fong-ruey & Brooks-Gunn, 1994). For these infants, it is hard to separate the effects of deficits in the home environment from those of problems caused by prematurity.

Research by Bradley and colleagues (1994) has underscored the importance of the home environment in the development of low-birth-weight children. Overall, the researchers found that low-birth-weight children born into poverty function poorly in all areas of development (Bradley et al., 1994). However, they also found that babies who did well had stimulating toys and materials available, responsive parents who understood and accepted the baby's behavior, and space for play and exploration. The low-birth-weight infant, then, may benefit from a home where parents are sensitive and attentive and provide a rich array of objects and persons for the child to interact with (Bradley et al., 1987).

Birth Defects and Developmental Disorders

In spite of all of the possible things that can go wrong in the prenatal period and during the birth process, most infants are born normal and healthy. About three babies out of 100, however, have some kind of anomaly or malformation at birth. Many of these congenital disorders or anomalies can affect the individual's development.

Congenital heart defects include hearts with openings between the chambers and hearts that are malformed. Sometimes heart disease is associated with other genetic anomalies such as Down syndrome. If the heart defect is severe, it can interfere with growth and development. The baby may need corrective surgery at some point.

Neural tube defects occur in one out of 500 births. A common neural tube defect is spina bifida. In this condition, one or more vertebra do not close over the spinal

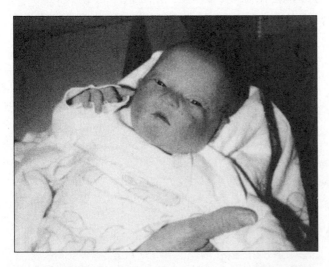

Children with Down syndrome often are not as active as normal newborns.

cord, leaving the cord uncovered in a portion of the spinal column. When the cord bulges through the opening, this increases the risk of fetal death and paralysis.

Several congenital conditions can affect an infant's brain. Hydrocephalus is a condition in which there is excess fluid in the baby's head. Because of the pressure of this increased fluid, hydrocephalus can result in mental retardation, paralysis and lack of coordination, and seizures. A shunt can be placed in the head to drain off the excess fluid. Infants with microcephaly have a much smaller than normal head. Because of a small brain, these infants can be mentally retarded. In anencephaly, the baby is lacking all or part of a brain, and the life expectancy of these infants is very short. The question has arisen regarding the ethics of using these infants as donors for organ transplants. Should an infant with no brain who will die in a matter of days or weeks be sacrificed to save the life of another child?

Several chromosomal abnormalities can affect development. The most common is Down syndrome or Trisomy 21, which results from an extra chromosome. Infants born with this disorder are at higher risk of heart defects and increased infant mortality. Babies with Down syndrome also have some degree of mental retardation, but the degree of retardation varies with each child. Early intervention programs can help these children reach their full potential. Many learn to read, hold jobs, and live in group housing. Babies born with other problems involving extra chromosomes, such as Trisomy 13 and Trisomy 18, usually do not live beyond 6 to 12 months.

Metabolic problems include phenylketonuria (PKU). A baby with this condition cannot metabolize a substance known as phenylalanine, found in protein. This substance builds up and can cause mental retardation. For this reason, babies are tested for PKU at birth. Children with this condition must eat a restricted diet and avoid foods containing phenylalanine.

Babies who acquire brain damage from lack of oxygen or intracranial bleeding, either before or during birth, can develop **cerebral palsy.** The major problems with this condition are paralysis, muscle weakness, and lack of coordination. Some children with cerebral palsy also have mental retardation. A high portion, 70–80%, have some combination of speech and hearing problems, visual problems, learning problems, and/or seizures.

FOCUS ON SOCIOLOGY

When the Baby Isn't Perfect

The birth of an infant with a disability can initiate a time of grief and loss for new parents. These parents have lost the baby they dreamed of and expected throughout the pregnancy. The perfect, fantasy baby died at birth, and they must now adjust to the reality of a less-than-perfect infant.

Parents of a child with a disability often go through an initial phase of grief, shock, and denial. Though faced with indisputable medical evidence of their child's condition, many parents attempt to minimize the seriousness of the disability (Jackson, 1985). One mother remembers thinking as the nurse checked her wristband before handing the baby over at discharge, "Please God, let her tell me I have the wrong baby."

As the parents develop a sense of awareness of the problem, they are often overcome by a sense of guilt and failure. They may feel they are being punished for past indiscretions or for wanting the baby to be of a particular sex instead of just a healthy baby. They may agonize over what they could have done to cause the disability. They may feel that they are biological failures for not being able to make a baby "right" (Jackson, 1985).

The sorrow and grief that accompany the birth of a child with a disability is chronic and pervasive (Kowalski, 1985). Parents of a child with a disability are faced with their loss every day. Each new crisis renews the feelings of intense sadness and guilt.

Such a situation increases stress for the family at a time when the family is also faced with added financial burdens. Families can feel lonely and isolated and cut off from former friends and acquaintances. The divorce rate in families with children with mental retardation is three times the national average (Kowalski, 1985). Investigators have found that families with children with developmental disabilities experience problems with adjustment, poor health, and family relations (Schilling, Gilchrist, & Schinke, 1984).

Research indicates that families with children with developmental disabilities need personal coping skills and an adequate social support network. Personal coping skills include problem-solving abilities, relaxation techniques, self-praise, and so forth. Adequate social support includes physical assistance, information, and emotional support. Supportive social networks are associated with increased personal well-being for the parents and enhanced development for the child (Dunst, Trivette, & Cross, 1986).

PSYCHOLOGICAL DIMENSION

Cognitive Development and Information Processing

True or False?

- Psychosocial development is a continuous process from about the 12th week of intrauterine life through the preschool years.
- There is a high correlation between intrauterine fetal activity and a newborn's level of activity.
- Babies of stressed mothers have higher levels of fetal activity and exhibit more problems after birth than babies of nonstressed mothers.
- Mothers with a fetus who becomes very active at bedtime should place a flashlight under the covers and turn it on.
- A fetus prefers Mozart to the Rolling Stones.
- Fetuses of all cultures really like the music of Boy George.
- A newborn responds to its mother's voice.

Surprisingly enough, recent research indicates that all the preceding statements are true. And yes, researchers have found that individual fetuses, not yet born into any culture, really do prefer the music of Boy George (St. James, 1987). It was once thought that before birth the fetus could not experience sensation, emotion, learning, personality, or thought. New ways of studying fetal behavior, however, have revolutionized thinking about the prenatal period. Advancements in ultrasound, intrauterine photography, measurement of fetal movement and heart rate, and the survival of infants at earlier and earlier stages of development in neonatal intensive care nurseries, have provided valuable insight into prenatal behavior. Information is gained through ultrasound; by recording changes in fetal movement, heart rate, and breathing motions; and by noting changes in swallowing and sucking behaviors in response to stimulation. Noting the responses of infants as early as 24 weeks' gestation in an NICU has provided information on the behavior of the fetus during the last 16 weeks of intrauterine development.

Because of this new information, psychosocial development is considered to be a continuous process from the 12th week of intrauterine life through the preschool years. And enough research now exists to allow us to look at the unborn child's various responses and capabilities.

There is much evidence that a fetus responds to various types of stimulation. For instance, the fetus has been observed to react to invasive obstetrical procedures. During amniocentesis, doctors have noted the fetus to respond by drawing away from the needle, decreasing breathing motions, and exhibiting an erratic heartbeat. Also, during intrauterine blood transfusions, doctors have noted signs of fetal distress, including vigorous body and breathing movements and increased fetal cortisol and B-endorphin levels, an apparent sign of hormonal stress response to needle invasion (Giannakoulopoulos et al., 1994).

The fetus also responds to light. Shining a bright light on the pregnant woman's abdomen causes an increase in fetal heart rate. In fact, it is now believed that the fetus may see light through the abdomen as a rosy glow. Many women report that the fetus becomes more active at bedtime; this increase in activity could be due to the darkness in the womb when the woman turns out the light and goes to bed. Placing a flashlight under the covers could serve as a nightlight for the fetus (Schuster & Ashburn, 1992).

The fetus seems to respond to touch. By the 17th week of gestation, almost all parts of the fetal body will react to being stroked by a hair. Many fetuses will kick back at a spot pressed on the pregnant woman's abdomen, such as by a book or an arm.

In addition, babies in the womb show a preference for certain tastes. Fetuses will increase their swallowing of amniotic fluid when drops of a sweet tasting substance are introduced into the womb, and they will stop swallowing when a bitter substance is introduced (Chamberlain, 1994b).

Communication

Much anecdotal evidence suggests that a fetus responds to sound. When a pregnant woman laughs or coughs, fetal movement increases. Many women report that the fetus is startled by loud noises such as a door slamming. Women at loud concerts or viewing violent movies report increased fetal activity. Researchers have found that fetuses seem to become more active in response to loud rock music, whereas classical music has an apparently calming effect (St. James, 1987). Research has shown that at 26 weeks' gestation, a fetus will respond to a sound vibration. After several repeats of the sound stimulus, the fetus will stop responding. This failure to respond after repeated stimulation is evidence of the ability of the fetus to habituate—a form of learning (Chamberlain, 1994a).

Fetal learning ability is also evidenced by the fact that a newborn responds to her mother's voice over another woman's and to music heard in the womb. Newborns also prefer to hear their native language (Mehler, cited in Chamberlain, 1994a). The fetus hears these familiar sounds, learns to distinguish them from others, and prefers them after birth. In fact, studies by DeCasper and Fifer (1980) found that newborns who had heard, in utero, their mothers read *The Cat in the Hat* twice a day, preferred that story over *The King, the Mice and the Cheese,* which they had not heard. (See the Focus section on page 177, How Do We Know Babies Prefer Boy George?)

Attitudes and Emotions

The mother's emotional state also seems to affect the fetus. Some evidence suggests that depressed or highly anxious women give birth to children with lower birth weights, higher levels of crying, and more neurological problems (Creno, 1994). Excessive crying and inconsolability of newborns has been linked to the mother's score on a depression scale during pregnancy (Zuckerman, cited in Chamberlain, 1994a).

Chamberlain (1994) reports that "current research reveals prenatal pain, preferences, interests, learning, memory, aggressive behavior, fear, crying, smiling and affection. . . . Observation from conception to birth reveals a continuum of prenatal and postnatal behavior in which sensory, motor, emotional and cognitive features are constantly intertwined" (p. 19).

A small but growing number of parents and mental health professionals now believe that a child's emotional health begins at conception. These parents and professionals believe that prenatal meditation and communication with the fetus increase bonding and result in the child's better emotional well-being (Creno, 1994). Whether or not these beliefs hold up under close examination, they can be used in work with expectant parents.

The practitioner can encourage the parents to talk, play music, read, and sing to their unborn child. Parents who see that the baby will kick back at a spot pressed on the mother's abdomen can experience the fetus as a real, interactive being. These activities can help the parents relate to the baby and may increase their level of attachment to their child. Some researchers believe that this early attachment may help prevent later child abuse.

FOCUS ON RESEARCH

How Do We Know Babies Prefer Boy George?

Researchers have come up with some ingenious ways to determine what very young infants prefer. Here's how DeCasper and his associates found out that babies prefer sounds heard in the womb. In one of their studies, these researchers had pregnant women read a passage from *The Cat in the Hat* twice a day during the last six weeks of pregnancy. When the baby was born, the researchers set up an experiment using a pacifier hooked up to a tape recorder. By sucking faster or slower the baby could control what was heard through a set of earphones. Some of the babies heard *The Cat in the Hat* when they sucked fast and heard *The King, the Mice and the Cheese* when they sucked slowly. For some babies, this was reversed so that they heard *The Cat in the Hat* when they sucked slowly. The researchers found that the babies would change their

rate of sucking to hear the familiar story. This was true even when a woman other than the baby's mother read the story. In similar studies, newborns would vary the rate of sucking to hear their mother's voice, their native language, and certain types of music.

Researchers have also devised a method using sucking to determine what an infant likes to look at. In these studies, an infant sucks on a nipple hooked up to a slide projector. Whenever the infant sucks, a new picture is projected for the baby to see. So, if the infant wants to look at a particular picture, he or she quickly learns to stop sucking. The researchers can gauge an infant's interest in a picture from the length of time the infant pauses in sucking to look at that picture.

Social Cognition and Regulation

At birth, a newborn infant is sensitive and responsive. During the first hour after delivery, the baby is usually in a state of quiet alertness and spends most of this time quietly listening and looking around with eyes wide open. A newborn can focus on objects about 8 to 12 inches away—the distance from a mother's arms, cradling the infant against her, to her face. In fact, studies have shown that newborns prefer looking at contrasting, complex patterns with curves—especially faces. Newborns will orient toward a sound, and they prefer high-pitched sounds, such as a female voice. They recognize their mother's voice and prefer it to that of another woman's. Newborns can discriminate tastes and prefer sweet over salty, acidic, or bitter. A 6-day-old baby knows its mother's smell and can distinguish her breast pad from another woman's.

Infants interact with their environment and begin learning from birth, and perhaps even earlier, as we have discussed. Research shows that a fetus is capable of basic types of learning. Infant preferences such as those mentioned above (mother's voice and specific foods) may develop in utero (Azar, 1997b). While researchers do not suggest that parents should begin teaching their babies prenatally, they do point out the importance of prenatal care on the baby's physical and cognitive development.

Newborn infants can imitate facial expressions such as sticking out the tongue. They also move in response to speech in a sort of rhythmic dance. In studies, 1-day-old infants were trained to turn their heads to the right upon hearing a bell for a reward of sugar water. They learned to discriminate the bell from a buzzer and not to turn at the sound of the buzzer. They were then trained to turn for the buzzer and not the bell (Klaus & Klaus, 1985).

NEWBORN STATES

A newborn infant spends most of its time in one of six states. Ten percent of each 24 hours is spent in the quiet alert state, listening and looking around. This time provides a good opportunity for making eye contact and interacting with an infant. The infant may also be in an active alert state—moving, looking around, and making small sounds. This state occurs when the infant is beginning to get hungry or fussy. When really hungry or uncomfortable, the infant enters the crying state—not at all hard to recognize. After feeding and before falling asleep, the infant is in the drowsiness state—relaxed and moving a little with eyes half-closed and unfocused. Then the newborn has two periods of sleep, which alternate every 30 minutes. In quiet sleep, the baby is relaxed, moves little, and breathes regularly. During active sleep, the baby's eyes move under the eyelids and may even flutter open; the baby moves around making faces and breathing rapidly. This state of sleep is also referred to as rapid eye movement (REM) and is comparable to adult REM sleep, in which dreaming occurs, although it is not known whether infants dream.

An infant spends most of its time in sleep states, though sometimes it does not seem that way to tired new parents. Infants also use sleep to control their environment. When overstressed or stimulated, they cope by going to sleep.

NEWBORN REFLEXES

Babies at birth are equipped with many reflexes and survival skills. When placed face down, infants will turn their head to the side or will turn away from something obstructing their breathing. If a scarf is placed over their face, infants will swipe at it with their hands and arms in an effort to remove the scarf. If you touch the side of a baby's face, the baby will turn toward the touch and open its mouth, displaying the rooting reflex. By touching the appropriate side of an infant's face, a breast-feeding mother can get the baby to turn toward her breast and open its mouth in preparation for feeding. Infants also have sucking and swallowing reflexes, which allow them to take in food and swallow it.

When pricked on the foot, babies will withdraw the limb to avoid the prick. When placed in an upright position with feet touching a hard surface, infants will place one foot in front of the other in a walking pattern. The crawling reflex is similar: When placed on their stomach, infants will push against something placed next to their feet. Babies also have a palmar grasp reflex and so will grasp hold of a finger or an object placed against their palm. This reflex would allow a newborn to grasp the mother's hair for security when being carried. When pulled to a sitting position, babies will open their eyes. This is a good way to wake a sleepy baby for a feeding. When startled, babies exhibit the Moro reflex—arching their back, throwing out their arms, and grasping with their fingers. When stroked on the bottom of the foot, babies exhibit the Babinski reflex, fanning out their toes. The tonic neck reflex, or fencing reflex, occurs in the following way. To help prevent the baby's head from falling, babies' neck muscles are linked to the babies' arms. So, when babies turn their head to the side, as happens when they lie on their back, they extend the arm and leg on that side while flexing the arm and leg on the opposite side. If you look closely at babies in this position, you will see that one hand is now directly in their line of sight. In fact, one of the first moving objects babies study closely is their hand. So regardless of the evolutionary significance of this reflex, by turning the head to the side and extending the arm, a baby has something interesting to look at.

THE BRAZELTON NEONATAL ASSESSMENT SCALE

The Brazelton Neonatal Assessment Scale (BNAS) can be used with infants up to 1 month of age to assess such items as the newborn's muscle tone and reflexes, as well as response to and control of stimulation (see Table 5.3). For instance, the practitioner pulls the baby to a sitting position and notes whether she holds her head steady or lets it fall back; or the

TABLE 5.3	Brazelton Neonatal Assessment Scale	
Items Assessed	**Examples**	**Scoring**
Neurological Items		
Elicited reflexes and movements	Plantar grasp Hand grasp Ankle clonus Babinski Standing Automatic walking Crawling Tonic neck reflex Moro Rooting Sucking Passive movements of both legs and both arms	These neurological items are rated on a three-point scale for low, medium, and high intensity of response; asymmetry and absence are also noted.
Behavioral Items		
Specific behaviors observed or elicited	Focusing and following an object Reaction to an auditory stimulus Reaction to persons Reaction to a voice Reaction to a person's face and voice	These behavioral items are rated on a nine-point scale. The midpoint of the scale denotes the expected behavior of a 3-day-old normal baby.
General behaviors observed	Degree of alertness Motor maturity Cuddliness Consolability with intervention Peak of excitement Irritability Amount of startles Self-quieting activity Hand-to-mouth facility Number of smiles	

(Based on Brazelton, 1973)

practitioner holds the baby upright on a table to elicit the walking reflex. In another test, the practitioner rings a bell to see whether the baby will turn toward the sound. Then the practitioner rings the bell to see how long it takes the baby to habituate and stop turning toward the bell. In all, the baby is evaluated on 37 behavioral items and 18 neurological reflexes.

The exam is especially helpful in looking at how babies use different responses and states of consciousness to control their reactions to environmental stimulation. A baby who has had too much stimulation may respond by averting his or her gaze, falling asleep, or crying. The practitioner can help the parents understand their infant by pointing out the baby's needs and preferences in interactions. The practitioner can frame the baby's response in a positive light: "Look at how she is telling you she has had enough; that's amazing." The parents can learn to look for signs that the baby is stressed or that the baby is ready for more interaction, and they can learn to vary the level of stimulation to make the interaction pleasant for both parents and baby.

Implications for Practice: Using the BNAS

Several studies have highlighted the benefits of using the Brazelton Neonatal Assessment Scale with new parents. After participating in the BNAS, mothers of high-risk infants show more responsiveness to their babies (Widmayer & Field, 1980). Other studies have shown that use of the assessment increases the parents' confidence in their care-giving abilities, increases the effectiveness of parent-child interactions, and increases the parents' understanding of their newborn's behavior (Myers, 1982). Fathers who participate in the assessment have shown more involvement in the care of their babies and more confidence in their parenting skills (Myers, 1982). Some studies tentatively conclude that use of the BNAS increases later cognitive development in infants (Tedder, 1991).

The assessment is inexpensive, and parents seem to enjoy participating. Some hospitals use the BNAS as part of their discharge teaching for new parents. Use of the assessment is a good way to introduce new parents to the individuality of their baby and to help them appreciate their newborn as a unique human being with strengths and resources.

Psychological Hazards

In the past, hospital routine separated mother and infant at birth. During the hospital stay, they were reunited every four hours for a feeding. Then, in 1972, pediatricians John Kennell and Marshall Klaus published a study indicating that mothers who received extra contact with their infants beginning immediately after birth exhibited better mothering skills than did mothers who received the routine hospital mother-infant contact. These pediatricians concluded that human mothers experienced a "**sensitive period**" just after birth for bonding with their infants in the same way that other species, such as goats, cows, and sheep, do.

Over the years, many articles have been published on the importance of early mother-infant contact. These findings have been important in changing hospital birthing practices to allow more contact between mothers and babies. In most hospitals now, healthy, full-term infants are handed to their mothers at birth for skin-to-skin contact. Face-to-face eye contact and breast-feeding are encouraged immediately after delivery. Many clinicians involve new parents in newborn examinations such as the BNAS in an effort to enhance parent-child interactions by introducing the parents to their baby's characteristics. Nurses in the NICU are trained to encourage interactions with premature and sick infants and their families. Some believe that early bonding can reduce child abuse and neglect.

These ideas of early contact helped change the way women give birth, but have these ideas set up unrealistic expectations for new families? What implications does this bonding issue have for the woman who has an emergency c-section and is not conscious immediately after birth? Or for the woman who lives in a remote area of an Indian reservation and has no transportation to go to the NICU for regular visits with her infant? Or for the woman who adopts a much-wanted infant when the baby is several months old?

Some practitioners now believe that the importance of early bonding should not be overemphasized to the exclusion of other social and emotional factors that can affect the mother-infant relationship (Eyer, 1994). For example, some of our accepted bonding practices may be in conflict with childbearing practices and rituals of other cultures (Symanski, 1992). In some cultures, other female family members assume the major care of the newborn while the new mother recovers from giving birth. In some Native American and Hispanic cultures, women do not attempt breast-feeding until their milk comes in. And, for cultural reasons, some mothers may not engage in extended eye contact with their newborns.

Research has failed to show that early contact has any long-term benefits for forming attachments (Goldberg, 1983; Grusec & Lytton, 1988). In fact, many researchers now believe that forming an attachment is an ongoing process and that the immediate postpartum period is not the only opportunity for establishing lifelong ties. Mothers of premature infants or adopted babies can and do love and care for their infants. And although evidence exists that early interventions such as introducing the baby to the mother by doing the BNAS enhances subsequent mother-infant interactions, this immediate postpartum period does not represent the only opportunity to enhance family relationships. Finally, early bonding is not the magical answer to child abuse and neglect. Bonding should not be overemphasized at the cost of dealing with the complex social and emotional problems of the family, such as poverty and social isolation (Eyer, 1994, p. 90).

THE BABY'S EXPERIENCE OF BIRTH

The use of medications has made labor and delivery less painful for the mother, but to what extent have obstetrical interventions made the process more painful for the baby? Potentially painful procedures for the infant include internal fetal monitoring, in which an electrode is placed under the baby's scalp, and fetal blood scalp sampling, in which blood is taken from the baby's head during delivery. Babies born by forceps delivery often have forceps marks on their faces for several hours after birth. Babies delivered vaginally often have elongated heads and facial bruising and swelling caused by the birth process. Is being squeezed through a small opening into a bright, cold world traumatic for the baby? What effect, if any, does birth trauma have on later development?

In 1929, Otto Rank described birth as a traumatic event that affected an individual's ability to cope with stress later in life. In particular, he believed that a long, complicated labor led to an anxious and neurotic adult.

In 1975, Frederick LeBoyer, a French obstetrician, wrote a book called *Birth Without Violence,* in which he advocated reducing the trauma of birth. At that time, infants were routinely delivered in brightly lit, cold operating rooms. After birth, the baby was struck to stimulate breathing and was often separated from the mother for several hours. LeBoyer suggested that the newborn receive gentle handling for the first 15 to 30 minutes of life. In the LeBoyer method, the infant is born in a quiet, warm, dimly lit setting. The physician places the newborn on the mother's abdomen and waits until the cord stops pulsing before cutting it. Shortly after birth, the baby is given a warm bath to simulate the amniotic fluid of the uterine environment.

The benefits of a gentle birth, however, are questionable. It is difficult to regulate the temperature of the bath, and it is hard for the physician and nurses to see in a dimly lit room. In addition, there is no evidence that these gentle techniques result in a happier, more well-adjusted child. One study looked at 385 neonates at a hospital in Quebec and found no evidence that gentle birth techniques or other perinatal circumstances, such as use of medication or delivery by c-section, had any effect on infant temperament in the first year of life (Maziade, 1987).

Despite the controversy over the benefits of gentle birth, many hospitals and physicians have adopted some of these techniques for routine births. As was previously described, in many hospitals, babies are born in homelike birthing rooms. Physicians no longer strike the infant to start its breathing, and, immediately after delivery, the baby is placed on the mother's abdomen. The mother can ask for a delay in administering silver nitrate or erythromycin drops to the baby's eyes to facilitate eye contact in the minutes following birth. The baby is often weighed and examined in a warm bed with the mother and father watching. Hospital procedures now encourage early contact between the new parents and the baby. But most hospitals do not give the baby a bath until several hours after birth.

Implications for Practice: The Birth Experience and Development

The birth process may be beneficial to the baby. The contractions of labor help clear the lungs of mucus; babies who are born by cesarean section have more respiratory difficulties than do babies born vaginally.

One study suggests that the increase in catecholamines—presumably caused by the stress of birth—enhances the neonate's chance of survival (Lagercrantz, 1986). However, some therapists believe that prenatal trauma and birth trauma have a profound effect on psychological development. Some research has suggested that a relationship exists between near-death experiences at birth and later suicide, and between barbiturate and opiate use in labor and later drug addiction (Jacobson, 1987; Roedding, 1991). Although these notions are controversial, you may still find it helpful to note the method of delivery and occurrence of any birth trauma when making an assessment.

THE NICU EXPERIENCE

What are the long-term developmental consequences of spending the first three months of life in a NICU? Do the stresses of painful procedures, separation from parents, and overstimulation have an effect on later personality development? At this point, there are no clear answers to these questions.

Some studies have shown that infants who spent time in special-care nurseries were at higher risk for child abuse (Lynch, Roberts, & Gordon, 1976). This increase in risk was attributed to the fact that the infant and parents were separated and did not form an attachment. Although Klaus and Kennel (1976) emphasized the importance of early contact for bonding in the postpartum period, other studies have failed to establish the existence of this "sensitive period." However, numerous studies have shown the importance of touch for the premature infant (Harrison, Leeper, & Yoon, 1991; Harrison & Woods, 1991). Parental touch results in increased weight gain, a better-developed nervous system, and more rapid development. Other studies have indicated that the high levels of stress and stimulation in the NICU affect the infant's blood oxygen level and contribute to chronic lung disease. The increased level of stimulation to the premature infant brain may also affect early brain development (Als et al., 1994).

Implications for Practice: Changes in NICU Practices

NICUs now allow more parent-infant interaction. NICU staff are encouraged to promote parental involvement in the baby's care. An innovative concept in the care of premature infants is Kangaroo Care. Instead of spending most of the time in an isolette, the baby lies in skin-to-skin contact with the mother's or father's chest while receiving NICU care. Proponents of Kangaroo Care claim that this procedure improves the baby's temperature regulation, heart rate, breathing patterns, weight gain and growth, behavioral states, emotional states, and interactions with parents (Ludington-Hoe & Golant, 1993).

A concept for reducing the high levels of stress and stimulation in preterm infant care is individualized developmental care (Als et al., 1994). In this approach, nurses are specially trained to recognize signs of stress (changes in skin color, pauses in breathing, finger splaying, arching, averting gaze) in premature babies and to help the infant with self-calming techniques. For instance, babies are placed in a flexed position for sleep to promote restfulness, and they are comforted before and after taxing or painful procedures. Babies are allowed to sleep, wake, and feed on their own individual schedules. The neonatal unit is kept relatively dark and quiet. Special equipment such as a hammock, soft nipple on a terrycloth strip, and terrycloth bunting is also used to help soothe the infant. Researchers found that these measures resulted in calmer infants with better medical and developmental outcomes than did routine care.

MULTIPLE GESTATION BIRTHS

The experience of having a baby is thrilling yet challenging. Parents may feel excited, while at the same time wondering if they will be able to live up to the tasks of parenting. Parents have these feelings when they come home from the hospital with one baby; imagine what it would be like to come home with two, three, or more babies. With multiple-gestation births on the rise (see Multiple Gestations, page 163), this situation is becoming a reality for more and more families.

Follow-up work with families having multiple births indicates that parents often experience more stress and depression than families with singleton infants (Wilcox et al., 1996). Leonard (1998) suggests that as many as 25% of parents, particularly mothers, experience depression or anxiety disorders, including panic attacks and obsessive-compulsive disorder. Such disorders obviously affect the parent; however, they also affect the infants. Studies show that infants of depressed mothers have increased heart rates, decreased muscle tone, and more sleeping and eating disturbances than infants of nondepressed mothers (Leonard, 1998).

A social worker can assist families of multiple gestation infants by providing a nonjudgmental environment for parents to talk about their experiences. In some situations, the social worker may need to discuss seeking mental health services that may include appropriate medications (Leonard, 1998).

SOCIAL DIMENSION

Families, Groups, Support Systems, and Communities

Each child is born into a family environment. What effect does that environment have on development? What is necessary for optimal development? Research by Bradley (1987) indicates that stimulation and support are the most important requirements in the home. New babies need parents who respond to them and talk to them. They need a structured, safe home with stimulating play and interesting toys. And new babies especially need a small group of adults who are warm and nurturing and eager to meet the infants' needs. (The next chapter will explore infants and families in more detail.)

PRENATAL INTERVENTION PROGRAMS: EVERY BIRTH A HEALTHY ONE

Adequate prenatal care is vital in ensuring the best pregnancy outcome. Yet in many poor communities access to health care is still a problem (Brooks-Gunn, McCormick, & Heagarty, 1988). Barriers to health care in poor neighborhoods include the large number of pregnant adolescents, the high number of non-English-speaking clients, and the prevalence of inadequate literacy skills. In addition, cultural ideas about health care practices may be hard to overcome, so that even when health care is available, pregnant women may not understand the need for early and regular prenatal care.

How then do we encourage pregnant women to seek care? One answer is to set up programs that use indigenous lay workers to recruit pregnant women into prenatal care. The idea behind such programs is that community members can have more influence on the health practices of their neighbors than can a health care professional. An example of this type of prenatal outreach program is Woman to Woman in Tucson, Arizona. This program uses trained lay health care workers in disadvantaged neighborhoods to locate and educate expectant mothers. These lay workers, or *promotoras,* are volunteers who receive 40 hours of training. Following the formal training period, the *promotoras* attend regular group meetings for ongoing training, case review, and support. Outreach workers recruit clients in the community by distributing flyers, putting up posters, and setting up booths at health fairs and other neighborhood events. After a woman is enrolled in the program, other workers visit her in her home to offer emotional support; help her get to medical and agency appointments, prenatal education, and information; help her make contact with community resources; and help her obtain services and information on problem-solving skills. Ideally, outreach workers in these programs can overcome some of the barriers to prenatal care in poor communities and help get better care for their neighbors.

POSTPARTUM EARLY INTERVENTION PROGRAMS

Many new families may be facing less-than-ideal conditions, and few programs exist to help them. After an uncomplicated vaginal birth, if the mother isn't bleeding and the baby is stable, both are discharged from the hospital to home after a 48-hour stay, whether or not they actually have a home. These new families can be dealing with problems such as homelessness, domestic violence, stress, poverty, and unemployment. A two-day hospital stay does not allow much time to deal with these problems, and unfortunately, taking a baby home to such an environment increases the risk of abuse and neglect (Belsky, Gilstrap, & Rovine, 1984).

Some researchers believe that early intervention programs that include home visitation can greatly benefit new families at risk for abuse and neglect. Evidence suggests that these programs improve poor children's cognitive development and school performance (Ramey & Ramey, 1998b) and reduce the incidence of delinquent behavior and conduct disorder (Fongruey & Brooks-Gunn, 1994; Zigler, Taussig, & Black, 1992). Seitz and colleagues (1985) found that, ten years after conducting a comprehensive early intervention program using home visitation, lasting positive outcomes could be observed in parental socioeconomic status, children's behavior and social adjustment, and parent-child relationship in comparison with a control group.

An example of a program that includes home visitation is Healthy Families Arizona (LeCroy et al., 1996). Healthy Start/Healthy Families began as a three-year demonstration project in Hawaii in 1985 with the primary goal of supporting the family's optimal functioning. Results from the Hawaii program showed that, out of the 241 intervention families, none had reports of child abuse or neglect.

The Arizona program screens families at the time of an infant's birth for risk factors that can cause high stress levels. Families at risk for abuse and neglect are then visited weekly by paraprofessional workers. The workers attempt to reduce each family's stress level by providing support, assisting parents to identify needs and solve problems, and coordinating with community services appropriate to the family's needs. Practical assistance is provided for obtaining food, housing, diapers, utilities, child care, and transportation.

The workers also seek to strengthen family functioning. They provide information and activities designed to improve the parent-child relationship and enhance parents' understanding of child development and appropriate discipline techniques. The worker encourages parents to provide the child with adequate nurturance and stimulation and helps parents find appropriate toys and other play materials.

The family support worker assists parents in developing social supports, managing stress and anger, and developing skills to avoid and resolve crises. The worker maintains contact with the family until the target child is 5 years old and ready to attend school.

FOCUS ON DIVERSITY

Fighting the Stereotype— Resilient Adolescent Mothers

My inner strengths are like when I make a goal, I always complete it. It's just something that I am real good at. And when I got pregnant, I—I wasn't thinking of myself anymore, I just was thinking of my daughter. And I did not want to be—I knew I was a statistic already, but I did not want to be one of the ones that was looked down on. I wanted to be one that you could look towards. You know it's already done, then let's see where we go on from there. Let's not just look towards the bad.
— V., an adolescent mother

In American society, adolescent pregnancies have typically been seen as social tragedies and a product of a spiraling intergenerational cycle. Adolescents have been described as "emotionally unstable with poor decision making skills and school failures," as well as being considered burdens on the country's resources due to their financial dependency. Research has focused on the problems of adolescent mothers but has not dealt as much with their strengths and resilience.

Who are the adolescents who are able to successfully adjust to their roles as mothers? What characteristics help them succeed as both students and mothers? Interviews with "successful" adolescent mothers have identified major areas of strength and resilience. These teens were found to have insight or a healthy realism about their situations and were able to recognize their weaknesses without giving up. They were proactive, taking charge of their lives and using the resources available to them in the community. Relationships also played a large role in the teens' success. Specifically noted were strong relationships with parents, families, teachers, peers, and the baby's father.

While these findings are clearly not meant to encourage pregnancy in adolescent girls, they do provide an interesting framework that could be included in parenting and intervention programs. Perhaps the outcomes for many teen mothers could be improved if they learned to focus on their strengths rather than on the reasons they are destined to fail.

Beth A. Auerbach-Dixon (Adapted from Carey, Ratliff, & Lyle, 1998)

Multicultural and Gender Considerations

Up to this point, we have looked thoroughly at the biological birth of the infant. But many cultures include another aspect of birth—the social birth of the child as a new member of the community. In fact, many cultural and ethnic groups have specific rites or ceremonies that welcome the child into the group. For instance, in many cultures during a special ceremony, someone other than the parents receives the child into the society and expresses the desire to help raise the child. In some cultures, godparents accept responsibility for the child. During a baptismal ceremony, an entire church congregation welcomes the child and vows to oversee the teaching and nurturing of the infant. In some cultures, circumcision is used as a birth ceremony. Removal of the foreskin of the penis is a symbolic act that establishes the child as a member of a particular culture or religion. Other cultures may have naming ceremonies to welcome the child into the community. In some Native American naming ceremonies, the new infant is held up to the rising sun as described in the following passage by Byrd Baylor (1977/1978).

> And high on a mesa edge in Arizona they were holding a baby toward the sun. They were speaking the child's new name so the sun would hear and know that child. It had to be sunrise. And it had to be that first sudden moment. That's when all the power of life is in the sky (p. 8).

INFANT MORTALITY: THE AFRICAN-AMERICAN–WHITE DISPARITY

Although medical advances have reduced the overall infant mortality rate in the United States, the current rate is still higher than that in many other developed nations. This variation is due in part to the powerful racial disparities that exist in U.S. infant mortality rates. In 1996, the infant mortality rate for white infants was 6.1 per 1,000, whereas the rate for African-American infants was more than twice as high, at 14.1 per 1,000 (National Center for Health Statistics, 1998). What factors are causing this alarming disparity?

For white infants, the leading cause of death is congenital anomalies, whereas for African-American infants, it is low birth weight. Although many consider poverty and lack of prenatal care to be contributing factors for low birth weight, after controlling for sociodemographic factors, the proportion of low-birth-weight babies is still twice as high for African-Americans as for whites (Eberstadt, 1991).

Interestingly, several studies have found that the Hispanic infant mortality rate is as low as or, in some instances, lower than Caucasian infant mortality, even though Hispanics tend to have a lower socioeconomic status, have less education, and encounter language and cultural barriers that make them three times less likely to receive prenatal care than non-Hispanics (Council on Scientific Affairs, 1991; Furino & Munoz, 1991; Rogers, 1989; Warner, 1991). So, even though Hispanic women have to deal with poverty and lack of prenatal care, their infant mortality rate is significantly lower than that of African-American women. Why?

It has been suggested that Hispanic women have favorable birth-weight distributions in part because of their low rates of smoking and drinking and their strong familial, cultural, and social ties (Rogers, 1989). In other words, Hispanic women have a strong social support network, which seems to mediate the effects of poverty and lack of prenatal care (Mason, 1991). If socioeconomic factors and lack of prenatal care fail to account for the infant mortality disparity, what then is the cause?

More than 90% of the excess risk of low birth weight among African-American infants is related to the mothers' increased risk for high blood pressure, placental problems, or premature labor (Davidson, 1992). These factors can all be seen as related to maternal health and behavioral practices that can be affected by stress. African-American women are segregated into black neighborhoods, lack social support, and experience increased problems owing to their ethnicity. All these factors increase the pregnant woman's level of environmental stress, and this increased stress can lead to poor health habits, such as abusing substances and failing to obtain adequate health care. These poor health habits, in turn, affect pregnancy outcome.

In conclusion, then, to reduce the infant mortality of African-American infants, the United States may need to focus more on social problems than medical ones. This implies taking measures to increase the social support and decrease the environmental stress in an African-American woman's life.

FOCUS ON MULTICULTURALISM

Cultural Differences of Newborns

How much of the cultural difference in temperament is learned and how much is inherited? Daniel Freedman tested infants from different cultures on their "defense reaction," measured by:

- The babies' reaction to a cloth pressed over their noses;
- How quickly the babies stopped crying when picked up;
- How long it took the babies to adapt to a light shown in their eyes; and
- How they reacted to a sudden loss of support of the head and neck.

In response to the cloth pressed over their noses, the white and African-American babies fought the cloth by turning away and swiping at the cloth with their hands. In contrast, Chinese and Navajo babies did not try to remove the cloth, but lay on their backs and breathed through their mouths. Also, crying Chinese and Navajo babies stopped crying immediately upon being picked up, whereas white babies cried for longer periods. Puerto Rican babies were also easier to console and were less likely to be startled in response to stress than white and African-American babies were. In response to the light shown in their eyes, white babies took longer to adapt than Chinese babies. In response to having head and neck support withdrawn, white babies became agitated and began crying, whereas Navajo babies remained calm and unconcerned.

Freedman concluded that what we consider cultural conditioning may in fact have a biological basis. Take, for example, the use of the cradleboard by Navajo mothers. Navajo babies are generally intro-duced to the cradleboard in the first month of life, but it is not forced on the baby—if the baby starts to fuss, he is released. However, most Navajo babies accept the cradleboard and do not begin protesting until after six months, with most babies giving up the cradleboard by one year. In contrast, a study by Chisholm of Caucasian infants raised on cradleboards found that these babies fussed and protested more than the Navajo infants. All the Caucasian babies were completely off the board before they were six months old. Although we have assumed that Asian and Native American mothers conditioned their children to be quiet and compliant, these children may actually have just been born that way.

(Adapted from Freedman & DeBoer, 1979)

CIRCUMCISION

Circumcision of newborn males is a controversial issue. For years, removing the foreskin of the penis shortly after birth was standard procedure in the United States. Circumcision was done for religious reasons, for hygienic purposes, and because many parents wanted their baby boy to resemble his father—and most of the other men in the United States. Other countries, though, had much lower circumcision rates. In 1975, the American Academy of Pediatrics (AAP) decided to no longer endorse circumcision of newborns. Their policy stated that there was no proven medical rationale for newborn circumcision.

Many began to argue against routine circumcision. Critics brought up the possible hazards of strapping a newborn baby boy down and removing a part of his anatomy while using no anesthesia. These critics also pointed out the possible complications of circumcision, including infection and bleeding. Some insurance plans began to refuse to pay for routine circumcision at birth. And the rate of circumcision of newborns began to decline.

In 1989, because of research that showed potential medical benefits such as lower risk of urinary tract infections, sexually transmitted diseases, and inflammation and infection of the penis, the AAP acknowledged the medical benefits to circumcision (American Academy of Pediatrics, 1999).

Then, in 1999, the AAP again revised its policy on newborn circumcision. The Academy's statement indicated that, despite the potential benefits of circumcision, there were no sufficient findings to recommend routine circumcision in newborns (American Academy of Pediatrics, 1999).

Physicians used to believe that newborns did not feel pain and that, even if they did, anesthesia carried too much risk for a newborn. However, babies do feel pain, and the procedure is painful. The Academy now recommends that some form of pain relief, such as topical or local anesthetic, should be used. Additionally, circumcision is appropriate only for infants who are healthy and stable (American Academy of Pediatrics, 1999).

In cases in which circumcision is not essential to the child's well-being, parents should be given sufficient information about the potential risks and benefits of the procedure to enable them to make an informed decision (American Academy of Pediatrics, 1999).

Social Hazards

In this chapter, we have focused mainly on the biological risk factors that can affect prenatal and perinatal development: gestational age, prenatal environment, genetic anomalies, and so on. Throughout the discussion, though, you may have noticed a strong undercurrent of associated risk—the social factors that can have a negative effect on developmental outcomes. Social risk factors include poverty, unemployment, lack of maternal education, parental mental illness, large family, absent father, adverse neighborhood, economic recession, and inadequate health care systems (Fongruey & Brooks-Gunn, 1994). Many of these risk factors have a common denominator: poverty.

Children born into poverty have an increased risk of health and developmental problems (Kliegman, 1992). Poverty is a factor in lack of prenatal care, low birth weight, prematurity, and poor maternal health habits. In particular, low income is strongly associated with child maltreatment (Jones & McCurdy, 1992), and children who are abused and neglected have a higher risk of developmental problems (Goldson, 1991). Of course, this does not mean that poor families love their children any less than affluent families

do. The high levels of environmental stress associated with pov-erty inhibit good parenting by preventing parents from providing a stimulating and nurturing environment (Bradley et al., 1994). In later chapters, we will continue to explore the effects of poverty on development.

DRUG-EXPOSED INFANTS

Newborns who were exposed in utero to drugs have a very low sensory threshold because of their fragile and disorganized nervous systems. These infants have trouble actively engaging in their environments. They very rarely reach and maintain a quiet and alert state. In response to stimulation, these infants spend a lot of time either sleeping or crying uncontrollably. Interactions with them can be difficult, because these infants are easily overwhelmed by the sight of a human face (Griffith, 1988).

The mother of the drug-exposed infant is or has recently been a drug user. Drug-addicted women often come from dysfunctional homes and, as a result, may have very low self-esteem and an exaggerated need for affection. Such women may have become pregnant to have someone—the baby—who will love them unconditionally (Griffith, 1988).

So what happens when such a mother tries to interact with this baby? The mother approaches the baby expecting love and acceptance or at least a smile, and the baby, upon seeing a human face, begins to cry uncontrollably. The mother now feels rejected and inadequate, and the baby is at risk for abuse and neglect. The mother may stop trying to interact with the infant and let him sleep all the time, or she may become angry when her attempts to soothe him fail to stop his constant crying.

Implications for Practice:
Long-Term Effects of Prenatal Drug Use

Little research has been done to verify the long-term effects of cocaine and other illegal substances on infants. Griffith (1992) describes the major risk factors for drug-exposed infants as being related to the fact that chronic substance-abusing women receive inadequate prenatal care and have poor prenatal nutrition. After birth, the major risk to the infant is having parents who continue to abuse drugs. Chronic drug abuse is also associated with an increased incidence of child abuse and neglect. Drug-abusing parents may fail to provide the child with adequate nutrition, appropriate medical care, or a stimulating learning environment.

Children who are removed from the home do not necessarily fare any better. These children may be shifted among foster homes for the first several years of life and may be at increased risk for failure to thrive and attachment problems.

Mothers of drug-exposed infants can be taught how to interact with their babies. Swaddling, use of pacifiers, vertical rocking, and control of intensity of stimulation can help these babies reach a quiet, alert state (Griffith, 1988). Although the effects of prenatal drug exposure are still unclear, some research (Griffith, 1992; Newman & Buka, 1991) suggests that, with early recognition, early intervention, and the benefits of a stable home environment, exposed children can achieve normal development.

FETAL ALCOHOL SYNDROME

Children with fetal alcohol syndrome (FAS) are at high risk for physical and sexual abuse, abandonment, and neglect. These children are hard to care for, even for nonalcoholic parents. FAS babies may be hyperactive, irritable, and may need to be fed hourly. An alcoholic home is often characterized by few economic resources and little emotional support. However, only a small percentage of FAS children remain in their own homes. A study of FAS individuals revealed that by the age of 6, 64% of FAS children were no longer with their biological mother. In this study, many of the mothers of FAS children had died from alcohol-related problems, and many FAS children were in the foster care system, where they experienced multiple home situations (Streissguth, LaDue, & Randels, 1988). Although early intervention can help with development, no amount of social services can reverse the devastating effects of prenatal alcohol abuse on children.

Implications for Practice: Preventing FAS

Prevention of fetal alcohol syndrome involves teaching pregnant women about nutrition and the harmful effects of drinking during pregnancy. Practitioners should screen for alcohol problems at the first prenatal visit and work with women through support groups and education classes to promote healthy pregnancy outcomes.

A manual from the U.S. Department of Health and Human Services states, "The birth of a child with FAS can be a pivotal point in a family's decision to seek alcoholism treatment" (Streissguth, LaDue, & Randels, 1988, p. 46). The authors note that extensive support services are needed for these families to help them deal with the tasks of overcoming alcoholism and parenting a child with a disability.

FOCUS ON SOCIOLOGY

Domestic Violence

Teri arrived in Labor and Delivery in premature labor brought on by cocaine use. Teri is 33 weeks pregnant and has had no prenatal care. After further questioning by the social worker, Teri disclosed that, although she has been abusing cocaine during the pregnancy, her contractions started shortly after her husband shoved her against the refrigerator. She claims that he often becomes violent after drinking and sometimes pushes or shoves her. Teri and her husband live in the desert in a pop-up trailer with no heat, no running water, and no indoor toilet. They have no car. Teri's husband makes it to his five-dollar-an-hour job during the week and often helps at night with the kids. But after work on Fridays, he starts drinking and, by the end of the weekend, usually ends up pushing Teri around some. Teri copes by using cocaine.

Domestic violence is a risk factor for a pregnant woman and her fetus. For many women, battering starts or becomes worse during pregnancy. Studies indicate that up to one in four women are physically abused at some point during gestation. Physical abuse during pregnancy increases the risk of miscarriage, preterm labor, and low birth weight (Bullock & McFarlane, 1989; Newberger et al., 1992). Because of social isolation, battered women have less access to prenatal care (Chambliss, 1994). In addition, because of the increased stress experienced in a violent relationship, battered women have a high incidence of poor

Prenatal Information to Obtain in Making an Assessment

GESTATION

Duration of pregnancy—was baby full term or premature?

History of maternal substance abuse

Medications taken by mother during pregnancy

Mother's nutritional status

Maternal illness during pregnancy

Maternal exposure to radiation, toxic wastes

Other maternal factors during pregnancy: fever, accidents, diabetes, toxemia, threatened abortion (vaginal bleeding), previous stillbirths

(Adapted from Willis & Holden, 1990)

BIRTH

Presentation of infant—was baby breech or normal?

Type of delivery—cesarean or vaginal?

Birth weight

Multiple or single birth

Complications—prolonged labor, fetal anoxia (fetal distress)

NEWBORN

Problems with newborn—hyperbilirubinemia (jaundice), hypoglycemia (low blood sugar), cerebral hemorrhage, infections

Duration of hospitalization (more than 48 hours or less)

---

health habits, such as cigarette use and drug and alcohol abuse, all of which can have adverse effects on a developing fetus (Newberger et al., 1992).

Women do not usually volunteer information about abuse; they need to be asked. During the interview, the woman should be separated from her male partner (McFarlane et al., 1992; Newberger et al., 1992). A woman is more likely to disclose abuse to another woman offering sympathy, help, and support. With a hesitant client, the interviewer should use open-ended questions such as, "When I see injuries like yours, often it is because someone has done it on purpose. I'm wondering if that's what happened to you."

The home situation also needs to be assessed. What is the level of violence? Are there any weapons in the home? Is the woman afraid of her partner? Is she afraid for her children? What previous experiences has she had with the police and courts?

The woman needs to develop a safety plan. Whom can she call? Where can she go? Can she put some money away? Does she have copies of identification for herself and her children (for example, birth certificates, social security cards, legal documents)? The battered woman needs information about shelters and emergency housing and referrals to legal and medical care and to counseling and support groups. Most of all, a battered woman needs to be reassured that no one deserves to be hurt by someone she loves.

Implications for Practice: Prenatal Considerations

In this chapter, we attempted to look closely at those prenatal and perinatal factors that can affect lifelong development of an individual. Complications of pregnancy and birth, hazards in the prenatal environment, maternal habits, prematurity, genetic abnormalities, and social influences are all risk factors for developmental problems. An adequate assessment of prenatal and perinatal risk factors may sometimes provide a clue to possible contributions to an individual's problem (see Box 5.1).

(text continues on page 192)

The Family of a Premature Infant*

Jessica and Travis asked to see the hospital social worker to discuss their concerns for their 2-week-old infant, who was in the hospital NICU. The baby had been born nine weeks' premature. The couple was displaying some fear and apprehension in interacting with their baby during his stay in the NICU. They were apprehensive about their ability to parent their infant. They were worried about how they would ever be able to care for the baby on their own at home. They were also concerned about future developmental problems for their child.

DEVELOPMENTAL HISTORY

Travis and Jessica had been attempting to have a baby for several years. Two previous pregnancies had ended in miscarriage. Fifteen months after her last miscarriage, Jessica became pregnant for the third time. She did not use alcohol or drugs during the pregnancy, but she did continue to smoke. After learning she was pregnant, though, she had managed to cut down to four or five cigarettes per day. Preterm labor began for Jessica in week 26 of her pregnancy, and she was placed on bed rest and medications at home to stop her labor. Several weeks later her cervix started to dilate, and she was hospitalized in the high-risk obstetrics unit for the duration of the pregnancy. Eric was born at 31 weeks gestation and weighed 1,134 grams (2 lb. 8 oz.). The Apgar scores were 6 at one minute and 7 at five minutes. Immediately after birth, Eric began to experience respiratory distress. After a brief viewing by his parents, he was transferred to the neonatal intensive care unit.

_____

*The cases in this book are loosely based on several actual cases. Names and other identifying details included in the cases in this book are fictitious.

BIOPHYSICAL CONSIDERATIONS

On admission to NICU, Eric was placed under an oxygen hood. He required cardiac and respiratory monitoring. Because he was too small to maintain his body temperature, he was placed in an incubator. He required intravenous lines for maintaining fluids and administering medications. Eric's very low birth weight and gestational age placed him at potential risk for continued respiratory difficulty, anemia, infection, intraventricular hemorrhage, jaundice, and retinopathy of prematurity.

Fortunately, Eric's condition improved quickly. His lungs were mature enough for his need for supplemental oxygen to end when he was removed from the oxygen hood three days after birth. He then developed jaundice (hyperbilirubinemia), but that was successfully treated with phototherapy (being placed under lights). Because he was born before his sucking reflex was well established, he required oral gavage feedings. Eight days after birth, he was transferred to the area of the NICU for "growing preemies," where he would remain until he had developed coordination to nipple- or breast-feed and had gained enough weight for discharge home.

PSYCHOLOGICAL CONSIDERATIONS

Jessica and Travis reported that, on entering the NICU for the first time, they found themselves totally unprepared for the sight of their baby. Alongside the machines and other technology, he appeared weak and vulnerable. Travis described his thoughts on that day: "We had lost control of the situation and felt completely intimidated. There were machines everywhere and he just looked so small." Travis and Jessica began to worry about possible complications for their baby. As do many families faced with high-risk perinatal situations, Jessica and Travis became focused on possible medical outcomes instead of on their new baby.

Worry and uncertainty over their child's fate began to interfere with parental attachment and bonding. Jessica and Travis found it difficult to bond with a baby they feared might die or be severely handicapped. Jessica described her bonding process with Eric as a roller coaster ride. "I loved him, but it felt like a risk."

Jessica felt she did not know her infant—that she had lost control of the baby to the NICU staff. She felt inadequate and incompetent in her ability to care for her very ill child. Jessica remembered those early moments following Eric's birth. "He was taken away so quickly, and we had no idea where they were taking him. I looked at Travis and started crying. It wasn't what we expected." Just minutes after finally becoming a new mother, Jessica had relinquished her role of primary caregiver to the nurses and medical staff. This feeling was further reinforced when Jessica attempted to hold her baby. He slept most of the time, and when he was awake he was irritable. When Jessica held him, he would cry, put up his hands, and turn away from her. Jessica felt that the baby was rejecting her.

SOCIAL CONSIDERATIONS

Family Situation

Jessica and Travis were in their mid-20s and had been married to each other for six years. Travis worked as a manager in a supermarket. Jessica worked as a medical transcriber in a hospital. They had recently purchased their first home. Jessica had planned to take three months off from work to care for her new baby, but because she was on bed rest for five weeks before the birth and had been visiting her baby in NICU daily since his birth, Jessica had already used up half of her maternity leave. Jessica was afraid of losing her job, but she did not see how she could return to work full-time with such a small baby to care for. In spite of this, the couple did not see how they could make their mortgage payments on just Travis's salary. They had little savings. There was a possibility that Jessica could work part-time and perhaps do some transcription at home.

Jessica's parents lived in town, and she reported having a warm and close relationship with them. Her mother had expressed a desire to help with the baby's care, but because of back problems, her participation would be limited. But her mother stated she might be able to come and watch the baby while Jessica was working at home.

Groups, Social Support Systems, and Communities

Travis and Jessica attended a Methodist church in their neighborhood. They had many church friends and neighbors who had offered support and prepared meals for them throughout the past six weeks. Jessica's friends from work had also helped out by throwing a baby shower a few days after the baby's birth and providing her with needed baby items.

The community in which the couple lived provided an early intervention program for low-birth-weight babies. The program offered weekly in-home visits as well as regular developmental follow-up in a clinic.

SUMMARY AND IMPRESSIONS

From the assessment, this family had the following problems:

1. Low-birth-weight infant because of prematurity
2. Medical complications of hyperbilirubinemia and respiratory distress with need for supplemental oxygen
3. Problems with parent-infant interactions
4. Unknown long-term prognosis for the infant
5. Family financial problems

Looking at the couple's strengths and resources showed that they had a stable home life with an adequate environment for a low-birth-weight baby. They had family and friends who were supportive and caring. The parents were interested in and willing to be involved in learning to care for and interact with their infant. The hospital staff was very supportive of the new parents and willing to be involved in enhancing

(continued)

positive parent-infant interactions. The community provided an early intervention program for parents of low-birth-weight infants.

After meeting with the social worker, Jessica spent time every day with Eric, initially just observing others caring for him. His primary nurse explained his capacity for interaction, "time out" signals, proper handling, and positioning. The nurse showed Jessica how to swaddle the baby and hold him quietly for a feeding. She taught Jessica to wait until the baby began to look around searchingly before trying to make eye contact and talk to him. The nurse explained that when Eric held up his hand and spread his fingers, he was signaling that he was tired and needed some time alone. Given information and support from the nurses and from the social worker, Jessica was able to interact positively with her infant.

As time went by, both parents learned about and participated in Eric's care. Their involvement helped establish and enhance their bond to the baby. They kept a calendar of events and took photos of Eric's days in the NICU—the transition from incubator to open crib, first tub bath, first attempts at feeding. Thus they were able to share their tiny son's struggles and accomplishments with friends and family.

After five weeks in the hospital, Eric weighed 1,843 grams (4 lb. 1 oz.), was breast-feeding well, and was ready to go home. Jessica and Travis were ready to accept the responsibility for him at home, but the excitement of discharge was still tempered with apprehension about the transition. The long-term effects of the baby's prematurity were still unknown. And though they were now independent in their caring for Eric, they still felt "dependent on the NICU staff for backup." They admitted to still feeling a bit incompetent and unsure of their ability to adequately care for their small son. Travis recalls that "leaving the hospital was almost as stressful as being there, but we were glad to be taking our baby home. Finally!"

(Cathy Jaworski R.N. provided information for this case.)

Hopefully you have begun to see the importance of prevention. Early prenatal care, identification and treatment of substance abuse, parent education, promotion of good health practices, and adequate social support can go a long way in optimizing development and dealing with problems before they start.

For high-risk infants and families, early intervention programs that are "intensive, comprehensive, well integrated into other community services and flexible in responding to a family's unique needs produce the most consistent and impressive outcomes" (Daro, 1991).

Given all the hazards and complications and all that can possibly go wrong, the birth of a healthy infant truly is a miracle.

Summary

DEVELOPMENTAL THEMES

During pregnancy, the couple goes through several stages in preparation for the baby's birth. At first, the couple must accept the reality of the pregnancy. As pregnancy progresses, the woman integrates the fetus as part of herself. She turns inward and begins to resolve her own identity crisis. Toward the end of pregnancy, the woman begins to prepare for the birth and to see the fetus as a separate being. At birth, the couple must reconcile the real baby with their fantasy baby.

BIOPHYSICAL DIMENSION

Biophysical Growth and Development

Conception occurs with the union of sperm and egg in the fallopian tube. From conception to implantation (about two weeks), the fertilized egg is known as a zygote. From two to eight weeks, it is an embryo. During the period of the embryo, most major organs and features are formed. At eight weeks, the embryo becomes a fetus. From this time until birth, the fetus grows and puts on weight. The birth process is divided into three stages. The first stage lasts 12–14 hours and ends with the cervix (opening to the womb) fully dilated (opened) and the woman ready to push the baby down the birth canal. The second stage is the actual birth and can last from minutes to three hours. The third stage is the delivery of the placenta, or afterbirth. Many births involve some form of pain-relieving medication, but long-term effects of these medications are still unknown. A normal newborn weighs between 5½ and 9½ pounds. Full-term pregnancy lasts 38–41 weeks. The Apgar score is an objective exam of the newborn's adjustment to life.

Biophysical Hazards

Complications of pregnancy may affect child development. These complications may include persistent vomiting, vaginal bleeding, toxemia or preeclampsia, and intrauterine growth retardation (IUGR). Several environmental factors may affect pregnancy outcome, including maternal age (mothers under 18 or over 35), multiple births, poor nutrition, illness, drug use, alcohol use, cigarette use, and stress. Alcohol use during pregnancy may cause the child to suffer from fetal alcohol syndrome (FAS), the leading known preventable cause of mental retardation in the Western world. Several tests screen for fetal problems, including ultrasound, alpha-fetoprotein blood screening, amniocentesis, and chorionic villus sample (CVS).

Birth complications may also affect later development. Such complications include anoxia, meconium aspiration, malpresentation, and a prolonged labor. Birth complications can necessitate birth by cesarean section, or birth through an abdominal incision. A major risk factor for newborns is low birth weight, either from intrauterine growth retardation (prenatal deprivation) or prematurity (birth before 38 weeks). Premature babies face many problems, such as breathing problems, feeding problems, and jaundice. Birth defects that may affect development include heart defects, neural tube defects, chromosomal abnormalities, phenylketonuria, and cerebral palsy.

PSYCHOLOGICAL DIMENSION

Cognitive Development and Information Processing

Research indicates that the fetus responds to stimulation. The fetus can see, hear, taste, and respond to touch.

Communication

Research by DeCasper found that newborns recognize their mother's voice, indicating fetal learning in utero.

Attitudes and Emotions

Research suggests that the woman's emotional state affects the fetus. Some professionals now believe that a child's emotional health begins at conception and that prenatal experiences affect emotional development.

Social Cognition and Regulation

Newborns interact with and respond to their environment. They recognize their mother's voice and her smell. They imitate facial expressions, and they can learn. Newborns experience several states, ranging from quiet alertness to fussiness to sleep. Babies are also equipped with reflexes and survival skills. The Brazelton Neonatal Assessment Scale measures a baby's responses to stimuli and ability to regulate those responses.

Psychological Hazards

In the past, many experts believed that there was a sensitive period for maternal-infant bonding in the first few hours after birth. This belief led to changes in hospital practices. However, many people now feel that the first few hours after birth are not so critical and that bonding is an ongoing process.

Gentle birthing procedures were developed by LeBoyer to make the birth process less traumatizing for the baby, but the benefits of gentle birth are questionable. The long-term effects of spending the first weeks or months of life in a neonatal intensive care unit are still unknown, but many NICUs now encourage parent-infant interaction and developmental care procedures.

SOCIAL DIMENSION

Families, Groups, Support Systems, and Communities

For optimal development, babies need adequate stimulation and loving, caring adults. Prenatal intervention programs attempt to get women into prenatal care. Postpartum intervention programs provide support to new families.

Multicultural and Gender Considerations

Many societies and cultures have welcoming rituals and rites to include the baby as a new member. Although the overall mortality rate is decreasing, the rate for African-Americans in the United States is still quite high. This high rate is attributed to risk factors that are influenced by environmental stress. The solution to this problem may need to include social as well as medical considerations. Even though the circumcision rate is falling, the majority of male infants in this country are circumcised at birth. But many people now question the practice of performing the procedure without anesthesia.

Social Hazards

Drug-exposed infants are disorganized and may have a low sensory threshold. They are difficult to care for and may be at risk of abuse and neglect. Early intervention may benefit these babies. Infants with fetal alcohol syndrome are also at increased risk for abuse and neglect. Parents who continue to abuse drugs and alcohol after the baby's birth may not provide an adequate environment for development. Poverty is also a risk factor for infant development.

🌐 Online Resources

La Leche League International
http://www.lalecheleague.org
> Provides information and encouragement to women who want to breast-feed. Site contains educational and self-help information and links to other pregnancy, birth, and health websites.

Centers for Disease Control (CDC)
http://www.cdc.gov
> The CDC's goal is to promote health and good quality of life through the control and prevention of disease, injury, and disability. This site contains a broad range of health and disease information, but it also has specific links to data and statistics related to pregnancy and birth.

Childbirth.org
http://www.childbirth.org
> Provides educational and self-help information regarding pregnancy, birth, and women's health in general.

Planned Parenthood
http://www.plannedparenthood.org
> The official website of Planned Parenthood Federation of America. Provides information regarding family planning, birth control, and reproductive health.

American College of Obstetricians and Gynecologists
http://www.acog.org
> Provides educational and self-help information for health care professionals, women, and teens regarding general health, pregnancy, birth, and birth control.

InfoTrac® College Edition

For interesting materials related to what you have just read, please go to the *InfoTrac College Edition* website and search using the following key words:

prenatal care fetal alcohol syndrome
genetic screening domestic violence
teen pregnancy

Key Terms

alpha-fetoprotein
blood screening
amniocentesis
anoxia
Apgar score
Brazelton Neonatal
Assessment Scale
(BNAS)

bronchopulmonary
dysplasia (BPD)
cerebral palsy
cesarean section
chorionic villus sample
(CVS)
fetal alcohol syndrome
(FAS)

gestation
gestational diabetes
hyperemesis
gravidarum
intrauterine growth
retardation
(IUGR)
malpresentation
meconium aspiration
neural tube defects

polyhydramnios
prematurity
prolonged labor
Rh incompatibility
sensitive period
teratogens
toxemia
ultrasound
vaginal bleeding

Developmental Themes

Stage: trust vs. mistrust. Formation of attachments, acquisition of knowledge, development of a sense of self.

Biophysical Dimension

Biophysical Growth and Development	Physical growth, brain development. Normal development: rapid growth and physical development, from lying down to standing and walking. Atypical development: any developmental disability, such as Prader-Willi syndrome.
Biophysical Hazards	Accidents, childhood illness and disease, lack of immunization, SIDS.

Psychological Dimension

Cognitive Development and Information Processing	Piaget's sensorimotor stage. Information processing techniques and ideas: attention, categorization, cross-modal transfer, memory.
Communication	Infant gestural communication, infants' acquisition of language, adults' infant-directed speech.
Attitudes and Emotions	Development of emotions, stranger anxiety, separation anxiety; differences in infant temperament and goodness of fit, different attachment patterns.
Social Cognition and Regulation	Development of a sense of self, understanding of standards of right and wrong, learn to say no.
Psychological Hazards	Separation and loss, disorders of attachment, failure to thrive, possible mental health issues.

Social Dimension

Families, Groups, Support Systems, and Communities	Interactions between infants and their families, fathers, grandparents, siblings, adoptive family members, peers, day care workers.
Multicultural and Gender Considerations	Issues involve developmental assessment of minority infants, cultural considerations in assessment, gender differences, sex stereotyping.
Social Hazards	Impoverished environment, poverty, infant abuse and foster care, lead poisoning, parents with mental illness, parents with a history of developmental delay, teen parents.

Infancy

DEVELOPMENTAL THEMES

Before modern times, the major developmental task of infancy was simply to survive it. In premodern Europe, 40% of all children died before they were 5 years old. And babies who did survive were not exactly treated like cherished little bundles of joy. Many families, hesitant to invest in someone with such a high probability of dying, sent their babies to be raised by wet nurses (women hired to breast-feed babies) for the first two years of life—until the babies had survived infancy. With improved nutrition and control of infection and childhood disease, the infant mortality rate improved dramatically. Over the years, there has been an accompanying increase in interest in babies and their development. Ideas of infant development changed during the 20th century, from the early belief that babies were "blobs" that could not see, hear, think, or feel to the more recent belief that babies are highly sensitive creatures whose experiences in early infancy affect personality and other characteristics for the rest of life. The first two years of life are now regarded as a special time of growth and development.

According to Erikson, infancy is the stage of trust. Infants are born totally dependent on their caregivers. They must receive appropriate and consistent care in order to develop a sense of security. Infants who have their needs met consistently in a warm and nurturing manner learn that the world is a safe place and that people are dependable. They learn trust. This trust allows babies to develop positive emotional bonds or social attachments to their caregivers. Babies who are neglected, rejected, and inconsistently cared for learn to be suspicious and fearful of the world around them. These babies develop mistrust, which can prevent or delay cognitive development and hinder movement into other stages (Schuster & Ashburn, 1992). A baby must also develop a sense of self, form an attachment to caregivers, and acquire knowledge (Kagan, 1984b). These tasks will be explored in depth in this chapter as we consider the physical, cognitive, emotional, and social development of a child from birth to age 2.

Biophysical Growth and Development

Here's how to have some fun with a 2-year-old: Measure her and predict her future size. At the age of 2, a child has already grown to half her adult height. During the first two years, she quadrupled her birth weight and now weighs between 27 and 30 pounds. As you can see, the first two years of life are a time of rapid growth and development. Several processes occur to take the child from being a sedentary infant to a busy and active toddler.

At birth, an infant's bones are soft and pliable. Over the period of infancy the bones harden, or ossify, to allow the child to stand and walk. The infant's skull comprises several bones that are not fused together, to allow

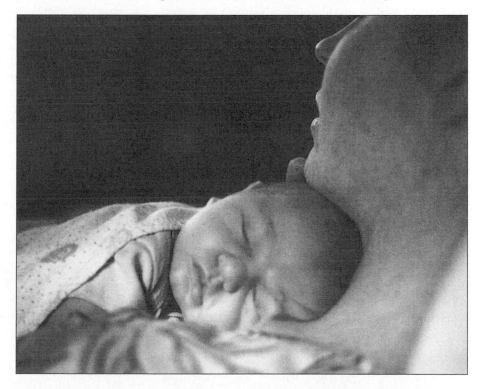

Attachment between infant and a primary caregiver is crucial for healthy development.

molding of the head for a vaginal birth. *Fontanelles,* or soft spots, mark the spots where the skull bones do not join. By the age of 2, these soft spots fill in and harden.

An infant's brain grows to more than half its adult size by the end of the first year. Indeed, it grows so rapidly that, between the seventh month of gestation and the age of 1, the brain gains 1.7 grams per day (Shaffer, 1993). Diet during this period of rapid brain growth is crucial. It takes a good amount of high-quality protein to sustain this rate of growth. Inadequate nutrition in infancy can have a detrimental effect on brain development.

Another concept of brain development is **myelinization,** which begins in the prenatal period and continues after birth. Myelin is a substance that forms around neurons and acts as insulation, allowing faster and more efficient transmission of nerve impulses. Myelinization occurs from the brain downward and from the spinal cord out to the extremities. Motor development follows the growth of this myelin sheath. Therefore, a baby's development is referred to as **cephalocaudal** (from the head to the feet) and **proximodistal** (from the spine to the extremities). So the baby gains control of its body in a downward and outward direction. For example, first the baby gains control of her head and neck and can lift her head up. Then she gains control of her trunk and can roll over. A baby can grasp an object in her palm before she can pick up an object with thumb and forefinger.

Motor development follows this sequence: hold up head, roll over, sit, roll from back or stomach to sit, crawl or creep, move from sit to crawl and back again, pull to stand, stand alone, cruise (walk holding onto furniture), walk. Table 6.1 lists typical ages for attaining motor development in infancy.

Although there are cultural variations in age norms, infants the world over obtain these motor milestones in the same sequence. This is evidence of a maturational theory of development—that developmental achievements are genetically programmed to occur in a particular sequence as the baby grows.

Implications for Practice: Recognizing Developmental Delay

How can you tell whether a baby is developmentally delayed? This is where knowledge of developmental norms becomes so important. To make an accurate as-

TABLE 6.1   Age Norm for Motor Development

	Age (in months) at which:	
Skill	50% of Infants Have Mastered Skill	90% of Infants Have Mastered Skill
Lifts head 90° while lying on stomach	2.2	3.2
Rolls over	2.8	4.7
Sits propped up	2.9	4.2
Sits without support	5.5	7.8
Stands holding on	5.8	10.0
Walks holding on	9.2	12.7
Stands alone momentarily	9.8	13.0
Stands well alone	11.5	13.9
Walks well	12.1	14.3
Walks up steps	17.0	22.0
Kicks ball forward	20.0	24.0

(Adapted from Frankenberg & Dodds, 1967)

sessment of developmental problems, you have to be able to contrast a child's current level of functioning with what is expected of typical children her age (Johnson & Goldman, 1990). Basically, infants may need developmental assessment if they fail to demonstrate a skill at an age when 90% of babies can perform that skill (refer to Table 6.1).

However, recently there has been an increased incidence of delay in babies learning to roll over and gain head and neck control. This delay is the result of a trend to place babies on their back or side to sleep instead of on their stomach, as was the old norm. Parents used to be encouraged to place a baby on his stomach in case the baby spit up while asleep. However, recent studies have suggested that babies who sleep on their stomach run a higher risk of dying from SIDS (American Academy of Pediatrics, 1992; American Academy of Pediatrics, 1996). (See Focus on Biophysics: SIDS, page 203.) Now pediatricians recommend that parents put babies to sleep on their back, and a resulting decrease in SIDS deaths has been observed. However, since infants spend less time on their stomach, they miss out on opportunities to strengthen their arms, head, neck, and trunk by not having the opportunity to roll over or push themselves up. Early intervention programs now recommend that parents allow a baby to have some "tummy time," or special time to play on his stomach, while awake.

FOCUS ON DEVELOPMENT

Early Intervention for Developmental Delay

Margaret's first baby was born with a severe neural tube defect. The baby had a meningocele, or an opening in the back of her head. Unfortunately, the problem was not detected prenatally, and after a long and difficult labor, the baby was delivered with forceps. The baby suffered brain damage. Margaret's doctor told her that the baby would be severely mentally retarded and would never learn to walk or talk or feed herself. He suggested placing the baby in an institution, but Margaret took her daughter home. The community in which Margaret lived provided an early intervention program for infants with disabilities, and the baby started a formal program at the age of 3 months. Margaret spent hours each day doing exercises and activities with her infant. And, although the child would never be completely normal, at the age of 6 Margaret's daughter could not only walk and talk and feed herself but also every day after school she would go outside and roller-skate around the block.

In the 1970s, there was an increase in infant stimulation programs for infants with disabilities. Before this time, parents were encouraged to institutionalize babies with mental retardation. But then information began to accumulate on the abilities of very young babies. Researchers learned that infants could process information from birth; newborns could see and hear and understand (Pines, 1982). So, programs were developed to begin interventions for infants with disabilities. In 1986, PL99-457 (Part H), Services for Infants and Toddlers with Handicapping Conditions, was enacted to provide special services to children with disabilities from birth.

Most communities now provide infant stimulation or early intervention programs for infants with disabilities and their families. In most cases, the parents are involved as the infant's teachers. The parents are taught exercises and activities to perform with the child at home to enhance the child's development. For instance, babies with Down syndrome have weak muscles and poor muscle tone. For this reason, these babies have delayed motor development. So, at an age when typical babies are lifting their heads, grabbing at interesting objects, and learning from these interactions, Down syndrome babies, who because of weak neck muscles cannot lift their heads, receive less stimulation and interaction. By exercising the baby's neck, parents can help strengthen the baby's muscles so the baby can lift its head. Helping babies with mental retardation lift their heads, reach for objects, move around, and interact with the environment enriches their experiences and enhances their cognitive development as well as their physical development.

What about other disabling conditions? Infants with visual impairments are delayed in their ability to reach for objects, crawl, and walk. Blind infants will not begin to crawl until their second year (Zigler & Stevenson, 1993). Parents of blind infants can be taught to use auditory and other forms of sensory stimulation to enhance their infants' development. Hearing-impaired infants often appear to develop normally for the first few months. These babies begin to vocalize and babble at the same age that unimpaired infants do. However, after nine months these infants show problems in learning language. The language deficit affects acquisition of other cognitive skills, and parents who do not know that their baby is deaf may think the child has some mental retardation. Early detection of and intervention for a hearing impairment can enhance this child's development.

Biophysical Hazards

To new parents, babies may often seem like accidents just waiting to happen. Infants climb on chairs that topple over, fall down stairs, eat poisonous plants, choke on small objects, and fall headfirst into buckets of water. Infants require constant attention to protect them from injury. Parents need to babyproof the house carefully and to anticipate possible hazards to their child. Parents should remember that not all homes are babyproofed, which means that, when visiting other people's homes, they should be alert to possible hazards such as swimming pools, medication bottles within the baby's reach, and exposed electrical outlets. Table 6.2 lists some considerations for preventing accidents and injury.

ILLNESS

Although babies are born with some natural immunity to rubella, measles, mumps, polio, and diphtheria, this immunity does not last past the age of 3 to 6 months. In addition, babies are susceptible to chicken pox, tetanus, whooping cough (pertussis), and strep infections during this time (Foster, Hunsberger, & Anderson, 1989). As stated at the beginning of this chapter, in the past many children did not survive infancy because of these diseases. In fact, pertussis is still a major problem in the United States; pertussis vaccine is the only vaccine that has not reached immunization levels of 90% (Teitelbaum & Edmunds, 1999). Immunization is an important issue for both parents and children; Table 6.3 lists the immunization schedule for childhood.

Babies are also very susceptible to upper respiratory infections (colds). Exposure to tobacco smoke can increase the risk of respiratory problems for infants, placing them at higher risk for bronchitis and pneumonia. Respiratory syncytial virus (RSV) is the most common respiratory pathogen in infants and children. RSV infection causes respiratory distress in infants and results in increased risk

of hospitalization for many infants, especially premature infants, during the winter months.

Meningitis, a bacterial infection of the lining of the brain, is especially hazardous to infants. This illness can result in a 1–5% death rate or in neurological complications, including learning disabilities. Babies with meningitis are irritable, run a fever, have a high-pitched cry, and often have bulging fontanelles.

Colic can develop between 2 and 6 weeks of age. Colic refers to patterns of sudden and unexplained outbursts of inconsolable crying. The outbursts typically occur at about the same time each day and spontaneously resolve. At other times the infant cries normally. Colic has been attributed to food allergies, an immature digestive system or immature nervous system, and to a nervous caregiver. To the relief of parents, babies outgrow this condition by about 3 months of age.

TABLE 6.2	Preventing Accidents and Injury in Infancy
Hazard	**Prevention**
Falls	Don't leave infant unrestrained on any surface. Even very small infants can move and fall off a bed or couch. Don't place a baby in an infant seat on a table. The baby may wiggle the seat off and fall. Avoid use of infant walkers.
Poisoning	Lock up all hazardous materials, including cleaning supplies and medications. Use childproof caps on medications. Keep poisonous plants out of reach. Keep number of poison control near phone.
Choking	Keep small objects out of reach. Don't tie anything around baby's neck, including the pacifier. Cut food into small pieces. Avoid hard foods such as nuts, hard candy. Parents and caregivers should learn the Heimlich maneuver.
Suffocation	Don't prop the bottle to feed. Keep plastic bags out of reach. Remove doors of old refrigerators. Don't shake baby powder onto baby (put in your hand and apply). Avoid use of pillows, soft toys, and several blankets in crib. Use approved crib. Watch for drapery or blinds cords near crib and within baby's reach throughout the house.
Drowning	Never leave baby unattended in bathtub. Keep toilet seat down. Be careful of all containers of water. Babies can drown in only a few inches of water in a bucket. Use pool safety gates. Never leave baby unattended near pool or any water. Parents and caregivers should take a CPR class.
Burns	Lower temperature of water heater to 120°–130°. Check temperature of bathwater with elbow. Push pot handles toward back of stove. Use nonflammable clothing. Install smoke detectors. Don't heat bottles in microwave.
Auto accidents	Always buckle child into approved car seat. Never place a baby in the front seat of a vehicle that has air bags.

TABLE 8.3   Immunization Schedule for Infants

Age	Immunization
Birth	Hepatitis B (Hep-B)
1–4 months	Hep-B
2 months	Diphtheria, tetanus, pertussis (DTP), polio (OPV), hemophilus influenza (Hib) (for meningitis), rotavirus (RV)
4 months	DTP, OPV, Hib, RV
6 months	DTP, Hib, RV
6–18 months	OPV, Hep-B
12–15 months	Hib, measles, mumps, and rubella (MMR)
12–18 months	Varicella (chicken pox)
15–18 months	DTP
4–6 years	DTP, OPV, MMR
11–12 years	Tetanus, diphtheria

(Based on recommendations by the Advisory Committee on Immunization Practices, the American Academy of Pediatrics, and the American Academy of Family Physicians, 1999)

FOCUS ON BIOPHYSICS

Sudden Infant Death Syndrome

At 4:00 in the morning, Dana woke sweating. Something was wrong. She had put her 2-month-old baby to bed at 7:00 P.M. the previous evening, and he was still asleep. He had never slept longer than six hours before. In fact, lately he had been sleeping poorly because he had a cold and had been waking often with a stuffy nose. Dana went to check on the baby and found him lying on his stomach, wedged up at the top corner of his crib. The sheet was crumpled, his blankets were kicked off, and there was a little blood on the mattress. Dana put her hand on the baby's back and discovered he was not breathing. Dana's screams woke her husband, John, and he called the paramedics. Unfortunately, efforts to resuscitate the baby failed, and he was pronounced dead at the hospital.

Sudden infant death syndrome (SIDS) refers to the unexpected death of an infant, for which no physical cause can be found. SIDS is the most common cause of death in the first year of life (Krugman et al., 1994). SIDS occurs in approximately 1 in 400 babies and re-

sults in 7,000 deaths each year. Although investigators still do not know what causes SIDS, several risk factors have been identified. SIDS occurs more often in male infants, low-birth-weight infants, premature infants, babies with low Apgar scores, babies whose sibling previously died of SIDS, and babies who sleep on their stomachs (Martinez, 1996). Several maternal factors also increase the risk of SIDS; these factors include young age, multiple births, smoking, prenatal drug abuse, low SES, no prenatal care, and closely spaced pregnancies (Martinez, 1996).

Several theories on what causes SIDS have been proposed, but none of these theories is conclusive. The latest evidence suggests that babies who die of SIDS have a problem with their lungs. Autopsies of SIDS babies often reveal changes in the airway. Many babies who die of SIDS had a viral infection. The majority of babies had blood-stained frothy secretions in their mouths and in the bed, which showed signs of a struggle (Berry, 1993). These clues—an infection, signs of a struggle, and changes in the airway—suggest that the babies do not just stop breathing in their sleep; something may be going on in the babies' lungs (Martinez, 1996). Other evidence contributes to this notion. Premature babies have more respiratory problems and a higher risk of SIDS. Breathing secondhand smoke can contribute to respiratory problems, and babies of mothers who smoke have a definite increase in risk of SIDS.

What about putting babies to sleep on their stomach? As mentioned previously, babies have been put to bed this way for many years. In 1992, the American Academy of Pediatrics began recommending that babies be put to sleep on their sides or backs, rather than on their stomachs. Since the release of the Academy's recommendations, there has been a 15–20% decrease in the number of SIDS deaths in the United States (American Academy of Pediatrics, 1996). In countries where this position has been discouraged for many years, the death rate from SIDS has been reduced by 50% (Willinger, Hoffman, & Hartford, 1994). In 1996, revisions to the Academy's original recommendations were made. These included comments that the supine position (sleeping on the back) confers the lowest risk, as opposed to the side position, and that soft sleeping surfaces and gas-trapping objects in the crib be avoided.

Note that the current recommendations are for healthy infants only. Infants with respiratory or digestive problems should be put to bed as recommended by their pediatrician (American Academy of Pediatrics, 1996). "Tummy time" is recommended during periods when the infant is awake and supervised to assist in motor development and to help avoid the formation of flat spots on the back of his skull, which may result from sleeping in a supine position.

Other evidence suggests that babies who fall into deep sleep may be at higher risk. As an example, babies who sleep alone can go into deep sleep, but infants who sleep with their caregiver adjust their sleep patterns to synchronize with the caregiver's. So, as the caregiver drifts in and out of deep and light sleep, the infant's sleep patterns follow. In fact, rates of SIDS are lower in countries where infants routinely sleep with their mothers (Stipp, 1995). However, a lack of scientific evidence in support of these observations has prevented the AAP from recommending bed sharing for SIDS prevention (American Academy of Pediatrics, 1997).

As yet, no one knows what causes babies to die unexpectedly, but parents who lose an infant this way often blame themselves and try to determine what they did wrong. The parents may believe that putting the baby down alone in the room with a cold for that long nap was the cause. Their grief is almost unimaginable. Parents coping with the loss of an infant to SIDS need much support. Although finding a cause for SIDS may help prevent future deaths, at present no particular cause has been identified.

PSYCHOLOGICAL DIMENSION

Cognitive Development and Information Processing

Suddenly a piece of space stands out. It's a pillar, thin and taut. It stands motionless and sings out a bright melody. Now, from close by, different notes drift in.

There is nearby another pillar of space. It, too, sings— but in harmony with the first. The two melodies mingle in a tight duet, one melody loud, the other quiet. . . . Then from somewhere else, sounds a different note. A shooting star, it flashes past and quickly disappears. (Stern, 1990, p. 32)

In this passage from *Diary of a Baby,* Daniel Stern describes a 6-week-old infant turning his head and seeing first one crib bar and then another. Try to imagine what the shooting star could be. It is the baby's hand passing through his line of vision.

People have long been intrigued with trying to determine what babies think about, what they perceive, and how they process information. In the past, theories of infant development were based on the clinical infant—a construct developed by the therapist working with adult clients trying to remember early experience. Theories of infant development from developmental psychology are based on the observed infant. In this case, researchers set up experiments and observe babies to determine their responses and capabilities (Stern, 1985). Jean Piaget was well regarded for his ability to observe human development.

PIAGET'S SENSORIMOTOR STAGE

Piaget developed his theories of cognitive development by closely observing first his own children and then others. He classified the time from birth to age 2 as the *sensorimotor stage.* During this stage, the infant goes from having mostly random reflex actions to displaying **goal-directed behavior.** For example, instead of just watching a hand shoot past her eyes, she learns to use that hand to push a chair over to the kitchen counter so she can climb up on the counter and get cookies. Goal-directed behavior, then, is putting together a series of actions to achieve a desired result. The infant in this stage also develops **object permanence**—the ability to hold an image of an object or person in one's mind. According to Piaget, very young infants forget an object as soon as they can no longer see it. For instance, if you show a 4-month-old infant a toy and then place that toy under a cloth, the baby will not lift the cloth to find the toy even if the baby saw you put it there. But 2-year-olds remember that those cookies are on the counter even though they can't see them. They hold the image of the cookies in their mind and thoughtfully solve the problem of how to get to them.

Piaget's sensorimotor stage is divided into six substages.

1. *Reflex activity (birth to 1 month):* Piaget believed that the reflexes present at birth are the basic building blocks for intelligent behavior. Touch the baby on the cheek, and the baby will turn toward the touch with open mouth. Place a nipple in the baby's mouth, and the baby will suck. Place an object in the baby's palm, and the baby will grasp it. Ring a bell, and the baby will look for it. These actions are not intentional but are the result of inborn reflexes. The baby quickly begins to learn about the environment through these random reflex actions.

2. *Primary circular reactions (1 to 4 months):* During this stage, the baby learns that certain reflex actions bring about pleasurable results. The baby then begins to repeat those actions. For instance, babies learn that sucking to eat reduces hunger and gives comfort. If babies accidentally place their hand in their mouth, they will suck on it and find this sucking comforting. They will then repeat placing the hand in the mouth for comfort. Through accidental reflex activity, the baby acquires new patterns of behavior. The baby is focused on its body (primary) and on repeated actions (circular). Piaget believed that babies in this stage could repeat actions only they themselves initiated and could not imitate actions of others.

3. *Secondary circular reactions (4 to 8 months):* Now babies' focus shifts from their own body to objects in the world (secondary). They learn to control not just their body but other things as well and will repeat random actions for their results. For instance, if a baby is lying in a crib looking at a mobile and the baby kicks its feet and the mobile moves (and the baby finds this movement interesting), the baby will kick its feet again to see whether the mobile will move. Babies at this stage will recreate actions to see interesting results.

4. *Coordination of secondary schemes (8 to 12 months):* In this stage, the baby learns to take several random activities and put them together to achieve a goal. This is known as **intentional means-end behavior.** Now the baby can begin to solve problems. The baby also begins to develop object permanence. If you hide a toy under a cloth, a 9-month-old baby will lift the cloth to find the toy. But if you then hide the toy under a different cloth, the baby will continue to search for the toy under the original one. Even if you show the baby you are hiding the toy in a new place, the baby will still look in the original hiding place. Another characteristic of this stage is that babies are able to imitate actions performed by others. If you show babies how to clap, they can repeat the action after watching you, but they cannot initiate the action on their own.

5. *Tertiary circular reactions (12 to 18 months):* Babies at this age are little explorers. They no longer rely on random activity but can now think up activities on their own. If you show babies at this age that you are hiding the toy under one cloth and then show them that you are hiding it under a second cloth, they will be able to find the toy. But if you put the toy under a box and then place the box under a cloth, then tip the toy out of the box and leave it under the cloth and return the box to its original location, the babies will search for the toy under the box. They will not look under the cloth even though they can see the bulge the toy makes in the fabric. Babies at this stage are said to be unable to understand **invisible displacements.**

6. *Beginning of representational thought (18 to 24 months):* Here babies make a transition from being action oriented to being symbol oriented. Babies now have full object permanence and can hold an image of an object or person in their mind and solve problems. So, they will search for a toy even if they didn't see you hide it. Babies will look for cookies in the cookie jar on the counter because they remember that is where the cookies are kept, even though they didn't see you place them there. Babies can keep the image of cookies in their mind and figure out how to get to them. Now babies can repeat actions without having to watch someone else, so they can clap for themselves when they are pleased with their accomplishment.

INFORMATION PROCESSING

New research is finding that babies may be more competent than Piaget ever imagined. Innovative techniques make it possible to observe infants much more closely than Piaget did. These techniques look at how babies actually process the information they receive through sensory stimulation.

One way of observing babies is by studying their attention patterns. Infants display **obligatory attention;** that is, they will look intently at or fixate on something interesting and not be distracted from it (Stern, 1990). Researchers can determine how babies process information by looking at how long it takes a baby to stop paying attention to the same stimulus (**habituation**) and how long it takes the baby to become interested in a new stimulus (**dishabituation**). Babies will look longer at something they find interesting. After becoming familiar or bored with that stimulus, they stop looking at it, or habituate; then they will pay attention to a new stimulus, or dishabituate.

Researchers have discovered that babies not only pay attention to stimuli they have never seen before, but they also pay more attention to events they have some control over, such as watching a mobile they can shake by kicking, and to events they did not expect to happen. Using this information, researchers have discovered some amazing capabilities of young infants.

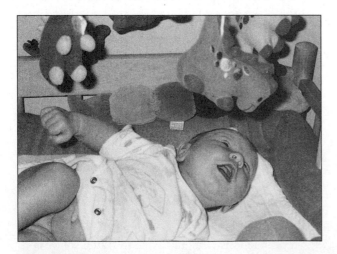

Mobiles are excellent devices for getting a baby to focus attention on objects in the external environment.

Cohen and Strauss (1979) found that 30-week-old infants were able to categorize (place objects into groups) on the basis of similarities. They habituated one group of infants to a single individual (Sally) by showing the babies a picture of a female face until they became bored with it and looked away. They habituated another group of infants to a series of individuals (Sally, Mary, Barbara, and Joan). These infants paid less attention to each subsequent picture of a new female face. Then each group was shown a picture of a new face (Elizabeth). The infants who had seen only Sally dishabituated to Elizabeth and looked intently at that picture. The infants who had seen the series of faces (Sally, Mary, Barbara, and Joan) were not interested in another female face and remained habituated—they would not look at the new face. Although the individual stimulus was new, these infants had formed a category for the series of female faces and were then habituated to the category. Research has shown that infants as young as 6 or 7 months display **categorization** (Bjorklund & Bjorklund, 1992).

Some research suggests that very small babies can transfer information gained from one sense to another sense. This process is referred to as **cross-modal transfer.** An example would be exploring an unseen object with your hands and then trying to recognize a picture of that object. Piaget had argued that babies learn this capability gradually through repeated associated actions such as watching their hands grasp objects. But current research suggests that this ability may be present in very young infants.

In one study (Meltzoff & Borton, 1979), 3-week-old infants were blindfolded and given a pacifier with an unusual nipple shape to suck (see Figure 6.1). The nipple was then removed and placed next to another unusually shaped nipple. When the blindfold was removed, the babies would look longest at the nipple they had sucked. These babies were able to detect the shape of the nipple in their mouths and then, based on that information, determine the visual appearance of the nipple. But wait, didn't we just state that babies who become familiar with an object, or habituate, prefer to look at an object they have never seen before? If this is true, then it would be expected that an infant shown two nipples would prefer to look at the one that they had *not* sucked. Yet in this study, the infants looked at the nipples they *had* sucked. This apparent

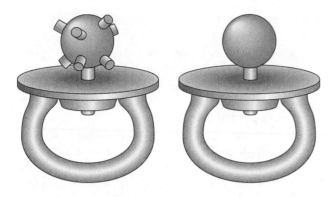

FIGURE 8.1   Pacifiers used to test cross-modal transfer (Meltzoff & Borton, 1979)

contradiction may be explained by the fact that the babies in the Meltzoff and Borton study were only 3 weeks of age. Some researchers argue that very young infants may take longer to habituate to a new stimulus and therefore would look at the same nipple they had sucked. As babies become older, they habituate more quickly, and their ability for cross-modal transfer becomes more developed (Rose et al., 1998).

Rose and colleagues (1998) found support for an interesting hypothesis regarding cross-modal transfer in infants and children. They found that cross-modal performance was better when tactile exploration was done with the left hand. Why would the left hand be better? First, sensory input from one side of the body goes primarily to the opposite hemisphere of the brain. Second, the right cerebral hemisphere, which is primarily processing the information taken in using the left hand, has a special ability for tactile processing. Taken together, these two factors produce the so-called left-hand advantage in cross-modal transfer. So, if a baby touches an object hidden in a box with the left hand, he will be able to identify it by sight more easily than if he touches it with his right hand.

Other research has found that infants have better memories than had been believed. Rovee-Collier and Colleagues (1980) placed 2½-month-old infants in a crib and attached a mobile to a leg or an arm with a ribbon. The babies learned to shake the mobile by moving that arm or leg. Two weeks later, when placed back in the crib with the same mobile, the babies tried to shake the mobile by moving the appropriate limb, even though the ribbon was not attached.

Indeed, studies seem to show that babies have an innate sense of how the world works. For example, in experiments conducted by Spelke (1994), babies attended more to unexpected physical actions, such as a ball seeming to roll through a solid barrier or a ball hanging in midair. Spelke found that babies can also recognize the position of a moving ball when it leaves their view and then look to where they expect the ball to be when it comes back into sight. Another researcher, Wynn (1992), discovered that babies seem to have a sense of addition and subtraction. In these experiments, researchers would show a 5-month-old baby a doll and then place the doll behind a screen. Then they would show the baby another doll and place that one behind the screen. They would then remove the screen to reveal either two or three dolls. The babies would look longer at the unexpected result of three dolls instead of two.

Sophisticated technology has also contributed to knowledge on information processing. Haith and Canfield (1991) had babies lie in a black box and look at a TV screen. The babies would see a sequence of colorful objects appear in different positions while the researcher watched the babies' eye movements with an infrared camera hooked up to a computer. After seeing a particular sequence five times, the babies would begin to predict where the next object would appear and look to that position. With practice, babies as young as 3 months could remember a four-step series. Two weeks later, when they were placed in the box, they still remembered that series.

This new research indicates that object permanence may occur much earlier than Piaget hypothesized; babies show surprise when objects disappear behind a screen or behave in unexpected ways (Baillargeon, 1987; Spelke, 1985). And babies may be able to imitate others earlier than Piaget believed possible (Meltzoff & Moore, 1977, 1983).

What does all this mean? Spelke (1994) suggests that, in addition to being born with basic reflexes, newborns have an innate core of knowledge of the world and how it works that begins to emerge very early in life. As more sophisticated methods for observing infants are developed, more knowledge about their information-processing capacities will become available. (See Focus on Research: IQ Testing in Infancy, page 208.).

Implications for Practice: Should Babies Learn to Read?

If babies are so brilliant, should parents devote time and energy to teaching young children to read or perform math problems? Should parents place note cards that name items around the house to encourage language development?

Parents who attempt structured teaching of young babies may become invested in the success of their endeavors. Such attempts at early enrichment may turn into stressful parent-child interactions. Babies involved for long periods in a structured teaching session may miss out on opportunities for free play and exploration. Most young babies do not need to know how to read or add—they have better things to do. In addition, no evidence suggests that enrichment programs create Superbabies (Zigler & Stevenson, 1993). Parents should be encouraged to provide an interesting environment for the child to explore; to provide stimulating play materials; and to talk to, play with, and enjoy their baby.

FOCUS ON RESEARCH

IQ Testing in Infancy

Do the capabilities of young infants have any predictive value for later cognitive performance? In general, scores of mental development in the first months of life do not predict later IQ. Prediction of later IQ becomes much more reliable after the baby is 2 years old and no longer an infant. Predicting future functioning in infants is most accurate for those who score significantly below average (Honzik, 1976). In other words, a baby who walks at 9 months may not be brighter than one who walks at 13 months; but a baby who does not walk until 22 months may have cognitive delays.

To date, the Bayley Scale of Infant Development (BSID) is one of the best measures of infant development available (Culbertson & Gyurke, 1990). As already stated, this measure does not predict later cognitive ability if the scores are average to above average. However, the measure is predictive of cognitive problems if the scores are significantly below average. Tests such as the BSID, then, are valuable in identifying develop-

mental problems. The BSID tests cognitive and motor skills of infants aged 2 months to 30 months. The infant is assessed on scales that cover memory, perceptual abilities, problem-solving skills, object permanence, verbal skills, gross and fine motor skills, and personal-social skills. Test administration requires special equipment and a trained clinician.

Interestingly, recent research suggests that measures of information processing in infancy may be more predictive of future learning problems than are tests such as the BSID. For instance, infants who fixate visual stimuli briefly and habituate quickly have been found to do better on cognitive scores when they are age 2 and 4 (Bornstein & Sigman, 1986) and also at age 12 (Sigman, 1991). When shown a series of pictures, these infants will study a new picture for a brief time only and then look for a new picture. As just stated, babies who do this score higher on later cognitive measures. Additional researchers have provided recent support for the speculations that speed, reaction time, and memory in infancy are predictors of later childhood IQ (Dougherty & Haith, 1997; Rose & Feldman, 1997). So, bright babies may be able to process visual information more quickly; that is, they learn more about the stimulus and retain the information in a briefer period of time than less bright babies do.

Some evidence indicates that the ability to demonstrate cross-modal transfer and object permanence predicts later IQ (Rose et al., 1998; Rose, 1991). In fact, Rose (1992) found that 6-year-old children at risk for learning disabilities had demonstrated low scores on processing visual information at 7 months of age and on performing cross-modal transfers at 1 year. Further research may make it possible to use information-processing measures to identify children at risk for later learning problems.

Communication

Although newborn babies cannot speak words, they can communicate and are born ready to respond to the human voice. Babies will move in synchrony to human speech in a kind of dance that is slow and rhythmic (Condon, 1975). Neonates prefer human speech to noise; they prefer their own language to others; they prefer baby talk to adult speech; they prefer a female voice to a male voice, and they prefer their mother's voice to another woman's. By the end of infancy, the baby begins to learn to speak a language. Anyone who has tried to learn a new language as an adult knows how hard this can be. But a baby does it quite well and in a consistent and predictable fashion. Babies all over the world and throughout time have developed speech in the same sequence.

CRYING AND COOING

The newborn communicates primarily by crying. At first crying is unintentional, simply a response to discomfort or need. But as the caregiver responds to the infant's cries, the baby learns to cry for specific reasons. New parents often ask, "Why does the baby cry?" Babies cry when they are hungry, tired, cold, wet, hot, scared, lonely, in pain, bored—whatever. Most caregivers learn to distinguish between cries, such as the loud, piercing cry of pain or the fussy, whiny sound of tiredness or boredom.

By the end of the first month (3 to 5 weeks), babies begin to coo or make vowel sounds such as "aaaaah" or "oooooh" (see Table 6.4). At around 3 or 4 months, the baby throws in some consonants such as "b" or "k."

BABBLING

Between 3 and 6 months, the baby puts vowel and consonant sounds together, repeats them over and over, and begins **babbling.** Common early babbling sounds include "mamama," "papapa," and "dadada." It is probably no coincidence that in many languages the common names ascribed to infants to refer to their mother and father are mama, dada, and papa.

Babies all over the world begin making these repetitive sounds at this age. Babbling seems to be a maturational process, because even deaf babies who have never heard language will begin to babble by 6 months; however, with no auditory reinforcement, they stop babbling by 8 months. (But if the hearing impairment is caught early and the parents communicate with the baby through sign language, the baby will repeat some signs over and over and "sign babble.")

Why do infants babble? Babbling may be a form of practice to develop the throat, lips, and tongue for producing sounds (Zigler & Stevenson, 1993). Or it may be

TABLE 6.4	Developmental Milestones for Speech and Language
Age (in months)	Milestone
2–3	Coos
3–6	Babbles
9–17	Says "mama" and "dada"
12–15	Uses two to three words besides "mama" and "dada"
15–18	Uses many words and can point to body parts
20–24	Uses two- to three-word sentences
24	Refers to self by own name

(Adapted from Willis & Holden, 1990)

a way for infants to begin to relate socially with family members and to learn the basic social skills of communication (Bjorklund & Bjorklund, 1992). For the first six months, infants vocalize at the same time as someone talking to them. By 7 or 8 months of age, though, the baby begins to take turns in vocalizing. Now the baby will listen while someone else is speaking and then respond with babbling. By 8 months, the infant takes on the accent of the native language, matches the speaker's tone of voice, and ends phrases with upward or downward inflection (Bjorklund & Bjorklund, 1992). The baby is learning the basics of communication.

The infant then begins to make sounds that refer to specific objects, people, or actions. For instance, the baby may make an "rrrrr" sound when seeing a truck or say "mmmmm" when seeing food. Babies also accompany their speech with gestures such as pointing to get their message across. A popular form of this type of communication is the scream-and-point method. Babbling increases until the age of 9 to 12 months, when babies say their first word.

Infants with hearing loss also use vocal prelinguistic communication. Some research suggests that infants with and without hearing loss use the same amount of vocal and gesticular communication (Spencer, 1993).

HOLOPHRASTIC SPEECH

Babies begin to say their first words by 9 to 12 months. At this point, their receptive language is better than their expressive language; in other words, they understand more words than they can say. By the time babies speak their first word, they can understand almost 100 words (Benedict, 1979). The baby begins to add new words slowly, one at a time, until she has a vocabulary of 10 words (Shaffer, 1993). Then the baby has a vocabulary spurt, or naming explosion, whereby new words are added rapidly (Zigler & Stevenson, 1993). By 20 months, a baby has a vocabulary of about 50 words; by 24 months, about 180 (Shaffer, 1993).

During the early-speech phase, the baby uses one word to express the meaning of a whole sentence, which is referred to as **holophrastic speech.** For instance, a baby may point to a pitcher, whine, and say "juice," meaning "I would like some juice to drink." When you pour a cup and hand it to him, he may smile and happily say "juice," meaning "Oh good, some juice to drink at last." When the cup tips and spills juice on his shirt, he may grab the shirt, cry, and say "juice," meaning "I've spilled juice all over me and now I'm wet and uncomfortable and I want a clean shirt." Babies at this age use one word in a fashion referred to as an **overextension.** This means that the word becomes generalized to include a larger category. For instance, babies often use the word "dog" to refer to any furry animal, but this overextension does not mean that the baby can't tell the difference between a dog and a cow. The baby can often accurately point out animals in a book before being able to name them. Remember, babies know more words than they can say; but when your usable vocabulary consists of four words, and you know the large mooing animal is not mommy, daddy, or ball, then dog is your best guess. Often the adult will then provide the proper name of the animal for the baby: "That's a cow. A cow goes moo. Can you say cow?" By mislabeling the animal, the baby has gained more knowledge and an increased vocabulary. So the baby now points to the cow and says . . . "dog." It may take a few tries to get it right.

What are the first words babies learn? Babies learn words that refer to things that interest them—often people or objects important to them, such as caregivers (mommy, daddy), toys (bear, doll), food (milk, cookie), and animals (dog, kitty). They also like things that move or make noise (airplane, truck) or that can be acted on (ball).

TELEGRAPHIC SPEECH

Between 18 and 24 months, babies begin to put words together to form simple phrases or sentences. Because these sentences are abbreviated, like the message in a telegram, they are referred to as **telegraphic speech.** When you have to pay for each word you use, as you do when sending a telegram, then you want to use only words that are absolutely necessary to convey your message. So, in telegraphic speech, babies use nouns, verbs, and adjectives. They omit auxiliary verbs, prepositions, articles, and pronouns. For example, 18-month-old Sarah had never said more than one word at a time. One day she was sitting quietly at her mother's feet looking at a lamp. After a few minutes, she climbed into her mother's lap and said, "Mommy, lamp, hot, burn, ouch." With a few words she had communicated the message that if you touched a hot light bulb you would burn yourself, and it would hurt.

This period of development is an exciting time. Parents begin to get a glimpse of what is going on in their child's mind. But what *is* going on in an infant's mind? Again, infants use words that are important to them: words that convey action (throw ball), possession (my truck), recurrence (more juice), nonexistence (all gone), location (doggie out), and naming and labeling (cow).

Implications for Practice: Recognizing Speech Problems

Although infants develop speech in a predictable sequence, the amount of speech individual children evidence at age 2 can vary greatly. Some 2-year-olds speak in simple two-word phrases, whereas others speak in longer sentences. Both are normal. But, as we mentioned earlier, it is important to recognize delays in speech, especially in the case of hearing-impaired children. If the hearing loss is caught early, children can learn sign language in the same progression as they would have learned spoken language. The problem is identifying hearing loss in an infant. Hearing loss is often undetected because the infant begins to babble on schedule. Parents should instead note how the infant responds to loud noises. A baby who does not startle when hearing a loud noise, or does not look to find the source of a noise, may have hearing problems.

As we have seen, to develop speech, infants need to hear spoken language. But even some infants without hearing impairments can have problems with adequate verbal stimulation. Parents with a lack of developmental information may assume that a 7-month-old infant doesn't understand speech and may thus fail to interact verbally with the baby. This can be a particular problem with teenage parents. Adolescent parents need to be encouraged to speak to the baby even if the essence of the speech is silly nonsense (see the following Focus section).

FOCUS ON DEVELOPMENT

How's My Little Schnookums?

What happens to mature, sophisticated adults when they see a baby? All of a sudden they begin speaking in a sing-song, high-pitched voice, using short phrases, asking lots of questions, using many repetitions, and adding exaggerated emphasis to certain words.

"How's daddy's little schnookums? What do you see? Is that a *doggie*? Yes? Where's the *doggie*? Hello, *doggie*. Nice *doggie*."

This kind of speech directed toward infants occurs in other cultures and is initiated by both sexes and people in various age groups, from elderly gentlemen to 4-year-olds. Some parents attempt to avoid talking to their baby using this infant-directed speech, or baby talk, fearing that their baby will end up talking this way. But new research suggests that failure to use baby talk may be a mistake. Babies love to listen to this type of speech and actually seem to learn language better when addressed in this fashion.

Anne Fernald (1987), the leading researcher in infant-directed speech, has suggested that babies prefer baby talk. She trained babies to turn their heads to hear different types of speech, and these babies turned to hear infant-directed speech more than they did to hear regular adult speech. In an effort to explain why babies prefer baby talk, Fernald is studying the musical qualities of infant-directed speech. The sounds in baby talk cover two octaves, with a sing-song quality that may help modulate infants' emotions. Also, this type of speech may help teach babies language, because it engages the babies' attention. Remember, babies prefer high-pitched sounds rather than low-pitched ones. (Babies are able to respond to vocally expressed emotion before they can respond to facial expressions of emotion.) In addition, certain sounds in baby talk have different meanings, such as high-pitched sounds stressing the importance of a particular word.

In another study by Fernald (1991), when an adult who used either baby talk or adult talk asked babies under 18 months to look at a picture of an object, the babies would recognize the name of the object only when the adult emphasized that word using baby talk (Adler, 1990). According to Fernald, then, baby talk is important for normal infant development. In fact, instead of just being silly chatter, it may be music to their ears (Adler, 1990).

Attitudes and Emotions

In the past, research concentrated on cognitive development, with emotion being seen as the outcome of cognitive activity. The baby would engage in activities and learn that some were pleasant, some were sad, and some were scary (Bremmer, 1988). Recent research, however, indicates that emotions have a strong biological component. If this is true, then babies do not learn to be afraid of unfamiliar situations; they enter a developmental stage in which they begin to exhibit fear of strange people and places.

Research by Izard (1982) and associates suggests that babies all over the world develop emotions at the same ages in a predictable sequence. Izard videotaped infants' expressions during various situations, such as being separated and reunited with their mothers, being approached by a stranger, hearing a balloon pop nearby, tasting lemon rind, and receiving scheduled inoculations. He then had independent observers classify the infants' expressions. This type of research has found that at birth babies display interest, distress, disgust, and happiness. Between age 2½ and 6 months, infants display other primary emotions of anger, sadness, surprise, and fear.

Fear is one of the emotions that develop during the first year of life. At 5 to 6 months, babies begin to show **stranger anxiety.** Before this age, if given time to warm up, babies will smile at anyone. At 8 months, though, babies will cry and turn away from an unfamiliar face. Between 8 and 10 months, babies begin to display **separation anxiety;** the baby now cries at being left by the primary caregiver. This fear begins to diminish at about 13 months, when the baby has acquired object permanence and can remember the mother when she is away and anticipate her return. At this time, the baby may also have developed a **transitional object**—a blanket, toy, or teddy bear the baby uses for comfort in the caregiver's absence. During the second year of life, babies add complex or secondary emotions of embarrassment, shame, guilt, and pride. These emotions may require that the child have a sense of self and knowledge of appropriate conduct; in other words, the baby would realize that "Baby has done something wrong." By 18–24 months, babies are fairly accomplished in the emotional area, being able to display a wide range of emotions and even to fake certain emotions, such as sadness, in order to manipulate others (Shaffer, 1993).

Research suggests that emotional expression in infancy is predictive of later childhood emotional characteristics. Shy babies grow up to be shy children. (See Focus on Psychology: Shy Children Are Born, Not Made, this page.) Huebner (cited in Trotter, 1987) had babies look at a human face, a mannequin face, and an inanimate object with scrambled facial features. Five years later, the babies who had looked longest at the human face were the most sociable, whereas those who had looked the least time at the human face were shy and withdrawn.

Many researchers have wondered whether babies can read facial expressions. Research on younger infants is inconclusive, but there is clear evidence that by 8 to 10 months of age, babies are affected by the moods of others (Shaffer, 1993). Termine (1988) found that babies of sad mothers exhibited a similar expression and showed less exploratory and play behavior than did babies of happy mothers. When confronted with strange situations, babies at this age look to the mother for emotional cues. For instance, if the baby sees a new toy that looks like a pink bunny noisily beating a drum, the baby will look to see how the mother feels about this object. If the mother smiles, the baby may approach the toy. By 12 months, babies will even look to strangers for cues on how to react. Looking to others for emotional information is known as **social referencing.** In a study by Klinnert and colleagues (1986), 12-month-old babies would play with an unfamiliar toy if a nearby stranger smiled at them but would not approach the toy if the stranger showed fear. Older babies, then, take cues from others as to which situations are safe or not.

Greenspan and Greenspan (1985) have described a developmental sequence for emotions from birth through age 4. The infant first takes an interest in the world, then in people, then falls in love with the caretakers, and later learns to dream, imagine, and fantasize.

FOCUS ON PSYCHOLOGY

Shy Children (and Uptight Monkeys) Are Born, Not Made

At a preschool in Silver Spring, Maryland, a mother tries to drop her 2-year-old son off at a Mother's Morning Out program only to find that he clings to her leg, cries, and adamantly refuses to enter the room, whereas other children rush into the room and begin playing with the toys. An hour away, on a five-acre wooded lot, a mother rhesus monkey is separated from her 2-month-old infant. This infant becomes very upset, shows signs of depression, and stops eating, whereas other monkey infants adjust easily to periodic separation from their mothers.

Jerome Kagan studies human infant development, and Stephen Suomi conducts developmental studies of monkeys. These researchers have found that extremely inhibited children and uptight monkeys often behave in similar ways when faced with novel situations. They found that these species have similar physiological reactions as well. Kagan believes that the limbic system—particularly the amygdala and hypothalamus—in these children and monkeys is activated more easily and that this overactivation is inherited. Kagan found that timid children show a pattern of excessive physiological responses to mildly stressful situations that do not occur in more easygoing children. Under stress, these children have dilated pupils, a more rapid heartbeat, and elevated blood cortisol. Suomi's uptight monkeys, when stressed during infancy by brief separations from their mothers, showed the same rise in blood cortisol and increase in heart rate. The researchers found that neither the monkeys nor the children tend to outgrow these abnormal physiological responses to stress.

Suomi and Kagan agree that this extreme timidity seems to have a genetic foundation. The monkeys were reared together in nurseries and in peer groups, so parenting was not influencing their individual reactions to stress. Research by Robert Plomin and David Rowe indicates that identical twins tend to exhibit the same reaction to strangers, supporting the notion that humans possess a biological predisposition to extreme shyness. About 20% of monkeys and 15% of children seem to be genetically predisposed to timidity. However, being born shy does not doom a child or monkey to lifelong social difficulties.

Suomi found that monkeys can be helped to overcome their stress responses through changes in how they are reared. Environmental influences such as having a nurturing mother can offset the genetic tendency toward shyness. Surrounding a monkey with friendly, outgoing peers and a nurturing foster mother or grandmother helps the monkey learn coping strategies. When stressed, this monkey can seek out a nurturing friend or mother figure. This activity prevents the normal high-stress physical response. Growing up with a nurturing mother figure often helps these monkeys respond better than their peers and become leaders in their group.

Kagan's studies of human children provide evidence that, although timid toddlers tend to stay shy, these children can overcome this tendency with help from their parents. Social workers can help parents of very shy children recognize the problem early, protect the child from too much stress, and help the child learn coping skills. Parents can help the child by inviting other children to the home to play with the child and by teaching the child how to cope with the physical response brought on by stressful situations.

The work of Suomi and Kagan has helped to clarify how heredity and environment interact to influence behavior and development. Some children may be born shy, but a supportive and nurturing environment can help them to later social success.

(Adler, 1989, 1990; Asher, 1987)

INFANT TEMPERAMENT

Though all babies seem to possess primary emotions at birth, those emotions vary in how they are exhibited among individual newborns. Some babies are easily comforted and sleep and eat on a regular schedule. Some babies are more difficult to comfort and have very unpredictable daily patterns. The characteristic pattern in which an infant responds to and interacts with the environment is referred to as **temperament.** Some consider temperament to be the basis of later personality development. And for the most part, temperament is thought to be biologically determined (Thomas & Chess, 1989).

In an extensive study of temperament, Alexander Thomas and Stella Chess conducted the New York Longitudinal Survey in the mid-1970s. They looked at 133 individuals from infancy through adulthood and identified nine dimensions of temperament, including activity level, rhythmicity, approach or withdrawal, adaptability, threshold of responsiveness, intensity of reaction, quality of mood, distractibility, and attention span and persistence. (See Box 6.1.)

Based on the data obtained from their work, Thomas and Chess (1977) determined that the combination of these nine dimensions described three types of children: the easy child, the slow-to-warm-up child, and the difficult child. Approximately 40% of the children in their sample fit the description of the **easy child.** This baby is characterized by regular, positive responses to new stimuli, high adaptability to change, and mild or moderately intense mood, which is usually positive. In other words, this infant is apt to easily accept new toys, foods, individuals, and settings. This baby has predictable eating and sleeping schedules and is usually happy and pleasant.

Fifteen percent of the children studied were classified as **slow to warm up.** As babies, these children exhibit a more sedate and less exuberant orientation to the world. They have more negative responses and are slower to adapt to new situations. Like the easy

BOX 6.1

Dimensions of Temperament

Activity level: Active babies are in motion most of the time, even while sleeping. Quiet babies can be placed almost anywhere, as they will not move much.

Rhythmicity: Some babies are very regular in the times they eat, sleep, and have bowel movements. Others are very irregular and unpredictable.

Approach or withdrawal: When presented with a new toy, some babies respond positively by smiling, vocalizing, and reaching for it. Other babies cry, turn away, or push the toy away.

Adaptability: Some babies adapt to changes in routine easily and quickly. They may be shy with a new sitter at first but accept the sitter after a brief time. Some babies become very upset at even slight changes. They may cry for days even if their familiar sitter changes hairstyle.

Threshold of responsiveness: Some babies sleep through loud noises and cry briefly when they fall down. Others wake easily in response to sounds and cry long and loud when even slightly hurt.

Intensity of reaction: Some babies cry softly and giggle gently. Others scream and kick and laugh out loud.

Quality of mood: Some babies are pleasant and contented most of the time. Others are fussy and irritable.

Distractibility: Some babies can be easily distracted from something they want. If you offer them a toy, they will stop trying to turn on the TV. Other babies are intent on figuring out how the TV works no matter what you do.

Persistence and attention span: Some babies are very persistent in their activities. If they are looking at a book, they need to turn every page before they will let you put on their shoes. Other babies turn a few pages of the book and move on to something else. Some children are temperamentally "difficult," displaying negative moods and sleep, eating, and elimination irregularities. These children are less adaptable, more vulnerable to adversity, and more likely to produce and elicit adverse responses.

---

child, the slow-to-warm-up child usually has predictable eating and sleeping schedules. Although these infants are wary of new experiences, such as visiting a new house, they are able to adjust over time, if not hurried or pushed during the transition.

In contrast to the other types, the difficult child has unpredictable daily habits. As babies, they wake up at a different time every day and do not establish a regular napping schedule. Their appetite also varies from day to day. These infants exhibit negative responses to new stimuli, adapt slowly or not at all, and usually express an intense, negative mood. These babies protest loudly when introduced to new toys, foods, people, or situations; throw temper tantrums when agitated or frustrated; and squeal loudly when excited. Ten percent of the children in the sample fit this description.

Since the work of Thomas and Chess, much research has been conducted to examine the validity of inborn temperament. Studies of twins have found temperament to be biologically determined to some ex-

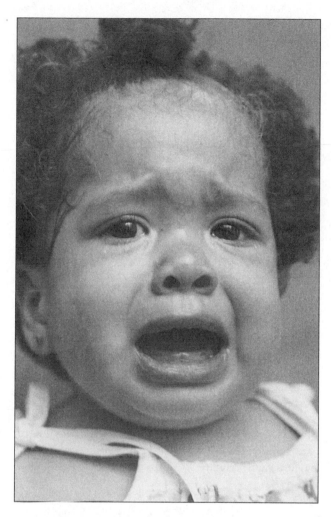

Some children are temperamentally "difficult," displaying negative moods and sleep, eating, and elimination irregularities. These children are less adaptable, more vulnerable to adversity, and more likely to produce and elicit adverse responses.

opment. One way that environment can affect personality development is through **goodness of fit.** Goodness of fit refers to how well the demands of the environment match the child's behavioral style. An active, intense baby with outgoing, high-energy parents who encourage loud play and exploration will have a better fit than will such a baby born to quiet, introspective parents who expect the baby to sit and look at books.

Research indicates that the family environment can play a role in the child's later development. Maziade and colleagues (1990) discovered that all 38 of the children in their study, who were identified at age 7 as having a difficult temperament and a poorly functioning family with little behavioral control, were diagnosed as having a clinical disorder in preadolescence or adolescence. A slow-to-warm-up baby may experience stress if the parents are highly sociable and always on the go. An easy child with a more difficult sibling may be ignored while the parents concentrate their energy on their other child.

Parents can be helped to understand their babies' different temperament styles and to alter the environment to fit that style and enhance the child's development. Researcher Alicia F. Lieberman (1993), author of *The Emotional Life of the Toddler,* focuses on all three temperament types described by Thomas and Chess, as well as an additional type, which she calls the *active child.* Lieberman makes recommendations as to how best to interact with each type of child. Parents of difficult children should not take the children's behavior personally, should keep a sense of humor about the children's behavior, should be patiently available to the children, should have clear guidelines for behavior, and should develop a support system that allows the parents time away from the children. Parents of active children should structure the house and yard to allow for robust play. Parents of slow-to-warm-up children should take special measures in introducing their children to new situations. Parents should essentially stay near the children until their mood has changed from caution to enjoyment, then step back. Lieberman reminds parents that easy children can be taken advantage of. They may not demand attention or complain even when they should and may therefore be ignored in the hectic pace of everyday life.

tent (Emde et al., 1992). Our review of studies by Kagan found that shy babies grow up to be shy children, and difficult babies grow up to be difficult adults. In Thomas and Chess's study, 70% of the difficult infants entered psychiatric treatment later in life, but only 18% of the easy infants did so.

Implications for Practice: Goodness of Fit

Although research has found that one's personality seems to be partially genetically determined, the environment shapes the balance of personality devel-

ATTACHMENT*

Anyone who has had the privilege of a friendship with a small child may have noticed changes in how the child interacts with you as he grows. Before 3 months, the baby will come to you, smile, and make eye contact. Around 4 months, the baby may frown at seeing your face, look to mother's face, and then back at you. It may take a few minutes of coaxing to get the baby to come to you. By 8 months, the baby may whine and turn away to hug mother when you approach. You may have to resort to bribing with a toy or treat to get the baby to come to you. But the baby may still refuse, obviously preferring mother now. Because of these actions, you may begin to feel the child no longer likes you. Then one day you go to visit your active toddler friend and you are greeted with a big grin. The child takes your hand, waves goodbye to mom, and wants to go home with you (see Table 6.5).

This scenario illustrates the process of **attachment,** or forming a strong emotional tie to a caregiver. Researchers have long been interested in what motivates a baby to form this close bond with a caregiver and to prefer that caregiver to other people. Early theories held that attachment was the result of need satisfaction. In other words, babies love their mother because she feeds and takes care of them. But classic research by Harlow on infant rhesus monkeys failed to support this idea. These monkeys were separated from their mothers at birth and raised in a cage with an inanimate surrogate mother made of either wire or cloth. Some monkeys were fed by the wire surrogates and some by the cloth ones. But when the infant monkeys needed someone to cling to, they preferred the cloth mother even when they had been fed by the wire mother. These monkeys showed no preference for the wire surrogate who had fed them.

*Ellen Blessington, MSW, contributed to this section.

TABLE 6.5	Bowlby's Phases of Attachment	
	Age	**Behaviors**
Phase 1	Birth–2 or 3 mos.	Displays indiscriminate smiling, cooing, clinging toward anyone.
Phase 2	2–3 mos. to 6–7 mos.	Begins selective interactions. Develops a true social smile directed at preferred caregivers. Compares a stranger's face with caregiver's.
Phase 3	6–7 mos. to 1 year	Clearly attached to primary caregiver. Cries when caregiver leaves. Crawls after caregiver. Wary of strangers and strange situations.
Phase 4	Second year of life	Has full object permanence. More secure in knowledge that caregiver exists when not in sight. More sociable with other people.

Today, attachment theory is most closely identified with psychiatrist John Bowlby (1958). According to his theory, attachment has a biological, evolutionary basis. A baby forms a close, intimate relationship with a caregiver to ensure its survival. In an evolutionary sense, when a predator threatens, someone needs to protect the vulnerable young. And infants need a particular caregiver to remember to pick them up when everyone else is running away.

This theory suggests that parents and infants may be biologically programmed to form an attachment. The caregiver and the infant each exhibit specific behaviors that facilitate the process of forming a bond.

THE PARENTS' BEHAVIORS

Parents of an infant engage in several activities meant to engage the baby's attention. They position their faces directly within the infant's visual field, about 22.5 cm away from the baby's face (Papousek & Papousek, 1992). This is a very interesting phenomenon considering that a newborn can focus on objects no more than 30 cm away. Parents seem to instinctively know how far the baby can see, so they attempt eye contact within that range. Parents also attempt to get the infant's attention through a series of facial expressions known as the "greeting response." In this response, parents tilt their head back, open their mouth halfway, and raise their eyebrows (Papousek & Papousek, 1987). Parents also use baby talk when addressing the infant. (See Focus on Development: How's My Little Schnookums?, page 211.) Research suggests that these behaviors are not conscious but intuitive in nature (Papousek & Papousek, 1992). Parents just seem to know what babies like and respond that way.

THE INFANT'S BEHAVIORS

The biggest contribution the infant makes in the attachment process is having "the look." Babies are cute. Adults just cannot seem to resist the rounded facial features and "babyishness" of infants. Adults are also drawn to babies' responsiveness. Parents like to feel recognized and needed, and newborns seem equipped to meet that need. Babies show a particular fondness for a human face and respond to adults with smiles and vocalizations. As we have already seen, babies recognize their mother's voice at birth. Newborns also respond by imitating facial expressions.

The infant's reflexes—in particular grasping, sucking, rooting, and turning—serve as responses to parental caregiving and also reinforce parental interaction. These infant behaviors make the parents feel needed. In addition, infants quickly learn who is caring for them and make responses that reinforce that care. For instance, within three days of birth, a newborn will respond to being placed in the feeding position by moving in the direction of the mother, turning toward the breast, and opening the mouth (Call, 1964).

OTHER ATTACHMENT IDEAS

Mary Ainsworth added information to ideas of attachment. According to Ainsworth and colleagues (1978), the infant uses the primary caregiver as a secure base from which to leave to explore the environment and to return to for comfort and security. Using this idea, Ainsworth developed a method of measuring attachment by observing the infant's response to various events occurring in a strange situation. This laboratory assessment procedure, known as the Strange Situation Procedure, involves eight structured episodes occurring over about 25 minutes:

- *Episode 1:* Mother and baby are introduced to a playroom.

- *Episode 2:* Mother and baby are left alone to explore the contents of the playroom.

- *Episode 3:* An unfamiliar woman joins them.

- *Episode 4:* The mother leaves the room and the stranger attempts to play with the baby.

- *Episode 5:* The mother returns.

- *Episode 6:* The child is left completely alone.

- *Episode 7:* The strange woman returns.

- *Episode 8:* The mother returns.

Analysis of the responses of infants in the strange situation led to a classification of attachment patterns. Ainsworth identified three levels of attachment.

1. *Secure attachment:* These infants use their mothers as a secure base from which to explore the playroom. They are aware of their mother's presence and keep checking to make sure she is available if needed. When their mothers leave them, these infants cry or protest. When the mothers return, these infants seek them out for comfort and physical contact.

2. *Anxious attachment:* These infants are clingy and reluctant to explore the playroom even with their mother present. When their mothers leave, these infants become extremely upset and cry for long periods of time. When their mothers return, these infants seek physical contact but also hit their mothers or pull away. They are not easily soothed by their mothers. According to Ainsworth, these infants do not trust their mothers to meet their security needs.

3. *Avoidant attachment:* These infants demonstrate a marked indifference toward their mothers. They do not use their mothers as secure bases but actually act as if their mothers are not present. They do not seek eye contact or attention from their mothers. They are not distressed when their mothers leave and show indifference upon their return.

Sixty-five percent of middle-class infants display secure-attachment behaviors. What factors influence the attachment process? How do 35% of infants end up not securely attached?

RISK FACTORS ASSOCIATED WITH ATTACHMENT FAILURE

Factors involving the baby, the mother, and the home can interfere with attachment. First of all, characteristics of babies can affect the mother-infant relationship. For instance, premature babies may be at risk for attachment problems; these babies are not as "cute" as full-term infants and also not as responsive. Preterm infants can be less engaged with their mothers and receive less enjoyment in mother-involved play activities (Field, 1983). In addition, preterm infants often spend an extended period of time in the neonatal intensive care unit, making contact with the mother difficult (Niven, Wiszniewski, & AlRoomi, 1993). However, this may only be a temporary interruption for the mother and infant, with attachment possible once the mother takes the baby home. In fact, a recent research study failed to show a difference in attachment patterns between extremely premature and full-term infants (Wintgens et al., 1998). Other infant-related factors that can affect attachment include drug exposure (Lester, 1992) and difficult temperament.

A parent-related problem that affects the attachment relationship can occur with adolescent mothers. These mothers on average engage in less verbal exchange with their children and have trouble interpreting and responding to their infant's cues (Crockenberg, 1981; Field, 1981; Hann et al., 1990). Another problem arises with depressed mothers, who may have more problems bonding with their babies. A depressed mother is wrapped up in her own feelings and may not be responsive to an infant. She may be so busy concentrating on her own pain that she misses the baby's social cues. The baby then tends to match the mother's mood even with other nondepressed adults. Research shows that the way a mother expresses her depression can influence the attachment pattern of the infant (Rosenblum, Mazet, & Benony, 1997). Depressed mothers who express themselves as stressed and anxious tend to have infants who develop insecure-ambivalent attachment. These babies appear anxious and restless when separated from the mother but show mixed behaviors when reunited with her. Infants often develop insecure-avoidant attachment when the mother expresses her depression by appearing disinterested and withdrawn. Babies with insecure-avoidant attach-

ment seem independent when separated from the mother and avoid contact when reunited. Other parental factors that may affect attachment include alcoholism, childhood abuse and neglect, and an unplanned pregnancy.

Factors in the home can also affect attachment. A mother with lots of small children may not have time to respond to a new infant. The marital relationship has an effect on the primary caregiver's interactions with an infant. When spouses or partners are supportive, mothers are more responsive and affectionate toward their babies (Crnic, 1984). And a mother's level of social support is critical, especially when she is parenting an irritable infant. A secure attachment is more likely when a mother has an adequate social support network (Crockenberg, 1981). High levels of environmental stress also influence mother-baby interactions (Booth et al., 1987). Mothers dealing with poverty, domestic violence, and their own personal trauma may not have enough emotional energy to engage an infant.

In fact, a new category of attachment failure has been suggested by Main and Soloman (1986, 1990): *disorganized/disoriented attachment*. Children in this category exhibit unclear, inconclusive, or contradictory attachment patterns. This category can include children who are hard to classify and do not fit into one of Ainsworth's three attachment patterns. Children with this pattern often come from families with the problems just mentioned.

Implications for Practice: Assessing Attachment Problems

Bowlby believed that a warm, intimate, and continuous relationship with the mother was vital for a child's later personality development. Recent research suggests that the quality of a child's attachment with a primary caregiver is an excellent predictor of later functioning (Cicchetti & Wagner, 1990). Securely attached children exhibit a healthy mix of self-reliance and the ability to ask for help from others (Stroufe, Fox, & Pancake, 1983). Children with secure attachments relate better to their peers than do those with insecure attachments (Lieberman, 1977; Matas, Arend, & Stroufe, 1978). A strong parent-child bond also seems to result in better self-knowledge (Pipp, Easterbrooks, & Harmon, 1992) and in better school performance (Jacobsen, Edelstein, & Hoffman, 1994).

If attachment is so important to development, what are the signs to look for in assessing children that would point to attachment problems? Children with attachment problems are believed to exhibit the following behaviors in interactions. They do not show a preference for a particular adult; they may seek affection and attention from anyone and run up to and hug total strangers. They will wander away from their caregiver—the caregiver is frequently losing the child in crowds and in public places. The child may be reckless and accident-prone, and excessively clingy or aggressive toward the caregiver. The type of behaviors that Zeanah and Emde (1994) believe are suggestive of an attachment difficulty in young children are listed in Table 6.6.

TABLE 6.6 Assessing Attachment Problems in Young Children	
Behaviors	**Signs of Attachment Disorders**
Showing affection	Lack of warm and affectionate interchanges across a range of interactions; promiscuous affection with relatively unfamiliar adults
Comfort seeking	Lack of comfort seeking when hurt, frightened, or ill; comfort-seeking in odd or ambivalent manner
Reliance for help	Excessive dependence, or inability to seek and use supportive presence of attachment figure when needed
Cooperation	Lack of compliance with caregiver requests and demands by the child as a striking feature of caregiver-child interactions, or compulsive compliance
Exploratory behavior	Failure to check back with caregiver in unfamiliar settings, or exploration limited by child's unwillingness to leave caregiver
Controlling behavior	Oversolicitous and inappropriate caregiving behavior, or excessively bossy and punitive controlling of caregiver by the child
Reunion responses	Failure to reestablish interaction after separations, including ignoring/avoiding behaviors, intense anger, or lack of affection

(Zeanah, Mammen, & Lieberman, 1993)

FOCUS ON MULTICULTURALISM

Cultural Considerations in Examining African-American Attachment Patterns

Practitioners should be aware that the cross-cultural validity of identified attachment behaviors has been called into question. As stated by attachment researcher Jacquelyne Faye Jackson (1993), "[b]oth execution of the 'strange situation' procedure and unequivocal classification of infant attachments have been technically difficult in cultures outside the USA (Sagi et al., 1985; Takahashi, 1986), and no transcultural distribution of types has been found (Van Ijzendoorn & Kroonenberg, 1988)" (p. 91).

Jackson (1993) presents a compelling argument that the African-American practice of sharing child-care responsibilities among relatives results in a negative misinterpretation of African-American infant-attachment patterns. Jackson explains that, as a consequence of discrimination, African-American mothers have, historically and currently, needed to work outside the home. As a result of this economic reality, African-American culture has developed a distinct, adaptive, cultural pattern to ensure that their children receive the nurturance and care they require.

This cultural pattern includes the exposure of the child to a multitude of extended-family caregivers. Jackson (1993) notes research (Young, 1970) indicating that, because of a cultural context that encourages the acceptance and development of caring interactions with a number of different caregivers across a variety of settings, African-American children develop an independent and outgoing orientation. Hence, she asserts that, when African-American children are assessed using the Strange Situation, they may be mistakenly viewed as not being securely attached because of their greater confidence in examining novel environments and their high level of trust as to the comings and goings of caregivers in general.

Jackson (1993), therefore, maintains that it is not surprising that a relatively high proportion of African-American children appear to be insecurely attached when assessed according to the standards for majority

Newborn babies display a special interest in the human face. A preference for seeing their mother's face develops rapidly and encourages social interactions between mother and baby.

of their expression of distress and their reunion behaviors. Moreover, given the infants' observed pleasant attitudes toward their mothers, it is also questionable whether these infants could be seen as fitting Ainsworth's typology for resistant or avoidant infants.

Because she believed that the Strange Situation is inadequate in assessing African-American infant-attachment patterns, Jackson (1993) conducted an exploratory study that employed a laboratory assessment procedure developed by Kotelchuck (1976). Kotelchuck's playroom strategy includes two attachment figures, in contrast to the Strange Situation, which includes only one. Jackson found that African-American infants use both their mothers and secondary attachment figures as secure bases from which to explore the environment. She also found that the majority of the African-American infants she studied were simply not upset by being left in a playroom for a brief time period with an amicable stranger. As a result of her exploratory study, Jackson believes that, although Kotelchuck's procedure is an improvement in assessing African-American infant attachment by the inclusion of multiple caregivers, it is not sufficiently stressful to activate distress reactions in African-American children. Hence, she concludes that culturally relevant assessment instruments need to be developed and that researchers should be cautious in arriving at negative conclusions regarding African-American infant-attachment patterns.

(Courtesy of Ellen Blessington)

children. In support of her contention, she cites the work of Hansen (1980), who also questioned whether the African-American children he had examined when employing the Strange Situation had experienced the degree of stress necessary to elicit attachment behaviors. The children he studied actively explored the playroom, did not demonstrate noteworthy distress at times of separation, and were not specifically solicitous of maternal attention at times of reunion. Furthermore, these children had an overall genial demeanor during the procedure. Thus, it can be argued that these children did not experience the Strange Situation in the same fashion as do majority children, both in terms

Social Cognition and Regulation

At what age does a baby know that she is a baby? Lewis conducted experiments to test babies' awareness of self (Lewis & Brooks-Gunn, 1979). He put a spot of rouge on the baby's nose and had the mother sit with her infant in her lap in front of a mirror. If the babies recognized themselves in the mirror, they touched their own nose. Babies under 1 year looked in the mirror but did not touch their nose. Some babies at 15 months would touch their nose; but by 18 months, 75% of the babies recognized themselves in the mirror and touched their nose. Further research by Lewis has suggested that most babies have a sense of self by 18 months.

Margaret Mahler felt that developing a sense of self as being separate from others was a major developmental process with a significant effect on personality development. In Mahler's view, the infant grows from being a newborn with no sense of self as separate from her caretaker to being an autonomous, independent individual. She termed this process **separation-individuation.** During the first month of life, infants are in the *normal autistic phase,* unaware of self, other people, or the world. At 1 to 5 months, the babies are in the *normal symbiotic phase,* aware that someone is caring for them but unaware of that person as being separate from themselves. At 5 to 9 months, in the *differentiation phase,* babies begin to get a sense of self and non-self. At this age, babies will sit in their mother's lap and explore the mother's face visually and tactually. As babies begin to crawl and then walk between 9 and 14 months, they enter the *practicing phase.* Now they can move away from the mother, but they need to check back often for emotional refueling (a look, a smile, a hug). The *rapprochement phase* occurs between 14 and 24 months. Babies know they are separate from the mother but still need to check back regularly. The *consolidation phase* occurs between the age of 2 and 3. Now babies can separate from the mother without becoming too upset.

Remember that Mahler's theories of separation-individuation are based on the *clinical infant,* the adult recalling the past in psychotherapy. In experiments involving information processing, Daniel Stern (1985) has done extensive research on the *observed infant.* On the basis of data from these experiments, Stern believes that infants have a sense of self from birth, that babies are always able to differentiate self from others. How? As we discussed in the Information Processing section of this chapter, babies are able at birth to accurately discriminate sensory input. Even newborns seem to have an innate core of knowledge about the world. They can tell when they are sucking their own or someone else's fingers. They can tell when they are moving their own arm or having it raised by someone to play "How big is baby?" And they can tell when they are causing actions or when someone else is.

In any case, by the end of infancy, children have a well-established sense of self as separate and indepen-

TABLE 6.7 Developmental Milestones for Social Behaviors	
Age (in months)	**Milestone**
0–2	Smiles in response to a voice or touch
3–5	Smiles spontaneously
3–5	Reaches for familiar people
9–11	Plays pat-a-cake and peek-a-boo
9–11	Becomes upset when separated from caregiver
20–23	Plays near but not with other children
28–31	Is aware of differences between sexes
32–35	Can identify own sex
32–35	Can separate easily from caregiver

(Adapted from Willis & Holden, 1990)

dent. This notion of self is important for later development. For instance, as you may remember, a baby must have a sense of self before being able to express more complex emotions, such as guilt and shame. More important, a sense of self is a necessary foundation for social development. "The acquisition of the self by the end of the second year not only facilitates the acquisition of social knowledge, but underlies social competence, peer relations, gender identity, and empathy" (Brooks-Gunn & Lewis, 1984, p. 234). Some important milestones in social development are listed in Table 6.7.

REGULATION

Somewhere around the age of 2, the baby learns to say "No!" This is a statement of independence and autonomy. The baby now has a sense of self and what that self wants and does not want. The ability to know right from wrong, good from bad, and want from not want begins to develop after the age of 18 months. Regulation can begin when the infant has adequate language skills, a sense of self, more complex emotions of guilt and shame, and a sense of autonomy (Lyons-Ruth & Zeanah, 1993). Even babies who have been "easy" up to this point may not be as compliant now. They are more difficult to distract. They can formulate certain goals and realize whether or not they have obtained them (Lyons-Ruth & Zeanah, 1993). And, in terms of moral development, they have internalized certain standards and become upset when those standards are not met. Where did they get these standards and ideas of right and wrong, good and bad?

These standards and ideas are based on the previous responses of others. Remember, babies engage in social referencing; that is, they look to an adult for guidance in how to respond in new situations. Babies learn through experience that, when they throw things on the floor and break them, mother becomes upset. They learn that when they pour their juice on the floor, father becomes upset. So now when babies break or spill something, they become upset. At this age, babies will often reach out for an object and then look to mother to see if she is going to stop them.

Babies at this age are also unsure of many standards, and they test parents to determine which actions are acceptable and which are not—usually more than once. "Will mother get mad at me if I eat the food in this bowl on the floor? She lets the cat eat it. But mother yelled at me last time I ate it. Why? Let's see what happens this time."

Through repeated experimentation, babies learn to be reasonably obedient in the presence of parents. But they do not possess the ability to obey when parents are not watching until about 36 months (Lyons-Ruth & Zeanah, 1993). To the 2-year-old, it's OK to eat cat food unless mom catches you. In this context, the reason to be good is to avoid displeasure from mom.

Implications for Practice: The Terrible Twos

During the second half of the second year of life, babies can become much more difficult. They begin to develop a sense of autonomy and independence. They want to do things for themselves, they want to do it now, and they want to do it their way. *No* becomes their favorite word. Even when asked whether they want ice cream, children may reply "No" and then cry when the parents don't provide the ice cream. Some parents become locked in power struggles with their children, sometimes erupting into food battles. Parents may try to force the child to eat only to discover that some children would rather starve than eat when coerced. And some parents allow the toddler to run the house. They hesitate to provide any structure for the baby, failing to set limits or establish regular routines. Even though toddlers struggle to obtain it, they are often afraid of their growing independence. Parents

should be encouraged to set limits and provide structure and routine for the child but to allow independence when appropriate and avoid power struggles.

Psychological Hazards

What exactly are the effects on psychological development of losing a caregiver at a young age or even of failing to establish a bond with a primary caregiver at all? Loss of a primary caregiver has often been referred to as *maternal deprivation,* which can occur through separation from the caregiver, failure of the caregiver to interact with the infant, or neglect or abuse of the baby. If the loss occurs before 6 months of age, it can interfere with the baby's forming an attachment to a caregiver. If the loss occurs after 6 months, it can disrupt an existing attachment (Bremmer, 1988).

FAILURE TO FORM AN ATTACHMENT

What happens to babies who fail to form an attachment? Research on this issue has to rely on separations that occur naturally, and it usually involves babies who have been institutionalized. A classic study was conducted by Spitz (1945) on children in orphanages in the United States and Germany. These babies received adequate medical attention, food, and physical care but they received little social interaction. Most of their time was spent in cribs with a sheet over the rails. The death rate for children under 2 in these institutions was high; many died from childhood diseases such as measles. The babies were emotionally apathetic and retarded in physical, mental, and social growth.

What about institutions that offer more stimulation? Tizard and Rees (1974) looked at good British orphanages that had a high caregiver-to-baby ratio and lots of interaction. These institutions provided stimulating toys and materials but had a high staff turnover. Some babies experienced 50–80 caregivers before preschool age. These children were normal in intellectual development but had problems socially and emotionally. At the age of 8, many were restless, disobedient, and unpopular with their peers and constantly sought attention. Tizard found that, the longer the babies were in the institution, the more trouble they had with peer relations.

Infants who move from one foster home to another can have attachment problems. What happens when these children grow up? Bowlby (1980) looked at adolescents who had spent their infancy and childhood in institutions or foster care, often with repeated moves. These adolescents, who were not loved consistently as babies, were unable to love as teens. They displayed a lack of empathy and affection for others. Many children who fail to form attachments as infants grow up to exhibit disturbed behavior such as delinquency, disregard for life, and lack of empathy. These are the children who kill animals—the ones who would stomp a cat to death (Trout, 1995).

So, early deprivation of a consistent caregiver can affect cognitive, emotional, and social development. But can these effects of early deprivation be reversed with good care at a later age? Quite by accident, Skeels (1936) had an opportunity to explore this question. Two infant girls aged 13 and 16 months from neglectful families were admitted to an overcrowded orphanage in Iowa. Because they appeared retarded and functioned at the age of 6 or 7 months, they were placed in a home for women with retardation. Six months later these girls were alert, lively, and functioning normally. Why? They had become the "darlings" of the women in the home and received a great deal of stimulation and interaction. Skeels followed these girls' development and found that they remained normal. He then conducted a study comparing children in the orphanage with children placed in the home for women with retardation (Skodak & Skeels, 1945, 1949). Even as adults, the children who had been placed with the attentive women functioned better than did those who had been in the orphanage.

Suomi and Harlow (1972) raised infant rhesus monkeys in social isolation for six months. These isolated monkeys displayed a lack of social skills. For "therapy" these monkeys were placed with a 3-month-old monkey for two hours a day, three days a week. Young monkeys were used as "therapists" because they would not know that the behavior of the isolated monkeys was abnormal and would not be as aggressive toward them as older monkeys would have been. Because the young monkeys learned social skills from the regular monkey colony in which they spent most of their time, they taught the isolated monkeys how to interact. After six months of this type of therapy, the isolated monkeys learned social skills similar to those of normal monkeys.

So it appears that the effects of early deprivation can be reversed to some extent. But what happens to infants who form an attachment to a caregiver and then lose that caregiver?

SEPARATION AFTER ATTACHMENT

Babies who are separated from their primary caregiver show immediate effects (Rutter, 1981). At first, they display acute distress by crying and complaining loudly. This is known as the *protest phase*. Then babies go into the *despair phase*, showing general misery and apathy. When the caregiver fails to return after a period of time, the baby becomes unconcerned and relatively peaceful once again. This is the *detachment phase*. The amount of distress a baby displays depends on the circumstances. For example, there is a difference between going to grandma's for a week and being admitted to the hospital for surgery. In the hospital, the baby may be separated from the whole family and experience scary and painful procedures. Children who are in another family situation—especially if with a sibling or other family member—adapt more easily (Bremmer, 1988).

How does loss of a caregiver affect the child after these immediate responses? Recent studies have corroborated what Anna Freud suggested, "that separation is always traumatic in one way or another, but that it is particularly so for the young child" (Gerard & Dukette, 1954). The most profound responses occur if the separation takes place when the child is between 6 and 28 months (Trout, 1995). These responses include a drop in developmental quotient (the child scores lower on standard developmental tests), low frustration tolerance, eating disturbances, depression, social withdrawal, inconsolability when left alone, and repeated efforts to make the lost object reappear (opening cabinet doors, waiting by doors). In particular, a *sudden* loss can be overwhelming for a small child and have long-lasting effects (Trout, 1995).

So which is worse, to have loved and lost (separation from a primary caregiver) or to have never loved at all (failure to form an attachment)? Rutter (1981) looked at children from homes broken by divorce and children from homes where the mother had died. For children, the effects of these two circumstances (death and divorce) can result in similar short-term and long-term consequences (Kastenbaum, 1977). Rutter found that children from broken homes displayed higher rates of delinquent behavior than did children from intact homes. But what was causing the behavior problems—the breakup or difficulties in the home that led to the breakup? Rutter found that there was more delinquency in children from homes with family problems that caused the breakup than in children from stable homes where the mother had died. So it may not have been the loss of the caregiver that caused the behavior problems but difficulties in the broken homes. In general, there appear to be more problems for children who fail to form an attachment than for those who lose their primary caregiver (Bremmer, 1988).

Implications for Practice: Fostering Secure Attachment

Labeling early loss or separation as maternal deprivation implies that the mother is solely responsible for her infant's well-being. However, there are actually few effects from the lack of attachment to a biological mother (Bremmer, 1988). What is important is the quality of stimulation the child receives and some sense of continuity. A baby needs care that is consistent and continuous (Zigler & Stevenson, 1993). Consistent care means that one caregiver is predictable and reliable over time so that the baby can form a bond with that person. The mother is not the only person qualified for this role. Fathers, grandmothers, adoptive parents, aunts, and friends can all serve as primary caregivers. In fact, babies can form attachments to more than one person. A baby who receives nurturing care from a few people can form several attachments (Bremmer, 1988).

But this care needs to be consistent during infancy. Separations from the caregiver should be well planned, because babies tolerate separations better if they are prepared for the separation in advance. Trout (1995) suggests that even a very young infant be given information about a pending separation over and over. The child should be told that he may feel afraid, lonely, and sad. Children in foster care should receive regular visits with parents unless the parents are dangerous or there is no possibility of a reunion. Babies separated from caregivers do better if they are placed in a family-like environment. In fact, spending some time away from the caregiver—at grandma's or a friend's home—may help children deal with later, more difficult separations (Stacey et al., 1970).

In general, recovery from early separation and loss depends on the child, the circumstances of the loss, and what occurs after the loss. With good, loving care, children may be able to overcome the effects of early deprivation. Although it was once believed that trauma and deprivation in infancy would scar a person for life, research shows that infants are extremely resilient. With an adequate environment, appropriate intervention, and care provided in an enduring fashion, children may recover from early loss and deprivation (Emde, 1987).

FAILURE TO THRIVE

By definition, **failure to thrive** occurs when a child's weight falls below the 5th percentile for his age. Many failure-to-thrive babies begin life at normal weight but then decrease their rate of weight gain significantly. Some babies may be constitutionally small and naturally fall into this weight range. But for these babies, their height and weight drop simultaneously. For failure-to-thrive babies, weight drops before their height or head circumference begins to decline (Frank, Silva, & Needlman, 1993).

Cases of failure to thrive are usually divided into two classifications—organic and nonorganic. In organic failure to thrive, there is an underlying medical condition such as congenital heart disease, cystic fibrosis, or renal disease that causes the growth decline. In nonorganic failure to thrive, no medical cause can be found. Cases of nonorganic failure to thrive have usually been attributed to emotional deprivation. Selma Fraiberg (1980) states that nonorganic failure to thrive "is almost universally associated with the impairment of the mother's capacity to nourish, both in the material and in the psychological sense of the word" (p. 104). In this instance, then, failure to thrive can be considered to have a psychological cause: maternal deprivation. And, in fact, many mothers of failure-to-thrive infants are found to have been deprived in some way in their own childhood. Many of these mothers report an unhappy childhood and a difficult relationship with their own mothers. These factors may interfere with a woman's ability to emotionally respond to her infant and adequately meet his needs. Some believe that this emotional deprivation causes a decrease in the amount of growth hormone produced in the infant's pituitary gland, resulting in slow growth. Emotional tension also may increase the likelihood of the infant having vomiting and diarrhea or loss of appetite (Schuster & Ashburn, 1992).

However, Dr. Deborah Frank and colleagues (1993) state that emotional disturbance in itself does not cause slow growth. According to Frank, although emotional stress may be a contributing factor, failure to thrive is a problem of inadequate caloric intake. And it is not helpful to label the condition organic or nonorganic. Babies with heart or lung disease may have a medical cause for slow growth, but they may have also developed a feeding problem. And babies with nonorganic failure to thrive may have a genetically determined temperament that makes them difficult to feed. Failure to thrive, then, would not just be the result of maternal deprivation but of an interaction between biologic and environmental factors.

Failure to thrive can happen in families in which parents obviously care about their children. Some babies are very difficult to feed—for instance, babies with cerebral palsy. An example would be the feeding scene from the movie *My Left Foot*, where a harried mom, in a very stressful family situation with a nondemanding child with cerebral palsy, spoons a couple of bites of mush into her child's mouth and then goes off to do a mountain of chores. Another situation occurs among premature babies. Twenty to forty percent of failure-to-thrive infants started out with low birth weight (Zigler & Stevenson, 1993). Low-birth-weight, premature babies can be difficult to feed. Remember, premature babies can be irritable and hard to care for. Also, some babies have chronic ear infections or sore throats. These babies may not feel well enough to eat most of the time. Because they have inadequate nutrition, they are more prone to be sick; and because they are sick, they are less likely to eat.

Family situations can also contribute to failure to thrive. Families with high levels of stress may have a chaotic lifestyle and may fail to establish regular mealtimes. Family members may be too preoccupied with problems of living to notice that the child is not eating. They may feed the child in front of the TV, which can be very distracting. Some parents may be too controlling and get into "food battles" with their toddler. In this situation, the child gains power by not eating. Some weight-conscious parents may think that fat is bad and switch the baby to low-fat milk. Some mothers may be struggling with their own eating disorder, such as anorexia nervosa or bulimia, and may fail to understand the caloric needs of small children. Some families are dealing with depression, substance abuse, or domestic violence. Parents with developmental delay may have trouble understanding nutritional requirements for babies. And of course, another contributing factor may be poverty. The Supplemental Food Program for Women, Infants and Children (WIC) provides only enough formula to meet 75% of an infant's daily needs. Some families may run out of money for food before the next TANF (Temporary Aid to Needy Families) check, packet of food stamps, or paycheck comes. These parents may dilute the formula to make it last longer. Poverty also contributes to overcrowding, disorganization, and increased distractions in the home, all of which can interfere with feeding an infant (Frank, Silva, & Needlman, 1993).

Implications for Practice: Treating Failure to Thrive

Infancy is a time of rapid growth, and good nutrition during this time is vital for optimal development. Nutritional deficits during infancy can have long-lasting effects, including growth deficits, decreased resistance to infection, later personality problems, learning disorders, poor academic performance, and mental retardation. But blaming the mother for her infant's slow growth only makes her defensive and resistant to help. Ephross (1982) states that failure to thrive is not the result of maternal emotional deprivation but is a problem of family dysfunction with multiple causes. Failure-to-thrive families are not "bad" families but people with problems who need help.

These families may need counseling to deal with depression, substance abuse, grief and loss issues, and environmental stress. Parents may need help in establishing techniques to deal with a difficult, hard-to-feed infant. Many parents need help in improving parent-child interactions, especially in establishing positive, rewarding feeding experiences that are free from coercion, food battles, and the distraction of television. Information on infant developmental norms and the nutritional needs of babies can benefit many new parents. Because of their risk for developmental delay, failure-to-thrive infants are often eligible for early intervention services. (See Focus on Development: Early Intervention for Developmental Delay, page 201.)

Infants with severe failure to thrive may require hospitalization, but many families require intensive outpatient and in-home treatment for many months from a team of professionals including a pediatrician, a nutritionist, and a social worker (Frank, 1993).

INFANT MENTAL HEALTH

On hearing the term *infant mental health,* many people laugh and ask how you do therapy with a baby. Does he lie in a crib and free-associate? Actually, in the last 20 years there has been a significant increase in the knowledge of the emotional, social, and cognitive functioning of infants. Along with this knowledge has come an interest in working with the problems of infancy. Infants are vulnerable creatures subject to abuse and neglect. Infants may withdraw from interactions and even seem to suffer from depression. They can also develop problems with feeding, sleeping, and behavioral regulation (Emde, 1987). But as we have seen, they are very resilient and can respond to appropriate intervention.

Problems in the infant-parent relationship can occur as the result of many different factors including previous pregnancy loss, postpartum depression, medical/developmental problems of the infant, drug use by parents, abuse of the infant, prolonged separations, family stress, mental illness of a parent, or a parent with a long-standing attachment disorder of his or her own.

Out of the concern for the psychological problems of infancy has come the multidisciplinary specialty of infant mental health. This specialty is concerned with the factors that affect the psychological health of infants and with development of methods to assess and treat these small clients (Lieberman, 1985). The traditional knowledge base and intervention skills of social workers are especially suited for work in this

field (Bonkowski & Yanos, 1992). The Education of the Handicapped Act Amendments of 1986 require that states provide family-based services for at-risk children from birth to age 3. This requirement opens opportunities for social workers to become actively involved in providing services to infants and their families.

Implications for Practice: Assessment and Interventions of Infant Mental Health

The University of Southern Maine has developed a tool to assess and enhance the emotional well-being of children from birth to five years. This brief assessment instrument is called AIMS, which is an acronym for:

Attachment—The emotional tie between a primary caregiver and an infant

Interaction—A communicative exchange of information between caregiver and child

Mastery—The child's development of increasingly complex physical, cognitive, linguistic, emotional, and social abilities

Social Support—A network of people, resources, and influences available to families that enhances healthy attachment, interaction, and mastery of developmental skills

The AIMS tool looks at children ages 2 weeks, 2, 4, 6, 9, 12, and 18 months, and 2, 3, 4, and 5 years of age. At each age level the tool offers guidelines for psychosocial practice, including interview questions and points of observation to use in assessing each of the AIMS areas of emotional development. The tool also suggests brief interventions to help strengthen each area of emotional development. The example below offers suggested interventions to help strengthen attachment of children aged 0–5 years.

1. Show admiration for the baby/child (appearance, personality, health, behavior) in the presence of the parent

2. Point out parent's ability to "hear" child's cries/ requests and to respond appropriately

3. Discuss the role of the other parent in caregiving

4. Discuss upcoming stages of infant/child development

5. Comment on how proud the parent must be to see the baby/child doing so well

For more information, contact: Project AIMS Human Services Development Institute, University of Southern Maine, 96 Falmouth St., Portland, Maine, 04103, (207) 780-4430.

Other specific interventions include:

- Speaking for the baby—expressing what you interpret the baby is trying to say to the parent, such as, "I would like to eat now"

- Watch, wait, and wonder—having the parent observe the infant and wonder what the infant is thinking or feeling or is trying to communicate

- Developmental play—guiding the parent in age-appropriate play activities with child

- Nurturing the dyad—encouraging the parent to engage in nurturing activities with infant (rocking, cuddling, massage)

SOCIAL DIMENSION

Families, Groups, Support Systems, and Communities

A baby is no longer seen as a passive creature controlled by his basic instincts but is viewed as an active participant in the family environment (Emde, 1987). Treatment of an infant cannot be separated from treatment of the family. Interventions with infants require a systems approach, because problems with a baby do not reside in the baby but in the interactions between the baby and a caregiver or the baby and the family. So, in working with infants, you do not concentrate on the baby alone or the parent alone but on their relationship and on relationships among other family members (Jennings, Wisner, & Conby, 1991).

In fact, many researchers now feel that an infant needs to be viewed less as an individual and more as a social product. Sameroff (1993) describes a transactional model of infant development: ". . . the develop-

ment of the child is seen as a product of a continuous dynamic interaction between the child and the experience provided by his or her family and social context" (p. 6).

FAMILY INFLUENCES

Factors in the family that can affect development include parental personality and temperament, parental mental illness, major family transitions such as death and divorce, and periods of parental unresponsiveness such as those that occur with depression (Crnic & Harris, 1990). Intergenerational patterns also often affect the family environment. Parenting styles are passed on from parents to children, who then use the same style with their own children (Lyons-Ruth & Zeanah, 1993). Parents who abuse their children were often abused as children themselves.

Interactions in the family seem to occur in a circular pattern. Parents who are satisfied with the marriage may interact positively with the baby and have a responsive infant. Stress in the relationship can preoccupy the parents and affect the quality of their interaction with the infant. Marital problems, then, can negatively affect the baby's development.

Ironically, one of the major sources of stress in the relationship can be the babies themselves. A demanding infant can increase the family stress level, which can then interfere with the parents' interactions, which in turn can affect the baby's responses.

Belsky (1981) describes these interactions as **circular influences.** He states that "what transpires between husband and wife might affect a parent's caregiving attitudes and/or behavior, which in turn could influence the infant's functioning, which, coming full circle, might affect the marital relationship." And Clarke-Stewart (1978) looks at this circular influence still another way. The mother's stimulating involvement with the infant enhances the infant's development. This responsive infant increases the father's participation in parenting. The father's interest in the infant further increases the mother's involvement with the baby.

Other family relationships can also play an important role in determining the quality of the family environment. In general, a mother's relationships affect

Fathers are an important source of sensory, affective, and social stimulation for infants.

how she cares for the infant, and this care affects the infant's development (Crockenberg, Lyons-Ruth, & Dickstein, 1993). The more support the caregiver receives, the better care the infant receives. As we have seen, social support is especially important for caregivers of handicapped infants, premature infants, and for caregivers with problems such as depression. Caregivers deal with stress better—whether it is from the infant or other factors of life—if there is adequate support (Crnic & Harris, 1990).

If we consider that the mother is usually the caregiver, where does she receive most of this support? A study by Levitt (1986) asked mothers of 13-month-old infants to identify individuals who supplied support for them. The top two people on the list were family members—the father of the baby and the maternal grandmother. These two family members, then, can indirectly affect the infant's development by supplying support for the mother, but what direct influence might they also have on the infant?

FATHERS AND BABIES

On the birth of his first son, one of the authors of this book asked "When do I get to throw him in the air?" Studies have found that this is a usual male response to interacting with an infant. In general, fathers spend less time with the baby than mothers do. When they do spend time with the baby, that time usually involves playing more than caregiving. Mothers actually play more with babies, but that is because they spend more time overall with the infant. And the quality of the play that fathers engage in with the infant differs from that of mothers. Mothers involve the infant in verbal interactions, whereas fathers are more physical

and rough with their babies. They tend to move the infant's limbs and bounce and lift the infant in the air (Yogman, 1982).

Belsky, Gilstrap, and Rovine (1984) found that fathers also spent more time reading and watching TV with infants, whereas mothers spent more time nurturing and caring for the infants. This does not mean, however, that fathers cannot be nurturing and sensitive caretakers. Fathers who do spend more time with babies and engage in caretaking activities can be sensitive to an infant's cues (Lamb, 1982). What happens when the father is the primary caregiver? The father is just as competent in giving care as the mother is (Parke & O'Leary, 1976), but the father still plays in a more physical way with the infant (Field, 1978).

Fathers, then, can be competent primary caregivers. Babies can form an attachment with fathers much the same as they do with their mothers (Lamb, 1982). The more fathers interact with infants, the greater effect they can have on development.

But what about a father who is not married to and not cohabitating with the mother of his baby? What sort of role will he have in raising his baby? Research has shown that roughly 90% of these fathers spend some time with their babies during the first 15 months of life, but contact tends to decrease over time (Vosler & Robertson, 1998). Single mothers often return to live with their parents, especially in the case of adolescent mothers. Sometimes, if there is not a strong relationship between the baby's father and the mother's family, the maternal grandmother can act as a barrier to the father's interaction with the baby (Vosler & Robertson, 1998). Additional factors, such as poverty, maternal depression, and minimal parental education can also contribute to father non-involvement in nonmarital co-parenting situations (Vosler & Robertson, 1998).

Here's an interesting question: Can fathers experience postpartum depression? While it is not termed as such, some research supports the notion, specifically for inexperienced fathers. Ferketich and Mercer (1995) found that inexperienced fathers evidence significantly more depression than experienced fathers do, largely because of the changes in identity and lifestyle that first-time parents experience.

GRANDPARENTS AND BABIES

Next to the baby's father, the maternal grandmother is the main source of support for most mothers. For single mothers, the maternal grandmother is often the first source of support. In the case of teenage mothers, the grandmother can even step in as the infant's primary caregiver.

Three out of five children see their grandparents at least once per week (Tinsley & Parke, 1987). Studies have found that infants who have frequent contact with their grandparents interact with grandparents in the same manner they do with their parents (Crockenberg, Lyons-Ruth, & Dickstein, 1993), and babies whose grandparents interact with them show higher developmental scores (Tinsley & Parke, 1987), much as they do when they have highly responsive parents. When the mother is struggling with difficulties that interfere with her ability to care for a baby, the grandmother can mediate the effect these maternal problems have on the infant. When the mother is young, single, mentally ill, addicted to drugs, or unable to care for the infant, the grandmother can provide consistent and nurturing care for the baby.

In addition, with so many mothers returning to work after the birth of their babies, many grandmothers are assuming child-care responsibilities (Lewis, 1987). This is especially true for lower-SES families. In some cases, because of parents' substance abuse, poverty, hopelessness, and disability from AIDS, grandparents are serving as primary caregivers and are raising the children. Oyserman, Radin, and Benn (1993) suggest that grandfathers can fill the role of absent fathers for children of single mothers. In fact, the American Association for Retired Persons (AARP) now publishes a newsletter for grandparents raising grandchildren; it also provides a grandparent information center.

SIBLINGS AND BABIES

Often the mother of an infant with an older sibling, when asked the age of her baby, will reply with something like, "He's 18 months, but he thinks he's 4." Infants with an older sibling may spend a large portion of their time in the company of that sibling. Spending so much time with another person can certainly influence development. Infants tend to imitate their older siblings. If the interactions with the sibling are positive, the baby can learn sharing and cooperation (Dunn, 1991). However, 25% of all interactions between 18-month-olds and their siblings involve conflict and aggression. Dunn and Munn (1986) found that the level of aggression of an older sibling was correlated to the level of aggression of the younger child six months later.

Crockenberg, Lyons-Ruth, and Dickstein (1993) state that because infants imitate older siblings, it is important to understand how siblings influence infant development. More research is needed in this area. Can a sibling help provide comfort and support when parents are emotionally or physically unavailable? Can an aggressive sibling teach the baby to be more aggressive in interactions with others?

BABIES AND THEIR PEERS

Young babies often interact by curiously poking each other in the eyes. Actually, babies really do interact with one another—at least to some extent. In the first year, babies look, smile, touch, and vocalize with one another (Mueller & Vandell, 1979). In the second year, toys become more important in interactions. Of course, many of these interactions involve babies taking toys away from each other. But babies can also play some simple games together (Mueller & Lucas, 1975). Babies will play contingency games, in which one will perform an action and the other will respond to it; say, one baby will throw a doll up in the air and the other will scream. At 20 months, babies begin to interact more fully with one another. They begin to take turns in an activity and may be able to roll a ball back and forth without running to retrieve the ball before it reaches the other baby.

PLAYING WITH BABY

Every baby is unique, and each may enjoy a different amount of stimulation through play. For new parents, as well as parents of special-needs babies, it can be difficult to know when and how much a baby wants to play. Following are a few guidelines that parents can keep in mind when they are playing with their baby (adapted from Griffith, D., 1992).

1. Never "force" a baby to play when he is distressed or disinterested. Look for signs such as distress due to overstimulation, baby averting his eyes, yawning, sneezing, skin color changes, rapid breathing, and crying. Stopping play at the first signs of distress can help a baby regain control, which aids in the development of self-regulation skills.

2. Calm baby immediately if she reaches a frantic state of crying. Swaddle the baby to help her relax and control body movements. Providing a pacifier for sucking can help a baby soothe herself.

3. Play with the baby at times when she is calm and alert. Avoid overstimulation by presenting only one toy at a time, keeping the toys relatively simple (for example, rattles, balls).

4. Increase intensity of play (duration, frequency, new objects) as the baby becomes more comfortable.

5. Unswaddle baby during play and times when he is awake and calm. This allows him the freedom to explore, as well as providing him with opportunities to develop motor control.

ADOPTION

California couple, financially secure, with much love and affection to offer, wishes to adopt white newborn to age 1. Suburban home, lots of pets. Can provide a secure and rewarding life for your baby.

Newspapers are full of such ads placed by couples looking for a baby to adopt. Many ads specify white newborns, but with the number of young girls who choose abortion or single parenting, the search for a white infant can be long and frustrating.

Adoptions can be arranged through an agency or a private source. Most states have agencies that handle adoptions in the state welfare department or department of children's services. Children can also be adopted through private agencies that are regulated by the state. However, the wait for an infant through an agency may take years, so some couples seek other adoption options.

In some states, private adoptions can be arranged through a physician or a lawyer. Adoptions can even be started through ads placed in a newspaper and then processed privately by a lawyer. However, more problems are connected with these private adoptions. Parents pursuing this type of adoption may receive less background information on the birth parents than they would through an agency, and birth mothers receive less counseling. The financial costs to the adopting couple can be high. And private adoptions may involve more legal problems than agency adoptions (Costin, Bell, & Downs, 1991).

Because the supply of white infants is so limited, some parents choose to adopt older children, special-needs children, or foreign infants. One-half of children adopted are over 2 years old. Special-needs children include those who have disabilities, and the state may provide a subsidy to adopting parents to help cover medical expenses. Ten percent of adoptions are international adoptions (Schuster & Ashburn, 1992).

OPEN ADOPTION

In years past, parents who adopted a child as an infant often debated whether or not to tell him or her about the adoption. Many children grew up not knowing they were adopted, and the birth mother's identity was kept secret from those who did know. Parents are now encouraged to be honest with the child from the beginning. In 1975, laws changed to allow adults who had been adopted to obtain information about their birth parents if those parents did not object. This change in attitude toward adoption information has led to **open adoptions.**

In this type of adoption, the birth mother and sometimes the birth father participate in choosing a family for their baby. That family may choose to attend childbirth preparation with the birth mother and be present at the baby's birth. The birth mother may stay in contact with the

Many families choose to adopt. This family has adopted two children of mixed race.

family as the child grows, exchanging letters and photographs. Sometimes visits are arranged between the birth mother and the child. In some cases these visits are arranged through the adoption agency and are limited to once or twice a year, whereas in other cases the birth mother may serve as the child's babysitter (Foster, Hunsberger, & Anderson, 1989).

Open adoptions can lead to problems, though. What about families with adopted children from different birth parents? What if one birth mother stays in contact with the child and the other does not? What if the birth mother ceases contact with the child at a later time? In addition, adoptive parents may agree to any conditions of the birth mother in order to have a baby. How does this affect their parenting abilities (Costin, Bell, & Downs, 1991)? Also, the birth mother may change her mind after the baby is born, leaving a couple—who may have waited through the pregnancy, furnished a nursery, and attended the birth—without a child. But when both sets of parents agree on the conditions of the open adoption, this arrangement can be satisfactory to all involved.

TRANSRACIAL ADOPTION

Adoption of children of a race different from that of the adopting family—**transracial adoption**—is highly controversial. The majority of couples looking to adopt a child are white, but many of the children available for adoption are not. This means that, without transracial adoption, many white couples remain childless while minority children wait in foster care for permanent homes twice as long as white children (Smith, 1995). But the National Association of Black Social Workers (NABSW) is opposed to transracial adoptions. They believe that African-American children raised in a white home will lose connection with their race and culture—that the children will grow up not fitting into either culture.

The Multiethnic Placement Act of 1994 prohibits adoption decisions based solely on race, color, or national origin. This law was developed in order to reduce the amount of time minority children wait to be adopted. (This law does not affect the Indian Child Welfare Act, discussed in the next section.) The National

Association of Social Workers (NASW) still states that efforts should be made to place a child in the home of parents who are of similar racial and ethnic background. The NABSW now recommends that transracial adoptions be considered only as a last resort.

Prospective foster and adoptive parents need to become familiar with and understand racial and cross-cultural issues before adopting a child of different race. Efforts need to be made to increase the number of prospective foster and adoptive parents from all races and cultures (Smith, 1995).

NATIVE-AMERICAN ADOPTION

Another controversy surrounds the adoption of Native-American children. In the 1950s and 1960s, 25%–35% of all Native-American children were removed from their families. Many of these children were taken from parents who were poor and lived in homes with no indoor plumbing. After adoption, these children were often raised in circumstances that deprived them of their culture and heritage. Many believed that this practice was threatening the future of Native-American tribes (Doyle, 1995).

In 1978, Congress passed the Indian Child Welfare Act, giving tribes control over adoption of Native-American children. Adoptions involving Native-American children require not only a release from the birth parents but also a release from the tribe. Even when the parents agree to the adoption by a non-Indian family, the tribe can veto the process and place the child with a Native-American family. Critics claim that children have been removed from adoptive parents and returned to a tribe even when the birth parents did not live on a reservation and had no tribal affiliation. Tribes argue, however, that to preserve heritage, Native-American children need to be raised by Native-American families.

BIRTH FATHERS

The rights of birth fathers is another area of concern. The well-publicized case of Baby Jessica illustrates this problem. Jan and Roberta DeBoer adopted a 1-week-old baby girl after the baby's birth mother agreed to the adoption and signed the release. However, the birth mother lied about the identity of the baby's father, claiming the father was her present boyfriend.

She changed her mind about the adoption after several weeks and told the real father of the baby—her ex-boyfriend, Dan Schmidt. He then petitioned for custody of the baby on the grounds that he had not signed a release for the adoption as the father of the infant. The DeBoers challenged the petition in court for two years. Finally, the Supreme Court refused to hear the case, upholding a lower-court decision giving custody of the baby to the birth parents, who had in the meantime married and given birth to another child. As the nation watched on television, Jessica, then 2 years old, was removed, crying, from the arms of her adopted mother and turned over to her birth parents.

In 1972, the Supreme Court ruled that unwed fathers could not be denied custody of their children unless they were proved unfit as parents. But how long a time period should an unwed father have to assert his parental rights? Some states allow six months, which is a long time for a baby to wait for a home. Some agencies will not consider an adoption unless the birth mother names the father of the baby so his release may be obtained. But some birth mothers will not name the father out of fear or because they do not want him to be involved (Foster, Hunsberger, & Anderson, 1989). Many men do not learn of the birth of a child until the child has been placed in an adoptive home. At that point, should the baby be removed from a home he may have lived in for several months and be turned over to the birth father? Or, if the man is not an unfit parent, should the birth mother be allowed to decide the fate of his child without his consent?

In 1983, the Supreme Court ruled that men could not claim rights to a child unless they had established a relationship with the child. How can a man establish a relationship, though, if the birth mother keeps the pregnancy and birth a secret from him? In response to this problem, New York and other states have established a putative father registry for unwed fathers. An unmarried man must register so that he can be notified of any adoption proceedings involving a potential offspring.

Implications for Practice: Making Difficult Decisions in Adoption Practices

Adoption brings up the question of what takes precedence: the best interests of the child or the rights of the birth parents, ethnic group, or tribe? Children have been removed from homes they have lived in for months because of issues of paternal rights, same-race placement, and tribal affiliation. Some claim that children's rights should be considered first and that the children should remain in homes where they have come to consider the adoptive parents their family. But the issue is very complicated. For instance, many were appalled that baby Jessica was removed from the only home she had ever known and given to total strangers who just happened to be her parents. But her birth father had petitioned for parental rights when she was only three weeks old. The DeBoers fought a long battle that lasted two years, but some believe that the best interest of the child would have been to surrender the baby in the beginning instead of keeping her until she was attached to her adoptive family.

Social workers need to consider these issues carefully. What are the rights of birth fathers? Should children be raised in same-race homes? How long should children wait in foster care for same-race families? Should tribes have the right to protect cultural heritage?

Another issue concerns children placed in foster care because of abuse or neglect. These children may wait for years for parental rights to be terminated to release them for adoption. Many believe that these children should be permanently removed from their parents and placed for adoption. Others favor family preservation efforts with the ultimate goal of reuniting children with their birth families. They believe that poor people are penalized by having their children taken away. Many birth mothers are poor and single, whereas couples wishing to adopt are financially secure and married. And sometimes children love their parents even though those parents are inadequate.

FOCUS ON SOCIOLOGY

How Are Adoptive Families Doing?

Approximately 25% of adopted children, as compared with 15% of non-adopted children, require clinical intervention for severe behavioral problems. However, research by psychologists reveals that adopted children and their adoptive families do quite well.

David Brodzinsky at Rutgers University has been studying adoption for more than 20 years, and he reports that approximately 75%–80% of adopted children are well within the normal psychological range. Adopted children are most often referred for clinical treatment for problems such as acting out or aggression starting at age 5 to 7 years, when they are just beginning to understand that they've lost their birth family as well as having gained an adoptive family. Brodzinsky found that coping styles affected their experiences; children in adoptive families that had a problem-focused, assistance-seeking style of coping fared much better than did those with an avoidant style of coping. He also found that adopted children have neither more nor less serious problems than do non-adopted children when their parents divorce—it affects both groups "in a serious way." Anu Sharma and her colleagues at the Search Institute in Minneapolis conducted a study of 181 adopted adolescents and found that most of the teens were functioning within the normal mental health range and that the teens described themselves as attached to their parents. Children from open adoptions, in which birth mothers have contact with their children, also seem to lack the confusion many had feared they would have about their parents' identity. Harold Grotevant at the University of Minnesota and Ruth McRoy at the University of Texas at Austin found that the children view their adoptive mother as their mother and view the birth mother as an aunt or friend.

The experience of adoption also brings adoptive parents closer together. Cornell University researcher Jeffrey Haugaard finds this to be especially true in cases in which the child has problematic behavior, because the parents come together to deal with this behavior. Haugaard also found that older adoptees form stronger attachments to their adopted fathers than to their adopted mothers; he speculates that this may be because they feel abandoned by their birth mother. Ellen Pinderhughes at Vanderbilt University is developing a family-systems model to research situations such as those in which birth mothers' maternal rights have been terminated owing to abuse or neglect.

Jane Wenk (Adapted from DeAngelis, 1995a)

DAY CARE

In Chapter 11, we discuss the fact that, in general, maternal employment may have a positive effect on children's development. But what about infants less than a year old whose mothers work full-time outside the home? Does maternal employment in the first year interfere with attachment? Do babies who grow up in day care suffer any ill effects? Many researchers have tried to answer these questions.

Belsky and Rovine (1988) looked at attachment in infants with working mothers. Their research suggested that babies whose mothers worked more than 20 hours a week were at risk of forming insecure attachments. However, Clarke-Stewart (1989) argues that such studies run into problems because they use the Strange Situation procedure to assess attachment. Children in day care may be more used to strangers and may not exhibit apprehension in a stranger's presence. When assessed using the Strange Situation procedure, then, these children would not be wary of the strange situation or the stranger and would therefore not receive secure attachment rating. In fact, other studies (Chase-Landsdale & Owen, 1987) have found no difference in attachment for children in day care. In relation to day care affecting attachment, Belsky and Rovine (1988) concluded that it is too hard to say what the effects are because it depends "on the child, the family, and the particular day care arrangements." (See Focus on Research: Who's Minding the Baby? this page.) In fact, some professionals are beginning to think that day care gives children a secure caregiver with whom to form an attachment when the home lacks a secure, reliable caregiver.

Implications for Practice: The Realities of Day Care

Although it is interesting to discuss the effects of day care on child development, many mothers do not have much choice about whether or not they return to work after the birth of a baby. Financially, many women need to work to pay the bills and buy the food. Some women return to work within weeks of giving birth. They must find care for their infants, and there just are not enough federally subsidized day-care centers for low-income women (Specht & Craig, 1987). Some studies have suggested that good day care can increase the cognitive and social functioning of disadvantaged children (Broberg et al., 1997; Brock, 1980; Devaney, Ellwood, & Love, 1997). One study examining the cognitive effects of the federal Head Start program found that children who attended Head Start showed more cognitive improvement than either children who did not attend preschool or children who attended a preschool program other than Head Start (Devaney, Ellwood, & Love, 1997). However, many jobs available to low-income women do not pay enough for them to afford good day care. Without federally subsidized care, these women must rely on other arrangements that may not be as beneficial to the baby's development.

FOCUS ON RESEARCH

Who's Minding the Baby?

More than half of the children living in the United States are in the care of someone other than their mother for significant periods of time. What type of child care is best in terms of a child's healthy psychological development? Until now the answer wasn't clear, but a study of child care conducted by the National Institute of Child Health and Human Development (NICHD) provides some revealing data.

In 1990, a team of NICHD researchers recruited 1,364 infants from two-parent and single-parent families across the United States representing a range of socioeconomic and sociocultural backgrounds. The study included a random sample of which approximately 60% had mothers who worked or attended school full-time, 20% had mothers who worked or attended school part-time, and 20% had mothers who stayed at home full-time. Parents of the infants studied chose a variety of child-care situations, including child care provided by the fathers and grandparents of the child, child care in a home setting, and child care in a day-care center.

Researchers find that children are most likely to receive higher-quality caregiving when there are fewer children being cared for and the child-to-adult ratios are low. This study also revealed that less authoritarian beliefs about child-rearing on the part of caregivers, as well as the provision of stimulating physical facilities, were most likely to result in higher-quality caregiving. According to the research, the highest quality of caregiving was provided by fathers and grandparents as well as in-home caregivers, whereas the lowest quality of caregiving was provided by child-care centers. However, regardless of care type, an adult-child ratio of 1 to 1 was the best predictor of high-quality caregiving.

(Adapted from Azar, 1995 by Jane Wenk)

Multicultural and Gender Considerations

When feeding their infants, mothers in Yorkshire, England, tell their children something about the spoonful of food "going to Auntie Mary's in Bradford." Mothers in Newfoundland tell small children that if they don't eat the crusts of their bread, the Crust Man will steal the children away. Many American mothers fly spoonfuls of food like airplanes into their childrens' mouths. In other cultures, such as the Malay, as soon as children learn to walk they are expected to feed themselves when they get hungry with no encouraging comments from mother (Dettwyler, 1989). These various feeding practices illustrate the fact that parents in different cultures bring different beliefs, attitudes, and practices to the raising of their children. Even in the United States, the child-raising practices and beliefs of ethnic groups can be quite different from those of the majority culture.

Minority infants are more likely to live in homes with younger mothers, single mothers, and large extended families (Coll & Myer, 1993). Minority families face problems including socioeconomic disadvantage, inadequate access to health care, residential segregation, substandard housing, and unemployment. Coll and Myer (1993) state that "if we recognize that these minority and ethnic families experience different cultural expectations, family constellations and access to economic and social resources, in addition to being subjected to prejudice, racism, classism, sexism, and segregation, we would expect that their world view and their infants' developmental outcome would be profoundly affected by these life experiences" (p. 60).

DEVELOPMENTAL ASSESSMENT OF MINORITY INFANTS

Of particular concern is the developmental assessment of minority infants, because the norms established for developmental assessment instruments are based on the majority of children in this country, who are Anglo. Compared with these norms, some minority children may appear abnormal. In particular, African infants appear developmentally advanced, whereas Native-American and Asian infants may be a bit reserved on standard measures. You may remember from the last chapter that there is some evidence that these characteristics may be genetic, but infant-care practices among cultures also vary and may contribute to this difference. African infants are handled vigorously by their mothers from birth. Their mothers place them in an upright position for most of the day and encourage early sitting, standing, and walking (Cintas, 1988). Native-American and Asian infants, in contrast, are more protected by their parents.

Cintas (1988) cautions that practitioners "working among a heterogeneous population such as that in the United States need to be cognizant that cultural variations in developmental patterns do exist. Further, since infant care practices appear to have some influence on neuromotor performance, North American therapists and families can perhaps benefit from knowledge of parent care methods in other cultures" (p. 17).

FOCUS ON MULTICULTURALISM

Understanding Different Cultural Beliefs

Understanding different cultural beliefs is important when working with minority families with infants. Coll and Myer (1993) discuss the clinical implications of working with families from minority cultures. First, the family with different attitudes and beliefs may not feel that a "problem"—whether biological, psychological, or social—exists. For instance, in some cultures, having a baby as a teen is a way to gain status and respect in the community. Dealing with the "problems" of teenage motherhood in this community, then, could be difficult if the community does not see it as a problem. In fact, Burton (1990) found that in one African-American community with a high level of male unemployment, teenage childbearing was encouraged; because the maternal grandmother would be caring for the infant, she (as the mother of the teenager) would be young enough to take care of and enjoy the baby. Families have different ideas as to the origin of a problem as well (Coll & Meyer, 1993). Some families may see a developmental problem as an act of God, as punishment for past sins, or as a test of faith. Some may turn to faith healers or religious leaders for a cure. Families also differ in their expectations of treatment. Play therapy to facilitate parent-infant interactions may be inappropriate for cultures that do not see the mother's role as including playing with her children. In those cultures, grandparents, siblings, and other children are expected to interact with infants. Asian mothers often take on the role of teacher of their infants (Coll & Meyer, 1993).

Coll and Meyer (1993) suggest a series of cultural assessment questions that can help provide an idea of how a family views a problem—what the problem is, how it originated, and what the family expects in terms of treatment.

1. What do you think caused your child's problem?
2. Why do you think it started when it did?
3. What do you think the problem does to your child? How does it work?
4. How severe is your child's problem? Do you expect it will have a short- or long-term course?
5. What kind of treatment do you think your child should receive?
6. What are the most important results that you hope to have your child receive from treatment?
7. What are the main things that the problem has caused for you and your child?
8. What do you fear most about your child's problem?

GENDER ISSUES

Some mothers joke that the first time you hand a baby boy a truck, he will push it on the floor and say, "rrrrrrr"

or some other appropriate truck noise, whereas a baby girl will try to feed it her bottle. Just how different are baby boys and girls, and how much of that difference is learned from their parents?

Although children do not label themselves as boys or girls until they are 2½ to 3 years old, they display gender differences in behavior from birth (Coll & Meyer, 1993). As summarized in Bjorklund and Bjorklund (1992), boys are more aggressive, more active, take more chances, are more demanding of parental attention, and get into more mischief as toddlers. Girls are more nurturing and more compliant at this age.

In the second year of life, infants begin to show toy preferences. By 18 to 22 months, boys play more with trucks and cars, and girls play with dolls and soft toys (Smith & Daglish, 1977). But to what extent do parents and others encourage children to play with these sex-associated toys?

Babies actually are treated differently from birth. Parents are more rough and active with baby boys and more verbally interactive with baby girls. Studies by Fagot (1978, 1991) show that fathers give fewer positive responses to boys who play with cross-sex toys, and mothers give more verbal instructions to girls. Parents encourage girls to participate in dancing, playing dress-up, and playing with dolls, whereas they encourage boys to play with blocks, trucks, and push-and-pull toys. Interestingly, children of parents who encourage sex-associated toy play can accurately label themselves as boy or girl sooner than other children (Fagot, 1989, 1992).

Even parents who want to be non-gender-specific in interactions with their infants may unconsciously alter their responses. For instance, consider a 14-month-old girl who brings a truck to show to her mother. Her mother wants to encourage her daughter to play with typically male toys, so she says, "What have you got there, a truck? That's good, honey." Then the baby approaches her mother with a doll and mother says, "What a pretty baby. Is she your baby? Is she hungry? Are you her mommy? Maybe you should feed her. Go get her bottle and give her some milk. You be the mommy and feed your baby." Which toy do you think the little girl has been rewarded for playing with? With the interactions that occur between babies, parents, and others, children may refuse to play with cross-sex toys by the age of 18 to 24 months (Shaffer, 1993).

Coll and Meyer (1993) offer this conclusion from the literature on gender and infants: "Gender differences in behavior from birth have been documented in a variety of cultures. . . . But more important than actual sex differences in behavior may be the caregivers' interpretations of an infant's behavior, development, and needs as a function of the infant's gender" (p. 59).

Social Hazards

As we discussed in the last chapter, poverty can have a detrimental effect on development. Infants in poor families are more likely to have inadequate nutrition and are also more likely to have increased blood lead levels (see the subsequent section on lead poisoning). Poor infants have more health problems and more injuries, and when abused or neglected they are more likely to be removed from their homes. Seventy percent of children in foster care are from poor families (Halpern, 1993).

Infants living in poverty are more likely to have an impoverished environment with irregular daily routines, overcrowding, little attention for the baby, and lack of parental responsiveness (Halpern, 1993). Poverty adds to the caregiver's stress and can contribute to depression, making it difficult to care for an infant (Sachs, Pietrukowicz, & Hall, 1997). The effects of prenatal poverty may have resulted in a premature birth or a baby with complications. This infant may need extra care and parental responsiveness, but the energy of the mother must go to dealing with the problems of living and not to the infant. Halpern states that "a fussy, disorganized, low-birthweight infant is likely to overtax the limited physical and emotional resources of an already overstressed mother" (p. 75). The mother may then avoid interacting with the infant.

Homeless infants are at highest risk. Having no home makes it very difficult to meet the needs of an infant. How does a homeless caregiver prepare bottles, store infant food, wash clothes, provide a safe environment to explore, find toys? Because of poverty, then, a difficult-to-care-for infant may be born to an overstressed mother with few resources. The infant adds to the mother's stress, and the baby is at increased risk of abuse and neglect.

ENVIRONMENTAL CONTEXT AND CHILD DEVELOPMENT

So far, in considering factors that can affect development, we have looked at the characteristics of the child and then of the family. A third variable that is important for optimal development is the type of environment the child experiences—in other words, the child's home. The quality of the home environment affects the health and development of an individual, and a poor environment may result in poor development. Halpern (1993) discusses aspects of the infant's environment that contribute to good developmental outcomes, including the cognitive, socioemotional, and physical environment of the home.

Cognitively, infants develop well if they receive rich and varied verbal interaction from their caregivers. The caregivers should place an emphasis on learning and provide a variety of stimulation for the baby. In the socioemotional realm, infants need parents who are responsive, warm, and nurturing. Harsh punishment can have negative effects for the baby. The physical environment should be safe and well organized. The baby should have adequate areas to explore. Appropriate and stimulating toys and play materials should be available for the infant to investigate and manipulate. Early intervention was mentioned previously in the chapter as a means of assisting infants who have developmental delay or mental retardation. But early intervention programs can also help infants who are at risk because of socioeconomic factors. Research shows that at-risk infants involved in early intervention between 0–3 years of age exhibit improved cognitive development and social competence (Ramey & Ramey, 1998a). And these benefits seem to be long-lasting. Positive effects of preschool-age and continued intervention can be maintained through age 12 (Campbell & Ramey, 1994).

Taking these factors into consideration, what is an impoverished environment? This would be a home that is overcrowded, noisy, and disorganized. The baby would have no set routine or predictability. Multiple caregivers would come and go. Siblings as young as 9 years old would be responsible for watching the baby (Sachs, Pietrukowicz, & Hall, 1997). Someone may calm the baby by handing the child a bottle filled with cola. The baby may be confined to a small area

Sample Items from the Home Inventory (Infant-Toddler Version)

EMOTIONAL AND VERBAL
RESPONSIVENESS OF PARENTS

Parent responds to the child's vocalizations with verbal response.

Parent caresses or kisses child at least once during visit.

ACCEPTANCE OF CHILD

Parent does not shout at child during visit.

Parent does not interfere with child's actions or restrict child's movements more than three times during visit.

ORGANIZATION OF THE PHYSICAL AND
TEMPORAL ENVIRONMENT

When parent is away, care is provided by one of three regular substitutes.

Someone takes child to grocery store at least once a week.

PROVISION OF APPROPRIATE PLAY MATERIALS

Child has some muscle-activity toys or equipment.

Parent provides toys or some interesting activities for child during visit.

PARENTAL INVOLVEMENT WITH CHILD

Parent consciously encourages developmental advance.

Parent structures child's play periods.

OPPORTUNITIES FOR VARIETY
IN DAILY STIMULATION

Father provides some caretaking every day.

Family visits or receives visits from relatives once a month.

(Adapted from Bradley & Brisby, 1990)

---

with few toys or interesting objects to manipulate. The baby would receive little or no verbal interaction or warmth from caregivers. Caregivers may fail to respond to or meet the baby's needs.

Unfortunately, the negative effects of the infant's environment can have a long-term effect. In one longitudinal study, Shaw, Keenan, Vondra, Delliquadri, and Giovannelli (1997) found that environmental and family problems, as well as infant temperament and parenting factors, contribute to internalizing problems seen in the child at age 5.

Implications for Practice: Assessing the Home Environment

Quality of the home environment should be considered when making an assessment. Researchers have developed various methods for measuring the quality of a child's home. The most widely used measurement is the Home Observation for Measurement of the Environment Inventory, or HOME Inventory (Caldwell & Bradley, 1984). This instrument is designed to measure

the quality and quantity of stimulation and support available to the child in the home. It consists of 45 items separated into six subscales: parental responsiveness, acceptance of child, organization of environment, play materials, parental involvement with child, and variety of stimulation (see Box 6.2). Assessment of the environment consists of observation of the home and a semistructured interview conducted in the child's home with a primary caregiver (Bradley & Brisby, 1990).

FOCUS ON RESILIENCY

Programs Targeted at Infants and Children Living in Poverty

As we have discussed, infants and children living in poverty are exposed to an array of problems that put them at risk for biological, psychological, and social difficulties. Poor nutrition, lack of health insurance, and poor or inconsistent caregiving are some risk factors that children in poverty consistently face. Federally funded programs have been instituted that specifically target risk factors such as these.

The Supplemental Food Program for Women, Infants, and Children (WIC) was mentioned in Chapter 5 as a source of supplemental nutrition for low-income pregnant women and their children up to 5 years of age. This program has proven to be highly successful in its goal of providing nutrition for low-income infants, with statistics showing close to 100% coverage of eligible babies. Unfortunately, only 57% of eligible children between 1 and 4 years are enrolled.

Medicaid was created in 1965 to provide health insurance for single mothers, infants, and children. Medicaid eligibility for children varies from state to state and is based on the family's income. However, eligibility was expanded in the 1980s to improve coverage for more low-income children. While efforts to provide low-income children with health insurance have increased, many children from working-class homes are uninsured because their parents make too much money to qualify for Medicaid but too little to afford private insurance.

Finally, there is project Head Start (see also Chapter 7), which was created in 1965 to improve the cognitive, intellectual, and social development of preschool-age children living in poverty. Head Start has grown to be the nation's primary federally funded child-development preschool program. In the 1990s, Early Head Start was created, which is a program that specifically targets children from birth to 3 years of age. Its goal is to enhance infant and toddler development by working closely with parents and families (Lally & Keith, 1997).

While programs such as WIC, Medicaid, and Head Start cannot eliminate the existence of poverty, they can help in counteracting many of its negative effects.

(Written by Beth A. Auerbach-Dixon; adapted from Devaney, Ellwood, & Love, 1997)

INFANT ABUSE

One-third of the child victims of abuse are less than 1 year old. Factors that put children at risk for abuse and neglect during the first year of life include poverty, minimal maternal education, maternal depression, presence of other young children in the home, and the mother's separation from her own mother before age 14 (Kotch et al., 1995). A common injury to babies at this age is head trauma. Infants who are difficult to soothe and who cry uncontrollably are at particular risk of this type of injury (Mrazek, 1993). Head trauma may occur from someone hitting the baby's head against a hard object, but a head injury can also occur if someone shakes the infant. This form of abuse is known as **shaken infant syndrome.** Some parents who would never dream of hitting a baby's head against a wall will pick a crying infant up and, out of sheer frustration, shake the baby. Difficult and demanding infants may be at a higher risk for this type of abuse. The frustrated parent shakes the infant to stop the infant's crying. Unfortunately, it works; the baby suffers a head injury, and possibly a concussion, and stops crying. The next time the infant cries, the parent is more likely to shake the infant again. But shaking an infant can cause severe injury. Babies have weak neck muscles and cannot control their heads well. When shaken, the head moves back and forth rapidly, and the brain hits the skull. There is usually no external evidence of injury, such as bruising, but there is usually bleeding of the brain and retinal hemorrhage. Many shaken infants suffer permanent neurological damage, seizure disorders, blindness, and deafness. Visible symptoms of a shaken baby include lethargy, crying, vomiting, loss of appetite, and seizures. Twenty-five percent die from their injuries.

Parents at risk of physically harming their infants need help. They need information on ways to deal with a crying infant. They need to understand that the baby's responses are not intentional; the baby is not out to get them. They need help in learning to control and modify their infant's responses, and they may need to adjust the level of stimulation the baby receives. They need to understand differences in temperament—that a difficult, demanding baby cannot help being that way. They may need help in dealing with stress in their lives and in finding adequate resources and social support. These parents need to know that, when they are at the end of their rope and on the verge of lashing out at the infant, they should put the baby in the crib, close the door, and take a break. They can call someone else to come over and deal with the baby for a while. They especially need to know to *never shake a baby*.

Another form of infant abuse is **Munchausen's syndrome by proxy.** In this form of abuse, the caregiver (usually the mother) induces symptoms of illness in her child. The mother may administer syrup of ipecac to the baby to induce vomiting or may place drops of blood in the infant's urine. Of particular concern are babies who seem to be suffering from apnea (episodes where breathing stops). This apnea may be a result of efforts by the mother to fabricate illness in the child by smothering the child and then seeking help to resuscitate the infant. This form of abuse places infants at high risk of death. Infants who are intentionally suffocated by the caregiver are sometimes dismissed as a SIDS death. Normally, a complete autopsy and death investigation must be conducted to determine a diagnosis of SIDS. Unfortunately, SIDS death and death from suffocation cannot be *distinguished* by autopsy (American Academy of Pediatrics, 1993). In fact, one study estimated that close to 5% of SIDS deaths were caused by abuse (American Academy of Pediatrics, 1994). Situational and familial factors play an important role in helping distinguish abuse from SIDS (for instance, history of apnea in the presence of one caregiver, death at an age greater than 6 months, and unexplained deaths of one or more siblings) (American Academy of Pediatrics, 1994). An example of child abuse mistaken as SIDS is the case of Marie Noe who, in 1999, confessed to suffocating eight of her babies between the years 1949 to 1968 (McCoy, 1999). At the time, each infant's death was attributed to "crib death."

Other evidence of abuse of infants includes bruising, skull fractures, broken bones, and burns. Box 6.3 discusses ways to differentiate between accidental and inflicted injuries.

FOSTER CARE

Infants who are abused or neglected may be removed from their parents and placed in foster care. In many cases, the aim is to return the child to the parents when the abusive or neglectful situation changes. Some children, though, remain in foster care for a long time, waiting to return home or to be placed for adoption. And some children move from one foster home to another. This lack of permanence and continuity of care can have detrimental effects on an infant. There is evidence that abuse, neglect, and late age of adoption placement increase emotional and/or behavioral problems in children (Dumaret, Duyme, & Tomkiewicz, 1997), which can influence the success of foster care placement. Dumaret, Duyme, and Tomkiewicz. suggest that foster and adoptive families be made aware of a child's history so they can be more sensitive to the child's needs.

Fahlberg (1991) suggests the following guidelines for children placed in foster care. The child's previous caregivers should participate in the placement decision. The caregivers should be included in a separation interview to help determine what type of placement would be best for the child. Caregivers should continue visiting the child in foster care; visitation allows the attachment relationship to continue and allows the caregivers to practice positive interactions with the child. Davis, Landsverk, Newton, and Ganger (1996) found that parents who visited their children as recommended by the courts had high rates of reunification, although compliance with visitation was not a predictor of which children remained in their parent's home after 12 months. Whenever possible, siblings should be placed in the same foster home.

LEAD POISONING

In older buildings, constructed before 1950, walls were painted with paint that contained up to 50% lead. As the buildings aged, the paint began to peel off the walls. In poor areas, many neglected, run-down dwellings have problems with peeling lead-based paint. It is estimated that more than one million children under the age of 6 live in these buildings ("Ongoing efforts . . . ," 1999). Infants will put anything in their mouths, including paint chips. Eating this paint causes lead to build up in their systems. Children with high lead levels in their blood may have problems with learning and with delayed growth and hearing loss. One out of six children in the United States has toxic blood lead levels that can affect intellectual functioning. The percentage of poor children with high lead levels is nine times higher than that of more affluent children. The lead levels of African-American children are

Accidental versus Inflicted Injuries (Child Abuse): What to Look for

ACCIDENTAL INJURY

The story of how the injury occurred is clear and consistent.

The resulting symptoms occur immediately after the accident.

The caregivers seek treatment for the infant immediately after the injury occurs.

The accident is witnessed by another person.

Someone knows the answer to "what happened" and "how did it happen?"

A major injury that is an accident is the result of a major event. For example,

- Major injuries occur outside the house;
- Falls are not a major cause of death or injury;
- Falls that cause injury are from a significant height (more than 10 feet).

The child is active and climbing.

INFLICTED INJURY

No one knows how the injury occurred and/or the story changes.

The symptoms occur up to days after the alleged injury.

The caregivers may delay seeking treatment for the symptoms.

No one saw the accident or it occurred while only one person was present.

The story is "the same old story"; that is, the baby fell off the couch or bed. (Police refer to "the killer couch.")

A major inflicted injury is described as being caused by a minor event, such as:

- A fall from a height of 2–3 feet;
- A sibling dropped the child;
- Several minor injuries occurred to explain the major injury.

The child is nonmobile.

---

six times higher than those of Caucasian children (Bellinger & Needleman, 1985).

Unfortunately, the lead does not even have to be directly ingested. Even in homes where the paint is not peeling off the walls, household dust can contain lead. In fact, the Community Lead Education and Reduction Corps has found that household dust, ingested unintentionally through normal hand-to-mouth contact, is the primary source of lead exposure for children ("Ongoing efforts . . . ," 1999). Studies have shown that daily exposure to even low levels of lead in the environment can result in inattention, hyperactivity, and irritability (Marlowe, 1985). Although older housing is the main source of lead exposure, lead in the environment is also produced through industrial emissions and from the exhaust of leaded gasoline. Drinking water can also contain lead.

Social workers need to be aware of programs to remove lead-based paint from older dwellings. But that is only part of the problem. Because lead is present in the environment from other sources, many children are at risk of lead poisoning. And now researchers are finding that even low lead levels can affect learning. For this reason, it is now being recommended that all children with learning disabilities or behavior problems be screened for lead exposure. Early identification and treatment reduces the risk of permanent damage, and an inexpensive blood test can identify lead exposure (Marlowe, 1985). An affected child should then be removed from the source of the exposure. If the lead level is high, medications can help remove lead from the body. Recommendations for reducing the potential for lead exposure include the use of air-filtration (HEPA) devices, washing walls, floors, and trim with lead-specific detergent, and monitoring children's hand-to-mouth activity and hygiene.

PARENTS WITH MENTAL ILLNESS

Children whose parents have a mental illness are more at risk of developing mental illness themselves (Seifer & Dickstein, 1993). Some of this risk is genetic, but some risk comes from the parents' behavior. The risk is particularly high if the parent has bipolar disorder or schizophrenia, is addicted to alcohol or drugs, or is depressed. These types of mental illness can interfere with parent-infant interactions.

For example, a depressed mother may fail to make eye contact when feeding the infant, may be less inclined to play with the infant, and may be less responsive to the infant. To a depressed mother, the infant may seem demanding and troublesome. Because the mother is more likely to be negative in her interactions with the baby, the baby then reflects the mother's mood and is more negative in interactions both with the mother and with other adults. As a toddler, the child of a depressed mother seems more negative and impulsive, engages in more conflict with the mother, and may exhibit an insecure attachment (Seifer & Dickstein, 1993).

Maternal depression is of particular concern because some women seem to suffer from a form of depression after giving birth. A large percentage of women experience some low feelings after having a baby; these feelings are usually attributed to changing hormones or fatigue. This *postpartum depression* clears up in a few days or weeks. But some women may display clinical signs of depression that last for months. Women who have postpartum depression have been shown to be less attuned to their infants and are less affirming of the infant's experience (Murray et al., 1996). The affective interaction of a depressed mother can also influence the infant's attachment. (See also Risk Factors Associated with Attachment Failure, page 218.) There is some question as to whether this type of postpartum depression is different from other forms of depression (Seifer & Dickstein, 1993). In fact, the DSM-IV classifies postpartum depression as Major Depressive Episode with Postpartum Onset if the depression occurs within four weeks of delivery. Women who experience postpartum depression should not pass the depression off as "baby blues" but should be encouraged to seek treatment.

PARENTS WITH A HISTORY OF DEVELOPMENTAL DELAY

Jill brought her 1-month-old daughter to the ER. The baby was having seizures and was admitted to the Pediatric Intensive Care Unit. Jill was a 20-year-old developmentally delayed (DD) mother. She lived with her daughter and the baby's father, who was also DD. Jill had proven to her DD case worker that she could manage her own finances, so her case was closed. However, after the birth of the baby, she had trouble making ends meet each month. She had been evicted three times in the past year for failing to pay the rent. By the end of each month, she was out of the WIC vouchers and money for food and milk. Jill's mother usually helped out with food for the baby. However, at the end of this month, Jill explained to the social worker that her mother was out of town and she had had no money to buy food or milk for the past week. As a result, the baby had not eaten or had milk to drink for the last two days.

Several problems can arise for infants of parents with a history of developmental delay. Many mothers with mental retardation have low self-esteem (Bromwich, 1985). They may not be emotionally available to the infant, and they may lack skills in reading and responding to the baby's cues. They may lack judgment about what is safe handling of an infant and may be rough with the baby. They may lack the ability to be flexible and adapt their responses to the changing needs of a growing child (Bromwich, 1985). They may be unable to budget and plan finances adequately or access resources in a crisis.

In-home help and parenting programs can benefit many parents who are developmentally delayed. Having another adult in the home can make a critical difference (Bromwich, 1985). Some parents with mental retardation live with their own parents, who provide support and help with child care.

Several issues need to be considered in this situation. Federal and state laws have assured equality to people with disabilities, including the right to have children (Bromwich, 1985). But what is in the best interests of the baby? Should a baby who is not growing be removed from the home? What if the baby is attached to the parents? What happens as the unimpaired child grows up with parents with mental retardation? Perhaps more programs need to be developed that address the needs of children living with such parents and that can help those parents provide adequate care for their children. Bromwich (1985) suggests that, as we protect the rights of parents with a history of developmental delay to have children, we must also protect the rights of those children "to be exposed to social and educational experiences that will foster their healthy growth and allow them to develop their own capabilities to the fullest" (p. 12).

TEEN PARENTS—CHILDREN HAVING CHILDREN

Nancy, a hospital social worker, was surprised to receive a request from the nurses on the postpartum unit for a social work visit to an 11-year-old new mother. She thought there must be some mistake. But on entering the room, she found a young girl holding a beautiful baby boy, watching *Barney* on TV.

Teen parents come with their own set of risks and problems. Adolescent parents are more likely to be living in poverty. In addition, they are at risk of developmental problems themselves that can interfere with their ability to interact with an infant. As we shall see in the chapter on adolescence, teens are in the developmental stage of identity formation. And, as in the preceding example, some teen mothers are still just children themselves and may have problems with establishing an identity while trying to care for an infant.

Compared to adults, teen parents are more prone to depression (Osofsky, Hann, & Peebles, 1993). In addition, as parents they are less verbally interactive with the infant and less responsive and so do not offer the baby enough cognitive stimulation. Many teens lack knowledge of developmental milestones. For instance, some adolescents may have unrealistically high developmental expectations for the baby, whereas some

may fail to recognize developmental problems. In general, compared to adults, adolescents perceive their infants as being more difficult and engage in more punitive child-raising practices. With toddlers, teens are less sensitive, more intrusive, and more negative in interactions. Infants of adolescent parents may have more problems with attachment (Osofsky, Hann, & Peebles, 1993).

Osofsky, Hann, and Peebles (1993) discuss factors that help teens succeed as parents of an infant. These factors include having support, being able to complete their education, and receiving help to cope with depression, increase their self-esteem, and understand their infant's temperament.

While there has been a decline in teen birth rates in recent years, down 13% between 1991 and 1995, the 1996 birth rate (54.7 live births/1,000 teen females)

(text continues on p. 246)

Teen parents and their infants may need additional support. Often, teen parents do not understand developmental milestones and offer limited cognitive stimulation to the baby.

Failure to Thrive

Roberto was referred to the Growth and Nutrition Clinic by his pediatrician. The social worker in the clinic completed the initial psychosocial assessment. The baby is a 15-month-old Hispanic male who weighs 19 pounds, 2 ounces. His rate of growth has been dropping since he was 2 months old and is now well below the 5th percentile for his age. Roberto's parents both have a history of developmental delay. His pediatrician is concerned about Roberto's lack of growth and his parents' ability to care for him adequately. For this reason, he has referred the case to Child Protective Services (CPS) for failure to thrive.

DEVELOPMENTAL HISTORY

This was the first pregnancy for Roberto's mother, Angelica. She carried the baby to term and had a normal vaginal delivery. Roberto weighed 5 pounds, 12 ounces at birth with Apgar scores of 8 and 9. Angelica denies any drug or alcohol abuse during the pregnancy. She reports that she experienced persistent vomiting throughout the first half of the pregnancy. Until her sixth month of gestation, she was almost unable to hold down any food or drink, and she was hospitalized three times for dehydration. She states that she and her husband, Raul, very much wanted a baby. Although she was very happy to be pregnant, she was so sick that she was glad when it was over.

At 15 months, Roberto is only now beginning to pull to stand. His mother is not sure whether he says any words other than "mama" and "dada."

BIOPHYSICAL CONSIDERATIONS

Since he was 2 months old, Roberto has suffered from almost constant ear infections. Roberto was bottle-fed, and his mother reports that he was a very slow eater, sometimes taking over an hour to finish a bottle. Often he would only take a couple of ounces at a feeding. Roberto is especially hard to feed when he is ill. Then he has a very poor appetite. The doctor believes that Roberto's failure to gain weight makes him more susceptible to illness.

PSYCHOLOGICAL CONSIDERATIONS

Cognitive Development

Roberto's development seems delayed; he does not walk alone yet. His mother reports that he did not sit alone until he was 9 months old. Roberto appears to be thin and sickly and quite wobbly on his feet even when holding on to something.

Communication

Roberto says no words other than an occasional "mama" or "dada." He does startle to loud noises. He sometimes appears to comprehend basic requests but often ignores them. He communicates mostly by pointing and grunting.

Attitudes and Emotions

Roberto's mother reports that as a baby he was loud and intense. He was very unpredictable in daily habits. He never has liked cuddling very much and has always been difficult to calm. On observation, when Roberto looks to his mother, she looks past him. When asked to hold the baby in her lap, she faces him away from her. He squirms to get down and screams until she lets him go. He plays well with his father. They make eye contact and smile at each other. His father talks to him, shows him interesting objects, wrestles on the floor with him, and changes his diaper when needed.

Social Cognition and Regulation

Roberto makes few social overtures to his mother or to the social worker during the interview. He ignores all requests from anyone. He seems interested only in exploring the room, and he can be distracted only by physical play with his father. According to his parents, Roberto is very hard to feed. He often refuses to eat. Roberto will sit in his high chair only for a few minutes before wanting to get down. His parents have been so worried about his lack of weight gain lately that they now spend over an hour trying to force the baby to eat. Mealtimes have become a nightmare for everyone. When Roberto does eat, he refuses to eat from his own plate but takes food from his mother's. In other areas, the baby seems to have no set routine. He has no regular bedtime or bedtime routine. His parents allow him to stay up until he falls asleep on the living room floor.

SOCIAL CONSIDERATIONS

Family

Roberto's parents are married and live in a one-room apartment in a poor section of town. They are both Mexican-American. Roberto's father is from Mexico and does not speak English. On standardized tests, both parents exhibit developmental delay. Roberto's father works as a food server in a Mexican restaurant, and his mother stays at home to care for the baby. Though she has poor reading skills, Angelica graduated from high school. Raul completed the sixth grade in Mexico. Angelica's mother and sister live in town, but all of Raul's family live in Mexico. Angelica thinks her baby is doing well. She says he is just not that interested in eating, but she feeds him when she can. As a child, Angelica says that she didn't have much of an appetite either, but that was good because her family did not have much to eat. She doesn't understand why everyone is so worried about her son's weight.

On observation, Angelica is a small, thin woman who looks sad most of the time. She does not even brighten when her baby comes up to her. Even when he smiles at her, Angelica avoids eye contact with her son.

Although they are developmentally delayed, Angelica and Raul have been doing well on their own. They maintain an apartment, hold a job, and pay the bills. Though they live in a poor neighborhood, the apartment is clean; the baby has few toys to play with. Also,

they have no transportation and rely on public transportation, which is somewhat lacking in their town. This lack of reliable transportation makes getting to appointments a long ordeal. Lunchtime is often spent in waiting rooms or on the bus.

Social Support

Angelica has a close relationship with her mother and sister. They babysit for her sometimes and come over to help out. Angelica and Raul attend parenting classes through the Department of Developmental Disabilities. They have an in-home parent aide who visits them once a week. They really don't have any friends, and although they are religious, they do not attend church on a regular basis. The local Child Protective Services has a day-care program. CPS will pay for the child to attend a day-care center full-time where he can experience a set routine, can receive up to three meals a day, and can observe other children eating and enjoying mealtimes.

Multicultural Considerations

When Roberto has been sick with ear infections, his parents have often used folk remedies. They say he doesn't like to take his antibiotics; in fact, he tries to spit out the medication. So Raul's grandmother suggested they feed the baby sweetened manzanita tea. He likes it and will drink it, and his parents think it helps with his fevers.

When asked what she thinks is wrong with the baby, Angelica replies emphatically that she had "nervous" during pregnancy. When asked to elaborate, Angelica explains that Raul lost his job when she was five months pregnant, and they had no money until Raul found his present job three months later. Angelica was under a lot of stress during this time and worried constantly about how they would support a baby. She is sure this is why Roberto is so irritable and hard to feed.

Because they are unable to get him to eat enough, the parents often light candles and recite prayers asking that they will get to keep their baby and not lose him to CPS. They pray that he will soon eat well, and grow, and walk on his own, so that everyone will think they are good parents and they can keep their son.

(continued)

Raul is the higher-functioning parent, but he does not speak English. Because no one at the clinic speaks Spanish, communication with Raul is through a volunteer interpreter. The interpreter often seems to be changing what was originally intended in the messages to Raul. The staff suspects that the interpreter is giving his own advice to the parents. On one occasion, a staff member with some understanding of the language thought she heard the interpreter tell Raul not to worry, that he just needed to make sure the baby drank "la leche" (milk). It is often difficult to tell whether the parents understand instructions about their baby.

SUMMARY AND IMPRESSIONS

Roberto seems to have the following problems:

1. Failure to thrive
2. Possible developmental delay, possibly due to inadequate food intake
3. Chronic ear infections, which may contribute to lack of appetite
4. Difficult temperament
5. Behavioral problems with feeding

Additional problems:

1. Parents with a history of developmental delay
2. Poverty

3. Possible poor environment
4. Lack of routine and order in care
5. Possible poor mother-infant interactions
6. Possible maternal depression

The parents have many strengths and resources. They are able to maintain an apartment on their own. Angelica and Raul obviously love and care for the infant. Though Angelica in particular may have some problems in interactions with the baby, she is very concerned about his health and development. The parents have kept all their appointments at the clinic. They cooperate well with the parent-training program and with the parent aide. The baby seems to be especially attached to his father.

Both parents are highly motivated to do whatever is necessary to keep their baby. They can follow simple written instructions regarding care and feeding of their child. They are keeping clear and accurate food logs about what Roberto eats each day. They are willing to work at establishing a schedule for the baby—to feed him six times a day and to establish a regular bedtime routine. They are also considering the daycare program for Roberto. The baby has been referred for developmental assessment. Several members of the clinic staff have signed up for an accelerated Spanish course.

---

was higher than the rate in 1980 (American Academy of Pediatrics, 1999). Social workers should consider teen mothers to be a population that continues to be in need of support and intervention.

Implications for Practice:
The Importance of Social Support

Infants need a safe and stimulating environment and nurturing, responsive caregivers. Several difficulties may interfere with a caregiver's ability to provide an adequate environment or to interact with an infant. As we

have seen, these problems include poverty, drug and alcohol addiction, mental illness, marital difficulties, adolescent parenthood, and developmental delay. In all these situations, we have stressed the importance of social support. Mothers interact more positively with their infants if fathers are supportive and help with child care. Single, teen mothers do better with the help of involved grandparents. Parents of handicapped infants and of difficult infants fare better when they have friends who call to ask how the parents are coping or who offer to sit for the child to give the parents a break.

New parents need the help of other people—family, friends, neighbors, churches, agencies, and community programs. You may hear this African proverb often in your career, but it describes social support so well: "It takes a whole village to raise a child."

Summary

DEVELOPMENTAL THEMES

According to Erikson, infancy is the psychosocial stage of trust versus mistrust. During infancy, babies learn to trust, they develop a sense of self, they form an attachment to a caregiver, and they acquire knowledge about the world and how it works.

BIOPHYSICAL DIMENSION

Biophysical Growth and Development

In the first two years of life, the infant grows to half his adult height. The infant brain also grows to more than half its adult size. Diet is important for optimal growth and development. Motor development follows the formation of the myelin sheath and progresses in a cephalocaudal and proximodistal direction. Motor development seems to be maturational. Infants may be developmentally delayed if they fail to demonstrate a skill at an age when 90% of infants that age can perform.

Biophysical Hazards

Accidents, illness, and disease are hazards of infancy. Babies should receive regular immunizations in the first two years.

PSYCHOLOGICAL DIMENSION

Cognitive Development and Information Processing

According to Piaget, infants are in the sensorimotor stage of development. During this stage, infants go from having mostly random reflex actions to displaying goal-directed behavior. Babies also acquire object permanence during this stage. The substages of this stage are reflex activity, primary circular reactions, secondary circular reactions, coordination of secondary schemes, tertiary circular reactions, and representational thought. Research using measures of information processing suggests that babies have more capacities than Piaget imagined. They can categorize objects into groups, transfer information from one sense to another, remember, and imitate. Recent studies seem to show that babies have an innate sense of how the world works.

Communication

The acquisition of language occurs in an orderly and predictable fashion, from crying and cooing to babbling, to the development of holophrastic and then telegraphic speech. Babies need to hear speech in order to acquire it. Hearing impairment and parents who fail to communicate with the baby can affect language development.

Attitudes and Emotions

As with motor development and language acquisition, the development of emotions seems to follow a maturational sequence. Babies first develop anger, sadness, surprise, and fear. Then in the second year, complex emotions—such as embarrassment, shame, guilt, and pride—develop. Emotional expression in infancy seems to predict later emotional characteristics. Babies display different temperaments from the easy child to the slow-to-warm-up child and the difficult child. Some add the classification of the active child. Goodness of fit can affect personality development. Babies attach or form an emotional bond with a caregiver. Bowlby's theory of attachment suggests that parents and infants are biologically programmed to form this attachment. Ainsworth developed the Strange Situation procedure to assess attachment. Her classifications of attachment include secure attachment, anxious attachment, avoidant attachment, and, more recently, disorganized/disoriented attachment.

Social Cognition and Regulation

Research suggests that most babies have a sense of self by 18 months of age. According to Mahler, development of a sense of self was a process that went through stages: normal autistic phase, normal symbiotic phase, differentiation phase, practicing phase, rapprochement phase, and consolidation phase. More recent research suggests that babies have a sense of self from birth. Regulation of self can begin when the infant has language skills, a sense of self, complex emotions, and a sense of autonomy.

Psychological Hazards

Failure to form an attachment and loss of or separation from a caregiver can have long-lasting effects on the child, some of which can be mediated by intervention and adequate nurturing. Repeated moves from one foster home to another can be detrimental in infancy. Failure to thrive has been described as a problem of attachment but is ultimately a problem of inadequate nutrition, often a result of a combination of biological, psychological, and social factors. Different family situations can contribute to the occurrence of failure to thrive.

SOCIAL DIMENSION

Families, Groups, Support Systems, and Communities

A baby cannot be studied only individually but must be looked at in the context of the family. Problems with an infant arise in the interaction with caregivers and other significant people. Interactions between infants and caregivers are referred to as circular influences. Social support enhances parent-infant interactions. Adoption procedures have changed over the years; many people now opt for open adoptions. Some question the ethics of adoption practices, especially in transracial adoption, Native-American adoptions, and those involving the rights of birth fathers. It is difficult to discuss the effect of day care in infancy. Ultimately it depends on the child, the family, and the particular day-care arrangements. However, quality day care is a necessary and important consideration.

Multicultural and Gender Considerations

Cultural and ethnic practices may affect development. Cultural variations in development exist. Male and female infants behave differently from birth, and they are treated differently.

Social Hazards

The home environment can affect development. Infants need verbal interaction; a variety of stimulation; warm, responsive caregivers; a safe, well-organized home and freedom to explore it; and appropriate and stimulating toys. Poverty can have a detrimental effect on development. Infants born in poverty to overstressed caregivers are at increased risk of abuse and neglect. Forms of infant abuse include shaken infant syndrome and Munchausen's syndrome by proxy. Lead poisoning from eating paint chips or absorbing environmental lead can cause learning problems and delayed growth and development. Children born to parents with mental illness, parents with a history of developmental delay, and teenage parents may be at increased risk for developmental problems. Early intervention and social support can mediate problems in these families.

🌐 Online Resources

American Academy of Pediatrics
http://www.aap.org
> Provides information for health care professionals and the public regarding AAP recommendations related to pediatric issues, such as vaccination and sleeping position guidelines. Also provides educational and self-help information for parents.

Head Start: Administration for Children and Families—U.S. Department of Health and Human Services
http://www2.acf.dhhs.gov/programs/hsb
> Information for providers, parents, volunteers, and community organizations regarding Head Start programs, specific services offered, and site locations.

Children's Bureau: Administration for Children and Families—U.S. Department of Health and Human Services
http://www.acf.dhhs.gov/programs/cb
> The Administration for Children and Families funds state, tribal, and community child welfare programs, such as child protective services, family preservation, and foster care. This site provides information regarding this agency's programs as well as information and statistics related to child welfare issues.

National Institute of Child Health and Human Development—National Institutes of Health
http://www.nih.gov/nichd
> Focus of the NICHD is on research and epidemiology related to child and human development.

Highlights of this site include relevant research publications, federal health program updates, and information regarding research studies, including information about participation in NICHD studies.

Lead Programs: Office of Pollution Prevention and Toxics—Environmental Protection Agency
http://www.epa.gov/opptintr/lead
Provides policy information and links to other relevant sites that address the issue of lead poisoning.

InfoTrac® College Edition

For interesting materials related to what you have just read, please go to the *InfoTrac College Edition* website and search using the following key words:

sudden infant death syndrome

children temperament

transracial adoption

day care

lead poisoning

fatherhood

Key Terms

attachment
babbling
categorization
cephalocaudal
circular influences
cross-modal transfer
difficult child
dishabituation
easy child
failure to thrive
goal-directed behavior
goodness of fit
habituation
holophrastic speech
intentional means-end behavior
invisible displacements
Munchausen's syndrome by proxy

myelinization
object permanence
obligatory attention
open adoption
overextension
proximodistal
separation anxiety
separation-individuation
shaken infant syndrome
slow-to-warm-up child
social referencing
stranger anxiety
telegraphic speech
temperament
transitional object
transracial adoption

Developmental Themes

Stage: autonomy vs. shame. Development of greater autonomy, physical ability, and language skills; mastery of basic self-help skills; increased social skills.

Biophysical Dimension

Biophysical Growth and Development
Ability to run, jump, climb, tumble, ride a tricycle, throw a ball; need for large-muscle activity; increase in fine-motor coordination; need for optimal nutrition

Biophysical Hazards
Asthma, leukemia.

Psychological Dimension

Cognitive Development and Information Processing
Piaget's preoperational stage. Longer attention span; infantile amnesia; memory; increase in information processing speed; task analysis, developmental waves.

Communication
Expansion of language abilities, syntax, grammar; increase in semantic skills; communication disorders.

Attitudes and Emotions
Fears, aggression, anger management, altruism/empathy, fantasy.

Social Cognition and Regulation
Self-concept, self-control, sociability of preschoolers, social skills training for preschoolers.

Psychological Hazards
Developmental disorders; diagnosis and assessment issues; elimination problems: enuresis, encopresis; anxiety disorders, depression, autism.

Social Dimension

Families, Groups, Support Systems, and Communities
Parenting, parenting styles, mother's role, father's role, sibling relationships, peer relationships, play, effects of TV. Education: value of preschool, kindergarten, Head Start.

Multicultural and Gender Considerations
Development of racial identity, gender role, and sexual identity role.

Social Hazards
Marital conflict/divorce, child abuse, poverty, coping and resiliency.

CHAPTER 7

Early Childhood

DEVELOPMENTAL THEMES

When Skyler's parents ask him a question, his response is a predictable "No, no, no!" "Skyler, you like ice cream?" "No, no, no!" He continues to shake his head. Grabbing his father by the finger, Skyler pulls him into the family room and demands that he put in a *Sesame Street* video. His father reluctantly complies. Afterward, Skyler is ready for refueling—obtaining some emotional closeness before moving on to his next activity.

Early childhood often represents a struggle for independence and self-mastery. Children expend a lot of energy striving for inner control. They are pushing for independence, yet at the same time they are overwhelmed with feelings of dependence. A critical task at this age is achieving a balance between these two forces. Perhaps one of the most amusing phases of development is the toddler/preschool years. The "terrible twos" are a result of this desire to establish autonomy. Even when offered something desirable, the toddler, like the child in the paragraph above, exclaims "No!" demonstrating how strong is the desire to be in control. The "No!" also confirms the toddler's ability to make his or her own decisions. Erikson refers to this toddler (2–3 years) stage as *autonomy versus doubt.* Children who successfully master this stage develop a sense of self-control and adequacy. Children at this age are fast becoming more independent, trying out all kinds of activities for themselves as well as learning many self-care skills that facilitate their autonomy. Children who do not realize a sense of independence and self-control at this age are likely to have feelings of shame and self-doubt about themselves instead.

During the toddler/preschool years, from age 2 to 5, children are transformed from infants and toddlers into little boys and girls. Physical and cognitive changes continue to unfold. Yet, perhaps the most profound changes during this period occur in children's social and emotional growth and language acquisition. Preschoolers are honing the skills they will need in preparation for formal education in the middle childhood years.

Children in this stage increasingly demonstrate greater autonomy, physical ability, and language skills in their activities and relationships. They revel in their sense of accomplishment and mastery in the areas of basic self-help skills such as toiletry, dressing, and hygiene and in recreational skills such as running, jumping, and bike riding. This mastery also extends to verbal skills used in expressing thoughts, singing, playing pretend games, and playing social games.

Older preschool children, ages 3–5, face the psychosocial crisis, which Erikson referred to as *initiative versus guilt.* Children at this period ideally initiate all kinds of activities for themselves, including motor, cognitive, fantasy, imaginative, and language activities, and they achieve some proficiency and mastery in these areas. Perfection is not important as a goal; however, feeling that their efforts will be encouraged and praised is crucial to developing a healthy sense of initiative. Children who feel that they can take on and participate in a task with the expectation that they will achieve some degree of mastery will be more ready to meet the challenges involved in learning at school.

The primary tasks of early childhood, between the ages of 2 and 5 years, include developing better coordinated gross motor skills, acquiring social skills to enhance relationships, and achieving immense growth in cognitive abilities and expressive language skills, all of which are fostered during play. Play is crucial to physical, cognitive, and emotional growth for preschool children. Learning and relationship skills are acquired through daily, active play. By the end of the preschool period, most children will have developed the necessary attention, coordination, and social skills to make the transition successfully to middle childhood, when school and peers will become the primary focus of children's days.

BIOPHYSICAL DIMENSION

Biophysical Growth and Development

Physical development refers to two processes. The first involves actual physical growth, and the second involves an increase in the ability to perform various motor tasks.

The average preschool child grows 2.5 inches and gains 5–7 pounds a year. Girls remain only slightly smaller and lighter than boys, a pattern that lasts through most of childhood until puberty. During early childhood, both boys and girls slim down, with their body fat percentages declining slowly. Girls tend to have more body fat than boys overall, and boys tend to have more muscle tissue than girls, even at this young age. As their body fat decreases and trunks lengthen, preschoolers lose their babyish look, although their heads are still relatively large compared with their bodies. By the time children turn 3 years old, they have doubled in height and are four times heavier than they were at birth.

GROSS MOTOR SKILLS

Early childhood is an exciting time for physical growth and motor development. At this age, children run, jump, climb, and tumble repeatedly for the sheer joy derived from challenging their bodies. They are stimulated and delighted by their accomplishments. The typical 3-year-old child can ride a tricycle, walk up and down stairs, throw a ball overhand, and catch a ball that is bounced. Many can even turn a forward roll and gallop. Catching a ball thrown through the air will still be a relatively difficult feat, but some children begin to practice with large balls. By age 4, children refine their coordination of large muscle groups and can jump higher and farther, run faster, throw a ball with more speed and precision, and hit a ball off a tee. They can hop on one foot and descend stairs with one foot on each stair. Five-year-olds can hit a ball pitched to them, jump rope, and roller skate (Skinner, 1979). Girls tend to develop both gross and fine motor skills slightly before boys do. Just as infants love "peekaboo," pre-schoolers never tire of "chase" and "hide and seek," games that allow them to shriek and run at high speeds with anyone and everyone in hot pursuit.

Three-year-olds exhibit the highest activity level of any age group. Just watching a 3-year-old play can be an exhausting experience for any adult. These children are seldom still even as they eat and sleep. The high levels of physical activity characteristic of this age necessitate daily physical exercise that uses the large muscles.

FINE MOTOR SKILLS

Fine motor coordination during early childhood progresses rapidly as well. However, children in this age group can be frustrated by the limitations in their precision and dexterity. Some projects are frustrating to preschoolers because the child can cognitively conceive of the goal but cannot achieve the intended result because of fine motor limitations. For example, a child might want to make a beautiful necklace but struggles to loop tiny beads on a string. That same child might want to build a tower as tall as his or her brother's only to watch it wobble and topple. We can imagine the frustration.

The average 3-year-old likes to build tall towers and enjoys large-piece puzzles and manipulating figures in cars and playhouses. Three-year-olds also strive to conquer zippers, snaps, and scissors. Four-year-olds enjoy building complicated towers and buildings and begin to understand basic structural and design requirements to accomplish the task. Four-year-olds can manage buttons and draw stick figures. Five-year-olds can print capital letters, simple letters, and numbers. Preschoolers learn to master scissors, paints, pencils, and crayons quite readily. They enjoy the tactile and creative expression afforded by these media.

This girl has developed the fine motor skills to brush her teeth. This skill will be refined as her development progresses.

The ability to eat independently—a major milestone of early childhood—is a task that challenges the fine motor skills of the child and the patience of her parents.

Preschoolers are often more adept at operating video players than are their parents. With the proliferation of CD and DVD players in home computers, many children also learn to successfully and fearlessly navigate educational and recreational software games. For this age group, computer-based programs that are interactive and "speak" to the child, without requiring any reading, are preferred sources of play and learning. Although children in this age group typically do not formally read, they can recognize letter patterns and logo designs as meaningful symbols in much the same way as they will later recognize letters and words.

BIOPHYSICAL HAZARDS

The fatal disorders of early childhood include birth defects, cancer, and heart disease. Fortunately, the number of deaths in developed countries have recently been reduced as a result of improvements in health care and treatment (Garrison & McQuiston, 1989). Prevention strategies to reduce the fatality rates for children under age 5 include adequate birth spacing, prenatal care, breast-feeding, immunizations, and special feedings before, during, and after serious illnesses.

ASTHMA

Asthma is another health concern for preschool children. Almost 5 million children under the age of 18 suffer from asthma, the leading chronic illness among children (National Center for Environmental Health, 1999). With recent advances in the knowledge and treatment of asthma, asthmatic children are no longer restricted in activity and can anticipate leading normal lives. Learning to manage asthma can prevent serious medical and psychological complications.

What is asthma, and how do we recognize an asthma attack? Asthma is a respiratory illness that makes breathing difficult because of narrowing of the bronchial tubes. The lung tissues swell, the muscle surrounding the bronchial tubes goes into spasms, and mucus accumulates within the air passages. Asthmatic children can be recognized typically by the wheezing sound produced when the air is squeezed out through the narrowed tubes. They also experience congestion or tightness in the chest, difficulty exhaling, and rapid breathing.

Although most incidences of asthma in early childhood are triggered by viral illnesses, allergens—such as dust mites, mold, and pollen—cold air, tobacco smoke, and smoke from a wood-burning fire can trigger or exacerbate episodes. Asthma is also considered to be hereditary, although the complex genetics of the disease are not fully understood (Sears, 1997). Risk factors associated with development of asthma in young children include maternal smoking during pregnancy, exposure of the child to second-hand smoke, and low birth weight (Sears, 1997). Researchers also believe that infants who are exposed to allergens in utero and early infancy may be more likely to develop allergies, wheezing, and childhood asthma (Sears, 1997). Treatment includes use of bronchodilators in young children to relax the muscles around the bronchial tubes and anti-inflammatory drugs to treat the swelling of the lung tissues. Reducing the exposure to allergens, even before birth, is recommended, especially for children who have a family history of asthma (Sears, 1997). A first or serious asthma attack can be a life-threatening event and is not something that can be managed without the care of a physician.

PSYCHOLOGICAL DIMENSION

Cognitive Development and Information Processing

Early childhood is a time of fanciful, creative, and imaginative thought. Children can think about themselves and others in new and important ways. Imaginative thought leads the way for the development of humor, empathy, and altruism. These features of psychological development will be discussed here.

Three-year-old children can use abstraction and symbols in increasingly complicated ways. They can classify objects according to one feature, such as color or shape, and recognize that cats and dogs fit into different categories. At about age 4, children can begin to categorize objects along two dimensions and understand that both cats and dogs fall into the larger category of animals. Numbers symbolize more than just words for the preschool child, who learns to understand the meaning and function of numbers and to use them in everyday tasks. For example, a child may count three books to read at naptime or ask for five more pitches before dinner.

Preschoolers can understand objects as ideas that exist mentally when the object is not physically present. Until children reach the age of about 5, they have little concept of time, past or future. They have diffi-

culty imagining something they have never experienced before. Without a concept of time, they cannot think logically about cause and effect. As a result, consequences of actions cannot be abstracted. However, around the time a child turns 5, a sense of time and logical thinking begin to take shape. Five-year-olds begin to imagine likely outcomes of their behavior. In addition, they have more experience on which to base these logical consequences.

PIAGET'S PREOPERATIONAL STAGE

Piaget's work laid important foundations for our thinking about what children know (Piaget, 1967). Piaget labeled the early childhood years, roughly from the age of 2 to about 7, the *preoperational stage* of cognitive development. Children in the preoperational stage cannot perform certain tasks mentally that older children can handle. Preoperational children cannot understand the meaning of properties like weight, volume, size, or height without a physical representation of the concept.

More about the meaning of operations according to Piaget will be discussed in the chapter on middle childhood, when children enter the stage of concrete operations. *Operations* conform to rules and principles of logic that preschool children do not comprehend. During the preschool years, mental reasoning, stable concepts, egocentrism, and magical beliefs emerge in children's thoughts as they make the transition from a simple use of symbols to more sophisticated use.

Piaget described two substages of preoperational thought, *symbolic function* and *intuitive thought*. What can we expect of children during these stages of development? Children between the ages of 2 and 4 typically possess abilities characteristic of the symbolic function substage. This means that they can now represent objects mentally that are not present in their immediate environment. At this stage, children can draw scribbles that represent an object or person (Gardner, 1980), play pretend games alone and with other children, and talk about people and things not present. They can begin to imagine whole scenarios about other people and themselves and incorporate these ideas into their play and language. For instance, children in the symbolic function stage can play "house" or "school," taking the roles of mom, dad, student, or teacher. Because they can now conceive of and share increasingly complex thoughts and ideas, their social interactions move to a deeper level of involvement and satisfaction.

Egocentrism is another characteristic feature of the symbolic function substage, according to Piaget's theory. Egocentric children cannot distinguish between their perspective and that of another's. For example, preschool children playing hide and seek will think that if they cannot see us, we cannot see them. They cannot understand that we have a vantage point different from their own. Another familiar example is that of preschoolers nodding their head on the phone without speaking, not realizing that the person on the other end cannot see them.

Animism, as Piaget described, refers to the belief that inanimate objects have lifelike qualities and abilities. Some developmentalists disagree that this is a general concept the child holds about the world. Instead, they argue that animism represents a child's lack of knowledge and understanding about features of the world (Dolgin & Behrend, 1984). We should also consider that many children's movies and stories depend specifically on this notion. So, we must ask ourselves, do children think this way independently, or is animism a function of the way we portray the world to them at this age?

Piaget's second substage of the preoperational stage, intuitive thought, develops between the ages of 4 and 7. Children in this substage employ primitive reasoning but not formal logic. During this substage, children typically ask a lot of questions, want to know the "how" and "why" of everything, and are sure of what they know but not certain of how they came to know something. As we have described above, some of Piaget's conclusions may be erroneous because they relied on assumptions made about children's thinking based on adult-oriented tasks and interpretations. Challenges to Piaget's theoretical assumptions are currently being examined in research labs.

INFORMATION PROCESSING

Research in the field of information processing focuses on how children come to know something rather than on what they know when. This emphasis complements the view espoused by Piaget and other stage theorists who are interested in the latter concern. Examples of information processes include developmental changes in attention and memory. During early childhood, children make great strides in both abilities.

As you will remember, infants' attention spans tend to be relatively short and wandering. Preschoolers, in contrast, develop the capacity to attend for longer and longer periods of time if they are motivated by the activity. For example, children at this age are interested in books that tell a story, especially about a favorite topic, can watch about a half-hour of a show such as *Barney* or *Aladdin,* and can play simple board games. By the time they begin school at age 6, children can attend for increasingly longer periods of time. This increased attention span is necessary for the child to benefit from formal education.

One of the limits in attention that preschool children demonstrate is an inability to attend to the relevant aspects of a task. This deficit imposes limits on children's problem-solving abilities, because children attend to the more exciting aspects instead, such as bright colors, lights, movement, and novelty. Developmentalists describe the process of learning to attend to relevant aspects as children's acquiring cognitive control of their attention. When this change occurs, preschool children act less impulsively and engage in more reflective thought (Paris & Lindayer, 1982).

A second important process in children's cognitive development involves retention of information over time. The process of information storage and retrieval depends heavily on how children understand and represent information (Ornstein, 1995). As we have mentioned, infants as young as 7 months old are capable of conscious memory.

However, most children have little or no memory for specific events before the age of 3. This phenomenon is known as **infantile amnesia.** Researchers believe that several cognitive developments in children during early childhood are responsible for changes in memory capabilities. These include a sense of self, which allows children to represent autobiographical material and is held largely responsible for the resolution of infantile amnesia (Howe, 1995).

Robin Fivush (1995) found that, starting at age 3, children begin to embellish their stories and recitation of memories. This embellishment adds details and feelings and puts the memory into context. These recountings enhance the child's organization of memories, which, in turn, promotes memory abilities. Although the methodology for this research has been criticized because of the reliance on correlational data (Brewer, 1995), defenders state that, by nature, most work with memory must be retrospective and correlational.

Stein (1995) has found that, when a particular event is relevant and meaningful to a child, children as young as 3 can recount the memory with as much description and complexity as a 14-year-old. Stein's work generally relies on children's memories of salient events that made them feel happy, sad, or scared. Stein concludes that emotionally charged events can be stored accurately even by young preschool children. In fact, before the advent of recorded public information people used this memory concept as a public record. When one person sold a piece of land to another they would gather a group of small boys from the area to observe the exchange of money for land. Then they would beat the boys so they would not forget the transaction as they grew older.

Memory processes involve both the storage and retrieval of information. Howe (1995) has found that, for children age 1 year to 11 years, problems in storage were three times greater than retrieval failure rates. In addition, preschoolers' memories fade faster than those of older children and adults. Researchers believe that either young children's memories are not completely stored or their ability to organize autobiographical events is not sufficient to guarantee storage.

The speed of processing information increases during early childhood, as do the abilities to rehearse, repeat, and identify items, all of which promote storage and short-term memory functions. These abilities have been assessed in children using the digit span task. The average 3-year-old child can repeat two digits in succession. Short-term memory functions increase during early childhood, so that by age 7 the average child can repeat five digits. Of course, individual differences in aptitude and IQ will influence a child's performance (Dempster, 1981).

TASK ANALYSIS

Task analysis is another way to study what children know. This method identifies the various components of the task the child is performing. Researchers have found that, when tasks are made simpler and more interesting, children tend to show greater cognitive maturity than revealed by the studies of Piaget (Hawkins et al., 1984). Nonsense words in syllogisms were used to demonstrate this position. Children were presented with two true statements and were asked whether the conclusion was then true. The use of nonsense words prevented children from answering based on previous experience with the items and appealed to the children's sense of fun. This study showed that preschool children do use reasoning, which Piaget had concluded was beyond their capacity (Hawkins et al., 1984). The numerous and varied questions preschool children ask provide clues about their cognitive efforts to reason and understand themselves, other people, and their world.

DEVELOPMENTAL WAVES

Until recently, developmentalists pictured children's cognitive development as proceeding in stages or steps. But the step model has posed problems in explaining the great variability in children's development and the change process of development. Questions still remained about how children shift from the use of one strategy to another and how children seem to use so many different strategies to complete the same task at any given time.

Traditional theories are being challenged by a new model that suggests that "overlapping waves," as opposed to steps, better account for how children learn and use strategies (Siegler, 1995). This theory is referred to as **developmental waves.** The waves represent the natural ebb and flow of the continuity and transitions in children's thinking. Siegler (1995) advocates a shift from emphasizing how children think at different ages to examining how many and what kinds of strategies children use at any age. This focus provides a means of analyzing a strategy by task framework. In addition, information about how children change the use of strategies can be gleaned from this focus.

Siegler's theoretical suppositions are supported by evidence from his research. These findings are as follows: Children learn a new strategy slowly and frequently revert to using the old strategy as they are learning the new; they tend to use older, more time-consuming strategies for difficult tasks; and they choose a correct strategy more often when approved by their partner while working in pairs. Also, children tend to use three or more strategies to solve problems such as telling time and as many as seven strategies when faced with moral-reasoning problems. Numerous studies support the notion that children always use more than one strategy to solve all kinds of problems. Although Siegler's work has introduced new ways of thinking about how development advances, his work does not discount the previous work put forth by stage or level theorists. These theoretical viewpoints may complement one another to broaden our understanding of children's cognitive development.

Communication

Preschool children's comprehension precedes their speech. They can understand much of what is said around them and to them before they can verbally express their ideas on the subject. The process of acquiring language skills proceeds in a relatively uniform way for most children, although the time frame may vary. Language acquisition during the preschool years is quite remarkable when we think of children advancing from putting one and two words together to, in just a few months' time, forming complex sentences and questions incorporating the correct morphology, syntax, semantics, and pragmatics of conversation.

What kinds of speech can we expect from preschool children? Three-year-old children have a vocabulary of about 900 words. By age 6, their vocabulary will have increased to between 8,000 and 14,000 words. In other words, they will have learned an average of 5–8 words a day since they were 1 year old (Carey, 1977). At about age 3, children can also converse about people, objects, and places not present. Once children have matured cognitively to achieve mental representation of things not physically present, they can think about them and talk about them.

Once children put two words together consistently, they begin to use morphological rules. We hear children at this age use plurals, possessives, and verb tenses—including the present-progressive tense (-*ing* endings). Children will make grammatical mistakes at this age and overuse the rules, which is referred to as *overregularization.* Examples include saying "mouses" for "mice" and "he goed" instead of "he went," which children may have said correctly earlier. These mistakes and overuse problems imply that children "know" the rules, yet their perception and understanding of the world is limited by their developmental level (Santrock, 1992). Berko (1958) demonstrated knowledge of morphological rules by asking preschool and first-grade children to read fictional words, recall the correct word, and apply the correct ending. Because the words were fictional, the children were forced to rely on rules and not memory. Preschool children could complete this task, as could first graders. During early childhood, children also learn to use articles such as "a" to refer to something initially and "the" for later references to the same noun.

Children also learn to apply the rules of syntax as their language skills progress. They first learn to add "wh" words, such as *where* and *what,* to the beginnings of sentences to form questions. Later, they learn to invert the subject and verb. Early preschool children will ask, "What we are going to do now?" and "Where my ball is?" As they approach the elementary school years, children speak in more complex ways, such as combining ideas in one sentence (Santrock, 1992). Negatives are learned in much the same manner. First, children place the negative marker at the beginning of the sentence, then place the negative close to the verb, and finally, use auxiliary verbs such as *was, do,* and *is* to modify the verb as adults do.

Children's semantic skills improve readily as well. We see children at this age learning the meaning of relationship words, such as *big/little, fast/slow, I/you,* and using them accurately in sentences. However, they do not use these words in the sense of true comparison until about age 4 or 5, when they can articulate comments such as "I am bigger than you." To carry on an effective conversation, children must know to use "I" as the speaker and "you" as the object. This semantic relationship appears to be one of the first ones that young children come to know.

In addition, children become increasingly skilled at the pragmatics of conversation during early childhood. Recent research suggests that preschool children are more adept at communicating comprehensible messages than earlier studies indicated (Revelle, Wellman, & Karabenick, 1985). For example, preschool children speak differently to younger children than they do to adults. Shatz and Gelman (1973) found that 4-year-olds spoke in short sentences to toddlers and elaborated, using more polite diction, when speaking to adults. Also, we see children at a very young age recognizing that they are more likely to have their requests met if they speak patiently and politely (Bates, 1976). Savvy 3-year-olds quickly rephrase "I wanna go now!" to "Please, can we go now?" We even see preschoolers correcting their own ambiguous messages when they are not understood. They will also let a speaker know when a message has not been clear enough for them to respond (Revelle, Wellman, & Karabenich, 1985). Clarifying ambiguous messages is a skill that develops more fully in middle childhood.

Language development also appears to be encouraged by the frequency and type of responses verbalized to children by adult speakers. Parents who ask their children lots of questions and initiate frequent verbal interaction tend to promote syntactical rule learning and longer utterances in their preschool children. These children tend to recognize more letters and numbers by age 5–6 and score higher on second-grade reading proficiency tests compared with children of parents who are less conversant (Hoff-Ginsberg, 1986).

In addition, children exposed to adults who speak in slightly more complex and longer sentences, and who both expand and recast the child's telegraphic statements into new grammatical forms, acquire syntactical principles faster than other children do (Hoff-Ginsberg, 1986). So, we can glean from these studies that, although children do not learn language simply by imitating adults, environmental exposure to slightly more advanced language provides an opportunity for language expansion in young children. (The following Focus section on Social Development looks at language as a form of social reinforcement.)

Research shows that preschoolers who are bilingual may learn to read faster than those who are monolingual (Bialystock, 1997). While preschoolers usually know the alphabet and can spell their names, they are often unable to read without the use of pictures. In a study by Bialystock (1997), 4- and 5-year-olds were shown pictures of objects along with the words that named the objects and then asked to name each word after the corresponding picture card was removed (cited in "Speaking Another Language . . . ," 1997). Bialystock found that the bilingual children scored twice as high as the monolingual children, illustrating the fact that the bilingual children understood the meaning of the written word independent of the object's picture. Bialystock concluded that children who know more than one language may learn to read faster because they have figured out the rules for two different language systems.

FOCUS ON SOCIAL DEVELOPMENT

Language as a Social Reinforcement

Language for the preschooler not only represents a means of expressing needs but it also becomes a social reinforcer. Language allows children to share and interact with others in ways not previously available to them. Language opens up a whole new world of secrets, jokes, cooperative play, and positive reinforcement. Furthermore, language skills facilitate independence, allowing children to respond to and initiate verbal requests.

The peer group is already a powerful socializing agent. Never mind that parents are mortified when their child screams at the top of his lungs to a departing friend, "Bye-bye, Butthead!" The other child roars with delight at the compliment and returns the salutation. Such is the social language of the preschool child.

COMMUNICATION DISORDERS

Language develops rapidly during the preschool years. For the most part, children learn language in an orderly, sequential fashion. Developmental delays can occur, however. Communication disorders we are likely to see in preschoolers include expressive language disorder, phonological disorder, and stuttering.

Expressive language disorder can be either developmental or acquired. The acquired type generally follows some known neurological insult, whereas the developmental type does not. The identifying features of this disorder will vary according to age of the child and severity of the disorder. These features include limited speech and vocabulary, shortened sentences, difficulty learning new words, misuse of words, limited and simple grammar, and slowed language acquisition. Language comprehension is usually normal (American Psychiatric Association, 1994).

Developmental expressive language disorder is usually evident by the time a child is 3 and occurs in 3%-5% of children. About half of these children outgrow the problem, whereas the remainder suffer long-term complications. Fewer children also exhibit mixed expressive-receptive language disorder, in which they experience difficulty understanding language as well (American Psychiatric Association, 1994).

Phonological disorder affects at least 2.5% of preschoolers and is more prevalent in males. The defining characteristics include difficulty articulating speech sounds, especially those learned later in the developmental sequence (such as *l, r, s, z, th, ch*), and making errors in the order of sounds in syllables or words, such as "aks" for "ask." Most children with mild cases recover by the early elementary years without intervention (American Psychiatric Association, 1994).

Attitudes and Emotions

No two preschoolers would ever be described exactly alike. As they wind their way through the early developmental years, most children are a mix of positive and negative attributes. However, some children possess qualities that make them easy and fun to be around, whereas appreciating other children requires more tolerance and work. The old axiom "Beauty is in the eye of the beholder" also applies to preferences in personality types. We cannot exclude the interpretive bias of the person ascribing value judgments to children's behaviors and qualities. For instance, some adults would describe a very active child with a mind of his own as exuberant and determined, whereas others would describe him as aggressive or hyperactive—terms that are pejorative and reflect, to a large degree, the qualities preferred by the adult speakers and not necessarily the "true" characteristics of the child.

FOCUS ON RESILIENCE

Emotion Coaching and Emotional Intelligence

"I want Zebra! I want Zebra!" she moaned again. Then she started to cry ... By now I was getting "do something" looks from the passengers, the airline attendants, from my wife, seated across the aisle ... I felt bad. Then it dawned on me: I couldn't get Zebra right now, but I could offer her the next best thing— a father's comfort ... "You wish you had Zebra now," I said to her. "Yeah," she said sadly ... "You're tired now, and smelling Zebra and cuddling with him would feel real good. I wish we had Zebra here so you could hold him" ... "Yeah," she said with a sigh. "I'm so sorry," I said, watching the tension leave her face. She rested her head against the back of her safety seat. She continued to complain softly a few more times, but she was growing calmer. Within a few minutes, she was asleep ... Finding out that I understood how she felt seemed to make her feel better ... it was a memorable testament to the power of empathy.
—GOTTMAN, 1997, PP. 69-70

This exchange between a father and his daughter represents what John Gottman (1997) calls "emotion coaching." Emotion coaching is a process by which a parent or caregiver assists a child in recognizing his emotions and then uses the experience as a way for the child to learn about himself and to problem solve. Gottman describes emotion coaching as consisting of five steps:

1. Become aware of the child's emotion;
2. Recognize the emotion as an opportunity for intimacy and teaching;
3. Listen empathetically, validating the child's feelings;
4. Help the child find words to label the emotion he is having;
5. Set limits while exploring strategies to solve the problem at hand.

Gottman has found that children whose parents used emotion coaching techniques were better able to regulate their own emotions, soothe themselves when they were upset, better focus attention, and respond well in difficult situations (for example, in conflicts with other children). Gottman believes that negative emotions are important for children to experience and that they can provide rich opportunities for teaching and relationship-building between a child and parent. Social workers can draw from Gottman's model when working with families as a way of assisting parents to understand their child's emotions and to help him or her develop adaptive coping skills.

(Beth A. Auerbach-Dixon, adapted from Gottman, 1997)

FEARS

Preschool children enjoy wonderfully exciting imaginations and fantasy lives. Firstborn children often invent an imaginary friend at this age to serve many purposes. An imaginary friend can try out negative, risky, and even miraculous behaviors and feelings, provide companionship, and foster creativity. Children's imaginary friends should be respected and, for the most part, allowed to be just that—the child's own imaginary friend.

A preschool child's emerging cognitive abilities and imagination also promote empathy and humor. However, the down side of these new cognitive abilities is the onset of fears and phobias. Fears and **phobias** become issues for preschool children, as do nightmares and **night terrors.** Fears of the dark, monsters, loud noises, and strange places crop up in imagination in ways that were not possible before the child was capable of symbolism and abstraction. Most children try to squelch these fears and strong emotions while awake, holding in their reactions so others will not be displeased. As a result, these fears will often surface at night when the child's conscious guard is down, especially during REM dream sleep. The dreams may be terrifying to the preschool child because they may portray aggressive feelings and actions the child has been trying to control in response to fears while awake.

Several steps can be taken to help children learn to handle negative feelings and fearful thoughts adaptively. Children benefit from discussions to prepare and reassure them about their fears and strong emotional responses. We can also teach children to talk about their feelings and act out their aggressive energy in safe ways, such as hard play, hitting something soft, and taking some time alone. Preschool children may not be able to act on these suggestions but will benefit from the discussion and may themselves generate some healthy coping strategies through the process (Brazelton, 1992).

AGGRESSION

Our connotations of aggression are usually negative and call up various images of violence. But how do we define **aggression** when we think of this concept in developmental terms? What forms might aggression take as children mature? What are the meanings of aggressive acts? And do these forms and meanings change over time with development?

To grow, develop, and survive, we must be equipped with a biological drive for aggression. Researchers have divided aggression into two forms, **hostile aggression** and **instrumental aggression** (Shaffer, 1989). The most accepted definition of aggression by researchers today includes an element of intention. Baron and Byrne (1984) refer to aggression as all acts intended to hurt another and include acts that were not successful. For example, a child knocking over another in the midst of a pillow fight would not be considered aggressive. Yet, a child who strikes at but misses a friend who has taken his ball would be considered aggressive. Behaviors designed to hurt another are referred to as *hostile aggression.* Behaviors designed to achieve a nonaggressive end but, nonetheless, hurt someone in the process are referred to as *instrumental aggression.*

In general, preschool aggressive acts diminish after age 4 as children learn better negotiating skills. They also learn to resolve differences verbally in tandem with the increased expectations of parents and teachers preparing children for elementary school.

What can research tell us about preschool children's aggressive behaviors? Studies by Florence Goodenough (1931) and Willard Hartup (1974) provide us with most of our knowledge of aggressive behaviors in preschool children. Goodenough's work analyzed mothers' diaries of their 2-to-5-year-olds' angry episodes and the suspected causes and outcomes. Hartup observed interactions of 4-to-6-year-olds and 6-to-7-year-

Children express aggression and problems sharing in many ways. Most preschool children have not developed social skills to control their aggressive behavior.

olds, recording the causes and consequences of inter-peer aggression. Their findings of normal preschool aggressive behavior are summarized as follows.

- The total amount of aggression tends to peak at about age 4, and then it decreases. Temper tantrums with no recognizable antecedent tend to decrease during the preschool period and are almost nonexistent after age 4.

- At about age 3, preschoolers increase their retaliatory aggression in response to frustration or attack.

- Young preschoolers, age 2–3, tend to behave aggressively after parents have set limits. Older children tend to act aggressively in response to peer conflict.

- Young preschoolers tend to kick and hit to get something they want, such as a toy. Their aggres-

sion is primarily instrumental. Older preschoolers tend to use verbal aggression in the form of teasing, name-calling, and tattling. They still argue over objects, but their aggressive acts become more hostile, designed to hurt another.

Implications for Practice: Curbing Aggression

With the increase in school shootings in recent years, added emphasis has been placed on watching for signs of aggression in children starting as early as preschool. The hope is that aggressive acts in later years can be avoided if aggression is curbed early in a child's life. Box 7.1 lists numerous warning signs for aggression and violent behavior in toddlers, preschool-age children, and school-age children.

Several strategies for decreasing hostile aggressive acts have been researched. We will describe each of these procedures briefly. Remember, the goal is not to deny or negate the preschool child's very real emotional experience. Rather, the goal is to help the child find adaptive ways of expressing and asserting needs and interacting with others.

- *Incompatible-response technique* (Brown & Elliott, 1965; Slaby & Crowley, 1977): This technique promotes prosocial behaviors and reduces aggressive acts by simultaneously ignoring all but dangerous, aggressive interchanges while positively reinforcing acts incompatible with aggression. This method has been shown to reduce verbal and physical aggression while promoting helpfulness. Another advantage lies in the avoidance of punishment and attention paid to aggressive acts. Therefore, children are not reinforced for attention-seeking aggressive acts, and aggression in the form of punishment is not modeled to the children.

- *Time-out procedure* (Parke & Slaby, 1983): This technique allows adults to attend to and prevent harmful acts of aggression in nonpunitive ways by removing the child from the activity and providing a safe place for the child to regain control of behavior. The adult does not unwittingly provide reinforcement for attention-seeking behavior because attention is withdrawn until appropriate behavior can be maintained.

BOX 7.1

Warning Signs for Violence and Aggression in Children

Toddler and Preschool-Aged Child

- Has multiple temper tantrums in a day, each lasting more than 15 minutes; child is not easily calmed by parent or caregiver
- Has frequent aggressive outbursts, often with no reason or cause
- Behaves impulsively and fearlessly
- Frequently refuses to follow directions and listen to adults
- Appears to not be attached to parents
- Spends a significant amount of time watching violent television shows
- Engages in play that has violent themes
- Acts cruelly toward other children

(Adapted from APA, 1996)

School-Aged Child

- Often disrupts classroom activities in school
- Gets into frequent fights at school
- Reacts to disappointment, criticism, or teasing with intense anger, blame, or revenge
- Watches violent television shows and/or plays violent video games
- Has few friends at school; is often rejected by other children because of his or her behavior; makes friends with other children known to be aggressive or unruly
- Does not listen to adults
- Does not exhibit sensitivity to the feelings of others
- Acts cruelly toward pets or other animals

- *Modeling and coaching strategies* (Richard & Dodge, 1982): This method relies on adults and other children to serve as models and teachers of nonaggressive conflict resolution strategies. Children are more likely to use these alternative strategies if they see someone else obtain success using these methods. This technique has proved effective with chronically aggressive children who have poor problem-solving skills.

- *Creating nonaggressive environments* (Feshbach, 1956; Hartup, 1974; Smith & Connolly, 1980): This method relies on the ingenuity of adults to create play spaces that minimize conflict and the need for physical contact. Large play spaces allow children to play vigorously without physically contacting each other. Play environments that have enough equipment for all the children also prevent conflict. Also, when aggressive toys are provided, children tend to get into more fights. Keeping aggressive toys out of the play areas of

young children can prevent aggressive behavior in the form of play and real fights.

The following Focus section examines what happens to children who were aggressive in preschool.

FOCUS ON DEVELOPMENT

▼

Handling Preschool Aggression— Do They Grow Out of It?

When he was 2, Doug's mother took him to a play group. He was not a popular addition to the group. After only two weeks he became known as "the biter." The other mothers would run to pick up their children whenever Doug approached them. When he was 3, his mother enrolled him in a preschool program. After the first month, the teacher called his mother in for a conference because Doug had pushed another child off the slide. When he was 4, his mother took him to Sunday school. The first day, someone came to get her out of the church service because Doug had gotten in an argument with another child and punched the child in the nose.

What happens to aggressive preschoolers? Research has shown us that aggression in preschoolers tends to be associated with aggression in middle childhood (Emmerich, 1966) and even adolescence (Olweus, 1980). Although stability in aggression has usually been considered a male attribute, recent research has documented stability of aggressive tendencies among females as well (Caspi, Elder, & Bem, 1987; Huesmann et al., 1984). Males tend to be more aggressive physically and verbally than females (Maccoby, 1980; Maccoby & Jacklin, 1974). In addition, aggressive attacks are likely to be less intense if the target of the aggression is a female (Barrett, 1979).

Yet, despite biological differences, families, society, and even the individuals themselves play a large role in the development and maintenance of aggressive characteristics and behavior (Olweus, 1980; Patterson, DeBarsyshe, & Ramsey, 1989). Olweus (1980) found that highly active, impulsive boys tended to be the most aggressive. Mothers of these boys were found to be more tolerant of their aggression, but when they could no longer ignore the behavior, they reacted with physical punishment to get their sons in line. Parents who fail to monitor and supervise their children effectively are frequently the parents of deviant adolescents, as discussed in Chapter 9.

In addition, Patterson and colleagues (1989) researched parent-child interactions in families with at least one aggressive child and found these home environments to be characterized as coercive. The researchers described coercive interactions as ways of making someone stop irritating another and included crying, whining, complaining, yelling, and hitting. Negative reinforcement, the removal of a noxious behavior, was also used to control family members. Social reinforcement, affection, and approval were rarely articulated in these families as a means of achieving and rewarding desired behavior. Children are also exposed to numerous incidences of violence in society via the television, sports, and superheroes. We will consider the effects of these social systems in a later section.

How can we alleviate the propensity for aggressive acts among preschoolers in our society? Assertive aggression often takes the form of separating from parents, achieving independence, and striving to master new skills, all of which are necessary if a child is to survive in the world. Hostile aggression, however, is often intended to hurt or coerce, physically or verbally, another child into doing what the aggressor wants. This kind of aggression is not favorably regarded, yet, for children, the meaning of the act must be understood before we can help them achieve their goals any other way.

There is always an underlying message when children use aggression of any kind. Say, for example, we see a preschooler wrestle another child to the ground to retrieve a toy. The meaning of the behavior may be to say to the other child, "See what I can do," or "I'll show you who I am," or "I'll do what I feel like doing." The child may be making a plea for attention from the other child or adults. All in all, preschoolers' aggressive behaviors are ways of defining themselves and asserting their independence.

Even when preschoolers cannot verbalize their rationale, we can model other appropriate, and more effective, ways of asserting ourselves. These include asking the children about their feelings and needs, acknowledging their feelings, and redirecting their energies toward more helpful ways of expressing negative feelings. Children should be encouraged to assert themselves in ways that help define themselves as unique individuals and establish their autonomy by setting personal limits in order to maximize their own growth and development, not to exploit or take advantage of others.

FOCUS ON RESEARCH

▼

Children's Coping with Background Anger

E. Mark Cummings has systematically explored how young children cope when exposed to anger—especially anger in the home. In one such study, Cummings

(1987) exposed pairs of 4- and 5-year-old same-sex friends to a series of 5-minute interchanges enacted by two adult women. The women were first friendly and greeted each other warmly. Then they simulated anger at each other and yelled but were not physically aggressive. Last, they reconciled, apologized, and parted amicably. Between each simulated session were 5-minute spaces without the adults present. The children watched from an adjoining room as they played. Following the angry sequences, the children were interviewed about their feelings and were observed playing together.

Cummings (1987) found that preschoolers showed increased arousal following the exposure to background anger. This increased arousal took the form of positive and negative behaviors, including more sharing and smiling as well as verbal and physical aggression.

Cummings (1987) concluded that children as young as 4 and 5 responded aggressively and with heightened arousal to a relatively tame incidence of anger. He underscores the implications of these findings for children living with marital conflict, which would have a more direct influence on the children.

ALTRUISM AND EMPATHY

For young children, **altruism,** helpful behaviors that arise out of a concern for the welfare of others, begins with sharing. Learning to share becomes much of the focus of social interactions during a child's first years. Eisenberg (1982) has studied children's sharing behavior extensively. She concludes that, by age 3, children generally share because sharing promotes fun in play. By age 4, children show more empathic sharing as they develop an ability to recognize and understand the feelings of others. In addition, through parental encouragement, 4-year-olds have internalized the belief that they have an obligation to share. This does not mean they always act on this knowledge, however. Sharing is a difficult concept to grasp, one that takes many years to develop. Still, children at this age do not share in an altruistic sense. Rather, they are usually motivated to share as a means of getting their way.

How do children learn to share and develop a sense of altruism? For the most part, peers provide the primary influence in this arena, above and beyond adult direction to share and give. Peers accomplish this by providing reinforcement through their responses to the give and take of social play (Eisenberg, 1982). When a child happily hands over the treasured racecar, there is nothing more powerful than the friend's exuberant smile to reinforce sharing. Additionally, research shows that children who observe others sharing are more likely to share themselves (Wilson & Piazza, 1990).

Each of us has an innate capacity for **empathy,** the ability to understand the feelings and attitudes of others. Children are predisposed to empathize with the emotions of others from a very young age. Even infants demonstrate this capacity to detect and model the feelings of another when they use social referencing. Children need adult encouragement to develop their natural capacity for empathy, however. Modeling can be an important tool for adults to use, including demonstration of empathetic responding, helping the child identify her own emotions, and pointing out the consequences of the child's actions for others (Barasch, 1998).

Preschool children cannot cognitively understand another person's feelings. Yet, they are equipped with the emotional ability to sense another's feelings, recognize them independently of their own, and match them with their own experiences. To match another's feelings, first a child needs to be able to identify the feeling. Preschoolers feel the basic emotions of happiness, sadness, and anger intensely and can empathize quite readily with these feelings in others. The terms *empathy* and *sympathy* are sometimes used interchangeably; however, they refer to two different aspects of emotional responding. Whereas empathy requires an understanding *of* another person's feelings, sympathy involves feeling sorrow or concern *for* another person (Eisenberg, Wentzel, & Harris, 1998).

Altruism has been found to be a highly stable attribute, similar to its counterpart, aggression (Rushton, 1980). Children who act prosocially in one setting are likely to do so in others. When sex differences are found, girls tend to be more helpful, but sex-difference findings in general tend to be controversial (Radke-Yarrow, Zahn-Waxler, & Chapman, 1983). Preschoolers also tend to act more altruistically toward other children of the same sex (Hartup, 1974), but need becomes a determinant as children develop. One factor found to contribute to children's altruistic behavior was opportunities to provide compassionate, helpful care to younger siblings (Radke-Yarrow, Zahn-Waxler, & Chapman, 1983). Compared with other societies, Western society places a higher value on competition and individual achievement. As a result, children from industrialized societies often score lower on measures of altruism compared with children from cultures in which the group is valued over the individual (Whiting & Whiting, 1975).

Implications for Practice: Helping Children Develop Empathy

How do we, as adults, encourage the development of empathy in children? First, we need to help children understand a range of emotions and to identify and label them accurately. To accomplish this task, we can honestly express our own emotions and provide children with word labels for their own future experiences. Praising prosocial behavior and talking to children about their feelings increases their emotional and cognitive understanding. When children do something that pleases us, we should be quick to let them know our feelings. We can also let children know that their concern for us makes us feel better. Sometimes children will laugh, not because seeing someone feeling bad strikes them as funny, but because they do not understand more complex emotions like frustration and embarrassment. They have usually felt this way at one time, too, but cannot identify or label the emotion when they see it in another person.

Social Cognition and Regulation

Preschoolers' self-concepts are largely determined by their physical characteristics and physical abilities. They learn to classify themselves and others according to age first, gender second, and then by what they can actively do, such as play baseball or climb a tree, and sometimes by what they physically possess. This method of classifying themselves is referred to as the **categorical self.**

During the preschool years, children become increasingly able to make finer distinctions between physical attributes. Yet, not until middle childhood do they consistently attribute psychological characteristics to themselves or to others. We should note, however, that parents tend to describe their children along these same dimensions, both to the children and to other adults. We can observe behavioral attributes of our children and only infer the psychological components. Furthermore, adults may describe children in this way to the children themselves in accordance with their perception of the children's understanding. In other words, children may be demonstrating cognitive limitations when they describe themselves along physical and activity dimensions, or they may be reflecting the characteristics they have always heard applied to themselves.

We hear 3- to 5-year-olds refer to themselves as little or big boys and girls, depending on how independent they feel at the moment. Edwards (1984) demonstrated through the use of photographs that preschoolers can recognize distinctions in other age groups such as babies, little boys and girls (ages 2–6), big boys and girls (ages 7–13), mommies and daddies (14–49), and grandmas and grandpas (50+). They are also likely to know that they are either boys or girls, although they may still believe these are transitory properties they could change if they wanted to (Kohlberg, 1969). By school age, children recognize gender as a fixed feature of identity and have some ideas of culturally sanctioned roles that parallel one's sexual identity. Gender development will be more fully addressed in a later section.

Preschool children can make basic distinctions between their private selves and public selves. They can understand that others do not know everything they think or feel. Preschool children have been shown to fake an emotion to manipulate another person, demonstrating their belief that only they have access to some personal information (Bretherton et al., 1986). They recognize that their own private talk, which accompanies many problem-solving tasks, is not the same as speaking to another person, as Vygotsky (1962) highlighted in his theory. Four- and five-year-olds, especially, know that thinking goes on in their heads; others cannot "see" what they are thinking, and inanimate objects do not think (Johnson & Wellman, 1982).

The following Focus section looks at a contemporary debate: Should we encourage self-esteem or competency in children?

▼

Self-Esteem versus Competency Debate

A recent debate has raged about the utility of promoting self-esteem versus competency. In fact, some developmental psychologists would argue that self-esteem is not the important ingredient in children's success (Damon, 1995; Seligman, 1996) and that false praise can actually do some harm (Seligman, 1996). Critics of the self-esteem movement offer several points in contention of praising kids indiscriminately for any effort put forth (Damon, 1995; Seligman, 1995; Stevenson, 1995).

First, they argue, the data legitimately shows positive self-esteem to be highly correlated with academic achievement; positive social skills; and resistance to drug involvement, early sex, gangs, and delinquency. However, they strongly assert that proponents of self-esteem as a "vaccine" to protect against social ills misinterpret the data to infer causality. Instead, the reverse conclusion is just as likely but cannot be inferred from existing data either. That conclusion states that self-esteem increases as a function of increased competency and mastery, better skills for dealing with problems, and an improved ability to evaluate oneself accurately.

Their second argument pertains to the practice of dispensing praise liberally and with no real basis. This practice can actually produce the opposite effect, causing children to distrust both adults' opinions and their own judgment. Furthermore, as a result of unwarranted praise, children do not learn to assess their strengths and weaknesses accurately.

In his book, *The Optimistic Child,* Seligman (1996) points out that "failure, in itself, is not catastrophic," it is the child's interpretation of the failure that can lead to problems such as depression (p. 14). The child's explanatory style, or the way he thinks about causes, can strongly influence how he thinks about the good and bad events that happen to him. Seligman

believes that a child who has an *optimistic* explanatory style is better equipped to deal with the ups and downs of life. Seligman conceptualizes explanatory style using three dimensions: permanence, pervasiveness, and personalization.

- *Permanence—Sometimes versus Always:* When bad events happen, a pessimistic child believes they are permanent. An example of a pessimistic statement regarding a negative event might be "I never do well on spelling tests." An optimistic child would explain a negative event as something temporary with the potential to change, saying, "I didn't do well on the spelling test today." In contrast, an optimistic child would explain a good event as having a permanent cause, such as, "I received good grades because I work hard," as opposed to a temporary cause, "My grades were good because Mom made me study."

- *Pervasiveness—Specific versus Global:* When causes are seen as pervasive, they are projected onto many aspects of life, not just a single episode. A global, or pessimistic, statement might be "Everyone hates me," whereas a specific, optimistic statement might be: "Mary doesn't like me." Regarding good events, optimistic statements are global ("I'm a smart person"), and pessimistic statements are specific to a situation ("I do well at reading").

- *Personal—Internal vs. External:* Personalization involves deciding who caused something to happen or, simply, who is to blame. Children can blame themselves (internal) or other people or situations (external). Children who continually blame themselves when bad things happen tend to have lower self-esteem. However, this does not imply that the way to feel good is to blame others; children must hold themselves accountable for their wrongdoings and faults. The key is for children to use behavioral, rather than general, self-blame. Behavioral self-blame is optimistic in nature (temporary and specific)—for example, "I was punished because I disobeyed the rules." General self-blame is pessimistic (permanent and pervasive): "I was punished because I'm a bad kid."

Seligman (1996) believes that, instead of helping children "feel good," parents, teachers, and social workers should assist children in "doing well," which involves developing the "ability to think and to cope with the basic challenges of life" (p. 32). Like Gottman (1997), Seligman feels that negative emotions and experiences are important to a child's emotional growth. Seligman would likely argue strongly against the recent trend in some schools to eliminate failing grades. In preventing children from failing, they are also missing the opportun-ity to experience normal and natural emotions, such as sadness, anxiety, and anger. By protecting children from failure, we make it more difficult for them to develop the skills of mastery, and this results, ironically, in lowered self-esteem.

SOCIABILITY OF PRESCHOOLERS

As children age, they naturally come into contact with a larger social audience that includes other adults, teachers, peers, siblings, and older children. Two- and three-year-olds still stay physically close to adults and seek physical affection. Older preschoolers tend to seek the attention and approval of their peers through antics and playful gestures (Hartup, 1983).

Researchers have examined the question of sociability among preschoolers from several angles. Baumrind (1971) has focused attention on features of parent-child relationships that promote sociability. She has found that warm, supportive parents who set reasonable standards and expectations for their children's social interactions tend to raise well-adjusted, socially competent children. However, permissive parents who do not set or enforce social rules tend to raise children who are more rebellious, aggressive, and uncooperative.

Shea (1981) observed 3- and 4-year-old children attending preschool over a period of about ten weeks. He concluded that children's social skills were enhanced by their participation in preschool. Over the course of the observational period, children began to interact more with one another than with the teacher and became more playful and outgoing as opposed to forceful and aggressive. Although preschool experiences have typically been shown to bolster children's sociability, children who are less sociable tend to miss more school (Pennebaker et al., 1981). Social-skills training becomes essential to bring these children up to speed, so to speak, so they too can reap the benefits of the preschool social environment. (See the following Focus section: Social Skills Training for Preschool Children.)

Longitudinal studies have produced data suggesting that sociability is a highly stable trait. By the age of 2, children's social behaviors are fairly predictable. The social behaviors assessed include reactions to play sessions, initiation of social interactions, and time spent interacting with other children. Measures of children's sociability at age 2 predicted sociability at age 3½ in preschool (Bronson, 1985). These findings are particularly salient when one is considering the long-term effects on unsociable children. Later on, in middle childhood and adolescence, peer rejection becomes a forceful determinant correlate of behavioral and emotional difficulties.

FOCUS ON SOCIAL DEVELOPMENT

Social Skills Training for Preschool Children

To develop sociability skills in children, we must first consider exactly what skills we would like to improve. Asher and Dodge (1986) defined these skills as initiating play activities; communicating effectively; cooperating; giving help, affection, and approval to their peers; and resolving conflicts. The development of effective social skills is exceedingly important, because poor peer relationships are often the result of poor social skills. Poor peer relations, especially rejection by peers, have been linked steadily with increases in delinquency, psychopathology, and low self-esteem.

Several therapeutic approaches have been designed to remedy social-skills problems in children. These approaches include reinforcement, modeling, and cognitive strategies. Reinforcement and modeling strategies may be necessary at first to make immediate gains and motivate children to pursue more complicated strategies, such as problem solving and role-play, that are associated with long-term gains.

To implement positive reinforcement strategies, two essential elements must be present. First, positive reinforcement in the form of verbal praise, attention, and even tangible rewards can be used to shape socially appropriate responses. For example, every time a child shares, praise can be bestowed. This works best if the praise is awarded consistently to every child who demonstrates desirable social behavior according to a group reinforcement plan (Combs & Slaby, 1977). In this way, unsociable children can see others rewarded for positive behavior as well. While positive social behavior is being rewarded, less desirable behaviors such as solitary play and aggressive behaviors are ignored as much as possible, so as not to reinforce them inadvertently.

Second, the environment often requires slight manipulation to provide and instigate social contact that can then be reinforced. We can structure a play setting relatively easily by introducing social games like tag and duck-duck-goose that draw in the less sociable children. In addition, children deficient in social skills can be given a valuable commodity such as treats to give out to playmates. This strategy creates a social interaction in which everyone will want to interact with the unsociable child.

Modeling techniques have also been shown to help socially shy or withdrawn children enter the play group with less fear. Models that work best are those who are like the unsociable children in that they appear initially hesitant to engage others socially. When the models' positive social behaviors and natural benefits are pointed out to the group, undersocialized children more often imitate the positive behaviors (Asher & Renshaw, 1981). Another unexpected gain resulted from this practice: Not only did the shy children engage in positive social behaviors like smiling, helping, and initiating contact, but so did the other children in the room. The benefits were reciprocal in that all the children responded in socially positive ways to one another (Cooke & Apolloni, 1976).

More complex social-skills-training approaches, such as teaching cognitive strategies, require more activity on the part of the unsocialized child. The child actively participates in thinking about and practicing scenarios to develop helpful tools for problem solving. In coaching, the therapist both demonstrates and provides the rationale for particular socially desirable behaviors. The child then practices the behavior with the therapist and, even better, in live settings where interaction and cooperation are encouraged (Oden & Asher, 1977).

Role-playing techniques represent another cognitive therapy strategy. In this case, children discuss hypothetical problems and generate potential solutions for them. Myrna Shure and George Spivack (1980) developed a ten-week program aimed at preschoolers. The children used puppets to act out problem scenarios and helpful solutions. Then the preschoolers were guided in discussing the feelings of all the characters involved in the problem situation. Gains were made not only in the puppet exchanges, which became less aggressive, but also in the kinds of solutions worked out by the students themselves in the classroom.

REGULATION

Young preschool children rely on physical means of expressing their emotions, both positive and negative. When preschoolers are happy, they are happy with their whole bodies, from smiling faces down to dancing feet. When they feel angry or frustrated, they strike out physically as well. They throw tantrums, hit, kick, throw objects, and even bite. These behaviors assert their autonomy in the only way they know.

As preschoolers develop better and better language skills, and as their adult role models set reasonable limits and model social cooperation as well as acceptable ways of expressing negative emotions, children begin to incorporate these skills into their repertoire of self-assertive techniques. They are displaying the first signs of self-control when they use words and not physical aggression to communicate their feelings (Spitz, 1966). However, the preschooler's first choice of words are rarely those that would win a peace prize. They use fighting words—words chosen to arouse a reaction in another child, not mediate the problem. Not surprisingly, for young preschoolers, much of the vocabulary of the day revolves around body parts and bodily functions. Verbally aggressive preschoolers will use "bathroom talk," use swear words and "I hate you" (Wolfgang, 1977). The content of the remark is not what is important at that moment, but rather the emotion conveyed. The content may be dealt with another time when the child is calm enough to hear what we say. We can tell children that those words hurt others' feelings, but they can't cooperate when their emotional energy is high.

Children who learn to use words instead of physical aggression will, eventually, learn to use more socially sanctioned verbal approaches as well (Wolfgang, 1977). The process of internalizing self-control takes time over the course of early and middle childhood (Fraiberg, 1968). Schuster and Ashburn (1992) have noted that children whose parents acknowledge the children's feelings and teach them to use alternate behaviors and means of expressing their feelings also learn cooperation and internalize self-control. Children who are taught to obey and comply regardless of how they feel do not learn to internalize cooperation skills. They may strike out, engaging in less mature behaviors when the threat of punishment is not there.

Psychological Hazards

Many disorders of childhood affect behaviors in very specific domains, such as eating, sleeping, eliminating, speaking, paying attention, and learning. Mood disorders, including anxiety and depression, and even the beginnings of antisocial conduct can be seen in children as they attempt to cope with normal developmental issues as well as situational and traumatic stressors. These disorders are considered developmental in that they represent an aberration in the normal course of development.

The disorders of childhood generally fall into one of three categories: developmental delays, developmental disorders, and developmental psychopathology. Developmental delays represent a slowed rate of skill acquisition, or normal behaviors such as bedwetting that occur at an inappropriate age. Delays can occur in almost any area of functioning; however, most children catch up before any real damage is done. Delays in critical areas, such as speech, tend to be more readily recognized and produce more profound negative effects for the child.

Developmental disorders occur in the areas of eating, sleeping, speech, eliminating, and attending (Bootzin & Acocella, 1988). These disorders are characterized by a disruption in the performance of these skills. As such, they tend to cause problems for those caring for the children as well as for the children themselves. Children with developmental disorders are more likely to be referred for treatment than are children who show delays in the acquisition of normal behaviors, unless the delays are extreme. Examples of developmental disorders include enuresis, encopresis, stuttering, attention deficit disorder, and night terrors.

Developmental psychopathology results when a child's healthy adaptation is impeded by an inability to rally resources and cope with stressors. Although the child's response may, in fact, be a reasonable response to an identifiable stressor, the child's functioning becomes impaired by an inability to cope with and recover from trauma. Instead of one behavioral domain being affected, multiple areas of the child's life are compromised, including peer and family relationships, school performance, activities, and developmental goals. In this sense, developmental psychopathology is pervasive. Examples of developmental psychopathology include mood disorders such as anxiety and depression. Although these disorders have counterparts in adult psychopathology, the etiology, course of the disorder, and prognosis are different for children.

DIAGNOSTIC AND ASSESSMENT ISSUES

Age is a critical factor in determining whether a particular behavior falls within an expected and normal developmental range. Children develop and change rapidly compared with adults, making a diagnosis of problem behavior difficult for parents and professionals. This difficulty is confounded by the fact that many normally developing children experience transitory problems from time to time and frequently adjust and grow out of the problem behavior just as quickly.

Children are dependent on adults not only to recognize the existence of a problem but also to seek help for them. Parents who have grown accustomed to a child's usual pattern of behavior, and those who do not have the opportunity to observe their child in the company of age mates, may not possess the requisite understanding of normal developmental behavior patterns to ascertain whether their child needs help. Furthermore, treatment of childhood disorders frequently involves the cooperation and participation of parents and family members, only some of whom are capable and willing.

In the following sections we will examine childhood disorders involving elimination, speech, attention, anxiety, and depression.

ELIMINATION

Problems in toilet training can arise from unreasonable parental expectations, because children must be physically, emotionally, and cognitively mature enough to master the task. In our culture, children are generally daytime toilet-trained by the time they enter the preschool years and nighttime trained about one year later. Girls' ability and motivation generally precede that of boys, and a wide normal range exists between children.

Enuresis is defined as a lack of bladder control after age 5 (American Psychiatric Association, 1994). Primary enuresis refers to bladder control that was never achieved by age 5, and secondary enuresis refers to a loss of ability after first achieving control. Sec-

ondary enuresis frequently occurs when feelings of jealousy or insecurity are triggered, such as following the birth of a sibling or a similar stressor. After a period of adjustment, toilet-training skills return to normal. Other times, the problem becomes more serious. Thirty percent of enuretic children were found to be aggressive, unresponsive to discipline, and have low frustration tolerances (Kaffman & Elizur, 1977). Fewer children showed signs of poor motivation, depression, and lack of assertiveness. During the normal course of the disorder, about 5%–10% of children spontaneously recover each year. It is believed that enuresis is a heritable disorder, with 75% of enuretic children having an immediate family member who once had the disorder (Geroski & Rodgers, 1998).

Encopresis is defined as a lack of bowel control after a normal age and is distinguished as either primary or secondary. Encopresis is not diagnosed before age 4. The disorder is more common in boys than in girls and occurs in about 1% of the 5-year-old population. About one out of four encopretic children are also enuretic. Factors associated with encopresis include inconsistent toilet training and psychosocial stressors, such as entering school or the birth of a new sibling. Encopresis rarely becomes chronic.

ANXIETY DISORDERS

Separation anxiety disorder, characterized by severe anxiety about leaving home or separating from the child's primary attachment figures, is not uncommon, occurring in about 4% of the population. Children typically fear harm will come to them or their family if separated, and they go to great lengths to prevent separations. Children develop somatic complaints, refuse to attend school, and behave in clingy, demanding ways with parents to ensure their closeness. These children also experience sadness, loss of interest in activities, withdrawal, and difficulty concentrating on school or play. In the course of normal development, separation anxiety peaks at about 1 year and gradually lessens with age. Separation anxiety is most frequently seen in very tight-knit families and following some sort of trauma for the child. In the general population, separation anxiety is more prevalent in females than males; however, gender rates are about equal in clinical samples (American Psychiatric Association, 1994).

A child's mastery of toilet training requires coordination of biophysical, psychological, and social domains of development.

Avoidant disorder, commonly called a fear of strangers and strange or new situations, can be socially debilitating to a child. This response is normal between the ages of 8 months and 2–3 years, but it may continue into childhood for some children. A child may severely limit involvement in social and academic settings to avoid this fear. As a result, the child may feel lonely and depressed and lose self-confidence, causing further avoidant behavior (Bootzin & Acocella, 1988).

Overanxious disorder or generalized anxiety disorder is distinguished from separation anxiety in that the child's fears have no specific focus. In the case of overanxious disorder, children anticipate something going wrong in almost any situation and worry about the possibility. Children with these unfocused worries doubt themselves and their abilities as well. Worries often center on school and sports performance, and children frequently redo tasks in an attempt to make sure they are good enough. Children living in homes where love and acceptance are granted for good behavior tend to be approval seeking and perfectionistic (American Psychiatric Association, 1994). A vicious cycle unfolds when children's performance is handicapped by worries and anxiety, which, in turn, causes them to fail and produces even more anxiety (Bootzin & Acocella, 1988).

Attention-deficit/hyperactivity disorder (ADHD) is characterized by persistent inattention and/or hyperactivity (American Psychiatric Association, 1994). While there are many children who meet the diagnostic criteria for this disorder, it is often difficult to diagnose in children younger than 5 years because of the behavior variation normally seen at this age (American Psychiatric Association, 1994). Additionally, until children begin kindergarten or elementary school, they do not typically have many demands on their attention, which makes an attention disorder difficult to recognize. Yet, there are many children as young as 4 or 5 years old who are diagnosed with ADHD and prescribed Ritalin or other pharmaceutical medication (Hancock, 1996). This phenomenon spurs the question: Do these children have actual attention and hyperactivity problems, or have adults simply lost patience with active children? Proponents for the use of medication in controlling ADHD believe that there are some children who cannot sit still without the help of psycho-pharmaceuticals such as Ritalin. Opponents, however, argue that using medication is simply an easier solution to the problem because it takes less time than sitting down and talking (Hancock, 1996). With roughly 1.3 million of America's 5 to 14-year-olds taking Ritalin (Hancock, 1996), it appears that this debate will continue.

CHILDHOOD DEPRESSION

Depression in children tends to co-occur in the presence of other psychological disorders (Garmezy & Rutter, 1983). The symptom pattern differs from that exhibited by adults. Children tend to display more than one symptom and can act clingy, disobedient, irritable, sad, and hopeless; refuse to attend school; and show a decreased interest in usual activities. Children are rarely suicidal, although this possibility increases in adolescence. Children who experience depression tend to have mood disorders as adults (Cantwell, 1982). Prevalence rates for prepubertal males and females are about equal, however, by the time girls reach adolescence and adulthood, they are twice as likely to report depression as males (American Psychiatric Association, 1994). Depressive episodes often result from a severe psychosocial stressor in a child's life, such as the loss of a loved one, separation, or other trauma. A more serious psychological disorder is discussed in the following Focus on Psychology section.

FOCUS ON PSYCHOLOGY

Childhood Autism—A Severe Developmental Disorder

Kevin's parents thought he was a little odd as a baby. He was rather fussy. When they fed him and tried to stroke his back, he would stop eating and fuss until they stopped the stroking. When they picked him up for play, he would often avert his gaze or look past them. As a toddler, he liked to play by himself. He would sit for long periods of time just watching a patch of sun on the floor or dropping blocks over and over. His language development seemed especially slow, but he was their first baby and they had no expectations for language acquisition. The pediatrician told them Kevin would learn to speak soon. When he went to preschool at the age of 3, however, the teacher called the parents in for a conference because Kevin would not play or interact with any of the children in the class. He spent most of his mornings sitting and rocking and he rarely spoke to anyone. In fact, the only thing the teachers had heard him say was "water" when he needed a drink.

Childhood **autism** is a pervasive developmental disorder with profound implications for the child's ability to function (American Psychiatric Association, 1994). Children with autism suffer psychological, cognitive, and social deficits that impair their functional capacities in nearly every realm of their lives.

Although the disorder is typically present at birth, autism is often not diagnosed until the child is about 3 years old, when language deficits can be distinguished from speech delays. It is these speech and language delays that distinguish autism from Asperger's Disorder, a pervasive developmental disorder in children that shares many of the diagnostic criteria with autism, but does not involve language delays (American Psychiatric Association, 1994).

Language deficits are prominent in autistic children. More than half do not speak at all, whereas others whine, scream, or demonstrate **echolalia,** repeating songs and phrases from others' conversations. These verbalizations are distinct from social communication because they are rarely intended as a means of interacting with or communicating information to another person. More often, verbal expression is used as a means of self-stimulation or for getting a simple need met. The severity of language deficits has been found to be the best predictor of the child's overall prognosis. Children who have developed recognizable speech by the age of 5 fare the best in terms of leading independent lives.

Mental retardation appears to be a stable feature of autistic disorder, with more than 70% of children testing at an IQ level below 70. Furthermore, their mental retardation does not improve with therapy (Rutter, 1985). Boys are three to four times more likely to develop autism than are girls.

Significant social deficits and poor relationship skills also characterize autism. These children typically react to others not as people but as objects in their environment. They do not relate physically, seek comfort, communicate, or otherwise interact with other people unless they need something they cannot manage themselves (Bootzin & Acocella, 1988). They prefer the company of inanimate objects, and when with other people, autistic children frequently do not respond to their own names, make eye contact, smile, initiate communication, or respond when spoken to. More often, autistic children will not acknowledge the presence of another human being.

We see autistic children play in rigid, unimaginative ways. They do not use make-believe or imitative play. Furthermore, they do not engage in social play, instead preferring to occupy themselves alone. They also engage in nonfunctional routines and rituals (APA, 1994). These children demand sameness and predictability in their environments and daily routines. They also exhibit distorted body movements. Autistic children can be seen flapping their arms, hands, and fingers, banging their heads, and twisting their bodies in unnatural ways.

Parenting an autistic child can be extremely difficult, frustrating, and sad. When a child does not respond or relate, the quality of parental and sibling interactions and stimulation can taper off. Treatment efforts result in slow, minimal gains. Behavioral therapy techniques have documented empirical support. These techniques include token economy strategies, modeling, social skills training, and language and speech training. B. J. Freeman (1993) proposes an individually based program, in which each child's developmental profile is considered and treatment components are designed accordingly.

SOCIAL DIMENSION

Families, Groups, Support Systems, and Communities

By the time a child reaches the period of early childhood, the family has undergone numerous changes. These changes are noted in the marital relationship,

Play increases social contacts, conversation, and social skills.

parent-child relationships, work, and family systems dynamics. The couple has become a family, and that family may continue growing again with the birth of another child. The developing child plays an active role in promoting healthy change in the family structure and dynamics while, at the same time, adjusting to the changes.

For the preschooler, parents and family remain the primary socializers and sources of companionship and comfort. However, as children progress through the preschool years, they relate to and rely on a larger circle of adults and peers because their needs no longer center so much on physical care. Preschoolers are growing, exploring, investigating, and refining motor, social, and emotional skills at an exhilarating and enthusiastic pace. They also discover new sources of anger, frustration, jealousy, and elation as they interact within a wider social environment.

Parenting roles and tasks shift from those involving physical care to setting limits, encouraging increasing amounts of independence in self-care and play skills, and using language and reason as methods of social control. Throughout all these very profound

changes in the preschooler's social environment, the family continues to provide the basis for support, attachment, and exploration. Children need their parents to be there for them whenever they need them.

FAMILY INFLUENCES

As we mentioned briefly, parenting roles begin to take on a different color as children traverse the preschool years. Children still need their parents as the primary sources of attention, care, love, encouragement, and security. Children living in homes where their changing needs are provided for can attend to their developmental tasks unencumbered with worries or fears for their safety and for that of their family members. Parents who are too preoccupied with their own identity issues, ambitions, or survival will struggle with child-rearing tasks that seem extremely demanding because they compete for energy with their other pressing needs.

Parents of preschoolers begin to shift their focus from physical care to encouraging self-care, greater independence, and compliance with rules of social systems such as the family, peer group, preschool, and society. Effective parents allow their children to try out new activities, develop some self-sufficiency, and set reasonable limits with their children. Parents who are too rigid or demanding impose unrealistic expectations on their children, causing them to feel as if they cannot measure up and to feel guilty for failing to accomplish something on their own.

According to Erikson's theory, the psychosocial crisis facing children during the preschool years is one of initiative versus guilt. The parent of a preschooler, much like the parent of the adolescent, must help the child discover personal and social abilities and limits while enjoying their accomplishments and sense of self-reliance. In this way, measured against the backdrop of peers and society, children continue to learn about themselves.

PARENTING STYLES

Diana Baumrind has investigated parenting styles over several decades (1971, 1991), and her research has described three styles of parenting and their consequent effects on children: *authoritarian, authoritative,* and *laissez-faire permissive.* Maccoby and Martin (1983) have further differentiated the permissive parenting style to include two distinct types, *permissive indulgent* and *permissive indifferent.* Erikson (1968) also theorized that parents differ along two dimensions of parenting he considered fundamental during the preschool years as parents begin to restrain and socialize their children. He labeled these dimensions parental warmth (warmth-hostility) and parental control (permissiveness-restrictiveness).

Parental warmth refers to the acceptance and approval shown to children across a number of different occasions. These parents offer their children encouragement and praise and are generous with affection. Hostile parents, on the other hand, tend to criticize, reject, or ignore their children and their bids for attention. Parents tend to be characterized as either warm and approving or hostile and rejecting, and these styles tend to be mutually exclusive.

The construct of parental control taps into the number of demands, restrictions, and limits that parents place on their children. Permissive parents encourage their children to explore and make independent decisions. Restrictive parents impose more demands and enforce more rules on their children, controlling their actions and decisions. Parents tend to become more permissive as children age and develop the experience and ability to make healthy decisions for themselves. All children need guidance and monitoring, which can be flexible and change according to the developmental needs of the child.

What effects do we see on children reared within the context of these distinct parenting models? Parents need to adapt their style of relating and interacting, as well as discipline, to their child's developmental level. As children enter the preschool years, parents can begin to rely on verbal exchanges, reasoning,

moral sanctions, and giving and withholding of special privileges. Table 7.1 highlights the features associated with each parenting style and the behavioral effects on the children. Discipline strategies that invoke logical and immediate consequences for preschool children tend to be the most effective because children are beginning to understand cause and effect. They also help a child develop an ability to think logically about actions and to make choices based on likely outcomes. Furthermore, the use of logical consequences helps avoid power struggles between parents who impose discipline (Dreykurs, 1964). Logical consequences just happen, because of their very nature, and the child begins to learn about problem solving in the real world.

Several researchers found few differences between mothers and fathers when disciplining their preschool-aged children. Mothers tend to verbalize more while fathers give more commands (McLaughlin, 1983; Yogman, Cooley, & Kindlon, 1988). Differences did emerge when researchers examined the interaction between parents and sons and daughters. Sons were provided more task-oriented, directive, and approval instructions than were daughters by both par-

TABLE 7.1   Effects of Parenting Styles on Children

Parenting Style	Characteristics	Effects on Children
Authoritarian	Restrictive, punitive style; sets firm limits and encourages effort; few verbal exchanges allowed.	Average social; cognitive competencies; fearful, unhappy, vulnerable to stress.
Authoritative	Warm, nurturing, accepting; encourages independence, but with limits; verbal exchanges using negotiating, compromise, and reason also encouraged; responsive to needs of child.	High social, cognitive competencies; cope well with stress; curious, self-controlled, cooperative with adults, energetic, friendly, self-reliant.
Permissive Indulgent	Very involved in child's life; few demands placed on child; lax control; allows freedom of expression, encourages creativity, confidence.	Low self control; difficulty focusing own behavior; expect to get their own way; allow poor social, cognitive competencies; not popular with others.
Permissive Indifferent	Very uninvolved in child; few demands placed on child; lax control; allows freedom of expression and impulses	Low self-control; poor social, cognitive competencies; rebellious, impulsive, aggressive.

ents (Frankel, 1983). Girls, on the other hand, were taught to be more cautious and cooperative and were provided feedback about their performance more than were boys. The subtle, but clear, messages to boys and girls from both parents convey stereotypical gender-role expectations. More aggressive behavior is tolerated, if not encouraged, in boys, whereas girls are taught cooperation and empathy through parental play and teaching (Power & Shanks, 1989).

Cultural Differences in Parenting Styles

Many researchers have documented the positive effects on children raised by parents who are warm and affectionate and who set consistent, reasonable rules for their children as opposed to those that behave in a punitive or aloof manner (Baumrind, 1971). Of course, most of this research has been conducted on middle-class, white families. These findings may neglect the fact that not all children are raised to participate and succeed in the same environment as the middle-class children represented in these studies.

Research studies of lower-income and lower-educational-status families suggest that these parents tend to be more authoritarian in their child-raising practices; they expect more obedience from their children, engage in less verbal exchange, and exhibit less warmth (Maccoby, 1980). But does this make lower-income parents less desirable or effective parents? Shaffer (1989) reviews several reasons why lower-SES parents may be more authoritarian with their children. They may be facing more stress, which makes it harder for them to be warm and caring. They may be preparing their children for the types of jobs the parents themselves hold, in which obedience and respect are positive attributes. The children themselves may be more difficult to parent. Many lower-income mothers are young and may not have received adequate prenatal care. As a result, these mothers may have delivered premature, low-birth-weight, or drug- or alcohol-exposed babies. As we have discussed, such babies are more difficult to care for. Also, lower-SES parents may feel that authoritarian parenting is necessary to protect their children from environments that are full of risks. These risks increase the likelihood of delinquency, school dropout, early pregnancy, and substance use. Children from risky environments may not be permitted the luxury of experimentation without dire consequences that children from more affluent environments are afforded. Some researchers have found that low-income, inner-city parents who are strict and set stringent rules for their children, yet also provide high levels of warmth, assist their children in resisting the negative influences in their school and neighborhood environments that lead to low achievement and delinquency (McLoyd, 1998).

As a result, children from lower-SES families may play by and adopt a different set of values according to the roles, goals, and relationships they aspire to. These ecological constraints are not always incorporated into the interpretations of findings on the most effective parenting style for children. We must remember that as the cultural context changes, so do expectations of behavior and beliefs. For example, Slaughter-Defoe (1995), reviewing her previous research regarding parenting by African-American women living in a low-income area of Chicago, found that these women used mothers' discussion groups and extended family for support and as protective factors for their children. Ethnocentric biases prohibit us from understanding which parenting styles promote competent children in differing cultures and subcultures (Laosa, 1981). But regardless of the parental style, or the reasons for that particular style, parental warmth and approval remain important ingredients in the parent-child relationship.

NONTRADITIONAL FAMILIES

In today's society, there are many different types of "non-traditional" families. For example, many children are now being raised in families with same-sex parents. These families are sometimes criticized by those who feel that gay or lesbian parents cannot raise a well-adjusted child. However, the literature does not support this belief. Studies show that children raised by gay or lesbian parents showed no psychological or adjustment differences than children raised in "traditional" families (Cavaliere, 1995; Chan, Raboy, & Patterson, 1998). The research states that the bottom line is that it is not the parent's sexual orientation that influences the child's adjustment, but rather the quality of the parent-child relationship and the relationship between the two parents that impacts the child (Chan, Raboy, & Patterson, 1998). The preceding Focus on Multiculturalism pointed out cultural differences in parenting styles.

MOTHER'S ROLE

Although preschool children need their mothers less for physical care than they did as infants, the need for emotional support and encouragement is just as great as ever (Hartup, 1989; Sears, Maccoby, & Leven, 1957). Still, much of a mother's time with her preschooler revolves around child-care duties (seven times more than fathers), whereas fathers tend to spend much less time in direct care and more time playing (Robinson, 1977).

What kinds of things do preschoolers learn from their mothers? Studies reveal that mothers tend to introduce soothing activities to their preschoolers, such as reading, drawing, and music. In this way, children are learning how to soothe and comfort themselves. Children also learn a great deal about feelings and relationships from their mothers. During play, mothers tend to be more verbal and visual with their preschoolers than fathers (Power, 1985). This interaction style during play may contribute to the child's understanding of relationships and coping strategies.

In addition, preschoolers are attuned to learning about the meaning of their gender and begin to identify with the same-sex parent, all the while learning how to relate to the opposite-sex parent. Preschoolers observe that males and females act differently. Research has supported the idea that males and females rely on different strategic approaches to solve problems. Males tend to focus on only one relevant aspect of the problem and base their decision on that aspect alone. Females, on the other hand, tend to gather lots of information and attend to the context of the situation before determining a solution. In this way, chil-

dren learn about diversity and alternative approaches to events in their lives.

FATHER'S ROLE

The relationship between preschoolers and their father broadens the children's perspective on the world. For the most part, even today, preschool boys and girls are raised in almost exclusively female environments. They spend most of their time with mothers and with babysitters and teachers, who are usually female. The child's father may be the only male figure with whom contact is regular.

As we discussed in the last chapter, fathers play differently with their children than mothers do. Remember, father play has been described as more provocative and vigorous, and less conventional and verbal than mother play (Yogman, Colley, & Kindlen, 1988). These differences were found to be especially true of play with preschoolers, and with sons more so than with daughters. Fathers who play physically and roughly with their children tend to raise children with increased social competencies (MacDonald, 1987; Parke et al., 1988). This physical play is important to children in that how they learn to cope with the exhilaration, challenge, and unpredictability of their fathers' physical play prepares them for later life experiences.

By watching and interacting with their fathers, children also learn that there are numerous ways to complete a task. The father may not do things exactly the way the child's mother does, and the child is shown another way to solve a problem. Of course, family structures and parenting styles vary. Mothers and fathers may assume complementary but nonstandard roles that work just as well for their children and family.

Around age 4 or 5, both boys and girls find their relationship with their fathers especially appealing and important, and they seek him out as a playmate more often than they seek their mother (Lamb, 1981). Adult males help young boys define their own developing masculinity by encouraging and supporting their accomplishments. Boys will model themselves after their fathers at this age. Girls also seek out fatherly attention and time. The father's role helps girls define their feminine side. Also, preschool girls may tend to be resentful and jealous of their mother's special relationship with their father. Involved fathers help preschool children understand more about themselves and the larger world.

Is There Such a Thing as "Quality Time"?

At 5:30 A.M., John wakes to hurriedly get ready for work in order to beat the 7 o'clock rush-hour—the children are still asleep when he leaves home for his downtown office. Michelle is up at 7:30 to get the kids up, feed them breakfast, and get herself ready for work. The babysitter arrives to take the oldest to preschool at 8:30 and to watch the youngest during the day at her home. By 6:00 P.M., Michelle's work day is done, and she picks the kids up from the babysitter's house; John is preparing to leave the office in order to be home by 7 o'clock. Michelle feeds the kids their dinner at 6:30 while she looks over some faxes that came through for her on their home fax machine during the day. John arrives home at 7:15, after negotiating his way through particularly heavy traffic. The kids watch TV while John and Michelle look over bills and the day's mail. At 7:45, John, Michelle, and the kids get together in the living room for their "quality time"—they ask the kids about their day and sit together to watch part of a Disney video. By 9, after taking baths, brushing teeth, and a bedtime story, the kids are asleep in their beds.

In today's busy world, the preceding scenario has become a frequent reality. Parents are expected to balance long hours at work with the time they spend with their family. Beginning in the early 1970s, the concept of "quality time" was developed, which touted the belief that it is not important how much time you spend with your children, as long as the time spent is high-quality. But is the belief that high-quality time is better than the amount of time spent with children accurate? Researchers and psychologists say that it is not.

Researchers have found that high-quality time is very important, but it should not be a substitute for spending "pure" time with children (Shapiro, 1997). The fact remains that children seem to do better, emotionally, psychologically, and socially, when they spend more time with their parents. This concept was supported in a study by Clarke-Stewart, who found that babies whose mothers spent more time actively involved, interacting verbally and physically, showed better cognitive and social development than babies whose mothers did not interact as actively with them (Shapiro, 1997).

Psychologists, such as Jeanne Brooks-Gunn, believe that when quality time is substituted for quantity time, parental monitoring of children also decreases. While this might not have an obvious impact for younger children, it can be apparent when children enter into adolescence and are faced with issues such as peer pressure, including pressure to try drugs, alcohol, and sex (Shapiro, 1997).

So how is a busy family supposed to balance careers, family time, and social activities? There does not appear to be an easy answer. Some companies are becoming more flexible regarding employee hours, allowing workers to have flextime or to job share. Some parents have made decisions to reduce their hours at work, accepting less pay in exchange for more time with their families. Kantrowitz (1997) presents the following suggestions for busy parents:

1. Slow down—If it is financially feasible, one parent can cut back on hours at work for a few years. Also, try to eat at least one meal a day together, whether it is breakfast or dinner.

2. Bargain for time—Pose the idea of alternatives, such as job sharing, flextime, or telecommuting, to employers.

3. Stay flexible—Not all solutions to time problems work out the first time. Parents should remain flexible and not get discouraged if their time strategy does not work out the first time.

4. Be consistent—Concentrate on the three Rs (routines, rituals, and the ridiculous). Routines, such as mealtimes, allow the family time to reconnect. Rituals can be anything from holidays to pizza night.

5. Celebrate everyday miracles—This is where the ridiculous comes in. Enjoy and cherish the spontaneous moments that happen when the family is together. These moments are often the foundations for stories that are retold year after year.

SIBLINGS

Most children grow up in a family enriched and complicated by the presence of siblings. In the United States and Britain, this figure is estimated to be about 80%. The birth of a sibling often occurs when the first or previous child enters the preschool years. The exact influence one sibling wields over another depends on many factors, including birth order, birth spacing, number of siblings, and gender.

Sibling rivalry tends to begin early. Frequently, an older child will have to make adjustments and concessions, willingly or not, as soon as the next baby arrives. Even before the birth of a sibling, mothers can be incapacitated during pregnancy and not able to perform all of their usual child-care responsibilities. For most children, the period of adjustment to a new sibling is relatively short. As the youngest becomes capable of responding to an older child, positive interactions between siblings soon begin to dispel the initial reaction of anger and resentment. The children also develop a relationship of their own, not contingent on the parents' involvement.

What do we know about sibling relationships? Aside from exploring all possible combinations of sibling dyads, we will consider differences compared with the parent-child relationship, age, and gender. The sibling relationship was found to differ from that of the parent-child relationship (Baskett & Johnson, 1982). In-home observations supported the contention that both parent-child and sibling-sibling relationships favored more positive than negative interactions. However, children demonstrated more affection, compliance, and positive social responses to parents than to their brothers and sisters. Instead, children directed more negative behaviors, such as teasing, hitting, and yelling at their siblings, than at parents. Older siblings were found to be both more aggressive and domineering as well as helpful and nurturant with younger siblings (Abramovitch et al., 1986). Fighting and rivalry among siblings provides a safe opportunity to practice resolving conflicts and, in fact, may toughen up children, making them less vulnerable to the pain and hurt that can be a part of peer relationships.

Same-sex siblings were found to be more aggressive and to struggle more over dominance than were cross-sex siblings (Minnett, Vanell, & Santrock, 1983). However, several other investigators found opposing results, concluding that same-sex siblings showed more prosocial behaviors to one another than did cross-sex siblings (Abramovitch et al., 1986; Dunn & Kendrick, 1982; Furman & Buhrmester, 1985a, 1985b).

When children live together as siblings, they contribute to each other's development in unique ways. They serve as teachers and models of both prosocial and negative behavior, communication partners, playmates, and rivals. Even children as young as preschoolers provide valuable and attentive emotional support to younger siblings, especially when they have been shown basic care skills and can identify the baby's source of distress (Stewart, 1983).

Siblings benefit from assuming the role of teacher or learner. Firstborn children with younger siblings, compared with only children, have been shown to excel in academic achievement, believed, in part, to stem from playing the role of tutor to younger siblings (Zajonc & Markus, 1975). Younger siblings benefit from instruction in social skills, negotiation, and learning academic basics like ABCs and 123s by playing games like "school." Children who do not have siblings display solid social adjustment gained through social interactions with peers and extended family.

While sibling rivalry may come and go between brothers and sisters, there are those siblings who seem as though they will never get along. Researchers hy-

Siblings offer challenges to the development of interpersonal relationships.

pothesize that, in these cases, there may be a "clash" in temperament between the two children that prevents their developing a quality relationship (Brody, 1998). The concept is similar to "goodness of fit," as discussed in Chapter 6, where the temperament of the baby is very different from the personality and lifestyle of the parents. With siblings who have very dissimilar temperaments, conflict can arise simply because each child's emotions, behaviors, and coping mechanisms are different. However, just because two siblings have very different temperaments does not mean that they will never have a quality relationship. Other factors, such as the parent-child relationship, parental management of sibling conflict, and a positive and prosocial family environment, can ameliorate the conflict between siblings (Brody, 1998).

PEER RELATIONSHIPS

During the early childhood period of development, children continue to rely heavily on their parents for social and emotional support, care, and companionship. However, the security fostered by healthy family relationships provides children with the stability necessary to initiate play and friendships confidently with peers (Hartup, 1989; Pettit, Dodge, & Brown, 1988). Throughout this period of development, peers play an increasingly important role in the child's life.

Just how important are peer relationships in early childhood? We see peers providing a different learning environment from that of the family. Compared with the nonegalitarian family atmosphere, peer relationships tend to be of equal status. Preschoolers need other peers close in age to compare skills and their own abilities, learn social skills and information, and try out ways of interacting in a safe environment. Through this comparison, children find out more about themselves and others (Shaffer, 1989). Peer relationships have been associated with normal social development, whereas peer isolation and rejection have been linked to a host of behavioral problems in children, including delinquency and schizophrenia (Cairns et al., 1989; Kupersmidt & Coie, 1990). Peer rejection has been shown to predict more deleterious effects than peer isolation (Cowen et al., 1973).

In a classic study epitomizing the importance of peer relations, Anna Freud (Freud & Dann, 1951) studied six children found in a concentration camp after World War II. The children had all lost their parents and had reared themselves with very little consistent contact from adults. The children were each other's constant companions and refused to tolerate separation. They shared easily and were more concerned for the others than for themselves. After 35 years, the children had all grown to lead successful lives, with no evidence of psychosis or criminality. The companionship, nurturance, and skills they learned from each other supplanted those received from adults in their early years.

Researchers have found that children as young as 5–6 years of age spend as much free time with peers as with adults (Ellis, Rogoff, & Cromer, 1981). How would we characterize preschool children's peer groups? Preschoolers typically play with children of the same sex, a pattern that develops as early as ages 1–2 and continues through middle childhood (Ellis. Rogoff, & Cromer, 1981). This observation should not come as a surprise to us, given that children are socialized by parents who may think boys should play with boys and girls with girls. Furthermore, because gender-role development and stereotypical behaviors and interests peak during these years, we would expect children to play with others who share their interests.

What kinds of influence do preschool friends exert on each other? Even preschoolers distinguish preferred playmates from acquaintances. They share more readily (Masters & Furman, 1981), are less hostile (Hinde et al., 1985), and make more personal sacrifices for the benefit of a friend (Kanfer, Stifter, & Morris, 1981). They also reinforce sex-appropriate behavior and extinguish behavior that does not conform (Lamb, Easterbrooks, & Holden, 1980). Preschoolers have also been observed to imitate and mimic a friend to instigate a positive social encounter and influence the other child (Dollinger & Gasser, 1981; Grusec & Abramovitch, 1982).

In addition, several factors were found to contribute to the popularity of preschoolers with their peers. These factors included secure attachment to authoritative parents, having an athletic build, facial attractiveness (Langlois, 1986), higher intelligence (Hartup, 1983), a pleasant name (McDavid & Harari, 1973), and behavioral characteristics such as outgoing, cooperative, and supportive (Langlois & Stynczynski, 1979). Obviously, children born without some of these innate characteristics may benefit from developing compensatory social skills to achieve positive status within their peer group.

PRESCHOOLERS' PLAY

As we have stated in previous sections, play is the primary medium for learning for preschool children. Play, for all ages, is a pleasurable activity, rewarding in its own right for the positive feelings engendered. In addition, frustrations, tensions, conflict, and anxiety can be reduced through play experiences. Play increases children's peer affiliations, social contacts, conversation, and social skills. Piaget (1967) observed that children's cognitive skills are exercised and promoted during play. Conversely, children's play is also limited by their cognitive abilities. Vygotsky (1962) also emphasized the importance of imaginative play for preschoolers in developing symbolic functions. Berlyne (1960) described how play fulfills a child's need for exploration, curiosity, surprise, and novelty. These opportunities provide children with information about themselves and their world.

Mildred Parten (1932) observed and categorized preschool children's play according to the amount of social interaction. Her findings are described in Table 7.2. Parten concluded that 3-year-olds engaged in more solitary and parallel play, whereas 5-year-olds were more frequently seen playing associatively and cooperatively. Barnes (1971) replicated Parten's study to find that play styles of children had changed over the decades. He found that children spent less time playing associatively or cooperatively than the children in the 1930s, perhaps due to the effects of TV and technological toys that require a single operator and less imagination.

Current research now looks at play as a function of both social interaction and cognitive ability (Bergin, 1988). Preschoolers were found to engage primarily in pretense/symbolic play (Bergin, 1988; Singer & Singer, 1987) and constructive play (Hetherington, Cox, & Cox, 1982). These current representations of children's play are described in Table 7.3.

EFFECTS OF TV ON PRESCHOOL CHILDREN

Television has been noted as an important socializing agent and influence on children's behavior. American children spend more time watching television than they do with their parents or in school, an average of 20 hours per week (Nielsen Media Research, 1998). The television has become a convenient babysitter. Parents often use television to hold children's attention so they can accomplish household chores. Many parents find that in today's fast-paced world, they have less time to interact with their children. Bronfenbrenner (1986) commented that TV becomes a negative influence not because of what is provided but, instead, because of what is prevented. He suggests that the presence of TV decreases the amount of time families spend actively participating in mutual activities requiring discourse, argument, and reciprocity—such as playing games, going on outings, and talking—that promote children's learning. The American Academy of Pediatrics (AAP) also agrees with the argument that TV decreases family time. In a press release, the AAP

TABLE 7.2	Preschool Children's Play Styles
Play Type	**Child's Behavior**
Unoccupied play	Unengaged with other children or activities, not goal directed, least frequent type of play.
Solitary play	Child plays alone, engaged in task but not with other children, typical of 2- to 3-year-olds.
Onlooker play	Child watches other children play and talks, asks questions, and participates verbally but does not engage in the play directly. Interested, but not involved.
Parallel play	Child plays with toys like those others are using, but does not play with other child. More common among younger children than older ones.
Associative play	Children play actively together. The interaction is more important than the task or organization of the play. Social skills such as turn-taking, follow-the-leader are objects of the play.
Cooperative play	Children play an organized activity with a lot of social interaction. Social games, formal activities arranged by a teacher, competitive games fall into this category. Not as frequent among preschoolers.

stated that, especially for babies and toddlers, direct interaction with parents and caregivers is needed to assist in healthy brain growth and psychological and social skills (American Academy of Pediatrics, press release, 1999).

Television has been criticized for negatively influencing children's lives—for example, by promoting increased passivity, because television is not an interactive method of learning. Another criticism is that television perpetuates unrealistic views and expectations incompatible with real life, such as fairy-tale endings. A third criticism is that television promotes aggressive behavior and flaunts gratuitous sex. (See the Focus section on Television and Aggression, this page.) Finally, television casts women, older people, and ethnic minorities in stereotypical roles, often unfavorably as victims, villains, criminals, and/or incompetents (Brody, 1987). In addition, Condry (1989) found that ethnic minorities tended to be underrepresented on TV compared with whites.

However, television has no doubt also brought advantages to children's lives. These advantages include educational programs that expose children to information, knowledge, and alternative lifestyles and points of view to which they would not normally have access. But the images and themes of entertainment television often erode these advantages.

Originally, educational television shows such as *Sesame Street* were developed and marketed to reach underprivileged children. The goal was to prepare children for school by helping them learn letters, numbers, colors, counting, classifying, and simple problem solving. Evaluations of *Sesame Street* confirmed the intentions of the show. Children who watched *Sesame Street* often made cognitive gains that lasted into the early elementary years. This finding was especially strong for 3-year-olds compared with 5-year-olds who already had some of the skills taught on the show

TABLE 7.3	Development of Children's Play
Play Category	**Activity Description**
Sensorimotor play	Typical of infancy, to explore sensorimotor abilities.
Practice play	A means of practicing new skills, developing motor coordination, mental mastery. A skill or behavior is repeated until the skill is mastered. Important for sports and other games. Common throughout life and accounts for about one-third of preschoolers' play time (Rubin, Fein, & Vandenberg, 1983).
Pretense/symbolic play	Sociodramatic play when children use the physical environment as symbolic of something else, pretend play, try out fantasy, and role-play. Begins between 9 and 30 months of age and peaks at about ages 4–5.
Social play	Social interaction with peers, rough-and-tumble play, running, chasing, wrestling, and jumping are examples.
Constructive play	Combines sensorimotor and symbolic play, games that are created by the children, or projects developed by the children themselves. Organized games with rules are more common in elementary school–aged children.

(Bogatz & Ball, 1972). The only criticism logged against *Sesame Street* is that children from advantaged homes tend to watch the show more than do the underprivileged children for whom it was originally intended.

How children are affected by television viewing is determined, to a large extent, by what they are watching. In addition, parents can discuss the themes, staging, cultural biases, and peddling of consumerism depicted on television with their children. Open, nonjudgmental discussions can teach children to be informed viewers and not just consumers of television hype.

FOCUS ON RESEARCH

Television and Aggression

Bandura (1965) was one of the first researchers to study the effects of watching television violence on children. In his experiment, one group of children watched a violent television show, and one group did not. He found that children who had been exposed to the violence on television were later more likely to hit a doll repeatedly than were those who had not.

In another study, Steuer, Applefield, and Smith (1971) observed preschool children playing outdoors at nursery school and paired these children according to how much aggressive behavior, like hitting and kicking, they displayed. One child in each pair was shown a violent television program every day for two weeks. The other child was shown a television show free of aggressive and violent acts. The researchers found that those children shown the violent show, despite their previous level of aggressive behavior, became more aggressive in their play.

From these studies, we can conclude that television violence promotes increased levels of aggressive behavior in the play of preschool children. Friedrich and Stein (1973) demonstrated that this effect was strongest for children who engaged in more aggressive behaviors before viewing violence on television. Children who were not rated as aggressive to start with were hardly affected by the television violence. So, although violent television may contribute to aggressive acts in children, it is only one of many factors.

PRESCHOOL ENVIRONMENT

Today, many preschoolers will attend preschool or day care for three to five years. The emphasis of preschool programs varies greatly, with some focusing primarily on cognitive, academic development and others focusing almost exclusively on social and emotional development. However, for a child to appreciate a preschool setting fully, the curriculum should closely match the child's developmental goals.

Overall, preschool children tend to perform well in school when they have learned some self-control and self-discipline. These skills allow them to work with others, delay gratification, and handle the frustration inherent in problem solving that accompanies school tasks. The family environment, and parents in particular, can create situations in which the child experiences frustration and mastery, as well as learns to accept no for an answer. Children will learn internal self-control by first learning to accept external control of their behavior imposed by parents. As a side effect that is beneficial to the child-teacher relationship, children learn to respect and cooperate with adults and those in authority but not to fear them. These skills smooth children's transition to formal educational settings.

KINDERGARTEN

The concept of kindergarten was first developed by Freidrich Froebel in the 1840s. He conceived of kindergarten as a "garden for children," where they would be carefully nurtured, like plants. However, over the course of shifting trends in social and educational practices, some kindergartens have become too focused and concerned with success and achievement as opposed to nurturing the developing child (Elkind, 1981, 1987). This approach also worries some developmental experts who fear that too much pressure is placed on children to succeed and achieve at the expense of real learning.

In response to this debate over delineating the most effective kindergarten environment, Ballenger (1983) described a child-centered kindergarten, organized around the child's needs, interests, and learning style. Ballenger's guidelines emphasize teaching the whole child, including the physical, cognitive, and social being. He argues that kindergarten programs should concentrate their efforts on the process of learning, not on what is learned. Ballenger stresses that kindergarten children learn most effectively through play incorporating direct experience with objects, people, and materials. He further describes as excellent those kindergarten programs that focus on the child's state of being, not becoming, through speaking, listening, experimenting, exploring, and discussing.

Although preschool and kindergarten are among the resources available to assist in preparing children for formal education, many developmentalists reiterate the fact that parents play the largest and most critical role in preparing their children for school. Only when parents are prevented from doing so do the other resources become especially important (Schuster & Ashburn, 1992).

PROJECT HEAD START

Project Head Start was spearheaded in 1965 as part of Lyndon Johnson's Great Society initiative. The overall goal was to break the cycle of poverty by providing a preschool experience for children from economically disadvantaged families at risk for school failure. Krown (1974) and Smilansky's research (1968), as well as Seligman's theory of learned helplessness (Seligman,

1975), have documented that children from disorganized, helpless families perform poorly in school. According to this research, parents in these families feel helpless to control events in their lives and, as a result, are detached from their environment and are unresponsive to their children's needs. They fail to teach their children ways of mastering their environment, and the children in essence inherit the attitude of helplessness. When the children cannot fulfill their own expectations to perform well in school, they become detached as well and feel helpless to succeed. Their natural curiosity and motivation are thwarted from the beginning.

To counteract this phenomenon, the program was first offered to 4- and 5-year-olds during the summer preceding their kindergarten year. Now the program is available for an entire year prior to enrollment in kindergarten. In some areas of the country, Early Head Start exists, which directs its interventions toward infants and toddlers in an effort to enhance development through the creation of partnerships with parents (Lalley & Keith, 1997). Head Start shares many features of other early intervention programs (Richmond, Stipek, & Zigler, 1979), yet it makes unique contributions in the areas of parent participation, health, and nutrition. The specific curriculum for each Head Start program is determined by the individual program, with about 2,000 programs existing in slightly different forms. However, all Head Start programs are committed to improving the quality of life for the children and family participants.

What have we learned over the past 30 years of administering Head Start and other early intervention programs? First, we have refined our evaluation skills. We have learned that specific goals must be outlined for any project to ensure a proper evaluation of the program's intended effects. Initially, the effects of Head Start were evaluated only in terms of increases in children's IQ scores. But this situation represents only one small factor in determining school success. Effects on the health and motivation of the children and parent component were not examined, although they clearly influence school achievement as well (Zigler & Trickett, 1978). As a result, the evaluation failed to measure change in the most prominent areas of the program and caused undue disenchantment with the program. An example of this dissatisfaction stemmed from the Westinghouse Learning Corporation's (1969) evaluation, which showed that, even after a full year of Head Start, children's IQ scores were initially increased only to decrease a short while later in elementary school. Head Start proponents have had to battle for funding and acceptance ever since. Fortunately, more comprehensive, better-designed follow-up evaluations of Head Start have shown that children who participated in this program were more likely to succeed at school and less likely to be placed in remedial education programs (Consortium for Longitudinal Studies, 1983). Additionally, research studies have found certain specific factors that, when included in early education/intervention programs, make a difference in positive child outcomes (Ramey, 1999):

- Two or more years of enrollment in preschool are better than one.

- More hours per day and more days per year provide greater benefits to children and often better meet the needs of families.

- Involvement of parents is critical for the child's success.

- Program effectiveness is greatly influenced by the quality and training of its teaching staff.

- Low-resource and special-needs families benefit from comprehensive support services.

- Program quality improves when there are low staff-to-child ratios.

Although Project Head Start has served about 7.5 million children during the first 15 years of operation, this number represents only about 20% of those eligible (Schuster & Ashburn, 1992). The program is still underfunded and cannot provide enrollment for all eligible children. Federal and local monies fund the program, which is provided free to all eligible children.

An effective evaluation of early intervention programs must also include a cost-benefit analysis. A cost-benefit analysis is an important consideration because policy makers usually depend heavily on this figure. The Committee on Economic Development (1987) has determined that every dollar spent on preschool intervention programs saves $4.75 in later expenses for remedial education, welfare, and crime.

FULL-SERVICE SCHOOLS

A handful of what are called "full-service" schools exist in the United States. A full-service school is one that brings together education, health, and social service agencies under one roof. In her book, *Full-Service Schools,* Dryfoos (1994) explains the need to bring community agencies, such as health care, child care, parent education, case management, and welfare, into the school. Doing this, she argues, would be responsive to the needs of the community and provide accessibility to those who need the services the most (Dryfoos, 1994). Proponents of full-service schools believe that these schools can improve education, improve access to services, and serve as a center for neighborhood revitalization (Dryfoos, 1994).

Multicultural and Gender Considerations

The preschool years are important for developing a positive and unique sense of self (Proshansky & Newton, 1968). Preschool children begin to recognize ethnic characteristics in appearance in themselves and in others. One of the early classic studies on racial awareness was conducted by the Clarks in 1939 (Clark & Clark, 1939). The researchers asked three 5-year-old African-American children to identify themselves from a series of drawings that included various animals, a clown, a white boy, and an African-American boy. They discovered that by age 4 children would begin to identify the African-American boy, and by age 5 their identification with the African-American boy was well developed.

Young preschoolers may not understand ethnicity as a fixed personal attribute until they have developed the concept of conservation, which occurs close to age 5. Preschoolers do not understand that these features may have a social significance beyond what is visible to the eye. Just as children cannot cognitively understand the meaning of sexuality, they cannot understand the social meaning of membership in one culture or another. As soon as they identify with one ethnic group, children learn who they are in comparison with others. They learn to evaluate themselves along the dimensions of appearance, ability, group

membership, and hopes for the future (Proshansky & Newton, 1968).

What preschool children come to know about their own heritage is largely determined by their parents and extended families. They have not often branched out into the larger community unprotected by caregivers. Children who feel valued in their own right learn to respect themselves and others. In addition, parents who teach their children the truth about racial inequality and discrimination may be preparing them to deal squarely with problem situations when they are encountered.

FOCUS ON MULTICULTURALISM

Cross-Culturally Adopted Children and Ethnic Identity Development

As we mentioned, children learn about their heritage and ethnicity largely through their parents and extended families. But what about a child who has been adopted into a culture that is different from his or her birth culture? What factors are involved in the development of this child's ethnic identity?

While very young children cannot cognitively understand the process of adoption, they are able to recognize that there are physical differences between themselves and their parents. Especially for internationally adopted children, there may be no opportunity to see or interact with people who share their culture of origin, and this can make ethnic identity formation more difficult. Unable to identify with either his birth culture or his adoptive culture, a child can find himself confused about where he belongs. This is especially true for adopted children of color who often realize that they are different because of comments and questions from teachers and friends.

How can social workers assist families who want their cross-culturally adopted child to develop a positive sense of identity? Generally, it is the new culture into which the child will assimilate. Research indicates ways in which parents can assist their child in developing a healthy ethnic identity. Social workers can assist the parents in including the following into their parenting practices and family environment:

- A nurturing home environment;

- Acknowledgment of the physical differences between themselves and their child, with emphasis on emotional, psychological, and social similarities;

- Exposure of the child to affirmative role models from their country of origin.

Although no distinct guidelines exist for raising a child in a culture different from his culture of origin, studies find that transracially and internationally adopted children do not differ in their self-esteem or adjustment compared to children adopted into same-race families, especially when the child is adopted at a young age. It does appear, however, that the child's environment, family and community play an important role in successful adjustment and ethnic identity formation.

Beth A. Auerbach-Dixon (Adapted from Friedlander, 1999)

GENDER-ROLE AND SEXUAL IDENTITY DEVELOPMENT

Gender-role development and sexual identity development are separate yet intrinsically linked processes. What factors contribute to gender and sexual identity development? As we discussed in the last chapter, babies show gender differences from birth, and certainly social and cultural expectations permeate child rearing from a very early age. Parents, families, teachers, peers, and physical and cognitive development all contribute to a child's sexual identity formation.

By the preschool years, boys will play with boys and girls with girls (Hartup, 1983). This represents the beginning of gender-role identity in that boys and girls tend to play differently during the preschool years. Preschool boys and girls already have strong notions of sex-typed play (Kuhn, Kohlberg, Langer, & Haan, 1977). They can identify whether boys or girls cook, play with cars, fight, climb trees, and kiss. Gender-specific toy preferences are also evident at this young age (Weinraub et al., 1984), and parents encourage sex-typed play in young children as well. This is especially true of fathers who tolerate tomboyish activities for girls but tend to express more concern about cross-sex activities for boys (Langlois & Downs, 1980). Boys adopt sex-typed behavior and toys earlier than girls do (Blakemore, LaRue, & Olejnik, 1979).

At this time, children also strengthen their identification with the same-sex parent. They will dress like them and engage in sex-stereotypic behaviors. They are busy exploring what it means to be a boy or girl in their world. Before ages 4 to 5, preschool children may think their sex is changeable. After this time, however, children realize they will always be either a boy or a girl. By age 3, children know what gender they are. By age 4, they can identify and recognize differences in boys and girls based on styles of behaving, playing, and dressing.

Sex play becomes more common in this age group and is usually nothing more than a healthy curiosity about their bodies. Children at this age are fascinated with everyone's body and bodily functions. Modesty and privacy are not concepts that have any meaning to them; curiosity wins out. Masturbatory play is also common during this period. The preschool years are an excellent time to introduce the notion of "private" and "public" selves. In addition, these concepts become useful in talking about safety and in preventing sexual abuse of children.

Although many gender-role qualities are learned, two characteristics appear to be genetically transposed: aggression and nurturance. Boys tend to be more aggressive than girls and engage in more aggressive play, from rough-and-tumble sports to "fights" with guns and superheroes (Maccoby & Jacklin, 1974). Girls display more nurturance than boys and play more games oriented to relationship themes (Maccoby, 1980). These qualities do not describe every boy or girl but, as we have stated before, they do tend to remain fairly constant over the course of development for most children.

FOCUS ON GENDER

The Effects of Sex Stereotyping

Tyrone's mother was determined to raise her children in a non-gender-specific way. In particular, she wanted her son to develop characteristics of warmth and nurturance, free from the constraints of sex stereotyping, so she discouraged aggressive play and aggressive toys. Tyrone spent most of his time at home with his mother and sister playing quietly. He often joined his sister in playing with her dolls and stuffed animals. Tyrone's mother did not become worried about him until he began wearing a dress-up skirt and pretending his name was Tara. Then she took him to a therapist who told her to forget the dolls, throw out the skirt, and buy him a cowboy outfit.

Many people argue that parents should not raise gender-neutral children because gender differences have real meaning and value in our society and to the children themselves. Studies by Fagot (1989, 1991) suggest that young children whose mothers have stereotypical attitudes toward sex roles in the family more easily learn labels for boys and girls; and children whose parents encourage sex-typed toy play can accurately label sex at an earlier age. Children may need to identify as one sex or the other not only in a physical sense as they learn about their bodies but also from a role standpoint as they learn about who they are in the larger society.

But what exactly are children learning about their sex roles in this society? By early childhood, children have been found to attribute greater competency to boys than to girls. In one study, 3- to 5-year-old children, when asked who was smart, pointed to the baby that was labeled the "boy" (Haugh, Hoffman, & Cowan, 1980). And parents tolerate a girl acting like a boy more readily than they do a boy acting like a girl. In fact, Emmerich (1959) suggested that girls spend their developmental years trying not to be babies, but boys spend these years trying not to be girls. Even children's literature makes being a boy more interesting than being a girl. In traditional literature, boys have adventures while girls get rescued and clean up after dwarfs. This same representation of gender-roles is also seen in television cartoon characters. Male cartoon characters outnumber female characters almost four to one, and, as in children's literature, the male characters are usually portrayed as powerful, strong, and smart, while the female characters are often portrayed as "damsels in distress" (American Psychological Association, press release, 1997).

Many people believe that these attitudes have contributed to inequality of women in our society, and they support teaching children to be androgynous. **Androgyny** refers to a combination of feminine and masculine attributes in the same individual. Advocates for androgyny argue that many girls and women have suffered from a loss of opportunity because of traditional sex stereotypes. Bem (1974) suggests that well-adjusted people possess qualities that are both masculine (assertiveness, competitiveness) and feminine (cooperation, nurturance).

However, preschool children have been found to be very rigid in their sex-type behaviors and attitudes (Maccoby, 1980). Maybe this rigidity is necessary for the child to develop a gender identity. After this identity has been well established, children can then alter their ideas about sex roles and characteristics. In fact, Hall and Halberstadt (1980) found that 27%–32% of 8- to 11-year-olds could be classified as androgynous.

Perhaps the real problem is not in gender-role differences but in the value assigned to those roles and sex-type characteristics by the culture.

Social Hazards

As discussed in the previous chapter, poverty and social class affect children's lives even before they are born. In 1994, it was estimated that 22% of the children in the United States were living in families with incomes below the federal poverty threshold (McLoyd, 1998).

How does poverty affect the preschool child's development? Children of lower-class families receive less exposure to language and cognitive stimulation in the home than do middle-class children. Children whose parents do not talk to them directly are hindered in their ability to use and understand language (Kagan, Kearsley, & Zelazo, 1978). Mastery experiences in the early years provide children with the confidence and motivation to try new experiences and expect to succeed. A positive sense of mastery is directly related to success in school (Kagan, Kearsley, & Zelazo, 1978). Hungry children cannot learn, and children who are not consistently cared for do not learn to care about themselves or to trust others. Additionally, research has shown that teachers perceive low-income children differently than higher-income children and often have lower achievement expectations, provide less positive attention, and give less positive reinforcement to them (McLoyd, 1998). So, it may often be the case that low-income children receive less cognitive stimulation not only in the home but also in school. The fundamental questions of preschool children center on their developing sense of mastery and worth. Through their behavior they ask, "Can I make a difference in my world?" and "Am I valued and loved for myself?" Children growing up in poverty depend heavily on their parents' ability to attend to their children's needs despite their own pressing worries. This is a formidable task, not easily met by any class of parents.

CHILD ABUSE

Child abuse, or the maltreatment of children, implies a range of conditions that violate social norms regarding the care, security, and safety of minors. Although state laws regulating the treatment of children vary, each state defines child maltreatment to include one or more of the following: physical abuse, sexual abuse, physical neglect, educational neglect, and psychological abuse (Pecora, Whittaker, & Maluccio, 1992).

Physical abuse involves injuries such as broken bones, serious and minor burns, head injuries, and bruises. In addition, there may be physical contact that does not cause noticeable injuries. Slapping, punching, and striking a child with a belt or a paddle does not always result in a visible injury.

Sexual abuse typically refers to various forms of touching, penetration, and exploitation. *Molestation* is the term used to describe inappropriate touching of minors, which may or may not involve genital contact. *Exploitation* refers to involving a child in sexual activities such as prostitution or pornography. Penetration includes oral, anal, or genital contact and can involve the use of body parts (fingers, penis) or objects.

Child neglect can include less explicit forms of abuse because it can refer to both active and passive behaviors from adults. Physical neglect includes abandonment, delay or refusal of health care, inadequate supervision, and inadequate provision of basic care such as food, housing, clothing, and personal hygiene. If each of these areas of neglect is to be avoided, then parents need continual support, resources, and initia-

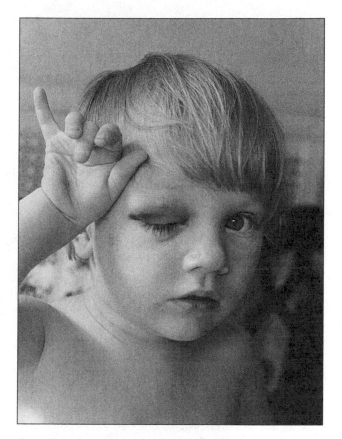

Child abuse is a serious problem in the United States—with far-reaching consequences.

tive in caring for their children. Often, child neglect is the result of severe lack of resources.

Educational neglect includes not enrolling a child in an educational program, allowing frequent absence from school, and refusing to respond to special educational needs. At times, parental values surrounding the role of formal schooling and the problems of handicapping conditions may come into conflict with the mandates of education laws and the values of special-education providers. These potential conflicts cloud the issues of educational neglect, thereby creating difficulty in substantiating negligence in some cases.

Psychological abuse refers to physical restraint, repeated threats, exploitation, rejection, and degradation. Although less concrete in its definition, descriptions of psychological abuse suggest that verbal messages are considered behaviors that should be regulated with regard to their effect on children's well-being. For example, negative labels and name-calling are forms of degradation.

People often think of child maltreatment as abusive behavior from a parent. In fact, the mistreatment of children can include any relationship in which an adult is responsible for the general well-being and supervision of minors. Thus, the adults potentially involved in child maltreatment may include parents, members of extended family, teachers, child-care providers, clergy, and so on.

FACTORS THAT CONTRIBUTE TO CHILD ABUSE

Several factors that contribute to child maltreatment have been identified, including family stress, child and family characteristics, interaction style, parent problems, and the value of violence. The most consistent factor is that parents who abuse or neglect their children were often abused or neglected in their own childhood. Another major factor in child maltreatment is substance abuse. The use of crack/cocaine or methamphetamines can seriously affect one's ability to care for children. Alcohol abuse also contributes to the risk of child abuse, especially when combined with other drug abuse. Children who are perceived as different, such as handicapped children and children with difficult temperaments, are at increased risk for abuse. Marital conflict, domestic violence, employment and financial stress, and social isolation all exacerbate negative interactions within a family that can increase the risk of child maltreatment (Child abuse and neglect clearinghouse, 1999). Many studies have established a strong relationship among poverty, social isolation, and child abuse or neglect (Garbarino, 1976; Garbarino & Kostelny, 1992; Garbarino & Sherman, 1980; Gelles, 1992). In addition, unemployment, lack of housing, daily stress, and community violence contribute to increased risk (Imery & Laumann-Billings, 1998). But, as we have pointed out in previous chapters, the presence of these factors does not automatically mean that the family will abuse its children. Specifically, Garbarino and colleagues have found that families who live in communities with little social support or lack of community identity have higher inci-

dences of child abuse and neglect, as well as juvenile delinquency, drug trafficking, and violent crime (Coulton et al., 1995).

INCIDENCE OF CHILD ABUSE

With the help of television and newspaper reporting, widespread awareness of child abuse and neglect has been achieved in recent years. It is not uncommon to learn of someone's personal experiences as a victim via a television talk show. As a result of this increased reporting, there *appears* to have been an alarming increase in physical abuse, sexual abuse, and neglect in the last two decades (National Center on Child Abuse and Neglect, 1994; Strauss & Gelles, 1986). But frequent reporting is difficult to distinguish from actual increases in new cases of child maltreatment. Incidence rates may vary depending on how the data are collected and on the channels used for reporting. Formal reports to child protective service agencies may only partly represent the actual rates of abuse (Strauss & Gelles, 1986).

According to the most recent statistics from the national report *Child Maltreatment 1996: Reports from the States to the National Child Abuse and Neglect Data System,* more than 2 million reports involving over 3 million children were made to Child Protective Services (CPS). This represents 44 per 1,000 children in the population. Almost 1 million children were identified as victims of substantiated or indicated abuse or neglect in 1996, an 18% increase since 1990. Seventy-seven percent of the perpetrators were parents, and 11% were other relatives of the child.

In 1996, there were an estimated 1,077 child deaths from abuse. Children under the age of 3 account for three-quarters of these deaths. The number of child fatalities from maltreatment has steadily increased over the last decade. However, the actual number of deaths may be underreported. Many deaths labeled as accidents or SIDS may in reality be the result of abuse.

The most common form of maltreatment is neglect (52%), followed by physical abuse (24%), sexual abuse (12%), emotional maltreatment (6%), and medical neglect (3%). Of the children abused, more than half were 7 years old or younger, and one-quarter were under the age of 4.

Reports of child maltreatment include people from all educational, economic, and ethnic backgrounds. However, poor people and minorities are more likely to be reported (Pecora, Whittaker, & Maluccio, 1992).

REPORTING CHILD ABUSE

Diane, a social worker in a clinic, sees a new client, a mother referred with a 14-month-old child diagnosed with failure to thrive. The doctors have been unable to find any medical reason for the child's slow weight gain, although he is well below the third percentile for his age. His head, however, is unusually large, and he is showing signs of developmental delay. Diane's task is to do a psychosocial assessment to see if there are any social reasons for the child's failure to thrive and to offer interventions. Diane quickly establishes a good rapport with the mother, and the mother begins to discuss her home life at length and in great detail. During the course of the interview, the mother divulges the following information:

- She has an older son, age 3, who was and still is failing to thrive with no medical reason.

- She has a daughter, age 4, who repeatedly runs away from home. In fact, the child needs constant supervision because she runs away whenever she gets the chance—for instance, if someone leaves the door unbolted. The police have been called several times to help find the child, and they have reported the family to Child Protective Services (CPS) three times. Lately, the mother has resorted to tying the child to a chair or to her person to keep the child from running away.

- She has a son, age 6, who has just been held back in kindergarten because of problems in school. He is very aggressive and has problems interacting with other children; he often hits or kicks them.

- Her husband is an alcoholic who has been arrested twice for domestic violence and once for child abuse when he struck the mother while she was holding their 4-month-old child, injuring the child. However, he is able to keep steady employment and earns a good income. He has agreed to go to counseling sessions with his wife.

- There is no open CPS case presently. The mother is obviously stressed and has little social support. She pays no notice to the child's attempts to gain her attention during the interview.

What is the social worker's legal obligation regarding contacting CPS in this case involving a severely malnourished child? In other words, should you call CPS to report this mother who has just confided this information to you, knowing that the child may be suffering from the social situation?

Deciding whether to report child maltreatment may be one of the most challenging situations that a person can face. Concerns about false reporting and the potentially negative or stigmatizing outcome for the children and families involved may create a predicament for the person making the decision.

Social workers, however, are mandated reporters. This means that they are legally obligated to report even a suspicion of child abuse or neglect to CPS. As a result, many cases that are reported involve suspected or mild abuse or neglect. CPS then investigates and determines whether the report is substantiated and if intervention is necessary. Remember, reports involving 3 million children are made each year. Of these reports, only one-third are substantiated. Of the cases that are substantiated, 40% receive no services as the result of limited time, money, and resources. Very few cases, less than 20%, involve any court action. Most families are encouraged to seek voluntary treatment (Emery & Laumann-Billings, 1998). So, in the preceding case involving a stressed mother who is seeking help for her child, what do you do? You are required to report the case if you suspect abuse or neglect; yet CPS may be unable to offer much help to the family, and a report may only undermine your therapeutic relationship with the mother. But remember, the rights of client-professional confidentiality (except attorney-client) are usually waived in child abuse and neglect reporting. And there *is* a penalty for failure to report. Mental health professionals face such dilemmas regularly when working with families.

INVESTIGATION OF CHILD MALTREATMENT

Child abuse is often difficult to substantiate. Confirming the history of child maltreatment requires comprehensive, time-consuming assessments, but child protection workers must often make immediate decisions with limited data. The child's safety must be ensured, but the rights of the parents and children involved must also be protected (Besharov, 1985).

Workers making child placement decisions are often faced with competing values—keeping the family together versus protecting the child (Pecora, Whittaker, & Maluccio, 1992). Often the worker has a poor history, little information, and limited time in which to come to a decision about whether to remove the child from the home.

People's mobility also contributes to the difficulty in substantiating abuse that has supposedly occurred over a long period of time. Such mobility may result in a lack of continuity from one agency to another in compiling necessary information. Mobility may also contribute to the delay of interventions and to a lack of effectiveness in helping families.

Child protection organizations use an assessment system that addresses the nature and severity of child maltreatment and the further risk to child safety. The collected information is used to determine what services are needed and what services are available, as well as the intervention's chances of producing a successful outcome (Pecora, Whittaker, & Maluccio, 1992).

In conducting the initial assessment/investigation, the primary issues to consider include (Child abuse and neglect clearinghouse, 1999):

- Did the child suffer maltreatment?
- Did a crime occur? (Many cases of physical or sexual abuse are reported to law enforcement.)
- Who is the alleged offender?
- Were there witnesses?
- Are there other victims?
- Is there any physical evidence?
- What is the risk of future maltreatment to the child?
- Is the child safe?
- What measures need to be taken to keep the child safe?
- Does the family have emergency needs?
- Can the agency offer continuing services to help protect the child and reduce the risk of future maltreatment?

Collecting this information is a time-consuming task. Thorough interviews of adults and children involved in child maltreatment require extensive time and skill. Often, the adults involved are not willing to divulge information concerning individual and familial history, the nature and extent of stress present in the family, negative feelings toward the child, and the possibility of irresponsible behavior on their part. Parents may be reluctant to discuss their situation fully for fear that the only outcome is losing their child.

Interviewing children to confirm abuse is very difficult because of several developmental concerns, including language, cognition, emotional growth, and attachment to significant adults. Before age 5, children's expressive language is still developing, and a child may not have the expressive vocabulary and sentence structure to describe experiences with accuracy and detail. The details concerning how the child felt and what happened where and when may be extremely difficult or impossible for many children to express. In particular, very young children have difficulty distinguishing real events from imagined ones. Children who are awakened from a deep sleep during an abusive incident may have difficulty orienting to time, place, and the authenticity of abusive behavior.

Feelings of guilt about the abuse are common among victims. Children who have been convinced that they are somehow responsible for an adult's reactions may internalize the blame or assume responsibility for abusive conditions. Some children may believe that if they could just be "good," the abuse would stop. The loyalty and bond between children and the significant adults in their lives may also contribute to a child's feeling guilty about disclosing abuse. Children may realize that disclosure of the abuse could break up the family. If dad is the sexual-abuse perpetrator and goes to jail as a result of the disclosure, the family may lose its main source of income.

THE EFFECTS OF CHILD ABUSE AND NEGLECT

Although it is difficult to pinpoint direct consequences of child abuse and neglect, there are effects that can be documented for some children. Infants who suffer head trauma or shaking can have long-lasting neurological deficits including blindness, deafness, mental retardation, and cerebral palsy. Children can also suffer psychological effects including bedwetting, tantrums, hyperactivity, low self-esteem, school problems, social withdrawal, oppositional behavior, compulsivity, and aggressive behaviors (Child Abuse and Neglect Clearinghouse, 1999; Cicchetti & Toth, 1995). Children who are physically abused exhibit more self-destructive behavior, such as suicide attempts and self-mutilation (Child Abuse and Neglect Clearinghouse, 1999). Children who have been maltreated are also at risk of attachment problems that can affect interpersonal relationships throughout life (Cicchetti & Toth, 1995).

FOCUS ON NARRATIVE

A Child Called "It"

The New York Times bestseller, *A Child Called "It,"* is the story of a young boy severely abused by his alcoholic mother. He is not allowed to interact with the rest of the family. He sleeps in the basement. His mother refuses to feed him for days at a time. When she catches him stealing food to survive, she makes him throw it up and then eat it again. She pushes his face into a soiled diaper. She cuts him with a knife. Here is his account of the psychological effect of years of abuse.

At the core of my soul, I hated myself more than anybody or anything. I came to believe that everything that happened to me or around me was my own fault because I had let it go on for so long. I wanted what others had but saw no way to get it, so I hated them for having it. I wanted to be strong, but inside I knew I was a wimp. I never had the courage to stand up to The Bitch, so I knew I deserved whatever happened to me. For years Mother had brainwashed me by having me shout aloud, "I hate myself! I hate myself!" Her efforts paid off. A few weeks before I started fifth grade, I hated myself so much that I wished I were dead.

School no longer held the exciting appeal that it had years ago. I struggled to concentrate on my work while in class, but my bottled-up anger often flashed at the wrong times. One Friday afternoon in the winter of 1973, for no apparent reason, I stormed out of the classroom, screaming at everyone as I

fled. I slammed the door so hard I thought the glass above the door would shatter. I ran to the bathroom, and with my tiny red fist I pounded the tiles until my strength drained away. Afterwards, I collapsed on the floor praying for a miracle. It never came.

(Pelzer, 1995, p. 21)

Implications for Practice: The Child Welfare Worker

Social workers have a long history of interest in the welfare of children and families. In recent years, the profession has shifted away from casework and has developed specific goals and interventions (Wells, 1995). But selecting and implementing these interventions for child abuse and neglect require highly skilled professionals (Brissett-Chapman, 1995), and, in the field of child abuse, these services are more often provided by paraprofessionals (Wells, 1995).

Collaboration among social workers, other human services providers, law enforcement, and the family's social support system is important when dealing with the complicated and multifaceted problems of child abuse. But few comprehensive and coordinated prevention and treatment programs exist, creating a vacuous situation for child protection workers and for families in crisis (Brissett-Chapman, 1995). In most child welfare organizations, the reality of shrinking financial resources results in few staff managing large caseloads. The workload often leaves little time for supervision or staff development. But in spite of the stress and difficulties associated with the job, children need protection, families need help, and people need support; and the role of the child welfare worker is an important and challenging opportunity for social work professionals.

RISK AND PROTECTIVE FACTORS

Research has identified risk factors that play a clear role in child development. These factors include exposure to parental psychopathology, low socioeconomic status, low IQ, large family size, marital discord and divorce, poor parent-child relationships, poor social support, perinatal trauma, biological disabilities, difficult

(text continues on p. 297)

Developmental Delay in a 4-Year-Old

DEVELOPMENTAL HISTORY

Missy, a 4-year-old white girl, was referred to the Speech and Language Center by her pediatrician. Missy's mother, Mrs. Jones, stated that she was not concerned about Missy until her relatives started commenting about her speech. She reported they would say things like, "Well, she'll probably be talking in whole paragraphs once she gets going." Other than this small problem, Mrs. Jones stated that Missy had been "pretty much average, just like my first daughter" in development. She reports no pregnancy or birth complications that she can remember. She added that she has not found her daughter to be a problem and that they get along well and "understand each other just fine."

BIOPHYSICAL CONSIDERATIONS

Missy is rather small for her age, appearing thin and tired. She has some trouble with gross motor coordination and cannot skip or throw a ball yet. Her fine motor coordination appears to be normal, although she is hesitant to initiate tasks and slow to complete them. At the teachers' request, Mrs. Jones had Missy's hearing tested a year ago. The examination concluded that Missy's hearing was within normal limits.

PSYCHOLOGICAL CONSIDERATIONS
Information Processing

Missy exhibits difficulties with information-processing tasks. Specifically, she is inattentive at times, staring out into space rather than paying attention to the task at hand. She appears easily distracted during conversation, but she plays the same games for hours on end at home, according to her mother. Her memory is poor

in testing; however, her mother says she can replay events over and over days after they happened. Mrs. Jones related that Missy attended preschool last year for a brief time, but she removed her because the school "wasn't right for her." When asked to elaborate about this, Mrs. Jones added that there was not enough structure in the school program, and Missy would just play imaginary games by herself all day. The teachers asked Mrs. Jones about hearing and speech difficulties. Mrs. Jones followed up with her pediatrician and had Missy's hearing tested.

The Wechsler Preschool and Primary Scale of Intelligence was administered to Missy, and she achieved a Full Scale IQ score of 92, placing her in the average range. Her Performance IQ score was 97 and her Verbal score was 80. Assessment of Missy's intellectual functioning revealed that her scores for expressive language development were below her overall intellectual functioning scores. Also, her scores on tests of her ability to understand language were in the normal range, significantly above her expressive language scores. Furthermore, her performance on the visual-motor tasks showed slight impairment.

Communication

Missy speaks when spoken to, hardly ever initiating communication. During the interview, her speech was slow and quiet. Her mother reports that she responds to questions at home but does not carry on lengthy conversations. Her mother added that Missy's older sister often completes sentences for her. Testing revealed Missy's vocabulary was limited for her age. In addition, she used the wrong tense in her responses to questions. Missy tended to hesitate when speaking, as if waiting for someone to help her. She nodded her head or gestured whenever possible.

Attitudes and Emotions

Missy's mother reports that Missy is a compliant child who usually does what she is told and does not argue or "sass back." Missy's demeanor is quiet, but she can become quite animated and insistent when playing with her dolls. Missy rarely cries or calls attention to herself in the family, Mrs. Jones recalls. To her, Missy looks content most of the time and is never demanding of attention. Her mother completed the Child Behavior Checklist (Achenbach & Edelbrock, 1983), and Missy's scores were in the normal range, with no elevations. However, her scores for internalizing behaviors were significantly higher than her externalizing behavior score.

When asked, Missy reports that she feels "fine." She states she rarely has upsets but admits to feeling sad much of the time, except when playing with her dolls. When asked if she cries very often, Missy says that she does not. She plays with her dolls or goes to the neighbor's house when she feels sad. When asked about her favorite activities, she listed playing with dolls and playing with the family dog alone outside in the backyard.

Missy agreed to draw a picture of herself for formal assessment. She did so hesitantly and slowly. Her picture was developmentally appropriate, although very small and in one corner.

Social Cognition and Regulation

Mrs. Jones reports that Missy has one friend she plays with in the neighborhood. Together, they play dolls. Usually Missy visits the friend's house and brings her dolls along. She is quite willing to share as long as her game is being played. Missy does not often play with her sister or her brother, but instead plays alongside them. Mrs. Jones noted that her oldest daughter spends a lot of time at her aunt's house next door. Mrs. Jones commented that Missy usually talks "baby talk" when playing dolls and her older sister complains about this when they do play together. Missy's older sister is often rude to Missy, too, according to her mother. She calls her names and teases her.

Missy relates that she likes her older sister but also likes it when she is away from home at her aunt's house, stating she doesn't have to "worry so much."

Missy never argues with her sister. Neither Missy nor Missy's mother report any incidences of verbal or physical aggression instigated by Missy. Her friend does not seek out her company but will usually play when asked. Missy often tries to convince the friend to play dolls when the friend wants to play another game instead.

In terms of Missy's self-care skills, she generally has no difficulties. She feeds herself, brushes her teeth, and dresses herself but does not fasten her own buttons. She sometimes has difficulty choosing clothing to wear and will wait until her mother comes in her room to ask for help. Mrs. Jones states that Missy goes to bed easily but often lies in bed for over an hour before falling asleep. Missy denies nightmares or fears associated with sleep. She admits to worrying about her family and says she "sometimes just waits and listens." She says she likes to have her dog sleep in her room with her at night. Mrs. Jones reports that Missy is not a big eater but will usually nibble at whatever she is served. Missy states her appetite is adequate but that she doesn't feel like eating very often.

SOCIAL CONSIDERATIONS

Family Situation

Missy lives with her mother, father, older sister, and younger brother in a small house owned by her father's sister. Mrs. Jones reluctantly admitted that her marriage is not perfect. She stated that she and her husband argue frequently about money, his help in the family, and the children. She added that he blamed her for the children's problems because she "partied too much and did too many drugs in high school." Neither she nor her husband finished high school, and both are currently unemployed. Mrs. Jones reported that her husband does not spend much time with the children, even though he is home most of the day. He yells at them when they are too loud, but he has never struck the children. She described the home as usually quiet, without anybody talking to the others unless something is wrong.

Mrs. Jones stated she has thought about leaving her husband but has nowhere else to go. Mrs. Jones

(continued)

added that she often feels trapped in the house; her husband will not let her go out without him very often, except to take the children to their appointments. Mrs. Jones conceded she spends little time recreating with her children because most of her time is spent performing household duties, child care, and taking her children to their appointments.

Missy stated she was closer to her mother but was afraid her father would be angry if he knew. In vague terms, Missy admitted to worrying about what will happen to her family. She says she likes to play at the neighbor's house and was happy going to school. Missy states that she plays dolls most of the time and stays in her room when home. She is not allowed outside to play very often, even though she lives near a school.

Groups, Social Supports, and Communities

Missy's family interacts primarily with social welfare institutions. Her family receives assistance in the form of temporary aid for needy families and food stamps. Her mother goes with the children to the appointments because her father will not attend, nor will he baby-sit the children when she is out.

Multicultural and Gender Considerations

Missy lives in a fairly homogeneous neighborhood and rarely has contact with people of a different ethnic background. Her family does not participate in community events, and the preschool she had attended briefly was also primarily white.

As for her gender development, Missy plays with stereotypical girl toys when she has the opportunity. She identifies herself as a girl and drew long hair and a bow on herself in her figure drawing.

SUMMARY AND IMPRESSIONS

Missy has several problems that became evident during the assessment.

1. Expressive Language Disorder—mild (American Psychiatric Association, 1994)
2. Poor peer relations and lack of social skills
3. Excessive worries interfering with sleep and appetite
4. Possible childhood depression
5. Inadequate self-system
6. Possible problems with coordination

Additional difficulties include the following:

7. Poor family communication
8. Inadequate social and peer opportunities
9. Marital conflict and possible abusive behavior directed toward her mother by her father
10. Inadequate gross motor play opportunities

Missy was cooperative with the social worker. However, her limited verbal skills, including poor vocabulary, inaccurate sentence structure and grammar, and reluctance to engage in conversation, made information gathering a difficult task. Some concern also exists about Mrs. Jones's ability to attend to Missy's physical and emotional needs. Furthermore, the Jones family does not appear capable of providing a sufficiently interactive and stimulating environment to promote healthy growth and remedy Missy's language delays.

On a positive note, Missy possesses adaptive skills in the sense that she can adjust her behavior to minimize the damage her environment imposes on her. She is quiet and does not make demands on a family already stressed by unemployment and marital conflict. In addition, she and her mother appear to have a close relationship compared with other family members. She also has a friend with whom she enjoys spending time and with whom her feelings are reciprocated to some degree. Last, she would most likely develop more friendships and improve her motor skills if given the opportunity.

temperament, and being born male (Pellegrini, 1990). This list puts many children at risk. Yet, in the face of such difficulties, some children thrive (Werner & Smith, 1982). These children are said to possess **resiliency,** the ability to recover from or adjust to stress. What factors influence the development of children who demonstrate resiliency? What helps some children of single, teenage mothers, or alcoholic mothers or depressed mothers, grow up to be well adjusted and productive?

The following qualities protect children against the traumas and adversities of life.

- Such children have good social skills; they have a positive mood and are friendly. Other people like them.

- They are able to interact with and engage other people. They approach and interact with adults outside the home. As a result, these children receive encouragement and support from teachers, other relatives, babysitters.

- They possess good problem-solving skills. As a result, they acquire a sense of mastery and learn to think for themselves.

- They have specific interests and are usually very creative.

Research has also identified protective factors that affect these children's early development:

- They had a good relationship with at least one caring adult, especially in the first year of life. Children cannot rear themselves.

- They faced challenges and were not over-protected.

- They did not have to deal with overwhelming stress. Children with one risk factor may do well, but with each added risk the likelihood of problems for the child increases (Pines, 1979).

Implications for Practice: Resiliency

Physical, psychological, and social stressors may impede some children's growth and development. Fortunately, most children are highly resilient, and with the help of knowledgeable and supportive adults in their environment, they can develop adaptive mecha-

nisms for coping with adversity. For others, the adversity may be too great, causing them to fall behind their peers developmentally. Accurate assessment and timely intervention are critical to healthy development in distressed children. When too much time goes by, children suffer complications that prevent them from learning new skills and catching up with peers. Prevention efforts include providing identified high-risk children with medical and educational programs to combat an unstable home environment.

Summary

DEVELOPMENTAL THEMES

Children in early childhood are developing greater autonomy. This is the Eriksonian psychosocial stage of autonomy versus shame and doubt (ages 2–3) and also of initiative versus guilt (ages 3–5). Children in this stage develop coordinated gross motor skills, acquire social skills, and achieve growth in cognitive and language abilities.

BIOPHYSICAL DIMENSION

Biophysical Growth and Development

Preschool children run, jump, climb, and tumble. They can ride a tricycle, walk up and down stairs, throw a ball, and catch a bounced ball. Fine motor skills also increase. Children learn to handle buttons and zippers and by age 5 can print letters. These children need time and room for physical activity.

Biophysical Hazards

Asthma is a leading chronic illness among children. Risk factors for asthma include having a family history of asthma, allergy problems, and exposure to second-hand smoke.

PSYCHOLOGICAL DIMENSION

Cognitive Development and Information Processing

Preschool children have increased attention spans. As they progress through this stage, they develop cognitive control of their attention and can attend to the relevant aspects of a task. Children usually do not remember much before the age of 3. As children develop a sense of self, their memory for past events increases. Speed of information processing increases during early childhood. Preschool children are in Piaget's preoperational stage. The substages of this stage are symbolic function and intuitive thought. Characteristics of thinking in this stage include egocentrism and animism. According to task analysis, when the task is interesting to the child, the child shows greater cognitive maturity. Other researchers feel development occurs in overlapping waves instead of discrete steps.

Communication

Children of this age understand more than they can express. They begin to learn the basic rules of language and communication. Language development is enhanced when the child receives appropriate verbal interaction from adults. During this time, communication disorders such as stuttering can arise.

Attitudes and Emotions

Preschool children have vivid and active imaginations. They may develop fears and phobias. Some experience nightmares and night terrors. Aggression can be described as either instrumental or hostile (with intent). Preschool aggressive acts diminish after age 4 as children learn to negotiate. In an effort to reduce aggression, children can be taught ways of expressing needs and interacting with others. When encouraged to identify and express their own emotions, children learn to be more empathic.

Social Cognition and Regulation

Preschool children learn to classify themselves by their physical characteristics and abilities. They usually know their gender and have some idea of cultural roles. Children begin to learn self-control at this age. They learn to use words instead of aggression. Children at this age begin to develop social skills. Having warm, supportive parents who set reasonable limits and having opportunities to interact with peers enhances children's social skills.

Psychological Hazards

Children in early childhood may encounter developmental delays, developmental disorders, and developmental psychopathology. Age is a crucial factor in assessing developmental problems. Some problems are normal, transitory behaviors for a particular age. Children may exhibit problems of elimination such as enuresis and encopresis. They may have anxiety disorders such as separation anxiety, avoidant disorder, and overanxious disorder. Children may become depressed from stressors in their life.

SOCIAL DIMENSION

Families, Groups, Support Systems, and Communities

Parenting styles fall into the categories of authoritarian, authoritative, and permissive (permissive indulgent and permissive indifferent). These styles have different behavioral outcomes for children. Parental warmth is an important consideration in any style. Mothers, fathers, siblings, and peers play important roles in the socialization of children. Play is the primary method of learning in early childhood. Play styles can be categorized according to the amount of social interaction occurring. Younger children engage in more solitary play, whereas older children play more cooperatively. Television is seen as an important socializing influence on children. Preschool programs should consider the developmental needs of the child. Project Head Start was developed to give underprivileged children a preschool experience and to enhance later school performance.

Multicultural and Gender Considerations

Children develop a racial identity as a fixed attribute by the age of 5. Parents and extended families influence children's knowledge of ethnicity and heritage. Preschool children learn gender identity and tend to play with same-sex peers and with sex-appropriate toys. Boys tend to be more aggressive, and girls more nurturing.

Social Hazards

Divorce results in particular stressors for children. These stressors can be taxing for children. Children of divorce must make many adjustments and benefit from support during and after the divorce. Child abuse includes physical abuse, sexual abuse, neglect, and psychological abuse. Family stress, social isolation, and parental history of abuse as a child all contribute to the risk of child abuse. Child welfare workers face difficult decisions regarding appropriate placement of abused children. Safety of the child must be weighed against family preservation. Poverty can affect children's sense of mastery and their ability to learn. Though many children face risk factors for development such as parental mental illness, poverty, large family, divorce, poor parent-child interactions, lack of social support, perinatal trauma, disability, and difficult temperament, many display resiliency and overcome these early stressors. In general, resilient children possess social skills and problem-solving abilities. These children had a nurturing caregiver in the first year of life. They faced difficulties, but were not overwhelmed by them.

🌐 Online Resources

National Institute of Mental Health
http://www.nimh.nih.gov

This is a searchable site that provides information on many psychological issues and disorders. Topics relevant to early childhood include ADD/ADHD, autism, and learning disorders.

American Psychological Association
http://www.apa.com

Contains information relevant to mental health professionals, the public, and students on broad and specific mental health topics. This is a searchable site that includes press releases and literature pertaining to early childhood development.

Prevent Child Abuse America
http://www.childabuse.org

This site provides information and resources regarding child abuse prevention. A broad range of information is available through this site, including information for reporting abuse, literature, statistics, and numerous links to other relevant sites.

Child Welfare League of America
http://www.cwla.org

This is the official website of CWLA, a non-profit organization that advocates for policies and programs meant to protect children of all ages. The website describes the mission of the organization, relevant programs, professional conferences and trainings, and searchable literature.

𝄞 InfoTrac® College Edition

For interesting materials related to what you have just read, please go to the *InfoTrac College Edition* website and search using the following key words:

childhood anxiety disorders	autism
self-esteem	parenting styles
social skills training	head start

Key Terms

aggression	empathy
altruism	encopresis
androgyny	enuresis
animism	hostile aggression
attention-deficit/hyperactivity disorder (ADHD)	infantile amnesia
	instrumental aggression
	night terrors
autism	overanxious disorder
avoidant disorder	phobias
categorical self	resiliency
child abuse	separation anxiety disorder
developmental waves	task analysis
echolalia	
egocentrism	

Developmental Themes

Stage: industry vs. inferiority. Adaptation to separation, greater interaction with peers, increased capacity to learn from others.

Biophysical Dimension

Biophysical Growth and Development
Ability to throw and catch a ball (age 6 years), play baseball (8–10 years), team sports (10–12); slow consistent growth until prepubertal years.

Biophysical Hazards
Greater risk for physical injury; potential for hearing and sight loss, physical abnormalities, and serious physical illness.

Psychological Dimension

Cognitive Development and Information Processing
Concrete reasoning, mental reversal of operations, capacity to think about two objects at the same time, decrease in egocentric thinking.

Communication
More correct and complex language, development of abstract connotations, reading and writing abilities refined.

Attitudes and Emotions
Development of a more differentiated self, better understanding of how others view them, evaluation of themselves against their peers to establish a sense of self, increase in sex-typed behaviors.

Social Cognition and Regulation
Development of self-reflective view, moral development moves from what's-in-it-for-me fairness to interpersonal conformity, cooperation and reciprocity in interpersonal awareness; at later stages (ages 11–13) role-taking skill can be evident, development of skills in friendship making.

Psychological Hazards
Learning problems, physical or sexual abuse, loneliness and isolation.

Social Dimension

Families, Groups, Support Systems, and Communities
Greater independence from family/parents as primary role models. Development of peer relationships, friendship, reciprocity, sharing, more formalized peer groups, less dependence on parental authority, mastery of academic and school demands.

Multicultural and Gender Considerations
Continued development of ethnic identification and gender roles.

Social Hazards
Poverty, family disruption, divorce, peer difficulties, school adjustment and learning difficulties.

Middle Childhood

CHAPTER CONTENTS

DEVELOPMENTAL THEMES

A white 1970 Volkswagen Beetle passes by. "Slug bug," says the 7-year-old sitting next to me and punches me in the arm. Ten minutes later, an old VW bug with a sunroof goes by. "Double slug bug." I get two more punches.

> "I pinch you, you can't pinch back, for I see a man in a white straw hat."
> "Oh, wow! Check it out! Made you look! Made you look!"
> "Roses are red,
> violets are blue,
> I'm going crazy
> just like you."

Middle childhood is characterized by a child culture—a whole reality of rules, reciprocity, and fairness (Konner, 1991). "Slug bug" is a very popular game for children in middle childhood, and its appeal comes from a long tradition. The game "I pinch you, you can't pinch back, for I see a man in a white straw hat" was a well-known game in the 1950s in England (Opie & Opie, 1987). "Made you look!" has been around as long as we can remember. It is great fun for kids because they can trick you into doing something, and they love that. "Roses are red, violets are blue"—this line fills many pages of yearbooks and provides an opportunity for wonderful poetic expression.

All these examples of games probably sound familiar to you. Although its nature and style may change, such play is universal for children in middle childhood. Why are these games so familiar? In middle childhood, games and play form a common children's culture—a culture that children can control and that belongs to no one but them (Konner, 1991). As children move from early childhood to middle childhood, their capacity to play such games unfolds. Their focus is on developing rules, ensuring fairness, and creating sanctions for rule-breakers. Children at this age can be in charge of the rules—in fact, they can create their own new rules. Piaget learned a great deal from children's games, referring to them as "the most admirable social institutions." Rousseau, the philosopher, said that the work of children is play. Play is their work, and they learn and grow from it. Such play seems particularly critical in the middle childhood years.

Middle childhood is the stage in life that begins at age 6 and ends at age 12, when adolescence begins. Children at this stage are ending their preschool years and beginning to learn new skills and competencies. This stage is often referred to by Erikson as one of industry, which means "to build," versus inferiority. Children in this stage develop competence in intellectual, social, and physical skills. Children who fail to gain this sense of competence may develop feelings of inferiority.

Many of the most important skills to children at this age are indicated by their daily pursuit of games, sports, reading, writing, and other school-related skills. This is a critical time for the development of coordination, physical strength, and flexibility. During this stage, children continue to make impressive cognitive gains in their intellectual functioning. As they move closer to adolescence, they develop some sophisticated logic and problem-solving abilities. The development of role-taking abilities becomes important as children's interactions with peers become more critical. Successful adaptation to friendships and peer groups is a major developmental task for this age group. Much of this adaptation is played out in the school system, because this is where the child now spends half of his or her waking hours. Successful adaptation can be complicated by psychological problems associated with learning or communication or by social problems such as peer difficulties or family disruption and divorce.

BIOPHYSICAL DIMENSION

Biophysical Growth and Development

Throughout middle childhood, children experience a slow but consistent growth pattern. This slow growth is sandwiched between the rapid growth of early childhood and the forthcoming growth spurt in the prepubertal years (10–13 years old for girls, 12–16 years old for boys). For instance, during the early and middle childhood years, children grow an average of 2 to 3 inches per year. The average 6-year-old child reaches almost 4 feet. Girls are generally shorter than boys at age 6, but by age 10, girls are slightly taller than boys. They continue to be taller through age 13. In terms of weight, girls weigh less than boys until age 11, when they have a growth spurt and end up weighing 3 pounds more than boys within the span of only one year. By age 14, boys exceed girls in weight and height and continue to do so throughout adulthood.

In middle childhood, fat tissue develops more quickly than muscle tissue, although through middle childhood there is actually a decrease in the growth of fatty tissue and an increase in muscle development. Girls retain the fat tissue longer, and boys develop muscle tissue more quickly. In physical appearance, girls are rounder, softer, and smoother than boys because of their greater amount of fatty tissue.

Motor development in middle childhood continues, and children become more coordinated and smoother in their responses. Development in both the large and small muscles facilitates changes in the child's coordination, agility, and smoothness. Whereas only one child in a thousand can hit a tennis ball over the net by age 4, by age 11 most children can learn to play tennis well (Santrock, 1996). Elementary school children become fascinated with many sports activities, such as climbing, throwing and catching a ball, swimming, skateboarding, and inline skating. At this age, gross-motor activity is emphasized. Often school-age children have difficulty controlling their impulses—they jump, run, bicycle, and climb everywhere. Such activity can sometimes lead to unrecognized fatigue that becomes exhibited in quarrelsome or crying behavior (Schuster & Ashburn, 1986). By 7 and 8 years of age, children, although still very active, develop more interest in sit-down games, because they have an increased attention span and better cognitive abilities. By 8 and 10 years of age, children are involved in activities that require longer and more concentrated attention and effort, such as baseball, gymnastic skills, or soccer. As children get to the end of middle childhood, they become more interested in peer-related physical activities.

During middle childhood, boys' gross motor development exceeds that of girls'. However, girls are better than boys at fine-motor skills. Boys' greater gross motor development may partially explain why boys are more interested in physical activity than girls are (Lefrancois, 1994).

Although children become increasingly adultlike, they are not miniature adults. Many of the child's physical elements are not completely developed. The child's optic nerve is not developed, and therefore the child cannot see as well as an adult. The child's bone growth and muscular development are far from complete. It is important to understand the child developmentally, because without such an understanding, we may expect certain behaviors at an age at which the child is not physically or intellectually prepared to perform them. The result is likely to be to discouragement on the part of the child. **Readiness** is an important concept in understanding human development. For example, if we give a child special reading lessons at the age of 4, he or she can learn over the course of one or two years, whereas the average 6-year-old will learn to read in a matter of weeks.

Children's physical development has received increased attention in recent years. The following Focus section discusses America's problem of overweight children.

FOCUS ON ACTIVITY

Our Nation's Kids Are Turning into Couch Potatoes

Although video games may help hand-eye coordination, there is nothing better to help a child develop than good old exercise. However, in America, older children are gaining weight and becoming increasingly sedentary. Physical activity is dropping off significantly during childhood and adolescence. For example, from the ages of 6 to 18, boys decrease their activity by at least 24% and girls by at least 36%.

Why is there such a marked decline in physical activity? Psychologists speculate that many children leave sports teams as athletics become more competitive, as academic demands take over, and as parents stop signing them up for sports classes and camps. Others cite children's fixation on video games and television. And many blame children's lack of knowledge about exercise's benefits and the failure of parents and physical education (PE) teachers to instill in children a life-long exercise ethic.

For example, if you observe a PE class, you may see most of the class standing around waiting for their turn while one or two children practice a skill. In one study, researchers found that elementary students spent only 8.5% of PE time in vigorous activities; middle school students spent 16% in such activities. These percentages are both much lower than the 50% active time standard set by the National Office of Disease Prevention and Health Promotion.

When asked about exercise, one child said, "running **is** boring, and then you pant." Because kids do not recognize the health benefits as adults do, adults must be creative. For example, exercising with a friend, making up stories while running, or seeing who can spot the most blue cars while bicycling may entice couch-potato children into getting outdoors. Additionally, PE programs should help make children fitter as well as teach them life skills, such as self-discipline and goal setting. The bottom line is this: If you do not train them while they are young, they won't exercise when they are adults.

Misha Marvel (Based on Murray, 1996)

Biophysical Hazards

Most of the children we see and interact with demonstrate the strong innate capability to grow in an orderly sequence that shows healthy development. However, both the rate and pattern of growth can be altered by adversity. When the child's environment is not meeting the child's fundamental needs, growth can be affected. Nutrition, amount of rest and sleep, opportunities to learn, amount of affection, extent of security—these and other factors can determine how fast and to what degree a child develops.

If we take a worldwide perspective, it is easy to discover that children suffering from poverty and lack of food are unable to achieve healthy development. Also, conditions that exist during times of war, such as lack of food, constant fear, and loss of or separation from parents, can lead to permanent physical damage. Although human development is marked by great resilience, there are environmental conditions that will produce marked changes in growth.

Consider the following conditions and their effect on development: Lack of iodine in community drinking water will lead to an increase in **cretinism,** a chronic disease characterized by physical deformity and dwarfism. **Rickets** is caused by a deficiency in vitamin D and produces permanent damage to the bones, resulting in a flat chest, deformed pelvis, and/or a crooked back.

Cognitive Development and Information Processing

Middle childhood represents an exciting period of study in terms of cognitive development. Piaget classified children in this age group as operating from concrete operational thought. This stage is characterized by becoming less egocentric. The child begins to decenter and demonstrates the operation of **reversibility.** Children at this stage also show conservation skills.

Piaget described the concrete operational stage as a series of operations or mental actions that are reversible. Such an operation is characterized by rules of logic. This stage is referred to as *concrete* because the child's thinking is limited to real objects. A child at this stage cannot use the logic of formal operations to compare the ideal with the actual or to think hypothetically.

The best way to understand these concepts is through the mind of Piaget himself. Piaget was a great observer of children, and he devised many ingenious experiments or tasks to test his ideas. His task of conservation is one of the most famous and is a hallmark of the concrete operations stage. **Conservation** has to do with the quantitative aspects of objects or things that do not change unless something has been added to or subtracted from the object, (although other changes may lead to perceptual differences).

Figure 8.1 shows tasks that can be used to measure conservation of number, mass, length, and area. Let's look at an example of conservation of mass. Suppose we give a child two equal balls of clay, then take one ball and roll it out into a long and narrow shape. The child is asked whether the snakelike object contains the same amount of clay as the original ball of clay. A child who is 5 or 6 will say that the long, narrow piece of clay contains more. However, a child of 7 or 8 is likely to reason that, although one ball of clay was rolled into a snakelike shape, it could be reformed into a ball and it would still contain the same amount of clay. This task also shows that the child can use the operation of reversibility. Rather than focusing exclusively

FIGURE 8.1
Tests of conservation (Weiten, 1995)

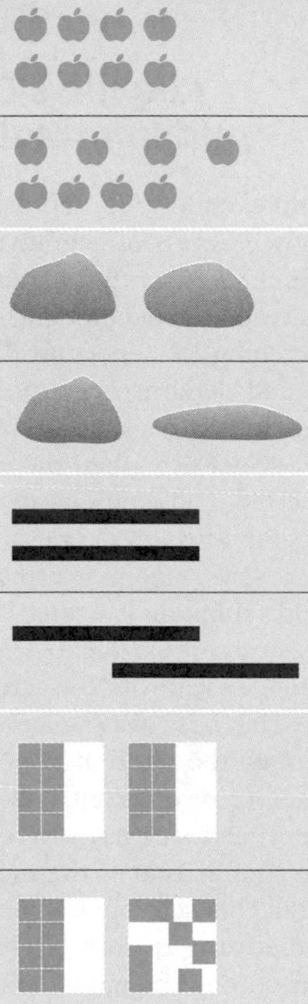

	Typical tasks used to measure conservation	Typical age of mastery
	Conservation of number Two equivalent rows of objects are shown to the child, who agrees that they have the same number of objects.	6–7
	One row is lengthened, and the child is asked whether one row has more objects.	
	Conservation of mass The child acknowledges that two clay balls have equal amounts of clay.	7–8
	The experimenter changes the shape of one of the balls and asks the child whether they still contain equal amounts of clay.	
	Conservation of length The child agrees that two sticks aligned with each other are the same length.	7–8
	After moving one stick to the left or right, the experimenter asks the child whether the sticks are of equal length.	
	Conservation of area Two identical sheets of cardboard have wooden blocks placed on them in identical positions; the child confirms that the same amount of space is left on each piece of cardboard.	8–9
	The experimenter scatters the blocks on one piece of cardboard and again asks the child whether the two pieces have the same amount of unoccupied space.	

on the physical characteristics of the objects, the child is able to coordinate information about both shapes of the clay, demonstrating concrete operational thinking (thought processes governed by rules of logic).

Although Piaget's influence on and contribution to understanding cognitive development is unmistakable, there are some important new developments in the field. In particular, Piaget argued that children's cognitive development proceeded according to a predetermined sequence of stages. However, recent research has discovered that there is tremendous individual variation in the performance of children of the same age

and supposedly the same stage. In addition, when the instructions for the task change even slightly, it can throw the results off considerably. Consequently, many of the researchers who continue in the Piagetian tradition now refer to "levels," which are considered less specific developmental milestones than "stages."

INTELLIGENCE AND INTELLIGENCE TESTS

Although we discuss and refer to intelligence often in our everyday world, the concept of intelligence is quite complex and difficult to measure. However, most people are familiar with Alfred Binet's concept of **mental age,** which is the age level at which the child scored on an intelligence test. Binet developed the first intelligence test in 1905. The Stanford-Binet is a well-known, widely used **intelligence quotient,** or IQ, test. Most of us think of the IQ test in terms of the following formula:

$$IQ = \frac{\text{mental age}}{\text{chronological age}} \times 100$$

IQ is calculated by comparing the child's mental age with the child's chronological age. Because IQ tests can have important implications in the planning of services for children, let's examine the two IQ tests commonly encountered in school reports or case records, the Stanford-Binet and the Weschsler.

Stanford-Binet

This test must be administered individually by a trained person. It is most often used with young children, although it is designed for individuals 2 to 18 years old. The Stanford-Binet is considered to be a verbal test of intelligence because it contains a large number of items that rely on verbal abilities. Table 8.1 gives examples of representative tasks used in the test.

The Stanford-Binet comprises four areas: *verbal reasoning, quantitative reasoning, abstract/visual reasoning,* and *short-term memory.* The IQ score is a composite score that is referred to as a measure of "adaptive ability." The Stanford-Binet has been administered to many people, and the results show that people's IQ scores form a normal distribution; most of the cases fall in the middle of the distribution. The Stanford-Binet has a mean of 100 and a standard deviation of 16. The mean refers to the average score, and the standard deviation is a measure of how much the scores vary. Reviewing some basic statistical concepts, one standard deviation from the mean constitutes 68% of the cases. The 68% is considered the average range, with scores ranging from 84 to 116.

Wechsler

Another popular test developed for use with children is the Wechsler Intelligence Scale for Children, third edition (WISC-III). This test is different from the Stanford-Binet in that it groups the test items into subsets that make up separate verbal and performance scales. The WISC-III is unique, because it taps both verbal and performance abilities, producing three values: a verbal IQ, a performance IQ, and a full-scale IQ. The verbal scale samples the degree of knowledge about general information; the ability to master concepts, think abstractly, and concentrate; use of judgment; and memory. The performance measure samples visual-motor skills, planning ability, attention to detail, and other attributes. The various subtests of this test allow the examiner to determine particular areas of strengths and weaknesses. In addition to this test, there is the Wechsler Preschool and Primary Scale of Intelligence-Revised (WPPSI-R), which has been developed for children between the ages of 4 and 6½.

Kaufman Assessment Battery for Children (K-ABC)

The K-ABC battery of tests is a new method of assessment based on a particular model of functioning referred to as the **Das-Luria model of cognitive functioning** (Das, 1984). The model is based on the notion that there are two modes of processing information: simultaneous processing and successive processing. Simultaneous processing is concerned with the immediate processing of related stimuli, whereas successive processing is concerned with the processing of stimuli that reflect a sequence, or ordering. From this perspective, intelligence is based on the ability to use both simultaneous and successive strategies effectively in goal-setting and planning behavior.

This test, like the WISC-III, comprises various subtests, each related to various abilities. Some of the subtests include the Mental Processing Composite Index, which assesses general intellectual functioning, and the Achievement Index, which assesses knowledge of facts, language concepts, and other school-related skills such as arithmetic, reading, and vocabulary. The developers of this test have provided extensive data in support of its reliability and validity.

The K-ABC may be of particular interest to social workers in the school, because one of the test's specific functions is to provide information to help plan teaching and remediation, especially with learning-disabled children. Central to the model is the ability to construct a cognitive map of a particular child so that

TABLE 8.1	Sample Tasks from the Stanford-Binet Test

Age	Sample Tasks
2	Identify parts of the body on a large paper doll. Place a circle, square, and triangle in the appropriate three holes of a form board.
5	Complete a drawing of a man. Fold a paper triangle in a manner similar to that modeled by examiner.
8	Answer questions about a story that has been read by the examiner. Indicate how objects are similar and different.
12	Define a number of words. Repeat five digits backward.

his or her specific strengths and weaknesses can be identified. Instructional strategies are then based on the results of the cognitive mapping.

INTELLIGENCE TESTS: GOOD OR BAD?

Since their inception, intelligence tests have been controversial. Early concerns about IQ tests centered on their use to label and classify children. It was common to find children labeled "average" if they scored 105 on a Stanford-Binet, "mentally retarded" if they scored 65, and "genius" if they obtained a score of 150. Such labels should not come from the results of a single test. Indeed, additional information should be carefully gathered and assessed if a child is going to be classified. Unfortunately, many children are still being classified by the results of a single test and will receive a label from their classification that will stay with them for many years.

Another major issue concerning the use of intelligence tests is whether they can be considered culturally biased. Many of the tests rely heavily on verbal intelligence that reflects a middle-class bias. Adrian Dove dramatized this point when he developed the Chitling Test. Sample items from this test included defining such things as a "gas-head," a "blood," and "Bo-Diddley" and knowing how long to cook chitlings. His point was clear: The emphasis on verbal abilities in many IQ tests reflected an environment that was familiar to white, middle-class children. Many of the IQ tests have attempted to improve their cultural fairness. For example, the Stanford-Binet, known for its emphasis on verbal abilities, is considered less accurate for

children whose language development is different from or slower than that of the average middle-class child. The latest edition of the test has been designed to ameliorate this problem. The more recently developed *Kaufman Assessment Battery for Children* is being promoted as more culturally fair than existing intelligence tests (Kaufman & Kaufman, 1983).

Are intelligence tests good or bad? Often it is not the intelligence test that is problematic but the misuse of the test. We must remember that intelligence is a complex concept. It is not fixed, and it cannot be measured easily. If a child is despondent and unmotivated when tested, this could easily influence the results. If an IQ test is administered in English and that is not the person's native language, the results are not likely to be accurate. Intelligence tests are not easily linked to success, and therefore their use should be carefully scrutinized. Social workers must ensure that children receive fair and accurate assessments. Understanding the benefits and weaknesses of intelligence tests is a start in this direction.

INFORMATION PROCESSING

Researchers are beginning to study how children process information about their social world. For instance, information processing may be linked to aggressive behavior. Consider the following scenario: Justin walks by Sean's desk and accidentally knocks a book off of his desk. Sean immediately jumps up and pushes Justin. The teacher runs over to break it up. The teacher is familiar with this scenario because Sean often gets into fights. Sean immediately responded to Justin as if Justin's actions were hostile, and this led him to an aggressive reaction. Kenneth Dodge studies boys like Sean because he believes they have skill deficits in their ability to detect social cues. In his study (Dodge et al., 1984), children viewed videotaped vignettes that depicted a social interaction in which one child provokes the other. Three different scenes were used that showed different intentions—hostile, prosocial, and accidental—and children were asked to differentiate among the intentions. The study found that children who were identified as being socially rejected did not perform as well as did children who were popular or average. Children who are deficient in

intention-cue detection are likely to make errors and view acts that are prosocial or accidental as hostile.

How we process information can be critical to our mental health and well-being, and so information processing has become a major approach to understanding the developing child. Three factors are fundamental to the information-processing approach: (1) how knowledge develops—its creation; (2) the processes and strategies that become part of the knowledge base or the processes used to retrieve information from the knowledge base; (3) the child's awareness of self as a knower able to use and evaluate strategies, also referred to as **metacognition,** which is knowledge about knowing. As we progress with the developing child, we will return to these early notions of information processing to examine the role of cognitive development.

The following sections posits that emotions and information processing, not IQ, may be the true measure of human intelligence.

THE SIGNIFICANCE OF EMOTIONAL INTELLIGENCE

Can you believe that a scientist can see the future by watching 4-year-olds interact with a marshmallow? The researcher invites the children, one by one, into a plain room and begins a gentle torment. You can have this marshmallow now, he says. But if you wait while I run an errand, you can have two marshmallows when I get back. And then he leaves.

Some children grab for the treat as soon as the researcher walks out the door. Some last a few minutes before they give in. But others are determined to wait. They cover their eyes; they put their heads down; they sing to themselves; they try to play games or even fall asleep. When the researcher returns, he gives these children their hard-earned marshmallows. And then, science waits for them to grow up.

By the time the children reach high school, something remarkable has happened. A survey of the children's parents and teachers found that those who as 4-year-olds had the strength to hold out for the second marshmallow generally grew up to be better adjusted, more popular, adventurous, confident and dependable teenagers (Shoda, Mischel, & Peake, 1990). The children who gave in to temptation early on were more likely to be lonely, easily frustrated, and stubborn. They buckled under stress and shied away from challenges. And when some of the students in the two groups took the SATs, the kids who had held out longer scored an average of 210 points higher. What does this mean?

It seems that the ability to delay gratification is a master skill, a triumph of the reasoning brain over the impulsive one. It is a sign, in short, of **emotional intelligence** (EQ) (Goleman, 1995; Gibbs, 1995). And EQ does not show up on an IQ test. The phrase "emotional intelligence" begins to describe qualities like understanding one's own feelings, empathy for the feelings of others, and regulating emotions in ways that enhance life. When it comes to predicting people's success, brain power as measured by IQ and standardized achievement tests may actually matter less than the qualities of mind once thought of as "character."

Some people are blessed with a lot of EQ and IQ, some with little of one or either. How do EQ and IQ complement each other? How does one's ability to handle stress, for instance, affect the ability to concentrate and put intelligence to use? Researchers are trying to answer these questions, but they generally agree that IQ counts for about 20%; the rest depends on such "nurture" topics as environment and experiences.

Perhaps the most visible emotional skills, the ones we recognize most readily, are the "people skills," such as empathy, graciousness, and the ability to read a social situation. Researchers believe that about 90% of emotional communication is nonverbal.

Like other emotional skills, empathy is an innate quality that can be shaped by experience. Infants as young as 3 months old exhibit empathy when they get upset at the sound of another baby crying. Even very young children learn by imitation; by watching how others act when they see someone in distress, these children acquire a repertoire of sensitive responses. However, if the feelings they begin to express are not recognized and reinforced by the adults around them, not only do they cease to express those feelings, but they also become less able to recognize them in themselves and others.

Nowhere is the discussion of emotional intelligence more pressing than in schools, where both the stakes and the opportunities seem greatest. Instead of constant crisis intervention, or declarations of war on drug abuse or teenage pregnancy or violence, preventative medicine should be the focus. Schools can implement an "emotional literacy" program, which teaches kids to learn to manage anger, frustration, and loneliness. Educators can point to many examples that support the importance of teaching the qualities that make up EQ. Students who are depressed or angry literally cannot learn. Children who have trouble being accepted by their classmates are two to eight times more likely to drop out than children who are accepted. An inability to distinguish feelings or handle frustration has also been linked to eating disorders in girls.

However, any campaign to refine emotional skills in children may end up teaching that there is a "right" emotional response for any given situation; for example, one should laugh at parades, cry at funerals, sit still in church.

Perhaps an ingredient is missing. Emotional skills, like intellectual ones, are morally neutral. Just as a genius could use his or her intellect either to cure cancer or to engineer a deadly virus, someone with great empathetic insight could use it to inspire colleagues or exploit them. Without a moral compass to guide people in how to employ their gifts, emotional intelligence can be used for good or evil. The knack of delaying gratification that makes a child one marshmallow richer can help him or her become a good citizen or—just as easily—a brilliant criminal.

FOCUS ON ASSESSMENT

Assessing Childhood Competency to Testify

Are children in the period of middle childhood cognitively competent to testify as a witness? Children are sometimes needed as witnesses to acts of crime and negligence. They are also victims of abuse, crime, or neglect. To testify in these matters, they must be able to truthfully and accurately communicate their personal knowledge of relevant facts. The law presumes that children under 10 or 12 years of age, depending on the jurisdiction, are incompetent to testify (Weithorn, 1984).

The justification for this presumption is the child's developmental immaturity. Although this presumption is refutable in most jurisdictions, it requires a solid understanding of a child's individual development.

The validity and reliability of a child's testimony has been challenged on a number of grounds: memory, cognitive development, moral development, and suggestibility (Melton et al., 1987). The memory issues relate to children's capacity to communicate their recollections of an event in response to questions presented in court. Will children describe "true memory" of an event, or will their memory of an event be the product of the suggestions from others with whom they have discussed the event? Will the child describe actual occurrences or occurrences based on fantasy? As you recall, fantasy and language are schemas used by preoperational children to adapt to their environment. Although there is concern that children may confuse fact with imagined experiences, a recent study indicates that children are no more likely than adults to confuse what is observed with what is imagined. Child abuse workers further recognize that "very young children do not fantasize or lie about having experienced sexual abuse" (Weithorn, 1984). These findings suggest that children's capacity to recall events is not limited by their development. They possess the capacity to recall events when given direct questions. However, research does support the viewpoint that children's developmental immaturity limits their capacity for free recall. Their memory of events must be prompted by objective questions.

Cognitive development affects the child's conceptualization or comprehension of events. Can a child conceptualize complex acts and order these acts in time and space? Does the child understand the meaning of terms and behaviors of relevance to a legal inquiry? The answers to each of these questions are influenced by knowledge from cognitive development. Children acquire cognitive competencies at different ages. Developmentalists also note inconsistencies in children's cognitive capacities across situations and tasks encountered by children in middle childhood.

Will children's immaturity influence their likelihood of being truthful in their testimony? This issue of moral development is often raised as a critical issue. Melton and colleagues (1987) point out that children are no more prone to lying than are adults. How development affects children's morality is in their ability to provide reasons or justifications for their behavior. Development also affects children's comprehension of terms such as oath, truth, and court. However, this type of comprehension has no bearing on their propensity to tell the truth. Data on suggestibility is less clear, although research has not found as many age differences as one might expect (Melton, 1987).

A primary fear is that children's testimony will be determined by their perceptions of adult expectations of how they should behave—that is, the type of testimony that the adult examiner is expecting of them. There is also a fear that children are more susceptible to leading questions. However, research by Marin, Holmes, Guth, and Kovac (1979) demonstrates that children are no less affected by leading questions than adults are. (Further research is needed, however.)

Each of these issues presents different assessment objectives for practitioners. Melton and his colleagues (1987) have provided the following guidelines for evaluating children's competency to testify.

Evaluators should assess the child's:

1. Understanding of the obligation to tell the truth;

2. Reliability of memory;

3. Ability to perceive reality accurately;

4. Vulnerability to suggestion.

These guidelines cannot be implemented without understanding the key cognitive developmental milestones for early and middle childhood.

Communication

Middle childhood is the period of linguistic refinement. In early childhood, the focus in language development is on such things as correcting the past tense of irregular verbs. Children's use of language becomes increasingly grammatically correct and more complex than the simple yes or no questions or the big "why" questions (Sigelman, 1999). Language develops in deaf children much as it does in hearing children. (The section on Developmental Aspects of Sign Language, page 312, gives a description of how sign lan-

guage develops.) As children develop, they become increasingly aware that words can have multiple meanings, and they understand the notion of abstract connotations. This ability to "go beyond the information" is referred to as **metalinguistic awareness** (Sigelman, 1999). As this ability develops, children begin to appreciate the humor in jokes, riddles, and puns. At about age 10, children can begin to understand and use metaphors such as "people who live in glass houses shouldn't throw stones" (Reynolds & Ortony, 1980). In studying language and middle childhood, the relationship between language and knowledge becomes important.

Language development is central to healthy development in children. (See the Focus section on Speech Disorders in Children, page 313, for a description of the effects of speech disorders.) Language is the door to obtaining information from others. It allows you to make requests of other people and makes a wealth of information accessible. In fact, early language researchers believed that language was necessary for thought (Whorf, 1956). However, most child developmentalists now believe that thought is a prerequisite to language.

Piaget's research led him to the conclusion that many logical concepts are learned before the development of the language that corresponds to those concepts (Lefrancois, 1995). For example, a child first learns the concept of bigger and then begins to use the language that describes the concept.

Recent research has found that difficulties in communication can result in the case of listeners who fail to detect **uninformative messages**—who don't ask for clarification of messages (Beal, 1987). Six to seven-year-olds will clarify an uninformative message they judge to be problematic. However, younger children, having at least some idea of what is meant by a statement, will overlook the problem in the message and assume that the speaker's intentions are clear. For example, "Bring me that toy" is an ambiguous statement when two toys are next to each other. A young child will hear the request and assume the speaker wants the closest toy, whereas 8- to 10-year-olds will question the ambiguity and ask for clarification.

We can teach children with communication difficulties better communication skills by having them learn to focus on the differences among the stimuli in their conversations (Pratt, McLaren, & Wickens, 1984). Also, we can teach children to be better listeners by having them evaluate what they hear and ask questions to clarify statements they don't understand.

Another important aspect of communication is the developmental theory of **verbal control** that came from the work of Russian psychologists Vygotsky and Luria (Luria, 1961; Vygotsky, 1962). They believe that speech develops through three successive stages: other-external, whereby the behavior of a child is controlled through the verbalizations of others; self-external, whereby the child's own overt verbalizations provide control over his or her behavior; and self-internal, whereby the child's behavior is controlled by his or her own covert *self-verbalizations*. This early work on the role of speech and behavior was groundbreaking, because it suggested the relationship between self-verbalizations and self-guidance. An important developmental aspect of speech and behavior was also discovered: Luria observed that, as children got older, they were able to inhibit behavior not only by following adult instructions (other-external) but also in response to their own self-instructions (self-internal). If, as the Russian researchers suggest, internal speech can control overt behavior, then why not teach children who lack self-control to use their own speech to gain more control over their actions? Their work laid the groundwork for the development of self-instructional training, a popular treatment approach for impulsive children who lack self-control.

Implications for Practice: Self-Instructional Training

Self-instructional training has become a major treatment modality for practitioners working with children who have difficulties with self-control. Researchers have developed a fairly specific sequence of training activities that include the following: (1) The therapist performs the task while asking questions aloud about the task, giving self-guiding instructions and making self-evaluations of the performance. (2) The child imitates the therapist's overt self-instructional sequence while doing the task. (3) The therapist repeats the task, this time using a whisper. (4) The child imitates the therapist's performance and self-instructions using a whisper. (5) The therapist models covert self-

instructions while performing the task. (6) The child imitates the therapist's covert self-instructions and performance. Research has found that it is important to perform tasks in ways that are not perfect and then teach children how to cope with errors in their performance (Kendall & Braswell, 1985).

One program (Camp et al., 1977) developed a "think-aloud" approach to working with aggressive, impulsive children. The approach uses the cognitive-behavioral techniques outlined in the previous paragraph to teach self-instructions for solving problems. Children were taught to ask and answer four questions: (1) What is my problem? (2) What is my plan? (3) Am I using my plan? (4) How did I do? The practitioners used various cognitive problems and interpersonal problem-solving games requiring the children to control their impulses to teach the self-instructional skills. In a similar manner, Kazdin and Frame (1983) worked with an aggressive 11-year-old boy and taught him problem-solving steps that could be used in everyday situations. Their training focused on the following set of questions and statements: What am I supposed to do?; I need to look at all my possibilities; I have to focus in (concentrate); I have to make a choice; How well did I do?

Social workers interested in applying such techniques should keep in mind the following recommendations (Kazdin & Frame, 1983). First, self-statements should be ones that children can understand and retain. The statements should be committed to rote memory, and practitioners need to keep them simple to avoid overburdening the child. Research has found that general self-statements ("I need to look at all my possibilities") are better than specific self-statements ("Just kick the ball, and don't get mad"). Last, keep the self-instructions geared to problems that represent difficulties in real life.

DEVELOPMENTAL ASPECTS OF SIGN LANGUAGE

Although we normally think of communication as exclusively verbal, this is not necessarily so. Many people communicate using sign language. Children who are born without the ability to hear and who therefore cannot communicate with an oral language often learn American Sign Language (ASL), an advanced sys-

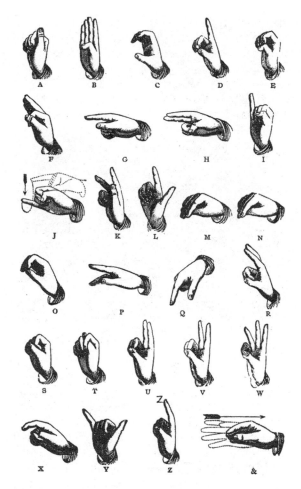

FIGURE 8.2   Sign language (courtesy of Ohio School for the Deaf)

tem of communication that includes the use of both hands in various gestures, like the ones in Figure 8.2.

Children learn ASL just as they would an oral language (Shaffer, 1993). Children who are born to deaf parents begin to learn to communicate with signs at a very early age. Most deaf children will learn their first sign at around 9 months of age, which is 3 months before hearing children begin to use words (Bonvillian, Orlansky, & Novack, 1983). Like hearing children, deaf children begin to communicate by "babbling," but they do it in signs that they have observed their parents using. As the children develop, they begin to use the

equivalent of one-word phrases—a single sign that communicates several messages. Interestingly, the kinds of signs that children first begin to use are essentially the same as the categories of words that speaking children first learn. Deaf children's ability to communicate continues to develop as they begin to combine signs similar to the telegraphic statements made by speaking children. Communication becomes increasingly refined as deaf children learn the complex rules inherent in communicating their thoughts and feelings.

ASL is a creative and advanced system of communication. Similar to oral language, signs combine to form declarative statements and ask questions. ASL users are fond of making a play on words (pun) just as oral communicators do. Many people argue for "total communication" among the deaf, so that they can use ASL and oral language. The movie *Children of a Lesser God,* for example, shows some of the issues involved in learning and using "total communication." Learning oral communication and ASL does not make it easier for children to learn the spoken language, but many people believe it enhances the quality of interactions between deaf and hearing people.

FOCUS ON DEVELOPMENT

Speech Disorders in Children

The development of a speech disorder can have a negative effect on a child's healthy development. It is not uncommon for children with speech disorders to have difficulties with intellectual and academic achievements, as well as emotional difficulties. Such children may be teased and as a result have low self-esteem. Family problems can also develop, especially if family members pressure the child.

There is a wide variation in the nature of speech disorders. Some are extremely mild and almost unnoticeable; others can be so serious that they affect day-to-day living. We don't know what causes the majority of speech disorders, but there can be a combination of physiological, psychological, or environmental circumstances. Speech disorders manifest themselves in a variety of forms, including articulatory problems, voice abnormalities, stuttering, or aphasia, the inability to speak. Speech disorders are more common among children who have hearing impairments, physical impairments (such as cerebral palsy), mental retardation, and emotional disturbances. Two of the more common speech disorders are stuttering and faulty articulation.

Stuttering refers to interruptions in communication produced by repetitions, hesitations, or other forms of "blockages" of sounds or words. Some children with more serious forms of stuttering also have overt indications of tension. Stuttering is four or five times more common in boys than in girls, and an estimated 5% of all children may suffer from a stuttering problem for various periods of time. Most cases of stuttering begin early—by age 4 or 5—and usually clear up spontaneously, but professional speech therapists are sometimes needed.

Most experts now believe that stuttering develops as a result of biological and environmental factors. Research from a biological perspective has found that the incidence of stuttering is higher when there is a family history of stuttering. Furthermore, research on the brain has demonstrated that the neural organization of stutterers is different from that of nonstutterers. However, other research supports environmental factors; for example, stuttering varies quite dramatically across cultures. Anthropologists have noted the relative absence of stuttering in cultures with permissive child-rearing practices. In contrast, industrial cultures that stress competition, pressure to speak at an early age, and standards of achievement have produced a higher incidence of stuttering. Most speech disorder experts believe that the causes of stuttering, like many other individual characteristics, develop from an interaction between biological and environmental factors.

Not all communication is verbal; many children must communicate using sign language. These children learn American Sign Language (ASL), a system of communication based on hand gestures.

BILINGUAL CHILDREN

Language and communication are difficult skills for children to develop. What happens when a child is spoken to in one language at home and taught another language in school? This is referred to as being **bilingual.** Researchers have found that there can be both negative and positive outcomes for bilingual children. For minority children whose first language is a minority language, learning a second language is a disadvantage for them. However, when children's first language is the majority language, learning a second language can be an advantage (Lefrancois, 1994).

Many Hispanic children in the United States have a negative experience with bilingualism because they become less functional in Spanish, their first language, as their language skills improve in English. Lefrancois (1995) believes that there are three reasons for this problem. First, the majority language, in our case English, is the dominant language used in the media and larger community, so Spanish receives little reinforcement outside the home. Second, the minority language (Spanish) is often discouraged in the home or by the children themselves. Third, the minority language (Spanish) used in the home is sometimes not a model of good use, especially when characterized by such factors as colloquialism and improper grammar. If Spanish is not part of the children's schooling, they are not likely to write or read it. For minority children, the minority language should be taught, and the majority language should be the second language (Lefrancois, 1995).

In other circumstances, when children's first language is the majority language, learning the second language has distinct benefits (Bialystok, 1988). Consider, for example, English-speaking children enrolled in Spanish-immersion programs. As Lefrancois (1995, p. 302) notes, "although most students who go through immersion schooling don't develop as high a level of proficiency as do native speakers, their language deficiencies don't seem to interfere with their use of the second language."

The results of a good bilingual program can be both a proficiency in the second language and a strengthening of the first language. Evaluation of bilingualism is complex, but Cummins and Swain (1986) argue that bilingualism can have positive advantages for both minority and majority children.

OTHER CULTURAL INFLUENCES ON LANGUAGE ABILITIES

A child's language abilities can be influenced by cultural experiences. Disadvantaged children stereotypically have a restricted vocabulary and construct sentences that are less grammatically correct than middle-class children's. Although lower-class children

People often think that exposing a child to languages will confuse the child and cause linguistic problems. These fears are unfounded.

score lower on tests of vocabulary and sentence structure, the issue of appropriate use of grammar is controversial. A distinction needs to be made between language performance and language competence (Ashburn et al., 1986). Grammatical "correctness" may be a relative or arbitrary issue. Children whose dialect differs from white, middle-class children may be using "structured grammatical systems through which they can express both emotional and logical thoughts" (Mussen, 1974).

When a child says, "Me and him ain't goin' to no movie," the child is speaking an imperfect sentence according to the American school system of the larger middle-class society. However, this construction is typical in African-American dialects in which the verb "to be" incorporates a tense, referred to as *habitual* (Seymour, 1974). The habitual tense expresses an action that occurs frequently or continually. Therefore, "He be playin' " in standard English is "He's still playing," "He's always playing," or "He's been playing." "He playin' " means "He is playing currently." Such nonstandard grammar might sound reasonable when spoken to other members of this person's culture. Children with this type of language are not necessarily deficient in the ability to learn to speak standard English; they are merely the product of their environment. So how should a child from this culture speak? When the child is in his or her cultural environment, it is appropriate and adaptive for him or her to speak using nonstandard grammar. When attempting to be biculturally adaptive, the child will need to speak "correctly," especially if the child is seeking socioeconomic advancement.

Disadvantaged children may use nonstandard grammar, but the more controversial question is, does nonstandard grammar lead to substandard language competence? According to the language deficit theory, this language is deficient and inferior. This deficiency affects students' academic achievement and their intellectual development. Subsequently, students' opportunities for employment advancement are limited. These language deficiencies are the result of impoverished environmental circumstances. The language difference theory argues the opposite—that nonstandard grammar does not reflect deficient language development. As noted earlier, the dialect, or use of nonstandard grammar, represents a well-ordered and highly structured language that differs from standard English.

The following Focus section examines the various challenges refugee children must face to succeed in their new American homeland.

FOCUS ON MULTICULTURALISM

Refugee Children: A New Life

Imagine traveling, sometimes by bus or boat, but mostly on foot, hundreds of miles with your family. But this isn't just a hiking trip—you are fleeing your home, village, and country from "bad people" who want to hurt you and your family. You are 7 years old. You often get hungry and tired, but there isn't much food and little time to stop and take rests. You are fleeing for your lives. How do you feel—what
do you think—when you cross the border and must begin a whole new life?

Within the field of child welfare, refugee children have received relatively little attention. These are children who have made international migrations because of political oppression in their home countries. Approximately 100,000 refuges are admitted into the United States each year—almost 1.3 million since 1982. Many of these refugees are children. Refugee children may arrive with immediate or extended family members or as unaccompanied minors who are placed with relatives or in foster care. The majority of these refugees have been fleeing from Southeast Asia, the former Soviet Union, Eastern Europe, Cuba, and Haiti after political upheaval in their respective countries.

On resettlement, refugee children face additional hardships. In addition to language barriers, a variety of unique stressors are experienced. First, for children who are with their families, there are often intergenerational problems. Frequently, children adopt the customs of the new country much more quickly than their parents do, resulting in a role reversal whereby children become translators of language and cultural norms for their parents. This frequently leads to a lack of respect for elders, which is an extremely important value in many of the original cultures. Second, problems may also develop with child discipline; some types of discipline used in the native culture may be considered child abuse in the Unites States. A third source of stress is strong expectations for achievement placed on children by their parents. Many older refugees have given up hope for their own achievement; however, they view their children's opportunity to live a better life as redeeming their own suffering.

Another common issue is post-traumatic stress disorder. A significant number of refugee children have witnessed death, torture, rape, and/or imprisonment of family members. Disease and starvation are also common. Many refugees leave their homeland in boats and are at sea for long periods without adequate food, water, shelter, or sanitation. Frequently, when they arrive in the United States, they undergo long stays in refugee camps that have poor housing and shortages of clothing and water. All these factors contribute to post-traumatic stress.

In addition to intergenerational conflicts and post-traumatic stress, refugee children experience difficulties with **acculturation** and cultural identity. In their homes they are expected to behave in accordance with the native culture, whereas in school, they are expected to behave as Americans. Thus, they must live a dual life for which they have no role models.

In recognition of some of the unique difficulties faced by refugee children, U. S. legislative policies have been developed and implemented to provide services to this population. From the post–WWII period to 1980, refugee assistance was provided on an ad hoc basis in response to crises in different parts of the world. The Refugee Act of 1980 and the refugee education assistance Act of 1980 established for the first time a set of comprehensive, permanent, and systematic policies for refugee assistance. These policies guide the provision of cash assistance, medical assistance, and social services to refugees. Services specifically for refugee children include special education, English language training, child welfare and health care.

Even though these policies represent an improvement, additional policy advances for refugee children and their families should be sought. Social workers who work with refugees must continue to advocate increased humanitarian treatment of refugee children. Policies should develop a long-term outlook in recognition that the achievement of refugee economic stability is a very lengthy process. Supportive services for refugee children should be aimed at promoting long-term adaptation as opposed to short-term "crisis stabilization." School-based programs for refugee children must address the multiple stressors experienced by these populations—specifically, intergenerational conflict, post-traumatic stress, and acculturation. One way to do this is through support groups that encourage children to share their feelings and experiences and develop healthy coping strategies. Intervention programs must be tailored to each ethnic group. Clearly, Soviet and Haitian children, for example, have had vastly different experiences.

Like all children, refugee children represent an investment in our nation's future. Equitable and effective policies and programs that improve these children's chances for success in adulthood will strengthen the well-being of the nation as a whole.

(Based on Potocky, 1996)

Attitudes and Emotions

As children enter middle childhood, their self-concepts begin to change as the result of children's increasing ability to understand how other people view them. Remember the theory of the looking-glass self, wherein one's self-concept is the image seen in the "looking glass"? This theory helps explain how children's self-concepts begin to change in middle childhood; they have a much better ability to look into that glass and see how their behavior can elicit certain reactions from others. Children begin to control their own actions depending on what kind of social self they want to display.

In early childhood, conceptions of self were limited to primarily physical qualities—motor skills, sex-type, and age. In middle childhood, conceptions of the self expand to include such things as ideal self, ethnic awareness, and conscience development (Konner, 1991). In addition to gaining an expanded self-concept, children at this age begin to have a more differentiated self-concept, a more individuated view of themselves, and their self-concept becomes increasingly stable (Santrock, 1996).

This differentiated view of oneself is a less global view than the one held previously. Children who earlier thought of themselves as "not talented" might now recognize that, although they are not very good at sports, they are better than most children at playing a musical instrument. Children's self-concepts also become more individuated, so that they begin to see themselves as different from others, as unique: "I am the fastest person in my school." Their self-concepts are developing into a more integrated sense of who they are. Self-concept will continue to change, but the early threads of the self are being sown as children continue to develop their more complete self.

Self-concept is complex and difficult to measure; however, Harter (1985) has developed a unique measure of self-concept called the Self-Perception Profile for Children (see Table 8.2 for examples of sample items). Her measure is based on children's evaluations of four areas of competence:

1. *Cognitive competence.* Being good at school work, remembering things, doing well in school, understanding what is read.

TABLE 8.2 Sample Items from the Self-Perception Profile for Children (measuring social competence, cognitive competence, physical competence, and general self-esteem)

Really True	Sort of True				Sort of True	Really True
☐	☐	Some kids find it hard to make friends.	BUT	For other kids it's pretty easy.	☐	☐
☐	☐	Some kids like school because they do well in class.	BUT	Other kids don't like school because they aren't doing very well.	☐	☐
☐	☐	Some kids feel they are better than others their age are at sports.	BUT	Other kids don't feel they can play as well.	☐	☐
☐	☐	Some kids think that maybe they are not very good people.	BUT	Other kids are pretty sure that they are a good person.	☐	☐

(Harter, 1985)

2. *Social competence.* Having a lot of friends, having other people like you, feeling well liked, being important to one's classmates.

3. *Physical competence.* Doing well at sports, being chosen for team games, liking games and sports.

4. *General self-worth.* Being sure of self, feeling happy the way I am, feeling like a good person, wanting to stay the same.

This measure has received a lot of praise because, unlike other measures that ask about a child's perceptions regarding his or her abilities in a variety of areas, Harter's scale breaks up the notion of self-concept into four areas. Each area then measures a child's self-concept in that domain.

Research using this scale has led to some interesting findings (Harter, 1982), the most important of which is that children make distinctions about their competencies in different areas. Therefore, a child's self-esteem depends on the situation or circumstance. A measure of a child's overall self-concept could be misleading because it may depend on the area being assessed. Children may have positive self-esteem in the classroom but a poor self-concept on the playground where sports games are played.

Also important is the finding that children's evaluations of themselves resemble the way other people perceive them. For example, a child whose self-rating was high on social competence was in fact found to have a lot of friends who considered her to be a good friend. In a similar manner, a child's self-evaluation of cognitive competence was related to how teachers evaluated the child's academic achievements. These research results provide continued support for the idea that how other people perceive us has a lot to do with who we are (Shaffer, 1993). In this case, the "looking glass" represents how others perceive a child's self-esteem, and, as the looking-glass theory would predict, it accurately reflects the child's own self esteem.

These findings also lend support to Erik Erikson's notion that the psychosocial crisis that 6- to 12-year-olds confront is *industry versus inferiority.* At this age, children measure themselves against their peers to establish a sense of who they are. The focus is on personal and social competence, or, according to Harter's research, on cognitive and social competencies. Children work hard to develop their cognitive skills—writing, reading, and arithmetic—as well as their social skills—cooperation, fairness, and receiving approval from others. Erikson's theory predicts that children who develop these skills will successfully master a sense of "industriousness," and they will be able to move on to the next stage of development, the identity crisis of adolescence.

Social Cognition and Regulation

One of the most important concepts in understanding human behavior comes from the field of social cognition. **Social cognition** refers to the level of awareness one has regarding other people's thoughts, feelings, and intentions. Social cognition has a tremendous effect on how children relate to other children and adults. As children mature and develop, their cognitive growth gives them a new understanding of themselves and other people. Perhaps most critical is the child's developing capacity concerning **role-taking abilities,** or perspective-taking skills.

Social role-taking ability, or the reduction of egocentric thought, is viewed as a critical aspect of healthy social development. Based on the early work of Piaget (1929), this concept refers to children's inability to decenter the focus of their conceptual efforts. In other words, children without role-taking abilities just can't see things from another person's perspective. Young children cannot empathize with the feelings of other people; this social cognitive capacity develops as the child grows older.

How does a child develop role-taking abilities? This skill matures through exposure to role-taking opportunities that involve an exchange of differing perspectives. Role-taking is related to moral development, which depends on a person's ability to perceive and comprehend the differing perspectives of other people. Role-taking should be considered a parallel stage to moral development; it is a necessary but not sufficient condition for moral reasoning. The next chapter discusses in greater detail aspects of moral development. For now, let's see why an understanding of role-taking has important implications for understanding and working with children.

Role-taking ability begins to change around 12 years of age, when the ability to think about oneself and one's social relations becomes more advanced (Selman, 1980; Shantz, 1983). As the child grows older, he or she can begin to infer others' feelings, thoughts, and intentions. Although cognitive abilities begin to expand during this developmental period, this period is still characterized by egocentrism, or the inability to assume another person's role or viewpoint.

Role-taking ability is closely related to the development of social skills in children. Role-taking is a prerequisite for the emergence of many social behaviors, such as cooperation and altruism. Various researchers (Piaget & Inhelder, 1969; Staub, 1984) have suggested that a variety of social behaviors are strengthened by a child's ability to take the role of another person. One researcher, Robert Selman, has expanded the concept of social role-taking to help explain how children's friendships and peer relationships develop.

INTERPERSONAL AWARENESS

Robert Selman's work has focused on what he refers to as interpersonal awareness—how the child conceives his or her own interpersonal relationships, particularly friendship and peer group relationships. Can distinctive ways of reasoning about such relationships be ordered along a developmental continuum? Furthermore, do children who have social and emotional problems reason at a different level compared with better-functioning peers? These are the questions that Selman sought to answer in his research. Before we reveal the answers, let's look a little closer at his theory of interpersonal awareness.

As we learned from the classical work of Piaget, children's physical-cognitive development proceeds according to specific stages:

0—preoperational
1—transitional preoperational
2—consolidated concrete operational
3—transitional concrete/early formal operations
4—consolidated formal operations

In a similar manner, Selman (1980) suggests that developmental levels can account for social perspective-taking abilities:

0—undifferentiated and egocentric perspective-taking skill
1—differentiated and subjective perspective taking
2—self-reflective and reciprocal perspective taking
3—third-person and mutual perspective taking
4—societal/symbolic perspective taking

At the first stage of perspective taking, children cannot differentiate between the physical and the psychological aspects of people. Beginning with level 1,

TABLE 8.3	Developmental Stages Across Impersonal and Interpersonal Awareness		
	Impersonal		**Interpersonal**
Stage	**Cognitive**	**Friendship**	**Peer Group**
0	Intuitive preoperational	Momentary physical playmate	Physical connections
1	Transitional preoperational/concrete operational	One-way assistance	Unilateral relations
2	Consolidated concrete operational	Fair-weather cooperation	Bilateral partnerships
3	Transitional concrete/early formal operational	Intimate-mutual sharing	Homogeneous community
4	Consolidated formal operational	Autonomous interdependence	Pluralistic organization

(Adapted from Selman, 1980; Selman, Jaquette, & Lavin, 1977)

children (ages 5–9) begin to differentiate the physical and psychological characteristics of individuals. For example, they can differentiate between intentional and unintentional behavior. By level 2 (ages 7–12), major advances occur, and children can take a self-reflective view of the self. Children recognize that there can be a difference between the physical self and the psychological self. Level 3 is known as the mutual perspective-taking level (ages 10–15), because children can take a third-person perspective; that is, they can truly see things from different perspectives. Level 4 emerges after age 12, but it may not be present until adulthood. At this level, one can think abstractly about the various levels of understanding and can recognize that each level can have a different point of view. Although this material is theoretically complex, you will see in the following section how it can be useful in understanding and working with children.

INTERPERSONAL AWARENESS AND INTERPERSONAL RELATIONSHIPS

Continuing with Selman's theory (1980; 1990), we can take interpersonal awareness and examine how the child conceives his or her own interpersonal relationships, particularly friendship and peer group relations. As Table 8.3 indicates, there are stages of friendship and peer group formation that relate to the physical-cognitive stages of development. For example, in the consolidated concrete operational stage, the corresponding stages are one-way assistance in friendship and unilateral relations in the peer group.

Selman's research sought to answer this question: Can distinctive ways of reasoning about relationships be ordered along a developmental continuum? Based on his research, he identified the stages shown in Table 8.4.

Let's look even more closely at how to apply his work. We can take one issue that is relevant to friendship—interpersonal trust—and see how the developmental stages of friendship apply (Selman, Jaquette, & Lavin, 1977). Table 8.4 shows the stage, level of friendship, and sample responses that would indicate the stage the child is in.

As Table 8.4 indicates, children reason differently about trust, depending on their level of interpersonal awareness. The researchers gathered these sample responses by presenting children with different dilemmas and then asking a series of questions, such as: What is trust? Why is it important for friends to trust each other in order to stay friends? With this kind of interviewing, they established the different stages of interpersonal awareness.

By studying the levels of interpersonal awareness of normal and emotionally disturbed children, Selman hopes he can develop a set of therapeutic and educational goals oriented to developing greater maturity of interpersonal awareness. Selman's research suggests that children who have experienced extremely inconsistent or disruptive interpersonal experiences, and who manifest severe difficulties in their interpersonal relations, do not develop through the domain of social reasoning as steadily as do children with more consistent, dependable, and mutual relations with friends or peers. A 15-year-old who defines a friend as "someone who does what I want him to do" is going to have difficulty establishing friendships with adolescents who perceive friendship as cooperation and reciprocal affection (Selman, Jaquette, & Lavin, 1977).

Implications for Practice: Pair Therapy

How can we help children develop better ways of reasoning about friendships and peer relations? The key is providing children with role-taking opportunities and encouraging them to think in ways that expand their social reasoning.

Lyman and Selman (1985) have described *pair therapy* as a means of enhancing the social reasoning of children who are experiencing peer conflict. In pair therapy, two children with interpersonal difficulties meet for weekly sessions with an adult who provides a forum for negotiation. The therapist helps the peers reflect on their different ideas and strategies. When children experience repeated negotiation, taking into consideration various and different perspectives, they are given new opportunities to develop insight and skills.

Pair therapy involves three basic dimensions: stage setting, structuring, and facilitating reflection. Stage setting is simply the development of specific opportunities for conflict within a conducive environment. The stage should provide an atmosphere of acceptance and safety in which the children are free to express themselves, share ideas and fantasies, and try out new ways of dealing with conflicts. Structuring involves mediating peer negotiations, providing incentives, setting limits, and becoming less involved as necessary. The structuring should provide the opportunity and the motivation to experiment with new and better ways of negotiating conflicts. To facilitate reflection, the therapist encourages the children to reflect on their own and their partner's behavior, helps facilitate peer feedback, and uses role modeling and

TABLE 8.4	Stages of Friendship Showing Sample Responses	
Stage	**Friendship**	**Sample Responses**
0	Momentary physical playmate	Alan, age 4, said he trusted his friend, Eric. When asked why, he said, "If I give him my toy he won't break it . . . he isn't strong enough."
1	One-way assistance	"I trust a friend if he does what I tell him."
2	Fair-weather cooperation	"Trust means if you do something for him, he will do something for you."
3	Intimate-mutual sharing	Trust is "when they can get it off their chest if they talk with you; things that are going on in your life and in the other person's life."
4	Autonomous interdependence	"Trust means that you've got to grow, the more you hold on to, the less you have. You have to have confidence in yourself as a good friend, then you'll have trust in your relationship."

(Based on Selman, Jaquette, & Lavin, 1977)

problem solving to encourage alternative strategies for conflict resolution. Reflection is encouraged both *in vivo,* while the children are together working on problems, and after the fact, so they develop retrospective reflection.

Psychological Hazards

Most childhood disorders can be classified into one of two categories: problems of undercontrol and problems of overcontrol. Undercontrol problems are often referred to as **externalizing problems,** and overcontrol problems are referred to as **internalizing problems** (Achenbach & Edelbrock, 1983). Externalizing problems consist of behaviors that reflect a tendency to "act out"—for example, aggressive behavior like fighting, acting defiantly, and hyperactivity. Internalizing problems consist of behaviors that reflect an "inner state," such as anxiety, loneliness, shyness, social withdrawal, and depression. Two of the most common problems of middle childhood are attention deficit hyperactivity disorder (ADHD), an externalizing problem, and depression, an internalizing problem.

The following Focus section shows how to use the Child Behavior Checklist and the internalizing and externalizing model developed by Achenbach.

Empirical Assessment—The Achenbach Child Behavior Checklist

An empirical approach to assessment gathers systematic ratings of children from significant others, parents, teachers, and/or practitioners. One well-known approach to empirical assessment is the Child Behavior Checklist developed by Thomas Achenbach. The Child Behavior Checklist is a standardized rating scale that is typically filled out by parents and teachers. It examines behavior across a number of domains or syndromes, such as depressed, obsessive compulsive, socially withdrawn, aggressive, and so forth. The items include statements such as "Can't concentrate," "Can't pay attention for long," and "Disobedient at home." The parent circles 2 if the item is always true or often true; 1 if the item is somewhat true or sometimes true; 0 if the item is not true.

The checklist is scored on the Child Behavior Profile (see Figure 8.3). Each of the syndromes of the profile (for example, anxious/depressed, aggressive behavior) were developed through extensive research (see Achenbach, McConaughy, & Howell, 1987). To score the profile, the 1s and 2s under the syndrome are summed to obtain a total score. This score is then charted on the profile. For example, on the profile for Jenny, there were several 1s and 2s under the withdrawn syndrome. When these scores are summed, Jenny receives a score of 8, which is entered as the total on the bottom of the profile and then charted. The Child Behavior Checklist is normed, which means one can compare scores against the scores obtained from a normal population of children. For example, Jenny's score of 8 on the social withdrawal scale is around the 98th percentile (normal range is marked on the left of the profile, and the dotted line represents the upper boundary of normal). This means that a score of 8 on the social withdrawal scale is higher than the scores obtained by 98% of the 4- to 18-year-old girls in the normative sample.

The behavior profile for Jenny led to the following observations: Jenny's mother completed the Child Behavior Checklist during her intake visit to the Child Guidance Clinic. Two of the scales from the Child Behavior Checklist suggest problems: socially withdrawn, anxious/depressed. The anxious/depressed scale showed scores on all the items. A score of 2 was listed on four items: lonely, worthless, sad, and worried. The social withdrawal scale had scores on six items: rather be alone, won't talk, shy, sulks, sad, and withdrawn. These results suggest some serious problems for Jenny, especially in the areas of depression and social withdrawal. The practitioner would want to seek additional information (teacher reports, observations, clinical interviews) to corroborate these results before reaching any conclusions (Achenbach, 1991). The next section discusses ADHD in more depth.

HYPERACTIVITY, OR ATTENTION DEFICIT HYPERACTIVITY DISORDER

Carlos was referred to the outpatient mental health clinic by his teacher, who demanded that Carlos get some help to control his behavior. Carlos, age 7, demanded the attention of almost everyone around him and constantly disturbed the other children in the class. The teacher noted that Carlos could not sit still, concentrate on his work, or complete his tasks. He was always on the move. Even when sitting in his seat, Carlos fidgeted and moved about, which disturbed other students next to him. His mother reported that he was a motor mouth; was unable to stick to any one chore, task, or game; and was often found away from the house where he was not allowed to be. She described several examples of Carlos's poor judgment and problem-solving abilities.

Carlos, of course, is a typical 7-year-old boy who suffers from **attention deficit hyperactivity disorder** (ADHD). Carlos has three important characteristics of the disorder: excess motor activity, impulsiveness, and inattention.

Although most researchers and clinicians who work with children like Carlos agree that there is a true syndrome or disorder in which you can classify such children, to do so in a reliable manner is problematic. Schwartz and Johnson (1985) point out some

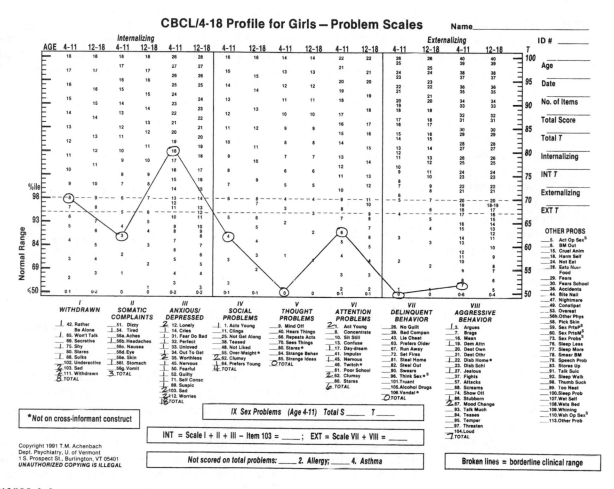

FIGURE 8.3   Revised Child Behavior Profile (Achenbach, 1991)

diagnostic problems. For example, the criterion "has difficulty sitting still or fidgets excessively" assumes that everyone will agree on what it means to fidget. But what is excessive fidgeting? Without any normative criteria (recorded observations of how much the average child fidgets), applying this criterion is difficult. Consider, for example, that in one study teachers of 8-year-olds classified 43% as having short attention spans (Werry & Quay, 1971). Children at this age are often considered "bundles of energy," and a certain amount of hyperactivity occurs in children who would be considered "normal." Therefore, behavior

problems in children must be considered within the context of developmental norms. A child with ADHD is developmentally abnormal; otherwise, many average children with "bundles of energy" would be classified as being hyperactive.

Despite these problems, checklists have been developed that can help in identifying children who are likely to suffer from ADHD. Usually parents or teachers are asked to fill out a checklist indicating which behaviors are characteristic of the child. A rating scale is then used in assessing ADHD in children. It is estimated that about 3% of children can be diagnosed as having ADHD and that, of those with the disorder, there are three ADHD boys for every one ADHD girl (American Psychiatric Association, 1994).

Researchers are still unclear about the causes of hyperactivity. It used to be thought that hyperactivity was caused by some form of brain dysfunction; in fact, hyperactivity used to be referred to as minimal brain dysfunction. Much research has been conducted to investigate the role of brain dysfunction and hyperactivity. A lack of activity in the frontal cortex and the basal ganglia has been observed in people with ADHD (Zametkin et al., 1990) Other researchers (Riccio et al., 1993) have found evidence that the right hemisphere may be malfunctioning. However, research has failed to demonstrate a clear relationship between ADHD and any neurological impairment. Researchers have turned their attention to an investigation of genetics and ADHD, and although the studies are not conclusive, the evidence does suggest there are genetic factors in ADHD.

Implications for Practice: ADHD and Medication

Many people are familiar with the pharmacological treatment of children with ADHD. A high percentage of children diagnosed with ADHD receive some form of medication (for example, Ritalin, Dexedrine, Cylert, Benzedrine). The majority of children are helped by the medication, which increases the child's ability to sustain attention. However, medications do not necessarily reduce activity levels, and they have little effect on school performance. Although it is clear that medication helps ADHD children in the short term, the long-term benefit of medication has been questioned. In addition, many practitioners are concerned about the side effects of medication on children. Two common reactions to medication for hyperactivity are appetite reduction and sleep disturbance (Loney & Ordona, 1975). In spite of these problems, medication seems to make children less distractible and less disruptive in class (Dulcan, 1986; Swanson et al., 1993). It also enhances the way classmates perceive the hyperactive child, which may produce important social benefits.

Most experts believe that medication should be supplemented by behavioral treatment. This hunch was confirmed by studies that have found that the combination of medication with cognitive-behavioral treatment produced the most benefit. Thus, it seems necessary to provide treatment beyond medication that will address academic performance, an aspect of behavior not affected by medication. Chase and Clement (1985) found that having children set goals for reading assignments and give themselves points to exchange for reinforcers increased both the amount of work completed and its accuracy.

FOCUS ON HEALTH

Are We Overmedicating Our Children?

Prozac now comes in peppermint flavor. Although the Food and Drug Administration (FDA) forbids the marketing of antidepressants, such as Prozac, for children, it is hard not to view candy-flavored pills as a move in that direction. Even with the FDA's mandate, physicians have prescribed Prozac to children for a number of "off label" uses. For example, in 1996, doctors wrote 735,000 prescriptions for Prozac, Ritalin, and other psychiatric medications for children ages 6 to 18—an 80% increase in two years.

Although some practitioners believe the trend means children are finally getting the treatment they need, others are concerned about inadequate research, the substitution of medications for behavioral treatments, and the fact that some psychotropic drugs do not seem to work on children. Physicians often lack crucial information on drugs' effects on children. They may not know the long-term effects on developing physiology or even the proper dosages to give. Opponents see the trend as an epidemic of inappropriate prescribing.

It is hard not to see an economic motivation behind all the prescriptions for children. A 100-tablet bottle of Ritalin, for example, costs about $50, making it far less expensive alternative than behavioral therapy and a far more attractive choice to insurers cutting costs. Further, many doctors are writing prescriptions without ordering psychological or educational tests.

A related problem is that, once the FDA approves a drug to treat a particular condition, any physician may prescribe it to any patient, regardless of age. And the push to put children on these drugs comes from everyday people—parents and teachers. Some overly rambunctious children have been sent home with a note from the principal saying they are not allowed back to school unless they have a Ritalin prescription. As mentioned in the previous section, teachers are given checklists of behavior that could be symptoms of ADHD, as though they can diagnose them. Effective treatment of ADHD is complicated, and we need to be open to both medical and behavioral treatment options.

Misha Marvel (Based on Clay, 1997)

SOCIAL DIMENSION

Families, Groups, Support Systems, and Communities

Family strength is an important concept that has dramatically influenced social work practice. Social workers are increasingly concerned about offering families opportunities to use their strengths. For too long, social workers did not recognize family strength and instead were concerned only with a family's pathology. Today, family strength is emphasized, because we recognize that the family environment holds the key to unlocking a child's capacity to grow and develop in a healthy manner.

A child can grow up in many different family contexts—as one of ten other children with little or no individual parental attention; in a family with an alcoholic parent; as the target of a stepparent's physical and sexual abuse; or in poverty where gang warfare and drug abuse are a part of everyday life. In contrast, children can also grow up in large families that care deeply about one another and work together to provide for themselves; in families where alcoholism afflicts one of the parents but an abiding love exists be-

tween the parents; in situations where child abuse has devastated and torn apart families but they have worked to create a new context in which they can live peacefully together; and in situations where poverty and drug abuse are all around but where enough love exists to protect against negative influences. All children are caught in the complex web of family relationships that significantly shape their future.

NORMAL FAMILY PROCESS

By the time children reach late childhood, they are spending much less time with parents and more time with peers. One study (Hill & Stafford, 1980) found that parents spend less than half as much time with their children between the ages of 5 and 12 than they did before. However, although less time is spent with the family, it continues to be an extremely important influence on the child. A parent's attitude about a child's ability is a more important influence than is the child's past performance (Parsons, Adler, & Kaczala, 1982a).

At this age, the family provides an important base for the child to continue growing and developing. Children need the safe, authoritative structure that parents can provide. Although children show less love and respect for their parents, they depend on parents for unconditional love and as sources of information and authority (Rapalje, Degelman, & Ashburn, 1986). The role of discipline continues to be critical to good parenting.

PARENTAL DISCIPLINE

Three major parental disciplinary strategies identified by Hoffman (1970) are **power assertive discipline,** which includes physical punishment, threat of punishment, and physical attempts to control the child's behavior; **love withdrawal,** which involves withdrawing love when the child's behavior is viewed as inappropriate; and **induction,** which involves the use of explanation and rationality in attempting to influence the child's actions.

What effects do these different strategies of parental discipline have on children? Research studies have shown that parents who use power assertion (punishment) increase their children's aggressive tendencies. There are several possible explanations regarding why punishment would lead to aggressive behavior in children. As you learned earlier, parents who act aggressively toward their children provide a model of aggressive behavior for the child to imitate. Also, children involved in physical confrontations with their parents learn that this is how disputes are resolved—through fighting, arguing, and threats of punishment. Have you ever observed a child being physically punished by his or her parents? You may also have noticed the child is embarrassed and ashamed, which demeans the child. Children with low self-esteem may be more likely to respond with aggressive behavior in the absence of more appropriate social skills.

Parents who use love withdrawal do so by verbally discounting children, threatening to send the children away, and indicating to the children that they are not loved because of their actions. Love withdrawal also includes such parental actions as persistently ignoring the child, refusing to talk with the child (the silent treatment), and generally not interacting with the child. Of course, this behavior is unfair and often makes the child fearful. Research has found that this form of parenting can lead to excessive anxiety in children and inhibit needed expression of emotions (Hoffman, 1970).

Consider the difference between these two types of parental discipline strategies: "Chen, get in this house right now! If you don't do as I say, I'll take the paddle to your butt" and "Chen, you need to come in and get ready for dinner. Your aunt is expecting us later tonight and we don't want to be late." How would a child feel in response to these two statements? The first response is likely to elicit anger and resentment, whereas the second response is more likely to elicit cooperation and understanding. The use of induction helps the child develop an understanding of why he or she should act in the requested manner. Other examples include telling a child, "Please don't climb on that wall because it isn't strong enough to hold your weight" (appeal to prevent injury); "You can't watch TV tonight because you broke our rule about no more throwing temper tantrums" (appeal to fairness); "Don't chew food with your mouth open—that's not appropriate at the dinner table" (appeal to standards of conduct).

Induction is an important parental strategy because it helps children develop internal moral standards (Lickona, 1983). Children disciplined by induction methods gain experience in exercising self-control and learn to display more consideration and generosity toward others when compared with children who have been disciplined with power assertion techniques (Dlugokinski & Firestone, 1974). Induction is really a strategy based on principles of moral development. Understanding a child's social, cognitive, and moral development is critical in successfully using such discipline strategies. An understanding of parental discipline styles is pivotal in helping parents learn effective parenting techniques.

Implications for Practice: Parent Training

Many social workers are called on to do some form of parent training. They may run parent-training groups for parents of noncompliant children, work directly with foster parents, or conduct parent-training classes to help prepare pregnant adolescents to become better parents. Indeed, parent-training courses have been introduced everywhere—in schools, hospitals, community mental health centers, and churches. Professionals approach parent training from many different perspectives, ranging from humanistic to psychoanalytic, and, although there are some similarities, there are also some important differences. Let's examine four of the more popular approaches to parent training that you will likely come across in your work: parent-effectiveness training (Gordon, 1970); parent-involvement training (reality therapy for parents, inspired by William Glasser); behavior modification (Forehand & Long, 1996; Barkley, 1998); and systematic training for effective parenting (Adlerian therapy for parents, originated by Dreikurs and best represented by the work of Dinkmeyer et al., 1997). We will briefly examine some of the fundamental principles involved in each of these approaches (based on Brown, 1976; Jaffee, 1991).

PARENT-EFFECTIVENESS TRAINING (P.E.T.)

This humanist approach to parenting emphasizes the need for respect between parent and child. Central to

Gordon's ideas about parenting is his complete rejection of parental power. P.E.T. encourages parents to give up, forever, the use of power. He argues two reasons for this. First, it is damaging to people and relationships, and, second, power undermines P.E.T.'s no-lose method of resolving conflicts. Another interesting concept in P.E.T. is its conceptualization of children's behavior. P.E.T. holds that there is no such thing as children's misbehavior; children simply behave. All behavior is aimed at getting needs met. The driving ideas behind P.E.T. are summarized in Table 8.5.

The first strategy is to encourage parents and children to enlarge the no-problem aspect of their relationships. This goal can be accomplished via such approaches as environmental modification—putting things where children can't reach them—or minding your own business, or relaxing and staying calm.

When this doesn't work, the parent turns to the critical techniques of P.E.T. The parent is taught to first ask the question "Who owns the problem?" If the child owns the problem, the parent learns to use active listening. For example, the child comes home and is upset because her homework was lost and so wasn't turned in to the teacher. The parent is taught to help the child understand, accept, and deal with her feelings: "You really look upset—it means a lot to you to get your homework turned in on time." Often a parent's inclination is to use other ineffective strategies, including getting mad at the child, attempting to reassure the child, or presenting rationalizations or solutions.

When the behavior is unacceptable to the parent, the parent owns the problem, and the first strategy is to use I-messages: "I really need some quiet time—could you please turn off the stereo?" Parents are taught to use this rather than the familiar you-message: "You always have to turn the stereo up too loud." These messages, according to P.E.T., only demean the child and can be damaging to the child's self-esteem.

When active listening and I-messages do not resolve the problem, the parent turns to the no-lose method of problem solving. The parent elicits the child's cooperation in problem solving and follows these six steps: (1) Define the conflict; (2) use brainstorming with the child to generate solutions; (3) evaluate the solutions on the list; (4) see if there is a solution that satisfies both parties, and, if so; (5) decide

TABLE 8.5	The P.E.T. Approach to Parenting	
Behavior acceptable to parent	Child owns problem	Use active listening
	No problem	
Behavior unacceptable to parent	Parent owns problem	Use I-messages, and if necessary, the no-lose method of problem solving.

(Gordon, 1970)

how to implement it; and (6) evaluate the solution later to see if it worked.

PARENT-INVOLVEMENT TRAINING (P.I.T.)

A large part of the P.I.T. program focuses on getting parents involved. The P.I.T. theory holds that no behavior change can take place without a helping relationship based on trust, warmth, and respect. You must believe in your child for any behavior or self-concept to change. P.I.T. uses direct strategies for getting kids involved, including teaching parents to stop what they are doing and attend to their children, especially if the children are upset. Other strategies involve specific instructions for such things as dinnertime conversations, games to play, and so forth. The program is based on the following seven steps:

1. Establish and maintain involvement. Strongly recommended is conversation—talking about topics of mutual interest.

2. Help the children see what their current behavior is and understand that it is something they have chosen. Although feelings are important, behavior is critical.

3. Suggest that the children evaluate their behavior. Self-judgment is stressed by asking the children whether what they are doing is helping them.

4. Help the children plan increasingly responsible behavior. Help the child set realistic goals and have a successful experience.

5. Get the children to make a commitment to the plan. Contracts like this increase the children's motivation and involvement.

6. Accept no excuses; if the children fail to meet the commitment, start again with step three.

7. Don't use punishment. This can cause the children physical or mental pain and may lead to loneliness, isolation, or hostility. Instead, use praise for successes—it will encourage involvement.

BEHAVIOR MODIFICATION

The use of *behavior modification* in parent training involves teaching parents how to apply the principles of behavior to their children. The principles of behavior include such concepts as reinforcement, punishment, extinction, differential reinforcement of other behaviors, and stimulus control. Parent-training programs usually start out by teaching parents how to define the behavior they would like to see changed. After learning how to define behavior precisely, parents choose a home project to begin to put the principles to work. Parents must choose a behavior, define it, and develop a method of tracking and record-keeping. If parents are working on reducing the number of temper tantrums, then they must define what a temper tantrum is and record this behavior. Often they chart the behavior for a week or more with graph paper in order to assess the extent of the problem and to have a comparison after introducing an intervention.

Parents are then taught ways to either increase behaviors or decrease behaviors. Most parents choose to implement a reinforcement program based either on praise (social reinforcement) or on a home-style token economy, where points are exchanged for tangible reinforcement (money, prizes, or special privileges). When working to decrease behaviors, parents are taught to use various forms of punishments. For example, a parent working on reducing bedtime crying may use extinction, which involves ignoring the behavior (because the parent's attention was what kept the child crying night after night). Two of the most widely used punishments are time-out and the withdrawal of privileges. Time-out is time without reinforcement, and the child must sit quietly in a chair in the corner of a room for 2–6 minutes. The strategy is to make the time-out boring and unrewarding to the child. Withdrawal of privileges is often used on older children in conjunction with token economies. When unacceptable behaviors continue, the child loses a predetermined privilege. For example, a parent trying to reduce sibling fights would withdraw the privilege of watching TV that night for any instance of fighting.

Most behavior modification programs work hard to teach parents the hidden value of using praise and reinforcement with their children. Parents are encouraged to increase the use of praise dramatically. They are taught to rewrite rules using positive language, to record and increase the number of times they use praise, to make and display cards to encourage praise (like "catch your child being good"), and to display charts proudly showing the progress that the child is making.

SYSTEMATIC TRAINING FOR EFFECTIVE PARENTING (STEP)

This approach to parent training rests on the belief that a misbehaving child is a discouraged child. The STEP program teaches parents that there are four goals to a child's misbehavior: attention, power, revenge, and inadequacy. STEP teaches parents to use techniques of encouragement and discipline. Encouragement strategies emphasize giving the child a lot of responsibility and avoiding overprotection and unnecessary service. Whereas most parents will serve the child by pouring the child's milk, STEP recommends letting the child pour his or her own milk. If the child spills it, wipe it up and let the child try it again. STEP strongly recommends that parents not be overprotective but allow children to learn from their own behavior. This is well demonstrated by the STEP approach to discipline.

Discipline involves the use of **natural and logical consequences.** Again, the idea is to get parents to allow children the opportunity to experience the effects of their choices and behavior—good and bad. Unlike behavior modification, in which parents reward and punish the child's behavior (which means the parents are responsible for the child's behavior), STEP says children should be allowed to make their own decisions. If their choice is good, they experience the benefits; if their choice is bad, they suffer the consequences. This encourages children's actions to become more responsible and adult oriented, guided by natural outcomes and not parental interference.

The idea behind natural consequences is that they follow directly from the child's behavior in the absence of parental intervention. For example, children who arrive home late and miss dinner will have to prepare their own dinner. Children who leave the house without a coat will have to deal with being cold. Children who miss the bus are expected to walk to school. These are natural consequences because they follow directly from the behavior. When this is not possible because natural consequences are not available or would be dangerous, STEP teaches parents to use logical consequences. For example, if the parent cannot trust the child to play outside, the child must play inside; or if the child colors on the wall with a crayon, the crayons are taken away. Natural and logical consequences are considered preferable to rewards and punishments because they avoid power struggles and give children the opportunity to learn from real-life consequences.

GROUPS, SUPPORT SYSTEMS, AND COMMUNITIES

In middle childhood, children begin to have an increasing preference for spending time with their peers. This shift is clearly illustrated by Figure 8.4, from a study by Ellis, Rogoff, and Cromer (1981). The figure reveals the dramatic increase of child companions from age 1 to age 8. This increase is accompanied by a similar decrease in the number of adult companions. Also interesting is the fact that these children actually spent less time with age-mates (children within one year of their age) than with children who were either younger or older.

What makes a peer group? Is it just a few children who are similar in age and who hang out together? Apparently not, since researchers have defined **peer groups** in a specific manner: a group of age-mates that is durable and involves interactions based on an established set of social relationships. Peer groups are defined by their shared values and goals. Often, children in

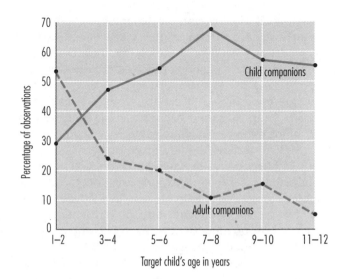

FIGURE 8.4 Developmental changes in children's companionship with children and adults (Ellis, Rogoff, & Cromer, 1981)

cliques are identified by their similar social prejudices, speech, and/or clothing styles. Within the group, each individual will have a certain role or status. Although formal groups often elect individuals to certain roles, like team leader, similar roles emerge naturally in informal peer groups. Let's examine the ways that peer groups are formed, as well as the social interactions within peer groups and their possible influences on members' behavior.

GROUP FORMATION

As children increase the number of stable encounters they have with age-mates, they begin to form groups. These groups often start when the child enters school and has increased regular contact with peers. Peer groups are important in the child's development throughout the life course, but their nature and function change as children get older. In early middle childhood, children are involved in informal groups that lack much structure. There are few rules that govern the behavior of the members, and there is a high turnover in membership. As a result, the influence of peer groups is reduced until the child reaches late childhood. Beginning with the junior high school years, group formation becomes increasingly important as peer relationships take on a new significance. At this age, groups become more formalized and roles emerge more clearly, as do the social rules that govern the groups—for example, "We only allow girls from our soccer group." Children begin to feel a cohesiveness that binds them to the group's values.

The most famous study of group formation was done by Sherif and colleagues (Sherif et al., 1961), who conducted a fascinating experiment with boys in a camp setting. The children were divided arbitrarily into two groups, and many of the boys resented being separated from their friends. As the groups participated in separate activities, group members' cooperation and cohesiveness with one another developed. Soon each group had developed its own rules of conduct, leadership hierarchy, and status relationships. The children in each group now identified more closely with peers from their own group. The experiment continued by bringing the two groups together for an intergroup conflict phase. The children were exposed to win-lose competition and planned frustration to increase the tension between the groups. These activities increased the level of animosity harbored by the two groups. In the last phase of the experiment, the researchers explored ways to reduce the intergroup conflict. When Sherif and colleagues sought to reduce the conflict, they brought the two groups together under noncompetitive conditions. However, this only heightened the conflict. When the two groups were brought together to work on a common goal that required cooperation (the researchers deliberately broke a water line so both groups would have to help), the boys were able to reduce the conflict.

This study has many important implications. First, the study illustrated the importance of cooperation and common goals in the formation of cohesive groups. The study also showed that groups independent of any previously shared interest can develop bad feelings and learn to discriminate against an "out" group. Second, the study found that competition and frustration could increase hostility between groups. Third, the study found that such hostility could be reduced when a common goal is introduced and groups are required to work together.

THE POWER OF PEERS

Early research by Merrill Roff (1963) was groundbreaking in its discovery of the importance of peers for healthy psychological development. Roff conducted a number of follow-up studies that examined children who had poor peer relationships and found that years later, as adults, these people had more than the usual number of mental health adjustments, had more problems adjusting to military service, and had more serious mental health problems.

Numerous studies now confirm Roff's early hunches that difficulties in social adjustment are likely to lead to poor mental health. Research by Cowen and others (1973) demonstrated the predictive power of not getting along with peers. His well-known study began by identifying first-grade children who were having poor peer relationships and were thought to be at increased risk for mental health problems. To test his idea, he followed several first-grade classes until the children reached early adulthood. He found that the children identified to be at increased risk because of poor peer relationships were disproportionately represented as suffering from psychiatric problems as adults.

Even more interesting for social workers was his finding that assessment of children's social competence by their peers is a more powerful predictor of later behavior problems than assessment by parents, teachers, or mental health practitioners. Indeed, we now realize that peers are critical to the healthy development of a child—perhaps second in importance only to the influence of parents.

Peers have always been considered an important aspect of childhood, but in the last 10–15 years we have learned much more about the effect that children can have on one another—both positive and negative. One thing is clear: Peer friendship is an important part of a child's development. People have an innate desire for human companionship, and peer friendship is critical if we are to feel connected and socially involved with one another. The absence of peer friendship speaks clearly to how important it is for healthy development. The following letter is from an adult who was deprived of peer friendships while growing up (Hartup, 1979, p. 155):

Peer groups are important throughout a child's development. In early middle childhood, they are informal and lack structure, but by late middle childhood peer groups become more formalized, with distinct roles and social rules that govern the group.

I am an only child, now 57 years old, and I want to tell you some things about my life. Not only was I an only child, but I grew up in the country where there were no nearby children to play with. My mother did not want children around. She used to say, "I don't want my kid to bother anybody and I don't want nobody's kids bothering me."

From the first year of school I was teased and made fun of. For example, in about third or fourth grade I dreaded to get on the school bus to go to school because the other children on the bus called me "Mommy's baby." In about the second grade I heard a vulgar word. I asked what it meant, and they made fun of me. So I learned a lesson—don't ask questions. This can lead to a lot of confusion to hear talk one doesn't understand and not be able to learn what it means . . . I never went out with a girl while I was in school—in fact I hardly talked to them. In our school the boys and girls did not play together. Boys were sent to one part of the playground and girls to another. So, I didn't learn anything about girls. When we got into high school and the boys and girls started dating, I could only listen to their stories about their experiences.

I could tell you a lot more, but the important thing is I have never married or had any children. I have not been successful in an occupation or vocation. I believe my troubles are not all due to being an only child . . . but I do believe you are right in recommending playmates for preschool children, and I will add playmates for the school-agers and not have them strictly supervised by adults. I believe I confirm the experiments with monkeys in being overly timid sometimes and overly aggressive sometimes. Parents of only children should make special efforts to provide playmates for [their children].

This letter supports various research studies that have documented the significance of good peer relationships. In reviewing this literature, Hartup (1983) summarized the importance of peer relations on child development:

- Poor peer relations are associated with discomfort, anxiety, and a general unwillingness to engage the environment.
- Children master their aggressive impulses within the context of peer relations.
- Sexual socialization cannot take place in the absence of peer interaction.
- Peer relations are related to role-taking ability, empathy, and moral reasoning.
- Children who are rejected by their peers are at greater risk for delinquency, school dropout, and mental health problems.

Children offer one another important knowledge and skills that are often unavailable from adults. Friendships are critical because they provide opportunities for learning social skills and a beginning sense of group belonging. The recent emphasis on peer relationships has stimulated research and program development in two areas, social skills training and social cognition. (See the Focus section concerning isolated children and social skills, page 333.)

Implications for Practice: Cross-Cultural Drug Abuse Prevention

No matter what a child's ethnic background, the factors that lead to drug abuse are largely the same. This fact is important when one is designing and implementing drug abuse prevention programs in "real world" America, because here we have many different ethnic groups living, working, and going to school together. After hundreds of years of the "melting pot," it is difficult to implement an intervention that focuses on one specific ethnic population.

"Life Skills Training" (Botvin, 1996) is a prevention program developed to determine the extent to which the essentially same intervention will work with many different kinds of kids. This school-based drug abuse prevention program has been shown to lower tobacco, marijuana, and alcohol use among white middle-class seventh graders as well as inner-city African-American and Hispanic youths. In addition, Life Skills Training works equally as well with boys as it does with girls. Because the program teaches skills to resist social pressures and fosters students' anti-drug attitudes and perceptions, it also lowers adolescents' intentions to use drugs in the future. Regular classroom instructors teach the program. They teach a range of social and personal skills that increase young people's ability effectively to handle the challenge of adolescent life and reduce the probability that they will use alcohol and drugs. The teachers are encouraged to change some of the role-play scenarios and use familiar language to make the role play real. The teachers that tailor the program to their class understand that the Life Skills Training curriculum's success depends on engaging the kids.

CULTURE AND COOPERATION

Cooperation is a critical concept in understanding peer interactions. Do children from different cultures respond to cooperation in different ways? Under certain circumstances—for example, when there is an element of competition—differences occur in the degrees of cooperation. Researchers have found that children from small Mexican villages are more cooperative than urban Mexican, Mexican-American, African-American, and white American children (Madsen & Shapira, 1970). Other similar studies have found differences between urban and rural children. These results point to the influence of simple, agrarian cultures that foster cooperation in children. Urban cultures that are more complex reward competition more.

Can Isolated Children Be Taught the Social Skills Needed for Friendship Making?

A study by Oden and Asher (1977) was designed to assess coaching as a method of training socially isolated children in social skills for gains in peer acceptance. Children (ages 9–10) were selected for this study on the basis of the results of a sociometric assessment. The sociometric assessment used a roster-and-rating questionnaire. Children rated each other in answer to two questions administered separately during the same session: "How much do you like to play with this person at school?" and "How much do you like to work with this person at school?" The children used a rating scale consisting of five points from 1—"I don't like to" to 5—"I like to a lot." Based on these results, children who were rated as less-accepted children became the participants in the study. The children were then randomly assigned to one of three groups: coaching, peer pairing, or control. The coaching group included instructions from an adult in social skills for friendship making; playing games with peers to practice social skills; and a postplay review session with the coach. In the peer-pairing group, isolated children played the same games with the same peers but did not receive instruction or review. In the control group, isolated children were taken out of the classroom with the same peers but did not interact or receive verbal instruction or review. To measure the effectiveness of the intervention, the researchers used the sociometric measure previously described and a "best friends" peer-nomination inventory in which children were asked to name one, two, or three of their best friends in the classroom. The overall results of the research found that the coaching procedure was effective in increasing isolated children's peer acceptance. In particular, the coaching group showed significant increases on the play sociometric rating from pretest to posttest when compared with the peer-pairing and control group. Also impressive in this research was the finding that the coaching

group continued to make gains far above the other two groups at a one-year follow-up. With regard to friendship nominations, the results found that the coaching group did increase the number of best-friend nominations, but this gain was not enough to produce statistical significance. The researchers point out that this measure would not be expected to show large differences since many children are unlikely to substitute a recently trained child for a long-standing friend. This study points to the potential for enhancing children's peer relationships when a direct intervention is implemented for isolated children.

SCHOOL INFLUENCES

School is a major socialization agent for our children. Children begin school by age 6 and spend five hours every weekday interacting with teacher and peers in ways that will affect their social and emotional development. When most of us think of schools, we think of the three Rs—reading, 'riting, and 'rithmetic. However, schools go far beyond academic basics. Children must learn to conform to the rules set forth in their school, respond to teacher demands, interact successfully with age-mates, and manage their day-to-day responsibilities. Schools often invite such opportunities as ganging up on peers, involvement in drugs, and new experiences with sex. Clearly, schools have a major responsibility in the proper socialization of children.

The following Focus section examines how, in today's increasingly hostile school environment, some children develop fears about attending school.

Why Are Children Afraid to Go to School?

Although many children look forward to going to school each morning, some hate leaving the comforts of home for the trials of school—a place where they might wear the wrong clothes or give the wrong answer in class. Some children even refuse to go to school, throwing tantrums or complaining of stomachaches, headaches, or nausea. These children suffer from what is commonly called **school phobia,** or school refusal. Broadly defined, school phobia is anxiety and fear related to being in school.

The development of school phobia in children is a serious concern among parents, teachers, and mental health professionals. This disorder affects 5%–10% of U.S. school children and can lead to serious problems with school absenteeism. Researchers have found that chronic absence puts students at risk for psychological problems later in life, such as alcohol abuse and criminal behavior, as well as underemployment and even marital difficulties (Last, 1990).

A closer look at what constitutes school phobia reveals several issues. Some children experience generalized anxiety about their abilities. Others have fears specific to a school-related activity, such as the walk down the hallway between classes. A related issue, social phobia, involves worry over peer relations and public speaking.

Most social phobias, such as school phobia, begin around ages 11 or 12, a time when children tend to insult and pick on one another most viciously. Some children are extremely fearful of being humiliated or embarrassed. Peers' opinions tend to be crucial, so children obsess over how others judge them. Particularly at risk for developing peer-related phobias are children harassed for physical traits, such as obesity and skinniness, or physical disabilities. Intellectual ability can also incite taunting from peers; some children suffer for their braininess, while others get ridiculed for their academic slowness.

There is hope, however. Overcoming the problem of social phobia requires a team effort involving teachers, parents, and school social workers. For example, teachers and school staff can encourage children to stay in class and urge them to check their anxiety by talking through it or using breathing exercises to calm rapid breathing. Calling parents from school should be the last resort. Parents, for their part, can more firmly set and enact rules about school attendance. Creating a regular morning routine prevents children from dwelling on anxiety and developing school-related aches and pains. Finally, therapy can be used to help children face their fears with the use of coping-skills training and other types of behavior-related therapy.

Misha Marvel (Based on Last, 1990; Murray, 1997)

DESIGNING MORE EFFECTIVE SCHOOLS

Research on the effects of different schools has produced some evidence that we can do a much better job at designing good and effective schools. Rutter and others (1979) gathered extensive data from schools on such factors as achievement tests, attendance records, and classroom behavior and found that schools differ in effectiveness. Students in the "better" schools attended school more regularly, exhibited fewer behavior problems, and made better academic progress than did students from the less effective schools. Particularly interesting was the finding that the initially poor students who attended the "better" schools scored just as high on the measure of academic progress as did the initially good students who attended the least-effective schools. Schools can and do make a difference in students' successes.

Perhaps surprising to many was the finding that many traditional measures of a good school did not enhance the school's effectiveness (MacIver, Reuman & Main, 1995; Wang, Haertal, & Walberg, 1993). Not important were factors such as monetary support, size of the school, staff-pupil ratios, or quality of the buildings (Hedger, Laine, & Greenwald, 1994; Hanushek, 1997; Rutter, 1983).

What does make for a good school? Most important to a school's effectiveness is the atmosphere of the school and its quality as a social institution (MacIver et al., 1995). Effective schools and classrooms are likely to:

1. Strongly emphasize academics (demand a lot from students, expect a lot, assign regular homework, set clear classroom objectives);
2. Focus on task-oriented behavior (reinforce good work, provide clear instructions, do not waste classroom time); and

3. Manage discipline problems effectively (be clear about the rules, use consequences consistently, avoid physical or excessive punishment).

Recent examination of several inner-city middle schools (Wulf, 1997) adds to Rutter's research. What makes a good school with today's changing neighborhoods and families? There are no stock answers, like mandated wardrobe or test scores or classroom size. But some universal truths have been identified. A good school is a community of parents, teachers, and students. A good school, like a good class, is run by someone with a vision, passion, and compassion. A good school has teachers who still enjoy the challenge, no matter what their age or experience. A good school prepares its students not just for the SATs or ACTs but also for the world beyond the school doors.

These conclusions come in the wake of the United States' concern for education. Although well-intentioned, this concern has manifested itself in an insistence on such standards as test scores, school dress codes, and class size. Such mandates must be applied gently. Too much testing will cut into the work that teachers and students should be doing; uniforms should not stifle efforts to bring out the individuality in each student; and a large class with an inspiring leader is far better than a small class with a mediocre teacher.

Some lessons learned from the inner-city schools encompass four ideas (Wulf, 1997). First, good after-school programs that engage the interests of both students and staff can extend and improve the regular school day's learning. Second, computers as a learning tool, in classrooms with teachers who are properly trained to integrate technology into curriculum, are vital for all children, not just those from families who can afford a home computer. Third, small classes work best for reading and math in the early primary grades because they allow increased personal interaction between students and teachers. Also, small classes tend to reduce paperwork, so teachers can spend more time planning lessons. And fourth, if we want to have high expectations for students, we have to have high expectations for teachers. Because teachers must be prepared for the challenge of today's classrooms, colleges are raising their standards, creating extended internships and developing partnerships with public schools. Once on the job, teachers should have opportunities to continue their education.

TEACHER EXPECTATIONS

One of the most famous educational research studies documented the well-known influence of teacher expectations on student performance. Rosenthal and Jacobson (1968) gave a group of students an IQ test and convinced their teachers that this test could predict which students would develop rapidly in intellectual growth. Teachers were then given the names of students who were likely to show such bursts of intellectual growth. In reality, the teachers had been given the names of ordinary students who were chosen at random. When the researchers retested these children, the "brightest" students showed significantly greater gains in IQ and reading achievement than did other students in the class. The effect of the teacher expectations was dramatic: Their expectations became self-fulfilling prophecies.

New research (Madon, Jussim, & Eccles, 1997) supports the theory that teachers' beliefs in students' abilities influence their performance. But, contrary to assertions that the teacher who underestimates a student's potential seriously undermines the student's performance, the study found that underestimating student achievement hurts students' test scores only marginally—10 percentiles. However, teachers with high hopes can raise students' test scores as much as 30 percentiles. The researchers believe that the average teacher *wants* his or her students to succeed and will help out as much as possible. Low-achievers respond well to prodding and prompting from teachers because most students want to do well; they just need encouragement.

The following section continues the discussion of students' self-perceptions with regard to learning.

SELF-EXPECTATIONS AND SCHOOL PERFORMANCE

Although the influence of teacher expectations on school performance has long been considered to be significant, more recent concern has focused on students' self-expectations (Lefrancois, 1994; Seligman,

1995). Research by Dweck (1986) examined students who could be classified as either mastery oriented, likely to attribute their successes to ability and effort; or helplessness oriented, likely to attribute their failures to luck or the difficulty of the task—causes over which they have no personal control. Studies that have looked at the differences between these two types of students have found that mastery students are confident in their performances on various tasks, whereas helpless students see themselves not only as helpless but also as lacking confidence in their abilities. They think they will likely confront failure in the future (Diener & Dweck, 1980). In one study (Dweck & Reppucci, 1973), the helpless children gave up after a single failure, although they had both the ability and the motivation to perform on subsequent tasks.

Although many children experience **learned helplessness,** research has demonstrated that these children can be taught to attribute their failures to insufficient effort rather than a lack of ability. This affects their sense of *self-efficacy,* and they learn to persist in spite of a failure (Seligman, 1995).

DISADVANTAGED CHILDREN AND THE PUBLIC SCHOOL SYSTEM

The public school system is a middle-class institution, and as a result, it can have a negative effect on disadvantaged children. Seligman (1999) outlines three barriers that low-income and minority students face in the school system: low parental expectations in school performance, lack of culturally relevant educational materials, and low teacher expectations for school performance.

Academic expectations may be quite different when we compare middle-class parents with low-income and minority parents. Whereas middle-class parents put value on the idea of "getting ahead," parents of disadvantaged children are often more concerned with "staying out of trouble." These varying expectations are likely to influence the academic behavior of children—working hard to get ahead or working just enough to get by. Sometimes disadvantaged parents inadvertently influence school performance; they simply participate less in school activities, and as a result their children place less value on school. However, when parents of disadvantaged children do get involved and expect good school performance from their children, their children are likely to do well (Comer, 1993). Social workers should keep in mind that parental involvement and interest in the child's school performance can make a difference.

The "relevance" of school material can also be a barrier for low-income and minority children. Imagine reading only stories about well-to-do white children when you are an African-American who lives in a low-income neighborhood. The stories might not be of much interest because they lack any cultural rele-

In the public school system, low-income African-American students can face significant barriers, including low parental and teacher expectations regarding school performance and lack of culturally relevant educational materials.

vance. One study that examined this issue found that Hispanic-Americans (who spoke only English) scored far below Anglo classmates in reading proficiency. The reading material dealt mostly with middle-class interests and values and was not culturally relevant. However, these same Hispanic-American students performed much better in comparison with white students on mathematical ability—the testing of which involves less culturally oriented material. Our schools need to do a better job of providing minority students with culturally relevant material.

Earlier we presented information about the importance of teacher expectations. If teachers hold negative expectations about low-income and minority children, they will build critical barriers to academic success. Unfortunately, it appears that teachers do have lower expectations for children from low-income families (Minuchin & Shapiro, 1983). A common practice in many schools is to advance students to the next grade regardless of their accomplishments. This action may represent teachers' negative expectations that these children are not going to do well anyway. Such "social promotions" may perpetuate social inequality by depriving children of the opportunity to acquire necessary academic skills.

Implications for Practice: Enhancing School-Community Relationships

Social workers, in particular school social workers, often have the opportunity to influence the way in which school systems, teachers, and school officials interact with community members. One goal of a school social worker in a low-income community might be to minimize the barriers, like those just described, that low-income and families of color confront. The social worker could act as a consultant to the school system and work with teachers to help them encourage better performance from minority students, work with families to help them get more involved in school activities and have more of a say in school materials, and work with school officials in an attempt to examine their school policies, such as "social promotions," to evaluate whether they truly benefit the children involved.

Often the primary role of the school social worker is to enhance school-community relations. Constable (1999) describes some of the remedial tasks school so-

cial workers are likely to perform in addressing school-community relations:

- Identify children or target groups of children needing alternative educational planning or programs and support services;
- Consult and collaborate with community representatives to identify the effects of interacting school/community/pupil characteristics and develop resources to meet needs of child or target group;
- Collaborate with community agencies in the development of alternative education programs and support services;
- Clarify and interpret specific roles and responsibilities of the community in promoting school attendance;
- Set objectives, monitor progress, and measure outcomes of service.

School social workers often provide a vital link between the community and the school. Often the child and his or her family need specialized services from other agencies—for example, health services, counseling, and respite care. School pupils also are sometimes involved in other major socialization agencies, such as the juvenile justice system or the child welfare system. The school social worker must interact with community agencies in efforts to provide needed planning (Constable, 1999).

SCHOOLS AND U.S. PUBLIC LAW 94-142

One of the most significant changes to affect schools was the adoption and implementation of U.S. Public Law (PL) 94-142, the Education for All Handicapped Act. This law has been referred to as a "bill of rights for the handicapped" because it established the right to a free, appropriate, public education for all "handicapped" children aged 3 through 21.

Children included under the provisions of this law are evaluated according to a multidisciplinary team. The team develops their objectives, and, together with special education and related services, provides each child with a written **Individualized Educational Plan (IEP)**. This law guarantees children the right to

Public Law 94-142 and other developments in education have contributed to the mainstreaming of children with physical and developmental disabilities.

special education and related services, including any service that helps the child benefit from special education. Services that are recommended in the IEP must be provided to the child and his or her family at no cost. Of particular interest to social workers is the fact that seriously emotionally disturbed children fall under the category of "disabled."

This law has provided, in essence, a legal mandate for school social work services. School social workers become involved in the development and coordination of the Individualized Educational Plan required for every student (Timberlake, Sabatino, & Hooper, 1999). The multiple tasks required of the school social worker point to the importance of understanding the school environment and its influence on children's de-

velopment. Indeed, it is critical to understand the school as a social organization. School social workers often must act as change agents within the school, working toward organizational change to meet the needs of the students they serve.

Multicultural and Gender Considerations

Imagine a child who turns on the TV Sunday morning and becomes engrossed in a TV series. He or she begins to identify with one of the characters on the show and imagines being that person. However, the characters in this TV program are all white. Suddenly, one day the child is not really sure he or she can be like this person and begins to realize that many people will consider him or her an outsider. The child is Hispanic, unlike the character in the TV program. The pervasive and subtle effects of racism are beginning to be felt in the everyday life of this child.

By middle childhood, racial identity is beginning to be formed. Children begin to think about who they are in terms of similar peer groups, their appearance, and their aspirations. How is the development of a child's self-concept affected by a society that imports negative meanings to being a minority? Do these children as a consequence develop feelings of self-doubt, inferiority, and low self-esteem?

Studies of Mexican-American children show that ethnic awareness develops after gender and race awareness. In looking at different ages of Mexican-American children, researchers (DeAngelis, 1994) found that young preschool children have limited knowledge of their ethnic identity. But, as they get older, their understanding of their heritage grows broader and more complex. In addition, bilingual Mexican-American children were found to be more aware of their ethnic identity than those who spoke only English. In fact, both ethnic and racial constancy are not attained until a few years after gender constancy. This finding contradicts the Piagetian view that, once children reach a concrete operational stage where certain relationships are viewed as stable regardless of appearance, these mental operations should lead to general social constancy.

The developmental findings highlight the need for teachers and others who work with ethnic-minority children to attend to the youngsters' developmental stages—for example, by developing educational materials aimed at the level of understanding of each child.

Researchers also found that families who identify more with their ethnic roots are more likely to teach their children about their ethnic background and that children's ethnic identity is related to ethnically based behavior, such as cooperation and respect. Also, the degree to which children identify with their Mexican heritage was based on their mothers' teaching.

During middle childhood, parents can no longer protect their children from the hostility caused by prejudice because of a child's color, appearance, attitudes, ethnic background, or neighborhood. However, parents and teachers can accentuate the child's strengths and abilities. Inner-city children can be remarkably self-reliant and independent. These children clearly grow up fast and develop functional characteristics to help them adapt to many of the hardships in life. Unfortunately, many teachers fail to recognize these abilities as strengths. Still, much progress has been made by parents, teachers, and others who recognize the strengths evident in all children. The benefits are clear: Children's identity and self-esteem can be strengthened by providing them with a sense of belonging and reassurance about their differences (Rapalje, Degelman, & Ashburn, 1986). Their differences need to be associated with positive attributes, not with the societal projections that attribute different with "bad" or "less worthy."

The following Focus section examines rites of passage that can help redirect young African-American men.

FOCUS ON MULTICULTURALISM

▼

Heritage-Based Rites of Passage for African-American Youth

In South Central Los Angeles, a 6-year-old boy from a low-income family walks to school in plastic flip-flops because his family cannot afford to buy him sturdy shoes. A young African-American man—ironically a member of a street gang—sees him on the street, picks him up, feeds him, gives him a pair of sneakers and drops him off at school.

This real-life scenario is not what mainstream society would consider typical. The media portray young African-American males as drug dealers and killers who do not want to learn to be responsible. The fact is that 90% of young African-American men are going to school and helping the community. A national movement is helping young black men cope with the difficulties they face from stereotyping and other societal pressures. Rites of passage and mentoring programs are providing solutions.

Through initiation rites, the programs reinforce values such as self-respect, responsibility, and dedication to family, community and one another. They meet several objectives: Youngsters develop a value orientation; adults gain a sense of empowerment and commitment through helping the children; and the sponsoring organizations improve the troubled status of young black males in the community.

Stereotypes can create an "invisibility syndrome": African-American males are often treated as if they do not exist or should be feared. The stereotypes represent a set of assumptions and expectations that create the lens through which African-American males are seen. Children experience the stereotypes of how they are viewed by some teachers and police. The media give the impression that African-American males do not want to make an honest living—that they just want to hang out on the street corners selling drugs. As a result, youth are put on the defensive. It is not uncommon for police to hassle innocent young black men just because they are young black men.

Culture, the entertainment industry, social networks, and adults give young black men negative messages about their capabilities and coping skills. Therefore, some youth become totally discouraged by the school experience because of how teachers treat them and decide to opt out, finding it too difficult. African-American boys also battle the attitude that, if they succeed in school, they are "copping out" or "being white." The gifted ones are then pressured to bury or underplay their talent to be accepted by their peers.

Rites of passage and mentoring programs have grown in the United States to assist young men in their fight against stereotypes. African-American institutions, including churches, fraternities, social clubs, and schools, are implementing the programs.

Teachers and community members identify the program's voluntary participants. They choose young men who demonstrate either negative or positive leadership over their peers. The goal is for the youth to form a network and rechannel some of the energies they might use to get into trouble into becoming a positive influence on others.

Parents must be willing to participate in the neighborhood programs. Community service, for example, is a program requirement. Parents and their children sign contracts that describe program expectations. If parents do not participate, the child is dropped from the program. Rites of passage will be successful only if the parents reinforce the programs at home.

Direct community involvement is another key to success of rites-of-passage programs. Parents and schools cannot do everything. The positive values that come from the rites-of-passage programs have to be reinforced in the community.

Western societies have lost the traditions used to initiate boys into manhood. Initiation rites now consist of getting a driver's license, getting drunk, and having sex. Rites-of-passage programs use traditional practices from Africa and adapt them to the contemporary needs of young men in urban communities. The programs instill a value system and a sense of pride and self-worth in the young men that encourage them to succeed. They emphasize leadership, critical thinking, decision making, and problem solving.

These programs have an Afrocentric value system. They promote, for example, "Nguzo Saba"—unity, self-determination, collective work, responsibility, cooperative economics, purpose, creativity, and faith. Nguzo Saba is the cornerstone of the African-American holiday Kwanza, in which communities give thanks for the past year and prepare for the new year.

Each member spends two years in the programs. On completion, a circle of elders returns as he graduates to the community in a formal ceremony. Each young man presents what he has learned from the program. The community is then asked to accept the young men as new members and support them in their roles. Teaching youth what is needed to make the

transition into adulthood successfully is vital to create a sense of responsibility and pride in their heritage, and to encourage them to succeed.

Misha Marvel (Based on Burnette, 1995)

SEX ROLES IN MIDDLE CHILDHOOD

During middle childhood, girls and boys begin to learn about their differing roles. With increasing expectations about what a boy or girl should think or do, children at this age must begin to incorporate such information into their self-concept. Middle childhood begins to have a significant effect on children's **sex-typed behavior.** Sex-typed behavior is the developmental process by which culturally assigned values and behaviors are considered appropriate for members of that sex.

With their increased ability to understand other people's expectations of themselves, children, especially boys, begin to show some changes in sex-typed behavior. The behavior and attitudes of boys become increasingly masculine oriented. However, girls at this age do not show a corresponding change toward femininity; in fact, they have a preference for masculine interests and activities (Richardson & Simpson, 1982). (Remember, this tendency began in the preschool years.) For example, in examining the Christmas wish list of boys and girls, Richardon and Simpson (1982) found that most requests were sex-typed but that more girls than boys asked for "opposite sex" items. What can account for this tendency for girls to show interest in masculine-oriented behavior? Shaffer (1993) suggests three possible reasons: (1) Girls are becoming increasingly aware that masculine behavior is more highly valued; (2) girls are permitted to engage in more cross-sex play than boys are; and (3) masculine games may simply be preferred because they are more action-oriented than playing with dolls and doll houses.

Children at this age also begin to develop **sex-role stereotypes.** Sex-role stereotypes reflect how we categorize people according to our general impressions of what we consider "male" and "female." What do you consider to be the major differences between men and women? Do you believe that women are more submissive, passive, less competitive, more home oriented, less adventurous, or less confident than men are? Do you believe that men are more aggressive, more objective, more active, more competitive, or more direct than women are? The ideas you have about such differences between men and women reflect your stereotypes. In previous chapters, we pointed out that sex differences exist from birth and are noticeable through the preschool years. However, disagreement exists about whether these differences result from biology or from socialization. In other words, how much of the early difference between sexes is due to genes and how much due to sex-role stereotyping? What are the true differences between men and women?

A famous review of more than 1,500 studies by Maccoby and Jacklin (1974) attempted to set the record straight. The results are surprising, because most of us have grown up with many myths about gender differences that reinforce our sex-role stereotypes. The results found only four gender-related differences:

1. Females have greater verbal ability.

2. Males have better visual/spatial ability.

3. Males have better mathematical skills.

4. Males are more aggressive.

Our myths about gender differences are quite strong, but as stated earlier, only four differences can be accounted for. The following list describes some of the more common myths about gender differences that you should review and consider rejecting. If this is difficult for you then you know firsthand how difficult it can be to change stereotypes.

- Boys are more active than girls.
- Girls are more suggestible than boys.
- Boys are more competitive than girls.
- Girls are more sensitive than boys.
- Boys are more dominant than girls.
- Girls are more social than boys.

One of the reasons it is hard for us to change our views about gender myths is because sex-role stereo-typing begins at a very early age. Recall the study by Haugh, Hoffman, and Cowan (1980), in which 3- and 5-year-olds watched a film with two babies playing, one identified as male and one as female. When asked to point to the baby that was "smart," the children almost always chose whichever one had been labeled a boy.

We learn to develop such stereotypes at home and at school. Parents often have different expectations of boys than of girls. In addition to reinforcing gender stereotypes, we are learning how parents can even affect their sons' and daughters' attributions about their academic achievements. Not surprisingly, one study (Parsons, Adler, & Kaczala, 1982b) found that parents expect their sons to do better in math than their daughters. However, these attitudes also affected their children's own assessments of their math abilities and their belief that they can be successful in the future. In other words, children's beliefs about their own math abilities were better reflected by their parents' beliefs in their math potential than by their own past experiences in math. A child's academic self-concept is strongly influenced by his or her parents' stereotypical notions about that child's academic potential. Add this type of influence to findings that show that teachers praise a boy's ability when he is successful but praise a girl's neatness and effort when she is successful (Dweck et al., 1978), and you can see why we have a long way to go to change sex-role stereotypes.

Social Hazards

The experience of childhood takes place in a social context—in the neighborhood and community where the child lives. The neighborhood is perhaps most critical to the middle child in molding the child's experiences and shaping how the child adjusts to the social world. The neighborhood opens up an important arena for exploration and social interaction and contributes to the child's physical and social development (Garbarino et al., 1992). As the child moves beyond the boundaries of the front yard, he or she is affected by who is in the neighborhood and how safe the neighborhood is. Consider the multitude of neighborhood factors that contribute to the child's development—

neighborhood safety, available health and social services, recreational activities, quality of the local schools, the surrounding economic conditions.

The notion of a "community" becomes increasingly critical to the child's healthy development. The nature and types of social interactions available influence the quality of life for families. Consider the difference between the types of social interactions that occur in a housing project in Chicago and in an upper-income suburb in Chicago. As you can see, consideration of the social hazards alerts us to how the community affects the development of the child. Indeed, studies have shown that, when a community's economy is negatively affected, rates of domestic violence increase (Straus, Gelles, & Steinmetz, 1980).

One reality not widely recognized is that children are more prone to victimization than adults. Sadly, in cases of family violence, adults report that they inflict almost twice as much severe violence on a child in their household than against their adult partner (Finkelhor & Dziuba-Leatherman, 1994). This violence includes beating, kicking, and hitting with a fist or an object. Further, when we add to family violence the frequent occurrence of peer and sibling assaults against younger children, we see a picture in which children are victims of violence far too often. Families that exist in high-risk neighborhoods and communities face a large number of stresses.

FOCUS ON MULTICULTURALISM

▼

Primary Prevention for Traumatized Khmer Children

In an innovative program to resettle Khmer refugee children in Tacoma, Washington, Duncan and Kang (cited in Williams & Berry, 1991) describe a creative and culturally sensitive treatment program. These children lived through the Pol Pot atrocities in Cambodia and were forced from their families when they arrived by themselves in Tacoma. They experienced trauma and loss that included the separation from families without the resolution of grief and loss. In addition, these children experienced serious acculturative stress.

Post-traumatic symptoms emerged soon after their arrival and included sleep disturbances, nightmares involving family members, and disturbing visits of spirits, including parents and grandparents.

The primary prevention program included three Theravada Buddhist ceremonies and rituals to honor the children's dead family. These included *Ban Skol,* a memorial for absent family members; *Pratchun Ban,* an annual family reunion of living and deceased relatives, and religious observances for absent family members that took place during the Khmer New Year's celebration. Also included was special consultation with Khmer Buddhist spiritual leaders. Last, the program included placements in ethnically similar foster homes.

The Ban Skol ceremony was a joint effort between the foster parents and the social service agency that was held at the child's foster home. A special meal was provided to the monks, family, guests, and agency staff. The child prepared a list of the family members and was instructed to burn it and to douse the ashes slowly with water. This symbolic cremation was prepared for those children who had witnessed dead bodies that were simply left to rot, and the refugee child was the primary focus of the ceremony. This ritual was intended to provide protective functions to the child. As Williams and Berry (1991, p. 637) point out, "through the process of the ceremony, the child was able to begin seeing the foster family, their friends, and the agency's caseworkers as sources of support."

During the ceremony, many of the children were either withdrawn or overcome with feelings of loss and grief. This allowed the foster family and others to console the children and offer support. There were anecdotal reports after the ceremony of decreased sleep problems, fewer spirit visits, increased bonding with the foster family, and greater grief resolution.

(Adapted from Williams & Berry, 1991)

MARITAL CONFLICT AND DIVORCE

Marital conflict and divorce constitute major impediments to the adjustment of children of all ages. Divorce rates of about 50% reflect increased societal acceptance of divorce. Nearly 1 million children will experience divorce each year. By the year 2000, one out of four children will live in stepfamilies. Half of all children will live in single-parent families for some part of their childhood (Jaffe, 1991); recent statistics show that 24% of children under 18 live with their mothers only, 4% with their fathers only (U.S. Bureau of the Census, 1997).

In this section, we will focus on the experience of divorce from the child's point of view. Although we tend to think of divorce as occurring at a fixed point in time, for the child and family, the real-

TABLE 8.6   Stressors That Occur with Divorce

Life Changes	Consequent Effects on Children
Hostilities between parents	Sadness, anger, loyalty conflicts
Distraught custodial parent	Anxiety, put in roles of parent, co-parent to custodial parent
Loss of relationship with noncustodial parent	Self-blame, low self-esteem, depression
Parent dating	Competitive feelings with parent's new partner, fear of loss of parent's affection, curiosity (for older children) about parent's sexuality
Remarriage	Sharing parents, accepting parents' intimacy, forming relationships with stepparents and stepsiblings, accepting new parent as authority, resolving issues of loyalty to new stepparent and parent of same gender
Poverty, associated	Downward economic mobility, emotional stresses, changes in residence, loss of peer relationships and familiar school environment, change in consistent caregivers

(Adapted from Kalter & Schreier, 1994)

ity of divorce looks and feels more like a succession of painful experiences (Hetherington, 1989; Wallerstein & Blakeslee, 1989). In fact, Kalter (1987; 1990) proposed that children experience a series of stressors when their parents divorce. The stressors outlined by Kalter and Schreier (1994, p. 308), in order of significance, are described in Table 8.6. In the presence of such extreme stressors, children's energy is diverted from their own needs to worries about security, safety, and survival for themselves and their loved ones.

Wallerstein (1988) describes three stages of divorce, all of which affect children's ability to focus on their developmental tasks. The *acute phase* is characterized by parental fighting, conflict, anger, depression, and the actual separation, which is often not mutual. This phase represents a crisis and often lasts for more than a year and is particularly difficult for children because they witness arguments and must live amidst household instability and parental neglect (Lorenz et al., 1997). Parents do not often consider the effects of their behavior on their children when they are embroiled in a heated, prolonged battle. During this phase, children usually bear the brunt of poor parenting, although the quality generally improves after a year (Hetherington, Cox, & Cox, 1982).

The second phase is described as the *transitional phase,* in which parents and children try to adjust to

their new life in a restructured family. The transitional phase usually lasts several years before the family settles into new roles and routines. In the third phase, the *stabilizing phase,* the family has typically adapted to the shifts in roles and allegiances. An optimal level of functioning is regained, and the family has moved on to tackle new changes. Not every family experiences each of these stages, however. Individual family members will vary in the level of functioning they achieve postdivorce.

Divorce is especially taxing on children because it disrupts one of the core relationships in their lives and dissolves the family structure they depend on for secure development (Amato, 1993). More often than not, children of divorce face adjustment issues throughout the course of their lives. As is true of the divorce process, the stresses evoked by divorce are not limited by time and will resurface in different forms as children develop. Although research has cited marital conflict as contributing more to children's distress than the actual divorce (Amato, 1993), many factors have been identified as determinants of children's adjustment (Amato & Booth, 1996). These factors include the personality and temperament of the child, the quality of the parent-child relationship pre- and postdivorce, stability of the custodial parent's household, financial security, and the postdivorce relationship between the ex-spouses (Amato, 1993; Hetherington, 1989; Wallerstein, 1988).

For all children, regardless of age or gender, the loss of a parent dredges up feelings of insecurity, loss of self-worth, loss of love and feeling lovable, anxiety, loneliness, anger, resentment, guilt, fear of abandonment, depression, and helplessness (Wallerstein & Blakeslee, 1989). Children must also face issues of relocation to new homes and schools; maternal employment; custodial parents who are themselves under stress, impatient, and overburdened; disorganization and unpredictability in daily events such as meals and bedtime; and difficulties in school performance and peer relationships. Unfortunately, just when children need their parents the most, parents' ability to attend to their children effectively is compromised (Amato, 1993; Wallerstein & Blakeslee, 1989).

So how do children fare when marital conflict and divorce become part of their life history? The age of the child at the time of divorce influences short- and long-term adjustment. Young children initially suffer more fear because they are more dependent on their parents and are more limited cognitively in their ability to understand the reasons for divorce; they tend to blame themselves. Because they are working on separation issues during the early childhood years, fears of abandonment become heightened with the reality of divorce (Hetherington, 1989). Wallerstein (1988) found that young children's adjustment tended to deteriorate during the year and a half following the divorce and continued to be poor even after five years. This was especially true for boys, who were more aggressive and disruptive at home and at school. Young children's development rests more completely on the quality of care in the home. Consequently, they suffer more than older children when the quality is diminished. Older children possess a larger coping repertoire with direct access to more resources than do younger children, which can buffer them from the initial hardships imposed by divorce (Cicchetti & Schneider-Rosen, 1986).

However, young children tend to have better long-term prognoses for adjustment when assessed ten years later. This finding may be the result of their limited recollection of specific traumatic events and consequent fears and their inability to incorporate the experience into their belief systems (Masten, Best, & Garmezy,

1991). Interestingly, children who were young at the time of the divorce fantasized about their parents reuniting even ten years after the divorce. These children reported feelings of sadness over the loss of their family and worries about future relationships and commitments, especially with the opposite sex. Younger children reported feeling more hopeful about relationships than did their older siblings. Adolescent girls reported the most anxiety (Wallerstein, Corbin, & Lewis, 1988).

Differences in adjustment outcome for boys and girls have also been noted and depend, to a large extent, on the sex of the custodial parent. Overall, girls tend to fare better following divorce than do boys. Most girls tend to adapt faster and better to divorce, with the exception of those who mature early at puberty. These girls were found to be less compliant, more argumentative, have lowered self-esteem and more problems in heterosexual relationships than on-time and late-maturing girls (Hetherington, 1988). Boys who resided with mothers who never remarried tended to experience the hardest adjustment from preschool through adolescence. Generally, children living with custodial parents of the same sex demonstrated increased self-esteem, social competencies, independence, security, and maturity (Santrock & Warshak, 1986).

These findings may be attributed to the fact that most children reside in the custody of their mothers and are provided with role models and sources of support. Some people believe that sons need fathers more than daughters do. In truth, girls may find role models in their mothers and learn relationship skills from them that boys need to learn from fathers. These findings may also reflect the difficulty that many single mothers of teenage boys confront when disciplining and controlling their sons. The power structure embedded in many cultures within our society attributes more value and autonomy to males than to females. As a result, mothers may have little authority over their sons, and daughters may have fewer rebellious aspirations.

Implications for Practice: Smoothing the Aftermath of a Divorce

Sigelman (1999) identifies five factors that can help smooth the path in the aftermath of a divorce:

1. *Adequate financial support:* Research studies confirm the notion that families do much better in adjusting to divorce when their finances are not seriously depleted (Simmons et al., 1993). The challenge is helping single-parent households retain a reasonable amount of financial support. Social policy experts have been encouraging states to pursue noncustodial parents who do not pay their child support. Unfortunately only about half of noncustodial fathers pay child support (Sorensen, 1997).

2. *Adequate parenting by the custodial parent:* Because parents are under increased stress and pressure, their parenting usually becomes less effective. However, if parents can be supported in these stressful times and encouraged to continue a relationship based on warmth and consistent discipline, their children will be less likely to experience problems (Simmons, et al., 1994).

3. *Emotional support from the noncustodial parent.* One serious consequence of many divorces is the intense hostility and anger that the spouses feel and express. As a result, children feel insecure, are torn between the parents, and are more likely to experience behavior problems (Amato, 1993). Also, many children lose contact with their noncustodial parent. In fact, about one-third of the children lose contact with their fathers (Seltzer & Bianchi, 1988). Research suggests that regular contact with supportive fathers can help children, particularly sons, adjust to the divorce (Amato, 1993; Simmons, et al., 1994). When children have supportive relationships with both parents and there is an effort to reduce the conflict between parents, they are more likely to make a positive adjustment to a single-parent household.

4. *Additional social support:* Social support also plays an important role in helping both parents and children adjust to the negative effects of divorce. Parents who have close friends are less depressed (Menaghan & Lieberman, 1986), and children benefit as well from close friends (Lustig, Wolchik, & Braver, 1992). Children who participate in divorce groups have an opportunity to share their feelings and learn positive coping skills (Kalter & Schreier, 1994). Also, adolescents in single-parent homes commit fewer delinquent acts when a relative helps with the childrearing and supervision (Dornbusch et al., 1985). Helping a family find social support can lessen the negative effects of divorce.

5. *A minimum of additional stressors:* The divorcing family may face many new changes—decreased income, moves to new neighborhoods, legal battles, and extended family complications. Not surprisingly, the ability to cope successfully with divorce can be facilitated by reducing the amount of stress (Amato, 1993).

Many factors influence how a family reacts to a divorce. The five factors just described represent a beginning point for thinking about how to help families who must face this crisis. Sigelman (1999) reminds us of how these factors demonstrate that the family is a social system within larger social systems. Adjustment to divorce must take into consideration how mother, father, and children all influence one another, as well as the family's experience in its interactions with the surrounding world.

Summary

DEVELOPMENTAL THEMES

As children end their preschool years, they begin to learn new skills and competencies. Middle childhood represents a stage of "industry," which means "to build." Children are building skills by playing games and are making large gains in their intellectual functioning. Successful adaptation to peer groups is a major developmental task.

BIOPHYSICAL DIMENSION
Biophysical Growth and Development

In middle childhood, boys and girls exhibit a slow but consistent growth pattern. Girls retain their fat tissue longer than boys do; boys develop muscle tissue more quickly. Continued development in the large and small muscles enhances the child's coordination, agility, and smoothness. Sports become popular as boys and girls enjoy climbing, throwing, swimming, skating, and in-line skating. Boys have greater motor development, and girls are better than boys at fine motor skills.

Biophysical Hazards

Environmental conditions can affect the child's health and development. Poverty and a lack of food can be very damaging. Impoverished conditions can lead to such problems as cretinism and rickets. Physical activity drops off significantly during childhood and adolescence, creating overweight children.

PSYCHOLOGICAL DIMENSION

Information Processing

Children at this age operate from concrete operational thought; that is, thought processes are governed by rules of logic. This stage is characterized by becoming less egocentric. Children can show reversible thought and conservation skills. For example, they understand that certain transformations do not change the quantitative features of objects. Although Piaget's ideas have withstood the test of time, it is now recognized that cognitive changes do not proceed according to predetermined sequences of stages. As a result, *levels* is a better conceptual notion than *stages*.

Information processing is also relevant to a child's social relationships. Research has found that skill deficits in how children process information may influence their behavioral interactions. Children's intelligence is often measured with an IQ test. IQ is measured by dividing mental age by chronological age and multiplying by 100. The Stanford-Binet is a widely used IQ test that includes four areas: verbal reasoning, quantitative reasoning, abstract/visual reasoning, and short-term memory. Other similar tests used with children include the Wechsler tests and the Kaufman Assessment Battery for children. Concerns about the use of IQ tests include the labeling and classification of children and cultural bias. Emotional intelligence (EQ) describes qualities such as understanding one's own feelings, empathy for the feelings of others, and regulating emotions in ways that enhance life.

Communication

Middle childhood is considered a period of linguistic refinement. As children develop their language skills, they become capable of metalinguistic awareness and appreciate humor in jokes, riddles, and puns. Children who are deaf learn language in much the same manner as hearing children. As communication becomes increasingly important for the social life of children, deficits in communication have social consequences. For example, speech disorders like stuttering can lead to academic as well as emotional difficulties.

Verbal control develops as children move from external control to covert self-verbalizations. Self-instructional training is a major treatment approach for children who have difficulties with self-control. Bilingual children can have both positive and negative outcomes, depending on how the two languages are used. A child's language abilities can be influenced by cultural experiences. Disadvantaged children have a restricted vocabulary and construct sentences that are less grammatically correct than those of middle-class students.

Attitudes and Emotions

Conceptions of self extend to include such things as ideal self, ethnic awareness, and conscience development, and a more differentiated self-concept emerges. This self-view is less global and more specific to who the child is as a unique being. One measure of children's self-concept is the Perceived Competence Scale for Children. Research has found that children's evaluations of themselves reflect the way other people perceive them.

Social Cognition and Regulation

Social role taking is the reduction of egocentric thought—egocentric thoughts being children's inability to decenter the focus of their conceptual efforts. Role-taking ability—to see things from another person's perspective—changes around 12 years of age, when a child can think about himself or herself and social relations become more advanced. A child's interpersonal awareness can be ordered along a developmental continuum, and concepts such as friendship
(text continues on p. 351)

Attention Deficit Hyperactivity Disorder

DEVELOPMENTAL HISTORY

Tommy is a 7-year-old African-American child who was referred to the Child Guidance Clinic by his teacher. Tommy's mother, Ms. Paul, reports that Tommy's birth was not planned and that Tommy's father was not pleased about her pregnancy. She was upset that Tommy's father did not want the child and concerned about what would happen. Ms. Paul reported that she was in labor for a very long time and that she was given Demerol during the birth process. Complications in pregnancy were mostly a result of her failure to dilate properly.

Ms. Paul noted that Tommy developed "normally" and began walking and talking at developmentally appropriate times. She noted that at about age 5 Tommy became much more difficult to manage. She began getting complaints about his behavior at school.

BIOPHYSICAL CONSIDERATIONS

At about age 5, Tommy developed problems with his eye muscles. He received optometric treatment for about a year. Ms. Paul reports that she had a very difficult time getting him to do his required eye exercises. Tommy stopped receiving treatment last year when Ms. Paul changed jobs and lost her health insurance.

PSYCHOLOGICAL CONSIDERATIONS

Cognitive Development and Information Processing

Tommy has difficulties with information processing. In particular, his attention span is exceedingly short. This has led to his diagnosis of attention deficit hyperactivity disorder (ADHD). Teacher reports indicate that constant supervision is required to keep Tommy from talking to the other children. Also, his teachers state that he "cannot sit still" and that he "cannot concentrate."

Tommy's school performance has gotten much worse over the last year. His teacher reports that he is at least one full school year behind. Achievement tests suggest this is true but that his poor performance may be caused by his impulsiveness.

The parent interview supported similar conclusions. Ms. Paul has difficulty managing him because he is "all over the place." She also indicated that he lacks judgment. He will apparently do things that disturb other children and not be aware he is offending them. She says that he does not come in from play when he is supposed to and that she cannot get him to take responsibility around the house. Ms. Paul completed a Child Behavior Checklist (see Focus on Assessment: Empirical Assessment—The Achenbach Child Behavior Checklist, page 322), and Tommy received an "often true" or "sometimes true" rating in 9 of the 11 items that assess hyperactivity. The items included the following: can't concentrate, can't pay attention long, can't sit still, confused, daydreams, destroys his own things, impulsive or acts without thinking, poor school work, and prefers playing with younger children. Tommy scored well above the clinical cutoff score for hyperactivity.

Tommy was referred for a psychological evaluation, and the psychologist noted that Tommy could not maintain his attention, although he did stay in his seat. During an IQ task, Tommy gave up very quickly, making the assessment difficult. He also had difficulty maintaining his focus in conversations with the psychologist.

The Wechsler Intelligence Scale for Children-III (WISC-III) indicated that Tommy's overall intelligence is in the average range (FSIQ = 98), with similar verbal (VIQ = 101) and performance ability (PIQ = 99). Tommy's achievement scores show he is slightly below average for his age.

(continued)

Communication

Ms. Paul reports that Tommy can communicate appropriately for his age. She complains that at times Tommy can become a "motor mouth" and will not stop talking after repeated requests for him to do so. Although Tommy has difficulty getting along with peers, he does appear to be able to communicate with them in an age-appropriate manner.

In the clinical child interview, Tommy spoke clearly and loudly to the social worker. Although his language appeared normal, Tommy had difficulty completing his thoughts when responding to questions.

Attitudes and Emotions

Ms. Paul describes Tommy as an unhappy child who has many social problems and gets angry easily. She says that Tommy does have difficulty "controlling his emotions." Ms. Paul reports that Tommy had numerous temper tantrums when he was younger and that he has problems with his anger. As an example, she described a recent incident when Tommy got angry and began throwing his toys against the wall. Ms. Paul noted that it took her at least 20 minutes to get Tommy under control. Ms. Paul reports that Tommy does not easily admit to feelings of sadness; however, he does get into crying spells that last for a long time. She reports no specific fears, saying that at times he appears "fearless." Ms. Paul believes that Tommy is very upset over his father's leaving the family, although he never wants to talk about it. She feels that much of Tommy's current difficulties stem from her divorce.

In the interview with Tommy, he denied feeling lonely or being sad about anything in his life. When asked if he was sad that his parents were no longer together, he said, "They just want to go off and be by themselves." He agreed that sometimes his anger gets him into trouble. "I can really get mad," he said with some pride. Tommy reported that he did have difficulty in school and that he was "bad at school most of

the time." He also did not see himself as able to please his mother at home: "I don't do what she wants me to do." When asked about games and sports, Tommy said, "I am sometimes the best on the team." In general, in many of the domains in Tommy's life, he sees himself as "bad" or "unsuccessful," which is affecting his sense of self-esteem. Themes in the semistructured interview indicated problems with anger, low self-confidence, poor peer relationships, and a lack of interest in school.

Social Cognition and Regulation

Ms. Paul reports that Tommy does not have good judgment. Often it appears that Tommy does not think through the consequences of his actions. On several occasions, Tommy has been excessively cruel to their pet dog. Ms. Paul has consistently tried to explain to Tommy that it is wrong to inflict pain on the dog, yet Tommy does not refrain from being cruel toward the dog. Ms. Paul also reports that Tommy has difficulty getting along with peers partly because he sees them as mean and "always bugging him." Tommy has a difficult time having successful long-term interactions with his peers.

Tommy does not appear to have reciprocal friendships. For example, he does not know anything specific about his best friend's likes or dislikes. When asked, "What is a friend?" Tommy stated, "When you are over at someone's house playing with their things." In the interview with Tommy, he recounted an incident that occurred between him and a neighborhood boy. Tommy was asked how his actions might have made the other boy feel. Tommy could not identify the feeling the other boy would have been likely to have. Tommy's social knowledge of others and his sensitivity to other people's feelings is apparently not well developed.

With regard to adaptive and self-help skills, Tommy seems to have no difficulties. Tommy functions well in terms of daily living skills—he feeds himself, brushes his teeth, and cares for his health. Ms. Paul states that sometimes Tommy has difficulty going to sleep at bedtime and has difficulty getting up in the mornings.

In the semistructured interview, Tommy was presented with a conflicted social situation and asked how he would resolve the problem. He generated two impulsive solutions and could identify only a few of the consequences associated with his solutions. In a role-playing situation that could easily incite a fight, Tommy was asked what he would say or do. His response showed he lacks the skills needed to avoid situations likely to lead to conflict.

On the social competence measure of the Child Behavior Checklist, Tommy scored within the normal range on the activities scale but above the clinical cutoff point on the social and school scales.

SOCIAL CONSIDERATIONS

Family Situation

Ms. Paul and Tommy live together in a low-income African-American neighborhood. Ms. Paul and Tommy's father divorced two years ago. Tommy is an only child. Tommy sees his father about every two weeks. Ms. Paul states that she believes Tommy and his father have a good relationship. Ms. Paul characterized her marriage before the divorce as always in a conflict or fight over something. She reports that Mr. Paul was not abusive toward her or Tommy. Currently, Mr. Paul is contributing money toward child support, although sometimes his payments are late.

Ms. Paul recently got a new job as a sales clerk. She reports that she is happy with her new job and that she has been in good spirits lately. Ms. Paul reports frequent episodes of depression in the past. She has never been hospitalized or received treatment for depression. Although Ms. Paul is involved with her extended family, she states she feels lonely and without close friends. Ms. Paul states she loves to cook and enjoys having others over for dinner. Weekends are often spent with the relatives, fishing, or other planned activities.

Ms. Paul sees Tommy's problems as a result of his poor adjustment to the divorce. She thinks Tommy may be "hyperactive" but is not sure and does not want to put Tommy on "any drugs." Although she has problems with his behavior at home, she believes the school has not really worked with Tommy to help him. Ms. Paul made it very clear that she is not happy with Tommy's school and how it has treated him. She has become increasingly concerned about her ability to manage Tommy. She feels "completely exhausted at having to deal with him after work" and complains of extreme tiredness.

Ms. Paul and Tommy spend a lot of time with Tommy's grandparents. Ms. Paul's mother has "pitched in and helped a lot." Ms. Paul says she doesn't know what she would do without her. However, Tommy's grandfather is a concern. Ms. Paul reports that he has a long-term drinking problem and that she does not like to see Tommy around him when he has been drinking. Although she has discussed this many times with her parents, her father continues to drink sometimes when Tommy is around.

When Tommy was asked to do a family drawing, he stated, "I don't have a whole family." Tommy drew a picture of his mother cooking and him watching TV. He then drew a solid black line and drew a picture of his father. He stated that he and his father don't get to watch TV much.

Groups, Social Supports, and Contexts

Ms. Paul describes Tommy as not well liked by his peers, although he does have a few good friends. She believes Tommy's aggressive behavior affects his ability to get along well with peers. Tommy was rated above the clinical cutoff for aggressive on the Child Behavior Checklist. Ms. Paul noted the following items were of concern: aggressive, brags, cruel to others, demands attention, destroys others' things, disobeys at home, disobeys at school, poor peer relationships, impulsive, shows off, excess talk, teases, temper, and loud. Teacher reports confirm Tommy's difficulty with aggressive behavior.

Ms. Paul and Tommy interact with several social institutions that are of significance. As already noted, Ms. Paul is concerned about Tommy's school. She has gone to a number of teacher conferences, and each time she has felt that the school is unresponsive to her.

(continued)

She believes the teacher is angry because she has not put Tommy on any medication for his hyperactivity. Ms. Paul perceives the school as too large to respond effectively to the needs of the students. Ms. Paul describes Tommy's class as unstructured and too large for one teacher to handle. She also believes that the expectations of students there are extremely low because of where the school is located. Tommy's school is in a low-income neighborhood and is well known for having many social problems. Drug abuse is not uncommon.

Ms. Paul and Tommy regularly go to church. Ms. Paul states this is a very important part of her life. She sees a few of her friends there but wishes she could spend more time getting to know others in the church. Ms. Paul would like to bring better role models into Tommy's life. She is concerned that he will never have a chance at a decent life unless he sees the success some people can attain. Ms. Paul has friends, but without child care she cannot afford to spend much time away from Tommy.

Multicultural and Gender Considerations

Ms. Paul and Tommy live in an old house that is badly in need of repair in a poor, urban African-American neighborhood. Ms. Paul reports that much of the paint inside and outside the house is cracked and peeling. The paint could be lead-based and might account for Tommy's hyperactive behavior (research has found a relationship between high lead levels and attention deficit hyperactivity disorder).

Many of Tommy's peers in the neighborhood have already had associations with the law owing to drug use and vandalism. This leaves few male peer models for Tommy. Ms. Paul is concerned about his lack of "appropriate friends and acquaintances." Much of Tommy's free time appears to be spent playing aggressive sports or watching violent TV shows. Ms. Paul reports she does not monitor the type of TV programs Tommy watches. Ms. Paul feels many of the types of activities and games Tommy plays contribute to his problems because there are no "normal recreational activities for him to play in the neighborhood."

Although Ms. Paul and Tommy live in a primarily African-American neighborhood, Ms. Paul is concerned about Tommy's experiences of prejudice and discrimination. There have been long-standing conflicts among several of the ethnic groups in the nearby neighborhoods. Tommy has been in a number of fights that have occurred because of racial issues. Ms. Paul is also angry that Tommy's school is underfunded and that the teachers have such low expectations of the students.

Ms. Paul and Tommy have limited access to a number of needed resources. Although Ms. Paul has a full-time job, the minimal pay has not allowed her to receive needed health care for Tommy. Their house is crowded, and the peeling paint may be a significant health hazard. Ms. Paul's income level does not allow her to meet her and Tommy's needs adequately. Mr. Paul's late and inconsistent child support payments make budget planning difficult.

SUMMARY AND IMPRESSIONS

Tommy has several problems that have become evident from the assessment:

1. Impulsive and overactive behavior—apparently attention deficit hyperactivity disorder

2. Aggressive behavior—possibly conduct disorder

3. Poor school progress

4. Poor peer relationships and lack of social skills

Additional difficulties include the following:

5. Inadequate health care for Tommy

6. Inadequate and possibly unhealthful living environment

7. Inadequate recreational opportunities

8. Lack of role models

Ms. Paul and Tommy do have a number of personal strengths and resources. Ms. Paul is clearly concerned and motivated to do her best in providing for Tommy. She displays caring and concern over his difficulties. Ms. Paul has successfully provided for Tommy, to the best of her ability. She is perceived as an intelligent, hardworking person who has a lot of concern for others. Ms. Paul has better-than-average parenting skills. Tommy continues to have a successful relationship with his father following his parents' divorce. Ms. Paul also has some social support—especially from the extended family. She is involved in her church and continues to maintain a number of friendships.

and peer groups can be viewed as a series of steps through which children progress. How children think and reason about such concepts can influence their adjustment. Children may benefit from training, such as pair therapy, that helps facilitate such reasoning.

Psychological Hazards

Childhood disorders can be divided into two categories: externalizing problems of overcontrol and internalizing problems of undercontrol. ADHD, an externalizing disorder, is a common disorder that affects a child's attention and activity level. Medication is commonly used to treat this disorder, although some practitioners are concerned about inadequate research, the substitution of medications for behavioral treatments, and the fact that some psychotropic drugs do not seem to work on children.

SOCIAL DIMENSION

Families, Groups, Support Systems, and Communities

By the time a child reaches late childhood, he or she is spending much less time with parents and more time with peers. Still, the family provides children with a safe, authoritative structure that children need. Discipline continues to be critical for good parenting. Three major parental disciplinary strategies are power-assertive discipline, love withdrawal, and induction. Parent training is recommended by social workers for families that are having problems. Four approaches to parent training include parent-effectiveness train-

ing, parent-involvement training, behavior modification, and systematic training for effective parenting.

Children begin to have an increasing preference for spending time with their peers. They begin to form peer groups, which are often referred to as cliques. The process of group formation can have important implications for peer cooperation and respect and peer conflict and/or discrimination. Children who are rejected by their peers are at risk for adjustment problems. The importance of friendships and positive peer relationships has been uncovered by several studies. Friendships may provide for unique learning of critical social skills. Children who are rejected by their peers can be taught the social skills needed for friendship making.

Schools are a major socializing agent. A good school is a community of parents, teachers, and students. Such attributes as good after-school programs, computers in all classrooms, smaller class sizes, high expectations for students as well as teachers, and opportunities for teachers to continue their education will contribute to excellent schools. Effective schools can be differentiated from less effective schools on the basis of their atmosphere and quality as a social institution. A small percentage of children experience school phobia, an anxiety and fear related to being in school. Teacher expectations and a child's self-expectations can influence school performance. Schools have not made many accommodations for disadvantaged students. School social workers must sometimes act as advocates in school-community relationships. U. S. Public Law 94-142, the "bill of rights for the handicapped," or people with disabilities, is a case in point.

Multicultural and Gender Considerations

By middle childhood, racial identity is beginning to form. Families who identify with their ethnic roots are likely to teach their children about their ethnic background. Children's ethnic identity is related to ethnically based behavior, such as cooperation and respect. The effects of racism can influence a child's sense of identity. Rites of passage and mentoring programs are helping young African-American men cope with the difficulties they face from stereotyping and other societal pressures. Through initiation rites, the programs reinforce values such as self-respect, responsibility, and dedication to family, community and one another. Sex-typed behavior begins at this age. Children also begin to develop sex-role stereotypes. Although many stereotypes exist about differences between the sexes, one review study found only four gender differences.

Social Hazards

As in early childhood, in middle childhood divorce is a significant social hazard. Divorce leads most families into a period of crisis and reorganization.

🌐 Online Resources

The Child Survivor of Traumatic Stress
http://www.ummed.edu/pub/k/kfletche/kidsurv.html
> Based on an annual newsletter of the same name, this site provides information for professionals who work with traumatized children. Articles on the site are selections from earlier issues of the newsletter, with some updated or expanded for online readers. Online links to other trauma-related websites are also provided.

National Clearinghouse for Bilingual Education
http://www.ncbe.gwu.edu
> Provide information on language education for minority students, bilingual education, and English as a Second Language (ESL).

The United States Department of Education
http://www.ed.gov
> Includes information on the Administration's priorities, funding opportunities, student financial aid assistance, research and statistics, news and events, and so forth.

Center for Effective Collaboration and Practice (CECP)
http://www.air-dc.org/cecp/default.htm
> This site provides ways to improve services to children and youth with emotional and behavioral problems.

National Information Center for Children and Youth with Disabilities (NICHCY)
Speech Delays and Disorders
http://pages.cthome.net/cbristol/capd-gnl.html
> NICHCY is an information and referral center that provides free information on disabilities and disability-related issues. It provides personal responses to specific questions, publications, informational searches, and technical assistance.

InfoTrac® College Edition

For interesting materials related to what you have just read, please go to the *InfoTrac College Edition* website and search using the following key words:

bilingual education	school performance
refugee children	childhood friendship
sign language	emotional IQ

Key Terms

acculturation	Das-Luria model of
attention deficit	cognitive
hyperactivity	functioning
disorder (ADHD)	emotional
bilingual	intelligence (EQ)
conservation	externalizing
cretinism	problems

Individualized Education
   Plan (IEP)
induction
intelligence quotient
intention-cue detection
internalizing problems
learned helplessness

logical consequences
love withdrawal
mental age
metacognition
metalinguistic awareness
natural consequences
peer groups

power assertive
   discipline
readiness
reversibility
rickets
role-taking ability
school phobia

sex-role stereotype
sex-typed behavior
social cognition
uninformative messages
verbal control

Developmental Themes

Stage: identity vs. identity confusion. Independence from parents, increased emphasis on peer-group relations, preoccupation with self, changing body image.

Biophysical Dimension

Biophysical Growth and Development	Increased intellectual and physical ability; stronger, greater coordination and endurance; development of secondary sex characteristics, onset of menstrual cycle/nocturnal emissions.
Biophysical Hazards	Obesity, acne, headaches, meeting the proper nutritional needs.

Psychological Dimension

Cognitive Development and Information Processing	Formal operations, more abstract thinking, hypothetical reasoning, logical consistency.
Communication	Renewed interest in language, use of metaphors and satire, more organized communication, journal writing for more personalized communication.
Attitudes and Emotions	Identity formation, increased emotional intensity and fluctuations, changes in self-esteem, increased self-awareness and self-reflection, identity and independence.
Social Cognition and Regulation	Moral development moves from interpersonal conformity to responsibility to the system, egocentric thought evidenced by the imaginary audience and the personal fable, growth of social awareness.
Psychological Hazards	Conduct disorder, antisocial behavior, depression, suicidal attempts or rumination, eating disorders.

Social Dimension

Families, Groups, Support Systems, and Communities	Family influences, control and autonomy within the parent-adolescent relationship, parenting styles, stronger peer-group affiliation, popularity, development of cliques and crowds, potential gang involvement, transition to middle schools, motivation in high school.
Multicultural and Gender Considerations	Gender-role development, heterosexuality and homosexuality.
Social Hazards	Adolescents at risk, adolescent pregnancy, adolescent fathers, sexually transmitted diseases, alcohol and other drug use, delinquency.

Adolescence

DEVELOPMENTAL THEMES

On a beautiful spring evening in San Francisco, I stood at the intersection of Sutter and Polk streets, a cheerful, crowded jumble of boutiques and bookstores, head shops and bead shops, restaurants, and bars. The corner was thronged with students and tourists, straights and gays, and bunches of teenagers leaning against the window of a pizza shop. They wore uniforms and insignia of their various tribes: leather-clad punks, California surfers, Eastern preppies, suburban gypsies, and born-again hippies. Boys and girls laughed and joked and jostled and pushed one another with the rough physical affection with which kids treat their friends and fellow tribes people (Hersch, 1990, p. 19).

America's adolescents attract a lot of attention in their exuberance to establish an identity. Adolescence represents the journey of discovery—Who am I? How am I different from others? What do I want to do with my life? Erikson's theory of adolescent identity recognized this almost universal phenomenon.

But what is life like for today's adolescents? Our society offers a wealth of opportunities for young people to explore their place in society; modern technology has brought endless hours of watching MTV, Internet connections to the world, better physical health, and improved education. Yet, young people must also face head-on the ills that modern society brings with it—

AIDS, violence, exposure to alcohol and drugs, bombardment of media images, and hopelessness.

In spite of our changing society, the tasks that adolescents face have remained stable. In essence, adolescents must carve out their place in the world. And many of the problems young people face are not problems with themselves but the result of reduced opportunities and lack of support from caring adults (Santrock, 1996).

Adolescence is typically defined as the period of growth beginning about 10–12 years of age and ending around 21–22 years of age. Researchers studying adolescent development believe it is important to consider adolescence in terms of early and late periods. Early adolescence begins around ages 10–15 and is characterized by important physical changes and significant cognitive and social changes (see Box 9.1). In particular, early adolescents place great importance on peer approval. Late adolescence begins around the ages of 16–18 and continues up to approximately 22 years of age. During late adolescence, two developmental tasks are considered important: independence from the family and the development of personal identity. Erikson refers to this stage as one of *identity versus identity confusion.*

Adolescence is a period when young people become concerned about their physical appearance. In addition, they are concerned about how other people perceive how they look. They become aware of the fact that their bodies are developing; girls will have their first menstrual cycle, and boys may have their first nocturnal emission.

BIOPHYSICAL DIMENSION

Biophysical Growth and Development

Boys and girls at this stage of development both experience what is referred to as an adolescent growth spurt, whereby rapid gains in height and weight occur. However, the growth spurt occurs two years earlier for girls than for boys. The growth spurt for girls begins at about age 10 and lasts for about two years. For boys, it begins at age 12 and also lasts for about two years.

Puberty	Adult appearance and size	Parents	Parental responses to adult size of adolescent
	Reproductive capacity		
	Timing (especially if off-time)		Sexual stimulation of newly pubertal child
	Internal endocrine changes		
	Asynchrony (among body parts, among adolescents		Implications for parent's aging
			Impending separation
Cognition	Capacity for abstract thought	Society	Hope and expectations for youth
Peer groups	Conformity		Occupational choices and opportunities
	Pressure to try new experiences		
School	Changing school structure and format	(Petersen, Kennedy, & Sullivan, 1991)	

There is considerable individual variability, so girls could begin the growth spurt as early as 7 and boys as early as 9. Adolescents gain weight at the same rate at which they gain height.

THE PUBERTAL PROCESS

Biologically, adolescence begins with the onset of puberty. This process defines sexual maturity, or the capacity to make babies. **Puberty** is identified by the combination of the growth spurt, the maturation of physiological mechanisms, and the development of secondary sex characteristics, such as pubic hair and breasts (Adams & Gullotta, 1989). Although menstruation is one indication of puberty for girls, there is no clear indication for boys. Wet dreams and facial hair can indicate puberty in boys, but they may go unnoticed. Table 9.1 summarizes the changes that take place for boys and girls in the pubertal period.

The onset of puberty for girls has been occurring at an earlier age since it was first recorded in the 1800s. In particular, records from Norway in the 1840s show that **menarche,** the first menstruation, occurred at age 17, whereas today it occurs at age 13. In the United States, the average age for menarche has declined to 12.45 years of age. This dramatic change in the age of menarche decreased an average of four months every ten years during the 20th century. Why are girls prepared for childbirth at an earlier

age today? Although there are no clear answers, most experts believe the earlier onset is a result of a better standard of living, medical advances, and improved nutrition.

The following Focus section examines how the Apache ceremony honors the young woman who reaches the childbearing years.

FOCUS ON MULTICULTURALISM

▼

The Apache Ceremony of the Changing Woman

When an Apache girl reaches childbearing years, she is honored with a traditional ceremony of the changing woman. This ceremony comes from the Apache goddess White Painted Woman, who declared this event significant in the lives of the people: "Let all the people come together. Let them eat and dance and have a good time. The Masked Dancers will come forth at night, and then the People will dance with each other, side by side and face to face."

The four-day ceremony is one of the tribe's most private ceremonies. In preparation, the father sends announcements to friends and family. The girl undergoes instruction from an attendant who guides the maiden

TABLE 9.1	Physical Changes of the Pubertal Period		
Step	Females	Both Sexes	Males
1		Apocrine gland development	
2	Increased diameter of internal pelvis	Pelvic changes	Thickening and strengthening of bone structure
3	Growth of ovaries and uterus	Growth in gonads	Growth of testes and scrotum
4		Breast enlargement	
5		Appearance of pubic hair	
6	Growth of labia and vagina	Growth of external genitalia	Growth of penis
7	Menarche	External puberty	Nocturnal emissions
8		Axillary hair	
9	Oogenesis, ovulation	True puberty	Spermatogenesis, sperm in urine and semen
10	Broadening of hips	Broadening of body frame; vocal changes	Broadening of shoulders

(Schuster & Ashburn, 1992, p. 499)

in proper behavior. A special dressmaker constructs the clothes based on the original garments worn by the White Painted Woman. The garments are dyed pollen yellow, a symbol of fertility. Food is gathered and made to accommodate all the guests.

The ceremony begins in the morning with the washing of the maiden's hair with yucca roots. The attendant gives traditional advice (Mildred & Hooper, 1993):

> Be happy so your people may be happy. Don't talk too much, or you'll always be a talker. Don't be cross, or you'll always be a nag. Don't laugh too much, or your face will wrinkle soon. Don't allow water to touch your lips, or the skies will weep and everybody will not have a good time. Don't think bad thoughts, or you'll have evil to the end of your days (p. 64).

The White Painted Woman's holy home, or wickiup, is made of four spruce poles that are lashed together. The maiden enters her home and is now the personification of White Painted Woman. She now has supernatural powers. She lies down on deerskin and is massaged to become supple and possess good health. The shaman and special dancers perform rituals. As the sun rises, the woman faces east, and the shaman paints her face with white clay, using an eagle feather. She becomes "White Painted Woman" and is again painted with pollen and runs in four directions. As she leaves the wickiup for the last time, it is pulled down and

pushed to the east. Favors are tossed to the children, and her parents can now accept marriage proposals.

(Mildred & Hooper, 1993)

HORMONAL CHANGES IN ADOLESCENCE

During adolescence, the **endocrine glands** produce **hormones** that create various bodily changes in the young person. Table 9.1 outlines the physical changes that take place in males, in females, and in both sexes. Hormones are powerful chemical substances that regulate various organs in the body. The endocrine glands that secrete the sex hormones are the pituitary gland and the sex glands, or gonads, referred to as testes in the male and ovaries in the female. The pituitary gland, or master gland, regulates a number of the other glands. Control of the pituitary gland rests with the **hypothalamus,** which "instructs" the pituitary gland on the optimal level of hormone secretion. The hormones secreted by the pituitary gland are known as **gonadotropins,** and they activate the **testes** and the **ovaries,** which are the parts of the endocrine system called the *gonads*. The gonads secrete hormones— **androgen** from the testes and **estrogen** from the ovaries. These hormones have an important effect on puberty in adolescence. Their effect is gradual as the hormones are gradually secreted and the child moves toward physical and sexual maturity. The hormonal changes take place about a year before changes in the body and sex organs are visible (Daniel, 1983).

Implications for Practice: Physical Changes and Psychological Consequences

Physical changes have psychological consequences for developing boys and girls. With girls, menarche is associated with increased social maturity, improved status among peers, increased self-esteem, greater self-awareness regarding one's body, and increased self-consciousness (Brooks-Gunn, 1986; Petersen, 1987). These psychological changes are convincingly described in the following entry from *The Diary of Anne Frank* (1952):

> I think what is happening to me is so wonderful, and not only what can be seen on my body, but all that is taking place inside. I never discuss myself or any of these things with anybody; that is why I have to talk to myself about them.
>
> Each time I have a period—and that has only been three times—I have the feeling that in spite of all the pain, unpleasantness, and nastiness, I have a sweet secret, and that is why, although it is nothing but a nuisance to me in a way, I always long for the time that I shall feel that secret within me again.

However, puberty can be related to both positive and negative emotions. In one study (Petersen, 1987), an early-maturing girl exclaimed, "I tried to hide it. I was embarrassed and ashamed." A study by Brooks-Gunn and Ruble (1983) found that an equal percentage of girls had positive emotions about menarche, negative emotions, mixed emotions, or neutral emotions. One factor that influences whether a girl's reaction will be positive or negative is early or late maturation.

Studies have found that, in general, it is better to be an early-maturing boy rather than a late-maturing one. Research has found that early-maturing boys perceived themselves more positively, had more successful peer relationships, and were more confident when compared with late-maturing boys (Petersen, 1987; Simmons & Blyth, 1987). For girls, early maturation seems to have mixed effects. Early-maturing girls (maturity defined as onset of menstruation) did not do as well academically and were more likely to have behavior problems than late-maturing ones. However, early maturity brought with it an advantage in terms of in-

dependence and opposite-sex relationships. Early development was initially related to a positive body image, but this pattern was reversed when the girls entered the ninth grade, which may be due to the fact that early-maturing girls are shorter and stockier, whereas late-maturing girls are often taller and thinner.

These studies clearly demonstrate that the physical changes that take place in boys' and girls' bodies can lead to positive or negative reactions. An explanation for many of the negative reactions is that the young people were not prepared for the changes they experienced (Brooks-Gunn & Ruble, 1983). Most girls describe their first period as "a little upsetting." Although girls often receive some preparation, boys receive little or no preparation for their experiences of nocturnal emissions and spontaneous erections. What can be done to better prepare young people for these impending changes in their bodies? Better information from sex education programs or from parents could be helpful in creating a more positive adjustment for adolescents. A cross-cultural perspective indicates that for girls menarche is a sign of womanhood (Weideger, 1976); therefore, it is surprising that in the United States we do not treat a girl's first menses as a **rite of passage.** A ritualized recognition may be beneficial in helping young persons experience their bodily change as positive (Adams & Gullotta, 1989). Consider the family ritual one girl reported (Shipman, 1968):

> When I discovered it, I called my mother and she showed me what to do. Then she did something I'll never forget. She told me to come with her and went to the living room to tell my father. She just looked at me and then at him and said, "Well, your little girl is a young lady now." My dad gave me a hug and congratulated me, and I felt grown up and proud that I really was a lady at last. That was one of the most exciting days of my life. I was so excited and happy (pp. 6–7).

Although puberty clearly has an effect on adolescent development, many researchers are concluding that the it is not as strong as it was once believed to be (Brooks-Gunn & Warren, 1985; Petersen, 1987). Within the overall framework of the life cycle, puberty clearly has a significant effect, but so do other phases of the life cycle. For some young people puberty is stressful, but for most it is not. New challenges result from the biological changes, but there are also cognitive, social, and environmental changes to be dealt with. Biological change may not be the single source of significant change.

Biophysical Hazards

Although adolescence is typically a period of good general health, it is also the beginning of some potentially serious health concerns. In particular, many adolescents experience problems with nutritional needs and eating habits, weight concerns, dysmenorrhea, acne, and headaches.

NUTRITIONAL NEEDS AND EATING HABITS

A proper diet and physical exercise are especially important for young people. The rapid development young people experience engenders an increased need for nutrients (Sallis, 1993)—witness the hungry teenager wolfing down a burger, fries, and a large shake. Adolescents need to increase their caloric intake to match their rate of growth. Their caloric intake can be so enormous that it often angers parents who have to provide the food. An adolescent male who is involved in sports may need as many as 6,000 calories in one day (Schuster & Ashburn, 1992). Thus, a critical question is whether the adolescent is getting his or her nutritional needs met. Often, adolescents do not get the proper nutritional diet. They frequently miss a meal, usually breakfast, and may fill up on high-energy snacks rather than eating a proper meal. In fact, it is estimated that up to one-third of a young person's calories come from snack foods (Marrale, Shipman, & Rhodes, 1986). Although adolescents may get the calories they need, it is not uncommon for them to lack the proper amount of fluid, protein, iron, and calcium.

Adolescents' protein consumption should make up 12–16% of their total daily energy intake (Schuster & Ashburn, 1992). Adequate calcium intake is also a concern. Boys may not get enough calcium during periods of rapid skeletal growth, and girls, when weight-conscious, may unknowingly reduce their calcium intake. Also, over-consumption of soft drinks may interfere with obtaining enough calcium. Studies have found that caffeine and sugar in a soda can cause a 30-mg calcium loss three hours after consumption

(Marrale, Shipman, & Rhodes, 1986). The female adolescent's iron levels may be low from blood loss during menses; an iron supplement may be recommended.

WEIGHT CONCERNS

Obesity can be a serious problem for adolescents. **Obesity** can be defined as a body weight of 20% or more above the recommended weight for one's height. It is a serious health problem that is associated with certain diseases, high blood pressure, and social and psychological problems. In adolescence, obesity is a serious social problem because of the name-calling, stigma, and rejection by peers that many obese young people experience. Many children prior to adolescence develop extra fat in response to the adolescent growth spurt and, once additional fats cells are formed, they may predispose the person toward obesity (Schuster & Ashburn, 1992). In fact, eating behaviors established in adolescence carry into adulthood; 80% of obese adolescents become obese adults (Sigman & Flanery, 1992).

DYSMENORRHEA

Dysmenorrhea is the experience of painful menstruation. It occurs in approximately 33% of adolescent females once ovulation occurs (Schuster & Ashburn, 1992). Dysmenorrhea is experienced as spasmodic uterine or lower abdominal and back pain during the first 12 to 24 hours of the menstrual flow. Dysmenorrhea is probably caused by contraction of the smooth muscles and lack of oxygen to the uterine muscles (Schuster & Ashburn, 1992). It often disappears after the female reaches 24 years of age, when the uterus is completely mature, or after the birth of a baby.

ACNE

A common problem in adolescence is acne, occurring in more than 80% of adolescents. Acne is the result of increased androgen levels at puberty, which stimulate the production of sebum by the sebaceous glands of the body, usually the face. Most adolescents start to experience a decline in acne sometime after their 20th birthday. Acne is associated with genetic predisposition, but it is also related to accumulated oils in the body. Acne can be a concern because it can lead to scarring of the tissue and can create embarrassment and social withdrawal. In recent years, antibiotics have been used to control the spread of acne.

HEADACHE

By the time people reach adolescence, they most likely have experienced a headache. In fact, headaches can begin to occur with some frequency—29% of boys and 32% of girls have at least one headache per month during adolescence (Linet et al., 1989). Approximately 5% of boys and girls experience migraine headaches during adolescence.

PSYCHOLOGICAL DIMENSION

Cognitive Development and Information Processing

Cognitive development in adolescence is identified with Piaget's last intellectual stage—formal operations. This period of development generally begins at around age 11 or 12. At this stage of development, the adolescent is capable of abstract thought; before this stage, the child could use only **concrete thinking.** Now a whole new world is opened up within the adolescent's mind—flexible and abstract thinking. Adolescents begin to understand abstract propositions and try to reason logically about them. This kind of logical problem solving is referred to as **hypothetical-deductive reasoning.** This problem-solving process uses hunches, or hypotheses, to solve a problem and follows a planned manner to test and evaluate the hypotheses until the best solution is discovered.

In fact, adolescents may begin to ponder the nature of their own thinking. They can think about why they were thinking about certain things. This kind of abstract thinking is also associated with idealism and thoughts about future possibilities.

Why do adolescents often concern themselves with such things as future life plans, their internal life, or developing their own ideology? Piaget (1972) would argue that this type of thinking is caused by the characteristics of formal operational thought, which leads adolescents to engage in such thoughts. They can now think beyond the real to the possible and reflect on the nature of thought itself. For example, an adolescent girl might think, "What would it be like if Jack and I were married? I shouldn't think about Jack that way; I should think about what I want from him now."

Formal operational thought is believed to occur in two distinct stages during adolescence. The first stage is characterized by a focus on the ideal, with unlimited possibilities. This stage is referred to as *assimilation*—the adolescent consolidates new information into existing knowledge. During middle adolescence, a better balance is obtained through the process of *accommodation*—the adolescent must adjust to the cognitive changes that have occurred. By the time of late formal operational thought adolescents test their reasoning against experience and their formal operational thinking matures (Lapsley, 1989). Table 9.2 presents a summary of the five major changes that occur with formal operational thinking (Keating, 1980).

Although Piaget's theory emphasizes a universal understanding of thought, individual variations do occur in adolescents' cognitive development. For example, research by Strahan (1983) found that only one out of three eighth-grade students is capable of formal operational thinking. A critical factor in such thinking is the adolescent's experience and knowledge in certain areas (Flavell, 1985). Children and adolescents gradually build up knowledge through experience and practice (Santrock, 1990).

FOCUS ON MULTICULTURALISM

Racial Differences and Intellectual Ability

Block and Moore (1986) conducted a study using the Armed Services Vocational Aptitude Battery, which is a measure of intellectual potential. Items from the test are based on general knowledge and information and problem-solving abilities. The test involved more

TABLE 9.2 Examples of Formal Operations and Logic in Adolescence	
Major Changes in Thinking	**Examples**
Thinking about possibilities	"I would like to get to know her even better—she could be a good friend, or I might decide she'd be good as a girlfriend. We like each other. We can work out a closer relationship."
Testing hypotheses	"She told me she wasn't interested in being my girlfriend. After that I thought girls just don't like me, that I'm not good enough looking or cool enough. But I've had other girlfriends and other girls have shown interest in me. Not all girls are going to like me—I just need to find the right girl for me."
Thinking about the future	"I have a girlfriend now, and we get along really well, but if we stay together, I won't know what it's like to be with other girls. In order to marry the best person, it seems that you need to have a lot of girlfriends."
Thinking about thoughts	"I keep thinking about how much other people like me. Am I really popular with other kids? But even if I'm not that popular, I've got a lot of good friends. I shouldn't worry so much about whether I'm popular and just keep the good friends I have."
Expansion of thought	"I was invited to a party, but my best friend, Tyler, wasn't. John, who's giving the party, doesn't like Tyler. If I tell Tyler, then he'll be mad at John—and John told me not to let him know. But if Tyler asks me, I don't want to lie to him. I don't know if I should keep my promise to John and lie to Tyler."

than 12,000 male and female adolescents from a national sample. The data provides a good comparison among the three largest sociocultural groups in the United States: Caucasians, African-Americans, and Hispanics. The results found considerable differences across the three adolescent racial groups; however, the minority adolescents scored, on the average, lower than the majority adolescents. When socioeconomic status was controlled for, less disparate results were discovered. The authors present a *community-norm* theory to explain the observed differences, which, they believe, are related to schools as part of a local community or ecological system. Community standards set a limit on what schools can achieve.

Block and Moore (1986) state:

Children whose horizons are limited respond primarily to the norms of the community in which they play their part. These norms determine most of their speech, conduct, interests, aspirations, and motivations. The average effect of such determinants of behavior can be greatly different in communities that, for historical reasons, have been separated from the majority culture by barriers of communication and cultural interchange for many generations (p. 175).

The differences observed among the groups can be understood by the different local norms that influence performance. Differences may also be explained by "academic disidentification," which is what happens when a student no longer feels encouraged by academic success or discouraged by academic failure. According to researchers (Osborne, 1997), this community norm explains what happens to young African-American males between middle school and high school. Osborne believes that, because these young men experience negative stereotypes about their academic abilities, they develop anxiety and therefore withdraw from schoolwork. Interestingly, as these boys' grades and test scores drop, their self-esteem remains stable. Self-esteem is instead tied to their peers' perceptions of them and their athletic success. In contrast, Osborne found that Hispanic girls became more invested in their academic performance during high school. Why is this happening?

Communication

Along with an improvement in thinking abilities in adolescence comes a greater capacity for effective communication. The manner of a person's thinking is logically related to his or her ability to use language. For example, the use of metaphors increases during this time period. A metaphor is a comparison of two ideas, such as "he has a heart of stone." To understand metaphors, one must think beyond concrete operations; therefore, fables or parables are not of interest to elementary school children (Elkind, 1976).

Also of particular interest in adolescence is the use of satire or ridicule (Santrock, 1996). Adolescents typically invent satirical labels for teachers, parents, and peers. For example, peers may be known as "klutz," "brain," or "Mr. Heavy Metal."

Writing becomes much more meaningful in adolescence. Indeed, this is the age when many young people begin a journal to record their inner thoughts and personal experiences. Younger children have difficulty writing because they do not have the type of logical thought processes needed to organize their ideas. Adolescents are able to accentuate the important points they are trying to communicate because they can think logically about what they want to say before they write it down.

During adolescence, the nature of boys' talk and girls' talk begins to become increasingly differentiated, as described by one adolescent boy (Eckert, 1990):

> I think girls must talk too much, you know, they— they—talk constantly between themselves and about every little thing. Guys, I don't think we talk about that much. (*What kinds of things do you talk about?*) Not much. Girls . . . cars, or parties, you know. I think girls talk about, you know, every little relationship, every little thing that's ever happened, you know (p. 91).

In general, it appears that boys talk more in terms of competitive conversation, comparing knowledge and experience, whereas girls talk more about themselves, their personal feelings, and their relationships.

Attitudes and Emotions

Adolescence is an important period for developing self-concept. Young people set out to discover "who they are" and "what they want to become." A significant part of this process results from a focus on self-reflection and thought. And indeed there is much for the young adolescent to think about. Adolescents obtain greater freedom in behavior and decision making, increased opportunities for both acceptance and rejection by peer groups, experience in dating and the awareness of their sexuality, and major decisions af-

fecting their movement into adult life. As these experiences are explored and reflected on, the adolescent develops a more integrated self.

The founder of developmental psychology, G. Stanley Hall, is well known for his characterization of adolescence as a time of "storm and stress." In her writings, Anna Freud argued that such storm and stress are simply a part of normal adolescence. Psychoanalyst Peter Blos also believed that adolescence was a period of uncontrolled sexual and aggressive impulses. However, these early notions about the craziness of the teenage years are now considered to be myth. Experts in adolescent psychology (see, for example, Adelson, Douvan, Offer, and Bandura) are increasingly concerned because the widespread idea that adolescence is a normal period of serious difficulty has mischaracterized the lives of millions of healthy adolescents. Daniel Offer, a psychiatrist specializing in adolescence, brought attention to this myth when he declared a "Defense of Adolescence." Although it is difficult for many people to believe, research has empirically supported the fact that the majority of adolescents are well adjusted, get along well with peers and parents, and cope well with their emotional processes and external environments.

For purposes of studying the issues with which social workers and mental health professionals come in contact most often, this chapter focuses mostly on the deviant behaviors and alternative attitudes of teenagers. However, we should remember that the majority of teens are not like the ones this text uses as examples.

ADOLESCENT SELF-ESTEEM

Self-esteem is a global evaluation of one's self, often referred to as *self-image* or *self-concept*. What does research on adolescent self-esteem tell us about adjustment in adolescence? In general, we find that self-esteem can vary depending on the stage of adolescence. It is during early adolescence (age 12–14 years) that self-esteem appears to be at its lowest point (Simmons, Rosenberg, & Rosenberg, 1973). During these years, young people are highly self-conscious, and their self-perceptions are easily influenced. This is especially true of girls making the transition to junior high school. The lowest self-esteem occurs among girls who mature early and start to date (Simmons, Rosenberg, & Rosenberg, 1973). However, overall, most adolescents emerge from this developmental phase with about the same amount of self-esteem as they had at the outset (Dusek & Flaherty, 1981).

One interesting study attempted to examine the emotional life of adolescents during their daily life. Researchers Csikszentmihalyi and Larson (1984) asked 75 adolescents to wear electronic pagers for one week. When they were signaled, about every two hours, they completed a log about where they were, how they felt, and what they were experiencing. One conclusion derived from the study was that adolescents experience a remarkable amount of diversity. They may be a student, a helper, an employee, a commuter, a child, a teammate, a friend, and more. Also remarkable is that the average adolescent can come down from extreme happiness or up from extreme sadness within 45 minutes.

This situation contrasts with adults, who often take hours to change from one mood to the next. The researchers suggest that adolescents must learn to come to terms with the downs as well as the ups. Instead of allowing the down to completely overtake them, they need to strive for greater balance and perspective. Many young people, in response to boredom, become involved in less productive and less satisfying activities like watching television. However, those who take up more challenging activities learn the positive feelings of personal fulfillment that can result from such challenges.

Foster children, who tend to move around often from one family unit to another, may have an even harder time adjusting to adolescence and therefore suffer in their self-image. The following Focus section discusses male foster care adolescents and their self-image.

FOCUS ON RESEARCH

Foster Care Adolescents' Self-Image

In adolescence, self-esteem has been shown to be influenced by parental support, parental control, and parental participation; perceptions of family cohesion; and a sense of belonging to one's family. Consistent with these findings, low self-esteem has been found to be a characteristic of foster care children, with weakened family ties being associated with low-self-esteem and identity confusion. The dismal fact is that more than 98% of foster care children enter care because of some family dysfunction.

There is some evidence that removal from a dysfunctional family may increase self-esteem because of a reduction in the inconsistent interactions and conflict that characterize many dysfunctional families. However, foster children are at a higher risk of both psychosocial and medical problems. These relate to the high incidence of behavior problems and school problems in this population. Because of these conflicting findings, there is controversy over recent social work practice and policy that view foster care as a last resort because of the perception that the harmful effects of removal from the home outweigh the benefits.

The pattern of loss experienced by foster care children, including the loss of family, peer relationships, and community, is likely to influence the way they view themselves. In fact, self-esteem, as a major determinant of general mental health, could play a role in the resilience of foster care youths. Given the controversy over the use of foster care as an intervention and the effects that this debate has on placement decisions, it would be valuable to know how foster care youths value themselves and perceive their foster care experience.

Researchers found that the pattern of loss typically experienced by foster care children is likely to influence the way they view themselves. Research shows that, when family support is low, social relationships gain importance. Therefore, removal from a high-conflict family situation and placement in foster care may provide the opportunity to develop other supportive relationships that can then be used to develop a positive image.

In addition, the number of placements was consistent as the strongest explainer of self-image in the domains of morals and family relations, consistent with research that shows that low self-esteem is related to multiple placements. For example, multiple placements may affect perception of morals by introducing inconsistent standards of behavior each time the youth changes placements. If the standards of "good" behavior keep changing, it is less likely that foster care youths will gain an awareness of their intrinsic value.

Length of time in the current placement was also a factor in self-image domains of morals and vocational and educational goals. A lengthy stay in a stable foster care placement was negatively related to self-image. One possible explanation is that, because the ultimate goal of foster care is to return the child to the family, a lengthy stay in foster care may be detrimental to the adolescent. It appears that, the longer a young person remains in care, the less likely he or she is to return to the family. As many as one in four adolescents will remain in foster care until late adolescence, when they "age out" of the system or exit care by means such as running away, being incarcerated, or entering a psychiatric hospital.

Academic achievement was an explainer of self-image in two domains: vocational and educational goals, and emotional health. Foster care adolescents who were behind in school had low self-image, supporting previous research that school achievement is positively related to self-concept. This is a particularly important finding with regard to foster care youths because of the increased risk of school failure in this population. In the face of family disruption and loss, academic achievement is often portrayed as a secondary problem for these youths and may be allocated less attention and fewer resources than are necessary to overcome this deficit. Earlier research (Festinger, 1986) has shown that, as adults, this population maintains an educational achievement deficit that affects income and standard of living, which makes it even more critical that this issue be addressed early on in care.

So, what are the implications of this research? In general, foster care placement as an intervention for older adolescents should be reconsidered as an alternative. Youths that are experiencing deficits in the realms of family relations and mental health should have resources that specifically address these issues. This is especially important if there is a relationship between poor self-image in the emotional health domain in adolescence and low adult functioning and sense of well-being. The results also support the belief that multiple placements can create risk. Efforts aimed at stabilizing placements need to be paramount in the placement decision process. Finally, stable placements that provide opportunities for adolescents to achieve and to form supportive relationships may even be able to compensate for problems in other life areas.

Misha Marvel (Based on Courtney & Barth, 1996; Lyman & Bird, 1996.)

Implications for Practice: Enhancing Adolescents' Self-Concept

There are four main strategies for enhancing adolescents' self-concept: (1) encouraging achievement, (2) promoting competencies in specific areas, (3) providing peer and parental support, and (4) developing coping skills. Adolescents can improve their self-concept so that it moves closer to the concept of their ideal self. Also, many young people need to challenge the reality of their ideal self. Is it realistic to hope for such high standards? Many adolescents begin the process of insisting on irrational standards of behavior. Believing in "shoulds" and "musts" can take the place of recognizing real accomplishments. Adolescents who are taught to recall positive thoughts and feelings about past events show an increase in self-esteem (Anderson & Williams, 1985).

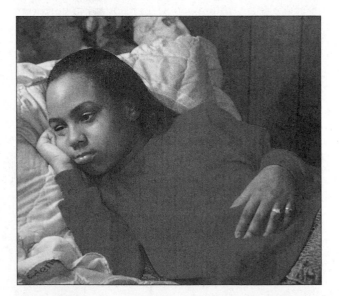

In early adolescence, young people who are self-conscious can easily develop negative self-perceptions. These self-perceptions sometimes lead to depression, a common problem in adolescence.

Adolescents can be guided to emphasize the areas in which they are likely to succeed. A less physically coordinated young person can become more skilled in playing a musical instrument or in playing a game that requires intellectual skills. The results of assertiveness-training studies with young people show an increase in self-esteem (Stake, DeVille, & Rennell, 1983). Sometimes adolescents need to work harder at achieving their standards of excellence or to accept a good performance instead of a perfect one (Schuster & Ashburn, 1992).

Self-esteem is also related to other factors such as peer group formation. Studies find that self-esteem is improved by both peer and parental support (Robinson, 1995) and by participation in community and school experiences (Harter, 1990). Such experiences through participation can enhance an adolescent's self-esteem.

Coping abilities relate to both enhanced self-esteem and reduced stress (Hetherington & Blechman, 1996; Lazarus, 1991). When adolescents use coping abilities to solve problems, the result is often positive self-evaluations and increased self-esteem. When taught coping strategies, adolescents learn to face problems realistically and honestly (Compas, 1995).

The following Focus section examines self-esteem of a particular group, African-Americans.

FOCUS ON MULTICULTURALISM

▼

Do African-American Adolescents Have Low Self-Esteem?

Although one might expect that African-American adolescents might have lower self-esteem than majority white youths, the issue is complex and not clear-cut. In the 1960s, during the period of school desegregation, it was believed that African-American children suffered damage to their self-esteem because they were in segregated schools. However, research that examined this issue found that there were no differences in self-esteem between African-American children in segregated and desegregated schools (Cook, 1979). Adolescents of color do experience greater discrimination, poverty, and social and educational barriers than

white youths do, and, as a result, we can predict more negative outcomes for African-American adolescents. However, as Gibbs (1990) points out, social workers must be careful about over-pathologizing and stereotyping all African-American youth as victims of their racial identity or social class status. The majority of African-American youth cope effectively with their ethnicity and social class status. Furthermore, research has found no differences in self-esteem between non-clinical samples of African-American youth and white youth (Gibbs, 1985; Rosenberg & Simmons, 1971). Chestang (1980) suggests that there is a dichotomy between "personal identity" and "racial identity." Self-esteem is related more closely to the various characteristics the adolescent subscribes to the self. Such things as physical attractiveness, peer popularity, and pride in identification with a religious or racial group have a strong influence on self-esteem. Family support is the best predictor of self-esteem.

More recent research (McCreary, Slavin, & Berry, 1996) notes that African-American adolescents constantly hear blacks described as criminals, drug users, absent fathers, and adolescent mothers. Adolescents who accept those negative views of African-Americans may be slightly more likely to act negatively and to have a lower self-esteem than those who don't hold these views. However, adolescents who hold positive attitudes about their own race may be partially protected against negative stereotypes and may be better prepared to withstand internal and/or external pressured to behave and feel negatively. Nonetheless, the problems facing African-American adolescents are multifaceted and complex. Thus, research must explore the role that contextual variables such as underemployment, lack of education, and crime play in stress and self-esteem in African-American adolescents.

Social Cognition and Regulation

Adolescence is believed to be an important time for the development of identity. Young people seek to answer important questions about themselves. Who am I? What is important to me in my life? These types of questions represent the stage of life that Erikson characterized as identity versus identity confusion. Young people enter what Erikson calls a **psychological moratorium**—a gap between childhood security and adult autonomy. Erikson's ideas were extended by James Marcia (1966), who developed a classification system for adolescent identity statuses, or modes of resolution:

TABLE 9.3	Examples of Questionnaire Items Used in Measuring Ego-Identity Status
Status	**Item**
Diffusion	I haven't chosen the occupation I really want to get into, but I'm working toward becoming a _____ until something better comes along.
Foreclosure	I've never really questioned my religion. If it's right for my parents, it must be right for me.
Moratorium	I just can't decide how capable I am as a person and what jobs I'll be right for.
Identity Achievement	A person's faith is unique to each individual. I've considered and reconsidered it myself and know what I can believe.

(Adams & Gullotta, 1989, p. 241)

- *Identity diffusion:* This is the least mature status for the adolescent to be in. Adolescents at this stage have not yet experienced a crisis; that is, they are not exploring meaningful alternatives. No commitments have been made to important attitudes, values, or plans for the future.

- *Identity foreclosure:* In this stage, adolescents have made a commitment to particular goals, values, and beliefs but have not yet experienced a crisis. Most often, in identity foreclosure, parents push a commitment on their adolescents in an authoritative manner (you will go to college or the army). Yet adolescents have not had the necessary opportunities to adequately explore their own perceptions, ideologies, and beliefs.

- *Identity moratorium:* This status describes adolescents who are currently experiencing a crisis—actively exploring values, ideologies, and beliefs. Their commitments may be either absent or only vaguely defined.

- *Identity achievement:* At this final stage, adolescents have undergone and resolved their crisis by making strong commitments to such things as an occupation, a sexual orientation, or a religious ideology.

Although the identity-status theory has had an enormous influence on the field of adolescent psychology, it has become increasingly criticized (Cote & Levine, 1988; Lapsley & Power, 1988). Most of the criticism revolves around Erikson's notions of crisis and commitment. Erikson emphasized questioning perceptions and expectations and developing an autonomous position within one's society, whereas the identity-status approach is concerned with simply evaluating whether one has thought about such issues. In their search for identity, young people are struggling with unresolved questions. Gullotta, Adams, and Markstrom (1999) present a variety of questionnaire items that represent an alternative to Marcia's interview technique in assessing identity status. Table 9.3 presents examples of the questionnaire items used in measuring ego-identity status.

Recent work in identity development suggests several important considerations. The idea of *crisis* may be misleading, in that identity development appears to be a lengthy process. The complexity of identity formation is becoming more recognized (Marcia, 1987), as is the notion that such a process does not begin and end in adolescence. Identity development is significant in adolescence because this is when physical development, cognitive development, and social development converge, creating the opportunity for a synthesis as the young person charts a path to adulthood (Santrock, 1996).

Marcia (1987) notes that critical issues for early adolescence are gaining confidence in parental support, developing a sense of industry, and achieving a self-reflective perspective about the future. However, research (Meilman, 1979) is finding that many of the most important identity changes take place in later adolescence, between the ages of 18 and 21. Furthermore, researchers (Adams, Abraham, & Markstrom, 1987) have found that changes toward a more advanced identity status are related to personality development and to social cognitive development.

The following Focus section examines identity considerations of Native-American youth.

FOCUS ON MULTICULTURALISM

Identity and Native-American Youth

Consider the following story about a conversation between a Native-American youth and an Anglo youth (Coles, 1986).

> "In school, I drew a picture of my father's horse. One of the other kids wouldn't believe that it was ours. He said, 'You don't really own that horse.' I said, 'It's a horse my father rides, and I feed it every morning.' He said, 'How come?' I said, 'My uncle and my father are good riders, and I'm pretty good.' He said, 'I can ride a horse better than you, and I'd rather be a pilot.' I told him I never thought of being a pilot."
>
> The boy is clear about the differences between himself and the Anglo youth he knows. "The Anglos I've met, they're different. I don't know why. Anglo kids, they won't let you get away with anything. Tell them something, and fast as lightning and loud as thunder, they'll say, 'I'm better than you, so there!' My father says it's always been like that."

The following poem of a 12-year-old youth reflects the development of his peaceful identity as a Native-American (Coles, 1986).

> Rivers flow. The sea sings.
> Oceans roar. Tides rise.
> Who am I?
> A small pebble on a giant shore;
> Who am I
> To ask who I am?
> Isn't it enough to be?

YOUTH OF COLOR
AND ADOLESCENT IDENTITY

Achieving identity in adolescence is a significant developmental task, and often it is an even more critical task for the adolescent of color. During adolescence, young people must integrate their image of being within an ethnic group while being exposed to values and images of the mainstream white culture. Young people often perceive a negative image from the white majority and then face the task of developing a positive identity as a member of an ethnic group (Spencer & Dornbusch, 1990). Because of their cognitive maturity, adolescents of color are often quite aware of how others are evaluating their minority status.

Issues that such youth face as they focus on identity development include racial stereotypes that affect their "looking-glass self"; cultural devaluation of the symbols and heroes of their group; and lack of successful role models with whom to identify (Spencer & Dornbusch, 1990).

Identity development during adolescence leaves many young people making comparisons between themselves and others. Eventually, adolescents of color must reconcile their lives from the standpoint of two contrasting cultural systems—their own ethnic and cultural values and the white majority cultural values. This challenge often leads to three options: alienation, whereby young people reject the majority culture and the opportunities it provides; assimilation, whereby they reject their ethnic values and strive to conform and assimilate to white majority values; and biculturalism, whereby they learn to negotiate both their ethnic values and the values of the dominant culture. In this case, the value structures of both groups are available, and the young people must negotiate which standards to use depending on the situation (Spencer & Dornbusch, 1990).

The following Focus section presents the voice of an African-American girl who identifies with the hip hop culture.

FOCUS ON NARRATIVE

An Open Letter to the World

Dear World,

I am a black child, a black child with pride, dignity, strength and courage and intelligence.

You wonder, "Is it possible for a black child to possess all those qualities?" And, of course, the realization that I do scares you to death. So . . . as you continue in your state of deep, never-ending denial of my will to survive, you deprive me of my heritage, misinform me of my accomplishments, omit my history from your schoolbooks, try to ban my musical education, tear down my community with drugs, disease, police brutality and more.

I have been oppressed and enslaved for many years. Every time you think you've won, I, and all of my brothers and sisters, rise to the occasion, and you lose again. I'm still here, and I'm still black.

I am a black child, here to return my people's dignity, to retrieve my people's history and, most of all, I am today's black child, striving to become tomorrow's black future.

—Shiela "Da Moon" Rose

(Taken from Carlip, 1995, p. 214)

Implications for Practice: Identity and Independence

Independence is related to developing an identity. To help a young person successfully develop an identity, issues of independence need to be carefully reviewed. Young people face many challenges as they attempt to establish an identity—making new commitments to friends, gaining greater independence from parents, and developing more intimate friendships and relationships. Also at this time, the young person is increasingly learning to reflect on his or her actions as he or she makes increasingly important life decisions.

Parents can be important influences in the adolescent's development of identity (Santrock, 1996). Research has found that the adolescent's connectedness to parents and the presence of a family atmosphere promotes individuation in the adolescent's identity development. **Connectedness** refers both to the adolescent's sensitivity to and respect for others' views and to the adolescent's openness and responsiveness to others' views. **Individuation** has two parts—separateness and self-assertion. Separateness is the expression of the individual's distinct self from others. Self-assertion refers to adolescents' expression of their viewpoints and their clear communication.

Consider the situation in which the adolescent's mother has not "let go" of her daughter. The girl is tied to the mother financially and emotionally in ways that do not let her mature independently. Under these cir-

cumstances, the girl could have difficulties in developing mature intimate relationships and in career choices (Santrock, 1996). She may turn down important opportunities for increased responsibility, doubting her abilities to be independent. Similarly, rather than confronting difficulties in her intimate relationships, she may turn to her mother for support and comfort. In working with adolescents, social workers need to be aware of their need for independence and help young people chart a course of increased maturity. This may involve working with parents or school staff on independence-granting skills to encourage responsibility and maturity. Too often, society sees the young person as immature and not ready for adult roles rather than systematically encouraging the young person to take increasing responsibility for mature behavior.

SOCIAL COGNITIVE MONITORING

Social cognitive monitoring refers to a person's ability to monitor and make sense of his or her social thoughts. This development of conscious self-awareness increases during middle childhood and adolescence. Such social awareness is indicated by thoughts like "I don't think I'm easily influenced by others" or "I'm going to have a difficult time talking to and getting to know this person." These kinds of thoughts exemplify how adolescents monitor their social world. As young people develop, they begin to recognize that social thoughts are difficult to assess. Also, experiencing different aspects of other people can decrease young people's accuracy in assessing social thoughts. For example, witnessing another person expressing strong emotions may lead to an inaccurate understanding of that person. As this process develops, children learn that people sometimes do not think accurately about others because they have caught them in a bad mood (Flavell, 1981). Flavell (1979, p. 910) states that "In many real-life situations, the monitoring problem is not to determine how well you understand what a message means but rather to determine how much you ought to believe it or do what it says to do."

REGULATION

A woman was dying of a particular type of cancer. However, there was one drug that doctors believed could save her. A druggist in the town where the woman and her husband lived had discovered this drug. Although the drug was expensive to make, the druggist was charging ten times what the drug cost him to make. He paid $200 for the drug and was charging $2,000 for a small dose of it. The woman's husband, Heinz, went to all their friends to borrow money for the drug; however, he gathered only $1,000—half the cost. He told the druggist that his wife was dying and asked him to sell it more cheaply or let him pay later. The druggist said, "No, I discovered the drug, and I am going to make money from it." So Heinz got desperate and broke into the druggist's store to steal the drug for his wife (Kohlberg, 1969).

This story raises a number of difficult moral questions. Should Heinz have stolen the drug? What is the right and wrong thing to do in this situation? Does the husband have a duty to steal the drug for his wife if he cannot get it in another way? Did the druggist have a right to charge so much for the drug?

This story and these types of questions can be used to investigate adolescents' moral judgments. How do adolescents think about moral dilemmas where there is no clear right or wrong answer? How a person reasons about whether to steal or not steal the drug would be an indication of his or her stage of moral development. **Moral development** refers to the rules of conduct people use in their interactions with others. For example, the adolescent could reason that he or she should not steal the drug because stealing is against the law. However, another line of reasoning might be that stealing the drug is acceptable because it is unfair to charge such a high price for the drug, and it is worse to have the wife die than it is to steal.

Kohlberg believes that rules of conduct develop as individuals progress through stages. Each stage represents a different way of reasoning about various rules of conduct. This model includes six separate stages of moral development. The stages, summarized in Box 9.2, begin in the preschool years and continue through adulthood. They can be thought of as theories of right and wrong that each of us carries around. Each stage has a different approach to what's right and a different idea why a person should be good (Lickona, 1983). As people progress through each stage, they get closer to a fully developed morality. The stages correspond to the preconventional and postconventional stages of moral reasoning as described by Kohlberg.

CRITIQUE OF KOHLBERG'S MORAL DEVELOPMENT THEORY

Although Kohlberg's theory of moral development has received considerable support, there have been a number of criticisms. Major questions have been raised concerning the link between moral thought and behavior, the quality of the research, and gender bias. To what extent is moral judgment associated with behavior? Do people who reason differently also decide to act on the basis of their judgments? These are difficult questions, and researchers have not found consistent results (see Emler, Renwick, & Malone, 1983; Lapsley, 1990). Perhaps moral reasoning does not directly affect behavior but may provide a sense of direction and ethical standards.

Criticism concerning the quality of the research in this area tends to focus on a couple of aspects. Most critical is how moral development is measured. Kohlberg uses a series of moral dilemmas, like the one presented earlier, and interviews subjects to arrive at a stage of moral development. Some researchers (Rest, 1986) would like to see alternative methods used in assessing moral development. Also, concerns have been raised about the content presented in the moral dilemmas; that is, the dilemmas do not reflect the subjects' lives. One developmentalist (Yussen, 1977) had adolescents generate their own moral dilemmas, and, indeed, the focus was oriented toward friends, acquaintances, and other issues as well as toward family and authority.

Another issue involving moral development has to do with gender bias. Most moral development research has been conducted with males. Carol Gilligan, a feminist scholar (1982, 1985), is well known for her criticism of Kohlberg. She contends that his theoretical perspective is based on a male-oriented **justice perspective,** in which the focus is on the rights of the individual. People are characterized as standing alone in their decision making. In contrast, Gilligan offers a theory based on a female-oriented **care perspective,** in which the focus is on people's connectedness to others; she focuses more on interpersonal communication. According to Gilligan, Kohlberg has underestimated the care perspective underlying moral development for both males and females. She believes that the highest level of moral development involves a search for moral equality between oneself and others.

BOX 9.2

The Stages of Moral Reasoning

Ages indicate reasonable developmental expectations for a child of normal intelligence growing up in a supportive moral environment.

Stage 0: Egocentric reasoning (preschool years—around age 4)

What's right: I should get my own way.

Reason to be good: To get rewards and avoid punishments.

Stage 1: Unquestioning obedience (around kindergarten age)

What's right: I should do what I'm told.

Reason to be good: To stay out of trouble.

Stage 2: What's-in-it-for-me fairness (early elementary grades)

What's right: I should look out for myself but be fair to those who are fair to me.

Reason to be good: Self-interest: What's in it for me?

Stage 3: Interpersonal conformity (middle to upper elementary grades and early to mid-teens)

What's right: I should be a nice person and live up to the expectations of people I know and care about.

Reason to be good: So others will think well of me (social approval) and I can think well of myself (self-esteem).

Stage 4: Responsibility to "the system" (high school years or late teens)

Stage 5: Principled conscience (young adulthood)

What's right: I should fulfill my responsibilities to the social or value system I feel part of.

Reason to be good: To keep the system from falling apart and to maintain self-respect as somebody who meets my obligations.

What's right: I should show the greatest possible respect for the rights and dignity of every individual person and should support a system that protects human rights.

Reason to be good: The obligation of conscience to act in accordance with the principle of respect for all human beings.

(Lickona, 1983, p. 12)

Implications for Practice: Adolescent Moral Development

To further illustrate how moral development can be used to better understand adolescence, we will use in-

dependence as an example. Most young adolescents are in stage 3, interpersonal conformity (see Box 9.2). At this stage, young people seek to be nice people—so that others will think well of them and they can think well of themselves. A significant challenge for parents is to confront the typical conformist reasoning apparent at this stage. This is best done by teaching the value of independence and strengthening the young person's ability to be her or his own person and resist the pressures of the peer group (Lickona, 1983). Lickona presents a parent's perspective on how to challenge adolescent thinking at this stage. He presents six ways to help adolescents break free of typical conformist reasoning:

1. *Be an independent person yourself:* Parents need to model independent thinking and behavior. When young people suggest the old standby "Other parents let their kids do . . ." parents need to resist the pressure to conform to parent peer pressure. Parents should suggest that what is important is not what others are doing but what they think is right.

2. *Talk about the value of being independent:* Parents need to help adolescents see that it is in their own interest to be independent. Lickona (1983) recommends that parents say such things as, "Be your own person. Do what you like to do, what *you're* interested in. If you're true to yourself, you'll be happy with yourself. You can't be happy trying to be what you're not" (p. 189).

3. *Help young people think of words to say:* Parents should help young people role-play the exact words they might use in resisting peer pressure; for example, to a boyfriend who's interested in sexual relations, the young person might respond to a statement such as "Everybody's doing it" with "Well, if everybody's doing it, then you shouldn't have any trouble finding somebody else" (Lickona, 1983, p. 189).

4. *Help young people understand themselves:* Young people will be better prepared to be independent if they understand the feelings that cause them to conform. Many young people experience feelings of inferiority, and those feelings lead them to seek peer approval through conformity.

5. *Help young people put popularity in perspective:* Peer popularity is what often keeps adolescents from being more independent. It is important for young people to realize that values change. Having a winning personality is valued at age 14 but may be less important in three or four years. Later, such values as sensitivity to others and being able to accomplish goals will become increasingly important.

6. *Challenge the "group morality" of stage 3:* Parents can challenge adolescents' conformist reasoning by helping them see that adhering to "group morality" isn't a very good way to solve moral problems.

Lickona (1983) presents an example of how parents can do this:

> Will, who was on the junior high school baseball team, told his mother that the coach had kicked a kid off the team. Kids who thought it was unfair were talking about boycotting practice.
>
> "Do *you* think it was unfair?" his mother asked.
>
> "I'm not sure," Will said. "I just heard about what happened from some other kids. I didn't see it. According to them, Mr. Thompson accused Eric Miller of goofing off when he wasn't doing anything wrong. Then he just told him he was off the team."
>
> "I see," his mother said, "So it's hard to be sure exactly what happened. What do you think of the boycott idea?"
>
> "I don't know," Will said.
>
> "How will you decide what to do?"
>
> "I'll find out what other kids are going to do."
>
> Will's mother tried to get him to examine the inadequacy of this kind of moral thinking. "What will you do then?"
>
> Will sighed and shrugged his shoulders.
>
> "So can you decide what's right on the basis of what the other kids are doing?"
>
> "I guess not," Will said.
>
> "Right," his mother said. "You have to use your own judgment. Think about what's fair, and what's going to help you, the coach, and the team. Would a boycott help matters?"
>
> "No, not really."
>
> "What else can be done?"
>
> Together, Will and his mother came up with the idea that he could go to Mr. Thompson privately the next day and ask if he would call a meeting of the team to talk about what happened (p. 190).

MORAL DEVELOPMENT: THREE THEORETICAL PERSPECTIVES

Adams and Gullotta (1989) describe three common theoretical perspectives used to help explain and understand moral development: cognitive-developmental, learning-theory, and psychoanalytic. The cognitive-developmental perspective is based on the notion of reciprocity between the individual and society. There is a norm of reciprocal respect that guides the individual in his or her moral conduct. A person's moral behavior is based on the manner in which the person justifies his or her actions. Therefore, the way a person reasons directly affects his or her behavior. In the learning-theory perspective, moral behavior results either from the reinforcement of behavior or through the observation of others' behavior (modeling). Individuals learn moral behavior through direct reinforcement and indirectly through observation of models. In the psychoanalytic perspective, moral behavior is the result of people's personalities, primarily their instinctual drives. People's instinctual drives are moderated by their ego development. Moral behavior is the result of people's personality—their early childhood experiences that have influenced their ego development.

The perspective provided by each theory would lead the practitioner to emphasize different things. For example, in understanding a young person's violent action, a cognitive-developmental perspective would seek to examine the person's reasoning—the person's moral justification for his or her actions. A learning-theory perspective would seek to examine what elements present in the young person's environment may be reinforcing his or her actions or what role models provide vicarious reinforcement. Last, a psychoanalytic perspective would focus on parental relationships, sense of guilt, and ego development to understand how desires and impulses are controlled.

EGOCENTRISM

"I hate eating at the swimming pool. Everyone just stares at you, I never know if I've got ice cream all over my face or if guys are just trying to look at my body," Janna said with a sense of desperation. Her friend, Anita, has a similar reaction: "I know, you can never look right at this place. I mean with wet hair and no makeup I think people are looking at me and saying, gosh I didn't think she looked that bad. I keep thinking that guys who might think I'm reasonable looking will come here and see me and never give me a second look."

This conversation between Janna and Anita at the local swimming pool represents what David Elkind

(1978) refers to as adolescent *egocentrism*. Egocentrism refers to a type of thought that is characterized by preoccupation with one's behavior, feeling, or thoughts in a self-conscious manner. It is the onset of formal operational thinking that is believed to lead to such egocentric thought. Elkind discusses two aspects of egocentric thought—the imaginary audience and the personal fable.

The **imaginary audience** is the belief that others are as preoccupied with the adolescent's behavior as he or she is. Adolescents harbor this notion that they are "on stage" and that everyone is their audience. Adolescents' preoccupation with their own bodies may be a result of their egocentric thinking. In the preceding conversation, both Janna and Anita believed that everyone's attention was directed at them, and therefore they were extremely concerned about their appearance.

The **personal fable** reflects adolescents' sense that they are indestructible and unique. In fact, they are so unique that no one can understand what it is like to be them. In their self-focus, they also come to believe that they are indestructible. Things simply are not going to happen to "them."

Recent work in adolescent egocentrism suggests that this phenomenon may be the result not only of formal thought, as Elkind hypothesized, but also of the adolescent's interpersonal understanding (Lapsley, 1990; Lapsley & Rice, 1988). Such an understanding reflects the ability to step out of oneself and perceive reactions from others in imaginative circumstances. This theoretical notion is similar to the perspective-taking theory presented earlier by Robert Selman (1980). As you will recall, Selman discusses how a child's perspective taking or role taking develops across five levels. By examining the way a child reasons according to different perspective-taking levels, you can better understand the child's behavior.

Psychological Hazards

A majority of psychological problems for boys and girls in adolescence involve *externalizing disorders.* This is particularly true for boys. Between the ages of 12 and 16, more than 25% of all boys and girls are referred to mental health clinics for problems of delinquency or conduct disorder (Achenbach & Edelbrock, 1983). *Internalizing disorders* are also well known in adolescence, as many young people become depressed and turn to suicide. Rarely does a person commit suicide without giving clues to others. However, over 5,000 young people between the ages of 15 and 24 commit suicide each year. The Western states have the highest rates among teens. (See the following Focus section.)

Depression is discussed in the chapter on young adulthood. Social workers interested in community mental health with children and adolescents need to become familiar with the problems associated with conduct disorder and delinquency, because these are major psychological hazards for young people.

FOCUS ON RESEARCH

Identifying Risk Factors for Suicide Attempts Among Navajo Adolescents

Suicide is the third most common cause of death in adolescents. The suicide rate for youths has tripled over the past 30 years. American Indians and Alaskan Natives have the highest suicide rates of all ethnic groups; it is more than double the rate for adolescents of all races. In a study conducted to identify the risk factors for self-reported suicide attempts by Navajo adolescents, more than 7,000 students in grades 6 through 12 on the Navajo reservation were surveyed. The study found that 15% of the sample (N = 971) reported a previous suicide attempt; more than half of those admitted to more than one attempt. The researchers wanted to discover what factors are likely to predict suicide attempts. Controlling for age, they used a regression model and found that the following factors predict the risk of suicide: history of mental health problems, alienation from family and community, having a friend who attempted suicide, weekly consumption of hard liquor, a family history of suicide or suicide attempts, poor self-perception of health, history of physical abuse, female gender, and sexual abuse. The authors conclude that efforts to prevent suicide attempts in Navajo adolescents should target individuals with the identified risk factors.

(Grossman, Milligan, & Deyo, 1991)

DELINQUENCY

A chapter on adolescence would also not be complete without a discussion about juvenile delinquency. How many of the individuals in your class do you think committed a delinquent act as a youth? If you guessed quite a lot, you are right. Studies have found that more than 80% of young people commit delinquent acts (Gold & Petronio, 1980), and studies of inner-city youth found that most delinquent acts occur at around age 15 to 16 years. Delinquent acts are more common among boys than girls, but the rate of delinquency for girls has been increasing over the past several years.

A lot of delinquent behavior is related to status in the peer group. Almost all (96%) young people committed at least one of ten common offenses (Farrington, 1995). Delinquent acts are committed both with peers and for peers (Sigelman & Shaffer, 1991). Minor delinquent acts are considered normal and appear to be motivated by the desire to be liked by peers and to enhance one's sense of self-esteem.

When deviant behavior occurs at early ages, it is viewed as conduct disorder. However, when the behaviors lead to illegal acts by juveniles, then the problem is identified as delinquency. Research has found that delinquency can be predicted from behavior displayed at early ages. For example, children who are identified as aggressive have a high probability of becoming delinquents in adolescence (Kazdin, 1987). Most criminals have a history of juvenile delinquency, but most individuals with a history of juvenile delinquency do not end up as criminals (Dryfoos, 1990).

Many studies have examined the antecedents of delinquency (Dryfoos, 1990). Delinquent adolescents often come from disturbed families where there is an absence of social and emotional support. This deficiency allows for negative peer influences to become more significant. Peer influence can lead to delinquent acts and ultimately to gang affiliation. Poor academic achievement is also related to delinquency. Young

TABLE 9.4   The Antecedents Associated with Delinquency

Antecedent	Association with Delinquency
Demographic	
Age	**Early initiation
Sex	**Males
Race/ethnicity	Conflicting and incomplete data
Personal	
Expectations for education	**Low expectations, little commitment
	*Low participation in school activities
School grades	**Low achievement in early grades, poor verbal ability
Conduct, general behavior, misconduct	**Truancy, "acting out," early stealing, lying
Religiosity	**Low attendance at church
Peer influence	**Heavy influence, low resistance
Conformity-rebelliousness	**Nonconformity, independence
Involvement in other high-risk behaviors	**Early, heavy substance use
	**Precocious sex
Psychological factors	**Hyperactivity, anxiety, aggressive behavior
Congenital defects	*Handicapping conditions
Family	
Household composition	*Inconsistent data
Income, poverty status	**Low socioeconomic status
Parent role	**Lack of bonding, repressive, abusive, low communication
Parental practice of high-risk behaviors	*Family history of criminality, violence, mental illness, alcoholism
Community	
Neighborhood quality	*Urban, high crime, high mobility
School quality	*Repressive environment
	*Tracking ability
	*Ineffective school management

*Several sources agree that this factor is a major predictor.
** Most sources agree that this factor is a major predictor.
(Dryfoos, 1990)

people who display limited problem-solving abilities and social skills are also more likely to be delinquent. Dryfoos (1990) summarizes the antecedents of delinquency based on numerous studies (see Table 9.4).

A survey conducted by the U.S. Department of Justice revealed that approximately 25,000 juveniles are in state correctional facilities. Characteristics of the juveniles in these facilities include the following: 93%

are male, 40% African-American, and 12% Hispanic; 75% are from divorced or single-parent families; more than 50% have had a family member incarcerated; and 60% had already been in jail.

Are criminals getting younger? Statistics say yes. In the mid 1980s, defendants in homicide cases averaged between ages 20 and 25. Today, defendants are typically ages 15 to 20 (Edwards, 1995). Depending on the state, some of these youths are being incarcerated in adult facilities. While some states have lowered the age restrictions, others have dropped the age restrictions entirely. And many states are spending more on prison cells and less on early intervention, family counseling and treatment. Instead of rehabilitation, jailed juveniles will be exposed to deviant peer groups and become more entrenched in the criminal community. What does this say about how we think of juvenile offenders? We support a combination of punishment and treatment, especially with first time offenders.

The following section discusses various ways to deal with juvenile offenders.

Implications for Practice:
Approaches to Treating Delinquent Youth

The approach to treatment of delinquent youth has changed over the last 20 years. In general, treatment has moved away from a psychiatric model focusing on intrapsychic conflict, emotional disturbance, and diagnosis to treatment models based on growth, behavioral change, skill acquisition, social learning and modeling, and responsibility for one's actions (Petr, 1998). In particular, behavioral approaches have been applied and evaluated with such young people. Treatment techniques emphasize reinforcement for appropriate behaviors, learning new social skills, token economies, modeling, and goal setting. Perhaps one of the most well-established treatment models is Patterson's parent-training model for aggressive children (Chamberlain & Patterson, 1985). This approach teaches child-management techniques to parents. Parents learn to define, pinpoint, monitor, and apply consequences to various child behaviors. Feldman, Caplinger, and Wodarski (1983) found support for behavioral methods in a community-based setting, and Alexander and Parsons (1982) integrated family systems and behavioral methods for delinquent youth. Behavioral methods became quite well known through the notoriety of Achievement Place, behavior modification programs for delinquent youths in a home-based residential setting (Fixsen et al., 1976). In the Achievement Place model, parents are taught to apply the principles of behavior modification. The young people follow a set of rules based on a token economy in which they earn privileges based on their daily behaviors. Six treatment methods appear to be the most widely used with delinquent youth: restitu-

tion and community service (teaches responsibility through direct or symbolic repayment of the victim); family intervention; token economies; fear, emotional shock, and avoid-ance training; wilderness training; and social skills training (White, 1989). Family intervention and social skills training appear to have the best results in reducing recidivism.

SOCIAL DIMENSION

Families, Groups, Support Systems, and Communities

The transition into adolescence involves some stress in most families, for both adolescent and parent. This stress may be due in part to the rapid developmental changes that take place; more occur during adolescence than any other period of the life cycle (Smetana et al., 1991). Three key developmental tasks for the family include the development of autonomy, resolution of parent-adolescent conflict, and parent-adolescent attachment (Steinberg, 1990).

FAMILY INFLUENCES: DEVELOPMENT OF AUTONOMY

Consider the following interaction between a mother and daughter:

DAUGHTER: Mom, get off my back! I know what I'm supposed to do around this house. I don't need you telling me every second.

MOTHER: I have to tell you every second or it just doesn't get done. If I could trust you to do it, I wouldn't have to keep after you.

This common interaction reveals an essential theme of the parent-adolescent relationship: control versus autonomy. Much of the stress in parent-adolescent relationships is related to struggles that revolve around control and autonomy. As young people move into adolescence, they begin the process of acquiring more independence, and parents need to begin the process of granting more independence.

Because parents have had full responsibility for their children up to now, the process becomes a difficult balance between letting go and retaining some control. Some parents successfully adapt to the adolescent's need for independence and are able to grant the young person more decision-making authority. However, other parents do not acquire the needed skills involved in independence granting and remain locked into a need for control over decision making. What is the result of these two different styles of parenting? Parents who hold tightly to their control and are authoritarian in their decision making are more likely to produce young people who have difficulty with autonomy. A democratic family structure that allows equal involvement of parents and adolescents, with parents retaining the final authority, appears to produce a young person with a healthy sense of autonomy.

PARENT-ADOLESCENT CONFLICT

The parent-adolescent relationship is not viewed, as it was in the past, as one of storm and stress, rebellion against parents, or a generation gap. The current thinking about the parent-adolescent relationship is that it is a transitional period characterized by minor conflicts and disagreements about the details of everyday life (Galambos & Almeida, 1992; Montemayer, 1983). Contrary to popular notions, most adolescents have warm and satisfying relationships with their parents, turn to parents for advice, and feel loved and appreciated by them (Offer, Ostrov, & Howard, 1981; Rutter et al., 1976). However, parent-adolescent disagreements are common; in fact, they appear to be a normative and adaptive aspect of the transition to adolescence (Smetana et al., 1991).

Researchers have discovered that it is during early adolescence when the conflict between parents and adolescents begins, and it is characterized by bickering and negative interactions, fewer shared activities, and less frequently expressed affection (Steinberg, 1990). Such conflicts often occur around the time of puberty. Some people interpret this situation to represent the family's adaptation to the adolescent's physical development (Hill et al., 1985). The frequency of conflict between parent and adolescent is about two times weekly—twice as often as a typical married couple (Montemayer, 1983). Contrary to many popular no-

tions, conflicts are not about values, politics, or social issues but about mundane everyday issues such as curfew, chores, and school—the same issues since studies began 60 years ago (Montemayer, 1983).

Is there a functional reason that adolescents and parents experience this increase in conflict? Many researchers believe that there is, and they base their ideas on the following theories (Steinberg, 1990):

1. Steinberg (1990) suggests that, based on a sociobiological perspective, conflict during adolescence ensures that young people will spend time separated from their family of origin and mate outside the natal group. This theory is based on the observation that conflict intensifies at puberty in other species of primates and that the underlying tension may be derived from an evolved basis. The adolescent is forced, through the bickering, to search for intimate companionship outside the family.

2. Holmbeck and Hill (1988, cited in Steinberg, 1990) explain the conflict from both psychoanalytic and social-learning theories. From an intrapsychic perspective, the conflict may facilitate the process of individuation. Furthermore, this intrapsychic emancipation allows the young person to develop a more realistic and mature appraisal of his or her parents. This leads to a more mutual relationship with them. The function of the disagreements is that adolescents must come to terms with their parents' fallibility and, as a result, lessen their dependence on their parents.

3. Smetana (1988) presents a cognitive-developmental perspective suggesting that parent-adolescent conflict can be best explained by the different manner in which adolescents and parents define family rules, events, and regulations. From a cognitive-developmental perspective, conflict in adolescence is related to the development of social reasoning. For example, instead of seeing an issue as one of social convention (everyone in this family must keep his or her room clean), it is perceived by the adolescent as an issue of personal choice (this is my room and I should decide how clean I want to keep it). Because parents maintain a conventional stance regarding such issues, conflict is the result. Also significant is that, at this early and middle adolescent period,

young people tend to perceive social conventions as arbitrary.

PARENT-ADOLESCENT ATTACHMENT

Is it better for adolescents to become detached from parents as they move toward independence, or is it better for them to remain attached? Just as it has been in infancy, secure attachment is becoming increasingly recognized as critical to adolescent healthy development. Yet, the psychoanalytic notion has been that adolescents who remain close to their parents will not show healthy developmental progress. Research has found that adolescents with secure attachments to their parents do better than their peers do in terms of self-reliance and independence, behavioral competence, and psychosocial well-being (Hill & Holmbeck, 1986; Maccoby & Martin, 1983; Steinberg & Silverberg, 1986). Furthermore, adolescents with secure attachments score lower on measures of social and psychological problems such as drug abuse, depression, and delinquency (McCord, 1990). As Steinberg (1990) points out, this finding is robust across socioeconomic and ethnic groups. He also points out that, contrary to some clinical notions, no research supports the hypothesis that the parent-adolescent relationship can be so cohesive that it is enmeshing.

PARENTING STYLES
AND ADOLESCENT DEVELOPMENT

Baumrind (1989) has identified three types of parenting styles: authoritative, authoritarian, and laissez-faire. She has found that the type of parenting influences the adolescent's behaviors.

Authoritative parenting, whereby there is warmth and affection coupled with demandingness, leads to psychologically healthy adolescents. Authoritative parents expect adolescents to be independent but still place limits and controls on their behaviors. Authoritative parenting is related to the young person's development of social competence—particularly self-reliance and social responsibility.

Authoritarian parenting is characterized by being demanding, restrictive, and punitive while showing low levels of warmth. This type of parenting is associated with anxiety concerning social comparison, ineffective social interactions, and inability to initiate activities.

Laissez-faire parenting has been recently suggested as representing two types—permissive indifferent and permissive indulgent. *Permissive indifferent* parents are uninvolved in their child's life such that they are neglectful and unresponsive. This type of parenting is associated with a lack of self-control on the part of the adolescent. *Permissive indulgent* parents are warm, accepting, and responsive but are undemanding. Such parents are actively involved in the adolescent's life but do not enforce rules and allow extensive freedom. Adolescents learn from this type of parenting that anything goes—they do not have to abide by rules. Research has found that responsiveness was the most important factor related to adolescents' social competence and, conversely, that parents who are indifferent or uninvolved are associated with adolescents with the greatest risk for psychological and social problems (Baumrind, 1989).

FOCUS ON NARRATIVE

An Adolescent's Perspective on Divorce

" 'Best years of your life,' someone once said. "I suppose it could be true if it wasn't for your parents. I know that sounds harsh, but imagine it: a teenage kid, going through the adolescent problems of anyone my age; boys, friends, changes physically and mentally; add to this 'O' level examinations, the piece of paper which could decide my future, school and family pressuring me into doing well (even though I realize it's for my own good); then suddenly it seemed as if my whole world as I knew it was collapsing around me and I couldn't do anything about it. I'm talking about divorce, affairs, separations, the whole horrible business rolled into one.

"It started when my father announced, with some bitterness I might add, that he was having an affair. It was so unexpected, so devastating even now, looking back, I can't see how my mother managed to hold herself together. She had always been so dependent on my father. Maybe that was one of the pressures that he tried to explain to me after the initial shock.

"They tried desperately to save their marriage, not once but several times, leaving a trail of bitterness and heartache behind them, but it wasn't working. My dad would sometimes leave for a few days in an attempt to gather his thoughts, sometimes returning for me, as we were always close, or maybe to relieve his guilt. Yet each time he was less like the father I had known. It was killing them both, and family life became so unhappy. I can remember many a blazing row, things were hurled, words were so blatantly said, and I was stuck in the middle of them both. I tried so hard to comfort both of them. First my mother, but when I was with her I was laden with guilt for not being with my father. I thought that he might think I didn't love him anymore, and vice versa. Yet as hard as I tried, I was inadequate; he finally left. Sitting at home night after night, wondering if my father was all right. Many a time the thought of my dad, or my mother for that matter, committing suicide came into my mind. Why didn't he phone? I would sit there willing the phone to ring just so that I would know he was OK."

(Goodings, 1987, pp. 157–58)

Implications for Practice:
The Power of Authoritative Parenting

Steinberg (1990) suggests that the power of authoritative parenting can be taught. The most relevant work in this area is based on the research of Patterson and colleagues at the Oregon Social Learning Center. They have developed specific treatment methods for working with families with aggressive, delinquent, and non-compliant children. Their social-learning model embraces many of the aspects of authoritative parenting—monitoring, supervision, clear limit setting and rules, and a warm relationship built on positive reinforcement. The focus of the program is on child management, not on interpersonal and underlying psychodynamics. The model teaches parents to communicate clear expectations for acceptable and unacceptable behavior, to carefully monitor target behaviors selected for modification, to consistently and contingently apply discipline (time-out), and to reinforce ac-

ceptable and positive behaviors. Research results have shown improvement in the target behaviors of children and improvement in the behavior of siblings as well (Patterson, 1986).

PEERS AND ADOLESCENT DEVELOPMENT

The notion of the "teenage" years is practically synonymous with peer relationships and peer groups. If we asked you to picture the first thing that comes to your mind when you hear the word *teenager* or *adolescent,* you'd probably picture one of the following scenes: a teenager talking on the telephone, two girlfriends sitting and talking with one another, a couple out on a date, a group of peers at the mall, or a group of teenagers at the movie theater. Such is the reality of most adolescents, who spend an increasing amount of time in the company of peers (Berndt & Ladd, 1989). Research has documented that, by the sixth grade, adults (excluding parents) account for only 25% of early adolescents' primary social network and even less (10%) when adolescents mature early (Garbarino, Burston, et al., 1978).

However, this time with the peer group is well spent. Adolescents are at a point in their development when they need to spend time with peers. This interaction provides important information that is usually not available within the family. Indeed, peer interaction is a critical source for personal and social competence development. Through interaction with peers, young people learn about sexual relations, compassion, leadership, conflict, and mutual problem solving, among other things. Locating a peer group that is supportive and compatible with one's interests is a psychological task of early adolescence. As discussed in earlier chapters, the effect of peer rejection and isolation can be critical to the adolescent's healthy development.

Good peer relations are also critical to one's popularity, and popularity is keenly sought after in adolescence. Young people strive to behave in a manner that will enhance their popularity. There are many factors that contribute to one's popularity: attractiveness, athletic ability, intellectual ability, social class, ethnic group membership, and special characteristics or talents. Attractiveness is a powerful force in determining one's popularity. This appears most critical at the

Adolescents spend more time with their peers—developing personal and social competence. Together they learn about sexual relations, leadership, conflict, and problem solving.

extremes—either very attractive or very unattractive—and is a determinant of social acceptance or rejection (Coleman, 1980).

PEER PRESSURE AND CONFORMITY

As one 15-year-old stated: "Kids need to look at peer pressure and ask, 'Do I want to do this?' Whether the answer is yes or no, they need to ask why" (Clasen & Brown, 1987). Peer pressure and conformity are strong pressures in adolescence. Peer pressure and conformity are the greatest in early adolescence, especially from the sixth to the ninth grades (Berndt, 1979). Adolescent thinking is often characterized by "if the group is doing it, it must be good and right." By late adolescence, conformity to antisocial behavior decreases, and parents and peers begin to experience greater agreement. As young people move toward independence, they rely less on peer and family influence. Perhaps this period of strict conformity to peers is a normal and important task of adolescence—to gradually come to terms with the influence of groups (Minuchin, 1977). We all have to learn to balance the need for personal autonomy with the desire for group participation.

Conformity, agreeing with the group opinion when pressured, can be both positive and negative (Santrock, 1996). Although we often view adolescent peer pressure and conformity through a negative lens, it is often positive or neutral. For example, many young people conform to dress, music, and hairstyle norms. Perhaps the greatest conformity is spending time with the peer group itself. Positive conformity and constructive peer pressure are exemplified by Students Against Drunk Driving (or SADD); members promise themselves, peers, and parents not to drink and drive (Clasen & Brown, 1987).

FRIENDSHIPS

In adolescence, increasingly complete friendships develop. Perhaps most significant is the capacity for intimacy in friendship. Intimacy in friendship refers to the sharing of personal thoughts. This personal knowledge about others leads to a greater sense of closeness. Although the intimacy of friendship is highly valued in adolescence, other important functions of friendship exist. Research by Parker and Gottman (1989) outlines six critical functions of friendship: companionship, stimulation, physical support, ego support, social comparison, and intimacy/affection. Consider the following description of a close friendship between two boys (Zolotow, 1968, p. 43):

> I know everything about John, and he knows everything about me. We know where the secret places are in each other's house and that my mother cooks better but his father tells funnier jokes. . . . We always stick together because I'm good at fights, but John's the only one besides my family who knows that I sleep with my light on at night. He can jump from the high diving board, but I know he's afraid of cats. . . . He saw me cry once, and the day he broke his arm I ran home and got his mother for him. We know what's in each other's refrigerator, which steps creak on each other's stairs, and how to get into each other's house if the door is

locked. I know who he really likes, and he knows
about Mary too. John is my best friend and I am his.

This quote clearly includes the six functions of friendship described above.

Implications for Practice:
Social Skills Training

Increasing emphasis is being placed on a social skills
or social competence model for understanding, preventing, and remedying the problems experienced by
adolescents. **Social skills training** assumes that problem behavior in young people can be understood in
terms of their not having acquired skills needed to
cope with various situational demands. The focus is on
discovering effective responses for resolving the demands of problem situations while minimizing the likelihood of future problems. This approach perceives
human development as a process of confronting a series of tasks and situational demands rather than as
movement through stages. The treatment model focuses on teaching the prosocial skills and competencies that are needed for day-to-day living, rather than
on understanding and eliminating pathological responses. The emphasis is on new learned behavior that
leads to positive consequences rather than on past behaviors that may have elicited negative consequences.

Promoting social competence in young people
can be an effective strategy for helping them confront
stressful and problematic situations. Adolescents need
to acquire numerous social skills, because during this
stage of life they develop new patterns of interpersonal relationships, confront new social experiences,
and need to learn new behavioral responses. Social
skills training has been applied to many different problem areas—for example, the specific problems Native-
American adolescents face (Schinke et al., 1985), school
adjustment problems (LeCroy & Milligan, 1996), aggressive behavior (Feindler & Guttman, 1994), preventing unwanted pregnancy (Barth, 1996), prevention of
substance abuse (Botvin, 1996), and peer mediation for
interpersonal conflict (Schrumpf, Crawford, & Usadel,
1991). Without adequate social skills, these experiences
can become avenues to such problems as unwanted
pregnancy, drug use, social isolation, and loneliness.

Depending on the goals of the program and the
type of problem situations being addressed, different
skills would be appropriate. For example, in a program
for juvenile offenders, Hazel and colleagues (1981) focused on the following skills: giving and receiving
feedback, negotiating and resisting peer pressure, and
problem solving. A program for pregnancy prevention
might focus on skills such as discussing birth control,
asking for information, refusing unacceptable demands,
and problem solving.

All social-skills programs break down skills into
component parts for easy teaching. For example, beginning conversational skills might include four parts:
greeting the other person, making small talk, deciding
whether the other person is listening, and bringing up
the main topic.

In teaching social skills, construct social situations
that demand the types of social skills you want to
teach. For example, LeCroy (1994) uses the following
situation in a social skills program:

> You went to spend the afternoon with some friends but
> agreed to be home by 4:00 P.M. since your family has
> plans to have dinner with some friends. You lost track
> of time and did not get home until 4:45 P.M. (p. 154).

The process of teaching social skills includes
seven basic steps that leaders should follow. Box 9.3
presents these steps and outlines the process for
teaching social skills (LeCroy, 1992). In each step, there
is a request for group-member involvement, because it
is critical that group leaders involve the participants
actively in the training. This keeps the learning process
interesting and pleasurable for the group members.

ADOLESCENT PEER GROUPS

Adolescent peer groups provide important functions
that extend beyond friendship. Groups provide an organized means of participation, a collective sense of
camaraderie, and group support for mastering the
tasks of adolescence. Group membership allows young
people to assess their individuality in light of group
pressure and norms. As young people continue their
search for identity, choosing to participate in a group
helps answer the question "With whom do I belong?"
Groups provide experience with difficult social expectations of inclusion and exclusion as well as conformity and independence.

It is during this period, late childhood through adolescence, that peer groups have their greatest impor-

BOX 9.3

Seven Basic Steps for Teaching Social Skills

1. Present the social skill being taught.
   a. Solicit an explanation of the skill.
   b. Get group members to provide rationales for the skill.
2. Discuss the social skill.
   a. List the skill steps.
   b. Get group members to give examples of using the skill.
3. Present a problem situation and model the skill.
   a. Evaluate the performance.
   b. Get group members to discuss the model.
4. Set the stage for role-playing the skill.
   a. Select the group members for role-playing.
   b. Get group members to observe the role-play.

5. Have group members rehearse the skill.
   a. Provide coaching if necessary.
   b. Get group members to provide feedback on verbal and nonverbal elements.
6. Practice using complex skill situations.
   a. Teach accessory skills—for example, problem solving.
   b. Get group members to discuss situations and provide feedback.
7. Train for generalization and maintenance.
   a. Encourage practice of skills outside the group.
   b. Get group members to bring up their own problem situations.

(LeCroy, 1992)

---

tance. As adolescents prepare for increasing independence, peer groups can provide needed support. For example, during this time sexual development and emotional development are critical, and peer groups help young people address these challenges. Ethnographic research by Fine (1980) reveals that sexual concerns are prominently dealt with in 9- to 12-year-olds.

CLIQUES AND CROWDS

Adolescents typically form small interaction-based groups in which they spend a great deal of time and develop close relationships. Such a group is referred to as a **clique.** In contrast, **crowds** are larger reputation-based collectives of similar young people who do not necessarily spend a lot of time together. *Reputation-based* refers to the adolescent's crowd affiliation, which suggests the attitudes or activities with which one is associated by peers (Brown, 1990). Typical crowds are commonly known as jocks, brains, partners, nerds, and druggies. Crowd norms reflect the stereotypic image that peers have of crowd members (Brown, 1990). These different types of crowds are commonly described in various studies and may be related to two basic dimensions on which adolescents could be rated—commitment to the formal reward system of the school (adult controlled) and commitment to the informal status system (peer controlled). This notion lead researchers Rigsby and McDill (1975) to identify four generic peer cultures: well-rounded, studious, fun culture, and uninvolved.

GANGS

Increasingly familiar are the gangs of the big cities— the Crips and the Bloods of Los Angeles and Chicago's Vice Lords and Black Gangster Disciples. The recent increase in gangs across the United States has received increasing attention from the media, popular writers, and scholars. Recent films such as *Colors,* about the Crips and the Bloods, and *Boyz in the Hood* have put the topic of gangs on the front pages of many newspapers. No longer are gangs associated only with New York, Chicago, and Los Angeles (Huff, 1993). How can we tell whether a person is a gang member? Defining what constitutes a gang is difficult. For example, what is the difference between a gang and a group? Gangs are usually differentiated from other groups on the basis of their delinquent activity, but the distinction is not just limited to delinquency. Huff (1993) provides a comprehensive definition of a youth **gang:**

> A collectivity consisting primarily of adolescents and young adults who (a) interact frequently with one another; (b) are frequently and deliberately involved in illegal activities; (c) share a common collective identity that is usually, but not always, expressed through a gang name; and (d) typically express that identity by adopting certain symbols and/or claiming control over certain "turf" (persons, places, things, and/or economic markets) (p. 4).

Gangs seem to be related to the developmental need for young people to associate with peer groups. Indeed, adolescents who have difficulties with peer relationships are often maladjusted (Huff, 1993). Because adolescence is a time when intense peer involvement is typical, it is not surprising that gangs are an outgrowth of that involvement. According to Huff (1993), because group experience is a normal part of the adolescent subculture, gangs can be considered an extreme manifestation of the need for peer group involvement and acceptance. Gangs often play an important function for young people by providing social support, bonding, and protection from rival gangs (Huff, 1993).

Growth in gang numbers is considerable. In Los Angeles, it is estimated that there are approximately 100,000 Crips and Bloods who account for more than 500 homicides every year. These two groups are the most discussed gangs because of their size, the extent of their violence, and their role in drug trafficking. Also, these gangs now exist throughout the United States and are not limited to Los Angeles. They began as primarily African-American and Hispanic street gangs in the late 1960s. The Crips are the original gang, and the Bloods formed as a means of protection against the Crips.

Gang members range in age from 15 to 30 years old, with the majority of gang members between ages 14 and 18. There is no centralized leadership, but groupings are based on a variety of factors, such as location. Gangs are often discussed in terms of three primary groupings: (1) leaders or original gangsters; (2) hard-cores, members committed to the gang and its criminal activities; and (3) wannabes, usually younger kids who want to be hard-core gang members. Gangs can often be identified by their symbols, clothes, or other ways of showing affiliation.

Gangs are not limited to males. Female gang involvement has increased and become more entrenched, more violent, and more and more oriented to male crime. For example, the number of serious crimes by teenage girls increased by more than 50% between 1968 and 1974; serious crimes by teenage boys increased less than 105 (Molidor, 1996). Why are girls joining gangs? Traditional theories about female gang participation focus on girls' social ineptness, physical unattractiveness, or psychological impairments. Does this mean that personal maladjustments create a female delinquent? Research (Molidor, 1996) has shown that the traditional theories do not show the entire picture. Themes that emerge include the lack of formal education because of falling through the cracks in the school system; a severely dysfunctional family life, including domestic violence, divorce and remarriage, with the birth parents never married; extensive alcohol and drug abuse by parents and extended family members; and severe physical or sexual abuse by relatives beginning at an early age. In addition, the majority of the young women's neighborhoods had widespread poverty, alcohol and drug use and distribution, and gang violence. Indeed, many members of gangs are victims long before they "choose" to join a gang. Interventions must start at an early age, before middle school, and must be focused on the family and the community.

The following section discusses another serious problem that young people face: the hopeless path of the runaway.

RUNAWAY YOUTH: A HOPELESS PATHWAY

Tim, at age 16, knows what it is like to be homeless. He's lived that way for the last five years. Where would you be most likely to find him? Look in abandoned buildings in downtown Phoenix, under highway overpasses, or in alleys filled with homeless men and women in the worst parts of the city. Tim is only one of an estimated 2 million runaways. What kinds of difficulties do these young people face? Are there common problems that most runaways have?

According to recent research, such homeless youth are frequently experiencing drug and alcohol abuse, prostitution, and thoughts of suicide. In an attempt to better understand runaway youth, Robertson, Roper, and Boyer (1985) conducted research interviews with youth, searching out abandoned buildings, fast-food restaurants, and the boulevards known to harbor such youth—Hollywood and Santa Monica. The interviews were conducted with young people aged 13 to 17, with an average age of 16.1 years. The majority of these young people were white (60.2%) and male (61.3%), and most had completed the ninth grade. The interviews revealed that these adolescents had previous experience with hopelessness (79%), and more than half had lived in foster homes or group homes. This history suggests a pattern of residential instability that began as early as age 5 or 6. Most of the youth were receiving money from friends, family, or short-term jobs. Young people are not eligible for welfare benefits, and shelters are not required to take them in. Additional sources of income included dealing drugs and prostitution.

In a profile of the runaway youth, almost 50% met the criteria for alcohol dependence; however, comorbidity was common. All the alcohol-dependent youth met the criteria for conduct disorder based on criteria from the DSM-IV. Robertson further found that more than one-fifth met the criteria for major depression. Nearly half the sample had attempted suicide at least once, and more than 50% had attempted suicide within the previous 12 months. Most of the adolescents in the sample had engaged in sex at least once. Moreover, only about half the sexually active adolescents reported that they had used a condom the last time they had sex. Almost half the girls reported one or more pregnancies.

Clearly, runaway youth face many health and social problems. Unfortunately, very few of these young people have the needed resources to address the problems they face. More than two-thirds of the sample had no medical coverage. Although many of these youth had been in state care, they had fallen out of care and were not receiving benefits they were entitled to through the state.

The following Focus section presents the voice of homeless youth.

FOCUS ON NARRATIVE

Homeless Youth

"It's strange, but I really like it when the lights go off in the movies, because then I'm no longer a 'homeless kid.' I'm just a person watching the movie like everyone else."

"A lot of the children at the hotel believe that they are 'hotel kids.' They've been told by so many people for so long that they are not important, that they live up to what is expected of them. It gets so some children have no dreams and live in a nightmare because they believe that they are 'hotel kids.' It's worse than being in jail. In jail you can see the bars and you know when you're getting out. In the hotel you can't see the bars because they're inside of you and you don't know when you're getting out."

(Berck, 1992, p. 6)

SCHOOL INFLUENCES

A functional match between schools and the adolescent is becoming an increasingly recognized idea that needs attention and reform. Indeed, many researchers and professionals believe that the middle school is not an effective institution for young people. Eccles and Midgley (1989) argue that a serious mismatch exists between the organization and curriculum of middle schools and the intellectual, social, and emotional needs of young adolescents. To address many of the educational issues of adolescents, we will examine three themes: the effect of schooling on adolescent development; the ecology of the schools; and a life-course perspective about schools (Entwisle, 1990).

Schooling has played an important role in influencing adolescent development. Perhaps most significant was the movement to make secondary schooling compulsory, putting adolescents in a submissive position and keeping them from the workforce in order to make employment more manageable. Although the emphasis in schools has changed over time, the basic function has remained stable since the 1900s (Sizer, 1983). That function is to provide a comprehensive curriculum to prepare young people for the diverse aspects of life. How this "comprehensive curriculum" is structured is a source of debate. For instance, the back-to-basics movement has gained prominence, but opponents argue that schools must also be responsive to young people's social and emotional lives.

Whatever the curriculum, the numerous hours that young people spend in school expose them to significant and life-changing events and experiences. Their identity formation, competence in social and academic abilities, career paths, and social relationships are all affected by their experience in school. In spite of this influence, many people have questioned whether schooling is effective. This question is evaluated from two vantage points: Does school affect cognitive abilities? Can schools compensate for the negative effects of poverty? (Santrock, 1996). Research suggests that schooled children can outperform unschooled children (Wagner & Stevenson, 1982). However, it is also true that average achievement-test gains are small in high school (Jencks, 1985). With regard to the second question, there is evidence, although not without controversy, that schools have little effect on the cognitive development of students in poverty. Furthermore, the effect of school quality produces small differences in students' achievements (Jencks, 1985).

Although students of color must confront institutional and individual discrimination, it is important to acknowledge diversity in the educational experience of different cultures and races. Some groups (for example, Asian-Indians and Chinese) perform better on the average in school and attain higher levels of formal education than whites do, whereas other groups (for instance, Puerto Ricans and Mexicans) do not compare as well (Mare & Winship, 1988). A significant predictor of educational success for youth of color is parents' level of education and father's occupation.

Our previous discussion focused on how young people's backgrounds and personal characteristics influence their school success, but also important are the social and organizational characteristics that influence adolescent development (Entwisle, 1990; Pawlak & Cousins, 1999). One of the major organizational factors that influence the relationship between school and adolescent development is the transition from elementary school to middle school and the transition from middle school to high school.

From 1970 to 1987, there was a 160% increase in the number of middle schools and a corresponding decline of 53% in the number of junior high schools (Alexander & McEwin, 1989). In most schools, the ninth grade has been included in the high school system, and most school systems now have middle schools that include either the seventh and eighth grades or the sixth, seventh, and eighth grades. The transition from elementary school to middle school is often a stressful one. As the Carnegie Council on Adolescent Development (1989) points out, it often represents a move from a small neighborhood school with the stability of one classroom to a large and impersonal institution, often more complex and bureaucratic. This shift may disrupt important support and comfort from peer groups and caring relationships from school teachers and staff. Furthermore, this transition occurs in tandem with puberty and other emotional and social changes (for example concerns about body image, decreased dependency on parents, changes in social cognition).

This stressful transition may be explained in part by the top-dog phenomenon observed by Simmons and Blyth (1987) in their study on the transition to adolescence. These researchers found that stress increases for young people as they move from being "top dog" (biggest, oldest, most powerful) in the elementary school to being "bottom dog" (smallest, youngest, least powerful) in the middle school. This study also compared the self-esteem of seventh-grade girls who had transitioned to junior high with girls who remained in a K–8 school. The junior high students were negatively affected by the transition: They experienced lower self-esteem, negative attitudes toward school, fewer leadership roles, and more victimization by boys. Despite the trend toward middle schools, there is no good evidence to support this change; in fact, some research suggests it would be better to keep the old school system of grades K–8 and 9–12.

The Carnegie Council on Adolescent Development has been extremely critical of the organization and curriculum of middle schools. The Council finds that middle schools fall short of meeting the educational, health, and social needs of young adolescents. They identify three essential qualities schools need to create a community for learning: (1) Schools need to be restructured to a more human scale, which means creating smaller learning environments; (2) schools need to create a small group of caring adults who work with one another to develop coordinated, meaningful, and challenging educational experiences and provide some stability with peer groups; and (3) schools need to create opportunities for each student to interact with at least one adult who can provide him or her with advice about academic matters and personal problems and emphasize the importance of succeeding in the middle school.

The high school also is not beyond criticism. One of the most prevalent images of the high school is that of the "shopping mall" (Powell, Farrar, & Cohen, 1985). Just as many shoppers wander aimlessly in the mall, average high school students are lost within the corridors and classrooms of the high school, according to an extensive study of 15 diverse high schools. Although high schools offer variety and choice, the result is a curriculum that is watered down and lacking in substance for most of the students. The researchers claim that the average students—neither on a "high" track nor a "low" track—are the forgotten students in the high school. Thus the shopping-mall high school promotes individualization but does not provide personalization.

HIGH-SCHOOL DROPOUTS

Although the high school dropout rate is considered to be a serious problem, the percentage of young people that do not finish high school has decreased considerably over the years. Fifty years ago, more than 60% of students had not finished high school. Today that percentage is approximately 14% (U.S. General Accounting Office, 1986). However, this figure varies dramatically depending on the city and region of the country. In Chicago, the dropout rate is 55%. Dropout rates of minority groups in urban cities, while declining, are still higher than those of white students. The gap between Hispanic and white young people who obtained a high school credential has remained at 31% from 1990 to 1996 (National Education Goals Panel, 1997). However, when students of color and white students with similar test scores and high school grades are compared, students of color may be somewhat *more* likely to graduate from high school (Entwisle, 1990). The poor academic preparation and disadvantaged economic background of students of color appear to account for their high dropout rate compared with the rate of white students.

Studies of the characteristics of dropouts have found several factors that predict dropout: living in poverty, being in a single-parent family, having parents who do not participate in decision making concerning the adolescent, delinquent behaviors, grade retention, poor grades, pregnancy, more than 15 hours of work per week, and urban lifestyle (National Research Council, 1993). Dropout prevention programs have focused on targeting at-risk students and improving academic performance, changing attitudes about school, and reducing absenteeism. Very few dropout prevention programs have been evaluated for their effectiveness. However, the trend is to begin dropout prevention strategies earlier than high school by focusing on middle schools and elementary schools. Also, because dropout rates in some schools are so high, the strategy is to improve those schools to help prevent dropout. It is estimated that 25% of urban schools have dropout rates of approximately 50% (National Research Council, 1993); therefore, an individualized approach is no longer feasible. The current focus of prevention is on school-wide practices that can reduce alienation from the educational process and increase motivation and interest in learning. One major change that can affect a young person's adjustment to school is a move from a familiar community to a new one.

Implications for Practice: Recommendations for a Smooth Family Relocation

Today's America seems to be getting smaller. Workers increasingly move their family from one state to another because of downsizing or a company merger. Extended family members live farther from each other and therefore are often unable to be the natural support system they are meant to be. According to the U.S. Census Bureau, each year more than 9 million children are uprooted as 17% of families change residence (Seppa, 1996). Several research findings show the effects on children of leaving home, school, friends, and being forced to start over. For many children, stresses are short term. However, relocation can have consequences later in life for at-risk children who have social adjustment problems, are slow in school, or move because of a family crisis, such as divorce. Fortunately, at-risk children who receive even a slight amount of special care in their new school adapt better than those left to do the best they can by themselves. This special care could take the form of a designated "special friend" who shows the new student around school and introduces him or her to peers. Or the care could extend to include special tutoring at school and at home to insure that the new student does not fall behind.

Multicultural and Gender Considerations

Many multicultural and gender considerations apply to adolescence (Stiffman & Davis, 1990). As young people experience a broader world, they become more aware of their unique qualities—what it means to be a person of color, an immigrant from another country, a boy or girl, a heterosexual or a homosexual.

PEER RELATIONSHIPS AND ADOLESCENTS OF COLOR

In adolescence, young people of color begin to interact with a more heterogeneous population, and as a result they become more aware of their ethnic status. Also, adolescents of color often have two sets of peer relationships—at school and in their neighborhoods (Santrock, 1996). Their neighborhood peers are more likely from their own ethnic group. In a study by Brown and Mounts (1989) of multiethnic high schools, between one-third and one-half of students of color were associated by peers with ethnically defined crowds—for example, rappers, African-Americans, or Hispanics. The remaining students, two-thirds to one-half, were classified into reputation-based groups such as populars or new wavers. Because adolescents of color may have two sets of peers, it is important to inquire about relationships both in school and in the neighborhood. Adolescents who may be isolated and rejected in school could be neighborhood stars (Gibbs & Huang, 1989).

THE ADOLESCENT IMMIGRANT

Thousands of adolescents immigrate to the United States with their families each year from countries all over the world—Mexico, Thailand, Vietnam, and Haiti, to name a few. How does immigration affect their long-term adjustment? A five-year longitudinal study (Arrendondo, 1984) suggests three factors that are important for a satisfactory adjustment. First, adolescents must address the issue of belonging versus estrangement. Many adolescent immigrants are quickly exposed to racial and ethnic discrimination; their minority status is heightened by differences in appearance, dress, and language. They can develop a sense of belonging through participation in their immediate community or through participation in educational and political activities. Second, critical to their adjustment is reliance on their earlier primary group's cultural values, because this can provide a foundation for their adjustment. By retaining their identification with earlier values, they can make new accommodations without the need to reject basic values. Last, the supportiveness of family relationships is necessary to provide positive expectations about their new adjustment to a different way of life. Encouragement that they can be successful and achieve their goals reduces the sense of self-doubt and feelings of being marginal and provides a basis for them to realize their aspirations. Immigrating adolescents face many unique challenges to successful acculturation.

Regardless of their cultural background, adolescent girls are confronted with special problems that arise solely because of their gender. The following Focus section explores the unique challenges that adolescent girls face.

FOCUS ON GENDER

Meeting at the Crossroads: A Study of Adolescent Girls

Carol Gilligan is well known for her feminist work *In a Different Voice,* which changed the way researchers view women's development. In her new work, *Meeting at the Crossroads,* with Lyn Mikel Brown, she examines the lives of adolescent girls and provides a new perspective about young girls' development. The central question the researchers sought to answer was, "What, on the way to womanhood, does a girl give up?" The way to womanhood was found to be accompanied by a falling away of the self. The researchers found that younger, preadolescent girls perceived conflict as a sign of healthy relationships, and they could more easily speak about their thoughts and feelings. At this stage of development, these girls were comfortable with feelings of anger, fighting in relationships, and disagreements. In contrast, girls approaching adolescence struggle with a preoccupation with perfection and are engulfed with idealized relationships. At this age, girls desire attention, love, and popularity, and in their pursuit to build relationships, they are expected to give up something—for example, expression of their real feelings of anger. These girls' accounts are documented with vivid anecdotes as they describe their losses and their inability to express themselves. The researchers refer to this phenomenon as a form of psychological repression. For example, Gail reflects on her life over the past year:

> "I think I've gotten along better with people . . . I don't disagree as much . . . and I don't get into fights as much. Like arguments with my friends." When the interviewer asks why, she responds, "Maybe because I can understand how they think now and accept them . . . accept what they think, instead of being just one-minded . . . I realized that I went along with that and I realized I was experienced I guess, because I realized that I should understand what they think also." Then the interviewer asks, "Do you think fighting or arguing is worthless?" and Gail offers a confusing statement and then concludes that yes, fighting is worthless because she's stopped fighting and she doesn't "have to think" (p. 93).

In this example, Brown and Gilligan comment: "Gail's response to her interviewer's questions about arguing exemplifies the intricate and subtle relationship between Gail's developing capacity to understand and appreciate and take in viewpoints different from her own and the fear that by continuing to speak in the presence of difference she will lose her relationship with her friends." Brown and Gilligan encourage practitioners to help strengthen healthy resistance and courage in girls. The major lesson is the importance of helping girls discover their lost voices.

(Brown & Gilligan, 1992)

GENDER ROLES

What does it mean to be a boy or a girl in today's society? In the past, indications were clearer about what boys did compared with girls—boys played rough and got dirty, whereas girls played quietly and kept clean. Today's culture allows greater diversity of gender roles and an increasing emphasis on equality or role sharing. Much of this change in gender roles is characterized as a move toward androgyny, which is the combination of masculine and feminine behaviors in the same person (Bem, 1977). An androgynous male adolescent is someone who is both assertive and sensitive to others; an androgynous female is dominant and assertive as well as nurturing. Various research studies on gender roles suggest that, in general, changes are taking place in the direction of greater role sharing.

Do you think you are an androgynous person? Box 9.4 shows a widely used measure of sex roles, the Bem Sex Role Inventory; you can make an assessment of yourself. There are four major gender-role classifications: androgynous, masculine, feminine, and undifferentiated. We have already defined *androgynous,* and you are familiar with the notions of masculine and feminine. The undifferentiated classification refers to a person who has neither masculine nor feminine characteristics. Although androgyny is a useful concept, researchers have had a difficult time defining the concept. Also, we must consider how the concept reflects the developmental level of the child (Santrock, 1996). What is feminine for a 4-year-old girl will be quite different from what is feminine for a 15-year-old. What aspects do you think best characterize masculinity and femininity during adolescence?

Recent work on gender roles has led to a greater understanding of the concepts involved. For example, Ford (1986) defines masculinity in terms of the concept of self-assertion and defines femininity in terms of integration. Self-assertion is composed of leadership, dominance, independence, competitiveness, and individualism. Integration refers to sympathy, affection, and understanding. An androgynous person has a high degree of both self-assertion and integration.

BODY IMAGE AND ADOLESCENT DEPRESSION FOR GIRLS

Body image in adolescent girls may explain their higher rates of depression. Depression is twice as high for girls as it is for boys. This may be the result of girls' significant unhappiness with their body image. In childhood up to puberty, more boys are depressed than

BOX 9.4

The Bem Sex Role Inventory

Instructions: Rate each item on the scale from 1 (never or almost never true) to 7 (always or almost always true).

1. self-reliant
2. yielding
3. helpful
4. defends own beliefs
5. cheerful
6. moody
7. independent
8. shy
9. conscientious
10. athletic
11. affectionate
12. theatrical
13. assertive
14. flatterable
15. happy
16. strong personality
17. loyal
18. unpredictable
19. forceful
20. feminine
21. reliable
22. analytical
23. sympathetic
24. jealous
25. has leadership abilities
26. sensitive to the needs of others
27. truthful
28. willing to take risks
29. understanding
30. secretive
31. makes decisions easily
32. compassionate
33. sincere
34. self-sufficient
35. eager to soothe hurt
36. conceited
37. dominant
38. soft-spoken
39. likable
40. masculine
41. warm
42. solemn
43. willing to take a stand
44. tender
45. friendly
46. aggressive
47. gullible
48. inefficient
49. acts as a leader
50. childlike
51. adaptable
52. individualistic
53. does not use harsh language
54. unsystematic
55. competitive
56. loves children
57. tactful
58. ambitious
59. gentle
60. conventional

Scoring: Masculinity score—add up ratings for 1, 4, 7, 10, 13, 16, 19, 22, 25, 28, 31, 34, 37, 40, 43, 46, 49, 52, 55, and 58. Divide the total by 20. The result is your masculinity score.

Femininity score—add up ratings for 2, 5, 8, 11, 14, 17, 20, 23, 26, 29, 32, 35, 38, 41, 44, 47, 50, 53, 56, and 59. Divide by the total by 20. That is your femininity score. *Note:* If your masculinity score is above 4.9 (the median score) and your femininity score is above 4.9 (the median score), then you would be classified as androgynous on Bem's scale.

(Hyde, 1985)

---

girls. Suddenly, in late adolescence, twice the number of girls as boys are depressed—a finding that continues through adulthood. Some research (Girgus, 1989) has examined a number of possible factors that could account for such differences, including body dissatisfaction, life events, popularity, and sex roles. However, the most significant factor related to depression is body image. Girls interpret their maturing bodies negatively because they desire to be thinner than they have been in the past. But whereas girls see their rounded curves as negative, boys perceive their own body changes as positive—as developing more muscles.

Girls and boys were equally likely to be depressed because of life events, but girls unhappy with their body images were more likely to be depressed. Also, girls who spend more time in "feminine activities"— such as makeup, cooking, shopping—were more inclined to be depressed. Girgus (1989) suggests that, because feminine stereotypical activities tend to be passive and may provide less mastery and autonomy, they may contribute to a tendency to depression.

Implications for Practice:
A Prevention Program for Adolescent Girls

The Go Girls program (LeCroy & Daley, 1999) seeks to address the unique challenges early adolescent girls encounter by providing them with practical instruction and skill-building exercises. The target population is seventh graders; the program hopes to "inoculate" them, in a way, with knowledge and skill early enough so that they may resist some of the common hazards of growing up in a culture that seems, in many respects, to be toxic to females. The program includes that following topics and sessions:

> WEEK ONE: *Being a girl in today's society*
> Session One: Introductory session/pretest
> Session Two: Being a girl in today's society
>
> WEEK TWO: *Establishing a positive self-image*
> Session Three: Rethinking self-statements
> Session Four: Body image
>
> WEEK THREE: *Establishing independence*
> Session Five: Problem-solving strategies
> Session Six: Assertiveness skills
>
> WEEK FOUR: *Making and keeping friends*
> Session Seven: Qualities of a friend
> Session Eight: Making and keeping friends
>
> WEEK FIVE: *When it all seems like too much*
> Session Nine: Straight talk about drugs
> Session: Ten: Where to go to get more help
>
> WEEK SIX: *Planning for the future*
> Session Eleven: Visions for a strong future
> Session Twelve: Closure/review/post-test

Some of the group sessions (such as the session on problem solving) emphasize skill building in areas equally pertinent to boys and to girls, but the examples and role-plays used to illustrate the skills emphasize girls as the major actors. Other sessions (such as the session on being a girl in today's society) are designed to address areas of special concern to adolescent girls—the profusion of negative images of women and girls common in popular media and the ability and confidence to critically challenge these cultural stereotypes. A randomized control-group experiment found that the program enhanced the skills and abilities of the participants significantly more than a control group of participants who did not receive the treatment (LeCroy & Daley, 1998).

FOCUS ON NARRATIVE

The Difficulty of Being a Girl in Today's Society

I cannot stop crying. Why won't the tears stop flowing? When I was little I'd just think of something, and then I'd be ok, but no happy thoughts pop into my mind at the moment. Crying is pointless. It gives me a headache, makes my eyes burn, makes my nose run and causes people to ask "What's the matter?" What do you expect me to say? Where would I begin?

How could I possibly explain how awful I feel about myself; how I can't remember the last time I was actually proud of myself; how I can't stand any of the people I used to call my "friends"; how I feel guilty about everything I do; how I hate being fat and wish I were thin; how I wish boys would like me even though I'm fat so I'd be happy with myself; how I wish I didn't depend on boys to raise my self-esteem; how I hate boys but want them anyway; how I know you don't really care what's the matter with me. Nobody cares. Maybe that's why I'm crying. Would you understand this? NO, BECAUSE YOU'RE SELF-CONFIDENT, POPULAR, AND THIN! YOU HAVE NO IDEA WHAT IT FEELS LIKE TO BE SO INFERIOR TO EVERYONE AROUND YOU! SO SHUT THE FUCK UP, WALK AWAY FROM ME, AND LET ME CRY IN PEACE!

(Carlip (1995), p. 53)

CONDUCTING ETHNOGRAPHIES TO STUDY ADOLESCENT BEHAVIOR

Ethnographic-type assignments can be used to learn how to integrate theories and information about human development. Peggy Quinn (1992) uses this technique in her Human Behavior classes. An ethnography is a study of people; the researcher studies how people make sense of their world. It has also been referred to as taking the client's perspective from the inside out (Watts, 1985).

Students were asked to select theories they perceived as appropriate for a given developmental stage. For example, some students chose to apply development theories to young teens. One good observational setting was the mall, where young people spend a fairly large percentage of their time. Students selected what aspect of the mall they would use—for example, the food court or the video arcade. Next, researchers developed a framework for observing teenagers' behavior, such as noting greeting behaviors, dress, conversational patterns, and so forth. Student observations included notes on peer pressures, efforts at differentiation, and the girls' flirtatious behavior. Students were expected to discuss their observations as reflecting various theories of human development.

As you read through this text on human development, take the time to conduct mini-ethnographies—observe a group of people and study their interactions. How does their behavior fit with various theories? What aspects of their behavior are difficult to understand? What meanings, besides the obvious, might explain their behavior? By asking questions and observing behavior, you can learn a great deal about people's unique behaviors and social relationships.

ADOLESCENT HETEROSEXUALITY

No discussion of adolescence would be complete without a section on adolescent sexuality. In adolescence, formation of a sexual identity is a major developmental task. From adolescence to young adulthood, young people begin the process of sexual exploration—a search for their sexual identities. Although this may sound like a sexual stereotype, it is during this time that boys aggressively search for sexual experience with girls, and girls eagerly desire romantic involvement with boys. For example, Cassell (1984) found that more girls than boys report being in love as the main reason for engaging in sexual intercourse. Adolescent boys recognize this socialization, and as a result, profess to be "in love" with a large number of girls. However, changes in sexual behavior in the last 20 years do show a decline in the sexual double standard. Incidence of sexual intercourse for adolescent girls has increased more rapidly than for boys, indicating greater acceptance of girls being sexually active. However, research on attitudes and feelings about sexual intercourse has found that twice as many boys as girls report positive feelings about their sexual experiences (Gordon & Gilgun, 1987). A related study found that both male and female adolescents accept that the role of the male adolescent is to be the aggressor in sexual relations and that the female adolescent's role is to set the limits of this behavior (Goodchilds & Zellman, 1984). Many aspects of adolescent sexuality have undergone rapid and considerable change, yet many other aspects have remained unchanged.

How sexually active are adolescents? Recent data suggests that they are quite active. Table 9.5 presents data from a sample of more than 46,000 young people in 25 states (Benson, 1990). As the table indicates, starting in the seventh grade, 22% of the boys and 10% of the girls have already experienced sexual intercourse. By the twelfth grade, 77% of the boys and 66% of the girls have experienced sexual intercourse. Contraceptive use shows a gradual increase from 33% at first intercourse in the seventh grade to 53% in the twelfth grade. Not quite half of the eighth- through twelfth-grade adolescents use contraceptives consistently after the first intercourse.

As might be expected, several factors influence the incidence of sexual activity among adolescents. For example, sexual activity is lowest for white adolescents, followed by Hispanic, and then African-American adolescents. The following factors have been found to significantly influence adolescents' sexual activity (see, for example, Miller, McCoy, & Olson, 1986; Newcomb, Huba, & Bentler, 1986):

- Living in a single-parent household is related to a higher incidence of sexual activity.
- Attending church and doing well in school discourages sexual activity.
- Good parent-adolescent communication discourages sexual activity.
- Early dating experience encourages sexual activity.
- Parental discipline—either too permissive or too strict—encourages sexual activity.

Petersen and Crockett (1992) identify four influences that they believe are associated with early sexual behavior and subsequent pregnancy:

1. *Biological influences:* Puberty is hypothesized to have a major influence on adolescent sexual behavior, leading to increased risk of pregnancy and childbearing. Pubertal development may affect adolescent sexual behavior in two ways: directly

through hormonal effects on the brain, and more indirectly through somatic changes that stimulate a more mature physical appearance, which in turn suggests expectations about more mature sexual behavior.

2. *Sexual abuse:* Prepubertal sexual abuse may have a significant effect on girls' subsequent sexual behavior. It is hypothesized that prepubertal sexual abuse is linked to earlier sexual behavior, earlier pregnancy, and earlier childbearing and that it is related to difficulties with childrearing skills. The reasons for this connection are complicated and not well understood.

3. *Deviance or problem behavior:* Adolescents that are involved in problem behaviors are more likely to have earlier sexual behavior and earlier pregnancy. Jessor (1992) identifies sexual behavior as one part of the problem behavior syndrome. Jessor speculates that involvement in problem behavior is related to psychological readiness to participate in adult behaviors. Or participation in one problem behavior may bring young people into contact with peer groups in which additional problem behaviors are modeled and encouraged. More simply, pregnancy and the sexual behavior of adolescents appear to be part of a "deviant lifestyle" characterized by multiple problem behaviors (Elliot, 1993).

4. *Normative expectations:* Transitions to subsequent life stages may be influenced by societal expectations. In other words, if an adolescent is expected to complete college, then marry, and then have children, these expectations are likely to influence the course of such events. Petersen and Crockett (1992) found that girls who are sexually active in junior high school anticipate making several adult transitions, such as finishing their education, starting a job, and marrying, at earlier ages than do girls who are not yet sexually

TABLE 9.5	Sexual Behavior, by Grade and Gender					
	Percentage Sexually Active				If Sexually Active, Percentage Using Contraceptives	
	One or More Times		Four or More Times		At First Intercourse (Partner or Self)	All the Time Now (Partner or Self)
Grade	Boys	Girls	Boys	Girls		
7	22	10	7	3	33	36
8	32	17	12	4	38	42
9	41	27	17	14	45	45
10	50	43	26	27	49	47
11	58	54	37	41	53	51
12	77	66	51	54	53	53

(Benson, 1990)

active. Also interesting is the finding of familial transmission of these expectations. Several studies have found a relationship between mothers' sexual experience as adolescents and the sexual experience of their adolescent child. This may be the result of a permissive attitude toward sex or the early maturity of both mother and daughter.

The following Focus section presents several adolescents' viewpoints on sex.

FOCUS ON NARRATIVE

Adolescents' Views on Sex

Santrock (1996, p. 384) quotes several adolescents about their sexual experiences:

I am 16 years old, and I really like this one girl. She wants to be a virgin until she marries. We went out last night, and she let me go pretty far, but not all the way ... It's getting hard for me to handle ... I feel I am ready to have sex. I have to admit I think about having sex with other girls too ... (Frank C.)

I'm 14 years old. I have a lot of sexy thoughts. Sometimes just before I drift off to sleep at night I think about this hunk who is 16 years old and plays on the football team. He is so gorgeous, and I can feel him holding me in his arms and kissing and hugging me ... (Amy S.)

Is it weird to be a 17-year-old guy and still be a virgin? Sometimes I feel like the only 17-year-old male on the planet who has not had sex. I feel like I am missing out on something great, or at least that's what I hear. I'm pretty religious and I sometimes feel guilty when I think about sex ...(Tom B.)

I'm 15 years old, and I had sex for the first time recently. I had all of these expectations about how great it was going to be ...We were both pretty scared about the whole thing. It was all over in a hurry. My first thought was, "Is this all there is?" It was a very disappointing experience. (Claire T.)

AIDS PREVENTION AND ADOLESCENT MALES

Given the high rate of sexual intercourse among adolescent boys, there is a great need for AIDS prevention among this population. AIDS, or acquired immune deficiency syndrome, is caused by the **human immunodeficiency virus (HIV).** This virus destroys the human immune system and leads to opportunistic infections. These infections are caused by agents such as bacteria and viruses that are usually harmless to a healthy individual. In the immune-compromised individual, however, these agents cause illness and, ultimately, death. Infection with HIV leads to a classification of the person as HIV-positive. Infection from this virus has been increasing at an alarming rate over the past several years. Of the new AIDS cases in young people ages 13–24 in 1996 and 1997, 52% were in young men who had sex with men.

It appears, however, that AIDS prevention is responding to the AIDS epidemic. From 1979 to 1988, the proportion of sexually active adolescent boys using condoms has doubled. A study reported by Sonenstein, Pleck, and Ku (1989) surveyed adolescent boys, ages 15–19, about their levels of sexual activity, use of contraception, and knowledge of AIDS. Using a comparison sample from 1979, they found that, despite the AIDS problem, the number of sexually active adolescents is on the rise. The researchers found almost a 20% increase from 1979 to 1988 in the number of 17-year-olds who say they had sexual intercourse. However, in 1979 only 21% of the sexually active adolescents used a condom the last time they had sex, whereas in 1988 58% reported using a condom. Furthermore, the percentage of adolescents who said they had used no protection during their last sexual intercourse fell from 51% in 1979 to 21% in 1988.

More encouraging is the level of knowledge the adolescent males had about AIDS. For example, most of the adolescents surveyed were knowledgeable about the way the virus is transmitted, and 82% realized that AIDS is not so uncommon that they don't have to worry about it. Also, most of the adolescents—75%—disagreed with the statement "using condoms to prevent AIDS is more trouble than it's worth." There are still some misconceptions; for example, 40% thought you could get AIDS from giving blood. However, progress in AIDS prevention appears to be paying off. As Ellen Stark (1989) reminds us, the trend of a round indentation in the wallet from carrying a condom is making a comeback.

Less encouraging is that young gay men aren't consistently practicing safe sex, although a majority of older gay men have changed to safe sex behavior. In one study of young gay men, 36% indicated they had had unprotected anal sex during the previous two months. Younger gay men see AIDS as something that happens to older gay men. Gay adolescents who are in foster care have often been victimized more than other children in the child welfare system. Additionally, youths identified as gay are often rejected from placement because of their sexual orientation (Sullivan, 1994). Other subgroups that represent high risk include youths in juvenile detention; in one study, all the jailed adolescents had experienced sex, and 78% had had two or more sex partners in the past year. Also, 13% had admitted using intravenous drugs. In a similar manner, homeless and runaway youths are at higher risk for AIDS. Because they are more concerned with daily survival, they do not view protecting themselves against AIDS as a priority (Sonenstein, Pleck, & Ku, 1989; Youngstrom, 1991).

ADOLESCENT HOMOSEXUALITY

Consider the following quotes from gay and lesbian adolescents (Hersch, 1990):

When all the guys are discussing their latest crushes, I play along. What a body Carol has. Look at those great tits on Marge. How can I tell them I dream of Dave? It would be all over the school in a flash. I'd be dead meat.

It's difficult to know what to wear, what to say, how to act with different people. You are so scared of being found out that you never know if you will ever be able to be yourself.

I don't understand what is going on with me. I want to kill myself. I'm scared of who I am. There is no one else like me. What am I going to do? It's not normal to be gay—normal is a man and a woman. Am I the only one?

These are the words of gay and lesbian adolescents. They are also words of secrecy and fear. They represent a world that homosexual adolescents must learn to live within. Life is difficult, if not dangerous, and many homosexual adolescents experience violence because of their sexual orientation. Indeed, adolescent homosexuality presents our society with many challenges. As Hersch (1990) aptly puts it, "to a culture already uncomfortable about adult sex, worried about adolescent sex, and downright hostile about homosexual sex, gay and lesbian adolescents pose a compounded threat—children who are sexual *and* deviant." Society has a difficult time accepting adolescents as sexually active and would rather deny the existence of homosexual adolescents. (See Focus on Diversity: Guidelines for Adolescents Who Want to Consider Coming Out, page 396.) Even sex education programs fail to address gay adolescents' needs or acknowledge their sexuality. This increases their sexual confusion and isolation (Murray, 1996) and may make them feel that their sexuality does not exist.

Yet, homosexual adolescents do exist. Chilman (1979) found that 3% of boys and 2% of girls report participating in ongoing homosexual relations during adolescence. However, that was more than 15 years ago. Today some experts estimate the gay and lesbian population at about 10%, although a recent national study reports that only 2.3% of males said they have had same-sex experience (Alan Guttmacher Institute, 1993). The estimated 4 million homosexual adolescents must confront many social problems.

Perhaps of most concern is the isolation, depression, and potential for suicide. Gay young people are two to three times as likely to attempt suicide as are other young people. In a study of homosexual adolescents (Remafedi, Farrow, & Deisher, 1991), 30% reported at least one suicide attempt. Twenty-one percent of the suicide attempts resulted in medical or psychiatric hospitalization, but almost three out of four attempts did not result in any medical attention. A significant number of the suicide attempts were related to personal turmoil about homosexuality. Many of these young people have a difficult time confronting the social isolation they experience, their concern about secrecy, and their fear of violence.

Often in adolescence, young people decide on a homosexual or heterosexual expression of their sexuality. Homosexual adolescents often experience alienation and face developmental problems because they may repress their identity, face peer rejection, and feel the pressure of cultural sanctions against intimate homosexual relations.

Several authors have explored the unique developmental challenges faced by gay youth in relation to the coming-out process. Adaptation to a homosexual identity is commonly conceived to span four stages, often sequentially, though progression may cease at any stage. However, while frameworks provide a helpful generic description of the developmental transition, the process is highly variable and rarely unfolds in an orderly, linear fashion (Schneider, 1991). It is characterized by diversions and detours and by individual differences, sex differences, and the historical context.

Troiden (1989) refers to the first stage of adaptation as *sensitization,* during which the individual becomes aware of feelings that makes him or her different according to social definitions. The next stage is *identity confusion,* whereby the person struggles with the implications of a homosexual identity. At this stage, individuals often try to make sense of their feelings without the advantage of accurate information and informed only by the negative and erroneous stereotypes of the dominant culture. Eventually, the strength of the feelings associated with sexual attraction lead to some degree of self-redefinition that may be associated with behaviors consistent with a homosexual identity. Troiden refers to this stage as *identity assumption*. Troiden describes the restructuring of the individual's social life to include a sustained, positive association with a community of like others that may follow as a final stage of *commitment*.

Unfortunately, many gay youths do not achieve comfortable acceptance of their sexual identity. In addition to the concern about depression and suicide, homosexual adolescents face a number of increased risks. Suffering destructive alcohol and drug abuse, being victims of crime, contracting sexual diseases including AIDS, and dropping out of school are some of the more prevalent risks associated with adolescent homosexuality. These risks can be compounded for the young person from a minority group. Gay and lesbian youth of color live within three communities: their ethnic community, the gay and lesbian community, and the majority community (McManus, 1991). They are thus susceptible to two types of prejudice: racism and homophobia. This lifestyle can require "a constant effort to maintain oneself in three different worlds, each of which fails to support significant aspects of a person's life" (p. 31).

FOCUS ON BEHAVIOR

▼

Can Changing a Child's Sex Change His Sexual Orientation?

He was one of a set of infant twin boys when, in 1963, his penis was damaged beyond repair by a circumcision that went awry. After seeking expert advise at Johns Hopkins Medical School, the parents decided that the child's best shot at a normal life was as an anatomically correct woman. The baby was castrated, and surgeons fashioned a kind of vagina out of the remaining tissue. When "she" grew older, hormone treatments would complete the transformation from boy to girl.

In the 1960s and 1970s, doctors believed that sexual identity existed on a continuum and that nurture was more important than nature in determining gender roles. Basically, experts believed that babies were born gender neutral, and, if you indoctrinate them early enough, you can make them either gender. Unfortunately for the child called "Joan," this theory did not prove true. Joan never really adjusted to her assigned gender. She spent her childhood and early adolescence rejecting life as a girl; ripping off dresses as a toddler, playing only with boys and stereotypical boys' toys and urinated standing up. Joan was sure she was a boy. But her doctors and psychiatrists kept pressuring her to act more feminine. At the age of 14, Joan gave up and decided she could either kill herself or live her life as a male. When she confronted her father, he tearfully told her the true story of her birth and sex change. "All of a sudden everything clicked . . . for the first time things made sense, and I understood who and what I was" (p. 83). With the support of her parents and different doctors, Joan underwent several surgeries to reconstruct a penis. "Joan" is now John, a happily married father of three adopted children.

This original landmark of modern science was, in actuality, a disaster. Although Joan became John in the late 1970s, no follow-up study reporting John's rejection of his original sex change was published. Dozens of other boys over the years have been needlessly castrated because of Joan's assumed success. Today's experts expect these boys-made-girls will reject their female identity by the time they reach puberty. But others are not so sure we have the answers. The final lesson is that adults need to listen to children as they develop and explore their sexual identity.

Misha Marvel (Adapted from Gorman, 1997)

FOCUS ON DIVERSITY

▼

Guidelines for Adolescents Who Want to Consider Coming Out

Many gay and lesbian adolescents will confront the decision about whether or not to come out and discuss their homosexuality. This is a difficult decision with a lot of serious consequences. Sauerman (1984) has produced a pamphlet for the Federation of Parents and Friends of Lesbians and Gays, Inc., that presents a series of questions that need to be considered before coming out:

1. Are you sure about your sexual orientation?
2. Are you comfortable with your gay sexuality?
3. Do you have support?
4. Are you knowledgeable about homosexuality?
5. What's the emotional climate at home?
6. Can you be patient?
7. What's your motive for coming out now?
8. Do you have available resources?
9. Are you financially dependent on your parents?
10. What is your general relationship with your parents?
11. What is their moral societal view?
12. Is this your decision?

Social Hazards

How can we understand the various factors that play a significant role in leading to adolescent risk behaviors or lifestyles? For several years, Richard Jessor (1987, 1992) has been studying adolescent problem behavior. Figure 9.1 shows five protective and risk factors that

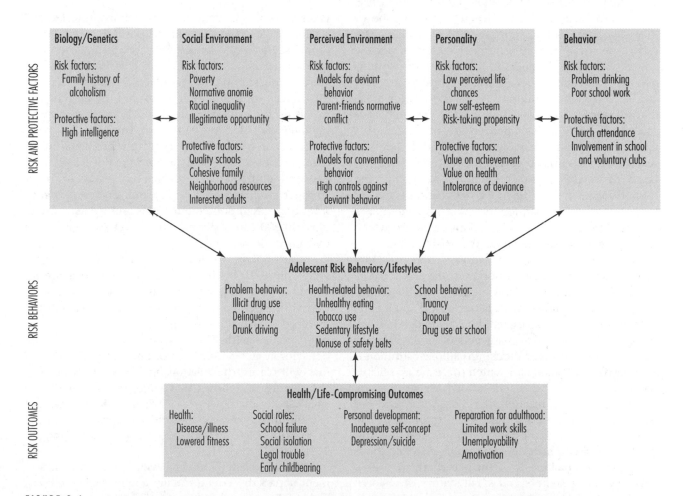

FIGURE 9.1 Conceptual framework for adolescent risk behavior using risk and protective factors (Jessor, 1992)

influence adolescent risk behavior: biology/genetics, social environment, perceived environment, personality, and behavior. Note that the influence of these concepts is bidirectional.

Before we begin to address various social hazards of adolescence, we must point out that many children and adolescents today are growing and developing in a violent world. Children and adolescents are being victimized on a daily basis more than we realize. Even in school, violence is a national problem. The media have recently focused on school violence as an epidemic, whereby students are being barraged by rapes, shootings, stabbings, and beatings. Consistent with the media's evaluation of the condition of schools, the American public has also viewed violence as the most important problem that schools face (Astor, Behre, Fravil, & Wallace, 1997). In fact, research has shown that 92% of the public supports violence training for school personnel. Seventy percent of school personnel report that potentially life-threatening events occurred in their school during the past year (Astor et al., 1997). Since children are in schools for a significant portion of their childhood, this research leads to the observation that children are potentially subjected to much more violence than adults are. Research supports this observation (Finkelhor & Dziuba-Leatherman, 1994). In fact, rates of assault, rape, and robbery against those aged 12–19 years are two to three times higher than for the adult population as a whole. Homicide is the only violent crime for which teens are somewhat less vulnerable than adults.

So, who is hurting our nation's children? Sadly, their families are. Adults report that they inflicted almost twice as much severe violence (which included beating, kicking, hitting with fist or object) on a child in their household than they did on their adult partner. Taking into account that many acts of family violence are not reported, this is shocking. Child prostitution is another national shame for which there are no reliable statistics.

When the victimization of children is considered as a whole, it prompts a number of questions. First, why is child victimization so common? Although this is obviously a complex question, some generalizations may apply (Finkelhor & Dziuba-Leatherman, 1994). Certainly the weakness and small stature of children and their dependent status put them at risk. They can-

not retaliate or deter victimization as effectively as can those with more strength and power. The social toleration of child victimization also plays a role. Society has an influential set of institutions, the police and criminal justice system, to enforce its relatively strong prohibitions against many kinds of crime, but much of the victimization of children is considered outside the purview of this system. A final generalization about why children are at high risk for victimization is that children have little choice about whom they associate with, less choice perhaps than any segment of the population besides prisoners.

BUILDING ASSETS FOR YOUTH: A COMMUNITY-BASED APPROACH

Peter Bensen, president of the Search institute, has led a nationwide effort to promote positive youth development. His work began with research describing youth assets and their effect on the at-risk behavior of youth reported in *The Troubled Journey* (Bensen, 1990). This approach attempts to shift the current emphasis on the crisis and problems of young people to building assets for and with them. The focus has been too much on trying to stop or prevent problems rather than on increasing young people's exposure to positive and constructive activities as a way to build stronger communities. The research on assets comes from more than 600 communities and is based on almost 50,000 young people. The survey (see Table 9.6) examined the presence of 30 assets.

The findings are revealing: high school students with only 1–10 of the 30 assets in their lives are involved in an average of 5.8 of 20 risk behaviors. However, young people with between 11 and 20 assets are involved in half the risk behaviors, only 3.4. Furthermore, youths with 26–30 assets show very little risk behavior at all. Examination of one of the risk behaviors will clarify the relationship between assets and risk. Figure 9.2 shows that young people with the smallest number of assets have the highest alcohol use and those with the most assets represent only 3% of youths with alcohol problems (Youth Update, 1994).

The approach to building assets is a growing movement across the country. Many communities, schools, and task forces are working together to develop a vision

TABLE 9.8	Thirty Assets for Youth		

External Assets

Support	Control	Structured Time Use
1. Family support	8. Parental standards	13. Involved in music
2. Parent(s) as social resources	9. Parental discipline	14. Involved in school extracurricular activities
3. Parent communication	10. Parenting monitoring	15. Involved in community organizations or activities
4. Other adult resources	11. Time at home	16. Involved in church or synagogue
5. Other adult communication	12. Positive peer influence	
6. Parent involvement in school		
7. Positive school climate		

Internal Assets

Educational Commitment	Positive Values	Social Competence
17. Achievement motivation	21. Values helping people	25. Assertiveness skills
18. Educational aspiration	22. Concerned about world hunger	26. Decision-making skills
19. School performance	23. Cares about other people's feelings	27. Friendship-making skills
20. Homework	24. Values sexual restraint	28. Planning skills
		29. Self-esteem
		30. Positive view of personal future

(Benson, 1990)

for positive youth development and to implement ways to build assets for youth.

YOUTH EMPLOYMENT

Most young people today will have had a part-time job by the time they finish high school. In today's world adolescents juggle school, friends, boyfriends or girlfriends, family and work (Pantiel, 1995). But is it good for teenagers to work? Research has found that the amount of hours involved in work can have positive or negative effects on adolescents. In general, working 15–20 hours per week improves a student's self-esteem and school satisfaction, and the student's grade point average is higher than nonworking peers (Steinberg, Fegley, & Dornbush., 1993). Research has found that adolescents working more than 20 hours per week experience negative effects. Adolescents who work this much show elevated levels of psychological distress, including low self-esteem (Steinberg, Fegley, &

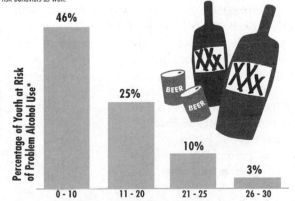

Building Assets Reduces Alcohol Abuse

This chart illustrates how building assets reduces problem alcohol use. Similar patterns occur for other at-risk behaviors as well.

*At risk in alcohol use is defined as drinking six or more times in the past month and/or having five or more drinks in a row, once or more in the past two weeks.

FIGURE 9.2　Building assets reduces alcohol abuse.

Dornbusch, 1993). These young people are more likely to get in trouble with the police and use drugs and alcohol (Crispell, 1995). In conclusion, adolescents who are involved in some work derive benefits that may encourage responsibility and autonomy and may provide important new opportunities in the future.

ADOLESCENT PREGNANCY AND CHILDBIRTH

A significant social hazard of the adolescent years is teenage pregnancy—a much-discussed topic in our society. Teenage pregnancy has become a national concern. Indeed, the act of being sexually active can take a young person down many new roads. Once an unplanned pregnancy occurs, there are many difficult decisions to confront: Should I have this baby? Should I give this baby up for adoption? Should I consider an abortion? The result of an unplanned pregnancy has many implications for the future of the young woman: involving the father, getting married, finishing school, dealing with parent relationships. It is as if the young person is thrust into a completely new reality. This section will examine the prevalence of adolescent pregnancy, the consequences of adolescent pregnancy, the adolescent father, and the implications for reducing adolescent pregnancy.

PREVALENCE OF ADOLESCENT PREGNANCY

The prevalence of adolescent pregnancy involves several factors. First, how many adolescents are sexually active? Second, how many of the sexually active adolescents are effectively using contraception? Third, if early pregnancy does occur, how many adolescents are obtaining abortions? Taking all these factors into consideration, one can see that the actual rate of births to adolescent parents has been decreasing over the last several years. Table 9.7 presents data on what changes have taken place for adolescent sexual behavior and outcome. As the data point indicates, sexual activity has clearly in-

creased over the years, but so has the use of contraception, which has slightly lowered the overall pregnancy rate (~1%). This lower rate, coupled with a small increase in abortion rate, has resulted in an overall decrease in the birthrate. Table 9.7 also makes clear that there are important racial differences in these statistics.

In general, there have been more than 1 million teen pregnancies in the United States since 1973, and about one out of every nine adolescent females conceives every year (Dryfoos, 1990). It is estimated that about one in four sexually active adolescents experiences a pregnancy during the year. Pregnancy of very young girls, under age 15, represents only 2% of the births of girls aged 15–19; thus it is considered a rare event.

FOCUS ON MULTICULTURALISM

Birth Rate of African-American Girls

Births among unmarried African-American girls have plunged to a 40-year low. In 1996, the birthrate among these women was 74.4 per 1,000, with the sharpest drop among 15- to 17-year-olds, whose birthrate has declined 20% since 1990. Why? What is causing this change?

Fear of AIDS may be the primary contributing factor. Although boys swagger just as much as ever when it comes to sex, girls are more insistent on condom use. AIDS has also led to more frank talk and pleas for abstinence from parents and school and community-center health classes.

TABLE 9.7   Percentage of Change in Rates of Sexual Behaviors and Outcomes for Girls 15–19 Years Old

	Sexual Activity 1982–1988	Contraception at First Intercourse 1982–1988	Pregnancy 1982–1987	Abortion 1982–1987	Birth 1982–1987
Total	+13%	+36%	–1%	+1%	–4%
White	+16%	+26%	–5%	–5%	–7%
Nonwhite	—	—	+4%	+11%	–1%
Black	+3%	+50%	—	—	+3%

(Hamburg & Dixon, 1992)

Another surprising possibility is that teens are again attaching the old stigma to unwed motherhood. A 15-year-old summed up teens' attitude with this comment "You lose a lot of friends . . . She had a baby shower and nobody came." The renewal of shame, if that is what it is, seems linked to the healthy economy. Whereas inner-city kids were once pessimistic about job possibilities, those who counsel them say they are now brimming with ambition. Experts point out that, although in 1965 there was a 20-point chasm between black and white high school graduation rates, the Census report in 1998 announced that it had disappeared. These young people seem to have a new outlook on life—one that includes self-respect and love of life.

Misha Marvel (Adapted from Edwards, 1998)

CONSEQUENCES OF ADOLESCENT PREGNANCY

The consequences of early pregnancy affect both the mother and the child. For the infant, consequences include low birth weight and an increased likelihood of infant mortality. Prenatal care is obtained by only one of every five mothers during the critical first three months of pregnancy. For the mother, especially young mothers, there are increased risks of complications and mortality. There is also a greater likelihood for young mothers to experience such complications as toxemia, anemia, and prolonged labor (Dryfoos, 1990).

The long-term consequences of early pregnancy find teenage mothers suffering many critical disadvantages. Not surprisingly, educational achievement is adversely affected mostly because of early dropout from school. This may contribute to the additional problems of low-status jobs, lower income, and welfare dependency. There are equally critical disadvantages in social relationships—high divorce rates, unstable relationships, and more subsequent unintended births. Long-term consequences for children of adolescents can include lower educational achievement, behavioral and emotional problems, a greater likelihood of themselves becoming teenage parents, and an existence based in poverty (Dryfoos, 1990).

Young women who terminate their pregnancy experience few negative consequences, although the later in the pregnancy the abortion occurs, the greater the risk of complications. The literature has not found significant psychological consequences associated with abortion. Similarly, there do not appear to be any serious psychological consequences associated with adoption, although adoption is rarely an alternative selected by teenage mothers.

ADOLESCENT FATHERS

The adolescent father is gaining increasing attention from society. What do we know about the adolescent father? In general, he may be more involved in parenting than previously thought. Research (Danziger & Radin, 1989) has found that fathers are willing and interested in participating in parenting. Many adolescent fathers have daily contact with their children, although

Adolescent pregnancy is an important risk factor because it decreases the likelihood that the mother will complete school and significantly reduces her chances for economic self-sufficiency.

in a recent study (Leadbetter, Way, & Raden, 1994) one-fourth of adolescent mothers reported the father having a close relationship with her and the child.

Being an adolescent father is associated with several disadvantages. For one, many adolescent fathers decide to provide financial support, and often this means quitting school. Having quit school, these fathers are eligible only for low-paying jobs.

Only recently have social service agencies recognized the need to respond to adolescent fathers. However, programs are springing up around the country that are specifically designed to help adolescent fathers cope and function effectively in their new role. One such program focuses exclusively on African-American fathers; the young men get together to take their children out for the day, provide emotional support for one another, and receive education about fathering and being an effective parent.

FOCUS ON GENDER

Including Adolescent Fathers

Social workers have been working with teenage mothers for many years now. The mother has often been the one who has made all the decisions regarding the baby. Teenage fathers have been left behind. Often they face hostility from their girlfriends' parents, as well as the myth that they don't want anything to do with their girlfriends or the baby once they find out about the pregnancy. Recent findings, however, are showing that an increasing number of fathers do not want to abandon their baby. Therefore, social workers need to consider including teenage fathers when decisions are being made (Anthony & Smith, 1994).

Teenage fathers face the same emotional struggles and dilemmas that teenage mothers do, and many fathers want a baby for the same reasons that teenage mothers want one. Like teenage mothers, fathers often imagine only the good times that lie ahead when they think of being a parent. And, not unlike teenage mothers, fathers often feel trapped once the reality sets in and they understand the totality of what is involved in raising a child.

Many fathers truly want to help support their girlfriends and their babies. Most fathers, even though they don't marry the baby's mother, tend to stay close during the first year of the baby's life. Social workers need to take this fact into account when working with teenage mothers and their children, since it is no longer just the two of them in the picture.

Unfortunately, fathers' involvement tends to taper off after the first year of the child's life, when the demands of hard work (required for supporting the child and girlfriend) and raising the child become too much for them to handle. It is important, therefore, that social workers pay attention to teenage fathers and offer them services during the second year of the baby's life as well. New programs are being offered that teach teenage fathers about nutrition and child care. Previously these classes were offered only to mothers; however, a recent trend is to offer coed classes.

Prevention is an important factor when looking at the problem of teenage pregnancies. Children need to be taught sex education early, which should include the proper use of contraceptives and a section on abstinence. Again, these classes are just as important for boys as for girls. One strategy in preventing teenage pregnancies is to have teenage fathers talk to the community about their experiences and encourage other teenagers to be more careful.

Marilyn Ramirez (Adapted from Robinson & Barret, 1985)

Implications for Practice: Reducing Adolescent Pregnancy

The consequences of adolescent pregnancy point to the need for a more effective means to reduce the incidence of unwanted adolescent pregnancy. How can it be done? A comprehensive approach at several levels is needed. Following are a few suggested approaches.

1. *Expanded sex education efforts.* The best model for sex education and the best data supporting the influence of the model on rates of pregnancy come from efforts outside the United States. The adolescent pregnancy rate in this country is the highest in the Western world. For example, the adolescent

pregnancy rate in the United States is twice as high as it is in England or Canada. It is three times as high as it is in Sweden. Yet, the adolescents in the United States are not any more sexually active than adolescents in these other countries. In fact, adolescents in Sweden are more sexually active at an earlier age and are more exposed to sexual activities through television. One difference may be that all children in Sweden, beginning at age 7, are enrolled in a sex education curriculum. The majority of parents appear to favor sex education in the schools.

In addition to sex education, decision-making skills, life skills, and life planning need to be emphasized. Barth (1996) has designed a school-based prevention program that emphasizes teaching young people problem-solving and assertiveness skills in addressing situations that include the risk of pregnancy.

2. *Increase access to birth control.* Many people believe that increased access to contraceptive devices would reduce the number of unwanted pregnancies. School-based clinics appear to be ideal because they can be community based, they can reduce stigma by providing a wide range of services, and their staff can work closely with other school officials and outside social service workers. A well-known example of a school-based clinic is Health Start, where primary and preventive services (physicals, emergency care, mental health, social work counseling) are offered during school hours at four schools (Dryfoos, 1990).

3. *Provide greater "life options" for young people.* Because many adolescent pregnancies are associated with social disadvantage, the implication is that changes in the social environment may be needed in order to enhance "life options" (Dryfoos, 1990). Increasingly, professionals are recognizing that adolescents have to become motivated to reduce their risk of pregnancy (Santrock, 1996). Edelman (1987) states the point succinctly: "The best contraceptive is a future."

4. *Enhance community involvement and support.* Too often, sex education and advice is seen as the parents' responsibility or the school's responsibility. In an important survey, Thornburg (1981) found that only 17% of adolescents' sex education comes from mothers and 2% from fathers. Yet we know that contraceptive use increases when there is greater communication between parent and adolescent about sex. But our efforts must go beyond the parents to a community-wide level (Blau & Gullotta, 1993). If we can change attitudes about sex education, we can enhance access to family planning services. In European countries where sex education is more open and without such conflict, adolescent pregnancy rates are much lower than they are in the United States.

SEX EDUCATION AND ADOLESCENT DEVELOPMENT

Does the adolescent's cognitive development have an influence on the success of sex education? Joan Lipsitz (1980) believes it does, because giving adolescents contraceptives is not enough. What does matter is adolescents' cognitive development—their acceptance of themselves and their sexuality. This level of acceptance depends on young people's emotional and cognitive development, or maturity. The prevention of adolescent pregnancy involves some very complicated features, including the ability to approach problem solving in a planned and organized way, the ability to anticipate consequences, the ability to delay gratification, and the ability to communicate in a direct manner.

However, many of these capabilities require the ability to solve problems and anticipate consequences—cognitive abilities that many adolescents are just beginning to develop. As a result, a lot of what is being used in prevention programs may not be appropriate for early adolescents. In late adolescence, there is some realistic and future-oriented thinking about sexual experiences. In middle adolescence, there is often much romanticizing about sexuality. And in early adolescence, sexuality is depersonalized in a manner that gives way to anxiety and denial.

Some researchers (Murray, 1996) recognize these differences in sexual maturity and assert that, to be effective, prevention programs should address sexual readiness and emerging sexual identities and orientations. The programs that teach only abstinence may be effective only for adolescents who refrain from sex anyway. Abstinence-only programs also fail to educate sexually active students about responsibility.

Precisely because adolescence is a time of sexual awakening, sexual feelings should be discussed, not ignored. Educators must realize that pubescent children need to understand their sexual feelings and changing bodies. Otherwise, unexplored, ill-defined sexuality can lead to frustration and irresponsible sexual behavior.

SEXUALLY TRANSMITTED DISEASES

Sexually transmitted diseases are an increasing concern among adolescents, particularly with the development of AIDS (acquired immune deficiency syndrome). AIDS is a disease for which there is no known cure. It is caused by a virus that attacks and destroys the body's immune system. The effects are both devastating and deadly. It is difficult to understand the incidence of AIDS in adolescence because it has a long incubation period that can last more than ten years from contraction of the HIV virus to clinical manifestation. We do know that the rate of AIDS is doubling every year and that the total current number exceeds 665,000—60,000 more than the number of American lives lost in the entire Vietnam War. It is estimated that one-half of all new HIV infections in the United States are among people under 25. Two minority groups, African-American and Hispanic, represent more than 50% of all adolescents with AIDS and 75% of all children with AIDS (Steel, 1988, cited in Dryfoos, 1990). According to the Centers for Disease Control, more than 90% of the adolescents surveyed understand that AIDS can be transmitted through sexual intercourse and sharing of needles; however, adolescents are also misinformed about contraction of the disease through blood tests and public toilets. More detailed information about other sexually transmitted diseases is discussed in the chapter on young adulthood.

ALCOHOL AND OTHER DRUG USE

No discussion of adolescent social hazards would be complete without a section on alcohol and other drug use. For many people—parents, teachers, and human service professionals—this is the number-one social issue facing young people today. Drinking is a big part of being an adolescent in today's world. One study found that almost all, 93%, of high school students had begun

drinking before graduating and that more than half, 56%, had begun drinking between the sixth and ninth grades (Johnston, O'Malley, & Bachman, 1985, 1988).

Binge drinking, typically defined as having five or more drinks in a row, is the most common problem behavior during adolescence and young adulthood (Schulenberg et al., 1996). A survey revealed that 28% of the nation's high school seniors and 40% of those 21 to 22 years old had engaged in binge drinking at least once within the previous two weeks (Johnston, O'Malley, & Bachman, 1994). There is little doubt that binge drinking, particularly if frequent, is an important health-compromising behavior. Specifically, frequent binge drinking makes one vulnerable to ongoing problems with alcohol, as well as other health-compromising behaviors, such as violence, use of illicit drugs, unprotected or unwanted sex, and driving while intoxicated (Schulenberg et. al, 1996), and it may reflect difficulties with the transition into young adulthood.

Another study found that 16% of eighth-graders had used marijuana, and 2.6% used cocaine. Thirty-five percent of twelfth-graders had used marijuana, and 4% had used cocaine (van Biema, 1995). In 1996, the U.S. Department of Health and Human Services released a study including almost 18,000 Americans and concluded that marijuana use among teens (ages 12 to 17) rose 105% from 1992 to 1994 and gained 37% between 1994 and 1995. Figure 9.3 shows the percentages of high school seniors using various drugs.

What causes young people to be more likely to abuse drugs? This question has undergone extensive research; several different factors play a significant role in drug use. In general, drug use by peers, drug use by parents, the belief that drugs lead to tension reduction, delinquent behavior, stress, a sense of power, and low self-esteem are often cited as key factors. Jessor (1987) suggests that problem behavior like drug use is linked to adolescents' attempt to assert their independence and become more adult-like. Also, drinking may be a learned mechanism for coping with frustration at the failure to attain more conventional goals.

Have you ever heard a parent proclaim; "Other teens drink, but not my kid." Are these parents stating a fact or a wish? Researchers in the Midwest (Bogenschneider, Wu, Raffaelli, & Tsay, 1998) studied almost 350 teens and their parents. All the teens admitted to

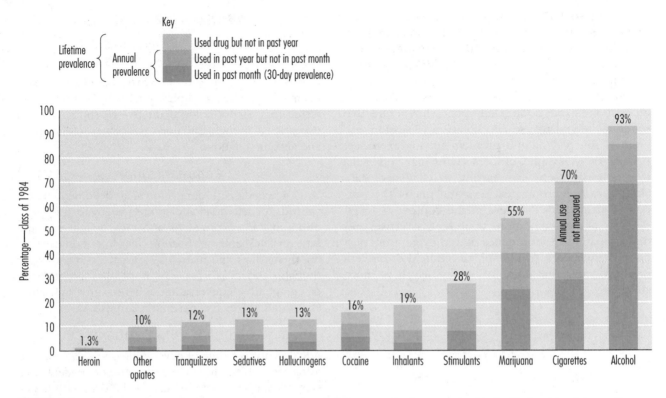

FIGURE 9.3   **Drug use among high school seniors (Johnston, O'Malley, & Bachman, 1985, for the National Institute on Drug Abuse, Publication No. ADM 85-1394)**

regular alcohol use, but less than a third of the parents were aware of it. Of those parents who were aware, they and their teenage children were more likely to discuss the risky behaviors associated with alcohol use, and parents were more likely to be realistic about their teen's friends' drinking behaviors. Do you think parental awareness helps protect teens from risky consequences?

In a 12-year longitudinal study of problem drinking among adolescents, Jessor (1987) found that three factors differentiated problem drinkers from other adolescents—their personal qualities, their social environment, and their other patterns of behavior.

In terms of personal qualities, problem drinkers were clearly alienated from conventional values. For example, they did not value academic achievement, religion, or conventional nondeviant behavior. In terms of their social environment, they perceived large differ-

ences between their parents' values and their friends' values, were more influenced by friends than parents, and had peers who also engaged in problem drinking.

Thus, problem drinking occurs within the context of other problem behaviors. In other words, problem drinkers were more likely than other adolescents to engage in additional problem behaviors, such as sexual activity and delinquency. Their behavior is part of a larger syndrome of norm-breaking problem behaviors. Therefore, adolescent drinking would predict other adolescent problem behaviors as well.

Implications for Practice: Combining Drug Prevention with Life Skills

But what about intervention programs aimed at preventing a variety of these problem behaviors? D.A.R.E. (Drug Abuse Resistance Education) is installed in 80% of America's school districts (van Biema, 1995). Police officers present 17 sessions on specific drugs and resisting peer pressure. Unfortunately, while immediately successful in preventing drug use, D.A.R.E. may not have a sustained effect on preventing drug use as the students grow older. However, a program named Life Skills (Botvin, 1980), originally designed to fight teen smoking, has additionally been shown effective to reduce teen drug use. Life Skills is a 15-session program of role-playing and problem solving exercises. Instead of uniformed officers (who may represent the authority teens are starting to challenge), Life Skills uses homeroom teachers and peers. The purpose is to present drug use in the context of social skills—making teens more confident, assertive, and discriminating about the messages they get from pop culture and peers. In the subjective field of prevention, programs that combine issues may have more success.

Summary

DEVELOPMENTAL THEMES

Adolescence represents a journey of discovery—a search to find out more about who one is. Peer approval is considered very important in early adolescence. By late adolescence, two developmental tasks are critical: independence from the family and the development of personal identity. Erikson refers to this stage as identity versus identity confusion. Many of the problems young people face are not with the youths themselves but a result of reduced opportunities and a neglect of support from a caring adult.

BIOPHYSICAL DIMENSION

Biophysical Growth and Development

Adolescents experience a growth spurt with rapid gains in height and weight. Biologically, adolescence begins with the onset of the pubertal process. This leads to hormonal changes in boys and girls. These physical and hormonal changes require psychological adjustment. Early-maturing boys have a positive self-image, while early-maturing girls may have difficulties. Some hazards include: eating habits, weight concerns, dysmenorrhea, acne, and headaches.

PSYCHOLOGICAL DIMENSION

Cognitive Development and Information Processing

Adolescence is a period of formal operations. Adolescents can now use complex and abstract thinking referred to as hypothetical-deductive reasoning. Formal operational thought includes two states: assimilation and accommodation.

Communication

In adolescence, communication skills become more advanced. For example, adolescents begin to use metaphors in their expressions and they delight in using satire. Adolescents can become very intent on expressing themselves, and many use journals to record their thoughts and ideas. In general, boys talk more in terms of competitive conversation, whereas girls talk more about themselves, feelings, and relationships.

Attitudes and Emotions

Adolescence is a time of developing one's self-concept. Adolescents begin to assume greater independent decision making, feel less pressure to conform with peers, experience dating and awareness of their sexuality, and begin to consider major decisions that affect their adult life. In essence, they develop an increasingly integrated self. In adolescence, self-esteem is influenced by parental support, parental control, and parental participation, perceptions of family cohesion, and a sense of belonging to one's family. Family support is the best predictor of self-esteem.

Although adolescence used to be considered a time of crisis, this notion is now considered to be a myth. Adolescents do, however, cycle through moods rapidly. Adolescence is also a time for the development of identity. Identity status theory describes four different identity stages that adolescents experience: diffusion, foreclosure, moratorium, and achievement. Adolescents of color may need to establish an identity in two different cultural systems—their own ethnic values and the values of the majority culture. One aspect of achieving an identity is seeking independence from one's family. There are four main strategies for enhancing adolescents' self-concept: (1) encouraging achievement, (2) promoting competencies in specific areas,

(text continues on p. 409)

A Depressed Adolescent

DEVELOPMENTAL HISTORY

Susie Lee, a 13-year-old Chinese-American female, was brought to the agency by her biological parents. Susie's parents are third-generation Chinese-Americans who live according to American cultural norms and values. Susie has two brothers and one sister, all younger than she.

Susie's parents discussed her early development, including pregnancy and childhood illnesses. Susie's mother reported that her pregnancy was normal with no complications. She also states that she was very careful throughout her pregnancy to avoid food, drink, medication, or illegal substances that could harm her developing fetus. The only medical problems out of the ordinary were Susie's seizures at the age of 5 as a result of influenza. Her mother reported no developmental delays and that Susie crawled, walked, and talked at the appropriate times.

BIOPHYSICAL CONSIDERATIONS

Susie often has trouble sleeping at night and reports periodic nightmares (one or two per month). She also has experienced *night eating syndrome*—being unable to sleep at night, she eats. Then by morning she does not feel like eating breakfast. She has a tendency to consume a large amount of food quickly and feels bad afterward about having done that. She does not eat a balanced diet. She denies any self-induced vomiting. This sequence of events often leads to severe self-criticism. Susie was an early-maturing female who had her first menses at 11 years of age. She has been diagnosed with *dysmenorrhea* (painful menstruation) and often complains about having stomachaches.

PSYCHOLOGICAL CONSIDERATIONS

Cognitive Development and Information Processing

Susie appears to be of average intelligence and performs well academically. Last year she had above-average grades of As and Bs. In discussing her self-criticism, Susie demonstrated abstract thinking ability as she commented introspectively about her own thought processes. She demonstrates complex thinking about the psychological processes she is experiencing. However, Susie is often unable to make simple decisions because she is literally thinking too much about a decision. Susie believes she is invulnerable—that no harm can come to her. Although this is an aspect of normal cognitive development, it can lead to negative outcomes if her thinking influences her behavior.

Communication

One of Susie's strengths is her ability to communicate her thoughts and feelings clearly and directly. She expresses concern about her eating habits and about feeling down and irritable much of the time.

Attitudes and Emotions

Susie expresses intense emotions that range from extreme anger to hopelessness. She describes feeling sad, irritable, touchy, "on edge," and depressed. She described some of her feelings as "I feel like I'm falling into a dark tunnel that I cannot climb out of; screaming all the way down but no one hears me." Sometimes she's deeply sad and spends a lot of time crying. Other days she's extremely irritable—everybody and everything bothers her. When asked about how she perceives herself, she reports feeling like the ugliest girl at school. She often looks in the mirror and sees a fat,

(continued)

ugly person. She is extremely preoccupied with how "bad" she thinks she looks. "I hate my body," she reports. A lot of her self-criticism is related to her binge eating and her negative body image. Susie scored in the depressed range on the Beck Depression Inventory. She admitted that she thought about suicide previously—especially after a friend had committed suicide. At present she denies any thoughts of suicide. She does not have access to a gun.

Social Cognition and Regulation

Susie expresses strong egocentric thoughts. She is preoccupied with her feelings and behaviors in a self-conscious manner. This is demonstrated in her body perceptions—she is very concerned about how others are going to view her body and looks. She feels self-conscious about not having a boyfriend at the present time. This style of thinking is an entry to more intensely self-critical statements. She reports being quite concerned about what her peers are saying and doing and has difficulty expressing any independence around them. Her parents report that she "gives in to peer pressure all the time and that this gets her into a lot of trouble." Her mother expressed specific concern that she would not be able to say no to sexual advances by boys. In the one-to-one interview with Susie, she discussed having been sexually active with a previous boyfriend. She reports inconsistent use of birth control methods.

SOCIAL CONSIDERATIONS

Family Situation

Susie experiences serious family conflict, including a highly conflicted relationship and lack of closeness with her father. Indeed, her father still spanks her. Furthermore, Susie suffered a major loss when her favorite grandfather died last year of cancer. In addition, she started junior high school this school year, and this has been a difficult transition for her.

Susie expressed concern over her inability to get along with her family. In particular, fairness is a big issue with Susie. She reports that her siblings are treated more fairly than she is. Her parents describe situations in which Susie feels she is being treated unfairly and throws a temper tantrum. For example, last week she threw a tantrum because she found a box from a fast-food meal that had been her brother's lunch, stating that it wasn't fair that he got one and she did not. She threw things around the living room, started yelling, and ran to her room crying. Susie reports being gruff and harsh with family members on a daily basis. Her oppositional behavior is also evident on a regular, but not daily, basis when she lies, loses her temper, argues with her parents, fights with her siblings, or refuses to do her chores. She says she "feels unimportant to this family" and that everyone sees her as a "bad" kid. She is angry at her father and believes he mistreats her—especially by spanking her. She also believes that her parents, particularly her father, do not love her.

Groups, Social Supports, and Communities

Susie feels like an outsider at school although she has three or four friends she regularly interacts with. Recently Susie has found it difficult to go to school. When she is in school, she feels empty and dull. Although she used to be involved in after-school activities, she has no extracurricular activities now. When asked if she has an adult she is close to, she said there was no one for her to talk with, especially since her grandfather died. Her parents are frustrated with her and do not provide her with much emotional support.

Multicultural and Gender Considerations

Susie disclosed concern regarding her identity. Although her family is very well acculturated, she has recently been questioning the significance of her Chinese-American background since meeting a student at school who is very involved in the Chinese culture. She has expressed concern about how others may be viewing her. For example, at school she believes teachers expect more from her than other students when she turns in assignments or takes exams. She resents the additional pressure she feels from her teachers and her parents. She wants to be treated "just like everyone else." Her parents are frightened that they are losing control over her, and Susie complains that her parents are not giving her enough freedom. Although Susie's family is highly acculturated, they are having a difficult time reconciling their family values with the values and norms of the dominant society.

SUMMARY AND IMPRESSIONS

As a result of assessment, it is apparent that Susie has several problems that need to be addressed:

1. Depression
2. Irritable with extreme mood swings
3. Resentful behavior toward siblings
4. Uncontrolled anger outbursts

5. Poor family relationships
6. Possible unresolved grief
7. Adjustment issues involving her developmental stage (for example, identity concerns)
8. High-risk behaviors such as unprotected sexual intercourse

Although the family members are experiencing difficulties, they do provide a stable, predictable living situation for Susie and her siblings. Susie's father earns a steady income that provides adequate resources. Susie's mother works part-time while the children are at school and states that she is usually home when they return from school. They have lived in the community for five years and have established a network of family friends and church support. In addition, both parents appear genuinely concerned and willing to evaluate their parenting techniques in order to work toward a positive outcome. Susie's strengths include her intellect and thoughtfulness, her good communication skills, and her desire for improved family relationships.

(3) provision of peer and parental support, and (4) developing coping skills.

Social Cognition and Regulation

Adolescents are continuing to develop their moral reasoning abilities. Kohlberg's theory of moral development suggests that adolescents are in stage 3, "interpersonal conformity"—their reason to be good is to have others think well of them and, so, they can think well of themselves. To do "what's right" is to be a nice person and live up to the expectations of others. By late adolescence, most young people move to stage 4, "responsibility to the system," and they reason that they should fulfill their responsibilities to the social system of which they are part. Related to moral development is adolescent egocentrism, whereby young people are preoccupied with their behavior and thoughts in a self-conscious manner. There are two aspects of egocentric thought: the imaginary audience and the

personal fable. Adolescents develop the ability to monitor their social thoughts—a conscious self-awareness.

Psychological Hazards

Adolescents can develop a number of behavior problems that are both externalizing and internalizing. One fairly common externalizing disorder is conduct disorder, or delinquent activity. When deviant behavior occurs at early ages, the problem is viewed as conduct disorder. However, when the behaviors lead to illegal acts by juveniles, then the problem is identified as delinquency. Delinquency can be predicted from behavior displayed at early ages. Delinquent adolescents often come from disturbed families in which there is an absence of social and emotional support. This deficiency allows negative peer influences to become more significant. Behavioral treatment approaches are commonly used with children who have delinquent behaviors. Examples of internalizing disorders are depression and suicide. Rarely does a person commit suicide without giving clues to others.

SOCIAL DIMENSION

Families, Groups, Support Systems, and Communities

Three key developmental tasks for the family include the development of autonomy, the resolution of parent-adolescent conflict, and parent-adolescent attachment. Three types of parenting styles have been identified: authoritative parenting, authoritarian, and laissez-faire (with two types: permissive indifferent and permissive indulgent). Research studies have supported the effectiveness of authoritative parenting.

Adolescence and peer groups go hand in hand. Peer group interaction is a critical source of development of personal and social competence for adolescents. Peer pressure and conformity are evident in the adolescent years. Friendships flourish, and adolescents become capable of sharing intimately with one another. Social skills training can be an effective method of addressing many problems that adolescents experience. Adolescent peer groups are usually organized according to cliques or crowds.

Gangs have become an increasing problem for adolescents, and they appear to be related to the developmental need for young people to associate with peer groups. In adolescence, many young people of color become more aware of their ethnic minority status.

Schools play a critical role in facilitating the development of adolescents. The social and organizational aspects of schools can influence adolescent development. Often the transition between schools (for example from elementary school to middle school) can be difficult for adolescents. Both middle schools and high schools could be better designed to meet students' needs. A serious problem in the schools is the high dropout rate.

Multicultural and Gender Considerations

The adolescent immigrant must overcome special problems. Adolescents are becoming increasingly identified with their gender roles; however, there is more acceptance of androgyny, which is the combination of male and female behaviors in the same person. Adolescent girls face some difficult issues, and many lose their voice or sense of self. Depression is also more common for girls and often has to do with their body image. The development of sexual identity is a major task during this period. Adolescents discover their heterosexual or homosexual tendencies. By the end of high school, the majority of adolescents have had experience with sexual intercourse. There are four factors related to early sexual behavior: biological influences, history of sexual abuse, experiencing other problem behaviors, and normative expectations. AIDS prevention takes on special significance in the adolescent years.

Social Hazards

Many children and adolescents today are growing and developing in a violent world. Children and adolescents are being victimized on a daily basis, at home and in school. Adolescent problem behavior theory helps us to understand adolescents at risk. This theory identifies protective and risk factors that influence adolescent risk-taking behavior. Adolescents juggle school, friends, boyfriends or girlfriends, family and work. The amount of hours involved in work can have positive or negative effects on adolescents. Adolescent pregnancy and childbirth are also concerns. The consequences of adolescent pregnancy are significant for both the mother and the child. Adolescent fathers are being recognized as playing a more critical role in the adolescent pregnancy problem. A clear need exists in developing methods to reduce the incidence of adolescent pregnancy. There needs to be improved sex education and education about sexual assault for adolescent boys, as well as for gay youth. Abstinence-only programs fail to educate sexually active students about responsibility. An additional concern about adolescent sexual behavior is sexually transmitted diseases. Binge drinking is the most common problem behavior during adolescence and young adulthood.

Online Resources

Center for Adolescent Studies: Indiana University
http://education.indiana.edu/cashmpg.html
This adolescent online directory is an electronic guide to information on adolescent issues, sponsored by the Center for Adolescent Studies at Indiana University.

The American Academy of Child Adolescent Psychiatry
http://www.aacap.org
> This site contains information on recent news, facts for families, clinical practice and managed care, and research and training.

Girls Incorporated
http://www.reeusda.gov/pavnet/pm/pmgirls.htm
> This national organization offers technical assistance to community leaders who wish to start local Girls' groups.

Studies in Moral Development and Education
www.uic.edu/~lnucci/MoralEd
> This page links educators, scholars, and citizens who want to share their work and learn more about research, practices, and activities in the area of moral development and education.

Fathers and Their Families—Gangs
www.kidscampaigns.org/whoseside/maddads/gangs.html
> The Office of juvenile Justice and Delinquency Prevention offers fact sheets and full reports on gang activity and community initiatives to suppress it.

Survivors of the System: Foster Children United
http://www.azstarnet.com/nmarier/sos
> Promotes the voices of youth involved in or coming from the foster care system.

Teen Pregnancy
http://www.angelfire.com/yt/teenhealthcore/teenpreg.html
http://www.teenpregnancy.org
http://www.notmenotnow.org
> These sites have information and resources about teen pregnancy.

Free to Be Me
http://www.freetobeme.com
> Becoming the person I want to be. FAQs about youth sexual orientation.

 ## InfoTrac® College Edition

For interesting materials related to what you have just read, please go to the *InfoTrac College Edition* website and search using the following key words:

adolescent peer groups	adolescent suicide
high school dropouts	adolescent ethnicity
adolescent body image	delinquency

Key Terms

androgen
authoritarian parenting
authoritative parenting
care perspective
clique
concrete thinking
conduct disorder
connectedness
crowd
endocrine glands
estrogen
formal operational thought
gang
gonadotropins
hormones
human immunodeficiency virus (HIV)
hypothalamus
hypothetical-deductive reasoning

imaginary audience
individuation
justice perspective
laissez-faire parenting
menarche
moral development
obesity
ovaries
personal fable
psychological moratorium
puberty
rite of passage
self-esteem
social cognitive monitoring
social skills training
testes

Developmental Themes

Stage: intimacy vs. isolation. Independence from parents; economic independence; friendships, career, and marriage; transition to parenthood.

Biophysical Dimension

Biophysical Growth and Development
Changes in reproductive systems during early adulthood, the impact of hormones on women, peak of physical development, loss of muscle and increase in fat weight, and development of health patterns.

Biophysical Hazards
Health hazards, cancer and self-examinations, unhealthful lifestyle and life expectancy.

Psychological Dimension

Cognitive Development and Information Processing
Formal thought, reduced egocentrism, abstract thinking, and postformal thought.

Communication
Miscommunication, intimacy in communication, gender and communication, communicating with the deaf.

Attitudes and Emotions
Development of intimacy, opportunities for love, possibility of isolation and loneliness, shyness, search for an identity, commitment to a sense of identity in multiple contexts.

Social Cognition and Regulation
Moral development, responsibility, morality of justice, morality of care.

Psychological Hazards
Major life decisions, serious mental disorders, depression.

Social Dimension

Families, Groups, Support Systems, and Communities
Marriage, selecting a partner, coming together, adjustment to marriage, marital expectations and myths, being single, gay or lesbian relationships, transition to parenthood, work life, women and work.

Multicultural and Gender Considerations
Gender roles, multicultural challenges, motherhood mandates, gender expectations and stereotypes, challenges for persons of color.

Social Hazards
Families with a disabled member, divorce, sexual harassment, sexually transmitted diseases, rape and sexual assault, spouse abuse and effects on the family.

CHAPTER

10

Young Adulthood

CHAPTER CONTENTS

DEVELOPMENTAL THEMES

"I want to be smart. I want to be somebody. I want to make money. I want to be a successful lawyer, but my personal life comes first. I want to be a lovely wife, do my husband's shirts, take Chinese cooking lessons, and have two children. . . . I want to have a briefcase in my hands. I want to look good and feel good and be happy in what I am doing."
—Nicole DiMarco

The preceding quote from Ruth Sidel's book *On Her Own* (1990), a study about young women today, describes the aspirations, challenges, and difficulties that many young adults face. Young adulthood, which is considered a major life transition, is a critical period that spans the ages of 22 to 34 years. In young adulthood, significant life roles become established. Young people move from a preoccupation with the self to a focus on intimacy that often leads to marriage, children, and the need to establish a stable career path. In many ways, everything that has taken place before this stage can be considered preparation for adulthood.

Perhaps two of the most critical developmental tasks at this age are economic independence and independent decision making. Often these two aspects are considered to be the hallmarks of the transition from adolescence to young adulthood (Santrock, 1996). Eco-nomic independence occurs as young people move from high school or college into the workforce on a full-time basis. This change entails major life changes, because living independently carries with it new responsibilities. Many of these new responsibilities lead to independent decision making: where to work, where to live, how to budget income, what kind of dates to go on, when to get married, and so forth.

Whereas adolescents are preoccupied with the self, young adults turn outward and focus on social and intimate relationships with others, as described by Erikson (1974):

In youth you find out what you care to do and who you care to be—even in changing roles. In young adulthood you learn whom you care to be with—at work and in private life, not only exchanging intimacies but sharing intimacy. In adulthood, however, you learn to know what and whom you can take care of (p. 124).

Levinson describes young adulthood as focusing on choices in love, occupation, friendship, values, and lifestyle. The following Focus section describes the stages of adulthood according to Levinson.

FOCUS ON DEVELOPMENT

Levinson's Eight Stages of Adult Development

Levinson and his colleagues (1978) were instrumental in developing a theory of adult development. On the basis of intensive interviews with adult men at different stages in the life cycle, Levinson set forth his ideas about the stages adults go through. More recently he has expanded his theory to include adult women (Levinson, 1985, 1986). Levinson outlined eight developmental stages in young and middle adulthood. Fundamental to his theory is his notion of "life structure." A life structure represents a basic pattern of an adult's life at a particular time. A person's life structure reflects the choices a person makes, such as marriage, childrearing, career, and so forth. According to Levinson, the stages of the adult life cycle alternate between stability and turmoil and transition. The stages are summarized as follows:

1. *Ages 17 to 22:* Leave adolescence; make preliminary choices for adult life.

2. *Ages 22 to 28:* Initial choices in love, occupation, friendship, values, lifestyle.

3. *Ages 28 to 33:* Change in life structure, either a moderate change or, more often, a severe and stressful crisis.

4. *Ages 33 to 40:* Establish a niche in society; progress on a timetable, both in family and in career accomplishments.

5. *Ages 40 to 45:* Life structure comes into question; usually a time of crisis in the meaning, direction, and value of each person's life; neglected parts of the self (talents, desires, aspirations) seek expression.

6. *Ages 45 to 50:* Choices must be made and a new life structure formed; the person must commit to new tasks.

7. *Ages 50 to 55:* Further questioning and modification of the life structure; men who did not have a crisis at age 40 are likely to have one now.

8. *Ages 55 to 60:* Build a new life structure; can be a time of great fulfillment.

BIOPHYSICAL DIMENSION

Biophysical Growth and Development

Physical development in young adulthood represents both the peak of physical development and its slow decline as the body gets older. Our physical performance is usually the strongest during the early 20s. An easy way to assess the body's performance is to examine the average ages of Olympic gold medalists. Only about 15% of Olympic medalists are over the age of 30

(Santrock, 1996). The peak of muscular strength occurs between age 25 and 30 years and decreases about 10% between age 30 and 60 years. As a result, the mid-20s are a good age for speed and agility. However, professional athletes perform well into their 30s when they are competing in endurance sports, such as long-distance running and weight lifting.

In young adulthood, many individuals begin a pattern of health-conscious behavior. Indeed, the workout frenzy is very popular among this age group. This is a particularly good time to begin a healthy lifestyle. Many individuals at this age realize their once teenage metabolism is slowing down, and they start putting on weight and may struggle to avoid excessive weight gain and obesity. During early adulthood, the percentage of body weight composed of muscle decreases. This represents not a loss of muscle but an increase in fat weight (Haywood, 1986). It is recommended that body fat be 15% to 18% for men and 20% to 25% for women. Women typically have more fat deposits in the buttocks, thighs, breasts, and shoulders, whereas men distribute their fat more evenly. Body composition reflects an individual's overall physical health.

Fat in the body is stored in adipose cells. As these cells fill, your hunger is satisfied. If the cells are empty, then you are going to be hungry. As people gain weight, they increase the size of fat cells in the body—and at this point, it becomes difficult to make them shrink. Obese people have an excessive amount of fat cells in their bodies. One reason that we gain more weight as we age is that our **basal metabolism rate,** which is the minimum amount of energy that we use in our resting state, decreases. The implication of the decrease is this: To maintain the same weight as we had in the past, we must eat less.

Although restrictive diets are popular, exercise combined with proper diet is a more effective means by which to lose weight. Exercise is important because it burns up calories and continues to raise the metabolic rate for several hours after the exercise. Exercise can be effective in weight loss because it lowers the body's set point for weight and makes it easier to maintain a lower weight. The most effective means to lose weight is to exercise *and* eat a low-fat, healthy diet. The American Dietetic Association recommends the following: 10–15 grams of fiber per day, limiting intake to 30% of daily calories from fat, and increasing to 50%–60% the daily calories derived from complex carbohydrates such as fruits, vegetables, and grains.

REPRODUCTIVE SYSTEM DURING EARLY ADULTHOOD

This stage of development is considered the best period for a woman to become pregnant. A woman in her early 20s has a mature reproductive system and is likely to produce fertile eggs. Also, her hormone production is relatively regular. Because her physical abilities are at her peak and her uterus is receptive to a pregnancy, this is an ideal time for a safe and healthy delivery of a baby (Schuster & Ashburn, 1992).

EFFECT OF HORMONES ON WOMEN

Although hormones influence both men and women, their effect on women is stronger. As women progress through the **menstrual cycle,** their hormones fluctuate. In particular, estrogen levels rise to their highest point when a woman is ovulating and then begin to decline as she approaches her menstrual period. After ovulation, progesterone levels begin to increase. When progesterone production is at its highest, about ten days before the beginning of the menstrual cycle, some women experience the set of symptoms known as **premenstrual syndrome (PMS).** PMS is associated with breast tenderness, a bloated feeling, irritability, and negative moods occurring just before the menstrual period.

Although women are affected by PMS, most are not incapacitated. Nevertheless, in one study, a small portion of women, less than 10%, believed that their PMS symptoms could be considered severe (Woods, Most, & Dery, 1982). Some women report mild forms of these symptoms, but many women do not experience any symptoms at all.

One particularly fascinating study sheds some light on the social as well as the biological factors that influence premenstrual and menstrual symptoms. In a study of college women, Englander-Golden, Sonleitner, Whitmore, and Corbley (1986) found that women report more symptom changes over a month if they know that their menstrual cycles are being studied

than if they are just reporting how they feel on certain days with no reference to their menstrual cycle. The implication from this research is that stereotypes of what women "should" experience during menstruation affect what they experience and subsequently report. Related to this research is the finding that women in more traditional roles report more negative emotions during premenstrual and menstrual cycles than do women in nontraditional occupations or women who are highly educated (Brown & Woods, 1986; Woods, Most, & Dery, 1982). However, significant symptoms should not be discounted. In fact, DSM-IV, the classification system for psychiatric disorders, includes as a condition for further consideration the new diagnosis of Premenstrual Dysphoric Disorder. Some women suffering from this disorder may benefit from antidepressants.

Biophysical Hazards

An important health hazard of the reproductive system for both women and men is cancer. Women are encouraged to develop the habit of breast self-examination. During their lifetime, more than one in nine women will develop breast cancer (Javroff, 1996). Conducting a self-examination is easy and can be a life saver. Women should choose the same time each month to conduct the exam, preferably after the menstrual period has ended. This time frame is important because the breasts vary in size and texture during the menstrual cycle, but after the menstrual period they are not swollen. Health professionals can instruct women how to conduct the exam, and the American Cancer Society has brochures that describe the procedure.

Men are also encouraged to conduct a self-examination of the testes. Testicular cancer is a common disease for men between 15 and 35 years old and is the most common cause of cancer death among young adult males. Self-examination is important because, when detected, testicular cancer is second only to skin cancer in terms of successful cure rate. Men should be taught by a health professional how to perform the exam.

Additional physical hazards include diseases such as AIDS and homicide—particularly for African-American men, as described in the following Focus section. Also, in early adulthood many men and women suffer from the consequences of excessive drinking. The subsequent Focus section on drinking describes efforts to combat the abuse of alcohol by young people.

FOCUS ON MULTICULTURALISM

▼

Life and Death for African-Americans

Consider the following statistics:

- Three African-American males between the ages of 15 and 44 die for every white American male.

- Homicide is the leading cause of death of African-American males between the ages of 15 and 24.

- Nearly one in every three black men between 20 and 29 years of age is behind bars, on probation, or on parole.

- African-American males contract AIDS at a rate of 29.9 per 1,000, whereas for white male Americans the rate is 9.7 per 1,000.

- For black men the average life expectancy is 65, eight years less than for white males.

This data graphically reveals that the life expectancy for the African-American male is actually declining. In addition, health care coverage is a serious problem for African-Americans. Almost one-quarter of all African-Americans are not covered by private health insurance. As a result, African-Americans have higher incidences of chronic disability and illness.

(Baruth & Manning, 1991; Lacayo, 1995)

FOCUS ON BIOPHYSICS

▼

To Drink or Not to Drink: Is That Really the Question?

Loaded. Plastered. Tanked. Smashed. College entrance exam vocabulary? Guess again. These are colloquial terms for the all-too-familiar collegiate phenomenon of getting drunk. Although research indicates that most students successfully mature past the period of heavy drinking, the college period is one of heightened vulnerability to the pressures associated with alcohol consumption. Traditional prevention efforts have relied on educating the population about the potential dangers of abusing alcohol, assuming that the individual will apply this information to his or her own personal situation. Recently, prevention has taken on a new focus: affecting people's motivation and desire to drink. This approach is being implemented on college campuses and in small towns.

From laboratory data collected over more than ten years, researcher Alan Marlatt has found that "peer pressure and expectancies about sexual arousal and social acceptance could increase the reported amount people drink" (Azar, 1995, p. 20). Marlatt also found factors that could decrease the reported amount people drink: exercise, meditation, and participation in community activities. Marlatt is now using the information he discovered in his field research. His energies are aimed not at preventing drinking but at preventing development of drinking problems and ensuing injuries in those individuals who already drink.

With these goals in mind, Marlatt developed a six-week cognitive-behavioral program that (1) challenges the glamorous portrayal of the effects of alcohol; (2) emphasizes awareness of one's drinking habits as a safety precaution; and (3) suggests plausible alternatives to drinking—exercise, nonalcoholic parties, and community work. A one-hour motivational interview emphasizing these areas was effective in reducing binge drinking among small groups of college students.

On the basis of this success, Marlatt and his colleagues began a longitudinal study in 1990, in which they followed 500 college students identified as high risk for problem drinking when they were high school seniors. Half the sample received no treatment, and the other half underwent the one-hour motivational interview when they started college. Students whose drinking problems persisted received the six-week program, and any students who showed signs of severe drinking problems were taken out of the study and given a referral for treatment.

Annual evaluations, even after three years, show that the program makes a significant difference in help-

Alcohol consumption in college has many negative ramifications, including unwanted sexual activity, negative altercations, and automobile accidents.

ing to accelerate "maturing out of drinking behavior" (Azar, 1995, p. 20). Marlatt has now targeted fraternities and sororities with the hope that the group format will foster group pressure toward behavior change.

Julianne Azimov (Based on Azar, 1995)

PSYCHOLOGICAL DIMENSION

Cognitive Development and Information Processing

According to Piaget, the formal operational thinking that occurs in adolescence is the last stage of cognitive development. Therefore, young adulthood is characterized by the same mechanisms of formal operational thought. You will recall that Piaget (1972) believed that formal operational thought consists of conceiving ab-

stract concepts, systematic thinking, and step-by-step logic. In late adolescence and young adulthood, people refine their formal operational approach to problem solving. The cognitive changes that take place in adulthood consist of cognitive operations that are applied to increasingly complex situations and problems.

Adults are better able to harness formal operational thinking because of their reduced egocentrism, and therefore adults approach problems with greater objectivity. Adults are also able to more effectively access past experiences and education in using the cognitive operations that are present. Labouvie-Vief (1985) suggests that a new integration in thought occurs in adulthood, but she believes that adulthood carries a pragmatic adaptive strategy that leads to decreased emphasis on the logical approach characterized in adolescence. Perhaps this pragmatic approach provides experience for adults in generating and considering an increased number of options and realistically hypothesizing the potential effects of each option—a facet of multidimensional thinking (Bornstein & Schuster, 1992).

Many people do not achieve the level of formal operational thinking. This could be the result of many factors, such as genetic limitations on their cognitive abilities or poor cognitive stimulation as children. Studies have shown that only 60%–75% of adolescents can solve any formal operational problems (Neimark, 1975), and no more than 30% of adults ever complete the transition to the highest levels of formal operational thought (Kuhn, Kohlberg, Langer, & Haan, 1977). This suggests that formal operational thinking is not universal and instead is achieved only by certain people who are perhaps trained in this type of thinking.

DEVELOPMENT OF POSTFORMAL THOUGHT

Labouvie-Vief (1985) used a scenario to examine the differences between adolescent and adult thinking. Compare the adult and adolescent responses to the following scenario (Labouvie-Vief, 1985). How is the thinking different?

> John is known to be a heavy drinker, especially when he goes to parties. Mary, John's wife, warns him that if he gets drunk one more time, she will leave him and take the children. Tonight John is out late at an office party. John comes home drunk (p. 13).

> Does Mary leave John? How certain are you of your answer?

The adolescent response is as follows (Labouvie-Vief, 1985).

> It's a good chance that she would leave him because she warns him that she will leave him and take the children, but warning isn't an absolute thing. . . . And, I'd be absolutely sure that, well let's see. . . I'm trying to go all the way. I'm trying to think of putting everything [together] so I can be absolutely certain of an answer. . . . It's hard to be absolutely certain. "If he gets drunk, then she'll leave and take the children." I want to say yes 'cause everything's in that favor, in that direction, but I don't know how I can conclude that she does leave John (pp. 17–18).

Here is the adult response (Labouvie-Vief, 1985):

> There was no right or wrong answer. You could get logically to both answers [yes or no] . . . It depends on the steps they take to their answer. If they base it on what they feel, what they know, and they have certain steps to get an answer, it can be logical (p. 41).

Which response seems more characteristic of formal operational thinking? In the adolescent response, there is an understanding of the ambiguity of the situation but also the need to search for the correct answer. The adult response does not search for a correct answer—there is tolerance of the ambiguity. It also presents a combination of logic and feeling in understanding the situation.

As Labouvie-Vief (1985) points out in this example, the adult would be scored as not having reached formal operational thought in this example. Does this mean that there is a decline in formal operational thought as one gets older? Perhaps it is not so much a decline as a qualitative shift in one's way of thinking.

Implications for Practice:
Rational Emotive Behavior Therapy
and The Americans with Disabilities Act*

If you had a disability, would you feel sorry for yourself? Albert Ellis, who developed Rational Emotive Behavioral Therapy, or REBT, in 1955, believes you would. He believes that people with disabilities are particularly prone to a "mindset of distorted self-deprecation" because they face criticism and scorn from others. Because they notice their own deficiencies and because many of their relatives and associates ignore or condemn them for it, they falsely tend to conclude, "My deficiencies make me a deficient, inadequate individual," says Ellis.

REBT's primary goal is to help people dispute their own irrational beliefs and to respond more effectively to the problems they encounter. He now challenges self-hatred with his disabled clients. Ellis helps his disabled clients recognize their worth; shows them how to minimize their self-pity, depression, and anger; and helps them accept the challenge of being productive and happy in spite of their disabilities. Clients in REBT learn a variety of cognitive remedies for their emotional pain, such as rational coping statements and positive visualization.

But are they really able to be productive in our prejudiced society? In 1992, disabled people successfully pressed for passage of the Americans with Disabilities Act. The specific goal was to provide America's 49 million physically and mentally disabled

---

*Misha Marvel (Adapted from Smolowe, 1995, & Sleek, 1995.)

people access to public areas and workplaces. The law's mandate requiring universal access to public buildings, transit systems, and communications networks made a once-intimidating world more navigable. Curb ramps, lift-equipped buses, and rest-room stalls for wheelchair users are now a common part of the American landscape.

But how are the disabled doing in the job market? Roughly two-thirds of all working-age disabled are still unemployed. This is the same proportion that was jobless when the law was passed. It is true that many will risk losing health benefits and government subsidies if they take jobs. But, this seems to go against the original spirit of the law, which was to "puncture the stifling isolation of the disabled and draw them into the mainstream of civic life" (Smolowe, 1995, p. 54). What would Mr. Ellis have to say?

Communication

In young adulthood, perhaps what is most pronounced about communication is the notion of *miscommunication*; young men and women can become quite focused on the differences in the way they communicate. Indeed, this notion is reflected in the popular culture. For example, Deborah Tannen's (1991) book *You Just Don't Understand: Women and Men in Conversation*, points out many of the significant ways in which women and men differ in their relationships with each other. Although gender differences do exist, much of our understanding of the differences between men and women boils down to sexual stereotyping. Often the prescription regarding differences is reduced to two conclusions: Men are in pursuit of power, and women are in pursuit of relationships. Such generalizations have yet to be supported by good studies.

However, many people have written about the different communication styles of men and women. Women obtain a much greater level of intimate communication with each other than men do. Women discuss more intimate topics and confide their personal lives more than men do. In fact, women often complain about their lack of intimate conversations with men. When men are with men, they seldom maintain an inti-

mate conversation. Men rarely confide in each other about their private lives in the same way women do.

Intimacy between a man and a woman does not always follow the pathway that seems most logical. It is not during a long drive to the country or during an evening's dinner that they speak intimately. Too often, it is only after a long fight or after one person explodes in frustration that they break through their normal communication and meet each other on a more intimate level.

Practitioners need to understand communication with a diverse range of clients. The following Focus section looks at communication with deaf individuals.

Communicating with the Deaf Requires More Than Just Signs

Social workers who work with deaf clients know that just using an interpreter does not address the whole picture. To be effective in working with deaf clients, social workers must understand the linguistic, cultural, educational, and service issues. Deaf people are different in that they represent a linguistic minority with a separate language—ASL (American Sign Language). Research in psycholinguistics has found that signing is not just gesticulation but that it has its own syntax and is well formed like other languages. What makes social work practice with deaf clients difficult is that one is working in a language that is not one's own. A common error in the assessment of deaf individuals lies in not understanding that they often read and write English at a much lower level than hearing students at the same age level. For example, a deaf high school graduate may have a reading level of only the fourth grade. For social workers attempting to evaluate deaf clients, they need to know how to evaluate a person with poor reading skills. Writing is also very different for the deaf because ASL and English have very different structures, styles, and syntax. As a result, deaf people can appear mentally disoriented when in fact they are not. Professionals are needed who specialize in deafness; however, few programs train professionals with a subspecialty in deafness.

Attitudes and Emotions

A major psychosocial task in young adulthood is the development of intimacy with others. Erikson referred to this stage as intimacy versus isolation. Indeed, many young adults become quite focused on building intimate relationships with others. Intimacy in this context refers to the ability to share one's true self—both the good and the bad parts. Developing intimacy involves taking a risk, sharing aspects about yourself while knowing that the other person can make judgments about what you share. Kiefer (1988, p. 131) describes the complexities involved in intimacy: "Any close relationship involves the exchange of demands and expectations, some of which are difficult and unpleasant. More importantly, getting to know someone intimately always involves hurt when illusions are dashed or expectations unfulfilled; and it always involves unpleasant insight into one's own weaknesses."

Experiences of intimacy may be quite different for men than for women. Carol Gilligan (1982) noted that, whereas for men, identity precedes intimacy, for women, these tasks seem instead to be congruent. Intimacy occurs hand in hand with identity, as the female comes to know herself through her relationship with others. Although Gilligan believes that men focus more on justice and women focus more on caring and relationships, she does see these perspectives as converging. She believes that the perspective between fairness, or justice, and care provides a better understanding of relations between the sexes and also provides a more comprehensive portrayal of adult work and family relationships.

The counterpoint to intimacy is isolation—the inability to share intimately with others. With a lack of such exchanges, you are robbed of the experience of having another person understand you from your point of view, insight and understanding of yourself, and support and encouragement concerning your actions and thoughts. Such isolation may lead to a deep sense of loneliness.

LOVE

One of the most prevalent emotions in young adulthood is love. Love takes on particular significance for the young adult, who begins to experience many meaningful emotional relationships. Indeed, such emotions of love are likely to lead to marriage in young adulthood. Erik Erikson identifies the core task of the early adult years as intimacy. As the task of identity is addressed, the individual moves toward preparation for intimacy. Those who cannot effectively resolve the tasks of intimacy are left to isolation and lack the ability to form reciprocal exchanges based on understanding, empathy, and support. A major developmental task of the young adult is to develop emotionally satisfying relationships—to experience love.

But what is love? This is a critical question asked by many young adults. A typical young adult scenario could be the following: Two young people meet, and they begin seeing each other. As their interest and excitement grows, they become increasingly obsessed with the other. They want to spend increasing amounts of time with each other, and they cannot get their sexual desires fulfilled, no matter how much they try. And although they are sharing what seem to be immense parts of themselves with each other, they do not know if this is *really* love. They realize that to keep the relationship going entails a certain amount of sacrifice and personal risk. They are unsure whether they should take the plunge and exclaim "I love you" to each other. They face an extremely difficult question that is quite common for young adults to ask: Is this love? How can I tell?

Is love something we can define and study? In the last 20 years, many researchers have set out to study love and achieve a more exacting understanding of this emotion. Most researchers begin by differentiating romantic love from "true" love. Robert Solomon (1988) describes three features common to romantic love: (1) it is sexual in origin and motivation; (2) it is spontaneous and voluntary—and not directly under our control; and (3) it is an emotion appropriate only between equals (for example, not between a mother and child).

Hatfield and Walster (1985) describe several myths that have resulted from our idealized concept of love:

- *Myth 1:* When you fall in love, you'll know it.
- *Myth 2:* When love does hit, you have no control over it.
- *Myth 3:* Love is a completely positive experience.
- *Myth 4:* True love will last forever.
- *Myth 5:* Love can conquer all problems.

Robert Solomon (1988, p. 17) describes the difficulty many of us have in understanding love: "The problem, the irony, is that in our obsession with love we have lost touch with what love is, and we have stopped thinking carefully about what it should be. Love, like happiness, may make itself more available to those who don't press it too hard, who don't expect too much, who aren't too impatient to see it through."

Some new theories of love may shed some light on how we can better understand this elusive concept. Sternberg's triangular theory of love (1988) suggests that love has three components: intimacy, passion, and commitment. In this theory, intimacy refers to the warmth and closeness shared in a relationship; passion refers to the intense feelings (included are both positive and negative) experienced in love relationships, including sexual desire; commitment refers to the decision and intent to maintain a relationship in spite of the difficulties encountered. The triangular theory of love posits eight types of relationships that emerge from the presence or absence of the three components of love (see Figure 10.1) (based on Sternberg, 1986):

- *Nonlove* is the absence of any of the three components and reflects casual interactions.

- *Liking* involves the experience of only one component of love—intimacy. We feel close but not passionate toward the other.

- *Infatuation* involves the experience of only one component of love—passion. Such passion views the person who is loved as an idealized object rather than a real person.

- *Empty love* is the third component of the triangle that represents commitment. In this case there is commitment but none of the other essential ingredients of love.

- *Fatuous love* is the combination of passion and commitment. An example is people who become quickly and intensely involved with each other and decide to marry.

- *Romantic love* is the combination of intimacy and passion. Romantic lovers are drawn to each other in an intimate way and have lots of passion, but there is no commitment. Romantic love may begin as infatuation.

- *Companionate love* is the combination of intimacy and commitment. This type of love is observed in long-term marriages where passion is no longer present. Most romantic love relationships will eventually become companionate love relationships as passion fades.

- *Consummate love* is the result of all three components of love—intimacy, passion, and commitment. Although most of us seek consummate love relationships, maintaining such relationships is quite difficult.

FIGURE 10.1
The triangular theory of love includes three basic components: intimacy, passion, and commitment. The figure shows the three basic components and possible combinations.

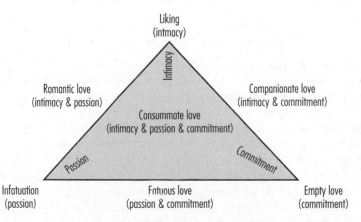

THE COUNTERPOINT OF LOVE: ISOLATION AND LONELINESS

Although many young adults actively seek emotionally satisfying friendships and romantic relationships, many others experience feelings of loneliness. In fact, research on the prevalence of loneliness (1) identifies adolescents and young adults as the loneliest age group and (2) finds that loneliness decreases with age, at least until late adulthood when marriage partners and friends begin to die (Peplau, Bikson, Rook, & Goodchilds, 1982; Rubenstein & Shaver, 1982).

Loneliness is a subjective feeling, and it is associated with social isolation, but it is not the *same* as social isolation. **Loneliness** is best defined as having fewer interpersonal relationships than *desired,* or not obtaining the desired level of personal satisfaction from interpersonal relationships. Loneliness, therefore, is not the same as spending time alone. Many people experience loneliness even though they may have many personal "friendships." However, many people desire solitude and want few personal relationships.

Loneliness in not one-dimensional; it appears to occur in different areas of one's life. For example, you could be satisfied with your relationship with your partner but not personally satisfied with your friendships. Research (Schmidt & Weiner, 1988) has identified four key areas where loneliness can be a problem: (1) romantic/sexual relationships, (2) friendship relationships, (3) family relationships, and (4) community relationships. Therefore, knowing what areas of loneliness are particularly problematic suggests a different focus for learning how to best address feelings of loneliness.

Implications for Practice: Coping with Loneliness

Most of the interventions developed to help people cope with loneliness focus on three areas: cognitive restructuring or changing negative self-talk; reducing anxiety and increasing comfort to help people stay engaged in social situations; and teaching people social skills like starting and maintaining a conversation. The appropriate intervention depends on the particular cause of the loneliness (Weiten & Lloyd, 1997).

Young (1982) identified a variety of different kinds of cognitions or self-talk that contribute to feelings of loneliness. His research identified six clusters of cogni-

TABLE 10.1 Cognitions and Behaviors That Lead to Loneliness	
Cognitive Clusters	**Behaviors**
I'm undesirable. I'm dull and boring.	Avoidance of friendships
I can't communicate with others. My thoughts and feelings are bottled up inside.	Minimal self-disclosure
I'm not a good lover. I can't relax, be spontaneous, and enjoy sex.	Avoidance of sexual relationships
I can't seem to get what I want from this relationship.	Lack of assertiveness in relationships
I won't risk being hurt again. I'd screw up any relationship.	Avoidance of potentially intimate relationships
I don't know how to act in this situation. I'll make a fool of myself.	Avoidance of other people

(Young, 1982)

tions that lead to different kinds of irrational cognitions and subsequent behaviors (see Table 10.1). Understanding a client's thinking processes can be helpful in planning different intervention strategies.

Social Cognition and Regulation

Although intimacy is a primary focus in young adulthood, independence also becomes an important developmental task. Although young adults are exploring aspects of intimacy, they are also recognizing their need for independence and freedom. Maturity and growth are reflected in the ability to experience both intimacy and dependence *and* freedom and independence.

In adolescence, young people are working to *develop* their identity; in young adulthood they are trying to *establish* their identity. Keniston (1971) refers to this developmental phase as "the continuing quest to operationalize a sense of identity." This often takes place as young adults begin to strengthen their own inner identity and clarify their beliefs and values. Still, it is common for people in this stage to struggle with doubts about independent decisions they must make. For example, they may be concerned about career choices or relationship commitments they are making.

This process of developing one's identity is often facilitated by how the young adult begins to shape a "dream." According to Levinson (1978), such dreams reflect what a person would like to accomplish as an adult. These dreams often start out being concrete and overly simplistic; then they mature into clear and realistic visions. Men's dreams tend to focus more on occupational goals, whereas women's dreams often include visions of both career and family (Levinson, 1986; Roberts & Newton, 1987).

Problems, however, can occur when people fail to establish their own identities. How can young people develop independent identities when they are still dependent on their parents for financial, personal, and emotional needs? Such dependency may lead to problems in developing intimate relationships with others or in developing independent career opportunities.

REGULATION

Kohlberg's theory of moral development was introduced in the chapter on adolescence. In young adulthood, moral development is further refined as young adults are able to address the cognitive complexities involved in resolving moral dilemmas.

Widely recognized in moral development theory is the controversy about whether there is a gender bias. Carol Gilligan (1982) is well known for her criticism of Kohlberg. What disturbed Gilligan was that most of Kohlberg's interviews regarding morality were conducted with men; in addition, the results of the interviews showed that women reason more at stage 3, whereas men reason more at stage 4. Gilligan challenged this finding because it suggested that women are considered morally inferior to men.

But what could account for these differences between men and women in the nature of their moral thoughts? Gilligan considered the differences between how boys and girls are socialized. Boys are taught to be assertive, independent, and achievement oriented, and this may lead them to perceive moral dilemmas as the result of conflicts between the rights of different parties (representative of stage 4). Girls, in contrast, are raised to be nurturing, concerned about the needs of others, and empathic, and this may lead them to perceive moral dilemmas as conflicts between individual needs and the needs and desires of others (representative of stage 3). Gilligan (1982) theorizes that these differences show a male perspective that emphasizes a justice perspective and a female perspective that emphasizes a care perspective. These contrasting views place a focus on morality in terms of laws that define rights and responsibilities as preeminent (male perspective) or in terms whereby the welfare of people is most central (female perspective).

Gilligan first set out to examine women's morality in her study of pregnant women facing the dilemma of whether to keep their babies or have abortions. She identified a series of stages that women go through:

- *Stage 1.* Self-interest is the key factor in decision making.
- *Stage 2.* Sacrificing self-interest for the welfare of others is the deciding influence.
- *Stage 3.* Avoiding hurting either the self or others is the guiding principle.

The last stage represents a morality of care or responsibility. An example of this stage of thinking would be:

> I would not be doing myself or the child a favor by having this child. . . . I don't need to pay off my imaginary debts to the world through this child, and I don't think that it is right to bring a child into the world and use it for that purpose. (Gilligan, 1977, p. 505)

The gender bias in moral thinking is still a controversy, and it has not been proved that Kohlberg's theory is biased against women (Sigelman, 1999). Some studies have found that women do reason in a similar manner to men (Walker, 1995; Wark & Krebs, 1996). In fact, one study (Garmon et al., 1996) found that females were quicker than males to reach the conventional level of moral reasoning. Nonetheless, Gilligan's work has raised awareness about the importance of considering gender in interpreting research results and has provided an important new direction in studying morality—an examination of both a morality of justice and a morality of care (Brabeck, 1983). For example, Gilgun (1995) recently examined the moral thinking of incest perpetrators using the concepts of both justice and care.

Psychological Hazards

Robert Havighurst (1972), a researcher who studies adulthood, has noted that the young adult years are one of the most difficult periods in a person's life. Indeed, young adults face many challenges during this period. They must make major decisions that include career and job choices, selecting a mate, extending education, and bearing and rearing children—these are major responsibilities for someone who is just entering adulthood. Many young adults become easily frustrated because they have not been adequately prepared for the life skills they now need. The large number of frustrations, coupled with immense responsibilities, often cause psychological problems. One devastating problem that a young person could have to face is learning to cope with a major mental illness.

SERIOUS MENTAL ILLNESS

Many of the major mental illnesses—in particular, **schizophrenia**—become evident in late adolescence and early adulthood. Those who suffer from schizophrenia can be grouped into three broad categories: (1) treated successfully with a full recovery, (2) partial recovery with a reasonably normal life, and (3) little or no recovery with repeated hospitalizations.

When a person suffers from an illness like schizophrenia, what factors might produce a favorable prognosis? Lehmann and Cancro (1985) have identified four factors that suggest the promise for recovery: (1) sudden rather than gradual onset, (2) onset that occurs at a later age, (3) good social and work environment before the onset of the disorder, and (4) informal support system within the patient's family.

What leads a person to develop a serious mental illness like schizophrenia? Most of the evidence points to heredity as the major explanation (Rieder et al., 1994). Studies have shown that relatives of a person with schizophrenia have an increased risk for developing schizophrenia, and the closer the relationship, the higher the risk. Figure 10.2 shows the association between the kind of relationship, the genetic relatedness, and the concordance rate, or lifetime risk. Being an identical twin of a schizophrenic person or the offspring of two schizophrenic parents creates almost a 50% risk for developing schizophrenia (Gottesman, 1991).

What causes schizophrenia? Many researchers now look to the influence of neurochemical factors. In particular, schizophrenia and other mood disorders are accompanied by changes in neurotransmitter activity in the brain. Most of the drugs that are effective in controlling the symptoms of schizophrenia act to restrain dopamine activity in the brain. Therefore, excess dopamine is believed to be the most likely cause of schizophrenia. Most recently, research (Davis et al., 1991) has linked schizophrenia to excessively high dopamine activity in subcortical areas of the brain but abnormally low dopamine activity in the prefrontal cortex area.

The National Alliance for the Mentally Ill (NAMI) has become a powerful advocacy group that promotes the well-being of people with schizophrenia and their families. Formed from a grassroots organization in 1979, today NAMI has chapters in most cities across the country. The organization is designed to serve in an advocacy role, bringing problems and issues to the attention of local, state, and government agencies. NAMI promotes research and knowledge that can be helpful to persons with mental illness and their families. For example, NAMI is particularly interested in research that would identify new ways to help clients readjust to the community, using the least restrictive environment as a guiding principle. NAMI is also involved in

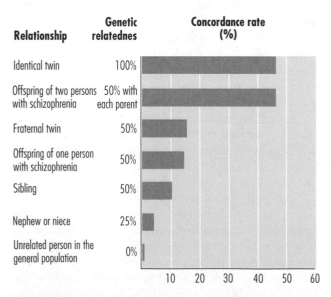

FIGURE 10.2   Genetic vulnerability to schizophrenic disorders (Nicol & Gottesman, 1983)

Serious mental illness—
from which people can suffer throughout their adult
life—often makes its first
appearance in young adulthood. Proper care and
treatment for persons with
mental illness are en-
hanced through case man-
agement services.

finding ways that would enable families to function more effectively and with less overall stress.

The following Focus section discusses case management services, which can be critical in providing effective care for persons with serious mental illness.

Case Management and Better Tracking Are Keys to Providing Better Care for Persons with Serious Mental Illness

Although case management and tracking systems are not new concepts, they are receiving renewed attention in the struggle to provide adequate care for persons with serious mental illness. Case management refers to the process of "managing" a case—linking individuals with needed services and coordinating existing services. In many cases, past efforts at case management failed because social workers were given extremely large caseloads and could not do the necessary advocacy work that would coordinate needed services.

Today, many states are finding that their case management systems need an overhaul. For example, New York has an intensive case management program in which approximately 4,000 adults with a history of inpatient care and poor follow-through have been assigned to the intensive unit. Here, the case managers have an average workload of about ten clients and are the single point of responsibility. In this model, caseworkers are responsible for providing the housing, job, and mental health care needs of the clients on a 24-hour basis. The state provides a total dollar amount of funds to be spent on each client's personal needs. This allows greater flexibility to meet the special needs of clients. For example, a client may not be taking necessary medication, but this failure could be partly the result of a substance-abuse problem that needs to be addressed.

Oklahoma, recognizing similar problems with their system of care for persons with mental illness, developed a centralized, statewide database to track its mentally ill clients. When clients enter the system, a confidential computer file is created that lists demographic data, diagnosis, treatment history, presenting problem(s), living arrangements, and payment source. All local community mental health centers and state hospitals can access the system. This system allows greater continuity of care for the clients. For example, when a client is discharged from the hospital, staff transmit key data to the community mental health centers. The center can then watch for the client and begin a treatment plan based on the client's individual history. Also, the tracking system can provide data to "flag" clients who may need further attention. For example, a report can be printed that lists all existing clients at each mental health center and identifies those clients who have not been seen for 40 days. Other reports can include a list of clients discharged from hospitals and referred to community mental health centers, with clients identified who never showed up at the centers, or a monthly list of clients who were readmitted to the hospital within two weeks of discharge—to identify clients who are not getting the services they need. The combination of improved case management and better tracking is providing better and more effective help for persons with serious mental illness.

(Youngstrom, 1990)

Implications for Practice: Assessment of Clients with Mental Illness

Social workers are often called on to provide necessary services for clients with mental illness. (Focus on Gender: Women and Depression, this page, looks at depression, one of the most common mental health problems for women in the United States.) Understanding the multifaceted aspects of mental illness is critical in designing and coordinating services. Some of the factors that social workers might want to consider in assessing the clients and their social situation are as follows (adapted from the National Institute of Mental Health, 1991):

PHYSICAL HEALTH STATUS

Physical functioning

Ability to perform activities for daily living

Extent of bodily pain

Quality of sleep

Level of energy and fatigue

QUALITY OF LIFE

Access to resources and opportunities

Fulfillment of life's roles and tasks

Overall well-being or life satisfaction

FAMILY AND PEER RELATIONSHIPS

Ability to maintain and develop relationships with others

Ability to maintain and develop relationships with family members

Extent of the family's burden

REHABILITATION STATUS

Social skills

Vocational status

Independent living skills

Although not complete, the preceding assessment list gives some idea of the complexity involved in working with people with mental illness. Understanding and helping these clients involves assessing multiple aspects of the social environment.

FOCUS ON GENDER

Women and Depression

Depression is one of the leading mental health problems for women in this country. It is estimated that more than 7 million women have diagnosable depression; indeed, women constitute 70% of those with depression. Unfortunately, many of these women will go without proper treatment, in spite of new treatment technologies that have reduced depressive symptoms in women by 80%–90%. Why do women experience such high rates of depression? This question, as you might imagine, generates a number of explanations, including the following:

- Approximately 37% of women have been victims of physical or sexual abuse before the age of 21.

- Seventy-five percent of the nation's poor are women.

- Depression is misdiagnosed an estimated 30%–50% of the time.

- There has been a 250% increase in suicide among women aged 15–24.

Most experts now agree that depression in women can be explained only from a biopsychosocial perspective. Research has identified a multitude of factors that influence the prevalence of depression, such as personal styles of women characterized as avoidant, passive, and pessimistic. These characteristics are related to sex-role expectations and socialization experiences. Also, women who suffer from depression often focus on their feelings, neglecting to take action to gain a sense of control over the conditions that may be leading to the depression.

Additional research has found that being unhappily married increases the chances for depression. For women, in comparison with men, being in an unhappy marriage increases the likelihood of depression threefold. When there are young children to care for in the home, women are more likely to be depressed. Similarly, the more children a woman has, the greater the likelihood of depression.

Other factors for depression include any physical and emotional abuse that a woman may have experienced. Many women in this country live in extreme poverty. Such adverse economic conditions contribute to the persistent depression many women feel. Other women may be further marginalized or socially stigmatized by their age, ethnicity, sexual orientation, or drug dependence.

(Jones, 1990)

SOCIAL DIMENSION

Families, Groups, Support Systems, and Communities

Marriage and the emergence of the "family" become one of the most significant life changes in young adulthood. The decisions whether to get married and to have children are fundamental struggles in this period. Newman and Newman (1995, p. 523) state: "[T]he most important social factors contributing to the creation of a lifestyle are whether one marries, the characteristics of one's marriage or intimate life partner, whether one has children and the characteristics of those children, and one's work. The extent to which one has a choice about each of these factors depends on cultural values and restrictions, societal norms and barriers, and socioeconomic factors, especially educational attainment. Each factor interacts with personality, interests, and life goals to shape a lifestyle."

MARRIAGE—FORMING A FAMILY

Although the institution of marriage has changed considerably over the past 30 or 40 years, most Americans still opt for marriage at least sometime in their lives—in fact, throughout the 20th century, only about 7% of women never married (Glick, 1984). Still, some distinctive changes have taken place with regard to marriage. Perhaps most significant is that young adults are postponing marriage until their late 20s; the percentage of single women between the ages of 20 and 24 rose dramatically from 28% in 1960 to 78% in 1987 (U.S. Bureau of the Census, 1989). In addition to the increase in the number of single women, there has also been an increase in the number of couples who choose to cohabit and not get married. Data from the U.S. Bureau of the Census (1990) shows that the number of couples cohabiting increased fivefold between 1970 and 1990. The upward trend in the divorce rate has also changed the way we view marriage. Marriage now takes place within the context of each marriage partner's own personal growth. As a result, people are less willing to sacrifice for the sake of the marriage. Today fewer stigmas are associated with divorce than in the past, partly because of the sheer numbers of people who eventually divorce. It is estimated that two out of every three marriages will end in divorce or separation (Wisensale, 1992).

In spite of these trends, many people still have an idealized notion of the "nuclear" family: a married couple with two or more children, the husband as the primary breadwinner, and the woman as the homemaker. Yet, it has been estimated that only 7% of American families achieve this ideal (Otto, 1988). Our image of the American family needs to change. We need to recognize the influence of single-parent families, childless families, unwed parents, gay couples, and dual-career families, which reflect the reality of the diversity of families.

SELECTING A PARTNER

Finding a partner to whom you are willing to make a serious commitment is usually a gradual process. This process involves moving through a series of phases that leads to a deepening attraction and commitment. Adams (1986) identified four phases that lead to marriage:

- *Phase I:* Opportunity, physical attraction, valued behaviors
- *Phase II:* Positive self-disclosure, rapport, sexuality, value concerns, salient homogeneity, similarity
- *Phase III:* Role compatibility, empathy
- *Phase IV:* The "right one" relationship, commitment escalators

In phase I, opportunity plays a critical role as a factor in determining who is available to choose from as a partner. Opportunity will be influenced by the values of the young person's culture, family, and social class (Schuster & Ashburn, 1992). For example, such cultural influences may produce opportunities for selecting a partner based on attendance at private schools, church groups, sporting events, or local neighborhood events. In the early stages, physical attraction and behaviors that are valued (for example, being outgoing) are also important determinants in the selection process.

By the time young people move to phase II, they are focusing on a process of more intimate discovery. They might reflect on such questions as, Who is this person, really? Is he (or she) similar to me? Through reciprocal self-disclosure, each person learns more about the other. The information gained is often assessed in terms of similarities. For example, many people would consider similarity in religious faith to be an important factor that would influence their selection of a mate.

The transition to phase III is similar but involves a deeper level of disclosure. Couples may share aspects about their sexual desires, personal fears, and life's dreams. In this phase, there is more trust and a greater level of risk as one shares increasingly intimate aspects of the self. This sharing leads to two central processes: role compatibility and empathy. The couple learns about the extent to which they are truly compatible and deepen their level of understanding about each other.

Finally, the couple reaches phase IV, where each partner is persuaded that this is the "right" relationship, and each person take steps to deepen his or her commitment to the other. Each partner has developed comfortable feelings and predictability. Furthermore, the couple is socially defined as being "together," so the costs of ending the relationship become much greater.

The following Focus section examines marriage for people with mental retardation.

FOCUS ON DIVERSITY

I Do, and I Will—Marriage as a Union of Souls and Determination

Getting to the church on time is the least of the obstacles facing Roger Drake Meyers and Virginia Rae Hensler on their wedding day, but you would never know it. Roger and Virginia, both born with mental retardation, are challenging the previously designated dependent role of adults with mental retardation. Their marriage is a reflection of their commitment to each other and their desire to free themselves from the often-inaccurate labels society imposes on individuals with mental retardation.

Determination of mental retardation is frequently based on IQ and social adjustment; difficulties in both areas appear before age 18 in people determined to have some form of retardation. About 89% of individuals with mental retardation have mild retardation and can have, with some assistance, an independent lifestyle. Early intervention programs involving intellectual and motor stimulation may enhance potential for this population.

Even with early developmental attention, how can we be sure that people like Roger and Virginia are ready for the rigors of marriage? In reality, we can never be sure that any couple, whatever its characteristics, is marriage-ready. The statistics suggest, however, that mildly retarded couples have as good a chance of navigating marriage as other couples. Marriage between such people occurs at roughly the same rate as marriage between members of any group within the nonaffected population. Couples' descriptions of their marriages are diverse: Some report creative, satisfying marriages; some describe a relationship characterized by poverty, depression, and violence; others see marriage as a "badge of normality and a way to 'pass' into the nonretarded community" (Meyers, 1978, p. 107).

Roger and Virginia see marriage as one way of finding a place within the larger community. In working toward complying with societal norms, they face many difficult marital issues. For example, they must decide whether to have children. Because neither Roger nor Virginia has congenital retardation, their children would have as much of a chance of not being retarded as would a child born to parents who have no retardation. Other difficulties relate to handling the well-intentioned but troublesome interference of their in-laws. With the help of a counselor, Roger and Virginia are able to address these issues effectively.

Both individually and as a couple, Roger and Virginia are excellent models of people who learn to work with and around a disability. They demonstrate the power of developing an individual's potential and of using personal strengths to move beyond societal labels.

Julianne Azimov (Based on Myers, 1978)

COMING TOGETHER— ADJUSTMENT TO MARRIAGE

Once a person has found the "right" partner, both must come together and begin the process of making an adjustment to marriage. This adjustment can be challenging, because it includes adapting to myths and expectations of marriage, learning how to effectively communicate with one's spouse, deriving satisfaction from one's relationship and learning how to deal with conflict, and accepting gender differences in how men and women relate to marriage.

MARITAL EXPECTATIONS AND MYTHS

Addressing marital expectations and myths is often a good place for couples to start adjusting to marriage. Too often, marriages go awry because one or both partners have unrealistic expectations. Larson (1988)

found that many college students are influenced by myths about marriage, and he developed a marriage quiz to assess such myths. The quiz includes items that are evaluated as either true or false. Some sample questions from the quiz areas follows:

1. A husband's marital satisfaction is usually lower if his wife is employed full-time than if she is a full-time homemaker.

2. In most marriages, having a child improves marital satisfaction for both spouses.

3. For most couples, marital satisfaction gradually increases from the first year of marriage through the childbearing years, the teen years, the empty-nest period, and retirement.

All of these items are false. Larson (1988) found that young adults answered almost half of the items on the marriage quiz incorrectly.

PREPARE (Premarital Personal and Relationship Evaluation) (Gleick, 1995) is a set of 125 questions used to assess a couple's compatibility, and it has been used with 500,000 couples for premarital counseling. The results are computer scored and can determine with 80% to 85% accuracy which couples will divorce.

Individuals are asked if they "Agree Strongly," "Agree," are "Undecided," "Disagree," or "Disagree Strongly" with statements such as the following:

- I believe most disagreements we currently have will decrease after marriage.

- I expect that some romantic love will fade after marriage.

- I am concerned about my partner's drinking/ smoking.

- I wish my partner was more careful in spending money.

- I am satisfied with the amount of affection I receive from my partner.

- My partner and I sometimes disagree regarding our interest in sex.

- I have some concerns about how my partner will be as a parent.

- We disagree on whether the husband's occupation should be a top priority in deciding where we live.

- I can easily share my positive and negative feelings with my partner.

- My partner is less interested in talking about our relationship than I am.

- We have some important disagreements that never seem to get resolved.

- I enjoy spending some time alone without my partner.

- At times I feel pressure to participate in activities my partner enjoys.

- My partner and I agree on how much we will share the household chores.

- We sometimes disagree on how to practice our religious beliefs.

Ten percent of couples who take the test are shocked by their poor scores and break their engagement (Gleik, 1995). Although this is painful, the immediate anguish is much less excruciating than a divorce with two kids. These results confirm the notion that, indeed, young adults may not be properly prepared to enter marriage with a realistic point of view. Adjustment to a new marriage requires a new set of tasks for each person. The following Focus section lists 20 of the new tasks a couple needs to address.

FOCUS ON FAMILY

▼

Tasks Associated with Adjustment to a New Marriage

Entering into a marriage is more complex than it might seem. Although individuals may come into a marriage with a lot of experience dating others, marriage brings a new set of tasks that the couple must work out. Kelly (1979) has identified 20 tasks that new couples face:

1. Establishing routines for daily living
2. Learning how to make purposeful decisions together
3. Building new friendships as a couple
4. Developing relationships with in-laws
5. Establishing a working family budget

6. Developing a "double-person" spending and shopping mentality
7. Establishing religious habits
8. Deciding on children and contraceptive methods
9. Learning how to negotiate conflicts
10. Learning the give and take of living together
11. Allocating responsibilities
12. Developing effective communication patterns
13. Establishing a shared core-value system
14. Identifying family "rules"
15. Creating common goals
16. Deciding on leisure-time activities and community involvement
17. Establishing financial credit
18. Developing a satisfying sex life
19. Establishing a balance between togetherness and respect for individuality
20. Establishing traditions as a family

NONVERBAL COMMUNICATION MAY BE MORE POWERFUL THAN YOU THINK

In well-known studies of nonverbal communication, Mehrabian (1969) and others have shown three dimensions represented in nonverbal expressions. (1) The *like-dislike* dimension is expressed through closeness or distance—for example, looking at or away from a person; (2) the *potency* dimension is expressed through one's expression—for example, standing straight rather than slumped or rapid versus slow movements; (3) the *responsiveness* dimension is expressed through one's facial movements, voice tone, and voice volume. Mehrabian (1972) is often noted for his observation that, of a total feeling conveyed in a message, 7% is verbal feeling, 38% is vocal feeling, and 55% is facial feeling. What's important about this observation is that, although we may restrict what we say in words, it is often more difficult to restrict our feelings from influencing our nonverbal responses. Therefore, nonverbal responses may contradict our verbal message. It is the nonverbal part of the message that will qualify what we are attempting to communicate verbally.

Problems in communication are of particular concern to couples. Beck and Jones (1973) discovered that communication problems were the most frequently identified issue of couples seeking counseling. Research (Fowers & Olson, 1989) has also found that happy and unhappy couples can be distinguished on the basis on three aspects of communication: comfort in sharing information with the other person, willingness to recognize and resolve conflicts as they occur, and quality of the couple's sexual life.

In a study that attempted to predict the likelihood of divorce, Buehlman, Gottman, & Katz (1992) studied communication and interaction styles while the couples discussed problem areas. Primarily on the basis of how the partners related to each other, the researchers were able to predict, with an accuracy rate of 94%, which couples would divorce three years later.

Implications for Practice: Empowering African-American Families

To be effective, social workers need to recognize the potential of the African-American's extended family, spirituality, religion, and the African-American community as a whole. Many practitioners who work with African-American clients are treating the wrong people. The people who come into therapy, women and children, are the least likely to affect change in the family. Instead, members of the extended family—the grandmothers and grandfathers, aunts and uncles, and fathers and boyfriends—should be targeted for change. For practitioners to be effective, they must work with the people who traditionally have the power in African-American families. Unfortunately, many African-Americans view therapy as something that "crazy, sick, white, or rich people" do—everyone but them. The challenge for social workers is to demonstrate to African-Americans that they have something to offer them. How can this be done? Two approaches are bringing spirituality and religion into practice and bringing families together as a key source of help.

For many African-American families, the psyche and the spirit are one. Therefore, some African-Americans view psychotherapy as antispiritual, because its theories do not include spirituality. Exploring religion in therapy and using it to help clients cope with trauma can be a key to working effectively with African-American families.

The pervasive threat of crime in poor African-American communities is a crisis that is leaving people feeling increasingly vulnerable and isolated. It is not enough for practitioners to do family therapy one family at a time. The challenge for social workers is to find a way to bring families closer together and capitalize on the strengths of the African-American community (Martin, 1995).

FOCUS ON FAMILIES

Families Under Stress

What do you think of as an "at-risk" family—a single-parent family, a family on welfare, or another kind? Would you consider a middle-class family with two working parents to be at risk? Many practitioners would not. But the fact remains that many families of all socioeconomic levels today are stressed out. Psychological health may be a greater concern to American families than previously realized. In a survey of 24,000 middle-class households in the northeastern United States, researchers found varying areas of concern, including heart disease, domestic violence, and substance abuse. In particular, the survey found that (1) 60% of the households had significant levels of stress and anxiety, (2) 9.1% of households said a member had been treated for drug or alcohol problems, compared with 5.3% nationally, (3) 19% had been treated for an emotional or psychological health problem, compared with 13% nationally, and (4) 4.4% of households said a member had displayed violent or abusive behavior toward another family member, compared to 2.8% nationally. Stressed households experienced much higher levels of drug and alcohol use, violent behavior, drunken driving, multiple sex partners, and suicide than did nonstressed households.

What does this mean to practitioners nationwide? According to a practitioner involved in the survey, "This is the first time I've left my office, looked at the community at large, and recognized the enormous psychological needs outside . . . what we are seeing in our practice is only the tip of the iceberg" (p. 35). Psychological health problems represented the overriding unmet health need. Additionally, the surveyed population would not traditionally be considered underserved, given its relatively high income. So why were so many households stressed? One likely reason was recent local corporate downsizing. The results of this research may expand our notion of who constitutes the underserved. Psychological well-being is a bigger problem than anybody imagined.

Misha Marvel (Adapted from Freiberg, 1996)

SATISFACTION AND CONFLICT IN MARRIAGE

What factors predict marital satisfaction? Researchers have attempted to answer this question for years. However, notions such as marital "satisfaction" or "success" are difficult to define. In spite of this problem, researchers have generally found the following factors to correlate positively with marital satisfaction:

- People whose parents were divorced are more likely to experience divorce themselves (White, 1990).

- Couples who marry young have a higher divorce rate (White, 1990).

- The longer the courtship, the greater the likelihood of marital success (Grover et al., 1985).

- Divorce is more common among the working and lower classes than among middle and upper classes, probably because of the greater financial stress in the world of the working and lower classes (Conger et al., 1990).

Is compatibility critical to marital success? Is the reduction of conflict critical to saving troubled marriages? Although many social work practitioners would answer yes, recent research found a different answer. Research by Gottman (1994) found that "it isn't the lack of compatibility that predicts divorce but the way couples handle their inevitable *incompatibilities,* not whether they fight all the time or never fight at all but the way they resolve conflicts and the overall quality of their emotional interactions" (p. 44). Indeed, Gottman and associates have discovered that what is critical in a marriage is the balance between the couple's positive and negative interactions—this is what determines their satisfaction. In fact, their research has

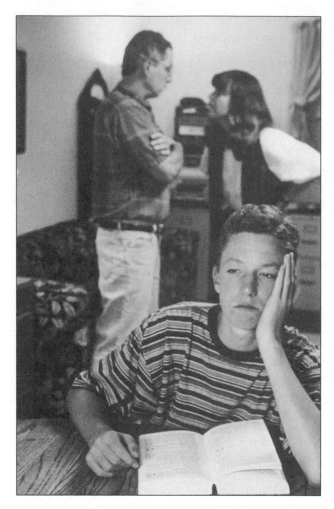

To have a successful marriage, couples must learn to communicate and resolve conflicts.

discovered that you can quantify the ratio of positive to negative interactions needed to maintain a healthy marriage. Gottman (1994) believes that "satisfied couples, no matter how their marriages stacked up against the ideal, were those who maintained a five-to-one ratio of positive to negative moments" (p. 44).

Conflict and fighting is part of married life. All marriages, including good ones, have a degree of conflict. It may be that such negativity serves a function in that it keeps the marriage dynamic rather than static. Gottman (1994) suggests that anger, if it is directed at a specific issue and expressed without contempt, can be healthy for marriages. However, not all negativity is equal, and the four factors that seem to lead to the worst outcomes for married couples include criticism, defensiveness, contempt, and stonewalling. In a functional marriage, anger and disagreements are directed at the other person's specific actions, whereas in a troubled relationship, criticism and contempt are directed at the person, rather than his or her actions. So it is not necessarily the anger but the insulting manner in which the anger is directed that makes the difference.

Insulting remarks often lead to intense fighting, and one spouse is likely to adopt the other processes that contribute to the negativity—for instance, stonewalling. Gottman (1994) found that about 85% of the stonewallers are male, and he believes this may be because of men's physiological reaction to conflict. When men face conflict, they get more intensely upset physiologically than women. More specifically, they experience increased heart rate and blood pressure and remain upset for longer periods of time than women do. One explanation for this response difference is that the male response may have served some evolutionary survival benefits: To protect the female and her young, perhaps he needed to remain physiologically responsive to external danger. However, as Gottman (1994) points out, "in modern life, the propensity to higher arousal is not nearly so adaptive; it feels terrible, and to avoid the acute distress it causes, men are likely simply to shut themselves down, refuse to respond, try, as much as possible, to turn themselves into unfeeling stone" (p. 46). This physiological gender difference may help us understand why men and women have such different approaches to conflict—women pursue the conflict with emotion, and men avoid the conflict through rationalizations, the "silent" treatment, and physically withdrawal.

GENDER DIFFERENCES IN COMMUNICATION

Gender differences in communication are often the source of much frustration and anger between men and women. Tannen (1991) describes how the process of socialization leads to many misunderstandings. Tannen believes that men are socialized to see the social world as basically hierarchical. As a result, men approach conversations as "negotiations in which people try to achieve and maintain the upper hand if they can and protect themselves from others' attempts to put

them down and push them around" (p. 25). In contrast, women are socialized to see the world as a community and to focus on their connections with others in the community. As a result, women approach conversations as "negotiations for closeness in which people try to seek and give confirmation and support, and to reach consensus. They try to protect themselves from others' attempts to push them away" (p. 25). The end result: Neither understands the other. What is it about men's and women's communication styles that makes them so different?

Some researchers identify men as using an instrumental style of communication and women as using an expressive style of communication. **Instrumental communication** refers to having a focus on identifying goals and finding solutions. **Expressive communication** involves the expression of emotions and having a perspective that is sensitive to how others feel. In general, men are more interested in having rational discussions and solving problems, and women are more interested in expressing emotions and feeling listened to and provided with support. The following scenario is a typical example of this kind of mismatch.

A young mother describes her worries and frustrations concerning appropriate child care for her son. She is using her expressive style and is most interested in having her partner listen to her and provide some support. However, the husband, using his instrumental style of communication, assumes she wants to solve a problem and begins to search for solutions. This mismatch in communication leads to serious problems. Because her husband is not listening to her and hence not providing her with the support she desires, she assumes he doesn't have any sympathy for her concerns. He is frustrated by what he perceives as her complaining and her inability to simply solve the problem.

This situation represents a classic mismatch because each person is talking at cross-purposes. Each person, in his or her own way, is attempting to respond appropriately. However, each is frustrating the other; she wants his sympathy, and he wants to help her solve a problem. In this context, each partner assumes that he or she knows what the other person wants, but this is clearly not the case.

Other differences in communication according to Tannen (1991) include women's use of **rapport talk,** which involves discussing similarities and matching experiences, and men's use of **report talk,** which involves discussing knowledge and displaying skill. What men and women talk about also varies considerably. Women usually prefer discussions about their personal lives and feelings, whereas men seem to prefer discussions about activities and events.

Differences also emerge in mixed-sex conversations, where women are more often *listeners* and men are more often *lecturers.* Tannen explains these differences by suggesting that this represents games that men and women learned to play in childhood. For men the game is "do you respect me?" and for women the game is "do you like me?" According to Tannen, mixed-sex conversation places women in a double bind, because men's style of conversation is dominant in most situations. Because the male style is used as the norm against which the woman will be evaluated, she is placed in this double bind; she is evaluated negatively if she adopts either a male or a female style. Tannen (1991) explains that "if they speak in ways expected of women, they are seen as inadequate leaders. If they speak in ways expected of leaders, they are seen as inadequate women" (p. 244).

Implications for Practice: Communication Skills for Men and Women

Communication Skills for Women   Often, in a discussion among men and women, men dominate the discussion. Women may need to "jump into" the conversation more forcefully than they are accustomed to doing. Good use of nonverbal behavior can be critical: making eye contact, using appropriate vocal tone and pitch, and maintaining good posture and orientation in space will command attention. When the content of a spoken message is inconsistent with the nonverbal message, the nonverbal message will have the greatest effect. Because nonverbal behavior can be so powerful, women should use both nonverbal and spoken messages to convey positive responses and should rely more on oral communication to express negative responses. Use of personal space can also influence the effect of a message. Many women need to become more visible by obtaining a good position for interaction with others.

Women are often less comfortable than men are in talking about themselves and their accomplishments.

Women for whom this is a problem might want to script a short biography that describes their specific accomplishments and states their areas of expertise. To feel more comfortable about sharing their point of view, women can also practice expressing opinions on a variety of topics.

Communication Skills for Men   Because men often tend to dominate a conversation, they should observe their patterns of communication and evaluate their tendency to dominate. If this is a problem for them, they can learn to catch themselves interrupting and politely encourage the other person to continue with his or her thoughts. Men can sometimes be difficult to talk with because they don't "carry" enough of the conversation; for example, they might provide only short answers to questions. Some men also need to work at being more conversational. A good technique to use for improving conversational skill is the two-question rule (Stuart, 1980). This rule keeps the conversation focused on the other person. It requires a speaker to ask an opening question and then to follow up that question with another inquiry. Often, people ask just one question, such as "How did you feel about that meeting?" and then proceed with their own analysis and reaction to the meeting. By contrast, asking a second, follow-up question demonstrates good listening and helps to keep the dominant person from launching into a lengthy monologue. In sum, many men need to practice being good listeners. Too often, women feel "talked at" rather than "talked with." Good listening requires concentration and sustained effort. A good balance of conversational give-and-take will facilitate good communication between men and women.

Men who do not usually use an expressive communication style can practice discussing their interests, feelings, and thoughts. To do so, rather than approach a conversation as an interaction about events and activities, men can focus on their *feelings* about various subjects.

DIVERSITY IN COMPANIONSHIP

Although marriage is a major developmental task for many young adults, increasing numbers of young adults are choosing alternatives to the traditional pathway of marriage and children. Many young adults choose to remain single, go through divorce and re-marriage, become part of a stepfamily, develop a committed relationship with a partner of the same sex, or cohabit. There are many ways that young adults can meet their needs for companionship.

REMAINING OR BECOMING SINGLE

Although some young adults remain single throughout their lives, many become single after being widowed, separated, or divorced. Being single has increased dramatically over the last 25 years. In the early 20s and mid to late 20s, the percentage of men and women who remain single has more than doubled. This trend is due to several factors. For example, young adults have increasingly delayed the age at which they marry, and this has increased the number of people who remain single before marriage. Also, the increased rate of divorce and separation has contributed to a larger number of men and women becoming single.

Many young adults who are single face difficult stereotypes and pressures. When the majority of the population marries, the question many single adults must confront is, "Why haven't you married?" Often the stereotype conforms to two alternatives (Keith, 1986): the assumption is either that the single people are uncommitted so they can pursue promiscuity, or they are single because they were not "good enough" to attract a mate.

Research studies have attempted to examine the differences between single and married people. Overall, single people do rate themselves as less happy than married people (Lee, Secombe, & Shehan, 1991). This seems to reflect the social expectation that it is better to be married. However, it is interesting to note that the differences have narrowed in recent years. Also, research finds single women to be happier than single men (Glenn & Weaver, 1988).

Being single may require some special adaptations. For example, socializing often occurs in couples, and the single person may feel left out. Many single people feel lonely because they lack the constant companionship available in a marriage or a committed relationship. Single people often complain about not wanting to go places or do things alone. A good network of friends can help eliminate these concerns.

HOMOSEXUAL RELATIONSHIPS

Use of the term *homosexual* can be traced back to 1869 (Money, 1988). Today, the term *gay* is more often used and is related to the gay-rights movement of the past 20 years. The term *gay* refers to males and sometimes females; however, the term "lesbian" refers exclusively to female homosexuals. More recently, references regarding homosexuals include gay, lesbian, bisexual, and questioning individuals.

In the late 1940s and early 1950s, Alfred Kinsey reported the sexual histories of thousands of Americans. His research found that 8% of men and 4% of women were exclusively homosexual for at least a period of three years. In addition, 4% of men and 2% of women were exclusively homosexual after adolescence. A much larger percentage of the population had some previous experience with homosexual behavior—37% of the men and 20% of the women reported at least one homosexual experience that led to orgasm.

The myth exists that individuals are either homosexual or heterosexual. However, Kinsey's sexual behavior studies showed that this is not accurate. Instead, one should view homosexuality and heterosexuality as a continuum. Figure 10.3 illustrates Kinsey's original idea that sexual orientation represented a seven-point scale.

More representative studies of the general population have estimated lower rates of homosexual behavior than did the early Kinsey studies. For example, one comparative analysis (Fay et al., 1989) found that, in both 1970 and 1988 studies, the portion of homosexual men in the general population during the preceding year was 2%. In a recent review of studies, Seidman and Rieder (1994) estimated that 2% of men are exclusively homosexual and that an additional 3% are bisexual. Diamond (1993) examined homosexuality for men and women throughout the world and estimated that 6% of men and 3% of women have engaged in same-sex behavior since adolescence. However, many experts believe that these estimates are low because the tremendous amount of social prejudice against homosexuals would preclude many from self-reporting homosexuality. Indeed, many experts place the estimate of homosexuals as high as 10% for both sexes. Furthermore, the way one defines homosexual behavior is going to have a large influence on how the prevalence is estimated.

FIGURE 10.3
Continuum of heterosexuality and homosexuality

Heterosexual		Questioning	Bisexual		Gay or Lesbian	
0 Exclusively heterosexual behavior	1 Incidental homosexual behavior	2 More than incidental homosexual behavior	3 Equal homosexual and heterosexual behavior	4 More than incidental heterosexual behavior	5 Incidental heterosexual behavior	6 Exclusively homosexual behavior

What determines sexual orientation? Some therapists believe it is biological factors—for example, hormones and neurological factors. Other researchers have focused on genetic factors as determinates of sexual orientation. The concordance rates for homosexuality in identical twins far exceed that of fraternal twins or adoptive siblings, suggesting a genetic contribution to sexual orientation (see Figure 10.4).

Many different studies have been conducted to determine whether homosexuals have a greater degree of psychopathology when compared with heterosexuals. Most studies using various methodologies have failed to find any differences (Gonsiorek, 1991). Furthermore, research on specific disorders, such as the sexual abuse of children, has not found an increased frequency of homosexual perpetrators (Groth & Birnbaum, 1978). This information has not provided support for the once-popular notion that detached or hostile fathers and castrating mothers are the link to male homosexuality. Indeed, most experts recognize that the origins of sexual orientation are multiple and diverse (Friedman & Downey, 1994).

There may be as many as 25 million gay people in the United States. How do gay couples differ from their heterosexual counterparts? In many respects, gay couples do not differ much from heterosexual couples. A study by Peplau (1991) compared homosexual and heterosexual men and women on what aspects of intimacy they valued and found that heterosexual men and women were quite similar to homosexual men and women.

Gay couples, however, do have to face a different reality concerning their relationship. Many couples want to legally bind their commitment but are unable to do so. Legal marriage is a nonreligious contract designed to support, encourage, and protect intimate relationships. Marriage law touches nearly every aspect of monogamous relationships, including domestic partner benefits, rights of visitation, medical decision-making, survivorship, child custody, immigration, and funerals. Since many couples have accepted the responsibilities of marriage, they feel they should get the rights as well. However, almost all states prohibit gay couples from legally marrying. Currently, employment benefits for domestic partners do not provide for full equity, and child custody and inheritance is also not covered. As a result, gay couples do not get the same economic benefits that heterosexual couples do (Rivera, 1991).

HOMOPHOBIA

Homophobia is an irrationally negative attitude toward homosexual people. Homosexual people are often depicted in terms of negative stereotypes; however, this tendency may have recently begun to lessen (Friedman & Downey, 1994). Still, a majority of people indicate that they would prefer to not be in a work setting with homosexual people (Herek, 1991). Factors that appear to be related to homophobia include authoritarian perspectives, highly religious views, being with others who share negative views toward homosexuals, and not having had any personal contact with gay or lesbian people. In recent years, homophobic attitudes as well as the fear of AIDS have led to many gays being harassed or even assaulted (Herek & Berrill, 1990).

Homophobia exists in all aspects of society. Many homosexual professionals, including doctors, social workers, and lawyers, believe that they need to conceal their homosexual identity. One study (Wisniewski & Toomey, 1987) found that social workers, like many other professional groups, show evidence of homophobia.

Although few studies on the subject are available, clearly many homosexuals remain "in the closet," and their colleagues and clients do not know their sexual ori-

FIGURE 10.4
Concordance rate for sexual orientation
(Based on data from Bailey et al., 1993)

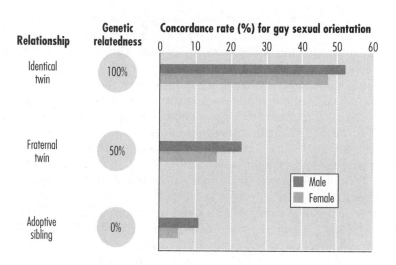

entation. Is AIDS affecting the number of homosexual men who come out? Marks (1988) found that today's young gay men continue to have a powerful gay identity that does not appear to be hampered by AIDS. In fact, in some ways AIDS has facilitated the process of coming out because individuals must address the consequences of the disease. What has changed, is the *way* people come out. The past image of gay men descending on the gay bar scene in search of sex is giving way to a stronger desire by gay men for more long-lasting relationships (Dregni, 1989).

INTERNALIZED HOMOPHOBIA

Why do some lesbians, gay men, and bisexuals seem to easily ignore society's prejudices toward their sexuality, while others absorb the bigotry to the point of self-loathing? This self-loathing, called **internalized homophobia,** exists when a gay man or lesbian has negative feelings about his or her own homosexuality or bisexuality. It can be associated with depression, low self-esteem, or extreme defensiveness, and it can impair a person's capacity for intimacy. Researchers (Sleek, 1996) have identified populations that have lower rates of internalized homophobia. They are (1) people who are more open about their homosexuality or bisexuality with their friends and acquaintances, particularly with heterosexuals, (2) women who have told their partners about their sexual orientation, (3) people who have a strong support system both within and outside the gay and lesbian communities, and (4) gay and bisexual men who told their mothers about their sexual orientation. Researchers note that internalized homophobia may actually be a common, albeit painful, path of development for gays, lesbians and bisexuals living in a homophobic society.

How can therapists help clients with internalized homophobia? Some approaches (Sleek, 1996) may include: (1) Discuss the patient's early experience and the ways he or she adapted to or repressed his or her homosexual feelings; (2) challenge the client's assumptions or beliefs about gender roles; (3) examine your own assumptions about gender roles, to make sure you are not presenting a traditional role as the only acceptable alternative for the client; and (4) be a role model. If you are gay or lesbian and have dealt with and overcome your own internalized homophobia or self-contempt, you provide a positive model for a gay client struggling with similar issues. Additionally, researchers admit that more research is needed on internalized homophobia to explore ethnic, cultural, and socioeconomic differences in internalized homophobia, as well as the role it plays in substance abuse, domestic violence, and suicide among gay men and lesbians.

TRANSITION TO PARENTHOOD

Carrying the baby horizontally across my chest like a football usually calms him and often puts him to sleep. But not tonight. He's still crying, cycling through his whole repertoire: the screechy fear cry; the lower, throaty demand cry; the pitiable gasping interspersed with slobbery whimpers. Kapa nursed him an hour ago at midnight, so he isn't hungry. Teething—always a suspect—doesn't seem to be the problem tonight: he isn't drooling much, nor is he clawing at his ears. I may give him a dropperful of Tylenol anyway, to help me relax (Goodrich, 1995, p. 12).

As this scene depicts, the transition to parenthood brings many changes and new challenges. Consider all the adaptations the new parent must make. Parents must now accommodate changes in priorities, as they have less time to spend on career and personal interests. Indeed, the loss of free time appears to be one of the most difficult adjustments for parents. How will the new household tasks be divided between the parents? Many parents struggle to find the time and energy needed to keep their own relationship satisfying in terms of intimacy and companionship. The transition must also include their adaptation to a new role—that of parent. What makes a good parent? What kind of parents do they want to be?

These life changes are usually accompanied by a significant increase in stress. The crying baby and the new demands of diapers, bottles, and laundry combine to create a stressful environment for many new parents. Mothers can be uniquely affected, and they often enter parenthood exhausted from the birth process. For older mothers and working mothers, the transition to parenthood is often more difficult. Women are particularly vulnerable to distress when they are the infant's major caretaker and when they have babies with difficult temperaments (Kalmuss, Davidson, & Cushman, 1992). Curran (1985) surveyed married couples and single mothers to identify what parents perceive to be the most stressful aspects of their lives. He identified the following top ten stressors listed in order of priority:

1. Economics, finances, budgeting
2. Children's behavior, discipline, sibling fighting
3. Insufficient couple time
4. Lack of shared responsibilities in the family
5. Communicating with children
6. Insufficient "me" time
7. Guilt for not accomplishing more
8. Spousal relationships (communication, friendship, sex)
9. Insufficient family playtime
10. Overscheduled family calendar

Implications for Practice: Preparing for the Transition to Parenthood

How can we make the transition to parenthood less stressful? Jay Belsky (1985) has recommended that parents be helped to reach realistic expectations about parental responsibilities. This recommendation is based on the finding that stress is highest in new mothers who have overestimated the benefits of their new mothering role and underestimated the difficulties associated with their new role. Mothers with optimistic perspectives about what it is like to be a parent tend to experience more distress, because their expectations need the greatest amount of realignment. Prospective parents could be greatly helped by better education about what parenting is like. Once parents understand that, although children are "bundles of joy," they can also be "bundles of stress," they can develop more realistic expectations and be in a better position to cope effectively with their new role as parents.

The following Focus section looks at the difficult issue of how to deal with parents of "crack babies."

FOCUS ON ETHICS

Parents of Crack Babies— Where Do We Draw the Line?

Jennifer Johnson of Florida was one of the first women convicted of child abuse as a result of her addiction to crack. She was sentenced to mandatory drug treatment and 15 years probation. As crack became increasingly popular, the media exposed the dramatic scenes of crack addiction known to many. Janee Chapman started using pot and alcohol when she was 12, and by the time she was 16, she was using cocaine. After her second pregnancy, she discovered crack. That caused social workers to remove her two children, but she still couldn't stop. Her crack baby was born with the "shakes," a common sign of drug exposure, and is developmentally delayed. Melinda East, a former crack addict, gave birth to a baby with the "shakes," but that did not stop her. She went back on the street as a prostitute to support herself and her habit. At times, she sold disposable diapers and milk back to the grocery store to obtain drug money.

The frustration and sadness of seeing crack babies has prompted many to ask, "When should we take their kids away?" The debate centers on the point at which child protective authorities should remove a child from the home. Many states now have child-abuse laws that consider it illegal for mothers to give birth to children with illegal drugs in their bloodstream. In some cases, this is considered delivering drugs to a minor. Frustrated policy makers have gone even further, some suggesting that female addicts be required to accept Norplant—a birth control implant that works for up to five years—if they want to avoid serving jail time. Many child advocates are impatient in considering the civil liberties of the mothers. They argue that the system is letting babies die, or at best, returning them to mothers who are ill equipped to parent them.

But what happens to the babies who are removed from their mothers? Many end up as wards of the court and are boarded in overcrowded hospitals. Other options include shifting the babies from one foster home to the next. Many experts believe many of these babies will end up suffering from the "failure to thrive" syndrome, whereby weight gain and normal development are negatively affected. Health policy officials are taking a closer look at the effect of such a punitive approach. Because many of these women do get pregnant again, and because they have already been treated negatively, many of them will be even less likely to seek health care again. Many communities are changing their initial strategy of removing all crack babies from their mothers. In Los Angeles, such an action would completely overwhelm the system. Instead, social workers must carefully assess the child's health and the mother's potential for rehabilitation when making court recommendations. Interestingly, one of the biggest factors in custody decisions is the presence of a grandmother. In some counties, grandmothers reportedly care for more than half of all crack babies.

Additional problems resulted from the policy to remove babies identified with drugs in their bodies. In a few cases there were mistaken assessments; for example, one mother had her child taken away after she received drugs for a cesarean delivery, which led to a false positive drug test. Also at issue is the fact that these social policies were implemented with women of color at public hospitals but not with white women in private hospitals. Such discrimination was exposed; along with the concomitant destruction of families as a result of this approach to the crack problem, it has led to renewed efforts to find other solutions—for example, the combination of offering addicted mothers intensive wraparound services with the threat of legal sanctions.

Addicted mothers need lots of help—detoxification, child pediatric services, counseling, social support, career and vocational help—backed up with the threat of legal intervention. For example, the Women and Infants Clinic in Boston offers comprehensive services but also requires women to submit to random urine tests each week. Other programs give mothers a choice: jail or treatment. Many experts believe that the ultimatum works well.

Social workers are also finding new ways to provide treatment for these women. For example, many social services professionals believe that it is not helpful to confront women about their lying and other problematic behavior as is often done in drug rehabilitation programs. What may be different about addicted mothers, compared with other addicted individuals, is that many of these women ended up in their situation because they were once sexually or physically abused or raped. This leads to a different treatment strategy than has typically been used in the past with addicts. The present approach is a combination of legal intervention and service delivery and the notion that, to save the child, we must also save the mother.

(Based on Cronin & Gorman, 1991)

VOLUNTARY CHILDLESSNESS

An increasing number of married couples choose not to have children (Seccombe, 1991). A review of U.S. Census Bureau data shows an increase in the number of women without children for all age groups. For women aged 25–29, the percentage without children went from less than 30% in 1970 to more than 40% in 1990. This change is most likely the result of women seeking career opportunities and marrying at a later age. The percentage of women who never expect to bear children is more than 9.4% (U.S. Bureau of the Census, 1992). Approximately one-third of childless couples decided before they married to remain childless (Veevers, 1980). In fact, many men and women decide while still adolescents to remain childless (Campbell, 1985).

WHEN COUPLES CAN'T
CONCEIVE: INFERTILITY

Infertility is defined as the inability to achieve pregnancy after one year of sexual intercourse with no contraception. The latest figures indicate that 20% to 25% of couples are infertile. This number is a significant increase over the 10% of couples unable to conceive only a generation ago. This rise in infertility is attributable to an increase in sexually transmitted diseases, which result in pelvic inflammation and adhesions, and also to the fact that couples now delay childbearing into their 30s. Female fertility decreases after age 30, and male fertility drops after age 45. Thus, couples who delay childbearing may pass up their most fertile years and later experience difficulties conceiving.

Infertility has several causes. Male abnormalities contribute to 40% of the cases of infertility, female problems another 40%; in the remaining 20% of cases there is no ascertainable reason the couple cannot conceive. In males, the problems of infertility involve having a low sperm count, having abnormally formed sperm, or having sperm with low motility; that is, the sperm are unable to make the journey through the cervix and uterus to the fallopian tube.

In females, menstrual cycles can result in infrequent or absent ovulation. Cervical mucus, which is hostile to sperm, can prevent migration of the sperm through the cervix. The fallopian tubes may become blocked, from past pelvic infection or inflammation from gonorrheal salpingitis or from the pelvic adhesions of endometriosis (a condition that arises when pieces of the lining of the uterus become attached to structures in the abdominal cavity including the fallopian tubes). Uterine problems such as fibroids, congenital malformations, and intrauterine adhesions can keep a fertilized egg from implanting.

Implications for Practice:
The Infertile Couple

Julie had always planned on having children. She had assumed she would get her degree, marry her boyfriend, work a while, and have a couple of children. After college, though, she went to graduate school and then began an exciting career. After eight years of an on-again, off-again relationship, her boy-friend left. After a couple of years of dating, at the age of 34, Julie fell in love, got married, and stopped taking birth control pills. Two years later, Julie has not conceived. At first she attributed her failure to conceive to having taken the pill for so long. But now, each month when she gets her period, Julie is increasingly worried. An infertility workup disclosed that her husband has a low sperm count. The couple's relationship is becoming strained as they consider their options for having a child.

Couples who receive the diagnosis of infertility may be in a crisis situation, and their emotions and reactions should be considered from this viewpoint. They are facing the loss of a lifelong dream—the end to their hopes and dreams of having a family. Often the first reaction is shock, followed by denial (this can't happen to us). The practitioner should allow the couple to express their feelings of isolation, guilt, depression, and anger. Because of the economic and emotional cost and low success rate of infertility treatment, Paulson and Sauer (1991) urge that counseling the couple should, from the beginning, include the option to stop the treatment. The social worker should help the couple differentiate treatment failure from personal failure. The practitioner's challenge is to reframe the meaning of infertility and the partners' view of themselves (Olshansky, 1992). Although the drive to become a biological parent may be strong, other options for fulfilling the need to nurture should be explored with the couple. The social worker should discuss the options of adoption and of leading a fulfilling life as a childless couple.

Ken Daniels feels that "social work, with its focus on the interaction of person/problem/situation, is ideally suited to respond to the psychosocial needs arising from infertility" (1993, p. 507). He notes that "a social worker providing counseling from a psychosocial perspective will be aware of the importance of the couple's support system and seek to enable them to utilize this vital source of support. This is in contrast to more traditional infertility counseling, where the focus is more likely to be on the individual or couple alone" (p. 509).

In addition to counseling for their emotional needs, the partners need assistance in using their social support system to help them through this crisis. The couple may have problems communicating with parents or employers at this time when they most need to talk with others. The social worker may need to hold sessions with the couple and with members of their extended family. Through role-playing and problem solving, the social worker can also enable the partners to explain to employers work-related problems caused by the infertility treatment.

The following Focus section examines what happens when a couple loses a baby.

FOCUS ON THE FAMILY

▼

Some Babies Die

Mei Ling and Kim were thrilled when they learned that Mei Ling was pregnant. Mei Ling told everyone—her co-workers, her friends, neighbors, and family—that she was pregnant. The couple began to look at baby items in stores and to plan how they would decorate the nursery. Eleven weeks into the pregnancy, however, late one afternoon at work, Mei Ling experienced some lower abdominal cramping. After dinner that night, she felt increased cramping and began to have vaginal bleeding. Mei Ling called her doctor, who told her to go to the hospital. There, later that evening, Mei Ling miscarried. Mei Ling and Kim were devastated by the loss, but their doctor assured them that they were young and could try again soon. The nurses gave Mei Ling a booklet about coping with fetal death, the number of a support group to call, and a satin-covered box containing a small gold ring. The couple was encouraged to name the baby and to have some kind of memorial. They hardly had time to cry. Kim returned to work two days later, and Mei Ling took a few days to recover. Two weeks after the loss, friends and family stopped asking Mei Ling how she felt. One month later, the couple had a major argument after Mei Ling accused Kim of not caring about their baby. After this blowup, they decided to attend the support group. Their first question was, "How long does this pain last?"

Often in a hospital or a clinical setting, a social worker is called on to support families who suffer a fetal loss. To many couples, an early miscarriage can signify the loss of a child. Even at the beginning of pregnancy, most couples have dreamed of and planned for their expected child. The mother, especially, has fantasized about the baby she will have, and the loss of that dream is very real and painful. At any stage of pregnancy, mourning a perinatal loss is difficult though, because there is so little concrete evidence of the child's existence. It is hard for a mother to identify with a child she has only interacted with through fantasy. It is hard for friends and family to understand the pain of the loss of someone they never knew. It is difficult to grieve for someone who never lived. As a consequence, many couples who experience a fetal loss lose not only their dream but also their right to mourn.

Often, because this situation involves coping not only with one's own grief but that of one's spouse, partners experience at least one episode of intense conflict following perinatal loss (Gilbert, 1989). Men and women grieve a fetal loss in different ways. Fathers report that intense grieving lasts less than one month, whereas mothers' intense grieving lasts up to one year (Hughes & Page-Lieberman, 1989). Because of the shorter period of intense grief that fathers experience, mothers may feel that their partner is unfeeling and not adequately mourning the loss, and fathers may feel that their partner is dwelling on her grief instead of getting on with life (Hughes & Page-Lieberman, 1989).

The couple needs to recognize that the fetal loss is the loss of a real baby and all the dreams and fantasies surrounding it. The couple should be encouraged to mourn adequately before attempting another pregnancy. Attempting to have a second pregnancy to replace a perinatal loss is likely to result in unresolved grief, which could interfere with subsequent bonding to the next child (Leon, 1992). First, the couple should be encouraged to see the body, name the baby, make a book of memories, and have a memorial service (Leon, 1986). The hospital can attempt to provide the family with evidence of the child's existence by providing a photograph, a lock of hair, a footprint, or whatever the couple wishes to keep. Most important, the couple should be allowed the time and opportunity to express their feelings about the loss. They should be helped to understand and accept that each person grieves loss in his or her own way. But for some who ask, "How long will the pain last?" the answer is often "A long time."

WORK LIFE

In young adulthood, a person's career or job can become a significant part of the person's self-identity. Often a person's self-definition is related to what he or she does. Levinson (1978) describes the process of young adults entering an occupation whereby they must develop an occupational identity and establish themselves in the work world. Each job carries with it a set of components that must be adapted to for successful adjustment in the workplace. Newman and Newman (1995) describe four of these components: the use of technical skills; the development of authority relations; adapting to special demands and hazards; and the development of interpersonal relationships with peers. As young adults make important inroads in their career, they may also be starting a family. Achieving a balance among one's career, leisure, and family life is a developmental task that needs to be addressed during this period.

The psychological importance of what people do varies, and it is important to understand the difference between a job and a career. Many people pursue a job in order to earn a living. Therefore, their job may not have much value to them from a psychological perspective. Other people pursue a career more as a way of life. Their career may have significant value to them because it is a central aspect of their life. Not everyone has the opportunity to pursue a career, so adapting to young adulthood can be very different depending on whether one is entering the workforce for a "job" or a "career."

WOMEN AND WORK

The role of women in the workplace has changed dramatically in recent decades. Sixty-two percent of married women with children under the age of 6 work outside the home (U.S. Bureau of the Census, 1995). Although the role of women has changed dramatically, the reality is that the workplace is still quite different for men than for women. Discrimination and inadequate opportunities remain significant obstacles for women (Eccles, 1987). Particularly significant is the fact that women still experience job segregation on the basis of gender. There are jobs that are considered "male" jobs and jobs that are considered "female" jobs. Many of the major professions—computer program-

ming, electrical engineering, accounting, and law—are dominated by men. And, of course, employees in female-dominated professions earn less than employees in male-dominated professions, even when skill levels and responsibilities are similar (Rukeyser, Cooney, & Winslow, 1988).

PEER RELATIONSHIPS— FORMING MENTORSHIPS

Levinson's theory of adult development describes the stage of entering the adult world. It is during this phase that the person begins to shape his or her "dream," or vision of what the person would like to accomplish as an adult. Often during this phase a special relationship is formed with a mentor—a person who serves as a role model, teacher, and adviser. This most often occurs in a work setting with a colleague. Mentors are usually about 10–15 years older than the individual and play a critical role in helping the young adult refine and achieve his or her dream. The use of mentors occurs more often for men than for women. Studies have found that, for career women, professional mentoring is less likely (Noe, 1988). This may be due to the lack of available mentors for young professional women. However, women have indicated that they often perceive older friends or relatives as role models. Often people volunteer to be a mentor for someone else. The following Focus section discusses volunteerism as a vital societal movement.

FOCUS ON COMMUNITY

Volunteerism and Social Services

Have you ever felt the satisfaction of knowing that you helped someone by your volunteer efforts? You are not alone. There are an estimated 93 million volunteers in America (Gerson, 1997). Volunteering confers many acknowledged benefits. It helps build a sense of community, breaks down barriers between people, and often raises quality of life for all involved. Some types of volunteer activities seem consistently successful, the most obvious example being the outpouring of help that occurs after natural disasters.

But we have to ask: If there are really 93 million volunteers in our country, why are our cities in worse shape than they have ever been? Because few of those millions, just 8.4%, work in "human services," a broad category that includes aiding the homeless, family counseling, serving as tutors or mentors, and so on. But the problems of troubled children, needy seniors, and the poor require exactly this kind of volunteering. It must be performed one on one, over a long period of time, and often in low-income neighborhoods. And for this type of assistance, there is a shortage of volunteers.

Why are supply and demand so misaligned? The simplest explanation is that volunteers sign up for reasons other than the urgency of social problems. Volunteers say they participate because (1) they were asked by someone, (2) they learned of an opportunity through an organization to which they belonged, or (3) a family member or friend would benefit as a result.

Economic realities also shape the choices volunteers can make. The backbone of volunteer involvement in the past was stay-at-home mothers with flexible schedules. Now, many families have both parents working, and whatever spare time is left over must go to the kids. "I don't think it is a question of people not wanting to volunteer; it is a question of how, where, and can I do it in a way that fits in my schedule," according to the vice chairwoman of City Cares of America, a group that hooks up busy people with appropriate volunteer opportunities (Gerson, 1997, p. 29).

Partly because the number, 93 million volunteers, is so impressive and inspiring, some politicians think that churches and charities, not government, should provide more of the social safety net for welfare reform. Supporters of turning over social programs to churches and charities say their plan will reawaken American passion. Religion is often crucial to turning lives around, and charitable organizations are often more efficient and effective than government programs. Americans gave 143.9 billion dollars to charities in 1995, up 7.8% from the previous year, which was the biggest increase in a decade. Opponents contend that counting on charity would ignore history. The social safety net grew precisely because churches and charities could no longer deal with the entrenched poverty of the late 20th century. Additionally, charities are already overburdened trying to respond to existing cuts in government spending for the poor, disabled, and needy. Finally, nonprofit organizations are not a substitute for government, because government already provides 37% of the funding for charities.

It is one thing to celebrate volunteers. It is another thing to depend on them to fill the gaps in welfare and other government programs. In this light, it is not the thought that counts. Volunteerism is often understood as a virtue, but now it should also be understood as a market. And viewed that way, it is an inefficient one. Most volunteers are not deployed effectively to solve the hardest, and most critical, problems. In fact, the majority of the 93 million volunteers do informal volunteering; babysitting for a neighbor, baking cookies for a school event, singing in the church choir, or serving on community boards. Volunteer management is often poor, and amazingly little is known about which volunteer programs really work. To an extent rarely acknowledged publicly, the volunteer sector is not ready for the responsibilities politicians want to thrust upon it.

Misha Marvel (Based on Gerson, 1997, and Shapiro, 1996)

Multicultural and Gender Considerations

Multicultural aspects of young adulthood are many and varied across different cultures. However, the development of one's career or livelihood is an important task that has clear multicultural aspects. In particular, unemployment rates are critical for the African-American, Hispanic, and Native-American groups. Many young adults in these groups value the family but are frustrated in their attempts to provide for their families because of limited opportunities. Baruth and Manning (1991) describe the following additional issues among different cultures as their members face adulthood: alcoholism among Native-Americans; acculturation of Asian-Americans; the stereotype of the African-American as violent; and the increasing significance of African-American females as the head of household. Table 10.2 presents some of the unique challenges that confront adults in Native-American, African-American, Hispanic-American, and Asian-American cultures.

TABLE 10.2 Challenges Confronting Ethnic or Racial Groups	
Ethnic or Racial Group	**Unique Challenges Confronting Adults**
Native-Americans	Many of their unique problems stem from a history of discrimination, broken treaties, and prejudice. Poor academic attainments (only 57% are high school graduates). Extremely high unemployment rates. Language problems have affected progress. Stereotypes promoted by TV and movies.
African-Americans	Dialect differences have challenged them. The stereotype of the "violent black" is influencing their social progress. Poor academic progress and lack of social progress. Social conditions that are detrimental to self-improvement like discrimination, racism, lack of opportunities.
Asian-Americans	Language problems have been a challenge. The "model minority" stereotype. With acculturation, family roles and expectations can conflict with the white American culture. Value changes in family relationships can lead to a schism between younger and older generations.
Hispanic-Americans	Language problems are critical because many Hispanics speak only Spanish. Poor academic progress and lack of social progress. Improvement in middle-paying and high-paying jobs. Lack of appropriate skills for coping in the dominant white society and with discrimination and prejudice.

(Adapted from Baruth & Manning, 1991)

BLENDING RELIGIONS

If you look at the world's major religions, there seem to be many paths to God. For the last 2000 years, when most people lived in villages, if those paths crossed, a holy war was more likely to break out than a wedding. But in America today we have a unique society in which the person next door may believe in one of many religious beliefs; our "paths" are crossing more than ever. The proportion of Jews who married Gentiles—about one in ten around the first half of the 20th century—doubled by 1960, doubled again by the early 1970s, and in this decade has leveled off at around 50%. Currently, one in three American Jews live in an interfaith household. The comparable figure for Catholics is 21%; Mormons, 30%; and Muslims, 40% (Adler, 1997). And, as these couples raise their children, they are, in effect, creating a new form of religious identity in America.

However, when it comes to the children, expecting children to choose their mother's or father's religions may put them in the position of rejecting one of their parents. These children may also feel they are not as good as their all-one-religion cousins or friends (Adler, 1997). To remedy this dilemma, some couples chose one religion to raise their children in, others expose the children to both or to a variety and let the

children choose, and still others blend their religions to make a third one.

The following Focus section gives us a view of one family's dilemma about how to raise their children.

FOCUS ON SPIRITUALITY

Spiritual Parenting

"The problem was, by the time I became a mother, I did not know what beliefs to 'subject' them to. I had thrown out my religious roots and did not know how to replace them. Even more to the point, I did not know how to define or talk about the spiritual connections I did feel . . . So our challenge became . . . how to raise two children to be compassionate, moral, and ethical people without returning to the very traditions we had rejected years ago.

"To me, spiritual parenting is more than bringing your kids up as good 'somethings'—Christians, Jews, Hindus, Muslims, Buddhists, Goddess devotees. It means giving them the tools they need to make their own choices and expand their own awareness. It involves being present to them in every aspect of their development. It means learning to speak their language, providing them the emotional foods they need to grow, and treating them with as much respect as you would an adult friend or family member. It means putting them first—above everything else in your life."

(Sparrowe, 1997)

GENDER ROLES

In young adulthood, women confront two significant role expectations (Weiten & Lloyd, 1997). In particular, two mandates characterize the traditional female role: the marriage mandate and the motherhood mandate.

The marriage mandate says that, to be a successful heterosexual female, you must find a marriage partner. In fact, part of being a young adult is that you have gotten married. Some researchers believe that the fact that a significant number of lesbians were previously married is evidence of the strength in the marriage mandate.

The motherhood mandate says that a successful adult woman also must bear children and become a mother. The mandate further suggests that it is important to have two children, with one of them being a son (Russo, 1979). The woman should also be a "good mother."

What is it like for women who do stay home to take care of the house and children? Tavris and Wade (1984) refer to this scenario as the "housewife syndrome." In general, women who stay at home have greater psychological adjustment problems compared with either employed husbands or employed wives (Steil & Turetsky, 1987). Women who experience the housewife syndrome have been found to be less happy, feel more discouraged, and be more self-critical than are employed single or married women (Nickerson & Pitochelli, 1978).

Two factors may help explain why women are less happy when they occupy the homemaker role. First, these women are socially isolated. It may be difficult, especially in our postmodern world, for them to find meaningful connections with others on a day-to-day basis. Second, the role of homemaker carries a negative connotation, and therefore the status of the homemaker is low. The important role of being a homemaker and good mother in the home is not highly val-

ued by our society, which makes it difficult for those who occupy this role.

Gender expectations and stereotypes can be negative and destructive for women and men. Many young adults are committed to discarding such expectations, focusing instead on qualities that are valued by everyone. For example, Carol Tavris (1992), in her book *The Mismeasure of Women,* examines the dominant male viewpoint and challenges this as a standard for what is normal for both men and women. She argues for an expanded view of what it means to be human and recommends a move away from the typical "us/them" perspective used when discussing gender issues.

The following Focus section looks at how men and women divide housework.

FOCUS ON GENDER

Housework—Are Men Doing Their Fair Share?

Because the roles men and women play in the family have changed dramatically in the last 30–40 years, many experts look to changes in child care and housework when assessing the significance of the changes. Do men share a greater role in child care and housework than they did in the past? Studies of the family in the late 1960s found that a husband's participation in family work was 1.1–1.6 hours per day compared with that of housewives, who worked 7.6 to 8.1 hours per day. But what if the wives were working outside the house? In this case, husbands increased their participation 0.1 hours per day when their wives were employed (Robinson, 1977). A few changes were noted in the 1970s. For example, Pleck (1985) found that husbands did family work 1.8 hours per day and housewives did family work 6.8 hours per day; employed wives did family work 4.0 hours per day. Studies have found that, yes, husbands have increased the amount of time they spend doing family work by about 25%. However, husbands' participation in family work continues to be about one-third that of their wives.

(Levant, 1990)

THE EFFECT OF MOTHER'S WORK ON CHILDREN'S DEVELOPMENT

As increasing numbers of women enter the workforce, an often-asked question is, "What affect does women's employment have on a child's development?" Hoffman (1987) has examined this question and pointed out two common assumptions: First, it is assumed that the more time that mothers spend with their children, the better the outcome. Second, it is assumed that full-time housewives in the past devoted more time to their children than the contemporary mother. Hoffman points out that negative effects can result from too much time together—for example, the development of unhealthy dependency. Furthermore, the technological developments of the last 20–40 years may mean that mothers today can spend about the same amount of time with their children that mothers did in the past.

Nonetheless, the popular belief holds that a mother's employment has a negative effect on the child's development. Interestingly, this notion may be unfounded, since many studies have discovered that maternal employment is *not* harmful to children (Demmo, 1992). Studies (Chase-Lansdale, 1981; Easterbrooks & Goldberg, 1985) have examined whether a mother's employment affects the quality of infant-mother interactions and emotional attachment and found no connection. What may be more important is the attitude of the parents. When families are satisfied with the wife's role in the family, the children are well adjusted (Easterbrooks & Goldberg, 1985). Strong attachments and commitment to children can clearly be a reality for working mothers.

Indeed, some recent research suggests that in some cases the effect of maternal employment may be positive. Children of working mothers have been found to be particularly self-reliant and responsible. This appears to be true more for girls than for boys. Hoffman (1987) concludes that daughters of working mothers achieve greater academic competence and higher career aspirations than daughters of stay-at-home mothers do.

The following Focus section looks at the changes that will be necessary worldwide for men and women to attain political and economic equality.

FOCUS ON GENDER

When Will Women and Men Be Equal?

According to the results of a new survey, it may take another 1000 years for women to match the political and economic clout of men. Based on the current rate of progress, it will take 500 years for women to hold equal managerial jobs and 475 years for women to reach equal political and economic status. These findings are based on the following types of statistical data:

- Women hold 41% of management jobs in the United States—11% high ranking and 3% top level.
- Women hold 40% of management jobs in Canada and Australia, 8.3% in Japan, and 4% in South Korea.
- Greece and Paraguay had a decrease in women managers.
- Only six of 179 members of the United Nations have a female head of state.
- Women occupy 3.5% of government cabinet posts worldwide.

(Sanchez, 1994)

Social Hazards

The William T. Grant Foundation (1988) became interested in examining how well American young people are making the transition from school to adult roles in work and family life. The results of their study found that the transition was particularly difficult for the forgotten half—the non-college-bound youth. A major focus of the study was on the declining economic fortunes of young adults. A disturbing finding was that "virtually all young male workers, despite their educational achievements, are, on average, far worse off than they were a decade ago, and minorities are substantially worse off than whites" (William T. Grant Foundation, 1988, p. 21). All males (except young African-American college graduates) suffered substantial earnings losses. This decline in earnings is a result of changes in the economy that have created a deterioration in real earnings.

How can there be earnings losses for Americans? This happens when the amount of money someone earns does not keep up with living costs. It simply costs a lot more to live today than it did 10 and 20 years ago—and how much you can buy for your money is substantially less. Consider some of the following statistics:

- In 1974, low-income families spent 35% of their income on rent and utilities. In 1983, that percentage had risen to 46%—almost half the family income.

- The average 30-year-old who owned a house in 1973 spent about 21% of his or her monthly income on home mortgage payments. However, by 1983 that same person was spending 44% of earnings to pay the mortgage.

- From 1974 to 1983, average housing costs and utility costs rose by 35%.

These facts mean that supporting a family is a lot harder for a larger percentage of American society today than it was in the past, particularly for young people who are not college bound. Coupled with this loss of earnings is the fact that good job opportunities are shrinking for young people. For example, in 1974 almost half of all jobs held by young African-Americans were blue-collar, craft, and operative occupations that paid enough to support a family. Only 12 years later, African-Americans held only 25% of these jobs. For noncollege youth, supporting a family is extremely difficult given these sharp declines in earnings. Decline in earnings is the primary reason the percentage of minority families that are below the poverty line has increased so dramatically.

American society needs to work toward better compensation for noncollege youth. The William T. Grant Foundation (1988, p. 24) concludes that "the American people should set as a conscious goal of public policy the improvement of employment and earnings levels for all workers, not the least those lacking college education." Although this recommendation seems logical, it is not without controversy. Congress did just pass an increase in the minimum wage, but many economists believe this will cost young people jobs even though it can increase their standard of living. Realistically, just how much will a minuscule increase in the minimum wage raise the standard of living for the working poor? The following Focus section discusses this issue.

FOCUS ON WELFARE REFORM

Barely Making Ends Meet

Millions of American families hold two or three jobs but still cannot afford necessities, and so they see little relief ahead. "Welfare reform" is on many people's lips, but the working poor receive little or no attention from politicians or policies. While welfare reform will hopefully lift millions of people off the dole and into the workforce, they will most definitely join the 10 million Americans who hover one rung above poverty on the nation's ladder of opportunity (Gibbs, 1995). These are the people who stretch groceries from one paycheck to another and have no savings, who ride the bus to discount stores and do not bother to clip coupons because the generic products are still cheaper, and, because they cannot afford health insurance, can be wiped out and pushed into poverty by even a minor medical problem. Two-thirds of the nearly 40 million Americans with no health insurance live in families with full-time workers.

In some cities, one-quarter of the people who call local homeless hotlines are working people: schoolteachers, chefs, computer maintenance workers, airline flight attendants. The standard recommendation is that a family should budget 30% of its income for housing. Among the working poor, 70% is more typical. The working poor may not expect much from government, but at a minimum, they wish the government would not make their hard lives even harder. Unfortunately, many of the working poor say that they are too discouraged to go out and vote because it is so easy for politicians to ignore them. As some people feel, "Now everything goes up except people's wages. Either you're rich or you're poor" (Gibbs, 1995, p. 17).

THE FAMILY THAT HAS
A CHILD WITH A DISABILITY

Having a child with a disability in the family can require many special adaptations on the part of family members (Schuster & Ashburn, 1992). Indeed, the care of a child with a disability often restructures the family's intentions and plans. The mother, who perhaps was looking forward to returning to work, may now decide that she needs to stay home to provide special care for the child. This decision, in turn, affects the financial status of the family and may compel the father to seek additional work to compensate for the loss of income. However, the father may also feel a need to be more available to the family (McConachie, 1986). The family may decide that services are not adequate in the area they live and may seek a new location that can better provide for the child. Many sacrifices are made as the family attempts to restructure and respond to the new demands placed on it.

The mother is often under enormous pressure and may become physically exhausted. She is often the person who must spend hours traveling to doctor's offices, following up on health insurance claims, seeking special education programs, and so forth. Going on a simple outing may require taking special equipment like a wheelchair, special eating utensils, and medications. Caring for a child with a severe disability is demanding and often leaves the mother stressed, socially isolated, and exhausted from the hard work (Pahl & Quine, 1987). Much of the stress results from the mother's inability to develop interests beyond the child's care. Critical to successful adjustment is the emotional support she can receive from her husband or significant others.

Parents of children with disabilities can benefit from respite service, so the parents can leave the child with others and get some time away. However, these services are not always available. And some parents have had so little time to themselves that, when they do get away, they do not know what to do (Schuster & Ashburn, 1992). The parents may spend their time fighting since they have not had any opportunity in their regular schedules to address their problems. For adjustment to take place, parents need to recognize

A family with a child who has a disability needs to make special efforts to provide the child with normal social experiences.

their responsibilities to each other as a couple as well as their responsibilities to the child as parents (Simons, 1987).

Does the increased stress and pressure result in a higher divorce rate among couples with a child with a disability compared with couples without such children? Although it would be logical to assume so, this is not the case. When divorce does occur, it is usually because of preexisting problems (Simons, 1987). Thomas (1987), who has studied family adaptation, reports that a common response among parents of children with a disability is a strengthening of their relationship and a perception that the experience of raising a child with a disability has helped them grow as individuals.

DIVORCE

As we mentioned earlier, for more than a century the percentage of marriages that end in divorce has been steadily increasing. However, it is difficult to determine the percentage of marriages that end in divorce. The often-quoted ratio of marriages in a given year to divorces in that year is considered misleading by researchers studying divorce. Regardless of the statistic used, divorce is becoming a fairly common event in American society. In 1993, the Bureau of Census projected that four out of ten first marriages would end in divorce. Factors associated with a high incidence of divorce include marriage at a young age, low educational attainments, and low income. Figure 10.5 presents the top ten reasons for obtaining a divorce by men and women.

Whatever the cause of the divorce, the emotional consequences are often dire for both

men and women. It is a dramatic change in one's life to go from being married to being divorced. Consider the following statement from Weiss's (1975) study on marital separation: "And then all of a sudden every goddamn thing, I'm back to zero. I have no house. I don't have a child. I don't have a wife. I don't have the same family. My economic position has been shattered. And nothing is recoverable. All these goals which I had struggled for, every goddamn one of them, is gone" (p. 75).

Research supports the negativity of divorce on husbands, wives, and their children. Many studies have found that divorce is associated with depression, anxiety, and drug use (Gotlib & McCabe, 1990; Schaefer & Burnett, 1987). Indeed, separated and divorced men and women have higher rates of psychiatric disturbance and admission to psychiatric hospitals. Some differences between men and women have been noted; for example, divorced men lose emotional support and ties to friends and relatives, whereas divorced women lose income (Gerstel, Reissman & Rosenfield, 1985; Smock, 1993). One study (Kiecolt-Glaser & Glaser, 1988) found that, in comparison with married couples,

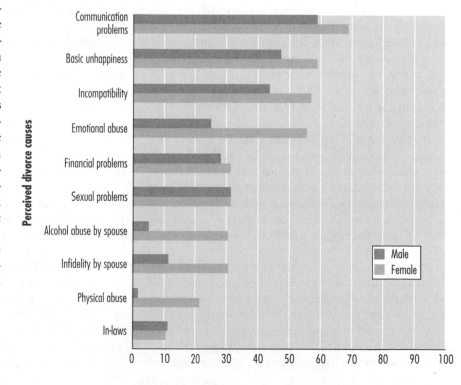

FIGURE 10.5
Reasons for divorce for men and women

individuals who were separated—and more stressed—had reduced their immune system's capacity to ward off infection and disease. Furthermore, studies have found that poor marital adjustment leads to depression and anxiety for women (Lorenz et al., 1997). Therefore, sticking it out in a conflicted and unhappy marriage may also lead to negative outcomes. The experience of a divorce is truly a crisis that can last a year or more (Booth & Amato, 1991; Lorenz et al., 1997) for the spouses, and it can take about two years for families to pull themselves back together.

Why do people divorce? Answers to this complex question must take into consideration a multitude of factors. One explanation has to do with the social changes that have occurred regarding the stigma associated with divorce. Divorce is not the evil phenomenon it was 50 years ago. Society as a whole has become increasingly tolerant of divorce—partly because of the increasing numbers of people who have experienced it. The institution of marriage underwent a particularly dramatic shift when women entered the workforce. People no longer necessarily have to stay married because of economic forces. According to researchers, we are in the midst of trying to renegotiate what the marriage contract is—what men and women are supposed to do as partners. Families have changed as well: The decline in fertility rates and smaller families enhance the likelihood of divorce when problems arise. Legal barriers to divorce have been reduced, and men and women are more likely to seek their own self-fulfillment rather than make sacrifices for each other (Yankelovich, 1981).

However, not all couples are calling it quits at the first sign of marital stress. As couples see the havoc divorce wreaks on divorced friends and acquaintances, many are now asserting a new effort to fight for their marriage. There is a growing recognition that marriages are not to be entered into—or dissolved—lightly because of the enormous social and economic costs (Gleick, 1995).

Almost no one disputes the many valid reasons for divorce—among them, domestic violence, child abuse and substance abuse. Mere incapability seems reason enough, when no children are involved. But the breakup of families is not considered to be only a social crisis. In the United States, the byproduct of what remains the world's highest divorce rate is millions of children thrown into poverty; despite their work outside the home, many women still suffer a severe income drop after divorce.

This may be why, suddenly, there seems to be so much attention being paid to preventing divorce. The past few years has seen a rise in the number of couples doing more to preserve and strengthen relationships. Some 4.6 million couples a year visit 50,000 licensed family therapists, up from 1.2 million in 1980 (Gleick, 1995).

But what happens to couples whose relationship is not recognized by the general society?

The following Focus section explores what happens when gay and lesbian couples break up.

FOCUS ON DIVERSITY

When Lesbian and Gay Couples Break Up

Surveys typically find that about 60% of all gay and lesbian adults are in couple relationships. In our survey of 1,266 couples, about three-quarters subscribed to a life-long commitment, and most of the remainder were committed "for a long time"—not unlike heterosexuals.

But lesbian and gay couples face many more obstacles than heterosexuals do in maintaining a relationship. Separation poses special burdens as well. Some couples must remain "invisible," a response to the threat of violence or lost jobs. Too often they enter relationships with problems, such as substance abuse and low self-esteem, that result from experiences of oppression.

Gay and lesbian couples also frequently lack support from immediate family. Instead of the typical blessings and presents awarded heterosexual unions, a same-sex wedding announcement may result in abandonment. Even the gay community has been slow to recognize family relationships. As one woman put it, "Gay friends I haven't seen in a while ask if we're still together—not 'How are you doing?'"

When relationships end, same-sex couples face the gender-blind pain of separation, property division, and lost contact with "in-laws" and common friends. Legally, they can mark the split-up by revising or destroying any documents that may have marked the relationship, such as powers of attorney, wills, and domestic partnership affidavits.

We believe lesbian and gay couples deserve the option to marry. Many already behave as married couples, but legalizing same-sex marriage would change the world around them and, we believe, make separation and divorce less likely.

(Bryant & Demian, 1990. Reprinted with permission.)

SEXUAL HARASSMENT

Sexual harassment is defined as unwelcome sexually oriented behavior. The behavior in question may be glares or "checking someone out," or it may involve physical touching, pressuring someone into sex, or sexual assault. It is being increasingly recognized in society as a problem, and it extends beyond the work setting—although this is where it usually occurs.

It is difficult to obtain accurate information about the prevalence of sexual harassment because many people don't recognize it and so hesitate to report it. However, it is estimated that as many as 50% to 75% of women have experienced sexual harassment on the job (Fain & Anderson, 1987), and 17% to 38% of women on college campuses report an experience with harassment (Dziech & Weiner, 1991).

From a legal viewpoint, there are two types of sexual harassment: **quid pro quo** and **environmental harassment.** *Quid pro quo* is a Latin phrase that means one thing is exchanged for something else. In the context of sexual harassment, a person in a position of power subjects a person of lower status to unwanted sexual advances. Furthermore, the person in power requires certain behaviors in exchange for a job, a promotion, a higher grade, and so forth. Fundamentally, some aspect of the person's job depends on her or his agreement to engage in some form of unwanted sex. Environmental harassment is when a hostile work environment is created by the person in power as a result of some unwanted sexual behavior. For example, telling work colleagues sexual jokes may create a hostile work environment.

Sexual harassment is not limited to sexual acts like intercourse. It includes a wide range of unso-licited and unwelcome actions like flirting, comments about another person's dress or anatomy, intrusive questions about another person's personal life, and descriptions of the harasser's own sexual experiences. Unwanted physical contact also includes a wide range of unwelcome behaviors such as touching, hugging, pinching, and slapping. Fundamentally, sexual harassment is an abuse of power by someone in a position of authority.

SEXUALLY TRANSMITTED DISEASES

Sexually transmitted diseases (STDs) are illnesses that are transmitted through sexual contact. STDs are being increasingly recognized as a serious social problem for adolescents and young adults. Many people think of STDs as one of three diseases: AIDS, syphilis, and gonorrhea. Actually, there are approximately 20 sexually transmitted diseases. Some can be easily treated, others cannot. Most, but not all, are transmitted through genital, oral-genital, or genital-anal contact; some do not require intercourse for transmission. For example, yeast infections can develop even when partners are monogamous.

The rate of STDs is increasing, and there are more than 13 million new cases each year. Gordon and Snyder (1989) present the increase in prevalence in a more dramatic fashion: If you are between the ages of 15 and 55, your chance of developing an STD other than AIDS is one in four during your lifetime. Box 10.1 describes the common sexually transmitted diseases. The following Focus section looks at how AIDS affects one ethnic group—Latinos.

AIDS AND PREVENTION

The effect of AIDS prevention programs in the United States was demonstrated in 1997 when the Centers for Disease Control and Prevention (CDC) reported a 6% decline in the estimated number of people diagnosed with AIDS in 1996 compared with that diagnosed in 1995—the first decline ever reported during the epidemic (Freiberg, 1998). This decline reflects the combined effect of successful prevention efforts, which have helped slow the infection rate in recent years, and new therapies in lengthening the healthy life span of people with HIV. The greatest decline

BOX 10.1

Common Sexually Transmitted Diseases

STD/TRANSMISSION/SYMPTOMS

ACQUIRED IMMUNE DEFICIENCY SYNDROME: Spread by sexual intercourse or anal intercourse. Can be spread by oral-genital sex, especially when semen is swallowed. Spread by nonsexual interaction through contaminated blood, for example, by sharing hypodermic needles used for drug injection. Typically there are no symptoms for approximately five years. After symptoms appear, death occurs soon afterward.

BACTERIAL VAGINOSIS: Most common is the transmission of *Gardnerella vaginalis* by sexual intercourse. Women experience a thin musty-smelling discharge. Most men are asymptomatic.

CANDIDIASIS: The growth of this fungus accelerates when the chemical balance of the vagina is disturbed; it can be transmitted through sexual intercourse. Described as a white "cheesy" discharge from the vagina, irritation of the vaginal tissue.

TRICHOMONIASIS: Can be transmitted through genital sexual contact or through less direct means—for example, from towels or bathtubs of infected people. Vaginal discharge that is white or yellow; unpleasant odor; vagina is sore and irritated.

CHLAMYDIAL INFECTION: The bacterium is transmitted primarily through sexual contact. It can be spread by fingers from one body part to another. For women, pelvic inflammatory disease can occur. This can disrupt the menstrual periods; elevate body temperature; lead to abdominal pain, nausea, vomiting, and headaches. In men, it can cause discharge from the penis and a burning sensation during urination. May be accompanied by heaviness in the affected testicles, inflammation of the scrotal skin, and swelling at the bottom of the testicle.

GONORRHEA: The bacterium is spread through genital, oral-genital, and genital-anal contact. In women, a greenish/yellow discharge; however, it often goes undetected. At a later stage, pelvic inflammatory disease may develop. In men, discharge from the penis and burning sensation during urination. Untreated complications can include inflammation of the scrotal skin and swelling at the base of the testicle.

SYPHILIS: The bacterium is transmitted from open lesions during genital, oral-genital, or genital-anal contact. In the primary stage, a chancre appears where the spirochetes entered the body. In the secondary stage, the chancre disappears, and a generalized skin rash appears. In the latent stages, there are often no observable symptoms. In the tertiary stage serious symptoms occur: heart failure, blindness, eventually death.

PUBIC LICE: Pubic lice are easily spread through body contact or through shared clothing or bedding. Lice invade the pubic hair area and cause persistent itching.

HERPES: The virus is transmitted primarily by genital, oral-genital, or genital-anal contact. An oral herpes virus is transmitted by kissing. Genital area develops small red, painful bumps. These papules are painful blisters that will rupture and form open sores.

GENITAL WARTS: The virus is spread primarily through genital, oral-genital, and genital-anal contact. Warts develop in the affected areas as hard yellow-gray bumps or soft, pinkish, cauliflower-like bumps in moist areas.

occurred among white gay and bisexual men, among whom prevention efforts initially started. Heterosexual incidence, however, has continued to increase—particularly among minority men and women. Even so, gay and bisexual men still account for almost half of those living with AIDS. Unsafe sex practices and HIV infections in these groups still remain high in many areas, with young gay men at particular risk (Freiberg, 1998).

A culturally specific intervention was developed to reduce the frequency of unsafe sex practices among African-American gay and bisexual men. Researchers believed that low self-esteem can promote riskier sexual behavior (Freiberg, 1998). In this study, researchers worked with 318 participants teaching assertiveness training, negotiation skills, and game-playing to improve knowledge of safe sex and effective condom use. Researchers reported that participants in the triple-session intervention greatly reduced their frequency of unprotected anal intercourse—from 46% to 20%. This reduction continued through the 12-month follow-up evaluation. The study demonstrated that African-American gay and bisexual men can reduce risky behavior if they are exposed to culturally relevant prevention messages (Freiberg, 1998).

Other AIDS prevention programs are designed specifically for women. One particular program (Freiberg, 1998) focused on teaching women negotiating skills, condom use, and the risks and barriers associated with their relationships with men. More than 200 single, pregnant inner-city women (57% African-American, 40% Caucasian, 3% other) were assigned to either an AIDS prevention group or one of two control groups—a general health-promotion group or a no-intervention group. The prevention group helped the women develop a health plan to curb their risk for HIV infection; the other group focused more broadly on improving the participants' general health. Women practiced assertiveness and negotiation skills with their partners and "cognitive rehearsal," imagining how they would solve a problem. Results indicated significantly greater condom use for the AIDS prevention group than for the no-intervention group; the health promotion group obtained more condoms than the no-intervention group but fewer than the AIDS prevention group.

AIDS AND THERAPY

How would you feel if your client told you he had AIDS? AIDS creates a variety of emotional dilemmas for practitioners. Practitioners who work with clients who are HIV positive say they face the prospect of continuous grief over the deaths of their patients (Sleek, 1996). Some report that they develop grand expectations of providing comfort, then feel unable to meet those expectations. They may feel guilt or shame at falling short of the demands they put on themselves to relieve their patients' feelings of fear, depression, or anger. Anger, in fact, may be the most unexpected emotion arising from therapy with people with HIV and AIDS. Conversely, other practitioners emotionally distance themselves from their patients to block out their own feelings of loss. Still others feel immense benefits while working with AIDS patients, especially those clients who want to make the most of their shortened life. The psychological work is considered more important now that drug companies are making advances in helping people with AIDS to live longer.

One of the most striking aspects of counseling AIDS patients is the need to bend the traditional therapeutic role. Many practitioners make home and hospital visits and run errands for clients who have grown too sick to leave the house.

A widespread myth about people with AIDS is that they have positive changes in their life perspective. However, those who counsel such patients find that many character issues remain, even in the face of death. HIV does not change people; it reveals them. People who do well in life are those who are able to reflect on their suffering, learn from it, and brace themselves so that in the future, they are not beaten down. As Sleek (1996) notes, to talk about what you could have done to prevent HIV/AIDS is futile. To talk about what you can do from now on is good.

AIDS INTERNATIONALLY

A United Nations report in 1996 found that AIDS cases have been underreported worldwide by as much as one-third. By the year 2000, it is estimated that 40 million people will be living with HIV. Prevention has been shown to reduce the spread of HIV. But practitioners have been focusing only on the individual and not enough on political systems and policy systems (Dunbar et al., 1998). Practitioners must address all the influences that can affect the spread of HIV—the community, the mass media, the schools, and the parents.

Educational programs are restricting the number of new cases in some countries. As Dunbar and colleagues (1998) point out, Australia has virtually no epidemic and can be used as a model of prevention. This country of over 20 million people reports only 500 new HIV infections a year. Part of the low infection rate is due to substance-abuse treatment on demand, explicit sex education for young people, and close collaboration with the gay community to promote safe sex.

The United Nation's "Report on the Global HIV/AIDS Epidemic" (Freiberg, 1998) concludes the following: 30.6 million people were infected with HIV at the end of 1997, which includes one in every 100 adults ages 15 to 49 worldwide and 1.1 million children under the age of 15. A few of the reported statistics are as follows:

- Most new infections worldwide occur in people age 15 to 24.

- About 16,000 new HIV infections took place every day in 1997, for a total of 5.8 million new infections during the year.

- More than 90% of HIV-infected people live in developing countries, and the vast majority of these do not know they are infected.

- The number of AIDS deaths since the beginning of the epidemic totals 11.7 million. Of the 2.3 million people who died of AIDS in 1997, 46% were women and 20% were children.

- Sub-Saharan Africa is the region with the fastest growing epidemic, with two-thirds of the total world number of HIV-infected people living there.

Tragically, the worst is yet to come. Treatment of people who are HIV positive in developing countries is hampered because they generally lack access to new antiretroviral drugs that can reduce the speed at which they develop AIDS (Freiberg, 1998). Even in developed countries, not everyone has access to the expensive new medications. And, drugs are not the cure. They are not effective in everyone, and it is not known how long their effects will last. Thus, as reported by Freiberg (1998), many of the 30 million people will die, if not in the near future, within the next decade.

Conditions in the United States are not much better. As of 1996, more than 70,000 women have been diagnosed with AIDS. In 1995 women accounted for 19% of new adult and adolescent AIDS cases, the highest yearly percentage ever. Women and, particularly women of color, are the fastest growing group of people with AIDS. HIV and AIDS affecting young and middle-age women in particular. As reported by Dunbar and colleagues (1998), the median age of women reported with AIDS is 35 years, and women aged 15 to 44 years account for 84% of all female cases. AIDS is the fourth leading cause of death in American women aged 25 to 44. AIDS is the leading cause of death for these women in 15 major cities.

FOCUS ON NARRATIVE

Spiritual Growth in Women with AIDS

By failing to recognize the personal growth experienced by some women with HIV, social work professionals can inadvertently minimize the strengths and power of their clients. This mind set tends to keep clients as victims and may impede ethical social work practice, which includes primacy of clients' interests, rights, and prerogatives.

When asked whether they had discovered any unexpected positive outcomes in the face of this very serious illness, 82% of infected women answered yes. These women spoke of rebuilt relationships, newfound values, a new sense of meaning and purpose, profound self-awareness and self-acceptance, and discoveries of connections with nature, God, and higher powers. They reported being able to use the pain and despair of the HIV diagnosis as an opportunity for self-awareness and growth, and some women described a profound healing in their lives that made room for a richer existence.

Five themes emerged: reckoning with death, life affirmation, creation of meanings, self-affirmation, and redefining relationships. The following are some quotes that express these themes (Dunbar et al., 1988):

Reckoning with death: "The only difference between me and you at this point . . . is that I know I might leave my body sooner that I thought I might. It only puts me closer to knowing that I'm mortal . . . I think AIDS brought the reality of death right home."

Life Affirmation: "I went though a process where I would see beauty in real simple things: flowers, a rainbow, these mountains, a rainstorm, a pond, a river. I never stopped to notice these things before. Yeah, you saw a rainbow, but now a rainbow represents to me the entire life force. It's a deeper appreciation . . . I think I've been on a steady course of becoming less materialistic . . . that is just not important anymore."

Creation of meaning: "Well, we're in a body, here on this earth. We have some sort of purpose for being here; it may not be clear to us in this whole lifetime what the purpose is, but we have a purpose. And it may not be some huge purpose. It may be only to learn patience, virtue, kindness."

Self-Affirmation: "You know, I think as a mother, as a woman, as a wife, I am always taking care of everybody else . . . But I finally realized that . . . if I don't start taking care of my own self, then I am not going to be around to take care of anybody else."

Redefining Relationships: "I am a lot harder on myself and on other people that I see . . . I don't try to fix people anymore . . . I don't wait around for it to happen . . . I'm very intolerant with people that I feel are wasting their life away . . . Who I choose as friends is different."

Many and probably most women living with HIV can describe positive psychological and spiritual growth, consistent with these five themes. These findings have direct implication for social workers, particularly those in clinical practice. There are at least seven ways a practitioner can help a client with a terminal illness: (1) anticipate, recognize, and encourage growth, (2) assist clients with death and dying issues, (3) identify and facilitate life affirmation, (4) recognize the importance of spiritual well-being and the creation of meaning, (5) encourage self-evaluation, self-affirmation, and self-care, (6) facilitate relationship resolution and the development of new relationships, and (7) keep biases in check. (Dunbar et al., 1998).

RAPE AND SEXUAL ASSAULT

There is no justification in this world for hurting me, for taking away what he tried to take away from me. . . . I cried, I know what rage lives inside of me. It's always been there—it always will be. It's OK. I went out and danced and got plowed last night. . . . I was drained the rest of the day and felt cruddy cuz of my hangover. . . . Tonight is my first night alone and I battle the "caged in" feeling. . . . I screamed in a loud voice in my front yard, "I am mad at the whole world. . . ." (from the diary of a 26-year-old rape victim, personal communication)

The prevalence of rape is so high that it is likely to touch everyone. It is now estimated that between two and three of every ten women will be a victim of rape—that's more than one rape every 6 minutes (Parrot & Bechhofer, 1991). Other experts estimate that up to 50% of women in the United States will be raped or subjected to attempted rape in their lifetime (Muehlenhard & Linton, 1987). Over the past 20 years, the incidence of rape in the United States has increased more than 20%, one of the largest increases for a major crime (Riesenberg, 1987); however, it is unclear whether the number of rapes is growing or the rate of reporting is increasing. Victims of rape are likely to be young, and only 20% of all rapes are committed by strangers.

The fear of rape has a direct effect on the quality of all women's lives. In their daily lives, women must take precautionary actions because of the fear. In particular, women must often isolate themselves—not go out after dark and certainly not go out alone.

Although victims of rape are predominantly women, men can be victims. Men raped by men suffer traumatic and long-term consequences, especially because they have never thought of themselves as possible rape victims. Also, rape is usually discussed in a heterosexual context, but homosexuals are also victims of rape. And, increasingly, men have reported being raped by women.

Two types of rape have been distinguished, **acquaintance rape** and **date rape** (Weiten & Lloyd,

1997). Acquaintance rape occurs when a woman is raped by someone she knows; date rape occurs when she is raped by someone she is dating. Date rape is different from the act of seduction. Seduction occurs when a woman is persuaded and *agrees* to have sex. Date rape occurs when a woman is forced into sexual intercourse without her consent.

Both men and women often fail to acknowledge that date rape has occurred. In one study (Koss, Gidycz, & Wisniewski, 1987) of men who admitted forcing a woman to have intercourse, none perceived this act as rape. Of the women who indicated sexual aggression that constituted a legal definition of rape, only 27% actually said that they had been raped. Why is there so little recognition that rape has occurred? Part of the answer lies in the myth that, for rape to occur, it has to be perpetrated by a stranger. However, stranger rape is less frequent than rape by an acquaintance or by a person the victim is dating. Koss (1985) refers to this as a "hidden crime," noting that the myth of stranger rape helps men deny their responsibility and causes women who have been raped to question and doubt their intentions.

Implications for Practice: Rape Trauma Syndrome

Regardless of the type of rape women experience, a common reaction is the **rape trauma syndrome.** As the quote at the beginning of the previous section reveals, women experience many intense emotions and reactions about being physically forced to have sex against their will. The crime is life threatening, the victim is helpless, she experiences a loss of control, and she has become the object of another person's rage. These reactions lead to overwhelming feelings of fear and stress. Women may develop a number of fears: fear of being alone, fear of men, fear of trusting a dating partner. Common feelings associated with rape include depression, anger, guilt, shame, and anxiety. Most rape survivors experience some of the following clusters of symptoms (Francis, 1993):

- **Disorganization phase:** This phase reflects the woman's immediate expressed or controlled reactions, physical reactions, and emotional reactions to the trauma. Common feelings in this phase are most likely fright, anger, and disbelief. A common

reaction is "second guessing"—for example, "what could I have done to avoid this?" Such questioning can lead to intense feelings of guilt and self-blame.

- **Controlled reaction:** In this phase, the rape victim achieves a more composed and calm perspective following the trauma. Although some women react in a physical manner by crying, shaking, and behaving hysterically, other women do not react this way. Even though the woman is experiencing a controlled reaction, she is still suffering from the trauma.

- **Reorganization phase:** This phase reflects the adjustment and adaptation that is necessary following the rape. In one study (Burgess & Holmstromm, 1985) of rape victims four years after the rape, three-quarters of the women felt recovered. Half the women felt recovered after several months; the other half indicated it took them years to recover following the trauma. A quarter of the women still did not feel recovered after four years. Reorganization needs to take place as women attempt to regain equilibrium in physical, psychological, social, and sexual areas. The recovery process follows a pattern similar to that of people who must adjust to grief. Francis (1993) identifies four issues that are important to the rape victim during the reorganization process:

1. Regaining a feeling of physical well-being and safety;

2. Working through fears and phobias;

3. Coming to terms with losses, such as loss of self-esteem and loss of trust;

4. Assimilating the event into one's sense of self (p. 680).

For many women, being in a support group is helpful because they can "tell their story" and begin the process of accepting what happened to them and learn how to assimilate their experience into their sense of self. However, many family therapists believe that the family can critically affect a rape victim's ability to recover from a trauma. For example, Pauline Boss notes that "I've come to believe that trauma survivors need more than to tell their story to the therapist . . . they have to tell it to someone who matters to them, someone who is willing to validate their pain" (cited in Markowitz, 1991). Often that person is a family member. As Markowitz (1991) notes, "the most powerful healing from a trauma comes from the love and support of family. Knowing they have someone they can count on, who loves them no matter what, helps survivors regain their confidence and trust in the world after a debilitating setback" (p. 32).

The following Focus section examines the global war against women.

FOCUS ON GENDER

The Global War Against Women

Violence against women—including assault, mutilation, murder, infanticide, rape, and cruel neglect—is perhaps the most pervasive yet least recognized human rights issue in the world. It is also a profound health problem, sapping women's physical and emotional vitality and undermining their confidence—both of which are vital to achieving important social goals, especially in the Third World.

In Bangkok, Thailand, a reported 50% of married women are beaten regularly by their husbands. In the barrios of Quito, Ecuador, 80% of women are said to have been physically abused. And in Nicaragua, 44% of men admit to beating their wives or girlfriends. Equally shocking statistics can be found in the industrial world. There are also less recognized forms of violence. In Nepal, female babies die from neglect because parents value sons over daughters; in Sudan, girls' genitals are mutilated to ensure virginity until marriage; and in India, young brides are murdered by their husbands when parents fail to provide enough dowry. This is not random violence. In all these instances, women are targets of violence because of their sex. The risk factor is being female. Most of these abuses have been reported in one or another country, at one or another time. But it is only when one begins to amass statistics and reports from around the world that the horrifying dimensions of this global war on women come into focus. For me, the revelation came only recently after talking with scores of women throughout the world. I never intended to investigate violence; I was researching maternal and child health issues overseas. But I would commonly begin my interviews with a simple question: "What is your biggest problem?" With unnerving frequency the answer came back: "My husband beats me."

(Heise, 1989. Reprinted with permission.)

DOMESTIC VIOLENCE IN THE FAMILY

Domestic violence is a serious problem in the United States. Families, often suffering from intense stress, conflicts, and maladaptive coping, fall prey to acts of violence (see Box 10.2). It is estimated that, over the course of their lives, more than 50% of women will at some point be a victim of battering. In many cases, the battering is life threatening; 2,000 to 4,000 women are beaten to death every year (Browne, 1987). Women are more likely to be killed by a husband, ex-husband, boyfriend, or acquaintance. Also, spouses and ex-spouses commit a much larger percentage of the homicides (18%) than do strangers (8.8%) (U.S. Department of Justice, 1995). Women aged 19 to 29 and women with incomes below $10,000 are more likely than other women to be victims of violence by a spouse or intimate (U.S. Department of Justice, 1995). Intimates causing the violence are more likely to injure women than strangers who victimize women. Such violence often leads to homelessness as women flee violent home situations. As many as one-third of homeless women have suffered domestic violence (National Council on Homelessness, 1995).

What would cause spouses and partners to resort to such gross mistreatment of each other? Of course, many factors relate to family violence, including intergenerational transmission of violence, poverty, social pressure and stress, social isolation and a lack of community involvement, serious personality problems, and psychopathology. When multiple risk factors are present, the family is vulnerable to maladaptive coping behaviors, and the family's welfare becomes threatened. Increasingly, researchers find that the minor, mutual slaps, kicks, and shoves depicted in television, movies, and comic strips are an all too common feature of real-life love and marriage (Sleek, 1998). Even though such acts may seem trivial compared with the type of

BOX 10.2

Violence Against Women in the United States

MURDER: Every day four women die as a result of domestic violence; this adds up to approximately 1,400 women a year. The number of women murdered by intimate partners exceeds the number of soldiers killed in the Vietnam War.

BATTERING: There are 572,000 reports of assault by intimate partners each year. A conservative estimate is that 2 to 4 million women are battered each year. Approximately 170,000 of those violent acts are so severe that women seek hospitalization, emergency room visits, or need a doctor's assessment.

SEXUAL ASSAULT: It is estimated that 132,000 women have been victims of rape or attempted rape, and more than half know their attackers. Anywhere from two to six times as many rapes are likely to happen that don't get reported. When one's former spouse or partner is the perpetrator, then the number of forcible rapes increased to 1.2 million.

THE TARGETS: Women are more than ten times more likely to be victims of violence perpetrated by an intimate than by a stranger. Women who are young, separated, divorced, single, low income, and African-American are more likely to be vic-

tims of assault and rape. Poverty is a significant factor in domestic violence, and spouse abuse is twice as likely when the spouse is unemployed. Violent attacks on lesbians and gays are growing at a very fast rate.

EFFECT ON CHILDREN: Violent juvenile offenders are four times more likely to have grown up in homes where there was a history of violence. Child witnesses of violence are reported to be five times more likely to commit or suffer violence when they become adults.

EFFECT ON HEALTH AND SOCIAL SERVICES: Battered women need more than twice the health care as nonbattered counterparts. Pregnant women who become battered (17% report being battered) are at risk for poor health outcomes such as miscarriages, stillbirths, and lowbirth-weight babies.

LEGISLATION: NOW, the National Organization for Women, helped secure passage of the Violence Against Women Act, which provides new revenue for addressing the issues of violence against women.

(National Organization for Women, 1995)

---

assaults that force women to seek safety in battered women's shelters, they are still abusive—to the psyche if not to the body. This initial type of aggression may lead to outright battering, in which the man usually has the physical advantage. Shockingly, many couples regard such actions as innocuous, even normal in any loving relationship. Even for mutually violent partners, therapy should focus first and foremost on ending the man's violent behavior, mainly because he can usually inflict more physical and psychological harm than the woman can. However, a practitioner should never question the spouses' strong bond with each other.

The couple often still shows evidence of mutual affection, empathy, and commitment.

Research (Sleek, 1998) has found similarities among romantic partners who exchange minor physical blows. They tend to (1) express a strong commitment to the relationship, (2) also engage in psychological abuse, such as insults and verbal threats, and (3) dismiss the physical fighting as minor, infrequent, or secondary to other problems.

If we could look back in time, we would see that many of these couples started exchanging shoves and slaps long before they exchanged vows. For this reason, reducing violence in dating relationships should be a focus for researchers and practitioners. As recommended in Sleek (1998), young people need to know how to resolve conflicts peacefully, become intolerant of physical abuse in romantic arguments, and minimize dominating and jealous behaviors toward a partner.

In addition to providing shelter to protect women from violence, many communities are attempting rehabilitation of the man who was the perpetrator.

THE ROLE OF SOCIAL WORKERS IN MANAGED CARE SYSTEMS

Managed care, as a cost-containing system of health care administration, is here to stay. However, this leaves the most vulnerable populations—poor people, people of color, women and children, and seniors—on the periphery. The populations in greatest need are often selected *out* of managed care systems because their high-risk status (poor nutrition, inadequate income, lack of prenatal care, substandard housing, minimal preventive care, and so on) ensures increased costs of care (Resnick & Tighe, 1997). Specific communities (certain rural and urban areas) are less likely to be served.

So what can social workers do? Between 20% and 80% of primary care visits involve the medicalization of presenting problems that are frequently psychosocial in origin (Resnick & Tighe, 1997). As Resnick and Tighe (1997) point out, physicians spend an excessive amount of time dealing with patients' psychological, social, and environmental concerns when their preference is to refer nonmedical issues to mental health practitioners. Physicians could make more effective use of their time by referring clients with the appropriate issues to social workers. Some of these issues include family issues; resource concerns; mental health issues; behavioral problems; medical noncompliance; and issues involving children, older adults, and people with mental retardation. In sum, social workers can play many vital roles as interdisciplinary team members working in community clinics under a managed health care system. Redirection of emotional, psychological, familial, and social concerns to social work professionals relieves other primary care staff from dealing with issues that may not best fit their area of expertise. Additionally, social work screening and case finding lessen the inappropriate use of valuable interdisciplinary professional time, thus increasing patient satisfaction.

THE FACTS: ALCOHOL, TOBACCO, AND OTHER DRUGS

In studies nationwide, alcohol, more than any other drug, has been closely associated with violence and aggression. In one study, respondents reporting either physical abuse or neglect of children were five times more likely to report alcohol abuse or dependence than were those who did not often report physical abuse or neglect. Alcohol is also involved in more than half of all rapes. Substance abuse brings out the worst in people and makes victims of us all.

This section focuses on issues compounded by substance abuse. The following facts and statistics make clear the need for preventing alcohol and other drug problems (adapted from the Center for Substance Abuse Prevention).

- After alcohol, tobacco and marijuana are the most frequently used drugs on college campuses. And the past few years have seen an increase in the use of LSD among college students.

- Alcoholism and child abuse, including incest, seem tightly intertwined. Not only do abusers tend to be heavy drinkers, but those who have been abused are subject to an increased risk of abusing alcohol and other drugs over the course of their lifetime.

- Alcohol consistently emerges as a significant predictor of marital violence. Alcoholic women have been found to be significantly more likely to have experienced negative verbal conflict with spouses than were nonalcoholic women. They were also more likely to have experienced a range of moderate and severe physical violence.

- Alcohol is present in more than 50% of all incidents of domestic violence.

- Alcohol, tobacco, and other drugs (ATOD) have been implicated as factors in many of the United

(text continues on p. 464)

Schizophrenia

Maria is a 24-year-old single woman who looks older than her stated age. She presented with symptoms of schizophrenia—prominent thought disorder, delusions, inappropriate affect or silly affect, and disorganized speech. The police brought Maria to the emergency room after neighbors complained of a young woman, who they feared might be dangerous, walking down the street laughing and talking to herself. Several days later, her brother called the police and reported Maria as a missing person. The police informed her brother that a young woman fitting his sister's description had been taken to the hospital and admitted to the psychiatric ward a few days ago.

Maria's family history revealed that she came from a problematic family. She was the second of three children and was often the victim of criticism and abuse from her father. Her father was abusive when he came home drunk. Maria's mother died when she was 13 years old, and Maria never "recovered." While she was living, Maria's mother had tried to protect the children from their father. Maria and her mother had been particularly close. When Maria's mother died, the children were placed in the custody of the state because of their father's inability to take care of them. The children were separated on several occasions during their tenure in foster homes, but separation took its toll on Maria.

Even when Maria was a young child, she experienced problems adjusting to minor changes and withdrew from her normal activities. Her school records supported the problems Maria had in trying to adjust to school routines and how traumatic it was for Maria to leave home and go to school. She had to compete with different children of different age groups while living in foster homes. She was beaten by some of these children and by some of the foster parents. Even before the foster homes, Maria had a history of "bizarre behavior" and was highly withdrawn. Her mother was hospitalized twice before she died, according to Maria's older sister. She told the attending physician: "My mother had emotional problems and was sent away."

DEVELOPMENTAL CONSIDERATIONS

Maria's problems started when she was very young— physical and psychological abuse, placement in foster homes, and lack of a sense of security. The first signs of her disorder were not detected until adulthood. However, she had a number of developmental issues often noted in the histories of persons who developed schizophrenia. Her early childhood and adolescence indicate that she had issues involving trust versus mistrust, separation-individuation, evidence of possible bonding difficulties, and identity difficulties during adolescence. The loss of her mother had a profound effect on Maria because her mother was Maria's only support system. Maria's symptoms of schizophrenia were undetected before the presentation of active psychotic symptoms. Her history of poor functioning in school and at work and her inability to adjust to life events contributed to Maria's disorder. Her disorder had an early and insidious onset. Given the characteristics of the onset, Maria were untreated until she moved into the active phase of schizophrenia.

BIOPHYSICAL CONSIDERATIONS

Maria's episode with schizophrenia may suggest that she had a predisposition for schizophrenia (genetic), which is supported by the finding that her mother had been hospitalized for emotional problems. Because structural changes in the brain are likely in neurotransmitter systems (namely dopamine), further confirmation for biophysical hypotheses can be found if brain imagery techniques show evidence of cortical atrophy.

PSYCHOLOGICAL CONSIDERATIONS

Maria manifested some deficits in the cognitive, affective, and behavioral domains. During the active phase of her disorder, she presented with disorganized speech, distorted perceptions (delusions and hallucinations), and distorted thought processes in the cognitive area. Her affective state is best characterized as inappropriate or silly. She laughed inappropriately throughout the admission process.

Communication

The communication process within Maria's family is unclear. The family demonstrates some signs of limited communication abilities within the family. Her bizarre behavior further aggravates her communication competence. She smiles inappropriately and does not demonstrate that she can share what she is experiencing.

Attitudes and Emotions

It is difficult at this time to assess Maria's attitudes and emotions; she is currently in the active phase of her illness, and the medication has not reduced her symptoms. Usually, her type of schizophrenia has a poor prognosis with a chronic course. Maria has isolated herself and rarely interacts with others. She does not appear to hold suspicious or bizarre delusions.

Family

Maria is 24. Before her mother died, Maria lived with her parents and two siblings. Maria's father was particularly abusive to her. The family believes that he singled her out because she looks like his paternal grandmother. Maria and her siblings lived in foster homes for about five years. Her sister, Ester, is 18 months her senior, and her brother, Mario, with whom she presently lives, is the youngest member of the family. She has no contact with her extended family.

Social Support

The most consistent support Maria ever had was her mother, who died when Maria was 13 years of age. Her mother's death undoubtedly contributed to many of Maria's problems in later life.

SUMMARY AND IMPRESSIONS

Maria is experiencing the following:

1. She developed schizophrenia, and the symptoms are currently in the active phase.
2. She had a prolonged history of social and psychological problems.
3. She was a victim of physical and psychological abuse.
4. The course of her disorder suggests a poor prognosis.
5. Her responses to neuroleptic medications has been marginal at best.
6. Her past medical record was essentially unremarkable.

Maria is a young adult who contracted a severe mental disorder known as schizophrenia, disorganized type. Her prognosis is poor with a chronic course. Her disorder is associated with possible structural changes in the brain—Type II schizophrenia. The etiology is unknown at this time. She may have had a predisposition for this disorder, as indicated by her family history. Her problems had been exacerbated by the interaction of biological, social, and psychological factors. These factors proved too much for her to handle. She cannot cope with these changes nor handle many other demands.

In the event of her discharge, she will need supervision and social support. It is imperative that her physician closely supervise her medication and be kept informed of Maria's status/relapse by those in charge of her custody. Her caregivers should be educated about Maria's disorder and attend at least some of her group sessions. Finally, it is critical that Maria's cultural background be taken into account in planning support services.

(Hubert Johnston)

States' most serious and expensive problems, including domestic violence, injury, HIV/AIDS and other sexually transmitted diseases, teen pregnancy, school failure, car crashes, escalating health care costs, low worker productivity, and homelessness.

- A large part of the U.S. national health care bill is for ATOD-related medical expenses. For example, 25% to 40% of all Americans in general hospital beds are being treated for complications of alcoholism.

- Alcohol is the drug most frequently used by 12- to 17-year-olds, and it causes the most negative health consequences. More than 4 million adolescents under the legal drinking age consume alcohol in any given month. Alcohol-related car crashes are the number one killer of teens.

- ATOD prevention does work; however, different ATOD prevention programs yield economic benefits at various times. For example, if alcohol- and drug-taking behavior is reduced among pregnant women, the payoff will be realized within a year. In contrast, the benefits of a successful preschool program may not accrue to society for a decade or more—when these youngsters become adolescents and begin making choices about ATOD use.

- Alcohol-related injuries alone cost an estimated $47 billion annually.

- The effect of ATOD-related injury and death takes a tremendous toll on our society. The number of potential years of life lost to ATOD-related injuries equals those lost to cancer and surpasses those lost to heart disease, the two leading causes of death in the United States.

- Approximately 10% of adult dementia in the United States is a result of alcohol-related brain damage.

- At least 90% of alcoholics are nicotine dependent.

- Alcohol consumption by a pregnant woman can result in her child being born with FAS, the most preventable cause of mental, physical, and psychological impairment in the Western world. According to research estimates, one to three of every 1,000 babies are born with FAS. There is no known safe level of alcohol consumption for a pregnant woman.

- Maternal smoking is a contributing factor in 14% of premature deliveries in the United States. There is also a direct correlation between the amount of smoking during pregnancy and the frequency of spontaneous abortion and fetal death.

- Adverse effects of secondhand smoke on children include: respiratory infections such as bronchitis and pneumonia, increased prevalence of fluid in the middle ear, reduced lung function, increased frequency and severity of symptoms in asthmatic children, and increased risk for asthma in children with no previous symptoms.

- Alcohol and other drug use may interfere with a parent's caregiver role; 50% to 80% percent of all child abuse and neglect cases substantiated by Child Protective Services involve some degree of alcohol and other drug use by the child's parents.

- ATOD weaken the immune system, thereby increasing susceptibility to infection and disease.

- According to the Centers for Disease Control Prevention, HIV/AIDS has been the sixth leading cause of death among 15- to 20-year-olds in the United States for more than three years. One in every five new AIDS cases diagnosed is in the 20- to 29-year age group, meaning that HIV transmission occurred during the teen years. Additionally, more than half the new cases of HIV infection in 1994 were related to drug use.

- For every death from suicide, experts estimate that eight suicide attempts are made. Suicide is now the second leading cause of death among persons 15 to 24 years of age. It is increasingly a problem among adolescents and elderly people.

- Suicide claims an estimated 900,000 years of life in America every year.

- High rates of alcohol involvement have been found among suicide victims who use firearms. Recent studies suggest that alcohol tends to be associated with impulsive rather than premeditated suicides.

- Crime is inextricably related to alcohol and other drugs. More than 1.1 million annual arrests for illicit drug violations, almost 1.4 million arrests for driving while intoxicated, 480,000 arrests for liquor law violations, and 704,000 arrests for drunkenness make a total of 4.3 million arrests for alcohol and other drug statutory crimes. The total accounts for more than one-third of all arrests in this country.

- The economic cost of ATOD-related crime is $61.8 billion annually.

- Alcohol is a key factor in up to 68% of manslaughter cases, 62% of assaults, 54% of murders/ attempted murders, 48% of robberies, and 44% of burglaries.

- The cost to arrest, try, sentence, and incarcerate those found guilty of offenses is a tremendous drain on U.S. resources.

- Lung cancer has now passed breast cancer as the leading fatal cancer for women. Lung cancer rates among females have increased sixfold in the past 40 years.

- Some women develop drug or alcohol dependencies as a way of coping with past abuse. For example, childhood sexual abuse is a strong predictor of later problem drinking.

- Workplace alcohol-, tobacco-, and other drug-related problems cost U.S. companies more than $100 billion each year.

- Up to 40% of industrial fatalities can be linked to alcohol consumption and alcoholism.

- Over a lifetime, each cigarette smoker costs approximately $10,000 more in medical expenditures than does a nonsmoker.

While alcohol and other drug use is neither an excuse for nor a direct cause of family violence, several theories might explain the relationship. For example, women who are abused often live with men who drink heavily, which places the women in an environment of potential violence. A second possible explanation is that women using alcohol and other drugs may not recognize assault cues, and, even if they do, they may not know how to respond appropriately. Third, alcohol and other drug abuse by either partner could contribute to family violence by exacerbating financial problems, child-care difficulties, or other family stressors.

Summary

DEVELOPMENTAL THEMES

Young adulthood is considered a major life transition. Most young adults move from a preoccupation with the self to intimacy with others, which leads to marriage, children, and a stable career path. Two of the critical developmental tasks are economic independence and independent decision making.

BIOPHYSICAL DIMENSION

Biophysical Growth and Development

Young adulthood represents the peak of physical development across the life span. During this time, a pattern of health-conscious behavior develops. Many young adults start putting on weight. This is because basal metabolism rate decreases as people get older. Women are in the prime time for pregnancy. Hormones can have a strong effect on women; many women experience premenstrual syndrome (PMS).

Biophysical Hazards

A health hazard of the reproductive system for both men and women is cancer. Women are encouraged to do breast self-examinations, and men are encouraged to do testicular self-examinations.

Schizophrenia is a major mental illness that occurs relatively frequently during this stage of life. There are many potential causes of schizophrenia; however, most researchers now look to the influence of neurochemical factors. Case management and tracking systems have received increased attention to help coordinate needed treatment for those with a serious mental illness.

PSYCHOLOGICAL DIMENSION

Cognitive Development and Information Processing

Formal operational thinking is typically present in young adulthood. The nature of formal operational thinking emphasizes problem solving, which represents a pragmatic adaptive strategy. Still, many young adults do not obtain the level of formal operational thinking.

Communication

Young adulthood is often focused on *mis*communication—in particular, the notion that men and women communicate differently. Women communicate more intimately with each other than do men.

Attitudes and Emotions

A major psychosocial task in young adulthood is the development of intimacy. The experience of intimacy may be different for men and for women. Ultimately the experience of intimacy is likely to lead to love. Romantic love must be differentiated from "true" love. There are many different kinds of love; but three components are critical to love: intimacy, passion, and commitment. Although many young adults pursue love, others must confront the pain of isolation and loneliness. Learning to cope with loneliness can be an important developmental task. Certain types of thinking processes may lead to behaviors that contribute to loneliness. Searching for an identity and seeking independence is also an important developmental task during young adulthood.

Social Cognition and Regulation

Moral development is increasingly refined in young adult women and men; women tend to emphasize a care perspective, and men may emphasize a justice perspective.

Psychological Hazards

The keys to good psychological health are prevention of and early detection of problems. Young adulthood is a period of making major life decisions and of taking on major responsibilities. Psychological health may be of greater concern to American families than previously realized. Young adults may be faced with depression after a job loss, conduct disorders, and the negative effects of divorce on children. Heart disease, domestic violence, and substance abuse are also problems. Depression, a serious mental illness, is one of the leading mental health problems among adult women.

SOCIAL DIMENSION

Families, Groups, Support Systems, and Communities

Marriage and the creation of a family most often occur in young adulthood. Many people still have an idealized vision of the "nuclear" family, when in fact families represent a great diversity of configurations. People go through four phases when selecting a partner to marry. Marriages often are problematic because they are based on unreasonable expectations and myths. Adjustment to a new marriage requires a new set of tasks and good communication. Certain factors have been found to predict marital satisfaction. Among them is not the amount of conflict in a relationship but the manner in which couples handle their incompatibilities. Important gender differences exist in how partners communicate with each other; men are more instrumental and women are more expressive, which has implications for teaching couples better communication skills.

Marriage is not the only option for young adults; many individuals remain or become single, and others develop homosexual or gay relationships.

When couples decide to raise children, the transition to parenthood can be difficult. An increasing number of couples find they cannot conceive and must face the issue of infertility.

In addition to a family, a young adult's career or job is often a significant part of his or her self-identity. Unfortunately, many young adults have had to face declining economic benefits owing to earnings losses. Women continue to face discrimination and inadequate opportunities in the workforce.

Volunteering brings many acknowledged benefits. Volunteers say they participate because they were asked to do so, they learned of an opportunity through an organization to which they belonged, or a family member or friend would benefit as a result.

Multicultural and Gender Considerations

In young adulthood, women face two significant role expectations or mandates: They must marry and they must be mothers. Although many new mothers do not work outside the home, research is finding that it may not be as harmful to the child as originally thought.

Ethnic or racial groups have unique challenges they must face as young adults. For example, Asian-Americans must deal with the "model minority" stereotype.

Young adults often begin to consider what role religion or spirituality will play in their lives. This concern intensifies when they become parents.

Social Hazards

Some families may require special adaptation techniques when they have a disabled family member. Just as young adults are building families, many are leaving families as a result of divorce. Divorce requires a significant adjustment for all family members. Additional social hazards include sexually transmitted diseases, rape and sexual assault, and domestic violence. The HIV/AIDS epidemic has been underreported worldwide. There are now 40 million people who will be living with HIV. However, there has been a decline in reported HIV cases recently, which reflects the combined effect of successful prevention efforts and new therapies to lengthen the healthy life span of people with HIV. The greatest decline occurred among white gay and bisexual men. Heterosexual incidence, however, has continued to increase, particularly among minority men and women.

Social workers can play many vital roles as interdisciplinary team members working in community clinics under the current managed health care system.

Online Resources

Cooperative Communication Skills—Internet Resource Center
http://www.coopcomm.org
> Self-help information, encouragement and teaching materials for better communication in work, family, friendship, and community.

Gay and Lesbian Alliance Against Defamation
http://www.glaad.org
> Working with the media, GLAAD aims to improve the public's attitudes toward homosexuals and put an end to violence and discrimination against lesbians and gay men. In English and Spanish, this website provides media alerts, policy updates, and links to other sites.

Planned Parenthood
http://plannedparenthood.org
> The official website of Planned Parenthood Federation of America. Planned Parenthood provides high-quality, affordable reproductive health care and sexual health information.

The International Council on Infertility Information Dissemination
http://www.inciid.org
> This site provides current information regarding the diagnosis, treatment, and prevention of infertility and pregnancy loss, as well as links to related websites.

National Domestic Violence Hotline
http:/www.ndvh.org
> Links individuals to help in their area using a nationwide database that includes detailed information on domestic violence shelters, other emergency shelters, legal advocacy and assistance programs, and social service programs.

InfoTrac® College Edition

For interesting materials related to what you have just read, please go to the *InfoTrac College Edition* website and search using the following key words:

serious mental illness	rape
premenstrual syndrome	infertility
divorce	

Key Terms

acquaintance rape	internalized
basal metabolism rate	homophobia
controlled reaction	loneliness
date rape	menstrual cycle
disorganization phase	premenstrual syndrome
environmental	(PMS)
harassment	quid pro quo
expressive	rape trauma syndrome
communication	rapport talk
infertility	reorganization phase
instrumental	report talk
communication	schizophrenia

Developmental Themes

Stage: generativity vs. stagnation. Adaptation to physical changes, to transition from parenthood, to aging parents; confronting mortality, reflections on work and family.

Biophysical Dimension

Biophysical Growth and Development

Adaptation to physical changes: changes in physical appearance, decrease in physical abilities, menopause, osteoporosis; possibility of need for estrogen replacement therapy.

Biophysical Hazards

Adjustment to sexuality in adulthood, women's health care, breast cancer, brain injury, physical illness.

Psychological Dimension

Cognitive Development and Information Processing

Cognitive focus on achieving goals, applying knowledge to real-world concerns, role-related achievement potential, concern over professional adolescence.

Communication

Reconnection with one's partner or spouse, communication on a deeper level, establishment of new relationships with others, forgiveness, concerns about illiteracy, communication with nonspeaking adults.

Attitudes and Emotions

Continued quest for identity, reexamination of expectations and roles, de-illusionment, death of the hero, midlife as a crisis.

Social Cognition and Regulation

Development of caring and socially responsible behaviors, establishment of mentor relationships, assumption of leadership roles, reflection on one's mortality.

Psychological Hazards

Alcohol and drug addiction, codependency, need for professional help, twelve-step programs.

Social Dimension

Families, Groups, Support Systems, and Communities

Blended families, launch of children into independence, empty nest syndrome, return to more intimate relationships, marital affairs, impact of adolescent children on middle-aged parents, changing relationships with adult children, addressing the needs of aging parents, caregiving, grandparenthood, the men's movement, men in therapy, satisfaction in work, balancing career and family.

Multicultural and Gender Considerations

Problems with generalizing adult development theories to women, gender differences at midlife, role strain and role conflict for women, ethnic identity in adulthood, balancing life in two cultures.

Social Hazards

Unemployment or job loss, homelessness, mental illness and homelessness, women and AIDS.

Middle Adulthood

DEVELOPMENTAL THEMES

Less than 100 years ago, only half of all Americans who reached age 20 lived to see the age of 65. And because their ancestors had little chance of living past 40, the concept of "middle age" as we now know it is new. In America today, most people survive well into their 70s or 80s. But midlife is still a mystery. Myths about psychological landmarks of midlife, such as the "empty-nest syndrome," the "midlife crisis," and the menopausal "change of life" continue to thrive in our society (Azar, 1996). However, many adults truly feel that they are at a crossroads at midlife, as aptly described by Margaret Atwood (1991) in her novel *Cat's Eye:*

> This is the middle of my life. I think of it as a place, like the middle of a river, the middle of a bridge, halfway across, halfway over. I'm supposed to have accumulated things by now: possessions, responsibilities, achievements, experience and wisdom (p. 13).

Midlife is different from other developmental phases in that it is less affected by biological maturation. Indeed, adults are most affected by their own experiences—and how they time those experiences. Even success or failure in life is shaped by personal and social factors. For some, midlife involves "launching" children and focusing on career development; for others, it may involve beginning a family and postponing career development. The effect of chronological age seems to become a less reliable indicator of what men and women are like at various points in their lives.

Midlife is often considered to begin at age 35 and continue until age 60—a span of 25 years. However, midlife is different for men and for women because of their differences in life expectancy. Therefore, more accurately, midlife begins at age 35 for men and age 39 for women (Baruch & Brooks-Gunn, 1984).

Adults at midlife are most typically characterized by a new perspective of who they are and a new perspective about their world, including a new definition of self, new expectations about what they want to accomplish, and new satisfactions in living. Because there is so much diversity in midlife, many experts refuse to identify a timetable for adult development. However, Gail Sheehy's (1976) book *Passages* reinforced the notion that adult lives are predictable and based on age-linked stages. In fact, the profound influence of Sheehy's book was that it set out a normative expectation that in middle adulthood there is a "midlife crisis" phase. What led to the enormous success of *Passages?* Many people want predictability and could relate to one of the phases Sheehy described. However, as midlife was studied further, the picture of development in adulthood grew more complex. Today, most experts see many of the problems seen in previous stage theories, and the idea of a universal midlife crisis has not found much empirical support. A recent study (McQuaide, 1998) found that 72% of women in midlife described themselves as happy or very happy.

Although stage theories have been commonly used to examine the life course, and midlife in particular, they are becoming increasingly less relevant (Goldstein & Landau, 1990). Many of the stages are simply not connected with the age ranges originally intended. "The identity crisis that Erikson thought should be resolved in adolescence now often persists well into the 20s; the bonding stage that is thought to typically occur in the mid-20s may be delayed until the 30s, or experienced more than once" (Goldstein & Landau, 1990, p. 20). Furthermore, societal changes for women have disrupted ideas of a life-stage approach. Women entering the workplace, delays in having children, changing patterns of career development—all these factors have wreaked havoc with attempts to generalize women's life patterns. Indeed, as Schlossberg (cited in Goldstein & Landau, 1990) noted, "give me a room of 40-year-old women and you have told me nothing" (p. 20).

Complicating the picture even further is the work of Neugarten, who has focused on the importance of changing times and how different expectations influence various "cohorts"—groups of people who are born in the same year or time period. For example, if you were born during the Great Depression, your perspective on midlife may be different than if you were born during more optimistic times. Neugarten argues that the social environment of a particular cohort will influence the social timetable of when people expect to accomplish major life tasks, such as having children or selecting a career. This situation implies that findings from one cohort may not apply to other cohorts. For this reason, it is difficult to make generalizations about people in middle age. In this chapter, then, we will attempt to explore the various ways individuals experience their middle years of life.

BIOPHYSICAL DIMENSION

Biophysical Growth and Development

Although the leading causes of death during middle age are cancer and heart disease, evidence suggests that these illnesses may not be purely physiological in origin. What other factor could be so powerful that it influences how a disease presents itself? *Stress.* Stress is linked to physical illness and may have an effect on how illness affects an individual.

A classic study sought to discover the causes of coronary disease. Friedman and Rosenman (1974) found that some individuals who were in good physical shape and should have avoided heart disease didn't, and others who were in bad physical shape successfully avoided heart disease. Eventually, they discovered that physical shape in addition to personality factors influenced the course of heart disease. They found people are of two personality types: **type A personality**—competitive, impatient, and sometimes hostile perfectionists; **type B personality**—relaxed, easygoing, and generally amicable individuals. Type B personalities are less easily agitated than Type A personalities are. Also, Type A behavior has been more often associated with heart disease and other health problems.

Researchers have attempted to measure Type A personality through a variety of methods, including checklists and interviews. It is still unclear what is the best approach to assessing Type A personality. Friedman and Rosenman (1974) describe a series of questions to help assess Type A personality—for example:

1. Do you find it difficult to restrain yourself from hurrying others' speech (finishing their sentences for them)?

2. Do you often try to do more than one thing at a time (such as eat and read simultaneously)?

3. Do you often feel guilty if you use extra time to relax?

4. Do you tend to get involved in a great number of projects at once?

5. Do you agree to take on too many responsibilities?

Several potential explanations link Type A personalities with heart disease and other health problems: (1) Type A personalities are more easily emotionally engaged in situations; they are quick to react, which affects their blood pressure and heart rate; (2) Type A individuals tend to push themselves beyond reasonable and healthy limits because of their perfectionist nature; (3) Type A individuals rely less on the support of other people and place more on themselves; and (4) Type A individuals tend to have poor health habits. The reactive nature of the Type A personality, both psychologically and physiologically, puts the individual at increased risk for health problems.

More recent research on Type A personality is pointing to hostility as the primary factor related to increased coronary risk (Booth-Kewley & Friedman, 1987; Smith & Pope, 1990). In particular, people who can be identified with **cynical hostility,** who are resentful, moody, and generally distrusting, have more problems with coronary disease, hypertension, and early mortality. These individuals display a quick temper and easily criticize others.

An important criticism of the studies on Type A personality and heart disease is that they have been primarily limited to people who were already ill. As a result, it is not clear whether the personality led to the disease or the disease led to the development of the personality. Groundbreaking research by Ronald Grossarth-Maticek (cited in Eysenck, 1989) examined a large group of individuals by administering personality tests and following them for ten years or more to see what health problems they might develop. This research identified different personality types: type 1, cancer-prone; type 2, coronary-heart-disease-prone; and types 3 and 4, healthy individuals who cope with stress in a nondestructive fashion. It also uncovered a strong relationship between personality and various health outcomes. For example, Grossarth-Maticek (cited in

Eysenck, 1989) was able to achieve 50% accuracy in predicting death from cancer. More specifically, he found that, of the type 1 individuals who died, half died from cancer and fewer than one-tenth died from heart disease. Of the type 2 individuals, one-third died from cancer, and one-fifth died from heart disease. However, individuals of types 3 and 4 showed few deaths. These basic conclusions have been replicated in other studies.

If we can understand more about why certain individuals develop health problems, can we prevent the problems? Eysenck and Grossarth-Maticek believe the answer is yes. They conducted an experimental study in which they taught cancer- and heart-disease-prone people to express their emotions more readily, use coping skills for stress, reduce their emotional dependencies, and become more self-reliant. In the study, they assigned 50 cancer-prone people to the therapy and 50 to a no-therapy condition. Their results showed a dramatic influence: In a 13-year follow-up, 45 of the original 50 in the therapy group were alive, but only 19 of the 50 in the no-therapy group were still living. They replicated these results with heart-disease-prone individuals and then again with women who had terminal breast cancer.

MENOPAUSE

> You know, it's kind of like when I was 10 years old, before puberty. I don't have to deal with all that female, sexual stuff anymore. I'm just me again.
> —A woman discussing her experience of menopause

Menopause occurs when a woman has not experienced a menstrual cycle for one year. Attitudes toward this event vary, depending on cultural connotations and on women's individual expectations. In societies in which the woman's role is mostly reproductive, inability to bear any more children is a loss of status. In cultures in which the wisdom and experience of older women is valued, menopause is seen as a positive life event (Borysenko, 1996). In general, young women and men view menopause more negatively, whereas women who have gone through the experience view it more positively. Individually, some women view the cessation of their monthly period as a sign of impending old age and mourn the loss of youth and beauty. Other women, as the one above, are glad to be rid of it.

In general, women who have gone through menopause view it more positively than men and younger women. Some women report increases in energy, self-confidence and assertiveness.

Menopause occurs when the ovaries stop functioning and no longer produce the hormones estrogen and progesterone. It is a gradual process that can take from 5 to 20 years. During premenopause, the time when hormone levels begin to fall until menstrual cycles stop, a woman may notice several changes: Her menstrual cycles may become irregular; she may experience a decreased monthly flow as well as increased spotting; symptoms of premenstrual tension such as breast tenderness and fluid retention may increase. The average age of menopause is 51.4 years; the vast majority of women reach menopause between 45 and 55 years of age (Schuster & Ashburn, 1992). Women who undergo early menopause, with the onset before about age 50, are at greater risk for developing heart disease, osteoporosis, and other chronic diseases than are women who reach menopause later (DeAngelis, 1997).

Falling estrogen levels affect women in different ways. The most universal symptom is the **hot flash;** a

TABLE 11.1	The Changes of Menopause	
When	**Symptom**	**Comments**
Before menopause	Irregular periods	Cycle may shorten or lengthen; flow may increase or decrease.
During menopause	Periods stop	
	Hot flashes	Skin temperature rises, then falls. Accompanied by sweating and sometimes heart palpitations, nausea, and anxiety. Occur anywhere from once a month to several times an hour. May begin 12–18 months before menopause and continue for some years thereafter.
	Insomnia	Sometimes caused by nightly bouts of hot flashes. Dream-rich REM sleep may also decrease, disturbing sleep.
	Psychological effects	Irritability, short-term memory loss, and problems with concentration are common. These symptoms may simply result from sleep deprivation.
After menopause	Changes in nervous system	The perception of touch can become more or less sensitive.
	Dry skin and hair	The skin can become thin, dry, and itchy. Hair may also thin out. Facial hair may increase.
	Incontinence	Tissue shrinkage in the bladder and weakening pelvic muscles may lead to problems with bladder control.
	Vaginal dryness	The mucous membranes and walls of the vagina become thinner, which may lead to pain on intercourse and susceptibility to infections.
	Bone loss	Increases dramatically.
	Cardiovascular changes	Blood vessels become less flexible. Cholesterol and triglyceride levels rise.

(Adapted from Davis, 1989)

wave of heat rises from the woman's chest to her neck, face, and arms. This feeling of heat may last from a few seconds to a minute or more (Borysenko, 1996; Dan & Bernhard, 1989). Hot flashes frequently occur at night, causing "night sweats." Recurrent night sweats can interfere with sleep. Another effect of estrogen loss is thinning and drying of the vaginal membranes. This problem occurs with less severity, though, if a woman stays sexually active. Loss of estrogen also affects the urinary tract and can result in an increase in the frequency of urination and in stress incontinence. This means that when a menopausal woman coughs, sneezes, or laughs she may inadvertently lose urine (Voda, 1993). Other physical changes include dry, itching skin and dry hair, and a heightened sense of touch (see Table 11.1). But the major physical effects of estrogen loss are cardiovascular changes, which put postmenopausal women at greater risk of heart disease, and increased bone loss, which puts them at risk of **osteoporosis** (thinning and weakening of the bones). As a result of this bone loss, postmenopausal women are at increased risk of bone fractures, especially of the

hip, and vertebral fractures (in the spine). Women most at risk of osteoporosis are white, slender, smokers with low calcium intake who don't exercise regularly. Although increased calcium intake can help prevent osteoporosis, the amount of calcium the body can use is limited without estrogen.

Psychological effects of menopause are unclear. Some women report increased energy, often referred to as "postmenopausal zest" (PMZ). Some attribute this increase in energy, confidence, and assertiveness not to biological events but to "the crisis and resolution of midlife women's psyche" (Apter, 1995, p. 201). In other words, menopausal women are struck by a sense of unmet goals or unfulfilled potential and experience "an increased capacity to resolve old conflicts and satisfy suppressed desires" (p. 202). Also, menopausal women no longer have a monthly loss of blood, and so their levels of iron may increase. Plus they no longer have periodic hormonal fluctuations and no longer have to deal with premenstrual syndrome.

A critical question is this: Do women become depressed and irritable at menopause? Because menopause occurs at a time in life when women may feel they are "getting old," it is difficult to differentiate the effects of menopause from the effects of aging (Dan & Bernhard, 1989). Apter (1995) states, "current research has found no significant changes in anger, anxiety, depression, self-consciousness, or worry about the body between women observed from the time they were premenopausal to the time they had become postmenopausal. This means that, in general, a woman's mood is not determined by menopause; but an individual woman may respond to it with increases in anger, anxiety, depression, or self-consciousness because of how she experiences or perceives its meaning" (p. 215). Some people argue that women who expect menopause to be a negative experience do indeed find it to be a negative experience. And some women who have a lot of symptoms may become depressed over the symptoms (Adler, 1991). Others believe that depression may occur as a result of the changes in a woman's life rather than because of hormonal loss. Women who think that to be valued they must be young and beautiful may become depressed over menopausal changes. Some women may feel sad as their children grow up and leave home.

So, many researchers believe that women who are emotionally stable before menopause experience no increase in depression or irritability. However, estrogen affects the production of **endorphins,** substances produced in the brain that make you feel good. A drop in estrogen results in a drop in endorphins (Davis, 1989), which can be depressive. In addition, menopausal women may experience insomnia as the result of night sweats, itching skin, and urinary frequency. And when they do sleep, it is not entirely restful because the amount of REM sleep (dream sleep) decreases. A sleep-deprived woman can be irritable and less able to concentrate and handle stress.

ETHNICITY AND MENOPAUSE

Researchers from the Study of Women's Health Across the Nation (SWAN) note that, at present, the base for understanding menopause is Caucasian women. One of the topics SWAN is studying is ethnic differences in the transition to menopause. They have found that women in different ethnic groups vary in the kinds and degree of menopausal symptoms they report. SWAN looked at two kinds of symptom clusters: estrogen-related symptoms, including hot flashes, night sweats, vaginal dryness, and urine leakage; and somatic symptoms, including difficulties in sleeping, headaches, a racing heart, and stiffness and soreness in the joints, neck, or shoulders. Table 11.2 presents generalizations of the findings within various ethnic and lifestyle groups.

SWAN also found that women's attitudes toward aging may explain who is using hormones and who is not (DeAngelis, 1997). Caucasian women may be using hormones to slow down the physical signs of aging. Interestingly, women of color get hysterectomies more often than Caucasian women. In particular, African-American women, for whom fibroid tumors are common, are twice as likely to have hysterectomies as white women. Hysterectomies are also common in women with less education. In sum, white, highly educated women are more likely to use hormone-replacement therapy than women of color.

Some women pass through menopause with few symptoms or effects; others experience severe problems. Although the occurrence of psychological changes at

TABLE 11.2	**Symptoms of Ethnic and Lifestyle Groups**
Ethnic or Lifestyle Group	**Symptoms**
African-American	Report more estrogen-related symptoms and fewer somatic symptoms than all other ethnic groups.
Hispanic	Report more urinary leakage and racing heart symptoms than all other ethnic groups.
Asian-American	Report fewer symptoms than all others.
Smokers	Within all ethnic groups, report more of both estrogen-related and somatic symptoms.
Education level	Less-educated women have more estrogen-related symptoms and more racing heart symptoms than others.
Physical Activity	Women who report getting less physical activity have more of all types of symptoms.

(Adapted from DeAngelis, 1997)

menopause is debatable, a woman experiencing any of these symptoms needs to believe that, whatever the cause, her complaints are being taken seriously and not being passed off as "all in her head." Women with physical symptoms may benefit from **estrogen replacement therapy (ERT)**, in which synthetic estrogen is taken to replace that lost through menopause.

ESTROGEN REPLACEMENT THERAPY

Recently, some literature has been encouraging women to accept menopause as a natural part of the life cycle. The writers claim that the medical profession has described menopause as a deficiency disease for which medication is prescribed. Such authors suggest that the cessation of menstruation is not an illness that needs to be treated but a part of the rhythm and flow of a woman's life. Some even claim an evolutionary advantage to menopause in that women can stop bearing children when they are still young enough and energetic enough to participate in raising older children (Dan & Bernhard, 1989).

This attitude, however, overlooks the fact that, just as recently as the 19th century, the average life expectancy of a woman was 48 years. So women who experienced the natural process of menopause may not have lived many years beyond that experience. Today, a healthy woman undergoing menopause at 52 can expect to live another 30 or more years (Davis, 1989). And research indicates that, as these years pass, the reduction in estrogen that occurs at menopause increases a woman's risk of heart disease, stroke, and osteoporosis. Evidence shows that estrogen replacement therapy (ERT) greatly reduces her risk for all these problems (Ravn, Rosenberg, & Bostofte, 1994). ERT helps with the symptoms associated with menopause such as hot flashes and vaginal dryness, too, but many women find these symptoms to be mild and easily remedied without the addition of daily hormones.

But heart disease is the leading cause of death in postmenopausal women, and hormone therapy with estrogen results in marked reduction in this risk (Stevenson, 1995). In addition, estrogen therapy has been shown to prevent the bone loss of osteoporosis for at least 15 years after menopause (Langer & Barrett-Connor, 1994).

Yet, despite this promising evidence, only 20% of women have had ERT prescribed for them, and only 40% of those for whom it is prescribed use it for more than one year (Hammond, 1994). The main reason for this failure to use ERT may be fear. Many women fear the increased risk of endometrial cancer and breast cancer that has been publicized to occur with ERT. Yet researchers have found that using progesterone in addition to estrogen for ten days during the month (hormone replacement therapy, or HRT) reduces the risk of endometrial cancer without affecting the benefits of estrogen (Ravn, Rosenberg, & Bostofte, 1994). The drawback is that adding progesterone to HRT causes some women to continue to menstruate. In addition, progesterone may cause symptoms associated with PMS, including fluid retention, and so a diuretic may be added to the daily medication regimen. Research is suggesting there is only a small risk, if any, of breast cancer from HRT, and then only after prolonged use of 15–20 years (Ravn, Rosenberg, & Bostofte, 1994). However, more recent studies found that the risk of breast cancer is 35% higher for women on HRT for five years or longer compared with nonusers (Lancet, 1997). Still, Ross and Whitehead (1995) contend that there are few medical reasons now to avoid HRT and that the choice should be up to the individual patient, depending on the severity of her symptoms and her risk of heart disease and osteoporosis. Women should also consider their personal risk of developing breast cancer when considering HRT.

So, is there really anything to fear from HRT? Not everything is known about the benefits and risks of HRT. Research lauding the benefits of HRT—as well that warning of the risks—may be based on inconclusive data (Azar, 1997). In fact, the most definitive finding from studies of HRT is that women are confused about its risks and benefits (Azar, 1997). Recent media reports tout HRT as a "miracle drug" that brings back or prolongs youth. However, some of the health benefits attributed to HRT, including prolongation of a woman's life, may actually be a function of how healthy the woman is *before* she chooses HRT. One reason why data is inconclusive is that few long-term studies have been done. Table 11.3 presents the benefits and risks of HRT.

SEXUALITY IN MIDDLE ADULTHOOD

The midlife years can often lead to problems for marital couples who do not understand some of the changes they are going through. Maggie Scarf (1992) notes the different physical changes that men and women go through during the middle years. A man's aging crisis can be related to the pressure he feels to "make it," and a woman's aging crisis can be related to concerns and anxiety she feels about her physical appearance. These changes have direct implications for their sexual relationship. Scarf (1992) describes how such changes affect the **sexual response cycle,** which includes three phases: desire, excitement, and orgasm. First, desire, being sexually motivated, can be affected by aging. For example, the side effects of diseases (such as diabetes or hyperthyroidism), of psychological difficulties (such as depression), or of medical concerns (such as hypertension) that require drug treatment can all negatively affect desire. In general, over time the sex drive declines, particularly for men. The male sex drive is also affected by a drop in testosterone, the male hormone.

Excitement, the second phase of the sexual response cycle, is the first physiological reaction to stimulation and results in blood engorgement of the genitals. As Scarf (1992) points out, "while earlier the mere thought of having sex might have made him erect, later on in life he will often require both *psychological and tactile* stimulation" (p. 54). This can make the man feel more vulnerable. In fact, without successful adaptation, both partners may end up humiliated—the man, who has to confront his slowed sexual response, and the woman, who may perceive his slowness as a sign of rejection and of her lack of attractiveness.

The last phase of the sexual response cycle, orgasm, also changes dramatically with age, primarily in the area known as the **refractory period**—the time between one orgasm and the physical capability to achieve another orgasm. The adolescent male can have as many as two orgasms per minute, but the midlife male may need as long as 24 to 48 hours between orgasms.

For the midlife woman, the sexual profile is quite different. Indeed, erotic interest often increases in the desire phase, primarily in response to changes in her biological makeup. When estrogen, the female hormone, declines, it allows her testosterone to have more of an influence. During menopause, the ovaries continue to produce small amounts of testosterone, and given the decline of estrogen, the effect of the testosterone is greater, leading to increased sexual desire (Scarf, 1992). However, in the excitement phase, lack of estrogen often leads to problems with vaginal dryness. Without proper treatment for this dryness, the sexual experience can be adversely affected. During the last phase, orgasm, the woman—unlike her male counterpart—has no refractory period and can

TABLE 11.3 Benefits and Risks of Hormone Replacement Therapy (HRT)	
Confirmed short-term benefits of HRT:	Eliminates vasomotor symptoms, including hot flashes.
	Improves vaginal lubrication.
Confirmed short-term risks and problems of HRT:	Breast tenderness.
	Continued menstrual bleeding (in women who take progesterone along with estrogen).
	Increases risk of endometrial growth (in women who do not take progesterone).
Confirmed long-term benefits of HRT:	Helps prevent osteoporosis.
	Decreases several risk factors for cardiovascular disease.
Confirmed long-term risks of HRT:	Increases risk of endometrial cancer if estrogen is taken without progesterone.
	Increases risk of deep-vein thrombosis; however, the risk is extremely low.
Unknown from current data:	Protects from full-blown cardiovascular disease.
	Protects from dementia.
	Increases risk of breast cancer.
	Increases sexual functioning.
	Increases longevity.

(Adapted from Azar, 1997)

Understanding the physical changes that affect sexuality in midlife can help men and women adapt and adjust.

have multiple orgasms. All the changes we have mentioned can make life difficult for sexual partners. As our sexual response system changes, we must be prepared to accommodate the changes and learn new ways of remaining sexually active.

Biophysical Hazards

SOCIAL WORK AND CANCER

Cancer is only second to heart disease as the most common cause of death in men and women. Since 1990 a diagnosis of cancer has been given to 12 million people, and 5 million people have died (National Cancer Institute, 1997). In the end, cancer will have taken the lives of one of every four Americans. But chances of recovery have risen from one out of two, ten years ago, to three out of four today. More than 8 million Americans have survived cancer for at least five years. Furthermore, the incidence of cancer fell 2.2% between 1992 and 1996; however, much of this decline is attributed to the increasing numbers of people who have quit smoking.

Types of cancer vary, as do the incidence and survival rates. Table 11.4 presents four common cancers and the percentage of the population developing the cancer according to age and gender. One of the biggest health fears of middle-aged women is breast cancer. In 1996, 184,000 women were diagnosed with breast cancer, and 44,300 women died of this disease. Women who live to age 85 have a 1-in-9 chance of developing cancer of the breast in their lifetime (Jaroff, 1996; Winawer & Shike, 1995). Not only is this risk high, it also represents a dramatic increase in breast cancer risk; in 1970, the risk was 1 in 16. What is causing this alarming increase?

Some medical experts believe that the increase is the result of heightened awareness of and earlier detection of the disease. This explanation might account for the fact that, although the rate of breast cancer has increased, earlier detection of the disease has improved the survival rates—so the mortality rate has remained stable or in some areas decreased (Winawer & Shike, 1995). Others argue that the increased incidence of breast cancer is the result of environmental factors. Some support for this idea comes from the fact that women who move from an area with low breast cancer rates to an area with high breast cancer rates experience an increase in their personal risk. Environmental factors that have been suggested as contributing to breast cancer include a diet high in fat, the presence of pesticides and other toxic chemicals in food and water, exposure to radiation from nuclear testing in the 1950s, and increased levels of stress (Clorfene-Costen, 1993).

Several factors that increase a woman's personal risk for breast cancer have been identified. One is age.

Although the overall chance of developing breast cancer is 1 in 9, this risk applies to an 85-year-old woman. A woman at age 30 has only a 1-in-2,500 chance and a woman at menopausal age a 1-in-50 chance (Winawer & Shike, 1995). Other risk factors include having a family history of breast cancer, undergoing menarche (the onset of menstrual periods) before age 12 or menopause (the cessation of menstrual periods) after age 50, being childless or having a first child after age 30, being overweight, having a sedentary lifestyle, drinking alcohol, and eating a diet high in fat.

Women are now encouraged to decrease their risk of breast cancer by lowering their intake of dietary fat, by increasing their physical activity, performing monthly breast examinations, and having annual mammograms (screening X rays of the breasts) after menopause (Friedenreich, 1995; Kerlikowske et al., 1995; Vantveer, 1994).

Early detection of breast cancer can reduce the need for extensive surgical intervention. In many instances, however, the treatment for breast cancer involves the surgical removal of part or all of the breast. Because of this disfiguring treatment, a woman may perceive breast cancer as a threat to her sense of herself as a feminine, sexual, nurturing being (Winawer & Shike, 1995). The psychosocial/psychosexual adjustments to the disease may be more difficult for a woman than the actual physical recovery from the surgery (Winawer & Shike, 1995). Women with breast cancer need support for their emotional as well as their physical well-being. Many women benefit from support groups for breast cancer patients. But some research suggests that the most important source of support is the family, in particular the woman's partner (Pistrang, 1995). The woman needs to be able to maintain good communication with her partner and to feel that her partner is empathic and will not withdraw from her because of disfiguring treatments. To mediate the psychological stress of breast cancer, social workers can help partners to continue to communicate with and support each other.

The implications of a diagnosis of breast cancer for women who lack a partner or other significant support are described in the following Focus section.

TABLE 11.4	Percentage of the Population Developing Cancer by Ages and Gender*				
		Ages			
		Birth–39	**40–59**	**60–79**	**Birth to Death**
Breast	Female	.44 (1/227)	3.94 (1/25)	6.89 (1/15)	12.52 (1/8)
Colon &	Male	.06 (1/1,667)	.88 (1/114)	4.19 (1/24)	5.88 (1/17)
Rectum	Female	.05 (1/2,000)	.68 (1/147)	3.18 (1/38)	5.72 (1/17)
Lung &	Male	.04 (1/2,500)	1.39 (1/72)	6.69 (1/15)	8.43 (1/12)
Bronchus	Female	.03 (1/3,300)	1.00 (1/100)	3.88 (1/26)	5.55 (1/18)
Prostate	Male	(Less than 1 in 10,000)	1.74 (1/57)	16.40 (1/6)	18.85 (1/5)

(National Cancer Institute Surveillance, Epidemiology, and End Results Program, 1997)

*Excludes basal and squamous cell skin cancers and in-situ carcinomas except bladder.

FOCUS ON NARRATIVE

An African-American Woman's Experience with Breast Cancer

"In July 1991, I was taking a shower, and all of a sudden there was this lump in my right breast. I'm fortunate because I only had a lumpectomy [the lump removed, instead of the whole breast]. It just put a little crease in the upper part of my right breast. They also took 25 lymph nodes out. Only two of them were cancerous, which was absolutely great. Then, I was in a state of denial, thinking, I'm fine now. But the doctors said, 'You have to have radiation and chemotherapy.'

"So I went for a bone scan. I'm looking up, and I see all these frigging signs that say, 'You are now entering a radiation zone.' That's when I became aware of what was really wrong with me. I started crying and could not stop. The doctor was totally detached. He was like: 'What's wrong with you? Why are you crying?'

"No one was with me. *Girlfriend, this whole thing has been by myself.* My mother had to work. My friends had to work. My daughter had to work. My children—two daughters and a son—couldn't really deal with it. I was dating a doctor at the time. He had been very supportive, but when I had my surgery, it took him an extra day to show up. I got out of the hospital, and he stopped communicating with me. I had to go through this alone.

"I got angry, because I kept getting these calls to go to support groups out of my area. All the groups that were available to women in Los Angeles are either on Wilshire Boulevard, which is in the financial district, or in Santa Monica, which is a good 20 miles from South Central L.A., where I live. It takes two hours to get to Santa Monica on a bus.

"My issues are different from the issues in the white community. My experience is, right now, all my bills are due. Some black women just started a job, won't get a paycheck for three weeks, and have no transportation. If women with children leave them at home, they have to pay someone.

"During my treatment, I started the Women of Color Breast Cancer Survivors' Support Group, which now has four sites in Central and South Central L.A. Our groups have three facilitators and me, trained through the National Black Women's Health Project. I make presentations about prevention. In the underserved community, you have women whose health gets pushed to the side. I enlighten them. It's about care of one's body. They don't even know they're at risk.

"And I want them to see my attitude. I'm overweight from the chemo, but you cannot tell I've had cancer, because everything about me exudes health, energy, and life."

(Viviansayles, 1993)

▼

Prostate Cancer

A disturbing silent issue for middle-aged men is prostate cancer. Although one in five American men will develop prostate cancer in his lifetime, most are only vaguely aware of the disease—its treatment and its consequences. Unlike women, who often talk freely among themselves about intimate health problems, most men shy away from discussion of their physical disorders, let alone problems involving a gland that produces seminal fluid and affects urinary flow. And they prefer not to undergo, or even think about, the digital rectal exam—the traditional test for detecting prostate problems.

However, whether a man is comfortable with these issues or not, the fact remains that prostate cancer is a common and deadly cancer. The American Cancer Society estimated that 41,400 men will die each year, just as 44,300 women will die from breast cancer. Why are so many Americans developing cancer? Simply, as the life span of Americans increases, so do the rates of cancers. More men are afflicted with prostate cancer because men are living longer, into the 70s and 80s, when the disease most often strikes. As men live longer and do not succumb to heart disease and stroke, more will die from prostate cancer.

In 1985, 85,000 men were told they had prostate cancer. By 1996, 317,000 cases were reported. By far the biggest factor in the high prostate-cancer diagnosis rate is the PSA test, which is a screening test for prostate-specific antigen in the blood, which in many cases can detect the disease early in its course, long before the tumor becomes palpable. Early detection and treatment will help reduce the number of prostate cancer deaths.

The prostate gland naturally begins to enlarge in a 50-year-old man, and the growing number of cells contribute to what is generally a steady but slight rise in the PSA count. But if the prostate cells become cancerous and begin multiplying, the PSA level jumps dramatically.

Because the average prostate cancer takes a decade to develop symptoms that seriously affect the quality of life, men either take a "watchful waiting" approach or receive treatment. Watchful waiting includes frequent blood tests, rectal exams, and an occasional biopsy, but no intervention unless the cancer becomes more aggressive. For those men who choose treatment, the options create dilemmas: Virtually all of them affect quality of life—hormones, radiation, cryotherapy (freezing the cancerous cells), and surgery may cause impotency, incontinence, or both. Although the decisions are ultimately the man's, doctors urge men whose life expectancy is ten years or more to get treatment.

(Adapted from Jaroff, 1996)

▼

Cancer Affects Us All

Two women discuss their experience with cancer and how painting helped them cope.

> In 1990, cancer became a catalyst for change in my family when my mother was diagnosed with an advanced endometrial tumor. Watching her struggle to maintain the consistency of her life against the inevitable force of her cancer was, for me, a difficult and unforgettable passage. In the aftermath of her death, I began to make paintings of my mother as a child, as a young woman, as an older woman, when she was ill. These reconstructed paintings not only helped me to deal with my grief, but they were also a tribute to her memory and a reminder of what there is both to lose and cherish.
> —Gail Skudera

> It took enormous discipline to alter my attitude more towards the positive, having suffered four cancer surgeries and follow-up treatments over a 20-year period. But I am now functioning better than ever, lavishing in my health. I paint as though I have only this day to touch paint and see color. I constantly make new discoveries by thoroughly indulging my curiosities.
> My paintings, better seasonal as I finally realize, document time through my study of color in the landscape. My reaction to facing the unknown, suddenly, and not recognizing myself in the mirror, and having pain, was to paint as though there was no tomorrow.
> —Lorna Ritz

(APA Monitor, June 1999, Volume 30)

A FAMILY-SYSTEMS LOOK AT COUPLES AND ILLNESS

When one spouse is sick, is it a family affair? It is, according to researchers Howard Liddle and Gail Dakov.

Liddle and Dakov studied patterns of coping in couples in which one spouse had cancer. Contrary to popular belief, they found that openly talking about the illness is *not* always the best coping mechanism. Instead, Liddle and Dakov conclude that what is important is not *how much* the couple communicates about illness-related concerns but how much "their desire to share is similar." This means that adjustment of partners who do *not* wish to discuss the illness is just as good as adjustment of spouses who wish to discuss concerns openly. Adjustment problems occur, however, when partners experience different levels of desire to talk about the illness.

Liddle and Dakov note that couples' adjustment to cancer is not based solely on communication styles but is also related to other factors. Relationship history, for example, plays a role in how couples adjust to illness. In many troubled couples, partners showed hostility toward each other after diagnosis. In happier couples, diagnosis reportedly brought spouses closer together.

Other research on couples in which the husband had a heart attack six months earlier looked at the emergence of overprotectiveness within the relationship. Researchers found that overprotectiveness, commonly thought to be hostile in origin, is actually a response to the well partner's desire to help when illness threatens a close relationship. The illness becomes an integral part of the system and emphasizes the interdependence of partners as key in understanding the dynamics of the dyad.

The following section examines how stress management interventions can help slow the progression of serious diseases.

Implications for Practice: Psychological Interventions for the Seriously Ill

Social workers would be quick to tell us that, while medical care for cancer patients has improved, psychosocial support is lacking. Such a conclusion is confirmed in a recent report, Ensuring Quality Cancer Care (1999), which found important differences in care provided by health care systems, health care providers, and insurance companies. Too often physicians do not recognize the psychological long-term effects of cancer and its treatment. For example, physicians do not accurately assess depression among cancer patients. Increasingly it has become recognized that pain management has been inadequate to meet the needs of patients.

Can stress management or psychosocial interventions slow down the progression of AIDS or cancer? It can, according to researchers throughout the United States. Psychological interventions such as teaching stress management, coping skills, relaxation training, problem solving, and fatigue management, as well as group support and social support, were tested in several states (DeAngelis, 1995; Sleek, 1995). The biological theory behind this holistic approach to healing is based on the hypothesis that discovering one has HIV or cancer may lead to social isolation and poor coping strategies that could suppress the immune system. Researchers have linked the amount of social support to changes in white blood cell (the natural "killer cell") activity, an indicator of how well the immune system is handling stress. Research also shows that relaxation techniques taught to cancer patients improve their moods, reduce emotional distress, and improve their ability to cope with their illness. For example, for women with breast or cervical cancer, group therapy allows them to express their feelings about their illness and treatment in a context of mutual support. By receiving group therapy as part of a medical treatment, women comply better with their treatment regimen and engage in healthier behaviors.

Group support and treatment is being widely used for cancer patients across the country. Studies have found that such treatment can improve the patient's quality of life, instilling a more positive mood, creating better interactions with family members, and increasing energy levels (Spiegel, 1999). In fact, one study (Spiegel, 1993) found that group treatment increased survival by 18 months for women with metastatic breast cancer. However, a replication of this study (Cunningham et al., 1998) did not find a longer survival rate for group therapy participants. At this point, additional studies are needed to confirm if group treatment can enhance a person's longevity.

Even homebound clients may want to participate in group therapy. Yvette Colon, a social worker, provides a telephone and online support group (Murray, 1999). She describes how people's increasing comfort with technology is expanding the available means of delivering client support. Telephone and online groups provide a forum for clients to address coping ability, emotional overload, fatigue, loss, and death.

For unknown reasons, not all women consider their health care in the same manner. In particular, low-income, minority women have lower rates of follow-up care than do higher-income, white women (Cancer Rates, 1998). This low follow-up rate may be a primary reason for the significant late-stage diagnosis and cancer fatalities among this population. Group support and therapy that takes into account the cultural, psychosocial, and systematic barriers encountered by these women as they obtain additional health care could greatly affect their chances for survival.

In general, stress-management and related interventions help patients to raise their awareness of stress symptoms and to challenge their negative thinking to better combat stress. Such interventions do not necessarily help people live longer or reverse the effects of serious diseases. However, research has shown that they help people to better cope with their illness and boost their immune functioning, which can improve quality of life for many people.

Unlike much research with social implications, there are hard outcomes to this type of health psychology (Sleek, 1995) because a person either has a disease or does not. Unfortunately, insurance plans often refuse to cover psychological services, even when the interventions are proven to be successful. Social workers and mental health professionals should lobby on clients' behalf for more holistic treatments. A healthy state of mind may be humankind's best medicine.

The following Focus section examines some of the dramatic health care changes that have occurred for women.

Women and Health Care: A Short History

Health care for women has changed dramatically over the last 25 to 35 years. Imagine the following: a woman being told that childbirth is better experienced in an unconscious state, natural childbirth being considered too dangerous and a friend—unexpectedly pregnant—having to fly to Mexico to obtain an abortion that is illegal in the United States (Boston's Women's Health Book Collective, 1992). These are the kinds of events that led to the 1970 publication of *Our Bodies, Ourselves.* This classic, first sold for 75 cents, sold more than 250,000 copies before it was commercially published. Women embraced the ideas that they could be experts on their own bodies and guide their own health care. They began to take action on policies that directly affected their health. For example, congressional hearings were disrupted as women voiced complaints about the side effects of the Pill. This crusade led to the development of a self-help movement that inspired the opening of dozens of women-controlled health centers. These efforts were largely in the service of white, middle-class women, but by the 1980s, women of color began to use their voices for change. They addressed issues such as the high incidence of sterilization abuse against poor women, especially women of color. By 1981, Bylle Avery, an African-American woman, was elected to the board of directors of the National Women's Health Network. Today, there are 150 chapters of the National Black Women's Health Project, as well as many chapters of associations such as the National Latina Health Organization, the Native-American Women's Health Education Resource Center, and the Asian Health Project—all the result of the grassroots effort to organize women at the community level with a commitment to self-help.

The results of this early movement led to changes that directly influence the lives of individual women. For example, midwives and nurse practitioners deliver babies in women's homes; the birth control pill no longer has excessive amounts of estrogen; women with breast cancer do not automatically lose their breasts; DES (diethylstilbestrol, a drug that produced offspring with increased cancer rates) is no longer given during pregnancy; abortions are readily available; and silicone breast implants are being phased out in favor of saline implants.

(Boston Women's Health Book Collective, 1992)

MIDLIFE AND THE WIDENING MIDSECTION
(Adapted from Dewitt, 1995)

"Super size;" "double gulp." Have you noticed how large American's food portions are? How many fast-food eateries do you drive by on your way to work? When was the last time that an 8-ounce carbonated beverage satisfied your thirst? According to the Agriculture Department, the food and restaurant industries spend $36 billion a year on advertisements designed to entice hungry people to abandon fruits and vegetables for chips, sodas, and Happy Meals. The average American watches 10,000 food ads on TV a year. What does this matter? Well, Americans are listening to the advertisements and getting fatter in the process. Drive-through windows and convenience stores have also contributed to our expanding waistlines. Why? (1) Take-out food tends to be high in fat, carbohydrates, sodium, and calories; (2) it tends to be eaten quickly, which means more of it is consumed; and (3) it tends to get eaten, all of it, no matter how much of it there is.

The number of Americans who are overweight jumped 30% from the 1960s to the 1980s. Currently, some 58 million people in the United States weigh at least 20% more than their ideal body weight, making them obese. Just when the country needs to reduce its health care bills, our eating habits may be pushing the costs higher. Overweight people are at a higher risk for diabetes, hypertension, heart disease, stroke, gout, arthritis, and some forms of cancer.

But all this talk of food ignores the other side of the weight-gain equation. Most Americans are bulging not because they consume too many calories but also because they burn off too few. In fact, people are eating less now than their ancestors did at the turn of the century, when the rate of obesity was much lower than it is today. A century of industrialization and invention, and with it new technology, has taken people out of the fields and put them behind desks and in front of computers. We are doing less manual work. Any exercise we get must be purposeful, and therefore scheduled into our hectic lives.

Are people taking the time to burn off those fast-food calories? Not many are. In 1991, 58% of U.S. adults said they exercised sporadically or not at all. The inactivity was especially marked among African-Americans,

Hispanics, low-income people, and the unemployed. The prevalence of obesity was nearly 50% for black and Hispanic women, compared with 35.5% for white women. In some Native-American communities, up to 70% of the adults are dangerously overweight. In all groups, genetic factors play a role. For example, scientists have known for years that identical twins separated at birth are far more likely to grow into the body types of their biological parents than of their adoptive parents.

So if we aren't exercising, what are we doing to try to fight the fat? Each year an estimated 80 million people go on a diet, but unfortunately, no matter how much weight they lose, 95% of them gain it back within five years. A major problem, nutritionists agree, is that most people think of diets as temporary restrictions imposed from the outside. They do not internalize their behavior change, so it is therefore temporary. How can one teach people to listen to their body? To eat when they're hungry, to eat appropriate portions, to move and stretch? Deep, long-lasting behavioral changes cannot be imposed from the outside; they must be internalized.

EFFECTS OF BRAIN INJURY ON THE FAMILY

In the movie *Regarding Henry,* a ruthless, high-priced lawyer suffers brain damage after being shot in the head. Following the injury, he remembers little of his former self or life. He is a very different man—one who moves slower, thinks slower, and cannot even remember how to read. He is unable to take up his old life again. At one point he comments, "I thought I could go back to my life . . . but I don't fit in." Henry cannot function as before in his job and ultimately quits. He loses most of his old friends, who cannot get used to the new Henry. Commenting on his recovery, his friends whisper at a party, "One minute you're an attorney. The next you're an imbecile." Henry and his family must learn to cope with a very different life.

What is the best way to cope with the brain injury of a loved one? Research suggests that there is no simple answer to this question. According to Betsy Zeigler, families who adjust well to the situation learn to see the post-injury person as distinct from the individual they previously knew. They are then able to let go of the old image of the family member and to integrate the new person into the family system. Although this perspective provides a practical goal for the family, the nature of brain injury makes this task difficult. The loss felt after a brain injury is in some ways harder to reconcile than the death of a loved one. Death is finite, but the extent and permanence of the loss with brain injury remains unclear. This fosters hope for recovery, but it also leaves family members in limbo: "After a death, you eventually get on with your life. [Brain injury] goes on forever, and you're dealing with it in one stage or another for the rest of your life" (Souza, cited in Mitiguy, 1990, p. 12).

Family members' grief may never quite be resolved, because of the unpredictable nature of brain injury. The injured individual remains a constant reminder of loss for family members, but society may not recognize the family's grief because the injured individual remains present in a physically familiar form.

Familial responses include denial and hope. Reactions to brain injury are not the same for any two individuals, but research suggests certain parental, sibling, son/daughter, and spousal similarities. For parents, children represent immortality through the perpetuation of family traditions and values. Although returning to the role of caregiver for a child with brain injury may recall an earlier nurturing role, this change in dynamics may also lead to overprotectiveness on the parents' part. Responses of mothers and fathers may differ owing to the differing nature of parent-child relationships. Injury can be both a binding and a divisive factor for parents.

Siblings' reactions to brain injury tend to vary according to age, prior relationship with the injured sibling, and role in the family. Sons and daughters of brain-injured parents also have diverse experiences, dependent on age, relationship with both the healthy and the brain-injured parent, and role changes within the family. Spouses of brain-injured individuals face challenges associated with the emotional, social, and physical aspects of the marital bond.

Although their feelings may not ever be completely resolved, many families do achieve a level of adjustment that incorporates a realistic perspective of the nature and the duration of loss. This facilitates the functioning of a family system that includes and changes with the brain-injured person.

Cognitive Development and Information Processing

Past researchers have attempted to study adult cognitive development based on the seminal ideas of Piaget. However recent researchers interested in adult development have discovered that using Piaget's child-oriented theory may not be the best approach for studying adult development. In fact, Piaget's work has contributed to the accepted social stereotype that childhood is the primary period for intellectual development (Willis, 1989). Childhood and adolescence have been seen as the time periods for acquiring the knowledge needed to operate successfully in adulthood. For a long time, it was believed that cognitive development or intelligence peaked in late adolescence and early adulthood. Of course, this belief appeared logical because there is an obvious shift of biological aging in middle adulthood, signaled most obviously by one's graying hair (Willis, 1989). A critical question related to the attempt to understand how cognitive development changes over the life course is this: Do individuals' cognitive abilities decline after young adulthood, as some stereotypes suggest?

A series of studies by Schaie has dramatically changed the way many people view cognitive development in middle adulthood. Schaie conducted longitudinal studies that discovered, for example, that verbal ability actually peaks in late middle age (Schaie & Strother, 1968). Figure 11.1 shows changes across the life span in five different aspects of cognitive ability: spatial visualization, reasoning, verbal ability, word fluency, and number ability. The overall conclusion from this data is that intellectual functioning is stable in middle age. Decline in intellectual ability begins only after age 60. Other interesting findings suggest that age-related declines occur earlier for some abilities—for example, numerical computations and spatial reasoning. The gender differences show that men perform at a somewhat higher level than women on spatial ability, but women perform at a somewhat higher level on reasoning ability.

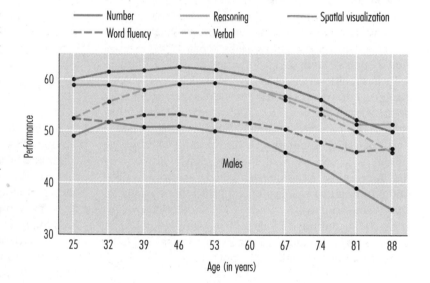

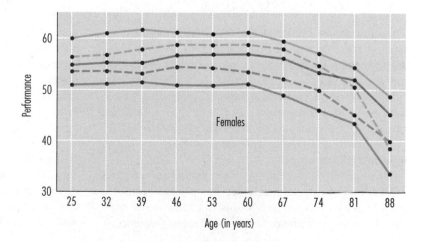

FIGURE 11.1
Intellectual performance across late adulthood (Schaie, 1983)

The results of these findings will probably be comforting to the many men and women at midlife who are required to perform at a very high level of intellectual competence. Adults in middle age are assuming major family, professional, and social responsibilities that demand sharp minds and the ability to acquire new skills and information (Willis, 1989). Schaie (1994) contends that this is why we must examine adult cognitive functioning in a different manner. Rather than using the child-focus, which involves how information is acquired, to study adult intellect, we need to examine how information is used. During adulthood, individuals are not exclusively concerned with acquiring skills but are concentrating more on achieving goals. This means that a majority of their cognitive abilities are focused on applying knowledge to real-world problems, which requires a new set of cognitive abilities—social and abstract cognitive skills. Schaie (1983) argues that cognitive and social functioning merge dramatically in midlife, when tasks have what Schaie calls "role-related achievement potential." Adults perform better at these tasks because the tasks are strongly related to the roles adults are assuming. This merging of social and cognitive functioning is also related to adults at midlife who are assuming more responsibility for others. Many adults become increasingly involved in civic and community organizations. Schaie's theory suggests that young adults move from "What should I know?" to the middle adulthood focus of "How should I use what I know?" to later adulthood, when the emphasis is "Why should I know?" (Schaie, 1977, p. 135).

EFFECT OF PROFESSIONAL OBSOLESCENCE

The concept of **professional obsolescence** may be particularly relevant during the midlife years (Willis, 1989). Professional obsolescence refers to the use of information, theories, and technology that are less useful in performing tasks than what is currently available in one's field of practice. As Dubin (1972) points out, obsolescence is not linked to age-related loss of ability but rather to an inability to learn and apply new information and techniques.

In our rapidly changing information society, it is critical to keep up with relevant knowledge. Adults in midlife have finished schooling but may need additional training to remain current on the job. As people's

life span grows, so does their longevity in the workforce. As a result, special efforts may be required to prevent professional obsolescence.

For example, almost all professional occupations now require some knowledge of computers. Few middle-aged adults received any formal training on how to use computers. However, given the rapid technological changes, adults will need new skills to remain competent in the workforce. Indeed, a person's professional half-life may be getting increasingly shorter as the information explosion expands. One's **professional half-life** is the time it takes for 50% of one's professional knowledge to become invalid or obsolete (Dubin, 1972). This varies according to one's career; for example, the professional half-life of a computer scientist is perhaps only two or three years (Willis, 1989). We can see that "learning is, indeed, becoming a lifelong process" (Willis, 1989, p. 109).

Communication

By midlife, the process of communication is clearly established. Communication at this stage is dominated by family and by friends. In terms of the family, this may be the period in life when one can truly reconnect with one's partner or spouse. After many years of raising children, many midlife adults are ready to establish more meaningful relationships with their spouse, adult children, and friends. Before middle adulthood, many adults are simply too busy managing family life to establish a strong network of friends. Also, at midlife adults begin the process of "life review"; they may reflect on communications that they would like to mend or at least make better. Midlife adults are seeking more meaning in their lives, and as a consequence, they are interested in communication on a deeper level. The friendships developed at this time are based on values such as honesty, sincerity, closeness, and mutual support.

THE FORGIVENESS PROCESS

In fact, many adults may become increasingly interested in engaging in the process of forgiveness as they reflect on relationships that may not have progressed the way they wanted. Beverely Flanigan (1992) has written a book on the topic, entitled *Forgiving the Un-*

forgivable. This book examines questions like the following: How long should a woman maintain anger at a husband who leaves her for a younger woman? Should she express rage toward the husband, and, if so, for how long after their divorce? How can she make things right in her own life after this unforgivable act?

By midlife, many people have accumulated a history of harms from persons with whom they have had close relationships. We have all heard of individuals who are not communicating with a sister, brother, child, parent, or close friend because of some unforgivable act. Flanigan illustrates how forgiveness is an essential mechanism for righting such wrongs. Many people are not at peace with themselves for not having asked the forgiveness of a loved one. Others remain angry at themselves for not being able to forgive a friend or a relative for some harmful action. If practitioners desire to help clients with forgiveness issues, Flanigan argues that they should have some understanding of the forgiveness process.

Flanigan (1992) has studied individuals who have "forgiven the unforgivable." From this research, she has identified six phases that appear to be involved in the journey of forgiving an unforgivable injury:

- *Phase one:* Naming the injury
- *Phase two:* Claiming the injury
- *Phase three:* Blaming the injurer
- *Phase four:* Balancing the scales
- *Phase five:* Choosing to forgive
- *Phase six:* The emergence of a new self

This process of forgiving begins with identifying and naming the injury and ends with the emergence of a new self. Although many people begin this process, all do not finish it. Forgiveness will not occur without a person making significant changes in his or her feelings and beliefs. "Forgiveness is a rational process; it is a conversion in the way you have thought about yourself and other people and about harm and vulnerability" (Flanigan, 1992, p. 72). At the end of this process, individuals do not wish any harm on their injurers and develop a new perspective about the causes of events in their lives.

In addition, research (Enright, 1996) shows that people who forgive someone who has hurt them seem to reap significant mental health benefits. And the act of forgiving appears to be one of the basic processes that keeps personal relationships functioning, according to studies of long-married couples (Azar, 1997). Forgiveness takes conscious effort, whereas the defensive mechanisms of resentment or revenge are somewhat automatic (Enright, 1996; McCullough, 1997). Forgiveness is not the same as reconciliation. Forgiveness involves only the person who was hurt. Reconciliation takes both people *and* requires a change in the person who did the hurting. Research (Enright, 1996) shows that forgiving can be liberating. Carrying around a desire for revenge or a need to avoid someone is not healthy. Hostility and aggression are linked to a multitude of health problems. However, people who are able to forgive benefit through a decrease in anxiety, depression, and hostility and an increase in hope, self-esteem, and existential well-being (Enright, 1996).

So what is the key to forgiveness? How do we begin to forgive someone who has hurt us deeply? McCullough's (1997) research says *empathy.* Empathy motivates forgiveness: people who feel empathy for the person who offended them are more able to forgive than people who do not. People are also more likely to forgive an offender if the offender apologizes—because the apology encourages empathy. In sum, an apology leads to empathy, and empathy mediates forgiveness.

But are there some situations in which not forgiveness but revenge lets people heal? The following Focus section discusses how many grieving families try to find comfort and closure in the execution of a loved one's murderer.

FOCUS ON SOCIOLOGY

Execution and Therapeutic Revenge

A murderer, strapped to a gurney, hooked up to intravenous tubes, and waiting for the deadly drugs to flow into his body turns to the grieving family of his victim and says, "I hope you can go on with your lives and we can put an end to this" (Browne, McGraw, & Vest, 1997). This is what many victims' family members hope to get out of an execution: an end to their suffering and grief. But do they find it?

Consistently since 1987, more than 70% of Americans polled say they support the death penalty. Although the percentages regarding capital punishment have not changed much within the last decade, the nature of the discussion has. The discussion used to be formed in terms of practicality: Was the death penalty effective in deterring crime? Was killing an offender the best way to protect society? But recently, the argument for the death penalty centers not on the criminal's "debt" to society but on the right of a victim's loved ones to gain peace of mind through his or her death. This is, in effect, therapeutic vengeance.

The impulse for revenge is potent and natural. The grieving process for a murder victim is similar to the grieving process many go through when they loose a loved one: disbelief, anger, grief, and finally, for some, acceptance. But loved ones of homicide victims rarely move through these stages easily. "Murder often taps a well of rage that can drown out all other emotions" (Browne, McGraw, & Vest, 1997, p. 28). Survivors often mistakenly think that if "justice is served" and the murderer is executed, they can move past the rage and get on with their lives.

In recent years, a victims-rights movement has lobbied to let victims testify directly to the accused during the trial and make statements about their pain and suffering during sentencing, and to allow victim's families to view executions. In some cases, allowing these rights does help the survivors heal, but, in others, survivors realize that revenge is not so sweet.

Misha Marvel (Based on Browne, McGraw, & Vest, 1997)

THE ILLITERATE ADULT

Many of us take for granted our ability to communicate through writing, reading, and speaking. However, as many as 20% of the adults in our society are functionally **illiterate**—they cannot read and write well enough to participate in society. The National Institute for Literacy (1998) estimates that 40 million or more American adults do not possess the reading skills needed to function independently in society. As modern society becomes more complex, concerns about illiteracy become increasingly critical.

The notion of being **functionally literate** originated in World War I when the U.S. Army found that many soldiers could read and write but not to an extent that would make them effective soldiers (Radwin, 1993). Programs were started to teach soldiers to be functionally literate.

Definitions of functional literacy vary widely and have changed over time. In the late 19th century, literacy was the ability to write one's name. The U.S. Bureau of the Census defines functional literacy as a sixth-grade reading level. The most common definition of functional literacy is the ability to perform everyday reading, writing, and arithmetic tasks. These different definitions produce different estimates of functional illiteracy that range from 13% to 50% (Radwin, 1993). Whatever the exact percentage, we do know that illiteracy afflicts mainly people who are poor, uneducated, under-educated and belonging to a minority. Many illiterate adults grew up in socioeconomically disadvantaged areas with family members who did not encourage reading skills and with no one else to help them learn essential literacy skills.

Where does the functionally illiterate adult come from? Most people who are illiterate completed elementary school, and many even received a high school diploma (Schuster & Ashburn, 1992). However, in school they did not learn some essential skills, such as writing letters, filling out applications, reading instructions on a package, reading the newspaper, and writing a check.

Functionally illiterate adults are often embarrassed that they do not understand essential communication. They are often concerned that people will "discover" that they are illiterate, and therefore they hide their inability to read and write. Disabled persons may be illiterate because they were denied proper educational services as a child. Parents may have lacked the confidence that the child could learn and so inadvertently contributed toward his or her illiteracy (Schuster & Ashburn, 1992).

NON-ENGLISH-SPEAKING ADULTS

In many respects, adults living in the United States who do not speak English may face similar difficulties. Often, immigrants who do not speak English face discrimination in employment. They may be highly educated and competent in their native language but unable to communicate in English, thus forced into low-paying jobs and lives of poverty. The immigrant may not have important functional skills such as reading street signs, advertisements, newspaper want ads, and so forth. Being shut off from one's surrounding world can lead to anger, frustration, and depression. Often non-English-speaking persons must become dependent on others to translate and communicate for them. This can lead to relationship problems and a difficult lifestyle wherein one cannot communicate with other people. "Feelings, fears, pleasures, observations must all be kept to oneself, creating a lonely, depressing existence" (Schuster & Ashburn, 1992, p. 596).

THE HARD-OF-HEARING ADULT

Imagine being 36 years old and noticing that you are having trouble understanding your friend when you are speaking on the telephone. At first you ask the speaker to repeat his statement, but as time goes on and friends and co-workers wonder why you are always so absent minded, you later find it easier not to initiate conversation. Such slow loss of hearing is a fact of life for many people in the United States. More than 28 million people are hearing impaired, according to the National Institute on Deafness and Other Communications Disorders (Seppa, 1997), and nine in ten are hard of hearing, or partially deaf. These people have little in common with profoundly deaf people, many of whom were born unable to hear, live in a deaf society, use sign language, and flourish in a rich culture of their own. On the contrary, hard-of-hearing people are at risk of isolation and withdrawal from society. They confront psychological issues different from those dealt with by deaf people, including the frustrations of having cultural and personal links to the hearing world as its sounds slip away.

Sadly, despite greater social acceptance and mainstreaming of people with disabilities, the stigma of hearing loss has endured over the years. Hearing loss and hearing aids are commonly associated with aging, being inadequate, or being incompetent (Seppa, 1997). Therefore, people often deny their hearing loss or avoid doing something about it. Practitioners can alert families to basic techniques that improve the lives of people with hearing problems, such as talking directly at them so they can see the speaker's face and read his or her expressions and lips. Speaking clearly and at an un-

rushed pace also helps the partially deaf to understand conversation. Connecting hard-of-hearing people with others who face the same disability provides a peer network of people who are not deaf but are not fully hearing. The best-known group for this is Self Help for Hard of Hearing People (SHHH), an international, educational consumer organization devoted to hard-of-hearing people and their relatives and friends who still want to participate in the hearing world (Seppa, 1997).

Implications for Practice: Clients with Hearing Loss

Hearing impairment is one of the most common of all chronic disabilities, and it affects people's lives in profound ways. People with hearing loss are subject not only to the particular difficulties that their disability creates but also to any social or psychological problems that might require social work intervention. It is important, then, that all social workers understand the differences among deaf and hearing-impaired people and have the tools for assessing the meaning of hearing loss for a particular client (Luey, Glass, & Elliott, 1995).

About 8% of all people have a significant hearing loss, and many more have losses classified as mild or moderate. Both prevalence and severity of hearing loss dramatically increase with age. The incidence of self-reported trouble with hearing is 33% for people aged 65 to 74% and 62% for people older than age 85. In contrast to the high prevalence of hearing impairment, only 1% of the population is profoundly deaf, and, of those, only 22% lost their hearing before age 19. People who were born deaf, then, actually constitute a very small percentage of the hearing-impaired population (Luey, Glass, & Elliott, 1995).

The most damaging thing about hearing loss is that it interferes with communication. Some people with hearing loss are able to understand speech by discerning meaning from fragments of sound, supplemented by visual clues from people's lip movements and facial expressions. This skill, speechreading, is difficult and taxing. Some people seem to have a talent for it, and others do not. At best, however, speechreading is demanding, tiring, and only partially accurate. Generally, the worse hearing becomes, the harder it is to speechread and the more likely it is for people to think of themselves as deaf rather than hard of hearing (Luey, Glass & Elliott, 1995).

People whose primary language is ASL tend to come together. Such groups have existed for many generations and have established a particular culture. Many people tend to marry within the culture and affiliate with formal and informal organizations that are a part of it. In addition to language, the culture includes particular behaviors, norms, and beliefs (Luey, Glass & Elliott, 1995).

Another significant difference between culturally deaf people and those that have become hard of hearing are their feelings about deafness itself. People in the deaf community and culture tend to perceive deafness not as a disability but as an alternative lifestyle and culture. In contrast, those who become deaf miss their earlier access to spoken communication, and they miss sound. For them, deafness is both a disability and a loss; it is something to be mourned (Luey, Glass & Elliott, 1995).

In recent years, people with onset hearing loss have formed groups and organizations to address their social, cultural, and political interests. Self Help for Hard of Hearing People (SHHH) largely comprises culturally hearing people with relatively severe hearing losses. SHHH members usually are not comfortable with the word "deaf" and generally communicate by speechreading aided by special amplifying devices. Few SHHH members use manual communication of any form, though some of them are beginning to use speech-to-text technology. SHHH members are largely middle-class and middle-aged or older (Luey, Glass, & Elliott, 1995).

So where do social workers come in? The first thing a social worker needs to do when meeting a deaf or hard-of-hearing client is to establish a way to communicate. What language does the client know and prefer? Because most hearing-impaired persons are not culturally deaf, most clients with hearing loss will have good speech ability and prefer English or the spoken language of their culture. If the client speechreads, the social worker can help by finding a quiet, well-lit place to talk. He or she should face the client; speak slowly and clearly; rephrase anything the client misunderstands; and offer to write key words, names, or specific information. Some clients with good speech and knowledge of English prefer to involve an interpreter for important interactions, and they are entitled to that accommodation. Professional interpreters for the deaf are able to use both signed English and ASL and to select the language suited to the individual and the situation (Luey, Glass, & Elliott, 1995).

LEGAL IMPLICATIONS

At least one of every 16 Americans has some degree of hearing loss and may use a variety of communication modes, including spoken English and ASL. One of every 100 Americans is profoundly deaf—that is, not able to hear speech well enough to understand it (McEntee, 1995).

The U.S. Rehabilitation Act of 1973 addressed the needs of disabled people at different ages. Title V was designed to ensure that programs receiving federal funds could be used by disabled individuals. The four major sections of Title V prohibit discrimination and require accessibility in employment; education; and health, welfare, and social services (McEntee, 1995).

To increase access to services, U.S. federal laws dictate the use of interpreters in mental health settings. Despite this, a survey of all mental health centers in one state found that 29% of the 28 respondents flatly stated that they were not accessible to deaf people. Additionally, 39% stated that they did not provide interpreters, even though 72% of the agencies indicated that they had served deaf individuals; of these 72%, only 25% had used certified interpreters (McEntee, 1995).

The Americans with Disabilities Act is far reaching, and its effects will undoubtedly touch the social work profession in diverse and profound ways. To be effective advocates, social workers need to be aware of the various pieces of legislation that affect the lives of clients. The profession also needs to be aware that services must be rendered in a different manner for deaf people and for hard-of-hearing people. Social workers need to be aware of their own communication modes and how to use support personnel and equipment.

Attitudes and Emotions

Many theorists believe that a midlife identity change takes place for most adults. Adults may begin to ask themselves, "What do I want to spend the rest of my life doing?" or "Are my relationships giving me the kind of satisfaction I want?" Such questions reflect identity changes that can have a strong influence on emotions. In particular, some adults may experience increased depression and anxiety. Why would these emotions become prevalent in midlife?

Goldstein and Landau (1990) argue that at midlife there is a "coming apart" that takes place in the continued quest for identity. This process of coming apart is facilitated by a review of the self in relation to work and family and a re-examination of expectations and roles that may no longer be valid. Goldstein and Landau believe that, for many adults, this process is linked to increased rates of depression and recognition of the reality of aging. And although many adults "come apart," this process ultimately leads to "coming together," whereby there is a renewal and reintegration of one's identity.

A significant part of the coming-apart process may be related to Levinson's (1978) notion of **de-illusionment,** which refers to the giving up of illusions from earlier periods of life and reflects the general loss of faith in people and ideas. In addition, many midlife adults experience what is referred to as the death of the hero. Many cultures emphasize hero myths (Campbell, 1988), and such heroes may provide us with important psychological benefits. For example, a hero provides a model to emulate. A hero may provide a mechanism for us to reflect on our own achievements or may provide an example of making successful transformations from difficult times to periods of renewal. Goldstein and Landau (1990) point out that, "as we approach midlife, our youthful hero is running out of steam and his mission is questionable" (p. 89). They believe that, for healthy adult development to proceed, the hero must die and eventually be replaced. This phenomenon may explain some of the depression and anxiety that is common in midlife.

MIDLIFE AS A CRISIS

Given the intense focus on reflection, is there a midlife crisis? The answer to this question is complex. Levinson's (1978) theory of adult development suggests that crisis is a normal part of adult development. However, work by Vallant (1977) found that only a small percentage of adults experience a midlife crisis. Apter

The 50th birthday is a key marker in the life course for most middle adults. They often realize at this point that they have completed two-thirds of their life and have only one-third remaining.

(1995) adds to the literature on women in midlife and believes that at midlife a crisis is likely to occur that includes a period of reflection and self-questioning. She suggests that men may no longer experience the midlife crisis but that women today engage in crisis as a normal developmental stage. Neugarten (1986) reminds us that development may be different, depending on the cohort; therefore, past studies may have been reflecting a cohort phenomenon rather than a stage. And although not all midlife adults will experience a "crisis," this period of life does seem to be a time for intense self-reflection.

So, particularly during middle age, adults are in a position to reflect on their lives. This reflection often influences important actions they may take. Levinson (1978) has presented the most compelling theory about the influence of such reflection on the behavior of men at midlife:

> A profound reappraisal of this kind cannot be a cool, intellectual process. It must involve emotional turmoil, despair, the sense of not knowing where to turn or of being stagnant and unable to move at all. A man in this state often makes false starts. He tentatively tests a variety of new choices, not only out of impulsiveness but, equally, out of a need to explore, to see what is possible, to find out how it feels to engage in a particular

love relationship, occupation, or solitary pursuit. Every genuine reappraisal must be agonizing, because it challenges the illusions and vested interests on which the existing structure is based (p. 23).

Why do midlife adults reflect on the importance of meaning in their lives? The process begins with recognition that youthful qualities are being lost, bringing reminders that one's physical functioning is decreasing while contact with problems of illness and exposure to death are increasing. Levinson suggests that much of this cognitive processing is in response to a subtle reflection of one's mortality.

Midlife can become painful for adults as a result of the growing realization of their mortality. As they reflect on the fact that their life will eventually end, they feel a corresponding concern about its meaning. Reflecting on their life, they have many questions and doubts about how meaningfully they have pursued it.

Social Cognition and Regulation

Although the preceding theories seem to suggest that at midlife there is a strong internal focus on oneself in which change is experienced as a crisis, Maas (1989) argues that midlife represents an increased opportunity to branch out and become involved in socially responsible activities. This branching out to more socially responsible behavior results from the natural transitions that occur in midlife. For example, children often leave the home, and spouses become increasingly removed from their roles as mother and father.

Most major theorists on adult development discuss this emphasis on social responsibility. Early on, Havighurst (1952) suggested that at midlife the major task was one of civic and social responsibility. Erikson's task of ego integrity reflects an emphasis on actions directed toward social causes. It is "an emotional integration which permits participation by followership as well as acceptance of the responsibility of leadership: both must be learned and practiced in religion and in politics, in the economic order and in technology" (Erikson, 1959, p. 97). Maslow (1962) describes the feelings of gratitude that arise following an individual's "peak experience," which often result in the person's desire to do something good for the world.

Maas (1989) defines the essence of social responsibility as based on two aspects. The first is the person's sense of obligation. Midlife adults can move beyond their narrow self-interest and begin to consider the general interest of others. "The obligation is based on a keen awareness of one's group memberships—ultimately, the human race—and of human interdependence in society" (Maas, 1989, p. 260). The second aspect of social responsibility is the person's ability to carry out his or her sense of obligation. By midlife, most adults have obtained a level of competence that allows them to be effective in undertaking their obligations. Over time, they develop the capacity to become socially responsible and fulfill their sense of obligation to society.

Psychological Hazards

As many of the adult development theories point out, midlife can be a difficult period, requiring many new adjustments. The new roles one must adapt to, the intense reflection about one's accomplishments, and the search for new meaning can lead to psychological hazards. In particular, alcohol and drug use may have progressed to the point of serious addiction.

ALCOHOL AND DRUG ADDICTION

Alcoholism is the consumption of alcoholic beverages to the extent that major aspects of a person's life, such as work, family, and friends, are affected. Alcoholism is considered a disease by many, meaning that it follows a prescribed course of physical, psychological, and social symptoms. Alcoholism is a progressive problem that can lead to irreversible damage and, ultimately, death. When an alcoholic person abstains from drinking, he or she is said to be "recovering."

An estimated 11 million Americans are alcoholics (The National Clearinghouse for Alcohol and Drug Information, 1996), and alcoholism touches all age and all sociocultural and economic groups. It is currently estimated that, of all alcoholics, the majority (75%) are men and a quarter (25%) are women. Alcoholism is one of the most serious social problems facing Americans. Weiten and Lloyd (1997) note that alcohol misuse is blamed in 64% of murders, 41% of assaults, 30% of suicides, 60% of child abuse, 45% of drownings, and 55% of arrests. Alcohol contributes to 100,000 deaths annually, making it the third leading cause of preventable mortality in the United States, after tobacco and diet activity patterns (McGinnis & Foege, 1993). It is estimated that as many as one family in three is affected in some way by a drinking problem (Caplan, 1993).

Identification and assessment of alcoholism is complex. Not all alcoholics drink every day, and many people who do have one or two drinks every day would not be considered alcoholics. Some people will react to a personal crisis and abuse alcohol as a means of coping for a period of time but not become alcoholics. Indeed, many young adults will abuse alcohol for a short time period but eventually develop a healthy pattern of social drinking. Distinguishing heavy drinking from the early stages of alcoholism can sometimes be difficult.

Assessment usually begins with a person's consumption levels and personal or family history of alcohol-related problems. Common assessment questions include (National Institute on Alcohol Abuse and Alcoholism, 1995): How long have you been drinking this amount? How many times a week (or month) do you have four or more drinks on one occasion? What is the most you have consumed on one occasion during the past year? And a family-history question: Have you or anyone in your immediate family ever had a drinking problem?

When individuals are currently experiencing alcohol-related problems and need to be assessed for being alcohol dependent, the CAGE is often used as an assessment instrument (National Institute on Alcohol Abuse and Alcoholism, 1995). Indications of dependence are three or four positive responses to the CAGE. The CAGE assessment is based on five questions:

- Are there times when you are unable to stop drinking once you have started?
- Does it take more drinks than before to get "high"?
- Do you feel a strong urge to drink?
- Do you change your plans so that you can have a drink?
- Do you ever drink in the morning to relieve the shakes?

Some common signs suggest someone is moving into the early stages of alcoholism. Many people increasingly use alcohol to cope with their personal problems. Others experience memory lapses or "blackouts" while drinking, craving for alcohol, and an increase in tolerance for alcohol. In the middle stages of alcoholism, there is an increase in memory problems from blackouts, and the person becomes increasingly physically dependent on alcohol. This dependence is first suggested when the person experiences early morning tremors and agitation that require a drink for relief. In the later and final stages, there are regular drinking bouts. Also during this stage, alcoholics experience **delirium tremens (DTs),** a withdrawal syndrome with symptoms including agitation, tremor, hallucination, and sometimes seizures.

Researchers still do not understand the causes of this complex problem; however, it is likely to include a combination of biological, psychological, and social factors. Recent attention has been directed to the incidence of alcoholism in families. Studies have shown that 50%–80% of all alcoholics have a close relative who is alcoholic (Littrell, 1991). As a result, researchers have begun to search for an inherited physical predisposition to alcohol addiction. Some research has suggested that alcoholism is related to a particular gene on chromosome 11. This gene is related to the production of receptor sites, on brain cells, of the neurotransmitter dopamine.

Many researchers have attempted to find a particular personality that would lead to the development of alcoholism, but results have not been encouraging. However, alcoholism does appear to be related to various types of emotional problems. For example, many alcoholics drink to help them cope with feelings of depression or anxiety. Other individuals drink as a means to release their inhibited feelings. Alcoholics may experience role conflicts in their work and family life.

Although in the United States many substance-abuse problems are related to alcohol, serious consequences are also associated with drug dependence. Drug dependence, or drug addiction, is defined by three characteristics (Goode, 1993). First, it is related to the length of time a person has been using the drug. Just how long a time is required to develop dependence is difficult to say and is related to the particular type of drug and the particular user's characteristics. Second, individuals who are dependent find it difficult to stop using the drug. A lot of effort is consumed with continuing to use the drug, including stealing to get needed money. Third, when dependent drug users do refrain from using, they experience physical pain or psychological stress, referred to as the *withdrawal syndrome.*

Drug dependence is associated with a large number of different drugs, ranging from nicotine found in tobacco products, Valium used as a sedative, angel dust (a street drug derived from horse tranquilizer), and hallucinogenic drugs (such as LSD and mescaline), to name only a few. There are six primary classifications of drugs: *narcotics,* like heroin and morphine; *sedatives,* like Seconal and Quaaludes, which include barbiturates and nonbarbiturates; *stimulants,* like amphetamines and cocaine; *hallucinogens,* like LSD and mescaline; *cannabis,* like marijuana and hashish; and *alcohol,* like wine and scotch.

FOCUS ON GENDER

Women and Drugs

When you think of a "druggie," is the picture that first comes to your mind a woman? Probably not. However, the use of alcohol, tobacco, and other drugs (ATOD) by women is a significant problem. It is estimated that 4.6 million women in the United States are alcohol dependent. Additional estimates guess that 5% of American women have used an illicit substance in the past 30 days. However, although the number of women abusing substances is significant, women appear to be less susceptible than men are to addiction to illicit substances. Interestingly, current evidence suggests that women view substance abuse more negatively and tend to be less tolerant of it than men. This may help explain why our idea of a drug addict rarely includes women.

Psychosocial factors associated with ATOD use and abuse also appear to be different for men and women. Addicted women are more likely than addicted men to suffer from affective disorders; are more likely to experience guilt, anxiety, and depression; and typically have lower self-esteem. Addicted women are more likely to have lower life expectations, less education, fewer job skills, and fewer financial resources. For these reasons, women in recovery may be better helped by groups that focus on building self-esteem and perceptions of personal power and that challenge sex-role stereotyping.

Many previously nonalcoholic young women typically began as "social drinkers." Therefore, to be affective, ATOD prevention must be relevant to and address the target population's beliefs about vulnerability to substance abuse. Women tend to believe that substance abuse is caused by biological and environmental influences. They view genetic disposition and family history as more strongly contributing to substance abuse. Similarly, women commonly identify relationship problems and stress as situational or environmental causes of substance abuse. Because women are more receptive to ideas about the influence of environmental and genetic factors in substance abuse, prevention programs should provide the opportunity to explore these issues in detail, especially those that influence women to initiate substance abuse. Examining how interpersonal influences increase women's vulnerability should be an integral part of prevention strategies. Additionally, given the reported incidence of addiction to psychotropic medications among women, an important aspect of prevention programs would be raising women's consciousness about addiction to these medications.

(Adapted from Kauffman, Silver, & Poulin, 1997)

FOCUS ON NARRATIVE

Goodbye, Johnnie Walker

"In the past year, I started drinking in the shower each morning. I was drunk by nine, drunk at noon, drunk at three, drunk at seven, and drunk at ten o'clock. I had pretty much stopped eating, although I still made dinner for my wife, our dogs, and myself and pretended to enjoy a fine meal in a fine little house on a pretty street in a nice little town. Eventually, my body started eating itself to stay alive. Ketosis is the medical term.

"Why my drinking got so out of control after so many years of my being a functioning and productive alcoholic remains a mystery to me. I just know that I had become (and still am) one sick son of a bitch just a step away from the grave because I suffer from the disease of alcoholism. I drank too much. It is as simple and as difficult as that. I find most books that deal with drinking and rehab somewhat smug and self-congratulatory. I am neither confident enough or sufficiently proud enough of getting through a day sober to take that attitude. Truth be told, I am confident only that I will have another drink at some point in my life. Maybe today."

(Davidson, 1998, p. 18)

Implications for Practice: Addiction and AA's 12-Step Program

The 12-step approach to addiction is so popular that it is now referred to as a social movement (Herman, 1988). In the 12-step approach—the core of Alcoholics Anonymous (AA)—people follow 12 carefully devised steps on the road to recovery. What exactly is the 12-step program, and how does it work?

The 12-step program is straightforward in its approach to alcoholism. Part of its success may be related to the clear model it sets out as necessary for the road to recovery. Essentially, members are expected to "work the steps." In the process, individuals must admit wrongdoing, admit their powerlessness, pray and meditate, and meet with sponsors outside the group meetings. AA is famous for its helpful slogans, such as "live one day at a time" and "let go and let God."

The program is delivered through a series of weekly meetings. Members are encouraged to go to the meetings, and many people keep a daily schedule of meeting attendance. Most meetings begin with an opening statement, then a speaker addresses the group telling his

or her own personal story, the members are invited to share, and then there is a closing statement. Members may speak about whatever they want, and the group must listen without interruption or subsequent comment.

Members are also encouraged to get involved with a sponsor. The sponsor is a kind of "buddy" who helps the member by providing advice and counsel about the program philosophy and structure. There is a strong emphasis on providing members with support. Sponsors and other members make themselves available 24 hours a day to help the person during times of crisis.

Although AA is recognized as one of the more effective approaches to alcoholism, it has come under increasing criticism. First, few studies have been able to clearly document AA's effectiveness, so many researchers are leery about its overall "success" rate. Equally critical are individuals who do not like AA's emphasis on religion and individual responsibility. For example, one of the 12 steps states, "[We have] made a decision to turn our will and our lives over to the care of God, *as we understood Him*" [italics added]. Many individuals also do not like the emphasis of putting the

Twelve-step programs, which attract many people who are seeking help, offer a social context for addressing problems, a group setting for social support, and a clear structure.

alcoholic's addiction completely on the alcoholic's shoulders. Because AA accepts a disease concept of alcoholism, the responsibility for both the disease and recovery rests with the individual.

What other contextual factors might relate to people becoming addicted? Increasing research is providing some support for the notion that there may be a genetic predisposition toward alcoholism. These explanations are not consistent with the AA philosophy. Because AA members must admit to "powerlessness," it is difficult to promote notions of empowerment with AA members.

Critics offer additional questions for thought: "Can all human pain be collected into one big bundle labeled addiction? Should it be? What about the feelings of pleasure that people derive from food, drugs, alcohol, sex, and a host of other substances and activities?" (Herman, 1988, p. 59). This "movement" of disease-related addictions raises concerns about turning self-destructive behaviors into diseases and normal people (with problems) into victims rather than promoting empowerment of the individual as a socially responsible member of society. Some of the dissatisfaction with the AA model has inspired new but related approaches such as Rational Recovery, Secular Organization for Sobriety, and Women for Sobriety. Fingarette (1988), an outspoken critic of the AA model, argues that alcoholism is a mythical disease. He notes that "what seems to be compassion done in the name of a 'disease' turns out to subvert the drinker's autonomy and will to change, and to exacerbate a serious social problem" (p. 64). Fingarette spells out the social and political pressure that continue to define alcoholism as a disease.

If there are so many problems with AA's model of addiction, why do so many professionals believe that it is an effective alternative for alcoholics? Regardless of all the criticism, AA does attract a large number of individuals who are looking for help and offers them something that appeals to their needs. There may be three primary reasons why AA works, at least for some people (Bufe, 1987; Herman, 1988):

1. *It provides a needed social context for addressing the problem.* In this social context is a safe haven for people to be understood and to be accepted for who they are. Many people in society are demoralized and lonely, and any program that can address those issues will be helpful to people.

2. *It provides a group setting for social support.* In most groups, a critical factor to success is having the feeling that you are not alone—that you are not unique. By expressing feelings and receiving emotional support, people gain confidence that they can take action to solve their problems.

3. *It provides a clear structure—a path to follow.* There is a self-determined behavioral routine that members follow, and this can be critical when your life is literally turned upside down. The steps provide a mechanism to focus one's energy.

CODEPENDENCY

As part of the self-help movement, the codependency movement has become very popular—"the chic neurosis of our time" (Lyon & Greenberg, 1991, p. 435). The term *codependency* refers to a pattern of behavior in which a person's sense of self-worth is based on external referents. Codependents have a strong need for personal validation that is met by excessive caretaking of others, often to the neglect of their own best interests. The excessive caretaking often results in a preoccupation with the other person's feelings. The end result is excessive guilt when the codependent does not act assertive, fears of abandonment, and anxiety over not hurting another's feelings. The term *codependency* was originally applied to the wives of alcoholic husbands who got enmeshed in their spouses' addictions in ways that supported their addiction. For example, a wife may lie to her husband's supervisor, who calls to find out why her husband has not yet arrived for work. In essence, she protects him from the natural consequences of his addiction. Today, the term *codependency* is used very broadly to refer to the general tendency to be preoccupied with another person's needs to the exclusion of one's own (Weiten & Lloyd, 1997).

Why would someone become codependent? The major theorists believe that codependents seek out dysfunctional relationships with troubled individuals so they can fulfill their need for excessive caretaking. Codependency is particularly a concern for women who have an overly strong need for affection and approval. Haaken (1990) suggests that women are more vulnerable than are men to codependency because they are socialized to value support, selflessness, and caretaking.

Similar to AA groups is Codependents Anonymous, a recovery program for people afflicted with codependency. In this context, codependency is seen as a disease, and recovery takes place when individuals admit that they have lost control over the disease (Weiten & Lloyd, 1994).

Weiten and Lloyd (1997, p.8) have reviewed literature on the codependency movement and summarized a number of criticisms that are worth noting:

1. There is no clear definition of *codependency*. In fact, Whitfield (1991) found 23 different definitions. The implication of this discrepancy is that it is difficult to determine who is codependent and who is not (Fischer, Spann, & Crawford, 1991).

2. At present, no good empirical studies exist to support many of the basic concepts of codependency (Wright & Wright, 1991). Also, it is difficult to determine whether codependency is equally relevant across different types of problems. Does codependency operate in the same way for people who are addicted to food, love, or sex?

3. Kaminer (1992) asserts that "every conceivable form of arguably compulsive behavior is classified as an addiction. We are a nation of sexaholics, rage-aholics, shopaholics, and rushaholics" (p. 10). This perspective may demean the concept of addiction.

4. All problems end up being traced back to codependency. For example, Beattie's (1987) book *Codependent No More* lists 234 symptoms of codependency. This is considered an oversimplification of a complex problem, because it seems unlikely that everything can be explained by the processes of addiction and codependency.

5. Some women have raised concerns about the label of codependency as it is applied to women. It may contribute to a pattern of self-blame regarding their own suffering, problems with men, and their husband's problems (Tavris, 1992).

6. Although recovery groups are suggested as the only viable treatment, alternative further research

may uncover additional treatment strategies that are helpful. Perhaps certain people will do better with recovery groups, and others will need to find alternative treatments.

Given these criticisms, is codependency a useful concept? The answer depends on one's perspective. However, it has helped practitioners to better understand complex relationships and how they are tied to addictive behaviors. Certainly, codependency is a popular concept, and to some extent it has accurately described the conflicts that many people feel. Furthermore, recovery groups like AA are likely to provide participants with needed social support to get additional help or learn how to cope better with their problems. Part of that help may be obtained through professional guidance from a social worker or other health professional.

Implications for Practice: When to Seek Professional Help

Under what circumstances would you recommend a person seek professional help? In general, individuals should be encouraged to seek professional treatment when they are under serious psychological distress. First, consider that other forms of social support may be helpful to the individual. These would include family members, church members, and personal friends. Sometimes a person's distress or conflict can be effectively dealt with by these types of natural helpers. However, other times it is best to encourage the person to obtain professional help. The type of help would vary—individual therapy, group therapy, or family therapy—depending on the nature of the concern. Some general guidelines for when to get help might include the following (Bruckner-Gordon, Gangi, & Wallman, 1988):

*   There are no friends or acquaintances to discuss or help the person with his or her problem.

*   The friends or acquaintances indicate that the person's problems are too difficult for them to handle.

*   The person feels extremely overwhelmed and helpless.

*   The person's daily life is affected by his or her psychological distress.

However, given the complexities we all face in modern life, individuals often seek professional help because they feel dissatisfied with life. The following Focus section examines the controversial false memory syndrome, stimulated by the large number of women who sought help for having been sexually abused as a child.

FOCUS ON PSYCHOLOGY

▼

False Memory Syndrome

One of the fascinating stories of the 1990s is the emergence of the False Memory Syndrome Foundation (FMSF). This foundation was established after thousands of women revealed that they had been sexually abused as children. In 1985, a *Los Angeles Times* poll reported that 22% of those sampled had been sexually abused before the age of 18. Many of these women sought refuge in *The Courage to Heal* (Bass & Davis, 1994), a self-help book that profiles more than 100 interviews with survivors of sexual abuse. Although this revelation shocked the country, a new development became equally shocking—the organization of a group of parents who believed that they had been falsely accused of sexual abuse. By 1992, more than 8,000 accused parents were involved with the False Memory Syndrome Foundation. These parents claimed their innocence and were exasperated in their attempts to meet with their sons' and daughters' therapists to tell their part of the story. They were angry about having become completely ostracized by their children and sought some scientific evidence that might help explain their sons' and daughters' misperceived judgments.

The interest in false memory syndrome intensified as several books were published, such as Elizabeth Loftus's *The Myth of Repressed Memory*, Richard Ofshe's *Making Monsters*, and (by a father accused of sexual abuse) Mark Pendergrast's *Victims of Memory*. As Butler (1995) describes it, "the 'incest recovery movement' turned into the 'recovered memory movement.' " Also contributing to the growing interest in the false memory syndrome (FMS) were the court cases won by the parents accused of sexual abuse against the therapists of women who recalled memories of sexual abuse. The validity of the memories were challenged, with the defense that many of the recollections were false creations, born of the patients' suggestibility and their therapists' leading questions (Gorman, 1995). Indeed, the therapists were found to have reinforced the false memories of their clients. By 1994, more than 300 women and men had "recanted" accusations of parental sexual abuse and contacted the False Memory Syndrome Foundation. Not surprisingly, these events raised far more questions than answers. Butler (1995) asks: "Why are a relatively small group of accused parents so close to setting the clinical agenda for millions of genuine abuse survivors and eclipsing public awareness of the more than 130,000 children who are newly sexually victimized each year" (p. 43)?

Butler believes these events may be partly the result of a backlash against therapy—against the idea that anybody can be a victim. And although many therapists may be contributing to this backlash through their ineffective practice, incest cannot be explained by bad therapy alone. As Butler (1995) argues, "it may be easier for the culture to focus its outrage on therapy than to face the larger issue—its failure to protect children, both yesterday's and today's, from real abuse" (p. 79). Child abuse is a real and enormous problem. More than 400,000 reports of verified sexual assaults are filed with authorities each year by teachers and doctors who deal with obviously battered and traumatized youngsters (Gorman, 1995).

(Adapted from Butler, 1995)

SOCIAL DIMENSION

Families, Groups, Support Systems, and Communities

Family diversity was discussed in the chapter on young adulthood, the stage when many adults are beginning their families. Divorce was also addressed, but divorce often leads to new relationships and often to new marriages—with the end result of a **blended family.** A blended family is a newly formed unit consisting of a husband and a wife, one or both of whom have children from a previous marriage. Blended families are a norm in our society today. In middle adulthood, many divorces and remarriages take place, creating blended families. More than 33% of all U.S. children are expected to live in a stepfamily before they reach the age of 18 (Martin, 1995). Adapting to a blended family may require facing unique tasks, because many changes must be confronted. Bray (in Martin, 1995) has found that children, after witnessing conflict, loss, new commitment, and overall transition after a divorce, are at a higher risk for emotional and behavioral problems.

BLENDED FAMILIES OR STEPFAMILIES

As we have seen, divorce and subsequent remarriage is increasingly common, and 60% of partners who divorce have children and become single parents. However, most single parents do not remain so for long. Indeed, within five years of a divorce, three-quarters of single-parent families will become blended families, or **stepfamilies.** Stepfamilies are families whose kinship is determined by remarriage. Many stepfamilies will procreate to add to the family.

Stepfamilies face significant changes as they must adapt to a new marital relationship, continue relationships with prior spouses, and help the children adjust to a difficult family transition. Families must begin with acceptance of loss and changes, readjust expectations about what a family is, facilitate role adjustment for all family members, and coordinate a lifestyle that juggles two family households.

How do such changes affect the children in stepfamilies? Research is just beginning to shed light on this question. In general, following remarriage of their parents, many children develop behavior problems (Santrock, 1992). Behavior problems are more likely in boys, whereas girls often experience an increase in emotional problems. Adolescents can pose special problems for the stepfamily because they are moving toward independence, and the increased stress associated with the stepfamily may adversely affect them. Younger adolescents (ages 10–14) have the most difficult time adjusting because they are wrestling with identity formation issues and tend to be oppositional.

Older adolescents (ages 15+) need less parenting and have less investment in family life (Martin, 1995). Younger children are the most accepting of a new adult, particularly if he or she is a positive influence on the newly formed family.

Of course, some benefits are also associated with a stepfamily. Moving from a single-parent family to a family with a stepfather or a stepmother can add a significant new relationship to the life of the child. In fact, boys seem to do less well in single-parent families than girls do, and when they gain a stepfather, they become less anxious, experience increased in self-esteem, and make a better adjustment in general (Martin, 1995). Girls do not seem to benefit as much in gaining a stepfather. Still, over time both boys and girls make an adjustment to being part of a stepfamily.

Research (Heatherington, 1988; Martin, 1995) suggests that the stepfather is most likely to gain acceptance by his stepchildren if he refrains from directly controlling the child's behavior; this is better left to the mother of the child. "Instead, the new father should first work at establishing a relationship with the child and support the mother in her parenting" (Heatherington, 1988, p. 311). After a stronger relationship is established, then the stepfather can engage in more authoritative parenting.

Adapting to the new stepfamily can be complex and may be assisted by professional counseling services. Couples need to bolster their marital relationship and work to adapt to the changes. Wald (1989) believes that it is essential for social workers to "understand that the characteristics inherent in the stepfamily do not reflect pathological dynamics but rather normal and transitional adjustments to a new situation" (p. 560). Even under the best conditions within the new family, it may take two to four years for the new family members to adjust to one another (Martin, 1995).

Bray (in Martin, 1995) conducted a nine-year longitudinal study to find out how mental health professionals can help families cope with the transition into a blended family. Five specific themes emerged from his study: planning for remarriage, marital relationships, parenting in stepfamilies, stepparent-child relationships, and noncustodial parent issues. Table 11.5 presents a summary of these five coping strategies for newly blended families.

TABLE 11.5	Stepfamily Issues, Coping Strategies, and Suggestions	
Issues	**Coping Strategies**	**Suggestions**
Planning for remarriage	Financial and living arrangements	Couples who hold a "one pot" philosophy about family money and move into a new home together report greater satisfaction.
	Resolve feelings with the previous marriage	Ex-spouses who reframe a remarriage as a "final emotional divorce" prevent further hurt and allow the new couple a fresh start.
	Anticipate parenting changes and decisions	Making decisions as a team will strengthen the new marital bond and defray some future conflicts.
Marriage quality	Give priority to building the marital bond	Couples who create a strong bond first will ultimately benefit the children by creating a stable home environment.
Parenting in stepfamilies	Recognize children's needs	The new stepparent should act as a "buddy" until a solid bond is formed. Negotiating family rules frees the stepparent from acting as disciplinarian.
Stepparent-child relations	Consider children's gender	Both boys and girls prefer verbal affection such as praises and compliments. Girls are uncomfortable with physical closeness. Boys accept a stepfather more quickly than girls do.
Noncustodial parent issues	Maintain positive relationship	The less a parent visits, the more abandoned a child will feel. Speaking against an ex-spouse undermines a child's self-esteem and puts the child in the unjust position of having to defend a parent.

(Martin, 1995)

MARRIAGE AND INTIMATE RELATIONSHIPS AT MIDLIFE

Many couples at midlife are launching their children into adulthood. For the partners who have been parents throughout much of their lives, this signals a significant change—often referred to as the *empty nest syndrome*. However, this reference confers some outdated notions on this stage of life. Originally, the empty nest syndrome was of particular concern for the mother who had devoted herself full-time to raising children. Of course, that picture has changed with the large increase in the number of working mothers. Studies have found that, rather than being "empty," this stage can be fulfilling for both men and women. So, rather than seeing marital satisfaction decline, research has found that it begins a steady climb upward in the postchildbearing years (Brubaker, 1990).

Why would satisfaction increase as children are launched into adulthood? Rollins (1989) believes that the stresses associated with children are due to "roles overload," whereby parents with children at home neglect their roles as married partners, and that this situation has a negative effect on marital satisfaction. Over-

load occurs in these families because communication and companionship are sacrificed in order to respond to the caregiving role as parents. The implication is that "professional helpers can be alert to marital problems of their clients at midlife that are related to poor communication and lack of companionship" (Hunter & Sundel, 1989, p. 181).

How do love and intimate relationships change at midlife? One common explanation is that the nature of intimacy changes and couples develop more affectionate and companionate love. Whereas, in young adulthood much of the focus on intimacy revolves around romantic love, physical attraction, and passion, by midlife many adults are more concerned about maintaining relationships from the perspective of mutual sharing, security, and loyalty (Reedy, Birren, & Schaie, 1981).

Is there such a thing as a good marriage that has survived? Judith Wallerstein (1995) notes that many people claim they have never seen a good marriage and cannot imagine how one would look. Her research examined the lives of affluent married couples who have experienced satisfying, enduring marriages. What she offers is confirmation that a good marriage requires a lot of hard work and dedication. Without a strong appreciation for the other person, a sense of companionship and loyalty, sexual attraction, and empathy, you are less likely to have a successful marriage.

Of course, many middle adults' lives move in different directions, and this creates distance between them. Each partner may be seeking different goals and commitments that make the development of mutual sharing difficult. For example, the wife may be seeking growth through work and other commitments, while the husband may be seeking stronger emotional support and shared activities. As Wallerstein (1995) points out, the survival of the marriage may depend on the commitment each spouse has attained over the years and each one's ability to appreciate and understand the other person's needs. In many respects, it is during middle adulthood that the couple may want to review and renew their commitment to the marriage. Although a couple may face important changes, divorce is much less likely to occur at midlife than at an earlier point in life (Rollins, 1989).

In middle adulthood, many individuals are not married or connected to a significant other or partner. They may be lifelong singles or recently divorced or widowed. However, at midlife, these individuals also seek relationships that are mutual, loyal, and companionate. As Lindsey (1982) found, most single adults have at least one significant other of the same or opposite sex who is part of their "adopted" family. Such support is critical to the individual's life satisfaction and mental health (Lindsey, 1982).

The following Focus section takes a closer look at marital satisfaction among African-Americans.

FOCUS ON MULTICULTURALISM

▼

Marital Satisfaction Among African-Americans

Most of the research on marital satisfaction has been conducted with couples who are white, middle-class, and affluent. However, African-Americans have a higher divorce rate compared with whites at every income level. Research by Broman (1993) sought to ex-

amine what factors predict marital quality among African-Americans. Results found that, for both husbands and wives, the perception that family income was adequate to meet the family's needs was predictive of marital satisfaction. For African-American women, economic adequacy was related to how positively they assessed their husband's role performance. In addition to economic adequacy, the following factors were also considered important: Providing emotional support predicted marital satisfaction and harmony for both men and women; for African-American men, having a smaller number of children was related to greater marital satisfaction, but for African-American women, it wasn't the number of children but the degree of problems associated with raising the children; personal development and the opportunity to express individual freedoms were positively related to marital satisfaction for both husbands and wives; and for African-American women, job satisfaction was correlated with marital satisfaction.

(Broman, 1993)

EXTRAMARITAL AFFAIRS

For many men and women who struggle with changes in midlife, an extramarital affair offers an opportunity to rediscover themselves. Married couples often have established routine patterns that become unexciting and boring. At midlife, they are often searching for something new and different, and an affair may offer them a unique opportunity to rediscover different aspects of themselves. Such affairs may be related to seeking greater fulfillment in personal relationships. An affair may emerge out of anxiety over physical aging and a need to perceive oneself as still attractive. For men, an affair may be an opportunity to deny their declining sexual performance. As Goldstein and Landau (1990) aptly put it, "if either a man or a woman is haunted by the sense of time running out, if either abruptly realizes that they have spent much of their lives doing what others wanted them to do, then either one is a likely candidate to follow wherever a forbidden impulse leads" (p. 189).

Santrock (1989) describes how, for the next generation of midlife women, sexual relationships outside of marriage are likely to continue to increase because of such factors as greater acceptance of women as sexual beings, family changes that leave many women without men, men's shorter life expectancy, and the changing role of women in the workforce. "Extramarital sex will frequently occur in the transition out of marriage and into new sexual and marital arrangements" (Santrock, 1989, p. 471). Midlife women may be increasingly interested in extramarital sex, not because they are unhappy in their marriage but because they are seeking excitement and variety in their sex lives. By participating in the workforce, married women become more equal partners in the marriage, and single women increase their opportunity to access potential partners. In addition, Santrock believes that, because of the above-mentioned changes, midlife women will enjoy solitary sex more frequently than their older sisters or mothers did.

How common are extramarital affairs or instances of nonmonogamy in couple relationships? Affairs are least likely to occur with wives; 14% reported having an extramarital affair since the beginning of a relationship. For men, the percentage was just 8% more; a total of 22% report having affairs (Americans for Divorce Reform, 1998). This represents 3% to 4% of all married relationships. For gay men, nonmonogamous relationships were extremely common—more than 80% report instances of such relationships. Lesbians were only a little more likely to have nonmonogamous relationships (28%) when compared with husbands and wives.

PARENT/ADULT-CHILD RELATIONSHIPS

Any discussion of the family in middle adulthood must address two aspects: how middle-aged parents relate to their adult children and how middle-aged parents relate to their aging parents. It is for this reason that middle adulthood is seen as the phase in life that provides continuity in the family's identity. Middle-aged adults become the critical link between their aging parents and their young adult children. They provide the foundation for the bridge that links the generations.

As in other stages in the family life cycle, the family continues to be a primary source of social support, with parents and their children providing important mutual assistance to one another (Lemme, 1995). The

mutual support comes in a variety of ways; for example, parents may provide needed baby-sitting when grandchildren are small, and children may provide needed care to parents during times of illness or hospitalization. As Lemme (1995) points out, "this reciprocal assistance may shift in direction over the life of the family, focusing more on children in the earlier stages and flowing more toward parents as they age" (p. 283). Social support is a critical link in the long-term relationship between middle-aged parents and their children and between middle-aged adults and their aging parents.

MIDDLE-AGED PARENTS AND THEIR ADOLESCENT CHILDREN

> When I was a boy of 14 my father was so ignorant I could hardly stand to have the man around. But when I got to be 21, I was astonished at how much he learnt in 7 years.
> —Mark Twain

Small children tend to see parents as all-powerful and all-knowing. When those children become adolescents, suddenly their parents no longer seem so competent or knowledgeable. Throughout this book, we have been concentrating on how parents influence their children's development; but how do children, especially adolescent children, influence their middle-aged parents?

Research by Laurence Steinberg (1995) has found that the most difficult time for parents is when their children are between the ages of 11 and 14. Steinberg states that parents' midlife crises develop most often when their children reach this age. In fact, 40% of parents experience a decrease in psychological well-being during their children's adolescence. Also, marital satisfaction declines during this time. What changes in the parents and the children account for these midlife problems?

For one thing, parents experience more economic problems during their children's adolescence because teenage children cost more. Parents may be dealing with career decisions and questioning life goals during this time. They also may be concerned with their health and appearance. Middle-aged parents may feel they are becoming less attractive while watching their adolescents become more attractive. One mother remarked, "You know you are a middle-aged woman when you go out in public and the men who used to flirt with you now flirt with your daughter."

Children are also going through changes at this time. Whereas younger children are more compliant and easy to handle, adolescent children become noncompliant, oppositional, and resistant to parental standards. They may question parental demands and challenge decisions. The child may become oversensitive to adult remarks. Adolescents begin to push for more independence and autonomy from parental control. Many adolescents become larger than their parents. A single mother may wonder how to control a son who towers over her.

All these changes lead to conflict and power struggles between adolescents and their middle-aged parents. And this conflict increases the stress level in the lives of these middle-aged adults. Steinberg has found that these problems occur in all family types. Single mothers have more problems with their sons, and they tend to let their sons go their own way when power struggles arise. In stepfamilies, more problems exist with daughters, who may feel a loss of closeness with the mother when she remarries. And in intact two-parent families, both parents may face a loss of control of their children, jealousy of their children's accomplishments, or fear of the children making the same mistakes the parents made (Dubin, 1994).

Steinberg has found that being involved in a satisfying career and having outside interests and activities help middle-aged parents cope with this difficult time. Patience and understanding become critical when parenting adolescents. As Mark Twain tells us, when children grow up, their parents amazingly regain their competence and knowledge.

MIDDLE-AGED PARENTS AND THEIR ADULT CHILDREN

By midlife, many parents have raised their children to adults and must now shift their relationship from one of parent-child to one of parent-friend. In large part as a result of longevity, parents and their children are likely to grow old together. This change is positive; most parents report an improved relationship with their sons and daughters as they become young adults. Most adult children feel "close" or "very close" to their parents. Middle-aged parents and their adult children have frequent contact and emotionally satisfying relationships, but exchanges of practical or financial assistance are uncommon. And while cultural differences in such relationships have been assumed, researchers have not been able to document consistent results (Lye, 1996).

However, at midlife, parents are often in the ironic situation of addressing the difficulties of raising children and at the same time discussing shared difficulties with difficult and impossible parents. It is in this sense that middle-aged adults are often referred to as the *sandwich generation.* Although many parents may perceive their children as friends when they become adults, does having a good relationship with one's parents make a difference on a young adult's psychological adjustment?

Baruch and Barnett (1983) studied middle-aged women to examine how a woman's overall well-being was related to her relationship with her mother. The results showed that middle-aged women are better adjusted psychologically when they have a positive relationship with their mothers. In particular, those women with positive relationships had greater self-esteem, were less anxious and less depressed than women who did not have satisfactory relationships with their mothers.

Middle-aged women also play an important role as *kinkeeper,* keeping the ties between families. It often becomes the middle-aged woman's role to bring the family together for family traditions and celebrations. This role is probably related to the strong mother-daughter bond that is consistent over the life span (Troll, 1986). Adult daughters are more likely than adult sons to live nearby and to exchange help with their mothers (Cicirelli, 1983). Daughters are also more likely to be the keepers of family symbols, photographs, and heirlooms than are sons.

MIDDLE-AGED ADULTS AND THEIR AGING PARENTS

It is too late to turn back. I have set in motion events that are tumbling me along like a broken branch in floodtide. I have run out of choices. I look at my 94-year-old mother. Her thin, hunched body is dwarfed amid a welter of crates, cartons of books, piles of possessions to take to the Salvation Army, and other stacks of worthless items too precious to leave behind. Her expression matches the disheveled room. She doesn't know it yet, but by this time next week, she will be in a nursing home in Colorado, a thousand miles from here, whatever life remains to her drastically changed. The cost of dying, particularly if one does it slowly, is prohibitive in California (Hartney, 1989, p. 39).

As the this quote points out, middle-aged adults must face the task of caring for their aging parents— a task that can sometimes be very difficult. With the increase in life expectancy, there is a greater need for adult children to care for their aging parents, who may need assistance with daily activities such as eating, dressing, housework, and finances. Since 1980, the number of individuals needing assistance has doubled (U.S. Bureau of the Census, 1990). Most often when an elderly parent needs some assistance, it is family members who provide the needed medical and personal care.

Not only has the number of older people who need caregiving increased, but the nature of caregiving required is also changing (Pearlin et al., 1990). Because of rapid medical advances, individuals are much less likely to die from acute causes and instead are more likely to die from a chronic illness, like cancer (Lemme, 1995). Furthermore, when an individual gets a chronic illness, he or she is more likely to live longer than in the past. The implication for middle-aged adults is that the caretaking role is extended over a longer period of time. Therefore, adult children provide not only longer care to their parents but also more difficult care (Brody, 1985).

Providing needed assistance is a shared expectation of both adult children and their aging parents. Harmon and Blieszner (1990) found that more than 85% of adult children agreed with the following responsibilities they should assume: help understand resources, give emotional support, talk over matters of importance, make room in home for emergency, sacrifice personal freedom, and be together on special occasions. Aging parents also endorsed these same responsibilities, but adult children had a greater sense of obligation than their parents expected of them.

Parent caring, as it is sometimes called, is most often left to the daughter in the family. In this culture, women are expected to assume the role of caretaker, managing and nurturing the family. Many women assume dual roles of both mother and grandmother, caring for elderly parents and helping adult children manage their families (Arlington & Troll, 1984). Most often, women play an essential role in making sure family members receive proper health care, providing transportation, arranging and planning family gatherings, providing emotional support to aging parents, and talking with family members to keep everyone abreast of new developments in the family.

This picture of the adult child caring for elderly parents has been refuted by media reports, which too often have portrayed the adult child as neglecting or abandoning his or her parents. Gerontologists have pointed to research that shows children attending to parents' needs and providing essential caregiving functions (Brody, 1981). Also, most of what we know about caregiving comes from research on middle-class European Americans, and there may be similarities and differences depending on the ethnic group studies. For example, Pueblo-Indian caregivers report similar experiences of role strain (Hennessy & John, 1995), conflict with the family, and difficulties in managing care as do European caregivers. However, the Indian caregivers do not experience social constraints, limits on personal freedom, or embarrassment.

Although we are emphasizing caregiving here, many older people remain in good or excellent health. Only 5% of adults who are 65 years and older suffer from organic brain syndrome, and only 10% show signs of dementia. Older persons like living alone and want to function quite independently (Lemme, 1995). In fact, research by Stueve and O'Donnell (1984) found that the notion of "caught in the middle" may be quite inaccurate for our understanding of parent-child relationships. This notion makes sense only in the context of a traditional life-cycle approach, and, as these researchers found, many women today do not fit into the typical life-cycle stages. For example, many women in their 40s and 50s may be parenting adolescent children, but an increasing number of women this age are also just beginning their families. Still, women are expected to provide care for elderly parents and often for other elderly kin as well—including parents-in-law (Stueve & O'Donnell, 1984).

In fact, Aneshensel and colleagues (1995) point out that parent care is best conceptualized as an unexpected career. A **caregiving career** often includes caring for children, caring for elderly parents and relatives, and providing care for a dependent husband. Caregiving is not simply a one-time, limited episode; indeed, caregiving has important implications for women who provide this care without receipt of wages, pension benefits, or other resources (Lemme, 1995). How the caregiving duties of middle-aged women is going to affect their participation in the labor force is an important consideration for their future. Beck (cited in Lemme, 1995) states that the average woman will spend 17 years caring for children and 18 years caring for aging parents.

FOCUS ON DISABILITIES

Families of Adults with Mental Retardation

As social workers or practitioners, we will most likely work with adults with disabilities in an institutional setting. Have you ever thought about people who are being cared for in their parents' home, long after they reach adulthood? Of the estimated 2 million people with developmental disabilities living in the United States, only 15.6% live in institutional settings. Of those living in non-institutional settings, the majority live with their families. Consequently, families play a significant role in the service delivery system. Family living often promotes community integration, employment, social relationships, and other benefits that are not easily provided in the social services system.

There are several reasons to become more knowledgeable about families who continue to care for their child past the age of 21. First, researchers have found that, although older caregivers of adults with mental retardation experience stress and personal burden, they have greater stability, better morale, and better health than caregivers of elderly people. Support resources have been found to play a significant role in reducing perceived caregiver burden. It has long been

known that strong formal or informal social supports can buffer the effect of stress. Research has shown that support services can have a positive influence on the family's ability to provide care to a child with developmental disabilities and can postpone the need for out-of-home placement.

There are several implications for social workers who work with families of adults with mental retardation and other developmental disabilities. First, social workers who work for public social services must continue to identify and serve the families with the greatest needs. Second, social workers must learn to listen to how the families define their situations, explore with them resources that are available to them, and support them in deciding which resources would be most beneficial. Third, social workers can connect families with parent support groups; these groups provide emotional support and teach parents to use their own strengths and develop coping skills that help them face their particular difficulties. Finally, social workers can serve as advocates for the development of services and support for families of adult children with mental retardation. Social workers can advocate within the social services agency on behalf of the families, connect families with legal advocates or attorneys, provide families with information, and train families to advocate on their own behalf.

(Adapted from Hayden & Goldman, 1996)

Implications for Practice: Adjusting to the Role of Caregiver

Being a caregiver can be a stressful experience. Although being a caregiver is most often a satisfying experience, it is also the kind of experience that provides constant stress and often produces mental and physical consequences for the caregiver (Aneshensel et al., 1995). Twenty years ago little was known about effective caregiving. Mace and Rabin's *The 36-Hour Day* (1981) was a breakthrough in documenting the difficulties of caring for a family member with dementia. Because so many older people will need caregivers in the future, Peak and Toseland (1992) refer to caregiving as a social problem. As they note, many caregivers are unprepared for their role. Also, depending on the nature of the illness, caregivers may need to be prepared for rapid degeneration of the person being cared for. Daily routines such as helping with feeding, toileting, and lifting can become difficult. From a psychosocial perspective, caregivers often feel abandoned by their friends and family members and may have feelings of depression, anxiety, self-blame, and general stress (Peak & Toseland, 1992).

An important source of support for caregivers is a social support group. Such a group may provide needed emotional support, teach coping skills, and reduce anxiety and stress. Toseland and Rossiter (1989) suggest that a support group can provide the following functions to caregivers.

- Provide a much-needed respite from caregiving
- Reduce isolation and loneliness
- Provide an opportunity to share feelings and experiences in a supportive atmosphere
- Affirm and validate feelings and thoughts about the caregiving situation
- Instill hope
- Educate caregivers about the effects of chronic disabilities and available community resources
- Encourage a mutual sharing of information about effective coping strategies
- Help caregivers to become motivated to use systematic problem-solving procedures and coping strategies to reduce or eliminate the stress they are experiencing

In caregiving support groups, social workers are expected to provide supportive interventions that stress such skills as ventilation of stressful experiences in an understanding and supportive environment, validation and confirmation of similar caregiving experiences, affirmation of members' ability to cope with the situation, praise for providing the care, and support and understanding of members' struggles with difficult situations (Peak & Toseland, 1992).

GRANDPARENTHOOD

Many parents have the opportunity to be grandparents. Indeed, given the longevity of older adults, most will live long enough to be involved with grandchildren, and some will live long enough to be involved with their great-grandchildren. Grandparents approach their new roles from different perspectives. Some are interested mostly in being fun-seekers, having mostly informal and playful interactions, while others are surrogate parents, assuming major child-care responsibilities (Neugarten & Weinstein, 1964). Grandparents can serve as important role models of aging and integrity (Kivnick, 1986). They offer the family a sense of continuity.

The role shift to grandparents can require relearning old skills and adapting to new ways of parenting. Grandparents may be called on to help calm a fussy baby, change a diaper, heat a bottle of milk, and teach toilet training to a toddler. Often the grandparent's approach is different from that of the parent, and the differences between them need to be worked out. Being a grandparent, therefore, involves new roles that affect family relationships (Severino et al., 1986). Grandparenting can be very rewarding if it is approached with experience and wisdom.

The experience of being a grandparent may offer a sense of completion to the middle-aged adult. Being a grandparent may reflect a person's influence across the generations, providing to him or her an affirmation of values and a sense of general satisfaction (Cherlin & Furstenberg, 1986). Grandparents often are able to share their experience and wisdom in childrearing, offer emotional support to the parents, and achieve satisfaction in their grandchildren's accomplishments (Neugarten & Weinstein, 1964). This new role offers new opportunities and new learning. The tasks of grandparenting can lead to self-reflection on one's own parenting history and call for new competencies.

SOME GRANDPARENTS BECOME PARENTS AGAIN—GRANDPARENTS RAISING THEIR GRANDCHILDREN

This situation brings forth special concerns (Kelly, 1993): It's like turning back the clock to 20 years ago, yet we're a lot older. We're back to finding a sitter if we have to go out. We're back to having very little, or should I say, no time to ourselves. I am too old for the young mothers, and the people I grew old with do not have grandchildren with them all the time. We have nothing in common anymore. This situation makes me feel like a misfit. I should be going to senior citizens' activities instead of parent-teacher meetings. What worries me most is what should happen to him if I should die.

When young parents cannot care for their children because of such factors as substance abuse, mental illness, criminal activity, poverty, homelessness, or AIDS, frequently it is the grandparents who end up raising the children. Though many grandparents willingly accept the responsibility for their children's children, this responsibility often brings added stress. Kelly (1993) discusses the stress associated with the demands of parenthood at a later age:

- Older adults raising their children's children face increased family stress at all levels. These grandparents may worry about their own children, who may be in trouble with addiction or illness. These older adults may also be coping with their own elderly parents who need care. Now they have small children to raise who may have been abused or neglected. These children may need extra care and support.

- In general, social support mediates stress for parents. But grandparents raising their grandchildren may lose their support network. They are often isolated from their peers, who are no longer raising children.

- The grandparents may worry about living long enough to raise their grandchildren or about becoming ill and being unable to care for their grandchildren.

Because of such stress factors, grandparents may experience problems in relating to their grandchildren. Such stress can lead to a decrease in caregiver-child interactions, which can then affect the children's development (Crnic & Greenberg, 1990).

Organizations such as the American Association of Retired Persons (AARP) have established formal support systems for grandparents raising grandchildren. AARP publishes a newsletter and offers a grandparent information center.

In general, grandparenting can play a critical role in adapting to the aging process. For many grandparents, this new role replaces impending retirement and concern over loss of responsibilities. Being a grandparent contributes to one's personal influences across the generations, and in this sense it may help grandparents become more comfortable with their own death. It provides an acceptable opportunity to pass on one's cultural heritage and communicate special meanings to grandchildren.

The following Focus section describes the role that African-American grandmothers play in multigenerational households.

FOCUS ON MULTICULTURALISM

African-American Grandmothers

What role do African-American grandmothers play in multigenerational households? Research by Pearson, Hunter, Ensminger, and Kellam (1990) sought to answer this question by examining the role grandmothers play when living with their grandchildren. The researchers found the following results.

- One-third of all families in the study were extended families, and 10% of the households included grandmothers.

- Grandmothers were most involved in parenting functions when there was no mother in the home. In general, parenting involvement differed as a function of family structure.

- Employment of the grandmother did not influence her participation in parenting.

The types of roles grandmothers played in their parenting functions included both authoritarian and nurturing.

THE MEN'S MOVEMENT

Almost everyone is familiar with the women's movement and its influence on American society, but we have only recently been exposed to the men's movement. Although the men's movement is current, it emerged in a different way from the women's movement. In

African-American men are actively examining positive black male role models.

particular, the men's movement seems aimed more toward personal change rather than external change (Graham, 1992). Perhaps best known in the men's movement is Robert Bly's book *Iron John* (1992). The story of *Iron John* is about a boy who helps a primitive man escape from the adults who are holding him captive and goes with him to a journey in the woods. Here the boy grows to manhood. This story is about the unavailability and the distance many men feel toward their fathers. Bly is addressing the influence of his own abusive and alcoholic father. Bly's concern is about the contemporary separation of boys from their fathers. He contends that many mothers look to their sons for the emotional satisfaction their husbands deny them. The son feels ashamed when he realizes he cannot soothe his mother, and at the same time he distrusts his father and other men. Bly's book highlights how our culture contributes to the separation of boys from their fathers, which has led to an absence of appropriate masculine identity. His book has spawned a movement of men who are seeking to recover their lost manhood by denouncing contemporary culture and rediscovering their lost masculine identity.

Similarly, Sam Keen's (1991) *Fire in the Belly* is about the process of being a man. Keen, like Bly, suggests that men must break free of cultural boundaries in

order to reassert their masculinity and male role. Keen states than men's problems result from the "primal power that women wielded over men because of the imperfect separation of man from the mother" (p. 17). Many theorists believe that, in childhood, boys prematurely dissociate from their mothers and enter the aggressive, competitive world of men. The boy desires to turn to his father but finds him emotionally distant and unavailable. The result is that his developing masculinity is defined by turning away from anything feminine.

The previous popular image was of the sensitive man. As Graham (1992) notes, "the sensitive-man model was accepted and emulated by few men, and it did not seem that many women found it completely satisfying" (p. 840). To Bly, this image of the sensitive man is what has robbed men of their righteous anger and their ability to act with certainty and has disconnected them from their identity and their instincts toward manhood (Graham, 1992).

The interest in men's issues is also being examined within specific ethnic groups. For example, in 1990 the National Council of African-American Men, an organization that fosters understanding of black males, was formed. More recently, as mentioned in the last chapter, there was the Million Man March, where African-American men bonded together and marched in Washington, D.C. Particularly relevant is the effect of racism on gender-role development. One program receiving increasing attention is the Afrocentric socialization model—whereby black youth are matched with positive black male role models to help them develop more effective coping responses.

Implications for Practice: Men in Therapy

Male and female stereotypes of men can have a significant effect on a man's use of social services. As Sleek (1994) states, "men are about as comfortable in therapy as penguins in the desert" (p. 6). Men seek mental health services about half as frequently as women do. When men do enter treatment, they often are uncomfortable with self-disclosure and emotional exploration. Bogard (1991), in her book *Feminist Approaches for Men in Family Therapy*, describes her experience of reaching an impasse with a defensive male client. Bogard confronted her stereotype that "men can't do more" when a colleague confronted her about why she stopped challenging the client. Bogard now argues that men's ability to grow is seriously untapped by mental health practitioners. Female practitioners often describe male clients as dependent, childlike, and distant. She found that women often do the emotional work for their male clients rather than challenging them to articulate their feelings.

Male practitioners also have negative stereotypes about their male clients. In a recent study by McPhee (cited in Sleek, 1994), therapists were asked to diagnose, based on individual vignettes, male and female potential clients with different jobs and income. Both male and female therapists diagnosed more serious problems—for example, affective or personality disorders—in the men than in the women, even though the vignettes described symptoms characteristic of adjustment disorder.

Mental health practitioners are now realizing the need to make treatment male-friendly. This can be accomplished through several avenues, such as helping the reluctant male client move toward instrumental changes rather than stressing emotional expression. And the process of seeking treatment can be reframed as a sign of strength. Also, many practitioners believe that men's therapy groups work better than individual therapy for many men. Recent books such as *Men in Groups* (Andronio, 1997) and a new psychotherapy for traditional men (Brooks, 1998) document the increasing emphasis of group work with men.

Attempts to make treatment more accessible to men may be critical to creating successful adjustment for many men. A recent program by Ivanoff (High rate of suicide among New York City police, 1994) attempted to respond to the high rate of suicide among personnel of the New York police department. Because most police officers are male, Ivanoff had to respond to the resistance of the officers to seeking treatment. Indeed, Ivanoff found that officers are trained not to show signs of weakness and not to discuss problems or feelings. The project had to encourage officers who needed help to seek it. The method used to address officers' reluctance included viewing a film that examines the lives of three officers who considered suicide. The reluctant officers reported that they were more willing to seek help for themselves and for fellow officers after having viewed this film and having participated in a training session.

CAREER DEVELOPMENT AND JOB SATISFACTION

Consider the following comments from Kyle, a 51-year-old man (Bergoquist, Greenberg, & Klaum, 1993).

> I have come through the printing industry, from apprentice to journeyman, learning the trade and going through the changes we have experienced in the industry. It's been quite an experience. But my success was moving through the management part of the job, and this has been most rewarding to me. It certainly broadened my scope, and being part of the challenges of the future has been a great lesson. . . . I'm where I am today because of the way I do my job, and I feel I have been recognized for that. This job is a continuing learning process. I don't happen to think that, just because I have this job, I have reached the goal I set for myself in life. I feel that there is a lot more for me to do and still a lot more for me to learn (pp. 120–121).

Development in work and career is a major context for adult development (Newman & Newman, 1995). Regardless of the nature of the work, unskilled or professional, it becomes a central focus around which adult life revolves. Indeed, work often provides a growing sense of satisfaction as one gets older (Warr, 1992). Our jobs may mean more to us, and as a consequence, we are more serious about our work and derive more satisfaction from it—which is aptly described in the preceding quote.

Unfortunately, more and more husbands and wives are in conflict over the amount of time men put into their work. Waters and Saunders (1996) consider this a conflict because families are no longer willing to consider the husband's contribution to the family in terms of financial support only. And, more and more men are uncomfortable with this concept as well, although they do not know how to "back off" from work without feeling less of a man. When put in the context of today's working world, which seems to "ask more for less," men's awareness that they need to be more accountable to their spouses and families for both active contributions and emotional awareness has the effect of putting them "right in the middle." Many men realize that they are less willing to brush off family needs for work demands, and at the same time, families are less willing to be brushed off.

Men tend to confuse what they do with who they are (Waters & Saunders, 1996). Historically, men have been able to express their manhood through their work. Therefore, letting up on work can imply being less of a man. Consider this man's dilemma: "If I put myself and my family seriously in the picture, I feel like I'm just not really trying at work, like everyone else is going to get ahead of me and I'm washed up. I know it's illogical, but it's like work is all or nothing—either I go 100% or I'm a has-been" (Waters & Saunders, 1996, p. 47).

WORK AS A WAY OF LIFE

What you do in your job is likely to have a major effect on your overall lifestyle. First, work is going to determine your **socioeconomic status.** Socioeconomic status is a common research variable that combines economic status or level of income, social status or level of education, and work status as measured by your occupation (Dutton & Levine, 1989). Our world is centered on our work—it determines where we live, who we socialize with, what schools we take our children to, and it contributes to our sense of self.

Our work also sets forth the kind of expectations that society has for us. It determines the social appropriateness of how we dress, behave, and evaluate ourselves (Lemme, 1995). So, our work is certainly more than just a job; it gives direction to our overall lifestyle and is central to our identity. Studs Terkel (1974), who interviewed men and women about their work, concluded that work is "a search for daily meaning as well as daily bread, for recognition as well as cash, for astonishment rather than torpor; in short, for a sort of life rather than a Monday through Friday sort of dying. Perhaps immortality, too, is part of the quest" (p. xiii).

FOCUS ON SPIRITUALITY

The Spirituality of Work

Matthew Fox, a priest and director of the Institute in Culture and Creation Spirituality, has provided an out-

line of a spirituality of work in his book, *The Reinvention of Work* (1994). He discusses how work and life are part and parcel of the same thing: "Life and livelihood should not be separated but flow from the same source, which is spirit, for both life and livelihood are about spirit. Spirit means life, and both life and livelihood are about living in depth, living with meaning, purpose, joy and a sense of contributing to the greater community" (p. 206). For Fox, developing a spirituality of work consists of bringing life and livelihood back together again. As Thomas Aquinas said, "to live well is to work well." Fox developed a spirituality-of-work questionnaire that helps people consider the role of spirituality in their work.

Some of the questions from the spirituality of work questionnaire include (Fox, 1994, pp. 309–310):

1. Do I experience joy in my work?
2. Do others experience joy or a result of my work?
3. Is my work actively creating good work for others?
4. How does my work connect to the Great Work of the Universe?
5. What inner work have I been involved in over the past five years?
6. What do I learn at work?
7. If I suddenly received an inheritance of $300,000, would I immediately cease my work?
8. What am I doing to reinvent the profession in which I work?
9. How can my family and I lead a simpler lifestyle, get along on less, and enjoy life more?
10. What is sacred about the work I do?

These are only 10 of 30 questions in the spirituality-of-work questionnaire. However, these questions do allow one to examine one's attitude toward spirituality and work.

CAREER CHANGES AT MIDLIFE

The popular idea holds that many individuals change their careers at midlife. Indeed, many fascinating stories have been written about people who gave up jobs earning hundreds of thousands of dollars to move to the country and reconsider their values. But how many people really make such dramatic life changes? Estimates are that only about 10% of men and women change jobs at midlife. What are some of the reasons that motivate men and women to change careers?

Newman and Newman (1995) have identified five reasons that may lead to a change in work-related goals. First, some careers may just end during middle adulthood; the individual cannot perform the duties of the job—for example, professional athletes. The second reason reflects the popular stereotype of the midlife crisis—that adults decide that their work is not meaningful to them anymore and go in search of a different, more meaningful, career. Third, midlife career change can occur because the individual believes he or she has succeeded as much as possible in a job, perhaps because changing technology has created the need for specialized training to keep up with the job. Fourth, particularly for women, a career change may come when children are "launched" and there is more time to commit to a career. Also, women may become **displaced homemakers,** forced into the job market by the circumstances of divorce or widowhood. Fifth, because of economic pressures, the workforce may be restructured, requiring that some workers be laid off.

The idea of the midlife career change is a central thesis in Levinson's (1978) theory of adult development. Levinson suggests that many adults become reflective about their experience in a job and must reconcile their idealistic hopes with realistic possibilities. Given the amount of time left in a career, can the individual reach his or her goals? When this issue becomes a central focus, it can be the motivating factor behind serious midlife changes, such as career changes, extramarital affairs, divorce, and alcoholism.

GENDER, WORK, AND THE FAMILY: DIFFERENT PATHWAYS

Typically, men have pursued a narrow career pathway for most of their adult lives. At midlife, they may begin to question their accomplishments at work, but they may also question their contribution to the family. At midlife, a common male reaction is to reevaluate one's role in the family in relation to one's commitment to

work. Men may regret not having spent more time with their children. For example, the reflections of Alex, a 50-year-old, are common:"We had a good family. It could have been much better if I had put much more into it. I've learned to take the important things more seriously than I had before. Too many times my family took a back seat to my work" (Bergquist, Greenberg, & Klaum, 1993, p. 93).

For women, the potential for midlife career changes is greater because they have not had such a narrow career pathway. Many women have had an **interrupted career** that began before motherhood, was interrupted by childrearing, and was then re-established when full-time work resumed (Golan, 1986). Other women start professional training while raising children and then move into a full-time career. The implication for this pattern is significant in terms of career progress and earning potential for later life (Hatch, 1990). Because retirement income is directly related to work history, women's earning potential has long-term economic consequences for them. This fact, coupled with increasing caregiving functions, is likely to contribute to poverty among older women (Davis, Grant, & Rowland, 1990).

When a midlife career or schooling change does take place, it is likely to have special significance. A number of benefits are enjoyed by many women who return to or start a career. Apter (1995), in her study of midlife women, explains it this way: "They not only learned new facts, but gained new perspectives. In learning how to run a business, for example, some women felt they were gaining access to an entire range of concepts that they had previously thought themselves incapable of mastering. In studying social theory or psychology or literature, they gathered new tools for reflecting on the problems that had long plagued them. Moreover, the new knowledge and new skills would, they hoped, lead to new opportunities for further friendships, further self-confirming experiences, and make further knowledge possible" (p. 154). Many women at midlife pursue schooling as a means of continued growth and change. The pursuit of learning does not just enhance one's education. It reflects something more personal—an opportunity to rediscover strengths and become empowered (Hohman, 1995).

These kinds of changes may create conflict within the family. This may be particularly true when a husband is pulling back from his career and wants to spend more time with his family and his wife wants to spend more time pursuing school or a career. Also, the woman's shift in direction may mean that she will put less emphasis on other more family-oriented roles. The degree to which work and family roles conflict depends in part on how the partners view each other's participation in the world of work (Newman & Newman, 1995). For example, in a traditional household, a husband may support his wife's new career only to the extent that it is viewed as supplementary to his own career. Successful adaptation will depend on how partners resolve the changes in roles and the flexibility with which they approach these changes.

Multicultural and Gender Considerations

Cavanaugh (1997) raises the question, "to what extent is it important or beneficial to maintain ethnic identity across adulthood" (p. 52)? In many respects, the notion of ethnic identity is contrary to the idea of assimilation into the larger society (Cool, 1987). Research with older adults has found that ethnic identity can serve as a source of support for the individual. At the point in life when people are becoming increasingly removed from society, ethnic identity is likely to provide a strong source of support (Royce, 1982). Indeed, research by Luborsky and Rubinstein (1987; 1990) found that ethnic identity became more important later in life than it was in early adulthood. Qualitative interviews with older widows uncovered the manner in which ethnic identity became stronger as the individual aged. For example, individuals discussed how, after the death of a spouse, they adopted the role of family historian. As a consequence, they reflected on the importance of family heritage and traditions, which often led to a rediscovery of the significance of their ethnic roots. Also, individuals discussed how reexamining the past had to be integrated with their current selves. This process becomes increasingly important as people age and move toward an overall sense of integrity in their life.

The following Focus section describes a Puerto Rican–American woman's experience of being a person of color who is a professional social worker.

FOCUS ON NARRATIVE

A Bicultural Life: Living in Two Worlds

"It is strange to have lived in the country for almost 40 years and have someone I've just met ask me, 'Where do you come from?' as if I had just arrived from the island. At those moments, I feel a sudden split in my being. How do I explain that I come from two worlds, and that most of the time I feel I am on a bridge shuttling back and forth between them? Despite my lush memories of growing up in Puerto Rico—the smell of the ocean, the sound of the breeze, and the taste of cornmeal with coconut milk and ripe plantains—sometimes it seems I have become a *gringa* in the way I think and live my life. Yet, that question about where I come from always reminds me that others see me as a foreigner, as someone who doesn't belong . . .

"It was not until I was 26 that I finally realized that much of my life would not be lived fully in either world but on the bridge. Most Latinos marry early and have children right away and that was what my Puerto Rican fiancé wanted. Instead, I decided to go to graduate school, even though that meant abandoning rules I had learned growing up about being a Latina. Despite the shame I felt admitting to my fiancé—and myself—that I did not immediately want children and my mother's life, my choice marked my liberation from the world of my childhood and my embrace of the part of me that had become a *gringa* . . .

"While I can't remember experiencing outright discrimination as a professional because of my race or culture, I have felt the subtleties of prejudice and the discomfort of tokenism. When I am asked to present at national conferences, or to be active in professional organizations, it is never clear to me whether I'm being asked for myself or because I represent a 'minority' group. Recently, while giving information about my professional experience over the phone to someone from a national professional organization, I had to explain over and over that my work as a family therapist wasn't limited to Latinos and that I gained my expertise working with adolescents and their families while directing an adolescent day hospital at a major mental health center ...

"What I offer beyond my skill as a therapist and my own experience of immigration, is my optimism. While never easy, I *know* it is possible to shuttle between these two worlds. When I help people construct the bridges they need for this journey between cultures, my own bridge becomes sturdier and wider."

(Garcia-Preto, 1994)

GENDER CONCERNS

Perhaps nowhere in the life cycle is the issue of gender differences more pronounced than in middle adulthood. Part of the reason for this disparity is that the classical research in this area was based exclusively on men but was generalized to women. For example, Daniel Levinson's well-known work on adult development is based on a small sample of all men. Yet, the purpose of his study was to create an overarching conception of development that would encompass the biological, psychological, and social factors that influence adult development. Carol Gilligan, in her work on women's development, found that many well-known theories and ideas about adult development were based on studies of men. She found clear examples of sexual stereotypes that emphasized either love or work. Expressive capacities are assigned to women, whereas instrumental abilities are assigned to men.

What, if any, are the differences between women and men when they reach midlife? Apter (1995) believes that women experience a crisis at midlife that is a normal part of their developmental growth, whereas for men, the midlife crisis is relevant to only a minority of them. Although women must suffer through some doubt and despair, a hope of new development sustains them. Apter (1995) explains it this way: "When women are freed of the supposition that someone else

has the answer, when they are no longer shadowed by a need to please a parent, when they are less anxious about standing in opposition to a partner, when the fantasy of the ideal of who they should be is shattered by the mature reflection in the mirror, they grow strong enough to listen to their own answers to the questions they pose" (p. 23). Therefore, even though there is a crisis, women become empowered to come up with their own answers. This newfound energy and self-assertion is what Apter refers to as the "secret path that women achieve at midlife."

A major difference between men and women is that men are often focused on their one primary role—whether it be worker, father, or lover—in midlife. They often find a new sense of relaxation about life, more expressiveness, and a general enjoyment of the fruits of their labor. In contrast, women's roles in midlife are characterized by their multiple roles—mother, wife, daughter, worker. Bateson (1990) refers to how women "compose a life" as they develop different themes. These themes result in more change over the life course in comparison with men. They move from their crisis to liberation and newfound energy as they confront a critical question: "Why did it take me so long to trust myself" (Apter, 1995, p. 27)?

To answer this question, women must do a lot of "midlife reconstruction." Men, however, appear not to have this need for the integration among the various parts of their selves. Their needs are less likely to conflict (Apter, 1995), whereas women must address conflicting needs—for example, pleasing self versus pleasing others, and private time versus development of outside relationships.

From a more theoretical perspective, women at midlife may be dealing with role strain and role conflict. Since women are searching for greater integration, this is likely to reflect attempts to adapt to each role and to the many segments of each social circle subscribed to that role. Indeed, women are often committed to four major roles: wife, homemaker, mother, and employee. In addition, women must relate to other roles—such as daughter, daughter-in-law, neighbor, and friend—which can lead to role conflict (Bernard, 1975, 1981). Lopata and Barnewolt (1984) believe that women at midlife must adapt to many conflicting social-role commitments. However, many men

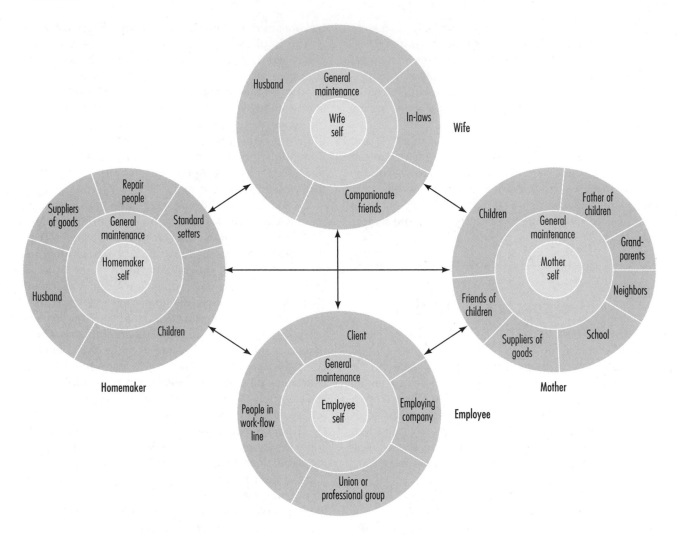

FIGURE 11.2   Four major social roles of women (Lopata & Barnewolt, 1984)

and women in midlife relinquish the role of parents, and, as the major duties of parenting decline, they are more free to break out of traditional sex roles.

Figure 11.2 presents the four major social roles of women in American society.

Although many similarities exist between middle adult men and women of different ethnicities, there are some distinctions that can have important implications. For example, Cavanough (1997) discusses some of the similarities and differences between African-American men and women and white men and women at midlife. For instance, he refers to research by Thorson (1995) that found African-Americans to be more likely than whites to come from backgrounds of poverty and to be more likely to age quickly and to be vulnerable to disorders related to poverty. Among all African-Americans across lower- and upper-income classes, hypertension is a common disorder in the middle adult years.

The fate of African-American men has an effect on African-American women. Because African-American men are more likely to suffer from poor health, African-American women are more likely than white women to face midlife as widows. Furthermore, African-American women have fewer opportunities for remarriage when compared with their white counterparts. These factors, and others, mean that many African-American women are single.

In addition, for many African-American women, midlife is a period of mothering—of her grandchildren or other children related to the extended family. Perhaps most significant is the fact that the "overwhelming majority of black women arrive at and live through the middle years burdened by economic problems" (Spurlock, 1984, p. 255). This is aptly summarized by poet Langston Hughes's (1970) statement that life "ain't no crystal stair."

Social Hazards

Employment is an important aspect of most adults' meaningful participation in life. Therefore, when adults become jobless, it can have significant physical, psychological, and social consequences. The individual's sense of worth and hope about the future declines. For men, employment has a strong cultural significance—this is how a man cares for his family. Loss of a job can be embarrassing and socially uncomfortable, especially given this country's emphasis on productivity. Joblessness can stimulate feelings of anger, guilt, and shame (Newman & Newman, 1995). African-Americans and Hispanic/Latino-Americans are more likely to experience unemployment—often chronic unemployment—than are white Americans.

Joblessness affects the entire community. For example, one study (Janosik, 1986) found that a 1% increase in unemployment resulted in the following consequences for the community: 5% more suicides, 3%–4% increase in hospitalizations for mental illness, 4%–6% increase in homicides, 6%–7% increase in prison incarcerations, and a 2% increase in the overall death rate. Braginsky and Braginsky (1975) conducted research that compared white-collar men who became unemployed with employed white-collar men. The results revealed the psychological

effect of unemployment. The men felt unwanted and insignificant, lacking a role in society. Many of the men harbored feelings of anger and bitterness. They felt isolated and looked down on by their friends. Particularly revealing was the finding that even after becoming reemployed they continued to suffer from feelings of low self-esteem.

The effect of joblessness is felt not just by the unemployed individual. If a family is involved, members face problems of increased conflict, loss of morale, violence, feelings of deprivation, and loss of roles (Schuster & Ashburn, 1992). The family's ability to cope with adversity is tested. Children can also be affected because they may no longer have the money to participate in special events or buy new clothes. Children may become depressed at their situation or angry toward their parents for not being able to provide them with certain necessities.

HOMELESSNESS

Imagine what it would be like to be homeless—no permanent place to call home. For many people, "home" is a makeshift structure in a washout in the desert, a county jail cell, or even a storm drain. Yet, every night as many as 760,000 people are without a home and end up sleeping wherever they can—often in public parks, bus stops, homeless shelters, or just in the street (National Center on Homelessness and Poverty, 1996). Approximately 7 million people experienced homelessness between 1985 and 1990 (Link et al., 1994).

Who are the homeless? The homeless are a diverse group of men and women that includes young people, single men and women, families, adults with mental illness, and older adults. They are often disabled or chronically sick individuals without support for housing, older persons on fixed incomes who have no family support, Vietnam veterans who have not adjusted to society, documented and undocumented immigrants, ex-prisoners without support for their return to society, and unemployed persons without adequate income (Peterson, 1993). According to studies conducted in homeless shelters, the majority of the homeless population is white, although African-Americans

The problem of homelessness has grown in recent years. A wide range of people can become homeless; common reasons for homelessness include loss of job, lack of family support, avoidance, substance abuse, and mental illness.

and Hispanic/Latino-Americans are overrepresented. Indeed, homeless people no longer fit the stereotype of the middle-aged alcoholic male; instead they are a heterogeneous group (Connell, 1987). In fact, owing in part to poor wages and a loss of buying power over the last several years, families are the fastest-growing group among the homeless.

What factors contribute to homelessness? The reasons for homelessness are as diverse as the homeless population. In general, homeless people get to that state after a long series of crises, poor decision making, and missed opportunities (Bassuk, 1991). Common factors related to homelessness include lack of employment opportunities, need to flee from vio-

lence, lack of family support, substance abuse, and mental illness.

Mental illness among the homeless is a serious problem in this country (Rochefort, 1997). Many people with mental illness have become homeless through failures in the mental health care system, the disabling effects of mental illness that has gone untreated, the combined influence of substance abuse and mental illness, and the inability of many people with mental illness to set realistic life goals. Also relevant is a loss of adequate income and diminished social supports. Many of the current problems of this segment of the homeless population are related to the effects of deinstitutionalization. When people with mental illness were categorically released from hospitals and care facilities, they were not provided adequate community support programs. E. F. Torrey (1988) has studied mental illness for years, and he describes many of the problems of deinstitutionalization:

- There are twice as many people living on the streets and in shelters as there are in public psychiatric hospitals.

- There are increasing numbers of people with serious mental illness in the nation's jails and prisons.

- People with serious mental illness are regularly released from hospitals with little or no provision for aftercare or follow-up treatment.

- Violent acts perpetrated by people with untreated mental illness are increasing.

- Housing and living conditions for people with mental illness in the community are grossly inadequate.

- Community mental health centers, originally funded to provide community care so people with mental illness would no longer have to go to state psychiatric hospitals, are almost complete failures.

- Laws designed to protect the rights of people with serious mental illness primarily protect their right to remain ill.

- The majority of the people with mental illness who were discharged from hospitals have been officially "lost."

PREDICTORS AND PREVENTION
IN INNER-CITY HOMELESS INDIVIDUALS

Between 1984 and 1986, a study funded by the National Institute of Mental Health (NIMH) engaged almost 400 homeless people in inner-city Los Angeles in extensive individual interviews (Koegel, 1989). Using this sample as representative of the skid row homeless population, researchers sought to gain insight into these individuals' experiences and characteristics, to learn the incidence of specific psychiatric disorders in this population, and to discover differences between homeless individuals with chronic mental illness and those who do not have mental illness.

Data from this study suggest that mental illness is more prevalent in the inner-city homeless population than in the greater Los Angeles community. About 28% of the targeted population suffered from "severe and chronic major mental illness," such as schizophrenia or bipolar disorder (Koegel, 1989, p. 16). Nearly half of these individuals were also chronic substance abusers. In addition, 34% of the population abused substances but did not have a major mental illness. This finding suggests an overall chronic substance abuse rate of 46%. Individuals who abused substances and/or had chronic mental illness were homeless more often and for longer duration than those without either condition.

Yet substance abuse and mental illness should not be isolated as solely responsible for homelessness. Urban demographics contribute as well: As the number of both employed and unemployed poor is increasing, the availability of low-income housing is decreasing. Poverty and the lack of affordable housing cause homelessness; mental illness and substance abuse increase vulnerability to homelessness.

This complex interaction of factors leading to homelessness suggests that effective intervention must take a comprehensive approach to helping this population. Mental health programs should take preventive steps on behalf of vulnerable individuals. In addition, attention must be given to the broader social issues that affect this population, such as social welfare and affordable housing. Effective outreach is critical to helping vulnerable populations.

The following Focus section describes the need for outreach programs for women at risk for AIDS.

FOCUS ON GENDER

Women at Risk for AIDS— Is There Hope?

"AIDS will become one of the four leading killers of women," reports Judith Cohen. It is already the number-one killer of African-American women in New York and New Jersey. Cohen notes that more than 70% of women with AIDS are African-American or Hispanic/Latino-American. With experts suggesting that the number of female AIDS deaths is around 14,000, it is clear that programs intended to prevent AIDS in at-risk female populations need to be aggressive in their efforts.

The best strategies for AIDS outreach include actively seeking these women out and addressing in some depth all the other issues that are affecting their lives. Outreach may involve services such as rape counseling, legal advocacy, and assistance with parenting issues. Another crucial element of the AIDS-prevention program is a focus on empowering women as individuals, building self-esteem and other inner resources that will help the women initiate and sustain changes in their lifestyle. External resources, such as day care and other community support mechanisms, can also be cultivated to help women maintain these changes and reduce their risk for AIDS.

A six-month evaluation of a demonstration program designed to reduce the risk of AIDS to women showed significant decreases in overall drug-injection frequency and in the frequency with which users shared injection equipment. The percentage of women who always use new needles doubled, and in the remaining women, incidence of needle-cleaning rose. Changes in sexual behaviors were also noted but were not as remarkable as the transformation in drug-related practices. With such positive results after only six months, it is clear that barriers to reaching this at-risk population are not insurmountable.

Julianne Azimov (Based on Freiberg, 1990)

(text continued on p. 521)

Alcoholism in Middle Age

Lee Park is a 54-year-old man who has an alcohol addiction. He began treatment at the Harborview Medical Center after his wife and children worked with a substance-abuse counselor who coached them in how to perform an "intervention" on Lee. The "intervention" consisted of a meeting among Lee, his wife, and their two children, in which they expressed to him their concern about his drinking and the negative consequences it had for them. Each family member spoke frankly about his or her fears and anxieties over Lee's drinking behavior. They gave carefully constructed examples of when he had acted inappropriately because of his drinking. They also pressured Lee to seek immediate treatment, and he agreed to go with them to the Harborview Medical Center that specializes in alcoholism treatment.

DEVELOPMENTAL CONSIDERATIONS

Lee began drinking socially as a young adult. He enjoyed entertaining and being in the company of others. His social drinking continued and slowly, over time, it grew more and more serious. Lee has also experienced bouts of depression. He becomes very withdrawn and loses all motivation for work. He becomes irritable and often does not get enough sleep during the night, and then he feels drowsy during the day.

Lee describes an eventful history that seems to have preceded his move into a serious drinking problem. Throughout his career, Lee had been loyal to one company and performed adequately as an electrical engineer. Slowly his job performance deteriorated, and although Lee still adequately conducted his job, his employer was unhappy with his results. Eventually Lee was "let go" from his job, and at 54 years of age, he did not have an easy time seeking new employment. Lee was unemployed for more than one year. At that time, he desperately searched for a new position; however, it seemed that employers were interested only in hiring younger workers. Lee's frustration at not being able to find work led to an increase in his rate of drinking. Drinking became a way for him to calm his anxieties and move from very unpleasant feelings of worry and concern to more pleasant feelings associated with the drinking. Lee was able to start a small business successfully, and it has been going well, although Lee reports feeling extremely nervous about his potential for continued success.

BIOPHYSICAL CONSIDERATIONS

Lee's alcoholism has developed into a physical dependence. His abstinence from alcohol in the hospital led to alcohol withdrawal, suggesting physical tolerance. He was observed to have coarse tremors of the hands. Family members report the presence of chemically induced alcoholic blackouts. Additional symptoms included insomnia and daytime drowsiness, increased psychomotor activity, and increased blood pressure.

Lee has been drinking for almost 30 years. He began drinking in his 20s, and it has gotten steadily more frequent and more intense. He drinks every day but most heavily on weekends. Lee primarily drinks scotch but also consumes beer. He estimated his drinking to be about "a pint of scotch" a day.

In spite of a long history of drinking, Lee's general health was rated satisfactory by the physician. He has a tendency toward high blood pressure, but the doctor does not consider it to be a medical concern at this time. Lee is 25 pounds overweight, owing primarily to a lack of exercise and excess calories obtained from drinking. All other indications suggest Lee does not have any other physical concerns.

PSYCHOLOGICAL CONSIDERATIONS

Cognitive Development and Information Processing

Lee is a college graduate with a B.A. degree in engineering. He presents himself as someone who has the capacity for good intellectual functioning. However, this is difficult to assess at times because of his lack of motivation and flat affect. In discussing his current work situation, Lee is able to articulate difficult business decisions he is grappling with. Moreover, he displays reasonable problem-solving abilities in relation to the tasks he is currently working on. For example, he recognizes that one of his difficulties is retaining good employees and keeping them motivated to work. Because he is feeling unmotivated, he is concerned about how his employees may be reacting to his lack of motivation. He has described several ideas for how to address this problem. In general, Lee's judgment about work issues shows careful consideration of consequences and forethought about the implications of his actions.

When discussing more personal issues, Lee appears to have difficulties with cognitive flexibility. In particular, he displays thinking styles characteristic of a depressed person. For example, when asked about how he could reach out to establish some new relationships with other men, he could think of no alternatives. And when asked about past relationships, he exclaimed, "I should have friends but no one really feels close to me." Such thoughts show minimization and all-or-nothing thinking patterns.

Communication

Lee has serious communication difficulties, particularly in the context of his family. He is reserved and has a timid, unassertive personality style. In family sessions, he often turns to his wife to let her speak for him.

His wife describes frustrating attempts to simply "talk to Lee about what is going on with him." He recognizes this and describes difficulties in "expressing my thoughts to my wife and children." Because the children have recently moved out on their own, Lee and his wife are readjusting to more time by themselves and with each other. Lee's wife wants him to become more involved with social activities and is motivated to push him to confront his drinking problem so "they can return to a normal life."

Attitudes and Emotions

Although alcohol drinking has been consistent since young adulthood, it became more frequent and more intense after Lee lost his employment. This loss was significant for Lee, because he felt he no longer had a significant role in his family. He reports feeling guilty about not being able to provide for the family. Lee reported a general sense of failure and hopelessness about the future following his employment loss. Although he now has a financially stable business, he reports feeling anxious and nervous about his future. Lee complains often of "low energy" and believes he is depressed much of the time. He states, "I do not have anything to look forward to." Lee is also beginning to wonder what the meaning of his life has been. He describes much of his life to date as "a failure." When asked what he would like to accomplish, he responded, "I don't feel I have anything I can accomplish or look forward to."

Social Cognition and Regulation

Lee's sense of self, or self-concept, is negative. He is focused on his limitations and inadequacies and has a great deal of difficulty when asked to discuss any positive attributes. This is probably related to his depression as described above.

Lee is beginning to accept the notion that he has a drinking problem. In the past when confronted with concerns about his drinking, he immediately expressed

(continued)

denial of any problems. In the last five years, his wife has been increasingly concerned and confrontational about his drinking. About one year ago, Lee had an alcohol- related accident; fortunately, no one was hurt. At one point, his wife challenged him to quit for three months to prove that he did not have a drinking problem. Lee was unable to meet the challenge. Also, family members, especially after working with a counselor, became better at letting Lee experience the consequences of his drinking behavior rather than covering up for him and assuming caretaking and enabling roles for him. Lee does acknowledge that his drinking is "a problem for other people in my family."

Lee does express much concern over "what he has left in his life." He appears concerned that family members and others perceive him as having made an important contribution. With regard to this issue, he expresses intense dissatisfaction: "I want others to feel I have done right by them, and I should get my act together for the benefit of others." He can express his frustration over wanting to "get more out of life," and it appears he is consistently thoughtful about what he wants to achieve in the future.

SOCIAL CONSIDERATIONS

Family

Lee has been married for 30 years and feels his marriage is one of convenience. He gets along with his wife, but she "isn't able to really understand my problems or help me." Although he presents the marriage in a negative light, he is observed to be caring and concerned with discussing his problems with his wife. She has been putting increasing pressure on Lee, which has resulted in an increasing conflict between them. She stated, "I told Lee I was tired of this and I did not want to live under these circumstances."

Lee's relationship with his children has also become increasingly strained. The children and his wife have been more confrontational, and this may explain the increase in family conflict. Lee believes the children should "stay out of this" and does not want them to be involved in his treatment. He appears embarrassed to admit that he has a problem and needs help. The children report feeling "cut off" from their father and "do not know how to separate who he is from his drinking problem."

Lee's parents live far away, and he has not been very involved with them in the past even though he is an only child. However, recently his father had a heart attack and he went to visit them. When he returned, he said he was "shocked" to see how old they were getting and realized that they may need help in the next several years. He reports additional stress and feels that this is not a burden he can take on right now.

Social Support

Lee's greatest social support is from his family. His wife and children are concerned about his behavior and are motivated to help him quit drinking. And even though he describes his relationships as strained, they are what he appears to care the most about. Lee has a strong sense of social responsibility toward his family, and he wants them to see him as a competent and effective husband and father.

Outside his family, Lee has one business friend that he spends a lot of time with. He describes this person as his only friend. His wife has encouraged him to attend AA meetings in the past, and within the last six months, he did attend AA meetings for about a month. He quit going, complaining that they were too religious and that the people there were "too screwed up to be of any help to me."

Multicultural and Gender Considerations

Lee comes from a family that has always been accepting and open toward drinking. He can remember drinking with his family of origin when he was only 17 years old. Both of his parents drank alcohol, but he says neither of them had a drinking problem.

Lee also comes from a middle-class family that values success through hard work. It is difficult to determine exactly when Lee's drinking became serious enough to constitute alcoholism. However, his loss of employment was very significant in his life, and he describes his most serious problems as having begun when he lost his job. For Lee, work gave him an acceptable role to play in his family and helped him feel he was making a contribution to society. When he lost that ability, he was not able to cope effectively and turned to alcohol for relief.

SUMMARY AND IMPRESSIONS

Lee is experiencing the following problems:

1. He has an alcohol addiction.
2. He has mild to moderate denial regarding the negative aspects of his alcohol use.
3. He is experiencing clinical depression.
4. He has serious self-doubts concerning his self-worth and experiences worry and anxiety over his future.
5. He needs to reestablish his relationship with his wife and children.

6. He has difficulty expressing himself and being assertive.

Lee is a high-functioning midlife male who has an alcohol addiction and is experiencing depression. It is difficult to assess the relationship between his feeling depressed and his drinking. He may have developed a serious drinking problem in his effort to use alcohol to cope with his depressive feelings. Lee's family is experiencing many concerns related to Lee's drinking and is actively involved in his treatment. They can offer him needed support and reassurance throughout his recovery. Although Lee has entered Harborview Medical Center for his alcoholism, he is still experiencing denial in relation to his alcohol use.

Exacerbating his problems are concerns that Lee has regarding his future and worries about his ability to succeed in life. He is increasingly concerned about his contribution in life. Lee's difficulties in communication and assertiveness make it difficult for him to make his needs known. Lee has some important strengths that will help his prognosis for treatment. He is an intellectually competent man with a successful business. His family is supportive and involved in his treatment. He is making progress on his denial and has agreed to a first step of seeking inpatient treatment.

(continued from p. 517)

ADAPTING TO MIDLIFE

The experience of reaching midlife affects individuals in different ways, depending on their expectations and their own life experiences. Some people may greet the approach of their later years with anxiety and dread, as exemplified by the following quote from Apter (1995): "From the very beginning of my awareness that this person who was 'me' would grow older, the prospect brought no eagerness, only dread. At some prehistory of the self, as I was attempting to adapt to a grotesquely conceived future, I plotted my

escape from aging. The simple solution I came to was that when I discovered my first grey hair, I would pull it out and then kill myself. I imagined how I would lie on the carpet of my childhood bedroom where this chill thought found me. I would be discovered, dead, before anyone could disclose the evil secret of my maturity" (p. 51).

Yet for others, for most, the prospect of maturity brings renewal and opportunity—not a last chance but a continuing chance to develop and grow, to leave one's mark in the world. In many instances, the old saying holds true: "Life begins at 40." As people's longevity increases, expectations of their productivity also increase, and they do more and demand more from midlife.

niques are taught to people with cancer, there is an improvement in patients' moods, lowered emotional distress, and an improvement in patients' ability to cope with their illness.

Summary

DEVELOPMENTAL THEMES

Middle adulthood is different from other life stages because it is less affected by biological maturation and most affected by adults' own experiences. Such experiences represent great diversity in middle adulthood, although for many adults this life stage involves launching children and focusing on career development. At midlife, many adults develop a new perspective about who they are as they reflect on their past years.

BIOPHYSICAL DIMENSION

Biophysical Growth and Development

The leading causes of death during middle age are cancer and heart disease. Stress, however, can have an influence on one's health, particularly if the person has a Type A personality. In middle age, women experience menopause. For some women this can lead to physical and psychological changes. These women may benefit from estrogen replacement therapy. Physical changes also lead to changes in the sexual response cycle.

Biophysical Hazards

During middle age, breast cancer becomes a significant concern for women (1 in 9 chance). Risk factors include age, family history, having menarche before age 12 or menopause after 50, being childless, being overweight, alcohol ingestion, sedentary lifestyle, eating a diet high in fat. For men, prostate cancer is a common (1 in 5 chance) and deadly cancer. Age is a factor in prostate cancer, and as more men live longer and do not succumb to heart attacks and stroke, more will die from prostate cancer. When relaxation tech-

PSYCHOLOGICAL DIMENSION

Cognitive Development and Information Processing

Intellectual functioning is stable in middle age. Adult intelligence is more related to adults' performing role-related tasks. Professional obsolescence may become relevant during this life stage.

Communication

Communication patterns often change as adults reconnect with their partner or spouse. As adults move closer to doing a "life review," they reassess their communication with others. For some, this leads to engaging in the process of forgiveness.

Many adults must adjust to the fact that they are functionally illiterate. Others must adapt as non-English-speaking persons. A slow loss of hearing is a fact of life for many others.

Attitudes and Emotions

Midlife may bring about an identity change, which requires a renewal and reintegration of one's identity. Although midlife does not necessarily result in a midlife crisis, midlife usually involves a period of reflection.

Social Cognition and Regulation

Midlife represents an increased opportunity to become involved in socially responsible activities. There is a stronger sense of one's obligation to society.

Psychological Hazards

One critical psychological hazard is the development of alcohol or drug addiction. The 12-step program is a self-help method of treatment for alcohol and drug dependence. The notion of codependency has become popular in recent years. It is helpful to know when individuals should seek professional help.

SOCIAL DIMENSION

Families, Groups, Support Systems, and Communities

Many middle-aged adults join blended or stepfamilies. Individuals in stepfamilies face significant change as they adapt to many new aspects of the family.

Marital relationships can be positively affected as children leave the home and marriage partners develop more companionate love. However, as adults reflect on their lives, many seek new experiences that can sometimes lead to extramarital affairs.

The relationship between middle-aged parents and their children changes as the children grow older. The adolescent years, when parents' general well-being decreases, can be especially difficult. As the children become adults, most families experience improvements in their relationships with one another.

Middle-aged parents must also begin the process of caring for their aging parents. Many adults, particularly women, do a significant amount of caregiving for their elderly parents. Many caregivers are unprepared for this role. At the same time, many parents of adult children become grandparents. The experience of grandparenting can offer new roles and may be helpful in adapting to the aging process.

The men's movement has provided new alternatives in the ways men see their roles and responsibilities. For many men, it has provided a new type of masculine identity. Male and female stereotypes of men can influence their use of social and psychological treatment.

There is a growing sense of satisfaction as one grows older. An individual's career or work gives direction to one's overall lifestyle and identity. Career changes at midlife are not as common as often thought. One's work or career can lead to different pathways for men and women. Men are often stepping back from their work, whereas women may be investing time in a new job or returning to school.

Multicultural and Gender Considerations

Gender differences may be pronounced in middle adulthood. Many of the original theories of adult development were based exclusively on men. Men often focus on one primary role, whereas women often juggle multiple roles. These multiple roles may lead women to search for a sense of integration in midlife. People also may find that their ethnic identity provides a sense of support as they get older.

Social Hazards

Adults can face significant hazards during midlife. Joblessness can take a strong social and psychological toll. Often, joblessness results in homelessness. Although the homeless are a diverse group, many homeless adults have mental illness and face difficult adjustments in the community.

🌐 Online Resources

The American Institute of Stress
http://www.stress.org
> The American Institute of Stress provides information on the role that stress plays in health and disease. The site is a clearinghouse for information on stress-related subjects.

The National Foundation for Depression
http://www.depression.org
> This site has information about depression. It provides information on the causes, symptoms, and treatment of depression.

National Organization for Women (NOW)
http://www.noworg/isser/violence
> This site is maintained by NOW and provides information about women and advocacy efforts to prevent violence.

Something Happened to Me or Someone I Know
http://www.victimservices.org/visitor/.htm
> This resource provided by New York Citizens Victims Services offers a Resource Center Help Line for victims and concerned others.

National Institute on Alcohol Abuse and Alcoholism (NIAAA)
http://www.niaaa.nih.gov
NIAAA is the information service of the Center for Substance Abuse Prevention of the Substance Abuse and Mental Health Services Administration in the U.S. Department of Health and Human Services. NIAAA is the world's largest resource for current information and materials concerning substance abuse.

National Institute on Drug Abuse
http://www.nida.nih.gov
One of the scientific institutes of the U.S. national institutes of Health, NIDA supports more than 85% of the world's research on the health aspects of drug abuse and addiction; it provides information on drug abuse and links to related websites.

Center for Substance Abuse Research
http://www.bsos.umd.edu/cesar/cesar.htm
This site was designed to disseminate information on substance abuse and related problems; includes publications and links to other sites.

Alcoholics Anonymous (AA)
http://www.alcoholics.anonymous.org
This site provides a self-recovery program for alcoholics. It also includes information for professionals.

American Cancer Society
http://www.cancer.org
This site has information on research, new findings, statistics and a searchable database on cancer-related topics.

The Kinney Institute for Research in Sex Gender and Reproduction
http://www.indiana.edu/kinsey
This site is from the famous Kinsey Institute. It includes research, publication paper and links to other sites.

Sexology Netline
http://www.netaccess.on.ca/sexorg

This is the Institute for Advanced Study of Human Sexuality Alumni Association of Professional Sexologists. It includes a variety of information on topics related to sex and responds to individuals' questions.

The National American Menopause Society
http://www.menopause.org
This site provides information about menopause. It includes information about the organization, suggested readings, and research.

American Men's Studies Association
http://www.cybersales.net
This site is a not-for-profit organization for people interested in the exploration of masculinity in modern society.

GLAAD: Gay and Lesbian Alliances Against Defamation
http://www.glaad.org
This site was designed to improve the public's attitudes toward homosexuality and address discrimination against lesbians and gay men.

NAACP (National Association for the Advancement of Colored People)
http://www.naacp.org
This site represents the oldest and largest civil rights organization in the United States. The NAACP promotes political, social, and economic equality among minority citizens.

Center for the Study of Group Processes
http://www.viowa.edu/grpproc
This sites provides information on group processes and is designed to promote interest and knowledge about how group process functions.

The National Institute for Literacy
http://novel.nifl.gov
By serving as a resource for the literacy community, the Institute assists in addressing urgent national priorities—upgrading the workforce, reducing welfare dependency, raising the standard of living, and creating safer communities.

InfoTrac® College Edition

For interesting materials related to what you have just read, please go to the *InfoTrac College Edition* website and search using the following key words:

menopause	false memory syndrome
forgiveness	caregivers
hearing loss	homelessness

Key Terms

alcoholism	cynical hostility
blended family	de-illusionment
caregiving career	delirium tremens (DTs)

displaced homemakers	professional half-life
endorphins	professional
estrogen replacement	obsolescence
therapy (ERT)	refractory period
functionally literate	sexual response cycle
hot flash	socioeconomic status
illiterate	stepfamily
interrupted career	Type A personality
menopause	Type B personality
osteoporosis	

Developmental Themes

Stage: integrity vs. despair. Management of changing status and roles, cultivation of new roles, need to cope with physical and emotional changes of aging, and to confront own mortality.

Biophysical Dimension

Biophysical Growth and Development	Need to face age-related changes in physical decline, increased vulnerability to chronic health problems and life-threatening illnesses, changes in sexuality and sexual relations, and health-enhancing behaviors.
Biophysical Hazards	Chronic health problems, arthritis, hypertension, and declining health.

Psychological Dimension

Cognitive Development and Information Processing	Fluid and crystallized intelligence, adjustment to changes in memory and learning.
Communication	Life review and communication of critical life events.
Attitudes and Emotions	Grief and loss, mourning, death and dying, fear of death, widowhood, loneliness and other related emotions.
Social Cognition and Regulation	Maintenance of a stable sense of self, successful aging.
Psychological Hazards	Alzheimer's disease, depression, suicide, assisted suicide.

Social Dimension

Families, Groups, Support Systems, and Communities	Family relationships, couples, parent-child relationships, caregiving for and by older people, grandparenthood, friendship, nursing homes, hospice, retirement.
Multicultural and Gender Considerations	Issues of gender and family minority groups.
Social Hazards	Abuse and neglect—physical, psychological, and material; stereotyping; ageism, sexism, racism; living on a fixed income.

Late Adulthood

by Shirley Patterson

DEVELOPMENTAL THEMES

A social worker was speaking at a weekly social meeting of a senior citizens' group. All the participants were at least 70 years old. The subject of the talk was the needs of older adults. To begin his presentation, the social worker asked how many people present considered themselves "older adults." No hands were raised.

The years from age 60 until death are considered late adulthood. Erikson termed this stage "old age," with the developmental task being to experience integrity or despair. According to Erikson, people in their later years tend to reflect on their lives and their accomplishments. If they believe their life has been meaningful and rewarding, they experience satisfaction that their life has been worthwhile and develop integrity. If, however, they are disappointed because of missed opportunities and unresolved crises, they may regret what they have done with their lives and fall into despair.

But what exactly is "old age"? The answer to this question is becoming increasingly difficult for the simple reason that people are living longer. "Old" keeps getting older. These days, 70-year-olds may not consider themselves old. And the stage of "old age" keeps lasting longer. Those people who are 85 and older make up the fastest-growing segment of the population in the United States and other prosperous nations. Between 1960 and 1990, while the overall U.S. population grew 39%, the ranks of those 85 and older jumped 232%. The U.S. Census Bureau projects that, by the year 2040, there will be 1.3 million Americans 100 years or older; some demographics put the figure at 4 million (Wallis, 1995). With increased life expectancy, it is not uncommon for individuals to live nearly a third of their lives in the arena of late adulthood. In the future, it may not be that uncommon for some individuals to spend almost half their lives in this span of development.

Many believe that Erikson's stages compress too many years into this life stage. For instance, Erikson's (1963) first six stages of psychosocial development cover a span of 34 years, whereas the other two stages, middle adulthood to old age, range from 35 years of age to death. Newman and Newman (1994) have revised Erikson's stages and have included two developmental descriptors for older persons: late adulthood (ages 60 to 75) and very old age (75 until death). Other theorists have divided the developmental stages into two to four subperiods, including the young-old, middle-old, old-old, and very old (Botwinick, 1984; Charness & Bosman, 1992; Neugarten, 1974).

Adding to the problem of defining the stage of late adulthood is the fact that, when people live longer, they have more opportunities to develop differently.

This older person is alert and vitally involved in life, enjoying new experiences while reflecting on past events.

According to some theorists (Bornstein, 1992; Germain, 1991; Neugarten, 1969), the amalgamation of a lifetime of forces (intrinsic and extrinsic) influences the development of people such that the longer they live, the more diverse they become. Hartford (1985) put it succinctly when she argued:

> There is a tendency to lump this entire age period into one set of characteristics called "old age." For no other age span have the social or behavioral sciences done this. Infancy, early childhood, later childhood, adolescence, young adulthood, middle age each cover a shorter period of time ranging from three or four years to a decade. The physiological changes, psychological changes, social experiences, and personal characteristics of people beyond early 60s are as dramatic in five- to ten-year age spans as they are earlier in life (p. 45).

TABLE 12.1	General Characteristics of Older Adults by Subperiod

Subperiod	Characteristics
Young-old (65–74)	Many may still be employed full- or part-time because of the extension of mandatory retirement age or personal wishes to work; other, more affluent individuals may be retired and pursuing long-term interests and activities; the phenomenon of women outliving their spouses begins to emerge; the young-old typically remain active in the community and maintain strong ties with families and friends; some may increase their recreation, adult education, and volunteer activities. Retirement often means the beginning of facing a series of losses, including status and income, with resulting decrease in activities that are costly. Loss through death of mates, friends, family members, and co-workers becomes more frequent. Chronic illness may develop and/or become more debilitating and depression is not uncommon. This age group may assume or continue the assumption of the caregiver role to an elderly relative. Most individuals in this age group maintain a good capacity to cope and use their talents productively.
Middle-old (75–84)	More in this age group experience chronic disease (arthritis, cardiovascular, respiratory, circulatory); added stresses through death of mates (an even greater number of males die), friends, relatives, and adult children. Generally, people in this age cohort tend to experience more physiological changes in terms of impairments in vision or hearing; problems with balance that may lead to loss of mobility (for example, walking, driving); slowing of response time and judgment of spatial relationships. These factors, combined with accrued losses, often have negative effects on older adults with respect to a more constricted life space and may result in withdrawal, depression, disorientation, and pseudo-dementia. Growing numbers of people in this age range, however, continue to manage well and contribute to the arts, literature, science, and politics. They are socially and physically active, in better health, better educated, and better able to function independently. Because of the noticeably different rates of change of individuals in this age group, they are even more diverse from one another than are the young-old.
Old-old (85+)	Although the 85+ age group is the fastest-growing population of any age group, they represented only 3.4 million of the 32.8 million elderly in 1993. A predominant number of this group is dependent, frail, and experiencing more disabilities and chronic illnesses. Social isolation tends to become greater for this cohort because they have more physical decrements and are more vulnerable to accidents, disabling diseases, and environmental impacts. Mobility becomes even more limited, and very few are employed, though some work independently or use their creative capacities for fulfillment. Mental disorders increase with age—a small proportion (5% to 7% of the total population and up to 20% of the 85+ group) of elderly show evidence of brain disorders or some form of dementia. Those elderly who have survived well continue to maintain daily routines, and live independently or with families, although the ratio of women to men (256:100) is much greater.

(Based on Hartford, 1985)

As a result of these factors (for example, longevity and diversity), there is significant difficulty in distinguishing the developmental tasks of particular subperiods in late adulthood. An 80-year-old with a hearty genetic inheritance who has maintained a healthy lifestyle may still be gainfully employed. This individual has not had to confront changes related to age in his or her work role and status. In contrast, a 65-year-old with a debilitating terminal illness has had to confront such losses as the work role, good health, and changes in body image, as well as the immediacy of mortality. Although it is difficult to delineate the characteristics of older people in different subperiods of late adulthood,

it is possible to suggest general characteristics for each subperiod (see Table 12.1). Practitioners, however, must look beyond these general characteristics and explore and identify the nuances of this population's diversity.

What are the factors that contribute to a person's longevity? According to researchers (Friedman et al., 1995), there are several. First, aspects of individual psychology are linked to longevity across the life span. In particular, ego strength, dependability, trust, and lack of impulsiveness are important. Second, both personality and social stress are predictors of longevity. In both childhood and adulthood, the trauma of divorce and family conflict predict premature mortality.

With late adulthood being such a lengthy stage with such divergent individuals, how can the tasks of this stage of life be defined? Butler, Lewis, and Sunderland (1991) have observed that older people have some special characteristics "connected with the unique sense of having lived a long time and having accepted the concept of life as a cycle from birth through death" (p. 79). According to the authors, these characteristics include the following:

- A desire to leave a legacy through children, grandchildren, work, art, memories, possessions. The notion of "legacy" provides a sense of continuity with future generations.

- The "elder" function, which is closely associated with the notion of legacy, in that older people have a predilection for sharing a wealth of accumulated knowledge, experience, and wisdom with the young.

- Attachment to familiar objects, which means an increasing emotional investment in familiar household objects, heirlooms, keepsakes, photo albums, and letters. Attachments to pets are characteristic particularly of old-old people and engender a sense of continuity, assist the memory, and provide both comfort and security.

- Change in the sense of time, which indicates that, although middle-aged adults may be concerned with time running out, older adults tend to live in the present and experience a sense of time as "now" with children, friends, nature, and closeness (physical and emotional).

- Creativity, curiosity, and surprise, which suggest that, with continued good health and adequate social and environmental supports, many older people retain a curiosity about life and all living things, and some develop or discover creative abilities. The adaptive qualities of curiosity, creativity, and surprise are likely to reflect lifelong personality traits that add richness to old age.

- A sense of consummation or fulfillment in life, which are those qualities of "serenity" and "wisdom" that emanate from a sense of having resolved one's personal conflicts and viewing one's life in a historical context that is generally positive and gratifying.

These brief summaries indicate that chronological age has little to do with one's ability to survive, persevere, and achieve fulfillment in life. In fact, even through adversity, some persevere and make significant contributions to others. Take, for example, Esther E. Twente, a little-known social worker and educator from the rural Midwest. Beset with serious vision, hearing, and arthritic problems, Twente, between her mid-60s and mid-70s, was engaged in the following activities: directed a two-year Ford Foundation Project, one of seven funded across the United States; was co-investigator of two sequential three-year research projects funded by the National Institute of Mental Health (NIMH); and published her first book, *Never Too Old* (1970), at age 75. Until six weeks before her death at age 76 from metastatic cancer, Twente continued to work on one of the NIMH research projects. Although Esther E. Twente is not a household name—even within her own profession of social work—she left a significant legacy to all who follow her and to students and

Esther Twente was a pioneer social work practitioner and educator who focused her writing on the capacities and potential of older people. *Never Too Old,* Twente's only book, was published when she was 75 years old, one year before her death.

colleagues who knew her. This legacy, among other things, includes contributions to the knowledge base of the "strengths perspective" in social work, particularly as this concept relates to older people. Twente was not a prolific writer, but she had a way of capturing the essence of ideas through her remarkable powers of personal observation.

Many older people have creative capacities. The repeated evidence may even lead one to speculate that the creative urge may possibly become stronger as life draws to a close—like the push for life in the old apple tree that produces an especially bountiful crop just before its death. The farmer remarks, "It overworked itself." But perhaps it was just trying to satisfy that final big desire (Twente, 1965, p. 106).

The following Focus section, written by Esther Twente, is an example of the strengths perspective.

Apple Trees, Strength, and Creativity

It was a cold, snowy day in January when I first met Mrs. Stanley. I was visiting old people because I thought they might be lonely. Mrs. Stanley is a 90-year-old widow. Her husband was a farmer, but like many others during the Depression, the Stanleys lost their land. They moved to a small town. Then Mr. Stanley died.

When I arrived, Mrs. Stanley was lying down. Her voice was weak. She was suffering from shingles in her face and she complained of dysentery. She was unhappy, neither the world nor anyone in it seemed to please her. After a while I said, "I hear you have a green thumb."

With that a great change came over her. Her expression brightened. Her voice became stronger. She told me of her interest in plants, her rare bulbs, the flowers she had furnished for three weddings, and her hopes for a garden for the coming summer. Then she said, "I have other interests."

I am sure you have, I replied, for by now I sensed the creative capacity of the old lady.

She got up, spry and enthusiastic, and showed me her collection of vases. Then she said, "Would you like to see my embroidery?"

Of course I would. And there it was, drawers-full. Many of the designs were of her own making, and every piece was carefully done.

I have kept in touch with Mrs. Stanley. We have discussed international relations and the John Birch Society. I have seen her during the summer pulling weeds and tenderly touching one flower after another. She wrote letters to me telling me when this lily was in bloom and that rose was about to open. Her granddaughter and I took pictures of her garden. In the fall slides of her flowers were shown at a meeting of a newly organized group of older people. Proudly she told about each plant.

Spring is here again. The wind is still cold but Mrs. Stanley is in her garden carefully planting her bulbs. "I like the fresh air," she says.

(Taken from Twente, 1965, pp. 107–108)

Biophysical Growth and Development

Given successful treatment of illnesses and accidental injuries, the potential life span of the human species could extend to 120 years of age (Schaie & Willis, 1986). Although **life span** represents the upper limit of human life, **life expectancy** refers to the number of years the average person may live who was born in a particular year (Santrock, 1997; Schaie & Willis, 1986). Moreover, owing to such factors as healthier lifestyles, better nutrition, decreased mortality rates, and technological advances in medicine, life expectancy has increased significantly in the last several decades. Data drawn from the U.S. Bureau of the Census, the American Association of Retired Persons (AARP), and the Administration on Aging (AOA) (1994) indicate the following:

- People who reached age 65 in 1992 had an average life expectancy of an additional 17.5 years—19.1 years for females and 15.5 years for males.

- In 1993, the 65-and-older population numbered 32.8 million and represented 12.7% of the population in the United States.

- In 1993, approximately one in every eight Americans were 65 and older.

- Because women tend to outlive men, the ratio of women to men increases with age, ranging from 122:100 at ages 65–69 to 256:100 after 85.

- It is estimated that by 2030 the older population will have grown to 70.2 million, nearly twice their number in 1993 and representing 20% of the total population.

- Between 2010 and 2030, the most rapid increase in population is expected when a generation of "baby boomers" reach age 65.

- By 2030, minority groups are projected to represent 25% of the older population, nearly double the percentage (13%) in 1990. In fact, the total minority population will grow at a much faster rate than the white non-Hispanic population age 65 and over (see Table 12.2).

There is as much variation among older people in the physical changes that occur with age as there is with their developmental tasks generally. Miller (1992) postulates that certain conclusions can be drawn from several biological theories of aging:

1. Biological aging occurs in all living organisms.
2. Biological aging is natural, inevitable, irreversible, and progressive with time.
3. The course of aging varies from individual to individual.
4. The rate of aging for different organs and tissues varies among individuals.
5. Biological aging is influenced by nonbiological factors.
6. Biological aging processes are different from pathological processes.
7. Biological aging increases one's vulnerability to disease (p. 804).

Because physical change and decline vary from individual to individual, chronological age cannot be used as a marker for biophysical change. Inevitably, however, physical change does occur in the following biological systems (see Table 12.3): skeletal, muscle, brain and nervous system, sensory, circulatory, respiratory, and integumentary (skin, hair, nails).

SEXUALITY

Large-scale research (Kinsey, Pomeroy, & Martin, 1948; Kinsey et al., 1953; Masters & Johnson, 1966; Starr & Weiner, 1982) on sexual behavior indicates that older adults maintain not only interest but also activity in sexual relationships in later life. Earlier research has been affirmed by a recent National Council on Aging Study (Duffy, 1998) of 1,292 older adults for whom sexuality continues to be a vital element in their lives. Before the sexual revolution of the 1960s, sexuality was not a common, everyday topic of conversation. Even today, when sexuality is more freely discussed, according to Butler and colleagues (1991), both young and old are amazed that 70-, 80-, and 90-year-olds are interested in making love. Members of this society assume that: (1) older people do not have sexual desires; (2) they could not make love even if they did want to; (3) they are too fragile physically and it might hurt them; (4) they are physically unattractive and therefore sexually undesirable; and (5) the whole notion is shameful and decidedly perverse (p. 219).

Physiological Changes and Sexual Activity

Physiological changes affect both female and male sexual activity to some extent. Most older women in good health can expect to continue sexual activities well into late life. As discussed in the last chapter, though, many older women may be coping with the postmenopausal changes brought on by estrogen depletion, including

TABLE 12.2   Projected Rate of Growth of Ethnic Older People (65+) Between 1990 and 2030

Ethnic Older People	Percent
White non-Hispanic	93
Hispanic	555
Non-Hispanic Blacks	160
American Indians, Eskimos, Aleuts	231
Asians, Pacific Islanders	693

(Based on AARP & AOA, 1994)

TABLE 12.3 Age-Related Changes in Biological Systems	
Skeletal system	Reduction in height of 2 to 4 cm per decade owing to decline of spinal discs, osteoporosis, and other age-related changes; bones become less dense due to osteoporosis—a gradual loss of bone mass (bone loss in women more accelerated owing to estrogen loss); joints are more restricted, resulting in a diminished range of motion in the upper arms, lower back, hips, knees, and feet; osteoarthritis, the most common form of arthritis, affects about 30% of older persons and is considered a universal aging phenomenon; foot problems (non-disease-related) may include bunions, heel spurs, hammer toes, and calluses.
Muscle system	Lean body mass decreases with the beginning of middle age, and body fat increases in males (50%) and females (33%); power and speed of muscular contractions gradually decreases with age; incontinence owing to slowed reflexes; there is a gradual decline in muscle strength and endurance, which results in muscle fatigue after briefer periods of activity or exercise.
Brain and nervous system	With age there is a loss of neurons (estimated to be between 5% and 10% until the 70s—may accelerate subsequently), the basic cellular unit of the nervous system; unless the blood supply is blocked, there may be little functional change; if, for example, there is diminished flow of blood to the brain, neurotransmitter changes, accumulations of cholesterol, and so on, these changes may affect reaction time and interfere with perception and cognition.
Sensory system	Gait and balance changes may occur because of combined effects of muscular, skeletal, and neurological changes, which may result in an increase in accidents and falls; owing to toughening of the skin, older people experience a decrease in tactile sensitivity and develop a higher pain threshold; there is a decline in a sense of smell owing to gradual degenerative changes in olfactory cells and a decrease in a sense of taste as a result of such factors as presence of dental or systemic disease, and so forth; changes in vision increase with age, often as the result of a reduction of the quality or intensity of light reaching the retina; very old age may be accompanied by degenerative changes in the retina, impairing one's ability to see; the ratio of legal blindness is 100:100,000 in individuals under age 21, but it increases to 1,400:100,000 in individuals age 69 and above; significant hearing impairment occurs with increasing age when degenerative changes affect the compartments of the ear and the auditory nerve pathway; high-pitched sounds are not heard as well, resulting in jumbled or distorted words and sentences.
Circulatory system	Age-related changes appear to include a slight enlargement of the left ventricle of the heart and thickening of the atrial endocardium and atrial ventricular valves; changes in the arteries (an increase in collagen and calcification of elastin fibers) make the arterial walls more vulnerable to disorders that cause their hardening and thickening (for example, the most common form of arteriosclerosis); such factors as obesity, lack of exercise, anxiety, illness, and hardening of blood vessels may cause an increase in blood pressure; with increasing age, veins become less elastic, thicker, and more dilated, causing valves in the large leg vein to become less efficient in returning blood to the heart.
Respiratory system	Between the ages of 20 and 80, lung capacity decreases 40%, even in the absence of disease; lungs lose elasticity, the chest decreases in size, and the diaphragm weakens; mouth breathing and snoring is the result of connective tissue changes that cause the nose to have a retracted septum; although air volumes are altered because of changes in the chest wall and in lung elastic recoil, total lung capacity stays essentially the same due to compensatory mechanisms.
Integumentary system	Age-related changes in the skin make the skin look paler, thinner, and irregularly pigmented; skin has diminished moisture content and less turgor, resulting in easier injury to the skin's surface; other indicators of age-related changes include wrinkling, sagging, and mostly harmless growths and lesions; nails become increasingly soft, brittle, and are likely to split; because of trauma or poor circulation, toenails may thicken; graying hair and baldness (most frequently in males) occurs with age; loss of body hair is progressively experienced by men and women in the pubic and armpit area; coarse hair, caused in part by hormonal changes, may grow on the upper lip and lower face of older women and the ears, nostrils, and eyebrows of older men.

(Based on Miller, 1992; Santrock, 1997; Zastrow & Kirst-Ashman, 1994) thinning and drying of the vaginal walls. This dryness may make intercourse more difficult for them. Estrogen creams and hormone replacement therapy can help alleviate the dryness. Plus, women who remain sexually active have less of a problem.

Older men typically are able to engage in sexual activity well into their 70s, 80s, and beyond. Unless there is physical illness or emotional difficulties, older men do not lose their facility for erection with age. Manual stimulation of the penis, however, may be required to initiate sexual activity. A decrease in the pressure to ejaculate is caused by a reduction in the volume of seminal fluid. In turn, orgasms, although still pleasurable, are experienced in a shorter one-stage period rather than in two stages, as experienced in earlier life. It may take from 12 to 24 hours for older men to achieve an erection following ejaculation. If older men lose interest in sexual activities or become impotent, a number of causes can account for these conditions, including extreme fatigue, alcohol abuse, overeating, boredom, depression, and fear of an inability to perform. Erectile dysfunction may be caused by such physical causes as cardiorespiratory, atherosclerotic, neurological, genitourinary, endocrine, hematological, and infectious disorders. Impotence also has been induced by such drugs as antihypertensive medication, tranquilizers, and antidepressants. Intractable physical impotence may be cured through penile implants or prosthesis. Most erectile problems, however, may be dealt with effectively through sexual therapy or through individual, couple, or group counseling (Butler et al., 1991).

Implications for Practice: The Need for Sexual Expression in Late Adulthood

The capacity for sexual expression in late adulthood has been well documented. It may diminish to some extent because of ill health, widowhood, or lack of access to suitable partners. Butler and colleagues (1991) noted that sex, a sense of self-esteem, and the self-image are closely related. Additionally, a study by Marsiglio and Donnelly (1992), which used a national probability sample that included 807 respondents 60 years of age or older, revealed that people's sense of self-worth/competence and partner's health status were significantly and positively related to the incidence of sex within the past month. To maintain good biopsychosocial health, older people need to recognize and understand the interrela-

tionship of physical and emotional needs and capacities. It is critical to understand that unsafe sex among elders, as well as young people, may give rise to AIDS. Nationally, more than 10% of all AIDS cases occur in people over 50, with 25% of those cases over 60 and 4% in people over 70 (Graham, 1998).

Biophysical Hazards

The processes of physiological aging increase the individual's vulnerability to various types of health problems. According to Santrock (1995), chronic disorders "are characterized by slow onset and long duration. Chronic disorders rarely develop in early adulthood, increase during middle adulthood, and become common in late adulthood" (p. 521). Many older people have chronic conditions, and the older one becomes, the more likely one is to have multiple conditions (see Figure 12.1).

CHRONIC HEALTH PROBLEMS

The two most common types of chronic disorders are arthritis and hypertension. *Arthritis* is a broad term that describes a wide variety of disease entities, the most common of which include rheumatoid arthritis and osteoarthritis. Generally, arthritis is located in the connective tissues of the body, primarily tendons, ligaments, and cartilage (Cohen, 1982). The tissues become inflamed, causing pain and difficulty in movement (Santrock, 1997). Rheumatoid arthritis, which is more common in females than in males, may appear to be a disease of the immune system because it can stimulate inflammation in such parts of the body as the heart, nerves, spleen, liver, and blood vessels. Both emotional and physical stressors facilitate the occurrence of the disease (Bullock & Rosendahl, 1988). Although some people have some form of disability the remainder of their lives, this condition can be treated with medication or surgery.

Osteoarthritis, a degenerative joint disease, is the result of repeated trauma or wear and tear on tissue, primarily in large joints such as the shoulder, knee, hip, and ankle. It involves the loss and destruction of cartilage that serves as a buffer between bones where they have contact with each other. Cartilage loss results in severe pain and impaired joint function (Burdman, 1986). Both

FIGURE 12.1   **Most frequently occurring chronic conditions per 100 non-institutionalized elderly in 1992 (Adapted from American Association of Retired Persons)**

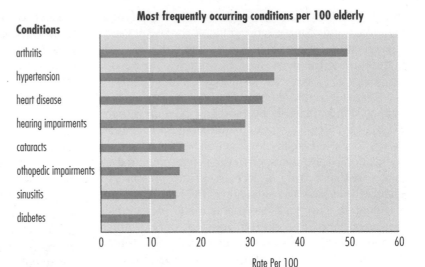

Conditions

arthritis

hypertension

heart disease

hearing impairments

cataracts

othopedic impairments

sinusitis

diabetes

Most frequently occurring conditions per 100 elderly

Rate Per 100

rheumatoid and osteoarthritis symptoms begin in middle age and become more marked with age. Osteoarthritis affects men and woman equally. Gross or fine motor impairments, joint deformity, and posture changes represent the more severe forms of this condition (Miller, 1992).

Genetics is a factor in the development of hypertension (high blood pressure) (Bullock & Rosendahl, 1988). Hypertension predisposes older people to stroke and heart disease. It poses a substantial risk even in moderate form. Hypertension in older people is most commonly caused by arteriosclerosis (hardening of the arteries) or atherosclerosis (clogging of the arteries with fatty deposits) and may affect the kidneys and blood vessels. This condition is more common and severe in African-Americans than in whites (Kent, 1980). Depending on the type and severity of the person's hypertension, as well as other medical problems, the condition may be treated by medication, by change in health habits, or by a combination of both (Tucker, 1980).

A large percentage (35%) of all hospital admissions for chronic and acute disorders were attributed to older people. And once admitted, older people tend to stay longer in the hospital—on average, 8.2 days compared with 5.1 days for people under 65. In addition, those over 65 averaged more contacts with doctors. A disproportionate amount of total personal health care expenditures are attributable to this age group. Out of $162 billion in expenditures, an average of $5,360 was spent per year on each older person, whereas an average of $1,290 was spent on younger persons. The largest share of health care expenditures for older persons was hospital expenses (42%), followed by physicians (21%), and nursing home costs (20%). Older adults rely more on government programs to pay for their health care. About two-thirds (63%) of health care expenditures for older people are covered by government benefit programs, including Medicare and Medicaid, whereas only 26% of

health care expenditures for people under 65 are subsidized by benefit programs (AARP & AOA, 1994).

The following section discusses how alcoholism affects people in later life.

ALCOHOLISM IN LATE ADULTHOOD

Stresses associated with retirement, along with age-related physiological changes, can increase the risk of problem drinking and alcoholism for elderly people. Differences exist among people who develop alcoholism while dealing with retirement and other stresses related to getting older. Retirees may be upset over the loss of their professional identities. They may discover that the social lives in their new retirement community revolve around "happy hour." They may be lonely or depressed about health problems. They may simply not have enough to do.

What many people do not realize is that drinking can become more physically hazardous with age (Clay, 1996). The amount of alcohol consumption that is associated with problem use is usually less for older people because metabolic changes associated with aging allows alcohol to be absorbed into the bloodstream much more rapidly. Also, the prescribed medications many older people take can interact adversely with alcohol. Dimming eyesight, loss of balance, and other age-related problems can dramatically increase the risk of physical injury during intoxication.

How can we identify and help older alcoholics? Treatment may be difficult not only because older alcoholics are hard to find but also because many of the symptoms of alcoholism can masquerade as depression, dementia, or other problems associated with aging. Many experts believe that older people need elder-specific treatment. For example, some Alcoholics Anonymous (AA) groups cater primarily to older people. Such programs can have added benefits for older drinkers. Attending AA meetings is a way to reduce their sense of social isolation, and finding a ready-made social group can be very helpful.

Implications for Practice:
Maintaining Good Health

Variations in age-related biophysical changes indicate the importance of having an adequate understanding of older people's health status. Thorough physical exams assist in discerning the biophysical needs and capacities of individuals within this age group. Good health and the maintenance of good health are dependent on such factors as exercise and better nutrition. Exercise has a significant effect on the heart, lungs, blood pressure, bones, muscles, and overall physical well-being of older adults. Moreover, exercise is positively associated with psychosocial health in terms of lessening depression, reducing stress, and enhancing intellectual functioning. Adequate nutrition promotes a higher level of wellness in late adulthood. Although nutrition requirements of older adults are not significantly different from those of middle-aged people, it is crucial that they eat high-quality foods that are low in calories. Daily diets must include the major food groupings with adequate amounts of fiber and fluids (Miller, 1992; Santrock, 1997).

Regular exercise helps older adults maintain or improve their physical and mental well-being.

PSYCHOLOGICAL DIMENSION

Cognitive Development and Information Processing

Determining the nature of intellectual decline in late adulthood is a complex issue influenced by the types of studies used to measure this phenomenon. Two major types of research strategies used are cross-sectional and longitudinal studies. On the basis of cross-sectional data, Horn (1982) concluded that although **crystallized intelligence** (accumulated information and verbal skills) increases with age, **fluid intelligence** (abstract reasoning ability) decreases with age. However, Schaie (1994) has conducted longitudinal research that indicated that, although moderate declines may occur for some, for others intellectual capacities may increase with age. Schaie (Schaie & Willis, 1986) criticized cross-sectional studies such as Horn's because the data collected compared different age groups (for example, 30-year-olds and 70-year-olds). Also cross-sectional studies do not take into account **cohort** effects.

As we have discussed earlier in the book, *cohort* refers to any group of people born within a specified short period. For instance, people born in 1920, in 1945, and in 1960 constitute distinct cohorts. Snapshots of them at the same age would reveal marked differences not only in appearance but also in many aspects of psychological functioning. Variation is inevitable because each cohort is exposed to a unique set of cultural and societal experiences as it travels through life (Belsky, 1990).

Further, Belsky explains that older cohorts, compared with younger cohorts, have not been exposed to an environment that promotes better health practices and emphasizes education. Younger cohorts, therefore, have distinct advantages over older cohorts because of these types of cohort differences. Cross-sectional studies do offer more reliable information about age differences at any point in time, but they do not offer more reliable information about age changes over the life span.

In the longitudinal approach, which focuses on age changes, one or more age cohorts are chosen and tested periodically over a number of years. It is preferable that the same measures are used in this process. Although this research strategy yields valuable data on age changes, it does not lead to easily made universal assumptions about aging. Conclusions can be drawn only about the age cohort selected "because each cohort is unique, and it may show an idiosyncratic pattern of change as it ages" (Belsky, 1990, p. 28). Other problems that occur with longitudinal research include such factors as cost, amount of time consumed, and the dropout rate due to illness, disinterest, migration, and the like (Santrock, 1997).

In the Seattle Longitudinal Study (Schaie & Willis, 1986), five primary mental abilities of respondents were tested, including verbal meaning, reasoning ability, word fluency, numerical ability, and spatial visualization. Frequency distributions covering seven-year age ranges were prepared to determine the proportion of people likely to decline at a given age. Abilities varied greatly in areas tested; however, by age 67, there was no more than a 25% decline; by age 74, about 33% decline; and by age 81, decline had risen to about 40%. The investigators pointed out that the large proportion who remained stable and the few who increased performance on some measures was remarkable. Although

the state of knowledge of intellectual decline is imperfect, it appears likely that decline is not a given with advancing age and that there is considerable variation in the loss of mental abilities.

INFORMATION PROCESSING, MEMORY, AND LEARNING

The speed of information processing to retrieve knowledge is dependent on sensory inputs from the eyes, ears, and other sensory organs. With age, the eye's ability to focus on nearby objects decreases, the amount of light required to see increases, and there is impairment in the ability to adapt from light to darkness and back to light. The ability to hear, particularly high frequencies, also decreases (Burdman, 1986). With sensory deficits, age seems to affect the quality of perception and the ability to receive, process, and act on information. This tends to lead to a slowing of behavioral responses in late adulthood (Burdman, 1986; Salthouse & Coon, 1993).

There is an interrelationship between memory and learning; that is, memory is the ability to retain what has been learned. Difficulties or impairments in this area may be caused by problems of perception, attention, or motivation. Burdman (1986) points out that the state of emotional and physical health can have a significant effect on memory functions. These types of impairments may be misdiagnosed when, as is often the case, they are transitory or reversible (see the following Focus section). In addition, a variety of drugs may affect memory function or mimic certain brain disorders (Butler et al., 1991).

FOCUS ON NARRATIVE

The Professor Prevails

Professor Frank Minkoff, a 70-year-old Russian immigrant with a university degree in engineering, was still teaching mathematics at an evening school. He was unmarried, was the only member of his family in the United States, and lived in an apartment crammed with books. Suddenly he became confused and disoriented. He was frightened and refused to leave his room. Concerned neighbors quickly called a doctor, who expressed his unwillingness to make a home visit, saying, "There is nothing I can do. He needs to be in a nursing home or a mental institution." The neighbors were unconvinced, remembering Mr. M.'s earlier good functioning. They pleaded with the doctor, and, under pressure, he angrily complied and visited the home. While there, he again repeated his conviction that Mr. M. needed "custodial" care. Mr. M. was coherent enough to refuse, saying he would never voluntarily go to a nursing home or mental hospital. He did agree to be admitted to a medical hospital. Admission took place and studies resulted in the diagnosis "reversible brain syndrome due to acute viral infection." Mr. M. was successfully treated and released to his home in good condition in less than a week.

(Butler, 1975, p. 5)

In the normal aging process, long-term memory loss rarely occurs, although losses in short-term and recent memory occur much more frequently. It is possible that current events do not have the significance for the older person that events of the past have for them. Exercising and keeping the mind stimulated and active assist memory functioning (Burdman, 1986). The Seattle Longitudinal Study (Schaie, 1983) showed that a significant number of older people do not decline intellectually even in their 80s. Schaie (1987) states that several factors characterize these octogenarians: They have no cardiovascular disease; they are average or above economically; they are actively involved in life; and their self-reports indicate they have been flexible in attitudes and behavior since the middle years. Overall, those who have a flexible attitude, adapt easily to change, enjoy learning new things, and like seeing new places show less mental decline in old age (Azar, 1996).

Implications for Practice: Changes in Mental Functioning

It is clear that intellectual capacity does not necessarily decline with age, although the speed of information processing tends to decline as a result of sensory and visual-motor changes. Problems with memory may be as a result of a number of factors, including health, perception, attention, and motivation. Other explanations may include differences in level of education and ability to reason abstractly (fluid intelligence) or both, instead of aging per se. Criticisms of testing methods (for instance, the requirement of completing trivial tasks in sterile laboratory settings) have been advanced as a barrier to performance. Studying how people complete practical tasks within their natural environments is a more appropriate approach (Santrock, 1997; Schaie & Willis, 1986).

Methods of retraining have been developed to assist older adults in sharpening their cognitive skills. Using a variety of training strategies (for example, modeling, individual practice, feedback, and group discussion), Willis and Nesselroade (1990) taught older adults how to identify the rule or pattern in problem solution. Following the cognitive training, in this seven-year longitudinal study, 70- and 80-year-old adults performed at a higher level than they had in their late 60s. Cognitive interventions (Schaie, 1994) were designed to remedy decline in the fluid abilities of inductive reasoning and spatial orientation. The cognitive training study results conducted with subsamples of longitudinal subjects suggest that declines in many older people are likely the result of disuse and are reversible in persons who have remained stable.

Cognitive well-being is an overriding concern for older persons and their families. Mental decline or impairment poses a great threat to individuals as they age. Yet, some common beliefs associated with mental impairment must be dispelled (see Box 12.1).

Communication

The purpose of **reminiscence** as a part of the normal life review process was articulated by Butler (1963) in response to the widespread notion that reminiscence was associated with short-term memory loss and, therefore, was an indicator of aging. He noted that reminiscence is a mental process that emerges when one realizes the inevitability of death. Reviewing one's life has the potential of bringing to consciousness past events, especially those in which conflicts have been unresolved and "that can be looked at again and reintegrated" (Butler et al., 1991, p. 112). The reintegration process serves the function of putting one's life in order and preparing for death. This process is seen as

BOX 12.1

Common Myths Associated with Mental Impairment

MYTH: Changes in mental capability and behavior such as confusion, forgetfulness, and depression are just signs of growing older.

FACT: There are distinct differences between changes occurring with "normal" aging and those of mental disorders. However, mild levels of impairment can and do occur when a normally aging individual is under stress or has a physical problem. Factors such as sensory loss and decreased ability to cope with stresses may affect the normal aging person as well.

MYTH: Old people who are forgetful or confused should never be left alone.

FACT: Older persons who exhibit symptoms of minimal impairment can and do function in the community. Constant surveillance and overprotective measures tend to reduce the older person's freedom and sense of self-control and should be held to a minimum, short of endangering the individual or others. Adequate support systems must integrate the resources of family, health care providers, and community. Adaptations of the older person's environment may be all that is required.

MYTH: Old people are uncooperative and unsociable.

FACT: Unusual behavior may often result from sensory deficits that can be corrected. The older person who cannot see or hear well is often unable to communicate effectively, and the resulting frustration may give rise to inappropriate behavior. Sadness or depression can also cause the older person to withdraw.

MYTH: Inability to concentrate, impaired attention span, and memory loss in an older person are signs of aging.

FACT: Depression as well as an organic mental dysfunction can cause impairments of mood and thought. Depression is the most common affective disorder in older persons. Because depression responds well to treatment, it should be targeted even when the diagnosis is uncertain.

MYTH: Older people should not be allowed to engage in work or activity that requires mental or physical effort.

FACT: Depriving older people of work or activity simply because of their age invariably results in a loss of self-esteem, which causes serious problems. Often older persons are patronized and/or excluded from significant social roles when in reality they have much to contribute. Allowing for responsibilities to match the abilities of older persons will enhance self-respect and help them to maintain a functional level well into later years.

MYTH: Older people need eight hours of sleep every night.

FACT: Sleep patterns change over time. Many older persons function well on five to six hours of sleep a day. Some prefer to sleep less at night and to rest when they feel tired during the day.

MYTH: Older people react to alcohol and drugs just as do younger adults.

FACT: The alteration in absorption, distribution, and excretion rates in older persons make them very sensitive to the actions of individual drugs. Also, older persons are prone to toxic reactions because of drug interactions. There is a need for conservative use of drugs, continuous monitoring to avoid side effects, and an awareness of the potential for alcohol-related problems.

(Burdman, 1986)

universal, spontaneous, and unselective. It occurs in other age groups but is most commonly observed in older persons who are near to death. Butler (1963) noted that it also may be more frequently observed in the aged because retirement allows time for reflection and contemplation. Reminiscence has the potential for assisting an older person to bring positive closure to life and often is a gift to the one who listens (see the following Focus section).

FOCUS ON DEVELOPMENT

Reminiscing with an Older Person

I do not live in the past; it is the past which is alive in me.
—Rene Dubos

Reminiscing, something we find ourselves doing more and more as we age, is normal and natural; it is part of the process of putting meaning to our lives. But there may be more to sharing memories for older people. In addition to helping them put their lives in order, reminiscence can be a socialization tool, as memories are shared with friends and relatives. It can help an older person orient to the present by getting a "good grip" on the past. As one reviews the events of one's life, past accomplishments and successes may be more appreciated in hindsight, whereas weaknesses and mistakes don't seem as serious as they did decades ago.

Reminiscence holds many rewards for the listener as well. We can gain great insight into "survivorship," the skills and traits developed over a lifetime to cope with adversity and life's challenges. If the speaker is a relative, the stories illustrate the characters of family members we may or may not have known, as well as the character of the family as a whole. We may learn the origins of the traditions and rituals we practice, gain clues to the way family members have been assigned roles within the family, and add to our sense of continuity, connectedness, and belonging.

Here are some tips for making the most out of listening to an older loved one's reminiscing:

• Suggesting a topic, such as family traditions, parent-child relationships, youthful passages, courtship

and marriage, the Depression, war years, education, and professions may help trigger vivid memories.

• Don't be afraid to talk about past losses and the death of long-ago loved ones. This may give you valuable insight into the speaker's feelings regarding his or her own approaching death and wishes regarding life-sustaining measures and funeral arrangements.

• Don't trust your own memory; write down the stories you hear, or use a tape recorder or videotape. These will all become priceless mementos.

• Bookstores carry specially bound volumes that are designed specifically for recording reminiscences and genealogical information.

• Even those suffering from dementia or other mental impairments have lucid moments when they can vividly recall the events of their life, and having an active and interested listener may help them feel less isolated and more anchored.

• Also be an "audience" for older persons to whom you are not related. They may have no close family with whom to share the stories of their lives.

• Reminiscence is a gift to the listener and a chance for the older person to reinforce his or her part of the continuum of life and feel unique, precious, and cherished.

(Based on Richardson, 1988)

Attitudes and Emotions

Loss, and its attendant issues, is one of the dominant factors that characterize the common emotional problems of older adults. In every aspect of late life, losses occur from the micro to the macro: death of a loved one; decline in health; loss of status, prestige, and active involvement in communal life. Older adulthood is marked by the expending of physical and emotional energy on grieving, grief resolution, adaptation, and recovery from loss (Butler et al., 1991). Multiple losses at any one point in time are not uncommon. The variety of factors that may affect

Factors That May Affect Experience, Behavior, and Adaptation in Loss

ENVIRONMENTAL OR EXTRINSIC FACTORS

Personal losses or gain: marital partners; other loved and significant figures (friends, children)

Social forces (losses or gain): status changes, prestige changes: in social groups other than family and as paterfamilias

SOCIOECONOMIC ADVERSITIES: INCOME DROP, INFLATION

Unwanted retirement: arbitrary retirement policies

Cultural devaluation of older persons: sense of uselessness, therapeutic pessimism, forced isolation, forced segregation

INTRINSIC FACTORS

Nature of personality: character structure (defensive and integrative mechanisms), life history, survival characteristics

Physical diseases: disease of any organ system; perceptual decrements; sexual losses; disease of integrative systems (hormonal, vascular, and central nervous systems); brain damage; arteriosclerosis; senile dementia, and so on; physical limitations (such as arthritis)

Age-specific changes (largely obscure and mysterious, but inexorable with the passage of time): losses of speed of processes and response; involuntary processes; others (heredity, survival qualities); changes in body size and appearance ("slipping" and "shrinkage")

Experience of bodily dissolution and approaching death (subjective passage of time)

(Butler et al., 1991)

---

individual experience, overt behavior, and level of adaptation are outlined in Box 12.2.

GRIEF AND LOSS

Grief, associated with loss, is the normative emotional reaction experienced by people in late adulthood. Death, as loss, is viewed as the most profound loss human beings endure because the dying process and death are accompanied by such losses as the following: the loss of people, the loss of experiencing, the loss of control and competence, the loss of the body, the loss of the capacity to complete projects and plans, and the loss of life's dream (Kalish, 1985). Grief may be expressed physiologically and emotionally. Physiological expressions of grief often include emptiness in the pit of the stomach, a feeling of suffocation or shortness of breath, weak knees, and a tendency to deep sighing (Butler et al., 1991). Emotional expressions of grief may include such reactions as depres-

sion, sorrow, sadness, relief, guilt, anger, and denial (Kalish, 1985). The loss of a spouse or a partner or other loved ones through death may have a profound effect on survivors, partly because there is less likelihood that the lost relationships will be replaced.

THE IMPORTANCE OF MOURNING

Jill lost her husband, Robert, to cancer in 1987. He had been ill for three years, and his death was no surprise. At the time of his death, Jill was busy with funeral arrangements and with putting her financial affairs in order. After the death, she was active in her church and in community organizations and filled her days with various civic and volunteer activities. She rarely mentioned her husband, and her friends were amazed at her courage and fortitude. Over the years, several men asked her out on dates, but she refused, saying no one could ever replace Robert. Then, last week, her cat died. He had been her pet for 14 years, and now Jill finds that she cannot stop crying. In fact, she is in so much emotional pain that she is having difficulty sleeping and often finds herself wishing she were dead. She feels foolish for being so upset over an animal, but eight years after the death of her husband, she feels terribly lost and alone.

William Worden (1991), in *Grief Counseling and Grief Therapy,* discusses the importance of working through grief. When people who experience the loss of a loved one do not deal with their pain and loss, problems can arise years down the road. Worden outlines four steps necessary in mourning a loss:

- *Accept the loss.* Initially, people deny the reality of a death, so the first task is to accept that the loved one is gone and will not return. Often people display searching behaviors, seeing the loved one in a crowd or hearing his or her voice.

- *Feel the pain.* Many ask after the death of a loved one, "When does this pain go away?" Many simply do not want to hurt so much, so they busy themselves in activities or go on a trip to avoid their feelings. But pain cannot be avoided, and, if not dealt with at the time of death, it may resurface when another loss occurs (such as the death of a pet). Bereaved individuals need to externalize the pain by talking about the death and the loved one. Group therapy situations are helpful.

- *Adjust to a new environment.* The bereaved person needs to realize that he or she can live in a world in which the loved one no longer exists.

- *Reinvest in new relationships.* Relationships are a risk. The bereaved person must work through grief before being able to enter new relationships and be willing to risk being hurt again.

How do you know when you have worked through the grief over loss of a loved one? When you can recall that person and it doesn't hurt.

DEATH AND DYING

The process people go through when facing imminent death has been described in various ways by different investigators (see, for example, Kastenbaum & Weisman, 1972; Kübler-Ross, 1969; Pattison, 1978). Perhaps

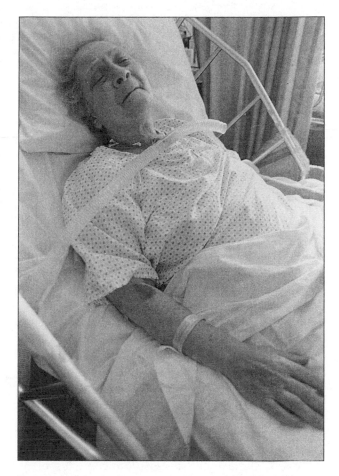

Preparing for death often means addressing emotional pain, grief and indignity. Grieving the loss of family and friends, as well as the loss of life, is part of the dying process.

the best-known investigator of the process of dying is Elisabeth Kübler-Ross, a Swiss-born psychiatrist who began a systematic study of death and dying at the University of Chicago's teaching-research hospital. After interviewing more than 200 dying patients, Kübler-Ross identified five stages (not necessarily sequential) in the dying process: (1) denial and isolation, (2) anger, (3) bargaining, (4) depression, and (5) acceptance.

1. *Denial and isolation* is the most common response in the initial stage of the process. It is characterized by feelings of shock, disbelief, and numbness. In the short run, denial serves as a healthy defense for dealing with a painful, difficult

situation. As a buffer, denial provides a brief respite to people, allowing them opportunity to confront the reality of dying and to mobilize other less radical defenses.

2. *Anger* provides people with the chance to vent their rage and resentment about dying. It is not uncommon for anger to be displaced on loved ones and caregivers, both formal and informal. The displacement typically is not personal, but it is a cry of anguish, perhaps at the untimeliness of death, over enviousness of those who experience good health, or about all that will be left uncompleted and unfulfilled.

3. *Bargaining* is an attempt to delay or postpone death's inevitability. Terminally ill people may believe they can bargain for an extension of life because rewards often follow good behavior (for instance, "I will quit smoking, drinking, and lose weight if I can live to see my granddaughter married").

4. *Depression* is characterized by a great sense of loss and consists of two types: reactive depression and preparatory depression. Reactive depression focuses on past losses and may be accompanied by guilt or shame (for example, for not confronting issues of estrangement with loved ones). In contrast, preparatory depression takes into account all the impending losses to come: loss of self, loss of relationship, and all that one has ever known or loved.

5. *Acceptance* of mortality is not resignation but a state in which people have an opportunity to consider the end of life with some dignity. If enough time is available to confront death, this stage allows the working through of prior emotional reactions. People during this stage may be weak, withdrawn, and uncommunicative with others.

As more people spend their remaining days in impersonal institutions it becomes more important to help dying patients to let go of life in peace. According to some professionals (Clay, 1997), interventions can assist the dying in accomplishing this task. For instance:

- To alleviate depression, help the dying review their lives and finish unfinished business;

- To ease the dying through this transition, reassure them that they have done everything they need to do and can let go now;

- To manage anxiety about health problems, utilize visualization or relaxation techniques;

- To modify fears of dying in agony, make sure patients have adequate pain medication properly prescribed.

The following Focus section discusses what happens when a person dies.

FOCUS ON BIOPHYSICS

The Dying Process

Death from a chronic illness does not usually come quickly; it may take weeks or months (Enck, 1992). Beginning one to three months before death, several changes occur in dying individuals. First they begin to withdraw and turn inward. This is the first step in separating from the world. They begin to sleep more and to interact with friends and family less. There may be a drop in food consumption.

The dying process begins about one to two weeks before death occurs. The dying person becomes disoriented and confused. He or she may talk to long-deceased loved ones or become agitated and pick at the bedclothes. Sleep increases, and food consumption falls to very little. The dying person may perspire more, and his or her skin color may change to pale yellow with bluish hands and feet. Breathing and pulse become irregular.

Days or hours before the death, all these signs intensify. However, the dying person may experience a surge of energy and be more alert, eating and socializing—almost as if he or she were getting the energy to say goodbye. Then the person usually slips into a coma. Hands, feet, and legs become blotchy and purplish. Pulse is weak and hard to find. Breathing becomes very irregular with long pauses between breaths. Then the dying person becomes unresponsive and breathing stops.

I am standing upon the seashore. A ship at my side spreads her white sails to the morning breeze and starts for the blue ocean. She is an object of beauty and strength. I stand and watch her until at length she hangs like a speck of white cloud just where the sea and sky come to mingle with each other.

Then someone at my side says: "There, she is gone!"

"Gone where?"

Gone from my sight. That is all. She is just as large in mast and hull and spar as she was when she left my side and she is just as able to bear her load of living freight to her destined port.

Her diminished size is in me, not in her. And just at the moment when someone at my side says: "There, she is gone!" there are other eyes watching her coming, and other voices ready to take up the glad shout: "Here she comes!"

And that is dying. (Anonymous)

(Adapted from Karnes, 1986)

CAUSES OF DEATH

The leading causes of death (in rank order) of Americans 65 years of age and older are (1) heart disease, (2) cancer, (3) cerebrovascular disease (stroke), (4) lung diseases, (5) pneumonia and influenza, and (6) diabetes (Santrock, 1997). Nearly half (48%) of non-institutionalized older women (8.6 million) were widows, whereas only 14% of non-institutionalized older men (1.8 million) were widowers, a ratio of nearly 5:1 (AARP & AOA, 1994).

Although we earlier made some generalizations with respect to grief reactions in response to death, patterns of grieving are not uniform. Widows and widowers, for example, may react or respond differently to the death of a spouse.

It is a myth that when one spouse dies, the other soon follows. In fact, the most recent research shows that, although this might be somewhat true for widows under age 50, those aged 60–69 have the same mortality rate as married women, and those over 70 show only a slightly higher mortality rate. For men, however, mortality rates seem to be significantly higher among widowers (Hesling & Szklo, 1981).

FEAR OF DEATH

One of the most common human reactions to death and the process of dying is fear. Attitudes toward death and dying vary over the life span and have been a topic of study. Nagy (1959) conducted a study of death anxiety, interviewing children between the ages of 3 and 10. She found that children 3 to 5 years of age did not know what death meant or have any sense of its reality; for those between 6 and 9, death was viewed as real but was perceived as relating to others rather than the self; and for those 9 and older, death was viewed as final and inevitable, even for the self. In adolescence and early adulthood, it is difficult to confront one's mortality, and the fear of death, or death anxiety, is relatively low.

In middle age, according to Neugarten (1968), both men and women have developed an awareness of the finiteness of time. Time-left-to-live for both men and women is more significant a perception than is distance-from-birth. Investigators (Kalish & Reynolds, 1976; Puner, 1974) have shown that the fear of death is a more prominent feature of middle age than it is in younger or older age groups. Middle age is a time when bodily changes begin to occur (for example, wrinkles, graying hair), chronic illnesses may begin to develop, concern for financing retirement becomes an issue, and/or a parent may die or suffer a terminal condition. These and other life events obviously have the power to generate fear and anxiety.

Fear of death, or death anxiety, is relatively low in old age. Dying is more of an everyday topic of conversation among the old, and late adulthood appears to be a time of life when one deals more directly with life's end. Older people have experienced a range of losses, including death of a loved one. A heightened awareness of death and its attendant issues is the result of such factors as the increased sophistication of modern medical technology, discussions about euthanasia and physician-assisted suicide, and the passage of The Patient Self-Determination Act of 1990 (PSDA). The purpose of this act is twofold: (1) to encourage competent adults to execute advance directives (for example, living wills, durable powers of attorney for health care) and (2) to identify previously admitted patients to acute or long-term care facilities who have completed advance directives. "Institutions that receive Medicare or Medicaid funding are required to ask patients about the presence of advance directives, to record responses, and to provide patients without such documents with information regarding their right to establish one" (Morrison et al., 1995, p. 478). The focus of the act is improved access to and increased execution of advance directives.

Several studies have provided evidence of lower death anxiety among older people compared with other adult age groups (see, for instance, Bascue & Lawrence, 1977; Bengston, Cuellar, & Ragan, 1977). Much of this evidence comes from the use of the Death Attitude Profile (DAP), which includes the following dimensions:

1. Fear of death (negative thoughts and feelings about the state of death)

2. Fear of dying (negative thoughts and feelings about the process of dying)

3. Approach-oriented death acceptance (death is viewed as a passageway to a happy afterlife)

4. Escape-oriented death acceptance (death is viewed as an escape from a painful existence)

5. Neutral acceptance (death is neither welcomed nor feared but simply accepted as reality) (p. 115)

Studies using the Death Attitude Profile have found that older respondents showed less fear of death and more acceptance of it (approach, escape, and neutral) than did their younger or middle-aged counterparts.

In Western societies, death has often been viewed as an unnatural interruption of or deviance in relation to life. Other cultures, however, have viewed loss and death as a natural and not uncomfortable part of the process of life and living (see the following Focus section). In the last several decades, societal changes have influenced attitudes toward death such that acceptance of its inevitability and normality are more prevalent. Today, people express more concern about quality-of-life issues than about dying—a one-time experience.

FOCUS ON NARRATIVE

▼

A Native-American Elder Contemplates Life's End

Today is a very good day to die.
Every living thing is in harmony with me.
Every voice sings a chorus within me.
All beauty has come to rest in my eyes.

All bad thoughts have departed from me.
Today is a very good day to die.
My land is peaceful around me.
My fields have been turned for the last time.
My house is filled with laughter.
My children have come home.
Yes, today is a very good day to die.

(Wood, 1984, p. 31)

WIDOWHOOD

Because widowhood is more common for women—because they generally live longer and may marry older men—women may be better prepared for this life change. Or perhaps women cope better because they are more likely to have a good network of support. Still another possibility is that widowhood may actually signify a time for growth in women's lives. Silverman (1987) sees widowhood as a change in the life cycle, necessitating adjustments in the way a woman relates to herself and to others and leading to a new identity: "When widowhood is seen as a stage in the life cycle, then it can also be understood not only as an ending but as a beginning as well" (p. 171).

Although widows of any age experience a period of bereavement and possibly fear and uncertainty, they seem to emerge from their pain with new strengths: increased decisiveness and feelings of self-reliance, autonomy, and freedom. They may feel a void for the rest of their lives, but, over time, "other selves and other relationships emerge that bring other satisfactions" (Silverman, 1987, p. 180). Some may recognize that they have spent most of their lives meeting others' needs, seeing life through their husbands' eyes, and speaking their husbands' words. They begin to rediscover—or discover for the first time—their own voices.

Widows seldom remarry, which has often been attributed to the fact that there are four widows for every widower in the United States (Bremmer & van den Bosch, 1995). But one study suggests that widows often choose to remain single (Gentry, Rosenman, & Shulman, 1987). Women in this study were asked to cite the resources they used to cope with the problems that arise from widowhood. The most frequently cited resource was the woman herself. Even remarried widows cited themselves as their most important resource, indicating that widowhood brings increased feelings of self-reliance and decreased dependence on others. Forty percent of the women reported no wish to remarry, "because, despite the difficulties, they enjoyed the independence that life without a spouse gave them" (p. 170). Perhaps the widow, emerging slowly from her dark chrysalis of pain and grief, finds new identity—even rebirth—in her last stage of life, as colorful and free as a butterfly.

In some respects, older men may be more vulnerable and fragile when they experience the death of a spouse. It is almost as though the center of life has died with the loved one. Death, as an alternative to living without a loved one, may be a welcome choice. In his book *Diary of an Old Man,* Chaim Bermant's (1966) main character, Cyril, recounts the events leading to the death of a widowed friend (see the following Focus section).

FOCUS ON NARRATIVE

The Death of a Widower

They buried old Harry this morning. I don't know why I call him old Harry, but old Harry it's been for as long as I've known him. He was 74—tried to make out he was only 73, but he was 74 if a day, and a nice old soul, but he didn't wear well. Some men don't begin to straighten out till they get widowed—as if the wife kept them from the sun; others fall apart. Harry was a faller-apart. He used to say: "It's all right for you, Cyril. You lost your Elsie when you were still a young man. You had time to get used to your own company. But Deirdre and me have been together for thirty-eight years. It's a bit late at my age to get used to myself." He went up to his bed straight after her funeral and never came down, at least not on his own legs.

(Taken from Bermant, 1966, p. 9)

OTHER RELATED EMOTIONS

Loneliness in late adulthood tends to be greater immediately following the death of a spouse or partner and may grow when there is an ever-diminishing circle of significant others who may not be replaced easily (Busse & Pfeiffer, 1977; Butler et al., 1991). Loneliness has been defined as "an awareness of an absence of meaningful integration with other persons or groups, a consciousness of being excluded from the system of opportunities and rewards in which other people participate" (Busse & Pfeiffer, 1977, p. 163). Although loneliness affects members of all age groups at some time, its presence may be especially poignant in the aged who fear they have no one to whom they can relate.

There appears to be little research on loneliness and the aged, but one early study (Shanas et al., 1968) examined the relationship between subjectively experienced loneliness and social isolation. Only half of those living alone stated that they felt lonely rarely or not at all, whereas three-fourths living with other people reported they were rarely or never lonely. Those who had been single all their lives were less lonely than those who were married, widowed, separated, or divorced. The investigators concluded that loss or desolation has a closer relationship with loneliness than isolation.

Nonetheless, when the elderly no longer have the rewards of work, and family members do not live nearby, their social and emotional needs may not be met. Pets, acquaintances, church, and hobbies assist in ordering one's life but are not enough to meet intimacy needs. There are still individuals who are "independent-pull-yourself-up-by-your-bootstraps-people" living alone and pursuing daily routines without much connection to life. Older people in group- or collective-oriented cultures have less of a sense of loss of independence or self-esteem.

Guilt, a sense of impotence and helplessness, and rage are other emotional reactions that may occur in old age. Although this period of life often is a time for positive reflection and reminiscence for some, for others remembrances of past estrangements and conflicts may surface. Just as one is attempting to find some kind of holistic meaning of life, guilt feelings arise. It is important to resolve these kinds of issues in this stage of life (Butler et al., 1991). Age also may bring with it a sense of helplessness and impotence for those who once held positions of power. Lack of control over one's life is both depressing and anxiety provoking. Those affected by a feeling of powerlessness and loss of self-esteem as they age are of lower socioeconomic classes, women, and members of some ethnic groups. White upper-class men in their 80s, who have the highest suicide rates, are also likely to experience emotional disorders (Butler et al., 1991; Schaie & Willis, 1986). Feelings of rage and anger may be manifested in those who experience the indignities and neglect of the "society that once valued their productive capacities" (Butler et al., 1991, p. 95).

Implications for Practice: Coping with Loss

Longevity brings with it both joy and sadness. When people live long enough, there is a certainty that age will bring with it a series of losses that may evoke a range of common human emotions. These emotions will vary depending on such factors as nature of the situation, closeness of a relationship, investment in a career, commitment to a belief system, gender, ethnic background, and socioeconomic status. Being aware of the types of losses associated with aging, the emotions that may follow, and the diversity of expression of these emotions provides guidelines for assisting older people to come to terms with life. There is no general formula for optimal aging, but one can help people in late adulthood find the formula that suits their own particular individuality.

Social Cognition and Regulation

A significant issue in the concept of sense of self for older adults is that they resist thinking of themselves as older adults (Schuster & Ashburn, 1992). "Old is always 15 years older than I am." Recall the senior citizens' group from the beginning of the chapter; not one person in this 70+ age group considered him- or herself to be "old." In fact, people begin to make the transition to defining themselves as old only when their health begins to fail. Yet, inside that frail, failing body, the older adult is still a young adult.

Another concept in older adults' sense of self is that they tend to think of themselves in terms of their former occupation. When introduced, many state what job they retired from. They also tend to keep the same behavior patterns they developed over the years (Schuster & Ashburn, 1992). Basically, as people age, they do not change their core sense of self. They do

Most older adults don't think of themselves as "old." They prefer to remain active and want to be seen as the individuals they are.

not become like other older adults but become more like themselves.

THEORIES OF SUCCESSFUL AGING

What are the dimensions of adjustment in late adulthood that maintain, decrease, or increase life satisfaction? An assumption made by social gerontologists in the early 1940s and 1950s was that continued involvement in activities and maintenance of social roles was a prescription for higher morale, although little research supported this assumption. In the early 1960s, however, an alternative view suggested that levels of life satisfaction are associated with a diminution of activities and relationships. In the ensuing years, these rival theories fueled both debate and research.

Disengagement theory was introduced initially by Cumming and Henry (1961) in the Kansas City

Study of Adult Life. This theory postulates that disengagement occurs in late adulthood through the process of mutual withdrawal of the person and of society, and the process could begin from either side. People choose to withdraw when they recognize a lessening of their capacities and distance from death, whereas society withdraws to maintain equilibrium by making room for younger people in the social system. Withdrawal was not viewed as a uniform pattern—for example, some people might be forced to retire rather than choose to retire. Although the variability of disengagement might decrease morale initially, once people had an opportunity to reorganize their lives and priorities, a higher level of morale could be established. Moreover, even with cultural and individual variations in timing, the process of disengagement was seen as universal and inevitable. The controversy over a theoretical approach proposing that people, at a certain point in life, became self-preoccupied and less interested in relationships and societal involvement stimulated research on life satisfaction and activity.

Activity theory focuses on the relationship between social activity and life satisfaction in late adulthood. The loss of roles through retirement, death, and distance (such as grandparenting when children and their offspring live far away) deprives people of roles that have been a major source of stability throughout life. The central assumption of this theory was that, the more activity one engaged in, the greater one's sense of life satisfaction would be (Lemon, Bengston, & Peterson, 1972). The researchers described three types of activities: (1) informal, which involved socializing with relatives, friends, and neighbors; (2) formal, including participation in voluntary groups; and (3) solitary, pursuing an activity independently, such as reading. Informal activities are the most intimate, followed by formal and then solitary activities. The hypothesis that informal activities would be the most reinforcing and would contribute to life satisfaction was partially supported by the research. A later replication of the study (Longino & Kart, 1982) provided substantial support for this hypothesis. Moreover, Longino and Kart found that informal activity was the type of activity most highly associated with life satisfaction. Informal (intimate) activity appears to reaffirm important roles and a sense of self-worth with others. This study showed that formal activity was associated

with decreased morale, whereas solitary activity had no influence on life satisfaction. The major implication of this study is that not all activities carry equal weight in terms of adjustment in late adulthood. Quality, more than frequency, of activities is important.

Neither disengagement nor activity theory focuses on individual differences in adjustment to aging. Instead, both theories are broad and offer a variety of patterns one might follow. For instance, forced retirement would not increase life satisfaction, but choosing to retire and focusing on one's most cherished activities would.

Psychological Hazards

Traditionally, mental disorders in late adulthood have been classified in two ways: as functional (psychiatric) disorders, with no known physical causes, and organic disorders, for which there are documented physical causes (Belsky, 1990; Butler et al., 1991). According to Butler and colleagues (1991), there is a blurring of the boundaries of the organic and functional disorders of the aged because research with respect to the "biochemical underpinnings of the 'functional' psychiatric disorders, and behavioral research in the 'organic' disorders is revealing multiple psychological and social factors which strongly influence clinical outcomes" (p. 115). Two of the most serious mental disorders that appear to affect older people are **dementia** (impairment or loss of cognitive abilities)—especially dementia of the Alzheimer's type—and depression (Belsky, 1990; Butler et al., 1991; Santrock, 1997; Schaie & Willis, 1986). In late adulthood, a variety of factors (for example, physical, cognitive, social, and emotional difficulties) may combine in such a way that diagnosis of a mental disorder may be confounded. Types of dementia, for instance, share common symptom presentation but have different etiologies. The DSM-IV (American Psychiatric Association, 1994) lists the following types:

1. Dementia of the Alzheimer's type
2. Vascular dementia
3. Dementia due to HIV disease
4. Dementia due to head trauma

5. Dementia due to Parkinson's disease

6. Dementia due to Pick's disease

7. Dementia caused by Creutzfeldt-Jakob disease

8. Dementia caused by other medical conditions

9. Substance-induced persisting dementia

10. Dementia caused by multiple etiologies

11. Dementia not otherwise specified

In addition, for example, early-stage Alzheimer's might "look like" depression, and vice versa (Belsky, 1990; Gruetzner, 1988). Moreover, even quite skilled diagnosticians may vary in their diagnoses, both in terms of type and whether the person has a mental disorder at all (Gurland et al., 1982). Psychological problems and symptoms may also appear to be different in old age than in younger ages (for instance, depression may be manifested by memory problems alone), and this cohort of people tend to underreport any negative symptoms (Belsky, 1990).

ALZHEIMER'S DISEASE

Alzheimer's disease, as distinct from the normal processes of aging (Gruetzner, 1988), has been defined as a "progressive, irreversible brain disorder characterized by gradual deterioration of memory, reasoning, language, and eventual physical function" (Santrock, 1997, p. 562). It is estimated that 2.5 million individuals in the United States have Alzheimer's disease (Butler et al., 1991; Gruetzner, 1988), and it is projected that, by 2025, 7-9 million people will suffer from this disease (Butler et al., 1991). Alzheimer's occurs more frequently in women than in men, probably because of women's longer life expectancy (American psychiatric Association, 1994; Butler et al., 1991).

Dementia of the Alzheimer's type (DAT) gradually causes deterioration in memory, intelligence, awareness, and ability to control bodily functions. At various stages, those affected by the disease often will lose the ability to communicate and will experience perceptual problems (for example, cannot read or follow simple directives), depression, agitation, suspiciousness, delusion, and hallucinations (Blazer, 1998). In the latter stages of the disease, progressive paralysis and breathing difficulties occur. Problems with breathing often result in pneumonia, the leading cause of death

for those afflicted with Alzheimer's (Zastrow & Kirst-Ashman, 1997).

The most current research on Alzheimer's disease in terms of causes, diagnosis, and treatment is summarized in the following sections.

Causes

Scientists have already found certain inherited abnormal genes that predispose an individual to early Alzheimer's (in the 30s or 40s). Currently, there is extensive work being conducted in the field of genetics, trying to pinpoint a gene that may cause Alzheimer's disease in old age.

A recent study involving older nuns indicates that the most highly educated and intellectually active of these subjects lived longer, maintained more agile brains, and seemed less likely to develop Alzheimer's, supporting a "use it or lose it" theory (Heilman, 1995).

Previous research that indicated a possible connection between aluminum exposure and Alzheimer's has not been supported by further study, and it appears unlikely that aluminum exposure is a factor.

Some scientists have suggested that Alzheimer's disease may be virally transmitted. There are some similarities between the disease and certain "slow" viruses—such as AIDS and Kuru, a neurological disorder documented in certain tribes in New Guinea—in which symptoms appear a considerable length of time after infection (Hinrichsen, 1990).

Diagnosis

At this time, autopsy is the only definitive method of diagnosing Alzheimer's. Diagnosis in a living patient requires a complex and costly battery of psychological and neurological tests whose combined results correctly diagnose Alzheimer's in about 90% of cases (Gordon, 1994); however, new tests seem promising.

Researchers at UCLA reported that it seems possible to use brain-imaging scans to see signs of mental deterioration in people with abnormal genes many years before Alzheimer's symptoms appear (Heilman, 1995). Researchers at the National Institute of Mental Health have found that a form of magnetic resonance imaging (MRI) called frequency-shifted burst imaging, can detect the lowered blood flow in the brain that is characteristic of those with Alzheimer's. This type of imaging is quick, can be performed with an ordinary scanner,

Alzheimer's disease brings significant challenges to the caregiver and family members because of the sufferer's extensive loss of memory, personality changes, loss of communication, and relinquishing of inhibitions.

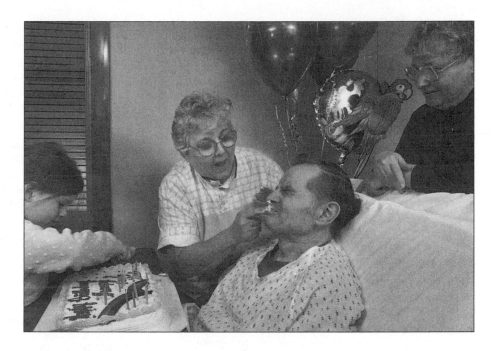

and does not require the use of radioisotopes, allowing the test to be performed frequently to monitor changes (Beardsley, 1995).

A simple eye test, using tropicamide to dilate the patient's pupils, may be the most promising diagnostic technique. Huntington Potter, a neurobiologist at Harvard University, looked for similarities between Alzheimer's sufferers and people born with Down syndrome (it was already known that those with Down syndrome often exhibit symptoms similar to Alzheimer's when they reach their 30s). Potter tested 58 people to see whether their eyes were as hypersensitive to the drug atropine (which comes from the belladonna plant) as are the eyes of those with Down syndrome. Nineteen of the subjects had probable diagnoses of Alzheimer's (the others had other dementias or no illness at all), and 18 of these showed a significantly wider and faster dilation of the pupil than that of the other subjects. It is hoped that further extensive testing of this method will begin soon, leading to commercialization of the test (Gorman, 1994).

Treatment

The only drug currently approved by the Federal Drug Administration (FDA) is tacrine, which can minimize Alzheimer's symptoms. But tacrine helps only a few people for a short period of time, has possible serious side effects, and does not stop progression of the disease.

Some common drugs may affect development of Alzheimer's. There is some indication that postmenopausal women who are given estrogen replacement therapy are far less likely to get Alzheimer's than are those who are untreated. Also being researched are anti-inflammatory drugs and vitamins E and C.

Although President Clinton lifted the ban on fetal tissue research in 1993, the current political climate makes it unlikely that there will be significant federal funding for this research in the future. There had been high hopes that healthy fetal brain cells would reveal the substances that stimulate the brain to make the chemicals needed for its survival, leading to a synthesized form of these substances that could revitalize the brains of Alzheimer's patients.

CytoTherapeutics, a biotechnology company, is investigating implanting a natural body chemical (Nerve Growth Factor) into the brain to protect cells from dying. Research has also begun at the University of California at San Diego, in which skin or muscle cells are taken from a patient's own body, stimulated to produce a crucial missing chemical, and then injected directly into the patient's brain (Heilman, 1995).

Nature may hold the key to an Alzheimer's cure. A chemist has synthesized a neurotoxin found in marine worms to make GTS-21, a compound that ameliorates some symptoms of Alzheimer's. A drug derived from a plant called a Caucasian snowdrop mimics the effects of the drug tacrine without the accompanying potential of liver damage (Lipkin, 1995).

Implications for Practice: Alzheimer's and the Family

In people with Alzheimer's disease, the individual's behavioral alterations (for example, physical and verbal aggression, delusions, suspiciousness, uncontrollable agitation, wandering) have an enormous effect on the family as well as on the individual. Providing care to a loved one with Alzheimer's is a challenging activity, even under the best of circumstances. Why one caregiver copes effectively whereas another becomes demoralized, unable to cope, and at risk for poor health is not well understood. There is evidence, however, that a person's perception of social support is critical in understanding how he or she copes with stress (Monahan & Hooker, 1995). When the disease is not advanced, individuals may show signs of depression, which tend to exacerbate cognitive deficits (Belsky, 1990). Group and individual counseling are available to persons with Alzheimer's and their caregivers. If the disease is not advanced, the person with Alzheimer's might benefit from a support group to discuss feelings, problems, and ideas for coping. Individual sessions might consist of cognitive training or reality orientation to help people remember important information and be reoriented to time, date, and place. Caregiver support groups and family treatment assist all (partners, spouses, children, close friends) who care for one who has Alzheimer's. The focus of either type of treatment might be on dealing with feelings and frustrations and providing practical tips for coping with the situation. Respite care consists of supervised adult daytime health care for the person with Alzheimer's and provides the caregiver with periods of rest and relief. In some communities, in-home respite care is available for evenings, weekends, or longer time periods (Hyman, 1987).

FOCUS ON RESEARCH

Predicting Alzheimer's

Would you want to know if you are at high risk of growing old with Alzheimer's? Doctors may soon be able to identify individuals in the earliest stages of the illness—years or even decades before any noticeable decline in intellectual ability. But such a test could create a dilemma of a different sort: Do people really want to know that Alzheimer's lies in their future when medicine can offer no cure?

The possibility of early diagnosis arises from advanced brain-mapping technology and new insights into the genetics of Alzheimer's. In recent years, researchers have learned that the disease is linked to the presence of a gene called Apo-E4. But the gene does not always trigger the illness; people with one copy of the gene have perhaps a 50% chance of getting Alzheimer's, and for those with two copies the likelihood rises to about 90% by age 80. In no cases can geneticists reliably predict at what age the disease will start.

(Nash, 1995)

DEPRESSION

A relatively small percentage of older people have major depressive disorders as classified by the DSM—(American Psychiatric Association, 1994). What is not clear is the prevalence of mild depressive symptoms in late adulthood. The estimate of its prevalence has ranged anywhere from 5% to more than 30% (Gurland et al., 1980; Waxman et al., 1985). It has been pointed out that late-life depression may be characterized by the following paradox: "Although the prevalence of depressive symptoms increases with age, the prevalence of major depressive disorders does not" (Kennedy et al., 1989).

Generally, it is difficult to distinguish between levels of depression. Depression is not the same as the sadness or unhappiness felt by people confronting everyday life. Symptoms of depression may include feelings of sadness and emptiness, withdrawal, self-neglect, changes in appetite, loss of sexual desire, and sleeping problems (Gruetzner, 1988). In older people, depressive symptoms are often associated with medical conditions that tend to mask the depression itself. Medical conditions commonly associated with depression include: (1) coronary artery disease—for example, hypertension, myocardial infarction; (2) neurologic disorders—for instance, cerebrovascular accidents, Alzheimer's disease; (3) metabolic disturbances—such as diabetes, hypo- or hyperthyroidism; (4) cancer—for example, pancreatic, breast, lung; and (5) other conditions—such as arthritis, sexual dysfunction, and deafness (Sunderland et al., 1988). Another study (Kennedy et al., 1989), using a representative sample of 2,137 older urban residents, found a hierarchy of characteristics associated with substantial levels of depressive symptoms: illness, disability, isolation, bereavement, and poverty.

Symptoms of depression have been treated through the use of medication and counseling. According to Belsky (1990), medication may work well with symptoms tied to physical signs of illness and less well when tied to events. Counseling is the treatment of choice when the focus is on changing the "depression-causing situation or modifying the person's depression-generating thoughts" (p. 276).

Implications for Practice: Assessing Depression in Older Persons

Physical health and functioning are key factors associated with depression in older people. Depression has a reverberating effect in that the process of recovery may be impeded if the person is not motivated to pursue adequate medical attention and rehabilitation, maintain medical regimens, and engage in self-care. This may be particularly true if there is no hope of regaining previous levels of functioning (DeAngelis, 1997). Interestingly, in a rural study (O'Hara, Kohout, & Wallace, 1985) that consisted of 3,159 older adults (aged 65 to 105 years), the data indicated that prevalence of significant depressive symptomatology (9%) was low for this sample. Those most at risk for depression were women, people who lived alone, and those with lower incomes. There was also evidence that those at lower risk for depression were married and had attained higher educational levels. The investigators speculated that high levels of social support available in rural communities account for low levels of depression.

The latter research suggests that social work practitioners should assist depressed older people in restoring broken social support systems or acquiring new systems through voluntary activities or special-interest groups, for example. For the older person who lives alone, home-sharing with a younger person who can assist around the house might be an option. Supportive approaches that emphasize the uncovering and mobilization of an individual's strengths to help them remain connected with life can be very

useful. There has been considerable success in using cognitive behavioral approaches that assist the depressed client in identifying and changing depression-generating thoughts or cognitions.

One "quick" method of assessing potential depression in older people is the Geriatric Depression Scale (GDS), a 15-item validated scale (Yesavage et al., 1983). In scoring the scale, assign one point for each answer given as follows: questions 1, 5, 7, 11, and 13 answered no, and the remainder answered yes. A normal score is 0–5; above 5 suggests depression (see Box 12.3).

SUICIDE

Suicide is a significant problem in late adulthood. Furthermore, although only a small proportion of depressed people commit suicide, most serious suicide attempts are made by depressed people (Belsky, 1990). Committing suicide because of depression over a lifetime of accumulated losses, debilitating terminal illnesses, isolation, loneliness, lack of a sense of control, and the like is not so surprising. When depression is defined all inclusively, it has been estimated that nearly 100% of older people who attempt suicide have depressive symptoms (Stenback, 1980).

The prevalence of suicide in any age group is difficult to determine with accuracy because suicides may be masked, for instance, as accidents or natural causes. A study (Manton, Blazer, & Woodbury, 1987) analyzing cross-temporal data on suicide (between 1962 and 1981) from the National Center on Health Statistics found that the suicide rate was highest in older white males, followed by nonwhite males, white females, and nonwhite females (see Figure 12.2). Note that the suicide rate for white men peaked in middle age; also, the suicide rate was highest for white women in middle age. For nonwhite males, the suicide rate was higher in young adulthood. Over time, the suicide rate for nonwhite females decreases with minor peaks. Another study (Rich, Young, & Fowler, 1986) indicated that the suicide rate per 100,000 people was 31.9% for males and 15.9% for females 65 and older.

Butler and colleagues (1991) speculate that the most preventable suicides are those related to depression since suicide "in these cases is a passive, desperate giving up" (p. 131). There are those, however, who choose their time of death before dependency and

Geriatric Depression Scale (GDS): Short Form (Example)

CIRCLE THE BEST ANSWER FOR
HOW YOU FELT OVER THE PAST WEEK.

1. Are you basically satisfied with your life? yes/no

2. Have you dropped many of your activities and interests? yes/no

3. Do you feel that your life is empty? yes/no

4. Do you often get bored? yes/no

5. Are you in good spirits most of the time? yes/no

6. Are you afraid that something bad is going to happen to you? yes/no

7. Do you feel happy most of the time? yes/no

8. Do you often feel helpless? yes/no

9. Do you prefer to stay at home rather than go out and do new things? yes/no

10. Do you feel you have more problems with memory than most? yes/no

11. Do you think it is wonderful to be alive now? yes/no

12. Do you feel pretty worthless the way you are now? yes/no

13. Do you feel full of energy? yes/no

14. Do you feel that your situation is hopeless? yes/no

15. Do you think that most people are better off than you are? yes/no

(Yesavage et al., 1983)

---

complete lack of control engulfs them. Some even advocate for **assisted suicide** (helping to provide the means to end a person's life) (see the following Focus section) or **euthanasia** (putting to death those with a painful or debilitating terminal illness) (see the subsequent Focus section on the right to die).

FOCUS ON ETHICS

Assisted Suicide: Murder or Mercy?

Dr. Jack Kavorkian, known as "Dr. Death," may be newsworthy in the United States, but he's actually part of a tradition that has been operational in the Netherlands for more than a decade. Moved and concerned by the moral burden posed by participating in euthanasia and assisted suicide, the Royal Dutch Medical Association has recently proposed some refinements to existing euthanasia guidelines. The Association's present rules address several crucial areas. First, the patient's request for euthanasia must be made independently and voluntar-

ily. In addition, the patient must have been well-informed about the alternatives and have a firm and lasting resolve to die. The patient's suffering must be experienced as hopeless and unbearable, with the physician concluding that the suffering cannot be remedied. The physician must have a consultation with at least one colleague familiar with euthanasia-related cases and issues; the proper written documentation, including the patient's medical history and the declaration that the preceding rules have been met, must be generated.

The new guidelines, put together by lawyers and ethicists as well as doctors, appear in a 39-page policy document sent out in August 1995 to the 24,000 members of the Royal Dutch Medical Association. Although the new rules do not propose any fundamental changes, they do impose some restrictions on the existent guidelines. The first refinement suggests that whenever possible, doctors should have terminally ill patients administer their own fatal drugs, as opposed to a physician administering an intravenous drip or injection. Second, the new rules stipulate that the outside consultation must be with a physician who does not have a preexisting professional or family relationship with the patient

FIGURE 12.2 **Suicide rates (Manton, Blazer, & Woodbury, 1987)**

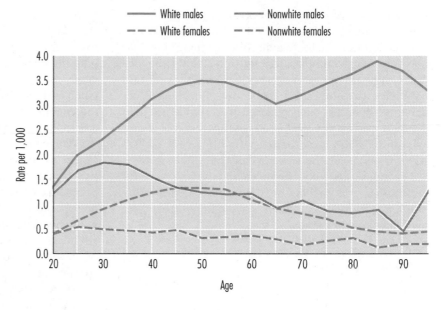

or the attending doctor. Finally, although no doctor is required to perform euthanasia, he or she is obligated to inform patients of his or her moral position so that a patient wishing to die might contact another physician for assistance.

It is the position of the Association and its proponents that the patient's participation in the termination of his or her own life helps diminish, if only slightly, the difficult moral and emotional burden experienced by the assisting physician. Opponents of euthanasia and assisted suicide suggest a perversity in the euthanasia logic that refusing to kill someone is considered cruel and that agreeing to kill the person is compassionate. One such opponent suggests that at the heart of the Netherlands' problem is a lack of facilities for palliative care, such as hospices, which could alleviate the pain and suffering that lead patients to wish to end their lives. But is this simply a way to ease the collective conscience of the living?

In a discussion of the ethics of assisted suicide from a social work value-based perspective (that is, client self-determination versus client well-being), Callahan (1994) concluded that assisted suicide is unethical. He referred to studies that indicated that most suicidal people have impaired judgment caused by depression or other mental illness. Moreover, he pointed out that the contagion phenomenon and the destigmatization of suicide may lead to higher rates of suicide among the young as well as the general population.

(Julianne Azimov, based on Simons, 1995)

THE LIVING WILL AND MEDICAL POWER OF ATTORNEY

If a person has a terminal illness that is not treatable or reversible, the **living will** allows that person to document that he or she does not want to be kept alive by artificial means but instead desires care only for comfort. The person states that he or she does not wish to be resuscitated if breathing stops or the heart stops beating.

The **medical power of attorney** applies to a person with any illness (not necessarily a terminal one). If an ill person loses the ability to make medical decisions regarding his or her care, the medical power of attorney designates someone to have the authority to make those decisions for the ill person.

Many hospitals give the patient the option to make a living will or to designate medical power of attorney on admission. Preparation of these documents does not require a lawyer or a notary; they require only a witness. These documents can be revoked in writing at any time.

FOCUS ON SOCIOLOGY

Right to Die

"Two years ago my mother, who was then 83, told me that she planned to end her life by taking an overdose of pills. Her health was failing rapidly and she was going blind. She didn't want to become weak and dependent. She had always been a fierce and active woman. She wrote her intentions in a letter to me—I was her only close family member—and she told two friends and her doctor. We all told her that we would not help her accumulate enough pills to do the job. And I think we all worked very hard to help her find new reasons to be happy to be alive. But finally I understood that she really wanted to do what she had planned, and in the end, after she gathered together enough pills and took them, I sat with her for the last 36 hours as she slipped away. I can't tell you how many of her friends and acquaintances told me how graceful my mother was in her life to the very end. For my mother, given her personality, staying in control of her own life made her graceful."

—A 41-year-old woman

(Howell, Allen, & Doress, 1987)

SOCIAL DIMENSION

Families, Groups, Support Systems, and Communities

Today's older people have experienced all the influences of neonatal development, infancy, childhood, adolescence, early adulthood, and middle age. The development and behavior of the young-old, the middle-old, and the old-old also have been shaped by different historic events over their life spans as well as by unique events that have influenced their lives positively or negatively. Development, however, does not stop with age. The context of older people's lives continues to influence their growth and development.

FAMILIES

Social work family theorists Hartman and Laird (1987) have defined two types of families, one that is created and one that is inherited: "A family [then] is created when two or more people construct an intimate environment that they define as a family, an environment in which they generally will share a living space, commit-

ment, and a variety of roles and functions usually considered part of family life. The second family, common to all human beings and psychologically important whether or not close ties have been maintained, is the family of origin—that family of blood or **bloodlike ties** (such as those that occur in adoption), both vertical (intergenerational) and horizontal (kinship), living and dead, close and distant, known and unknown" (p. 576).

The behavior of older adults is influenced to some extent by the patterns present in their families of origin. To their created or chosen family forms, older people have brought with them certain sets of values, beliefs, and varied ways of interacting with others and with their environments. Created family forms in late adulthood are as diverse as they were in other periods of development. Some older adults live with their spouses of 40 years or more; others are newlyweds; some are widowed, single, or never married; and others are gay men or lesbians. In a sense, those who reside in nursing homes can count other residents and staff as family as well as adult children and other relatives. For non-institutionalized older people, other relatives with whom they live may include parents, children, siblings, nieces, or nephews. Older people living with nonrelatives may include gay or lesbian partners, friends, or "roommates." Those who live alone may count as family a circle of friends, as well as children and other relatives. It is obvious that the configurations of created family forms among older people are both diverse and complex. For purposes of this discussion of family, however, we shall include only relationships between marital partners, gay male and lesbian partners, parents and children, grandparents and grandchildren, and friends.

COUPLES

Most of the studies on satisfaction with marital relationships have used cross-sectional approaches, which tend to measure cohort differences rather than relationships over time. More longitudinal studies are needed to accomplish the latter. Early studies (Blood & Wolfe, 1960; Pineo, 1969) showed that marital satisfaction decreased over time, particularly after children were born. However, later studies (Miller, 1976; Orthner, 1975; Rollins & Feldman, 1970), have shown that, although marital satisfaction drops when children are born, it tends to rise to previous highs in the postparental period. Marital partners have the opportunity to rediscover and renew their relationship and have the time to spend with each other in pursuit of joint interests. There is some evidence (Atchley & Miller, 1983) that people of higher socioeconomic status and levels of education experience greater marital satisfaction than do those who are less well off and less well educated (Depner & Ingersol-Dayton, 1985). Marital satisfaction for those who remarry in old age appears to be quite high (McKain, 1972). These individuals typically are in good health and are seeking others with whom they can enjoy such activities as travel and leisure.

Studies (Atchley & Miller, 1983; Duvall & Miller, 1985) have shown, though, that when one of the marital partners becomes ill, the other partner's morale declines. However, the illness does not appear to erode the bond between husband and wife (Johnson, 1983). Indeed, the healthy spouse becomes the primary caregiver and rarely seeks outside help (Cantor, 1983; Johnson, 1983). As with other age groups, satisfaction or happiness with marriage differs among the old; some remain close and in love and others do not.

PARENT-CHILD RELATIONSHIPS

Increased health and longevity have complicated parent-child relationships. In the normal course of events, cohort (generational) differences cause conflicts between parents and children over the life span. A younger adult child, for instance, may have little patience or understanding of the experience of a parsimonious older parent who lived through the Depression. The complexity of parent-child relationships increases even more when aging parents have older adult children. Children who themselves are approaching retirement age, with all its constraints and concerns (for instance, income, health), may have to care for older parents as well. Caregiving of elderly parents by aging children is a common phenomenon in today's society. And, for some aging children, responsibilities (for example, financial, emotional) have not ceased for their own young adult children.

Caregiving, typically, is the responsibility of the adult daughter rather than the son. Brody (1981), a social worker, and her colleagues coined the phrase "women in the middle," which implies that such women are in middle age, in the middle from a generational standpoint, and in the middle in that the demands of their various roles compete for their time and energy. To an extent unprecedented in history, roles as paid workers and as caregiving daughters and daughters-in-law to dependent older people have been added to women's traditional roles as wives, homemakers, mothers, and grandmothers (p. 471).

Although most research has focused on daughters as caregivers of elderly parents, some investigators (Delgado & Tennstedt, 1997) have begun to examine the role of sons as primary caregivers. In this study of caregivers, the researchers found that Puerto Rican sons assumed the caregiving role out of a sense of responsibility and when other potential caregivers were unavailable owing to circumstances or distance.

More than half of elderly people now live near one of their adult children. Practitioners find that an elderly parent's move to be closer to family can have positive effects. The adult children may get help with their own youngsters. And their elderly parents gain a sense of security at a time of vulnerability. However, many conflicting emotions arise because of these relocations. They fear and look forward to the move—the dichotomy of leaving familiar surroundings and going to live near family. After they have moved, many older people want to help their adult children with their families but are afraid of intruding on their children's lives. Reunified families often struggle with how to set boundaries while integrating one another's social worlds (Seppa, 1996). And when adult children assume caregiving duties for an aging parent, the role reversals can be upsetting to all involved.

Caregiving of older parents is an issue that has had and will continue to have an enormous effect on families in the future. Current literature abounds on the intricacies of caregiving; for instance, a small list includes gender and caregiving (Baruch & Spaid, 1989; Young & Kahana, 1989); dementia and caregiving (Dura, Haywood-Niler, Kiecolt-Glaser, 1990; Hinrichsen & Ramirez, 1992); and stress and the burden of caregiving (Cattanach & Tebes, 1991; Stephens, Kinney, & Ogrocki, 1991). Caregiving can be extraordinarily stressful for any adult child, but the burdens of homosexual and single adults caring for an older parent may have additional consequences if they have never been married or had children of their own.

Take, for example, the situation of a 57-year-old gay man who cares for his 90-year-old mother in the home. Ricardo, as we shall call him, has schizophrenia, is stabilized on medication and supportive treatment, and has 15 years of sobriety from alcoholism. His mother is bedridden and needs constant personal care. According to his social worker, Ricardo and his mother live in the family home and are supported by their disability and social security income. Ricardo is a bright, well-read, articulate individual who cultivates a large vegetable garden each year and cares for his mother with tenderness and concern. Ricardo's caregiving role has kept him from pursuing other interests and relationships, but he does not complain. There are times when he speculates about what will happen after the death of his mother and when he reaches old age. There will be no one left in the family to call on.

Because the issues of caregiving are so complex and overwhelming, it often is easy to view older people as always the recipients rather than the givers of help. A growing body of research (see, for example, Cantor, 1979; Patterson, 1987; Quam, 1983) indicates that older people provide a remarkable amount of help not only to relatives but also to friends and neighbors. In her study of **natural helpers** (relatives, friends, and neighbors to whom one turns in time of need), Patterson (1987) found that older respondents assisted relatives, friends, and neighbors with a range of life transitional, environmental, and interpersonal relationship difficulties. The relatives helped were not just adult children, grandchildren, and their own parents but also siblings, in-laws, and other relatives (aunts and uncles, nieces and nephews, cousins). Thus, the informal caregiving role should be expanded to include a wider variety of helpers (neighbors and friends) as well as the old people themselves. Moreover, the scientific basis for the mediating effect of social support on both mental and physical health problems is overwhelming (Cobb, 1976; Ornish, 1998).

GRANDPARENTHOOD

For many older people (80%), grandparenthood is a role in which they find joy in their relationships with grandchildren. Moreover, most view grandparenting as easier than being a parent (Brubaker, 1985). Even if there are infrequent contacts with grandchildren,

Grandparents can be important figures in a child's life and can play a significant role in transmitting cultural and family values to children.

grandparents state that being a grandparent has significant meaning in their lives (Wood & Robertson, 1978). According to Hagestad (1985), grandparenting has many meanings, some which are intangible: Grandparents serve as symbols of connectedness within and between lives; as people who can listen and have time to do so; as reserves of time, help, and attention; as links to the unknown past; as people who are sufficiently varied, flexible, and complex to defy easy categories and clear-cut roles (p. 48).

Grandparenting appears to have different functions in some families, depending on such factors as ethnicity and culture. For instance, Hagestad (1985) found that grandmothers were closer to both their children and grandchildren than grandfathers and provided more personal advice to them. Robertson (1976) found that young adult working-class grandchildren perceived their grandparents positively, and their primary expectation of the grandparents was to provide emotional gratification and nurturance. About two-thirds of the young adults viewed their responsibility toward the grandparents as helping without payment. In a study of African-American, white, and Mexican-American grandparenting relationships, Bengston (1985) found that Mexican-American grandparents and grandchildren had closer relationships with one another than the white and African-American respondents had with their grandchildren. Furthermore, these grandparents had more frequent contact with their grandchildren and assumed more supportive roles to them and their parents.

FRIENDSHIPS

Old age is not the time of loneliness and desolation that many people think it is. Elderly people do not *lose* their social lives, they *alter* them (Murray, 1997). Friends play an important, supportive role in old age. While it is true that younger people socialize more frequently, the contact is more with acquaintances and professional contacts. Older adults, by comparison, seek social contact with a select few close friends and family members. Older adults' recognition that they have fewer years left is the catalyst for this shift (Fredrickson, 1990). The concept is that if you perceive many years ahead of you, you will probably try meeting new people to enrich your life. But if your future seems limited, you will more likely spend more time with your family and close friends. These ideas are part of Fredrickson's (1990) "socioemotional selectivity" theory, which posits that the perception of time governs the social motives people pursue. Because our chronological age colors the way we view the amount of time we have left in life, stage of life is importantly associated with our social needs.

Sandmaier (1995) states that the bond of friendship is elective, more fragile than ties with kin, and has no formalized rituals. And, she writes further, "as we move through our lives, the friends we've made and kept over time take on an increasingly vital role as curators of our emotional histories" (p. 34). Litwak and Szelenyi (1969) identified three types of primary group structures: kin, neighbors, and friends, each with different functions. Ties of kinship are characterized by the permanence of relationship and/or legal responsibility. Thus kin are more likely to exchange support and resources in situations requiring long-term commitment, such as the care of an aged member or financial aid during prolonged unemployment. Ties among neighbors are based on face-to-face contact and immediate proximity and, in urban life, tend to lack permanence in this era of mobility. Thus neighbors are more likely to exchange resources and services that do not require a long-term commitment (such as short-term babysitting or transportation for shopping or medical appointments). Ties among friends lack, to some degree, the permanence of kinship ties and often the proximity of neighbors. But because friendship rests on mutual regard and often affection, friends are more likely to exchange guidance, advice, and emotional support. In her study of the support systems of 400 women over 50 (Mn = 66 years), Quam (1983) found that friends were most likely to be called on for expressive support (for example, listening to personal/family problems) and unlikely to be called on for instrumental support (for instance, financial). Frauenhofer and colleagues (1987) quote a 75-year-old woman who aptly describes the importance of social support in later adulthood:

> The greatest pleasure of growing old is remaining in contact with friends from church and in the community. I'm treasurer of the Older Women's League chapter here, and also the Black Caucus on Aging. I kept contact with my friends from childhood. I love people, all kinds of people. I don't give up a relationship easily. I only gave up one in 72 years, someone who really, really hurt me. I am friends with my ex-husband's second wife and went to see her on my vacation. She was so glad to see me (p. 129).

Friendships have a special significance for gay men, lesbians, single adults, and those who have moved to retirement communities, often some distance from children, grandchildren, and other relatives. For instance, one group known as the Body Limerick evolved into a close-knit cadre of friends when they started a limerick group to "put a little humor in their lives." The group members range in age from 55 to 95 and meet frequently for potluck dinners and limerick construction. Once a year, the group takes a trip together to such places as Santa Fe and San Diego, and one year they rented a houseboat on Lake Powell. The group has become emotionally close and supportive and has unlimited abilities to laugh at themselves. A 72-year-old member penned the following:

> There was an old man in Sun City
> Who really was smart and quite witty,
> But he was blind as a bat,
> And so was his cat,
> How in the heck can we end such a ditty?
>
> (V. Wood, 1996, personal communication)

RELIGION AND SPIRITUALITY

There is a renewed interest in the significance of religion and spirituality in the lives of older people as well as in the general population (Zastrow & Kirst-Ashman, 1997). George Gallup, Jr. (1990) found that most Americans (95%) believe in God, evidencing greater interest in religion than other Western democracies. Further, African-Americans tend to be more religious than other Americans, women more religious than men, and older people more religious than younger people. In a review of research concerning religious commitment and mental health status of older people, Koenig (1990) found that studies indicated a positive relationship between religious beliefs, attitudes, coping behaviors and mental health. Levin and Vanderpool (1987) reviewed 27 studies with respect to the correlation between religious attendance and better health. Of the 27 studies, some 22 found that attendance was associated positively with health status.

According to Reed (1987), spirituality refers to those views and behaviors that exemplify a sense of relatedness to something other than the self. Spirituality connotes a level of awareness that goes beyond ordinary physical and spatial boundaries. Schuster and Ashburn (1992) suggest that the spiritual domain completes the holistic view of people in their environments. Spiritual and health beliefs are highly integrated in most American-Indian cultures (Coggins, 1990). Related to the idea of treatment of disease among many tribes is the notion that human beings are made up of a body, mind, and spirit (Locust, 1988). One cannot physically treat only the body but also must consider any disharmony in the three domains of body, mind, and spirit.

Religion and spirituality appear to be important aspects of the physical, psychological, and social lives of older people. In assessing the needs of older people and in working directly with them, it is key to understand their belief systems and the role these systems play in their lives.

NURSING HOMES

Long-term care can be defined as medical and social interventions for those who have chronic illnesses or impairments. These interventions are geared toward helping a patient live as satisfactorily as possible and may be provided in a number of settings, including normal private homes, supportive housing, and nursing homes or other institutions.

About 5% of older people live in long-term-care facilities, and many feel that a nursing home is a "last resort," when other resources have been exhausted or the situation has become desperate. Actually, nursing homes may be more realistically viewed as a specialized resource for those who need a higher level of care than can be provided at home.

The decision to move to assisted living can be a difficult one for families and individuals. Many older adults wish to remain independent as long as possible. Many family members wish to provide care for older relatives for as long as possible. Some older people have no one to provide needed care. When an older adult becomes confused and disoriented, wanders off without warning, is incontinent, or is bedridden, help becomes necessary. The problem then becomes finding appropriate placement. Custodial care of older people is not covered by most insurance. The cost of nursing homes or assisted living can be more than many older adults' monthly income from Social Security or a pension. Older adults living on a fixed income may have to exhaust their resources and savings to become eligible for state- or federal-government-funded placement. Social workers are often involved in helping older adults obtain adequate care at home or appropriate placement. Social workers can also challenge the conventional concept of nursing homes as primarily medical institutions and advocate for fulfilling residents' social and emotional needs (Levenson, 1998).

The following Focus section describes guidelines that can be used for choosing a nursing home.

FOCUS ON SOCIOLOGY

Choosing a Nursing Home

Federal reforms passed in the late 1980s mandate that nursing home operators work to attain the highest level of physical, mental and psychosocial well-being of each patient as possible. They were established in response to widespread and sometimes heinous physical and emotional neglect of residents. Although these national standards have led to a high level of quality in most nursing homes, here are some guidelines for those seeking an excellent facility for a client or loved one:

- Be sure the nursing home is licensed. Medicare and Medicaid eligibility may also be an indication of basic quality, but some excellent facilities accept only private payments. Also check for membership in the American Health Care Association, which sets high standards for quality.

- Walk through the facility and smell the air. Occasional odors from incontinence and other medical conditions are unavoidable, but a persistently bad-smelling facility is probably poorly run.

- Check the fee schedule. Be sure you understand exactly what services are included, and beware of hidden charges.

- Request a full tour, including the kitchen. Be suspicious of any facility that denies this request.

- Talk to staff members at every level, especially the aides who have the most contact with residents. Watch them interact with residents.

- Ask about a backup plan for medical emergencies. If the patient's regular doctor is not available, what happens?

- Observe the residents. Do they appear well cared for?

- Be sure the rules about visitors and residents leaving the vicinity for outside activities are reasonable and flexible.

- Ask about choices for residents. Are they allowed to choose activities, foods, furnishings? Can they bring treasured belongings from home?

(Adapted from Roth & Atherton, 1989)

HOSPICE

Up until World War II, death was a part of the human experience and of the life of the community. People died at home in the presence of friends and family. Everyone, including children, saw and experienced death as an integral part of life (Munley, 1983). Today, many people live in areas separated from extended family. Many adults have never seen a dying person or experienced a death.

In fact, modern medicine has almost made death an isolated phenomenon affecting older people. Those over 65 account for two-thirds of all deaths; and the majority of total deaths occur from diseases of older adults, such as stroke, cancer, and heart disease. Instead of occurring at home in the midst of loved ones, most of these deaths now occur in a hospital. Today more than 50% of Americans die in hospitals, and nearly 20% die in nursing homes. For some, the final days are spent in isolation, fear, and pain (Clay, 1997).

This movement of death from the home to the hospital occurred shortly after World War II. According to Kastenbaum (1981), attitudes toward death then changed, as though people were trying to pretend death did not exist. Efforts to provide an alternative to hospital death resulted in the **hospice** movement. Hospices became important in treating terminal patients when families, patients, and caregivers found hospitals were not meeting their needs. In contrast to the goals of a hospital, the aim of hospice care is to care for and support the dying. Whereas the major focus of the hospital is to cure, the major focus of hospice care is pain and symptom control.

Individuals are eligible for hospice care when they have less than a six-month life expectancy and agree to give up seeking a cure for their illness. Hospice care is provided in the patient's home and sometimes in a special hospice unit in a hospital or community agency. Many hospice patients are older persons, and many are dying of cancer. But, increasingly, hospice patients are young people with AIDS. The purpose of the hospice is to allow the patient to experience death, not in isolation but in an atmosphere of love and acceptance.

RETIREMENT

Retirement occurs when one leaves the workforce and begins living on some kind of pension. Often, retirement is thought of as the period at which people begin to receive social security or other pension benefits. Although most people think of retirement as occurring around age 65, it arrives earlier for many people. In fact, some people plan to retire in their 50s. This trend has been increasing as many companies offer a package of early retirement to entice people to retire, often done to free up personnel money for new workers. However, many older workers are not ready to jump on the early-retirement bandwagon. In fact, research shows that most people underestimate older people's ability and willingness to work (Clay, 1996). An unintended result of early retirement is that there is increasingly a long interval between the end of working and the end of life.

What would it be like to go from working on the same job or in a similar job for 30–40 years to becoming retired? No schedule to follow, no alarms to set, no need to be in rush-hour traffic, no performance or work reviews, none of the familiar behaviors that are associated with work. For many older adults, retirement can be a difficult period of adjustment. Being forced to retire can be devastating. Whether the cause is ill health, mandatory retirement laws, or subtle pressures from employers or co-workers, involuntary retirement can result in both psychological and physical problems—especially for those adults who derived most of their sense of identity from their work, where the job is the only real interest in life; the friends were mostly colleagues. When a person such as this retires, there is nothing much left. This single-mindedness about work is not the only personality trait that can lead to problems once people are no longer working. People prone to rigidity may also have difficulty adjusting (Clay, 1996). In fact, for a long time many theorists thought that retirement automatically led to a crisis. From this perspective, retirement was considered negative, hazardous to one's physical and mental health. Now research has found that this is not the case and that, although retirement may require some special adjustment, it does not have to be a crisis. In fact, there are several factors that can help determine how well a person adjusts to retirement. Retiring gradually is one way to avert a crisis. Cultivating interests and friendships unrelated to work is another important factor in adapting successfully to retirement (Clay, 1996).

Still, retirement involves a major shift in one's family roles, daily activity, social interactions, and financial resources. How one anticipates these changes can affect how successfully one retires. Atchley (1976) identifies a process of adjustment to retirement that moves through a series of changes. Individuals begin at the *preretirement phase,* which is an opportunity to begin to think and plan for retirement. Just after retirement, individuals often move into a *honeymoon phase,* wherein they discover newfound freedom and they enjoy increased opportunities for visiting family and friends and enjoying leisure time, sports activities, gardening, and so forth. Not surprisingly, the honeymoon phase ends and leads to a *disenchantment phase,* wherein retirement does not seem as pleasant as before. Last, the individual moves to a *reorientation phase* and becomes more realistic about retirement and learns to make the necessary adaptations. Researchers (Ekerdt, Bossé, & Levkoff, 1985) have found that these phases are accurate. Men recently retired were satisfied and optimistic about the future, but 13 to 18 months later they were disenchanted with their lives, and men in long-term retirement were satisfied and reoriented.

So far, we have been talking about retirement mostly in terms of how it affects men. Many women cannot afford to retire, especially if they are uncoupled. Those who manage to retire may suffer extra stress owing to financial worries. With women's longer life expectancies, they may be terrified of outliving their money. Other women find themselves pressured to retire prematurely by spouses who have already retired. Often married to older men, these women may just be hitting their stride at work when their husbands insist it is time to start traveling and enjoying themselves. Once they retire, women may find that retirement does not offer them the same opportunities as their male counterparts. They may, for example, give up their paid employment only to face years of providing care for ailing parents or husbands.

Retirement can strain marriages. Conflict is especially common in couples living by traditional gender roles—couples who suffer the most disruption when the husband abruptly intrudes on the wife's routines. In the best-case scenario, the couple eventually works things out. Growing closer together, they may even move toward androgyny as the wife becomes more assertive and the husband more nurturing. In the worst case, however, the forced intimacy of retirement unsettles the marriage.

Retirement is made more difficult for individuals who have little income to begin with and must then adjust to a reduction in income. Many older adults become embarrassed and uncomfortable with the notion that they have little money and cannot provide for their family as they may have done in the past.

The following Focus section discusses how some cultures have no retirement.

▼

Some Cultures Have No Retirement

If you were living among the !Kung San of the Kalahari Desert in Africa, you would not understand the concept of retirement. As adults get older, rather than being put into retirement they are considered important people who have respect in the community. They take on a number of critical roles in the community: (1) stewards of water rights and resources in the area; (2) keepers of knowledge, skills, and lore; (3) teachers and caretakers of children; (4) spiritual teachers and healers; and (5) privileged community members. In many respects, these roles are based on reciprocal obligations across the life cycle (Biesele & Howell, 1981). There is no retirement here. Men continue to perform hunting and healing functions, and women remain gatherers and healers. As they grow old, men move to less taxing responsibilities such as trapping, gathering, visiting, and telling stories. Women move to less physical activities as well, including child care and production of handicrafts.

Multicultural and Gender Considerations

Greene (1994) states that "members of an ethnic group think of themselves as a 'people' ... with diverse lifestyle, languages, histories, and cultural strengths and supports" (p. 6). To work with different ethnic groups, social workers must acquire informed, competent, and culturally sensitive services. Because there is such diversity in minority groups, difficulties often are generated in health and mental health services as a result of inflexibilities in these systems. Successful service provision to minority older people (Cuellar, 1980) is de-

pendent on whether services are located in the ethnic community and are easily accessible, have an informal and personalized environment, have a client-oriented staff that helps them get all the services needed, and have bilingual or indigenous outreach workers who are culturally sensitive and concerned about the people and the community they serve. One common factor that appears to be present in diverse Native-American tribes is the concept of the extended family. This form of family may be influenced by residence (urban or reservation), acculturation, socioeconomic factors, and varied family circumstances. Younger family members seek both advice and support from their elders. In assuming a central role in the family, older Native-Americans provide spiritual, cultural, and behavioral guidance for younger family members. Grandparenting is viewed as an important responsibility, and it is not uncommon for older people to take over complete child-rearing responsibilities for their adult children. In exchange for these kinds of help, older Native-Americans are respected and cared for if they become unable to care for themselves (Shoemaker, 1989). Informal support is more plentiful on reservations than in urban areas because of the close proximity of family members.

In the past, a certain set of role behaviors was expected of males and females in traditional Indian culture. It is likely that gender-role expectations are maintained among the oldest Native-Americans. For instance, older women assumed responsibility for such expressive functions as "kin-keeping," whereas men retained the employment role. With rapid societal changes, impoverishment, and acculturation, more middle-aged to young-old women are assuming leadership roles than in the past (Hanson, 1980).

To understand African-American families, it is critical to investigate an array of factors: African cultural influences, racial oppression, social class differences both within and between groups, and family and kinship networks (Dodson, 1988). For instance, in one study (Johnson & Barer, 1990) of families and networks among older inner-city African-Americans, the investigators found that both African-Americans and whites used formal support systems when they needed help, but African-Americans had more active informal support networks than whites did, despite the low incidence of child and spousal support. The investigators postulate that African-American families expand their network membership through the creation of fictive kin, which can consist of friends, godparents, children in other families, church members, and the like. In effect, such individuals assume the rights and obligations found among kin. This phenomenon was referred to by Hartman and Laird (1987) in their definition of family of origin as that family of blood or "bloodlike" ties. Thus, family boundaries are broadened in African-American cultures and reinforced by the use of such familial terminology as "brother," "sister," "aunt," and "uncle" when these individuals may not be related by blood.

There is a growing highly educated middle class emerging in the African-American culture that is represented in high occupational ranks, yet a disproportionate number of African-Americans are illiterate and impoverished, including older people (Markides & Mindel, 1987). African-American men have been stereotyped in this country as irresponsible, criminal, and lacking in masculinity, whereas African-American women have been viewed as the backbone or strong person in the marital dyad (Staples, 1988). Marital relationships have been influenced by socioeconomic and educational factors such that the divorce rate among African-Americans is twice that of whites (Ho, 1987). Over time, middle-aged and older African-American women have been a source of strength to their families. A qualitative study (Allen & Chin-Sang, 1990) has shown that, within the context of lifelong work histories, older African-American women have followed a pattern of unpaid agricultural work in childhood, paid domestic and service work as adults, and volunteer work in church and senior centers as retirees. By incorporating their lifetime of hard work into leisure activities and service to self and others, African-American women have continued a history of self-reliance in old age.

The notion of extended family is a strong orientation among all populations of Hispanics (Applewhite, 1988), although their migration histories differ (Gelfand & Barresi, 1987). The Hispanic family, which also includes close friends and godparents, is viewed as a warm, nurturing circle of people who foster a sense of belonging. Traditionally, the Hispanic family has designated certain family roles and functions by generation and sex. In terms of the male in the family,

the nature of *machismo* has taken many varying forms, from head of the household, decision maker, breadwinner, authority over spouse and children to provider of protection and the one responsible for those who cannot care for themselves. The opposite tradition, *marianismo,* refers to the self-sacrificing female who, as wife and mother, complements the traditional male role. The person's age, coupled with individual personalities and degree of acculturation, determines the actual extent to which Hispanic men and women assume these roles (Applewhite, 1988).

Older people in Hispanic families are viewed as wise, knowledgeable, and deserving of respect from the young. Respect of elders emphasizes past labor for the family and providing continuity for its members over the life cycle. When they can no longer assume paid work roles, older Hispanics become transmitters of their culture, nurturers and protectors of small children, family historians, and teachers of the faith (Bacerra, 1988).

GENDER ISSUES

Hess (1990) summed up the major issue with respect to gender and age: "Because the life course is played out within systems of stratification, sex and race distinctions will remain crucial to understanding the process of aging in any society as long as gender and racial equality remain distant goals" (p. 15). Women tend to have a longer life expectancy than men do, but women experience more chronic and disabling diseases than do their male counterparts, who have more fatal diseases (Markides, 1990). As noted earlier, 17% of women, contrasted with 7% of men, live alone. This isolation, coupled with potential chronic disabilities, makes women prime candidates for institutionalization, whereas men with disabilities are most likely to be cared for by a spouse—55% compared with 18% of women (Hess, 1990). According to the U.S. Senate, Special Committee on Aging (1988), three out of four nursing home residents are women, three-fourths are over age 80, 84% are unmarried, and 93% are white. Women of color are more likely to be cared for by a relative. If nursing home placement is necessary, it is critical for social work practitioners and family members to thoroughly investigate the facility and its policies.

Social Hazards

The social hazards of late adulthood may take many forms. Older people are particularly vulnerable to being victimized. Victimization may take a violent form, for example, mugging and robbery, or it may take a more subtle direction, such as fraudulent money "scams" or selling people goods and services that are unneeded. Two particular types of hazards older adults may experience are abuse and stereotyping.

ELDER ABUSE

Battering or abuse typically is perpetrated on older persons by family members and home-care workers or in institutions where they reside. Five different types of **elder abuse** have been identified and delineated by Wolf and Pillemer (1989): (1) physical abuse, causing pain or injury (for instance, broken bones, burns); (2) psychological abuse, causing mental or emotional anguish (for example, threats, intimidation, shaming); (3) material abuse, illegal or improper use of the person's resources; (4) active neglect, refusal to care for the older person, deliberate attempt to place physical and emotional stress on the person (such as leaving an incontinent person alone, denial of food); and (5) passive abuse, refusal or failure to care for the older person because of inadequate knowledge or own disabilities.

As with any family secret, the prevalence of abuse is difficult to determine but may be as much as 4% a year. It has been estimated that as many as 1 million older people have been abused at some point. Spousal abuse is the most prevalent form of abuse, followed by abuse perpetrated by an adult child. Abuse often is associated with the caregiver's mental illness, chronic disease, or alcoholism. According to Breckman and Adelman (1988), the risk factors for mistreatment or abuse include the presence of one or more of the following:

- Presence of family member's mental illness, dementia, retardation, or drug or alcohol abuse;
- A history of family violence;
- Older person's dependency on others to meet all physical and emotional needs;
- Older person's isolation from others and activities of choice;

- Stressful life events such as financial loss, death, divorce;
- Older person who lives with caregiver.

Hooyman and Lustbader (1986) have outlined the areas of assessment social workers should cover when poor care is evident:

- *What has been the nature of the long-term relationship between family members and the older person?* Were the adult children physically or sexually abused earlier in life? When forced to be caregivers, those with unresolved resentments may consciously or unwittingly use the situation to get back at the parent. The power to withhold needed help to a physically vulnerable parent offers adult children a position of superior strength, which can play into past and current battles.

- *What current life problems unrelated to the care needs are pressuring family members?* Are financial constraints interfering with compliance with medical recommendations? Is the primary caregiver overwhelmed by demands from several dependent people at once? Job stresses, personal health limitations, and worries about their own children are examples of problems that may affect caregivers' capacities to meet care demands constructively.

- *What difficulties are resulting directly from the older person's care needs?* How much rest are caregivers getting? What personal sacrifices are caregivers making to serve the person's needs? How much constant surveillance is involved in the caregiving tasks? Is the care especially stressful or repugnant? How drastically has the older person's personality changed in response to illness? When difficult care needs are present, the availability of extra help and professional support become critical determinants of family members' ability to sustain nonabusive care (p. 104).

STEREOTYPING

Individual and family development occurs within a context influenced by economic, historical, cultural, and social factors. By examining these factors over time, we have seen the birth, growth, and development of ageism, sexism, and racism. It is highly likely that every American will experience one or more prejudiced acts if they reach late adulthood. On the basis of income and health alone, it is clear that older women of color are in triple jeopardy (Edmonds, 1990), carrying the burdens of **ageism,** racism, and sexism. Robert Butler (1990) called ageism a disease in which prejudices and stereotypes are applied to older people simply on the basis of their age. Despite the discriminatory assaults experienced by older adults, they tend to prevail and continue to enrich the lives of those around them.

LIVING ON A FIXED INCOME

In 1993, although the median income of families headed by persons 65 and over was $25,821, the range in income was wide; approximately 21% of family households with an older person as head had incomes of less than $15,000, whereas 41% had incomes of $30,000 or more. And for nonheads of households, 45% of persons living alone or with nonrelatives had incomes below $10,000. In fact, approximately 3.8 million older people were below the poverty level (in 1993, $8,740 for an older couple or household and $6,930 for an individual), and another 2.3 million were classified as "near-poor." In 1993, 11% of whites, 28% of African-Americans, and 21% of Hispanic older people were impoverished (AARP & AOA, 1994).

Many individuals in other stages of life can look to the future with the hope of increasing their income in various ways (promotion, new job, spouse returns to work, kids leave home). But for many older people, retirement means living on a **fixed income,** which does not increase from year to year. Often that income is reduced after retirement by one-third or one-half (Schuster & Ashburn,

1992). These older adults then need to adjust their lifestyle to cope with the reduced availability of financial resources. Adjustments range from eating out less often to substantially reducing food intake; from moving to a smaller home to forgoing necessary home repairs and doing without heat and air conditioning. Even those who saved money for retirement may find their resources greatly reduced after a prolonged illness. For women, the problem may be even more severe because twice as many women as men tend to fall below the poverty level (Hess, 1990).

Summary

DEVELOPMENTAL THEMES

It is difficult to define the developmental themes of late adulthood, because this period covers such a long span of years. In addition, people are living longer and old keeps getting older. As people live longer, they become more diverse. Erikson describes this stage as one of integrity versus despair. Late adulthood is a time where people tend to reflect on their lives and accomplishments.

(continued on page 572)

Often older adults live on a fixed income—for many this means poverty.

Depression in an Older Woman

Esther Rodriguez is a 77-year-old widow who broke her hip three months ago. After a two-week hospital stay for emergency hip replacement surgery and four weeks in a convalescent facility for strengthening and mobility training, she is staying in her daughter and son-in-law's home because she was not fully capable of caring for herself independently when her need for skilled services (and thus her Medicare coverage) ended at the convalescent facility. She was referred to Catholic Social Services by her daughter, who wanted help in making long-range plans for her mother's care.

Mrs. Rodriguez has lived in the same house for nearly 50 years. She raised two sons and a daughter there. Her husband, who died five years ago, worked for the railroad. Mrs. Rodriguez was primarily a home-maker, but she supplemented the family income by selling her homemade tortillas and tamales to neighborhood restaurants. Mrs. Rodriguez's older son died, at age 52, of cancer two years ago. Her younger son lives in another state with his second wife and their children. Mrs. Rodriguez's daughter, Ana Clark, 50, and Ana's, husband, Joe Clark, are purchasing the modern townhouse that they moved into five years ago. It is located on the opposite side of town from Mrs. Rodriguez. Ana is a self-employed C.P.A. She and her husband own their own accounting firm. They have two grown children and three grandchildren. One of their sons, age 24, is living in their home while he seeks employment.

DEVELOPMENTAL HISTORY

Mr. and Mrs. Rodriguez had made a comfortable adjustment to retirement and had about seven years together before his death five years ago. Mrs. Rodriguez's activities had not changed as much as her husband's, but she spent less time in church activities with the other women and more time gardening and working around the house with her husband. Once a week, however, she had lunch with three of her best high school friends while her husband played bingo with his retired friends at church. On Sundays, her daughter Ana and son-in-law Joe came for dinner. Her husband's death was very hard for her. It took her nearly two years before she felt she could wake up and not ache from feeling lonely. Following her son's death two years ago, she again had a very hard time. Ana reported that her mother never seemed to be her old self after that.

The current circumstances of Mrs. Rodriguez and her daughter's family are stressing the natural stages of family and individual life cycle development. Mrs. Rodriguez's role with her older son (wise parent, loving mother) has been prematurely interrupted, as has his role with her and his sister (responsible son who can help with maintenance of family home, validation of parental wisdom and elder's value). Ana is just into the stage of launching children and moving on, but her son's return home and now her mother's living with her is requiring a return to more caretaking and home-management demands. Ana and her mother have been arguing daily about Mrs. Rodriguez returning to her own home. Ana is worried that her mother will forget to take her blood pressure medicine, fall down, or even wander away. She doesn't think her mother will bother with eating or, worse still, may forget to turn off the stove and set fire to her house. This role reversal with her mother (daughter taking more parental responsibility for adult parent and parent being more dependent) is magnified by the fact that her mother is living in Ana's home, and it is hard for Ana to learn to support her mother without overfunctioning for her. Their arguing represents what a considerable strain this is for both mother and daughter. Ana also has confessed that she and her husband have been arguing frequently. They are having to renegotiate their marital relationship to accommodate both the younger and older generation living in their family space. Ana also is feeling pressure to put in

(continued)

more hours at work as tax season is approaching, and her husband is expecting her to keep up with her part of their business.

Ana becomes tearful as she confesses to feeling "trapped." She is worried about her mother's current well-being, but she is also fearful that Mrs. Rodriguez may have an incurable problem, such as Alzheimer's disease, and that she will never be able to return to living in her own home. Ana seems to be feeling some resentment of the fact that she has become her mother's chief caretaker, even though she works full-time, has raised her own children, and has a brother who should be equally responsible for their mother. Ana has had several telephone conversations with her brother to discuss optional living arrangements for Mrs. Rodriguez. Her brother expresses concern, but he poses distance and his own family responsibilities as barriers to his being an integral part of any solution. He has offered some limited financial help and has given his approval to whatever plan his sister and mother work out.

BIOPHYSICAL CONSIDERATIONS

Mrs. Rodriguez is not frail and is of above-average intelligence. She had been completely independent in her own home before she broke her hip. She was able to do all her activities of daily living in her familiar environment. She needed partial help with only two instrumental activities of daily living. Following her husband's death, she had asked Ana to help her manage the lump-sum life insurance money from her husband's railroad life policy, and she needed help with transportation for shopping because she had never learned to drive.

Chronic medical problems for Mrs. Rodriguez include arthritis, hearing loss, high blood pressure, digestive difficulties, and osteoporosis. The osteoporosis was a major factor contributing to her broken hip. Whether she fell and the soft bone in her hip broke or whether the hip broke and caused her to fall is not known; either way, the brittleness of her bones puts her at great risk for further broken bones resulting from slight falls

and for compression fractures in her spine, which can occur without provocation.

Mrs. Rodriguez is well-known to her family doctor, whose office is in her neighborhood. He has treated her for several years, since his father, who delivered her three children, died. A telephone conversation with the doctor has revealed that Mrs. Rodriguez has managed her chronic medical problems well. She has been compliant in taking her blood pressure medication and comes in for periodic checkups. Her chronic conditions are stable. However, since being at Ana's, Mrs. Rodriguez complains of chronic pain "all over." She frequently refuses to take her daily walk, citing pain in her (artificial) hip as the reason. She has frequent headaches and seems tired most of the time. Ana reports that the orthopedic surgeon who replaced her mother's hip states she is healing well and, with time and normal activity, the soreness in her hip should decrease. Because Mrs. Rodriguez is now so far away from her doctor's office, she has not seen her regular doctor since she left the hospital. Ana is trying to decide whether to find a doctor near her own home to take over her mother's care or to transport her mother across town to see her regular doctor.

Cognitive Development and Psychological Hazards

Ana reports that her mother "is just not with it." She had always enjoyed watching the news and discussing current events with others, but Ana can no longer engage her in discussion. Mrs. Rodriguez cannot seem to concentrate on the news stories, and she becomes agitated and frustrated when Ana tries to talk with her. "She just doesn't seem to care about anything," Ana says. Ana also reports that her mother has significant short-term memory deficits. She becomes upset with Ana if Ana is late getting home from work, even after Ana calls before leaving the office to tell her that she's stopping for groceries. She often asks what day it is, only to ask the same question 10 minutes later. She tells Ana that she ate the meal Ana left for her, although Ana finds it untouched in the refrigerator. Ana reports that her mother began exhibiting these memory problems a few weeks after she entered the nursing home.

In an effort to sort out whether Mrs. Rodriguez's cognitive difficulties are organic or more psychological and related to a significant depression, the social worker completed a Mini-Mental Status Exam. At first, Mrs. Rodriguez had difficulty comprehending what was being asked of her, but then the social worker decided that perhaps a part of the problem was Mrs. Rodriguez's hearing loss. The social worker began using a voice amplifier attached to earphones that Mrs. Rodriguez was asked to wear, and Mrs. Rodriguez responded much better to the questions and appeared much brighter. She scored 25 out of a possible 30 points. She had the most difficulty with attention/calculation and recall sections. This score is strongly suggestive of a pseudodementia caused by depression, rather than an organic, irreversible dementia.

When the social worker asked Mrs. Rodriguez to take the self-administered Geriatric Depression Scale, she scored 7, which suggests that depression may be the root of her cognitive and memory difficulties and her generalized physical pain.

Attitudes and Emotions

The significant losses that Mrs. Rodriguez has experienced in the last few years (losing her husband and eldest son to death; another son to distance; her own hearing and now mobility) have taxed her abilities to adjust and cope. One coping strategy she has used is to maintain a sense of normality by continuing to perform routine activities of housekeeping, gardening, going to church, and visiting neighbors. These are now difficult for her because of her physical limitations and because she resides in a household that is not her own. The loss of her husband, though devastating, was more in the expected process of life, whereas the son's death before her own is more unnatural. This fact may be making bereavement more complicated for Mrs. Rodriguez. She often said she would much rather have gotten cancer herself and gone to be with her husband than for her son to have to leave this life so soon.

Ana believes that her son, who is recovering from substance abuse, may be using his grandmother as an excuse to avoid looking for employment. However, Mrs. Ro-driguez states that she has developed a "new" and close relationship with this 24-year-old grandson. They have shared a common struggle to recover from different difficulties, and both are concerned that the other succeeds. They may be a newfound resource for each other to cope with loss and the new challenges in their lives.

Support Systems, Contexts, and Multicultural and Gender Issues

Mrs. Rodriguez's home is in a historic part of town, populated by mostly Hispanic families. Many of these families have lived in the neighborhood for three or more generations. Mrs. Rodriguez has many friends in the neighborhood, which remains largely intact with a corner grocery, a pharmacy, a school and an active Catholic church. Mrs. Rodriguez has enjoyed cooking with the churchwomen who provide food for weddings, funerals, and special celebrations. She still takes pride in her tortilla-making. She has a number of close neighbors who have known her for years. She has provided them with support (babysitting, cooking, emotional support) many times in the past.

The church remains a central focus for the life of this community as well as for Mrs. Rodriguez. Attending mass on Sunday and religious holidays has always been an important part of her self-identity. She considers the parish priest her adviser on all matters of living and has spoken to him several times about personal matters since her husband died.

Ana's husband is white. Ana has left much of her cultural upbringing behind but continues to attend a Catholic church near her current home. Ana's children have become even more assimilated into the dominant culture. Although Ana and her mother are bilingual, Ana rarely speaks Spanish to her mother because she feels this would be inconsiderate to her husband and son, who speak only English. These cultural differences make Ana's home unfamiliar and, in many ways, uncomfortable for Mrs. Rodriguez. Mrs. Rodriguez's presence in Ana's home has brought up old conflicts for Ana around her Hispanic identity and heritage that Ana thought she had put to rest long ago.

Ecomaps demonstrate the changes in Mrs. Rodriguez's life context from before her husband died (see Figure 12.3) to the present time (see Figure 12.4).
(continued)

This assessment tool shows the severe constriction of her life space since her husband's death and her surgery. Many nurturing support systems—priest, church, friends, neighbors—and activities are no longer a part of her everyday existence. These accumulated losses will add to her depression and confusion, and her current living situation will only exacerbate the stressful relationship between Mrs.

FIGURE 12.3
Ecomap before husband's death (Hartman, 1978)

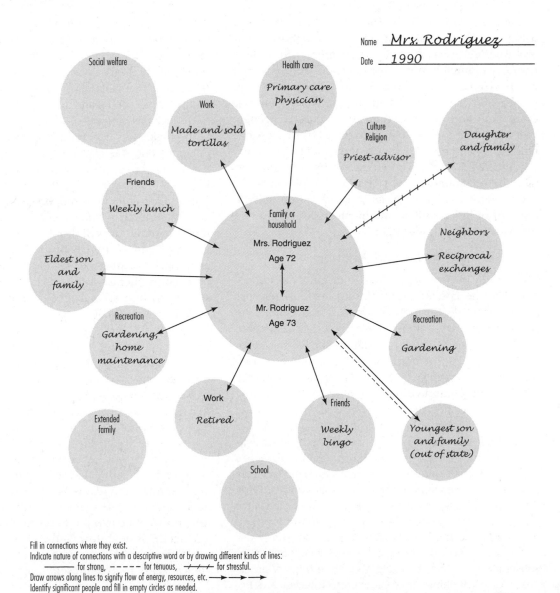

Name *Mrs. Rodriguez*

Date *1990*

Social welfare

Health care
Primary care physician

Work
Made and sold tortillas

Culture Religion
Priest-advisor

Daughter and family

Friends
Weekly lunch

Family or household

Mrs. Rodriguez
Age 72

Mr. Rodriguez
Age 73

Neighbors
Reciprocal exchanges

Eldest son and family

Recreation
Gardening, home maintenance

Recreation
Gardening

Extended family

Work
Retired

Friends
Weekly bingo

Youngest son and family (out of state)

School

Fill in connections where they exist.
Indicate nature of connections with a descriptive word or by drawing different kinds of lines:
————— for strong, – – – – – for tenuous, ⊬⊬⊬ for stressful.
Draw arrows along lines to signify flow of energy, resources, etc. ➤ ➤ ➤
Identify significant people and fill in empty circles as needed.

Rodriguez and her daughter, Ana. Restoration of Mrs. Rodriguez to her home and neighborhood, with appropriate formal supports, is the preferred goal of treatment.

Social Hazards

Impoverishment may be a hazard for Mrs. Rodriguez. She owns her home and has several thousand dollars in a saving account, but her income is fixed and just meets her regular expenses. She has Medicare but has not felt she could afford the cost of a supplemental health insurance policy on her fixed income. She has been able to manage comfortably, but added expenses for a prolonged period could quickly deplete her savings and leave her home as her only financial asset.

(continued)

FIGURE 12.4
Ecomap at present
(Hartman, 1978)

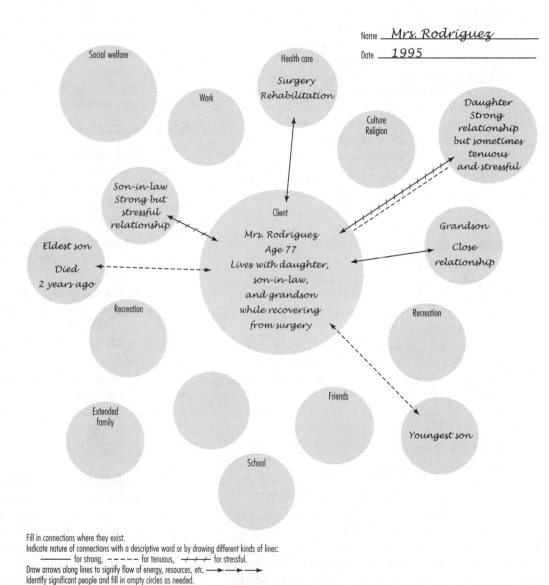

Name __Mrs. Rodriguez__

Date __1995__

Social welfare

Work

Health care
Surgery Rehabilitation

Culture Religion

Daughter Strong relationship but sometimes tenuous and stressful

Son-in-law Strong but stressful relationship

Client
Mrs. Rodriguez Age 77 Lives with daughter, son-in-law, and grandson while recovering from surgery

Grandson Close relationship

Eldest son Died 2 years ago

Recreation

Recreation

Extended family

Friends

Youngest son

School

Fill in connections where they exist.
Indicate nature of connections with a descriptive word or by drawing different kinds of lines:
———— for strong, – – – – for tenuous, ⁄–⁄–⁄ for stressful.
Draw arrows along lines to signify flow of energy, resources, etc. ——▶—▶
Identify significant people and fill in empty circles as needed.

SUMMARY AND IMPRESSIONS

Problems needing intervention:

- It is likely that depression has caused Mrs. Rodriguez's cognitive deterioration. Both medical and nonmedical interventions are suggested because there are important issues of loss and grief that Mrs. Rodriguez needs help in resolving, as well as physical signs of depression. With treatment for her depression, Mrs. Rodriguez should suffer less from "generalized pain," be motivated to continue rehabilitating her hip, and be able to make the necessary adjustments to continue her independent living, though with more supports.

- Hearing impairment may be creating more cognitive deficits and adding to Mrs. Rodriguez's depression. This needs to be further evaluated through an audiologist.

- Confusion as to the source of Mrs. Rodriguez's memory and concentration problems has produced anxiety and catastrophic thinking in Ana and hindered her ability to have accurate information needed for appropriate planning for her mother's future needs.

- Mrs. Rodriguez will need help with certain activities of daily living, such as bathing, dressing, and heavy housework because her mobility is still limited from the hip surgery.

- Ana is experiencing increasing stress owing to physical and time demands of caring for her mother and managing all of her other responsibilities.

- Ana's family is experiencing stress and role strain with the new demands on Ana at a time when the family is facing other demands in the business and needs of the younger son for emotional support to progress to the next stage in his life.

- Ana and Mrs. Rodriguez are experiencing role strain as Mrs. Rodriguez becomes more dependent.

Strengths identified:

- There is a strong family bond and commitment to looking for solutions that address everyone's needs.

- Mrs. Rodriguez has been flexible in adapting to earlier changes in her life and has coping skills that should continue to help her adapt.

- Mrs. Rodriguez lives in a supportive, close, culturally homogeneous neighborhood where she feels safe and important.

- Mrs. Rodriguez has built many reciprocal relationships among her neighbors, which may make it more probable that they can help her in ways that can enable her to return to living in her own home.

- Mrs. Rodriguez has a close relationship with former high school friends with whom she enjoys leisure-time activities.

(continued from page 566)

BIOPHYSICAL DIMENSION

Biophysical Growth and Development

Life expectancy has increased significantly in the last several decades. Physical change and decline vary from one person to another, but as the body ages, changes do occur in many biological systems. Older adults remain interested in and capable of sexual activity.

Biophysical Hazards

Aging can result in increased chronic health problems. The most common disorders are arthritis and hypertension. Arthritis involves inflammation of the connective tissues in the joints of the body and results in pain and difficulty in movement. Hypertension or high blood pressure can lead to stroke and heart disease. Alcoholism can be a major concern and a physical hazard, because metabolism slows with age. Good nutrition and adequate exercise can contribute to wellness in late adulthood.

PSYCHOLOGICAL DIMENSION

Cognitive Development and Information Processing

Mental decline varies among individuals. Many older adults retain mental abilities into advanced ages. Sensory deficits in late adulthood contribute to a slowing of behavioral responses. Long-term memory loss is rare, and short-term memory loss is more frequent in older adults. Problems of memory may be caused by several factors, including health, perception, attention, or motivation.

Communication

Reminiscing in old age may serve to put one's life in order and prepare one for death. Reminiscing with an older person helps the person bring closure to life and provides insight and rewards to the listener.

Attitudes and Emotions

Loss is a common theme for older adults. Grief is a normal reaction to loss, especially to loss that occurs as the result of death of a loved one. Kübler-Ross identified five stages in the dying process: denial and isolation, anger, bargaining, depression, and acceptance. The leading causes of death are heart disease, cancer, stroke, lung disease, pneumonia, influenza, and diabetes. Fear of death is stronger at younger ages than in older adulthood. Though widows experience a period of bereavement, many emerge with self-reliance and autonomy. Men who lose their wives have a more difficult adjustment than women who lose their husbands. With the loss of a partner and of other family members and friends, loneliness can be a problem for older adults. Life review may bring feelings of guilt and anger for some over missed opportunities and an increasing sense of powerlessness.

Social Cognition and Regulation

Older adults resist considering themselves old. They tend to continue thinking of themselves in terms of their former occupation. People's core sense of self does not change as they age. Rival theories explain the process of aging. Disengagement theory suggests that people tend to withdraw from society because of diminished capacities, while society withdraws from older individuals to make room for younger adults. Activity theory suggests that, as people are deprived of former roles through the process of aging, they must become engaged in other activities to retain life satisfaction.

Psychological Hazards

Dementia and depression are two serious disorders for older adults. One form of dementia is Alzheimer's disease. This disease results in deterioration of memory, reasoning, language, and physical function. Cause of and effective treatment for the disease are still undetermined. Factors that may be associated with depression among older people include illness, disability, isolation, bereavement, and poverty. Helping an older adult expand available social support may help with depression. Suicide is a risk for older depressed adults. Some advocate for assisted suicide among the elderly with terminal illness. The living will allows a terminally ill person to document that he or she does not want to be kept alive by artificial means. The medical power of attorney appoints someone to make medical decisions concerning care for an ill person.

SOCIAL DIMENSION

Families, Groups, Support Systems, and Communities

Forms of families are as diverse in older adulthood as in younger years. Marital pairs may become closer as partners have the opportunity to rediscover their relationship and pursue common interests. Some remain close, whereas others do not. With increased life expectancy, adults nearing retirement may be caregivers for their parents. Caregiving of older parents affects the family significantly and may cause stress. Older adults can also be helpers to others. Grandparenthood can be a fulfilling role for older adults, but this role may vary among different cultures and ethnic groups. Friends play an important, supportive role in old age. Some older adults will require the additional care offered by nursing homes and adult-care facilities. Hospice is an alternative for individuals with less than a six-month life expectancy. Instead of focusing on cure, hospice provides symptom and pain control. For many older adults, especially those who put an emphasis on their life's worth in work, retirement can be a difficult time of adjustment. Retirement can be especially difficult for women, because they may be unwilling to retire when their husbands do or may be financially unable to retire.

Multicultural and Gender Considerations

Women live longer than men do but suffer more disabling diseases. These factors give women a higher chance of being institutionalized in late adulthood. Three out of four nursing home residents are women. Services for older people need to be sensitive to cultural and ethnic considerations. Extended family is important for many ethnic groups. Older Native-Americans have more informal support on reservations than in urban areas. In the African-American culture, family boundaries are broadened to include close friends as brother, sister, aunt, or uncle. Older persons are respected in the extended families of the Hispanic culture.

Social Hazards

Elder abuse may be perpetrated by family members, home-care workers, or workers in institutions. Abuse may include physical abuse, psychological abuse, material abuse, neglect, and passive abuse. Older people may be discriminated against on the basis of age. Many older people live on a fixed income. These adults may have to adjust their style of living to accommodate a lower income from year to year. Prolonged illness may deplete financial resources. Poverty can cause problems with options for care for older adults.

🌐 Online Resources

American Association for Retired Persons
http://www.aarp.org
> The nation's leading organization for people ages 50 and older. Information and research (health, security, independent living, consumer issues, technology, work and economic), volunteer and community programs, issues and advocacy.

Assisted Living Networks Information and Advice About Assisted Living
http://www.alfnet.com/index.htm
> This site provides assisted living general information, assisted living facilities, etc.

Alzheimer's
http://www.alzheimers.com
> A comprehensive information resource and support network for Alzheimers' caregivers, with the latest news and research, and a Community Board for sharing tips and support.

Eldercare Web
http://www.elderweb.com
> Online source book with more than 4,000 reviewed links to information about health financing, housing, aging, and other issues related to the care of the frail elderly.

GriefNet
http://www.griefnet.org/index.html
> This site is an Internet community consisting of more than 30 e-mail support groups and two websites. Integrated approach to online grief support was developed to provide support to people working through loss and grief issues of all kinds.

National Institute on Aging (NIA)
http://www.nih.gov/nia
> Part of the National Institutes of Health, the principle biomedical research agency of the United States Government.

InfoTrac® College Edition

For interesting materials related to what you have just read, please go to the *InfoTrac College Edition* website and search using the following key words:

> elder abuse
>
> depression elderly
>
> widowhood
>
> ageism
>
> long-term care

Key Terms

activity theory

ageism

assisted suicide

bloodlike ties

cohort

crystallized intelligence

dementia

disengagement theory

elder abuse

euthanasia

fixed income

fluid intelligence

grief

hospice

life expectancy

life span

living will

medical power of attorney

natural helpers

reminiscence

EPILOGUE: THE JOURNEY OF LIFE

We have now come to the final pages of this book—moving from birth to death. We hope that the framework and information we have provided can help you make some sense of this lifelong progression. And yet, on a deeper level, is it possible for us to make sense of life? After taking this journey, perhaps this is an appropriate time to pause and reflect on the meaning of life. What is the real sense of it all?

Great minds have struggled with this question. Kierkegaard informs us that "life is lived forward, but understood backwards." Socrates was cheerful in his answer to this question—we are here to be happy. And for Socrates, the path to happiness was through knowledge. Other philosophers, such as Epicurus, would simply state that our existence is to cultivate pleasures. Religious philosophers place the focus of our existence on faith. If we have faith, we can be assured to have a special place in God's kingdom. According to Lao-tzu, our existence should be focused on knowing the inner harmony of Nature's Way. Bob Dylan sings "...all you can do is do what you must. You do what you must do and you do it well."

Though we can present the facts and theories of human development in the social environment, and philosophize at length, defining the purpose of life is a difficult task—maybe a lifelong task. In the end, perhaps it is up to us individually to make sense of our lives and to make life something very real and very meaningful. As we pause, then our personal reflections on life may provide our own sense of meaning. These reflections might bring forth images about our origin and our start in life, our growth and struggles throughout life, our hopes and our fears, our achievements, our love, and ultimately our death:

We whisper a new baby's name to the rising sun,
we laugh as the child mistakes a cow for a dog,
we call each other "buttface,"
we learn and grow,
we dye our hair purple as we struggle to establish a unique identity,
we work and we love and sometimes we cry,
we stand at the crossroads and hesitate for just a moment before moving on,
we stare as the shoreline recedes and the ship sails away before finally turning to hear the voices calling from the other shore.

Glossary

Abstraction   The ability to recognize the meaning of symbols.

Accommodation   The cognitive process of modifying the existing cognitive schema to allow for the admission of new information.

Acquaintance rape   When a woman is raped by someone she knows.

Activity theory   A theory of aging that holds that older people who remain active and involved experience greater life satisfaction.

Adaptation   Refers to the ability to respond to the demands of the environment. Includes the processes of assimilation and accommodation.

Affect   A person's instant emotional state.

Ageism   Prejudice against and stereotypes applied to people on the basis of their age.

Aggression   Acts that intend to hurt another.

Alcoholism   The consumption of alcoholic beverages to the extent that major aspects of a person's life, such as work, family, and friends, are affected.

Allele   One of a pair of genes for a specific trait.

Alpha-fetoprotein blood screening   Blood test used to detect neural tube defects.

Altruism   Helpful behaviors that arise out of concern for the welfare of others, without regard for personal gain.

Amniocentesis   A prenatal screening procedure in which a needle is inserted through the mother's abdomen into the uterus to collect a sample of amniotic fluid for chromosome testing.

Androcentricity   A perspective whereby men are considered the norm.

Androgen   The hormone secreted from the testes.

Androgyny   A combination of masculine and feminine behaviors in the same person.

Angina pectoris   A coronary condition involving pain and tightness in the chest.

Animism   The belief that inanimate objects have lifelike qualities and abilities.

Anoxia   Insufficient oxygen to the fetus during delivery.

Apgar score   A newborn assessment scale developed by Virginia Apgar that looks at the newborn's adaptation to life in the first minutes after birth. Scores are recorded at 1 minute and 5 minutes after delivery.

Assimilation   The cognitive process of consolidation of new information into existing knowledge.

Assisted suicide   Helping to provide the means for an individual with a terminal illness to end his or her life.

Associationism   One of the oldest constructs in psychology that involves the formation of mental associations that are registered or stored in the mind.

Attachment   The process by which an infant forms a strong emotional tie to a caregiver.

Attention   The ability to focus on a specific stimulus without distraction by irrelevant stimuli.

Attention deficit hyperactivity disorder (ADHD)   A psychiatric disorder in which a person shows signs of developmentally inappropriate inattention, impulsivity, and hyperactivity.

Attitude   A learned evaluative response.

Authoritarian parenting   A parenting style based on low levels of warmth and a demanding, restrictive, and punitive approach.

Authoritative parenting   Encourages warmth and affection; encourages independence but with limits and controls on the child.

Autism   Pervasive developmental disorder in which children suffer psychological, cognitive, and social deficits that impair functioning in almost all areas of life.

Autosomes   Chromosomes other than sex chromosomes.

Avoidant disorder   Fear of strangers and strange or new situations.

Axons   Long fibers that carry impulses from the cell body of a neuron to other cells.

Babbling   Early communication in which a baby puts vowel and consonant sounds together and repeats them over and over.

Basal metabolism rate The minimum amount of energy that we use in our resting state.

Behavioral intention Our subjective estimate of how likely we are to engage in a specific behavior.

Beliefs In social psychology, information about objects.

Bilingual The ability to speak two languages.

Biophysical dimension Refers to the biochemical, cell, organ, and physiological systems that represent the material substance of a person.

Blended family A newly formed unit consisting of a husband and wife, one or both of whom have children from a previous marriage.

Bloodlike ties Refers to different ethnic and cultural definitions of family, including situations such as adoption.

Brazelton Neonatal Assessment Scale (BNAS) Newborn assessment used to measure the baby's muscle tone and reflexes and how the baby responds to and controls stimulation.

Bureaucracy An organization that is ruled by officials.

Canalization The process by which persons inherit general pathways that constrain their growth and developmental processes.

Caregiving career Refers to the substantial caregiving functions women have that include caring for children, elderly parents, and a dependent husband.

Care perspective Reasoning about moral dilemmas with a focus on the connectedness to others; concern for others is paramount.

Categorical self Process by which preschoolers classify themselves, first according to age, then to gender, then to activities and possessions.

Categorization The ability to place objects into groups on the basis of their similarities.

Central nervous system The brain and spinal cord.

Cephalocaudal Development that progresses from the head to the feet.

Cerebral palsy Brain damage resulting from lack of oxygen during birth or from bleeding in the brain. Can cause paralysis, muscle weakness, and incoordination. Also may result in mental retardation and speech difficulties.

Cesarean section Delivery of a baby through an incision in the mother's abdomen.

Child abuse Child maltreatment that includes physical abuse, sexual abuse, physical neglect, educational neglect, and psychological abuse.

Cholinergic Refers to any nerve that releases the neurotransmitter acetylcholine at its synapse.

Chorionic villus sample (CVS) A prenatal screening procedure in which a catheter is inserted into the uterus through the vagina to obtain a piece of the developing placenta.

Circular influences Process by which family interactions affect interactions with the infant and affect the infant's interactions with the caregivers, which then affects family interactions.

Classical conditioning The strengthening of an association between a stimulus and a response through the presentation of a second stimulus.

Clique Small interaction-based group with close relationships.

Codependency A pattern of behavior in which a person's sense of self-worth is based on external referents.

Cognition Obtaining, organizing, and utilizing sensory and perceptual information from activities such as plans and strategies.

Cohesive group A group in which individual members have strong bonds with one another and to the group itself.

Cohort A group of people of about the same age, born around the same time.

Communication patterns How members of a group communicate verbally and nonverbally.

Concentration A person's ability to sustain inner mental operations without disruption.

Concrete thinking The ability to perform operations such as logical reasoning, which replaces intuitive thought as long as it is applied to concrete examples.

Conduct disorder DSM-IV term that refers to a cluster of behaviors that reflect oppositional, noncompliant, and delinquent actions, such as stealing, robbery, and assault.

Connectedness Refers to both a person's sensitivity to and respect for others' views and the person's openness and responsiveness to others' views.

Consciousness Our awareness of internal and external stimuli.

Conservation The recognition that properties of a substance do not change when its appearance is altered in some manner.

Continuity Associations occurring in the mind because two events occur together in time or space.

Controlled reaction A phase of rape trauma syndrome in which the rape victim assumes a more composed and calm perspective following the trauma.

Coping Active efforts to master, reduce, or tolerate the demands created by stress.

Creolization The process of maintaining original identities but incorporating customs and practices from other groups or cultures into the original identities.

Cretinism A chronic disease due to absence of, or deficiency in, normal thyroid secretion. Cretinism is characterized by physical deformity and dwarfism.

Cross-modal transfer The ability to transfer information gained from one sense to another sense. An example would be picking out a picture of something you had only felt with your hands.

Crossover A division process that involves an exchange of chromosome parts.

Crowd Larger than clique; reputation-based group of similar young people who do not necessarily spend a lot of time together.

Crystallized intelligence Accumulated information and verbal skills.

Culture A system of meanings and values shared by a population and transmitted to future generations.

Cynical hostility Tendencies toward being resentful, moody, and generally distrusting. Related to an increased tendency toward coronary disease, hypertension, and early mortality.

Cystic Fibrosis A serious disease of the exocrine gland that causes secretion of excess, thick body fluids.

Das-Luria model of cognitive functioning Understands cognitive functioning based on two modes of processing information: simultaneous meanings and successive processing.

Date rape When a woman is raped by someone she is dating.

De-illusionment The process of giving up illusions from earlier periods of life.

Delirium tremens (DTs) A withdrawal syndrome from alcoholism that includes agitation, tremor, hallucination, and sometimes seizures.

Dementia Impairment or loss of cognitive abilities, including memory impairment.

Dendrites The branched fibers on the cell body that bring messages to the cell body of the neuron.

Development The refinement or improvement of body components.

Developmental waves The idea that children learn in overlapping waves instead of in steps.

Diastolic pressure The measure of the blood's flow during the relaxation of the heart.

Differentiation theory Contends that all information needed to interpret sensory input is contained in the sensations themselves.

Difficult child A baby characterized by unpredictable daily habits, negative intense mood, and slow adaptability.

Discrimination Applying prejudice or bias to a person on the basis of some particular characteristic.

Disease Any classifiable set of symptoms and signs stemming from disturbed bodily function and associated with findings from laboratory and other tests.

Disengagement theory A theory of aging that holds that people and society withdraw from each other in old age—people because of their diminished capacity and society to make room for younger people.

Dishabituation The process by which an individual attends to a new stimulus after habituating to a previous stimulus.

Disorder A syndrome of behavioral, physical, or psychological dysfunctions less clearly defined than a disease primarily because etiology of the dysfunctions are unknown.

Disorganization phase A phase of rape trauma syndrome that reflects the woman's immediate expressed or controlled reactions, physical reactions, and emotional reactions to the trauma.

Disoriented states Whenever individuals experience significant deviations in their levels of awareness of time, place, and person.

Displaced homemakers Women who are forced into the job market because of divorce or widowhood.

Dominant gene A gene that is always expressed for a trait, in paired genes.

Dopamine A neurotransmitter whose generalized function is to activate other neurotransmitters and aid in exploratory and pleasure-seeking behaviors.

Easy child A baby characterized by regular, positive responses to new stimuli, high adaptability to change, and mild or moderately intense mood, which is usually positive.

Echolalia Repeating words, songs, and phrases heard in other people's communications.

Ecomap A tool used in social work to highlight the points of connection between systems influencing a person's life.

Ego According to Freud, the executive branch of one's personality that makes rational decisions.

Egocentrism   Being unable to distinguish between one's own perspective and another's.

Elder abuse   Maltreatment of older persons, which can include physical abuse, psychological abuse, material abuse, active neglect, and passive abuse.

Empathy   Possessing the ability to understand the feelings and attitudes of others.

Encopresis   Lack of bowel control after age 4.

Endocarditis   An infection or other factor that damages the heart's valves.

Endocrine glands   Glands, namely the pituitary gland and male and female gonads, that secrete chemicals into the bloodstream that help control bodily functioning.

Endorphins   Substances in the brain that are related to feeling good.

Enrichment theory   Contends that the information we receive through our senses is formless and we must augment this information to make sense of it.

Enuresis   Lack of bladder control after the age of 5, which results in bedwetting or daytime accidents.

Environmental harassment   Exists when a hostile work environment is created by the person in power as a result of some unwanted sexual behavior.

Epigenetic principle   The biological blueprint that dictates how an organism grows and reaches maturity.

Estrogen   The hormone secreted from the ovaries.

Estrogen replacement therapy (ERT)   A synthetic estrogen that is given to women to replace that lost through menopause.

Euthanasia   Assisting the death of those with painfully debilitating or terminal illness.

Exosystems   The larger institutions of society that influence our personal systems.

Expressive communication   The expression of emotions and having a perspective that is sensitive to how others feel.

Externalizing problems   Problems of overcontrol, such as aggressive behavior, fighting, and overactivity.

Failure to thrive   When the child's weight falls below the 5th percentile for age.

Family   A composition of people who decide to live together.

Family structure   The manner in which each family organizes itself into interactional patterns.

Fetal alcohol syndrome (FAS)   A set of birth defects that occur when a pregnant woman consumes alcohol. It is the leading known cause of mental retardation. Physical signs include small head, small eyes, thin upper lip, short nose, flattened midfacial area, and poorly developed philtrum (the part of the face between the nose and upper lip).

Fixed income   Income that does not increase from year to year though inflation and other factors may raise the cost of living.

Floating family   A family with a formless array of familial relationships that are in a continuous state of flux.

Fluid intelligence   Abstract reasoning ability.

Folkways   Group ways of solving problems and of doing things.

Formal operational thought   Thought processes characterized by adolescents' abilities to think about their own thought and to recognize both possibility and actuality.

Formal organization   Any large social group that is designed to rationally achieve a specific objective.

Formed groups   Groups created by an outside influence or intervention and convened for a particular purpose.

Fragile X syndrome   A serious form of mental retardation that is identified in karyotype studies by a constriction at the end of the long arm of the X chromosome.

Frontal lobe   The portion of the brain that participates in body movements, thinking, feeling, imagining, and making decisions.

Functionally literate   Able to perform everyday reading, writing, and arithmetic tasks.

Gang   "A collectivity consisting primarily of adolescents and young adults who (a) interact frequently with one another; (b) are frequently and deliberately involved in illegal activities; (c) share a common identity that is usually, but not always, expressed through a gang name; and (d) typically express that identity by adopting certain symbols and/or claiming control over certain 'turf'—persons, places, things, and/or economic markets" (Huff, 1993, p. 4).

Gender   The social definitions of male and female.

Gender polarization   The organizing of social life around male and female distinctions.

Genotype   The actual genes an individual carries for a specific trait.

Gestation   Length of time in the womb or fetal age. Full term is 38–41 weeks, premature is before 38 weeks, postmature is longer than 41 weeks.

Glia   The supporting cells that make up the bulk of the brain.

Goal-directed behavior   Putting together a series of actions to achieve a desired result.

Gonadotropins   Hormones secreted by the pituitary gland that activate the testes and ovaries.

Goodness of fit   Refers to how well the demands of the environment match the child's behavioral style.

Grief   The normal, emotional reaction to loss.

Groupthink   Occurs in a cohesive group that emphasizes consensus at the expense of critical thinking.

Growth   A technical term that refers to the addition of new biophysical components such as new cells or an increase in body size.

Habituation   The process by which an individual stops responding to a stimulus.

Hemophilia   A condition that is due to a defective gene on the X chromosome that causes a deficiency in the blood coagulation factor VIII.

Heterozygous genes   When two genes in a specific pair are different for a specific trait.

Hierarchy   Dimension of social space that includes all the elements in a society's system of social stratification.

Holophrastic speech   Using one word to express the meaning of a whole sentence.

Homeostasis in families   The self-regulating mechanism of a family system.

Homophobia   The fear and hatred of sex with a same-sex partner.

Homozygous genes   When two genes in a specific pair are the same for a specific trait.

Hormones   Chemical substances in the body that regulate various body organs.

Hospice   An alternative to hospital care for terminally ill patients. Hospice focuses on comfort and relief of symptoms instead of cure.

Hostile aggression   Behaviors designed to hurt another.

Hot flash   A sudden feeling of heat experienced by some women during menopause.

Human immunodeficiency virus (HIV)   A virus that destroys the human immune system and leads to the set of opportunistic infections commonly referred to as acquired immune deficiency syndrome, or AIDS.

Human relations school   A school of organizational theory that focuses on understanding the influences of informal networks on all forms of organizational activities.

Huntington's chorea   A disorder involving a dominant autosomal gene and characterized by progressive chorea

(purposeless motions) and the eventual development of dementia (mental deterioration).

Hyperemesis gravidarum   Persistent and unrelenting vomiting during pregnancy.

Hyperplasia   The type of growth that involves an increase in the number of cells.

Hypertrophic growth   The type of growth in which increases are observed in the size of cells.

Hypervigilance   An excessive focus on outward factors in the environment.

Hypothalamus   The part of the brain that controls the level of hormone secretion from the pituitary gland.

Hypothetical-deductive reasoning   The problem-solving process that tests and evaluates hypotheses to find the best solution.

Id   According to Freud, the instinctive component of personality that operates from the basis of the pleasure principle.

Ideal type   An abstract description derived from real cases that were analyzed to determine their essential features.

Illiterate   Inability to read and write well enough to participate in society.

Illness   A person's subjective perception of being unwell.

Imaginary audience   The belief that others are as preoccupied with an adolescent's behavior as he or she is.

Immediate memory   Information retained for up to 10 seconds.

Individuation   A process by which a person develops a stronger sense of autonomy.

Induction   Use of explanation and/or rationalizing in an attempt to influence a child's actions.

Infantile amnesia   Refers to the fact that children have little or no memory for specific events before the age of 3.

Infertility   Inability to achieve pregnancy after one year of sexual intercourse with no contraception.

Information processing   The theory that examines the uptake, selection, coding, and storage of information.

Instrumental aggression   Behaviors designed to achieve a nonaggressive end, which hurt someone in the process.

Instrumental communication   Having a focus on identifying goals and finding solutions.

Intelligence quotient   Mental age divided by chronological age, multiplied by 100.

Intentional means-end behavior   The process by which a child takes several random activities and puts them together to achieve a goal.

Intention-cue detection Ability to correctly perceive another person's intention; for example, differentiating prosocial, accidental, or hostile acts.

Internalizing problems Problems of undercontrol, such as anxiety, loneliness, shyness, and/or social withdrawal.

Interrupted career Began as a regular career and was interrupted by child-rearing and then reestablished when full-time work resumed.

Intrauterine growth retardation (IUGR) Growth slow-down in the prenatal period. Occurs when the fetal weight falls below the 10th percentile for gestational age.

Invisible displacement In testing for object permanence, moving a toy from one hiding place to another without letting the baby view the process of moving the toy.

Justice perspective Reasoning about moral dilemmas with a focus on the rights of the individual to independently make moral decisions.

Klinefelter's syndrome A condition in which a male is born with an extra X chromosome (XXY).

Lability The rapid shift from one emotion to another within a very brief period of time.

Laissez-faire parenting A parenting style representing two types: permissive indifferent parenting and permissive indulgent parenting. Permissive indifferent parents are uninvolved in their child's life; they are neglectful and unresponsive. Permissive indulgent parents are warm, accepting, and responsive but are undemanding.

Learned helplessness Learning to attribute failures to luck or the difficulty of the task.

Lesch-Nyhan syndrome A disorder that involves a gene on the X chromosome and is characterized by mental retardation, spasticity, and self-mutilation.

Libido According to Freud, the energy that drives all human behavior.

Life expectancy The number of years the average person born in a particular year may expect to live.

Life span The upper limit of years humans can live.

Living will A document that allows a terminally ill person to state that he or she does not want to be kept alive by artificial means.

Loneliness A state of feeling as though one has fewer interpersonal relationships than desired or not obtaining the desired level of personal satisfaction from interpersonal relationships.

Long-term memory Retention of information for days to months.

Love withdrawal Involves withdrawing love when a child's behavior is viewed as inappropriate.

Macrosystem Represents the larger subcultural and cultural contexts in which the microsystem, mesosystem, and exosystem are located.

Malignant tumors Tumors that are not self-contained.

Malpresentation Birth presentation other than head down (i.e., feet first, butt first, shoulder first).

Meconium aspiration Inhalation of fetal waste in the amniotic fluid during delivery. May result in later respiratory problems.

Medical power of attorney A document that allows an ill person to designate someone to have the authority to make decisions regarding medical care for the ill person.

Meiosis The process of cell division that creates the sex cells.

Menarche The first menstruation in pubertal females.

Menopause When a woman stops experiencing a menstrual cycle for a continuous period of time; her ovaries stop functioning and no longer produce the hormones estrogen and progesterone.

Menstrual cycle The series of changes in a nonpregnant female involving the preparation of the endometrium to receive a fertilized ovum, or, if no fertilization occurs, a portion of the endometrium is shed.

Mental age An intelligence test score that indicates the chronological age at which a child functions cognitively.

Mesosystems The network of personal settings in which we live our lives.

Metacognition Knowledge about knowing. A person's awareness of self as a knower able to use and evaluate strategies.

Metalinguistic awareness The ability to think about language and its properties.

Microsystems Any systems that involve face-to-face or direct contact among the system participants.

Mitosis The cellular process in which a body cell reproduces itself by dividing and producing two new daughter cells.

Mitral valve prolapse A valvular disease of the heart involving the protrusion of one or both cusps of the mitral valve back into the left atrium.

Mood A prevailing and enduring emotional state.

Moral development The rules of conduct people use in their interactions with others.

Mores   Folkways that are considered the right or wrong way of doing things.

Morphemes   Represent the smallest unit of meaning in any language system.

Multiplex relationship   A relationship in which a person has more than one type of exchange with another person.

Munchausen's syndrome by proxy   Child abuse in which the caregiver induces symptoms of illness in the child.

Mutations   Random events that distort key characteristics in an organism's growth and development.

Myelinization   The process of coating the nerve cells with myelin, a substance that forms around neurons and acts as insulation, allowing faster and more efficient transmission of nerve impulses.

Myocardial infarction   The condition in which insufficient oxygen is directed to the heart's muscle.

Myocarditis   An infection or other factor that damages the heart's muscle.

Natural groups   Groups created by naturally occurring events, interpersonal attraction, or the mutual needs of the individuals involved.

Natural helpers   Relatives, friends, and neighbors to whom one turns in time of trouble or need.

Neural tube defects   Birth defects of the brain or spinal cord that include the following: spina bifida, in which one or more vertebrae do not close over the spinal cord—if the cord bulges through the opening the baby has a meningocele; hydrocephalus—excess fluid in the head resulting in a large head; microcephaly—a much smaller than normal head; anencephaly—absence of all or part of the brain.

Neurons   The cells in the nervous system involved in conveying information from one cell to another.

Neurotransmitters   Chemicals that are synthesized inside the neuron.

Night terrors   A sudden awakening from sleep with intense feelings of panic.

Norms   Expectations and beliefs about appropriate behavior in a group.

Obesity   Having a body weight 20% or more above the recommended weight for one's height.

Object permanence   The ability to hold an image of an object or person in one's mind.

Obligatory attention   Describes the fact that babies will attend to something they find interesting and not be distracted from it.

Occipital lobe   Located below the parietal lobe and involved in the receiving and sending of visual information.

Open adoption   Adoption in which the birth mother and sometimes birth father participate in choosing the adoptive family, and often remain in contact with the child after adoption.

Operant conditioning   The acquisition of new responses because of their effects on the environment.

Organization   According to Piaget, a tendency held by all species to systematize their processes into coherent systems.

Osteoporosis   The thinning or weakening of bones.

Ovaries   Part of the female reproductive system. The ovaries produce the ovum, or egg, and the female hormones estrogen and progesterone.

Overanxious disorder   Fears that have no specific focus. Children with this disorder worry that something will go wrong in almost any situation.

Overextension   Using one word to include a larger category. An example is referring to all furry creatures as a dog.

Parasympathetic nervous system   The branch of the nervous system that counteracts the activities of the sympathetic nervous system and conserves body resources.

Parietal lobe   Portion of the brain that is primarily involved in the process of integrating sensory information.

Peer group   A group of age-mates that is durable and composed of interactions based on an established set of social relationships.

Perception   The interpretation of information detected by the senses.

Perceptual set   Whenever people perceive objects as having only their most common or recent functional significance.

Pericardium   The thin sac that encloses the heart.

Peripheral nervous system   All those nerves that lie outside the brain and spinal cord.

Personal fable   The adolescent's belief that he or she is indestructible and unique—so much so that no one can understand what it is like to be him or her.

Phenotype   The trait expressed by genes in the individual.

Phobias   Irrational fears.

Phonemes   The basic identifiable sounds in the language system.

Phonology   The component in language studies that examines the system of sound in languages.

Polyhydramnios   Excess amniotic fluid, the presence of which may indicate a problem with the fetus, such as anencephaly.

Power   In a group, a person's ability to obtain control through reward, coercion, expertise, personal characteristics, and legitimacy.

Power assertive discipline   A punitive style of discipline that includes physical punishment, threat of punishment, and/or attempts to control the child's behavior.

Pragmatics   The study of the rules that specify how language is used across social contexts.

Prejudice   A generalized negative attitude that is directed toward another person's membership in a socially defined group.

Prematurity   Birth before the 37th week of gestation.

Premenstrual syndrome (PMS)   A set of symptoms some women experience about ten days prior to their menstrual period. The symptoms may include breast tenderness, a bloated feeling, irritability, and negative moods.

Primary process thinking   Based on irrational, illogical, and fantasy-oriented notions.

Problem solving   The ability to sort out relevant from irrelevant information and to adopt a strategy or plan for completing the task.

Professional half-life   The time it takes for 50% of one's professional knowledge to become invalid or obsolete.

Professional obsolescence   The use of information, theories, and technology that are less useful in performing tasks than what is currently available in one's field of practice.

Prolonged labor   One lasting longer than 24 hours for a first-time mother or more than 12 hours for a woman who has previously given birth.

Protein   Any organic compound that has a large combination of amino acids.

Proximodistal   Development that progresses from the spine outward to the extremities.

Psychological dimension   The systems that contribute to the organization and direction of an individual's mental processes.

Psychological moratorium   A gap between childhood security and adult autonomy.

Puberty   A period in development that is characterized by maturation of physiological mechanisms, including reproductive capacity and the development of secondary sex characteristics.

Quid pro quo   Latin phrase meaning something is exchanged for something else.

Race   A large number of people who, for social or geographical reason, have interbred over a long period of time and developed visible physical characteristics and regard themselves and are regarded by others as a biological unit.

Racism   Any attitude, action, or institutional structure that subordinates a person because of his or her race.

Rape trauma syndrome   A cluster of symptoms experienced by rape victims.

Rapport talk   A style of communication that involves discussing similarities and matching experiences.

Readiness   Refers to the point in time when a child's developmental maturity allows him or her to quickly learn a needed skill or ability.

Recent memory   Refers to the retention of information within the last 24 hours.

Recessive gene   The gene that is not expressed in a trait unless paired with a similar or homozygous gene.

Reciprocal interaction   An interaction in which both parties can influence each other. For example, an infant can influence its mother and the mother can influence the infant.

Refractory period   The time between one orgasm and the physical capability to achieve another.

Relational space   The degree of intimacy between people as indicated by factors such as number and type of interactions between them, the intensity and length of their relationship, and the nature of their ties.

Reminiscence   The process of remembering the past and reviewing one's life that may arise when one realizes the inevitability of death.

Remote memory   Retention of information occurring several weeks or months in the past.

Reorganization phase   The adaptation and adjustment phase a rape victim experiences after a rape.

Repetition   A factor in association that assumes that ideas are likely to be associated when they occur together often.

Report talk   A style of communication that involves discussing knowledge and displaying skill.

Resiliency   The ability to recover from or adjust to problems, adversities, and stress in life.

Reversibility   The ability to reverse an action by mentally performing the opposite action.

Rh incompatibility   Occurs when the mother has Rh negative blood and the fetus has Rh positive blood. The mother makes antibodies that attack the fetal blood cells, resulting in anemia and possible fetal death or brain damage.

Rickets   A deficiency in either diet or sunshine that can induce permanent damage to the body, such as flat chest, deformed pelvis, or a crooked back.

Rite of passage   A ritualized recognition of a person's transition from one life stage to another, such as childhood to adolescence.

Role   A pattern of expected behavior that a person acts out in a group.

Role-taking ability   The mutual ability to see things from another person's perspective. It involves the reduction of egocentric thought.

Schema   An internal cognitive structure that facilitates adaptation.

Schizophrenia   A psychological disorder marked by disturbances in thought that spill over to affect perceptual, social, and emotional processes.

Secondary process thinking   Based on realistic and rational approaches to problem solving.

Semantics   The area in language studies that deals with meaning.

Sensation   The process in which receptors detect information that is transmitted to the brain.

Sensitive period   Based on the idea that humans experience a period of time immediately following birth in which the mother and infant bond. Researchers now believe this postbirth bonding is not as important as once thought.

Separation anxiety   Distress displayed by an infant in the absence of the primary caregiver. Usually begins around 8–10 months.

Separation anxiety disorder   Severe anxiety about leaving home or separating from the primary caregivers.

Separation-individuation   Developmental process proposed by Margaret Mahler in which the infant grows from having no sense of self as separate from the caregiver to being an autonomous, independent individual.

Sex   The biological status of being female or male.

Sex-role stereotype   How we can categorize people according to our impressions of what we consider "male" or "female."

Sex-typed behavior   The developmental process by which culturally assigned values and behaviors are considered appropriate for members of that sex.

Sexual response cycle   The three stages that culminate in sexual satisfaction: desire, excitement, and orgasm.

Shaken infant syndrome   Infant abuse in which an adult shakes the infant, causing brain damage.

Short-term memory   Memory of an event that can be maintained for about 20 to 30 seconds.

Signs   Have a valid relationship with the thing for which they stand.

Similarity   A factor in associationism that refers to associations being formed because events or ideas that occur close together have features that are similar.

Single-gene disorders   Inherited dysfunctions or defects that result from dominant, recessive, or X chromosome–linked genes.

Slow-to-warm-up child   A child who exhibits a sedate, less exuberant orientation to life. These babies are slow to adapt to new situations and many times have negative responses.

Social cognition   The level of awareness one has regarding other peoples' thoughts, feelings, and intentions.

Social cognitive monitoring   A person's ability to monitor and make sense of his or her social thoughts; a conscious self-awareness.

Social dimension   The systems of social relationships that the person interacts with individually or in a group.

Social distance   The nearness in relationships between people.

Social functioning   All the factors influencing the performance of roles that enable individuals to achieve a reasonable degree of fulfillment and to function as productive and contributing members of society.

Social integration   The quantity of ties that a person has to major social institutions.

Social learning theory   Assumes that people can learn by observing events that they do not directly experience or perform.

Social marginality   The absence of ties to major social institutions.

Social referencing   The process by which an infant looks to others for emotional information about how to respond in an unfamiliar situation or to an unfamiliar person or object.

Social skills training   A treatment program that assumes problem behaviors can be understood in terms of not having the skills needed to cope with situational demands.

Social support systems   Continuing social aggregates that provide individuals with opportunities for feedback about themselves and for validations for their expectations about others, which may offset deficiencies in these communications in larger community contexts.

Socioeconomic status   The combination of one's economic status or level of income, social status or level of education, and work status as measured by one's occupation.

Status   The ranking of each member's position in a group relative to the other members.

Stepfamily   Families whose kinship is determined by remarriage.

Stereotypes   Oversimplified or prejudicial beliefs about a target group held by nonmembers of that group.

Stranger anxiety   Distress displayed by an infant at the sight of an unfamiliar face. Usually begins around 5–6 months.

Subjective norms   Beliefs about what important people or significant others think about an object.

Superego   According to Freud, the moral guidance that helps balance the drives associated with the id.

Symbols   Stand for other things or ideas, but do not have a direct relationship with them.

Sympathetic nervous system   The branch of the nervous system that mobilizes the body for emergencies.

Symptoms   Subjective complaints like "my head hurts."

Synaptic cleft   The space between any two neurons or between a neuron and another cell.

Syndactyly   The total fusion of fingers and toes.

Syndrome   Any cluster of signs and symptoms.

Syntax   The component of language studies that focuses on the rules that govern the way words are combined to form sentences.

System   Any set of elements that affect or influence one another.

Systolic pressure   A measure of the heart when it is constricting and pumping blood out and through the body.

Task analysis   A method of studying what children know by identifying the various components of the task the child is performing.

Task groups   Groups that have as their primary purpose to complete the work for which the groups were convened.

Tay-Sachs disease   A neurodegenerative disorder that is characterized by progressive mental and physical retardation.

Telegraphic speech   Using only words that are absolutely necessary to convey a message.

Temperament   The characteristic pattern by which an infant responds to and interacts with the environment.

Temporal lobe   The portion of the brain involved in emotions and human motivation.

Teratogens   Substances that cause birth defects and anomalies.

Testes   Part of the male reproductive system. The testes produce sperm and the male hormone testosterone.

Toxemia or eclampsia   A serious complication of pregnancy, which can result in maternal death, fetal death, or fetal brain damage. Early stages are referred to as preeclampsia. Symptoms include elevated blood pressure, swelling of hands and face, weight gain, protein in urine.

Transitional object   Something (a blanket, toy, or teddy bear) the infant uses for comfort in the absence of the primary caregiver.

Transracial adoption   Adoption in which the child is of a different race than the adoptive parents.

Treatment groups   Groups that seek to meet members' socioemotional needs.

Trial and error   The sequential application of possible solutions to problems.

Triangulation   Occurs in families when two family members experience conflict and "triangulate," or involve, a third member to regulate the stress and conflict between them.

Tumor   What is formed when cell growth leads to the buildup of masses of purposeless tissue.

Turner's syndrome   Occurs when a female is born with only one X chromosome (X0).

Type A personality   Competitive, impatient, and sometimes hostile perfectionists.

Type B personality   Relaxed, easygoing, and generally amicable individuals.

Ultrasound   A prenatal screening procedure in which high- frequency sound waves are passed through the mother's abdomen to form a picture of the developing fetus.

Uninformative messages   Messages that do not clarify the exact meaning being communicated.

Uniplex relationship   A relationship in which a person has one type of exchange with a person.

Vaginal bleeding   A complication of pregnancy that may be associated with spontaneous abortion or with placental complications.

Values   Abstract goals that do not have specific objects or reference points, such as beauty, freedom, or health.

Verbal control   The development of speech through three successive stages: other-external, self-external, and self-internal; the idea that self-verbalizations are related to self-guidance.

Vigilance   The capacity of sustaining outward attention over a prolonged period of time.

References

Abel, E., & Sokol, R. (1987). Incidence of fetal alcohol syndrome and economic impact of FAS-related anomalies. *Drug & Alcohol Dependence, 19,* 51-70.

Abel, R. L. (1982). *The politics of informal justice: Vol. 1. American experience.* New York: Academic Press.

Abramovitch, R., Corter, C., Pepler, D. J., & Stanhope, L. (1986). Sibling and peer interaction: A final follow-up and comparison. *Child Development, 47,* 217-229.

Abuelo, D. N. (1983). Genetic disorders. In J. L. Matson and J. A. Muilick (Eds.), *Handbook of mental retardation.* New York: Pergamon Press.

Achenbach, T. M. (1991). *Child behavior checklist.* Burlington, VT: Department of Psychiatry.

Achenbach, T. M., & Edelbrock, C. (1983). *Manual for the child behavior checklist and revised child behavior profile.* Burlington, VT: University of Vermont Department of Psychiatry.

Achenbach, T. M., McConaughy, S. H., & Howell, C. T. (1987). Child/adolescent behavioral and emotional problems: Implications of cross-informant correlations for situational specificity. *Psychological Bulletin, 101,* 213-232.

Adams, B. N. (1986). *The family: A sociological interpretation* (4th ed.). San Diego: Harcourt Brace Jovanovich.

Adams, G. R., Abraham, K. G., & Markstrom, C. A. (1987). The relations among identity development, self-consciousness, and self-focusing during middle and late adolescence. *Developmental Psychology, 23,* 292-297.

Adams, G. R., & Gullotta, T. (1989). *Adolescent life experiences.* Pacific Grove, CA: Brooks/Cole.

Adler, H., Davies, S. P., Bane, F., Reeves, M., & Lewis, M. (1932). *Social Services Review, 6,* 429-451.

Adler, J. (1997, December 15). A matter of faith. *Time,* 49-54.

Adler, T. (1989, August). Shy monkeys are born, not made. *APA Monitor,* p. 5.

Adler, T. (1990, July). Genes and behavior: Old tune in a new key? *APA Monitor,* pp. 8-9.

Adler, T. (1990, December). Melody is the message of infant-directed speech. *APA Monitor,* p. 9.

Adler, T. (1991, July). Women's expectations are menopause villains. *APA Monitor,* p. 14.

Ainsworth, M. D. S., Blehar, M., Waters, E., & Wall, S. (1978). *Patterns of attachment.* Hillsdale, NJ: Erlbaum.

Ainsworth, M. D. S., & Eichberg, C. (1992). Effects of infant-mother attachment on mother's unresolved loss of an attachment figure or other traumatic experience. In P. Morris, J. Stevenson-Hinde, & C. Parkes (Eds.), *Attachment across the life cycle* (pp. 160-183). New York: Routledge.

Ajzen, I. (1987). Attitudes, traits, and actions: Dispositional prediction of behavior in personality and social psychology. In L. Berkowitz (Ed.), *Advances in experimental social psychology.* New York: Academic Press.

Alan Guttmachev Institute (1993). *National survey of the American males' sexual habits.* New York: Author.

Alexander, J. F., & Parsons, B. V. (1982). *Functional family therapy.* Pacific Grove, CA: Brooks/Cole.

Alexander, W. M., & McErwin, C. K. (1989). *Schools in the middle: Progress from 1968-1988.* Reston, VA: National Association of Secondary School Principals.

Allen, K. R., & Chin-Sang, V. (1990). A lifetime of work: The context and meanings of leisure for aging black women. *The Gerontologist, 30,* 734-740.

Allen-Meares, P., & Deroos, Y. (1997). The future of the social work profession. In M. Reisch, & E. Gambrill (Eds.), *Social work in the 21st century* (pp. 376-386). Thousand Oaks: Pine Forge Press.

Allport, G. W. (1935). Attitudes. In M. Murchison (Ed.), *Handbook of social psychology.* Worcester, MA: Clark University Press.

Als, H., Lawhon, G., Duffy, F., McAnulty, G., Gibes-Grossman, R., & Blickman, J. (1994). Individualized developmental care for the very low birth weight preterm infant: Medical and neurofunctional effects. *JAMA, 272,* 853-858.

Amato, P. R. (1993). Family processes and the competence of adolescents and primary school children. *Journal of Youth and Adolescence, 18,* 39-53.

Amato, P. R., & Booth, A. (1996). A prospective study of divorce and parent-child relationships. *Journal of Marriage and the Family, 58,* 356-365.

American Academy of Pediatrics. (1992). Positioning and sudden infant death syndrome (SIDS). *Pediatrics, 89,* 1120-1126.

American Academy of Pediatrics. (1993). Investigation and review of unexpected infant and child deaths. *Pediatrics, 92,* 734-735.

American Academy of Pediatrics. (1994). Distinguishing SIDS from child abuse fatalities. *Pediatrics, 94,* 124-126.

American Academy of Pediatrics (1996). Positioning and SIDS: Update. *Pediatrics, 98,* 1216-1218.

American Academy of Pediatrics. (1997). Does bed sharing affect the risk of SIDS? *Pediatrics, 100,* 272.

American Academy of Pediatrics. (1998, November 2). Press release: Declines in teen pregnancy and abortion rates [online]. Available at http://www.aap.org/advocacy/archives/novpre.htm.

American Academy of Pediatrics. (1999a). Adolescent pregnancy—Current trends and issues: 1998. *Pediatrics, 103,* 516-520.

American Academy of Pediatrics. (1999b, August 2). Press release: AAP discourages television for very young children [online]. Available at http://www.aap.org/advocacy/releases/augdis.htm.

American Academy of Pediatrics Task Force on Circumcision. (1999). Circumcision policy statement. *Pediatrics, 103,* 686-694.

American Association of Retired Persons & Administration on Aging. (1994). *A profile of older Americans.* Washington, DC: Author.

American Psychiatric Association. (1994). *Diagnostic and statistical manual of mental disorders* (4th ed.). Washington, DC: Author.

American Psychiatric Association. (1995). *Psychiatrists' viewpoints on religion and their services to religious institutions and ministry: Task force report 10.* Washington DC: Author.

American Psychological Association (1996). Potential warning signs for violence in children. From http://helping.apa.org/family/warning.htm.

American Psychological Association. (1997, August 17). APA news release: Cartoons still stereotype gender roles [online]. From http://www.apa.org/releases.cartoon.html.

Ancelet, B. J., Edwards, J. D., & Pitre, G. (1991). *Cajun country.* Jackson: University of Mississippi Press.

Andersen, M. L., & Collins, P. H. (1995). *Race, class and gender: An anthology.* Belmont, CA: Wadsworth.

Andersen, M. L., & Collins, P. H. (1998). (2nd ed.). *Race, class and gender: An anthology.* Belmont, CA: Wadsworth.

Anderson, H. I., & Goolishian, H. A. (1992). The client as expert: A not-knowing approach to therapy. In S. McNamee and K. Gergen (Eds.), *Therapy as social construction* (pp. 25-39). Newbury Park, CA: Sage.

Anderson, R. E., & Carter, I. (1990). *Human behavior in the social environment: A social systems approach* (4th ed.). New York: Aldine.

Anderson, S. M., & Williams, M. (1985). Cognitive/affective reaction in the improvement of self-esteem: When thoughts and feelings make a difference. *Journal of Personality and Social Psychology, 49,* 1086-1097.

Andreason, N. C. (1984). *The broken brain: The biological revolution in psychiatry.* New York: Harper & Row.

Andreason, N. C., & Black, D. W. (1991). *Introductory textbook of psychiatry.* Washington, DC: American Psychiatric Press.

Andrews, D. A., & Bonta, J. (1994). *The psychology of criminal conduct.* Cincinnati: Anderson Publishing.

Andrews, D. A., & Bonta, J. (1998) (2nd ed.). *The psychology of criminal conduct.* Cincinnati: Anderson Publishing.

Andronico, M. P. (1996). *Men in Groups.* Hyattsville, MD: American Psychological Association.

Aneshensel, C. S., Pearlin, L. I., Mullan, J. T., Zarit, S. H., & Whitlach, C. J. (1995). *Profiles in caregiving: The unexpected career.* San Diego: Academic Press.

Anthony, I., & Smith, D. C. (1994). Adolescent fathers; A positive acknowledgment in the school setting. *Social Work in Education, 9,* 26-32.

Apgar, V. (1953). A proposal for a new method of evaluation in the newborn infant. *Current Research in Anesthesia and Analgesia, 32,* 260-267.

Aponte, H. J., & Van Deusen, J. M. (1981). Structural family therapy. In A. S. Gurman & D. P. Kniskern (Eds.), *Handbook of family therapy.* New York: Brunner Mazel.

Appetite suppressant found in brain, researchers say. (1996, January 4). *USA Today.*

Applewhite, S. R. (Ed.). (1988). *Hispanic elderly in transition.* New York: Greenwood Press.

Apter, T. (1995). *Secret paths: Women in the new midlife.* New York: Norton.

Arlington, D. E., & Troll, L. E. (1984). Social change and equality: The roles of women and economics. In G. Baruch & J. Brooks-Gunn (Eds.), *Women in midlife.* New York: Plenum.

Arrendondo, P. M. (1984). Identity themes for immigrant young adults. *Adolescence, 19,* 977-993.

Ashburn, S. S., Schuster, C. S., Grimm, W. A., & Goff, S. M. (1986). Language development during childhood. In C. Schuster & S. S. Ashburn (Eds.), *The process of human development: A holistic life-span approach* (pp. 257-276). Boston: Little, Brown.

Asher, J. (1987, April). Born to be shy? *Psychology Today,* 56-64.

Asher, S. R., & Dodge, K. A. (1986). Identifying children who are rejected by their peers. *Developmental Psychology, 22,* 444-449.

Asher, S. R., & Renshaw, P. (1981). Children without friends: Social knowledge and social skill training. In S. R. Asher & J. M. Gottman (Eds.), *The development of children's friendships.* New York: Cambridge University Press.

Ashford, J. B. (1994). Child maltreatment interventions: Developments in law, prevention and treatment. *Criminal Justice Review, 19,* 271-285.

Ashford, J. B., & Littrell, J. (1998). Psychopathology. In J. Figueira-McDonough, F. E. Netting, A. Nichols-Casebolt (Eds.), *The role of gender in practiced knowledge: Claiming half the human experience* (pp. 127-159). New York: Garland Publishing, Inc.

Astor, R. A., Behre, W. J., Fravil, K. A., & Wallace, J. M. (1997). Perceptions of school violence as a problem and reports of violent events: A national survey of school social workers. *Social Work, 42,* 55-68.

Atchley, R. (1976). *The sociology of retirement.* New York: Halsted Press.

Atchley, R. C., & Miller, S. J. (1983). Types of elderly couples. In T. H. Brubaker (Ed.), *Family relationships in later life.* Beverly Hills, CA: Sage.

Atwood, M. (1991). *Cat's eye.* London: Virago.

Avard, D. (1985). Risks and benefits of obstetric epidural analgesia: A review. *Birth: Issues in Perinatal Care and Education, 12,* 215-225.

Azar, B. (1995a, May). Avoiding alcohol in real-world settings. *APA Monitor,* p. 20.

Azar, B. (1995b, June). Data released from child-care study. *APA Monitor,* p. 18.

Azar, B. (1996a, November). Project explores landscape of midlife. *APA Monitor,* p. 26.

Azar, B. (1996b, November). Some forms of memory improve as people age. *APA Monitor,* p. 27.

Azar, B. (1997, October). More study needed on hormone replacement. *APA Monitor,* p. 33.

Azar, B. (1997 November). Forgiveness helps keep relationships steadfast. *APA Monitor,* p. 14.

Azar, B. (1997a, December). Learning begins even before babes are born scientists show. *APA Monitor,* 17.

Azar, B. (1997b, December). Maternal emotions may influence fetal behaviors. *APA Monitor,* p. 15.

Bacerra, R. M. (1988). The Mexican American family. In C. H. Mindel, R. W. Habenstein, & R. Wright (Eds.), *Ethnic families in America: Patterns and variations* (3rd ed.). New York: Elsevier.

Baillargeon, R. (1987). Object permanence in 3 1/2 and 4 1/2 month-old infants. *Developmental Psychology, 23,* 655-664.

Balaskas, J. (1992). *Active birth: The new approach to giving birth naturally.* Boston: Harvard Common Press.

Baldwin, J. R., & Hecht, M. L. (1995). The layered perspective of cultural (in)tolerance(s). In R. L. Waiseman (Ed.), *Intercultural communication theory.* Thousands Oaks, CA: Sage.

Bales, R. F. (1958). Task roles and social roles in problem-solving groups. In E. E. Maccoby, T. M. Newcomb, & E. L. Hartley (Eds.), *Readings in social psychology.* New York: Holt, Rinehart & Winston.

Ballenger, M. (1983). Reading in the kindergarten: Comment. *Childhood Education, 59,* 187.

Bandura, A. (1965). Influence of models' reinforcement contingencies on the acquisition of imitative responses. *Journal of Personality and Social Psychology, 1,* 589-595.

Bandura, A. (1971). *Social learning theory.* Englewood Cliffs, NJ: Prentice Hall.

Bandura, A. (1977). *Social learning.* Englewood Cliffs, NJ: Prentice Hall.

Bandura, A. (1989). Social cognitive theory. In R. Vasta (Ed.), *Annuals of child development: Vol. 6. Theories of child development: Revised formulations and current issues.* Greenwich, CT: JAI Press.

Bandura, A., Ross, D., & Ross, S. (1963). Vicarious reinforcement and imitative learning. *Journal of Abnormal and Social Psychology, 67,* 601-607.

Bank, B. A., Seri, I., Ischiropoulos, H., Merrill, J., Rychik, J., & Ballard, R. A. (1999). Changes in oxygenation with inhaled nitric oxide in severe bronchopulmonary dysplasia. *Pediatrics, 103,* 610-619.

Banton, M. (1994). *Discrimination.* Buckingham: Open University Press.

Barash, D. P., & Lipton, J. E. (1985). Sociobiology. In H. Kaplan and B. J. Sadock (Eds.), *Comprehensive textbook of psychiatry* (Vol. 4). Baltimore: Williams & Wilkins.

Barasch, D. S. (1998). Empathy and compassion: How a child develops through the years. *Family Life,* 54-57.

Barkley, R. (1998). *Your defiant child; 8 steps to better behavior.* New York: Guilford Press.

Barnard, C. I. (1938). *The functions of the executive.* Cambridge, Mass.: Harvard University Press.

Barnes, K. E. (1971). Preschool play norms: A replication. *Developmental Psychology, 4,* 99-103.

Baron, R. A., & Byrne, D. (1984). *Social psychology: Understanding human interaction.* Newton, MA: Allyn & Bacon.

Barrett, D. E. (1979). A naturalistic study of sex differences in children's aggression. *Merrill-Plamer Quarterly, 25,* 193-203.

Barth, R. P. (1996). *Reducing the risk: Building skills to prevent pregnancy STD and HIV* (3rd ed.) Santa Cruz, CA: ETR Associates.

Bartlett, H. (1970). *The common base of social work practice.* Washington, DC: National Association of Social Workers.

Baruch, A. S., & Spaid, W. M. (1989). Gender differences in caregiving: Why do wives report greater burden? *The Gerontologist, 29,* 667-676.

Baruch, G. K., & Barnett, R. C. (1983). Adult daughters' relationships with their mothers. *Journal of Marriage and the Family, 45,* 601-606.

Baruch, G. K., & Brooks-Gunn, J. (1984). The study of women in midlife. In G. Baruch & J. Brooks-Gunn (Eds.), *Women in midlife*. New York: Plenum.

Baruth, L. G., & Manning, M. L. (1991). *Multicultural counseling and psychotherapy*. New York: Merrill.

Bascue, L. O., & Lawrence, R. E. (1977). A study of subjective time and death anxiety in the elderly. *Omega, 8,* 81–90.

Baskett, L. M., & Johnson, S. M. (1982). The young child's interactions with parents versus siblings. *Child Development, 53,* 643–650.

Basow, S. A. (1992). *Gender: Stereotypes and roles*. Pacific Grove, CA: Brooks/Cole.

Bassuk, E. L. (1991). Homeless families. *Scientific American, 265,* 66–74.

Bates, E. (1976). *The emergence of symbols*. New York: Academic Press.

Bateson, M. C. (1990). *Composing a life*. New York: Plume.

Baumgartner-Papageorgious, A. (1982). *My daddy might have loved me: Student perceptions of differences between being male and being female*. Denver: Institute for Equality in Education.

Baumrind, D. (1971). Current patterns of parental authority. *Developmental Psychology Monographs, 4* (1, Pt. 2).

Baumrind, D. (1989). Parenting styles and adolescent development. In J. Brooks-Gunn, R. Lerner, & A. C. Petersen (Eds.), *The encyclopedia of adolescence*. New York: Garland.

Baumrind, D. (1991). Effective parenting during the early adolescent transition. In P. A. Cowan & E. M. Hetherington (Eds.), *Advances in family research (Vol. 2)*. Hillsdale, NJ: Erlbaum.

Baylor, B. (1977/1978). *The way to start a day*. New York: Macmillan.

Beal, C. R. (1987). Repairing the message: Children's monitoring and revision skills, *Child Development, 58,* 920–928.

Beardsley, T. (1995, February). Putting Alzheimer's to the tests. *Scientific American,* 12–13.

Beattie, M. (1987). *Codependent no more*. New York: Harper Collins.

Beck, C. M., Rawlins, R. P., & Williams, S. R. (1988). *Mental health psychiatric nursing: Holistic life cycle approach*. St. Louis: C.V. Mosby.

Beck, D. F., & Jones, M. A. (1973). *Progress on family problems: A nationwide study of clients' and counselors' views on family agency services*. New York: Family Service Association of America.

Beckett, J. O., & Johnson, H. C. (1995). Human development. *The Encyclopedia of Social Work, 2,* 1385–1405.

Begley, S. (1996). Your child's brain, *Newsweek,* 55–61.

Begley, S. (1988, March). All about twins. *Reader's Digest,* 80–85.

Bellah, R., et al. (1996). *Habits of the heart*. Berkeley: University of California Press.

Bellinger, D., & Needleman, H. (1985). Prenatal and early postnatal exposure to lead: Developmental effects, correlates, and implications. *International Journal of Mental Health, 14,* 78–111.

Belsky, J. (1980). Child maltreatment: An ecological integration. *American Psychologist, 35,* 320–335.

Belsky, J. (1981). Early human experience: A family perspective. *Developmental Psychology, 17,* 3–23.

Belsky, J. (1985). Exploring differences in marital change across the transition to parenthood: The role of violated expectations. *Journal of Marriage and the Family, 47,* 1037–1044.

Belsky, J. (1990). *The psychology of aging: Theory, research, and interventions* (2nd ed.). Pacific Grove, CA: Brooks/Cole.

Belsky, J., Gilstrap, B., & Rovine, M. (1984). The Pennsylvania infant and family development project: 1. Stability and change in mother-infant and father-infant interaction in a family setting at 1, 3, and 9 months. *Child Development, 55,* 692–705.

Belsky, J., & Rovine, M. (1988). Nonmaternal care in the first year of life and the security of infant-parent attachment. *Child Development, 59,* 157–167.

Bem, D. J. (1967). Self-perception: An alternative interpretation of cognitive dissonance phenomena. *Psychological Review, 74,* 183–200.

Bem, S. L. (1974). The measurement of psychological androgyny. *Journal of Consulting and Clinical Psychology, 42,* 155–162.

Bem, S. L. (1977). On the utility of alternative procedures for assessing psychological androgyny. *Journal of Consulting and Clinical Psychology, 45,* 196–205.

Bem, S. L. (1993). *The lenses of gender: Transforming the debate on sexual inequality*. Binghamton, NY: Vail-Ballou.

Benedict, H. (1979). Early lexical development: Comprehension and production. *Journal of Child Language, 6,* 183–200.

Bengston, V. L. (1985). Diversity and symbolism in grandparental roles. In V. L. Bengston & J. Robertson (Eds.), *Grandparenthood*. Beverly Hills, CA: Sage.

Bengston, V. L., Cuellar, J. B., & Ragan, P. K. (1977). Stratum contrasts and similarities in attitudes toward death. *Journal of Gerontology, 12,* 76–88.

Benson, P. L. (1990). *The troubled journey: A portrait of 6th–12th grade youth*. Minneapolis: The Search Institute.

Bergin, D. (1988). Stages of play development. In D. Bergin (Ed.), *Play as a medium for learning and development*. Portsmouth, NH: Heinemann.

Bergoquist, W. H., Greenberg, E. M., & Klaum, G. A. (1993). *In our fifties: Voices of men and women reinventing their lives*. San Francisco: Jossey-Bass.

Berko, J. (1958). The child's learning of English morphology. *Word, 14,* 150–177.

Berlyne, D. E. (1960). *Conflict, arousal, and curiosity*. New York: McGraw-Hill.

Berman, P. S. (1997). *Case conceptualization and treatment panning: Exercises for integrating theory with practice*. Thousand Oaks: Sage Publications.

Bermant, C. (1966). *Diary of an old man*. Holt, Rinehart & Winston.

Bernard, J. (1975). *Women, wives, mothers: Values and options*. Chicago: Aldine.

Bernard, J. (1981). *The female world*. New York: Free Press.

Berndt, T. J. (1979). Developmental changes in conformity to peers and parents. *Developmental Psychology, 15,* 608–616.

Berndt, T. J., & Ladd, G. W. (1989). *Peer relations in child development*. New York: Wiley.

Berrick, J. D., & Gilbert, N. (1991). *With the best of intentions: The child sexual abuse prevention movement*. New York: Guilford Press.

Berrueta-Clement, J., Schweinhart, L., Barnett, W., Epstein, A., & Weikart, D. (1984). *Changed lives: Effects of the Perry Preschool Program on youths through age 19*. Ypsilanti, MI: High/Scope Press.

Berry, P. (1993). Pathological findings in SIDS. *Journal of Clinical Pathology, 45,* 11.

Berthold, S. (1989). Spiritism as a form of psychotherapy. *Social Casework, 70,* 502–509.

Besharov, D. J. (1985). Right versus rights: The dilemma of child protection. *Public Welfare, 42*(2), 19–27.

Beutler, L., & Harwood, T. (1995). Prescriptive psychotherapies. *Applied & Preventive Psychology, 4,* 89–100

Bialystok, E. (1988). Levels of bilingualism and levels of linguistic awareness. *Developmental Psychology, 24,* 560–567.

Bialystock, E. (1997). Speaking another language may help children master reading. *APA Monitor,* p. 8.

Biesele, M., & Howell, N. (1981). The old people give you life: Aging among !Kung hunter-gatherers. In P. T. Amoss & S. Harrell (Eds.), *Other ways of growing old: Anthropological perspectives*. Stanford, CA: Stanford University Press.

Bjorklund, D. F., & Bjorklund, B. R., (1992). *Looking at children: An introduction to child development*. Pacific Grove, CA: Brooks/Cole.

Black, D. (1993). *The social structure of right and wrong*. San Diego: Academic Press.

Black, D. J. (1976). *The behavior of law*. New York: Academic Press.

Blakemore, J. E. O., LaRue, A. A., & Olejnik, A. B. (1979). Sex-appropriate toy preference and the ability to conceptualize toys as sex-role related. *Developmental Psychology, 15,* 339–340.

Blashfield, R. K. (1984). *The classification of psychopathology: Neo-Kraepelian and quantitative approaches*. New York: Plenum.

Blau, G. M., & Gullotta, T. P. C. (1993). Promoting sexual responsibility in adolescence. In T. P. Gullotta, G. P. Adams, & R. Montemayor (Eds.), *Adolescent sexuality*. Newbury Park, CA: Sage.

Block, R. D., & Moore, E. G. (1986). *Advantage and disadvantage: A profile of American youth*. Hillsdale, NJ: Erlbaum.

Blood, R. O., & Wolfe, D. M. (1960). *Husbands and wives*. New York: Macmillan.

Blumstein, P., & Schwartz, P. (1983). *American couples*. New York: Simon & Schuster.

Boardman, S. K., & Horwitz, S. V. (1994). Constructive conflict management and social problems: An introduction. *Journal of Social Issues, 50,* 1–12.

Boehm, W. W. (1958). The nature of social work. *Social Work, 3,* 10–18.

Boehm, W. W. (1959). *Objectives of the social work curriculum of the future (Vol. 1)*. New York: Council of Social Work, Education.

Bogard, M. (1991). *Feminist approaches for men in family therapy*. New York: Haworth Press.

Bogatz, G. A., & Ball, S. (1972). *The second year of* Sesame Street: *A continuing evaluation*. Princeton, NJ: Educational Testing Service.

Bogenschneider, K., Wu, M., Raffaelli, M., & Tsay, J. C. (1998). "Other kids drink, but not my kid": Does parental awareness of adolescent alcohol use protect adolescents from risky consequences? *Journal of Marriage and the Family, 60,* 356–372.

Bonkowski, S., & Yanos, J. (1992). Infant mental health: An expanding field for social work. *Social Work, 37,* 144–148.

Bonvillian, J. D., Orlansky, M. D., & Novack, L. L. (1983). Development milestones: Sign language acquisition and motor development. *Child Development, 54,* 1435–1445.

Booth, C. L., Barnard, K. E., Mitchell, S. K., & Spieker, S. J. (1987). Successful intervention with multiproblem mothers: Effects on the mother-infant relationship. *Infant Mental Health Journal, 8,* 288–306.

Booth-Kewley, S., & Friedman, H. S. (1987). Psychological predictors of heart disease: A quantitative review. *Psychological Bulletin, 101,* 343–362.

Bootzin, R. E., & Acocella, J. R. (1988). *Abnormal psychology: Current perspectives*. New York: McGraw-Hill.

Bornstein, M., & Sigman, M. (1986). Continuity in mental development from infancy. *Child Development, 57,* 251–274.

Bornstein, R. (1992). Psychosocial development of the older adult. In C. S. Schuster & S. S. Ashburn (Eds.), *The process of human development: A holistic life-span approach* (3rd ed., pp. 831–850). New York: Lippincott.

Bornstein, R., & Schuster, C. S. (1992). Cognitive development during the adult years. In C. S. Schuster & C. Ashburn, *The process of human development*. New York: Lippincott.

Borysenko, J. (1996). *A woman's book of life: The biology, psychology, and spirituality of the feminine life cycle*. New York: Riverhead Books.

Boston Women's Health Book Collective. (1992). When yogurt was illegal. *Ms., 3,* 38–39.

Botvin, G. J. (1996). Substance abuse prevention through life skills training. In R. D. Peters, & R. J. McMahon (Eds.), *Preventing childhood disorders, substance abuse, and delinquency*. Thousand Oaks, CA: Sage.

Botvin, G. J., Baker, E., Dusenbury, L., Botvin, E. M., & Diaz, T. (1995). Long-term follow-up results of a randomized drug abuse prevention trial in a white middle-class population. *JAMA 273(4),* 1106–1112.

Botwinick, J. (1984). *Aging and behavior* (3rd ed.). New York: Springer.

Bouchard, T. J., Jr., Lykken, D. T., McGue, M., Segal, N. L., & Tellegen, A. (1990). Sources of human psychological differences: The Minnesota study of twins reared apart. *Science, 250,* 223–228.

Bourne, L. E., Ekstrand R. R., Dominowski, R. L. (1971). *The psychology of thinking*. Englewood Cliffs, NJ: Prentice Hall.

Bowen, M. (1978). *Family therapy in children practice*. New York: Jason Aronson.

Bower, T. G. R. (1982). *Development in infancy*. San Francisco: Freeman.

Bowlby, J. (1958). The nature of the child's tie to his mother. *International Journal of Psychoanalysis, 39,* 350–373.

Bowlby, J. (1969). *Attachment and loss: Vol. 1. Attachment*. New York: Basic Books.

Bowlby, J. (1980). *Attachment and loss: Vol. 3. Loss, sadness and depression*. New York: Basic Books.

Brabeck, M. (1983). Moral judgment: Theory and research on differences between males and females. *Developmental Review, 3,* 274–291.

Bradley, R. (1987). Providing a stimulating and supportive home environment for young children. *Physical and Occupational Therapy in Pediatrics, 7,* 77–89.

Bradley, R., & Brisby, J. (1990). Assessment of the home environment. In J. Johnson & J. Goldman (Eds.), *Developmental assessment in clinical child psychology* (pp. 219–250). New York: Pergamon Press.

Bradley, R., Caldwell, B., Rock, S., Casey, P., & Nelson, J. (1987). The early development of low-birthweight infants: Relationship to health, family status, family context, family processes and parenting. *International Journal of Behavioral Development, 10,* 301–318.

Bradley, R., Whiteside, L., Mundfrom, D., Casey, P., Kelleher, K., & Pope, S. (1994). Contribution of early intervention and early caregiving experiences to resilience in low-birthweight, premature children living in poverty. *Journal of Clinical Child Psychology, 23,* 425–434.

Braginsky, D. D., & Braginsky, B. M. (1975, August). Surplus people: Their lost faith in self and system. *Psychology Today, 9,* 68–72.

Brazelton, T. B. (1973). Neonatal behavioral assessment scale. In *Clinics in Developmental Medicine*, No. 50, Philadelphia: J. B. Lippincott.

Brazelton, T. B. (1992). *Touchpoints: Your child's emotional and behavioral development*. Reading, MA: Addison-Wesley.

Breckman, R., & Adelman, R. (1988). *Strategies for helping victims of elder mistreatment*. Newbury Park, CA: Sage.

Bremmer, J. (1988). *Infancy*. Great Britain: Page Bros.

Bremmer, J. N., & van den Bosch, L. (1995). *Between poverty and the pyre: Moments in the history of widowhood*. New York: Routledge.

Brennan, A. (1985). Participation and self-esteem: A test of six alternative explanations. *Adolescence, 20,* 445–466.

Bretherton, I., Fritz, J., Zahn-Waxler, C., & Ridgeway, D., (1986). Learning to talk about emotions. *Child Development, 57,* 529–548.

Brewer, W. (1995, June). New cognitive research makes waves. *APA Monitor.*

Brieland, D. (1987). History and evolution of social work practice. In A. Minahan (Ed.), *Encyclopedia of social work* (18th ed.) (pp. 739–754). Silver Spring, MD: National Association of Social Workers.

Brim, O. (1975). Macro-structural influences on child development and the need for childhood social indicators. *American Journal of Orthopsychiatry, 45,* 516–524.

Brissett-Chapman, S. (1995). Child abuse and neglect: Direct practice. In *Encyclopedia of Social Work* (19th ed.) Washington DC: NASW Press.

Broberg A. G., Wessels, H., Lamb, M. E., & Hwang, C. P. (1997). Effects of day care on the development of cognitive abilities in 8-year-olds: A longitudinal study. *Developmental Psychology, 33,* 62–69.

Brock, W. M. (1980). *The effects of day care: A review of the literature*. (ERIC Document Ed. 195–348) Los Alamitos, CA: Southwest Regional Laboratory for Educational Research and Development.

Brody, E. M. (1981). "Women in the middle" and family help to older people. *The Gerontologist, 21,* 471–480.

Brody, E. M. (1985). Parent care as a normative family stress. *The Gerontologist, 25,* 19–25.

Brody, G. H. (1998). Sibling relationship quality: Its causes ad consequences. *Annual Review of Psychology, 49,* 1–25.

Brody, J. E. (1987, January 21). Guidelines for parents on children's TV viewing. *New York Times.*

Brofenbrenner, U. (1996). Foreward. In R. B. Cairns, G. H. Elder, Jr., & J. Costello. (Eds.), *Developmental Science* (pp. ix–xvii). New York: Cambridge University Press.

Brofenbrenner, U. (1999). Environments in developmental perspective: Theoretical and operational models. In S. L. Friedman, & T. D. Wach (Eds.), *Measuring environment across the life span* (pp. 3-28). Washington, DC: American Psychological Association.

Broman, C. (1993). Race differences in marital well-being. *Journal of Marriage and the Family, 55,* 724-732.

Bromwich, R. (1985, December). Vulnerable infants and risky environments. *Zero to Three,* 7-12.

Bronfenbrenner, U. (1977). Toward an experimental ecology of human development. *American Psychologist, 32,* 513-531.

Bronfenbrenner, U. (1986). Ecology of the family as a context of human development: Research perspectives. *Developmental Psychology, 22,* 723-742.

Bronson, W. C. (1985). Developments in behavior with age mates during the second year of life. In M. Lewis & L. A. Rosenblum (Eds.), *The origins of behavior: Friendship and peer relations.* New York: Wiley.

Brooks, G. R. (1998). *A new psychotherapy for traditional men.* San Francisco: Jossey Bass.

Brooks-Gunn, J. (1986). Pubertal processes and girls' psychological adaptation. In R. M. Lerner & T. T. Foch (Eds.), *Biological psychosocial interactions in early adolescence: A life-span perspective.* Hillsdale, NJ: Erlbaum.

Brooks-Gunn, J., & Lewis, M. (1984). The development of early self-recognition. *Developmental Review, 4,* 215-239.

Brooks-Gunn, J., McCormick, M., & Heagarty, L. (1988). Preventing infant mortality and morbidity: Developmental perspectives. *American Journal of Orthopsychiatry, 58,* 288-295.

Brooks-Gunn, J., & Ruble, D. N. (1983). The experience of menarche from a developmental perspective. In J. Brooks-Gunn & A. C. Petersen (Eds.), *Girls at puberty.* New York: Plenum.

Brooks-Gunn, J. & Warren, M. P. (1985). The effects of delayed menarche in different contexts: Dance and nondance students. *Journal of Youth and Adolescence, 14,* 285-300.

Brooks-Gunn, J., & Warren, M. P. (1989, April). *How important are pubertal and social events for different problem behaviors and contexts.* Paper presented at the biennial meeting of the Society for Research in Child Development, Kansas City.

Brower, A. M., & Nurius, P. S. (1993). *Social cognition and individual change.* Newbury Park: Sage.

Brown, B. B. (1990). Peer groups and peer cultures. In S. S. Feldman & G. R. Elliott (Eds.), *At the threshold: The developing adolescent* (pp. 171-196). Cambridge, MA: Harvard University Press.

Brown, B. B., & Mounts, N. (1989, April). *Peer group structures in single versus multi-ethnic high schools.* Paper presented at the biennial meeting of the Society for Research in Child Development, Kansas City, MO.

Brown, C. C. (1976, November). It changed my life. *Psychology Today,* 48-112.

Brown, L. M., & Gillian, C. (1992). *Meeting at the crossroads.* New York: Ballantine Books.

Brown, L. N. (1991). *Groups for growth and change.* New York: Longman.

Brown, M. A., & Woods, N. F. (1986). Sex role orientation, sex typing, occupational traditionalism, and premenstrual symptoms. In V. L. Olesen & N. F. Woods (Eds.), *Culture, society, and menstruation.* Washington, DC: Hemisphere.

Brown, P., & Elliott, R. (1965). Control of aggression in a nursery school class. *Journal of Experimental Child Psychology, 2,* 103-107.

Brown, R. (1958). *Words and things.* Glencoe, IL: Free Press.

Brown, R. H. (1994). Reconstructing social theory after the postmodern critique. In H. W. Simons & M. Billig (Eds.), *After postmodernism: Reconstructing ideology critique.* London: Sage.

Browne, A. (1987). *When battered women kill.* New York: Free Press.

Brownlee, S., McGraw, D., & Vest, J. (1997, June 16). The place for vengeance. *U.S. News and World Report,* 25-32.

Brubaker, T. H. (1985). *Later life families.* Newbury Park, CA: Sage.

Brubaker, T. H. (1990). Families in later life: A burgeoning research area. *Journal of Marriage and the Family, 52,* 959-982.

Bruckner-Gordon, F., Gangi, B. K., & Wallman, G. U. (1988). *Making therapy work: Your guide to choosing, using, and ending therapy.* New York: HarperCollins.

Bryant, S., & Demian. (1990, May/June). When lesbian and gay couples break up. *Partners Newsletter for Gay and Lesbian Couples.*

Buck, R. (1984). *The communication of emotion.* New York: Guilford Press.

Buehler, C. A., Hogan, M. J., Robinson, B. E., & Levy, R. J. (1985). The parental divorce transition: Divorce-related stressors and well-being. *Journal of Divorce, 9,* 61-81.

Buehlman, K. T., Gottman, J. M., & Katz, L. F. (1992). How a couple views their past predicts their future: Predicting divorce from an oral history interview. *Journal of Family Psychology, 5,* 295-318.

Bufe, C. (1987, November). AA: Guilt and god for the gullible. *The Match! An Anarchist Journal.* Excerpted in *Utne Reader* (1988, November/December), 54-55.

Bullis, R. (1996). *Spirituality in social work practice.* Washington DC: Taylor & Francis.

Bullock, B. L., & Rosendahl, P. P. (1988). *Pathophysiology: Adaptations and alterations in function* (2nd ed.). Glenview, IL: Scott, Foresman.

Bullock, L. F., & McFarlane, J. (1989). The birth-weight/battering connection. *American Journal of Nursing, 89,* 1153-1155.

Burdman, G. M. (1986). *Healthful aging.* Englewood Cliffs, NJ: Prentice Hall.

Burgess, A. W., & Holmstromm, L. L. (1985). Rape trauma syndrome and post traumatic stress response. In A. W. Burgess (Ed.), *Rape and sexual assault: A research handbook* (pp. 46-60). New York: Garland.

Burnette, E. (1995, June). Black males retrieve a noble heritage, *APA Monitor,* pp. 1, 32.

Burnette, E. (1996, January). Researchers work to prevent social ills. *APA Monitor,* p. 32.

Burton, L. (1990). Teenage childbearing as an alternative life-course strategy in multigenerational black families. *Human Nature, 2,* 123-143.

Buss, D. M. (1995). Evolutionary psychology: A new paradigm for psychological science. *Psychological Inquiry, 6,* 1-30.

Buss, D. M. (1996). The evolutionary psychology of human social strategies. In E. T. Higgins & A. W. Kruglanski (Eds.), *Social psychology: Handbook of basic principles.* New York: Guilford Press.

Busse, E. W., & Pfeiffer, E. (1977). *Behavior and adaptation in late life.* Boston: Little, Brown.

Butler, K. (1995, March/April). Caught in the crossfire. *Family Therapy Networker,* 25-29.

Butler, R. (1959). *An orientation to knowledge of human growth and behavior in social work education (Vol. 6).* New York: Council of Social Work Education.

Butler, R. M. (1970). *Social functioning framework: An approach to the human behavior and social environment sequence.* New York: Council on Social Work Education.

Butler, R. N. (1963). The life review: An interpretation of reminiscence in the aged. *Psychiatry, 26,* 65-76.

Butler, R. N. (1975). *Why survive? Being old in America.* New York: Harper & Row.

Butler, R. N. (1990). A disease called ageism. *Journal of the American Geriatric Association, 38,* 178-180.

Butler, R. N., Lewis, M., & Sunderland, T. (1991). *Aging and mental health: Positive psychosocial and biomedical approaches* (4th ed.). New York: Macmillan.

Cairns, R. B., Cairns, B. D., Neckerman, H. J., Ferguson, L. L., & Gariepy, J. L. (1989). Growth and aggression: Childhood to adolescence. *Developmental Psychology, 25,* 320-330.

Caldwell, B., & Bradley, R. (1984). *Home observation for measurement of the environment.* Little Rock: University of Arkansas Press.

Call, J. D. (1964). Newborn approach behavior and early ego development. *International Journal of Psychoanalysis, 45,* 286.

Call, J. D. (1974). *Psychological and behavioral development of children.* Brennemann's Practice of Pediatrics, Harper and Row.

Callahan, J. (1994). The ethics of assisted suicide. *Health & Social Work, 19,* 237-244.

Calvert, S., & Calvert, P. (1992). *Sociology today.* London: Harvester/Weatsheaf.

Camp, B. W., Blom, G. E., Herbert, F., & Van Doorninck, W. J. (1977). "Think aloud": A program for developing self-control in young aggressive boys. *Journal of Abnormal Psychology, 5,* 167-169.

Campbell, E. (1985). *The childless marriage: An exploratory study of couples who do not want children.* New York: Tavistock.

Campbell, F. A., & Ramey, C. T. (1994). Effects of early intervention on intellectual and academic achievement: A follow-up study of children from low-income families. *Child Development, 65,* 684-698.

Campbell, J., with Moyers, B. (1988). *The power of myth.* New York: Doubleday.

Canda, E. (1989a). General implications of shamanism for clinical social work. *International Social Work, 26,* 14-22.

Canda, E. (1989b). Religious content in social work education: A comparative approach. *Journal of Social Work Education, 25,* 15-24.

Canda, E. (1990). An holistic approach to prayer for social work practice. *Social Thought, 16,* 3-13.

Cantor, M. H. (1979). Neighbors and friends: An overlooked resource in the informal support system. *Research on Aging, 1,* 434-463.

Cantor, M. H. (1983). Strain among caregivers: A study of the experience in the United States. *The Gerontologist, 23,* 597-604.

Cantwell, D. P. (1982). Childhood depression: A review of current research. In B. B. Lahey & A. E. Kazdin (Eds.), *Advances in child clinical psychology.* New York: Plenum.

Caplan, G. (1964). *Principles of preventive psychiatry.* New York: Basic Books.

Caplan, G. (1974). *Support systems and community mental health.* New York: Behavioral Publications.

Caplan, R. (1993). Alcoholism. *Grolier Electronic Encyclopedia.*

Carey, G., Ratliff, D., & Lyle, R. R. (1998). Resilient adolescent mothers: Ethnographic interviews. *Families, Systems and Health, 16,* 347-364.

Carey, S. (1977). The child as word learner. In M. Halle, J. Bresman, & G. A. Miller (Eds.), *Linguistic theory and psychological reality.* Cambridge: Massachusetts Institute of Technology Press.

Carlip, H. (1995). *Girl Power: Young women speak out.* New York: Warner Books.

Carnegie Council on Adolescent Development. (1989). *Turning points: Preparing youth for the 21st century.* New York: Carnegie Corporation.

Carnegie Task Force on Meeting the Needs of Young Children. (1994). *Starting Points.* New York: Carnegie Corporation.

Carolina Consortium on Human Development, The. (1996). Developmental science: A collaborative statement. In R. B. Cairns, G. H. Elder, Jr., & J. Costello (Eds.), *Developmental Science* (pp. 1-6). New York: Cambridge University Press.

Carstensen, L. (1990). *Psychology and Aging, 5,* 355-347.

Carter, B., & McGoldrick, M. (1988). *The changing family lifecycle: A framework for family therapy* (2nd ed.). New York: Gardner.

Cartwright, D. (1968). The nature of group cohesiveness. In D. Cartwright & A. Zander (Eds.), *Group dynamics: Research and theory* (3rd ed.). New York: Harper & Row.

Caspi, A., & Bem, D. (1990). Personality continuity and change across the life course. In L. Pervin (Ed.), *Handbook of Personality: Theory and Research.* New York: Guilford.

Caspi, A., Elder, G. H., & Bem, D. J. (1987). Moving against the world: Life-course patterns of explosive children. *Developmental Psychology, 23,* 308-313.

Cassell, C. (1984). *Swept away: Why women fear their own sexuality.* New York: Simon & Schuster.

Castillo, R. (1997). *Culture & mental illness: A client centered approach.* Belmont: Brooks/Cole publishing.

Castillo, R. (1998). *Meanings of Madness.* Belmont: Brooks/Cole Publishing Company.

Cattanach, L., & Tebes, J. K. (1991). The nature of elder impairment and its impact on family caregivers' health and psychosocial functioning. *The Gerontologist, 31,* 246-255.

Cavaliere, F. (1995, July). Society appears more open to gay parenting. *APA Monitor,* p. 51.

Cavanaugh, J. C. (1997). *Adult development and aging* (3rd ed.). Pacific Grove, CA: Brooks/Cole.

Center for Substance Abuse Prevention; Substance Abuse and Mental Health Services Administration. (1995, Spring). *Prevention works!* National Clearinghouse for Alcohol and Drug Information.

Centers for Disease Control. (1997, November 21). Update: Perinatally acquired HIV/AIDS—United States, 1997. *Morbidity & Mortality Weekly Report, 46,* 1086-1093.

Chaikin, A. E., Sigler, E., & Derlega, V. (1974). Non-verbal mediators of teacher expectancy effects. *Journal of Personality and Social Psychology, 30,* 144-149.

Chamberlain, D. (1994a). Intelligence before birth: Ethical implications for birth professionals. Manuscript submitted for publication.

Chamberlain, D. (1994b). *Observations of behavior before birth: Current findings.* Manuscript submitted for publication.

Chamberlain, P., & Patterson, G. R. (1985). Aggressive behavior in middle childhood. In D. Shaffer, A. A. Ehrhardt, & L. L. Greenhill (Eds.), *The clinical guide to child psychiatry.* New York: Free Press.

Chambliss, L. (1994, Fall). Domestic violence—What is the health care provider's responsibility? *Samaritan Airevac News for Physicians and Managers,* 1-3.

Chan, R. W., Raboy, B., & Patterson, C. J. (1998). Psychosocial adjustment among children conceived via donor insemination by lesbian and heterosexual mothers. *Child Development, 69,* 443-457.

Chapkis, W. (1986). *Beauty secrets: Women and the politics of appearance.* Boston: South End Press.

Chapman, J., Siegel, E., & Cross, A. (1990). Home visitors and child health: Analysis of selected programs. *Pediatrics, 85,* 1059-1068.

Charness, N., & Bosman, E. A. (1992). Human factors in aging. In F. I. M. Craik & T. A. Salthouse (Eds.), *The handbook of aging and cognition.* Hillsdale, NJ: Erlbaum.

Chase, S. N., & Clement, P. W. (1985). Effects of self-reinforcement and stimulants on academic performance in children with attention deficit disorder. *Journal of Clinical Child Psychology, 14,* 323-333.

Chase-Lansdale, P. L. (1981). Maternal employment and quality of infant-mother and infant-father attachment (Doctoral dissertation, University of Michigan). *Dissertation Abstracts International, 42,* 2562B.

Chase-Lansdale, P. L., & Owen, M. (1987). Maternal employment in a family contest: Effects on infant-mother and infant-father attachments. *Child Development, 58,* 1505-1512.

Cherlin, A., & Furstenberg, F. F. (1986). *The new American grandparent.* New York: Basic Books.

Cherry, F., & Deaux, K. (1978). Fear of success versus fear of gender-inappropriate behavior. *Sex Roles, 4,* 97-102.

Chestang, L. (1980). Character development in a hostile environment. In M. Bloom (Ed.), *Life span development.* New York: Macmillan.

Child abuse and neglect clearinghouse—Online publications. (1999, September). Available at: http://www.calib.com/nccanch/pubs/index.htm.

Chilman, C. (1979). *Adolescent sexuality in a changing American society: Social and psychological perspectives.* Washington, DC: Public Health Service, National Institutes of Mental Health.

Cho, S. A., Freeman, E. M., & Patterson, S. L. (1982). Adolescents' experience with death: Practice implications. *Social Casework, 63,* 88–94.

Chu, C. E., Cooke, A., Stephenson. J. B., & Tolmie, P. (1994). Diagnosis in Prader-Willi syndrome. *Archives of Disease in Childhood, 71,* 441–442.

Churchman, C. W. (1978). Foreword. In J. P. Van Gigch. *Applied general systems theory.* New York: Harper & Row.

Cicchetti, D., & Schneider-Rosen, K. (1986). An organizational approach to childhood depression. In M. Rutter, C. Izard, & P. B. Read (Eds.), *Depression in young people: Developmental and clinical perspectives.* New York: Guilford Press.

Cicchetti, D., & Toth, S. L. (1995). A developmental psychopathology perspective on child abuse and neglect. *Journal of the American Academy of Child and Adolescent Psychiatry, 34,* 541–566.

Cicchetti, D., & Wagner, S. (1990). Alternative assessment strategies for the evaluation of infants and toddlers: An organizational perspective. In S. J. Meisels and J. P. Shonkoff (Eds.), *Handbook of early childhood intervention* (pp. 246–277). New York: Cambridge University Press.

Cicirelli, V. G. (1983). Adult children and their elderly parents. In T. Brubaker (Ed.), *Family relationships in later life.* Beverly Hills: Sage.

Cintas, H. (1988). Cross-cultural variation in infant motor development. *Physical & Occupational Therapy in Pediatrics, 8,* 1–20.

Clark, K. B., & Clark M. K. (1939). The development of consciousness of self and emergence of racial identification in Negro preschool children. In R. Wilcox (Ed.), *The psychological consequences of being a black American: A sourcebook of research by black psychologists.* New York: Wiley.

Clarke-Stewart, K. A. (1978). And daddy makes three: The father's impact on mother and young child. *Child Development, 49,* 466–478.

Clarke-Stewart, K. A. (1989). Infant day care: Maligned or malignant? *American Psychologist, 44,* 266–273.

Clarke-Stewart, K. A. (1991). A home is not a school: The effects of environments on development. In M. Lewis & S. Feinman (Eds.), *Social influences and socialization in infancy* (pp. 41–61). New York: Plenum.

Clarke-Stewart, K. A., & Fein, G. G. (1983). Early childhood programs. In P. H. Mussen (Ed.), *Handbook of child psychology* (4th ed., Vol. 2). New York: Wiley.

Clasen, D. R., & Brown, B. B. (1987). Understanding peer pressure in middle school. *Middle School Journal, 19,* 21–23.

Clausen, J. A. (1986). *The life course: A sociological perspective.* Englewood Cliffs: Prentice Hall.

Clausen, J. A. (1991). Adolescent competence and the shaping of the life course. *American Journal of Sociology, 96,* 805–842.

Clausen, J. A. (1993). *American lives: Looking back at the children of the Great Depression.* New York: Free Press.

Clay, R. A. (1996a, December). Older alcoholics isolated, yet in need of treatment. *APA Monitor,* p. 38.

Clay, R. A. (1996b, December). Some elders thrive on working into late life. *APA Monitor,* p. 35.

Clay, R. A. (1996c, December). Retirement can offer new start. *APA Monitor,* pp. 1, 37.

Clay, R. A. (1996d, December). Retiring poses different challenges for women. *APA Monitor,* p. 36.

Clay, R. A. (1997a, April). Helping dying patients let go of life in peace. *APA Monitor,* p. 42.

Clay, R. A. (1997b, December). Are children being over medicated? *APA Monitor,* pp. 1, 27.

Clorfene-Costen, L. (1993, May/June). The environmental link to breast cancer. *Ms.,* pp. 52–56.

Cobb, S. (1976). Social support as a moderator of life stress. *Psychosomatic Medicine, 38,* 300–314.

Coggins, K. (1990). *Alternative pathways to healing: The recovery medicine wheel.* Deerfield Beach, FL: Health Communications.

Cohen, D. (1983). *Piaget: Critique and reassessment.* London: Croom Helm.

Cohen, D. (1988). Social work and psychotropic drug treatments. *Social Services Review, 62*(4), 576–599.

Cohen, G., Yeast, J., & Hu, D. (1994). Epidural analgesia in labor and cesarean delivery for dystocia. *Obstetrical & Gynecological Survey, 49,* 362–369.

Cohen, S. (1982). Arthritis—But what sort? *Geriatrics, 37,* 49–51.

Cohen, S., & Strauss, M. (1979). Concept acquisition in the human infant. *Child Development, 50,* 767–776.

Coleman, J. S. (1980). The peer group. In J. Adelson (Ed.), *Handbook of adolescent psychology.* New York: Wiley.

Coleman, J. S., Campbell, E., Hobson, C., McPartland, J., Mood, A., Weinfield, F., & York, R. (1966). *Equality of educational opportunity.* Washington, DC: U.S. Government Printing Office.

Coles, R. (1986). *The political life of children.* Boston: Little, Brown.

Coll, C., & Meyer, E. (1993). The sociocultural context of infant development. In C. Zeaneh (Ed.), *Handbook of infant mental health* (pp. 56–69). New York: Guilford Press.

Colletti, L. (1979). Relationship between pregnancy and birth complications and the later development of learning disabilities. *Journal of Learning Disabilities, 12,* 659–663.

Collins, A. H., & Pancoast, D. L. (1976). *Natural helping networks.* Washington, DC: National Association of Social Workers.

Comas-Diaz, L., & Greene, B. (1994). *Overview: An ethnocultural mosaic.* In L. Comas-Diaz & B. Greene (Eds.) Women of color: Integrating ethnic and gender identities in psychotherapy. New York: Guilford Press.

Combs, M. L., & Slaby, D. A. (1977). Social skills training with children. In B. B. Lahey & A. E. Kazdin (Eds.), *Advances in clinical child psychology.* New York: Plenum.

Comer, J. (1993). *School power* (rev. ed.). New York: Free Press.

Comer, R. J. (1999). *Abnormal psychology.* (3rd edition). New York: Freeman and Company.

Committee on Economic Development (1987). *Children in need: Investment strategies for the educationally disadvantaged.* Washington, DC: Committee for Economic Development.

Compas, B. F. (1995). Promoting successful coping during adolescence. In W. M. Rutter (Ed.), *Psychological disturbances in young people.* New York: Cambridge University Press.

Condon, W. (1975). Speech makes babies move. In R. Lewin (Ed.), *Child alive!* (pp. 75–85). Garden City, NY: Anchor Books.

Condry, J. C. (1989). *The psychology of television.* Hillsdale, NJ: Erlbaum.

Conger, R., Elder, G., Lorenz, F., Conger, K., Simons, R., Whitbeck, L., Huck, S., & Melby, J. (1990). Linking economic hardship to marital quality and instability. *Journal of Marriage and the Family, 52,* 643–656.

Connell, S. (1987). Homelessness. In *Encyclopedia of social work* (pp. 789–795). Silver Spring, MD: National Association of Social Workers.

Conners, K. (1989). Conners' Teacher Rating Scale—39-item version. (*CTRS-39*). North Tonawanda, NY: Multi-Health Systems.

Consortium for Longitudinal Studies (1983). *As the twig is bent.* Hillsdale, NJ: Erlbaum.

Constable, B. (1983). The individualized educational program: content, process, and the social worker's role. In B. Constable & J. Flynn (Eds.), *School social work: Practice and research perspectives.* Pacific Grove, CA: Brooks/Cole.

Constable, R. (1999). The individualized educational program and the IFSP: Content, process and the social workers' role. In R. Constable, S. McDonald, & J. P. Flynn (Eds.), *School social work: Practice, policy and research perspectives.* Chicago: Lyceum.

Cook, S. W. (1979). Social science and school desegregation: Did we mislead the Supreme Court? *Personality and Social Psychology, 5,* 418–428.

Cooke, T., & Apolloni, T. (1976). Developing positive social-emotional behaviors: A study of training and generalization effects. *Journal of Applied Behavior Analysis, 9,* 65–78.

Cool, L. E. (1987). The effects of social class and ethnicity on the aging process. In P. Silverman (Ed.), *The elderly as modern pioneers* (pp. 211-227). Bloomington: Indiana University Press.

Cooley, C. H. (1922). *Human nature and the social order.* New York: Scribner's.

Cooper, C. R., & Grotevant, H. D. (1989, April). *Individuality and connectedness in the family and adolescents' self and relational competence.* Paper presented at the biennial meeting of the Society for Research in Child Development, Kansas City, MO.

Corah, N., Anthony, E., Painter, P., Stern, J., & Thurston, D. (1965). Effects of perinatal anoxia after seven years. *Psychological Monographs, 79,* 3.

Coren, S., & Searleman, A. (1985). Birth stress and self-reported sleep difficulty. *Sleep, 8,* 222-226.

Costin, L., Bell, C., & Downs, S. (1991). *Child welfare: Policies and practices.* New York: Longman.

Cote, J. E., & Levine, C. (1988). A critical examination of the ego identity status paradigm. *Developmental Review, 8,* 147-184.

Cotterrell, R. (1984). *The sociology of law: An introduction.* London: Butterworths.

Coulton, C. J., Korbin, J. E., Su, M., & Chow, J. (1995). Community level factors and child maltreatment rates. *Child Development, 66,* 1262-1276.

Council on Scientific Affairs. (1991). Hispanic health in the United States. *Journal of the American Medical Association, 265,* 248-252.

Council on Social Work Education. (1990). *Psychopharmacology in social work education.* Alexandria, VA. Authors.

Council on Social Work Education. (1992). Curriculum policy statement for baccalaureate degree programs in social work education. In *Handbook of accreditation standards and procedures.* Alexandria, VA: Author.

Courtney, M. E., & Barth, R. P. (1996). Pathways of older adolescents out of foster care: Implications for independent living services. *Social Work, 41, 1,* 75-83.

Cowen, E. L., Pederson, A., Babigan, H., Izzo, L. D., & Trost, M. A. (1973). Long-term follow-up of early detected vulnerable children. *Journal of Consulting and Clinical Psychology, 41,* 438-446.

Creno, C. (1994, April 19). Bonding before birth: Child's mental health begins at conception, small-but-growing group insists. *The Arizona Republic,* E1.

Crispell, D. (1995). Why working teens get into trouble. *American Demographics, 17,* 19-20.

Crnic, K. (1984). Maternal stress and social support: Effects on the mother-infant relationship from birth to eighteen months. *American Journal of Orthopsychiatry, 54,* 224-235.

Crnic, K., & Greenberg, M. (1990). Minor parenting stresses with young children. *Child Development, 61,* 1628-1637.

Crnic, K., & Harris, V. (1990). Normal development in infancy and early childhood. In J. Johnson & J. Goldman (Eds.), *Developmental assessment in clinical child psychology* (pp. 15-33). New York: Pergamon Press.

Crockenberg, S. (1981). Infant irritability, mother responsiveness, and social influences on the security of infant-mother attachment. *Child Development, 52,* 857-865.

Crockenberg, S., Lyons-Ruth, K., & Dickstein, S. (1993). The family contest of infant mental health: II. Infant development in multiple family relationships. In C. Zeanah (Ed.), *Handbook of infant mental health* (pp. 38-55). New York: Guilford Press.

Crohan, S. E., & Antonucci, T. C. (1989). Friends as a source of social support in old age. In R. G. Adams & R. Blieszner (Eds.), *Older adult friendships.* Newbury Park, CA: Sage.

Cronin, M., & Gorman, C. (1991, May 13). Should we take away their kids? *Time,* pp. 62-63.

Cronin, M., Ludtke, M., & Willwerth, J. (1991, May 13). Innocent victims. *Time,* pp. 56-60.

Csikszentmihalyi, M., & Larson, R. (1984). *Being adolescent.* New York: Basic Books.

Cuellar, J. (1980). *Minority elderly Americans: A prototype for area agencies on aging.* San Diego, CA: Allied Home Health Association.

Culbertson, J., & Gyurke, J. (1990). Assessment of cognitive and motor development in infancy and childhood. In J. Johnson & J. Goldman (Eds.), *Developmental assessment in clinical child psychology* (pp. 100; 131). New York: Pergamon Press.

Cumming, E., & Henry, W. E. (1961). *Growing old: The process of disengagement.* New York: Basic Books.

Cummings, E. M. (1987). Coping with background anger in early childhood. *Child Development, 58,* 976-984.

Cummins, J., & Swain, M. (1986). *Bilingualism in education: Aspects of theory, research and practice.* London: Taylor & Fry.

Cunningham, A. J., Edmonds, C. V. I., Jenkins, G. P., Pollack, H., Lockwood, G. A., Warr, D. (1998). A randomized controlled trial of the effects of group psychological therapy on survival in women with metastatic breast cancer. *Psycho-Oncology, 7,* 508-517.

Curran, D. D. (1985). *Stress and the healthy family.* Minneapolis: Winston Press.

Damon, W. (1995, May). Is self-esteem really all that important? *APA Monitor.*

Dan A., & Bernhard, L. (1989). Menopause and other health issues for midlife. In S. Hunter & M. Sundel (Eds.), *Midlife myths: Issues, findings and practice implications* (pp. 201-217). Newbury Park, CA: Sage.

Dangel, R. F., & Polster, R. A. (1988). *Teaching child management skills.* Elmsford, NY: Pergamon Press.

Daniel, W. A. (1983). Pubertal changes in adolescence. In J. Brooks-Gunn & A. C. Petersen (Eds.), *Girls at puberty.* New York: Plenum.

Daniels, K. (1993). Infertility counselling: The need for a psychosocial perspective. *British Journal of Social Work, 23,* 501-512.

Dannefer, D. (1984). Adult development and social theory: A paradigmatic reappraisal. *American Sociological Review, 49,* 100-116.

Danziger, S. K., & Radin, N. (1989, April). *Absent does not equal uninvolved: Predictors of fathering in teen mother families.* Paper presented at the biennial meeting of the Society for Research in Child Development, Kansas City, MO.

Daro, D. (1991). Child sexual abuse prevention: Separating fact from fiction. *Child Abuse & Neglect, 15,* 1-4.

Darwin C. (1859/1958). *The origin of species by means of natural selection or the preservation of favored races in the struggle for life.* New York: New American Library (Mentor Books).

Darwin, C. (1872). *The expression of emotions in man and animals.* New York: Philosophical Library.

Das, J. P. (1984). Intelligence and information integration. In J. Kirby (Ed.), *Theory and research in learning disabilities.* New York: Plenum.

Davidson, E. (1992). Racial disparity in infant mortality. *New England Journal of Medicine, 327,* 1022-1023.

Davidson, M., & Jamison, P. W. (1983). The clinical social worker and current psychiatric drugs: Some introductory principles. *Clinical Social Work Journal, 71,* 134-150.

Davidson, N. (1998). Goodbye, Johnny Walker. *The Sun,* July, pp. 18-21.

Davis, I. P., Landsverk, J., Newton, R., & Ganger, W. (1996). Parental visiting and foster care reunification. *Children and Youth Services Review, 18,* 363-382.

Davis, K., Grant, P., & Rowland, D. (1990). Alone and poor: The plight of elderly women. *Generations, 14,* 43-47.

Davis, K. L., Kahn, R. S., Ko, G., & Davidson, M. (1991). Dopamine in schizophrenia: A review and reconceptualization. *American Journal of Psychiatry, 148,* 1474-1486.

Davis, L. (1989). The myths of menopause. In L. Fenson & J. Fenson (Eds.), *Human development 90/91* (pp. 237-241).

De Anda, D. (1984). Bicultural socialization: Factors affecting minority experience. *Social Work, 29,* 172-181.

DeAngelis, T. (1994a, August). Psychological concerns raised by genetic testing. *APA Monitor,* p. 28.

DeAngelis, T. (1994b, October). Kids develop ethnic awareness in stages, *APA Monitor,* p. 35.

DeAngelis, T. (1995a, January). How adoptees fare. *APA Monitor.*

DeAngelis, T. (1995b, October). Improving quality of life for the seriously ill. *APA Monitor,* 19.

DeAngelis, T. (1997a, October). Elderly may be less depressed than the young. *APA Monitor,* p. 25.

DeAngelis, T. (1997b, November). Menopause symptoms vary among ethnic groups. *APA Monitor,* pp. 16-17.

Deaux, K., Dane, F. C., & Wrightsman, L. S. (1993). *Social psychology in the 90s.* Pacific Grove, CA: Brooks/Cole.

DeCasper, A. J., & Fifer, W. P. (1980). Of human bonding: Newborns prefer their mothers' voices. *Science, 208,* 1174-1176.

Delgado, M., & Tennstedt, S. (1997). Puerto Rican sons as primary caregivers of elderly parents. *Social Work, 42,* 125; 134.

Demmo, D. H. (1992). Parent-child relations: Assessing recent changes. *Journal of Marriage and the Family, 54,* 104-117.

Demmo, D. H., & Acock, A. C. (1988). The impact of divorce on children. *Journal of Marriage and the Family, 50,* 619-648.

Dempster, F. N. (1981). Memory span: Sources of individual and developmental differences. *Psychological Bulletin, 89,* 63-100.

Denisoff, R. S., & Wahrman, R. (1979). *An introduction to sociology* (2nd ed.). New York: Macmillan.

Dennis, W. (1960). Causes of retardation among institutional children: Iran. *Journal of Genetic Psychology, 96,* 47-59.

Dennis, W. (1973). *Children of the creche.* East Norwalk, CT: Appleton-Century-Crofts.

Dennis, W., & Dennis, J. (1940). The effect of cradling practices upon the onset of walking in Hopi children. *Journal of Genetic Psychology, 56,* 77-86.

Depner, C. E., & Ingersol-Dayton, B. (1985). Conjugal social support: Patterns in later life. *Journal of Gerontology, 40,* 761-766.

Dettwyler, K. (1989). Styles of infant feeding: Parental/caretaker control of food consumption in young children. *Research Reports, 91,* 696-703.

Devaney, B. L., Ellwood, M. R., & Love, J. M. (1997). Programs that mitigate the effects of poverty on children. *The Future of Children: Children and Poverty, 7,* 88-112.

Devita, V. T., Hellman, S., & Rosenberg, S. A. (1989). *Cancer principles and practice of oncology* (Vol. 1, 3rd ed.). Philadelphia: Lippincott.

DeVito, J. (1970). *The psychology of speech and language: An introduction to psycholinguistics.* New York: Random House.

DeWitt, P. E. (1995, January 16). Food is now dished out in humongous portions that would satisfy Godzilla. *Time,* 58-65.

Diamond, M. (1993). Homosexuality and bisexuality in different populations. *Archives of Sexual Behavior, 22,* 291-310.

Diamond, M., & Karlen, A. (1980). *Sexual decisions.* Boston: Little, Brown.

Dick, J. P. R., Guiloff, R. J., Stewart, A., Blackstock, J., Bielawska, C., Paul, E. A., & Marsden, C. D. (1984). Mini-mental status examination in neurological patients. *Journal of Neurology, 47,* 496-499.

Diener, C. I., & Dweck, C. S. (1980). An analysis of learned helplessness: II. The processing of success. *Journal of Personality and Social Psychology, 39,* 940-952.

DiMatteo, M. R., (1991). *The psychology of health, illness, and medical care: An individual perspective.* Pacific Grove, CA: Brooks/Cole.

Dinkmeyer, D. (1991). *The parent handbook: Systematic training for effective parenting.* New York: Random House.

Dinkmeyer, D., & McKay, G. D. (1983). *Systematic training for effective parenting: The parent's guide.* St. Paul, MN: American Guidance Service.

Dinkmeyer, D., Sr., McKay, G. D., Dinkmeyer, D.,. Jr., & Dinkmeyer, D. (1997). *The parent's Handbook: Systematic training for effective parenting.* St. Paul, MN: American Guidance Service.

Dion, K., Miller, N., & Magnan, M. (1970). Cohesiveness and social responsibility as determinants of risk taking. *Proceedings of the American Psychological Association, 5,* 335-336.

Dlugokinski, E., & Firestone, I. J. (1974). Other centeredness and susceptibility to charitable appeals: Effects of perceived discipline. *Developmental Psychology, 10,* 21-28.

Dodge, K. A., Pettit, G. S., Murphy, R. R., & Buchsbaum, K. (1984). The assessment of intention-cue detection skills in children: Implications for developmental psycho-pathology. *Child Development, 55,* 163-173.

Dodson, J. (1988). *Conceptualizations* of black families. In H. P. McAdoo (Ed.), *Black families* (pp. 77-90). Beverly Hills, CA: Sage.

Dohrenwend, B. P. (1978). Social stress and community psychology. *American Journal of Community Psychology, 6,* 1-14.

Dohrenwend, B. P. (1998). *Adversity, stress, and psychopathology.* New York: Oxford University Press.

Dolgin, K. G., & Behrend, D. A. (1984). Children's knowledge about animates and inanimates. *Child Development, 55,* 1646-1650.

Dollinger, S. J., & Gasser, M. (1981). Imitation as social influence. *Journal of Genetic Psychology, 138,* 149-150.

Dornbusch, S. M., Carlsmith, J. M., Bushwall, S. J., Ritter, P. L., Leiderman, H., Hastorf, A. H., & Gross, R. T. (1985). Single parents, extended households, and the control of adolescents. *Child Development, 56,* 326-341.

Dougherty, T. M., & Haith, M. M. (1997). Infant expectations and reaction time as predictors of childhood speed of processing and IQ. *Developmental Psychology, 33,* 146-155.

Dowdy, Z. (1998, July 5). Racial bias in coverage by media of kids who kill. *Sacramento Bee,* Metro Final, p. F1.

Doyle, P. (1995, August 7). Custody fights in adoptions test Indian tribes' power. *Arizona Daily Star,* pp. 1, 8.

Dregni, M. (1989, September/October). Coming out in the age of AIDS. *Utne Reader,* pp. 19-20.

Drews, C. D., Murphy, C. C., Yeargin-Allsopp, M., & Decofle, P. (1996). The relationship between idiopathic mental retardation and maternal smoking during pregnancy. *Pediatrics, 97,* 547-553.

Dreykurs, R. (1964). *Children the challenge.* New York: Hawthorne Books.

Drucker, P. F. (1954). *The practice of management.* New York: Harper & Row.

Dryfoos, J. G. (1990). *Adolescents at risk: Prevalence and prevention.* New York: Oxford University Press.

Dryfoos, J. G. (1994). *Full-service schools.* San Francisco: Jossey-Bass.

Dubin, M. (1994). Aggravating adolescent years often will hit parents hard. *Arizona Daily Star,* p. 1D.

Dubin, S. (1972). Obsolescence or lifelong education: A choice for the professional. *American Psychologist, 17,* 486-498.

Dubos, R. (1978). Health and creative adaptation. *Human Nature, 1,* 74-82.

Dudley, J., & Helfgott, C. (1990). Exploring a place for spirituality in the social work curriculum. *Journal of Social Work Education, 26,* 287-294.

Duffy, J. A. (1998, September 29). Older adults enjoy sex, too, poll says. *The Arizona Republic,* p. A6.

Duffy, K. G., & Wong, F. Y. (1996). *Community psychology.* Boston: Allyn and Bacon.

Dulcan, M. K. (1986). Comprehensive treatment of children and adolescents with attention deficit disorders: The state of the art. *Clinical Psychology Review, 6,* 539-569.

Dumaret, A. C., Duyme, M., & Tomkiewicz, S. (1997). Foster children: Risk factors and development at a preschool age. *Early Child Development and Care, 134,* 23-42.

Dunbar, H. T., Mueller, C. W., Medina, C., & Wolf, T. (1998). Psychological and spiritual growth in women living with HIV. *Social Work, 43, 2,* 144-154.

Dunker, K. (1945). On problem solving. *Psychological Monographs, 58*(5, Whole No. 270).

Dunn, J. (1991). Sibling influences. In M. Lewis & S. Feinman (Eds.), *Social influences and socialization in infancy* (pp. 97-109). New York: Plenum.

Dunn, J., & Kendrick, C. (1982). *Siblings.* Cambridge, MA: Harvard University Press.

Dunn, J., & Munn, P. (1986). Sibling quarrels and maternal intervention: Individual differences in understanding and aggression. *Journal of Child Psychology and Psychiatry, 27,* 583-597.

Dunst, C., Trivette, C., & Cross, A. (1986). Mediating influences of social support: Personal, family, and child outcomes. *American Journal of Mental Deficiency, 90,* 403-417.

Dura, J. R., Haywood-Niler, E., & Kiecolt-Glaser, J. K. (1990). Spousal caregivers of persons with Alzheimer's and Parkinson's disease dementia: A preliminary comparison. *The Gerontologist, 30,* 332-336.

Durham, W. H. (1991). *Coevolution: Genes, culture, and human diversity.* Stanford, CA: Stanford University Press.

Dusek, J., & Flaherty, J. (1981). The development of the self-concept during the adolescent years. *Monographs of the Society for Research in Child Development, 46* (Serial No. 191).

Dutton, D. B., & Levine, S. (1989). Overview, methodological critique, and reformulation. In J. P. Bunker, D. S. Gomby, & B. H. Kehrer (Eds.), *Pathways to health* (pp. 29-69). Menlo Park, CA: Henry J. Kaiser Family Foundation.

Duvall, E. M. (1971). *Family development* (4th ed.). Philadelphia: Lippincott.

Duvall, E. M., & Miller, B. C. (1985). *Marriage and family development* (6th ed.). New York: Harper & Row.

Dweck, C. S. (1986). Motivational processes affecting learning. *American Psychologist, 41,* 1040-1048.

Dweck, C. S., Davidson, W., Nelson, S., & Enna, B. (1978). Sex differences in learned helplessness: II. The contingencies of evaluative feedback in the classroom, and III. An experimental analysis. *Developmental Psychology, 14,* 268-276.

Dweck, C. S., & Reppucci, N. D. (1973). Learned helplessness and reinforcement responsibility in children. *Journal of Personality and Social Psychology, 31,* 674-685.

Dwyer, K. P. (1995, May). Is self-esteem really all that important? *APA Monitor.*

Dziech, B. W., & Weiner, L. (1991). *The lecherous professor: Sexual harassment on campus.* Urbana: University of Illinois Press.

Eagly, A. H., & Wood, W. (1991). Explaining sex differences in social behavior: A meta-analytic perspective. *Journal of Sex Research, 36,* 424-435.

Easterbrooks, M. A., & Goldberg, W. A. (1985). Effects of early maternal employment on toddlers, mothers, and fathers. *Developmental Psychology, 21,* 774-783.

Eberstadt, N. (1991). America's infant mortality puzzle. *The Public Interest, 105,* 30-47.

Eccles, J. S. (1987). Gender roles and achievement patterns: An expectancy value perspective. In J. M. Reinisch, L. A. Roseblum, & S. A. Sanders (Eds.), *Masculinity/femininity.* New York: Oxford University Press.

Eccles, J. S., & Midgley, C. (1989). Stage/environment fit: Developmentally appropriate classrooms for early adolescents. In R. E. Ames & C. Ames (Eds.), *Research on motivation in education* (Vol. 3). New York: Academic Press.

Eckert, P. (1990). Cooperative competition in adolescent "girl talk." *Discourse Processes, 13,* 91-122.

Edelman, M. W. (1987). *Families in peril: An agenda for social change.* New York: Alan Guttmacher Institute.

Edmonds, M. (1990). The health of the Black aged female. In Z. Harel, E. A. McKinney, & M. Williams (Eds.), *Black aged.* Newbury Park, CA: Sage.

Edwards, C. (1984). The age group labels and categories of preschool children. *Child Development, 55,* 440-452.

Edwards, C., Johnson, A., Knight, E., Oyemade, U., Cole, O., Westney, O., Jones, S., Laryea, H., & Westney, L. (1994a). Maternal stress and pregnancy outcomes in a prenatal clinic population. *Journal of Nutrition, 124,* 1006-1022.

Edwards, C., Johnson, A., Knight, E., Oyemade, U., Cole, O., Westney, O., Jones, S., Laryca, H., & Westney, L. (1994b). Pica in an urban environment (African-American women and their pregnancies). *Journal of Nutrition, 124,* 9545-9554.

Edwards, D., Porter, S., & Stein, G. (1993). A pilot study of postnatal depression following caesarean section using two retrospective self-rating instruments. *Journal of Psychosomatic Research, 38,* 111-117.

Edwards, R. (December, 1995). The search for a proper punishment. *APA Monitor,* p. 30.

Eells, T. D. (1997). Psychotherapy case formulation: History and current status. In T. D. Eells (Ed.), *Handbook of psychotherapy: Case formulation* (pp. 1-25). New York: Guilford Press.

Eisenberg, N. (Ed.). (1982). *The development of prosocial behavior.* New York: Wiley.

Eisenberg, N., Wentzel, N., & Harris, J. D. (1998). The role of emotionally and regulation in empathy-related responding. *School Psychology Review, 27,* 506-522.

Eisendrath, S. J. (1988). The mind and somatic illness: psychological factors affecting physical illness. In H. H. Goldman (Ed.), *Review of general psychiatry.* East Norwalk, CT: Appleton & Lang.

Ekerdt, D. J., Bossé, R., & Levkoff, S. (1985). Empirical test for phases of retirement: Findings from the Normative Aging Study. *Journal of Gerontology, 40,* 368-374.

Elias, M. (1991). A multilevel action research perspective on stress-related interventions. In M. E. Colten & S. Gore (Eds.), *Adolescent stress.* New York: Aldine de Gruyter.

Elder, G. H., Jr. (1974). *Children of the great depression.* Chicago: University of Chicago Press.

Elder, G. H., Jr. (1985). *Life course dynamics: Trajectories and transitions. 1968-1980.* Ithaca: Cornell University Press.

Elder, G. H., Jr., (1991). Lives and social change. In W. R. Heinz (Ed.), *Theoretical advances in life course research* (pp. 58-86). Weinheim: Deutscher Studien Verlag.

Elder, G. H., Jr. (1996). Human lives in changing societies: Life course and developmental insights. In R. B. Cairns, G. H. Elder, Jr., & E. J. Costello (Eds.), *Developmental science* (pp. 31-62). Cambridge: Cambridge University Press.

Elkind, D. (1976). *Child development and education: A Piagetian perspective.* New York: Oxford University Press.

Elkind, D. (1978). Understanding the young adolescent. *Adolescence, 13,* 127-134.

Elkind, D. (1981). *The hurried child.* Reading, MA: Addison-Wesley.

Elkind, D. (1987). *Miseducation: Preschoolers at risk.* New York: Knopf.

Elliot, D. S. (1993). Promoting the health of adolescents: New directions for the twenty-first century. In S. Millstein, A. C. Petersen, & E. O. Nightingale (Eds.), *Adolescent health promotion.* New York: Oxford University Press.

Ellis, S., Rogoff, B., & Cromer, C. C. (1981). Age segregation in children's social interactions. *Developmental Psychology, 17,* 399-407.

Emde, R. (1987). Infant mental health: Clinical dilemmas, the expansion of meaning, and opportunities. In J. Osofsky (Ed.), *Handbook of infant development* (pp. 1297-1320). New York: Wiley.

Emde, R. N., Plomin, R., Robinson, J., Corley, R., DeFries, J., Fulkner, D. W., Reznick, J. S., Campos, J., Kagan, J., & Zahn-Waxler, C. (1992). Temperament, emotion, and cognition at fourteen months: The MacArthur Longitudinal Twin Study. *Child Development, 63,* 1437-1455.

Emery, R. E., & Laumann-Billings, L. (1998). An overview of the nature, causes, and consequences of abusive relationships: Toward differentiating maltreatment and violence. *American Psychologist, 53,* 121-135.

Emler, N., Renwick, S., & Malone, B. (1983). The relationship between moral reasoning and political orientation. *Journal of Personality and Social Psychology, 45,* 1073-1080.

Emmerich, W. (1959). Parental identification in young children. *Genetic Psychology Monographs, 60,* 257-308.

Emmerich, W. (1966). Continuity and stability in early social development: II. Teacher's ratings. *Child Development, 37,* 17-27.

Enck, R. (1992, July/August). The last few days. *The American Journal of Hospice and Palliative Care,* 11-13.

Englander-Golden, P., Sonleitner, F. J., Whitmore, M. R., & Corbley, G. J. M. (1986). Social and menstrual cycles: Methodological and substantive findings. In V. L. Olesen & N. F. Woods (Eds.), *Culture, society, and menstruation.* Washington, DC: Hemisphere.

Enright, R. D., & Freedman, S. R. (1996). Forgiveness as an intervention tool for incest survivors. *Journal of Consulting and Clinical Psychology, 64(5),* 983-992.

Entwisle, D. R. (1990). Schools and the adolescent. In S. S. Feldman & G. R. Elliot (Eds.), *At the threshold: The developing adolescent* (pp. 197-224). Cambridge, MA: Harvard University Press.

Ephross, J. (1982). A social work perspective on families with infants who fail to thrive. In P. J. Accardo (Ed.), *Failure to thrive in infancy and early childhood* (pp. 331-347). Baltimore: University Park Press.

Erickson, J. (1996, May 6). Obstetric anesthesia safety called remarkable. *The Arizona Daily Star,* 1B, 4B.

Erikson, E. (1959). Identity in the life cycle. [monograph 1]. *Psychological Issues, 1.*

Erikson, E. H. (1963). *Childhood and society* (2nd ed.). New York: Norton.

Erikson, E. H. (1968). *Identity: Youth and crisis.* New York: Norton.

Erikson, E. H. (1974). *Dimensions of a new identity.* New York: Norton.

Erikson, J. M. (1988). *Wisdom and the senses.* New York: W. W. Norton.

Etzioni, A. (1993). *The spirit of community: Rights, responsibilities, and the communitarian agenda.* New York: Crown Publishers.

Evans, C., & Dion, K. (1991). Group cohesion and performance. *Small Group Research, 22,* 175-186.

Ewalt, P. L., & Perkins, L. L. (1979). The real experience of death among adolescents. *Social Casework, 60,* 547-551.

Eyer, D. (1994). Mother-infant bonding: A scientific fiction. *Human Nature, 5,* 69-94.

Eysenck, H. J. (1989, December). Health's character. *Psychology Today,* 28-32, 34-35.

Fagot, B. (1978). The influence of sex of child on parental reactions to toddler children. *Child Development, 49,* 459-465.

Fagot, B. (1989). The young child's gender schema: Environmental input, internal organization. *Child Development, 60,* 663-672.

Fagot, B. (1991). Observations of parent reactions to sex-stereotyped behaviors: Age and sex effects. *Child Development, 62,* 617-628.

Fagot, B. (1992). Gender labeling, gender stereotyping, and parenting behaviors. *Developmental Psychology, 28,* 225-230.

Fahey, M., & Phillips, S. (1981). The self-concept in middle childhood: Some baseline data. *Child Study Journal, 11,* 155.

Fahlberg, V. (1991). *A child's journey through placement.* Indianapolis, IN: Perspectives Press.

Fain, T. C., & Anderson, D. L. (1987). Sexual harassment: Organizational context and diffuse status. *Sex Roles, 17,* 291-311.

Farrington, D. P. (1995). The challenge of teenage antisocial behavior. W. M. Rutter (Ed.), *Psychological disturbances in young people.* New York: Cambridge University Press.

Fay, R. E., Turner, C. F., Klassen, A. D., & Gagnon, J. H. (1989). Prevalence and patterns of same-gender sexual contact among men. *Science, 243,* 338-348.

FBI: Racism cause of most hate crime. (1993, January 5). *Tempe Daily Tribune,* p. A3.

Feinbloom, R. (1993). *Pregnancy, birth and the early months: A complete guide.* Reading, MA: Addison-Wesley.

Feagin, J. R., & Feagin, C. B. (1997). *Social problems: A critical power-conflict perspective.* (4th ed.). Upper Saddle River, NJ: Prentice Hall.

Feindler, E. L., & Guttman, J. (1994). Cognitive-behavioral anger control training. In C. LeCroy (Ed.), *Handbook of child and adolescent treatment manuals.* New York: Lexington Press.

Feingold, B. (1975). *Why your child is hyperactive.* New York: Random House.

Feinman, S. (1991). Bringing babies back into the social world. In M. Lewis & S. Feinman (Eds.), *Social influences and socialization in infancy* (pp. 281-320). New York: Plenum.

Feld, S., & Radin, N. (1982). *Social psychology for social work and the mental health professions.* New York: Columbia University Press.

Feldman, R. A., Caplinger, T. E., & Wodarski, J. S. (1983). *The St. Louis conundrum: The effective treatment of antisocial youth.* Englewood Cliffs, NJ: Prentice Hall.

Fellin, P. (1995). Understanding American communities. In J. Rothman, J. L. Erlich, & J. E. Troman (Eds.), *Strategies of community intervention* (5th ed.) (pp. 114-128). Itasca, NY: F. E. Peacock Publishers, Inc.

Ferketich, S. L., & Mercer, R. T. (1995). Paternal-infant attachment of experienced and inexperienced fathers during infancy. *Nursing Research, 44,* 31-37.

Fernald, A. (1987). Acoustic determinants of infant preference for motherese speech. *Infant Behavior and Development, 10,* 279-293.

Fernald, A. (1991). Prosody and focus in speech to infants and adults. *Developmental Psychology, 27,* 209-221.

Ferrante, J. (1995). *Sociology: A global perspective.* Belmont, CA: Wadsworth.

Feshbach, S. (1956). The catharsis hypothesis and some consequences of interaction with aggressive and neutral play objects. *Journal of Personality, 24,* 449-461.

Festinger, L. (1950). Informal and social communication. *Psychological Review, 57,* 271-282.

Festinger, L. (1957). *A theory of cognitive dissonance.* Stanford, CA: Stanford University Press.

Festinger, T. (1983). *No one ever asked us: A post-script to foster care.* New York: Columbia University Press.

Festinger, T. (1986). *Return to care.* Child Welfare League of America.

Field, T. (1978). Interaction behaviors of primary versus secondary caretaker fathers. *Developmental Psychology, 14,* 183-184.

Field, T. (1981). Early development of the preterm offspring of teenage mothers. In K. Scott, T. Field, & E. Robertson (Eds.), *Teenage parents and their offspring* (pp. 145-175). New York: Grune & Stratton.

Field, T. (1983). High-risk infants "have less fun" during early interactions. *Topics in Childhood Special Education, 3,* 77-87.

Field, T., Schanberg, S., Scafidi, F., Bauer, C., Nitza, V., Garcia, R., Nystrom, J., & Kuhn, C. (1986). Tactile/kinesthetic stimulation effects on preterm neonates. *Pediatrics, 77,* 654-658.

Field, T. M., Woodson, R., Greenberg, R., & Cohen, D. (1982). Discrimination and imitation of facial expression by neonates. *Science, 218,* 179-181.

Figel, H. (1960). Mind-body, not a pseudoproblem. In S. Hook (Ed.), *Dimensions of mind: A symposium.* New York: New York University Press.

Fine, G. A. (1980). The natural history of preadolescent male friendship groups. In H. C. Foot, A. J. Chapman, & J. R. Smith (Eds.), *Friendships and childhood relations.* New York: Wiley.

Fingarette, H. (1988). *Heavy drinking: The myth of alcoholism as a disease.* Berkeley: University of California Press.

Finkelhor, D., Dzuiba-Leatherman, J. (1994). Victimization of children. *American Psychologist, 49,* 173-183.

Finn, J. (1995). Computer-based self-help groups: A new resource to supplement support groups. *Social Work with Groups, 18,* 109-117.

Finn, J. (1996). Computer-based self-help groups: On-line recovery for addictions. *Computers in Human Services, 12.*

Fischer, J. L., Spann, L., & Crawford, D. W. (1991). Measuring codependency. *Alcoholism Treatment Quarterly, 8*, 87-100.

Fishbein, M., & Ajzen, I. (1975). *Belief, attitude, intention and behavior.* Reading, MA: Addison-Wesley.

Fivush, R. (1995). New cognitive research making waves. *APA Monitor.*

Fixsen, D. L., Phillips, E. L., Phillips, E. A., & Wolf, M. M. (1976). The teaching family model group home treatment. In W. E. Craighead, A. E. Kazdin, & M. J. Mahoney (Eds.), *Behavior modification.* Boston: Houghton Mifflin.

Flanigan, B. (1992). *Forgiving the unforgivable.* New York: Macmillan.

Flavell, J. H. (1979). Metacognition and cognitive monitoring: A new area of psychological inquiry. *American Psychologist, 34*, 906-911.

Flavell, J. H. (1981). Monitoring social cognitive enterprises: Something else that may develop in the area of social cognition. In J. H. Flavell & L. Ross (Eds.), *Social cognitive development: Frontiers and possible futures.* New York: Cambridge University Press.

Flavell, J. H. (1985). *Cognitive development* (2nd ed.). Englewood Cliffs, NJ: Prentice Hall.

Fong-ruey, L., & Brooks-Gunn, J. (1994). Cumulative familial risks and low-birthweight children's cognitive and behavioral development. *Journal of Clinical Child Psychology, 23*, 360-372.

Fontaine, P., & Toffler, W. (1991). Dorsal penile nerve block for newborn circumcision. *American Family Physician, 43*, 1327-1333.

Ford, M. E. (1986). A living systems conceptualization of social intelligence: Outcomes, processes, and developmental change. In R. J. Sternberg (Ed.), *Advances in the psychology of human intelligence* (Vol. 3). Hillsdale, NJ: Erlbaum.

Forehand, R. L., & Long, N. (1996). *Parenting the strong-willed child: The clinically proven five-week program for parents of two- to-six-year olds.*

Forsyth, D. R. (1999). *Group dynamics* (3rd ed.). Belmont: Wadsworth Publishing Company.

Foster, R., Hunsberger, M., & Anderson, J. (1989a). *Family-centered nursing care of children.* Philadelphia: Harcourt Brace Jovanovich.

Foster, R. L., Hunsberger, M. M. & Anderson, J. T. (1989b). *Family-centered nursing care of children.* Philadelphia: Saunders.

Foucault, M. (1980). *Power/knowledge: Selected interviews and other writings.* New York: Pantheon Books.

Fowers, B. J., & Olson, D. H. (1989). ENRICH Marital Inventory: A discriminant validity and cross-validation assessment. *Journal of Marital and Family Therapy, 15*, 65-79.

Fowler, J. W. (1981). *Stages of faith: The psychology of human development and the quest for meaning.* San Francisco: Harper and Row.

Fraiberg, S. H. (1968). *The magic years: Understanding and handling the problems of early childhood.* London: Methuen.

Fraiberg, S. H. (1980). *Clinical studies in infant mental health.* New York: Basic Books.

Francis, S. (1993). Rape and sexual assault. In B. S. Johnson, *Adaptation and growth: Psychiatric nursing.* Philadelphia: Lippincott.

Frank, A. (1952). *The diary of a young girl.* Garden City, NY: Doubleday.

Frank, D., Silva, M., & Needlman, R. (1993, February). Failure to thrive: Mystery, myth, and method. *Contemporary Pediatrics*, 114-133.

Frankel, M. (1983). Does mother know best? Mothers and fathers interacting with preschool sons and daughters. *Developmental Psychology, 19*, 694-702.

Frankenberg, W., & Dodds, J. (1967). Denver Development Screening Test. *Journal of Pediatrics, 71*, 181-191.

Frauenhofer, D., Scott, L., Doress, P. B., & Rosenthal-Keese, K. (1987). Relationships in middle and later life. In P. B. Doress, D. L. Siegel, & The Midlife and Older Women Book Project (Eds.), *Ourselves, growing older: Women aging with knowledge and power* (pp. 79-98). New York: Simon & Schuster.

Fredrickson, B. L., & Carstensen, L. L. (1990). Choosing social partners: How old age and anticipated endings make people more selective. *Psychology and Aging, 5*, 335-347.

Freedman, D. G., & DeBoer, M. M. (1979). Biological and cultural differences in early child development. *Annual Review of Anthropology, 8*, 579-600.

Freeman, B. J. (1993). The syndrome of autism: Update and guidelines for diagnosis. *Young Children, 6*, 1-11.

Freiberg, P. (1990, November). Outreach helps women at risk for AIDS. *APA Monitor,* pp. 28-29.

Freiberg, P. (1996, May). Study sparks war on emotional poverty. *APA Monitor,* p. 35.

Freiberg, P. (1998a, February). Prevention studies take a variety of tacks. *APA Monitor,* p. 33.

Freiberg, P. (1998b, February). We know how to stop the spread of AIDS: So why don't we? *APA Monitor,* p. 32.

Freidman, H. S., Tucker, J. S., Tomlinson-Keasey, C., Martin L. R., Wingard, D. L., & Criqui, M. H. (1995). Psychosocial and behavioral predictors of longevity. *American Psychologist*, 69-78.

French, J., & Raven, B. (1959). The bases of social power. In D. Cartwright (Ed.), *Studies in social power.* Ann Arbor: Institute for Research, University of Michigan.

Freud, A., & Dann, S. (1951). An experiment in group upbringing. *Psychoanalytic Study of the Child, 6*, 127-168.

Freud, S. (1953). *The future of an illusion.* New York: Liveright.

Friedenreich, C. (1995). A review of physical activity and breast cancer. *Epidemiology, 6*, 311-317.

Friedman, S. L., & Wach, T. D. (Eds.). (1999). *Measuring environment across the life span: Emerging methods and concepts.* Washington, DC: American Psychological Association.

Friendander, M. L. (1999). Ethnic identity development of internationally adopted children and adolescents: Implications for family therapists. *Journal of Marital and Family Therapy, 25*, 43-60.

Friedman, M., & Rosenman, R. F. (1974). *Type A behavior and your heart.* New York: Knopf.

Friedman, R. C., & Downey, J. I. (1994). Homosexuality. *The New England Journal of Medicine, 331*, 923-930.

Friedrich, L. K., & Stein, A. H. (1973). Aggressive and pro-social television programs and the natural behavior of preschool children. *Monographs of the Society for Research in Child Development, 38.*

Frosh, S. (1987). *The politics of psychoanalysis: An introduction to Freudian and post-Freudian theory.* New Haven, CT: Yale University Press.

Furino, A., & Munoz, E. (1991). Hispanic health: Time for data, time for action [Editorial]. *Journal of the American Medical Association, 265*, 253-257.

Furman, W., & Buhrmester, D. (1985a). Children's perceptions of their personal relationships in their social networks. *Developmental Psychology, 21*, 1016-1024.

Furman, W., & Buhrmester, D. (1985b). Children's perceptions of the qualities of sibling relationships. *Child Development, 56*, 448-461.

Galambos, N. L., & Almeida, D. M. (1992). Does parent-adolescent conflict increase in early adolescence? *Journal of Marriage and the Family, 54*, 737-747.

Galinsky, M., & Schopler, J. (1977). Warning: Groups may be dangerous. *Social Work, 22*, 89-94.

Gallagher, W. (1993). *The power of place: How our surrounding shape out thoughts, emotions, and actions.* New York: Poseidon Press.

Gallup, G., Jr. (1990). *Religion in America: 1990.* Princeton, NJ: Princeton Religious Research Center.

Gallup, G., & Castelli, J. (1989). *The people's religion.* New York: MacMilian Publishing Co.

Garbarino, J. (1976). A preliminary study of some ecological correlates of child abuse. *Child Development, 47*, 178-185.

Garbarino, J. (1995). *Raising children in a society toxic environment.* San Francisco: Jossey-Bass Publishers.

Garbarino, J. (1999). *Lost boys: Why our sons turn violent and how we can save them.* New York: Freepress.

Garbarino, J., & Abramowitz, R. H. (1992a). Sociocultural risk and opportunity. In J. Garbarino, *Children and families in the social environment* (2nd ed.). New York: Aldine de Gruyter.

Garbarino, J., & Abramowitz, R. H. (1992b). The family as a social system. In J. Garbarino, *Children and families in the social environment* (2nd ed.). New York: Walter de Gruyter.

Garbarino, J., Burston, N., Raber, S., Russel, R., & Crouter, A. (1978). The social maps of children approaching adolescence: Studying the ecology of youth development. *Journal of Youth and Adolescence, 7,* 417–428.

Garbarino, J., Galambos, N. L., Plantz, M. C., & Kostelny, K. (1992). The territory of childhood. In J. Garbarino (Ed.), *Children and families in the social environment* (2nd ed.). New York: Aldine de Gruyter.

Garbarino, J., & Kosteiny, K. (1992). Child maltreatment as a community problem. *Child Abuse and Neglect, 16,* 455–467.

Garbarino, J., & Sherman, D. (1980). High-risk neighborhoods and high-risk families: The human ecology of child maltreatment. *Child Development, 51,* 188–198.

Garcia-Preto, N. (1994, July/August). On the bridge. *Family Therapy Networker,* 35–37.

Gardner, H. (1980). *Artful scribbles: The significance of children's drawings.* New York: Basic Books.

Garmezy, N., & Rutter, M. (Eds.). (1983). *Stress, coping, and development in children.* New York: McGraw-Hill.

Garrison, W. T., & McQuiston, S. (1989). *Chronic illness during childhood and adolescence.* Newbury Park, CA: Sage.

Gartner, A., & Riessman, F. (1977). *Self-help in the human services.* San Francisco: Jossey-Bass.

Garvin, C. D., & Seabury, B. A. (1984). *Interpersonal practice in social work.* Englewood Cliffs, NJ: Prentice Hall.

Gaylin, W. (1986). *Rediscovering love.* New York: Viking Penguin.

Gelfand, D. E., & Barresi, C. M. (Eds.). (1987). *Ethnic dimensions of aging.* New York: Springer.

Gelles, R. J. (1987). *Family violence.* Newbury Park, CA: Sage.

Gelles, R. J. (1992). Poverty and violence toward children. *American Behavioral Scientist, 35,* 258–274.

Gentry, M., Rosenman, L., & Shulman, A. D. (1987). Comparison of the needs and support systems of remarried and nonremarried widows. In H. Lopata (Ed.), *Widows: Vol. II. North America* (pp. 158–170). Durham, NC: Duke University Press.

Gerard, M., & Dukette, R. (1954). Techniques for preventing separation trauma in child placement. *The American Journal of Orthopsychiatry, 24,* 111–127.

Gergen, K. J. (1991, September/October). The saturated family. *Family Therapy Networker,* 27–35.

Gerhart, U., & Brooks, A. (1993). The social work practitioner and antipsychotic drugs. *Social Work, 28,* 454–460.

Germain, C. B. (1991). *Human behavior in the social environment: An ecological view.* New York: Columbia University Press.

Geronimus, A. (1991). Teenage childbearing and social and reproductive disadvantage: The evolution of complex questions and the demise of simple answers. *Family Relations, 40,* 463–471.

Geronimus, A. (1992). Teenage childbearing and social disadvantage: Unprotected discourse. *Family Relations, 41,* 244–248.

Geroski, A. M., & Rodgers, L. A. (1998). Collaborative assessment and treatment of children with enuresis and encopresis. *Professional School Counseling, 2,* 128–135.

Gerson, M. J. (1997, April 28). Do do-gooders do much good? *Time,* pp. 26–37.

Gerstel, N., Reissman, C. K., & Rosenfield, S. (1985). Explaining the symptomatology of separated and divorced women and men: The role of marital conditions and social network. *Social Forces, 64,* 84–101.

Gesser, G., Wong, P. T. P., & Reker, G. T. (1987-88). Death attitudes across the life-span: The development and validation of the death attitude profile (DAP). *Omega, 18,* 113–128.

Giannakoulopoulos, X., Sepulveda, W., Kourtis, P., Glover, V., & Fisk, N. (1994). Fetal plasma cortisol and B-endorphin response to intrauterine needling. *Lancet, 344,* 77–81.

Gibbs, J. T. (1985). City girls: Psychosocial adjustment of urban black adolescent females. *SAGE: A Scholarly Journal of Black Women, 2,* 28–36.

Gibbs, J. T. (1990). Mental health issues of black adolescents: Implications for policy and practice. In A. R. Stiffman & L. E. Davis (Eds.), *Ethnic issues in adolescent mental health.* Newbury Park: Sage.

Gibbs, J. T., & Huang, L. N. (1989). A conceptual framework for assessing and treating minority youth. In J. T. Gibbs & L. N. Huang (Eds.), *Children of color.* San Francisco: Jossey-Bass.

Gibbs, N. (1995a, July 3). Getting nowhere. *Time,* pp. 17–20.

Gibbs, N. (1995b, October 2). The EQ factor. *Time,* pp. 60–68.

Gibson, E. (1984). Development of knowledge of visual-tactual affordances of substance. *Child Development, 55,* 453–460.

Giddens, A. (1989). *Sociology.* Cambridge, MA: Polity Press in association with Basil Blackwell.

Giel, R. (1998). Natural and human-made disasters. In B. P. Dohrenwend (Ed.), *Adversity, stress and psychopathology* (pp. 66–76). New York: Oxford University Press.

Gilbert, K. (1989). Interactive grief and coping in the marital dyad. *Death Studies, 13,* 605–626.

Gilchrist, L. E., Schinke, S. P., & Blythe, B. J. (1985). Preventing unwanted adolescent pregnancy. In L. D. Gilchrist, L. E., & S. P. Schinke (Eds.), *Preventing social and health problems through life skills training.* Seattle, WA: Center for Social Welfare.

Gilgun, J. F. (1995). We shared something special: The moral discourse of incest perpetrators. *Journal of Marriage and the Family, 57,* 265–281.

Gilligan, C. (1977). In a different voice: Women's conceptions of self and morality. *Harvard Educational Review, 47,* 481–517.

Gilligan, C. (1982). *In a different voice: Psychological theory and women's development.* Cambridge, MA: Harvard University Press.

Gilligan, C. (1985). *Response to critics.* Paper presented at the biennial meeting of the Society for Research in Child Development, Toronto.

Ginsburg, H. P. (1985). Jean Piaget. In H. I. Kaplan & B. J. Sadock (Eds.), *Comprehensive textbook of psychiatry.* (Vol. 4, pp. 178–183). Baltimore: Williams & Wilkins.

Girgus, J. (1989, October). Body image in girls pushes rate of depression up. *APA Monitor,* p. 33.

Gleick, E. (1995, February 27). Should this marriage be saved? *Time,* pp. 48–56.

Glenn, N. D., & Weaver, C. N. (1988). The changing relationship of marital status to reported happiness. *Journal of Marriage and the Family, 44,* 317–324.

Glick, P. C. (1984a). American household structure in transition. *Family Planning Perspectives, 16,* 205–211.

Glick, P. C. (1984b). Marriage, divorce, and living arrangements: Prospective changes. *Journal of Family Issues, 5,* 7–26.

Golan, N. (1986). *The perilous bridge.* New York: Free Press.

Gold, M., & Petronio, R. J. (1980). Delinquent behavior in adolescence. In J. Adelson (Ed.), *Handbook of adolescent psychology.* New York: Wiley.

Goldberg, S. (1983). Parent-infant bonding: Another look. *Child Development, 54,* 1355–1382.

Goldenberg, R. (1991). Maternal psychological characteristics and IUGR. *Pre and Perinatal Psychology Journal, 6,* 129–134.

Goldman, R. (1968). *Religious thinking from childhood to adolescence.* New York: Seabury.

Goldson, E. (1991). The affective and cognitive sequelae of child maltreatment. *Pediatric Clinics of North America, 38,* 1481–1496.

Goldstein, E. G. (1984). *Ego psychology and social work practice.* New York: Free Press.

Goldstein, R., & Landau, D. (1990). *Fortysomething.* Los Angeles: Tarcher.

Goleman, D. (1995). *Emotional intelligence.* New York: Bantam Books.

Gondolf (1989). *Men who batter: How they stop their abuse.* Paper presented at the second National Conference for Family Violence Researchers, Durham, NH.

Gonsiorek, J. C. (1991). The empirical basis for the demise of the illness model of homosexuality. In J. C. Gonsiorek & J. D. Weinrich (Eds.), *Homosexuality: Research implications for public policy* (pp. 115-137). Newbury Park, CA: Sage.

Goodchilds, J. D., & Zellman, G. L. (1984). Sexual signalling and sexual aggression in adolescent relationships. In N. M. Malamuth & E. D. Donnerstein (Eds.), *Pornography and sexual aggression.* New York: Academic Press.

Goode, E. (1993). Drug abuse. *Grolier Electronic Encyclopedia.*

Goodenough, F. (1931). *Anger in young children.* Minneapolis: University of Minnesota Press.

Goodings, C. (1987). *Bitter-sweet dreams: Girls' and young women's own stories.* London: Virago Press.

Goodrich, C. (1995, February). Fathering in the night. *The Sun,* pp. 12-14.

Goodwin, A. J., & Scott, L. (1987). Sexuality in the second half of life. In P. B. Doress, D. L. Siegel, & The Midlife and Older Women Book Project (Eds.), *Ourselves, growing older: Women aging with knowledge and power* (pp. 79-98). New York: Simon & Schuster.

Goodyear, I. M. (1990). *Life experiences, development, and childhood psychopathology.* New York: Wiley.

Gordon, M. R. (1994, November 6). In poignant public letter, Reagan reveals that he has Alzheimer's. *New York Times,* pp. 1, 47.

Gordon, S., & Gilgun, J. F. (1987). Adolescent sexuality. In V. B. Van Hasselt & M. Hersen (Eds.), *Handbook of adolescent psychology.* New York: Pergamon Press.

Gordon, S., & Snyder, C. W. (1989). *Personal issues in human sexuality: A guidebook for better sexual health.* Boston: Allyn & Bacon.

Gordon, T. (1970). *Parent effectiveness training.* New York: Wyden.

Gorman, C. (1994, November 21). An eye on Alzheimer's. *Time,* p. 89.

Gorman, C. (1995, April 17). Memory on trial. *Time,* pp. 54-55.

Gotlib, I. H., & McCabe, S. B. (1990). Marriage and psychopathology. In F. D. Fincham & T. N. Bradbury (Eds.), *The psychology of marriage: Basic issues and applications.* New York: Guilford Press.

Gotlib, I. H., & Wheaton, B. (1997). *Stress and adversity over the life course: Trajectories and turning points.* New York: Cambridge University Press.

Gottlieb, S., & Barrett, D. (1986). Effects of unanticipated cesarean section on mothers, infants, and their interaction in the first month of life. *Developmental and Behavioral Pediatrics, 7,* 180-185.

Gottman, J. M. (1994, May/June). Why marriages fail. *Family Therapy Networker,* pp. 41-48.

Gottman, J. M. (1997). *The heart of parenting: Raising an emotionally intelligent child.* New York: Simon & Schuster.

Graham, B. (1998, June 4-10). Age of AIDS. *New Times,* p. 4.

Graham, S. R. (1992). What does a man want? *American Psychologist, 47,* 837-841.

Granvold, D. K. (1995). Cognitive treatment. *The Encyclopedia of Social Work, 1,* 525-538.

Grebb, J. A., Reus, V. I., & Freimer, N. B. (1988). Neurobehavioral chemistry & physiology. In H. H. Goldman (Ed.), *Review of General Psychiatry.* East Norwalk, CT: Appleton & Lang.

Green, J. W. (1995). *Cultural awareness in the human services: A multi-ethnic approach.* Boston: Allyn & Bacon.

Green, R. G., Beatty, W. W., & Arkin, R. M. (1984). *Human motivation.* Boston: Allyn & Bacon.

Greene, R. R. (1994). *Human behavior theory: A diversity framework.* New York: Aldine de Gruyter.

Greenspan, S., & Greenspan, N. (1985). *First feelings: Milestones in the emotional development of your baby and child.* New York: Viking Press.

Grief, G., & Porembski, E. (1988). AIDS and significant others: Findings from a preliminary exploration of needs. *Health and Social Work,* 259-265.

Griffith, D. (1988). The effect of prenatal exposure to cocaine on the infant and on early maternal-infant interactions. In I. J. Chasnoff (Ed.), *Drugs, alcohol, pregnancy, and parenting.* Lancaster, U.K.: Kluwer.

Griffith, D. (1992, September). Prenatal exposure to cocaine and other drugs: Developmental and educational prognoses. *Phi Delta Kappan,* pp. 30-34.

Grinnell, R. M., Jr., Kyte, N. S., Bostwick G. J., Jr. (1981). Environmental modification. In A. N. Maluccio (Ed.), *Promoting competence in clients: A new/old approach to social work practice.* New York: Free Press.

Gross, M. D., Tofanelli, R. A., Butzirus, S. M., & Snodgrass, E. W. (1987). The effects of diets rich in and free from additives on the behavior of children with hyperkinetic and learning disorders. *Journal of the Academy of Child and Adolescent Psychiatry, 26,* 53-55.

Grossman, D. C., Milligan, C. B., & Deyo, R. A. (1991). Risk factors for suicide attempts among Navajo adolescents. *American Journal of Public Health, 81,* 870-874.

Groth, A. N., & Birnbaum, H. J. (1978). Adult sexual orientation and attraction to underage persons. *Archives of Sexual Behavior, 7,* 175-181.

Grover, K. J., Russell, C. S., Schumm, W. R., & Paff-Bergen, L. A. (1985). Mate selection processes and marital satisfaction. *Family Relations, 34,* 383-386.

Gruetzner, H. (1988). *Alzheimer's: A caregiver's guide and sourcebook.* New York: Wiley.

Grunwald, L., & Goldberg, J. (1993, July). The amazing minds of infants. *Life,* 46-60.

Grusec, J., & Abramovitch, R. (1982). Imitation of peers and adults in a natural setting: A functional analysis. *Child Development, 53,* 636-642.

Grusec, J., & Lytton, H. (1988). *Social development: History, theory and research.* New York: Springer-Verlag.

Guernsey, J. (1993). *Abortion: Understanding the controversy.* Minneapolis: Lerner.

Gullotta, T. P., Adams, G. R., & Markstrom, C. A. (1999). *The adolescent experience* (4th ed.). San Diego, Academic Press.

Gundara, J. S. (1993). Multiculturalism and the British nation-state. In J. Horton (Ed.), *Liberalism, multiculturalism, and toleration.* London: Macmillan Press.

Gunnar, M. (1984). Coping with aversive stimulation in the neonatal period: Quiet sleep and plasma cortisol levels during recovery from circumcision. *Child Development, 56,* 824-834.

Gupta, G. R. (1993). *Sociology of mental health.* Boston: Allyn and Bacon.

Gurin, G., Veroof, J. J., & Felds, S. (1960). *Americans view their mental health: A nationwide interview survey.* New York: Basic Books.

Gurland, B. J., Dean, L. L., Copeland, J., Gurland, R., & Golden, R. (1982). Criteria for the diagnosis of dementia in the community elderly. *The Gerontologist, 22,* 180-186.

Gurland, B. J., Dean, L. L., Cross, P., & Golden, R. (1980). The epidemiology of depression and dementia in the elderly: The use of multiple indicators of these conditions. In J. O. Cole & J. E. Barrett (Eds.), *Psychopathology of the aged.* New York: Raven Press.

Haaken, J. (1990). A critical analysis of the co-dependence construct. *Psychiatry, 53,* 396-406.

Hagan, J. (1995). *Delinquency and disrepute in the life course.* Greenwich, CN: JAI Press.

Hagestad, G. (1985). Continuity and connectedness. In V. L. Bengston & J. Robertson (Ed.), *Grandparenthood.* Beverly Hills, CA: Sage.

Hahn, N. (1993). Why children and parents must play while they eat: An interview with T. Berry Brazelton, M.D. *Journal of the American Dietetic Association, 93,* 1385-1387.

Haith, M., & Canfield, R. (1991). Young infants' visual expectations for symmetric and asymmetric stimulus sequences. *Developmental Psychology, 27,* 198-208.

Haley, J. (1990). *Problem-solving therapy.* San Francisco: Jossey-Bass.

Hall, J. A., & Halberstadt, A. G. (1980). Masculinity and femininity in children: Development of the Children's Personal Attributes Questionnaire. *Developmental Psychology, 16,* 270-280.

Halpern, R. (1993). Poverty and infant development. In C. Zeaneh (Ed.), *Handbook of infant mental health* (pp. 73-86). New York: Guilford Press.

Hamark, B., Uddenberg, N., & Forssman, L. (1995). The influence of social class on parity and psychological reactions in women coming for induced abortion. *Acta Obstetricia et Gynecologica Scandinavica, 74,* 302-306.

Hamburg, B. A., & Dixon, S. L. (1992). Adolescent pregnancy and parenthood. In M. K. Rosenheim & M. F. Testa (Eds.), *Early parenthood and coming of age in the 1990s.* New Brunswick, NJ: Rutgers University Press.

Hamdani, R. J. (1974). *Exploratory behavior and vocational development among disadvantaged inner-city adolescents.* Unpublished doctoral dissertation, Columbia University, New York.

Hammond, C. B. (1994). Women's concerns with hormone replacement therapy—Compliance issues. *Fertility & Sterility, 62,* 157-160.

Hancock, L. (1996, March 18). Mother's little helper. *Newsweek,* pp. 51-56.

Hann, D. M., Osofsky, J. D., Barnard, K. E., & Leonard, G. (1990). Maternal emotional availability in two risk groups [Special ICIS issue]. *Infant Behavior and Development, 13,* 404.

Hansen, J. F. (1980). *Children's attachment to mother figures and the social development of black infants and young children.* Unpublished manuscript, University of California, Berkeley.

Hanson, W. (1980, October). The urban Indian woman and her family. *Social Casework,* 476-483.

Harmon, R. R., & Blieszner, R. (1990). Filial responsibility expectations among adult child-older parent pairs. *Journal of Gerontology: Psychological Sciences, 45,* 110-112.

Harris, M. J., & Rosenthal, R. (1985). Mediation of interpersonal expectancy effects: 31 meta-analyses. *Psychological Bulletin, 97,* 363-386.

Harrison, L., Leeper, J., & Yoon, M. (1991). Preterm infants; physiologic responses to early parent touch. *Western Journal of Nursing Research, 13,* 698-713.

Harrison, L., & Woods, S. (1991, July/August). Early parental touch and preterm infants. *JOGNN,* pp. 299-305.

Harter, S. (1979). *The perceived competence scale.* Denver, CO: University of Denver.

Harter, S. (1982). The perceived competence scale for children. *Child Development, 53,* 87-97.

Harter, S. (1985). *Self-perception profile for children.* Denver, CO: University of Denver.

Harter, S. (1990). Self and identity development. In S. S. Feldman & G. R. Elliott (Eds.), *At the threshold: The developing adolescent.* Cambridge, MA: Harvard University Press.

Harter, S. (1995, May). Is self-esteem really all that important? *APA Monitor.*

Hartford, M. E. (1985). Understanding normative growth and development in aging: Working with strengths. *Journal of Gerontological Social Work, 8,* 37-54.

Hartman, A. (1978). Diagrammatic assessment of family relationships. *Social Casework, 59,* 465-476.

Hartman, A., & Laird, J. (1983). *Family-centered social work practice.* New York: Free Press.

Hartman, A., & Laird, J. (1987). Family practice. In A. Minahan (Ed.), *Encyclopedia of social work* (18th ed., Vol. 1, pp. 575-587). Silver Spring, MD: National Association of Social Workers.

Hartney, L. L. (1989, September/October). My mother's keeper. *Family Therapy Networker,* 38-41.

Hartup, W. W. (1974). Aggression in childhood: Developmental perspectives. *American Psychologist, 29,* 336-341.

Hartup, W. W. (1979). Peer relations and the growth of social competence. In M. W. Kent & J. E. Rolf (Eds.), *Primary prevention of psychopathology: Vol. 3. Social competence in children.* Hanover, NH: University Press of New England.

Hanushek, E. A. (1997). Assessing the effects of school resources on student performance: An update. *Educational Education and Policy Analysis, 19,* 141-164.

Harre, R. (1983). *Personal being.* Oxford: Blackwell Publishers.

Hartman, A. (1994). Social work practice. In F. Reamer (Ed.), *The foundations of social work knowledge.* New York: Columbia University Press.

Hartup, W. W. (1983). Peer relations. In P. H. Mussen (Ed.), *Handbook of child psychology* (4th ed., Vol. 4). New York: Wiley.

Hartup, W. W. (1989). Social relationships and their developmental significance. *American Psychologist, 44,* 120-126.

Hastorf, A. H., & Isen, A. M. (1992). Social knowledge. In A. H. Hastorf & A. M. Isen (Eds.), *Cognitive social psychology.* New York: Elsevier/North Holland.

Hatch, L. R. (1990). Gender and work: At midlife and beyond. *Generations, 14,* 48-51.

Hatfield, E., & Walster, G. W. (1985). *A new look at love.* New York: University Press of America.

Haugh, S. S., Hoffman, C. D., & Cowan, G. (1980). The eye of the very young beholder: Sex-typing of infants by young children. *Child Development, 51,* 598-600.

Havinghurst, R. (1948/1954). *Developmental tasks and education.* New York: McKay.

Havighurst, R. J. (1952). *Developmental tasks and education.* New York: David McKay.

Havighurst, R. J. (1972). *Developmental tasks and education* (3rd ed.). New York: David McKay.

REF: Hawkins, J., Pea, R. D., Glick, J., & Scribner, S. (1984). "Merds that laugh don't like mushrooms": Evidence for deductive reasoning by preschoolers. *Developmental Psychology, 20,* 584-594.

Hay, L. (1984). *You can heal your life.* Santa Monica, CA: Hay House.

Hayden, M. F., & Goldman, J. (1996). Families of adults with mental retardation: Stress levels and need for services. *Social Work, 41, 6,* 657-667.

Hayes, N., Stainton, M., & McNeil, D. (1993). Caring for a chronically ill infant: A paradigm case of maternal rehearsal in the neonatal intensive care unit. *Journal of Pediatric Nursing, 8*(6), 355-360.

Haywood, K. M. (1986). *Life span motor development.* Champaign, IL: Human Kinetics.

Hazel, J. S., Schumaker, J. B., Sherman, J. A., & Sheldon-Wilder, J. (1981). The development and evaluation of a group skills training program for court-adjudicated youths. In D. Upper and S. M. Ross (Eds.), *Behavioral group therapy, 1981:* An annual review. Champaign, IL: Research Press.

Hazen, C., & Shaver, P. (1987). Romantic love conceptualized as an attachment process. *Journal of Personality and Social Psychology, 52,* 511-524.

Hearn, G. (1979). General systems theory and social work. In F. J. Turner (Ed.), *Social work treatment: Interlocking theoretical approaches* (2nd ed.). New York: Free Press.

Heatherington, E. M. (1987). Family relations six years after divorce. In K. Pasley & M. Ihinger-Tollman (Eds.), *Remarriage and stepparenting today: Current research and theory.* New York: Guilford Press.

Heatherington, E. M. (1988). Parents, children, and siblings: Six years after divorce. In R. A. Hinde & J. Stevenson-Hinde (Eds.), *Relationships within families: Mutual influences* (pp. 311-331). New York: Oxford University Press.

Heatherington, E. M. (1989). Coping with family transitions: Winners, losers, and survivors. *Child Development, 60,* 1-14.

Heatherington, E. M., Cox, M., & Cox, R. (1979). Play and social interaction in children following divorce. *Journal of Social Issues, 35,* 26-49.

Hecht, M. (1993). *African American communication: Ethnic identity and cultural interpretation.* Newbury Park, CA: Sage.

Hedger, L. V., Laine, R. D., & Greenwald, R. (1994). Does money matter? A meta analysis of studies of the effects of differential school inputs on student outcomes. *Educational Researcher, 23,* 5-14.

Heilman, J. R. (1995, August 13). The good news about Alzheimer's. *Parade,* 12-13.

Heiney, S., Hasan, L., & Price, K. (1993). Developing and implementing a bereavement program for a children's hospital. *Journal of Pediatric Nursing, 8,* 385-391.

Heinz, W. R. (1991a). *Theoretical advances in life course research.* Weinheim: Deutscher Studien Verlaz.

Heinz, W. R. (1991b). Status passages, social risks, and the life course: A conceptual framework. In W. R. Heinz (Ed.), *Theoretical advances in life course research.* Weinheim: Deutscher Studien Verlaz.

Heinz, W. R. (1996). Introduction. In A. Weymann and W. R. Heinz (Eds.), *Society and biography: Interrelationships between social structure, institutions, and the life course.* Weinheim: Deutscher Studien Verlag.

Heise, L. (1989, March/April). The global war against women. *World Watch.*

Heller, K., Price, R., Reinharz, S., Riger, S., & Wanderman, A. (1984). *Psychology and community change: Challenges of the future.* Pacific Grove: Brooks/Cole Publishing.

Hennessy, C. H., & John, R. (1995). The interpretation of burden among Pueblo Indian caregivers. *Journal of Aging Studies, 9,* 215-229.

Hepworth, D. H., & Larsen, J. A. (1989). *Direct social work practice* (3rd ed.). Belmont, CA: Wadsworth.

Hepworth, D. H., & Larsen, J. A. (1993). *Direct social work practice* (4th ed.). Pacific Grove, CA: Brooks/Cole.

Herek, G. M. (1991). Stigma, prejudice, and violence against lesbians and gay men. In J. C. Gonsiorek & J. D. Weinrich (Eds.), *Homosexuality: Research implications for public policy.* Newbury Park, CA: Sage.

Herek, G. M., & Berrill, K. (1990). Violence against lesbians and gay men: Issues for research, practice and policy. *Journal of Interpersonal Violence, 5.*

Herman, E. (1988, Summer). The twelve-step program: Cure or cover? *Out/Look: National Lesbian and Gay Quarterly.* Excerpted in *Utne Reader* (1988, November/December), pp. 52-63.

Hersch, P. (1990, July/August). The resounding silence. *Family Therapy Networker,* pp. 18-29.

Hesling, K., & Szklo, K. (1981). Mortality after bereavement. *American Journal of Epidemiology, 144,* 42-52.

Hess, B. B. (1990). Gender & aging: The demographic parameters. *Generations, XIV,* 12-15.

Hess, R. O., & Hollaway, S. D. (1984). Family and school as educational institutions. In R. D. Parke (Ed.), *Review of child development research: Vol. 7. The family.* Chicago: University of Chicago Press.

Hetherington, E. M., & Blechman, E. A. (1996). *Stress, coping, and resiliency in children and families.* Manwah, NJ: Lawrence Erlbaum Association.

Hetherington, E. M., Cox, M., & Cox, R. (1982). Effects of divorce on parents and children. In M. Lamb (Ed.), *Nontraditional families: Parenting and child development.* Hillsdale, NJ: Erlbaum.

Heymans, P. G. (1994). Developmental tasks: A cultural analysis of human development. In J. J. FuterLaak, P. G. Heymans, A. I. Podol'skij. (Eds.), *Developmental tasks: Towards a cultural analysis of human development* (pp. 3-33). Dordrecht: Kluwer Academic Publishers.

High rate of suicide among New York City police. (1994, November). *NASW News,* p. 9.

Hilgard, E. R. (1987). *Psychology in America: A historical survey.* San Diego: Harcourt Brace Jovanovich.

Hill, C. R., & Stafford, F. P. (1980). Parental care of children: Time diary estimate of quantity, predictability, and variety. *Journal of Human Relations, 15,* 219-239.

Hill, J. P., & Hombeck, G. N. (1986). Attachment and autonomy during adolescence. *Annals of Child Development, 3,* 145-189.

Hill, J. P., Hombeck, G. N., Marlow, L., Green, T. M., & Lynch, M. E. (1985). Pubertal status and parent-child relations in families of 7th grade boys. *Journal of Early Adolescence, 5,* 31-44.

Hinde, R. A., Titmus, G., Easton, D., & Tamplin, A. (1985). Incidence of "friendship" and behavior toward strong associates and nonassociates in preschoolers. *Child Development, 56,* 234-245.

Hinrichsen, G. A. (1990). *Mental health problems and older adults: Choices and challenges.* Santa Barbara, CA: ABC-CLIO.

Hinrichsen, G. A., & Ramirez, M. (1992). Black and white dementia caregivers: A comparison of their adaptation, adjustment, and service utilization. *The Gerontologist, 32,* 375-381.

Ho, M. K. (1987). *Family therapy with ethnic minorities.* Newbury Park, CA: Sage.

Hoff-Ginsberg, E. (1986). Function and structure in maternal speech: Their relation to the child's development of syntax. *Developmental Psychology, 22,* 155-163.

Hoffman, L. (1987). The effects on children of maternal and paternal employment. In N. Gerstel & H. Gross (Eds.), *Families and work.* Philadelphia: Temple University Press.

Hoffman, L. W. (1989). Effects of maternal employment in two-parent families. *American Psychologist, 44,* 283-293.

Hoffman, M. L. (1970). Moral development. In P. H. Mussen (Ed.), *Carmichael's manual of child psychology* (Vol. 2). New York: Wiley.

Hoggett, P. (1997). *Contested communities: Experiences, struggles, policies.* Bristol: The Policy Press.

Hohman, M. (1995). *Self-efficacy and empowerment: A study of women in recovery from alcoholism.* Unpublished doctoral dissertation, School of Social Work, Arizona State University.

Holm, B. A., Cassidy, S. B., et al. (1993). Prader-Willi syndrome: Consensus diagnostic criteria. *Pediatrics, 2,* 398-402.

Honzik, M. (1976). Values and limitations of infant tests: An overview. In M. Lewis (Ed.), *Origins of intelligence* (pp. 59-95). New York: Plenum.

Hooyman, N. R. (1994). Diversity and populations at risk: Women. In F. G. Reamer (Ed.), *The foundations of social work knowledge.* New York: Columbia University Press.

Hooyman, N. R., & Lustbader, W. (1986). *Taking care: Supporting older people and their families.* New York: Free Press.

Horn, J. L. (1982). The theory of fluid and crystallized intelligence in relation to concepts of cognitive psychology and aging in adulthood. In F. J. M. Craik & S. Trehub (Eds.), *Aging and cognitive processes* (pp. 237-278). New York: Plenum.

Horton, J. (Ed.) (1993a). *Liberalism, multiculturalism, and toleration.* London: Macmillan Press.

Horton, J. (1993b). Liberalism, multiculturalism, and tolerance. In J. Horton (Ed.), *Liberalism, multiculturalism, and toleration.* London: Macmillan Press.

Horwitz, A. V. (1990). *The logic of social control.* New York: Plenum.

Hothersall, D. (1984). *History of psychology.* Philadelphia: Temple University Press.

Howard, D. V. (1983). *Cognitive psychology: Memory, language, and thought.* New York: Macmillan.

Howe, M. (1995, June). New cognitive developments make waves. *APA Monitor.*

Howell, M. C., Allen, M. C., & Doress, P. B. (1987). Dying and death. In P. B. Doress, D. L. Siegel, & The Midlife and Older Women Book Project (Eds.), *Ourselves, growing older: Women aging with knowledge and power* (pp. 392-403). New York: Simon & Schuster.

Hoyenga, K. B., & Hoyenga, K. T. (1988). *Psychobiology: The neuron and behavior.* Pacific Grove, CA: Brooks/Cole.

Huesmann, L. R., Eron, L. D., Lefkowitz, M. M., & Walder, L. O. (1984). Stability of aggression over time and generations. *Developmental Psychology, 6,* 1120-1134.

Huff, C. R. (1993). Gangs in the United States. In A. P. Goldstein & C. R. Huff (Eds.), *The gang intervention handbook* (pp. 3-20). Champaign, IL: Research Press.

Hughes, C. B., & Page-Lieberman, J. (1989). Totality of bereavement, 25-56-year-old fathers who experienced perinatal loss of infant. *Death Studies, 13,* 537-556.

Hughes, L. (1970). Mother to son. In A. Bontemps and L. Hughes (Eds.), *The poetry of the Negro, 1746-1970.* Garden City, NY: Doubleday.

Hunter, S., & Sundel, M. (Eds.). (1989). *Midlife myths: Issues, findings, and practice implications*. Newbury Park, CA: Sage.

Hutchison, E. D., Charlesworth, L. W. (1998). Human behavior in the social environment: The role or gender in the expansion of practice knowledge. In J. Figueira-McDonough, F. E. Netting, A. Nichols-Casebolt (Eds.), *The role of gender in practiced knowledge: Claiming half the human experience* (pp. 41–80). New York: Garland Publishing.

Hyde, A. B., & Murphy, J. (1955). An experiment in integrative learning. *The Social Service Review, 29*, 358.

Hyde, J. S. (1985). *Half the human experience: The psychology of women* (3rd ed.). Lexington, MA: Heath.

Hyman, J. (1987). Memory lapse and memory loss. In P. B. Doress, D. L. Siegel, & The Midlife and Older Women Book Project (Eds.), *Ourselves, growing older: Women aging with knowledge and power* (pp. 380–391). New York: Simon & Schuster.

Ianniruberto, A., & Tajani, E. (1981). Ultrasonographic study of fetal movements. *Seminars in Perinatology, 5*, 175–181.

Infant Health and Development Program. (1990). Enhancing the outcomes of low-birthweight premature infants. *Journal of the American Medical Association, 263*, 3035–3042.

Institute of Medicine's National Cancer Policy Board. (1999). *Ensuring quality cancer cure*.

Isen, A. M., & Hastorf, A. H. (1982). Some perspectives on cognitive social psychology. In A. Hastorf and A. Isen (Eds.), *Cognitive social psychology* (pp. 1–23). New York: Elsvier/North Holland.

Izard, C. (Ed.). (1982). *Measuring emotions in infants and children*. London: Cambridge University Press.

Jackson, J. F. (1993). Multiple caregivers among African Americans and infant attachment: The need for an emic approach. *Human Development, 36*, 87–102.

Jackson, P. (1985, April). When the baby isn't perfect. *American Journal of Nursing*, pp. 396–399.

Jacobsen, T., Edelstein, W., & Hoffman, V. (1994). A longitudinal study of the relation between representations of attachment in childhood and cognitive functioning in childhood and adolescence. *Developmental Psychology, 30*, 112–124.

Jacobson, B. (1987). Perinatal origin of adult self-destructive behavior. *Acta Psychiatrica Scandinavica, 76*, 364–371.

Jacoby, L. L., & Witherspoon, D. (1982). Remembering without awareness. *Canadian Journal of Psychology, 36*, 300–324.

Jaffe, M. L. (1991). *Understanding parenting*. Dubuque, IA: Wm. C. Brown.

James, W. (1884). What is emotion? *Mind, 19*, 188–205.

Janis, I. L. (1972). *Victims of groupthink*. Boston: Houghton Mifflin.

Janis, I. L. (1973, January). Groupthink. *Yale Alumni Magazine*, 16–19.

Janis, I. L. (1982). *Groupthink: Psychological studies of policy decisions and fiascoes*. Boston: Houghton Mifflin.

Jannke, S. (1994). Mandatory drug testing of pregnant women. *Childbirth Instructor, 4*(4), 12–18.

Janosik, E. H. (1986). *Crisis counseling: A contemporary approach*. Boston: Jones & Bartlett.

Janzen, C., & Harris, O. (1986). *Family treatment in social work practice* (2nd ed.). Itasca, IL: Peacock.

Jaroff, L. (1996, April 1). Prostate cancer: The battle. *Time*, pp. 58–65.

Jason, J., & van de Meer, A. (1989). *Parenting your premature baby*. New York: Henry Holt.

Jedrychowski, W., & Flak, E. (1996). Confronting the prenatal effects of active and passive tobacco smoking on the birth weight of children. *Central European Journal of Public Health, 4*, 201–205.

Jencks, C. (1985). How much do high school students learn? *Sociology of Education, 58*, 128–135.

Jennings, K., Wisner, K., Conley, B. (1991). Serving the mental health needs of families with children under three: A comprehensive program. *Infant Mental Health Journal, 12*, 276–290.

Jessor, R. (1987). Problem-behavior theory, psychosocial development, and adolescent problem drinking. *British Journal of Addiction, 82*, 331–342.

Jessor, R. (1992). Risk behavior in adolescence: A psychosocial framework for understanding and action. In D. E. Rogers & E. Ginzburg (Eds.), *Adolescents at risk: Medical and social perspectives* (pp. 19–34). Boulder, CO: Westview Press.

Jilik, W. G. (1994). Traditional healing in the prevention and treatment of alcohol and drug abuse. *Transcultural Psychiatry Research Review, 31*, 291–258.

Johnson, C. L. (1983). Dyadic family relationships and family supports. *The Gerontologist, 23*, 377–383.

Johnson, C. L., & Barer, B. M. (1990). Families and networks among older inner-city Blacks. *The Gerontologist, 30*, 726–733.

Johnson, C. N., & Wellman, H. M. (1982). Children's developing conceptions of the mind and brain. *Child Development, 53*, 222–234.

Johnson, D. W., & Johnson, R. (1989). *Cooperation and competition: Theory and research*. Edina, MN: Interaction Book Company.

Johnson, H. C. (1980). *Behavior, psychopathology, and the brain*. New York: Curriculum Concepts.

Johnson, H. C., Atkins, S. P., Battle, S. F., Hernandez-Arata, L., Hesselbrock, M., Libassi, M. F., & Parish, M. S. (1990, Spring/Summer). Strengthening the "bio" in the biopsychosocial paradigm. *Journal of Social Work Education, 109*–123.

Johnson, J., & Goldman, J. (1990). *Developmental assessment in clinical child psychology*. New York: Pergamon Press.

Johnson, J., Johnson, M., Cunningham, J., Ewing, S., Hatcher, D., & Dannen, C. (1982). *Newborn death: A book for parents experiencing the death of a very small infant*. Omaha, NE: Centering Corporation.

Johnson, J. H., & Fennell, E. (1983). Aggressive and delinquent behavior in childhood and adolescence. In E. Walker & M. Roberts (Eds.), *Handbook of clinical child psychology*. New York: Wiley.

Johnston, L. D., O'Malley, P. M., & Bachman, J. G. (1988). *Illicit drug use, smoking, and drinking by America's high school students, college students, and young adults, 1975–1987*. Washington, DC: National Institute of Drug Abuse.

Johnston, L. D., O'Malley, P. M., & Bachman, J. G. (1994). *National survey results on drug use from the monitoring the future Stusy, 1975–1993*. Rockville, MD: National Institute on Drug Abuse.

Jones, E., & McCurdy, K. (1992). The links between types of maltreatment and demographic characteristics of children. *Child Abuse and Neglect, 16*, 201–215.

Jones, J. (1990, November). APA report puts focus on women, depression, how to treat it. *APA Monitor*, p. 33.

Jones, S., & Raag, T. (1989). Smile production in infants: The importance of a social recipient for the facial signal. *Child Development, 60*, 811–818.

Jones-Witters, P., & Witters, W. (1986). *Drugs and society: A biological perspective*. Boston: Jones & Bartlett.

Jordan, C., & Franklin, C. (1995). *Clinical assessment for social workers*. Chicago: Lyceum Books.

Joseph, M. (1988). Religion and social work practice. *Social Casework, 69*, 443–452.

Kaffman, M., & Elizur, E. (1977). Infants who become enuretics: A longitudinal study of 161 kibbutz children. *Monographs of the Society for Research in Child Development, 42*.

Kagan, J. (1978). On emotion and its development: A working paper. In M. Lewis & L. A. Rosenglum (Eds.), *The development of affect*. New York: Plenum.

Kagan, J. (1984a). The idea of emotion in human development. In C. E. Izard, J. Kagan, & R. B. Zajonc (Eds.), *Emotion, cognition, and behavior*. New York: Cambridge University Press.

Kagan, J. (1984b). *The nature of the child*. New York: Basic Books.

Kagan, J., Kearsley, R. B., & Zelazo, P. R. (1978). The effects of infant daycare on psychological development. *Evaluation Quarterly, 1*, 143–158.

Kalat, J. W. (1992). *Biological psychology.* (4th ed.). Pacific Grove, CA: Brooks/Cole.

Kalat, J. W. (1995). *Biological psychology* (5th ed.). Pacific Grove, CA: Brooks/Cole.

Kalat, J. W. (1998). *Biological psychology* (6th ed.). Pacific Grove, CA: Brooks/Cole.

Kalish, R. A. (1985). *Death, grief, and caring relationships* (2nd ed.). Pacific Grove, CA: Brooks/Cole.

Kalish, R. A., & Reynolds, D. K. (1976). *An overview of death and ethnicity.* Farmingdale, NY: Baywood.

Kalmuss, D., Davidson, A., & Cushman, L. (1992). Parenting expectations, experiences, and adjustment to parenthood: A test of the violated expectations framework. *Journal of Marriage and the Family, 52,* 516-526.

Kalter, N. (1987). Long-term effects of divorce on children: A developmental vulnerability model. *American Journal of Orthopsychiatry, 57,* 587-600.

Kalter, N. (1990). *Growing up with divorce.* New York: Free Press.

Kalter, N., Kloner, A., Schreier, S., & Okla, K. (1989). Predictors of children's post divorce adjustment. *American Journal of Orthopsychiatry, 59,* 605-619.

Kalter, N., & Schreier, S. (1994). Developmental facilitation groups for children of divorce: The elementary school model. In C. W. LeCroy (Ed.), *Handbook of child and adolescent treatment manuals.* New York: Lexington Books.

Kaminer, W. (1992). *I'm dysfunctional, you're dysfunctional.* Reading, MA: Addison-Wesley.

Kaminski, H., Stafl, A., & Aiman, J. (1987). The effect of epidural analgesia on the frequency of instrumental obstetric delivery. *Obstetrics & Gynecology, 69,* 770-773.

Kanfer, F. H., Stifter, E., & Morris, S. J. (1981). Self-control and altruism: Delay of gratification for another. *Child Development, 52,* 674-682.

Kanter, R. M. (1977). Women in organizations: Sex roles, group dynamics, and change strategies. In A. Sergeant (Ed.), *Beyond sex roles.* St. Paul, MN: West.

Kantor, D., & Lehr, W. (1975). *Inside the family.* San Francisco: Jossey-Bass.

Kantrowitz, B. (1997, May 12). Beating the clock. *Newsweek,* p. 71.

Karnes, B. (1986). *Gone from my sight: The dying experience.*

Kastenbaum, R. (1977). Death and development through the life span. In H. Feifel (Ed.), *New meanings of death* (pp. 18-45). New York: McGraw-Hill.

Kastenbaum, R. (1981). *Death, society and human experience.* St. Louis: C.V. Mosby.

Kastenbaum, R., & Weisman, A. D. (1972). The psychological autopsy as a research procedure in gerontology. In D. P. Kent, R. Kastenbaum, & S. Sherwood (Eds.), *Research planning and action for the elderly: The power and potential of social science* (pp. 214-216). New York: Behavioral Publications.

Katz, P., & Zalk, S. (1978). Modification of children's racial attitudes. *Developmental Psychology, 14,* 447-456.

Kaufman, A. S., & Kaufman, N. L. (1983). *Kaufman assessment battery for children: Interpretive manual.* Circle Pines, MN: American Guidance Service.

Kaufman, S. E., Silver, P., & Poulin, J. (1997). Gender differences in attitudes toward alcohol, tobacco, and other drugs. *Social Work, 42(3),* 231-241.

Kazdin, A. E. (1987). *Conduct disorders in childhood and adolescence.* Newbury Park, CA: Sage.

Kazdin, A. E., & Frame, C. (1983). Aggressive behavior and conduct disorder. In R. J. Morris & T. R. Kratochwill (Eds.), *The practice of child therapy.* New York: Pergamon Press.

Kearney, C. A., Weyermann, A. G., & Durand, V. M. (1995). *Instructor's manual: Abnormal psychology.* Barlow/Durand. Pacific Grove: Brooks/Cole Publishing.

Keating, D. P. (1980). Thinking processes in adolescence. In J. Adelson (Ed.), *Handbook of adolescent psychology.* New York: Wiley.

Keefe, T. (1986). Mediation and social work treatment. In F. J. Turner (ED.), *Social work treatment* (pp. 155-180). New York: The Free Press.

Keen, S. (1991). *Fire in the belly: On being a man.* New York: Bantam Books.

Kehoe, M. (1989). *Lesbians over 60 speak for themselves.* New York: Harrington Park Press.

Keith, P. M. (1986). The social context and resources of the unmarried in old age. *International Journal of Aging and Human Development, 23,* 81-96.

Kellner, D. (1990). The postmodern turn: Positions, problems and prospects. In G. Rutger (Ed.), *Frontiers of social theory* (pp. 255-286). New York: Columbia University Press.

Kelly, R. K. (1979). *Courtship, marriage, and the family* (3rd ed.). New York: Harcourt Brace Jovanovich.

Kelly, S. (1993). Caregiver stress in grandparents raising grandchildren. *IMAGE: Journal of Nursing Scholarship, 25,* 331-337.

Kendall, P. C., & Braswell, L. (1985). *Cognitive-behavioral therapy for impulsive children.* New York: Guildford Press.

Keniston, K. (1971). *Youth and dissent: The rise of a new opposition.* New York: Harcourt Brace Jovanovich.

Kennedy, G. J., Kelman, H. R., Thomas, C., Wisniewski, W., Metz, H., & Bijur, P. E. (1989). Hierarchy of characteristics associated with depressive symptoms in an urban elderly sample. *American Journal of Psychiatry, 146,* 220-225.

Kent, S. (1980). Advances in hypertension research. *Geriatrics,* 103-104.

Kerlikowske, K., Grady, D., Rubin, S., Sandrock, C., & Ernster, V. (1995). Efficacy of screening mammography: A meta-analysis. *Journal of the American Medical Association, 273,* 149-154.

Kiecolt-Glaser, J. K., & Glaser, R. (1988). Behavioral influences on immune function. In T. Field, P. McCabe, & C. Schneiderman (Eds.), *Stress and coping across development.* Hillsdale, NJ: Erlbaum.

Kiefer, C. W. (1988). *The mantle of maturity: A history of ideas about character development.* Albany: State University of New York Press.

Kiesler, S. (1978). *Interpersonal processes in groups and organizations.* Arlington Heights, VA: AHM Publishing.

Kietzman, M. L., Spring, B., & Zubin, J. (1985). Perception, cognition, information processing. In H. I. Kaplan & B. J. Sadock (Eds.), *Comprehensive textbook of psychiatry* (Vol. 4, pp. 157-178). Baltimore: Williams & Wilkins.

Kimmel, D. C. (1978). Adult development and aging: A gay perspective. *Journal of Social Issues, 34,* 113-130.

Kinsey, A. C., Pomeroy, W. B., & Martin, C. E. (1948). *Sexual behavior in the human male.* Philadelphia: Saunders.

Kinsey, A. C., Pomeroy, W. B., Martin, C. E., & Gebhard, P. H. (1953). *Sexual behavior in the human female.* Philadelphia: Saunders.

Kirk, S. A., & Kutchins, H. (1992). *The selling of the DSM: The rhetoric of science and psychiatry.* New York: Aldine de Gruyter.

Kirk, S. A., & Kutchins, H. (1994, June 20). Is bad writing a mental disorder? The *New York Times.*

Kivnick, H. Q. (1986). Grandparenthood and a life cycle. *Journal of Geriatric Psychiatry, 19,* 39-55.

Klaus, M., & Kennell, J. (1976). *Maternal-infant bonding: The impact of early separation or loss on family development.* St. Louis: C.V. Mosby.

Klaus, M., Kennell, J., & Klaus, P. (1993). *Mothering the mother: How a doula can help you have a shorter, easier, and healthier birth.* Reading, MA: Addison-Wesley.

Klaus, M., & Klaus, P. (1985). *The amazing newborn.* Reading, MA: Addison-Wesley.

Kleigman, R. (1992). Perpetual poverty: Child health and the underclass. *Pediatrics, 89,* 710-713.

Kleinman, A. (1988). *The illness narratives: Suffering, healing, and the human condition.* New York: Basic Books.

Kline, M., Tschann, J. M., Johnston, J. R., & Wallerstein, J. S. (1989). Children's adjustment in joint and sole physical custody families. *Developmental Psychology, 25,* 430-438.

Klinnert, M., Emde, R., Butterfield, P., & Campos, J. (1986). Social referencing: The infant's use of emotional signals from a friendly adult with mother present. *Developmental Psychology, 22,* 427-432.

Koegel, P. (1989). Mental illness among the inner-city homeless. *Journal of the California Alliance for the Mentally Ill, 1,* 16-17.

Koenig, H. G. (1990). Research on religion and mental health in later life: A review and commentary. *Journal of Geriatric Psychiatry, 23,* 23-53.

Kohlberg, L. (1969). Stage and sequence: The cognitive-developmental approach to socialization. In D. A. Goslin (Ed.), *Handbook of socialization theory and research.* Chicago: Rand McNally.

Konner, M. (1991). *Childhood: A multicultural view.* Boston: Little, Brown.

Koss, M. P. (1985). The hidden rape victim: Personality, attitudinal, and situational characteristics. *Psychology of Women Quarterly, 9,* 193-212.

Koss, M. P., Gidycz, C. A., & Wisniewski, N. (1987). The scope of rape: Incidence and prevalence of sexual aggression and victimization in a national sample of higher education students. *Journal of Consulting and Clinical Psychology, 48,* 460-468.

Kotch, J. B., Browne, D. C., Ringwalt, C. L., Stewart, P. W., Ruina, E., Holt, K., Lowman, B., & Jung, J. W. (1995). Risk of child abuse or neglect in a cohort of low-income children. *Child Abuse & Neglect, 19,* 1115-1130.

Kotelchuck, M. (1976). The infant's relationship to the father: Experimental evidence. In M. E. Lamb (Ed.), *The role of the father in child development* (pp. 329-344). New York: Wiley.

Kowalski, K. (1985, April). The impact of chronic grief. *American Journal of Nursing,* pp. 398-399.

Kozol, J. (1985). *Illiterate America.* Garden City, NY: Anchor Books.

Krown, S. (1974). *Threes and fours go to school.* Englewood Cliffs, NJ: Prentice Hall.

Krugman, R., Bays, J., Chadwick, D., Kanda, M., Levitt, L., & McHugh, M. (1994). Distinguishing SIDS from child abuse fatalities. *Pediatrics, 94,* 124-126.

Kubick-Balicheski, P., Martinez, R., & Walsh, B. (1994, January/February). Coordinating transitions in care for improved perinatal outcomes: The RIMM project. *Discharge Planning Update,* 1-7.

Kubler-Ross, E. (1969). *On death and dying.* New York: Macmillan.

Kuhn, D., Kohlberg, L., Langer, J., & Haan, N. (1977). The development of formal operations in logical and moral judgment. *Genetic Psychology Monographs, 95,* 97-188.

Kulwicki, A. (1987). *An ethnographic study of illness perception and practices of Yemini-Americans.* Unpublished doctoral dissertation, Indiana University, Indianapolis.

Kupersmidt, J. B., & Coie, J. D. (1990). Preadolescent peer status, aggression, and school adjustment as predictors of externalizing problems in adolescence. *Child Development, 61,* 1350-1363.

Labassi, M. F. (1990). *Pscyhopharmacology in social work education.* (Contract No. 89MF7003901d). Washington, DC: National Institute of Mental Health.

Labouvie-Vief, G. (1986). Intelligence and cognition. In J. E. Birren & K. W. Schaie (Eds.), *Handbook on the psychology of aging* (2nd ed.). New York: Van Nostrand Reinhold.

Lacayo, R. (1995, October 30). I, too, sing America. *Time,* 33-36.

Lagercrantz, H. (1986). The stress of being born. *Scientific American, 254,* 100-107.

Lalley, J. R., & Keith, H. (1997). Early head start: The first two years. *Bulletin of Zero to Three: National Center for Infants, Toddlers, and Families, 18,* 3-8.

Lamb, L. (1994, November/December). Selecting for perfection: Is prenatal screening becoming a kind of eugenics? *Utne Reader,* pp. 26-28.

Lamb, M. E. (1981). The development of father-infant relationships. In M. E. Lamb (Ed.), *The role of the father in child development* (2nd ed.). New York: Wiley.

Lamb, M. E. (1982). *Nontraditional families: Parenting and child development.* Hillsdale, NJ: Erlbaum.

Lamb, M. E., Easterbrooks, M. A., & Holden, G. W. (1980). Reinforcement and punishment among preschoolers: Characteristics, effects, and correlates. *Child Development, 51,* 1230-1236.

Lancet (1995). *Breast cancer and hormone replacement therapy: Collaborative reanalysis of data from 51 epidemiological studies of 52,705 women with breast cancer and 108,411 women without breast cancer.*

Langer, R. D., & Barrett-Connor, E. (1994). Extended hormone replacement: Who should get it, and for how long? *Geriatrics, 49,* 20-29.

Langlois, J. H. (1986). From the eye of the beholder to behavioral reality: Development of social behaviors and social relations as a function of physical attractiveness. In C. P. Herman, M. P. Zanna, & E. P. Higgins (Eds.), *Physical appearance, stigma, and social behavior: The Ontario Symposium, Vol. 3.* Hillsdale, NJ: Erlbaum.

Langlois, J. H., & Downs, A. C. (1980). Peer relations as a function of physical attractiveness: The eye of the beholder or behavioral reality. *Child Development, 50,* 409-418.

Langlois, J. H., & Stynczynski, L. (1979). The effects of physical attractiveness on the behavioral attributions and peer preferences in acquainted children. *International Journal of Behavioral Development, 2,* 325-341.

Laosa, L. (1981). Maternal behavior: Socio-cultural diversity in modes of family interaction. In R. W. Henderson (Ed.), *Parent-child interaction: Theory, research and prospects.* New York: Academic Press.

Lapsley, D. K. (1985). Elkind on egocentrism. *Developmental Review, 5,* 227-236.

Lapsley, D. K. (1989). Continuity and discontinuity in adolescent social cognitive development. In R. Montemayer, G. Adams, & T. Gullota (Eds.), *Advances in adolescent research* (Vol. 2). Orlando, FL: Academic Press.

Lapsley, D. K. (1990). Continuity and discontinuity in adolescent social cognitive development. In R. Montemayor, G. Adams, & T. Gullotta (Eds.), *From Childhood to adolescence: A transitional period?* Newbury Park, CA: Sage.

Lapsley, D. K., Olson, L. M., Flannery, D., & Quintana, S. M. (1984). Moral judgment, personality, and attitude to authority in early and late adolescence. *Journal of Youth and Adolescence, 13,* 527-542.

Lapsley, D. K., & Power, F. C. (Eds.). (1988). *Self, ego, and identity.* New York: Springer-Verlag.

Lapsley, D. K., & Rice, K. G. (1988). The "new look" at the imaginary audience and personal fable: Toward an integrative model of adolescent ego development. In D. K. Lapsley & F. C. Power (Eds.), *Self, ego, and identity: Integrative approaches.* New York: Springer-Verlag.

Larson, J. H. (1988). The marriage quiz: College students' beliefs in selected myths about marriage. *Family Relations, 37,* 3-11.

Lasby, K., Newton, S., Sherrow, T., Stainton, M., & McNeil, D. (1994). Maternal work in the NICU: A case study of an "NICU experienced" mother. *Issues in Comprehensive Pediatric Nursing, 17,* 147-160.

Last, C. (1990). School phobias. *Journal of the American Academy of Child and Adolescent Psychiatry, 29, 1,* 31-35.

Laub, J. H., & Sampson, R. J. (1993). Turning points in the life course: Why change matters to the study of crime. *Criminology, 31,* 301-325.

Lawson, W. B. (1986). Racial and ethnic factors in psychiatric research. *Hospital and Community Psychiatry, 37,* 50-53.

Layder, D. (1994). *Understanding social theory.* London: Sage.

Lazarus, R. S. (1991). *Emotion and adaptation.* New York: Oxford University Press.

Lea, S. E. G. (1984). *Instinct, environment, and behaviour.* London: Methuen.

Leadbetter, B. J., Way, N., & Raden, A. (1994). *Barriers to involvement of fathers of the children of adolescent mothers.* Paper presented at the Society for Research on Adolescence, San Diego.

Leahey, T. H. (1987). *A history of psychology: Main currents in psychological thought.* Englewood Cliffs, NJ: Prentice Hall.

LeCroy, C. W. (1992). Promoting social competence in youth. In K. Corcoran (Ed.), *Structuring change* (pp. 167-180). Chicago: Lyceum Books.

LeCroy, C. W. (1994). Social skills training. In C. W. LeCroy (Ed.), *Handbook of child and adolescent treatment manuals.* New York: Lexington Books.

LeCroy, C. W. (1999). *Case studies in social work practice* (2nd edition). Pacific Grove, CA: Brooks/Cole.

LeCroy, C. W., Ashford, J. B., Krysik, J., & Milligan, K. B. (1996). *Healthy Families Arizona: Evaluation Report.* Unpublished manuscript.

LeCroy, C. W., & Daley, J. (1998). *Empirical validation of a primary prevention program for early adolescent girls.* Unpublished manuscript.

LeCroy, C. W., & Daley, J. (1999). Girls together: Building strengths for the future. In C. W. LeCroy (Ed.), *Case studies in social work practice.* Pacific Grove: Brooks/Cole.

LeCroy, C. W., & Milligan, K. B. (1996). Promoting social competence in the schools. In R. Constable, J. Flynn, & S. MacDonald (Eds.), *School social work: Practice and research perspectives.* Chicago: Lyceum Books.

Lee, G. R., Seccombe, K., & Shehan, C. L. (1991). Marital status and personal happiness: An analysis of trend data. *Journal of Marriage and the Family, 139,* 839–844.

Lefrancois, G. R. (1989). *Of children: An introduction to child development.* Belmont, CA: Wadsworth.

Lefrancois, G. R. (1994). *Of children: An intro to child development.* Canada: Van Vostrand Reinhold.

Lefrancois, G. R. (1995). *The lifespan.* Belmont, CA: Wadsworth.

Lehmann, H. E., & Cancro, R. (1985). Schizophrenia: Clinical features. In H. I. Kaplan & B. J. Sadock (Eds.), *New perspectives in schizophrenia.* New York: Macmillan.

Lembau, J. R. (1988). Emotional sequelae of abortion: Implications for clinical practice. *Psychology of Women Quarterly, 12,* 461–472.

Lemeshow, S. (1982). *The handbook of clinical types in mental retardation.* Boston: Allyn & Bacon.

Lemme, B. H. (1995). *Development in adulthood.* Needham Heights, MA: Allyn & Bacon.

Lemon, B. W., Bengston, V. L., & Peterson, J. A. (1972). An exploration of the activity theory of aging: Activity types and life satisfactions among in-movers of a retirement community. *Journal of Gerontology, 27,* 511–523.

Leon, I. (1986). Psychodynamics of perinatal loss. *Psychiatry, 49,* 312–322.

Leon, I. (1992). Perinatal loss: choreographing grief on the obstetric unit. *American Journal of Orthopsychiatry, 62*(1), 7–8.

Leonard, L. G. (1998). Depression and anxiety disorders during multiple pregnancy and parenthood. *Journal of Obstetric, Gynecologic and Neonatal Nursing, 27,* 329–337.

Leslie, G. R., Larson, R., & Gorman, B. L. (1973). *Order and change: Introductory sociology.* New York: Oxford University Press.

Lester, B. M. (1992). Infants and their families at risk: Assessment and intervention. *Infant Mental Health Journal, 13*(1), 54–66.

Levant, R. F. (1990). Men's changing roles. *The Family Psychologist, 6,* 4–6.

Levav, J. (1998). Individuals under conditions of maximum adversity. The holocaust. In B. P. Dohrenwend (Ed.), *Adversity, stress, and psychopathology* (pp. 13–33). New York: Oxford University Press.

Levenson, D. (1998, February). Nursing homes: More than just medical. *NASW News,* p. 3.

Levine, M., & Perkins, D. V. (1997). *Principles of community psychology* (2nd ed.). New York: Oxford University Press.

Levinger, G. (no date). *The interpersonal involvement scale.* University of Massachusetts, Amherst.

Levins, J. S., & Vanderpool, H. Y. (1987). Is frequent religious attendance really conducive to better health?: Toward an epidemiology of religion. *Social Science and Medicine, 24,* 589–600.

Levinson, D. J. (1978). *The seasons of a man's life.* New York: Knopf.

Levinson, D. J. (1985). The life cycle. In H. I. Kaplan & B. J. Sadock (Eds.), *Comprehensive textbook of psychiatry* (Vol. 4). Baltimore: Williams & Wilkins.

Levinson, D. J. (1986). A conception of adult development. *American Psychologist, 41,* 3–13.

Levinson, D. J., Darrow, C. M., Klein, E. G., Levinson, M. H., & Levitt, M. (1986). Social network relationships as sources of maternal support and well-being. *Developmental Psychology, 22,* 310–316.

Levitt, M. (1986). Social network relationships as sources of maternal support and well-being. *Developmental Psychology, 22,* 310–316.

Lewis, M. (1987). Social development in infancy and early childhood. In J. Osofsky (Ed.), *Handbook of infant development* (2nd ed., pp. 419–493). New York: Wiley.

Lewis, M. & Brooks-Gunn, J. (1979). *Social cognition and the acquisition of self.* New York: Plenum.

Libassi, M. F. (1990). Psychopharmacology in social work education (Contract No. 89MF700390ID). Washington, DC: National Institute of Mental Health.

Lickey, M. E., & Gordon, B. (1983). *Drugs for mental illness: A revolution in psychiatry.* New York: W. H. Freeman.

Lickona, T. (1983). *Raising good children.* New York: Bantam Books.

Lieberman, A. (1985). Infant mental health: A model for service delivery. *Journal of Clinical Child Psychology, 14,* 196–201.

Lieberman, A. F. (1977). Preschoolers' competence with a peer: Relations with attachment and peer experience. *Child Development, 48,* 1277–1287.

Lieberman, A. F. (1993). *The emotional life of the toddler.* New York: Free Press.

Limbo, R., & Wheeler, S. (1986). *When a baby dies: A handbook for healing and helping.* LaCrosse, WI: Resolve Through Sharing.

Lindemann, E. (1944). Symptomatology and management of acute grief. *American Journal of Psychiatry, 101,* 141–148.

Lindgren, H. C. (1969). *An introduction to social psychology.* New York: Wiley.

Lindsey, K. (1982). *Friends or family.* Boston: Beacon Press.

Linet, M. S., Stewart, W. F., Celentano, D. D., Ziegler, D., & Sprecher, M. (1989). An epidemiological study of headaches among adolescents and young adults. *Journal of the American Medical Association, 261,* 2211–2216.

Link, B., et al. (1995). Lifetime and five-year prevalence of homelessness in the United States: New evidence of an old debate. *American Journal of Orthopsychiatry, 65,* 347–354.

Lipkin, R. (1995, April 8). Sea worms and plants spur new drugs. *Science News,* p. 212.

Lippa, R. A. (1994). *Introduction to social psychology.* Pacific Grove, CA: Brooks/Cole.

Lipsitz, J. (1980). *Sexual development in young adolescents.* Invited speech given at the meeting of the American Association for Moral Education, Pittsburgh, PA.

Little, R., & Ervin, C. (1984). *Alcohol problems in women.* New York: Guilford Press.

Littrell, J. (1991). *Understanding and treating alcoholism.* Hillsdale, NJ: Erlbaum.

Littrell, J. & Ashford, J. B. (1994). Duty of social workers to refer for medications: A study of field supervisors. *Social Work Research, 18,* 123–128.

Littrell, J., & Beck, E. (2000). Perceiving oppression: Relationships with resilience, self-esteem, depressive symptoms, and reliance on God in African-American homeless men. *Journal of Sociology and Social Welfare, 26,* 137–158.

Litwak, E., & Szelenyi, I. (1969). Primary group structures and their functions: Kin, neighbors, and friends. *American Sociological Review, 34,* 465–481.

Locust, C. (1988). Wounding the spirit: Discrimination and traditional American Indian belief systems. *Harvard Educational Review, 58,* 315–330.

Loftus, E. F. (1993, May). The reality of repressed memories. *American Psychologist, 48,* 518–537.

Loney, J., & Ordona, T. (1975). Using cerebral stimulants to treat minimal brain dysfunction. *American Journal of Orthopsychiatry, 45,* 564–572.

Long, N., & Forehand, R. (1987). The effects of parental divorce and parental conflict on children: An overview. *Journal of Development and Behavioral Pediatrics, 815,* 292–296.

Longino, C. F., & Kart, C. S. (1982). Explicating activity theory: Formal replication. *Journal of Gerontology, 37,* 713–722.

Longres, J. F. (1995). *Human behavior in the social environment.* Itasca: Peacock.

Lonner, W. J., Thorndike, R. M., Forbes, N. E., & Ashworth, C. (1985). The influence of television on measured cognition abilities. A study with native Alaska children. *Journal of Cross-Cultural Psychology, 16,* 355–380.

Lopata, H. Z., & Barnewolt, D. (1984). The middle years: Changes and variations in social-role commitments. In G. Baruch & J. Brooks-Gunn (Eds.), *Women in midlife.* New York: Plenum.

Lorenz, F. O., Simons, R. C., Conger, R. D., Elder, G. H., Jr., Johnson, C., & Chao, W. (1997). Married and recently divorced mothers' stressful events and distress: Tracing change across time. *Journal of Marriage and the family, 59,* 219-232.

Los Angeles Times (1996). Series. *The brain: A work in progress.* http://www.csaf.org/brain.

Lowenberg, F. (1988). *Religion and social work practice in contemporary American society.* New York: Columbia University Press.

Lowery, E. H. (1993). *Freedom and Community: The Ethics of Interdependence.* Albany: State University of New York Press.

Lozoff, B. (1983). Birth and bonding in non-industrial societies. *Developmental Medicine and Child Neurology, 25,* 595-600.

Luborsky, M., & Rubinstein, R. L. (1987). Ethnicity and lifetimes: Self-concepts and situational contexts of ethnic identity in late life. In D. E. Gelfand & C. M. Barresi (Eds.), *Ethnic dimensions of aging.* New York: Springer.

Luborsky, M. R. & Rubinstein, R. L. (1990). Ethnic identity and bereavement in later life: The case of older widowers. In J. Sokolovsky (Ed.), *The Cultural Context of Aging* (pp. 229-240). New York: Bergin & Garvey.

Ludington-Hoe, S. & Golant, S. (1993). *Kangaroo care: The best you can do to help your preterm infant.* New York: Bantam Books.

Ludwig, A. M. (1986). *Principles of clinical psychiatry* (2nd ed.). New York: Free Press.

Luey, H. S.; Glass, L., & Elliott, H. (1995). Hard-of-hearing or deaf: Issues of ears, language, culture, and identity, *Social Work, 40,* 2, 177-182.

Lukes, S. (1991). *Moral conflict and politics.* Oxford: Clarendon Press.

Lumsden, C. J., & Wilson, E. O. (1981). *Genes, mind, and culture: The coevolutionary process.* Cambridge, MA: Harvard University Press.

Lunneborg, P. (1992). *Abortion: A positive decision.* New York: Bergin & Garvey.

Lupsey, D. K. (1991). Egocentrism theory and the "new look" at the imaginary audience and personal fable in adolescence. In R. M. Lerner, A. C. Petersen & J. Brooks-Gum (Eds.), *Encyclopedia of Adolescence.* New York: Garland.

Luria, A. (1961). *The role of speech in the regulation of normal and abnormal behaviors.* New York: Liveright.

Lustig, J. L., Wolchik, S. A., Braver, S. L. (1992). Social support in cumships and adjustment in children of divorce. *American Journal of Community Psychology, 20,* 393-399.

Lye, D. N. (1996). Adult child-parent relationships. *Annual Review of Sociology, 22,* 79-102.

Lyman, D. R., & Selman, R. L. (1985). Peer conflict in pair therapy: Clinical and developmental analyses. In M. W. Berkowitz (Ed.), *Peer conflict and psychological growth* (New directions for child development, No. 29). San Francisco: Jossey-Bass.

Lyman, S. B., & Bird, G. W. (1996). A closer look at self-image in male foster care adolescents. *Social Work, 41,* 85-96.

Lynch, M., Roberts, J., & Gordon, M. (1976). Child abuse: Early warning in the maternity hospital. *Developmental Medicine and Child Neurology, 18,* 759-766.

Lyon, D., & Greenberg, J. (1991). Evidence of codependency in women with an alcoholic parent: Helping out Mr. Wrong. *Journal of Personality and Social Psychology, 61,* 435-439.

Lyons, P., Wodarski, J. S., & Feit, M. D. (1998). Human behavior theory: Emerging trends and issues. *Journal of Human Behavior in the Social Environment, 1,* 1-21.

Lyons-Ruth, K., Connell, D. B., Grunebaum, H. U., & Botein, S. (1990). Infants at social risk: Maternal depression and family support services as mediators of infant development and security of attachment. *Child Development, 9,* 225-235.

Lyons-Ruth, K., & Zeanah, C. (1993). The family context of infant mental health: I. Affective development in the primary caregiving relationship.

In C. Zeanah (Ed.), *Handbook of infant mental health* (pp. 14-37). New York: Guilford Press.

Lyotard, J. F. (1984). *The postmodern critique: A report on knowledge* (G. Bennington and B. Massumi, Trans.). Minneapolis: University of Minnesota Press.

Lytle, L. D., Messing, R. B., Fisher, L., & Phebus, L. (1975). Effects of long-term corn consumption on brain serotonin and the response to electric shock. *Science, 190,* 692-694.

Maas, H. (1989). Social responsibility in middle age: Prospects and preconditions. In S. Hunter and M. Sundel (Eds.), *Midlife myths: Issues, findings, and practice implications.* Newbury Park, CA: Sage.

Maccoby, E. E. (1980). *Social development: Psychological growth and the parent-child relationship.* San Diego: Harcourt Brace Jovanovich.

Maccoby, E. E., & Jacklin, C. N. (1974). *The psychology of sex differences.* Palo Alto, CA: Stanford University Press.

Maccoby, E. E., & Martin, J. A. (1983). Socialization in the context of the family: Parent-child interaction. In P. H. Mussen (Ed.), *Handbook of child psychology* (4th ed., Vol 4). New York: Wiley.

MacDonald, K. (1987). Parent-child physical play with rejected, neglected, and popular boys. *Developmental Psychology, 23,* 705-711.

Mace, N. C., & Rabins, P. V. (1981). *The 36-hour day.* Baltimore: Johns Hopkins University Press.

Macht, M. W., & Ashford, J. B. (1991). *Introduction to social work and social welfare.* New York: Merrill/Macmillan.

MacIver, R. M. (1948). *The more perfect union: A program for the control of inter-group discrimination in the United States.* New York: Macmillan.

MacIver, D. J., Reuman, D. A., & Main, S. R. (1995). Social structuring of the school: Studying what is, illuminating what could be. *Annual Review of Psychology, 46,* 375-400.

Madon, S., Jussim, L., Eccles, J. (1997). In search of the powerful self-fulfilling prophecy. *Journal of Personality and Social Psychology, 72,* 791-809.

Madsen, M. C., & Shapira, A. (1970). Cooperative and competitive behavior of urban Afro-American, Anglo-American, Mexican-American, and Mexican village children. *Developmental Psychology, 3,* 16-20.

Magnusson, D., & Cairns, R. B. (1996). Developmental science: Toward a unified framework. In R. B. Cairns, G. H. Elder, Jr., & Costello, (Eds.), *Developmental Sciences* (pp. 7-30). New York: Cambridge University Press.

Magnusson, D., & Torestad, B. (1992). The individual as an interactive agent in the environment. In W. B. Walsh, R. H. Price, & K. H. Craik (Eds.), *Person-environment psychology: Models and perspectives* (pp. 89-127). Hillsdale, NJ: Lawrence Erlbaum Associates.

Main, M., & Solomon, J. (1986). Discovery of an insecure, disorganized/disoriented attachment pattern: Procedures, findings, and implications for the classification of behavior. In M. Yogman & T. B. Brazelton (Eds.), *Affective development in infancy* (pp. 95-124). Norwood, NJ: Ablex.

Main, M., & Solomon, J. (1990). Procedures for identifying infants as disorganized/disoriented during the Ainsworth Strange Situation. In M. T. Greenberg, D. Cicchetti, & E. M. Cummings (Eds.), *Attachment in the preschool years* (pp. 121-160). Chicago: University of Chicago Press.

Maluccio, A. N. (1981). *Promoting competence in clients—A new/old approach for social work practice.* New York: Free Press.

Manton, K. G., Blazer, D. G., & Woodbury, M. A. (1987). Suicide in middle-age and later life: Sex and race specific life table and cohort analyses. *Journal of Gerontology, 42,* 219-227.

Marcia, J. (1966). Development and validation of ego-identity status. *Journal of Personality and Social Psychology, 3,* 551-558.

Marcia, J. (1987). The identity status approach to the study of ego identity development. In T. Honess & K. Yardley (Eds.), *Self and identity: Perspectives across the lifespan.* London: Routledge & Kegan Paul.

Mare, R. D., & Winship, C. (1988). Ethnic and racial patterns of educational attainment and school enrollment. In G. D. Sandefur & M. Tienda (Eds.), *Divided opportunities* (pp. 173-195). New York: Plenum.

Marin, B. V., Holmes, D. L., Guth, M., & Kovac, P. (1979). The potential of children as eyewitnesses. *Law and Human Behavior, 3,* 295-305.

Markezich, A. (1996). Learning windows and the child's brain. Available at: http://supcrkids.com/aweb/pages/features/early1/early1.shtml.

Markham, L. R. (1984). De dog and de cat: Assisting speakers of Black English as they begin to write. *Young Children, 39,* 15-24.

Markides, K. S. (1990). Risk factors, gender, and health. *Generations, 14,* 17-21.

Markides, K. S., & Mindel, C. H. (1987). *Aging and ethnicity.* Newbury Park, CA: Sage.

Markowitz, L. M. (1991, November/December). After the trauma. *Family Therapy Networker,* pp. 30-37.

Marks, R. (1988, Spring). Coming out. *Out/Look.*

Marlowe, M. (1985). Low lead exposure and learning disabilities. *Research Communications in Psychology, Psychiatry and Behavior, 10,* 153-169.

Marrale, J. C., Shipman, J. H., & Rhodes, M. L. (1986). What some college students eat. *Nutrition Today, 21*(1), 16-21.

Marsiglio, W., & Donnelly, D. (1992). Sexual relations in later life: A national study of married persons. *Journal of Gerontology, 46,* 334-338.

Martin, S. (1995 October). Interventions that work for stepfamilies. *APA Monitor,* pp. 34-36.

Martin, S. (1995 October). Practitioners may misunderstand black families. *APA Monitor,* p. 36.

Martin, T. C., & Bumpass, L. L. (1989). Recent trends in marital disruption. *Demography, 26,* 37-51.

Martinez, F. (1996, May). *Can SIDS be prevented?* Presented at the Pediatric Specialty Conference, University Medical Center, Tucson, Arizona.

Maslow, A. H. (1962). *Toward a psychology of being.* Princeton, NJ: Van Nostrand.

Mason, C. & Elwood, R. (1995). Is there a psychological basis for the couvade and onset of paternal care? *International Journal of Nursing Studies, 32,* 137-148.

Mason, J. (1991). Reducing infant mortality in the United States through Healthy Start. *Public Health Reports, 106,* 479-483.

Masten, A. S., Best, K. M., & Garmezy, N. (1991). Resilience and development: Contributions from the study of children who overcome adversity. *Development and Psychopathology, 2,* 425-444.

Masters, J. C., & Furman, W. (1981). Popularity, individual friendship selection, and specific peer interaction among children. *Developmental Psychology, 17,* 344-350.

Masters, W. H., & Johnson, V. E. (1966). *Human sexual response.* Boston: Little, Brown.

Matas, L., Arend, R. A., & Stroufe, L. A. (1978). Continuity of adaptation in the second year: The relationship between quality of attachment and later competence. *Child Development, 49,* 547-556.

Matejcek, A., Dytrych, Z., & Schuller, V. (1979). The Prague study of children born from unwanted pregnancies.

Mattson, S. N., & Riley, E. P. (1998). A review of the neurobehavioral deficits in children with fetal alcohol syndrome or prenatal exposure to alcohol. *Alcoholism: Clinical and Experimental Research, 22,* 279-294.

Mawson, A. R., & Jacobs, K. W. (1978). Corn, trypotopha, and homicide. *Journal of Orthomolecular Psychiatry, 7,* 227-230.

Maxmen, J. S. (1986). *Essential psychopathology.* New York: Norton.

Maxmen, J. S., & Ward, N. (1995). *Essential psychopathology and its treatment.* New York: Norton.

Maxwell, M. (Ed.). (1991). *The sociobiological imagination.* Albany: State University of New York Press.

May, K., & Perrin, S. (1985). Prelude: Pregnancy and birth. In S. M. Hanson & F. W. Boxelt (Eds.), *Dimensions of fatherhood* (pp. 64-91). Beverly Hills, CA: Sage.

Maziade, M. (1987). Influence of gentle birth delivery procedures and other perinatal circumstances on infant temperament—Developmental and social implications. *Annual Progress in Child Psychiatry and Child Development,* 291-295.

Maziade, M., Caron, C., Cote, R., Merette, C., Bernier, H., Laplante, B., Boutin, P., & Thivierge, J. (1990). Psychiatric status of adolescents who had extreme temperaments at age 7. *American Journal of Psychiatry, 147,* 1531-1536.

McCamman, S., Rues, J., & Cannon S. (1988). Prader-Willi syndrome intervention approaches based on differential phase characteristics. *Topics in Clinical Nutrition, 3,* 1-8.

McCarthy, K. (1990, November). If one spouse is sick, both are affected. *APA Monitor,* p. 7.

McConachie, H. (1986). *Parents and young mentally handicapped children: A review of research issues.* Brookline, MA: Brookline Books.

McCord, J. (1990). Problem behaviors. In S. Feldman & G. R. Elliott (Eds.), *At the threshold: The developing adolescent.* Cambridge, MA: Harvard University Press.

McCoy, C. R. (1999, June 29). Mom pleads guilty to killing 8 kids: 70-year-old gets house arrest, probation. *The Arizona Republic,* p. A1.

McCreary, M. L., Slavin, L. A., & Berry, E. J. (1996). Predicting problem behavior and self-esteem among African American adolescents. *Journal of Adolescent Research, 11(2),* 216-234.

McCullough, M. E., Worthington, E. L., Everett, L. Jr., & Rachal, K. C. (1997). Interpersonal forgiving in close relationships. *Journal of Personality and Social Psychology, 73(2),* 321-336.

McDavid, J. W., & Harari, H. (1973). Stereotyping in names and popularity in grade school children. *Child Development, 37,* 453-459.

McEntee, M. K. (1995). Deaf and hard-of-hearing clients: Some legal implications, *Social Work, 40, 2,* 183-187.

McFarlane, J., Parker, B., Soeken, K., & Bullock, L. (1992). Assessing for abuse during pregnancy: Severity and frequency of injuries and associated entry into prenatal care. *Journal of the American Medical Association, 267,* 3176-3178.

McGinnis, J., & Foeye, W. (1993). Actual causes of death in the United States. *Journal of the American Medical Association, 270,* 2208-2218.

McGrath, J. E. (1984). *Groups: Interaction and performance.* Englewood Cliffs, NJ: Prentice Hall.

McGregor, D. (1960). *The human side of enterprise.* New York: McGraw-Hill.

McIntosh, P. (1995). White privilege and male privilege: A personal account of coming to see correspondences through work in women studies. In M. L. Andersen & P. H. Collins (Eds.), *Race, class, and gender: An anthology.* Belmont, CA: Wadsworth.

McKain, W. C. (1972). A new look at older marriages. *The Family Coordinator, 21,* 61-69.

McKee, B. (1974). The psychosocial development of men in early adulthood and the midlife transition. In D. F. Ricks, A. Thomas, & M. Roff (Eds.), *Life history research in psychopathology* (Vol. 3). Minneapolis: University of Minnesota Press.

McLaughlin, B. (1983). Child compliance to parental control techniques. *Developmental Psychology, 19,* 667-673.

McLemore, S. D. (1991). *Racial and ethnic relations in America.* Boston: Allyn & Bacon.

McLoyd, V. C. (1998). Socioeconomic disadvantage and child development. *American Psychologist, 53,* 185-204.

McManus, M. C. (1991). Serving lesbian and gay youth. *Focal Point, 5,* 1-4.

McNeil, D. (1992). Uncertainties, waiting, and possibilities: Experiences of becoming a mother with an infant in the NICU. *Neonatal Network, 11,* 78.

McQuaide, S. (1998). Women at midlife. *Social Work, 43,* 21-32.

Mehrabian, A. (1969). Significance of posture and position in the communication of attitude and status relationships. *Psychological Bulletin, 71,* 359-372.

Mehrabian, A. (1972). *Nonverbal communication.* Chicago: Aldine-Atherton.

Meilman, P. W. (1979). Cross-sectional age changes in ego identity status during adolescence. *Developmental Psychology, 15,* 230-231.

Melton, G. B., Petrila, J., Poythress, N. G., & Slobogin, C. (1987). *Psychological evaluations for the courts.* New York: Guilford Press.

Meltzoff, A., & Borton, R. (1979). Intermodal matching by human neonates. *Nature, 282,* 403-404.

Meltzoff, A., & Moore, M. (1977). Imitation of facial and manual gestures by human neonates. *Science, 198,* 75-78.

Meltzoff, A., & Moore, M. (1983). Newborn infants imitate adult facial gestures. *Child Development, 54,* 702-709.

Menaghan, E. G., & Lieberman, M. A. (1986). Changes in depression following divorce: A panel study. *Journal of Marriage and the Family, 45,* 371-386.

Meredith, H. V. (1978). Research between 1969 and 1970 on the standing height of young children in different parts of the world. In H. W. Reece & L. P. Lipsitt (Eds.), *Advances in child development and behavior* (Vol. 12). New York: Academic Press.

Meyers, D. G., & Jeeves, M. A. (1987). *Psychology through the eyes of faith.* San Francisco: Harper and Row.

Meyers, J. S. (1972). *An orientation to chronic disease and disability.* New York: Macmillan.

Meyers, R. (1978, November). A couple that could. *Psychology Today,* pp. 99-108.

Mildred, S., & Hooper, C. R. (1993, July/August). The ancient Apache ceremony of changing woman. *Southwest Passages,* p. 64.

Miller, B. (1992). Adolescent parenthood: Economic issues and social policies. *Journal of Family and Economic Issues, 13,* 467-475.

Miller, B. C. (1976). A multivariate developmental model of marital satisfaction. *Journal of Marriage and the Family, 38,* 643-657.

Miller, B. C., McCoy, J. K., & Olson, T. D. (1986). Dating age and stage as correlates of adolescent sexual attitudes and behavior. *Journal of Adolescent Research, 1,* 361-371.

Miller, C. A. (1992). Biophysical development during late adulthood. In C. S. Schuster & S. S. Ashburn (Eds.), *The process of human development: A holistic life-span approach* (3rd ed., pp. 804-830). Philadelphia: Lippincott.

Miller, G. A. (1956). The magical number, seven, plus or minus two: Some limits on our capacity for processing information. *Psychological Review, 63,* 81-97.

Minnett, A. M., Vanell, D. L., & Santrock, J. W. (1983). The effects of sibling status on sibling interaction: Influence of birth order, age, spacing, sex of the child, and sex of the sibling. *Child Development, 54,* 1064-1072.

Minuchin, P. P. (1977). *The middle years of childhood.* Pacific Grove, CA: Brooks/Cole.

Minuchin, P. P., and Shapiro, E. K. (1983). The school as a context for social development. In P. H. Mussen (Ed.), *Handbook of child psychology: Vol. 4. Socialization, personality, and social development.* New York: Wiley.

Minuchin, S. (1974). *Families and family therapy.* Cambridge, MA: Harvard University Press.

Mitchell, J. (1993). *Pregnant, substance-using women.* Rockville, MD: U.S. Department of Health and Human Services, Substance Abuse and Mental Health Services Administration.

Mitiguy, J. S. (1990, Fall). Coping with survival. *Headlines: The Brain Injury Magazine,* pp. 2-8.

Mitrushina, M., & Satz, P. (1991). Reliability and validity of the mini-mental status exam in neurologically intact elderly. *Journal of Clinical Psychology, 47,* 537-543.

Moffitt, L. C. (1996). *Connected community: Subtle forces in a systematic web.* New York: Nova Science Publishers, Inc.

Moffit, T. E., Lynam, D. R., & Silva, P. (1994). Neuropsychological tests predicting persistent male delinquency. *Criminology. 32,* 277-300.

Molidor, C. E. (1996). Female gang members: A profile of aggression and victimization. *Social Work, 41, 3,* 251-257.

Mollica, R., Streets, F., Boscarino, J., & Redlich, F. (1986). A community study of formal pastoral counseling activities of the clergy. *American Journal of Psychiatry, 143,* 323-329.

Monahan, D. J., & Hooker, K. (1995). Health of spouse caregivers of dementia patients: The role of personality and social support. *Social Work, 40, 3,* 305-314.

Monat, A., & Lazarus, R. S. (1977). *Stress and coping: An anthology.* New York: Columbia University Press.

Money, J. (1988). *Gay, straight, and in-between: The sexology of erotic orientation.* New York: Oxford University Press.

Montemayer, R. (1983). Parents and adolescents in conflict: All families some of the time and some families most of the time. *Journal of Early Adolescence, 3,* 83-103.

Morey, L. C., & Ochoa, E. S. (1989). An investigation of adherence to diagnostic criteria: Clinical diagnosis of the DSM-III personality disorders. *Journal of Personality Disorders, 3,* 180-192.

Morris, R. (1996). The world is a box of crayons. In P. R. Popple & L. Leighninger (Eds.), *Social work, social welfare, and American society* (pp. 645-647). Boston: Allyn & Bacon.

Morrison, R. S., Olson, E., Mertz, K. R., & Meier, D. E. (1995). The inaccessibility of advance directives on transfer from ambulatory to acute care settings. *Journal of the American Medical Association, 274,* 478-482.

Mrazek, P. (1993). Maltreatment and infant development. In C. Zeaneh (Ed.), *Handbook of infant mental health* (pp. 73-86). New York: Guilford Press.

Muehlenhard, C. L., & Linton, M. A. (1987). Date rape and sexual aggression in dating situations: Incidence and risk factors. *Journal of Counseling Psychology, 34,* 186-196.

Mueller, E., & Lucas, F. (1975). A developmental analysis of peer interaction among toddlers. In M. Lewis & L. Rosenglum (Eds.), *Friendship and peer relations.* New York: Wiley-Interscience.

Mueller, E., & Vandell, D. (1979). Infant-infant interaction. In J. D. Osofsy (Ed.), *Handbook of infant development.* New York: Wiley.

Munley, A. (1983). *The hospice alternative.* New York: Basic Books.

Murray, B. (1996, July). Getting children off of the couch and onto the filed, *APA Monitor,* pp. 42-43.

Murray, B. (1997a, September). School phobias hold many children back. *APA Monitor,* pp. 38-39.

Murray, B. (1997b, October). Elderly people alter their social priorities as they age. *APA Monitor,* p. 25.

Murray, B. (1999). Via the telephone, group support reaches cancer patients who might otherwise go without it. *APA Monitor.*

Murray, L., Cowley, A. F., Hooper, R., & Cooper, P. (1996). The impact of postnatal depression and associated adversity on early mother-infant interactions and later infant outcome. *Child Development, 67,* 2512-2526.

Mussen, P. H. (1974). *Child development and personality* (6th ed). New York: Harper & Row.

Mutryn, C. (1993). Psychosocial impact of cesarean section on the family: A literature review. *Social Science and Medicine, 37,* 1271-1282.

Myers, B. (1982). Early intervention using Brazelton training with middle-class mothers and fathers of newborns. *Child Development, 53,* 462-471.

Myers, B., Jarvis, P., & Creasey, G. (1987). Infants' behavior with their mothers and grandmothers. *Infant Behavior and Development, 10,* 245-259.

Nagy, M. H. (1959). The child's view of death. In H. Feifel (Ed.), *The meaning of death* (pp. 79-98). New York: McGraw-Hill.

Nakagawa, M. (1993). Community leaders, police talk, hate crimes. *Asian Week,* p. 12.

Nash, J. (1997, February 3) "Fertile minds." *Time, 149,* 48-56.

Nash, J. M. (1995, April 3). To know your own fate. *Time,* p. 62.

Nash, M. (1989). *The cauldron of ethnicity in the modern world.* Chicago: University of Chicago Press.

National Cancer Institute Surveillance, Epidemiology End Results Programs. (1997). National Cancer Institute.

National Center for Environmental Health. (1999, August 1). Asthma: A public health response. Available at: http://www.cdc.gov/nceh/programs/asthma/default.htm.

National Center for Health Statistics. (1998, August 27). Update on risk factors for infant mortality. [On-line]. *Supplement, Infant Mortality Statistics From the 1996 Period Linked Birth/Infant Death Data Set, 46,(12)*.

National Center on Child Abuse and Neglect. (1994). *Child maltreatment 1992: Reports from the states to the National Center on Child Abuse and Neglect*. Washington, DC: Government Printing Office.

National Council on Hopelessness. (1995). *Domestic violence and hopelessness*. National Council Fact Sheet on the Internet.

National Education Goals Pavel (1997). Survey. http://www.gwu.edu.

National Institute of Mental Health. (1991). *Caring for people with severe mental disorders: A national plan of research to improve services* (DHHS Publication No. ADM 91-1762). Washington, DC: U.S. Government Printing Office.

National Institute on Alcohol Abuse and Alcoholism (1995). *The physicians' guide to helping people with alcohol related problems*. Washington, DC: United States Department of Health and Human Services.

National Law Center on Homelessness and Poverty. (1996). *Mean sweeps: A report on anti-homelessness laws, litigation and alternatives in 50 United States cities*. Washington, D.C.: National Law Center on Homelessness and Poverty.

National Organization for Women. (1995). *Violence against women in the United States*. NOW home page on the Internet.

National Research Council. (1993). *Losing generations: Adolescents in high-risk settings*. Washington, DC: National Academy Press.

Neason, S. (1994). *Prader-Willi syndrome: A handbook for parents*. St. Louis, MO: Prader-Willi Syndrome Association.

Neimark, E. D. (1975). Longitudinal development of formal operational thought. *Genetic Psychology Monographs, 91*, 171-225.

Netting, F. E., Kettner, P. M., McMurtry, S. L. (1993). *Social Work Macro Practice*. White Plains, NY: Longman.

Neugarten, B. L. (1968). The awareness of middle age. In B. L. Neugarten (Ed.), *Middle age and aging* (pp. 93-98). Chicago: University of Chicago Press.

Neugarten, B. L. (1969). Continuities and discontinuities of psychological issues into adult life. *Human Development, 12*, 121-130.

Neugarten, B. L. (1974). Age groups in American society and the rise of the young old. *Annals of the American Academy of Political and Social Science*, 187-198.

Neugarten, B. L. (1986). The aging society. In A. Pifer & D. L. Bronte (Eds.), *Our aging society: Paradox and promise*. New York: Norton.

Neugarten, B. L. & Weinstein, K. (1964). The changing American grandparent. *Journal of Marriage and the Family, 26*, 199-204.

Newberger, E. H., Barkan, S. E., Lieberman, E. S., McCormick, M. C., Yllo, K., Gary, L. T., & Schechter, S. (1992). Abuse of pregnant women and adverse birth outcome [Commentary]. *Journal of the American Medical Association, 267*, 2370-2372.

Newcomb, M. D., Huba, G. J., & Bentler, P. M. (1986). Determinants of sexual and dating behaviors among adolescents. *Journal of Personality and Social Psychology, 50*, 428-438.

Newman, B. M., & Newman, P. R. (1987). *Development through life: A psychosocial approach* (4th ed.). Pacific Grove, CA: Brooks/Cole.

Newman, B. M., & Newman, P. R. (1991). *Development through life: A psychosocial approach* (5th ed.). Pacific Grove, CA: Brooks/Cole.

Newman, B. M., & Newman, P. R. (1995). *Development through life: A psychosocial approach* (6th ed.). Pacific Grove, CA: Brooks/Cole.

Newman, B. M., & Newman, P. R. (1999). *Development through life: A psycholosocial approach* (7th edition). Belmont: Brooks Cole/ Wadsworth.

Newman, B. S. (1994). Diversity and populations at risk: Gays and lesbians. In F. G. Reamer (Ed.), *The foundations of social work knowledge*. New York: Columbia University Press.

Newman, L., & Buka, S. (1991, Spring). Clipped wings: The fullest look yet at how prenatal exposure to drugs, alcohol and nicotine hobbles children's learning. *American Educator*, pp. 27-42.

Newsweek (1988). December 5, pp. 24, 29.

Nickerson, E. T., & Pitochelli, E. T. (1978). *Learned helplessness and depression in married women: Marriage as a depressing life style for women*. Paper presented at the meeting of the Eastern Psychological Association, Washington, DC.

Nicol, S. E., & Gottesman, I. I. (1983). Clues to the genetics and neurobiology of schizophrenia. *American Scientist, 71*, 398-404.

Nielsen Media Research. (1998). *1998 report on television*. New York: Author.

Nieto, A., Matorras, R., Villar, J., & Serra, M. (1998). Neonatal morbidity associated with disproportionate intrauterine growth retardation at term. *Journal of Obstetrics and Gynecology, 18*, 540-544.

Niven, C., Wiszniewski, C., & AlRoomi, L. (1993). Attachment (bonding) in mothers of pre-term babies. *Journal of Reproductive and Infant Psychology, 11*, 175-185.

Noe, R. A. (1988). Women and mentoring: A review and research agenda. *Academy of Management Review, 13*, 65-78.

Norton, D., Brown, E. F., Brown, E. G., Francis, E. A., Murase, K., & Valle, R. (1978). *The dual perspective: Inclusion of ethnic minority content in the social work curriculum*. New York: Council on Social Work Education.

Nuckolls, K. B., Cassel, J., & Kaplan, B. H. (1972). Psychosocial assets, life crises, and the prognosis of pregnancy. *American Journal of Epidemiology, 95*, 431-441.

Nurcombe, B., & Gallagher, R. M. (1986). *The clinical process in psychiatry: Diagnosis and management planning*. London: Cambridge University Press.

Oden, S., & Asher, S. R. (1977). Coaching children in social skills for friendship making. *Child Development, 48*, 495-506.

Offer, D., Ostrov, E., & Howard, K. (1981). *The adolescent: A psychological self-portrait*. New York: Basic Books.

O'Hara, M. W., Kohout, F. J., & Wallace, R. B. (1985). Depression among the rural elderly: A study of prevalence and correlates. *The Journal of Nervous and Mental Disease, 173*, 582-589.

Okun, B. F. (1984). *Working with adults: Individual, family, and career development*. Pacific Grove, CA: Brooks/Cole.

Olds, D., & Kitzman, H. (1990). Can home visitation improve the health of women and children at environmental risk? *Pediatrics, 86*, 108-116.

Olsen, J. (1980). Social and psychological correlates of pregnancy resolution among adolescent women: A review. *American Journal of Orthopsychiatry, 50*, 432-445.

Olshansky, E. (1992). Redefining the concepts of success and failure in infertility treatment. *NAACOGS Clinic Issues in Perinatal and Women's Health Nursing, 3*, 13-319.

Olweus, D. (1980). Familial and temperamental determinants of aggressive behavior in adolescent boys: A causal analysis. *Developmental Psychology, 16*, 644-660.

Ongoing efforts to prevent childhood lead exposure. (1999, June). *Journal of Environmental Health, 61*, 44-45.

Opie, I., & Opie, P. (1987). *The love and language of schoolchildren*. New York: Oxford University Press.

Ornish, D. (1997). *Love & survival*. New York: Harper-Collins.

Ornstein, P. (1995, January). New cognitive research making waves. *APA Monitor*.

Orthner, D. (1975). Leisure activity patterns and marital satisfaction over the marital career. *Journal of Marriage and the Family, 37*, 91-102.

Osborn, J. W. (1997). Race and academic disidentification. *Journal of Educational Psychology, 89*, 728-735.

Osofsky, J., Hann, D., & Peebles, C. (1993). Adolescent parenthood: Risks and opportunities for mothers and infants. In C. Zeaneh (Ed.), *Handbook of infant mental health* (pp. 106-119). New York: Guilford Press.

Ostrom, T. (1984). The sovereignty of social cognition. In R. S. Wyer & T. K. Srull (Eds.), *Handbook of social cognition* (Vol. 1, pp. 1-32). Hillsdale, NJ: Erlbaum.

Otto, L. B. (1988). America's youth: A changing profile. *Family Relations, 37*, 385-391.

Ouchi, W. (1981). *Theory Z: How American business can beat the Japanese challenge.* Reading, MA: Addison-Wesley.

Oyserman, D., Radin, N., Benn, R. (1993). Dynamics in a three-generational family: Teens, grandparents, and babies. *Developmental Psychology, 29,* 564-572.

Page, D. S. (1981). *Principles of biological chemistry* (2nd ed.). Boston: Willard Grant Press.

Pahl, J., & Quine, L. (1987). Families with mentally handicapped children. In J. Oxford (Ed.), *Treating the disorder, treating the family* (pp. 39-61). Baltimore: Johns Hopkins University Press.

Pancoast, D. L., & Collins, A. (1987). Natural helping networks. In *Encyclopedia of Social Work* (18th ed., pp. 177-182). Silver Spring, MD: National Association of Social Workers.

Pancoast, D. L., Parker, P., & Froland, C. (1983). *Rediscovering self-help: Its role in social care.* Beverly Hills, CA: Sage.

Pantiel, M. (1995). Should your teen work? *Better Homes and Gardens, 73,* 226-228.

Papousek, H., & Papousek, M. (1982). Integration into the social world: Survey of research. In P. M. Stratton (Ed.), *Psychobiology of human newborn* (pp. 367-390). New York: Wiley.

Papousek, H., & Papousek, M. (1987). Intuitive parenting: A dialectic counterpart to the infant's integrative competence. In J. Osofsky (Ed.), *Handbook of infant development* (2nd ed., pp. 669-720). New York: Wiley.

Papousek, H., & Papousek, M. (1992). Beyond emotional bonding: The role of preverbal communication in mental growth and health. *Infant Mental Health Journal, 13,* 43-53.

Papousek, M., Papousek, H., & Bornstein, M. H. (1985). The naturalistic vocal environment of young infants: On the significance of homogeneity and variability in parental speech. In T. Fields & N. Fox (Eds.), *Social perception in infants* (pp. 269-297). Norwood, NJ: Ablex.

Paris, S. C., & Lindayer, B. K. (1982). The development of cognitive skills during childhood. In B. B. Wolman (Ed.), *Handbook of developmental psychology.* Englewood Cliffs, NJ: Prentice Hall.

Parke, R. D., MacDonald, K., Beital, A., & Bhavangri, N. (1988). The interrelationships among families, fathers, and peers. In R. D. Peters (Ed.), *New approaches to family research.* New York: Brunner/Mazel.

Parke, R. D., & O'Leary, S. (1976). Family interaction in the newborn period: Some findings, some observations and some unresolved issues. In K. Riegel & J. Meacham (Eds.), *The developing individual in a changing world: Vol. 2. Social and environmental issues.* The Hague: Mouton.

Parke, R. D., & Slaby, R. G. (1983). The development of aggression. In P. H. Mussen (Ed.), *Handbook of child psychology* (4th ed., Vol. 4). New York: Wiley.

Parke, R. D., & Tinsley, B. (1987). Family interaction in infancy. In J. Osofsky (Ed.), *Handbook of infant development* (2nd ed., pp. 579-641). New York: Wiley.

Parker, B., McFarlane, J., Soeken, K., Torres, S., & Campbell, D. (1993). Physical and emotional abuse in pregnancy: A comparison of adult and teenage women. *Nursing Research, 42,* 173-177.

Parker, J. G., & Gottman, J. M. (1989). Social and emotional development in a relational context: Friendship interaction from early childhood to adolescence. In T. J. Berndt & G. W. Ladd (Eds.), *Peer relations in child development.* New York: Wiley.

Parrot, A., & Bechhofer, L. (1991). *Acquaintance rape.* New York: Wiley.

Parsons, J. E., Adler, T. F., & Kaczala, C. M. (1982a). Socialization of achievement attitudes and beliefs: Parental influences. *Child Development, 53,* 308-318.

Parsons, J. E., Adler, T. F., & Kaczala, C. M. (1982b). Socialization of achievement attitudes and beliefs: Parental influences. *Child Development, 53,* 322-329.

Parten, M. (1932). Social play among preschool children. *Journal of Abnormal and Social Psychology, 27,* 243-269.

Partners Task Force. *Legal marriage?* Box 9685, Seattle, WA 98109.

Pasui, K., & McFarland, K. F. (1997). Management of diabetes in pregnancy. *American Family Physician, 55,* 2731-2739.

Paternoster, R., & Brame, R. (1997). Multiple routes to delinquency? A test of developmental and general theories of crime. *Criminology, 35,* 49-84.

The Patient Self-Determination Act of 1990, 4206, 4751 of the *Omnibus Reconciliation Act of 1990,* PL No. 101-508 (November 5, 1990).

Patterson, G. R. (1982). *A social learning approach to family interventions: Vol. 3. Coercive family process.* Eugene, OR: Castalia.

Patterson, G. R. (1986). Performance models for antisocial boys. *American Psychologist, 41,* 432-444.

Patterson, G. R., DeBarsyshe, B. D., & Ramsey, E. (1989). A developmental perspective on antisocial behavior. *American Psychologist, 44,* 329-335.

Patterson, J. M., & McCubbin, H. I. (1987). Adolescent coping style and behaviors: Conceptualization and measurement. *Journal of Adolescence, 10,* 163-186.

Patterson, S., Brennan, E., Germain, C., & Memmot, J. (1988). The effectiveness of rural natural helpers. *Social Casework, 69,* 272-279.

Patterson, S. L. (1987). Older rural natural helpers: Gender and site differences in the helping process. *The Gerontologist, 27,* 639-644.

Pattison, E. M. (1978). The living-dying process. In C. A. Garfield (Ed.), *Psychosocial care of the dying patient* (pp. 145-153). New York: McGraw-Hill.

Paulson, R., & Sauer, M. (1991). Counseling the infertile couple: When enough is enough. *Obstetrics and Gynecology, 78,* 462-464.

Pavenstedt, E. (1965). A comparison of the child-rearing environment of upper-lower and very low lower—class families. *American Journal of Orthopsychiatry, 35,* 89-98.

Pawlak, E. J., & Cousins, L. (1999). School social work: Organizational perspectives. In R. Constable, S. McDonald, & J. P. Flynn (Eds.), *School social work: Practice, policy and research perspectives.* Chicago: Lyceum Press.

Peak, T., & Toseland, R. W. (1992). Friends don't really understand: The therapeutic benefit of social group work for caregivers of older persons. In C. W. LeCroy (Ed.), *Case studies in social work practice.* Pacific Grove, CA: Brooks/Cole.

Pearlin, L. I., Mullan, J. T., Semple, S. J., & Skaff, M. M. (1990). Caregiving and the stress process: An overview of concepts and their measures. *The Gerontologist, 30,* 583-594.

Pearson, J. L., Hunter, A. G., Ensminger, M. E., & Kellam, S. G. (1990). Black grandmothers in multigenerational households: Diversity in family structure and parenting involvement in the Woodlawn community. *Child Development, 61,* 434-442.

Pecora, P. J., Whittaker, J. K., & Maluccio, A. N. (1992). *The child welfare challenge: Policy, practice and research.* New York: Aldine de Gruyter.

Pederson, F., Cain, R., & Zaslow, M. (1982). Variation in infant experience associated with alternative family roles. In L. Laosa & I. Sigel (Eds.), *The family as a learning environment.* New York: Plenum.

Pedro-Carroll, J. L., & Cowen, E. L. (1985). The children of divorce intervention program: An investigation of the efficacy of a school-based prevention program. *Journal of Consulting and Clinical Psychology, 53,* 603-611.

Pellegrini, D. S. (1990). Psychosocial risk and protective factors in childhood. *Developmental and Behavioral Pediatrics, 11,* 201-209.

Pelton, L. H. (1981). *The social context of child abuse and neglect.* New York: Human Services Press.

Pelzer, D. (1995). *A child called "it."* Deerfield Beach, FL: Health Communications, Inc.

Penfield, W., & Perot, P. (1963). The brain's record of auditory and visual experience. *Brain, 86,* 595-696.

Pennebaker, J. W., Hendler, C. S., Durrett, M. E., & Richards, P. (1981). Social factors influencing absenteeism due to illness in nursery school children. *Child Development, 52,* 692-700.

Peplau, L. A. (1991). Lesbian and gay relationships. In J. C. Gonsiorek & J. D. Weinrich (Eds.), *Homosexuality: Research implications for public policy.* Newbury Park, CA: Sage.

Peplau, L. A., Bikson, T. K., Rook, K. S., & Goodchilds, J. D. (1982). Being old and living alone. In L. A. Peplau, L. A., & D. Perlman (Eds.), *Loneliness: A sourcebook of current theory, research, and therapy.* New York: Wiley-Interscience.

Perlman, H. H. (1959). The role concept and social casework: Some explorations: II What is social diagnosis? *Social Services Review, 33,* 409-414.

Perrow, C. (1978). The short and glorious history of organizational theory. In J. M. Shafritz & P. H. Whitbeck (Eds.), *Classics of organization theory* (pp. 313-323). Belmont, CA: Wadsworth.

Perry, B. D., Pollard, R., Blakely, T., Baker, W., & Vigilante, D. (1995). Childhood trauma, the neurobiology of adaptation and use dependent development of the brain: How states become traits. *Infant Mental Health Journal, 16,* 271-291.

Petersen, A. C. (1987, September). Those gangly years. *Psychology Today,* pp. 28-34.

Petersen, A. C., & Crockett, L. J. (1992). Adolescent sexuality, pregnancy, and child rearing: Developmental perspectives. In M. K. Rosenheim & M. F. Testa (Eds.), *Early parenthood and coming of age in the 1990s.* New Brunswick, NJ: Rutgers University Press.

Petersen, A. C., Kennedy, R. E., & Sullivan, P. (1991). Coping with adolescence. In M. E. Colten & S. Gore (Eds.), *Adolescent stress.* New York: Aldine de Gruyter.

Peterson, D. R. (1992). Interpersonal relationships as a link between person and environment. In W. B. Walsh, R. H. Price, & K. H. Craik (Eds.), *Person-environment psychology: Models and perspectives* (pp. 127-155). Hillsdale, NJ: Lawrence Erlbaum Associates.

Peterson, K. (1993). The homeless mentally ill. In B. S. Johnson (Ed.), *Psychiatric-mental health nursing* (3rd ed., pp. 589-601). Philadelphia: Lippincott.

Petr, C. G. (1998). *Social work with children and their families.* New York: Oxford University Press.

Petri, H. L. (1986). *Motivation: Theory and research* (2nd ed.). Belmont, CA: Wadsworth.

Petrinovich, L. (1995). *Human evolution, reproduction and morality.* New York: Plenum Press.

Pettit, G. S., Dodge, K. A., & Brown, M. M. (1988). Early family experience, social problem-solving patterns, and children's social competence. *Child Development, 59,* 107-120.

Pfohl, B. (1995, May). Is self-esteem really all that important? *APA Monitor.*

Piaget, J. (1929). *The child's conception of the world.* New York: Harcourt Brace.

Piaget, J. (1967). *The child's conception of the world.* Totowa, NJ: Littlefield, Adams.

Piaget, J. (1972). Intellectual evolution from adolescence to adulthood. *Human Development, 15,* 1-12.

Piaget, J., & Inhelder, B. (1969). *The psychology of the child.* New York: Basic Books.

Pindell, T. (1995). *A good place to live: America's last migration.* New York: Henry Holt and Company.

Pinderhughes, E. (1994). Diversity and populations at risk: Ethnic minorities and people of color. In F. G. Reamer (Ed.), *The foundations of social work knowledge.* New York: Columbia University Press.

Pinco, P. (1969). Developmental patterns in marriage. *Family Coordinator, 18,* 135-140.

Pines, M. (1979a). Head start in the nursery. *Psychology Today, 13,* 56.

Pines, M. (1979b, January). Superkids. *Psychology Today,* pp. 53-63.

Pines, M. (1982, June). It's changing the lives of handicapped kids: Infant stimulation. *Psychology Today,* pp. 48-53.

Pipp, S., Easterbrooks, M. A., & Harmon, R. J. (1992). The relation between attachment and knowledge of self and mother in one-to-three-year-old infants. *Child Development, 62,* 738-750.

Pistrang, N. (1995). The partner relationship in psychological response to breast cancer. *Social Science and Medicine, 40,* 789-797.

Pleck, J. H. (1985). *Working wives/working husbands.* Newbury Park, CA: Sage.

Plomin, R. (1990). *Nature and nurture: An introduction to human behavioral genetics.* Belmont, CA: Wadsworth.

Plomin, R. (1994). Nature, nurture, and social development. *Social Development, 3* (1), 37-53.

Plomin, R., & Daniels, D. (1987). Why are children in the same family so different from each other? *Behavioral and Brain Sciences, 10,* 1-16.

Plomin, R., DeFries, J. C., & McClearn, G. E. (1990). *Behavioral genetics: A primer* (2nd ed.). New York: W. H. Freeman.

Potocky, M. (1996). Refugee children: How are they faring economically as adults? *Social Work, 41, 4,* 364-373.

Powell, A. G., Farrar, E., & Cohen, D. K. (1985). *The shopping mall high school: Winners and losers in the educational marketplace.* Boston: Houghton Mifflin.

Power, T. G. (1985). Mother- and father-infant play: A developmental analysis. *Child Development, 56,* 1514-1524.

Power, T. G., & Shanks, J. A. (1989). Parents as socializers: Maternal and paternal views. *Journal of Youth and Adolescence, 18,* 203-220.

Pratt, M. W., McLaren, J., & Wickens, G. (1984). Rules as tools: Effective generalization of verbal self-regulative communication training by first-grade speakers. *Developmental Psychology, 20,* 893-902.

Pritchard, J., MacDonald, P., & Gant, N. (1985). *Williams obstetrics.* Norwalk, CT: Appleton-Century-Crofts.

Proshansky, H., & Newton, P. (1968). The development of Negro self-identity. In M. Deutsch, A. Jensen, & I. Katz (Eds.), *Race and social class in psychological development.* New York: Henry Holt.

Puner, M. (1974). *To the good long life: What we know about growing old.* New York: Universe Books.

Puri, B. K., Lacking, P. J., & Treasaden, I. H. (1996). *Textbook of psychiatry.* New York: Churchill Livingstone.

Quam, J. K. (1983). Older women and informal supports: Impact on prevention. In S. Simson, L. B. Wilson, J. Hermalin, & R. Hess (Eds.), *Aging and prevention: New approaches for preventing health and mental health problems in older adults.* New York: Haworth Press.

Quam, J. K., & Whitford, G. S. (1992). Adaptation and age-related expectations of older gay and lesbian adults. *The Gerontologist, 32,* 367-374.

Quinn, P. (1992). Ethnographic-type techniques in life-span human development courses: Integrating information and developing skills. *Family Relations, 41,* 59-64.

Radke-Yarrow, M., Cummings, E. M., Kuczynski, L., & Chapman, N. (1985). Patterns of attachment in two- and three-year olds in normal families and families with parental depression. *Child Development, 56,* 884-893.

Radke-Yarrow, M., Zahn-Waxler, C., & Chapman, M. (1983). Children's prosocial dispositions and behavior. In P. H. Mussen (Ed.), *Handbook of child psychology* (Vol. 4). New York: Wiley.

Radwin, E. (1993). Literacy and illiteracy. *The new Grolier multimedia encyclopedia* [CD ROM].

Ragozin, A. S., Bashan, R. B., Crnic, K. A., Greenberg, M. T., & Robinson, N. M. (1982). Effects of maternal age on parenting role. *Developmental Psychology, 18,* 627-634.

Raine, A., Brennan, P., & Mednick, S. (1994). Birth complications combined with early maternal rejection at age one year predispose to violent crime at 18 years. *Archives of General Psychiatry, 51,* 984-988.

Ramey, C. T., & Ramey, S. L. (1998a). Early intervention and early experience. *American Psychologist, 53,* 109-120.

Ramey, C. T., & Ramey, S. L. (1998b). Prevention of intellectual disabilities: Early intervention to improve cognitive development. *Preventative Medicine, 27,* 224-232.

Ramey, S. L. (1999). Head Start and preschool education: Toward continued improvement. *American Psychologist, 54,* 344-346.

Ramirez, M. (1978). A mestizo world view and the psychodynamics of Mexican-American border populations. In S. Ross (Ed.), *Views across the border:*

The United States and Mexico. Albuquerque: University of New Mexico Press.

Ramos, S. (1975). *Profile of man and culture in Mexico.* Austin: University of Texas Press.

Rapalje, J., Degelman, D., & Ashburn, S. S. (1986). Psychosocial development during the school-age years. In C. S. Schuster & S. S. Ashburn (Eds.), *The process of human development: A holistic life-span approach.* Boston: Little, Brown.

Rauch, J. (1988). *Genetic content for graduate social work education: Human behavior and the social environment.* Washington DC: Council of Social Work Education.

Ravn, S. H., Rosenberg, J., & Bostofte, E. (1994). Postmenopausal hormone replacement therapy—Clinical implications. *European Journal of Obstetrics, Gynecology, and Reproductive Biology, 53,* 81-93.

Reed, P. (1987). Spirituality and well-being of terminally ill hospital adults. *Research on Nursing and Health, 10,* 335-344.

Reeder, S., Mastroianni, L., & Martin, L. (1983). *Maternity Nursing* (15th ed.). Philadelphia: Lippincott.

Reedy, M. N., Birren, J. E., & Schaie, K. W. (1981). Age and sex differences in satisfying relationships across the adult life span. *Human Development, 24,* 52-66.

Reiss, I. R. (1980). *Family systems in America* (3rd ed.). New York: Holt, Rinehart & Winston.

Reissland, N. (1988). Neonatal imitation in the first hour of life: Observations in rural Nepal. *Developmental Psychology, 24,* 464-469.

Remafedi, G., Farrow, J. A., & Deisher, R. W. (1991). Risk factors for attempted suicide in gay and bisexual youth. *Pediatrics, 87,* 869-875.

Renninger, K. A., & Amsel, E. (1997). Change and development: An introduction. In E. Amsel and K. A. Renninger (Eds.) *Change and development: Issues of theory, method, and application.* Mahwah: Lawrence Erlbaum Associates, Publishers.

Resnick, C., & Tighe, E. G. (1997 January). The role of multidisciplinary community clinics in managed care systems. *Social Work, 42, 1,* 91-98.

Rest, J. R. (1986). *Moral development: Advances in research and theory.* New York: Praeger.

Revelle, G. L., Wellman, H. M., & Karabenick, J. D. (1985). Comprehension monitoring in preschool children. *Child Development, 56,* 654-663.

Reynolds, B. C. (1942). *Learning and teaching in the practice of social work.* New York: Farrar & Rinehart.

Reynolds, R. E., & Ortony, A. (1980). Some issues in the measurement of children's comprehension of metaphorical language. *Child Development, 51,* 1110-1119.

Riccio, C. A., Hynd, G. W., Cohen, M. J., & Gonzalez, J. J. (1993). Neurological basis of attention deficit hyperactivity disorder. *Exceptional Children, 60,* 118-124.

Rich, C. L., Young, D., & Fowler, R. C. (1986). San Diego suicide study. *Archives of General Psychiatry, 43,* 577-582.

Richard, B. A., & Dodge, K. A. (1982). Social maladjustment and problem-solving in school-aged children. *Journal of Consulting and Clinical Psychology, 50,* 226-233.

Richardson, D. K. (1988). The importance of reminiscence and family tradition. In J. Norris (Ed.), *Daughters of the elderly: Building partnerships in caregiving* (pp. 32-36). Bloomington: Indiana University Press.

Richardson, J. G., & Simpson, C. H. (1982). Children, gender, and social structure: An analysis of the contents of letters to Santa Claus. *Child Development, 53,* 429-436.

Richardson, K. (1988). *Understanding psychology.* Philadelphia: Open University Press.

Richmond, J. B., Stipek, D. J., & Zigler, E. (1979). A decade of Head Start. In E. Zigler & J. Valentine (Eds.), *Project Head Start: A legacy of the War on Poverty.* New York: Free Press.

Richmond, M. (1917). *Social diagnosis.* New York: Russell Sage Foundation.

Ridgeway, C. L. (1983). *The dynamics of small groups.* New York: St. Martin's Press.

Riesen, A. (1947). The development of visual perception in man and chimpanzee. *Science, 106,* 107-108.

Riesen, A., Chow, K., Semmes, J., & Nissen, H. (1951). Chimpanzee vision after four conditions of light deprivation. *American Psychologist, 6,* 282.

Riesenberg, D. (1987). Treating a societal malignancy—Rape. *Journal of American Medical Association, 257,* 899-900.

Rigsby, L. C., & McDill, E. L. (1975). Value orientations of high school students. In H. R. Strub (Ed.), *The sociology of education: A sourcebook* (pp. 53-75). Pacific Grove, CA: Brooks/Cole.

Ritter, M. (1996, January 2). Genetic missing link to personality found. *The Arizona Daily Star,* pp. 1, 7.

Rivera, R. R. (1991). Sexual orientation and the law. In J. C. Gonsiorek & J. D. Weinrich (Eds.), *Homosexuality: Research implications for public policy.* Newbury Park, CA: Sage.

Roberts, P., & Newton, P. M. (1987). Levinsonian studies of women's adult development. *Psychology and Aging, 2,* 154-163.

Robertson, I. (1977). *Sociology.* New York: Worth.

Robertson, J. F. (1976). Significance of grandparents: Perceptions of young adult grandchildren. *The Gerontologist, 16,* 137-140.

Robertson, M. J., Ropers, R. H., & Boyer, R. (1985). *The homeless of Los Angeles County: An empirical evaluation.* Los Angeles: UCLA School of Public Health.

Robin, A. (1994). Problem-solving training. In C. W. LeCroy (Ed.), *Handbook of child and adolescent training manuals.* New York: Lexington Books.

Robins, L. N., & McEvoy, L. (1990). Conduct problems as predictors of substance abuse. In L. N. Robins and M. Rutter (Eds.), *Straight and devious pathways from childhood to adulthood.* New York: Cambridge University Press.

Robins, L. N., & Rutter. M. (Eds.) (1990). *Straight and devious pathways from childhood to adulthood.* New York: Cambridge University Press.

Robinson, B. E., & Barret, R. L. (1985, December). Teenage fathers. *Psychology Today,* 66-70.

Robinson, J. P. (1977). *How Americans use time: A social-psychological analysis of everyday behavior.* New York: Praeger.

Robinson, N. S. (1995). Evaluating the nature of perceived support and its relation to perceived self-worth in adolescents. *Journal of Research on Adolescence, 5,* 253-280.

Robinson, W. P. (1965). The elaborated code in working-class language. *Language and speech, 8,* 243-252.

Robson, W. L., & Leung, A. K. (1992). The circumcision question. *Postgraduate Medicine, 91,* 237-242, 244.

Rochefort, D. (1997). *From poorhouse to homelessness: Policy analysis and mental health care.* New York, Auburn house.

Roedding, J. (1991). Birth trauma and suicide: A study of the relationship between near-death experiences and later suicidal behavior. *Pre- and Perinatal Psychology Journal, 6,* 145-169.

Roff, M. (1963). Childhood social interaction and young adulthood psychosis. *Journal of Clinical Psychology, 19,* 152-157.

Rogers, R. (1989). Ethnic and birth-weight differences in cause-specific infant mortality. *Demography, 26,* 335-341.

Rollins, B. C. (1989). Marital quality at midlife. In S. Hunter & M. Sundel (Eds.), *Midlife myths: Issues, findings, and practice implications.* Newbury Park, CA: Sage.

Rollins, B. C. & Feldman, H. (1970). Marital satisfaction over the life cycle. *Journal of Marriage and the Family, 32,* 20-28.

Roobeek, A. J. M. (1995). Biotechnology: A core technology in a new techno-economic paradigm. In M. Fransman, G. Junne, & A. Roobeek (Eds.), *The biotechnology revolution?* (pp. 62-84). Oxford and Cambridge, MA: Blackwell.

Roots of addiction. (1989, February 27). *Newsweek,* pp. 37-46.

Rose, S. (1991). Information processing at 1 year: Relation to birth status and developmental outcome during the first 5 years. *Developmental Psychology, 27*, 723-737.

Rose, S. (1992). Infant information processing in relation to six-year cognitive outcomes. *Child Development, 63*, 1126-1141.

Rose, S. A., & Feldman, J. F. (1997). Memory and speed: Their role in the relation of infant processing to later IQ. *Child Development, 68*, 630-641.

Rose, S. A., Feldman, J. F., Futterweit, L. R., & Jankowski, J. J. (1998). Continuity in tactual-visual cross-modal transfer: Infancy to 11 years. *Developmental Psychology, 34*, 435-440.

Rose, S. D. (1989). *Working with adults in groups: A multi-method approach.* San Francisco: Jossey-Bass.

Rosen, R. (1979). Some crucial issues concerning children of divorce. *Journal of Divorce, 3*, 19-26.

Rosenberg, M., & Simmons, R. (1971). *Black and white self-esteem: The urban school child.* Rose Monograph Series. Washington, DC: American Sociological Association.

Rosenblatt, A. (1962). The application of role concepts to the intake process. *Social Casework, 43*, 8-14.

Rosenblum, O., Mazet, P., & Benomy, H. (1997). Mother and infant affective involvement states and maternal depression. *Infant Mental Health Journal, 18*, 350-363.

Rosenhan, D. L. (1973). In being sane in insane places. *Science, 179, 4070*, 250-258.

Rosenthal, R., & Jacobson, L. (1968). *Pygmalian in the classroom.* New York: Holt, Rinehart & Winston.

Ross, D., & Whitehead, M. I. (1995). Selecting patients for HRT: Positive indications. *British Journal of Clinical Practice, 49*, 92-94.

Roth, L. L., & Atherton, C. R. (1989). *Promoting successful aging.* Chicago: Nelson-Hall.

Rothblum, E. D., & Franks, V. (1983). Introduction: Warning! sex-role stereotypes may be hazardous to your health. In V. Franks & E. D. Rothblum (Eds.), *The stereotyping of women: Its effects on mental health.* New York: Springer.

Rousseau, M. F. (1991). *Community: The tie that binds.* Lanbarn: University Press of America, Inc.

Rovee-Collier, C., Sullivan, M., Enright, M., Lucas, D., & Fagan, J. (1980). Reactivation of infant memory. *Science, 208*, 1159-1161.

Royce, A. P. (1982). *Ethnic identity: Strategies of diversity.* Bloomington: Indiana University Press.

Rozee, P. D., Bateman, P., & Gilmore, T. (1991). The personal perspective of acquaintance rape: A three-tier approach. In A. Parrot & L. Bechhofer (Eds.), *Acquaintance rape: The hidden crime.* New York: Wiley.

Rubenstein, C. M., & Shaver, P. (1982). The experience of loneliness. In L. A. Peplau & D. Perlman (Eds.), *Loneliness: A sourcebook of current theory, research, and therapy.* New York: Wiley.

Rubin, K. N., Fein, G. G., & Vandenberg, B. (1983). Play. In P. H. Mussen (Ed.), *Handbook of childhood psychology* (4th ed., Vol. 4). New York: Wiley.

Rubin, R. (1970). Cognitive style in pregnancy. *American Journal of Nursing, 70*, 502.

Rukeyser, L., Cooney, J., & Winslow, W. (1988). *Louis Rukeyser's business almanac.* New York: Simon & Schuster.

Ruse, M. (1991). Epistemology. In M. Maxwell (Ed.), *The sociobiology imagination.* Albany: State University of New York Press.

Rushdie, S. (1982, December). The new empire within Britain. *New Society*, p. 9.

Rushton, J. P. (1980). *Altruism, socialization, and society.* Englewood Cliffs, NJ: Prentice Hall.

Russo, N. (1979). Overview: Sex roles, fertility, and the motherhood mandate. *Psychology of Women Quarterly, 4*, 7-15.

Rutter, M. (1981). *Maternal deprivation reassessed.* Harmondsworth, Eng. Penguin Books.

Rutter, M. (1983). School effects on pupil progress: Research findings and policy implications. *Child Development, 54*, 1-29.

Rutter, M. (1985). Resilience in the face of adversity: Protective factors and resilience to psychiatric disorder. *British Journal of Psychiatry, 147*, 598-611.

Rutter, M. (1993). *Developing minds: Challenge and continuity across the life span.* New York: Harper Collins.

Rutter, M., Graham, P., Chadwick, F., & Yule, W. (1976). Adolescent turmoil: Fact or fiction? *Journal of Child Psychology and Psychiatry, 17*, 35-56.

Rutter, M., Maughan, B., Mortimore, J., & Ouston, J., with A. Smith (1979). *Fifteen thousand hours: Secondary schools and their effects on children.* Cambridge, MA: Harvard University Press.

Ryan, W. (1971). *Blaming the victim.* New York: Vintage Books.

Sachs, B., Pietrukowicz, M., & Hall, L. A. (1997). Parenting attitudes and behaviors of low-income single mothers with young children. *Journal of Pediatric Nursing, 12*, 67-73.

Sagi, A., Lamb, M. E., Lewkowicz, K. S., Shoham, R., Dvir, R., & Estes, D. (1985). Security of infant-mother, -father, and -metapelet attachments among Kibbutz-reared Israeli children. In I. Bretherton & E. Waters (Eds.), *Growing points of attachment theory and research* (pp. 257-275). Monographs of the Society for Research in Child Development, *50*(1-2, Serial No. 209).

Saleebey, D. (1985). In clinical social work practice, is the body politic? *Social Service Review, 59*, 578-592.

Saleebey, D. (1992a). Biology's challenge to social work: Embodying the person-in-environment perspective. *Social Work, 37*, 112-119.

Saleebey, D. (1992b). *The strengths perspective in social work practice.* New York: Longman.

Sallis, J. (1993). Promoting healthful diet and physical activity. In S. G. Millstein et al., *Promoting the Health of Adolescents.* New York: Oxford University Press.

Salthouse, T. A., & Coon, V. E. (1993). Influence of task-specific processing speed on age differences in memory. *Journal of Gerontology, 48*, 244-255.

Sameroff, A. (1993). Models of development and developmental risk. In C. Zeanah (Ed.), *Handbook of infant mental health* (pp. 3-13). New York: Guilford Press.

Sanchez, S. (1994). Equality of sexes? Give it 1000 years. *USA Today.*

Sandmaier, M. (1995, July/August). The gift of friendship. *The Family Therapy Networker*, pp. 23-34, 66-68.

Santrock, J. W. (1986). *Life-span development.* Dubuque, IA: Wm. C. Brown.

Santrock, J. W. (1989). *Life-span development* (3rd ed.). Dubuque, IA: Wm. C. Brown.

Santrock, J. W. (1990). *Adolescence* (4th ed.). Dubuque, IA: Wm. C. Brown.

Santrock, J. W. (1992). *Life-span development* (4th ed.). Dubuque, IA: Wm. C. Brown.

Santrock, J. W. (1995). *Life-span development* (5th ed.). Madison, WI, & Dubuque, IA: Brown & Benchmark.

Santrock, J. W. (1996). *Adolescence.* Madison, WI: Brown & Benchmark.

Santrock, J. W. (1997). *Life-span development* (6th ed.). Madison, WI, & Dubuque, IA: Brown & Benchmark.

Santrock, J. W., & Warshak, R. A. (1986). Development, relationships and legal considerations in father custody families. In M. E. Lamb (Ed.), *The father's role: Applied perspectives.* New York: Wiley.

Sanzenbach, P., Canda, E. E., & Joseph, M. (1989). Religion and social work: It's not that simple. *Social Casework, 70*, 571-575.

Sarton, M. (1984). *Letters from Maine, new poems.* New York: Norton.

Sauerman, T. H. (1984). *Read this before coming out to your parents.* Washington, DC: Federation of Parents & Friends of Lesbians and Gays, Inc.

Saussure, F. D. (1966). *Course in general linguistics* (W. Baskin, Trans.). New York: McGraw-Hill.

Scarf, M. (1992, July/August). The middle of the journey. *Family Therapy Networker*, pp. 51-55.

Scarr, S., & McCartney, K. (1983). How people make their own environments: A theory of genotype-environment effects. *Child Development, 54*, 424-435.

Schachter, F. F. (1981). Toddlers with employed mothers. *Child Development, 52,* 958-964.

Schaefer, E. S., & Burnett, C. K. (1987). Stability and predictability of quality of women's marital relationships and demoralization. *Journal of Personality and Social Psychology, 53,* 1129-1136.

Schaie, K. W. (1977). Toward a stage theory of adult cognitive development. *Aging and Human Development, 8,* 129-138.

Schaie, K. W. (Ed.) (1983a). *Longitudinal studies of adult psychological development.* New York: Guilford Press.

Schaie, K. W. (1983b). The Seattle longitudinal study: A twenty-one-year exploration of psychometric intelligence in adulthood. In K. W. Schaie (Ed.), *Longitudinal studies of adult psychological development* (pp. 64-135). New York: Guilford Press.

Schaie, K. W. (1987). Intelligence. In G. L. Maddox (Ed.), *The encyclopedia of aging* (pp. 357-358). New York: Springer.

Schaie, K. W. (1994). The course of adult intellectual development. *American Psychologist, 49,* 304-313.

Schaie, K. W., & Strother, C. R. (1968). A cross-sequential study of age changes in cognitive behavior. *Psychological Bulletin, 70,* 671-680.

Schaie, K. W., & Willis, S. L. (1986). *Adult development and aging* (2nd ed.). Boston: Little, Brown.

Scheff, T. (1999). Shame and the social bond: A sociological theory. Available at: http://sscf.ucsb.edu.scheff/2.html.

Scheibel, A. B. (1997). Embryological development of the human brain. Available at: http://www.newhorizons.org.

Scheiber, B. (1981). *One step at a time.* Washington, DC: U.S. Government Printing Office.

Schein, E. H. (1980). *Organizational Psychology.* Englewood Cliffs, NJ: Prentice Hall.

Schilling, R., Gilchrist, L., & Schinke, S. (1984). Coping and social support in families of developmentally disabled children. *Family Relations, 33,* 47-54.

Schinke, S. P., & Gilchrist, L. D. (1983). Coping with contraception: Cognitive and behavioral methods with adolescents. *Cognitive Therapy & Research, 7,* 379-388.

Schinke, S. P., Schilling, R. F., Gilchrist, L. D., Barth, R., Bobo, J. K., Trimble, J. E., & Cvetkovich, G. T. (1985). Preventing substance abuse among American Indian youth. *Social Casework, 66,* 213-317.

Schmidt, G., & Weiner, B. (1988). Measuring loneliness in different relationships. *Journal of Personality and Social Psychology, 44,* 1038-1047.

Schoem, D., Frankel, L., Zuniga, X., & Lewis, E. A. (Eds.). (1993). *Multicultural teaching in the university.* Westport, CT: Praeger.

Schoen, J., & Fischell, A. (1991). Pain in neonatal circumcision. *Clinical Pediatrics, 30,* 429-432.

Schriver, J. M. (1995). *Human behavior and the social environment: Shifting paradigms in essential knowledge for social work practice.* Boston: Allyn & Bacon.

Schulz, R., Visintainer, P., & Williamson, G. M. (1990). Psychiatric and physical morbidity effects of caregiving. *Journal of Gerontology, 45,* 181-191.

Schneider, M. (1991). Developing services for lesbian and gay adolescents. *Canadian Journal of Mental Health, 10, 1,* 133-151.

Schrumpf, F., Crawford, D., & Usadel, H. C. (1991). *Peer mediation: Conflict resolution in the schools.* Champaign, IL: Research Press.

Schulenberg, J., Wadsworth, K. N., O'Malley, P. M., Bachman, J. G., & Johnston, L. D. (1996). Adolescent risk factors for binge drinking during the transition to young adulthood: Variable- and pattern-centered approaches to change. *Developmental Psychology, 32, 4,* 659-674.

Schuster, C. S., & Ashburn, S. S. (1986). *The process of human development: A holistic life-span approach* (2nd ed.). Boston: Little, Brown.

Schuster, C. S., & Ashburn, S. S. (1992). *The process of human development: A holistic life-span approach* (3rd ed.). Philadelphia: Lippincott.

Schwartz, S., & Johnson, J. H. (1985). *Psychopathology of childhood.* New York: Pergamon Press.

Schwitalla, A. M. (1930). Proceedings of the National Conference of Social Work (pp. 544-551). Chicago: University of Chicago Press.

Sears, M. R. (1997). Epidemiology of childhood asthma. *The Lancet, 350,* 1015-1021.

Sears, R. R., Maccoby, E. E., & Leven, H. (1957). *Patterns of childrearing.* New York: Harper & Row.

Seccombe, K. (1991). Assessing the costs and benefits of children: Gender comparisons among child-free husbands and wives. *Journal of Marriage and the Family, 53,* 191-202.

Segal, J., & Yahraes, H. (1978a). *A child's journey: Forces that shape the lives of our young.* New York: McGraw-Hill.

Segal, J., & Yahraes, H. (1978b, November). Bringing up mother. *Psychology Today,* pp. 90-96.

Seidman, S. N., & Rieder, R. O. (1994). A review of sexual behavior in the United States. *American Journal of Psychiatry, 151,* 330-341.

Seifer, R., & Dickstein, S. (1993). Parental mental illness and infant development. In C. Zeanah (Ed.), *Handbook of infant mental health* (pp. 120-142). New York: Guilford Press.

Seitz, V., Rosenbaum, L. K., & Apfel, N. H. (1985). Effects of family support intervention: A 10-year follow-up. *Child Development,* 376-391.

Seligman, M. E. (1975). *Helplessness: On depression, development and death.* San Francisco: W. H. Freeman.

Seligman, M. E. (1995a). *The optimistic child.* New York: Harper Perennial.

Seligman, M. E. P. (1995b, May). Is self-esteem really all that important? *APA Monitor.*

Seligman, M. E. (1996). *The optimistic child: A proven program to safeguard children against depression and build lifelong resilience.* New York: Harper Perennial.

Selman, R. L. (1980). *The growth of interpersonal understanding.* New York: Academic Press.

Selman, R. L. (1990). *Making a friend in youth: Developmental theory and pair therapy.* Chicago: University of Chicago Press.

Selman, R. L., Jaquette, D., & Lavin, D. (1977). Interpersonal awareness in children: Toward an integration of developmental and clinical child psychology. *American Journal of Orthopsychiatry, 47,* 264-274.

Seltzer, J. A., & Bianchi, S. M. (1988). Children's contact with absent parents. *Journal of Marriage and the Family, 50,* 663-677.

Selye, H. (1936). A syndrome produced by diverse nocuous agents. *Nature, 138, p32.*

Selye, H. (1956). *The stress of life.* New York: McGraw Hill.

Selye, H. (1982). History and present status of the stress concept. In L. Goldberger, & S. Breznitz (Eds.), *Handbook of stress: Theoretical and clinical aspects.* New York: Free Press.

Sennett, R., & Cobb, J. (1972). *The hidden injuries of class.* New York: Vintage Books.

Sepkoski, C. (1992). The effects of maternal epidural anesthesia on neonatal behavior during the first month. *Developmental Medicine & Child Neurology, 34,* 1072-1080.

Seppa, N. (1996, December). When one's parents become neighbors. *APA Monitor,* p. 34.

Seppa, N. (1997, July). Hard-of-hearing clients often hide their disability. *APA Monitor,* p. 28.

Severino, S. K., Teusink, J. P., Pender, V. B., & Bernstein, A. E. (1986). Overview: The psychology of grandparenthood. *Journal of Geriatric Psychiatry, 19,* 3-17.

Seymour, D. Z. (1974). Black children. Black speech. In F. Rebelsky & L. Dorman (Eds.), *Child development and behavior* (2nd ed.). New York: Knopf.

Shaffer, D. R. (1989). *Developmental psychology: Childhood and adolescence* (2nd ed.). Pacific Grove, CA: Brooks/Cole.

Shaffer, D. R., (1993). *Developmental psychology: Childhood and adolescence* (3rd ed.). Pacific Grove, CA: Brooks/Cole.

Shafritz, J. M., & Whitbeck, P. H. (1978). *Classics of organization theory.* Oak Park, IL: Moore.

Shanas, E., Townsend, P., Wedderburn, D., Friis, H., Milhoj, P., & Stehouwer, B. (1968). *Old people in three industrial societies.* New York: Atherton.

Shantz, C. U. (1983). Social cognition. In P. H. Mussen (Ed.), *Handbook of child psychology* (4th ed., Vol. 3). New York: Wiley.

Shapiro, J. (1996, September, 9). Can churches save America? *U.S. News and World Report,* pp. 46–53.

Shapiro, L. (1997, May 12). The myth of quality time. *Newsweek,* pp. 62–69.

Shatz, M., & Gelman, R. (1973). The development of communication skills: Modifications in the speech of young children as a function of the listener. *Monographs of the Society for Research in Child Development, 38*(5, Serial No. 52).

Shaw, D. S., Keenan, K., Vondra, J. I., Delliquadri, E., & Giovannelli, J. (1997) Antecedents of preschool children's internalizing problems: A longitudinal study of low-income families. *Journal of the American Academy of Child and Adolescent Psychiatry, 36,* 1760–1767.

Shaw, M. E. (1981). *Group dynamics: The psychology of small group behavior.* New York: McGraw-Hill.

Shaw, M. W. (1981). *Group dynamics: The psychology of small group behavior* (3rd ed.). New York: McGraw-Hill.

Shea, J. D. C. (1981). Changes in interpersonal distances and categories of play behavior in the early weeks of preschool. *Developmental Psychology, 17,* 417–425.

Sheehan, G. J., & Martyn, M. (1970). Stuttering and its disappearance. *Journal of Speech and Hearing Research, 13,* 279–289.

Sheehy, G. (1976). *Passages.* New York: Dutton.

Sheridan, M., Bullis, R., Adcock, C., Berlin, S., & Miller, P. (1992). Serving diverse religious client populations: Issues for social work education and practice. *Journal of Social Work Education, 28,* 190–203.

Sherif, M., Harvey, O. J., White, B. J., Hood, W. R., & Sherif, C. W. (1961). *Intergroup conflict and cooperation: The Robber's Cave experiment.* Norman, OK: Institute of Group Relations, University of Oklahoma.

Sherman, E. (1987). *The meaning of midlife transitions.* Albany: State University of New York.

Shipman, G. (1968). The psychodynamics of sex education. *Family Coordinator, 17,* 3–12.

Shoda, Y., Mischel, W., & Peake, P. K. (1990). Predicting adolescent cognitive and self-regulatory competencies from preschool delay of gratification. *Developmental Psychology, 26,* 978–986.

Shoemaker, D. J. (1989). Transfer of children and the importance of grandmothers among the Navajo Indians. *Journal of Cross-Cultural Gerontology, 4,* 1–18.

Shure, M., & Spivack, G. (1980). Interpersonal problem solving as a mediator of behavioral adjustment in preschool and kindergarten children. *Journal of Applied Developmental Psychology, 1,* 37–52.

Sidel, R. (1990). *On her own: Growing up in the shadow of the American dream.* New York: Viking Penguin.

Siegler, R. S. (1995, January). New cognitive research making waves. *APA Monitor.*

Sigelman, C. K. (1999). *Life-span development* (3rd ed.), Pacific Grove, CA: Brooks/Cole.

Sigelman, C. K., & Shaffer, D. R. (1991). *Life-span development.* Pacific Grove, CA: Brooks/Cole.

Sigelman, C. K., & Shaffer, D. R. (1995). *Life-span development.* Pacific Grove, CA: Brooks/Cole.

Sigman, M. (1991). Continuity in cognitive abilities from infancy to 12 years of age. *Cognitive Development, 6,* 47–57.

Sigman, G. S., & Flanery, R. C. (1992). Eating disorders. In D. E. Greydanus & M. C. Wolraich (Eds.), *Behavioral pediatrics.* New York: Springer-Verlag.

Silverman, P. R. (1987a). Mutual aid groups. In *Encyclopedia of Social Work* (18th ed., pp. 1171–1176). Silver Spring, MD: National Association of Social Workers.

Silverman, P. R. (1987b). Widowhood as the next stage in the life course. In H. Lopata (Ed.), *Widows: Vol. II. North America* (171–190). Durham, NC: Duke University Press.

Silverstein, B., & Krate, R. (1975). *Children of the dark ghetto: A developmental psychology.* New York: Praeger.

Simmel, G. (1904). Fashion. *American Sociological Journal of Sociology, 62,* 541–559.

Simmons, R. G., & Blyth, D. A. (1987). *Moving into adolescence.* Hawthorne, NY: Aldine.

Simmons, R. G., Rosenberg, F., & Rosenberg, M. (1973). Disturbance in self-image at adolescence. *American Sociological Review, 38,* 553–568.

Simmons, R. L., Beaman, J., Conger, R. D., & Chao, W. (1993). Stress, support, and antisocial behavior trait as determinants of emotional well being and parenting practices among single mothers. *Journal of Marriage and the Family, 55,* 385–398.

Simmons, R. L., Whitbeck, L. B., Beuman, J., & Conger, R. D. (1994). The impact of mothers' parenting, involvement by nonresidential fathers, and parental conflict on the adjustment of adolescent children. *Journal of Marriage and the Family, 56,* 356–374.

Simons, M. (1995, September 11). Dutch doctors to tighten rules on mercy killings. *New York Times International.*

Simons, R. (1987). *After the tears.* San Diego: Harcourt Brace Jovanovich.

Singer, D. G., & Singer, J. L. (1987). Practical suggestions for controlling television. *Journal of Early Adolescence, 7,* 365–369.

Singer, L., & Yamashita, T. (1997). A longitudinal study of developmental outcomes of infants with bronchopulmonary dysplasia and very low birth weight. *Pediatrics, 100,* 987–994.

Siporin, M. (1986). Contribution of religious values to social work and the law. *Social Thought, 12,* 35–50.

Sizer, T. R. (1983). High school reform: The need for engineering. *Phi Delta Kappan,* 679–683.

Skeels, H. M. (1936). The mental development of children in foster homes. *Pedagogical Seminary and Journal of Genetic Psychology, 49,* 91–106.

Skinner, B. F. (1953). *Science and human behavior.* New York: Macmillan.

Skinner, L. (1979). *Motor development in the preschool years.* Springfield, IL: Charles C. Thomas.

Skodak, M. (1939). Children in foster homes: A study of mental development. *University of Iowa Studies in Child Welfare, 16*(1).

Skodak, M., & Skeels, H. (1945). A follow-up study of children in adoptive homes. *Journal of Genetic Psychology, 66,* 21–58.

Skodak, M., & Skeels, H. (1949). A follow-up study of one hundred adopted children. *Journal of Genetic Psychology, 75,* 85–125.

Skolnick, A. (1986). *The psychology of human development.* New York: Harcourt Brace Jovanovich.

Slaby, R. G., & Crowley, C. G. (1977). Modification of cooperation and aggression through teacher attention to children's speech. *Journal of Experimental Child Psychology, 23,* 442–458.

Slaughter-Defoe, D. T., (1995). Revisiting the concept of socialization: Caregiving and teaching in the 90s—A personal perspective. *American Psychologist, 50,* 276–286.

Sleek, S. (1994, November). Therapists, both male and female, fall victim to stereotypes of men. *APA Monitor,* pp. 6–7.

Sleek, S. (1995, October). Coping with disabilities the Albert Ellis way. *APA Monitor,* pp. 47.

Sleek, S. (1995, December). Battling breast cancer though group therapy. *APA Monitor,* p. 24.

Sleek, S. (1995, December). Rallying the troops inside our bodies. *APA Monitor,* pp. 1, 24.

Sleek, S. (1996, June). AIDS therapy: Patchwork of pain, hope. *APA Monitor,* pp. 1, 31.

Sleek, S. (1996, October). Research identifies causes of internal homophobia. *APA Monitor,* p. 57.

Sleek, S. (1998, April). Innocuous violence triggers the real thing. *APA Monitor,* pp. 1, 31.

Smart, B. (1993). *Postmodernity: Key ideas.* London: Routledge.

Smetana, J. G. (1988). Adolescents' and parents' conceptions of parental authority. *Child Development, 59,* 321-335.

Smetana, J. G., Yau, J., Restrepo, A., & Braeges, J. L. (1991). Conflict and adaptation in adolescence: Adolescent-parent conflict. In M. E. Colten & S. Gore (Eds.), *Adolescent stress.* New York: Aldine de Gruyter.

Smilansky, S. (1968). *The effects of sociodramatic play on disadvantaged preschool children.* New York: Wiley.

Smith, P., & Daglish, L. (1977). Sex differences in parent and infant behavior in the home. *Child Development, 48,* 1250-1254.

Smith, P. K., & Connolly, K. J. (1980). *The ecology of preschool behavior.* New York: Cambridge University Press.

Smith, R. (1995, July). The adoption equation, minus race. *NASW News,* p. 3.

Smith, T. W., & Pope, M. K. (1990). Cynical hostility as a health risk: Current status and future directions. *Journal of Social Behavior and Personality, 5,* 77-88.

Smolowe, J. (1995, July, 31). Noble aims, mixed results. *Time,* pp. 54-55.

Society for Neuroscience. (1995). Neuron migration and brain disorders. Available at: http://www.sfn.org/briefings/neuron.html.

Solomon, R. C. (1988). *About love: Reinventing romance for modern times.* New York: Simon & Schuster.

Sonenstein, F., Pleck, J., & Ku, L. (1989). Sexual activity, condom use and AIDS awareness in a national sample of adolescent males. *Family Planning Perspectives, 21,* 152-158.

Sorensen, E. (1997). A national profile of non residential fathers and their ability to pay child support. *Journal of Marriage and the Family, 59,* 785-797.

Southern Poverty Law Center. (1994). The intelligence report, August. Atlanta, GA: Southern Poverty Law Center.

Sparrowe, L. (1997). The heart of parenting. *Yoga Journal,* pp. 178-179.

Specht, R., & Craig, G. (1987). *Human development: A social work perspective.* Englewood Cliffs, NJ: Prentice Hall.

Spelke, E. (1985). Perception of unity, persistence, and identity: Thoughts on infants' conception of objects. In J. Mehler & R. Fox (Eds.), *Neonate cognition.* Hillsdale, NJ: Erlbaum.

Spelke, E. (1994). Initial knowledge: Six suggestions. *Cognition, 50,* 431-445.

Spencer, L. J. (1989). *Winning through participation.* Dubuque, IA: Institute of Cultural Affairs.

Spencer, M. B., & Dornbusch, S. M. (1990). Challenges in studying minority youth. In S. Feldman & G. R. Elliott (Eds.), *At the threshold: The developing adolescent.* Cambridge, MA: Harvard University Press.

Spencer, P. E. (1993). Communication behaviors of infants with hearing loss and their hearing mothers. *Journal of Speech and Hearing Research, 36,* 311-322.

Spiegel, D. (1993). Psychosocial intervention in cancer. *Journal of the National Cancer Institute, 85,* 1198-1202.

Spiegel, D. (1999). Healing words: Emotional experiences and disease outcomes. *Journal of the American Medical Association, 281,* 1328-1338.

Spitz, R. (1945). Hospitalism: An inquiry into the genesis of psychiatric conditions in early childhood. *Psychoanalytic Study of the Child, 1,* 53-74.

Spitz, R. A. (1966). *No and yes: On the genesis of human communication.* New York: International Universities Press.

Sprich-Buckminster, S. (1993). Are perinatal complications relevant to the manifestation of ADD? *Journal of the American Academy of Child and Adolescent Psychiatry, 32,* 1032-1037.

Spurlock, J. (1984). Black women in the middle years. In G. Baruch & J. Brooks-Gunn (Eds.), *Women in midlife.* New York: Plenum.

Stacey, N., Deardon, R., Pill, R., & Robinson, D. (1970). *Hospitals, children, and their families: The report of a pilot study.* London: Routledge & Kegan Paul.

Stainton, C., McNeil, D., & Harvey, S. (1992). Maternal tasks of uncertain motherhood. *Maternal-Child Nursing Journal, 20,* 113-123.

Stake, J. E., DeVille, C. J., & Rennell, C. L. (1983). The effects of assertiveness training on the performance self-esteem of adolescent girls. *Journal of Youth and Adolescence, 12,* 435-442.

Staples, R. (1988). The Black American family. In C. H. Mindel, R. W. Habenstein, & R. Wright (Eds.), *Ethnic families in America: Patterns and variations* (3rd ed.). New York: Elsevier.

Stark, E. (1989, October). Teen boys get condom sense. *Psychology Today,* p. 63.

Starr, B. D., & Weiner, M. B. (1982). *The Starr-Weiner report on sex and sexuality in the mature years.* New York: McGraw-Hill.

Staub, E. (1984). Steps toward a comprehensive theory of moral conduct: Goal orientation, social behavior, kindness, and cruelty. In W. M. Kurtines & J. L. Gewirtz (Eds.), *Morality, moral behavior, and moral development.* New York: Wiley.

Steil, J. M., & Turetsky, B. A. (1987). Is equal better? The relationship between marital equality and psychological symptomatology. In S. Oskamp (Ed.), *Family process and problems: Social psychological aspects.* Newbury Park, CA: Sage.

Stein, N. (1995, June). New cognitive research making waves. *APA Monitor.*

Steinberg, L. (1990). Autonomy, conflict, and harmony in the family relationship. In S. Feldman & G. Elliot (Eds.), *At the threshold: The developing adolescent* (pp. 255-276). Cambridge, MA: Harvard University Press.

Steinberg, L. (1995). *How your child's adolescence triggers your own crisis.* New York: Simon & Schuster.

Steinberg, L., Fegley, S., & Dornbush, S. M. (1993). Negative impact of part time work on adolescent adjustment: Evidence from a longitudinal study. *Developmental Psychology, 29,* 171-180.

Steinberg, L., & Silverberg, S. (1986). The vicissitudes of autonomy in early adolescence. *Child Development, 57,* 841-851.

Steiner, R. F., & Pomerantz, S. (1981). *The chemistry of living systems.* New York: Van Nostrand Reinhold.

Stenback, A. (1980). Depression and suicidal behavior in old age. In J. E. Birren & R. B. Sloane (Eds.). *Handbook of mental health and aging.* Englewood Cliffs, NJ: Prentice Hall.

Stenfels, P. (1994, February 10). Psychiatrists' manual shifts stance on religious and spiritual problems. *New York Times.*

Stephan, W., & Stephan, C. W. (1996). *Intergroup relations.* Boulder: Westview Press.

Stephens, M.A.P., Kinney, J. M., & Ogrocki, P. K. (1991). Stressors and well-being among caregivers to older adults with dementia: The in-home versus nursing home experience. *The Gerontologist, 31,* 217-223.

Stern, D. (1985). *The interpersonal world of the infant: A view from psychoanalysis and developmental psychology.* New York: Basic Books.

Stern, D. (1990). *Diary of a baby.* New York: Basic Books.

Sternberg, R. J. (1986). A triangular theory of love. *Psychological Review, 93,* 119-135.

Sternberg, R. J. (1988). Triangulating love. In R. J. Sternberg & M. L. Barnes (Eds.), *The psychology of love.* New Haven, CT: Yale University Press.

Steur, F. B., Applefield, J. M., & Smith, R. (1971). Televised aggression and interpersonal aggression of preschool children. *Journal of Experimental Child Psychology, 11,* 442-447.

Stevenson, H. (1995, May). Is self-esteem really all that important? *APA Monitor.*

Stevenson, J. C. (1995). *British Journal of Clinical Practice, 49,* 87-90.

Stevenson, L. (1974). *Seven theories of human nature.* New York: Oxford University Press.

Stevenson, L. (1981). *The study of human nature:* Readings. New York: Oxford University Press.

Stewart, R. B. (1983). Sibling Interaction: The role of older child as teacher for the younger. *Merrill-Palmer Quarterly, 29,* 47-68.

Stewart, R. B., Mobley, L. A., Van Tuyl, S. S., & Salvador, M. A. (1987). The firstborn's adjustment to the birth of a sibling: A longitudinal assessment. *Child Development, 58,* 341-355.

Stiffman, A. R., & Davis, L. E. (1990). *Ethnic issues in adolescent mental health.* Newbury Park, CA: Sage.

Stipp, D. (1995, May 24). Our prehistoric past casts ills in new light, some scientists say. The *Wall Street Journal,* pp. 1, 5.

St. James, J. (1987). *Inside baby's head.* Burton, OH: Palamora.

Stoner, J.A.F. (1961). *A comparison of individual and group decisions involving risk.* Unpublished master's thesis, Massachusetts Institute of Technology, Cambridge.

Stott, D. (1971). The child's hazards in utero. In J. G. Howells (Ed.), *Modern perspectives in international child psychiatry.* New York: Brunner/Mazel.

Stoudemire, A. (1994). *Clinical psychiatry for medical students* (2nd edition). Philadelphia: J. B. Lippincott Company.

Strahan, D. B. (1983). The emergence of formal operations in adolescence. *Transcendence, 11,* 7-14.

Strauss, M., Gelles, R., & Steinmetz, S. (1980). *Behind closed doors.* New York: Doubleday.

Strauss, M. A., & Gelles, R. J. (1986). Societal change and change in family violence from 1975 to 1985 as revealed in two national surveys. *Journal of Marriage and the Family, 48,* 465-479.

Street, E., & Soldan, J. (1998). A conceptual framework for the psychosocial issues faced by families with genetic condition. *Families, Systems, and Health, 16,* 217-232.

Streissguth, A., LaDue, R., & Randels, S. (1988). *A manual on adolescents and adults with fetal alcohol syndrome with special reference to American Indians.* Rockville, MD: U.S. Department of Health and Human Services.

Stringer, G. M., & Rants-Rodriguez, D. (1987). *So what's it to me?* Renton, WA: King County Rape Relief.

Stroufe, L. A., Fox, N. E., & Pancake, V. R. (1983). Attachment and dependency in developmental perspective. *Child Development, 54,* 1615-1627.

Stuart, R. B. (1980). *Helping couples change.* New York: Guilford Press.

Stueve, A., & O'Donnell, L. (1984). The daughter of aging parents. In G. Baruch & J. Brooks-Gunn (Eds.), *Women in midlife.* New York: Plenum.

Sullivan, T. R. (1994). Obstacles to effective child welfare service with gay and lesbian youths. *Child Welfare, 73,* 4, 291-304.

Sumner, W. G. (1906/1960). *Folkways.* New York: New American Library.

Sunderland, T., Lawlor, B. A., Molchan, S. E., & Martinez, R. A. (1988). Depressive symptoms in the elderly: Special concerns. *Psychopharmacology Bulletin, 24,* 567-576.

Suomi, S., & Harlow, H. (1972). Social rehabilitation of isolate-reared monkeys. *Developmental Psychology, 6,* 487-496.

Super, D. E., Kowalski, R., & Gotkin, E. (1967). *Floundering and trial after high school.* Unpublished manuscript, Columbia University, New York.

Swanson, J. M., McBurnett, K., Wigal, T., Pfieffer, E. J., Lerner, M. D., Williams, L., Christian, D. L., Tamm, L., Willcut, E., Crowley, K., Clevenger, W., Khouzam, N., Woo, C., Crinella, F. M., & Fisher, T. D. (1993). Effect of stimulant medication on children with attention deficit disorder: A "review of reviews." *Exceptional Children, 60,* 154-162.

Swinburne, R. (1986). *The evolution of the soul.* UK: Clarendon Press/Oxford University Press.

Symanski, M. (1992). Maternal-infant bonding: Practice issues for the 1990's. *Journal of Nurse-Midwifery, 37,* 67-73.

Symons, D. (1987). If we're all Darwinians, what's the fuss about? In C. Crawford, M. Smith, & D. Krebs (Eds.), *Sociobiology and psychology: Ideas, issues, and applications* (pp. 121-146). Hillsdale, NJ: Lawrence Erlbaum Associates, Inc.

Tajfel, H. (1978). Social categorization, social identity, and social comparison. In H. Tajfel (Ed.), *Differentiation between social groups* (pp. 61-76). New York: Academic Press.

Tajfel, H. (1982). *Social identity and intergroup relations.* Cambridge: Cambridge University Press.

Tajfel, H., & Turner, J. C. (1979). An integrative theory of intergroup conflict. In S. Worchel, & W. G. Austin (Eds.), *Psychology of intergroup relations.* Monterey, CA: Brooks/Cole.

Tajfel. H., & Turner, J. C. (1986). The social identity theory of intergroup behavior. In S. Worchel & W. G. Austin (Eds.) *Psychology of intergroup relations* (2nd ed. pp. 7-24). Chicago: Nelson Hall.

Takahashi, K. (1986). Examining the strange-situation procedure with Japanese mothers and 12-month-old infants. *Developmental Psychology, 22*(2), 265-270.

Takaki, R. (1993). *A different mirror: A history of multicultural America.* Boston: Little, Brown.

Tannen, D. (1991). *You just don't understand: Women and men in conversation.* New York: Morrow.

Task Force on Homelessness and Severe Mental Illness. (1992). *Outcasts on main street.* (DHHS Publication No. ADM 92-1904). Rockville, MD: Department of Health and Human Services.

Tavris, C. (1992). *The mismeasure of women.* New York: Simon and Schuster.

Tavris, C., & Wade, C. (1984). *The longest war: Sex differences in perspective.* New York: Harcourt Brace Jovanovich.

Taylor, F. W. (1947). *Scientific management.* New York: Harper & Row.

Taylor, I. (1976). *Introduction to Psycholinguistics.* New York: Holt, Rinehart & Winston.

Tedder, J. (1991). Using the Brazelton neonatal assessment scale to facilitate the parent-infant relationship in a primary care setting. *Nurse Practitioner, 16,* 26-36.

Teitelbaum, M. A., & Edmunds, M. (1999). Immunization and vaccine-preventable illness, United States, 1992 to 1997. *Statistical Bulletin,* 13-20.

Tellegen, A., Lykken, D. T., Bouchard, T. J., Wilcox, K. J., & Rich, S. (1988). Personality similarity in twins reared apart and together. *Journal of Personality and Social Psychology, 54,* 1031-1039.

Terkel, S. (1974). *Working: People talk about what they do all day and how they feel about what they do.* New York: Pantheon Books.

Termine, N. (1988). Infants' responses to their mothers' expressions of joy and sadness. *Developmental Psychology, 24,* 223-229.

Thoma, S. J. (1986). Estimating gender differences in the comprehension and preference of moral issues. *Developmental Review, 6,* 165-180.

Thomas, A., & Chess, S. (1977). *Temperament and development.* New York: Brunner/Mazel.

Thomas, A., & Chess, S. (1989). Temperament and personality. In G. A. Konnstamm, J. E. Bates, & M. K. Rothbart (Eds.), *Temperament in childhood* (pp. 249-261). New York: Wiley.

Thomas, R. B. (1987). Family adaptation to a child with a chronic illness. In M. H. Rose & R. B. Thomas (Eds.), *Children with chronic conditions: Nursing in a family and community context* (pp. 29-54). Orlando, FL: Grune & Stratton.

Thornburg, H. D. (1981). Sources of sex education among early adolescents. *Journal of Early Adolescence, 1,* 171-184.

Thorpe, J. A., & Breedlove, G. (1996). Epidural analgesia in labor: An evaluation of risks and benefits. *Birth, 23,* 63-83.

Timasheff, N. S. (1967). *Sociological theory.* New York: Random House.

Timberlake, E. M., Sabatino, C. A., & Hooper, S. N. (1982). *School social work: Practice and research perspectives.* Pacific Grove, CA: Brooks/Cole.

Tinsley, B., & Parke, R. (1987). Grandparents as interactive and social support agents for families with young infants. *International Journal of Aging & Human Development, 25,* 259-277.

Tizard, B., & Rees, J. (1974). A comparison of the effects of adoption, restoration to the natural mother, and continued institutionalization on the cognitive development of four-year-old children. *Journal of Child Psychology and Psychiatry and Allied Disciplines, 16,* 61-73.

Tolman, R. M., & Bennett, L. (1992). Group work with men who batter. In C. W. LeCroy (Ed.), *Case studies in social work practice.* Belmont, CA: Wadsworth.

Tong, R. (1993). Euthanasia in the 1990s. *Current Issues, 354,* 27-34.

Torrey, E. F. (1988). *Nowhere to go: The tragic odyssey of the homeless mentally ill.* New York: Harper & Row.

Toseland, R., & Hacker, L. (1982). Self-help groups and professional involvement. *Social Work, 27,* 341-347.

Toseland, R. W., & Rivas, R. F. (1995). *An introduction to group work practice* (2nd ed.). Needham Heights, MA: Allyn & Bacon.

Toseland, R. W., & Rossiter, C. (1989). Group interventions to support caregivers: A review and analysis. *The Gerontologist, 29,* 438-448.

Towle, C. (1945). *Common human needs:An interpretation for staff in public assistance agencies.* Washington, DC: U.S. Government Printing Office.

Towle, C. (1960). A social work approach to courses in growth and behavior. *Social Service Review. 34,* 402-414.

Towle, C. (1987). *Common human needs.* (Rev. ed.). Silver Spring, MD: National Association of Social Workers. (Original work published in 1945).

Troiden, R. (1989). The formation of homosexual identities. *Journal of Homosexuality, 17, 1-2,* 43-73.

Troll, L. E. (1986). *Family issues in current gerontology.* New York: Springer.

Troll, L. E., & Bengtson, V. L. (1982). Intergenerational relations throughout the life span. In B. Wolman (Ed.), *Handbook of developmental psychology* (pp. 890-911). Englewood Cliffs, NJ: Prentice Hall.

Trotter, R. (1987, May). You've come a long way, baby. *Psychology Today,* 34-47.

Trout, M. (1995, October). Infant attachment: Assessment, intervention and developmental impact. Workshop presented by M. Trout, Director of the Infant Parent Institute, Tucson, AZ.

Tucker, R. M. (1980). Is hypertension different in the elderly? *Geriatrics, 35,* 28-32.

Turner, J. (1972). *Patterns of social organization:A survey of social institutions.* New York: McGraw-Hill.

Turner, J. (1991). *The structure of sociological theory.* Belmont, CA: Wadsworth.

Turner, R. J., & Avison, W. R. (1985). Assessing risk factors for problem parenting: The significance of social support. *Journal of Marriage and the Family,* 881-892.

Twente, E. E. (1965). Aging, strength, and creativity. *Social Work, 10,* 105-110.

Twente, E. E. (1970). *Never too old.* San Francisco: Jossey-Bass.

Tyler, T. R. (1989). The psychology of procedural justice: A test of the group value model. *Journal of Personality and Social Psychology, 57,* 830-838.

Unger, D. G., & Wandersman, L. P. (1985). The importance of neighbors: The social, cognitive and affective components of neighboring. *American Journal of Community Psychology, 41,* 29-45.

U.S. Bureau of the Census. (1987). *Annual report of fertility rates.* Washington, DC: U.S. Government Printing Office.

U.S. Bureau of the Census. (1989). *Statistical abstract of the United States, 1989.* Washington, DC: U.S. Government Printing Office.

U.S. Bureau of the Census. (1990a). Need for personal assistance with everyday activities. Current *population reports,* Series P-25, No. 19. (Publication No. S/N 803-044-00007-4). Washington, DC: U.S. Government Printing Office.

U.S. Bureau of the Census. (1990b). *Statistical abstract of the United States, 1990.* Washington, DC: U.S. Government Printing Office.

U.S. Bureau of the Census. (1991). *Statistical abstract of the United States: 1991.* Washington, DC: U.S. Government Printing Office.

U.S. Bureau of the Census (1997). *Statistical abstract of the United States* (117th ed.), Washington D.C.: U. S. Government Printing Office.

U.S. Department of Health and Human Services. (1985). The child abuse and treatment amendments of 1984 (public Law 98-457). *Federal Register, 50,* 14878-14901.

U.S. Department of Justice. (1995). *Women usually victimized by offenders they know.* Bureau of Statistics, the Internet.

U.S. General Accounting Office. (1986). *School dropouts:The extent and nature of the problem.* Report to Congressional Requesters.

U.S. Senate, Special Committee on Aging. (1988). The long-term care challenge. *Developments in aging: 1987* (Vol. 3). Washington, DC: U.S. Government Printing Office.

Vale, J. R. (1980). *Genes, environment, and behavior:An interactionist approach.* New York: Harper & Row.

Vaillant, G. E. (1977). *Adaptation to life.* Boston: Little, Brown.

Valzelli, L. (1980). *An approach to neuroanatomical and neurochemical psychophysiology.* Torino, Italy: C. G. Edizioni Medic. Scientifiche.

Van Biema, D. (1995, November, 6). Full of promise. *Time,* pp. 62-63.

Van Den Bergh, N. (1986). Renaming:Vehicle for empowerment. In J. Penfield (Ed.), *Women and language in transition.* Albany: State University of New York Press.

Van Den Bergh, N., & Cooper, L. B. (1987). Feminist social work. In A. Minahan (Ed.), *Encyclopedia of social work.* Silver Spring, MD: NASW Press.

Vandenbosche, R. C., & Kirchner, J. T. (1998). Intrauterine growth retardation. *American Family Physician, 58,* 1384-1391.

Van Ijzendoorn, M. H., & Kroonenberg, P. M. (1988). Cross-cultural patterns of attachment: A meta-analysis of the strange situation. *Child Development, 59*(1), 147-156.

Van Strien, J., Bouma, A., & Bakker, D. (1987). Birth stress, autoimmune diseases and handedness. *Journal of Clinical and Experimental Neuropsychology, 9,* 775-780.

Vantveer, P. (1994). Diet and breast cancer: Trial and error. *Annals of Medicine, 26,* 453-460.

Vasconcellos, J. (1927). *Indologia: Una interpretación de la cultura ibero-americano.* Barcelona: Agencia Mundial de Liberia.

Veevers, J. E. (1980). *Childless by choice.* Toronto: Butterworths.

Verdoux, H. (1993). A comparative study of obstetric history in schizophrenics, bipolar patients and normal subjects. *Schizophrenia Research, 9,* 67-69.

Vetter, H. J. (1969). *Language behavior and communication:An introduction.* Itasca, IL: F. E. Peacock.

Visher, E. B., & Visher, J. S. (1988). *Old loyalties, new ties.* New York: Brunner/Mazel.

Viviansayles, P. J. (1993, May/June). The politics of breast cancer. *Ms.,* pp. 54-55.

Voda, A. M. (1993). A journey to the center of the cell: Understanding the physiology and endocrinology of menopause. In J. C. Callahan (Ed.), *Menopause:A midlife passage.* Bloomington, ID: Indiana University Press.

Vygotsky, L. S. (1962). *Thought and language.* Cambridge: Massachusetts Institute of Technology Press.

Wagner, D. A., & Stevenson, H. W. (1982). *Cultural perspectives on child development.* San Francisco: W. H. Freeman.

Wald, E. (1989). Family: Stepfamilies. In *Encyclopedia of social work* (pp. 555-561). Silver Spring, MD: National Association of Social Workers.

Walker, L. J. (1989). A longitudinal study of moral reasoning. *Child Development, 60,* 157-166.

Wallerstein, J. S. (1984). Children of divorce: Preliminary report of a ten-year follow-up of young children. *American Journal of Orthopsychiatry, 57,* 199-211.

Wallerstein, J. S. (1988). Children of divorce: Stress and developmental tasks. In N. Garmezy & M. Rutter (Eds.). *Stress, coping, and development in children.* Baltimore: Johns Hopkins University Press.

Wallerstein, J. S. (1995). *The good marriage:How and why love lasts.* Boston: Houghton Mifflin.

Wallerstein, J. S., & Blakeslee, S. (1989). *Second chances.* New York: Ticknor & Fields.

Wallerstein, J. S., Corbin, S. B., & Lewis, J. M. (1988). Children of divorce: A ten-year study. In E. M. Hetherington & J. Arasteh (Eds.), *Impact of divorce, single-parenting, and step-parenting on children.* Hillsdale, NJ: Erlbaum.

Wallis, C. (1995, March 6). How to live to be 120. *Time,* 85.

Wang, M. C., Haertel, G. D., & Walberg, H. J. (1993). Toward a knowledge base for school learning. *Review of Educational Research, 63,* 249-294.

Wang, S. Z., & Forsyth, K. D. (1998). Asthma and respiratory syncytial virus infection in infancy: Is there a link? *Clinical and Experimental Allergy, 28,* 927-935.

Wapner, S., Demick, J., Yamamoto, T., & Takahashi, T. (1997). *Handbook of Japan-United States Environment-Behavior Research.* New York: Plenum Press.

Warner, D. C. (1991). Health issues at the US-Mexican border. *Journal of the American Medical Association, 265,* 242-247.

Warr, P. (1992). Age and occupational well-being. *Psychology and Aging, 7,* 37-45.

Warren, K. (1985). Alcohol-related birth defects: Current trends in research. *Alcohol Health and Research World, 10,* 4.

Waters, D., & Saunders, J. T. (1996). I gave at the office. *Networker,* pp. 44-50.

Waters, M. (1994). *Modern sociological theory.* London: Sage.

Watson, J. B. (1925). *Behaviorism.* New York: Norton.

Watts, T. (1985). Ethnomethodogy. In R. M. Grinnell (Ed.), *Social work research and evaluation* (pp. 357-369). Itasca, IL: F. E. Peacock.

Waxman, H. M., McCreary, G., Weinrit, R. M., & Carner, E. A. (1985). A comparison of somatic complaints among depressed and non-depressed older persons. *The Gerontologist, 25,* 501-507.

Weick, A. (1992). Building strengths perspective for social work. In D. Salcebey (Ed.), *The strengths perspective in social work practice.* New York: Longman.

Weideger, P. (1976). *Menstruation and menopause.* New York: Knopf.

Weinman, J. (1987). *An outline of psychology as applied medicine.* Bristol: John Wright.

Weinraub, M., Clemens, L. P., Sockloff, A., Ethridge, T., Gracely, E., & Myers, B. (1984). The development of sex-role stereotypes in the third year: Relationships to gender labeling, gender identity, sex-typed toy preferences, and family characteristics. *Child Development, 55,* 1493-1503.

Weiss, R. S. (1975). *Marital separation.* New York: Basic Books.

Weiten, W. (1992). *Psychology* (2nd ed.). Pacific Grove, CA: Brooks/Cole.

Weiten, W. (1995). *Psychology: Themes and variations.* Pacific Grove, CA: Brooks/Cole.

Weiten, W., & Lloyd, M. A. (1997). *Psychology applied to modern life* (5th ed.). Pacific Grove, CA: Brooks/Cole.

Weiten, W., (2000). *Psychology: Themes & Variations.* (4th edition, briefer version). Pacific Grove: Wadsworth Brooks/Cole.

Weithorn, L. A. (1984). Children's capacities in legal contexts. In N. D. Reppucci, L. A. Weithorn, E. P. Mulvey, & J. Monahan (Eds.), *Children, mental health, and the law.* Beverly Hills, CA: Sage.

Wells, S. J. (1995). Child abuse and neglect overview. In *Encyclopedia of social work* (19th ed.). Washington DC: NASW Press.

Werner, E. E., & Smith, R. S. (1982). *Vulnerable but invincible: A longitudinal study of resilience and youth.* New York: McGraw-Hill.

Werry, J. S., & Quay, H. C. (1971). The prevalence of behavior symptoms in younger elementary school children. *American Journal of Orthopsychiatry, 41,* 136-143.

West, D. J., & Farrington, D. P. (1973). *Who becomes delinquent?* London: Heinemann.

Westinghouse Learning Corporation. (1969). *The impact of Head Start: An evaluation of the effects of Head Start on children's cognitive and affectional development.* Report to the Office of Economic Opportunity. Washington, DC: Learning House for Federal Scientific and Technical Information.

Weymann, A., & Heinz, W. R. (1996). *Society and biography.* Weinheim: Deutscher-Studien Vertag.

Wheaton, B., & Gotlib, I. H. (1997). Trajectories and turning points over the life course: Concepts and themes. In I. H. Gotlib, & B. Wheaton (Eds.), *Stress and adversity over the life course: Trajectories and turning points* (pp. 1-25). New York: Cambridge University Press.

White, J. L. (1989). *The troubled adolescent.* New York: Pergamon Press.

White, L. K. (1990). Determinants of divorce: A review of research in the eighties. *Journal of Marriage and the Family, 32,* 904-912.

White, R. W. (1959). Motivation reconsidered: The concept of competence. *Psychological Review, 66,* 297-333.

White, R. W. (1966). *Lives in progress* (2nd ed.). New York: Holt, Rinehart & Winston.

Whitfield, C. L. (1991). *Co-dependence: Healing the human condition.* Deerfield Beach, FL: Health Communications.

Whiting, B. B., & Whiting, J. W. M. (1975). *Children of 6 cultures: A psychocultural analysis.* Cambridge, MA: Harvard University Press.

Whittaker, J. K., & Garbarino, J. (1983). *Social support networks: Informal helping in the human services.* Hawthorne, NY: Aldine.

Whol, T. (1963). Correlation of anxiety and hostility with adrenocortical function. *Journal of the American Medical Association, 183,* 133-144.

Whorf, B. L. (1956). *Language, thought, and reality.* New York: Wiley.

Widmayer, S., & Field, T. (1980). Effects of Brazelton demonstrations on early interactions of preterm infants and their teen-age mothers. *Infant Behavior and Development, 3,* 79-89.

Widom, C. S. (1989). Does violence beget violence? A critical examination of the literature. *American Psychologist, 106,* 3-28.

Widom, C. S. (1998). Childhood victimization: Early adversity and subsequent psychopathology. In B. P. Dohrenwend (Ed.), *Adversity, stress, and psychopathology* (pp. 81-95). New York: Oxford University Press.

Wigfield, R. (1994). SIDS: Risk reduction measures. *Early Human Development, 38,* 161-164.

Wilcox, L. S., Kiely, J. L., Melvin, C. L., & Martin, M. C. (1996). Assisted reproductive technologies: Estimates of their contribution to multiple births and newborn hospital days in the United States. *Fertility and Sterility, 65,* 361-366.

William T. Grant Foundation (1988). *The forgotten half: Non-college youth in America.* Washington, DC: Youth and America's future: The William T. Grant Foundation on Work, Family and Citizenship.

Williams, C. L., & Berry, J. W. (1991). Primary prevention of acculturative stress among refugees. *American Psychologist, 46,* 632-641.

Williams, J. B. W., Karls, J. M., & Wandrei, K. (1989). The person-in-environment (PIE) system for describing problems of social functioning. *Hospital and Community Psychiatry, 40,* 1125-1127.

Willinger, M., Hoffman, H., & Hartford, R. (1994). Infant sleep position and risk for sudden infant death syndrome: Report of meeting held January 13 and 14, 1994, National Institutes of Health, Bethesda, Md. *Pediatrics, 93,* 814-819.

Willis, D., & Holden, E. (1990). Etiological factors contributing to deviant development. In J. Johnson & J. Goldman (Eds.), *Developmental assessment in clinical child psychology* (pp. 38-57). New York: Pergamon Press.

Willis, S. L. (1989). Adult intelligence. In S. Hunter and M. Sundel (Eds.), *Midlife myths: Issues, findings, and practice implications.* Newbury Park, CA: Sage.

Willis, S. L., & Nesselroade, C. S. (1990). Long-term effects of fluid ability training in old age. *Developmental Psychology, 26,* 905-910.

Wilson, C. C., & Piazza, C. C. (1990). Investigation of the effect of consistent and inconsistent behavioral example upon children's donation behaviors. *Journal of Genetic Psychology, 151,* 361--377.

Wilson, E. O. (1985). *Sociobiology: The new synthesis.* Cambridge, MA: Harvard University Press.

Wilson, K. J. (1987). *Anatomy and physiology in health and illness.* New York: Churchill Livingstone.

Wilson, W. J. (1987). *The truly disadvantaged: The inner city, the underclass and public policy.* Chicago: University of Chicago Press.

Wilson, W. J. (1996). *When work disappears: The world of the new urban poor.* New York: Knopf.

Winawer, S., & Shike, M. (1995). *Cancer free: The comprehensive cancer prevention program.* New York: Simon & Schuster.

Wine, J. D., & Smye, M. D. (1981). *Social competence.* New York: Guilford Press.

Wintgens, A., Lepine, S., Lefebvre, F., Glorieux, J., Gauthier, Y., & Robaey, P. (1998). Attachment, self-esteem, and psychomotor development in extremely premature children at preschool age. *Infant Mental Health Journal, 19,* 394-408.

Wise, M. G. (1986). Working with medicated clients: A primer for social workers. *Health and Social Work, 11,* 36–41.

Wise, P. (1992). Infant mortality as a social mirror. *New England Journal of Medicine, 326,* 1558–1559.

Wisensale, S. K. (1992). Toward the 21st century: Family change and public policy. *Family Relations, 41,* 417–422.

Wisniewski, J. J., & Toomey, B. G. (1987). Are social workers homophobic? *Social Work, 32,* 454–464.

Wolf, R. B., & Pillemer, K. A. (1989). *Helping elderly victims.* New York: Columbia University Press.

Wolfgang, C. H. (1977). *Helping aggressive and passive preschoolers through play.* Columbus, OH: Merrill.

Wood, N. (1974). *Many winters.* Santa Fe, NM: William Gannon.

Wood, V., & Robertson, J. F. (1978). Friendship and kinship interaction: Differential effect on the morale of the elderly. *Journal of Marriage and the Family, 40,* 367–375.

Wood, W. (1987). Meta-analytic review of sex differences in group performance. *Psychological Bulletin, 102,* 53–71.

Woodman, N. J., & Lenna, H. R. (1980). *Counseling with gay men and women: A guide for facilitating positive life-styles.* San Francisco: Jossey-Bass.

Woods, N. F., Most, A., & Dery, G. K. (1982). Prevalence of premenstrual symptoms. *American Journal of Public Health, 72,* 1257–1264.

Worden, W. (1991). *Grief counseling and grief therapy: A handbook for the mental health practitioner.* New York: Springer.

Wright, P. H., & Wright, K. D. (1991). Codependency: Addictive love, adjustive relating, or both? *Contemporary Family Therapy: An International Journal, 13,* 435–454.

Wulf, S. (1997, October, 27). How to teach our children well. *Time,* pp. 62–69.

Wyer, R. S., & Srull, T. K. (Eds.). (1984). *Handbook of social cognition* (Vol. 1). Hillsdale, NJ: Erlbaum.

Wynn, K. (1992). Addition and subtraction by human infants. *Nature, 358,* 749–750.

Yalom, I. (1985). *The theory and practice of group psychotherapy* (3rd ed.). New York: Basic Books.

Yankelovich, D. (1981). *New rules: Searching for self-fulfillment in a world turned upside down.* New York: Bantam Books.

Yesavage, J. A., Brink, T. L., & Rose, T. L., et al. (1983). Development and validation of a geriatric depression rating scale: A preliminary report. *Journal of Psychiatric Research, 17,* 37–49.

Yogman, M. (1982). Development of the father-infant relationship. In H. Fitzgerald, B. Lester, & M. Uogman (Eds.), *Theory and research in behavioral pediatrics* (pp. 221–279). New York: Plenum.

Yogman, M. W., Cooley, J., & Kindlon, D. (1988). Fathers, infants, and toddlers. In P. Bronstein & C. P. Cowan (Eds.), *Fatherhood today: Men's changing role in the family.* New York: Wiley.

Young, J. E. (1982). Loneliness, depression and cognitive therapy: Theory and application. In L. A. Peplau & D. Perlman (Eds.), *Loneliness: A sourcebook of current theory, research, and therapy.* New York: Wiley.

Young, R. F., & Kahana, E. (1989). Specifying caregiver outcomes: Gender and relationship aspects of caregiving strain. *The Gerontologist, 29,* 660–666.

Young, V. H. (1970). Family and childhood in a southern Negro community. *American Anthropologist, 72*(2), 269–288.

Youngstrom, N. (1990, October). Seriously mentally ill need better tracking. *APA Monitor,* pp. 18–19.

Youngstrom, N. (1991a, September). Drug exposure in home elicits worst behaviors. *APA Monitor,* p. 23.

Youngstrom, N. (1991b, October). Warning: Teens at risk for AIDS. *APA Monitor,* p. 38.

Youth Update (1994). *Building assets for youth.* Minneapolis, MN: Lutheran Brotherhood.

Yule, W. (1981). The epidemiology of child psychopathology. In B. Lahey & A. Kazdin (Eds.), *Advances in clinical child psychology* (Vol. 4). New York: Plenum.

Yussen, S. R. (1977). Characteristics of moral dilemmas written by adolescents. *Developmental Psychology, 13,* 162–163.

Zajonc, R. B. (1980). Feeling and thinking: Preferences need no inferences. *American Psychologist, 35,* 151–175.

Zajonc, R. B. (1984). On the primacy of affect. *American Psychologist, 39,* 117–123.

Zajonc, R. B., & Markus, G. B. (1975). Birth order and intellectual development. *Psychological Review, 82,* 74–88.

Zametkin, A. J., Nordahl, T., Gross, M., King, A. C., Semple, W. E., Rumsey, J., Hamburger, S., & Cohen, R. M. (1990). Cerebral glucose metabolism in adults with hyperactivity of childhood onset. *New England Journal of Medicine, 322,* 1361–1366.

Zastrow, C., & Kirst-Ashman, K. K. (1997). *Understanding human behavior and the social environment* (4th ed.). Chicago: Nelson-Hall.

Zausmer, E. (1978). Gross motor developmental stimulation. In S. M. Pueschel (Ed.), *Down syndrome: Growing and learning* (pp. 88–105). New York: Andrews, McMeel & Parker.

Zeanah, C. H., & Emde, R. N. (1994). Attachment disorders in infancy and childhood. In M. Rutter, E. Taylor, & L. Hersou (Eds.), *Child and adolescent psychiatry: Modern approaches* (pp. 490–504). Oxford: Blackwell Scientific.

Zelazo, R., Zelazo, N., & Kolb, S. (1972). "Walking" in the newborn. *Science, 176,* 314–315.

Zellman, G. L., & Eisen, M. (1984). Factors predicting pregnancy resolution decision satisfaction of unmarried adolescents. *Journal of Genetic Psychology, 145,* 231–234.

Ziegler, J. A. (1994). *Experimentalism and institutional change: An approach to the study of improvement of institutions.* Lanham: University Press of America.

Zigler, E. (1973). Project Head Start: Success or failure? *Learning, 1,* 43–47.

Zigler, E., & Finn-Stevenson, M. (1992). Applied developmental psychology. In M. E. Lamb & M. Bornstein (Eds.), *Developmental psychology: An advanced textbook* (3rd ed.). Hillsdale, NJ: Erlbaum.

Zigler, E., & Stevenson, M. F. (1993). *Children in a changing world: Development and social issues* (2nd ed.). Pacific Grove, CA: Brooks/Cole.

Zigler, E., Taussig, C., & Black, K. (1992). Early childhood intervention: A promising preventive for juvenile delinquency. *American Psychologist, 47,* 997–1006.

Zigler, E., & Trickett, P. E. (1978). IQ, social competence, and evaluation of early childhood intervention programs. *American Psychologist, 33,* 789–798.

Zigler, E., & Valentine, J. (1979). *Project Head Start: A legacy of the War on Poverty.* New York: Free Press.

Zimbardo, P. G. (1987). *Shyness.* New York: Jove.

Zolotow, C. (1968). *My friend John.* New York: Harper & Row.

Zuravin, S. J. (1989). The ecology of child abuse and neglect: Review of the literature and presentation of data. *Violence and Victims, 4,* 101–120.

Credits

This page constitutes an extension of the copyright page. We have made every effort to trace the ownership of all copyrighted material and to secure permission from copyright holders. In the event of any question arising as to the use of any material, we will be pleased to make the necessary correction in future printings. Thanks are due to the following authors, publishers, and agents for permission to use the material indicated.

Chapter 1: 14, Fig 1.1, from *The Dual Perspectives*, by D. Norton et al. Copyright © 1978, Council on Social Work Education. Reprinted with permission. **23,** Fig. 1.2, from a model of psychosocial stress from B. S. Dohrenwend (1978), social stress and community psychology. *American Journal of Community Psychology 6*, 1–14. Copyright 1978, Plenum Publishing Corporation.

Chapter 3: 73, Fig. 3.1, adapted from "Reflections on Dr. Borg's Life Cycle," by E. H. Erikson, in "Adulthood," *Daedalus, 105*, No. 2, Spring 1976, p. 43. Copyright © 1976 American Academy of Arts and Sciences. Adapted with permission. **85,** Fig. 3.5, from *Cognitive Psychology: Memory, Language and Thought*, by D. V. Howard, p. 18. Copyright © 1983. Reprinted by permission of Prentice Hall, Upper Saddle River, NJ. **93,** Fig. 3.8, from "Attitudes, Traits, and Actions," by I. Ajzen, 1987, *Advances in Experimental Social Psychology, 20*, 1–63. Copyright © 1987 Academic Press, Inc. Reprinted with permission.

Chapter 4: 106, Fig. 4.1, adapted from C. B. Kopp and J. B. Krakow, *Child Development in the Social Context* (Figure 12.1, p. 648). Copyright © 1982 by Addison-Wesley Longman Publishing Company, Inc. Adaptation appears in *Life-Span Human Development*, 2nd ed., by C. K. Sigleman and D. R. Shaffer, p. 88, Brooks/Cole Publishing, 1995. **107,** Fig. 4.2, from *Clinical Assessment for Social Workers*, by C. Jordan and C. Franklin, p. 23. Copyright © 1995 Lyceum Press. Reprinted with permission. **109,** Fig. 4.3, from "Early Human Experience," by J. Belsky, 1981, *Developmental Psychology 17*, 3–23. Copyright © 1981 American Psychological Association. Reprinted with permission. **110,** Table 4.1, adapted from The Changing Family Lifecycle, by B. Carter and M. McGoldrick, p. 15. Copyright © 1988 Allyn & Bacon. Adapted with permission. **127,** Focus on Theory, from *Modern Sociological Theory*, by M. Waters. Copyright © 1994 Sage Publications Ltd. Reprinted with permission. **111,** Fig. 4.4, from "Marital Satisfaction over the Family Life Cycle," by B. C. Collins & H. Feldman, 1970, *Journal of Marriage and the Family, 32*, 20–28. Copyright © 1970 National Council on Family Relations, 3989 Central Ave. NE., Suite 550, Minneapolis, MN 55421. Reprinted with permission. **116,** Box 4.1, adapted from "Functional Roles of Group Members," by K. D. Benne & P. Sheats, 1948, *Journal of Social Issues, 4* (2), 41–49. Copyright © The Society for the Psychological Study of Social Issues. Used with permission. **119,** Box 4.2, reprinted with permission of the Free Press, a division of Simon & Schuster, from *Decision Making: A Psychological Analysis of Conflict, Choice, and Commitment*, by Irving L. Janis and Leon Mann. Copyright © 1977 The Free Press. **129,** Table 4.3, from W.G. Ouchi, *Theory Z: How American Business Can Meet the Japanese Challenge*, p. 58, copyright © 1981 Addison-Wesley Publishing Company, Inc. Reprinted by permission of Addison-Wesley Publishing Company, Inc.

Chapter 5: 159, adapted from *Before We Are Born: Basic Embryology and Birth Defects*, 4th ed., by K. L. Moore. Copyright © 1989 by W. B. Saunders. Adapted by permission. Adaptation appears in *The Psychological Development of Children*, by F. B. Steuer, p. 148, Brooks/Cole Publishing, 1994. **189,** Box 5.1, adapted from "Etiological Factors Contributing to Deviant Development," by D. Willis and E. Holden. In J. Johnson and J. Goldman (eds.), *Development Assessment in Clinical Child Psychology*, p. 39. Copyright © 1990. All rights reserved. Adapted by permission of Allyn & Bacon.

Chapter 6: 200, Table 6.1, adapted from "The Denver Development Screening Test," by W. K. Frankenberg and J. B. Dodds, 1967, *Journal of Pediatrics, 71*, 181–91. Copyright © 1967 C. V. Mosby Company. Used with permission. **202,** Table 6.2, from *Family-Centered Nursing Care of Children*, by R. Foster, M. Hunsberger, and J. Anderson. Copyright © 1989 Harcourt Brace and Company. Reprinted with permission. **207,** Fig. 6.1, reprinted with permission from *Nature, 282*, "Intermodal Matching by Human Neonates," by A. Meltzoff and R. Borton, 403–404. Copyright © 1979 Macmillan Magazines Limited. **209,** Table 6.4, adapted from "Etiological Factors Contributing to Deviant Development," by D. Willis and E. Holden. In J. Johnson and J. Goldman (eds.), *Development Assessment in Clinical Child Psychology*, p. 5. Copyright © 1990. All rights reserved. Adapted by permission of Ally & Bacon. **219,** Table 6.6, from "Disorder of Attachment" by C. Zeanah, O. Mammen, and A. Lieberman. In C. Zeanah, Jr. (ed.), *Handbook of Infant Mental Health*, p. 346. Copyright © 1993 The Guilford Press. Reprinted with permission. **221,** Table 6.7, adapted from "Etiological Factors Contributing to Deviant Development," by D. Willis and E. Holden. In J. Johnson and J. Goldman (eds.), *Development Assessment in Clinical Child Psychology*, p. 5. Copyright © 1990. All rights reserved. Adapted by permission of Allyn & Bacon. **233,** Focus on Sociology, adapted by Jane Wenk from an article by Tori DeAngelis for the APA *Monitor*, January 1995, p. 36. Copyright © 1995 American Psychological Association. Adapted with permission. **234,** Focus on Research, adapted by Jane Wenk from an article by B. Azar for the APA *Monitor*, June 1995, p. 18. Copyright © 1995 American Psychological Association. Adapted with permission. **238,** Box 6.2, adapted from *Pediatric Nursing, 14*(2), 1988, p. 98. Reprinted with permission of the publisher, Jannetti Publications, Inc., East Holly Avenue Box 56, Pitman, NJ 08071-0056; Phone (609) 256-2300.

Chapter 8: 318, Table 8.2, reproduced with permission from S. Harter, *Self-Perception Profile for Children*, University of Denver, 1985. **320,** Table 8.3, adapted from "Interpersonal Awareness in Children," by R. L. Selman, D. Jaquette, and D. Lavin, 1977, *American Journal of Orthopsychiatry, 47*, 264–74; and from *The Growth of Interpersonal Understanding*, by R. L. Selman, copyright © 1980 Academic Press. Adapted with permission. **323,** Fig. 8.3, from the *Manual for the Child Behavior Profile*, by T. M. Achenbach. Copyright © 1991 T. M. Achenbach. Reproduced by permission. **327,** Table 8.5, from *Parental Effectiveness Training*, by Dr. Thomas Gordon. Copyright © 1970 by Thomas Gordon. Reprinted by permission of David McKay, Co., a division of Random House, Inc. **329,** Fig. 8.4, from "Age Segregation in Children's Social Interactions," by S. Ellis, B. Rogoff, and C. C. Cromer, 1981, *Developmental Psychology, 17*, 399–407. Copyright © 1981 American Psychological Association. Reprinted with permission. **333,** Focus on Research, by B. Murray, from an article titled "School Phobias Hold Many Children Back" in the APA *Monitor*, September 1997, pp. 38–39. Copyright © 1997 by the American Psychological Association. Reprinted by permission. **339,** Focus on Multiculturalism, by

Photo Credits

Photo Credits

Name Index

Subject Index

(continued